# FRENCH CHEESE
## BOOK

'The best (and crustiest) friend the farmhouse cheese-maker ever had'
*Guardian*

**Patrick Rance** has been a lover of cheese since early childhood, when his mid-morning treat was a 'buttery crust crowned with hunks of nutty-flavoured Cheddar.' For more than thirty years, cheese has been his vocation and passionate concern, and he has travelled widely throughout Britain and the Continent on his crusade for Real Cheese.

His *Great British Cheese Book* – now available in a revised second edition – has been acclaimed as 'our definitive cheese guide' and was chosen by Elizabeth David as one of her four favourite food books.

Pat and his wife Janet own the famous cheese shop Wells Stores in the Berkshire village of Streatley. It is now run by their son Hugh, one of seven children, all of them brought up on cheese.

*By the same author*

The Great British Cheese Book (1982)
(second revised edition 1988)

# THE FRENCH CHEESE BOOK

## Patrick Rance

### foreword by Jane Grigson

**M**
PAPERMAC

To my friend and mentor,
Pierre Androuët,
whose masterly work in the
cause of traditional cheese
can never be surpassed

Copyright © Patrick Rance 1989

All rights reserved. No reproduction, copy or transmission
of this publication may be made without written permission.
No paragraph of this publication may be reproduced, copied
or transmitted save with written permission or in
accordance with the provisions of the Copyright Act 1956
(as amended). Any person who does any unauthorised act
in relation to this publication may be liable to criminal
prosecution and civil claims for damages.

First published 1989 by Macmillan London Limited

First published in paperback 1991 by
PAPERMAC
a division of Macmillan Publishers Limited
Cavaye Place London SW10 9PG
and Basingstoke

Associated companies in Auckland, Delhi, Dublin, Gaborone,
Hamburg, Harare, Hong Kong, Johannesburg, Kuala Lumpur,
Lagos, Manzini, Melbourne, Mexico City, Nairobi, New York,
Singapore and Tokyo

ISBN 0–333–41360–1

A CIP catalogue record for this book is available from the British Library

Designed by Robert Updegraff

Maps by Hilary Evans

Typeset by Bookworm Typesetting, Manchester, England
Printed in Hong Kong

# Contents

ACKNOWLEDGMENTS vii
FOREWORD BY JANE GRIGSON ix
HOW TO USE THIS BOOK xiii
MAP xiv
INTRODUCTION xv

1  *Normandy, Maine and Brittany*   1
2  *Touraine, Orléanais and Berry*   57
3  *Poitou and Angoumois*   97
4  *Périgord and Quercy*   113
5  *The Pyrenees and Western Languedoc*   127
6  *Rouergue and Roquefort*   173
7  *Auvergne and other pays of the Massif Central*   201
8  *The North*   257
9  *Alsace, Bar and Lorraine*   277
10 *Brie, Champagne and the Île de France*   299
11 *Burgundy*   343
12 *Lyonnais*   371
13 *The Pays of the Ain*   381
14 *La Franche-Comté*   393
15 *Savoie and Bas Bugey*   413
16 *Dauphiné*   441
17 *Corsica*   467
18 *Provence and Eastern Languedoc*   481

APPENDIX 1: LISTERIA MONOCYTOGENES AND LISTERIA 523
APPENDIX 2: CHEESE AND HUMAN HEALTH 531
APPENDIX 3: BUYING, KEEPING AND SERVING CHEESE 532
GLOSSARY 537
BIBLIOGRAPHY 543
INDEX 545

# Acknowledgments

My first and greatest debt is to Pierre Androuët, co-founder of the Guilde des Fromagers, and indispensable authority for all students of cheese. His friendship and support strengthened my resolve to pursue this study of the historical background of French cheese and survey of its present state. He has done me the generous service of reading and correcting my typescript.

I would also like to thank the following:

My journalist wife Janet, vital companion, co-taster and interviewer on our cheese-hunting travels.

Our son Hugh, whose timely offer to take over the running of our shop, Wells Stores, Streatley, made the writing of this book possible. He has made independent forays to French farms, which have enhanced my knowledge, as well as enriching his range of French cheeses.

Simone Guet, and her husband Gabriel Guet of Nature & Progrès, who started as encouragers. They volunteered invaluable help, particularly with details of organic farming and historical accounts of cheese. Simone became a researcher for the book, as well as decoder and corrector of my manuscript mysteries. She transformed my illegible pages into typescripts which so raised my morale that finishing the book in my lifetime no longer seemed a remote dream.

Ninette Lyon, European food writer marvellously alive to the importance of cheese, and most penetrating in her discoveries of treasures new and old.

At the Guilde des Fromagers, Monsieur Jan Bachot, affable Keeper of the Seal, and the Guilde's secretary and archivist Madame Chantal Meunier; and many other members of the Guilde, particularly Maître Fromager Gérard Paul, who runs our Provençal branch.

Madame Catherine Manac'h (in London) and Madame Simone Cointat (in Paris) of Food From France (SOPEXA), who have given me much help and documentation.

Michael Alcock and Nick Chapman, who commissioned this book for Macmillan, both being cheese-lovers.

I owe a special debt to my Macmillan editor Brenda Thomson. She survived avalanches of typescript, bringing order out of chaos with a sensitive mixture of firmness and enthusiasm.

Other invaluable helpers at Macmillan were Kyle Cathie, Ann Cooke, Beverley Cousins, Hilary Evans, Hazel Orme, Elizabeth Pitman, Jo Stanfield and Robert Updegraff.

The index was prepared by Edward Leeson, and the proofreader was Ron Spall.

I am grateful to the following kind hosts and helpers who eased our path of research and made it more pleasurable: Michel Agodi of Dieppe, Albert Alric of Roquefort, Susan and Ian Anstruther, Madame Bernardi of Metz, Richard Binns, Jean-Louis Bloquet of Neufchâtel (Vallée de Bray), Edouard and Robert Cénéri of Cannes, Monsieur Clouet of Gunsbach, Dany and Philippe Condamine of Salon, Caroline Conran, Sandra Donzeau of Draveil near Paris, Nicolas Dreyfus of Fromagerie des Chaumes, Sally Fitzwater,

Clothilde and Eddie Gadler of Fontvieille, Geneviève and Claude Genisson of Douai, Marthe and Georges Girard of Fontvieille, Joseph Giudicelli of Corsica, Jenny Greene, Jane Grigson, Père Pierre Harymbat of the Pays Basque, Maurice Janier of Lyons, Professor Juillard of La Roche sur Foron, Monsieur Larcher of Sainte-Maure, Pierre Laur of Roquefort, Mary and David Lodge of the Agenais, Ninette and Peter Lyon of Paris and Provence, Carole Mansur, Claudia and Robert Maxtone Graham, Virginia and Stephen Minot, Monsieur and Madame de Murard of Brancion, Claude Olivier of Dieppe and Philippe Olivier of Boulogne, Gérard Paul of Aix, Simone Porcheret of Dijon, Veronica Pratt, Bettina and Gino Segré, Susan and Jean-Michel Vaillant of Strasbourg, Claude Veillet-Lavallée of Paris, Monsieur Verlaguet of Besse.

My warm thanks go to the hundreds of other helpful informants, cheesemakers and merchants, chefs, restaurateurs and hoteliers, who gave generously of their time and expertise. Most of their names will be found in the chapters and lists which follow.

# Foreword

My first encounter with Patrick Rance was in 1975. The family was organising a party for my husband's seventieth birthday, and I ordered the cheese course – for fifty people – from Wells Stores in Streatley. The magnificent and odoriferous spread of cheeses that arrived could have been supplied by no one else in the country at the time, with the possible exception of Paxton & Whitfield of Jermyn Street in London. Soon afterwards Richard Boston, founding voice of the campaign for real ale (CAMRA), took us to Streatley. It was an extraordinary visit, the unthinkable range of cheeses, the cellars where they were stored until perfectly ripe and ready for eating, the enthusiasm and excitement of it all. Most of the cheese came from France, but the revival of British cheese was beginning – a slow movement perhaps (Patrick Rance had been trying to halt the decline in the grand cheeses, and encourage new cheeses, from the mid-1950s) but one with a great future.

Patrick Rance is one of the few who truly deserve the title of 'guru'. Myself, I prefer the word 'champion', for he is a doughty campaigner (the word guru suggests a bearded sage sitting on a mountain or under a bo-tree, too passive a role). He has never been afraid to challenge the big battalions who have gradually and ineluctably set themselves the task of destroying any small pocket of good cheesemaking that had somehow managed to survive. A lamentable tale. These great molochs have slowly and quietly sabotaged such quality as remained, quite rightly assessing that the public would not notice such gradual destruction. When at last it became obvious, we would feel powerless and unable to do anything. This was the way that our bread and our ale had been ruined; cheese was the next victim.

Occasionally when something looks hopeless, a David comes to judgment and takes on Goliath. In the case of cheese, our David is Patrick Rance. There are, of course, other discriminating cheese sellers and *affineurs*, but they have not taken on the campaigning role. Most food writers and food producers are quietist, anxious to get on with their work which occupies all their energies. This, of course, is why big food business and food officialdom manage to get away with ruining our good things.

Patrick Rance's knowledge and energy are so vast that he has been able to move into the public sphere and challenge this destruction effectively. He knew that the processes of cheesemaking remain the same, whether one produces good, bad or indifferent cheese: it follows that the choice of end result depends on the character and intentions and financial condition of the maker. He set himself to encourage and sell good British cheeses, without turning his back on the glorious cheesemaking of France. So often in Britain people try to promote our good things foolishly, by decrying or ignoring foreign expertise rather than learning from it. For centuries the British have been saying that French skill with sauces – which they could not deny – was essential to disguise the poor quality of their meat and fish. What rubbish! The only way we can improve our food is to look to the best, wherever it turns up, learn all we can, then apply the knowledge to our own situation. This should not mean slavish copying, or the downgrading of foreign products to suit British taste, but turning out good products of our own through nice adjustment and informed judgment.

We tend to say 'Cheddar is the best cheese in the world'. And this may well be true of a fine, genuinely farm-produced Cheddar, made from the milk of a known herd or group of herds. How much of the so-called Cheddar on sale comes into this category? What percentage of world production does it represent? I remember trying a rather unsatisfactory goat cheese from a Hampshire farm. When discussing it on the telephone, I mentioned the similar but far better cheeses made in our district of France. It emerged that this cheesemaker in Hampshire, living right by Portsmouth and Southampton, had never taken the trouble to visit the goat-cheese heartland of France in Poitou-Charentes to study their methods, and, more important, their results.

This kind of insularity is completely alien to Patrick Rance. He knows that when one wishes to practise a craft, one should study the best exponents of it. How else can the standards be set? How else can one know what one is aiming at? This is the whole problem of food in Britain.

For cheesemakers, France is obviously the standard-setter. The problem has been the inaccurate logging of the cheeses they make. We do not know what exists now, what has disappeared, what has been reborn, what has been altered, what new cheeses have been developed over the last thirty years. The truth of the matter is that the French are careless with regard to the recording of their specialities. I would say that if we need to take standards of food production from them, they need to study our standards of research, record and indexing: in matters of cheese, they could well study this book – and I think they will.

When we first set up house in Trôo, a small village in Loir-et-Cher, in 1961, I found that a cheese was made there, a goats'-milk cheese. Or at least I found it in the reference books. On the ground, I rapidly discovered that there was one old lady, Mère Marie, with a small flock of goats: she made cheeses only for the family and a few close friends. 'Le petit Trôo', a nice little cheese in a pretty wrapper, came from a small dairy across the river Loir in the *commune* of Saint-Jacques: it was made entirely of cows' milk and had been for a fair number of years. Owing to the folly of the local mayor, we lost the dairy to Montoire, 6 kilometres away, where 'le petit Trôo' is still made, indeed on a larger scale, still of cows' milk, in the small *zone industriel* on the road to Savigny.

Since 1961 there has been an enormous revival of goat-cheese making, which has spread from the heartland to its fringes, including our gentle countryside of the Bas-Vendômois. When Patrick and Janet Rance came to visit me there in 1987, while they were working on this book, we were able to visit farm after farm making goat cheeses. After two days we were all exhausted, but we had not exhausted all the possibilities. Interestingly, we had run the gamut of production from the Montoire petit Trôo producer to the girl who had brought her flock of 200 goats from Alsace to Authon just so that she could make her cheeses, as it were, on the sacred ground: shrewdness as well as piety had directed her move to the 'right' area, and now she invents a new cheese every year to keep the smart restaurateurs of Paris happy (her production goes straight to Rungis, the great central market of France on the outskirts of Paris). Variety consists in new shape and new name rather than an entirely new type of cheese, it must be said; or it may mean the usual cheese rolled in a new coating: chopped herbs, or peppercorns for instance. We also visited a rural pair full of sudden mirth – they were the only people I have ever met who literally and uninhibitedly were laughing all the way to the bank – at their 'discovery' by Parisians with second homes in the district. They are now deemed *biologique* (organic). 'We've always farmed this way!' they chortled. 'Just like father!' Their up-to-date farming neighbours had been decidedly snooty about them, on account of the weeds and the chickens running around. Now they have the last laugh, putting up their prices, investing in a few stainless-steel utensils, increasing production without huge investment.

In this book Patrick Rance describes such areas as ours, areas of small cheeses that over the years come and go on the market stalls. He also describes the grand productions, the Emmentals and Cantals, the Roqueforts. He has discovered places that make fine cheeses using the latest hi-tech machinery. This shows, as I have said, that the decision to make fine cheese is personal and moral and, with intelligence, good business; that the modernisation of the millennial process does not have to mean a decline in the end product. Why should it not mean an improvement – in consistency of quality, for instance? Though, of course, with cheese one should not expect similarity all year round: the seasonal round, the effect of climate on pastures as the year proceeds, means that fine cheese can vary, but it should vary within a certain standard.

This new book, *The French Cheese Book*, is not only ammunition for the fight, any more than *The Great British Cheese Book*, recently republished in a revised edition, was intended purely as slingshot. It is a source of pleasure and expeditions. When you go to France, keep it in the car along with the Michelin guides and maps. Cheesemaking seems to occur in good gastronomic regions, which means you can rely on good eating generally – charcuterie, for instance, goes with cheesemaking as pigs were and are fed on the whey. Good gastronomy usually indicates good churches, châteaux, an interesting local life and an enjoyable landscape. By pursuing cheese you will make more discoveries than you had ever dreamed of, especially by way of geology and the flora. Patrick Rance often observes that he counted forty or fifty species in the pastures of certain famous cheese districts: that means pretty sites for picnicking and a beautiful bunch of flowers in your hotel room.

The shop at Streatley is now managed by the Rances' son, Hugh, one of their seven children. The parents live mainly in Provence, at Fontvieille, almost in the shadow of Daudet's mill, which is now a museum. Daudet was an enthusiast for good food; he knew a lot about it, as his Tartarin books, and the more serious novels, indicate. Whenever I read *'Soupe au fromage'*, from his *Contes du Lundi* (1873), I think of Patrick Rance. The story begins with the soup bubbling away on the hob in an empty room, then expands to describe the room, gradually revealing the trade of the absent occupier. He emerges as an actor, who sets his soup going so that when the curtain falls he has a meal to go home to, and a room full of its delicious smell. In my mind I always clothe that actor in Patrick Rance's envelope, imagining the glint of pleasure on the monocle, the widening grin as he walks up the stairs to the wonderful and increasing aroma of *soupe au fromage*, the reward of his hard day.

Jane Grigson
December, 1988

# *How to Use This Book*

France's most important cheeses were born of her old provinces, not her modern *départements*. I have therefore given a chapter to a province, or to a group of provinces interlocked by history, geography and related cheeses.

At the end of each provincial section is an alphabetical list of cheeses, places or districts where they are made or where they originated, and other items of local interest.

Map references in the cheese lists refer to Michelin standard 1:200,000, 1cm:2km, yellow maps, available in both England and France. Map numbers are followed by *pli* numbers, set in bold type. (*Pli* means fold, and each Michelin yellow map has twenty sections corresponding to the spaces between the folds.) For example, the village of Camembert is on map 55, *pli* **13**.

To help find obscure places, the abbreviations L, R and C (for Left, Right and Centre) give general direction to the eye, within the *pli*. Cardinal points (N, SW, WNW, etc.) give bearings from the centre of the *pli*, or from some other prominent point of reference. Where necessary, I have added road numbers (e.g. N10, D252) and river names (e.g. R. Loire).

*Pays* and *département* names are given just before the map references. Thus, La Boulette de Papleux is to be found at: Papleux, NW of La Chapelle; Thiérache/Aisne; 53 **16**, upper L.

I have specified whether the cheese is farm-made (*fermier*), artisan-made (*artisanal*), from a larger dairy (*laitier*), or creamery (*industriel*). Cheese from organic farms is listed as *biologique*. The next entry (e.g. 45% m.g.) means percentage of fat matter in solids. Next comes the type of milk: cows' (*vache*), goats' (*chèvre*), or ewes' (*brebis*), and whether it is raw (*cru*), heat-treated (*thermisé*), or fully pasteurised (*pasteurisé*).

Please read the Glossary before you set off on your journey through the book, and refer back to it when you meet any terms not explained elsewhere.

When you have finished this study of French cheeses, I hope that you will feel drawn to hunting them out on the ground; and that, if you did not already know the French cheese terms, you will find them slipping off your tongue as you talk to the splendid people who make and sell the cheeses.

# The Old Provinces and Modern Départements of France

### Départements

01 Ain
02 Aisne
03 Allier
04 Alpes-de-Haute-Provence
05 Hautes-Alpes
06 Alpes-Maritimes
07 Ardèche
08 Ardennes
09 Ariège
10 Aube
11 Aude
12 Aveyron
13 Bouches-du-Rhône
14 Calvados
15 Cantal
16 Charente
17 Charente-Maritime
18 Cher
19 Corrèze
20A Corse-du-Sud
20B Haute-Corse
21 Côte-d'Or
22 Côtes-du-Nord
23 Creuse
24 Dordogne
25 Doubs
26 Drôme
27 Eure
28 Eure-et-Loir
29 Finistère
30 Gard
31 Haute-Garonne
32 Gers
33 Gironde
34 Hérault
35 Ille-et-Vilaine
36 Indre
37 Indre-et-Loire
38 Isère
39 Jura
40 Landes
41 Loir-et-Cher
42 Loire
43 Haute-Loire
44 Loire-Atlantique
45 Loiret
46 Lot
47 Lot-et-Garonne
48 Lozère
49 Maine-et-Loire
50 Manche
51 Marne
52 Haute-Marne
53 Mayenne
54 Meurthe-et-Moselle
55 Meuse
56 Morbihan
57 Moselle
58 Nièvre
59 Nord
60 Oise
61 Orne
62 Pas-de-Calais
63 Puy-de-Dôme
64 Pyrénées-Atlantiques
65 Hautes-Pyrénées
66 Pyrénées-Orientales
67 Bas-Rhin
68 Haut-Rhin
69 Rhône
70 Haute-Saône
71 Saône-et-Loire
72 Sarthe
73 Savoie
74 Haute-Savoie
75 Paris
76 Seine-Maritime
77 Seine-et-Marne
78 Yvelines
79 Deux-Sèvres
80 Somme
81 Tarn
82 Tarn-et-Garonne
83 Var
84 Vaucluse
85 Vendée
86 Vienne
87 Haute-Vienne
88 Vosges
89 Yonne
90 Territoire-de-Belfort
91 Essonne
92 Hauts-de-Seine
93 Seine-St-Denis
94 Val-de-Marne
95 Val-d'Oise

PARIS REGION

# Introduction

## The cheeses and pays of France

A slice of good cheese is never just a thing to eat. It is usually also a slice of local history: agricultural, political, or ecclesiastical. Knowledge of this enables us to distinguish the genuine from the imitation; it adds to our appetite for the cheese and to the relish with which we savour it.

The cheeses of France are redolent of her history. Her traditional cheeses and *pays* are endless, inseparable mysteries. Only a young fool in love would be mad enough to try to embrace them all in a lifetime, let alone in a single volume.

In 1984, five years after commissioning my *Great British Cheese Book*, Macmillan London threw down just such a challenge. I was an old fool by this time, but still too blindly smitten to resist picking up the glove. The deciding factor in my acceptance was probably the prospect that my wife and I would have the felicitous duty to live and travel in France for several years to come.

My passion indeed set me two impossible tasks. First, I like to be definitive on any subject I tackle, but no definitive account of French cheese can ever be arrived at. French cheeses are in a constant state of flux. Some go by a multitude of names; other names cover a multitude of varieties. Some of the rarest and most succulent bear no name at all.

The most famous story about the number of French cheeses comes from a meeting between Winston Churchill and General de Gaulle. The General is said to have exclaimed: 'How can anyone be expected to govern a country with 324 cheeses?' Referring to this story, the academician Georges Duhamel consoled himself by asking how a country with 324 cheeses could ever die?

A popular saying claims that there is a French cheese for every day of the year. A more instructed count was made by a former head of the Dairy School at Mamirolles in Franche-Comté, Monsieur Roy, who reached 456. This was topped by Curnonsky, elected Prince of Gastronomes in 1927 in Paris, who asserted that 483 were recognised by connoisseurs of cheese in France. Pierre Androuët, in his 1971 *Guide du Fromage*, reached nearly 500. In the course of researching and writing this book, I came to my own conclusion, as I shall explain (see p. xix).

My second impossible task is hinted at in the apparently flippant, yet rational association of multiplicity of cheeses with ungovernability: I had to face the tangle of ancient *pays* which are the nurseries of those rebellious cheeses. The country called France is much too rich in geological, climatic, human and agricultural variety to suit the convenience of bureaucrats in Paris or Brussels. It expresses this in its rich pattern of former seigneuries, baronnies, viscomtés, comtés, principautés, dauphinés, duchés and even royaumes. These are often *pays* within *pays*, ancient divisions with their own human clans or races, their own well-tried systems of dairy farming and dairy breeds. These have been vindicated by the best agricultural research of the last few years as not only admirable but preferable for modern needs. As Georges Duhamel wrote in his preface to *The Provinces of France* (ed. Ogrizek): 'The frequent subdivisions of the agricultural land reveal the deep-rooted individualism of the people.' The number of French cheeses is one of the satisfactory results.

The old boundaries have been altered or overlaid by later political changes, but those old *pays*, with their hold on local loyalties, have survived even the Procrustean superimposition of the Revolutionary departmental system. This chopping up of so many provinces, however, makes it hard after 200 years always to be sure on which side of an Ancien Régime boundary one is standing. I have done my best to unravel this tangle, out of respect and affection for the peoples and their *pays*. Loyalty to local methods and traditions among farmers and cheesemakers, and among those who mature and distribute their produce, is the key to the integrity and virtue of their cheeses.

To any reader from a doubtful borderline area who finds that I have misnamed his *pays*, I offer my apologies and regrets. I feel very deeply on the subject; humanity is always the poorer for the disappearance of local languages, loves and loyalties. Their nurturing should stand first in the political programme of any regime which truly believes in local government.

Lest I be accused of romanticising, let me again quote Georges Duhamel. He was concerned for 'national unity', he esteemed French-language teaching as the principal unifying factor; but he stressed: 'For France to remain France, it is essential that each of its component provinces should preserve its traditions, its customs, graciously adapted to the exigencies of the soil, its colourful dialects often enriched, embellished and extolled by the local poets'. And by the local *paysans*, I will add, particularly the *éleveurs* of old breeds, and the makers and sellers of traditional cheeses.

## The roots and evolution of French cheese

The origins of the oldest cheeses are prehistoric. In the Pyrenees a ewes'-milk cheese, now officially called Iraty, has been made 'for ever', as the Basques say, by that timeless people, probably the longest-settled race in Europe. Centuries before the Romans came to eat and praise them, cheeses like today's Cantal, Salers, and blue *fourmes* were being made by the Arvernes; and Laguiole and Roquefort by the Gabalitains and their neighbours in the Massif Central. Likewise, the cheese now called Beaufort was being made by the Centrons in the Tarentaise. Up to a millennium separated their beginnings from the invaders who imposed on their makers the new kingdom of the Franks in the fifth century AD. Fifteen hundred years later, these cheeses still flourish as gems in the select range of the French Appellations d'Origine Contrôlées.

A new wave of dairy farming and cheesemaking followed the brush- and forest-clearances of the mediaeval monks. (Newly cleared lands, *essarts* (variously spelt), are widely commemorated in French place-names.) Cheeses started by or stimulated by monastic enterprise include Maroilles in the North, Meaux in Brie, Chaource on the Champagne–Burgundy border, Époisses in the heart of Burgundy, and Comté and Bleu de Gex in the Jura. There were other more anonymous monastic cheeses, especially in Benedictine and Cistercian communities. The greatest monastery in the west, at Cluny, boasted a thick-walled tenth-century cheese-tower, and there were satellite farms to keep it filled.

The aftermath of the Revolution suppressed and destroyed the monasteries, but not those cheeses, all still famous today.

By the end of the sixteenth century, despite slowness of transport, the known range of French cheeses was surprisingly broad in its scope. The great agriculturalist Olivier de Serres wrote in 1600: 'As for cheese, cows, although abundant, do not produce a result as delicate as the product of goat and ewe. It is nevertheless in great demand ... when climate and pasture give it a good name. For such reason the cheeses of the Auvergne are renowned all over France from coast to coast, whither they are despatched in large quantities. In various other parts of this Kingdom, there are also mountains rich in cows'-milk cheeses because of their exquisite pastures ... there are to be found odd corners of mountain, coast and plain, in numerous quarters of the provinces, celebrated for their good cheese of divers kinds and different milks. Brie, among others, for its good cheeses called *angelots*, and "les-baux-en-Provence" for the delicacy of its little *fourmageon* are much prized, and fertile in milk and cheeses; and similarly the province of Brittany.'

The *fourmageons* were probably of ewes' milk. Brittany's 'much prized' cheeses have sunk without a trace. Angelots are explained in Chapters 1, 8 and 10. The Norman contenders for the name, Pont-l'Évêque, Livarot and Camembert, became widely known under their newer names in the eighteenth century. Brie de Meaux won European homage of the Congress of Vienna in 1815.

The advent of the railways in the nineteenth century made the transport of perishable cheeses easier, but also drew off much of the milk to towns, and eventually to the big *laiteries*. This started the reduction in farmhouse cheesemaking, exacerbated later by two world wars. In recent decades the milk-buying power of modern industrial creameries has almost extinguished farmhouse production of soft cows'-milk cheeses. This trend now shows signs of being arrested, but the revival of farmhouse cheesemaking has not yet reached the Brie region.

# FRENCH CHEESES AT THE END OF THE 1980s

France makes a million and a quarter tonnes of cheese every year, five times the total British production. About one-fifth of the French total is made of raw milk. Goats'-milk cheese accounts for over 42,000 tonnes, ewes'-milk cheese for over 22,000 tonnes and cheeses of mixed milk for an undefined quantity. The rest, aproaching 1,200,000 tonnes, is made of cows' milk.

## *Chèvres*

In his indispensable *Guide du Fromage*, Pierre Androuët told us that there are 'hundreds of goat cheeses' to look out for in full season. He and Ninette Lyon described about 150 of them in their 1978 *Guide Marabout des Fromages*, mainly old-established cheeses in traditional strongholds of the goat. The rest of those 'hundreds' are little-known, often delectable cheeses to be found in every corner of France. When I ask their makers what they call them, I am usually left none the wiser. *'Je ne suis que petit fermier, je n'ai pas le droit de donner un nom à mes fromages'*, was the answer of one young goat-keeper in the Lochois. He seemed intimidated by being squeezed between two famous sources of goat cheese, Sainte-Maure de Touraine and Valençay in Berry. Most of his *confrères* and *consœurs*, puzzled by the question, just exclaim: *'Mais c'est chèvre!'*, meaning, 'It's goat cheese, of course, what do you think it is?' To the artisan whose only concern is to keep the goats happy and make a good cheese, classification must seem a collector's fad.

Among well over 300 named and un-named chèvres in this book, I have detected at least something individually characteristic in over 270, without having tasted the cheeses of numerous further farms, listed undescribed for you to explore; let alone having tasted them all at every stage or season.

## *Brebis*

Forty-six ewes'-milk cheeses were named by Henri Viard, with Ninette Lyon's assistance, in his *Fromages de France*. Some of these are extinct, but new ones have appeared since. My estimate in 1988 is that there are over sixty brebis of distinctive character. Roquefort is dominant, with over 16,000 tonnes, all made of unpasteurised milk from a million dairy ewes.

## *Fromages de vaches*

Well over 300 French cows'-milk cheeses are named in the *Guide Marabout*, but I have found many local variations of older cheeses; and new industrial inventions must bring the total to well over 400 today. Most of the new industrial cheeses are in the class of the soft, white-mould-injected, thick-crusted, everlasting range. They vary in fat content from over 60 per cent *matières grasses* down to the very low-fat slimmers' cheeses, dullest of all this dull collection. There are some good newcomers among the dross, for example La Brouère and Gourmelin, both made from the milk of selected local farms.

## Mixed-milk cheeses

This category includes *mi-chèvre* (at least 50 per cent goats' milk), *lait de mélange* (at least 25 per cent goats' milk) and other *mixtes*. The latter include cows' milk, goats' milk and ewes' milk, the mixtures and proportions varying with the seasons and the type of milk available. These seem to me to be too variable and unpredictable to quantify with any certainty. Altogether there are probably well over forty mixed-milk cheeses of all kinds in regular seasonal production.

I started on my book with a list of over 500 French cheese-names, and memories of many anonymous tastings. I finished with over 750. There is one certain fact about French cheeses: practically speaking, they are innumerable. I should have liked to produce a more comprehensive book, but life is too short. In any case, no book can be a substitute for personal experience. I hope the gaps I have left will spur my readers on to fresh explorations and discoveries.

## FARMING AND DAIRYING FOR FINE CHEESE

The most exciting and reliable cheeses come from naturally fertilised soils and ancient, variegated pastures and meadows. Just as old vines give the richest wines, old pastures yield the richest milk. The best dairy breeds are those either long established in the *pays*, or coming from a similar *pays* elsewhere. The pastures may harbour from twenty to fifty species of plant. Variety is healthy for the pastures themselves, which are disease-resistant, and healthy and appetising for the cows. Their aromatic esters enrich good meat and good cheese.

Good pastures and good cows deserve good dairying. What matters in milking parlour, dairy, cheese-room and *cave* is what has traditionally been rated next to godliness: cleanliness. Cleanliness preserves untainted the local plant- and breed-characteristics of the raw milk, so that they can be passed on into the cheese to give it aroma, flavour and texture. Hygiene does not exclude the presence and natural exploitation of local moulds. They can be healthy, even prophylactic, and are best exemplified in the Auvergne cheese Saint-Nectaire. This cheese also provides proof of the destruction of character by pasteurisation of the milk. The importance of organic farming to the standard of product, and to the health of the beast, can be further understood by reading on to the next section, on modern problems and poisonous farming (unfortunately not an exaggerated term today). The tale of the Burgundy farm of l'Abbaye de la Pierre-Qui-Vire touches on most of the factors involved, and provides a warning and an object lesson.*

## Tradition and the Appellations d'Origine Contrôlées

In cheesemaking, the traditional ways of doing things still set the finest standards. The proof lies in the all-time peak in production and popularity of

---

*Readers wishing to go more deeply into basic farming and dairy facts will find them treated at length in my *Great British Cheese Book*, Macmillan, revised edn, 1988.

some of France's oldest cheeses, now protected by effective AsOC. Their virtues arose from centuries of experience, observation and understanding of local soils, pastures and breeds of cattle, and of the resulting milk. Franche-Comté and Savoie provide living evidence that this traditional foundation for success is not only still viable, but superior to any modern system of farming and manufacture devised by science and industry. It is also infinitely more suited today, economically and environmentally, to the well-being of Europe.

Fortunately, the wisdom of ages was codified in the village co-operative dairies, the *fruitières*, of Franche-Comté and Savoie. These receive the milk and make the cheese for the farmers who do not have the scope or vocation to make their own. The farmers are bound to follow the proven practices of pasture management and winter feed laid down, and to keep to the customary breed of cattle. These rules, and the *fruitières'* methods of making, were sensibly perpetuated in the national AsOC and the regulations for regional *appellations* ('*labels*').

The 1976 AOC rules for Comté prescribe that 'Milk shall come solely from cows of the breeds Montbéliarde or Pie-rouge de l'Est, nourished according to established practices, codified in the statutes of the *fruitières*, on pastures lying within the defined region of production, feed to exclude silage, or any other fermented product.' This means permanent pastures, organically managed, and hay from local sources.

Every year 40,000 tonnes of Comté are produced from raw milk. Over 80 per cent of this is still based on the modestly sized, immemorial *fruitières*, of which there are over 300. Comté's two off-shoots, the regionally protected Morbier and the winter Mont d'Or, Vacherin du Haut-Doubs, with its national AOC, have flourished and expanded production rapidly without compromising authenticity. They are made in the *fruitières* and a few farms.

The national AsOC for the production of Reblochon and Beaufort in Savoie have similar rules, their breeds being Abondance and Tarine respectively. Their combined production of over 8000 tonnes exceeds the total raw-milk cheese-production of Great Britain.

Even more astonishing is the annual output of nearly 80,000 tonnes of regionally protected Emmental Grand Cru de l'Est. Much of it comes from the raw milk of those same regional breeds which provide the milk for Comté.

So it is still possible to produce quantity without sacrificing quality, provided tradition is thoroughly respected, and given the force of law.

## *Flavour, aroma and pasteurisation*

The milk for all the protected cheeses mentioned so far must, by the rules, be used raw. There is even prohibition of any apparatus in the dairy which could raise the temperature of milk above 40°C.

It has long been known that pasteurisation kills over 99 per cent of the bacteria, including all the good, without destroying all the bad. Recent investigation of the bacterium *Listeria monocytogenes* seems to show that even if, as claimed by disciples of pasteurisation, only an insignificant amount of *Listeria* is left after the operation, the denaturing of the milk makes it more vulnerable to infection or re-infection by the bacterium than raw-milk cheese (see Appendix 1).

So far as the flavour and aroma of cheese is concerned, the most significant factor in pasteurisation is its destruction of the aromatic esters. These are the vital sources of aroma and flavour, conducted by plant oils into the body fat and mammary glands of the dairy beast, and thence by those fats into the milk and cheese. This is conclusively demonstrated by the case of, again, Saint-Nectaire. Every element in the nature of the milk, the making, and the *affinage* of Saint-Nectaire from farm and from *laiterie* is identical, except one: the *laiteries* pasteurise their milk. The consequent failure of aroma and flavour in *laiterie* cheeses has been detected by both expert and amateur consumers, quite unaware that the cheeses they were eating came from pasteurised milk, and differed in origin from the farm cheeses to which they had been accustomed. (See Chapter 7, pp. 214–17.)

An industrial chemist told me in 1988 that his company had 5000 different bacterial cultures taken from milk produced in different parts of Europe. This makes for better matching of starters with milk (though the best starter will always be the local culture made on the spot). If the milk it is to start has been pasteurised, however, the best culture in the world will do little for flavour and aroma of the subsequent cheese, because the greater part of these factors lies not in the bacteria, but in the aromatic esters, nullified by pasteurisation. Clean dairying and milk which can be used raw are best, not factory cultures.

## Modern problems in the cheese world

### *Poisonous farming and its effects*

The European Economic Community's rigid imposition of the Milk Quota since 1984 has been a curse to many a good farm cheesemaker; but it has served to expose the cost of subsidising quantity at the expense of quality and variety in the dairy world. It has also made us think harder about pollution of land and water, and of our own bodies, by harmful chemicals. The heavy use of chemical fertilisers and sprays, and the change from the milk of the traditional dairy breeds to the higher-yield, low-protein milk of Frisonne-Holstein has had the following consequences.

**a.** *Pollution of soil and water by nitrates*. In 1987, the EEC began legal action over pollution in Britain. A letter from the EEC Commission to the British government warned us that 'Over-use of nitrogen fertilizers has contaminated drinking supplies with nitrates, which it is believed may cause blue baby syndrome, and cancer in adults.'[*] The French Ministerial Seventh *Inventaire* on Water of 23 February 1988 reported that about 8 million people in rural France received water of doubtful quality. Nitrates of agricultural origin were 'notably' at fault. An earlier test showed that one-third of 2000 sources of animal drinking water were of bad quality.

[*] Quoted in *The Times*, 8 August 1987.

Nitrates were penetrating wells and water-table. This was worst where most fertilisers were used. Human effects included loss of appetite and excessive urination. Cattle and other beasts were affected by nitrites (salts from nitrates), which can fix on haemoglobin and cause asphyxia.

In January 1988 Britain's Anglian Water Authority pointed to the pollution of water by chemical fertilisers, the pollution of the environment by straw-burning, the erosion of the soil by intensive farming, and the pollution of the sea by sewage-dumping. The Authority suggested remedying all four by composting of straw and sludge, which not only help as fertilisers but also in the building up of the topsoil.*

**b.** *Pollution of food by poor cattle-feeds, insecticides and abuse of antibiotics.* As the Basque *curé-fromager* of Saint-Jean-Pied-de-Port said to me: 'The [French] Ministry of Agriculture pushed for the greatest production of milk, no matter what they fed the cows on. When your wife breast-feeds the baby, give her some poor wine to drink and it's the baby that gets the colic. It's the same with the cows. They are given any old thing to eat, so their milk has to be pasteurised.'

Use of concentrates instead of hay is bad for cheese flavour and can pass on Salmonella. This is found, for instance, in bone-meal and fish-meal not sufficiently heat-treated. Overcrowding of cattle in intensive farming spreads the Salmonella.

Silage has become more fashionable in France since the early 1970s. It has long been ruled out in the best cheese farms and *fruitières* because of flavour-taint. *Listeria* reports give a health reason for avoiding it (see Appendix 1).

Beyond the water pollution already referred to, chemical residues from fertilisers and sprays can directly affect the health of worker and beast on the farm, can poison pastures and leave traces in food. Dr Leon Burmester, of the University of Iowa School of Preventive Medicine, has found a clear relationship between exposure to pesticides and cancers, including leukaemia, non-Hodgkins Lymphoma, and multiple Myeloma (although farmers in general have a lower rate of cancer because they smoke less than other groups). The United States Department of Agriculture figures show that crop losses to pests grew by over 15 per cent between 1945 and 1984, despite the enormous use of pesticides. Dozens of pest species developed immunity.

On 22 May 1988 the *Daily Telegraph* quoted a House of Commons Select Committee on Agriculture Report: 'Agrochemicals ... neurotoxins, many biocides (pesticides, herbicides, fungicides) are highly poisonous to the brain and nervous system.'

Excessive use of antibiotics, including their use as prophylactics, is self-defeating. It produces a high proportion of antibiotic resistance in cattle, which may be passed on to human beings. Antibiotic residues in milk can interfere with its coagulation.

**c.** *Surplus milk production.* Fertilisers and the use of Frisonne-Holstein dairy cattle have produced an unsaleable surplus of milk, much of it of too

---

*The Times, 18 November 1988.

low a quality to make good cheese. The EEC has dealt with this by the clumsy Milk Quota. This ordered that production be cut across the board, so that the clean, organic farm producing good milk, and sought-after raw-milk cheese, was cut as severely as the farm producing low-grade milk by polluting chemical methods.

## Reduction of farm and artisan cheesemaking

The farmer is prevented from expanding his cheese production because the milk supply for his cheese must come from his own farm and is reduced by the Milk Quota. The industrial cheesemakers are not affected by the Quota. They have always been able to increase their milk supply. They buy up artisan dairies which have milk contracts with dairy farms. They then close each artisan enterprise, kill its cheese, and send the milk to their own factories. This process has cost France old treasures such as Excelsior, Le Magnum, Fromage de Monsieur Fromage, and the last *artisanal* Brie de Montereau. Most of the industrially produced cheese which has taken their place consists of variations in shape and size on one theme: soft, white-coated, bland and characterless products, designed to last up to two months in supermarket cold-counters.

## Loss of traditional dairy breeds

Breeds producing milk responsible for the character of many local and regional cheeses are being allowed to die out. The Picarde in Brie, the Flamande in the North, and the Ferrandaise in Auvergne have almost disappeared. The vital Salers of Auvergne, still featured in publicity as a source of the character of Auvergnat cheese, is fast going the same way. The Vosgienne of Alsace and Lorraine has seriously diminished, although again it is credited with providing the virtue in Munster. Even the great Normande dropped from 28 per cent of the French dairy herd in 1970 to under 14 per cent thirteen years later. This caused loss of texture and richness in the cheeses of Normandy and Brie (Chapters 1 and 10 have more on this subject).

## Lower cheese standards

A French government decree of 26 October 1953 stipulated: 'The denomination "cheese", accompanied or not by a qualification or a *nom de fantasie* [invented name], is reserved for the product, fermented or not, of coagulation of milk, cream, skimmed milk, or a mixture of them, followed by *égouttage* [draining of the curd].' This decree laid down the minimum dry matter in weight of cheese at 23 per cent (plus 77 per cent water). Certain *fromage frais* were allowed to state on the label 'more than 85 per cent water'. Analyses have shown that this is now a common level, which often reaches nearly 90 per cent.

The 1953 law excludes methods which separate the solids from the milk by centrifugal force or ultra-filtration (use of a very fine-membrane filter) because such methods are not followed by the obligatory *égouttage*. This explains loss of consistency in some modern 'cheese', as for example Le

Pavé d'Affinois. Much cheese texture is owed to the nature and timing of *égouttage*. According to *Que Choisir?* (equivalent to Britain's *Which?* magazine)*, other so-called 'cheeses' are now being made by methods outside the legal definition. These are coyly sold as *specialités fromagères*. *Que Choisir?* mentions Saint-Morêt, Crème des Près and Chanteneige, which have a shelf-life of two months although they are termed *fromages frais*.

There are other soft white *croûte-fleurie* cheeses with a month or more of shelf-life, explained in the words of Bongrain, the makers of Petit Délice de France: 'It is a *stabilised* cheese which means that it will stay evenly mild and creamy during its long shelf-life of thirty-seven days. What is a stabilised cheese? ... It does not ripen from the outside towards the centre ... as with Brie or Camembert, but a natural lactic ferment spread into the curd allows a much more rapid ripening and gives a mild flavour with a soft, homogeneous texture which will not run.'

Such convenience foods cannot be termed natural, and must be considered as tending at least halfway towards processed cheese. Their crusts are too white and too thick, formed by mould-injection, instead of the natural acquisition of the mould from spores in the air. The crust keeps down acidity, adding to the interior blandness of the cheese. This has proved to be the type of cheese most vulnerable to *Listeria monocytogenes* (see Appendix 1). It can turn ammoniac when taken in and out of refrigeration.

The industrial producers would have you believe that traditional cheese has a very brief period of proper ripeness and a long period of being too smelly and too strong. In fact, a clean, well-made, fat, traditional soft cheese, kept at moderate temperature, develops gently as it swells towards its peak, and subsides very gradually. Even when under-ripe, it is refreshing, not dull, and it is good eating for seven to ten days for general tastes, with a further week of pleasure for stronger palates. Many soft and semi-soft traditional cheeses have subtle, not strong flavours, and textures which melt in the mouth, unattainable by the mass-produced factory cheeses.

Mechanised cheesemaking has caused loss of control by the cheesemaker. The good traditional cheesemaker sees what is going on in his open vat, tests the curd with his hand, measures acidity when necessary, and adjusts his timing of operations accordingly. Nature is allowed to take its course, and have its time, varying with the daily differences of pasture and weather.

The industrial cheesemaker works by blind navigation and fixed timing. He cannot hesitate or adjust to exceptional conditions. Modern New Zealand dairies have found whole batches of cheese faulty because of this. What is more, bulk tanking of milk, and production in a continuous stream, make it impossible to pin faults on a particular source of milk.

The character of some admirable and very individual blues has been almost lost in recent years. Pasteurisation of the milk was the first mistake. This disposed of local flavour not attributable to blueing. It also inhibited the blueing itself, which has led to deleterious artificial remedial practices.

*No. 207, June 1985

The next mistake was the abandonment of artisan methods by too many makers. This changed the traditional consistency of the cheese.

The third mistake was the acceptance of standardised factory *Penicillium roquefortii*, which tends to be used for any blue cheese. Formerly, cheeses were distinguished by the natural mould they acquired from the *caves* in which they were matured. Even Bleu de Gex and Septmoncel have succumbed to the fashion. Their dose of *P. roquefortii* is small, but one of the reasons for putting it there is to combat or pre-empt other moulds. It must therefore be supplanting the native mould to which old farmhouse cheesemakers attributed the cheeses' blueing. (See Chapters 11 and 13.)

The fourth mistake concerns the crusts. With the honourable exception of a few artisan-made cheeses, blues that should be hard-crusted are no longer exposed to local influences during the early period of ripening. The crusts of the *fourmes*, when allowed to develop, are frequently encased in foil. This destroys their natural tough crispness and changes the consistency of the interior from firmly fresh to soggy. Some modern *fourmes* have the consistency of the new soft blues of the Bresse region, and a flavour far removed from their ancestors' inimitable nuttiness.

We have admired the *appellations* of Franche-Comté and Savoie for their perpetuation of traditional farming and cheesemaking. Unfortunately, fifteen of the twenty-seven AsOC enacted up to 1988 condone pasteurisation or *thermisation*, obviously as a sop to industrial cheesemakers. The AsOC for chèvres allow not only pasteurisation but even the use of frozen milk or curd, or powdered milk, when fresh goats' milk is unavailable from December to March. The resulting cheese tends to be granular in texture, poor in flavour, and of short keeping-quality. It is liable to collapse into unpleasantness after limited exposure to normal temperatures, like any other frozen food.

The AsOC have failed to protect traditional breeds of cattle in the rules for Saint-Nectaire and other Auvergne cheeses, harming the Salers breed. In Brie and Normandy the Normandes and Picardes have not been specified, and the use of milk from Frisonnes has undoubtedly contributed to the loss of the traditional rich texture of these cheeses. The Roquefort AOC has good points, but does not deal effectively with the conditions of *affinage*. Very low-temperature storage undoubtedly spoils the character of many of the cheeses (see Chapter 6).

The use of calcium chloride (*chlorure de calcium*) is permitted at least in Maroilles. This serves to overcome difficulties in coagulation and *égouttage*, which cause excess moisture in curd. It is not a welcome additive in cheese, being in fact salts of hydrochloric acid.

## Erosion of standards through EEC policy

The EEC condoned excessive production of often indifferent milk by its purchase at guaranteed prices and storage at our cost of unsaleable dairy products, so encouraging factory farming. Small farms converting all their own high-grade milk into fine cheese not only gained nothing, but saw the unwanted factory cheeses being sold at give-away prices.

When the EEC tried to remedy this costly farce in 1984, instead of working to eliminate low-grade milk it decided to cut the good with the bad. This reduced the already inadequate amount of true farm cheese available (and made some herds uneconomic), while not restricting the milk available to cheesemakers buying milk from other producers.

The EEC is further undermining standards by attacking those enshrined in existing national laws and international treaties. In a judgment of 22 September 1988 the European Court in Luxembourg ruled that France could no longer exclude imports of substandard German 'Edam' of 34.3 per cent *matières grasses* in conformity with the Stresa Convention,* although 40 per cent *matières grasses* was the standard laid down there, and the German cheese was also in conflict with the rules of the Codex Alimentarius established by the UN Food and Agriculture and World Health Organizations.

The Court thus put Article 30 of the EEC Treaty not only above French law, but above the binding terms of earlier international agreements, and above the rules of guidance for consumer protection of the United Nations Organization.

This is ominous evidence of the arrogance and ignorance in dairy and consumer interests of the Brussels bureaucracy. This is also shown in the EEC's ill-directed panic reaction to the Listeriosis problem. Although the guilty bacteria (*Listeria monocytogenes*, see Appendix 1) have been firmly identified only in heat-treated cheese (in all but two cases fully pasteurised, and predominantly of largest scale industrial origin), resulting EEC measures threaten to price farm and artisan cheesemaking out of existence. The venerated farm and dairy of the Abbaye d'Entrammes has been forced to close, although its cheese has been impeccable so far as I know (see Chapter 1, p. 44). Pierre Androuët came to the conclusion in October 1988 that all small-scale cheesemaking was at risk.

## Listeriosis†

The sad irony is that the panic stemmed from the serious incidence of Listeriosis in Switzerland related to contaminated *pasteurised* Vacherin; whereas 500 international tests on the *un*pasteurised French Vacherin (they are made in the same Mont d'Or region, separated only by the frontier) proved clear of infection. Despite the evidence that soft pasteurised factory cheeses are vulnerable (no raw-milk cheese had been scientifically indicted up to November 1988), there continues to be a drive to pasteurise and a misguided encouragement to the trade and the consumer to go for pasteurised cheese.

Research has failed to trace the time and source of infection in recent European cases. Despite earlier Scandinavian research placing blame on imperfectly made or protected silage for dairy and meat cases, Dr

---

*The convention was signed in Rome on 9 May 1952 by Austria, Denmark, France, Holland, Italy, Norway, Sweden and Switzerland. Britain had no protected cheese then (the law came to Stilton's support years later). French cheeses were listed in this order: Roquefort, Camembert, Brie, Saint-Paulin and Gruyère (covering Swiss and French usages). French protection for Edam and Gouda (both Dutch, of course) is mentioned in this book.
† See also Appendix 1.

McLauchlin at Colindale writes: '... the fact that many wild animals and birds also contain *L. monocytogenes* suggests that this has little to do with silage'.* Earlier, Scandinavian research stressed the relevance of soil contamination, which explains infection of rabbits and birds, and the likelihood of silage as a conductor between soil and farm cattle (another scientist working on Listeriosis volunteered to me that plastic covering of silage made it vulnerable to penetration and infestation).

It would be of interest to subject traditionally made raw-milk soft cheeses and their industrial nominal counterparts to equal exposure in laboratory conditions to *L. monocytogenes*, and examine them periodically over a month for differences in rate and degree of contamination. The industrial cheeses might be left for the full term of their advertised shelf-life (sometimes up to seventy days).

## Remedies

European consumer organisations and national parliaments, particularly those in Westminster and Paris, have a duty to examine and call in question the disastrous powers of the EEC under Article 30. These tend to encourage deception and piracy, and, unless curtailed, will demolish existing laws protecting cheese-names and standards, instead of increasing and strengthening them in the desirable ways enlarged on in the following pages.

This is not just my private opinion. 'In fact, the alarm must be sounded for artisan and farm cheeses. I fear that the Community laws are in the process of exterminating them; and now we have to expect in 1992 the abolition of Appellations d'Origine Contrôlées, which will simplify matters for counterfeiters everywhere. Terms defining origin, type of milk, breed of cattle, etc., are on their way to being outlawed.' These words were written to me in October 1988 by Pierre Androuët, whose knowledge, expertise and vocation have known no equal in the history of French cheese. I hope they will move our French and British legislators into a renewed Entente Cordiale, working to arrest the rot; and into working with other signatories for incorporation of the Stresa Convention into Community law, and its broadening in the interests of all Europe.

The most urgent task is the amendment of EEC Article 30 to reinstate national powers to guard cheese-names and standards, and the channelling then of EEC energies towards helping and protecting farm cheesemakers and their raw-milk products instead of harassing them. Reform needs to begin literally at the grassroots. The EEC's concern for pollution and excess production should lead to encouragement of a return to traditional, organic farming methods, and to the use of the more interesting traditional breeds of cattle. Where multi-species pastures have been lost, they should be revived. Nitrogen-fixing clovers and other legumes make nitrogen fertilisers redundant. Milk pricing should acknowledge the virtues not only of clean, high-protein milk, but of the special dairy breeds, in the cause of good

*See p. 524. Cleaning up of silage practices in Scandinavia has been reported as having eliminated Listeriosis there.

cheesemaking. (This is a view put to me unsolicited by experts working for Fromageries des Chaumes, the great industrial concern.) National and regional AsOC, of which more are needed, should follow the example of the best existing ones, for example those in Franche-Comté and Savoie. Like those, they should prescribe the breeds of cow, and insist on traditional forms of nourishment and pasture management. Silage, cattle cake and roots should be excluded for reasons of flavour as well as health.

Some large dairy firms already see it in their interest to impose such a regime on dairy farms under contract to them. The family firm of Girod in the Haute-Savoie, who have made the unpasteurised Beaumont since 1881, provide an example.

Natural ripening of milk and the use of rennet from the appropriate animal (calf, kid or lamb) should be encouraged. Where starters are customary, they should be cultivated from local milk, preferably from the farm itself for farm cheese. The re-establishment of raw-milk cheese and natural mould crusts should be encouraged generally, and especially in AOC rules. These should also lay down strictly traditional methods of making, and eliminate existing compromises with industrial interests. Condonation of pasteurisation or other heat treatment should cease. So should the use of frozen curd or milk or powdered milk for winter chèvres. Brie de Meaux is an example of an AOC cheese rendered unrecognisable by bending of the rules for treatment of curd, and by the use of industrial surface moulds.

Salting of AOC cheeses should be much more rigorously controlled: over-salting is common, even when 'lightly salted' is the rule on paper.

Threatened breeds of dairy cattle should be specified in AsOC and regional labels. They include the following: Aubrac for Laguiole; Salers for Cantal, Salers and Saint-Nectaire; Villard-de-Lans in the Vercors for Bleu de Sassenage, not yet protected by an AOC; Ferrandaise at least for Fourmes de Rochefort-Montagne (still made exclusively from Ferrandaise milk in 1969).

The Flamande should be revived and specified in the AOC for Maroilles. One Maroilles farm does keep them, and I am told that they are milked for the making of that other old northern classic, Bergues.

The Normande should obviously be prescribed for Camembert, Livarot and Pont-l'Évêque. Brie, if it cannot revive its native race, should officially adopt the Normande and Picarde (both long used there) for Brie de Meaux, Brie de Melun and any future AsOC in the region.

The Montbéliarde is used in Burgundy at the Abbaye de Cîteaux, and the Brune des Alpes at the Abbaye de la Pierre-Qui-Vire. At over 500 metres' altitude the Brune des Alpes proved itself in competition with the Frisonne in toughness, and in yield, as the story of the *abbaye*'s farm in Chapter 11 shows. As the old *Grande Blanche* Burgundy dairy breed has virtually disappeared, these two immigrants should be considered alongside La Tachetée de l'Est' (Simmental crossing of the old *Grande Blanche* created this breed) if an AOC is planned for Époisses (which would benefit from protection against factory counterfeits).

Other breeds mentioned to me by the staff of Chaumes as worthy of revival are La Bazace, or Bazadoise, in the Bordeaux region; the Albret in the

Landes; La Blonde des Pyrenées; and La Rodez in Rouergue and southern Languedoc.

These changes for the better cannot happen by decree overnight. A transitional period of a few years is needed for revival of breeds, and for farms to go over to this gradually and change completely to organic management of pastures and meadows.

If AsOC are extended, care should be taken to avoid over-standardisation causing loss of a rich variety of local tradition. This occurred with Crottin de Chavignol, where young cheeses should be allowed once more to carry local names such as Le Sancerrois.

Some of the great dairy companies have shown commendable interest in farming and cattle breeding and in the making of raw-milk cheese. They might consider a further suggestion: investing money in cattle breeding and cheesemaking on individual farms, while there are still representatives of the breed alive, and cheesemakers with the authentic experience. Brie de Meaux, Brie de Melun and Brie de Montereau would be near the top of my list for rescue.

With the surge in demand for cheese of high quality made of raw milk from organic sources, such a revival could enable these companies to market farmhouse cheeses as stars on their lists. From being regarded by gourmets as the villains of the cheese world, they could become its heroes.

In over forty years of travel in France as a cheese-lover, thirty-five of them also as a cheese-merchant, I have found my views shared by all who have a true vocation in the world of dairy farming and cheese. With their love and understanding of the land and the animals which provide the milk for their cheeses, the makers of farmhouse cheese are the best guardians and restorers of the natural unpolluted countryside. Their products offer the richness and limitless variety of unspoilt local and seasonal flavour and aroma. They raise cheese above the level of an all-year-round, standardised, utilitarian factory food. Their cheese is a gourmet's heaven of ever-beckoning delights. May this book lead you on to them.

Fontvieille<br>January, 1989

MANCHE
Guernsey
Jersey
Belle Île
HAUTE-NORMANDIE
SEINE-MARITIME
PICARDIE
OISE
AMIENS
Dieppe
Fécamp
LE HAVRE
Yvetot
Neufchâtel-en-Bray
Forges-les-Eaux
Buchy
ROUEN
Gournay-en-Bray
Gisors
Seine
Honfleur
Deauville
Trouville
Pont-Audemer
Pont-l'Évêque
Beuvron-en-Auge
Lieurey
Elbeuf
Cabourg
Troarn
CAEN
Bayeux
Isigny
Carentan
Cherbourg
Valognes
Bricquebec
Ste-Mère-Église
MANCHE
Coutances
St-Lô
Tessy
Villedieu-les-Poêles
Le-Bény-Bocage
Vire
CALVADOS
St-Pierre-s-D
Livarot
Lisieux
Orbec
EURE
Evreux
Clécy
Falaise
Vimoutiers
BASSE-NORMANDIE
ÎLE-DE-FRANCE
VAL D'OISE
PARIS
YVELINES
Sourdeval
Avranches
Flers
Putanges
Écouche
ORNE
L'Aigle
Thymerais
Le Perche
Domfront
La Ferté-Macé
Bagnoles-de-l'Orne
Louvigné-du-Désert
Fougères
Javron
Mayenne
Alençon
EURE-ET-LOIR
Chartres
Beauce
St-Malo
Dinan
Perros-Guirec
Lannion
Ploudalmézeau
BREST
Guingamp
St-Brieuc
FINISTÈRE
CÔTES-DU-NORD
Gouarec
Caulnes
Montauban
RENNES
Quimper
Pontivy
Rohan
MORBIHAN
Josselin
Ploërmel
ILLE-ET-VILAINE
Janzé
MAYENNE
MAINE
Laval
LE MANS
SARTHE
La Ferté-Bernard
Montmirail
Connerré
Lorient
Ste-Anne d'Auray
Auray
Vannes
BRETAGNE
Château-Gontier
Châteaubriant
La Flèche
ORLÉANAIS
LOIR-ET-CHER
ORLÉANS
ANJOU
ANGERS
INDRE-ET-LOIRE
TOURS
TOURAINE
LOIRE-ATLANTIQUE
La Baule
St-Nazaire
NANTES
Loire
MAINE-ET-LOIRE
Vienne
VENDÉE
Sarthe
Mayenne
N1
N28
N29
N15
N14
N13
A13-E05
N12
N26
N175
N176
N137
N164
N165
N12-E50
N24
N65
N23
A11-E50
A81-E50
A11
N138
D963
N10
A10-E05
N20
N152
A71
A11-E05
N76
N147
N160

# Normandy, Maine and Brittany

## Normandie

North-west France has so long been a battlefield for invaders by land and sea that the permanence of the boundaries of the province we know as Normandy is astonishing. They have remained virtually unchanged from the fourth century AD, when the Emperor Gratian defined them.

The Romans had been there since 56 BC, when they found Iberians and Ligurians to the west and Celts and Belges to the east. Christianity came to these peoples in the third century, and the conquering Franks encouraged monastic enterprise among them in the seventh and eighth centuries (Mont-Saint-Michel dates from AD 709). Standards of agriculture and dairy are likely to have risen with the leadership of the *abbayes*, but monastic life and farming suffered in the ninth century when the destructive Normands (mainly Norsemen, with some Danes) started to swarm up the river estuaries. By 886 Paris was under siege. In 911 Charles III le Simple, retaining suzerain rights, conceded present-day Normandy to the Normands' leader, Rollon, from the River Epte in the east to Brittany in the west (from Seine-Maritime to Manche, in modern departmental terms). By intermarriage with and support from the reigning house of Capet, the ducs of Normandy achieved suzerainty over Le Vexin français and Pontoise in the east, and over Brittany. In 1066 Guillaume conquered England, asserting over Harold the right of succession to the throne conceded by Edward the Confessor. The Queen of England still reigns as duchesse de Normandie in the Channel Islands.

Despite disputes over succession, Henry I, Henry II and Richard Cœur de Lion were accepted in the duché, but when King John abducted Isabelle d'Angoulême he was condemned to forfeit his French lands and gained his title John Lackland (Jean-sans-terre). By 1204 his lands were in the hands of the French King Philippe Auguste. In the next century there were revolts against the French, pacified by restoration of Norman rights in 1315. Within fifty years, however, the see-saw struggle of the Hundred Years' War had started. Normandy changed rulers several times and was not permanently part of France until 1450. Until the seventeenth century the feudal and municipal privileges granted as *ducs* by the English kings were recognised; but Normandy suffered from being cut off from the English wool trade and from the wines of Poitou and Guyenne, still not parts of France. The latter deprivation benefited Normandy in the long run by encouraging her reliance on cider, which every traveller should try as accompaniment to her fish and her cheeses.

## Basse-Normandie
### MANCHE – CALVADOS – ORNE

When we travelled into Normandy in 1985, we made for the Pays d'Auge, in the heart of Norman dairy country, to see for ourselves what survived of its centuries-old dairy tradition. The countryside is still a delight to the eye, and proof that good dairy farming is the best way of conserving the landscape. Here there is a cosy intimacy and quiet liveliness, in contrast to the eye-and-heart-killing desert created by factory farming. The red-brown and white Normandes cows, with their endearingly irregular markings, close-graze small multi-species pastures enclosed by hedges and trees. Often accompanied by a few sheep and assorted fowl, they also explore the orchards, which provide not only more shelter for them, but also the cider that goes so perfectly with the cheeses in which their milk will end up. Farms and farm buildings are still predominantly of close vertical timber with infillings of lathe or wattle and daub, their colours matching the cows. The picturesque frailty of these buildings descends to sadness when they are neglected or patched up with corrugated iron, but this is the exception in the apparently flourishing Pays d'Auge, compared with the less fortunate fringes of Normandy.

By the eleventh century the Augelot or Angelon cheeses, products of the ancient Pays d'Auge, had taken shape, probably with monastic guidance. Later the name of a coin, *l'angelot*, became attached to them; it pictured a young angel defeating a dragon (see also Chapter 8). The earliest mention of Angelot as a cheese occurs in the first part of *Le Roman de la Rose* by Guillaume de Lorris, published about 1236. Augelots appear in 1560 and 1588 publications, in the latter *'bons fromages qu'on appelle "Augelots"'*.[*] Robert Courtine thinks Augelots may have preceded Angelots.

Such were the roots (possibly already branching off into variations) of Pont-l'Évêque and Livarot. It is surprising in a dairy *pays* of such stable boundaries that cheese records should be so scanty. For centuries only Augelot and Angelot were mentioned, still a source of dispute between some Brie, Camembert, Pont-l'Évêque and Livarot supporters. Robert Courtine considers Livarot to be one of the most ancient of cheeses. The officially sponsored booklet *Les fromages d'appellation d'origine* (ANAOF/Nathan, 1984) says that Pont-l'Évêque was originally called Angelon, before its thirteenth-century mention as Angelot. But the earliest recorded use of its present name came in the seventeenth century alongside Angelot by an

---

[*] Augelot is mentioned in *De re Cibaria* by La Bruyère-Champier, 1560, and *Recherches et Antiquités de la Province de Neustric* by Charles de Bougueville, 1588.

Abbot of Maroilles, which implies that they were not the same cheese, a difference suggested also by their respective shapes (see Chapter 8). Pierre Androuët believes that Pont-l'Évêque was originally round, but changed its shape, while Livarot stayed round. The idea that these two cheeses may originally have been alike comes up against the view held by some Pont-l'Évêque makers (notably Monsieur Touzé, see below) that their cheese was traditionally a brushed-crust cheese and that the washing of its crust was adopted only within the last century or so.

The first mention of Livarot by its present name known to me was by Pommeren de la Bretesche, Intendant, reporting in 1693 that Livarot was current on the Paris market. The next reference comes in the 1708 publication *Dictionnaire Universel Géographique et Historique*. The author, Thomas Corneille, was born in Rouen, much younger brother of the illustrious dramatic poet Pierre, and himself a respected dramatist and journalist. He wrote that excellent cheeses from Camembert and Livarot were on sale in Vimoutiers at its Monday market (which still flourishes). Thomas Corneille was eighty-three at this time and could well have known these cheeses for many years. Monsieur de Lamartinière's *Dictionnaire* of 1741 confirmed Corneille's information. It was still true in 1950.

## CAMEMBERT

The Livarot of 1708 was probably like today's; but we know that at least some of the Camemberts being made as late as the 1790s were only 5 centimetres in diameter, half their present size, and rather stodgy compared with Brie. It was in that disturbed decade that the excesses of the Revolutionary Terror occasioned the revolution in Camembert's cheese which produced its modern shape and internal texture. The crust retained the traditional blue coat given by the spores of the indigenous mould present in the *hâloirs* and *caves* of Basse-Normandie.

On the evening of 23 August 1792 seven priests died in the Terror at Meaux. A young colleague of theirs, the Abbé Gobert, unwilling to compromise his beliefs, was advised by his bishop to escape to England. He went on his way with an introduction to the bishop's cousin, *née* Marie Fontaine, who had been born in Roiville in 1761, and had worked there, or in the nearby village of Camembert, all her life. She was now married to a farmer called Harel near Vimoutiers.

Marie received the young priest and undertook to shelter him until the political atmosphere had calmed down. In return, the *abbé* watched her making cheese, his interest enlivened by his having observed parishioners making Brie de Meaux. Gobert thought the little Harel cheeses rather under-drained, and sad in their yellow-brown aspect, compared with his native Brie. Marie was receptive and tried the Brie method as he remembered it: patience with the curd, and leaving it unbroken until it went into the mould (draining the moulds on a slight slope may have come in then too). Marie's new, more succulent cheese went well on the market at Vimoutiers, and she decided to have bigger moulds made, 11 centimetres in diameter, thus inaugurating the modern size of Camembert. I have read that when Napoleon first met the cheese in Normandy he kissed the waitress who served it to him.

The Harel's daughter, also called Marie, learned the art of cheesemaking from her mother, and married Thomas Paynel of Champosoult, a parish adjoining Camembert and Roiville. They were very active and must, I believe, have made cheese, or had it made for them, on a farm in the parish of Camembert itself (perhaps one belonging to the Harel family). When Napoleon III opened the Paris–Granville railway in 1863, Marie Paynel presented him with one of her cheeses. Like any true cheese-lover, he asked where it came from. 'Camembert' was her answer, and 'Camembert it shall be called' was his response, together with the appointment of her son Victor as *fournisseur* to the Imperial Court. I do not think Marie Paynel would have presented a cheese unless it were made on her own or one of her own farms. (Another version of the story has the venue of the exchange as the Paris Exposition Universelle of 1855, the year her mother, Marie Harel, died.)

Railways eased the carriage of cheese to the Paris market, but also eased competition from imitators far away and encouraged the setting up of larger *fromageries*. Of the earliest factories for Camembert, one was founded by a goddaughter of Thomas Paynel in 1870, another by Monsieur Auguste Lepetit in 1872. (This Lepetit dairy at Cléville, closed in 1984, comes into the history of another cheese, Le Fromage de Monsieur Fromage: see p. 10 The Lepetit family, rich in medals for past Camemberts, is still making *lait cru* cheeses at Bretteville-sur-Dives and at another old stronghold of theirs, Saint-Maclou.) The factories drew much of their milk from farms which had previously made their own cheese, as did the urban *laiteries* now able to receive by train liquid milk fresh enough to sell to townspeople, and to hotels for the growing summer tourist trade. It is notable that now women were not only cheesemakers on the farm, where such a duty had long been assumed or imposed by marriage contracts, but until the 1950s also worked as *maîtres fromagers* of the growing number of Camembert factories.

The invention in 1880, probably by Auguste Lepetit, of the chipboard cheese-box, and its manufacture by an engineer called Ridel, further expanded the range of the market. Boxed cheeses were far more secure against rough handling and fly damage than the naked cheeses exposed on beds of straw in the traditional slatted wooden trays (though, given today's temperature-controlled vehicles, this is how I should prefer to receive them, their crust development undisturbed by wrapping and restricted air).

In 1910 another dramatic development literally changed the face of Camembert, and inevitably altered its external aroma and internal flavour. *Penicillium candidum* was introduced by Monsieur Roger Lepetit from the Pays de Bray in Haute-Normandie to replace the traditional natural surface blue (*penicillium glaucum*) of Camembert and Angelot. I am not quite old enough to have known them both, so I should like to see a batch of Camemberts *lait cru* from the same vat divided for *affinage*, half of them subjected to modern *hâloir* and *cave*, the other half to *affinage* in old premises where the original mould still flourishes. My guess is that the old method would produce a novelty on the modern market so exciting that *affineurs* would find both methods worth presenting. What is more, it would not be easy for modern factories to imitate, so it could give an extra boost to the honest *lait cru* trade.

Two world wars and too much big business nearly brought Camembert to its grave, except in name; and this name had been brought into contempt by failure to protect it against the masses of pasteurised factory distortions of the formula, perpetrated over almost all of France and abroad. Only among knowledgeable gourmets did Camembert still stand for the *lait cru* cheese of the Pays d'Auge. In 1981 in the market at Rouen I heard from a relative of his that the last Camembert farmer in the Auge had retired from making his cheese at Saint-Germain-de-Montgommery, just north of Vimoutiers. (His honoured name was Daniel Courtonne, and he came of a deep-rooted Norman family: within 20 kilometres of his farm are villages called Courtonne-la-Meudrac and Courtonne-les-Deux-Églises.) The Appellation Nationale d'Origine Contrôlée for Camembert de Normandie came into effect only two years later.

On our journey through the Pays d'Auge, we paused in Vimoutiers to pay our respects to Madame Harel. Her memorial there is owed to American respect and generosity: first that of Dr Joe Knirim, who cured stomach patients in the 1920s by prescribing doses of Camembert and Pilsner. Grateful to the inaugurator of modern Camembert for his success, he arrived at the *mairie* in Vimoutiers in 1928 with a bunch of flowers to put on her grave, only to find that no one could trace it. The statue commissioned at his expense from Eugène L'Hoëst to remedy the lack of commemoration was badly damaged in a 1944 bombardment, and moved to a nearby garden (where a notice gives a different date of birth for Marie Harel: 1781). A new American initiative paid for its replacement after the war with contributions from 400 workers at Van Wert's cheese factory in Ohio, the biggest American source of cheese in Camembert style.

Five or six kilometres south of Vimoutiers, along the little valley of the River Viette on the road to Trun, is a crossroads where the turn to the right leads over a bridge to the village of Camembert. In the south-west angle of the crossing is another memorial to 'Mme Harel née Marie Fontaine 1761–18 – qui inventa le Camembert'; an obelisk unveiled on 20 April 1925 by the then Maire de Camembert and Dr Dentu, Sénateur and Maire de Vimoutiers. If the *mairie* of Vimoutiers had been less ignorant or negligent in 1928, Dr Knirim could have been escorted with his flowers to this monument, and would have been saved the expense of setting up his statue in Vimoutiers. The municipality did not deserve it, but the charm of the figure on Dr Knirim's newer monument and its post-war replacement save us from regretting the failings of municipal bureaucracy.

About 2 kilometres further south of the crossroads, near a fork in the road, we found Monsieur Robert Durand's farm, La Héronnière, of picturesque traditional construction and in family occupation since 1937. Camembert-making had been resumed there in March 1981. So farmhouse Camembert had not died out when Daniel Courtonne gave up that year a few miles away. It continued here and, as we were soon to see, at La Ferme du Tourdouet next door, where the Delorme family had stopped selling their milk to a *laiterie* and taken up Camembert-making in the same year.

At La Héronnière, in addition to the ducks and geese in the farmyard, there were seven Normandes and twenty-one Frisonnes-Holsteins producing enough milk to make 1000 Camemberts a week in 1985. They were being sold *affinés* on the farm and to shops, or *demi-affinés* to one or two *fromagers–affineurs*. The intention was to expand the herd to forty, yielding enough milk for 200 cheeses a day. Meanwhile, cheese was made only every other day. We were given one of the smaller cheeses, of excellent Camembert aroma and flavour, still succulent, yet not too runny even after a week's travel. Being extremely sensitive to salt and having so much enjoyed this cheese, I was astonished that a Durand cheese (apparently straight from the farm) had been found bitter and over-salt by a Gault Millau panel in February 1986. From Christian Millau's own comment, this must have been a completely immature cheese with a fine *pâte*, as the panel agreed, yet already adorned with red mould. Christian Millau wondered what a good *affinage* might have done for it, and I think my words above give the answer.

At the neighbouring Ferme du Tourdouet we were greeted by assorted ducks, happy pigs, and an array of Camemberts at the *hâloir* stage taking advantage of a fine March day to spend a few hours healthily in the fresh air. They were coated in a thick white forest of mould. The herd, in the background, was twenty-four strong in milkers, and Monsieur Michel Delorme made cheese every day.

We bought a Delorme Camembert to take on our journey south. When we cut into it three days later its crust and texture were perfect and its flavour rich: a little on the salt side for my palate, but most enjoyable. We arrived at our Provençal cottage in Fontvieille after ten days on the road and it still had that moist, rich, clotted consistency, now gold right through, which is the mark and strength of the old farmhouse Brie we no longer see. This is something cheesemakers should seek after. Not only is it far more interesting and satisfying than the customary more liquefactious *pâte* of today, but the period over which it is agreeable to eat it is far less ephemeral, as our experience showed. Ten days after we bought it, our cheese was enthusiastically demolished over two or three days by a Camembert addict of more mature years than mine.

Christian Millau's view is that Camembert is not ready to eat until all trace of white at the centre has disappeared. This is a matter of taste. One of the features of the best traditionally made *lait cru* Brie and Camembert is that even the young, white *pâte* is never 'chalky' in the sense that second-rate cheese is when young. It always has a certain moisture, which naturally increases as the outer part ripens and closes in on the centre. To my taste, the most delicious stage of the cheese is when there is still a trace of that white at its heart in a moist but not melted state. This is called *l'âme*, the spirit or soul of the cheese, in Brie. The combination of the two consistencies and flavours is as delightful to the palate as the aroma is to the nose. For me this is the smell of heaven; Léon-Paul Fargue particularised it as *'les pieds de Dieu'*.

Gault Millau's February 1986 tasting, perverse in its choice of season, would nevertheless have given more satisfaction than it did if the AOC regulations had been doing their job. Most complaints were about neutrality of flavour, and only Monsieur Waroquier's Camembert from Le Moulin de Carel, presented by Marie-Anne Cantin, came through with flying colours.

## Livarot

Monsieur Michel Touzé's farm at Le Bôquet, near Vieux Pont, has been the temple of a succession of the faithful. Emmanuel, of the great Lepetit clan, was there from 1880, winning medals for his Camembert until he had to stop when the First World War broke out. Monsieur Touzé's father and mother were there from 1935, as makers and *affineurs* of Livarot. Between the wars, three-quarters of the farms making Livarot sold their cheese at the *blanc* stage to forty *affineurs*, working mostly in Saint-Pierre-sur-Dives, Livarot, Saint-Michel-de-Livet, Boissey, Montviette and Vimoutiers. There had been 200 of them in the 1870s, maturing over 2200 tonnes of Livarot a year, when it was eaten more than any other Norman cheese. The two world wars saw a steady diminution of farm cheesemaking of all kinds. By 1960, when Monsieur Touzé's father died, there were only two Livarot *affineurs* left, and they were not kept busy for much longer.

Livarot is a plump, rosy, big drum of a cheese laid on its side, twice the volume of Camembert. The *pâte* is firmer and stronger than that of Camembert. The milk of the previous day's two milkings is used, slightly skimmed to achieve 40 per cent *matières grasses*. The curd is cut large, and drained for twenty-four hours. It then rests in the moulds for a further twenty-four hours' drainage before hand-salting. Full-sized cheeses are given their first washing in brine of traditional formula on the twelfth day, and two further *sauçages* (washings) in their remaining forty-eight days of *affinage*. The Graindorge *fromagerie* at La Ferme de la Perrelle makes a first selection halfway through, eliminating imperfect crusts: too flat, too thick, or discoloured by grey mould. At this point they apply the five *laîches* of *typha latifolia*, cut in 1-centimetre strips like raffia, to the approved cheeses. They are given a final inspection before being boxed for despatch. The three smaller sizes of cheese are given fifteen to thirty days' *affinage* and rate three or four *laîches*. The *pâte* of the finished cheese is creamy-golden and smooth with many tiny apertures. The crust is pinky to reddish-gold, and bears marks of straw and of the metal grid on which it rested in the earlier stages of drainage. The aroma of the cheese is stronger than the flavour of the *pâte*, unless it has been kept for a very long time or in very warm conditions. Madeleine Kamman, a food expert whose mother had sold cheese, was one day fingering and smelling a Livarot at a stall in the Marché Saint-Honoré in Paris when a frizzle-haired, powdered customer with a pointed nose and mouth enquired, 'How's that Livarot?' 'Oh, fine,' Madeleine answered. 'As smelly and ready as can be.' The other customer reached her hand out for the cheese and bought it. She was Colette.

The first Livarots I sold in my shop at Streatley came from Saint-Michel-de-Livet, just north of Livarot, where Colas-Lebailly had made their cheese, suitably labelled *'au Délice des Gourmets'*, since 1867. The gourmet on the label was a well-filled young blood with black brilliantined hair and a monocle, tucking zestfully into his Livarot on a sunlit terrace. On the lawn behind, a bonneted dairymaid watched him anxiously, awaiting the verdict on her cheese. With the passing of Colas-Lebailly around 1970, alas, our gourmet's knife is poised forever in unfulfillable anticipation.

Another maker, the late Monsieur Moutarde, also gave up making his Livarot in Saint-Michel-de-Livet about that time, but his successor's cheese is good, Monsieur Lambert of Livarot tells me.

In Livarot itself the name of Georges Bisson, whose family made cheese for many years in the rue Gambier, is commemorated only by the Place Georges Bisson, which houses his old *mairie*. Sadly, his *fromagerie* was bought by Besnier and closed down in 1980 so that the giant concern could divert milk from the farms contracted to supply Bisson for his real Normandy cheeses, to expand the production of machine-made 'Camembert' Président. A Conservatoire des Techniques Fromagères Traditionnelles with a museum and library has long been planned in Normandy. Part of it, set up in 1987 within the old abbey walls of Saint-Pierre-sur-Dives, received 15,000 visitors in its first year. I had hoped that the scheme would embrace the old Bisson *fromagerie*, with its original equipment, cheese-boxes and labels, with active cheesemaking for demonstration and instructional purposes; but even if six-month courses are already being run at Saint-Pierre-sur-Dives, I hope this is still a possible extension. It is proposed to look into lost cheeses, so I commend to the Conservatoire my suggestion above (pp. 4–5) that the old *croûte-bleutée* of Camembert should be revived.

In 1976 Livarot was given its AOC, within the confined region of the Pays d'Auge between the Rivers Touques and Dives. However, AOC or no AOC, the Graindorge *fromagerie* kept Livarot production from sinking to an insignificant level at the start of the 1980s. From 750 tonnes in 1975 it fell to 590 tonnes in 1980. The Syndicat des Fabricants de Pont-l'Évêque et Livarot apparently blushed at the subsequent figures and ceased to publish them. They must have improved in the middle 1980s, as Graindorge alone made 650 tonnes in 1983. Livarot was being made in 1987 outside the town by Monsieur Moutarde's successor at Saint-Michel-de-Livet; by Madame Désirée Bisson et Fils (not related to Georges) at Sainte-Marguerite-de-Viette on a farmhouse scale; since 1980 by Monsieur C. Guyot's *fromagerie* at Notre Dame de Fresnay; and by Monsieur Denis Thébault (affiliated to Fromageries Triballat) at La Houssaye at Boissey. I am assured that there is a revival of interest in the cheese.

One measure which could help shops and foreign importers to widen Livarot's availability would be to offer the full-size cheese in cases of three and the smaller cheeses in sixes. I hope too that the joint Syndicat will actively encourage the use of Normandes and their natural feeding for production of milk for Livarot and for Pont-l'Évêque. Gault Millau did not include Livarot in their 1986 tasting, but did complain both of excessive neutrality of flavour and of off-flavours in their various Pont-l'Évêques. 'The milk of the Normandes is the foundation on which all Norman cheeses rest,' as Michel Touzé put it (we shall come back to him as maker of Pont-l'Évêque, Pavé d'Auge and his unique Vieux Pont au Calvados).

## Pont-l'Évêque, Pavé d'Auge and Vieux Pont au Calvados

We have covered the scant early records of Pont-l'Évêque (see pp. 2–3). In its making, full-cream milk is used warm from the cows, which the 1976 AOC rules allow to be pastured anywhere in Normandy's five *départements*, and even in the Maine *département* of Mayenne, which includes a corner of Anjou. This is stretching the old Pays d'Auge beyond reason, presumably to meet the claims of *laiteries*, but at least we can be grateful that it embraces the Manche, and with it one of the most respected individuals and families in Pont-l'Évêque history: Grillard of Rauville-la-Bigot. The AOC shows inexcusable laxity, however, by allowing *laiteries* to use *lait thermisé*, and does not appear to exclude pasteurisation.

The warm milk (the AOC specifies *'non acide'*), 3–3.5 litres for each cheese, used to be renneted, with rennet prepared from the *caillette* on the farm, at 32–33°C, but higher temperatures are now prevalent. Factories go up to 40°C to speed up the development of the curd. The curd is broken, unlike that of traditionally made Brie or Camembert. Some makers (including Monsieur Touzé) still pile up the cut curd crosswise under cloth and knead it to hasten drainage before it goes into the 10.5–11.5-centimetre square moulds for two days. Salting by hand with dry salt, or in *saumure*, is done on the fifth day after making. Cheeses remain in the *saloir* for two more days on a *battoir* (a straw-covered grid). There, and in the following period in the *hâloir* or *cave*, they are turned daily. The *pâte* of the ripe cheese is soft and golden, but not runny until it melts inside the mouth. It should taste rich but not sharp, and a good crust should give an agreeable edge to the flavour. Washed crust is smoother and more russet in colour. Brushed crust is often more granular (a touch of *morge*) and paler in colour: fawn to oatmeal, with sometimes a touch of pink. Monsieur Touzé's Pont-l'Évêque is dry-salted and brushed. He likes the atmosphere in the *hâloir* to be slightly drier than that of the cheese, but humid enough to leave it unctuous, and gives the cheese four to five weeks of *affinage*. He considers the dry *affinage* for *'fleur de croûte'* to be traditional, and believes that *saumure* was introduced in comparatively modern times. 'A *cave* doesn't just *happen*,' he said. 'You must keep an eye on the moulds.' One of these, to which the characteristic flavour of the old *pavés* was sometimes attributed, is *monilium candidum*. It is looked on with distaste by some cheesemakers, which accounts for the now prevalent practice of washing the crust of Pont-l'Évêque, as this discourages most mould development.

*Pavés* are an old tradition, in which Moyaux was the most familiar name. In the 1960s they seemed to be disappearing, but a growing demand for big cutting cheeses revived their making, as the long list at the end of this section proves. They tend to be more of the *croûte-brossée* type than *croûte-lavée*, thicker and slower ripening than their smaller cousin, Pont-l'Évêque, and two to six times the weight. For his Pavé d'Auge of 550 grams, Michel Touzé uses 6 litres of milk (against 3.5 for his Pont-l'Évêque). His *caillé* is 'worked on more in the cloth' than the *caillé* for Pont-l'Évêque, and ripened for 1½–2½ months, emerging with an oatmeal-coloured coat. We first found the *pâte* open-textured and gentle, but full of character. When we finished it, in Provence ten days after leaving Vieux Pont, it was still excellent in flavour and texture; obviously richer, but neither salty nor over-strong. This reinforced my experience that well-made traditional cheese has a far longer agreeable eating life than any factory products (for all their long-keeping claims), and stands up far better to poor conditions.

Michel Touzé makes one other cheese, achieved by a special *affinage* of some of his 320-gram *demi-pavés*, which take 100 litres of whole milk for thirty cheeses. They are washed in Calvados twenty-four hours after *démoulage*, and twice more during the first fortnight of their four to five weeks of *affinage*. He sells the result as Le Vieux Pont affiné au Calvados.

## Vanished cheeses

The Norman cheeses whose disappearances I mourn are not very old, but they filled two needs: one for a very small, soft *croûte-fleurie* cheese, and the other for a soft cheese much larger than Camembert and more agreeable at the *fromage frais* stage. The very small cheese was Le Fromage de Monsieur Fromage, a nineteenth-century innovation. Monsieur Fromage was a real *fermier*, with a real great-granddaughter, a friend of mine, to bear witness (regrettably, she is not a cheesemaker). This 150-gram double-cream cheese was 5–6 centimetres across, and I remember it vividly as being a little higher than it was wide, though some authorities contradict me. It was rich, with a very thin crust, and would melt rather quickly in warm weather, but this was no worry because it was made to be demolished at one sitting. On the box 'Monsieur' was romanticised in a top hat and a red swallow-tail coat. The Lepetit family kept him alive at their old Cléville factory until the early 1970s, when demand no longer paid for his keep. No attempt to imitate Monsieur has since come anywhere near to him.

Sadly, the cheese closest to Monsieur among his contemporaries has also expired. This was Le Ranchy, a *triple-crème* made by the Fromagerie de Ranchy, which also made Saint-Martin (labelled Saint-Pol by Lanquetot-Pigny of Rungis). This was a delightful flat, round cheese of almost Brie de Melun proportions, usually sold at the *fromage frais* stage. The dairy closed some time after 1977. I wish some enterprising dairyman with good sources of milk from Normandes would seek out the legatees and acquire the right to revive those excellent cheeses. The kilo-size cheeses now made in some Camembert dairies are not at all the same thing.

## Chèvres

I first met Saint-Martin at the cheese shop in Vire, which also introduced me to two interesting goat farms, years ago, when they were more rare in Normandy than now. I cannot say whether the young *chevrière* with several children and rather more goats is still making her tiny bell-shaped Chevrotins at Le Reculey, near Le Beny Bocage, but they were meltingly delicious, as were their bigger brothers. The other *chevriers* I discovered were Roger Legoupil and his son, of Moyon, who received customers on the farm for their beautiful, sweet Moyonnais *pavés*, in the form of base-of-pyramid, either square or extended for cutting. They are sold white as *fromages frais*, or coated with powdered charcoal when salted. They had won a gold medal in Paris in 1974, not long before my visit, and showed me a card of congratulation and appreciation of their cheese from Monsieur Grillard, the great Pavé d'Auge and Pont-l'Évêque maker.

## THE FUTURE OF NORMANDY'S CHEESES

As follows from Monsieur Touzé's words, the fundamental need, to put the seal on the future of Normandy's cheeses, is first, the restoration of the *race normande*. This high-yielding cow is second in numbers and yield to the Frisonne-Holstein (the national herd of Normandes was 1,358,600 in 1985, 280,000 down on 1982), but the nature of its milk is far more suitable for traditional cheeses, where richness of texture and flavour is of primary importance. In 1986 Normande milk had 4.17 per cent fats and 3.31 per cent non-fat solids, compared with 3.89 per cent fats and 3.06 per cent non-fat solids (worst of seventeen breeds recorded in France) for Frisonnes. Not surprisingly, Normandes produce milk of the colour and richness of our Channel Island cows. An AOC-directed programme over a period of, say, ten years should establish the Normande as the unique source of milk for Camembert, Pont-l'Évêque and Livarot. The reduction in yield per cow could, incidentally, be compensated for by more intensive grazing, which has been found at its optimum level to raise pasture production by 15 per cent. The Norman AOCs should also follow the example of the AOCs for the cheeses of Franche-Comté and Savoie (see Chapters 14 and 15), which lay down the hay of the region as winter feed and exclude silage. I have little doubt that the disagreeable odours and off-flavours detected by the Gault Millau panel in February 1986 could be traced to wrong winter feed. Such errors give ammunition to the opponents of *lait cru* cheese. The 'neutral' complaints cannot be attributed to pasteurisation, or even thermisation, if the AOC rule against bringing milk to a temperature higher than 37°C is being observed. I can only suggest that the blame could be distributed between the wrong breed of cattle, hay from meadows neutralised by chemical fertilisers, and the replacement of permanent multi-species grassland by one- or two-species leys.

Such pastures were described to me as 'the junk-food of the cow' by the director of the Commonwealth Bureau of Agricultural Botany at England's old Grassland Research Institute in 1979. Variety is not only best for us: it is also best for the health of the cows. It is essential to guard the rich local herbage on the old pastures and meadows, to which we owe the flavours passed on to the cheeses by their aromatic esters. These are neutralised by chemical farming and killed by pasteurisation (see Introduction). Standardisation should be left to factories extruding pasteurised fodder with a month or more of shelf-life. Great food made from fresh ingredients is never exactly the same twice running, whether it comes from chef or *fromager*, because the best raw materials are natural, alive and constantly changing. Honey flavours vary with the seasonal flowers or the placing of the hives. So, with pastures, one side of the hill is different from the other; the top of the hill is different from the bottom; and experienced Camembert *amateurs* of other days with local knowledge could detect not only which farm but which part of the farm had provided the milk for the cheese they were eating.

If AOC rules are tightened up and more farms resume cheesemaking, Camembert can return to the glory of its former untrammelled variety. As Michel Touzé insists: 'Cheesemaking is a vocation. You have to invest your faith in it from the start.'

## Cheeses of Basse-Normandie

### Abbaye de Bricquebec

**Trappiste de Bricquebec or Providence.** 1400g, 22cm × 5cm deep, and small size; semi-soft; *croûte-lavée*; *affiné* 2 months; yellow to gold colour; formerly made by monks at the Abbaye de Notre Dame de Grâce (an offshoot of the Abbaye d'Entrammes, Abbaye de Notre Dame du Port du Salut, Maine), this cheese has been made in plumper form at the Laiterie Coopérative de Valognes since the early 1960s; it is now frankly dull, and not improved by keeping. In 1987 I was told that the Abbaye had no intention of following the Entrammes example (see pp. 43–4), where the commercial enterprise was also sold, but smaller-scale cheesemaking was resumed by the monks. Male visitors only. N.B. See RAUVILLE-LA-BIGOT (8km N of Bricquebec) for farm with outstanding Pont-l'Évêque, Pavé.
45% m.g.; *laitier*; *vache pasteurisé*.
Manche; 54 **2**.

### L'Aigle

Tuesday market.
Orne; 60 **5**.

### Alençon

Friday and Sunday market. Fromages Blancs: Maigres, Gras, Battus, Lisses. See HÉLOUP.
Orne; 60 **3**.

### Angelon, Angelot

See pp. 2–3.

### Annebault

Market daily (except on out-of-season Wed). M. Pierre Gohier, *fermier*, Groupement des Agriculteurs de la Côte Fleurie: *fromage blanc*, *fromages de vache*, *de chèvre*, cream, yoghurt, butter, eggs, cider, calvados, honey, vegetables, conserves, poultry; also 'pommeau'.
*fermier*; *vache/chèvre cru*.
Calvados; 55 **3**, Pont-l'Évêque W 15.5km N175 crossroads.

### Auge

Pays d'Auge or Vallée d'Auge (Calvados and Northern Orne) is one of the most favoured dairy regions of France, in and between the valleys of La Dives and La Touques; the homeland and still the heart of Pont-l'Évêque, Livarot and Camembert. See MOYAUX for *pavé*.

**La Route du Fromage.** Names of cheese villages and towns on route with entries, in clockwise order, starting in the west; St-Pierre-sur-Dives (to SW is Bernières; to S 3km Lieury; to N by D16 Bretteville-sur-Dives, St-Maclou), Vieux-Pont-en-Auge (Le Bôquet), Boissey (La Houssaye), Ste-Marguerite-de-Viette, Livarot, Fervaques, St-Martin-de-Bienfaite, Orbec, Notre-Dame-de-Courson, Vimoutiers (to N, see Fermes-Auberges, and to W, Notre-Dame-de-Fresnay).

### Augelot

See pp. 2–3.

### Avranches

Saturday market.
Manche; 59 **8**.

## BAGNOLES DE L'ORNE

Tuesday and (better) Saturday market.
Orne; 60 **1**.

## BANVOU

**Fromages de Chèvre.** M. Lecamus makes at Le Vieux Bourg.
*fermier; chèvre cru.*
Orne; 60 **1**, 10km S of Flers between D962 and D18.

## BAYEUX

Saturday market (fish daily, afternoons).
Lion d'Or, 71 rue Saint-Jean (tel. 31 92 06 90); interior courtyard, good food, splendid cheeses from Pays d'Auge, in which staff are interested, if you are.
Cheese factors: Éts Jean-Jacques, N side of N13 (Bayeux to Caen), Saint-Martin-des-Entrées.
Calvados; 54 **15**.

## LE BÉNY-BOCAGE

Thursday market.

**Chevrotins du Reculey.** Tiny, bell-shaped cheeses, melting and delicious. I enjoyed them years ago but can't guarantee survival.
*fermier; chèvre cru.*
Calvados; 59 **9**, NE of Vire 13km Le Reculey.

## BERNIÈRES

**Camembert de Normandie AOC.** B. and Ph. Le Boucher make *lait cru* cheese *moulé à la main*, of good report (Gault Millau, February 1986), and Petit Falaisien Extra Doux.
45% m.g.; *fermier; chèvre cru.*
Calvados; 55 **12**, R on D511 S of Bernières Jort.

## BEUVRON-EN-AUGE

Old market converted to restaurant where Mme Engel (tel. 31 23 25 00) serves the morning's fish, poulet Vallée d'Auge, *jambon au cidre*, and farm cheeses.
'La Ferme de Beuvron' (tel. 31 79 29 19) 10.00–13.00, 14.30–19.00. Farmhouse cheeses sold daily in season and in school holidays; weekends out of season; the following cheeses are sold: Camembert (Durand of Camembert); *Pavé d'Auge* (Touzé of Vieux Pont); *Pont-l'Évêque* (GAEC Le Grand Plain, Saint-Pierre-du-Jonquet); *fromage blanc*, chèvre. All *lait cru*, fermier. At G. A. B. du Calvados (and in Caen market) Michel Foulon sells assorted cheeses, all *lait cru, fermier, biologique Nature & Progrès.*

**Camembert; Pont-l'Évêque; Chèvre; Fromage Blanc.** At Bures-sur-Dives, Mesnil de Bures (tel. 31 23 21 53) Groupement Gie des Marais, M. and Mme Thomine sell daily in afternoons.
*fermier; vache/chèvre cru.*

**Chèvre, Fromages de.** At Cambremer, Ferme de la Mimarnel on D50 (tel. 31 63 00 50). M. Jacques-Antoine Motte sells chèvres daily (except out-of-season Fri).
*fermier; chèvre cru.*
At Janville, Ferme aux Bonnements (tel. 31 23 28 63) on D78 Troarn road to Janville: M. Henri Porcher sells daily.
*fermier; chèvre cru.*

**Pont-l'Évêque AOC.** M. et Mme Dominique Demaris (tel. 31 79 23 05) at Putôt-en-Auge sell daily (except Sundays) up to 17.00 their own cheese, butter and cream.
*fermier; vache cru.*
La Route du Fromage, attainable from Beuvron via Crèvecœur by D16 to Saint-Pierre-sur-Dives (W extremity of tour); see AUGE.
Calvados; 55 **13/12**, high, 5km S of N175 near D400 junction on D49.

## BOISSEY

See LA HOUSSAYE.

## LA BOUILLE, BONDARD, BONDON

See p. 29 and p. 33.

## BONNEVILLE-LA-LOUVET

On D534 8km W of Pont-l'Évêque daily July–September, at weekends rest of year: roadside farm shop with range of produce, including Pont-l'Évêque, *fromage blanc*, pear and apple cider, Calvados.

## BONNEVILLE, CARRÉ DE

Succulent, piquant cheese, formerly made from 6l of milk (= 2 × Pont-l'Évêque) ripened 4 months (Courtine, 1973), grey-brown crust (Courtine, 1973): 'between Pont-l'Évêque and Pavé de Moyaux', and already 'disparu' (Marabout, 1978).
*fermier; vache cru.*
Calvados; 55 **4**, low.

BONNEVILLE, CURÉ DE

*Fromage frais de* Normandie (Lindon, 1961).
*laitier; vache.*
Calvados; 55 **4**, low.

BRETTEVILLE-SUR-DIVES

**Camembert AOC.** Éts Lepetit (founded 1872).
45% m.g.; *laitier; vache cru.*
Calvados; 55 **13**, far L of C.

BRICQUEBEC

See ABBAYE DE.

BRILLAT-SAVARIN

See p. 32.

BRIOUZE

Market.
Laiterie Saint-Hilaire-de-Briouze; M. Gillot makes *lait cru* Camembert and Le Fin Normand, and pasteurised Camembert.
Orne; 60 **1**, R; 3.5km to E, 60 **2**.

BRIQUE

See BRIQUETTE, p. 34.

CABOURG

Daily market in summer; Wednesday and Friday in winter.
Calvados; 55 **2**, on coast.

CAEN

Daily market except Monday; Bureau de Tourisme (leaflets for Route du Fromage); Syndicat des Fabricants de Camembert de Normandie, 82 rue de Bernières.
Calvados; 55 **11/12**.

CAILLÉ CAMPAGNARD

*Fromage frais* in tubs *moulé à la louche* by Graindorge at Livarot.
*laitier; artisanal; vache cru.*
Calvados; 55 **13**.

CAMEMBERT

Fête du Camembert last Sunday in July.

**Camembert Fermier.** For history, see pp. 3–4.
In the 1980s two farms are making Camembert in the *commune* on two adjacent farms, where D246 crosses the Camembert village road. They are on the left of the road, one before and one after the fork towards the neighbouring *commune*, Champosoult.
M. François Durand, La Héronnière (open daily 10.00–12.00, 14.00–18.00; on D246, 2km from Camembert tel. 33 39 08 08) makes 1000 Camemberts a week, and a few smaller-sized cheeses, selling a quarter on farm, the rest to shops and *marchands-affineurs.* (See pp. 5–6.) M. Michel and Mme Andrée Delorme Le Tordouet, open Mon to Fri 14.00–18.00; 3km S of Camembert, next farm beyond La Héronnière (tel. 33 39 12 56 if you wish to see cheese-making); they make around 140 full-sized Camembert every day.

**Le Camembert de Normandie AOC.** (31 August 1983). A Government decree of 31 August 1983 established the following method: 2–2.3l of milk for one cheese; 250–270g; 10.5–11cm diameter, 3cm deep; *caillé* obtained solely by renneting (15cl per 100l indicated by one artisan); 45–60 minutes after coagulation curd is hand-ladled into moulds (10–12cm × 13–14cm high) *moulé à la louche*, which is of same diameter as mould to avoid curd breaking; 4–5 ladles go into the mould, at hourly intervals; it is important to start taking curd from edge of vat, working concentrically over surface one ladle deep towards centre, to avoid unnecessary breaking of curd (which leads to 'leafy' consistency; moulds left to drain on gently sloping surface until curd has sunk halfway down, then fitted with base and turned (4–10 hours after end of filling) and left for rest of 24 hours (some advise second turn during this period) before turning out and salting on top face and sides, then on other face (7g per cheese); 24 hours in *saloir* at 12–18°C (one artisan I knew left cheeses 2 days at 10–11°C under fan to reduce humidity and gas after salting); he said, 'too little salt and mould doesn't develop; too much and surface mould becomes too thick'); 15 days' *affinage* at about 14°C, preferably 'in nice mouldy room in an old stone building with a dryish atmosphere' (eleventh and twelfth days on base with further 10–12 days for best cheeses at 8°C); factory cheeses are sprayed with suspension of mould in distilled water (*penicillium candidum*).
*Affinage*: at least 16 days from day of making must take place at the dairy of origin, within the region of the five

*départements* of Normandie. AOC cheeses do not have to state the *matières grasses*, nor the place of making (only the responsible person or company); but most labels do, and all should. Industrial cheese is given starter as well as rennet (to give back some of the bacteria killed by pasteurisation; but the destroyed aromatic esters cannot be replaced); curd is put into moulds in one operation (not 4–5 operations over 4–5 hours); salting is by brine bath; drainage takes a few hours; mould is sprayed on; *affinage* 12 days.

In 1982 10,450 tonnes of cheese would have qualified for the AOC, a mere 6.22 per cent of all French production under the name of Camembert.

*Sources of Camembert AOC.*
M. Michel Delorme and M. François Durand (see CAMEMBERT FERMIER) started in 1981.
Ferme de la Gambette, Montreuil-La-Cambe, Orne, 61; third in Gault Millau test February 1986 (started 1985); highly praised; stocked by Tradition Fromagère at Rungis for trade buyers and P. Olivier at Boulogne.
*fermier.*
Auge/Orne; 55 **13**, 15km SW of Vimoutiers.
See BEUVRON-EN-AUGE, farm shops and neighbourhood.
*fermier.*
Auge/Calvados.
M. Varrocquer, Le Moulin de Carel makes excellent *lait cru* cheese, which scored highly in a Gault Millau test in February 1986 from Christian Millau and three other judges. It was supplied by Marie-Anne Cantin of Paris. Real old-fashioned cheese: 'remarquable' (Millau).
*artisanal; vache cru.*
Auge/Calvados; 55 **13**, St-Pierre-sur-Dives S on D511.
B. and Ph. Le Boucher (see BERNIÈRES). Their cheese came fourth in a February 1986 Gault Millau test (see pp. 7 and 11).
Union Coopérative d'Isigny-Ste-Mère, Isigny-Ste-Mère 2 rue du Dr Boutrois 14230; a 270g Camembert Sainte-Mère supplied by G. Pascaud (Paris) came second, and one from Isigny supplied by M. R. Barthélémy came fifth in the Gault Millau test; some criticism of lack of character, yet violent odour. Millau thought it characteristic of *thermisation*,* but this is not permitted by AOC rules as it means raising milk to 65°C against AOC maximum of 37°C. Others on the panel liked the cheeses. Those who least liked the winner preferred these (the Sainte-Mère scored 6½/10, the Isigny 6/10). Various Isigny Camembert labels are in use, so look for one marked *'au lait cru'*.
Isigny supplies Sainsbury's *lait cru* Camembert and is hoping to see English sales of such cheese go up 20 per cent per annum. Professional visits to factories can be arranged.
Calvados; 55 **12**.
J. Gillot make *lait cru* Camembert Étendard Normand Vache Medaille at Laiterie de St-Hilaire-de-Briouze, 61220 Briouze (tel. 33 66 00 55).
Orne; 60 **1**.
Laiterie Maurice Lanquetot makes Camemberts *lait cru* Domaine d'Orbiquet laitier and Tradition. The Orbiquet has its *lait cru* sticker on the cheese inside the box. I have found them consistently satisfactory in development of crust, aroma and flavour when properly treated: not too low temperature, regular turning; (the old Orbiquet dairy on D519 is now used for other purposes; St-Martin is very close).
Calvados; 55 **14**.
Éts Pierre Lanquetot (100 years in the family) 8 rue de Vimoutiers, 14290 Orbec (tel. 31 32 80 02) have four *fromageries* making over 60,000 Camemberts daily under Duc Normand and local labels (e.g. Ferme d'Antignac) all *lait cru*, *moulé à la louche* (in 1985 two-fifths of all AOC cheese), and make 10 tonnes of butter daily at Isigny. No sales to public at dairies, but Bottin Gourmand says visits can be arranged.
Calvados; 54 **13**, 55 **13/14**.
Laiterie Coopérative de Périers makes *lait cru* Camembert Périers d'Isigny.
Manche; 54 **12**, E of Périers.
Éts Lepetit make *lait cru* Camembert, as they have done since 1872 (their old Cléville *laiterie* closed in 1984 (see MONSIEUR);

---

*The label Isi Camembert Isigny Sainte-Mère is now used on a 250g cheese, 45% m.g., which only an internal wrap reveals as made from *lait thermisé*, so Millau was probably right; this rules out AOC qualification.

pioneer *laitiers* in Camembert world, they have won fifty-eight or more medals.
Calvados; 55 **13**, far L of C on and E of D16 Bretteville-sur-Dives, Saint Maclou.
Henri Vallée et Fils of Clécy (established 1930, see below) make *lait cru* Camembert Ferme du Grand Béron at this farm *fromagerie* in the Suisse normande near Berjou. Christian Cantin of Paris supplied one for the Gault Millau test, awarded 5.7 out of 10 and criticised only for lack of individual character. I wonder whether this was because of slight lack of maturity, having eaten many an aromatic and full-flavoured cheese from this stable in my time. The methods were classic when I visited in 1977, and I would not expect them to have changed. La Fosse is another label used by Vallée for *lait cru* cheese. Confusingly Le Grand Béron, a 1000g cheese of Camembert-type *pâte* and crust, made at Clécy by Vallée, is pasteurised, so watch out.
Orne; 55 **11**, low C N of Berjou on Calvados boundary.

### Carentan

A name formerly renowned in Camembert circles for farm cheeses coming from the Douve-Taute area. The milk is all used by the Isigny or Sainte-Mer *laiteries* now.
Manche; 54 **13**, 11km W of Isigny.

### Carré

See BONNEVILLE-LA-LOUVET, PAVÉS.

### Carré de Bray

See HAUTE-NORMANDIE.

**Carré Choisy.** 220g soft *croûte-fleurie*, by Coopérative de Périers (see CAMEMBERT AOC sources (St-Sébastien-de-Raids)).
50% *m.g.*; *laitier*; *vache pasteurisé*.

### Castel

*Fromage frais* noted by Lindon, 1961.

### Cendré Normand de Grand Papa

200g round cheese, between Olivet and Cendré d'Aisy in style; by Rigaud who also makes a Fromage au Foin and Dôme (Taupinière type of Vendée).
45% *m.g.*; *laitier*; *vache*.
Orne; 60 **1**, L of C Champsecret.

### Chèvres

See BANVOU, LE BÉNY BOCAGE, HONFLEUR, JANVILLE, NOIRVILLE, NOTRE-DAME-DE-FRESNAY, STE-FOY-DE-MONTGOMMERY. A *chevrier* in Orne told me there were at least ten in his *département* and more in Calvados. Chèvres are also sold at Beuvron-en-Auge and Bures-sur-Dives (see BEUVRON-EN-AUGE).

### Chevrette

See HAUTE NORMANDIE.

### Chevrotin

See LE BÉNY-BOCAGE.

### Clécy

HQ and large *laiterie* (pasteurised cheese) of Henri Vallée et Fils since 1930. Telephone (31 69 07 04) to visit, or to Ferme du Grand Béron (see CAMEMBERT AOC LAIT CRU). As well as Camemberts, they make a 180g Vallée cheese *lait cru*. Le Grand Béron, 1000g cheese of Camembert-type curd, made at Clécy, is pasteurised.
Calvados; 55 **11**, lower C on D562.

### Coeur

See HAUTE-NORMANDIE for COEURS DE BRAY, DE NEUFCHATEL.

### Coeur de Camembert au Calvados

(Made specially for one or two shops.)
*fermier*; *artisanal*; *vache*.

### Coeurmandie

*Not* from Normandie. See p. 42.

### Condé-sur-Sarthe

Fromagerie Lutin, 20 rue de Saint-Germain, Jean Verrier, *maître fromager* (tel. 33 26 22 55 for visit) makes Camembert and Grand Rustique (1kg soft cheese, same *pâte* and *croûte*).
*laitier*; *artisanal*; *vache cru*.
Orne; 60 **3**, 1.5km W of Alençon.

### Coulommiers type, Président

Made by machine in Besnier factory.
*industriel*; *vache pasteurisé*.
Orne; Barberey.

### Le Coutançais

Soft double-cream cheese (gold medal Paris, 1980). Made by Union Laitière Normande at Coutances, where they also make pasteurised Camembert.
60% *m.g.*; *laitier*; *vache pasteurisé*.
Manche; 54 **12**.

## Coutances

Monday and Thursday market.

## Deauville

Tuesday and Thursday market; July to mid-September daily market; La Ferme Normande, *fromager*, Place du Marché, 09.00–13.00, 15.00–20.00, mid-June to mid-Sept.
Calvados; 55 **3**.

**Deauville.** 300g; flat with rounded sides; semi-soft; *croûte-lavée* (source not discovered).
*artisanal; vache cru.*
Calvados; 55 **3**.

## Dôme

Cheese in Taupinière style by Rigaud (see CENDRÉ NORMAND).
*laitier; vache.*

## Domfront

Saturday market; and see FERMES-AUBERGES.
Orne; 59 **10**.

## Écouché

Friday market.
Orne; 60 **2**.

## Edam Français, Cotentin, Cotentinette

Any use of name Edam is illegal as name for French cheese (by Franco-Dutch agreement), but made and so-called by Union Coopérative Laitière Isigny-Ste-Mère:
1. In red-waxed cannonball form, to sell 'tendre' (mild).
2. Natural crust, hardening to pale oatmeal, pitted, with age; medium (*demi-étuvé*) to mature (*étuvé*).
3. Also sold *tendre* in red-waxed loaf form as Cotentin and Cotentinette.
*40% m.g.; laitier; vache pasteurisé.*
Calvados; 54 **13**.

## Excelsior

See HAUTE-NORMANDIE.

## Falaise

Wednesday and Saturday market.
*Fromager*: Michel Delorière, 5 rue du Docteur Turgis (tel. 31 90 12 90).
Calvados; 55 **12**.

## Fermes-Auberges

Mme Duduit, Manoir Caudemone (tel. 31 63 53 74) serves local produce 1 May–1 November.
At neighbouring Ste-Foy-de-Montgommery's fifteenth-century *manoir*, open every day, M Lesdain has goat cheeses 'to eat on spot'.
Calvados; 55 **13**, 3km S of Livarot.
M. et Mme Albert Mottier, La Nocherie, St-Bômer-Les-Forges, 61700 Domfront (tel. 33 38 63 68); inn at former farm bakery, where sixteenth-century bread oven is still used for cooking, and *eau-de-vie-de-poire* is distilled.
Orne; 52 **10**, 6km N of Domfront.

## Le Fermier

Name of large Pavé by Michel Touzé (see VIEUX PONT).

## La Ferté Macé

Thursday market.
Orne; 60 **1/2**.

## Fervaques

**Pont-l'Évêque.** Albert Lallier, La Moissonnière (tel. 31 32 31 23), afternoons except Saturday, Sunday. M. Rioult, *épicier-fromager* (closed Mon).
*fermier; vache cru.*
Calvados; 55 **13**, far R of C.

## Fin-de-Siècle

See HAUTE-NORMANDIE.

## Flers

Wednesday market (and see BANVOU, 10km S, for Chèvre).
Orne; 60 **1**.

## Fleurette

'Crème parfumée' from first skimming of milk; 'Fromage de Commande Fleurette': special order for cheese (e.g. Pont-l'Évêque, made from new milking with added Fleurette).

## Foin

**Fromage au Foin Grand Papa.** Made by Rigaud, see CENDRÉ NORMAND.
*laitier; vache.*
Orne; 60 **1**.

## Fromages Blancs

**Fromages Blancs: Maigres, Gras, Battus, Lisses.** See ALENÇON, HÉLOUP.
*fermier; biologique; vache cru.*

**Fromage Blanc Caillé or à la Crème.** Prepared for retailers, sometimes by themselves (and see BONNEVILLE-LA-LOUVET).
*laitier; vache.*
Orne.

## Fromages Fermiers

See ALENÇON, AUGE (Route des Fromages), BEUVRON-EN-AUGE, CAMEMBERT, CHÈVRE, LIVAROT, PAVÉ, PONT-L'ÉVÊQUE.

## Fromages Frais

**Fromage Frais.** 5kg, in buckets, made at Ferme de Treillebois, Vardon, 61430 Athis de l'Orne.
*40% m.g.; fermier; vache.*

**Fromages Frais Isigny-Ste-Mère, Maigre, Lisse, Campagnard.** *Maigre*, low-fat; *lisse* is smooth;* *campagnard* is rustic. 500g pots; 5kg and 10kg buckets (see ISIGNY).
*0%, 4%, 20% m.g.; laitier; vache pasteurisé.*
Orne; 55 **1**, bottom.

## Fromage de Monsieur Fromage

This delicious 150g little deep drum of double-cream cheese had a rich, clotted, ultimately melting interior, and thin *croûte-fleurie* crust, much less substantial than Camembert. It was unlike any other cheese and its demise has left a gap no imitator has yet (1987) succeeded in filling. It was invented by a Camembert maker, M. Fromage (a Gaston Fromage made Camembert at Le Mesnil-Bacley 1km SW of Livarot.) A top-hatted red-cutaway coated figure was in the centre of the red label used by the Lepetit family, who took it over from the inventor's successor, M. Herselin, and made it at Cléville, where they made cheese from 1872 for more than a century. The Cléville dairy closed in 1984, but Fromage de Monsieur had become *feu Monsieur* (the late Monsieur) early in the 1970s. The Lepetit family continue to make Camembert *lait cru* (see CAMEMBERT AOC) at Bretteville-sur-Dives and St-Maclou (an old stronghold of theirs). There has been talk of Monsieur's resurrection, but nothing I have seen comes near the original. The somewhat similar Le Ranchy (see p. 25) has also died out.
Calvados; 55 **12**, high, far R.

## Gauville

Like a strong Livarot *fermier*, but probably extinct by 1980s. In 1973 Courtine could still find it on one or two farms in the season (*Larousse*). In 1978 Androuët and Ninette Lyon reported it on one farm, but asked, 'How long?' In 1982 Androuët could no longer find it.
*fermier; vache cru.*
Orne; 55 **14**, bottom R, 33km SE of Vimoutiers.

## Gouda Français

Another illegal name (see EDAM); 2–3kg cheese made by Union Coopérative Laitière Ste-Mère, and by Laiterie de Valognes.
*48% m.g.; laitier; vache pasteurisé.*
Manche.

## Gournay

See HAUTE-NORMANDIE.

## Goutu

Emmental-Gouda cross made by Laiterie de Valognes (see p. 27).
*laitier; vache pasteurisé.*
Manche; 55 **2**.

## Le Grand Béron

1000g; 22cm × 4–5cm deep; Camembert-style *pâte* and *croûte*; by Henri Vallée et Fils at Clécy. (Camembert Ferme du Grand Béron is *lait cru* cheese made in farm of the name at Cambercourt, Berjou by the Vallée family.)
*45% m.g.; laitier; vache pasteurisé.*
Calvados; 55 **11**, on D562.

## Grande Clotte

M. Ch. H. Grillard makes this 1kg *pavé* at Domaine de la Chesnée. Excellent, succulent consistency and fine flavour (1986), see RAUVILLE.
*45% m.g.; fermier; vache cru.*
Manche; 54 **1**, far R, 8km N of Bricquebec, Rauville-la-Bigot.

## Grand Papa

*Marque* of Rigaud at Champsecret, making Cendré Normand, Fromage au Foin and Dôme.

### Le Grand Pont

M. Graindorge makes this 18cm square, 3cm deep *pavé* in Pont-l'Évêque style at his *fromagerie*, La Ferme de la Perrelle, Livarot.
45% m.g.; *artisanal; vache cru.*
Calvados; Livarot.

### Grand Rustique

Fromagerie Lutin makes this 1000g cheese of Camembert character at Condé-sur-Sarthe (gold medal Paris, 1980).
45% m.g.; *artisanal; vache cru.*
Orne.

### Grand Sainte-Mère

Large, solid, industrial Brie-type cheese made by UCL Isigny-Ste-Mère.
45% m.g.; *laitier industriel; vache pasteurisé.*
Manche; 54 **13**.

### Hayons

See HAUTE-NORMANDIE.

### Héloup

*Fromages blancs; maigres, gras, battus, lisses.*
Orne; 60 **3**.

### Honfleur

Saturday market.
*Fromager*: La Fromagerie de l'Auge: M. Jean Louis Dubos sells Camembert Moulin de Carel, Pont-l'Évêque from Vieux Pont (see p. 27), Livarot from Livarot, local goat cheese, and many others.
Baker: La Paneterie; Louis David makes seven-grain bread *à l'ancienne*, rye-bread, local *pain brié* (salt-less, dense white), excellent accompaniments to cheese.
Cheese wholesaler: Éts Demars-Foucault et Cie, Équemauville-Honfleur.
Calvados; 55 **3/4**.

**Fromage de Chèvre.** Made near Honfleur by M. François Hue-Hermier, sold by M. Dubos (see above).
*fermier; chèvre cru.*
Calvados; 55 **3/4**.

### La Houssaye

**Livarot, Pont-l'Évêque, Pavé.**
*artisanal; vache cru.*
Fromager Denis Thébault (tel. 31 20 64 00) daily 08.30–16.30 except Saturday, Sunday; strong cheese (see LIVAROT sources, and PONT-L'ÉVÊQUE AOC).
Calvados; 55 **13**, SW of C, S of Boissey.

### Isi Blanche; Isi d'Or; Isidoux

See ISIGNY, Union Coopérative, below.

### Isigny-sur-Mer

Market every other Saturday.
One of *fromageries* Pierre Lanquetot (see CAMEMBERT AOC *lait cru.*
Union Coopérative Laitière Isigny-Ste-Mère has a large factory here and one to the E in Manche at Ste-Mère; 70% of its production in 1985 was Camembert *lait cru* (see CAMEMBERT AOC but a Camembert Isigny Sainte-Mère, 45% m.g. is now made of *lait thermisé*, so is not AOC, see p. 15), 8% is Grand Ste-Mère (see above) or Isidoux (*lait cru*), 2% Pont-l'Évêque. The rest included Dutch style (see EDAM, GOUDA) Mimolette, Pavé Sainte-Mère (*lait cru*), Raclette, Saint-Jouvin or Isi d'Or (grander version of Saint-Paulin), Saint-Paulin, and a white industrial cheese called Sainte-Mère or Isi Blanche. Important exports, including Sainsbury's Camembert *lait cru.*
Calvados, 54 **13**.

**Camembert lait cru Périers d'Isigny.**
Laiterie Coopérative de Périers makes this one and pasteurised cheeses including Carré Choisy, *croûte-fleurie*, of Carré de l'Est (see Chapter 10, p. 328) type.
*laitier; vache cru/pasteurisé.*
Manche; 54 **12**, St-Sebastien-de-Raids.

### Janville

**Fromage de Chèvre.** M. H. Porscher, Ferme
aux Bonnements, open daily (tel. 31 23 38 63).
*fermier; chèvre cru.*
Calvados; 55 **12**, upper R on D78 SE of Troarn.

### Lieury

On Route du Fromage; M. Rioult, *épicier-fromager* (not Mondays).
Calvados; 55 **13**.

### Lisieux

Saturday market.

**Lisieux; Le Petit Lisieux.** Flatter, therefore lighter version of Livarot, ripened 2

months; same diameter as full-size cheese (11–12cm), 'fruité' (Courtine), milder (other writers). I have not eaten it, but judgments need to specify age of sample to signify anything.
*artisanal; vache cru.*
Calvados; 55 **13**.

LIVAROT

Syndicat d'Initiative, Place Georges Bisson (tel. 31 63 54 39) shops: Mme Esnouf, Ferme du Héricourt, rue Marcel Gambier (closed Sun p.m., all Mon); good local cheese; knowledgeable, helpful; M. Françoise, 14 rue Maréchal Foch (closed Wed). Ask at any of above for details of Route du Fromage. Fromagerie de la Perrelle, Bernard Graindorge et Fils, open Mon–Fri (tel. 31 63 50 02) makes: Livarot AOC, Pont-l'Évêque AOC, Le Grand Pont (*pavé*) and La Perrelle (1500g cutting cheese of Livarot *pâte* and *croûte*).

Éts Georges Bisson, 66 rue Marcel Gambier was bought by Besnier and closed in 1980, but there is hope that the *fromagerie*, with equipment, boxes and labels will be reopened as part of the new Conservatoire des Techniques Fromagères Traditionelles for Normandy.

**Le Livarot AOC (1975/1980); Le Trois-Quarts Livarot; Le Petit Livarot, Le Quart Livarot.** *Région d'origine*: Pays d'Auge, in and between valleys of the rivers Dives and Touques, mostly in Calvados, but extending into Orne around Vimoutiers. 5 l of milk go into a 500g Livarot. The milk is lightly *écrémé*.

Le Livarot: 350–500g, 12cm × 5cm deep; *trois-quarts*: 270g Graindorge, 10.6cm wide; Petit: 225g Graindorge, 9cm wide; Quart: 110g Graindorge, 7cm wide. Soft cheese; *croûte-lavée*; golden-orange to pink crust, circumference bound with five *laîches*, strips of raffia, originally *typha latifolia* (recently revived at La Ferme de la Viette), designed to hold weaker cheeses in shape; now decorative and keeping up the rank of colonel, nickname of the cheese because of its five stripes.

*Method*: Raw milk is left to ripen naturally for up to 24 hours before being raised to 34–37°C and rennetted. Curd when formed is cut large, lightly stirred and drained for up to 24 hours before moulding. Moulds (formerly strips of wood clipped into circular form, now tall metal hoops) are turned several times in the following 24 hours. Cheeses removed from moulds are salted all over between third and seventh day after making (according to speed of drainage), and one day after salting removed to *cave* for at least 3 weeks (4 weeks total *affinage* is minimum), where they are washed with pure or slightly salted water at least three times, with turnings. The *saumure* (brine) used by Graindorge is a traditional formula. The five stripes are applied by hand during this period.

Full-sized cheeses are ripened for 60 days by Graindorge, smaller cheeses 15–30 days. Cheeses were formerly laid on rag-lined shelves. They now rest direct on the wood in the *caves*.

For history, see pp. 2–3.

*Sources of Livarot AOC.* 110g quart; 225g petit or demi; 270g trois-quarts; 450g Livarot. M. Bernard Graindorge and his son Thierry buy 14 million l of milk per year from 100 local farms, with great attention to purity and minimum fat and non-fat protein levels of 3.8% and 3.2% for Grade A (80% of suppliers). Bonuses are paid for each 0.1% improvement of constituents over Grade A. Nine million l were used for cheese in 1983 (650 tonnes of Livarot, 150 tonnes of Pont-l'Évêque). They now remove much of the water from the milk before it goes into the 95 l vats to receive starter and rennet.

Selection of cheeses is done halfway through *affinage* to eliminate imperfect crusts (too flat or too thick or discoloured by grey mould). After this they are promoted to colonel, if deserving. The best cheeses go out under the old red and blue Graindorge label. Seconds still qualifying for AOC are labelled Livarot de la Perrelle.

Non-AOC cheeses from Graindorge are sold cheaply as *Roger Bernard*.

Éts. Georges Bisson made prize cheese at Livarot (see p. 8).

Colas-Lebailly made excellent cheese on the northern outskirts of Livarot at Saint-Michel-de-Livet from 1867 until the early 1970s (label, '*Le Délice des Gourmets*'). See also p. 8.

Mme Désirée Bisson et Fils have been making Livarot and Pont-l'Évêque at La Fromagerie de la Viette for some years, on

farmhouse scale, and find demand growing (1987); open daily except Saturday p.m. and Sunday (tel. 31 20 60 37).
Pays d'Auge; 55 **13**, SW of C, Ste-Marguerite-de-Viette.
M. Denis Thébault (affiliated to the Groupe Triballat) makes Livarot, Pont-l'Évêque and Pavé. Livarot is aged on damp fir-wood shelves for at least 8 weeks in *cave humide*. He restored an old dairy in 1982, open 08.30–16.30 Monday–Friday.
Pays d'Auge; 55 **13**, SW of C, S of Boissey, La Houssaye.
M. C. Guyot has made Livarot and Pont-l'Évêque at the Fromagerie de Fresnay since 1980 (tel. 31 20 63 34).
Pays d'Auge; 55 **13**, SW of C on R. Oudon, Notre-Dame-de-Fresnay.

### Lucullus

Name invented by Androuët for *triple-crème* (75% m.g.) cheeses made of whole cows' milk enriched by extra cream.
Normandie; Île-de-France.

### Le Marbray

Neat drum, about 2.5kg, firm-crusted, with four layers of blue, made by Fromageries Bel in Normandie. '*Spécialité fromagère*' (see p. 46).
15% m.g.; *industriel*; *vache pasteurisé*.

### Maromme

See HAUTE-NORMANDIE.

### Mesnil

Unexciting *fromage frais* noted by Lindon (1961) without detail.
*laitier; vache.*

### Mignot Blanc; Mignot Passé

*Blanc*: Strong soft cheese fermented in enclosed space, eaten *frais* spring to early autumn; made from mid-nineteenth century around Vimoutiers.
*Passé*: Same cheese ripened. Courtine compared it with Livarot and said it had almost disappeared (1973). Androuët and Ninette Lyon found one in a market in summer, 350–400g, soft, fat, with natural crust (resembling Camembert), ripened one month; 'rich flavour, penetrating bouquet'; they thought the *fermière* selling it might be the last maker; dates from mid-nineteenth century.

### Mimolette Française

2.5–3kg; slightly flattened ball; semi-soft to hard, red-orange *pâte*; natural crust, rubbed, becoming hard and slightly pitted; mild to mellow: never strong, because of pasteurisation, but sometimes enriched by *affineurs* with port (see Chapter 8, pp. 265 and 266, ARRAS and BEUVRY); sold *jeune* (under 6 months), *demi-vieille* (6–12 months), *vieille* (12 months), *extra-vieille* (18 months). By UCL Isigny-Ste-Mère and Besnier (Le Président), at Ste-Mère-Église; Valco make it, labelled simply Mimolette Valco, at Valognes (see p. 27).
Mimolette comes from *demi-molle*, semi-soft, description of the young cheese, and was originally used for North Dutch cheeses of the type described above. It has been made in France, with other Dutch types, since Colbert encouraged such cheesemaking in Louis XIV's reign, to reduce imports.
40% m.g.; *laitier/industriel*; *vache pasteurisé*.
Manche; 54 **13**; 13km N of Carentan, Ste-Mère-Église, 54 **2**, Valognes.

### Monsieur

See FROMAGE DE MONSIEUR FROMAGE.

### Moyaux

See PAVÉ.

### Moyon

**Le Petit Moyonnais.** 1500g *Lingot*, 900g *pavé*, 180g *bondon* or *chabis*; as *fromages frais*, or *affinés*, coated in powdered charcoal; staring white, firm, but melt-in-mouth *pâte*; sweet, full flavour. Made by Roger Legoupil and his son (who trained at Château-Puyraux in Angoumois); sold on farm daily until 17.00; for a small charge visitors can go round the farm and dairy. The farm is E of the St-Lô-Tessy road (D28) opposite the turning (to the W) for Moyon (between Le Mesnil Opac and Fervaches). Roger Legoupil, 50 Moyon (tel. 33 56 32 42).
m.g. *non précisée*, min. 45%; *fermier*; *chèvre cru*.
Manche; 54 **13**, from Tessy-sur-Vire NW 6km.

### Noirville

**Fromages de Chèvre.** 1. Method Picodon-de-la-Drôme: *frais*, soft; *demi-sec*; *sec*,

with natural surface moulds; 2. Method Sainte-Maure: log; 3. Soft creamy *banon*-type.
*fermier; chèvre cru.*

**Fromage de Vache.** Neat drum, striated top; *pâte* of Romans type (see Chapter 16, p. 460).
*fermier; vache cru entier.*
All these made by Mme Smets, who sells on farm at Noirville (where 'known by everyone') and at Putanges market on Thursday.
Orne; 60 **2**, top from Putanges 6km NE.

NOTRE-DAME-DE-COURSON

M. Vigneau, *épicier-fromager* (closed Wed).
Calvados; 55 **13/14**.

NOTRE-DAME-DE-FRESNAY

**Fromage de Chèvre.** Mme Branelec-Bouillé makes and sells on farm, Le Val; also available to eat on spot at M. de Lesdain's house at Ste-Foy-de-Montgommery (5km S of Livarot).
*fermier; chèvre cru.*

**Livarot AOC; Pont-l'Évêque AOC; 'La Varinière'.** 350g cheese made by M. C. Guyot, Fromagerie de Fresnay (started 1980); visit Monday to Friday (tel. 31 20 63 34).
*artisanal; vache cru.*
Calvados; 55 **13**, SW of C on R. Oudon.

ORBEC

Wednesday (if Wed is holiday, Tues), and good Saturday markets. Pierre Lanquetot factory making *lait cru* Camembert AOC, (see p. 14), no sales retail.
Calvados; 55 **14**, C.

ORBIQUET

Old dairy no longer in use as such; close by, St-Martin-de-Bienfaite, where M. Maurice Lanquetot makes Domaine de l'Orbiquet (see CAMEMBERT AOC).
Calvados; 55 **14**, 1km N of Orbec.

ORÉ

200g soft flat drum, sold *frais*; source not traced.
40% m.g.; *vache.*

PARFAIT

'Nom de fantaisie' used for rich *triple-crème* cheese in inter-war and immediate post-war period (see FIN-DE-SIÈCLE).
*laitier; vache.*

PAVÉS DE NORMANDIE, OR CARRÉS

Pavés in Normandy are larger, usually much thicker versions of Pont-l'Évêque and other old golden-crusted cheeses (not necessarily washed-crust), with the curd sometimes more worked on outside the vat, in cloth, than with Pont-l'Évêque; crusts can be pale gold, pinky gold, or russet (*croûte-lavée*), or a pale fawn, matte surface (brushed crust).
Pays d'Auge/Calvados; Lisieux-Lieury district including W Eure; 55 **13/14**.

**Carré de Bonneville.** See BONNEVILLE. Le Fermier is larger 45% m.g. version of M. Touzé's Pavés d'Auge Fermier (see below). See also GRANDE CLOTTE and GRAND PONT.

**Pavé d'Auge.** Cheese, size of 2–3 Pont-l'Évêques, made at St-Julien-Le-Faucon.
*artisanal; vache cru.*
Calvados; 55 **13**, NW of C on D511.

**Pavé d'Auge le Fermier; Mini-Pavé d'Auge Fermier.** 550g (6 l of milk) and 320g; thick square; pale golden brushed crust; open texture (curd worked under cloth during drainage before putting in mould); flavour full of character, not strong; even after 10 days' travel our cheese still had excellent consistency and rich flavour (not salty, not sharp); see VIEUX PONT, M. Michel Touzé.
50% m.g.; *fermier; vache cru.*
Calvados; 55 **13**, L of C.

**Pavé d'Isigny.** 1700g; rectangular; *croûte-lavée*, reddish gold; by Union Coopérative Laitière d'Isigny-Ste-Mère (see ISIGNY).
50% m.g.; *laitier; vache cru.*
Calvados; 54 **13**.

**Pavé or Carré de Moyaux.** Most renowned of thick old Pavés, sometimes (here, at Fervaques and at Lieury) almost cubes.
50% m.g.; *fermier; artisanal; vache cru.*
Calvados; 55 **14**, high, on D510 NE of Lisieux, Moyaux.

**Pavé Normand.** 1kg, thick rectangular cheese, with white mould crust; 2kg thick round cheese, soft-ripened, by Henri Vallée et Fils, Clécy.
50% m.g.; *laitier; vache pasteurisé.*
Calvados; 55 **11**, S of C on D562.

**Le Pavé (Carré) du Plessis (Launay).** About 500g boxed washed-crust cheese made in the Fromagerie du Plessis started by a branch of the originally Huguenot family of du Plessis (from Midi, later Burgundian), who also made Pont-l'Évêque. They are now made there by Paul Launay, who won a gold medal in Paris for his Pont-l'Évêque in 1982, and recently renamed the dairy *Fromagerie de Noards*. Lieury, near by, used to feature an almost cubic Pavé in former days (see PAVÉ DE MOYAUX) remembered by Androuët.
*artisanal; vache cru.*
Eure; 8km E of Calvados border, 55 **14**, high R, S of Lieury, Noards.

**Pavé de Pont-l'Évêque.** Formerly made from 10 l of milk; 1kg cheese ripened 5–6 months, washed-crust; brown coat, some *monilium candidum* mould; very strong and individual.
*fermier; vache cru.*

**Pont d'Auge.** 1500g, square, deep Pavé, washed-crust (formerly by Pierre Levasseur), Gautier-Levasseur near Lisieux, who also make Pont-l'Évêque. Now larger scale.
*45% m.g.; laitier; vache (no longer cru).*
Calvados; 55 **14**.

**Le Tourgeville.** Pavé made by Lepeudry, Veuve Rigaud, Lanquetot; good Pont-l'Évêque (*croûte-lavée*) makers at Fromagerie de la Buissonnaye, Tourgeville.
*50% m.g.; artisanal; vache cru.*
Calvados; 55 **3**, 2km S of Deauville.

**Vieux Pané.** See p. 49.

LA PERRELLE

About 1500g, circular, washed-crust, Livarot style *pâte*, for cutting, by Graindorge, La Ferme de la Perrelle, Livarot (see p. 20), where they also make Pont-l'Évêque AOC.
*40% m.g.; laitier; vache cru.*

**Livarot de la Perrelle.** Seconds of Graindorge Livarot, still good enough for AOC. See LIVAROT.
*40% m.g.; laitier; vache cru.*

PETIT-SUISSE

See HAUTE-NORMANDIE.

PIQUETTE DE L'AVRANCHIN

Rennet 1 l milk (enough rennet to make it coagulate slowly); drain 24 hours and turn into a terrine; beat in 50cl of milk; add 20cl cream and beat again, and serve chilled. This is Ninette Lyon's recipe, and she adds that rennetting used to be done with a thistle stem or fig juice. (Greek and, following their example, Sicilian shepherds used, and still use, a branch fresh cut off a fig tree to stir the milk for making *pecorino*.)
*fermier; vache cru.*
Manche; 59 **8**, Avranches district.

POIDS PLUMÉ NORMAND

Camembert-size cheese made by Rigaud (see GRAND PAPA) for slimmers.
*25% m.g.; laitier; vache.*
Orne; 60 **1**, L of C.

PONT AUDEMER

Monday and Friday all-day markets; Fromagerie Jollit 08.45–12.30, 14.15–19.30 (except Tues and Sun p.m.).
Eure; 55 **4**.

PONT-L'ÉVÊQUE

Monday market.
Section Pont-l'Évêque du Syndicat des Fabricants de Pont-l'Évêque et Livarot.
Auge/Calvados; 55 **3**.

**Pont-l'Évêque AOC (1976/1980); Petit Pont-l'Évêque; Demi-Pont-l'Évêque.** Monstrously, the AOC does not demand *lait cru*, nor protect the proper area of origin, the Pays d'Auge, including all the Norman *départements* and Mayenne. The characters of cheeses from Haute-Normandie, Maine and Anjou are very different from that of the real *pays d'origine*.
*Pont-l'Évêque*: 300–400g; 10.5 to 11.5cm square; *Petit*: 220g; 8.5–9.5cm square; *demi*: 10.5–11.5cm × 5.2–5.7cm; half weight of maker's full-size cheese (cut into two rectangular half cheeses). For making, see p. 9.
Pont-l'Évêque, possibly of early twelfth-century monastic origin, and said to have been at first a round cheese, has claims on the twelfth-, thirteenth-century name Angelot (see pp. 2–3).
*Sources of Pont-l'Évêque AOC Lait cru* in Calvados to be found on map 55 **13**, unless otherwise stated, and within reach of, or on Route du Fromage. Gault Millau tested Pont-l'Évêque cheeses in February 1986 (out of season). Cheeses tested have notes preceded by 'GM'.

**Pont-l'Évêque AOC.** 1. 220g (*petit*) and 360g washed-crust, much lighter than Livarot, made by Graindorge father and son at La Ferme de la Perrelle in Livarot (see p. 20), open Monday to Friday. (GM: praised for good crust and fine *pâte*, but jury would have liked more characteristic flavour: perhaps too young a cheese, as marks varied less than in most cases).
45% m.g.; *laitier; artisanal; vache cru.*
Livarot, Calvados; SW of C.
2. AOC cheese made by Mme Désirée Bisson et Fils on farm scale for some years at la Fromagerie de la Viette on the Route du Fromage (also Livarot; tel. 31 20 60 37).
*artisanal; vache cru.*
Ste-Marguerite-de-Viette, Calvados; SW of C.
3. Lepeudry, Veuve Rigaud, Lanquetot et Cie make 360g *croûte-lavée* cheeses and give them 25 days' *affinage* at Fromagerie de la Buissonnaye, Tourgeville (see PAVÉS) (tel. 31 87 96 49); gold medal (Gault Millau winner with marks from 7 judges of 8/10 or more; praised for looks, for '*croûte-délicieuse*', fine *pâte* and much character). It is paler than most *croûte-lavée* cheeses. The Lepeudry name is over 100 years old here; 3 million litres of raw milk make 900,000 cheeses a year (324 tonnes).
Cheese can be bought at La Ferme de Beuvron and Gie des Marais, Bures-sur-Dives (see BEUVRON-EN-AUGE and neighbourhood); and on Route du Fromage, see AUGE.
50% m.g.; *artisanal; vache cru.*
Calvados; 55 **3**, near coast S of Deauville by D27.
4. *Croûte-lavée* cheese made by Pierre Levasseur, Gautier-Levasseur, St-Desir-de-Lisieux; I knew this as a neat, pleasant cheese while it was still 'Pierre Levasseur', *artisanal* and *lait cru*; I understand that it is now made on a larger scale of heat-treated milk.
45% m.g.; *laitier; vache (no longer cru).*
Calvados; 55 **13**, W edge of Lisieux.
Union Laitière du Pays d'Auge makes a 340g Pont-l'Évêque 45% m.g. at St-Désir-de-Lisieux, but the label 'Le Dauphin', which I have, does not declare *lait cru* or AOC.

**Pont-l'Évêque les Écussons Normands AOC.** 360g; *croûte-brossée* (*méthode* L. Foyer), very pale crust; very succulent interior with good flavour in March cheese (Gault Millau tasted three December or early January cheeses, perhaps all before maturity, as jury praised look of cheese and texture, but wished for more strength). Made by M. Charles Henri Grillard, Ferme de la Chesnée, Rauville-La-Bigot (see p. 25) noted for many years, and his father before him; prize winner since 1902 (and see LA GRANDE CLOTTE). I have had endless recommendations for this cheese, and it is praised in his preface to *Le Brie* (by Androuët and Chabot) by Michel Piot, Président de l'Association Professionnelle des Chroniqueurs et Informateurs de la Gastronomie.
45% m.g.; *artisanal; vache cru.*
Manche; 54 **1**, far R, 8km N of Bricquebec.

**Pont-l'Évêque Fermier.** Made by Robert Féret, found in Pont-l'Évêque market by Robert Freson (*The Taste of France*, 1981).
Calvados; 55 **3**, low R, 2km NW of Pont-l'Évêque, Coudray-Rabut.

**Pont-l'Évêque Fermier.** 1. Made by M. Martin; sold also at Bonneville-La-Louvet (see p. 13).
*fermier; vache cru.*
Calvados; 55 **3**, low 12km W of Pont-l'Évêque Bourgeauville.
2. 350g (3 l of milk), brushed-crust, pale gold; made and *affiné* by M. Michel Touzé (see PAVÉ D'AUGE FERMIER and VIEUX PONT) at Le Bôquet; open 08.00–12.00 daily except Sunday (tel. 31 20 78 67).
50% m.g.; *fermier; vache cru.*
Calvados; L of C, E of Vieux Pont.
3. 300g *croûte-lavée*, made by M. Albert and Mme D. Lallier, at Ferme de la Moissonnière, Fervaques (tel. 31 32 31 23) (GM: liked by judges who enjoyed Isigny and Ste-Mère Camemberts with strong aroma and neutral flavour; criticised by others for stretchy consistency and lack of flavour.
50% m.g.; *fermier; vache cru.*
Calvados; far R of C.
4. Made by GAEC de Grand Plain; sold also at Beuvron (see p. 13).
*fermier; vache cru.*
Calvados; 55 **12**, high 5.5km E of Troarn, St-Pierre-du-Jonquet.
5. Washed-crust; M. et Mme Dominique Demaris make 100 cheeses a day at Putôt-en-Auge, where established since 1950s; sale on farm up to 17.00, except Sunday (also butter, cream).

*fermier; vache cru.*
Calvados; 55 **12**, top R, 1km S of N175.

**Pont-l'Évêque Laitier Artisanal.** 330g brushed-crust *affiné* 1 month, made by Denis Thébault, Fromagerie Thébault, La Houssaye (open Mon–Fri 08.30–16.30) (GM 6.5 out of 10 from four judges, 6 from another, who liked the Fervaques cheese; the others thought the Thébault cheese too bitter and strong; they should have had a younger cheese to test before the strong example). This dairy was revived by M. Thébault in 1982, after twenty-five years of disuse. He collects milk from 12 farms.
*artisanal; vache.*
Calvados; SW of C, S of Boissey.

**Pont-l'Évêque Launay AOC.** 330g; made by Paul Launay, Fromagerie de Noards (and see PAVÉ DU PLESSIS) in a famous old *pavé* district, well E of Route du Fromage.
*45% m.g.; artisanal; vache cru.*
Eure; 55 **14**, 8km E of Calvados border, S of Lieury.

**Pont-l'Évêque la Varinière AOC.** 350g; made by M. C. Guyot, Fromagerie de Fresnay, Notre-Dame-de-Fresnay (tel. 31 20 63 34), started 1980.
*artisanal; vache cru.*
Calvados; 55 **13**, SW of C on R. Oudon.

PRÉSIDENT

Name on all Besnier cheeses in 'factories specialised for every sort of manufacture . . . optimal productivity uniquely due to the suppression of all *manutention* [untouched by human hand], thanks to the ultimate in automation . . . covering Camembert this specialisation has been pushed to the extreme to take account of the different tastes of consumers according to their regional customs'. These 'Camemberts' are made in ten factories in Normandy, and 'keep for 37 days'. The quotations are all from Besnier leaflets. They constitute a warning which leaves nothing for me to add.´

PROVIDENCE

Name used for Abbaye de Bricquebec cheese (see p. 12).

PUTANGES

Thursday market.
Orne; 60 **2**, high.

LE QUÉTON D'ISIGNY

1kg flat round soft cheese, *croûte-fleurie*, with aspect of young Brie de Montereau, by UCL Isigny; see ISIGNY.
*laitier; vache cru.*
Calvados.

RACLETTE

12kg Elle et Vire cheese by Union Laitière Normande (see VIRE).
*45% m.g.; laitier; vache pasteurisé.*
Calvados.

**Raclette Valco.** 6kg cheese of Alpine type for heating and scraping (variation on Fondue) made by Laiterie Coopérative Valco de Valognes (see p. 27), and now, at 1000 tonnes per year, forming half its production.
*45% and 48% m.g.; laitier; vache pasteurisé.*
Manche; 54 **2**.

LE RANCHY (dormant)

About 150g small, deep, upright drum, the nearest any other cheese has come to Monsieur (see p. 18), but fatter and more fragile; formerly made by Fromagerie de Ranchy.
*75% m.g.; artisanal; vache cru.*

**Saint-Martin or Saint-Pol.** *Triple-crème* cutting cheese of Brie de Melun proportions (about 1500g and 4cm deep), of clotted consistency and excellent unsalty rich flavour, called Saint-Martin (or Saint-Pol, as formerly distributed by Lanquetot-Pligny at Rungis). Unfortunately the Fromagerie de Ranchy closed down some time after 1977 and these fine, rather individual cheeses were lost. Before it is too late some keen artisan should trace the recipes and revive them (Triballat's Tyrou comes somewhere near).
*75% m.g.; artisanal; vache cru.*
Calvados; 54 **15**.

RAUVILLE-LA-BIGOT

M. Charles Henri Grillard's famous and widely respected family farmhouse cheese enterprise started 1902; many medals; see LA GRANDE CLOTTE, and PONT-L'ÉVÊQUE AOC (Rauville) Domaine de la Chesnée, 50121 Rauville-La-Bigot.
Manche; 54 **1**, far R 8km N of Bricquebec.

### Ribotte
Skimmed milk renneted and coagulated.

### Roger Bernard
Minimum 225g cheeses from Graindorge. See LIVAROT.

### Saint-Jouvin
2kg golden crusted, semi-soft; by UCL Isigny (see p. 19).
St-Mère; Manche.

### St-Lô
Tuesday and Saturday market.
Manche; 54 **13**.

### St-Maclou
Long-established Laiterie Lepetit for *lait cru* Camembert (see pp. 15–16).

### Ste-Marguerite-de-Viette
Fromagerie de la Viette; see LIVAROT, PONT-L'ÉVÊQUE.

### Saint-Martin or Saint-Pol
See LE RANCHY.

### St-Martin-de-Bienfaite
Éts Maurice Lanquetot, *lait cru* Camembert (see p. 15).

### Ste-Mère-Église
Union Coopérative Laitière Isigny Ste-Mère (see ISIGNY), which uses Ste-Mère in numerous cheese names.
Manche.

### Saint-Michel
Name given to *quart* Livarot formerly by Colas-Lebailly at St-Michel, see LIVAROT. Successor to M. Moutarde makes Livarot here.

### Saint-Morgon
200g cheese of Camembert type.
50% m.g.; *laitier*; *vache*.
Eure.

### Saint-Paulin
About 1500g; semi-soft, washed-crust, poor man's version of old monastic Abbaye de Notre Dame du Port du Salut, the original of Port du Salut (see pp. 43 and 46); see ISIGNY-SUR-MER.

### Saint-Philippe
Name given by Philippe Olivier of Boulogne (see p. 267) to soft drum-shaped cheese of 450g made for him on an undisclosed farm in Normandie.
*fermier*; *vache cru*.

### St-Pierre-sur-Dives
Monday market; Abbaye de St-Pierre-sur-Dives: eighteenth-century buildings taken over by *commune* in 1980s for Conservatoire des Fromages de Normandie; six-month courses; research into extinct cheeses; open to public on Route du Fromage; see CAMEMBERT (Moulin de Carel).
Calvados; 55 **13**.

### Saint Pol
Name formerly given by *affineur* to Saint-Martin (see RANCHY).

### Ste-Foy-de-Montgommery
Fifteenth-century *manoir* open daily serves *chèvres*.
Calvados; 55 **13**, 5km S of Livarot on Route du Fromage.

### Serans
Where P. Lavalou used to make a delicious *véritable* Camembert de Normandie (*label-rouge*) called Jour de Fête. The lid of the box was adorned with *belle-époque* figures, men in white ties, and full-dress uniforms, about to receive their Camembert from a white-gloved butler.
Orne; 60 **2**, high by Écouché.

### Sourdeval
Tuesday market; M. Alain Dupas used to make his *lait cru* Camembert here from organically produced milk, including Le Méray, until he was bought up by a bigger concern.
Manche; 59 **9**.

### Sû
A term for *lait écrémé* in the Cotentin.
Manche.

### Suprême
An old 'nom de fantaisie' applied to a *triple-crème* cheese between the wars, and later used for a bland industrial cheese.

## Tomme Grise
Tomme Normande *affinée* in Savoie.
20% m.g.; *laitier; vache pasteurisé.*

## Tourgeville
See PAVÉ, PONT-L'ÉVÊQUE.

## Trappiste
See BRICQUEBEC.

## Trouville-sur-Mer
Wednesday and Sunday market; daily from Easter to September.
Brasserie les Vapeurs (12.00–24.00 Feb to mid-Nov); fine fish and sea food; *lait cru* Camembert and Pont-l'Évêque (Lepeudry).
Calvados; 55 **3**, S of C.

**Le Trouville.** Local cheese formerly so named (1961), like Pont-l'Évêque.
*fermier; artisanal; vache cru.*
Calvados; 55 **3**, S of C.

## Truté
Term for skimmed milk around Condé-sur-Noireau, 14km N of Flers.
Calvados.

## Tyrou
*Triple-crème* cutting cheese a little reminiscent of Saint-Martin (see p. 25), made by Triballat.
75% m.g.; *laitier; vache.*

## Valognes
Tuesday and Friday market.
Laiterie coopérative Valco, 111 rue de Poterie, makes Trappiste de Bricquebec or Providence (see ABBAYE DE), Gouda Français, Goutu, Mimolette, Raclette, Saint-Paulin.
Manche; 54 **2**.

## Le Vieux Pont Affiné au Calvados
M. Michel Touzé and Mme Thérèse Touzé (assistant *fromager* Patrick Bove); some of their Mini Pavés of 320g are given three washings in Calvados in first two weeks of *affinage*, which totals 4–5 weeks, to achieve Le Vieux Pont. They also make this Demi-Pavé plain, 550g full size Pavé d'Auge, 350g *croûte-brossée* Pont-l'Évêque and a large cutting *pavé* called Le Fermier.
50% m.g. (except Le Fermier, 45% m.g.); *fermier; vache cru.*
Calvados; 55 **13**, L of C near Route du Fromage.

## Villedieu
See HAUTE-NORMANDIE.

## Villedieu-les-Poêles
Tuesday market.
Manche; 59 **8**.

## Vimoutiers
Monday afternoon and Friday market.
Syndicat d'Initiative (Route du Fromage leaflets). Memorial to Marie Harel (see pp. 3–5).
Auge/Orne; 55 **13**, lower R near Calvados border.

## Vire
Friday market. There is a good cheese shop near the place du 6 Juin (town centre).
Union Laitière normande, route d'Aunay-sur-Odon (its *marque* is Elle-et-Vire); well known for yoghurts and butter (90,000 tonnes per year); Raclette (see p. 5) is among its cheeses (74,000 tonnes per year of all kinds); this giant concern, formed from seventeen small co-operatives in 1945, has twenty-two liquid-milk dairies and factories, disposing of 800 million litres of milk annually, with an American subsidiary selling 3000 tonnes of French cheese. In 1984 it started exporting long-life milk to Britain.
Calvados; 59 **9**.

# Haute-Normandie
## SEINE-MARITIME – EURE

Haute-Normandie has only two *départements*, but they produce 4 per cent of French milk and 8 per cent of French cheese. Most of that cheese is industrial, such as the Mimolette and related cheeses of Lillebonne, Bongrain's Boursin of Bonneville-sur-Iton and Pacy-sur-Eure, and the ultra-modern soft products of Gervais, of which there is more to say when we come to Petit-Suisse. Gervais started making cheese in the Pays de Bray, the part of Haute-Normandie of most interest to us.

The Pays de Bray is one of the ancient cradles of French cheesemaking which has remained true to its traditions. A dozen or so small rivers rise in this fertile *pays*, running north-west to the Channel, north-east and east to the Bresle, and south towards the Seine. The land is green and pleasant rather than exciting. The comfortable brown-patched white of the Normande cattle is now jarringly punctuated by the black-and-white of the intruders, still called Frisonnes, although American Holstein sires have dominated the breed for generations.

## Frometon and Gournay

This has been dairy country for a thousand years and more. In 1050 Hugues de Gournay granted to the Abbaye de Sigy, to the north-west of Gournay, *'la dîme des Frometons'*, a tithe of the local cheese. At that time, monks were usually the exemplars and stimulators of cheesemaking, but here it seems they were fed 'lay' cheeses from outside their own demesnes. Frometon was still the cheese-name used when a basketful was given to Napoleon in 1805: it is a pity that a name lasting so long should have died so recently.

A longstanding local practice of keeping part of one day's cheese to ensure the development of the next day's led to the adoption of the term *caudiau* for cheese set aside for use in whole or in part for that purpose. Any not needed would be eaten fresh. It was, as it were, the tail (*caudia*, or *coda*) of the previous batch, perpetuating its strain of fermentation from one cheesemaking to the next.

Curd was drained on rush mats, locally called *caserettes*, and cheeses were sold under that name, still on the mats, as unsalted *fromage blanc*, or at the *fromage frais* stage. These flat, round cheeses were the standard Frometons in the southern part of the Pays de Bray around Gournay and Gournay has now been their name for over a century. Many were, and are, kept long enough to become *moussés*, coated with the soft, furry white *moisissure* provided by the abundant indigenous *penicillium candidum*. A few cheeses were ripened long enough to develop a rosy crust and reminded some observers of Camembert, but their aromas and internal textures and flavours were very different.

The cheese now called Gournay has for some years been made only in *laiteries*. In the middle of the last century it acquired a new name, Malakoff, through a distributor in Paris. He could have been directly celebrating the successful French assault on the Russian fort of Malakoff in the Crimea in 1855 (some flat, round fortresses do, perhaps, recall such a cheese), or could have been an inhabitant of the new Paris suburb given that name. The name Malakoff is still in use for the round, shallow *bonde platte* mould supplied to its members by the Syndicat for Neufchâtel cheeses.

## NEUFCHÂTEL CHEESES

Old basic methods including slow drainage and the addition of one cheese from an earlier batch to the new curds, persist in the Neufchâtel cheeses made in a belt across the centre of the Pays de Bray. They long ago developed a range of shapes, of which the Malakoff is the least used. Still the most common after centuries of existence is the Bondon or Bonde, meaning a bung, and the Bondard or Double-Bonde, *bondard* being the large bung used in a cider *barrique*.

Bondon was the mother of another cheese, fathered in 1850 by a Swiss *fromager* at the *laiterie* of Madame Hérould at Villiers-sur-Auchy, east of Gournay. He suggested adding cream to the slowly developed curd prepared for her Bondons to make it into a richer cheese which could be sold at the unsalted *fromage blanc* stage. (It was an old custom to add cream to Double-Bondes on the farm; this made them milder, but they were not usually eaten *blanc* or *frais*.) The result so excited the customers that a *commis* in the firm handling the cheeses in Les Halles decided to set up a factory to make them. His name was Charles Gervais and his first *laiterie* was in Ferrières on the eastern outskirts of Gournay, beside the railway station. Express distribution of the cheese, which was called Petit-Suisse, was done in Paris in yellow-wheeled cabriolets with bells. Madame Hérould's fortune was soon made.

Other cheeses were made by Gervais, and all the curd was drained in the traditional way in piled-up sacks. Sacks of curd left on top of the piles to drain more slowly were used, with the added cream, for making Petit-Suisse. It was packed in waxed boxes of six tiny cylinders, wrapped in thick paper, and was of delicious freshness and creamy consistency when the paper was peeled off. It is true that neglected or over-age Petits-Suisses dried up or took mould, but bought and used with due care and speed they were delicious. Another, later spin-off from regional tradition was the Demi-Sel, derived from the Carré Neufchâtel, and sold at the crustless *fromage frais* stage. Both these cheeses were later also produced by the Bray firm of Pommel.

Meanwhile, the use of heart-shaped moulds was spreading to Neufchâtel farms from the North. By the early 1900s Cœurs Neufchâtel were current on the Paris market, alongside the familiar little Bondons, the rectangular Briquettes and the Carrés.

Since then farms have almost given up making Bondons. I learned why when I first visited Monsieur Jacques Bailleux and his family in May 1977 at Mesnil-Mauger, where he had farmed and made cheese since 1953. His mother still farms at Le Fossé, where the family name is borne by the Neufchâtel cheeses made by Bernard Bailleux. Jacques Bailleux was producing Briquettes, Cœurs and Double-Bondes, but had given up Bondons because they were so labour-intensive to make and mature in the traditional way. All but three farms now share this view and leave the bulk of Bondons to the mechanised multi-mould world of the factories.

At Mesnil-Mauger I watched the patient interlocking of waiting and watching with laborious hand-and-finger work necessitated by Neufchâtel's uniquely prolonged procedure. It is slower than goat-cheese making and far removed from its simplicity. First came the covering of the vats containing yesterday's two milkings, then the renneting of that morning's milking, which would remain uncovered all day. This was fair May weather, and the time from renneting to withdrawal of curd for *égouttage* was running at about twenty-four hours (twelve hours is the fastest on any farm in summer, forty-eight hours the slowest in winter). The curd of yesterday's morning milk was now poured on to sacking cloths, wrapped in them and placed on a metal ladder-type *bannette* in a large tub, a *faisselier*, to drain. There it would remain for the rest of its second twenty-four hours, with periodic shifting of the bundles to share out fairly the time spent in top and bottom berths. The bundles of curd from two days before were now put under pressure of boxes of stones laid on planks for twenty-four hours. (Times for *égouttage* on the *bannette*, and pressure under direct weight or leverage, each vary with the amount of rennet and with the season, from two hours on one farm to between six and twenty-four hours on the rest.)

Now it was the turn of the curd of both milkings from three days before, already relieved from *pression* (the weights and planks having been placed on the next day's curd) to be turned out from its sacking on to a large table for *malaxage*. This means the thorough mixing of the two curds, the evening one a little moister than the morning one, and their enrichment by the broken-up fragments of a *fromage moussé*, a cheese on which the *penicillium candidum* was in full bloom. (Sometimes in winter the Bailleux would not mix the two curds together; the very slow timing might mean their being incompatible.) As soon as the *pâte* was evenly mixed and unctuous, Monsieur Bailleux hand-packed it into his Double-Bonde, Briquette and heart-shaped copper moulds. (Most moulds of all shapes are now of plastic, supplied to farms by the Syndicat to standardise cheeses to AOC sizes.) The moment the last mould was filled, the first was turned out and the cheese lightly salted on all surfaces, ready for the *cave*. There it would spend at least twelve days at 12–14°C with back-up heating ready to compensate for any sudden drop in temperature. The atmosphere was humid enough to keep happy and active the *couches* of *penicillium candidum* which darken walls and vaulting. Most Bailleux cheeses spend fifteen days there, and those for family and local trade twenty-one or more.

Within a few days the spores shot out by the lively black tapestry would start coating the new cheeses with the white surface which is traditional for Neufchâtel, an inheritance it has generously shared with Camembert since 1910 (see p. 4). Cheeses can be considered *à point* when they are *moussés* with an unbroken, deep-piled white velvet, rather thicker than Camembert's in proportion to the size of cheese. The *pâte* is then soft and slightly apertured, and looks deceptively almost granular, evidence of the laborious work put in to amalgamate the slowly developed curds.

The aroma on first impact is of the freshly blooming white mould. When the cheese is cut, a certain lactic sharpness is added. The flavour confirms the aroma, setting a unique fresh tartness against the creamy blandness of the crust, and then revealing the deeper richness which results from the prolonged ripening of milk and curd, and the mixing of two stages of curd with an already *moussé* cheese.

Goat cheeses share the slow initial stages of Neufchâtel; but England's Lancashire comes nearer, with its even longer, more laborious repeated hand-breaking and pressing of the curd, and its mixture of two curds from separate days, combining four milkings. Traditional Lancashire, too, has a tart edge to its flavour, unlike that of any other cheese, and most of it is sold at the same age as Neufchâtel. Though technically classified as a hard cheese, Lancashire is in fact a very large semi-soft cheese, mellowing quickly because of the unusual treatment and mixture of the curds, and softening as it ripens.

Some Neufchâtel is matured by the braver natives to a stage when its white surface bloom has retired into a newly formed black *couche*, which will soon generate its own spores. The cheese becomes exceedingly sharp, and the coat almost truffly on the palate, but a good deal stronger. Neufchâtel in this state is claimed by those who love it to be a supreme challenge to the most powerful wines, enhancing the taste of any which can meet it.

We visited Neufchâtel again eight years later, in 1985, and were kindly received and brought well up to date by Monsieur Bloquel at the *mairie*. As secretary of the Syndicat de Défense et de Qualité du Fromage de Neufchâtel, he thought that the last decade, including the institution of the AOC in the year of our previous visit, had not seen much change. The thirty-four active farms of which the Syndicat had details were producing a steady 350 tonnes of cheese a year, mainly in Cœurs, Briquettes and Double-Bondes. Only ten made Carrés and only three made any Bondons. The gap in Bondons was filled by the two laiteries, whose production appeared to have increased from between 450 and 500 tonnes in 1982 (Crémerie Française figures) to 660 tonnes in 1984.

Farm production was starting to grow again, but when I revisited Jacques Bailleux he said that new entrants to the Syndicat were hard to come by. The essential traditional methods (see pp. 37–9) put off any cheesemaker without a vocation, and there are still almost unavoidable faults which can creep in and ruin the production of one or several days. The commonest are *oïdium* (which forms a greasy surface and inhibits the taking of the vital *penicillium candidum*) and *penicillium glaucum*. The latter is the old blue surface mould for Camembert, all wrong for Neufchâtel, though still welcome in the *caves* of *affineurs* of some *chèvres*, and of the cows'-milk cheese of the Orléanais termed bleus for their crust colour (see Chapter 2).

The AOC rules bow to the *laiteries* in allowing the use of pasteurised milk, and in demanding a mere ten days' minimum time from renneting to sale. The Bailleux (now father and son in the GAEC d'Orson) consider three weeks the shortest respectable time, and say that two months is thought ideal to suit family and local tastes. *Grossistes* (wholesalers) take their cheeses at fifteen days. I noticed that the Bailleux repertoire now included a 500-gram Cœur.

## Lost cheeses: Excelsior, Le Magnum and Petit-Suisse

There are three casualties to mourn in the Pays de Bray, affecting a further two cheese-names. In the mid-1970s I found I could no longer buy Excelsior and Le Magnum. These were both cream-enriched cheeses of remarkable clotted texture, with gold to red *croûtes-fleuries*, which had been on my Wells Stores list since the 1950s (I have a January 1976 list still featuring Le Magnum at £2.20). The 220-gram Excelsior of 72 per cent *matières grasses* had been made by the Dubuc family at Rouvray-Câtillon near Forges-les-Eaux since 1890, latterly also in a 110-gram size. Le Magnum, a 500-gram *triple-crème* of Coulommiers form, was an inter-wars extension of Excelsior into a size important enough to provide a presentable single-cheese course at dinner. Dubuc made it at Forges-les-Eaux. Henri Androuët (Pierre Androuët's father) named the fully matured Excelsior 'Fin-de-Siècle' and the full-blooded Magnum 'Brillat-Savarin'. They richly deserved their titles.

Sadly, deaths in the Dubuc family led to the closure of their two establishments, and their two originals had had no worthy successors. The right to use the various names, including Brillat-Savarin, was bought up with Dubuc's milk-supply contracts by Besnier, to whom the preservation of those notable cheeses obviously meant nothing. (They also bought the Cléville milk and Monsieur Fromage's name, but I look in vain for his credible resurrection: see p. 10.) For some years the name Brillat-Savarin was used by makers of 500-gram *triple-crèmes* in various parts of France, but Besnier eventually clamped down on them (leading to such regrettable distortions as 'Brivarin'), and confined its use to the Fromagerie de Pansey in Brie Champenoise. This large *laiterie* did make its cheeses (including a passable Brie de Meaux AOC) of *lait cru*, but started pasteurising in the mid-1980s. I have not found any of these latter-day Brillat-Savarins, legitimate or pirate, justifying the original intention of Henri Androuët: to honour a cheese of extraordinary interior richness of texture and savour at the roseate-gold stage of its external *floraison*. So the disappearance of Excelsior and Le Magnum has also deprived the names Fin de Siècle and Brillat-Savarin of their meaning and purpose in life.

The third casualty of this *pays* is the Petit-Suisse. I have recounted its origin and history, to which it remained true until 1976 (see p. 29). Since then this delicious cream-enriched, 60 per cent *matières grasses double-crème* has been killed, and its name misapplied to an industrial 40 or 60 per cent *matières grasses* amalgam of milk solids and whey, separated from the rest of the milk without benefit of rennet, by centrifugal force, and without added cream. Léone Bérard wrote in 1978 that they no longer had the *onctuosité* of the really fresh Suisses of former days: 'and I have never rediscovered the taste at once mild and acidulated of the *froumagets* bought every Thursday in my childhood from the *paysanne* who called them out in the street from door to door in her donkey cart.'* I am not sure, technically speaking, that the new product even merits the name of cheese. It is certainly a mere shadow, or rather a watery dilution, of its former self. The continued use by the centrifuge-operators of the name Petit-Suisse for this travesty is a libel on the Swiss inventor and a betrayal of the trust of customers who used the original cheese for their recipes. This product might more reasonably now be sold as 'Petit-Swizz'. The only hope for discriminating former users who have not yet found an alternative is this: there are artisans making Petit-Suisse in the Tarn, Laiterie Sagne at Mazamet and Laiterie Boineau at nearby Lacalmilhe (see Chapter 5). They should find ready takers for their cheeses at Rungis, but if prosperity comes to them, I pray that they do not let it turn their heads or their cheese from the paths of righteousness: integrity is all.

## Cheeses of Haute-Normandie

### Beaussault

See NEUFCHÂTEL FERMIER.

### Bondard or Double-Bonde (AOC)

Neufchâtel, also called Fromage à Tout Bien and Fromage du Propriétaire (see NEUFCHÂTEL for type of *pâte*); min. 200g cylinder 5.8cm diameter 8cm long (AOC measurements for Double-Bonde) made by twenty-four farms out of thirty-four; or 300g 7cm × 9cm long (not AOC); soft; *croûte-fleurie*; *bondard* means bung, of the size for the enormous cider vat (*barrique*); Bondard or Double-Bonde (has been resumed in recent years). Gros-Bondards or Triple-Bondes (see p. 40) are sometimes made on farms for family occasions. Double-Bondes are an old custom on the farms, milder than most Neufchâtel cheeses. They formerly included cream added to the curd at the *malaxage* stage, and were called *Double-crème*.
50–60% m.g.; *fermier*; *vache cru entier*.
Seine-Maritime.

### Bonde-Platte

See MALAKOFF.

### Bondon or Bonde Neufchâtel (AOC)

(See NEUFCHÂTEL for type of *pâte*.) Min. 100g cylinder, 4.5cm diameter, 6.5cm long (AOC measurements), soft, *croûte-fleurie*; made by three farms and machine-made by the *laiteries*. Bondon is the older name and this is the oldest form of Neufchâtel cheese; *bondon*, still normally used, means a small bung, while *bonde* just means bung. Few farms make it because it is labour intensive and a tricky keeper, with so much exposed surface in relation to volume of cheese.
45–50% m.g.; *fermier*; *vache cru entier*.
Seine-Maritime.

### Bouelles

See NEUFCHÂTEL FERMIER.

### La Bouille

220g, 8cm across, 5–5.5cm deep; about 500g about 12cm × 5.5cm and recently 1000g (approx) cutting cheese; double cream; thick *croûte-fleurie*; rich aroma and flavour.
Androuët attributes this cheese to M. Fromage, an invention of the early 1900s (see p. 18), but I have never liked it as much as the original Little Monsieur and think it a post-M. Fromage invention. La Bouille is the Roumois word for *bidon*, milk-churn.
60% m.g.; *laitier/artisanal*; *vache enrichi de crème*.
Seine-Maritime.

### Boursin, Boursin-à-l'Ail-et-aux-Fines-Herbes, Boursin au Poivre

225g drum, 8cm × 4.5cm deep (and in miniatures); *fromage frais*, no crust; plain,

---

*Léone Bérard, *Le Livre des Fromages et de leurs à-côtés*, 1982.

or with garlic and *fines-herbes* mixed in *pâte*, or coated with coarsely crushed peppercorns (the most cheese-like and satisfactory version to my mind). Boursin invented this cheese after the Second World War, and it is now managed by Bongrain from Bonneville-sur-Iton, 8km W of Evreux.
75% m.g.; *industriel; vache pasteurisé*.
Eure; 55 **17**, 18km E of Evreux.

### BRILLAT-SAVARIN

This name was first given by Henri Androuët between the wars to a cream-enriched cheese made by Dubuc of a larger size than their Excelsior (see p. 35), usually after more than the minimum three weeks' ripening. This was called Le Magnum (see p. 36) in its normal guise on the market. Unfortunately the Dubuc dairies closed after deaths in the family in the early 1970s. The name was subsequently used in Basse-Normandie by Lepetit (at St-Maclou), by at least two *laitiers* in Burgundy, by Mme Soulié in Rouergue, and by makers elsewhere, for thick drums of white-coated *triple-crème*, usually sold in a very young state. These cheeses were and are very different from the rich, clotted textured, red and golden coated Magnum. Besnier had the right to the name, presumably in buying up the old Dubuc milk supplies and other interests, and suppressed its use by the *laitiers* mentioned above, who now use other titles, such as Vatel, Brivarin. Brillat-Savarin is now legally made as such by Fromageries de Pansey in the Brie region, and is of the thick, *croûte-fleurie* variety, rarely brought to full *affinage*.
75% m.g.; *laitier/artisanal; vache cru*.

### BRIQUETTE NEUFCHÂTEL

(See NEUFCHÂTEL for nature of *pâte*.) Min. 100g, 7cm × 5cm rectangular, 3cm deep; soft, *croûte-fleurie*; made by twenty-seven out of thirty-four farms in 1985.
45% m.g.; *fermier; vache cru*.

### BUCHAIL

1kg log, *fromage frais* mixed with garlic and herbs, made by Lhernault SA, rue des Abreuvoirs, Neufchâtel-en-Bray.
Seine-Maritime; 52 **15**.

### BUCHY

Monday market.
Seine-Maritime; 55 **7**, high.

### CARRÉ DE BRAY, CARRÉ NEUFCHÂTEL (AOC)

(For type of *pâte* see NEUFCHÂTEL.) 100g, 7cm square, 2cm deep; soft, *croûte-fleurie*; ripened 2 weeks in *cave humide*; an old local form of Neufchâtel cheese, from which (in the *fromage frais* stage) *demi-sel* has descended (and see CIBOULETTE). Ten out of thirty-four farms were making *carrés* in 1985.
45–50% m.g.; *fermier; laitier; vache cru/pasteurisé*.

### CASERETTE

120g, round, 7–8cm × 3cm deep; *fromage frais*, unsalted; one of oldest regional forms, after Caudiau (see below) and before Gournay (see p. 36). This size of Gournay has often been called Malakoff. La caserette was the rush mat on which the cheeses used to be drained and sold.
50% m.g.; *fermier; vache cru entier*.

### CAUDIAU

Old Bray cheese started with piece of previous day's cheese, not renneted; eaten *frais* or used as source of starter for next day's cheese.
*Cauda = coda = queue* = tail, signifying '*queue de fermentation*'. This cheese became Caserette, precursor of Gournay.
m.g. *non-précisée; fermier; vache cru entier*.
Seine-Maritime.

### CHEVRETTE FROMAGERIE DES NEIGES

About 1kg log; soft; no crust; with garlic and herbs; by Compagnie Fermière et Fromagère Normande, St-Germain-sur-Avre.
0% m.g. with added cream; *chèvre*.
Plaine de St-André/Eure; 60 **7**, high, N of N12 and R. Avre.

### CIBOULETTE NEUFCHÂTEL

Carré Neufchâtel Frais coated with *ciboulette* (chopped chives) and/or *ciboules* (spring onions); not within AOC range; it may be allowed to develop its white mould surface before sale.
45–50% m.g.; *fermier; vache cru*.
Seine-Maritime.

## Cœur de Bray or Cœur Neufchâtel (AOC)

(For type of *pâte* see NEUFCHÂTEL.) Minimum 200g heart, 8–10cm across, 2.5–3cm deep; soft; *croûte-fleurie*; late nineteenth-century invention, available in Paris markets early this century; thirty out of thirty-four farms were making it in 1985.
Double and Triple Cœurs are sometimes made on farms for family celebrations, and occasionally sold (see NEUFCHÂTEL FERMIER (Mesnil-Mauger)).
45–50% m.g.; *fermier; vache cru entier.*
Seine-Maritime.

## Dampierre St-Nicolas

*Fromager mi-gros* (cheese factor) with Rungis connections: M. Jean-Pierre Leroy.
Seine-Maritime; 52 **4**, 13km SE of Dieppe.

## Demi-Sel

67g; 6–7cm, square, 2cm deep (or 6cm × 25cm square); at *fromage frais* stage, no crust. M. Pommel developed this cheese in the later nineteenth century from the *frais* stage of Carré Neufchâtel, with simplified treatment of curd; Gervais took it up as well. It needs to be eaten very fresh, and has a slightly acid tang. In recent years importers outside France have been wary of stocking it because of 'sell by' dates, which certainly need examination before accepting the cheese. Perhaps the trouble is partly due to new methods of making (see PETIT-SUISSE).
40% m.g.; *industriel; vache pasteurisé.*
Seine-Maritime; 55 **8**, 52 **16**, Gournay-en-Bray.

## Demi-Suisse

See PETIT-SUISSE. Legal definition: *fromage frais* of renneted cows' milk, homogeneous *pâte*, firm, salt 2%, 40% m.g. minimum in dry matter, 30% minimum dry matter in whole cheese.

## Dieppe

Markets: Tuesday and Wednesday (small, two cheese stalls with local produce), Thursday and Saturday (good).
*Fromager/affineur*: M. Olivier, 16–18 rue Saint-Jacques. An excellent range of cheeses, issuing from fine, well-managed *caves*; plenty of other good food and drink.
(M. Olivier's grandfather sold cheese in Rouen in 1896; his father has retired, but still gives a hand; his brother Philippe is at Boulogne, see Chapter 8, p. 267.)

## Double-Bonde

See BONDARD NEUFCHÂTEL.

## Double-Cœur

See CŒUR.

## Elbeuf

Tuesday, Thursday, Saturday market.
*Fromager/affineur*: Jollit, Fromager de Tradition, rue du Maréchal Leclerc.
Roumois/Seine-Maritime; 55 **6**, bottom.

## Esclavelles

See NEUFCHÂTEL FERMIER.

## Excelsior (dormant)

110g and 220g (latter 9.5cm across, 3.5cm deep); 2 weeks in *hâloir*; rich clotted consistency and flavour; *croûte-fleurie* turning golden; invented 1890 by M. Dubuc at Rouvray-Catillon, and made there until family died out in early 1970s. I know of no existing cheese quite like it, but, at its best, Rouzaire's Comte-Robert comes nearest (see also LE MAGNUM).
72% m.g.; *artisanal; vache cru enrichi de crème.*
Pays de Bray, Seine-Maritime; 55 **8**, 7km SW of Forges-Les-Eaux, Rouvray-Catillon.

## Fécamp

Market last Saturday in month.
Seine-Maritime; 52 **12**, on coast.

## Fin de Siècle (dormant)

Name given between the wars by Henri Androuët to Excelsior (see p. 34).
72% m.g.; *artisanal; vache cru enrichi de crème.*
Seine-Maritime.

## Forges-les-Eaux

Thursday market; and see LE MAGNUM.
*Fromager* (*demi-gros* and retail): B. Buisson, 30 rue du Maréchal Leclerc, featuring Neufchâtel farm cheeses.
Seine-Maritime.

## Le Fossé

See NEUFCHÂTEL FERMIER.

### Frometon

The original cheeses of the region were known as Frometons. In 1050 Hugues de Gournay granted a tithe of Frometons (La Dîme des Frometons) to the Abbaye de Sigy (which is just S of Forges-Les-Eaux, about 22km NW of Gournay). Frometon–Caudiau – Caserette – Gournay – Neufchâtel is thought to be the line of development in the Pays de Bray.
Seine-Maritime.

### Froumaget

Name used for farmhouse versions of Petit-Suisse (see pp. 39–40).

### Gisors

Monday and Friday market.
Eure; 55 **8 9**, 25km S of Gournay.

### Gournay-en-Brie

Tuesday (best), Friday and Sunday market. Earliest known centre of cheesemaking in region (see FROMETON).

**Gournay.** This name became attached to round farm cheeses of the region developed from Caserette, Caudiau and Frometon, to become the type now called Neufchâtel or Malakoff; usually sold young, but sometimes *affiné* and slightly resembling Camembert. The term Gournay is now used for the industrial version of the flat round original type of the locality, 100–120g, 8cm diameter, 2.5cm deep; ripened just long enough to 'mousser', i.e. to acquire its fluffy coat of *penicillium candidum*. In its freshest state it was commonly called Malakoff in the Paris markets, and this name is still used. It can be kept 2–3 weeks in same conditions as Neufchâtel cheeses, and acquires a rosy crust.
45% m.g.; *fermier/industriel; vache cru/pasteurisé*.
Seine-Maritime; 52 **16**, 55 **8**, R of C.

### Gros-Bondard

See TRIPLE-BONDE.

### Le Havre

Tuesday, Thursday and Saturday market.
Caux, Seine-Maritime; 55 **3**.

### Les Hayons

*Fromage frais* recommended by Courtine as best accompanied with cider. The name (if a locality) is not in the Code Postal, nor on my map.
*vache*.
Seine-Maritime.

### Incheville

Name still used in 1950s for local cheeses of Neufchâtel type.
*fermier; vache cru*.
Seine-Maritime; 52 **5**, SE 6kms on D49, Incheville.

### Lillebonne

Wednesday market; *laiterie* making Cœur Rollot (see Chapter 8, p. 273 for type), Mimolette (*pasteurisé*).
Caux; 55 **4/5**.

### Le Magnum (dormant)

500g, round 13.5cm × 3.5cm; 3 weeks ripened; clotted *pâte*, *croûte-fleurie* deep golden and red; rich flavour; the original source of Brillat-Savarin (see p. 34); finished when Dubuc family died out in early 1970s (and see EXCELSIOR). I seem to remember some occasional Magnums of even higher fat content than 75%.
75% m.g.; *artisanal; vache cru enrichi de crème*.
Seine-Maritime; 55 **8**, Forges-Les-Eaux.

### Malakoff, Bonde-Platte

100–125g *fromage frais* stage of Gournay (see above); flat round, 8cm across, 2.5cm deep; this form and name is also used for some Neufchâtel cheeses.
45% m.g.; *laitier; vache pasteurisé*.
Pays de Bray, Seine-Maritime.

### Le Maromme

Saturday p.m. market.

**Maromme.** Name formerly found on local cheeses of Neufchâtel type, already disappearing in early 1960s.
*fermier; artisanal; vache cru*.
Seine-Maritime; 55 **6**, NW outskirt of Rouen.

### Mesnil-Mauger

See NEUFCHÂTEL FERMIER.

### Nesle-Hodeng

See NEUFCHÂTEL FERMIER.

NEUFCHÂTEL-EN-BRAY
Tuesday and (particularly lively) Saturday market. Syndicat de Défense et de Qualité du Fromage de Neufchâtel AOC, Mairie, BP 40, 76270 Neufchâtel-en-Bray (tel. 35 93 00 88); *Secrétaire*: M. Bloquel; formed by farmers, industrial cheesemakers, *collecteurs* and *affineurs*.
Seine-Maritime.

**Fromage de Neufchâtel (AOC 1977).**
AOC forms and number of farms making: *Le Bondon/La Bonde* (AOC), 100g cylinder, 6.5cm long × 4.5 diameter, 100g (min.) three farms, *laiteries*; Briquette (AOC), 7 × 5cm rectangle, 3cm deep, 100g (min.) twenty-seven farms; Carré (AOC), 6.5cm square, 2.4cm deep, 100g (min.) ten farms; Cœur (AOC), 8.5cm from cleft to point, 10cm from side to side, 3.2cm deep, 200g (min.) thirty farms, two *laiteries*; *Double-Bonde* (AOC) or *Bondard*, 8cm long, 5cm diameter, 200g (min.) twenty-four farms; *Parallélépipède* (AOC), modern rectangular development for cutting 1kg (min.) 27.5cm long, 7cm wide, 5cm deep.
See entries under all the above names (Double-Bonde, see BONDARD).
Non-AOC forms made on farms for family occasions or special orders: *Bonde-Platte* or *Malakoff*; *Double Cœur*, 400–500g, Triple Cœur about 600g; *La Pipette*, extended *briquette* for cutting; abandoned because it was too crumbly, and replaced by Parallélépipède (above); *Triple-Bonde* about 450g.
*Région d'origine:* centred on Londinières, Neufchâtel, Forges-Les-Eaux (all communes in these cantons). N: from Meulers NE to Grandcourt (excluding Douvrend, Les Ifs); NW: Grandcourt SE to Aumale (excluding Réalcamp, St-Martin-au-Bosc); E: Aumale S to Ferrière-en-Bray within Seine-Maritime boundary (excluding Beaufresne, an odd enclave); S: Ferrière E to La Feuille; W: La Feuille NNW to Buchy, St-Saens, Freuleville, Meulers (excluding St-Lucien, Rebets, Estouteville, Rocquemont, Rosay, Ardouval, Les Grandes-Ventes).
*Industrial:* Centrale laitière de Haute-Normandie makes curd for Lhernault (*lait pasteurisé*).
*Laiteries:* Lhernault and Isidore Lefebvre produce about 660 tonnes per year (1985).
*Farmhouse method:* whole milk fresh from cow (maximum acidity 18° Dornic).

Breeds 1985: fourteen farms all Normandes, eleven mostly Normandes, seven farms all Frisonnes-Holsteins, two mostly Frisonnes. Herds: from eight to ninety-eight cows; average twenty-nine cows; three are hand-milked; twenty-three farms have a regular or occasional surplus of milk collected by *laiteries*. Milk is placed in plastic or alloy bins or buckets (stoneware formerly, or churns).
*Mould:* Some makers put a few drops of *penicillium candidum* in the milk with the rennet; more comes into the curd at the *malaxage* stage (see below), but most comes from the black mould-rich ceiling and walls of the *caves*.
*Renneting:* Milk is renneted at temperatures varying from a little under 28°C in the cold season to 33°C or near in summer (when some makers wait an hour or two to let it cool before renneting); commercial rennet (1:2500 or 1:5000) is used in amounts usually judged by habit according to milk and room temperature (not usually tested by thermometer). In cold weather straw is sometimes wrapped round the container. Some farms have both strengths of rennet in selected strains, and use half the amount in summer compared with winter.
*Caillage:* usually starts within 1–1½ hours and lasts 12–48 hours according to temperature and dosage of rennet (in winter, it can be twice the time needed in summer on the same farm). Vat may be left uncovered first day, covered second day.
*Égouttage:* when the curd is judged ready it is poured into sacks or sacking on *bannettes* (wooden drainage frames in hamper or ladder form, except on three farms using metal) resting in the *faisselier* of wood (majority of farms), of cement or of steel (three farms just use sacks). Whey is exuded at 10° of acidity (Dornic scale) for 2–24 hours according to dosage of rennet. The packs of curd may be moved from time to time to improve drainage of whey, and may be put under pressure (screw press, lever press with stone counter-weight; or simple boxes of stones on planks over the sacking). Some makers keep the curd under pressure for 24 hours (including M. Jacques Bailleux in 1977).
*Malaxage:* mixing, once daily, of two batches of curd (one morning, one evening milking), which, according to rate of *cail-*

*lage* and *égouttage*, are likely to be from at least 2 days before, and may be 3 days old in winter. The two curds, the evening one normally a little moister than the other, are spread out on a table and sprinkled with the broken-up crumbs of one or more ripe cheeses chosen for the fullness of their bloom (when a farmer lacks such cheese through making difficulties or over-selling, it may be begged from a more provident neighbour). Some farms do not always mix curds of separate milkings in winter.

The whole is stirred up carefully, first in a general sweep, then with attention to successive parcels of curd, and finally collected together in one mass. The aims are: 1. to produce a *pâte* homogeneous in moisture and fat; 2. to spread the *'vaccin'*, the *penicillium candidum* from the older cheese; 3. to unite the *pâte* in an unctuous and malleable whole. Nine farms use a *moulinet* (curd-mill) for *malaxage*. Eleven farms produce their own *vaccin*, seventeen use an outside one (eight of these buying laboratory mould), six change method whenever they meet problems. Twelve never buy *penicillium*.

*Moulage:* Moulds of AOC and some other measurements (including Malakoff) are now sold by the Syndicat to the farms, to help with conformity to rules. The *pâte* is pressed into the *moules* by hand.

*Salage:* Some makers wait an hour after *moulage* has been completed to let surface of cheeses dry a little, but most begin salting as soon as last cheese is *moulé*. It is done by hand-sprinkling fine salt on both faces of the cheese held in the other hand. Some makers mix *penicillium candidum* with the salt to ensure working of *vaccin*. Salted cheeses are placed on dry wooden planks, on a slight incline to facilitate further expulsion of whey provoked by *salage*. If drainage appears insufficient, cheeses are turned and placed on metal grids, or on dry straw over a wooden frame.

*Affinage:* Done by five farms full-time, ten farms according to demand; by twenty *collecteurs-revendeurs*; and by two *laiteries industrielles*. When whey is drained cheeses are taken to *cave humide* at 10–12°C with heating available in cold spells to keep *penicillium* happy.

1. Lactic phase: lactic ferments work on the milk from the moment it leaves the cow, their effect being accelerated by renneting, transforming lactose into lactic acid, and easing the expulsion of whey. This is more vital for Neufchâtel than for Camembert because *caillage* and *égouttage* take much longer. This activity continues into the next phase.

2. Development of surface flora, moulds and yeasts. Yeasts *torula* and *mycoderma* flourish on the *pâte*'s acidity from soon after salting, as do milk flora (diplocci and bacilli); on second day *oïdium* starts to form fatty surface and mycelium of *penicillium candidum* may appear. Latter is apparent on third day. Fourth day *oïdium* should be slowing down, surface should be drying and *penicillium candidum* should be apparent to naked eye all over cheese, growing in following days into thick velvety coat.

*Faults:* Occasionally, mucor spore-cases appear (*'poil-de-chat'*, cat's hair). Presence of mycelium of *penicillium glaucum* means contamination with unwanted blue (the old-time Camembert surface mould), either spotting or completely blueing the crust. Insufficient or belated salting can cause *oïdium* to continue its development and exclude *penicillium candidum* or make it appear only in spots, a fault called *'dessalage'*, desalting.

*Penicillium candidum* establishes itself in the *cave* in a thick black coat on walls and ceiling, ensuring natural acquisition of mould by ripening cheeses. It degenerates on the surface to black after excessive keeping, and then gives birth to new white colonies. Laboratories use Neufchâtel as a source of cultures of *penicillium candidum* for commercial production. *Oïdium* and *penicillium glaucum* can also establish themselves with natural consequences affecting cheeses ripened in their presence.

3. Bacterial phase: bacteria, particularly *bacterium linens*, start during the second phase to break down the casein into edible cheese, the essential part of *affinage*.

*Matière grasse, Matière sèche:* AOC cheeses must have at least 45% m.g. in dry matter and 40% dry matter in the whole cheese, but the whole milk of this *pays* produces 48–62% m.g. and 41–59% of dry matter in cheese. Seasonal variations in fat are normal; but these figures suggest imperfect drainage, which leads not only to a less rich cheese, but to the development of other faults encouraged by excessive moisture. They must be ripened in the restricted region of origin for at least 10 days from rennetting, but most makers who mature their own regard 12–15 days as minimal.

*Production:* figures were being kept secret in the early 1980s, but *La Crémerie française* in December 1983 gave 350 tonnes of farm cheeses (an average of 10 tonnes per farm) and 450–500 tonnes for the two *laiteries industrielles*.

*Aspect and flavour:* Neufchâtel cheeses are sold at the peak of their thick white surface florescence, when the cheese is still young in appearance by the standards of other *croûtes-fleuries*. The aroma is slightly lactic and of fresh mould, the consistency smooth and soft, and the flavour distinctively tart. Unfortunately it is also often over-salt, no doubt because of anxiety about *oïdium* (see at *affinage* above). The best farm cheeses have a bold refreshing sharpness unlike any other cheese. *Cidre bouché* suits them admirably. Some amateurs of extremes like to keep their cheeses until the *penicillium candidum* has gone black, and then to use them to set off the strongest wines they can get hold of. I can imagine that the surface would have something of the truffle about it, and how much cheaper than the truffle.

*Sources of farmhouse cheese:* the Syndicat (see above at head of Neufchâtel entry) can supply locations where visitors are welcomed. In 1985 all the active farms not listed below were between the line Bully-Boc–Mesnil–Sommery SW of Neufchâtel in a belt running E and NE (including Gaillefontaine and Conteville) to the line St-Léger aux Bois (in the NE) and Aumale (in the E). In 1985, thirty-eight farms made cheese; 350 of them were commercially active, of which thirty-four had given full details of methods to the Syndicat (total farm production 350 tonnes 1982).

**Neufchâtel AOC Fermier.** Directions and distances given are from Neufchâtel, 52 **15**, and places noted are in the département of Seine-Maritime.

M. Bernard Bailleux makes cheese, including Carrés, at Le Fossé (and see FORGES-LES-EAUX).
SE 20km, 2km E of Forges-Les-Eaux.

MM. Jacques (*père*) and Philippe (*fils*) Bailleux (medallists) make cheese including 500g *cœurs* (not AOC) at le Gaec d'Orson, Mesnil-Mauger; Jacques' mother farms at Le Fossé, where the family name is kept up (see last entry and pp. 29 and 31). Gaec d'Orson farm gate is third on L (E of D1314) from Neufchâtel after Mesnil-Mauger turn). Bailleux tel. 35 90 59 03 (*père, mère*); 35 90 85 38 (*fils; cave* is on his farm); they sell at markets: Buchy (Mon), Gournay (Tues), Forges-Les-Eaux (Thur), Dieppe (Sat).
SE 9km off D1314.

M. Bolanchon makes cheese at Nesle-Hodeng.
SE 6km off D135, straight extension of D1314.

Mme Colette Hardicourt (medallist in Paris, including Briquette) makes cheeses at Bouelles.
SE 4km off D1314.

Mlle Colette Legendre has won medals in Paris (gold in 1980 for Cœur) for cheeses made at Neuville-Ferrières.
S 3km on D117.

M. Claude Monnier has won silver medals in Paris in recent years for his cheeses, made at Esclavelles.
SW 6km, off N28.

Mme Roland Poulet makes cheese, including 400g Double-Cœur (not AOC), at St-Maurice, 76870 Gaillefontaine (tel. 35 90 95 69).
SE 15km on D135.

M. Maurice Villiers makes 200g Double-Bondards, Cœurs and Carrés at Beaussault.
SE 10.5km off D135.

NEUVILLE-FERRIÈRES

See sources of NEUFCHÂTEL FERMIER.

PARALLÉLÉPIPÈDE – NEUFCHÂTEL (AOC)

See NEUFCHÂTEL AOC.

PETIT-SUISSE

See also DEMI-SUISSE.
50g sealed plastic and foil cups usually sold in sixes; very soft unsalted fresh cheese, formerly all cream cheese; now usually only 40% m.g. Made by Gervais, and a few scattered small dairymen (see Chapter 5, Mazamet, p. 167). A *double-* or *triple-crème* cheese until recently.

Since the 1970s the *pâte* has been produced from part-skimmed milk subjected to centrifugal force to release solids. The result now often is a lower-fat cheese, if it can be called a cheese, of no interest (see pp. xxiii–xxiv).

Present legal definition: *Fromage frais*, wrapped, homogeneous *pâte*, soft, unsalted, cylindrical, 60g, from renneted cows' milk; minimum 40% m.g. in dry matter; dry matter at least 23% in whole cheese of 40% m.g.; at least 30% if 60% m.g., curd is still supposed to be only from lactic fermentation and to be drained slowly. Milk must be pasteurised except by *fromager* with due veterinary clearance using his own farm milk.
40–60% m.g.; *laitier*; *industriel*; *vache pasteurisé*.

## Pipette – Neufchâtel (non AOC)

See NEUFCHÂTEL FERMIER.

## Rouen

Markets: Tuesday to Sunday, place du Vieux Marché, Friday, Saturday (all day), Sunday, place Saint-Marc.
Fête de Jeanne d'Arc: Sunday closest to 30 May.
Le Salon Normand des Équipements et de l'Alimentation annually in mid-March has cheese competitions for makers of Camembert, Livarot, Neufchâtel and Pont-L'Évêque.
*Fromagers*. In Vieux Marché (inside Pavillon Jeanne d'Arc): Pierre Allais, good selection of *lait cru* cheese from Normandy and elsewhere; Philippe Jollit, *fromager-affineur* (also at Elbeuf; his father Robert was *maître fromager* in Guilde); specialises in farm cheeses and wines; Maison Lefaucher (also poultry, game; has branch rue Armand Cassel) 1, Place du Vieux Marché: Au Faisan Doré, cheese and poultry, especially good for chèvres and cheeses of Nord; Alimentation Leroux, *affinage* in *caves naturelles*; butter salters (thigh-high casks of farmhouse butter); spirits; knowledgeable; 40 rue de l'Hôpital, 1517, rue Tour de Beurre.
Eating in Rouen at reasonable prices is best done in the Place du Vieux Marché, with fish and Norman cheeses as first choices (and do not forget cider as a fine accompaniment to both).
Seine-Maritime; 55 **6**.

## Rouennaise

Name formerly found (up to 1950s) on varieties of Neufchâtel cheese.
45% m.g.; *fermier*; *vache cru*.

## St-Maurice near Gaillefontaine

See NEUFCHÂTEL FERMIER.

## Suprême

Pre-war name given by some Parisian cheese merchants to *triple-crème* cheese from Bray (Courtine specifies Excelsior). It has been used since 1945 by one or two large *laitiers* for unexciting cheese, e.g. Suprême des Ducs (see Ducs, p. 364).

## Triple Bonde or Gros Bondard, Triple Cœur

Large (450–600g) versions of the cylindrical Bonde or Bondon and of the heart-shaped Neufchâtel, not within AOC measurements, but made on some farms, mainly for family occasions and special orders. Triple Bondes or Gros Bondards might be made 5 or 6 months ahead for end of year and New Year celebrations. By the time they were eaten their *pâte* would be brown and very sharp; the crust would have flowered white, blackened and reflowered more than once, with a greyer, grizzled final face.
45–60% m.g.; *fermier*; *vache cru*.
Seine-Maritime.

## Villedieu

Name formerly used on local cheese of Neufchâtel type (up to 1950s); the location is not on my Michelin maps, nor in postcode (the nearest is Villedieu-les-Poêles in the Manche, see p. 27).

## Yvetot

Wednesday market.
Seine-Maritime; 55 **5**, high.

# Le Maine
## MAYENNE – SARTHE

In pre-Roman times this region was the home of the Aulerques or Aulerces, a name covering a number of different tribes. When the Romans left it became Pagus Cenomauensis, the Cénomans being a Celtic people. They suffered Breton and Norman invasions before Hugues I established hereditary rule over Maine for his house in AD 955. The comtes d'Anjou and ducs de Normandie disputed suzerain power until, in 1126, Anjou acquired the province by marriage. So, when Henri d'Anjou became Henry II, Maine came under the crown of England, only to be lost by King John to Philippe Auguste of France. It changed hands again, coming back finally to the French crown when Charles V d'Anjou died in 1481. Various royal princes were subsequently ducs du Maine.

Maine stretches from the western hills of the Perche and the Vendômois fringe of the Paris basin through the forests of Sarthe in the north and the rich vales of the Loire in the south to the green country of Mayenne on the edge of the Breton *massif armoricain.* The southernmost part of the Mayenne *département* and a fraction of the Sarthe are strictly outposts of Anjou, centred on Maine-et-Loire. The Rivers Mayenne and Sarthe feed La Maine in Anjou.* There is a pleasing tradition in town and farm of crisp roofs of small slate over neat, sometimes severe stone buildings, grey-brown in colour. In the centre of the Sarthe and over most of Mayenne there are dairy and stock-raising pastures. The low-yielding, red-pied cattle of Maine–Anjou are receding as a dairy breed (67,400 in 1982, 44,300 in 1985). They have a balanced level of fats and solids in milk, but a short lactation, averaging 2698 litres in 1986. The province produces a great quantity of milk and factory cheese from the Frisonnes invaders and from numerous Normandes in the north.

## Frère Alexandre, Carré de Rouez-en-Champagne and Cœurmandie

At Chardigné, the firm of Besnier, whose Camembert factory has been touched on in the Basse-Normandie section (see p. 8), makes Saint-Paulin, and the smaller Frère Alexandre. The latter, with its pious label, exploits the monastic image of Maine's genuine Cistercian cheese traditions. These are maintained by the Abbaye d'Entrammes south of Laval, and its daughter convent in Laval, the Abbaye de la Coudre, which we shall be visiting.

Besnier also makes a small square cheese of Carré de l'Est-type called Carré de Rouez-en-Champagne, and a soft, white, heart-shaped cheese (big heart and little) called Cœurmandie, at Rouez in eastern Sarthe. The names are inventive. The term *champagne* is used for various pasture regions of France, first and most famously by the Champagne east of Paris, which

---
*Le Maine is the province, La Maine the river.

invented the bubbly wine. That area includes Brie *champenoise*, and is a respectable source of Carré de l'Est. Rouez is not given its 'champagne' by map or post office, only by Besnier. 'Cœurmandie' suggests heart of Normandy, but its nearest connection with Normandy is that it lies some way south of a Maine section of the well-dispersed Parc National de Normandie–Maine.

## Pré Clos, Vieux Pané, La Curieuse

The old family firm of the Perreault Frères (now part of the Bongrain group) presents a different face of large-scale cheesemaking. They make over 15,000 tonnes a year from cows' milk, under nine labels, at Château-Gontier. In the 1970s they invented the brown, grainy-coated, semi-soft Pré Clos, and Vieux Pané, first of the expansive cheeses of Pont-l'Évêque-type made by a big dairy. Both pleased my customers, so I went to investigate on my next visit to France.

Madame Fonteneau received us warmly at Bazouges on the outskirts of Château-Gontier, took us round the dairies and gave us some history of the firm. (She also took us to Château-Gontier's early Monday morning *marché des veaux*, the biggest market for calves in France.) For many years the Perreault family had been making Camembert, Saint-Paulin, and Pont-l'Évêque, under the attractive label of the inquisitive brown cow, 'La Curieuse' (not to be confused with the vulgar '*Vache Qui Rit*' of the Bel company). They were already using 24 million litres of milk in 1958, enough for 2500 tonnes of cheese. Though not yet bold enough to forgo pasteurisation, they had started to launch new cheeses. The successful, firm yet creamy *pâte* of Pré Clos (as it was then written; it is now Préclos) was explained by the laborious treatment of the curd after coagulation (see p. 9). The attractive *morge*-like crust was the edible result of rubbing this *croûte-lavée* cheese with toasted wheat flour.

The making of La Curieuse had been moved to a new dairy in the Vallée de l'Erve, birthplace of Vieux Pané. The surfaces of the cheeses had to be sprayed with powdered mould (and later *annatto*), but the *fromager* in charge explained that the mould would become established on the *hâloir* walls in time, and its naturally circulating spores would render the spraying operation redundant. This dairy and the old one at Bazouges have since been closed, as we learned on our next visit, in 1985. This time Françoise Guy looked after us hospitably and brought us up to date. Production had gone up by 35 per cent in five years, and all the milk was now *thermisé*. This is not as good as using *lait cru*, but is much gentler than pasteurisation. The old Saint-Paulin had departed, giving way to a fatter (double-cream) Grand Veneur, and to a low-fat version called Régitome.

I am not convinced that the modern centralised system produces cheeses with the same individuality as the older dairies. It also worries me that such long dates of keeping, forty-two to seventy days from wrapping date, are promised for them at temperatures of 4–6°C (37.5–42°F). These cheeses have a certain point at which their freshness of texture and particular flavours can charm customers. Earlier the flavour is absent; later the texture becomes stodgy rather than fresh, especially at below 40°F. Only the most soulless of machine-made dairy products deserve such treatment (and *they* have no flavour, texture or life to kill).

## Port-du-Salut

North from Château-Gontier, just over halfway to Laval, the old village of Entrammes with its former river-port, Port Ringeard, bears witness to the persistence of monastic endeavour and the fruitfulness of monastic enterprise. 'Enter Amnes', the Romans called this place, and between the waters it is, close to the Rivers Ouette and Jouanne, by a ford over the Mayenne where timeless highways meet. Boats could safely be drawn up there, whence its name and use as a port.

There was a Benedictine monastery here at least as early as the ninth century. The priory buildings were confiscated in the Revolution in the 1790s, but they were bought by a returned émigré who had benefited from the monks' hospitality in his exile. In 1815 the first post-Revolutionary Cistercian house was installed there and renamed in gratitude Notre Dame du Port-du-Salut (Haven of Salvation). A daughter house was founded at Bricquebec, which made a cheese until recent years, surviving as Bricquebec *laitier* today.

In 1830 Dom François d'Assise Couturier was elected *abbé* at Entrammes. To exploit the dairy side of the *abbaye*'s farm he inaugurated the *fromagerie*, which was enlarged and endowed with *caves* in 1850, when collection of additional milk from local farms began. The monks made a large, semi-soft, washed-crust cheese called Port-du-Salut. The *fromagerie* and mill at Entrammes were further developed by the Abbé Dom Henri in the 1860s, and the Abbaye de la Double was founded at Échourgnac in the Dordogne, a cheesemaking offspring which survives today. Notre Dame de Melleray, near the differently spelt Meilleraye, and Notre Dame de Timadeuc (or Thymadeuc) in Brittany are further Cistercian outposts of Port-du-Salut cheese (see p. 52).

Dom Henri's success led him to approach a Paris cheese-factor named Mauget about selling Port-du-Salut. They started in 1873 with three deliveries a week by rail. The announcement *'Arrivée de Fromage'* was posted up by Monsieur Mauget the moment the cheese came from the station, and he was sold out within a few hours of each delivery. Port-du-Salut was prudently registered as a trade name in 1874. Imitators already on the scene, and those to come, had to use the unprotected name Saint-Paulin, which covered 55,000 tonnes of cheese made all over France in 1984.

Port-du-Salut's ever-growing success finally made the *fromagerie* and the business too big for the *abbaye* to man and manage in the 1950s. First the monks gave the marketing exclusively to a Belgian company, AGICA, then in 1959 they sold it with the trade name Port-du-Salut to the Société Anonyme des Fermiers Réunis (SAFR), together with the contracts with local farms for milk supplies. The *abbaye* then re-established its own dairy farm with a herd of Frisonnes, including fifty milkers, kept up year by year with the farm-born progeny of Holstein sires. A smaller dairy and *cave* were set up in existing *abbaye* buildings, and in 1962 the monks went back to cheesemaking in the original style. Their cheese, made to the same old recipe, was at first called 'Fromage de l'Abbaye d'Entrammes, *lait cru*', with a discreet note at the foot of the label that it was the original of Port-du-Salut. Even this gesture towards tradition soon disappeared, presumably at SAFR's request, and the cheese was called simply Fromage de l'Abbaye, *lait cru, croûte-naturelle, fabrication artisanale*. Very good it was too, a world apart from the bright orange Port-Salut which SAFR tactfully made in the Barrois, not on the *abbaye*'s doorstep.

In Entrammes, Le Rouy, a plump, reddish, washed-crust cheese in small and cutting sizes, formerly made in the Barrois, now emerges from the monks' old *fromagerie* under SAFR's label. It derives from a small dairyman's adaptation of the Saint-Rémy of north-eastern France (see Chapter 8), and still bears that dairyman's name.

For the moment, alas, that is the only cheese made in Entrammes. On 26 October 1988 the monks sold their herd. 'Draconian' new EEC regulations resulting from the Swiss pasteurised Vacherin disaster of the previous winter killed their impeccable raw-milk Fromage de l'Abbaye. The monastery could not find 400,000 Francs for capital expenditure and 5000 Francs a month for bacterial tests, and had to close the *fromagerie* which had supported them and served discriminating cheese-lovers so well (see pp. xxv–xxvi).

## Véritable Trappe

On my last visit to the *abbaye*, when they heard that I was writing this book, the monks asked me to visit their sister house at Laval, L'Abbaye de la Coudre. We were directed to go north on N162 and turn left in Laval as for Fougères and Ernée on N157, which becomes the Boulevard des Trappistines. A spire on the left and traffic lights warn of the junction with rue Saint-Benoît, down which lies the convent. We were met in the courtyard by the smiling *sœur postière*, who, when she knew our purpose, found the bursar (*sœur économe*, or *cellerière*), Sœur Myriem, and the *sœur fromagère*, Sœur Pascale. In their fresh-faced, glowing company we were sustained by delicious tea and madeleines as we listened to the story of their *abbaye* and its cheese.

The convent was established in 1816 at Laval's old Prieurie de Sainte-Catherine by nuns who had been the neighbours in exile of monks from Entrammes. In the course of the years, daughter convents were founded at home and abroad, including Chambarand in the Dauphiné, and Sainte-Anne-d'Auray in Brittany (later transferred to Campénéac: see p. 51), both of which are still thriving cheese-producers. Thriving is the word, for cheese earns three-quarters of the revenue needed to maintain this and several other *abbayes*.

By 1859 the Trappistines of Sainte-Catherine had outgrown their old priory and moved to new buildings at La Coudre, on the outskirts of Laval. A *fromagerie* was started there in 1868 and given the monks' Port-du-Salut cheese recipe, which the nuns still use. To start with the nuns had their own little herd for milk, but the opening of the *fromagerie* necessitated collection of milk from local farms, now 12,000 litres a day, still collected in *bidons*. This is enough for 5 tonnes of cheese a week, 300 large and 2000 small cheeses every day, and keeps thirty-six to forty nuns busy in the *fromagerie*.

After pasteurisation the milk goes into round copper vats of the Jura style and is renneted. When the curd has formed it is cut fine, put in the moulds and pressed. On removal from the moulds, the 295- and 390-gram cheeses spend four hours in the brine bath, the full-sized cheeses eight hours. During their minimum of fifteen days' *affinage* in the *cave* at constant temperature and humidity, they are re-washed and rubbed to achieve the naturally golden and grainy crust called *morgée*.

The cheeses are known as Véritable Trappe. This name is part of the history of the Cistercians, who stemmed from the order founded by St Benedict between AD 525 and 530 at Monte Cassino. At the Benedictine Abbaye de Cîteaux in Burgundy, St Bernard was professed in 1113 and started the reforms which gave birth to the Cistercian order. Cîteaux's circumflex implies Cisteaux, whence Cistercians. In 1662 Dom Armand de Rancé, *abbé* of La Trappe (the Cistercian house at Soligny in Normandy), instituted the new reformed *'étroiste observance de La Trappe'*. This was the rule followed by Trappist monks and Trappistine nuns, kept alive at Valsainte and Darfeld during the Revolution and revived in France at the Restoration in 1815 and 1816 by the monks of Entrammes and the nuns of Laval. In 1892 all the Cistercian houses were united under the 'Ordre des Cisterciens de la Stricte Observance'. 'La Trappe' was no longer in the official title, but 'Trappiste' and 'Trappistine' persist as *surnoms* (nicknames) for monks, nuns and cheese.

We saw the gold medals won by the nuns' cheese in Paris at the Concours Général Agricole, one in 1984, and heard of their arrangements for distribution through friendly SAFR, and Rouzaire, and at Rungis (see p. 41). When I arrived home in Streatley I found that my son already had Véritable Trappe in stock.

We had asked to attend Vespers, and finished our extended 'working tea' just in time for the service. The nuns' voices and faces during the singing of Gregorian chant were equally serene and memorable. It was not an onerous way of giving thanks for what the Abbayes d'Entrammes and de la Coudre have done to enrich France's cheese heritage here in Maine, and in their several daughter houses elsewhere.

We turned next to Brittany, where the seeds of this lively Trappist cheese tradition have borne fruit on stony ground, although native talent has tended to turn its back on cheese.

## CHEESES OF LE MAINE

ABBAYE DE LA COUDRE

The convent has a *hostellerie* for visitors wishing to stay. The public can attend daily Mass at 07.00, Vespers 17.30, Compline 19.30.

**Véritable Trappe.** (Gold medal, Paris,

1984; previously medals 1875, 1878.) 295g Petit Touriste, 390g Grand Touriste, 1650g cutting cheese; soft round cheeses; *croûte-morgée*: first *lavage* 4 hours for small, 8 hours for large after removal from moulds; further *lavages* in *cave* during 15 days' *affinage*, followed by *frottage* to achieve the *croûte-morgée* (see Chapter 15, p. 414). Pleasant, fairly mild cheese made by nuns; 36–40 Trappistines Cisterciennes in *fromagerie* producing 2000 small, 300 large cheeses per day (5 tonnes per week). *Sœur Fromagère* (1985): Sœur Pascale. Recipe from Abbaye du Port-du-Salut, Entrammes, the parent community, when dairy was set up in 1868. Rungis: De Sailly-Maricou; Rouzaire (Rouzaire Société Fermière, 10 rue de la Madeleine, 77220 Tournan-en-Brie). Wholesale and export (cases of 6 large, 12 small).
W and NW France: distributed by SAFR.
40% m.g.; *artisanal*; *vache pasteurisé*.
Mayenne; 63 **10**, Laval on S side of Bvd des Trappistines (N157) on rue St Benoît.

### ABBAYE DE NOTRE DAME DU PORT-DU-SALUT

**Fromage de l'Abbaye (original Port-du-Salut from 1830s to 1959).** 235g and 2000g; round about 10cm and 28cm across respectively, 4cm deep; semi-soft, pressed; *croûte-lavée*, gold, natural colour; pale golden-cream, close-textured *pâte*; refreshing flavour and consistency against crisp crust; made by Cistercian monks from milk of their own herd of sixty Frisonnes-Holsteins from 1962 to October 1988.
SAFR tactfully made their Port-du-Salut cheese in Barrois (see p. 294), and Le Rouy (ex-Champagne) at Entrammes.
Impossible demands of EEC regulations (post-*Listeria* panic) forced the *abbaye* to cease production and to sell its herd on 26 October 1988 (see p. 44).
50% m.g.; *fermier*; *artisanal*; *vache cru*.
Entrammes; 63 **10**, Laval, S 10km by N162, turn W at modernised road junction for monastery.

### BEL

Fromagerie Bel at La Tournerie (tel. 43 95 04 60) receives visitors, if you wish to see high-powered industrial cheesemaking.
Sarthe; 64 **1**, Sablé.

### BESNIER

The giant Besnier company makes (at its untouched-by-human-hand-style factory) Saint-Paulin, smaller Frère Alexandre and white Tome des Alpes or Charchigné. It makes Carré de Rouez and Cœurmandie at Rouez.
Mayenne/Sarthe; 60 **1/2**/60 **12**; Javron W 5km Charchigné/Sillé le Guillaume S 6km Rouez.

### LA BOLOTTÉE, LA BOUINE, LE CANIQUET

Terms for *fromage blanc* in Sarthe.
*vache cru*.
Sarthe.

### CAMEMBERT

Soft cheese was being made under this name in Anjou in the eighteenth century (*Le Gazettin du Comestible*, 1780); Mayenne is within the AOC region but most cheese made there is pasteurised and industrial, remote from the type.

### CARRÉ DE ROUEZ EN CHAMPAGNE

200g; square, soft; *croûte-fleurie* factory-product; the 'en Champagne' embellishment of the name is neither in the postal code, nor on the map; see also BESNIER.

### CHAMOIS D'OR

2300g; round 24cm across; lightly pressed, close-textured, almost white, creamy *pâte*; *croûte-fleurie*; mild, melting cheese by Perreault Frères (see CHÂTEAU-GONTIER); claims to keep 50 days from making at 4–6°C. It needs to sell quickly, appealing to people who are put off by a soft cheese which starts to look ripe.
62% m.g.; *laitier*; *vache thermisé*.
Mayenne; 63 **10**, Château-Gontier.

### CHÂTEAU-GONTIER

Thursday and Saturday market.
Restaurant Le Faisan, Hôtel Bel-Air; local cheese and lambs (proprietor, M. Gilbert Delanoë is sheep breeder); friendly Routier establishment, tel. 43 07 11 97.
Fromageries Perreault, Zone industrielle Bellifourne 53204 Château-Gontier (tel. 43 07 90 98); see CHAMOIS D'OR, FINE DES PRÈS, GRAND VENEUR, PETIT and GRAND PONT-L'ÉVÊQUE, RÉGITOME, TROIS AMIS, VALEMBERT, VIEUX PANÉ; they also market a chèvre made in Poitou.
Other cheeses near: see ABBAYE DE NOTRE

DAME DU PORT-DU-SALUT, ABBAYE DE LA COUDRE, CHÈVRE, DIABLOTIN.

## CHÈVRE, FROMAGES DE

*fermier; chèvre cru.*
1. Mayenne; 63 **10**, from Château-Gontier, N 8.5km by N162 towards Laval; E at St-Germain-L'Homel, on road towards Ruillé-Froid-Fonds; 2. From Château-Gontier, S 12kms or more by N162 towards Angers; on E side of road; 3. Sarthe; 60 **15**, near Lannay, from *autoroute* crossing of D1, S 6km and E 250m along D125 towards Montmirail.

## CŒURMANDIE

200g and large cutting version, heart-shaped; soft, white *croûte-fleurie* industrial cheese. See BESNIER.
60% *m.g.; industriel; vache pasteurisé.*
Sarthe.

## CRÉMET D'ANGERS

Formerly *crème fraîche*, whipped, rennetted; served as *fromage blanc* with or without cream, on its own, or with pepper, salt, fresh herbs, or chives. Today usually prepared from whole milk rather than cream.
*vache.*

## CONNERRÉ

Local cheese noted without detail by Lindon (1961) as rare or *'disparu'.*
Sarthe; 64 **14**.

## DIABLOTIN

420g *croûte-lavée* cheese by Laiterie de Craon.
40% *m.g.; laitier; vache pasteurisé.*
Mayenne; 63 **9**, from Château-Gontier W 19km.

## ENTRAMMES

See ABBAYE DE NOTRE DAME DU PORT DU SALUT.

## LA FERTÉ BERNARD

Monday market.

**La Ferté Bernard.** Local cheese noted by Lindon in 1961 as rare, or *'disparu'.*
Sarthe; 60 **15**.

## FINE DES PRÈS

1600g; 20cm across, hexagonal; *croûte-fleurie;* soft, open-textured *pâte*, mild, low-fat; keeps 42 days from date of making at 4–6°C; by Perreault Frères.
20% *m.g.; laitier; vache thermisé.*
Mayenne; 63 **10**, Château-Gontier.

## LA FLÈCHE

Wednesday and Saturday market.
Sarthe; 64 **2**.

## FOUGEROLLES-DUPLESSIS

Friday market; and dairy, see GRAND SIÈCLE.

## FRÈRE ALEXANDRE

400g; tubby-round; washed-crust, semi-soft of Saint-Paulin type, which is also made here in full size by the Besnier machines; a pseudo-monastic try-on with a pious picture on the label. See BESNIER.
40% *m.g.; industriel; vache pasteurisé.*
Mayenne.

## FROMAGE BLANC

Names used in Sarthe; LA BOLOTTÉE, LA BOUINE, LE CANIQUET, LA FROMAGÉE, LA FROMAGÉE SALÉE.
*vache cru.*
Sarthe.

## LA FROMAGÉE, LA FROMAGÉE SALÉE

1. *Fromage frais* with salt and pepper; 2. *Fromage sec* grated, mixed with salt, pepper, shallots, marinated in *eau-de-vie*, or wine at least 4 days. It may be eaten by ladling it on to bread; 3. Chèvre broken into cows' milk, heated in the oven; rounds of frying onion added and cooked on slow heat.
An old Maine Christmas custom requires the inclusion of *fromagée* among the gifts brought to the infant Jesus in the crib.
*vache/chèvre cru.*
Maine/Mayenne and Sarthe.

## GRAND SIÈCLE

2kg; semi-soft cheese; *croûte-lavée;* by GALAC Claudel Roustang, Fougerolles-Duplessis.
60% *m.g.; laitier; vache pasteurisé.*
Mayenne; 59 **19**, from Louvigné du Desert E 7km.

## GRAND VENEUR

2100g, 24.5cm diameter; *croûte-lavée* with grid markings; softer than most *croûte-lavée* cheeses; new 1985 by Perreault Frères; *veneur* means huntsman, *grand*

*veneur* master of hounds.
60% m.g.; *laitier; vache thermisé.*
Mayenne; 63 **10**, Château-Gontier.

### Laval

Tuesday and Saturday market.
See ABBAYE DE LA COUDRE.
Mayenne; 63 **10**.

### Le Mans

Daily market except Monday.
Sarthe; 60 **13** or 64 **3**.

### Pont-l'Évêque La Curieuse, Petit Pont-l'Évêque La Curieuse

225g (9cm square), 335g (11cm square); washed-crust (for type see PONT-L'ÉVÊQUE, pp. 23–4); these cheeses and the one that follows are marked AOC (the *appellation d'origine contrôlée* includes Mayenne with Normandie, and does not specify *lait cru*). All are made by Perreault Frères.
45% m.g.; *laitier; vache thermisé.*
Mayenne; 63 **10**, Château-Gontier.

**Pont-l'Évêque Doux Trois Amis.** Mild version of Petit Pont-l'Évêque by Perreault Frères.
45% m.g.; *laitier; vache thermisé.*
Mayenne; 63 **10**, Château-Gontier.

### Port-du-Salut

See ABBAYE DE NOTRE DAME DU PORT-DU-SALUT.

### Préclos

2600g, 25cm diameter; pressed curd; washed-crust and treated with toasted wheat flour, giving a matte brown surface; close-textured, cream-coloured *pâte*, agreeable and refreshing if it has not been overchilled; makers, Perreault Frères, give it 70 days' life from making if kept at 4–6°C; but I think this treatment explains a certain dullness in Préclos compared with its impact when first made at Bazouges, although it was then made of fully pasteurised milk and is now made of *lait thermisé.*
The firm, yet creamy and melting nature of its curd then was achieved by leaving the curd in the vat 2 hours from rennetting, and then draining it on mats for 50 minutes, of which 15 minutes were under pressure, before placing in moulds for 20 minutes; it was removed for wrapping, turned and replaced in moulds for 15 minutes before second turning and another 15 minutes in moulds. Removed from moulds for 3 hours' pressure followed by 4 hours more in moulds at lower temperature. Twelve-hour bath in *saumure* at 14°C, followed by 24-hour rest at 15°C and *affinage* in *cave* at 13°C, with slightly salt *lavage* after 48 hours and further *lavage* a day later; daily turning, and periodic rubbing with toasted flour during *affinage*. The present Perreault fact sheet on methods of making suggests that the stages between first placing of curd in moulds and the 3 hours of pressure have been eliminated.
50% m.g.; *laitier; vache thermisé.*
Mayenne; 63 **10**, Château-Gontier.

### Régitome

1600g, 20cm diameter, soft low-fat; pale, natural to gold-coloured crust; Perreault Frères say it will keep for 60 days at 4–6°C; a slimmer's Saint-Paulin.
20% m.g.; *laitier; vache thermisé.*
Mayenne; 63 **10**, Château-Gontier.

### Le Rouy, Le Grand Rouy

About 200g, and large square cutting version; types Carré de L'Est *croûte-lavée*, industrial Pavé de Moyaux; ruddier, rougher crust than Pont l'Évêque; made by Société Anonyme des Fermiers Réunis, formerly in Champagne, now at Entrammes (see p. 46).
50% m.g.; *industriel; vache pasteurise.*
Mayenne; 63 **10**, S of Laval.

### Sablé-Solesmes

See BEL for industrial cheese.

### Saint-Paulin

A non-regional cheese of which nearly 60,000 tonnes is sold annually. Industrial semi-soft washed-curd (see p. 43) washed-crust cheese based originally on imitations in the nineteenth century of l'Abbaye de Notre Dame du Port du Salut at Entrammes (see p. 46); Besnier (see p. 46) make it at Rouez and the smaller Frère Alexandre (see p. 47); Perreault Frères make low-fat version (see RÉGITOME); Saint-Paulin is not, as factory methods have left it, one of France's masterpieces.
40–60% m.g.; *industriel; vache pasteurisé.*

### Tome des Alpes

Large rounded, white mould-coated indus-

trial cheese. See BESNIER.
*45% m.g.; industriel; vache pasteurisé.*
Mayenne.

### TROIS AMIS

3 Amis on label. See PONT-L'ÉVÊQUE.

### VALEMBERT

Another large, unexciting plump round soft to semi-soft white cutting cheese; from Perreault Frères.
*50% m.g.; laitier; vache thermisé.*
Mayenne; 63 **10**, Château-Gontier.

### VENEUR

See GRAND VENEUR.

### LE VIEUX PANÉ

2200g, 25cm square; soft; *croûte-lavée*, golden; first, I think, of the industrial large Pavés, Pont-l'Évêque style, and second most popular of Perreault cheeses; started in the 1970s in the Vallée de l'Erve, now made at Château-Gontier; 60-day life from date of wrapping at 4–6°C, but I think this too low to do justice to the cheese, which can be quite succulent and interesting if kindly treated; in contrast to this, it sometimes reaches shop counters in too unripe a state to be of interest.
*50% m.g.; laitier; vache thermisé.*
Mayenne; 63 **10**.

# Bretagne

## CÔTES-DU-NORD – FINISTÈRE – ILLE-ET-VILAINE – MORBIHAN – LOIRE-ATLANTIQUE

Brittany is wet, windy and rock-strewn, yet just as productively green and beautiful as Maine, in her own wilder fashion. Despite all those rocks, and with a mere fifteenth of the total land surface of France, Bretons care for one in five of French dairy cows, produce more than a fifth of French milk and make nearly a third of French butter. Cheese is a different story: 'They consume salted pork, pressed sardines, milk dishes and butter. They do not know about cheese.' Such was the report of a *préfet* of Bonaparte's in 1801.

One explanation of this Breton aberration may be that most of Armorica is a peninsula and its inhabitants are never far from the sea. They are the stock of waterborne settlers over the millennia. They have always known the sea, looked to it for defensive purposes, and turned to it for a living, whether as shipbuilders, seamen, merchant adventurers, privateers or fishermen. Their haul of fish is as great as that of the rest of France put together.

Early Armoricains left their permanent memorials in dolmens, tumuli and menhirs. In 57 BC the Romans found numerous tribes, but the seafaring Vénètes predominated. They remained rebellious subjects of the Roman province of Lyonnaise. In the fifth and sixth centuries Gaelic Celts, fleeing Britain to escape from invading Angles and Saxons, reached Armorica by sea in such large numbers that it became known as Little Britain or Brittany. One of its provinces became and remains Cornouaille (Cornwall at the tip of England they call Cornouailles). The use of Gaelic spread eastwards to a line between Saint-Nazaire and Mont-Saint-Michel. Brittany was nominally in the Merovingian kingdom, and was called La Marche de Bretagne under the Carolingians; but the Bretons were irrepressible.

Recognised by Charlemagne's son Louis le Pieux as a *duché* early in the ninth century, Brittany re-established its independence after he died, but was weakened by Norman invaders, and the Gaelic language was soon lost in the east. By the end of the ninth century, under the comte de Rennes, Brittany was a French fief disputed between the comtes d'Anjou and the ducs de Normandie. The final heiress of the House of Cornouaille married Geoffroi (son of Henry II of England), comte de Bretagne from 1171 to 1186. His heir, Arthur, also rightful heir to England's Richard Cœur de Lion, was murdered by his uncle John Lackland. Thereafter King Philippe Auguste seized Brittany and gave it to the House of Dreux. Again a duché, it was a fief disputed between England and France until the mid-fifteenth century. In 1532 it came finally to France after the death of the last duchesse, Claude, François I's first queen, and mother of the Dauphin Henri. As Henri II of France, he unfeelingly reduced it to the status of a province.

Bretons, nevertheless continued to give trouble to kings. At the Revolution they proved equally anti-republican, and resisted the anti-clerical laws until Bonaparte's Concordat with the Pope in 1801. Their language suffered under the centralised education of the Third Republic, which suppressed the tongues of Bretons, Basques, Provençaux and others outlandish enough not to cherish French as their first language. This policy was not significantly softened until the 1980s under President Mitterrand.

Whether they use their language or not, Bretons still behave independently, love bagpipes and boats, and get on famously with other Celts, even with non-Celtic Britons who share their tastes; and France still begins only where Brittany ends. 'You are nearly in France,' a Breton told a friend of mine quite naturally, just as some Cornishmen still say 'I'm going up to England,' before crossing the Tamar to Devon.

Nothing underlines this separation from France more than the respective attitudes towards cheese in the two countries. The commonest Breton cheese dish, Crémet, scarcely gets beyond the cream stage: *crème fraîche*, which is just towards the sour stage compared with English fresh cream, is whipped and the white of an egg is beaten *en neige*. The two are slowly mixed under continued whipping, moulded and cooled. Turned out of the moulds, the mixture is covered with whipped cream and *sucre vanillé* (not to be found in many English larders). Maingaux (variously spelt) is a Crémet without the egg, a sort of cream mousse, to make puff pastries more exciting.

Caillebotte and Jonchée (treated in more detail in Chapter 3), Gros Lait, Lait à Madame and Lait Ribot, are preparations from unsalted curd. They are eaten fresh, on their own, with fruit or with potatoes. We begin to see what that *préfet* meant about the Bretons and their 'milk dishes'.

No Breton cheeses are native in origin. The recipe for the most famous, 'Fromage Nantais, dit du Curé', was introduced to a *fromagère Nantaise* in the disturbed early 1790s by a refugee priest from the Vendée. It is a pleasant, sometimes powerful, washed-crust cheese, not found often enough locally (years ago I tried several shops in Nantes without success).

Other cheeses in this class, but larger and firmer, are the monastic descendants of Maine's Port-du-Salut, first made at Entrammes in the 1830s (see p. 43). They are made by the Cistercian monks of Melleray and Timadeuc, and by nuns of the same order who moved to Campénéac from Sainte-Anne-d'Auray. This was an offshoot of the Abbaye de la Coudre at Laval, which has used the recipe from Entrammes since 1868 (see pp. 45–6).

These and a scattering of pleasant goat cheeses, mainly the products of more recent invaders of Brittany, are what Breton restaurateurs could serve today, but usually do not.

Emmental and Saint-Paulin are the local caterers' standbys, as travelling food writers complain. They are representative of Brittany only in the sense that most of the Breton milk used for cheese does indeed go into these featureless factory products, devoid of any roots in the duché's soil, on which 88,000 tonnes of cheese is made every year, the bulk of it the dullest of pasteurised Emmental. Most of this is sent to the endless *caves* of Annecy, whence it emerges in vast containers bound for America, to be sold as 'Swiss Cheese'.

It is sad that native talent has not flowered into anything nearer cheese than Crémet and Maingaux; that, with minimal exceptions, restaurateurs have so little nose or thought for cheese that they just let factory fodder be landed on them and pass it on to unhappy guests. It is appropriate, though, that such a Catholic country should owe its decent immigrés of the cheese world to a *curé* from the Vendée and monks from Maine.

## Cheeses of Bretagne

### Abbaye de Campénéac Trappiste

2kg, 25cm × 4cm; smooth ochre *croûte-lavée*; *pâte* semi-soft, fine apertures, Entrammes type made by *Trappistines cisterciennes* of Abbaye de la Joie Notre Dame (tel. 97 74 12 04). This community, formed in 1921 from l'Abbaye de la Coudre, Laval, at Ste-Anne-d'Auray, inherited the recipe from the monks of l'Abbaye du Port-du-Salut, via their mother house in Laval, l'Abbaye de la Coudre.
40–42% m.g.; *artisanal*; *vache*.
Morbihan; 63 **4**, from Ploermel 8km E on N24.

### Abbaye de Melleray

**Trappiste de Melleray.** 2kg, 25cm × 5cm; smooth *croûte-lavée frottée*, colour straw to ochre; from Entrammes recipe, made by Cistercians of l'Abbaye de Notre-Dame de Melleray; nearby La Meilleraye *is* spelt differently (tel. 40 81 60 01).
45% m.g.; *artisanal*; *vache*.
Loire-Atlantique; 63 **7 8**, from Châteaubriant S 21km.

### Abbaye de Ste-Anne-d'Auray

The cheese formerly made at this convent is now made at Campénéac (see above), to which the Trappistine community moved some time back. Auray markets: Friday, second and fourth Monday.
Morbihan, 63 **2**.

### Abbaye de Timadeuc Trappiste

Semi-soft *croûte-lavée* monastic cheese from Entrammes recipe made by Cistercians of l'Abbaye de Timadeuc (tel. 97 51 50 29). Milk from their own herd.
*artisanal*; *vache cru*.
Morbihan; 58 **19**, from Pontivy 25km E via Rohan.

### Auray

Market: Friday, second and fourth Monday (and see ABBAYE DE STE-ANNE).

### La Baule

L'Hermitage serves 'superb cheeses' (Gault Millau magazine, Feb 1986).
Loire-Atlantique; 63 **14**.

### Brest

Markets: Monday, Tuesday (starred by Patricia Wells), Thursday, Friday; Kérédorn Saturday.
Finistère; 58 **4**.

### Bridelcrem

1600g round white cheese by Laiterie Bridel, Retiers.
52% m.g.; *industriel*; *vache pasteurisé*.
Ille-et-Vilaine; 63 **7**, from Janzé, 11km SE.

### Caillé Rennaise or Gros Lait

Heat milk to 30°C, add a few drops of rennet diluted in cup of same milk. Put into terrine and keep it moving; keep for 12 hours at 20°C. When coagulated strain in muslin. It can be drained in a bowl of fresh milk or covered with *crème fleurette* and served as is, or sweetened.
*vache*.
Ille-et-Vilaine, Rennes; 59 **17**.

### Caillebotte Bretonne, Caillebotte de Rennes Jonchées

*Caillé* drained in baskets lined with aromatic reed from *marais* (*acore jucundus*), served fresh, with or without whey beaten in; for serving with potatoes or *soupe à la galette de sarrasin* (cut into pasta-like strips). See also LAIT CUIT, LAIT À MADAME, LAIT MARRI, LAIT RIBOT.

### Camembert

GAEC de Gwenroc'h, La Guiguais sells its Camembert and butter on farm daily, except Sundays; and in Rennes market Saturdays, except July, August (tel. 96 83 43 12).
45% m.g.; *fermier*; *biologique*; Nature & Progrès; *vache cru*.
Finistère; 59 **15**, from Caulnes 7km NE on D766.

Laiterie E. Bridel at L'Hermitage.
Ille-et-Vilaine; 59 **17**, Rennes 11km W on D125 L'Hermitage.
Laiterie Triballat at Noyal-sur-Vilaine.
45% m.g.; *laitier*; *vache cru*.
12km E of Rennes N157 Noyal-sur-Vilaine.
Note: Camembert de Normandie AOC is restricted to *départements* within Normandie. See FOUGÈRES.

## CAMPÉNÉAC

See ABBAYE DE.

## CARRÉ BRETON

About 150g and 2kg, semi-soft, square, *croûte-lavée*; Curé style (see below), by Laiterie Triballat, Noyal-sur-Vilaine.
40% m.g.; *laitier*; *industriel*; *vache pasteurisé*.
Ille-et-Vilaine.

## CHÂTEAUBRIANT

Wednesday market.
Loire-Atlantique; 63 **7/8**.

## CHÈVRES

See ST AGATHON.

**Fromage de Chèvre.** Gérard Orsoni, Ferme Rouvrean 9.00–19.00 (tel. 97 22 27 51).
*fermier*; *biologique*; *Nature & Progrès*; *chèvre cru*.
Morbihan; 63 **4**, Josselin, S side Guegon.

**Fromages de Chèvre.** Chevrier de la Vallée à Plougesnat.
*fermier*; *chèvre cru*.
Côtes-du-Nord; 59 **2**, from Guingamp N 15km Plouec-du-Trieux.

**Fromages de Chèvre Fermier.** Gaec de la Ruée, La Ruée, Boisgervilly sells (with fruit and vegetables) on farm Tuesday, Friday 18.00–20.00; markets: Rennes, (Ste-Thérèse) Wednesday, (Lices) Saturday.
*fermier*; *biologique*; *Nature & Progrès*; *chèvre cru*.
Ille-et-Vilaine; 59 **15**, from Montauban 4km S.

**Fromage Fermier (Bûche).** Ropartz, Élevages Les Salles, Lanvallay.
*fermier*; *chèvre cru*.
Côtes-du-Nord; 59 **15**, E of Dinan.

**Fromages de Chèvre, de Vache.** Père Mané Lebras, *curé* of Mellionnec (tel. 96 24 23 91).
*fermier*; *biologique*; *chèvre/vache cru*.
Côtes-du-Nord; 58 **18**, from Gouarec 13.5km SW.

## CRÉMET BRETON, DE NANTES, NANTAIS

*Old version*: *crème fraîche* whipped then slowly mixed (still whipping) with white of egg (beaten *en neige*) and put in moulds, covered and allowed to drain in cool; serve turned out and covered with unwhipped cream and *sucre vanillé*. *Industrial*: whole milk renneted; when *caillé* formed, drained, then beaten with or without cream, and moulded in various shapes or sizes. *Another definition*: unpasteurised fresh cream into which whipped cream has been folded.
*domestique*; *industriel*; *vache entier*.
Loire-Atlantique/Nantais; 67 **3**.

## CURÉ DE NANTES, CURÉ NANTAIS, NANTAIS DIT DU CURÉ

200g square and 500g round (original form) *croûte-lavée*, semi-soft cheese, achieving strength; crust needs immediate unwrapping and aerating on straw to preserve it from sogginess, and from loss by adherence to wrap. See CARRÉ BRETON and p. 51.
*laitier*; *vache*.
Loire-Atlantique; 67 **3**, from Nantes, E 7km St-Julien-de-Concelles.

**Fromage du Pays Nantais, Dit du Curé.** Alexandre and Joan Jamin, St-Père-en-Retz.
*fermier*; *vache*.
Loire-Atlantique; 67 **1**, 10km N of Pornic.

## EMMENTAL

Many of the 85,000 tonnes of Breton-produced cheese consist of industrial pasteurised Emmental, some served to unfortunate restaurant customers in Bretagne, most sent to Annecy (Haute-Savoie) to mature in natural *caves*, and finally sent to the USA to be sold as 'Swiss Cheese'.

## FOUGÈRES

Saturday market.
I am told that Mme Nazart makes *lait cru* Camembert and butter at Laiterie Nazart, 35301 Fougères.
Ille-et-Vilaine; 59 **18**.

**Fromage Blanc à la Pie.** Caillebotte, see p. 52, in various forms.
*fermier*; *biologique*; *Nature & Progrès*; *vache cru*.

Finistère; 58 **3**, from 6km ENE of Ploudalmézeau.

## Fromage Frais

Over 82% moisture. By Triballat, Noyal (see p. 55).
*industriel; vache pasteurisé.*
Ille-et-Vilaine.

## Fromage Fermier

See CHÈVRES, CURÉ, FROMAGE BLANC.

## Gros Lait

Term for Caillé Rennaise (see p. 52).

## Guingamp

Friday (specially good) and Saturday market; and see CHÈVRES and SAINT-AGATHON.
Côtes-du-Nord; 59 **2**.

## Jonchée, Jonchée Rennaise

See CAILLEBOTTE.
*Jonchée* is a scattering (e.g. rushes for carpeting); here of rushes or reeds lining the basket in which the cheese is drained. Formerly Jonchée might be of ewes' milk.
*vache/brebis cru.*

## Josselin

Saturday market.
Morbihan; 63 **4**.

## Lait Cuit

Fresh milk coagulated by renneting and placing near hearth, skimmed before it coagulates. The whey is extracted after *caillage*, and what remains served on *galettes de sarrasin*.

## Lait à Madame

Put Lait Ribot (see below) in warm earthenware pot. Pour it out, leaving a little in the pot, to act as starter. Add fresh milk, wrap the pot in cloth soaked in hot water and place in bottom of cupboard until next day, when *caillé* will be ready to eat.

## Lait Marri

Bring milk to boil; as soon as surface froths add a spoonful of acid whey; let cool; when curd has formed serve with fresh milk, plain or sweetened.

## Lait Ribot

*Ribot* = the vertical instrument which beats cream to make butter in the churn. Buttermilk used to moisten and flavour mashed potatoes, or potatoes mashed with the fork on the plate.

All the above *laits* are used as terms for Caillebotte, of which they are variants.

## Lannion

Thursday market.
*Fromager-affineur*: Jean-Yves Bordier.
Côtes-du-Nord; 59 **1**.

## Lize, Tomme de

20cm diameter *tomme grise* (see p. 55) marked with weave of cloth, made in Bretagne (but source not traced) *affiné* Beaune (Bourgogne).
40% m.g.; *laitier; vache pasteurisé.*

## Maingaux, Maingeaux Rennais, Mingaux, Mingots

Mme Simone Morand, *Gastronomie Bretonne*: 'Take half-litre of cream from overnight milk and keep cool 3 days; put it in a terrine, add ¼l fresh cream (of that day), whip together. As mousse forms, lift it with strainer into another terrine, still beating original mix until cream is finished.' Served with puff pastries, etc.
*domestique; crémier; fermier; vache.*
Ille-et-Vilaine; Rennes; 59 **17**.

## Matignon

Wednesday market.
Finistère; 59 **5**.

## La Meilleraye-de-Bretagne, Melleray, Fromage de l'Abbaye de

See ABBAYE DE MELLERAY.

## Merzer, Fromage Allégé de Bretagne

Slimmer's cheese, St-Paulin type, by Triballat, Noyal.
20% m.g.; *industriel; vache pasteurisé.*
Ille-et-Vilaine; 59 **17**.

## Mingaux, Mingots

See MAINGAUX.

## Le Montalbanais

**Montauban de Bretagne.** Old Saint-Paulin type from 1950s.
*industriel; vache pasteurisé.*
Montauban-de-Bretagne; Ille-et-Vilain; 67 **3**.

### MORBIER

Imitation Morbier is made here, matured in Savoie or Jura and much is exported (see Chapter 14, pp. 407–8).
*industriel; vache pasteurisé.*

### NANTAIS

See CURÉ.

### NANTES

Daily market, Saturday outstanding. Fromagerie du Val d'Or, 5 rue Contrecarpe.
Loire-Atlantique; 67 **3**.

### NOYAL-SUR-VILAINE

Tuesday market. Laiterie Triballat, rue Julien Neveu; see CAMEMBERT, CARRÉ BRETON, FROMAGE FRAIS, MERZER.
Ille-et-Vilaine; 59 **17**.

### PLOERMEL

Monday market.
Morbihan; 63 **4**.

### QUIMPER

Wednesday and (better) Saturday market.
Finistère; 58 **15**.

### RENNES

Daily market (Sat best); also Ste-Thérèse Wednesday; Place des Lices Saturday.
*Fromager-affineur*: Mme Sava, 5 rue Nationale; range includes chèvres *du pays*.
Ille-et-Vilaine; 59 **17**.

### SAINT-AGATHON

Small flat, round cheese found by Lindon; invention of an Italian woman; not made since 1942. A Breton told Courtine it was aphrodisiac.
*fermier; chèvre cru.*
Côtes-du-Nord; 59 **2**, Guingamp.

### SAINTE-ANNE-D'AURAY

Cheese formerly made at convent here, now made at Campénéac (see Abbaye de Campénéac, p. 52). Auray, 6km S, has market Friday and second and fourth Monday.
*artisanal; vache.*
Morbihan; 63 **2**.

### ST-BRIEUC

Wednesday, Friday, Saturday market (Saturday starred by Patricia Wells).
Côtes-du-Nord; 59 **3**.

### ST-GILDAS-DES-BOIS

**Saint-Gildas.** 200g, 7–8cm × 5–6cm deep; melting *triple-crème*; *affiné* 2 weeks; *croûte-fleurie*; made by *laiterie–ferme–école* at St-Gildas.
*75% m.g.; laitier; vache pasteurisé.*
Loire-Atlantique; 63 **15**.

### ST-LUNAIRE

Sunday market.
Finistère; 59 **5**.

### ST-MALO

Market: Tuesday, Wednesday, Friday in town; Monday, Thursday, Saturday Rocabey (Patricia Wells stars Wednesday, Friday, Saturday market).
*Fromager-affineur*: Jean-Yves Bordier, 9 rue de l'Orme.
*lait cru, fermier, artisanal.*
Ille-et-Vilaine; 59 **2**.

### ST-NAZAIRE

Market daily, except Monday.
Loire-Atlantique; 63 **15**.

### SAINT-PAULIN

Semi-soft, orange-crusted factory cheese of no charm, helping Emmental (see p. 53) to use up cows' milk in factories. Washing curd during making deprives its consistency and flavour of any interest that might have survived pasteurisation and industrial methods; yet restaurateurs blot the Breton name by serving it as cheese.
*industriel; vache pasteurisé.*

### TIMADEUC (OR THYMADEUC)

See ABBAYE DE.

### TOMMES

See LIZE.

**Tomme Blanche.** This now ubiquitous cheese is factory-made in Bretagne.
*industriel; vache pasteurisé.*

**Tommes Grises.** 1500g–2kg cheeses imitating Tome de Savoie, sent to Beaune or Annecy for *affinage*; many sold there.
*30–40% m.g.; laitier; industriel; vache pasteurisé.*

### TRAPPISTE

Made at Abbayes de Campénéac, de Melleray, de Timadeuc from original recipe of Port-du-Salut-des-Trappes started at Entrammes (see pp. 43–4) in the 1830s.

ÎLE-DE-FRANCE
PARIS
SEINE-ET-MARNE
YVÉLINES
Brie
TROYES
BOURGOGNE
Le Perche
Dreux
Longny
Mortagne-au-Perche
Alençon
ORNE
Chartres
Beauce
EURE-ET-LOIR
Illiers-Combraye
Voves
Authon
Châteaudun
Pithiviers
ORLÉANAIS
ORLÉANS
Montargis
Châtillon-Coligny
LOIRET
Olivet
Beaugency
Sully
Gien
Châtillon-s-L
YONNE
ILLE-ET-VILAINE
RENNES
MAINE
SARTHE
LE MANS
Trôo
Montoire
Vendôme
LOIR-ET-CHER
Blois
Château-du-Loir
Segré
LOIRE-ATLANTIQUE
BRETAGNE
ANGERS
Baugé
Noyant
ANJOU
Les Rosiers
MAINE-ET-LOIRE
Saumur
Fontevraud
NANTES
INDRE-ET-LOIRE
TOURS
Onzain
Chaumont
Amboise
Contres
Montrichard
Montlouis
Bourgueil
Azay-le-Rideau
Cormery
Chinon
TOURAINE
Ste-Maure-de-T
Loches
Ligueil
Sologne
Romorantin
Selles-sur-Cher
Vierzon
Cosne-Cours-s-Loire
Sancerre
Sancerrois
NIVERNAIS
NIÈVRE
Valençay
Graçay
BOURGES
CHER
Levroux
Vatan
Issoudun
Châtillon-s-Indre
Palluau-sur-Indre
Mezières-en-Brenne
BERRY
Châteauroux
St-Amand-Montrond
Brenne
POITOU
Pouligny
Le Blanc
INDRE
La Châtre
BOURBONNAIS
ALLIER
VENDÉE
DEUX-SÈVRES
POITIERS
VIENNE
Loire
Seine
Yonne
Sarthe
Cher
Indre
Vienne

CHAPTER TWO

# Touraine, Orléanais and Berry

## ANJOU – TOURAINE – ORLÉANAIS – LE PERCHE – BEAUCE – THIMERAIS – BERRY

The natural threads drawing this region together are the Loire and its tributaries, the Loir, the Indre and the Cher. Man has added another copious stream, also rich in its varied tributaries: that of the region's wines. All the *pays* except Berry were in the Roman province of Lyonnaise, and suffered the common upheavals of the post-Roman era until the advance of the Saracens in the eighth century, which was halted at the Loire.

In the north, both Anjou, country of the Andecaves, and Orléanais, the *pays* named by the Romans Pagus Aurelianensis, were early *domaines* of the Capet family. Before the foundation of the French hereditary monarchy, two sons of Robert Capet le Fort, comte d'Anjou, were elected king: Eudes in 888 and Robert in 922. The Orléanais adjoined the duché de France, the heart of the kingdom, but Anjou was left in the charge of a Plantagenet vicomte whose successor became comte d'Anjou in the tenth century. The Plantagenets assumed hereditary control of Anjou, recovered Maugé which had been lost to Brittany in Merovingian times, and gradually took over the neighbouring Touraine, *pays* of the Turons in Gaul, which had become a comté in the tenth century. Comte Geoffroi le Bel d'Anjou married Mathilde, daughter of Henry I of England. In 1154 their son succeeded as Henry II, England's first Plantagenet king. His marriage to Eleanor of Aquitaine (Aliénor in France) brought England and most of northern and western France together.

Anjou was eventually taken by Philippe Auguste of France in 1205, and Touraine with Blois was conceded to Louis IX (Saint-Louis) in 1259. These two monarchs started and finished the château at Angers. The comtés suffered earlier from Norman incursions and later from the Anglo-French struggles of the Hundred Years' War. Nevertheless, Touraine was noted in the thirteenth and fourteenth centuries for its prosperity and elegance. The French monarchs loved their châteaux on the Loire, of which Blois was the main royal seat outside Paris until Henri IV's reign, and the seat of Parliament. (Versailles gained its hold on the Court in the seventeenth century under Louis XIII.)

The Perche, tucked in between Normandie, Maine and the Orléanais, was an ancient comté ruled by the House of Bellême. It passed from its last independent comte to the Crown of France in 1226. Berry came into Roman Aquitaine after short resistance to Caesar from the native Bituriges in 52 BC, and became an independent comté in the Carolingian era. In 1100 its ruler, Eudes Harpin, vicomte de Bourges, sold his part to King Philippe I, and France gradually acquired the rest of Berry. This was about all poor Charles VII inherited in 1422; he was known as *'le roi de Bourges'*.

As royal *domaines*, the Perche remained a comté, but Anjou, Orléanais (as Orléans) and Berry became duchés. They were granted as *apanages* (almost entirely to princes of the blood), coming back to the Crown as cadet lines died out, for later revival. The first duc de Berry, in 1360, was Jean de France. He was a great patron of the arts, and the illuminations of his *Très Riches Heures* have given much joy, as well as perpetuating views of the landscape, architecture, dress, and working and social habits of his time. The title of duc d'Orléans lives on today in a son of the comte de Paris, main pretender to the French throne. The present duc d'Anjou is another pretender, descendant of Louis XIV through the Spanish Bourbons.

## Dairy farming in Anjou and Le Perche

We must go back to much earlier history to explain the broad pattern of dairy animals and cheese in the whole region. When the Saracen invaders from Spain were stopped and driven back from the Loire in the eighth century, some of them stayed behind with their goats and their cheesemaking arts. The Loire has remained a fairly sharp dividing line between cow and goat country for over 1200 years. Facing north, the goat frontier is guarded on the left by the familiar log-shaped (*bûche*) Sainte-Maure; then by the outposts of the dark pyramid, Valençay, and the charcoal-coated base-of-cone Selles-sur-Cher; and on the right by the tiny rounded drum, Crottin de Chavignol, pushed beyond its old territory in recent years.

North of the Loire cheeses used traditionally to be made from cows' milk, except for a Vendômois pocket of chèvres around Trôo, Montoire and Villiers-sur-Loir, and isolated Gien in the Gâtinais orléanais. There has been a modern incursion of small-scale goat-farming into regions of France formerly devoted entirely to cow dairy.

Anjou remains essentially cow-dairy country, but most of its cheese is mass produced, typified by Besnier's 'Brie', Le Président. The curd for this is made and extruded by machine at Doué-la-Fontaine, south-west of Saumur, untouched by human hand and, thanks to pasteurisation, unenriched by any of the milk's original bacteria. There is no traditional pattern in Anjou, other than Crémet d'Anjou and the longstanding habit among *laitiers* small and large of copying Camembert from Normandy, Carré de l'Est from further east, and a few familiar forms of goat cheese from elsewhere, at the expense of local integrity and interest. Now Besnier, the biggest dairyman of them all, has added his version of Brie to the derivative repertoire of the duché.

The Perche looks to be idyllic dairy country, with its small hills, plentiful hedges, trees and orchards, with Normandes grazing under the fruit trees. On the roadsides and in the forests the height of the ashes, poplars, plane trees and beeches is striking. I have found only one cheese made in the Perche, though, and that a chèvre. The inhabitants of this beautiful comté offer to their guests generous quantities of Camembert, Pont-l'Évêque and Feuille de Dreux (the last usually from Madame Bizieau in faraway Dreux: see p. 61) as local fare.

Goats are comparatively new here. My guess is that the original Petit Perche cheese was one of the Dreux or Olivet type, which died out when the *laitiers* began collection of milk from the dairy farms and house cows virtually disappeared from the other farms. The land had always been pasture, but it used to serve an important non-dairy purpose: horse-breeding. Percherons (as the inhabitants are called, however many legs they have) used to include such large numbers of sturdy grey horses that Percheron means horse to most outsiders. They were originally lighter, but foreign demand led to the heavier modern breed, whose studbook registered over 100,000 animals between 1823 and 1914. In this mechanically ordered world they have largely given way to cattle; but they do survive, and I hope they are benefiting from the growing revival of interest in heavy horses, not just for show.

## Cheesemaking in La Petite Beauce

East of Anjou, along the right bank of the Loire, the Blésois and Vendômois include a part of the Beauce called La Petite Beauce. The big Beauce beyond, around Chartres, leads to the Thimerais in the north and to the Gâtinais orléanais in the east (see p. 61).

Even before modern maize-farming methods disfigured the landscape, the whole area was more attuned to cereals than to dairy or beef-raising. Most farms kept enough pasture for house cows to provide cream, butter, and cheese made from the leftover skimmed milk. This had to make up for lack of meat protein in feeding the family and living-in help; it had also to leave a surplus of cheese in the flush season to be preserved as food for extra labour in the harvest and the household in the winter.

The type of cheese made was related to that of the neighbouring Île de France and Brie to the east: soft, naturally crusted cheeses of Coulommiers proportions or smaller, but less fat and often a little slimmer. Pierre Androuët believes that the earliest cheeses of this kind in the Orléanais were made on farms around the monastery of Saint-Benoît-sur-Loire, east of Chateauneuf-sur-Loire, and that their growing reputation led to similar cheeses being produced on farms throughout much of the region. Cheeses for daily consumption were ripened in the *cave* where they acquired the natural native blue mould (which used to coat Camembert, until its makers were taught to tame *penicillium candidum*: see Chapter 1). The flush season surplus was placed in boxes of hay, chestnut leaves or *cendres de bois*, which protected the cheeses from each other as well as insulating them against temperature changes. The crusts formed naturally and the cheeses developed slowly enough to remain edible for months and to preserve them until the eating seasons, which were harvest, late autumn and winter.

Farms producing more than enough for their own needs sent cheeses to market. This stimulated a demand which gave employment to *affineurs*, especially in Orléans, rich in *caves* cut out of the *tuffeau* for wine. The *affineurs* collected surplus cheeses from farms and, no doubt, encouraged the better makers to keep a few more cows (as I have done in Britain when rare cheeses have tickled my taste-buds).

The *affineurs* began collecting the cheeses very young and selling them after weeks or months of *affinage* in one or more of the ways described above. Apart from having attractive additions to the seasonal repertoire, they must have been delighted to have good local cheeses to sell out of season. There were sold *bleu*, *cendré*, *au foin* or *à la feuille*. Crusts were entirely natural, *bleutées* by the old mould, made grey to gold by the wood-ash (from *sarments*, preferably) or coated with strands of fine hay over the mould. Leaves would make less impression on the crust, unless they were rather tightly packed; but some browning and sweetening would occur, and the cheeses were dressed in leaves for market. The number, arrangement and type of leaf varied from place to place.

Modern cheeses with white *penicillium candidum* crusts, rolled in ash, charcoal or hay just before distribution, are different animals altogether. *Cendré* properly means that the cheese has spent most of its period of *affinage* within the ash. *Au foin* and *à la feuille* likewise imply that hay and leaves are not just Sunday-go-to-market clothes, but have served to bed the cheeses down during their *affinage* and hibernation.

## Cheeses of Gâtinais orléanais

To the east, in the southern Gâtinais orléanais on the Loire, Gien or Giennois, having gone through a *lait de mélange* stage, survives as a chèvre. These days it is coated in charcoal powder, more like Selles-sur-Cher. North-east of Gien, towards Montargis, on the Rivers Vernisson and Loing respectively, Boismorand and Châtillon-Coligny once fathered fatter *bleutés* or *cendrés* cheeses; these are thought to have died out in the 1970s or earlier. The cheese called Montargis disappeared long ago. West of the town, which is capital of the Gâtinais orléanais, is Pannes, once selling a *cendré* cheese of its own, also believed lost before 1980. To the north-west, Bondaroy, now the northern part of Pithiviers, was still the source of Bondaroy au Foin from farm and artisan in 1970. Pithiviers gradually supplanted Bondaroy as the generic name for cheeses of the region ripened *au foin*, but neither name has been evident in recent years on cheeses from their locality. Pithiviers is still used, sometimes, as the class name for cheeses of any provenance ripened *au foin* in the Orléanais.

## Cheeses of the Drouais

In the Thimerais, north of Chartres, lies the Dreux district, the Drouais. Two or three chestnut leaves on each side are the traditional bedding for the local, Coulommiers-scale cheese during its *affinage* (though present practice tends to use fewer). There are reports of a good cheese made at Marsauceux, across the Eure east of Dreux, but Pierre Androuët's 1984 *Livre* d'Or reports it as pasteurised. North-east of Dreux, at Saint-Lubin-de-la-Haye, Madame Bizieau has been making her version, *'Spécialité au lait cru affinée aux feuilles de châtaignier'* for some years. It ripens to a good rich flavour, but in warm weather it should be bought in a young state as it becomes *coulant* rather quickly. In 1973 Robert Courtine found one *chèvre* in this area, called Beauceron by its maker; but on the whole this corner of our region has stayed true to its traditions: except that the *fromages à feuille* are no longer made of skimmed milk, unless the old 30 per cent *matières grasses* cheese of Simon Fissou survives at Bu.

## Cheeses of La Beauce

La Beauce covers a large part of the Orléanais, but if we exclude Beauceron, made in the Drouais, and the cheese of La Petite Beauce, which lies in the Vendômois and Blésois, Voves is the only cheese name which comes to mind. Crossing the bare Beauce now, with never a hedge and scarcely a blade of grass or roadside flower, we cannot be surprised at this. Pierre Androuët's 1971 *Guide du Fromage* listed Voves Cendré (*fermier*) as being matured for a month in a humid *cave* before undergoing two or three more months in *cendres de bois*; but he warned readers that it was disappearing and that over-ripe cheeses from Dreux were being substituted for it on the market. Robert Courtine kept Voves in his 1973 *Larousse des Fromages*, reporting that it was also ripened *au foin*. Henry Viard confirmed this in his 1980 *Fromages de France*; but Pierre Androuët and Ninette Lyon had been unable to find it when preparing their *Guide Marabout* of 1978. This moved them to a sad funeral oration on Voves, its fellow farm cheeses of the Orléanais in their traditional form, and the countryside from which they had sprung: 'Cereal growing has become an industry and they have no time for pastures or milking cows. There are even places in this granary of France where there is neither chicken nor rabbit on the farms.'

Olivet, in the same tradition as Voves, was mentioned in the Parisian *Gazetin du Comestible* in 1780. Olivet Bleu, Olivet-au-Foin and Olivet Cendré survive as names. They are borne, however, by smaller cheeses, usually slimmer than their forebears, some made within the region at Onzain; but too often they are made outside the Orléanais. One Petit Olivet-au-Foin is made at Valençay. These cheeses are usually brought to the *caves* of Orléans for *affinage* (as, for example, the Silors *marque*, made in Touraine). The *cendrés* examples do have a genuine wood-ash well ingrained in the crust; but the very fine green strands of hay on most Olivets-au-Foin appear more like post-*affinage* decorations on an untraditional white crust than evidence of their having contributed genuinely to the *affinage*.

Frinault or Chécy, invented by Monsieur Frinault in 1848 at Chécy, a wholemilk version of Petit Olivet Bleu, is still with us. Although now pasteurised, it is fruity when fully ripe. Patay, which still appears in books as a farmhouse cheese, *bleuté* or *cendré*, was reported as disappearing in 1971 by Androuët, and as missing in 1973 by Courtine. It has not come my way.

## Cheeses of Vendômois and Blésois

Vendômois and Blésois are at first sight more encouraging. A farm in Le Perche Vendômois provides Le Petit Perche (also made in the Gâtine Tourangelle). Vendôme is made on a number of farms. Le Petit Trôo is made at Trôo itself and at Montoire. Villiers is still made at Villiers-sur-Loir, and Villebarou survives at Onzain, near its place of origin. Yet when we looked into these cheeses we found that, whatever their virtues, all but one are different from the cheeses that bore their names up to the post-war period. Those appear to have died out in the 1960s and 1970s.

We discovered this by visiting the green vales and riverside cliffs of the Vendômois, where homes have been carved out of the *tuffeau* for human beings, wine and mushrooms. More conventional houses have arisen below them on the river banks and slopes, but there are still troglodytes, of whom the notable English food expert and writer Jane Grigson is one. With her exhilarating help we tasted local cheeses in Trôo and set out to explore farms and markets for all the cheeses listed above.

The cheese called Trôo is unusual north of the Loire in having long been listed as a chèvre, and is also an exception in still surviving on its original home ground. The goats of Trôo are few, so the privilege of eating the cheese is confined to family and friends of Madame *la chevrière*. There is also a cows'-milk version, started in 1963 as a co-operative enterprise by Monsieur Jacky Charpentier beside the Loire at Trôo. A few years ago, unable to get protection against flooding, he moved his dairy to Montoire, still using milk produced on the same farms from about a hundred Normandes. Unfortunately he can collect the milk only every other day and has to pasteurise. The Petit Trôo which results is a small, white, mould-coated drum, on the salt side when young and soft but within three weeks developing a firmer consistency and a richness of savour which counterbalances the salt. The same basic cheese is also coated in powdered charcoal and sold *frais* as Fromage Cendré.

Jane Grigson took me from this clinically tidy dairy to more rural Saint-Rimay, where Madame Simone Lefèvre milks her hundred Alpines and nine Saanens goats and makes a Vendômois. Her farmyard is a delightfully old-fashioned affair, swarming with free-range fowl and adorned by a pair of peacocks. Her Vendômois looks like a generous size of Selles-sur-Cher, tasting rich but slightly salty. It is but one of over a dozen chèvres in the farm's repertoire. These are to be seen, with some cheese or other at every stage from *faisselle* to *passé*, on the markets at Montoire and Vendôme on four days of the week (see list, pp. 83 and 91).

At Villiersfaux, Madame Hubert Petit keeps fifty tidy Alpines on her farm, Les Morines, where she was born and has made cheese for over thirty years. Her father made wine there, her grandmother cheese. Madame Petit's unnamed charcoal-coated chèvre is similar to other Vendôme farm cheeses. Between the *frais* and *demi-sec* stages I found it sweet and slightly winy, but once the *demi-sec* stage was established I found the salt spoiling the flavour, as so frequently happens when ready-mixed salt and charcoal is used.

We went on to La Gennetière at Naveil, just outside Vendôme, to find Madame Yves Gillard. Madame Gillard's mother kept three or four goats and made cheese, and she herself has always had a few, starting to make cheese herself in 1962. In 1970, with concern for animal and human health, she decided to go over to organic methods, and has not regretted it (see list, p. 92). The ambience is simple and earthy. Her fifty Alpines provide milk for Le Vendômois, over a litre for every cheese. Of Selles-sur-Cher appearance, but with slightly more sloping sides, it is coated in powdered charcoal, mixed by Madame Gillard with sea salt. At the *demi-sec* stage it had a pleasantly tacky texture and full flavour, a little salty but less so than most of its rivals.

We had to go to the Laiterie Taillard at Villiers-sur-Loir to find a Petit Vendôme still made of cows' milk. The milk from a hundred farms in the Loir valley comes mainly from Normandes and is *thermisé*. Monsieur Fichepin at the dairy compared the cheese with Chaource. In its soft, young state it is splendidly unsalt, loose-textured and creamy. It is still creamy, but the salt is more evident, at the *demi-sec* stage. I use this term because the cheese is made like a chèvre, coagulation taking twenty-four hours. Monsieur Fichepin talked of the former Vendôme-Villiers, noted above all other Vendômois cheeses, which was one of those ripened in coffers of *cendres de sarments de vignes*. The present cheese starts acquiring a natural white-mould surface within a week, not the *croûte-bleutée* of old. The dairy also turns out a Rond pur Chèvre de Villiers coated in powdered charcoal, for which the milk is pasteurised. I have seen it in the market as a neat young black drum, and also rustically *bleuté*, weighing about 100 grams.

Monsieur Fichepin said that the farmhouse cheeses of Villiers and in the Blésois around Villebarou were finished. The present 400-gram, 52 per cent *matières grasses* Villebarou of the Onzain Laiterie resembles a mild young Brillat-Savarin (see Chapter 1). Farms near Blois in Villebarou, Marolles and Saint-Denis-sur-Loire used to make a slightly heavier, wider and slimmer cheese with a crust naturally *bleutée* to grey-blue over its rich gold surface.

With Jane Grigson in the market at Montoire, we had a last search for Vendômois we had not already seen. A young *chevrière* was selling a Vendôme *fermier* of generous drum size, pleasantly light, moussey in texture, and in flavour refreshing but for its too obvious saltiness. I saw no cows'-milk Vendôme from any farm. Another Vendôme *fermier* I heard about, made by Guy Renvoisé at Coulommiers-la-Tour, turned out to be chèvre. It is praised by Pierre Androuët and others for its quality and *goût-de-noisette* (hazelnut).

It would be unwise to be categorical about any cheese's survival, or disappearance. I can only say that I have found no evidence of the survival in 1987 of Bondaroy or Pithiviers au Foin. Nor have I tracked down Vendôme, Villebarou or Villiers-sur-Loir in their old internal succulence and their traditionally acquired coats of blue or *cendres de sarments*. I hope I have missed something; or else that some keen traditionalists among regional *fromagers* will revive the local joys we have lost.

## SELLES-SUR-CHER

Over the Loire lies the natural region of the Sologne, abundant in woods and waters, a paradise for addicts of field-sports and poaching. The Sologne orléanaise extends to the River Cher as far as Châtres in the east, where the Sologne Berrichonne fills the north-west corner of the *département* of Cher. In and around this region chèvres have been plentiful for centuries, and the simple *rond* (so named by Pierre Androuët in the mid-1930s) was the local form of cheese, probably strained in terracotta moulds, and unnamed until well after the railways came. Selles-sur-Cher was a marketing centre, and gradually during the last century a common form of tinplate base-of-cone mould was introduced in the area. By 1987 the more standardised cheese was becoming known as Selles-sur-Cher, a cheese given its Appellation d'Origine Contrôlée in 1975. Makers tell me that it has always been coated in wood-ash, latterly in the form of powdered charcoal. It must have ten days of *affinage*, at which stage it is soft, sweet and refreshing, unless it has been oversalted. Further *affinage* enriches the flavour, but exacerbates any oversalting, of which Robert Courtine was already complaining in 1973.

The region includes the cantons of Montrichard, Contres, Romorantin (which had a *rond* of its own) and Mennetou in the Orléanais; and Saint-Aignan, Selles-sur-Cher, Valençay, Graçay, Lury and Issoudun-Nord south of the River Cher in Berry. In 1985, about 110 tonnes of cheese was produced by three big *laiteries* using 143 farms, and six or seven independent *éleveurs*. The rest, under 10 tonnes that year, was made on sixty-seven smaller farms whose cheeses were collected by *affineurs*. Two years later Monsieur Jacquin, *laitier* and *affineur* at La Vernelle, told me that the rate of production had been increasing by 15 per cent a year since 1985, and that about 200 small farms were now selling to *affineurs*.

If the *affineurs* encourage their *chevriers* to keep their goats out for as long as possible on natural, preferably organically farmed grazing and browsing, and check their salting practices, much good, sweet cheese should come of this growth in farm production.

## CROTTIN DE CHAVIGNOL AND SANCERROIS

In the far eastern corner of the Sologne the extension of the *zone d'origine* of Crottin de Chavignol up to the Loire has created another point of contact between Orléanais and Berry. This cheese has also established a Burgundian bridgehead east of the Loire in the canton de Cosne and a few *communes* on its borders. The original source of the cheese, Chavignol, at the heart of the Sancerrois, is still an active centre of *affinage*.

Mentions of goat cheese here go back to 1573. That is over 800 years after the introduction of goats to Poitou by the Saracens (see Chapter 3), so there were probably some in Berry long before the sixteenth century. *Crottin*, the locals' traditional term for the fully ripe state of their cheese, which has the shape of a pistol bullet, came in with the Franks from Germany and was first used in France in the early fifteenth century. The word means dung, particularly a horse or mule dropping, a fair description of the cheeses I remember thirty to forty years ago. Pierre Androuët, who would like the cheese to adopt a kinder name now, recalls it as often 'shrunken, black, hard to the extreme limit of edibility'. The name Crottin de Chavignol was officially adopted in 1829, a move instigated by a Monsieur Gaston-Dubois, whose descendants are still ripening farmhouse Crottins at Chavignol. The cheese was usually reserved for household consumption and for the labourers in the *vendange*. Many *vignerons* had their goats, and some still do. It is said that the importance of pruning vines was first taught to monks accidentally by goats, which got loose in the vineyard after the *vendange*. The shocking devastation they left behind them was transformed next year into the blessing of unprecedented growth and weight of vintage; but most modern *vignerons* would feel that the goat was too crude a pruning weapon.

For all this, Crottin was a venerated French institution, which had to be represented in my Streatley shop. For years kindly importers let me have them by the half-dozen. They reached me on a loose bed of straw in the little slatted wooden box from which the other six cheeses had been sold to a less distant customer. Even this handful did not always sell, until *nouvelle cuisine* made it fashionable to serve a warm Crottin in a salad. There was no more need to split cases.

Growth in demand led to the despatch of younger and younger cheeses, belying the descriptive nature of their old name. This was taken to the extreme in the 1970s, when instead of my dozen Crottins I received thirty fluffy babies three times Crottin size. Like cuckoo chicks, they dwarfed the adult Crottin; and Crottins they were not (nor could they be called so today). I nearly sent them back, but their infant glory won me over. Their refreshing consistency and flavour were irresistible to me and my customers. I re-ordered them on purpose, as well as Crottins, and learned that they were properly called Sancerrois. They sold readily for a few years, and then suddenly Rungis ceased to meet my order; neither Sancerrois nor explanation were ever forthcoming from trade sources.

A year or two later we crossed the Loire from Burgundy to Sancerre, and stopped round a bend at an attractively old-fashioned-looking *épicerie* on the left of the road. There were bottles of Sancerre Blanc in his window, but no Sancerrois visible among his Crottins and other *berrichons* cheeses. I had only to go in and ask. The *épicier* was delighted to descend to his cellar where the Sancerrois were reposing in peaceful *fraîcheur*, ready to be brought upstairs to meet faithful friends. Never have I enjoyed a picnic more than ours of that day, the perfect combination of a cool, but not cold wine and the young *fromage du pays*, with *pain de campagne*. Alas, that was probably the last Sancerrois I shall ever be allowed to eat.

In 1987 I learned from Monsieur Crochet, *affineur* of farmhouse Crottins de Chavignol at Bué, that the AOC of 1976 is responsible. It is interpreted not only, rightly, as forbidding the sale as Crottin de Chavignol of any cheese made outside the defined region, or not of due quality; it is also taken to exclude the association within the region of any of the other old territorial names with Crottin: we may no longer buy Sancerre, Bué, Crézancy, Santranges, except disguised under the name of Chavignol. What is more, no such cheeses may be sold at less than the minimum time of *affinage*, even under the traditional name of Sancerrois. That may explain why my Sancerre *épicier* had none on show, and it certainly accounts for their non-arrival latterly at Rungis.

Monsieur Crochet's grandfather had made and sold Sancerrois and made and sold his own Crottins as Crottins de Bué, but that was in an era less tiresomely regulated. I would like to see more AOCs, and stricter AOCs so far as animal and pasture management, salt-levels and techniques of making and *affinage* are concerned; but I cannot fathom why *fromagers* who are happy and proud to sell their cheeses under a local name, and at the *fromage frais* stage if they wish, should not be allowed to do so. It is like suppressing the names of the vineyards of Burgundy or Bordeaux. Such oppressive standardisation impoverishes the great French repertoire of cheeses instead of enriching it. The Chavignol AOC is particularly vulnerable to this criticism, because it specifically and shamefully allows the use of frozen curd, and stipulates only ten days' *affinage*, which makes nonsense of its appellation.

On this last point, however, I concede that the younger cheeses, which come a little nearer to my late lamented Sancerrois, undoubtedly win many new friends; but the cheese which wins them over is further from the old Crottin than it is from Sancerrois. As Pierre Androuët would like, the younger Crottins should be given a new name or, better, allowed to use their old ones. Crottins proper (or improper) should start at twenty-one days. Many of their old devotees would think even that far too soon. (All the stages of the cheese are described on pp. 77–8.)

As for impropriety, I have just read of a more genteel derivation of Crottin produced by Monsieur Touzery for the Syndicat in 1983. He claimed that the Flemish word *crot*, meaning a hole dug for a drinking pond, was adopted for a terracotta oil lamp; and because the ripe cheeses were similar in shape and colour to the lamp, but smaller, they were given the diminutive name Crottin. My guess is that Flemish *crot* is also French *crotte*, and that the oil lamps were named for the same reason that the cheeses were: they looked like horse dung.

## POULIGNY-SAINT-PIERRE

South-west from the Sancerrois, beyond la Champagne Berrichonne, is a smaller Sologne, with more heath and water, La Brenne. Close to the Poitou border, within the district of Le Blanc, is the AOC region of Pouligny-Saint-Pierre, thought to be the most venerable of Berry's pyramids. It is also the tallest, recalling the architecture of termites rather than of Egyptians in its rusticity, until the Eiffel Tower was built and the cheeses made around Pouligny acquired that structure as their first collective name, 'Tour Eiffel'. Pierre Androuët first classified them under Pouligny-Saint-Pierre when listing cheeses at his father's premises in the 1930s.

Pouligny shares with a few Sainte-Maures *fermiers* the distinction of retaining an old-fashioned goatiness and *croûte-bleutée*. It must be said, though, that the crust usually achieves this through injections of *penicil-*

*lium glaucum* after the drying stage, rather than from the natural surroundings of its *affinage*. Most of the cheeses, including a small quantity of farmhouse, undergo *affinage* (at least two weeks in the zone under AOC rules, and normally four to five) at the large Couturier or smaller Courthial establishments at Pouligny-Saint-Pierre.

*Lait cru* Pouligny AOC is made by the small Laiterie Coopérative de Tournon-Saint-Martin, which also makes the local half-cone-shaped chèvre named after this town, of similar *pâte* and crust.

## Levroux, Liniez and Vatan

Back in the Champagne Berrichonne, farms around Levroux, Liniez and Vatan have produced pyramidal cheeses more squat than Pouligny, sold outside the locality under those place-names in modern times. Robert Courtine regards this as the original pyramidal cheese and gives the originator of Levroux as a poor nineteenth-century *chevrière paysanne*, who visualised a potential rival to Pouligny, perhaps, as she looked at her pyramidal cake cases, and decided to use them as cheese-moulds. The cheeses which emerged so appealed to the public that by 1910 she could no longer satisfy demand. Her cake-shaped cheeses were imitated by farm after farm and their making spread north to Valençay.

## Valençay cheeses

West of Valençay in the Forêt de Loches is a series of slim pyramids (more Cleopatra's needle, or Pouligny cheese, than Valençay shape) erected as rendezvous for meets of hounds for *la chasse à courre*\* in the eighteenth century. Most of them have ecclesiastical names, such as Pyramide des Chartreux and the inevitable Pyramide de Saint-Hubert, eighth-century bishop and protector of the stag, paradoxically appointed by the hunting-and-shooting fraternity as their patron. The one lay exception is the Pyramide de Genillé. This stands west of the village where Madame Charlot makes her chèvre *pyramide* with its untreated natural crust, which she sells in the market at Loches. Three other local *chevriers* sell their charcoal-coated Valençay *pyramides* there. The association between monument and cheese is talked of, but without any documentation.

Monsieur Jacquin of La Vernelle is within the zone for the local appellation Valençay de l'Indre, recently defined by the regional promotion committee at Orléans as the Département de l'Indre. La Vernelle is within 11 kilometres of Valençay itself. He has a local story to account for Valençay's pyramidal cheeses: Talleyrand, famous for his interest in cheese (see Chapter 10), bought the Château de Valençay in 1805. Not long afterwards he was entertaining Napoleon there, and perhaps some cheese brought from Pouligny suggested the teasing topic of pyramids (Napoleon having had to retreat rather fast from Egypt in 1801, it could have been a sore subject). The discussion is said to have been good-humoured enough, nevertheless, to spawn the beginnings of Valençay.

\*hunting with a pack of hounds

What it comes to is that pyramidal moulds may have been with us for a century or two, or for much longer, but the names attached to the cheeses are of modern date. As was true of families before surnames, it was only when cheeses left their native villages that they started to be distinguished by the names of the villages whence they came; and for most cheeses such travel began only with the railways. Valençay is probably one of the most recent to be classified, however plausible the stories.

At its best Valençay can charm first as a sweet, young, soft, moussey cheese, staring white against its black charcoal coat at eight days, the minimum time of *affinage* demanded by the regional code of appellation. In the further three weeks given to the average cheese by the *affineurs*, it becomes ivory-coloured, firm but not hard inside, and acquires white or, more rarely, blue surface mould. It gains in strength and richness of flavour, with nuttiness and still some sweetness if the salt has not been overdone. Unfortunately this is often the case with the common use of factory-mixed powdered charcoal and salt, so buy where you can taste first. Red labels should now mean *laitier* cheese; green is for *fermier*. The *laitier* cheeses are injected with *penicillium candidum*. The authentic cheese naturally acquires *pencillium album*, which turns its surface blue.

The use of the name Valençay de l'Indre is now legally restricted to cheeses made in the *département*, but Valençay *tout simple* is still used by nearby farm cheesemakers in the Lochois, our gateway to the Touraine.

## Sainte-Maure de Touraine

The goats of Touraine and Poitou go back, as we have seen, to the eighth century, when the Saracens stopped at the Loire and were defeated at Sainte-Maure. From the Saracens who stayed behind, the Tourangeaux bought their first goats and the Tourangelles are said to have learned the art of dairy. From the new settlers' word *chebli* for goat came *chèvre* and *chabi*, with all the variants on the latter for goats' cheese. The form of Arab cheese I know is Labna or Labneh, like a young *banon* in appearance, and of similar size to the young Chabichou in its flatter form, as still made south of Poitou (see Chapter 3).

The symbol of goats' cheese for people outside chèvre territory, though, is the *bûche* (log) and the most familiar name is Sainte-Maure. The origin of the shape is lost in antiquity. The name comes from the ancient town, which has always been the marketing centre for the cheese, but which has only been used to denote the cheese in modern times. Locally it was *le chèvre* or *le fromage long*.

On our first visit to Sainte-Maure, in the 1950s, we looked for the inn we had heard about, Le Veau d'Or (Golden Calf), then classed in Michelin as *restaurant avec chambres*. Having put our motor in the outer yard marked as its car park, we found ourselves directed through an inner stableyard, where next week's veal was still on the hoof, surveying us with round-eyed innocence from the stalls. That welcome raised gastronomic expectations which the dining room did not disappoint. The next day, Friday, we found the distinguished old market hall, legacy of the Rohans, seigneurs until

1789. We plunged through a sea of live kids and poultry to the endless stalls of chèvres. The colours of those Sainte-Maure cheeses dominated the market and remain vivid in my memory after thirty years: gold, pink, deep rose, grey, pale to dark blue; but, above all, the glistening reds of cheeses which appeared to have just emerged from a bath of Chinon Rouge. The richness of those exteriors did not belie the flavours within.

Nearly two decades later, in 1973, Robert Courtine, conceding that true Sainte-Maure was *'délicieux'*, regretted that its name had not been protected and that there was so much oversalting. He deplored the mass of factories far outside Touraine, already extruding for winter cheese endless tubes of miscalled Sainte-Maure from curd frozen in the true goat-season's flush. In 1984 Pierre Androuët criticised the substitution of charcoal *cendres* for natural blueing of the surface of chèvres, saying, 'there is no such thing as a chèvre *cendré'*. This term promised that the cheese has actually been ripened in *cendres de bois*, not just coated with them (or with the factory-made powdered charcoal now almost ubiquitous), and had been properly applied to cows'-milk cheeses so ripened, particularly in the Orléanais, as we have seen. Chèvres, on the other hand, have traditionally been surface-blued by mould naturally present in the *affineur's cave*.

In 1986, returning to the Sainte-Maure region through the Lochois, we settled at the Hôtel de France, protected by the walls and towers of Loches and regaled with satisfying local dishes, cheeses and wines at table. Next morning I consulted our host, Monsieur Yves Barrat, who thoughtfully asked his excellent Solognot chef to join the discussion. Monsieur Barrat's mother and grandmother had kept goats on natural feeds, always outdoors for as much of the year as possible. They used little salt in their cheese, and what *cendres* they used were of their own making from *sarments*. These practices achieved 'cheese of sweet richness, strengthening in flavour with time to suit strong palates'.

'Now', Monsieur Barrat went on, 'you don't see goats out any more in Berry and Touraine. They're all indoors on artificial feed; and the *cendres* aren't real any more: they're powdered charcoal pre-mixed with salt. Even farm cheeses now are generally oversalted; the taste of the salt, not of the cheese, lingers on the tongue'. The chef agreed and welcomed the recent renaissance of small *chèvreries*: 'The locals say it is a good thing to find their sweeter cheeses on the market and in the shops'.

These views were later confirmed by the *fromager–affineur* Pierre Jacquin, who said the *grands éleveurs* kept their goats stabled, and on made-up feed, but their number was diminishing. (Pierre Androuët told me later that faults such as oversalting arose from such establishments' being too large to pay proper attention to the details of cheesemaking.) There was not enough cheese reaching the *affineurs* to meet demand. There were now more small *éleveurs* with under 200 goats, selling retail on the farm and in the market rather than to the *affineurs*.

In Loches market later that morning we talked with half a dozen of these smaller *chevriers*, men and women, mostly on the younger side. The Lochois is indisputably in Touraine, but what I saw and heard gave me the feeling of a border *pays*. Valençay and Selles-sur-Cher, by name, as well as anonymous *ronds*, bore witness to the eastward pull of Sologne and Berry, while the same makers' *bûches* looked west to the nearer native Sainte-Maure. Three named their logs Sainte-Maure, one called hers *rouleau*. Most of them used bought-in salted charcoal, but Monsieur Moreau made his own *cendres* from wood-ash. We tasted many of the cheeses and found them soft and white inside and refreshingly sweet, with one exception where the over-generous use of bought-in charcoal had produced too salt a flavour.

We had our last luncheon in the Touraine back at Sainte-Maure in the old Veau d'Or, remembered with affection from the 1950s. There was no longer a guard-of-honour of calves for arriving guests, but Monsieur Lalubin, *chef-de-cuisine–propriétaire*, and Madame did not disappoint us with either their welcome or their food. Indeed, when we thought to leave we were not allowed to. Our host, aware of our interest in cheese, and himself then secretary of the Sainte-Maure cheesemakers, was on the telephone seeking his president, Monsieur Larcher, at home, office and bank, to ask him to come and meet us. He eventually succeeded, and we spent a happy afternoon devouring Sainte-Maure at varying stages from different farms to the sound and savour of constantly flowing Chinon Rouge. This wine is Sainte-Maure's nearest neighbour and best companion, in most cheesemakers' opinion, though some addicts of Sainte-Maure do insist on Vouvray.

Monsieur Larcher brought us up to date on the state of the cheese. Its name still has no national recognition, but at the beginning of the 1970s the makers formed La Commanderie des Fromagers de Sainte-Maure, and a zone of origin was defined with regional authority. The first Grand Maître was the late Monsieur Marc Desaché, then mayor of Sainte-Maure, since when the Commanderie's base has been the Hôtel de Ville. The old annual cheese fair, dating back to 1881 but long dormant, was revived in 1971 and has won the status of a Foire Internationale de Gastronomie. Two competitions are held for Sainte-Maure cheesemakers on successive days. One is on the usual lines, with a panel of experts judging cheeses selected for entry by their makers. The other submits to the judges cheeses bought at random off the competitors' stalls: an excellent test of general, as opposed to selective, standards. There were nearly forty competition entries in 1985, and the number of Commanderie members was approaching fifty.

My hope is that the Commanderie's efforts to restore proper quality standards and territorial associations to the cheese of Sainte-Maure will be rewarded with an AOC. To serve the interests of the public and genuine cheesemakers its rules should allow no compromise with time- and trouble-saving industrial practices: pasteurisation, use of milk powder, frozen curd (so shamefully permitted to makers of Crottins de Chavignol), *penicillium candidum*, ready-mixed salt and powdered charcoal, or skimped *affinage*. Salting should be rigorously controlled if Sainte-Maure is to retain its discriminating *aficionados* and to charm new customers. Sainte-Maure is particularly vulnerable to this fault because of the large surface area to which the salt is applied in relation to the size of the cheese. This also makes it dry out more quickly, and raises the proportion of salt to remaining curd. Natural development of the *croûte-bleutée* and minimum length of *affinage* should be specified.

My last concern with Sainte-Maure is the stout piece of straw on which it is often impaled. This is practical, not decorative, and should be retained, with enough straw protruding at each end to facilitate handling without breaking the cheese or spoiling its surface with finger marks. Suggestions that it is unhygienic must be dismissed by sterilising the straw, which is done elsewhere in the chèvre world. I do recommend withdrawing the straw (with a fork over it to hold the end of the cheese as you pull) when the cheese is to be cut, so that full, not-too-thin circles of Sainte-Maure can be enjoyed, rather than a crumble.

The example of the best AOC practices elsewhere, not so far followed by AOCs for chèvres, shows the importance of laying down a natural local summer *régime* for the dairy animals, and restricting winter feed to dried feed from the same sources. Until this is done, it is either ignorant or dishonest for syndicats to boast of the natural local flavour of their chèvres. To appease industrial interests, the AOC regulators have descended to ineffectual amateurism.

This seems the right note on which to leave the still lively *chevriers* of Berry and Touraine, in whose hands the integrity of France's most sought-after chèvres can be restored or destroyed. Let them guard their cheeses from becoming indistinguishable from the imitations of Poitou, whither we now turn to look for the gold still remaining in the dross.

## Cheeses of Touraine, Orléanais and Berry

### Amboise
Friday and Saturday market.
Leonardo da Vinci's last home nearby.
Touraine/Indre-et-Loire; 64 **14**.

### Angers
Daily market (except Mon); city rich in treasures; La Maison Lemaire for organic farming advice and supplies, e.g. *sel gris* (natural salt), *présure*, etc.
Fédération Européenne des Syndicats d'Agrobiologistes, Les Loges, 49480 St-Sylvain-d'Anjou; tel. 41 43 69 15; send ff10 for information.
Anjou/Maine-de-Loire; 63 **20**, 64 **11**, Saint Sylvain top L NE of Angers.

### Anjou
See below and STE-MAURE-AMY-BIQUE.

**Le Biqueton.** Small flat drum; by M. Bénéteau at La Tessonalle, Cholet.
*artisanal; chèvre.*
Cholet; 67 **5/6**.

**Bûchette d'Anjou.** Small log made at La Morlière, St-Barthélémy.
*artisanal; chèvre.*
Anjou/Maine-et-Loire; 64 **11**, high L E of Angers.

**Crémet d'Anjou.** See CRÉMET.

**Fromage Blanc.** Sold, with yoghurt and milk by Michel and Françoise Menard at La Gemmerie (tel. 41 92 57 79).
*fermier; biologique; Nature & Progrès; vache cru.*
Le Bourg d'Iré; 63 **9**, 8km W of Segré.

**Fromage Blanc, Affiné.** Marie-Odile and Thierry Mercier sell at Pont l'Arche on farm; cheese, butter, cream, milk, cereals sold retail and wholesale (tel. 41 48 42 98 first); Angers Saturday market, place Général Leclerc; camping on the farm.
*fermier; biologique; Nature & Progrès; vache cru.*
Bouchemaine; 64 **11**, 63 **20**, N of Angers.

**Fromages de Chèvre.** 1. Cheese (and vegetables in season, apples, apple-juice, honey, jam) sold by Jean-Paul Bouc on farm Les Chupinières and at Angers on Saturday

market; camping at the farm.
*fermier; biologique; chèvre cru.*
Montpollin; 64 **2**, low, 5km N of Bauge off N138.
2. Cheese (and onions, garlic, vegetables in season) sold by Daniel Baudry on farm Le Theil all day Saturday; camping on the farm.
*fermier; biologique; chèvre cru.*
Le Guédéniau; 64 **12**, high R, SE of Baugé.

**Fromages Frais, Tome de Vache.** Jean Jemet sells on farm at Préau on Mondays; and on Wednesday and Saturday markets at Lafayette, Angers.
*fermier; biologique; Nature & Progrès; vache cru.*
Avrillé; 63 **20** on N167 NW edge of Angers.

**Fromages de Vache.** J. Frette sells organic cheese and butter at Chigne on farm and at Marché Biologique Beaujardin, Tours, Wednesday and Saturday.
*fermier; biologique; Nature & Progrès; vache cru.*
Maine-et-Loire; 64 **3** N of Noyant, bottom L.

### Anjouin

Coopérative de Berry d'Anjouin, Groupement des Producteurs de Fromage de Chèvre de la Vallée du Cher (*affinage* and distribution; e.g. Bûche Paillée, Selles-sur-Cher, Valençay de l'Indre).
Coopérative Fromagère Anjouin, St-Christophe-en-Bazelle, 36210 Chabris, makes pleasant versions of all Tourangeaux and Berrichons cheeses, under Saint-Christophe label, in the Vallée du Cher.
Berry/Indre; 64 **18/19**, low.

### Apéri

See AUTHON.

### Authon

La Chevrerie d'Authon, M. and Mme P. François (since 1985); tel. 54 80 32 24). During cheesemaking the curd is left at least 24 hours in the vat. The following cheeses are made here (and available from Delon at Rungis).

**Apéri.** Tiny dome 3cm high, 3cm wide, pierced with cut straw; moussey texture, slightly acid.

**Bigoton.** 170g oval, 12–13cm × 5cm × 4cm deep; at one week moussey texture on dry side but melts in mouth; tasty lactic flavour.

**Brie-type.** Larger version, round, 18cm diameter × 4cm deep (in Coulommiers shape), ripened for 8 weeks.

**Chabichou.** This has won gold and bronze medals in Paris.

**Chabis Blanc.** *Cendré* to order. Topped cone 4cm × 7–8cm × 5cm at base; sold *frais*.

**Cœur Cendré.** Made from curd expelled from Sainte-Maure and the miniature cheeses when straws are inserted; coated in charcoal.

**Croque Chèvre Frais.** Apéri coated with or containing within it paprika, *poivre, persil* (parsley), *oignon.*

**Croque-Chèvre Mirabel.** Dried mirabelles soaked in *eau-de-vie*, then rolled individually in croque-chèvre curd; filled curd soaked 24 hours in *eau-de-vie de mirabelle*, and sold in tiny *petit-four* cases; the fruit keeps its flavour.

**Crottins.** Most are sold *frais*; I tasted one *sec* and found it very tasty and admirably unsalt.

**Petit-Perche.** Deep base of cone, smaller than Selles-sur-Cher (which is 140–150g), and lightly *cendré*.

**Pyramide.** Pouligny-type (but outside AOC zone) 10cm tall, 3cm at top, 6cm at base; I tasted a *non-cendré* cheese of 5 weeks, and found it pleasingly sharp, yet sweet and unsalt.

**Sainte-Maure AOC.** Traditional log with straw inserted through middle when cheese is removed from mould (see CŒUR above).

**La Tomme.** 1500g; 25cm × 10cm deep; white at *frais* stage, gold at 4 weeks; fully ripe at 10 weeks, hard, crumbly, close texture, sweet and rich in flavour.
45% *m.g.; fermier; chèvre cru.*
Gâtine-Tourangelle; near Vendômois–Touraine border/Loir-et-Cher; 64 **5** low, far R off D71.

### Les Aydes Bleu or Cendré

Name used by Androuët, rue Amsterdam, Paris, for Olivet type cheese made at Chécy by Frinault.

50% m.g.; *artisanal; vache pasteurisé.*
Orléanais.

## Azay-le-Rideau

Wednesday market; wine fair last weekend in February; notable moated château.
Touraine/Indre-et-Loire; 64 **14**.

## Baies Roses

Red berries used to cover the tops of young chèvres of Selles-sur-Cher size (seen at Philippe Olivier's shop in Boulogne, and in Arras at Jean Claude Leclercq's).

## Beauce

N of region around Chartres: La Petite Beauce extends S to the Loire in the Vendômois and part of the Blésois.
See LA PETITE BEAUCE (BEAUCERON), CHARTRES, CHÂTEAUDUN, ILLIERS-COMBRAY, VOVES.

## Beauce, La Petite

1. Crottin-sized, ripened in *cendres*, wrapped in vine leaf; fine-textured *pâte*, like Trôo (see p. 91) and Montoire (see p. 83) (Lindon, 1961).
*fermier; vache cru.*
Loiret.
2. Coulommiers-size soft cheese; natural *croûte-bleutée*; presented in plane leaves.
45% m.g.; *fermier; vache cru.*
Vendômois (Petite-Beauce-Blésois/Loir-et-Cher).

## Beauceron

250g cheese with delicate interior.
*fermier; artisanal; chèvre cru.*
Thimerais/Eure-et-Loire; 60 **7**, high Dreux area.

## Beaugency

Saturday market.
Orléanais, Sologne/Loiret; 64 **8**.

**Boisgency.** Cheese made here in seventeenth century, when it was praised by the Abbé de Maroilles.

## Berry

See ANJOUIN, BERRYCHON, BILLY, BIQUE, BOURGES (market), BRUÈRE ALLICHAMPS (cheese fair), BÛCHE PAILLÉE, CABIC, CABRETTE, CAPRIN, CHABI, CHABICHOU, CHABIQUET, CHABRIS, CHÂTEAUROUX (market), CHÂTILLON-SUR-INDRE (market), CŒUR, CORNILLY, CRÉZANCY, CROTTIN, DÔME, FONGOMBAULT, GRAÇAY, LA JONCHÈRE, LEVROUX, MALLESSUI, MÉZIÈRES, MEUSNES, PAVÉ, PERLE, PETITS-SUISSES, POULIGNY NOTRE-DAME, POULIGNY-SAINT-PIERRE, PYRAMIDE, RIANS, ROULÉ, ST-AMAND-MONTROND, SAINT-CHEVRIER, SAINT-CHRISTOPHE, SANCERRE, SELLES-SUR-CHER, SELECT, TOURNON-ST-MARTIN, TOMME, TOUR-EIFFEL, VALENÇAY, VATAN, LA VERNELLE, VIERZON (market).

## Le Berrychon

Sainte-Maure-type *cendré, affiné* at La Vernelle (see p. 93).
45% m.g.; *fermier; chèvre cru.*
Berry.

## Le Bichonnet

Sainte-Maure and Pyramide by Bernard Ferrand at Anché, 37500 Chinon (tel. 47 93 11 50); bronze, silver and gold medals at Paris.
45% m.g.; *fermier; chèvre cru.*
Touraine/Indre-et-Loire; 67 **9**, 64 **13** bottom R, Anché.

## Bigoton

See AUTHON.

## Billy, le Petit

Like a smaller version of Selles-sur-Cher (see p. 89); it used to be ripened in plane or vine leaves in earthenware pots (Courtine, 1973).
45% m.g.; *fermier; chèvre cru.*
Berry/Indre; 64 **18**, L, Billy N of Selles-sur-Cher.

## Bique, La Pointe de

320g; tall *pyramide*, between Pouligny and Valençay in shape, *frais* or *fleuri (bleuté)* by Jacquin, La Vernelle (see p. 93).
45% m.g.; *laitier; chèvre.*
Berry/Indre.

## Biqueton, le

See ANJOU.

## Blésois

Blois district; see CHAUMONT, ONZAIN, PAVÉ, VILLEBAROU; strictly speaking, the Blésois is all on the right (north) bank of the Loire, and includes part of La Petite Beauce.

**Pavé du Blésois (or de la Sologne).** 10–11cm square × 2.5cm deep, on straw; or 750g truncated *pyramide* for cutting; soft;

one month's *séchage*; thin natural *croûte-bleutée*; light nutty flavour (Androuët, *Livre d'Or*, 1984; he thinks it is derived from Selles-sur-Cher recipe, apart from its form, which is more reminiscent of Valençay).
45% m.g.; *artisanal*; *chèvre*.
Loire-et-Cher.

### Bleu

In this region *bleu* signifies natural colouring of the crust of cheeses by surface mould (*croûte-bleutée*, or *fleurie*), as, for example, in Olivet Bleu, Vendôme Bleu. Properly this applies to Pouligny, Sainte-Maure, and other traditional *chèvres* when fully matured, but they are often coated now with powdered charcoal (ready mixed with salt, too often too much of it). This keeps the cheese young, white and mild inside, and virtually crustless, quite different from the more powerful original with its natural blue coat.

### Blois

Tuesday, Wednesday, Thursday and Saturday market, Sunday mornings; starred town.
Crémerie Riby, 90 rue du Commerce; Crémerie Seurre, 10 Port Chartraine; Ets Rogier, Saint-Gervais-la-Forêt (SE edge of Blois) are all recommended especially for Selles-sur-Cher.
Blésois/Loir-et-Cher; 64 **7**.

### Boisgency

See BEAUGENCY.

### Boismorand

See CHÂTILLON-COLIGNY. Fat cheese made from spring to autumn by farmers of the domaine de Bellecourt (commune Ste-Geneviève-des-Bois). Cheeses were conserved in *cendres de bois* for winter, eaten *sec* after some months, even *très sec* after a year or two. Thought to have ceased production by 1978 (*Marabout*).
*fermier*; *vache cru*.
Gâtinais/Loiret; 65 **2**, W of C, and district to E.

### Bondaroy au Foin

Here and in the nearby countryside farms made this soft, flat, round cheese (250–300g, 10–12cm deep) and conserved the surplus from the spring flush (May and June), and any later spare cheeses, in hay boxes for 5 weeks. The hay kept the cheeses apart, allowed natural crust to develop, and imparted its own agreeable flavour. The basic cheese was of the type originating at St-Benoist (see p. 86). Bondaroy has long been swamped by its larger neighbour Pithiviers (see p. 85), but I have seen neither cheese in later years. Their type is represented by Olivet au Foin (see p. 83), which is sometimes labelled as Pithiviers because Pithiviers dominated the class for years.
40–45% m.g.; *fermier*; *vache cru*.
Gâtinais/Loiret; 60 **20**, SE of C, E of Pithiviers.

### Bourges

Capital of Berry; daily market; cathedral and a great deal else: La Laiterie Bonneau makes Crottins de Chavignol AOC (see p. 77), among other cheeses.
Berry/Cher 69 **1**.

### Bourgueil

Tuesday market.
Touraine/Indre-et-Loire; 64 **13** SW of C.

### Brie

Cheese called Brie Président is manufactured at Doué-la-Fontaine by the entirely automated Besnier concern, helping to account for the enormous tonnage of cheese produced in Anjou and Maine with so little interest to show for it.
Anjou/Maine-et-Loire.

### Bruère Allichamps

Fourth week Sept.: foire aux fromages.
Berry/Cher; 69 **1**, low on N144 and R. Cher.

### Bûche

Means log, form of Sainte-Maure-de-Touraine, whose name has been borrowed for *chèvres* made far afield in the round shape. Flattened base or rectangular form usually indicates mixed-milk cheese: *mi-chèvre*, at least 50% goats' milk, or *lait-de-mélange* which should have at least 25% of goats' milk.

**Bûche Mi-Chèvre, Lait-de-Mélange.**
Usually rounded top, flat base, e.g. those of Coopérative Reignac-sur-Indre.
*laitier*; *vache/chèvre pasteurisé*.
Touraine/Indre-et-Loire; 64 **15/16**.

**Bûche Paillée.** 180g log in traditional Sainte-Maure form, with a straw (*paille*) through the middle. Groupe des Producteurs de Fromage de Chèvre de la Vallée du Cher, Anjouin. Many farmhouse Sainte-Maure cheeses have this straw lengthwise through the middle to facilitate handling without breaking, or spoiling the crust, e.g. Authon (see p. 72). See also SAINT-CHRISTOPHE.
*45% m.g.; artisanal; chèvre cru.*
Berry/Cher/Anjouin.

### CABIC

The names following, beginning Cab, Chab, derive from the Arabic *chebli* for goat (see POITOU), while words such as Caprin derive from the Latin *capra* for goat.

**Cabic du Berry.** 60g truncated cone (taller than it is wide) by Hubert Triballat at Rians.
*45% m.g.; laitier; chèvre.*
Berry/Cher; 65 **12**, low L.

**La Cabrette.** About 150g, of Selles-sur-Cher proportions; soft; rustic natural crust, rather orange in colour; by Couturier, *fromager* and *affineur* at Pouligny.
*45% m.g.; laitier; chèvre.*
Berry/Indre; 68 **16**, high NE of Le Blanc.

**Cabri, Cabri Blanc.** Base of cone, or small drum in shape; 120g at blanc stage, 70g when *affiné* to achieve rustic gold to grey-blue crust; farm cheese of Touraine in Selles-sur-Cher style, to be found in markets, especially at Tours.
*45% m.g.; fermier; chèvre cru.*
Touraine.

### CAMEMBERT-TYPE

Made at Saint Clément des Levées by Marcillat. See also VERNEUIL.
*artisanal; vache cru.*
Anjou/Maine-et-Loire; 64 **12**, 4km SE of Les Rosiers N bank of Loire.

### LE CAPRIN, GRAND CAPRIN

320g and 1600g long chèvres with triangular section; sold *frais* or *fleuri*; made by Jacquin *fromager–affineur* at La Vernelle (see p. 93).
*45% m.g.; laitier; chèvre.*
Berry/Indre.

### CARRÉ GOÛT DU JOUR

200g soft, white-coated; Coopérative Agricole Laitière de Champigny-sur-Veude.
*40% m.g.; laitier; vache pasteurisé.*
Touraine/Indre-et-Loire; 68 **3**, high far R.

### CENDRÉ

See FROMAGE CENDRÉ.

### CHABI

This is a commonly used name for goat cheese in Anjou (see p. 71), Touraine (see p. 90), and Poitou (see p. 103), and adjoining *pays* (see CABIC).

**Chabi Fermier.** 100–120g upright cylinder, tending towards conical; early in *affinage* crust goes crinkly and acquires blue surface mould. Here Chabi is short for Chabichou, which gets taller as it gets further north from its most earthy Cabécou roots in Périgord, Quercy and Rouergue. Chabis are found in markets, e.g. Tours.
*45% m.g.; fermier; chèvre cru.*

**Le Chabi.** 150g version of Chabi Fermier, *affiné* by Couturier, Pouligny-St-Pierre (see p. 85).
*45% m.g.; artisanal; chèvre.*
Berry/Indre.

### CHABICHOU

130g; truncated tall cone; farm cheese *affiné* by P. Hardy (*cendré* and *bleuté*), at Meusnes (see p. 83); and see AUTHON.
*45% m.g.; fermier; chèvre cru.*
Berry/Loir-et-Cher (*affinage*); Touraine-Poitou (making); on R. Vienne.

### LE CHABIQUET

160g version of Chabis (like Chabi), by Jacquin, La Vernelle (see p. 93).
*45% m.g.; laitier; chèvre.*
Berry/Indre.

### CHABIS

Like Chabi above, made in Berry (e.g. Le Chabiquet above), Gâtine Tourangelle (see AUTHON), and in Touraine (e.g. La Coopérative Fromagère Anjouin (see ANJOUIN).
*45% m.g.; laitier; chèvre.*
Berry/Indre; Touraine/Indre.

**Chabis Fermier.** Truncated cone, natural crust, *affiné* by Courthial Père et Fils, Pouligny-St-Pierre (see p. 85) *Collecteur-affineur* of farm cheeses from the Chabris

district: J.C. Audion.
45% m.g.; fermier; chèvre cru.
Berry/Indre/Touraine.

CHABRIS

160g chèvre of Camembert consistency and crust, affiné at Chabris.
45% m.g.; fermier; chèvre cru.
Berry/Indre; 64 **18**, 8km from Selles-sur-Cher.

LE CHAMPCOU

50g soft chèvre (1st prize winner in International Food Show London, 1979) made by La Coopérative Fromagère Anjouin (see p. 72).
45% m.g.; laitier; chèvre cru.

CHARTRES

Tuesday, Wednesday and Saturday market; historic and beautiful oasis in the maize-desert the modern Beauce has become.
Beauce/Eure-et-Loir; 60 **7/8**.

CHÂTEAU DU LOIR

Saturday market.
Sarthe; 64 **4**.

CHÂTEAUDUN

Tuesday, Thursday, Saturday market.
Beauce/Eure-et-Loir; 60 **17**, low.

CHÂTEAUROUX

Saturday market (cattle on Mondays).

**Châteauroux.** A cheese of this name was recorded by Lindon in 1961.
Berry/Indre; 68 **8**.

CHÂTILLON-COLIGNY

Cheese of the Bondaroy type (see p. 74) made locally years ago (see BOISMORAND).
fermier; artisanal; vache cru.
Gâtinais/Loiret; 65 **2**, far R of C.

CHÂTILLON-SUR-INDRE

Thursday market.
Berry; 68 **6**, R.

CHAUMONT-SUR-LOIRE

**Le Chaumont.** 200g round 'fromage blanc à l'ancienne' (not related to the Langres-like Chaumont of Champagne (see Chapter 10, p. 330)); the only example I have met was made by the Laiterie Fromagère d'Onzain on the opposite bank of the Loire, and very lightly salted (1986). This dairy also makes Olivet (see p. 83) Villebarou.
artisanal; vache.
Sologne Blésoise/Loir-et-Cher; 64 **16/17**, S bank of Loire.

CHAVIGNOL

See CROTTIN DE.

CHÉCY, FRINAULT

130g; flat round; 9cm × 2cm deep; affiné 3 weeks in humid cave, croûte-naturelle-bleutée, thin; like Olivet. One of the descendants of Saint-Benoist (see p. 86). Chast et Voy report a Chécy Cendré affiné 4 weeks in cendres de bois (1984). This cheese was started by M. Frinault at Chécy in 1848 and is still made there by the Frinault laiterie. It has also been known as Frinault (even as Frinot).
50% m.g.; laitier; artisanal; vache pasteurisé.
Orléanais/Loiret; 64 **9**, 10km E of Orléans on Loire.

CHÈVRES

See ANJOU (including BÛCHETTE) BIQUETON, AUTHON (APÉRI, BIGOTON, CHABICHOU, CHABIS, CŒUR, CROQUE-CHÈVRE, MIRABEL, CROTTIN, PETIT PERCHE, PYRAMIDE, SAINTE-MAURE, TOMME), BERRYCHON, BICHONNET, BILLY, BIQUE (LA POINTE DE), BLÉSOIS (PAVÉ DU), BÛCHE, CABIC, CABRETTE, CABRI, CAPRIN, CHABI, CHABICHOU, CHABIQUET, CHABIS, CHABRIS, CHAMPCOU, CHOUZE, CORNILLY, CRÉZANCY-SANCETTE, CROTTIN, FROMAGES FERMIERS, FROMAGE BLANC DE CHÈVRE, GIEN, GIENNOIS, GRAÇAY, LEVROUX, LIGUEIL, MALESSUI, MEUSNES (affineur), MONTOIRE, PERCHE, POULIGNY, PYRAMIDE, RIANS (laitier-affineur), ROND, SAINT-CHEVRIER, SAINTE-MAURE, SANCERROIS, SELLES-SUR-CHER, SELECT, SOLOGNE (see BLÉSOIS), TOMME, TOURNON, VALENÇAY, VATAN, VENDÔME, LA VERNELLE (laitier-affineur), VERNEUIL, VILLEBAROU, VILLIERS.

CHINON

Thursday, Saturday and Sunday market.
Touraine/Indre-et-Loire; 67 **9**.

CHOUZÉ-SUR-LOIRE

**Chouzé.** Soft cheese with thick penicillium candidum crust (Viard, 1980).
45% m.g.; laitier; chèvre.
Touraine/Indre-et-Loire; 64 **13**, S of Bourgueil.

## Cœur de Rians a la Crème

250g cheese at *faisselle* stage, probably by Triballat (see AUTHON and RIANS).
Berry/Cher; 65 **12**, low L.

## Contres

Friday market (Selles-sur-Cher country). Sologne/Loir-et-Cher; 64 **17**, NE of C.

## Cormery

A local *fromager* is using part of the refectory of the eighth-century *abbaye* as *affinoir* for his cheeses.
Touraine/Indre-et-Loire; 64 **15**, SE of Tours N143.

## Corne d'Or

Base of cone, like Selles-sur-Cher in appearance (see LIGUEIL, Unicoop).
45% m.g.; *laitier*; *chèvre*.
Touraine/Indre-et-Loire.

## Cornilly

250g soft, slightly conical; *frais* or *fleuri*; by Jacquin, La Vernelle.
45% m.g.; *laitier*; *chèvre*.
Berry/Indre; 64 **18**, lower L, S of Selles-sur-Cher.

## Crémet d'Anjou

Whip 125g of fresh cream and beat one white of egg; mix with care, continuing to beat; put into moulds, covered with muslin, to drain in cool temperature; to serve turn out the moulds and cover the Crémets with *crème fraîche* (preferably *fermière*) and vanilla sugar (*sucre vanillé* in France).

## Crézancy-en-Sancerre

80–100g young cheese of Crottin family (see SANCERROIS); stocked by MM. Cénéri at Cannes (see Chapter 18, p. 510). Courtine says Crézancy is fatter than Crottin de Chavignol (see below), but M. Crochet (*affineur* at Bué near Sancerre) tells me that it was one of many versions of Crottin named after local *communes*, a practice now forbidden in the Crottin de Chavignol region (strictly speaking since 1976, the year of the AOC).

## Croque-Chèvre

See AUTHON.

## Crottin

**Crottin de Chavignol, AOC 1976.** As packed by *affineurs*: 60–70g rounded drum; 4–5cm diameter × 5cm deep (shrinking steadily with further *affinage*); made in moulds slightly conical (5.5cm (top) × 5cm (base) × 7cm (depth) from which cheese emerges '*mou*' weighing 140g (see SANCERROIS), before normal 3 weeks of *affinage* at 13° in 80% humidity, achieving light coating of *penicillium*; it starts to show flavour at the '*coudre*' stage, after 8 days; at 12 days it is '*bleuté*' and very pleasant, and the Syndicat says it has now become '*le véritable* Crottin de Chavignol'. It is certainly delicious (if not oversalted) at these earlier stages; but the true, rich Crottin flavour and short texture comes later. The Syndicat says: '*Très sec* at 20 days, it is becoming brittle under the knife and has a full flavour.' The term '*repasse*' applies to cheeses, already *très sec*, further matured by a few makers in earthenware pots, in which they turn soft again with time. The Syndicat comments that on meeting one 'it would be indiscreet to ask it how old it was'.

*Method, most common:* 0.6 to 1 l of milk is required for one cheese. It is put in pails or basins of 10–50 l capacity. Rennetting is done while the milk is warm from the goats on the farm, and raised to 30°C in *laiteries*: 5ml of animal rennet diluted 1/5000 for 100 l of milk in full season, up to double that amount early and late in the season, when some makers add 2–3% of starter (*sérum* reserved from the previous cheesemaking). The curd takes from 24 to 48 hours according to season or weather. Some makers still use earthenware pots, which are noted by the Syndicat for giving 'an excellent regularity in the quality of the curd'. Unlike the practice anywhere else in the well-known goat-cheese world, draining is most often done on cloths laid on basket-work where it remains several hours, according to weather conditions, until ready to ladle into the moulds. Some *éleveurs* pour the undrained curd straight into the moulds. Most makers take the cheeses from the moulds within 24 hours, salt them lightly, and place them on the straw mats or trays on which they will travel to the *affineurs*. At this stage they are 5–5.5cm across and at least 5.5cm high, and must weigh 140g, including at least 37g of dry matter, to merit the AOC. Most large herds are stabled throughout the year these days, so the official claim that the Crottin's flavour is the result of Berry's pastures is disingenuous. Unfortunately (as Courtine was already complaining in 1973) *crottins laitiers* are oversalted. This is particularly ill-advised in a cheese which dries as it matures to less than half its *faisselle* weight.

The name Crottin de Chavignol was adopted with official encouragement in 1829. The Dubois, active *affineurs* of farmhouse cheeses, claim that their ancestor was the instigator of the naming.

In 1862 there were 14,559 goats in the Cher, a number nearly doubled by 1972. Production has risen steadily from 674 tonnes in 1980 to between 950 and 1000 tonnes in 1984 (providing about 6 million 60g farm cheeses and 7 million *laitiers* cheeses.

In late 1985, according to the Syndicat, *lait-cru* Crottin de Chavignol was being made by three *laiteries*, eight large farms (*éleveurs*, whom Androuët classes as *laitiers artisanaux*), and by an unspecified number of small farmers. It was reckoned at 400 in 1983 by *La Crémerie Française* (issue 1238/9 15–30 December), but M. Crochet estimated 150 in 1987. AOC cheeses are collected, ripened and distributed by eight *affineurs*, listed below, of whom Dubois-Boulay and Crochet devote themselves entirely to farmhouse cheeses. The use of individual commune or district names other than Chavignol is now forbidden (e.g. Bué, Crézancy, Sancerre and Sancerrois, formerly associated with young cheeses before they reached the Crottin stage). The AOC is criticised for not specifying *lait cru*, although I am assured that all the production controlled by the Syndicat is *lait cru*, and no uncontrolled cheese can be legally sold as Crottin de Chavignol. It is also criticised for extending the permitted *région d'origine* in the north into Sologne and the Orléanais, from the original Pays Fort and Sancerrois. The southern part of the region is the Champagne Berrichonne, the centre third of the Département du Cher. Across the Loire from Sancerre there is a bridgehead of the region in the Nivernais.

45% and 60% m.g.; *fermier artisanal*; *chèvre entier (cru)*.

Sources of AOC *fromages fermiers*: Nivernais: J. Pasquet, *éleveur*, Domaine de Cadoux, 58440 La Celle-sur-Loire (Nivernais/Nièvre, 65 **13**, N of Cosne). Pays-Fort: Godard, *affineur*, Blancafort (Pays-Fort/Sancerrois/Cher, 65 **11**, high R). Sancerrois: P. Bertrand, *affineur*, and Chamaillard, *affineur*, Santranges (Sancerrois/Cher, 65 **12**, high R, near Léré, which is on Canal de la Loire); Claude Crochet, *affineur* at Bué of Crottins de Chavignol *fermiers* (Sancerrois/Cher, 65 **12**, SW of Sancerre); M. Denizot, *affineur* (he also ripens *laitier* cheese, so specify *fermier*), Chavignol, packed at 70g; Dubois-Boulay, *affineurs* at Chavignol of Crottins de Chavignol *fermiers*, packed at 65g (Sancerrois/Cher, 65 **12**, R, W of Sancerre); Philippe Jay, La Forêt, 18260 Thou (Cher, not Loiret), silver medal Paris in 1980s (Sancerrois/Cher, 65 **12**, NW of C on N723). Sologne: B. de Renty, Les Grands, 18410 Argent-sur-Sauldre (Sologne/Cher, 65 **11**, top).

*Laitiers making AOC cheese 60g*: La Laiterie Bonneur, 170 avenue de St Amand, 18000 Bourges, 'Caprice'; Champagne Berrichonne/Cher; 69 **1**. La Fromagerie Hubert Triballat, Rians. 50% m.g. (won gold medal Paris in recent years) and see Denizot above. In 1985 I saw a triple-Crottin (triple length; standard diameter), made for restaurateurs to cut for salads and other items on the menu; Sancerrois/Cher; 65 **12**, low L.

CROTTINS (NON AOC)

**Crottins de Chèvre**

1. Coopérative Fromagère Anjouin (see p. 72); Berrychons ripened at Anjouin (rich; moist, open texture when young; on salt side later) and their own 60g, as de Bique (see p. 73).
*laitier; chèvre pasteurisé.*
Berry/Cher.

2. Pierre Jacquin, *fromager affineur*, La Vernelle (see p. 93) 60g Le Champignou.
*laitier; chèvre pasteurisé.*
Berry/Indre.

**Crottins Frais.** 110g Crottin sold soon after *faisselle* stage, by Triballat, Rians (see above CROTTIN DE CHAVIGNOL, LAITIERS AOC).
45% m.g.; *laitier, chèvre.*
Berry/Cher.

**Crottins au Lait-de-Mélange.** In December 1983 *La Crémerie Française* reported that three *fromagers* were collecting from

550 milk producers goat's and cows' milk which they mixed and made into Crottins.
*laitier; chèvre/vache pasteurisé or thermisé.*
Berry.

**Double-Crottin.** Double depth cheeses, made from chèvre curd from within the region but not of AOC size, so not allowed to bear the name Chavignol. I have seen triple depth cheeses, virtually logs, under the Crottin label (see CROTTIN DE CHAVIGNOL, LAITIERS AOC).
*chèvre; laitier.*

DÔME

**Dôme Cendré.** 180–200g cheese of above type, *cendré*; neat dome when young, rustically irregular, shrunken top when *affiné* (and see LOCHOIS (BEAUREPAIRE)).
*chèvre.*
Berry/Indre.

**Dôme de Chèvre.** 110g cheese reminiscent of La Taupinière (see Chapter 3, p. 111) made or *affiné* by Couturier, Pouligny.
*45% m.g.; laitier; chèvre pasteurisé.*
Berry/Indre; 68 **16**, high L on D975.

DREUX

Friday and Sunday market (inhabitants Drouais or Durocasses).

**Dreux à la Feuille; Feuille de Dreux; Fromage de Dreux.** 300–500g; 16–18cm × 2–3cm deep; 2–3 weeks in humid *cave*; *croûte-fleurie*; full-flavoured, soft cheese of Coulommiers shape, but usually thinner, ripened traditionally in boxes among chestnut leaves, and usually presented with three leaves on each face of crust.
Androuët recommends cheese made at Marsauceux (*Livre d'Or*, 1982, 1984), across the R. Eure, east of Dreux, and mentions that of Nogent-le-Roi (1982) 18km south-east up-river. He gives the cheese as *pasteurisé*.
*30–45% m.g.; laitier; artisanal; vache pasteurisé.*

**Spécialité au Lait Cru.** Another good cheese of the type, made by Mme Lucien Bizieau at St-Lubin-de-la-Haye; marked *affiné sous feuilles de châtaignier* (ripened under chestnut leaves); I have eaten and sold it for years, and enjoyed its rich flavour and oozy texture many times; a bare 2cm deep, it should not be kept long once it is ripe.
M. Simon Fisson made Fromage de Dreux some years ago at Bû (12km NE of Dreux), but I do not know whether it is still produced there. At 30% m.g. it would be more traditional, as cheeses of this type were made of milk already part-skimmed for cream and butter. They were kept in chestnut leaves on the farm for the family and staff. Household numbers were greater in former days, and the cheeses were larger than today's, and kept longer (30–45 days).
*45% m.g.; artisanal; vache cru.*
Thimerais/Eure-et-Loire; 60 **7**, high, 60 **8**, top on D933.

EIFFEL, LA TOUR

Nickname for Pouligny-Saint-Pierre (see p. 85).

LA FAISSELLE DE RIANS

*Fromage blanc maigre* by Triballat (see RIANS). See LOCHOIS (BEAUREPAIRE) for chèvre.
*82% moisture; laitier; vache.*
Berry/Cher; 65 **12**.

LA FERTÉ, LA FERTÉ BERNARD

1. Chèvre *lait cru* probably extinct (Lindon, 1961, as Ferté).
2. Vache *lait cru entier*, as La Ferté Bernard. Last mention Larousse 1973, still being made. Attributed to Perche but seems rather too far W; may have been made E of La Ferté but marketed there.
Maine/Perche/Sarthe; 60 **15**, W of C.

LE FONTGOMBAULT

L'Abbaye de Notre Dame makes a *pâte fraîche*, sold *en faisselle* (200g, 500g, or as required) on the farm, on weekdays only.
*artisanal; vache cru.*
Berry/Indre; 68 **16**, high L, on R. Creuse and D950.

FONTEVRAUD L'ABBAYE

Wednesday market; remarkable *abbaye*. Sometimes spelt Fontevrault.
Maine-et-Loire; 64 **13**, low far L.

FRINAULT, FRINOT

See CHÉCY.

## Fromage Blanc, Fromage Blanc Battu

See ANJOU, AUTHON (CHABIS BLANC), FAISS-ELLE, LOCHOIS (BEAUREPAIRE); TRÔO (FROMAGE BLANC BATTU), LA VERNELLE (for TÔME BLANCHE).

## Fromage Cendré

See AYDES, BOISMORAND, CHÂTILLON-COLIGNY, CHÉCY (including FRINAULT), OLIVET, PANNES, PATAY, PENNES, PERCHE (AUTHON), LA PETITE BEAUCE, SAINT-BENOIST, SILORS, TRÔO, VENDÔME, VILLIERS-SUR-LOIRE, VOVES. *Cendré* strictly implies *affinage* in *cendres de bois*, not mere charcoal-coating as usually practised today.

## Fromagée; Fromage Fort du Berry

*Demi-secs* to *passés* cheeses; in Drouais, local cheeses (see DREUX) marinated in cider to resoften. Then, used in *casse-croûte*; in Berry, chèvres well drained and finished, mixed with crushed garlic, *fines-herbes*, dry white wine and left in sealed pot for some weeks; eaten as a four o'clock snack by *chevriers-vignerons* (Androuët, *Livre d'Or*, 1984).
Thimerais-Drouais/Berry.

## Fromage Fort de Trôo

See TRÔO.

## Fromage Frais

**Fromage Frais Campagne.** See TRÔO.

**Fromage Frais Rians Plumé.**
0% m.g.; *laitier*.

**Fromage Frais Salé.** Made by Triballat at Rians (see p. 86).

**Fromage Frais Pur Chèvre.** Made by Mme Jacquet (see LOCHOIS, SENNEVIÈRES).
*fermier; chèvre cru*.
Berry/Cher.

## Fromages Fermiers

See ANJOU, AUTHON (TOURAINE), LA PETITE BEAUCE, BEAUCERON, BERRYCHON, BICHONNET (TOURAINE, SAINTE-MAURE), VALENÇAY, BILLY (BERRY), BOISMORAND (GÂTINAIS), BONDAROY (GATINAIS), CABRI (TOURAINE), CHABI, CHABICHOU (TOURAINE), CHABRIS (BERRY), CHÂTILLON-COLIGNY (GÂTINAIS), CRÉZANCY (BERRY), CROTTIN (BERRY, S. ORLÉANAIS, SOLOGNE), FONTGOMBAULT (GÂTINAIS), GIEN (GÂTINAIS), LEVROUX (BERRY), LOCHOIS, PERCHE (ORLÉANAIS, VENDÔMOIS), POULIGNY (BERRY), PYRAMIDE, SAINT AMAND (BERRY), SAINT-BENOIST (ORLÉANAIS), SAINTE-MAURE-DE-TOURAINE, SANCERRE (BERRY), SELLES-SUR-CHER (BERRY), TOURAINE, VALENÇAY (BERRY), VENDÔME (ORLÉANAIS).

## Gâtinais Orléanais

See BOISMORAND, BONDAROY, CHÂTILLON-COLIGNY, GIEN for FROMAGES FERMIERS, MONTARGIS, PANNES, PITHIVIERS (NE of region, E of Beauce, where it becomes Gâtinais Français in Seine-et-Marne and NW Yonne).

**Fromages de Chèvre.** André Fouchard, Les Veillères, 45460 Bray en Val (tel. 38 35 55 90), sells on farm before noon and after 18.00; and in Sully-sur-Loire (65 **1**, L) Monday market.
*fermier; biologique; chèvre cru*.
Loiret; 61 **12**, lower, far R near Les Bordes.

## Géant

**Le Sainte-Maure Géant.** 450g size (non-AOC), *frais* or *fleuri*, by Jacquin. See LA VERNELLE.
Berry/Indre.

## Gien

Wednesday and Saturday market; château with Musée International de la Chasse.

**Le Gien, le Giennois.** 200g, truncated cone (6cm top × 5cm deep × 8cm base), cylinder, or base of cone, like Selles-sur-Cher (see p. 89); *affinage*: in chestnut leaves or *cendres de bois* (Viard, 1980); 3 weeks *séchage* then 4 weeks in powdered charcoal or plane leaves (Androuët, 1984), or straw (Viard, 1980). Ninette Lyon and Viard also record it as made with *lait de mélange* (1978, 1980). Ninette Lyon found good cheeses further north around Les Bordes in the Gâtinais (the cheese described above is in that area). Probably originally a cows'-milk cheese in the Orléanais tradition (see SAINT-BENOIST); Viard gives its crust after *affinage* as *bleutée et fine* (chèvre) or thicker and pale grey (*lait-de-mélange*).
40–50% m.g.; *fermier*; *chèvre/lait de mélange cru*.
Gâtinais/Orléanais/Loiret; 65 **2**, lower L.

## Graçay

450g base of cone (10cm base, 6cm deep);

soft; natural *croûte-bleutée* and *cendrée*, traditionally 6 weeks *séchage*. Graçay is rich in old houses; it lies not far from Valençay, and Selles-sur-Cher (which cheese it resembles).
*45% m.g.; fermier; chèvre cru.*
Champagne-Berrichonne/Cher; 68 **9**, top L, 64 **19**, bottom L.

## Huppemeau

One of the traditional-type soft cheeses of the Orléanais, last mentioned by *Larousse-Gastronomique* in 1961 and described as similar to Brie. Possibly a trade name.
Orléanais.

## Illiers-Combray

Friday market; town so bound up with Marcel Proust that it adopted his fictional name for it, Combray.
Beauce/Eure-et-Loire; 60 **17**, upper L.

## La Jonchère

Triple-crème by Triballat of Rians.
*75% m.g.; laitier; vache pasteurisé.*
Berry/Cher; 65 **12**, low L.

## Levroux

Monday and Friday market; good source of pyramidal cheeses in shapes between the more pointed top of Pouligny (see p. 85) and the more truncated Valençay, which dominates the market. Sometimes still marketed as Levroux by a number of farms (1987). For history, see p. 67 (but see also LOCHOIS, GENILLÉ, and VALENÇAY).
Berry/Indre; 68 **8**.

**Levroux.** 250–300g *pyramide tronquée*, starting white, achieving thin natural *croûte-bleutée* and nutty flavour with 3 or more weeks of ventilated *affinage*. Viard tells us that the collectors of these cheeses for the *affineurs* also look for eggs and poultry, and are locally known as *coquassiers* (egg cups, more usually *coquetiers*, an old nickname for egg and poultry wholesalers).
Farm 20km from Levroux: *élevage de chèvres* on north side of N143 west (within 2km of Buzençais at Claise (not marked on map).
*45% m.g.; fermier; artisanal; chèvre cru.*
Berry/Indre; 68 **7**, SW of C.

## Ligueil

Monday market; Androuët was disappointed with local cheeses (formerly respected) on his 1982 tour.

**Ligueil, or Ligueil Bleu.** 1. 200g (*blanc*), 175g (*affiné*) cheese of Sainte-Maure type, formerly farmhouse with natural *croûte-bleutée*; now *laitier*, made by Uni-Coop-Ligueil, with thicker *croûte-fleurie* or *cendré*.
*45% m.g.; fermier; laitier; chèvre cru/pasteurisé.*
2. The name has also been used for a 200g, thin round *croûte-fleurie* cheese of Camembert consistency; Uni-Coop-Ligueil make 75g and 180g versions with mixed milk.
*60% m.g.; laitier; lait de mélange.*
Laiterie Uni-Coop-Ligueil, 37240 Indre-et-Loire; (tel. 47 59 60 17); visits 8.30–11.00, 15.30–16.30. Uni-Coop collected 3,850,000 l of goats' milk in 1984 for use in about 450 tonnes of soft chèvres and lait-de-mélange cheeses. In 1985 they were using 25,000 litres a day to produce 3000kg of cheese (equiv. to nearer 6 million litres a year), although they were expecting the return on cheese to drop. They were investing ff7 million (£700,000) in modernising the already mechanised *fromagerie*, and doubling their capacity for UHT milk production (sad, this; it was 23 million litres in 1984).
This *laiterie* makes: Corne d'Or (see p. 77), Sainte-Maure types (see LIGUEIL 1), *croûte-fleurie* soft round cheese (see LIGUEIL 2 above) and BÛCHE, see below, and does *affinage* of others, e.g. POULIGNY, see below.

**Bûche.** 1kg cutting log.
*45% m.g.; laitier; pur chèvre; lait-de-mélange.*

**Pouligny-Saint-Pierre AOC.** Further *affiné* at Ligueil after the obligatory 2 weeks *affinage* in La Brenne in Berry (Indre), the *région d'origine*.
*50% m.g.; artisanal; chèvre cru.*
Touraine/Indre-et-Loire; 68 **5**, high R.

## Liniez

Valençay style chèvre; village between Levroux and Vatan.
*artisanal; chèvre cru.*
Berry/Indre; 68 **8**, R on D926.

## Loches

Wednesday and Saturday market, with local farm cheeses; delightful medieval

château city; Hôtel de France, 6 rue Picois, 37600 Loches (tel. 47 59 00 32), M. and Mme Yves Barrat (he has worked at the Berkeley in London); good *accueil*, food including cheese, drink.
Touraine-Lochois/Indre-et-Loire; 68 **6**, top; Lochois 64 **16**, bottom.

**Chèvre Pyramide.** The Pyramide de Genillé is half-way to the village where M. and Mme Charlot make their white Pyramides; it is one of a number in the Forêt de Loches; others commemorate St-Quentin, Les Chartreux and St Hubert.
*fermier; chèvre cru.*
Indre-et-Loire; 64 **16**, low, on R Indrois 10.5km NE of Loches by D764.

**Fromage Blanc Pyramide; Sainte-Maure; Rond (like Selles-sur-Cher); Valençay.** Messrs Garceault Père et Fils, *producteurs-éleveurs* at Ferme de l'Aubertin (tel. 54 38 78 69) and Ferme du Châtaignier Fleuri (tel. 54 38 74 30) 36700 Cléré du Bois (both farms on SW of village; enquire, as roads go in all directions). They have 160 goats, and sell their cheeses, all *cendrés*, on the farms, and in the markets at Loches and at Palluau-sur-Indre (68 **7**, W of C) on Wednesdays and Saturdays, and at Châtillon-sur-Indre (68 **6**, NE of C) on Saturdays.
*fermier; chèvre cru.*
Indre; 68 **6**, C, 28km SSW of Loches W of D975.

**Fromages de Chèvre.** Pieralin and Marithé Meignan-Gareil make organic cheese at 17 La Villatte, Villeloin-Coulange, 37460 Montrésor (tel. 47 92 77 56).
*fermier; biologique; Nature & Progrès; chèvre cru.*
Indre-et-Loire; 64 **17**, bottom L, 68 **7**, top L 27km E of Loches by D760.

**Fromages de Chèvre Cendrés; Sainte-Maure; Valençay; le Rond Bleu; Crottin.** M. J.-C. Moreau makes these cheeses throughout the year (goats stabled), all *cendrés* with his own powdered ash from *feu-de-bois*, and matured 15 days, at Les Roches, 37600 Saint-Senoch (tel. 47 59 15 09). From Loches take D31 SW (Ligueil-Châtellerault) for 9km; turn south (left) through Varennes; 500m beyond Varennes turn east (left) for Château le Moutier; past château walls and three houses, Les Roches is at end of track. Le Rond Bleu is similar to Selles-sur-Cher.
*fermier; chèvre cru.*
Indre; 68 **5/6**, high 7.5km SW of Loches.

**Fromage Frais (in square tubs); Rouleau, Croûte-Naturelle or Cendré; Valençay Cendré.** Mme Jacquet makes these cheeses at Les Pennets at Sennevières, 37600 Loches, tel. 47 94 73 09 about 12.00 or after 18.00 any day of the week, to catch her when not machine-milking, making, or in the fields. She sells on farm after 18.00 daily, and at Loches market (Weds, Sats); her goats graze the fields by day and sleep in stables. The Rouleau crust, when not *cendrée*, turns a beautiful pinky-gold.
45% *m.g.; fermier; chèvre cru.*
Indre; 68 **6**, high, 8–10km SE of Loches by D760(E), D89(S).

**Fromage pur Chèvre; Sainte Maure; Fromage Blanc.** Follow D760 W direction Manthelan over crossroads at 5.5km (with sign N to Manceaux) and within 2km look for Fromage Pur Chèvre sign by dirt track on N side of road, to Château de Beaurepaire; *chevrerie* is behind château; *chevrier* M. Philippe Bennoin (1985), making Sainte-Maure (200g *sec*); 165g (*sec*) small cylinder, domed top rustic crust; and a larger, attractive Rond; *fromage blanc en faisselle*.
*fermier; chèvre cru.*
Indre-et-Loire; 64 **15 16**, bottom, 68 **5 6**, top W of Loches.

**Loches.** Soft cheese reported (undescribed) by Chast et Voy, 1984; as can be seen under Lochois below, there are a number of unnamed farm cheeses in Loches market; except for the obvious big names such as Sainte-Maure and Valençay, local farmers are reluctant to name their cheeses other than by shape or just as chèvres.
*Laiteries* at Ligueil (see p. 81) and Verneuil (see p. 93); only professional visits, unless groups with appointment).
The Forêt de Loches has a number of monumental pyramides.
45% *m.g.; chèvre.*
Touraine-Lochois/Indre-et-Loire; 68 **6**, top, Lochois 64 **16**, bottom.

LONGNY-AU-PERCHE
Wednesday market.
Orne; 60 **5**.

MALESSUI
Berrrichon word for cheese going runny

between *croûte* and *pâte*, slipping its coat, as we say in England (from *mal essuyé*, badly wiped, poorly finished).

MARSAUCEUX

Source of good Feuille de Dreux (see p. 79). Thimerais/Eure-et-Loir.

MEUSNES

M. Hardy, *affineur* of Sainte-Maure and other chèvres.

**Le Meusnois.** Chèvre, presumably of M. Hardy's *affinage* (stocked by MM. Cénéri in Cannes (see Chapter 18, p. 510). *laitier; chèvre.*
Berry/Loir-et-Cher; 64 **17 18**, on D17, 6.5km SW of Selles-sur-Cher.

MÉZIÈRES EN BRENNE

Thursday market; La Brenne is the AOC region of Pouligny-Saint-Pierre (see p. 85), between the Indre and the Creuse.
Berry/Indre; 68 **6**, lower R.

MIRABEL

See AUTHON.

MONTARGIS

Wednesday and Saturday market. Montargis cheese has long disappeared. Capital of Gâtinais Orléanais/Loiret 61 **12**, bottom, 65 **2**, top.

MONTLOUIS-SUR-LOIRE

Thursday market; wine fair third weekend in February; good white wine from Pinot de la Loire grape.
Touraine/Indre-et-Loire 64 **15**, 12km W of Tours on south bank.

MONTOIRE-SUR-LE-LOIR

Wednesday market from 11.30; Saturday market; good range of local farm cheeses (see VENDÔMOIS); centre for cheeses of Vendômois (see pp. 91–3). Coopérative Laitière de la Région de Montoire, zone industrielle, Route de Savigny, see TRÔO.

**Montoire.** Small cylindrical or flat round cheese, or truncated cone; *croûte-bleutée*, like some Vendôme or Selles-sur-Cher cheeses; flat-topped cone, about 5cm high and wide, weighing 100g, has light ochre or grey-blue crust (Viard, 1980). The Coopérative mentioned above makes a small flat drum of a chèvre at Montoire, coated with charcoal and sold *frais* (see TRÔO).
45% m.g.; artisanal, chèvre cru.
Orléanais/Vendômois/Loir-et-Cher; 64 **5**.

MONTRICHARD

Monday market; old town.
Orléanais/Loir-et-Cher; 64 **16/17**.

MORTAGNE-AU-PERCHE

Saturday morning market.
Orne; 60 **4**.

OLIVET BLEU/CENDRÉ/AU FOIN

This cheese was never made in Olivet but *affiné* in Olivet *caves*, and later in those of Orléans too. It was formerly of Coulommiers size; 200–300g; 10–13cm × 2.5cm deep; soft; one month in natural *cave humide* of *tuffeau* produces thin natural *croûte-bleutée*, and a week or two more brings on melting softness and a rich flavour. The *cendré* cheese is in grey-brown ash (originally from *sarments*), not black charcoal. Formerly they were often presented in plane leaves. The *foin* is hay from very fine grass, which coats the cheese; *cendres* and *foin* traditionally surround the cheese in wooden coffers during *affinage*. This is one of the class of cheeses probably descending from Saint-Benoist, which spread throughout the province and beyond. Until fairly recent years they were made of part-skimmed milk, which had provided cream or butter. The high season's surplus was preserved in the ways described above to meet the extra demands of harvest time, and the needs of winter. For many years *affineurs* with *tuffeau* caves in Orléans collected some of the farm surplus and did the *affinage* themselves. The use of hay probably originated at Bondaroy (see p. 74) and became widely familiar with Pithiviers (see p. 85).

Olivet is made by several *laitiers*, 230g, 45% m.g. by Laiterie Fromagère at Onzain (see below), and some by *laitiers* outside the Orléanais (e.g. see LE PETIT SILOR, PETIT OLIVET), who send their cheeses to the region for ripening; but many of the *caves* are now empty. SILOR mature cheeses in *cendres de bois* and hay at 8 rue des Halles, 45000 Orléans.
See also LES AYDES and CHÉCY.
40–45% m.g.; artisanal; laitier, vache.
Orléanais.

### Onzain
Laiterie Fromagère d'Onzain (see CHAUMONT, OLIVET, VILLEBAROU).
Blésois/Loir-et-Cher; 64 **16**.

### Orléans
Tuesday, Wednesday, Thursday, Saturday (covered) markets, strongly recommended. Comité de Promotions Centre-Val de Loire Berry Crac, 17 rue des Huguenots (has made a regional AC for Valençay).
Loiret.

### Orléanais
See AYDES, BEAUGENCY, CHÉCY (FRINAULT), CROTTIN, HUPPEMEAU, MONTARGIS (including GÂTINAIS-ORLÉANAIS and VENDÔMOIS), MONTOIRE, MONTRICHARD, OLIVET, PANNES, PATAY, PENNES, PETIT-PERCHE, ROMORANTIN-LANTHENAY, SAINT-BENOIST, SAINT-DENIS-DE-L'HÔTEL, SILORS, VENDÔME, VILLIERS SUR LOIR (see GÂTINAIS and THIMERAIS for neighbouring *pays* to N and E).

### Paillaud, Royal
200g cheese of Olivet au Foin type, but much fatter, by La Fromagerie des Forges, 36600 Valençay, which also makes Le Petit Olivet au Foin (see p. 83).
60% m.g.; *laitier, vache.*
Berry/Indre; 64 **18**, bottom.

### Palluau-sur-Indre
Wednesday and Saturday market.
Berry/Indre; 68 **7**, L of C.

### Pannes, Pannes Cendré
300g, 12cm × 2.5cm deep; another local cheese of the Olivet type, made west of Montargis, ripened for 3 months in chests of wood-ash; made in spring and summer (recorded by Viard, 1980, and Chast et Voy, 1984, although Lindon thought it had gone by 1961, and Androuët said it had disappeared long before 1982).
20–30% m.g.; *fermier; artisanal; vache.*
Gâtinais Orléanais; 61 **12**, lower L.

### Patay
500g, 2.5cm × 2.5cm (between Dreux and Olivet in character of *pâte*), eaten naturally *bleuté* in late spring and early summer, *cendré* later in season (Viard, 1980; Ninette Lyon thought it had disappeared by 1978; Courtine, in 1973, had already deemed it 'as forgotten as the battlefield').
25–45% m.g.; *fermier; artisanal; vache.*
Orléanais/Loiret; 68 **18**, low R.

### Pavé
**Le Pavé.** Rustic-looking square, deep, natural-crusted cheese by Laiterie Coopérative Pouligny-St-Pierre, 36300 Le Blanc (see also under BLÉSOIS, MONTOIRE, VENDÔMOIS, BRIQUES).
*laitier; chèvre.*

**Pavé de Jadis.** Extended truncated *pyramide, frais* or *croûte-fleurie*, of Valençay type *pâte*; by Jacquin (see LA VERNELLE).
*laitier; chèvre.*
Berry/Indre; 68 **16**, N of Le Blanc.

### Pennes, Pennes Cendré
This further variant on Olivet was noted by Chast et Voy in 1984. I traced no Pennes in the region, and wondered whether it was a corruption of Pannes; but Stobbs specified it as 250g 25% m.g. cheese ripened 1 month with natural crust to full flavour and attributed it to Blésois, in 1985.
20–30% m.g.; *fermier; vache cru.*
Orléanais/Blésois.

### Le Perche
See LONGNY-AU-PERCHE, MORTAGNE, LE PETIT PERCHE below. The ancient *comté du* Perche runs from southern Orne into south-eastern Eure-et-Loir and northern Loir-et-Cher.
Orne/Eure-et-Loir/Loir-et-Cher.

**Le Petit Perche.** 1. 270g round, soft chèvre by Michel Ponnet, Elevage Caprin de la Cohu, 41360 Savigny-sur-Braye (whence came monks who started Wensleydale cheesemaking, sent by the Abbé de Savigny at William the Conqueror's request). M. Ponnet's cheese has won a silver medal in Paris.
45% m.g.; *fermier; chèvre cru.*
Orléanais-Vendômois/Loir-et-Cher; 64 **5**, upper R.
2. 140–150g, base of cone; similar to Selles-sur-Cher (see p. 89), made by the François family at Authon (see p. 72).
Gâtine-Tourangelle; near Vendômois border 64 **5**, far R.

### La Perle du Berry
170g Selles-sur-Cher type *affiné* at La Vernelle (see p. 93).
45% m.g.; *fermier; chèvre cru.*
Berry.

## Petit

See also BEAUCE and PERCHE.

**Petit Olivet au Foin.** 200g cheese made by Fromagerie des Forges, 36600 Valençay, who also make Royal Paillaud (see p. 84).
*45% m.g.; laitier; vache.*
Berry/Indre.

**Petits Suisses.** *Fromage frais*, creamy, made by Triballat at Rians.
*laitier; vache pasteurisé.*
Berry/Cher.

**Petit Trôo.** See TRÔO.

## Pithiviers au Foin

See BONDAROY, where the cheese is thought to have started; close and larger neighbour Pithiviers took over the cheese for a long period. It has been dormant there in recent years, although the name has been used for Olivet au Foin and similar successors made elsewhere.
*artisanal; vache cru.*
Gâtinais/Loiret.

## Pouligny-Notre-Dame

**Fromage de Chèvre.** Antoine Aben, Las Sets, 36160 Pouligny-Notre-Dame (tel. 54 30 25 23).
*fermier; biologique; chèvre cru.*
Berry/Indre; 68 **19**, R of C 11km S of La Châtre.

## Pouligny-St-Pierre

**Le Pouligny-Saint-Pierre AOC (1976).** Making and *affinage* confined to La Brenne: twenty-two *communes* listed below in the district of Le Blanc.
225–250g, tall *pyramide*; 2–2.5cm across top, 8–9cm high, 6.5–8cm at base; the milk (2 l per cheese on average) is cooled before being lightly renneted; the curd is left to form naturally for 18–24 hours; within the whey it breaks apart into two or three sections with smooth, close-textured surfaces; it is ladled as unbroken as possible into iron pyramidal moulds. The moulds are topped up from reserves of curd put to drain in large *faisselles*; after draining for 48 hours cheeses are removed from moulds and lightly salted; they are dried on wicker or straw mats in a dark, airy and cool *hâloir*; once they are dry, the crusts are wiped and they are injected with *penicillium glaucum*. They stay at least 2 weeks (AOC minimum), but normally 4 or 5, at 10–12°C in a humid *cave* or store. The crust formed should be thin and *bleutée* (it can be pinky-gold under the *bleu*), the ivory-coloured *pâte* firm, yet giving; a goaty aroma and earthy flavour. Some cheese lovers have kept it longer, wrapped in plane leaves in pots with marc. It is judged the best of chèvres by those who like to be left in no doubt that it is goat cheese they are eating.

From May to November you can enjoy cheeses made when the goats are outdoors. Androuët, who was responsible for naming the cheese in the 1930s, could not find farm cheeses in 1982, but commended a local *laitier industriel*. Production that year was 167 tonnes, about 5% up on 1980 and 1982. In 1983 the Syndicat des Producteurs de Fromages de Pouligny-Saint-Pierre claimed two *fromageries*, two *affineurs* and ten other producers.

The *communes* are Azay-le-Ferron, Le Blanc, Ciron (68 **17**), Concremiers, Douadic, Fontgombault (see p. 79), Ingrandes, Lingé, Lurais, Martizay and Lureuil (68 **6**), Mauvières, Mérigny, Mézières-en-Brenne (68 **6**, lower R, has Thursday market), Néons-sur-Creuse (68 **5**), Pouligny-St-Pierre, Preuilly-la-Ville, Rosnay, Ruffec, St-Aigny, St-Hilaire-sur-Benaize, Sauzelles, Tournon-St-Martin (68 **6**, has Tuesday market). *Affineurs* at Pouligny-St-Pierre: SA Couturier (tel. 54 37 13 04) *affineurs* of numerous cheeses, including farmhouse, and makers. Courthial, Père et Fils (tel. 54 37 26 95).

The small Laiterie Coopérative de Tournon-St-Martin makes *lait cru* Pouligny AOC and other cheeses (see TOURNON-ST-MARTIN) (tel. 54 37 53 22).

Uni-Coop-Ligueil (see p. 81) advertises 50% m.g. Pouligny AOC presumably further *affiné* after the obligatory two weeks in the *Région d'origine*.

I have not found written claims for Pouligny's origin earlier than the last century but Berrichons I have talked to feel that it goes back centuries further.
*45–50% m.g.; fermier; artisanal; chèvre entier cru.*
La Brenne, W; N Berry/Indre; 68 **16**, high on D975.

## Purebique

200g Sainte-Maure type by Laiterie de la Cloche d'Or, Pont-de-Ruan; the actual

*laiterie* is in Vienne, Poitou.
50% m.g.; *laitier; chèvre pasteurisé*.
Touraine/Indre-et-Loire; 64 **14**, R on D17 and R. Indre.

PYRAMIDE

Cheeses of this form, to be seen magnified in monuments in the Forêt de Loches (see LOCHOIS: GENILLÉ, SENNEVIÈRES, CLÉRÉ DU BOIS) have long been made in Berry, e.g. Pouligny-Saint-Pierre ('Tour Eiffel') Levroux, Valençay and Vatan. They originally developed natural *croûte-bleutée*, but in the case of Valençay, are now often *cendrés*. They have been copied in Poitou and Angoumois by large *laiteries*, using either *penicillium candidum*, which achieves an uncharacteristic thick white crust, or powdered charcoal (ready-salted), which inhibits the normal skin and *pâte* development of the cheese. Only Pouligny has a national AOC, as the doyen of the cheeses, but regional protection has now been provided for Valençay, as Valençay-de-l'Indre, see p. 91. See also AUTHON. The various names were given to the cheeses in this century by *fromagers* such as Androuët, for convenience in descriptive listing, deriving from the local centres of marketing.

RIANS

*Fromager-affineur*: Hubert Triballat (see CROTTINS FRAIS, FROMAGES FRAIS, LA JONCHÈRE, PETITS-SUISSES, ROULÉ, SELLES-SUR-CHER (later period of *affinage*, after 10 days at least in *Région d'origine contrôlée*).
Berry/Cher; 65 **12**, low L.

ROMORANTIN-LANTHENAY

Wednesday, Friday and Saturday market; Musée de Sologne; old houses. (See ROND below.)
Orléanais-Sologne/Loir-et-Cher; 64 **18**.

ROND

*Rond* is an old general term for smaller round cheeses, usually straight-sided, not the base-of-cone shape of Selles-sur-Cher.

**Le Rond, le Super Rond.** 170g and 200g small round chèvres, frais or *croûte-fleurie affinés*, made by Jacquin at La Vernelle (see p. 93).
*laitier; chèvre*.
Berry/Indre.

**Le Rond Bleu.** See LOCHOIS, VARENNES.

*fermier; chèvre cru.*
Touraine-Lochois.

**Rond de Chèvre Fermier de Sainte-Maure.** About 150g; rounded, tubby cheese; grey-blue to brown crust.
*fermier; chèvre cru.*
Touraine, Sainte-Maure region.

**Rond pur Chèvre de Villiers.** 100g drum seen with *croûte-bleutée* and *croûte-cendrée* (and see VILLIERS-SUR-LOIR).
*artisanal; chèvre thermisé.*
Orléanais/Vendômois.

**Rond de Romorantin.** Local cheese remembered by Androuët, before Selles-sur-Cher's AOC of 1975.
*artisanal; chèvre cru.*
Orléanais/Sologne; 64 **18**.

ROULÉ

Swiss-roll of a cheese, with garlic and *fines-herbes*.
*laitier; vache pasteurisé.*
Berry/Cher.

ROULEAU

See LOCHOIS, SENNEVIÈRES.

ST-AMAND-MONTROND

Wednesday and Saturday market.

**Saint-Amand.** Crottin type, made locally, well south of the Crottin de Chavignol AOC (see p. 77) regional boundary (Courtine, 1973).
*fermier; artisanal; chèvre cru.*
Berry/Cher; 69 **1**, 69 **1 11**.

LE SAINT-BENOIST, SAINT-BENOÎT

350g–400g; 13–15cm diameter; resembling Coulommiers in scale, texture and taste; ripened for 10–15 days in summer, or for 20–30 in late autumn or winter in *hâloir*; or for longer keeping in wood-ash or in hay; originally a domestic product for the farm and its family and staff, surplus cheeses in the flush season being conserved *cendré* or *au foin* for extra labour in harvest, and for winter use; now rare. Androuët believes it to be centuries old, and the original of all the numerous regional cheeses of this type (typified by Olivet today, but in fatter form than the original cheese); Courtine said it had been well-known for 150 years (Larousse, 1973); (Marabout, 1978). Androuët and Ninette

Lyon wrote that it was disappearing. My monastic informant insists that it has never been made by the monks, despite strong tradition to the contrary.
*up to 40% m.g.; fermier; vache cru.*
Orléanais/Loiret; 64 **10**, R.

## Saint-Chevrier

1.4kg cutting cheese by Triballat of Rians (see p. 86).
*laitier; chèvre pasteurisé.*
Berry/Cher.

## Le Saint-Christophe

280g Sainte-Maure type with straw, either *frais* or *cendré*, becoming *bleuté*; pleasant cheeses (see anjouin).
*45% m.g.; laitier; chèvre.*
Berry/Indre; 64 **18**, low R.

## St-Denis-de-l'Hôtel

Sunday a.m. market; cheese fair first Sunday in June.
Orléanais/Loiret; 64 **10**.

## St-Laurian

Fromagerie St-Laurian, 36150 Vatan, makers and *affineurs* of cheeses of this region and from Poitou and the Angoumois; particularly chèvres.
Berry/Indre; 68 **8/9**.

## Saint-Lubin-de-la-Haye

See dreux, spécialité lait cru.

## Ste-Maure-de-Touraine

Friday market; centre for local cheese and butter; (see touraine for cows'-milk cheese). Commanderie des Fromages de Ste-Maure-de-Touraine, Hôtel de Ville, with about fifty active cheesemaking members.
First Sunday in June: Annual Foire de Fromages which has become Foire Internationale Gastronomique. Hôtel-Restaurant Le Veau d'Or. M. Lalubin, welcoming *chef-propriétaire* is secretary of the Commanderie.
Indre-et-Loire; 68 **4 5**, top.

## Sainte-Maure

(Region locally defined, but not yet legally protected.)
250–300g *bûche* of 15cm × 4cm, often impaled on a straw, which makes it easier to handle. Milk (2–3 l per cheese) is renneted at 15–20°C (from 1 drop per l in summer up to 2 drops in winter if necessary; at 1:2500 dilution) and takes 18–24 hours to form the curd, which is gently ladled into 24–30cm, slightly conical iron moulds (of which the effect is visible, one end of the log being perceptibly narrower than the other); 30cm moulds are becoming standard. Multiple moulds (*multi-moules*) in sets of thirty or fifty, used by some makers, ease the tricky job of filling without breaking the curd, which is shovelled on to a pierced tray fitted over the moulds, shaped to feed them by gravitation. After drainage at 15°C for about 24 hours (but can need much longer; it is quicker with *multi-moules*), the mould is turned on to a mat to complete drainage before dry salting at 1 per cent. *Affinage* lasts 3–4 weeks on straw in an airy *cave*, still at 15°C; this forms a thin *croûte-bleutée*, sometimes *rosée* to *rouge*, unless the cheese has been rolled in powdered charcoal. The latter was treated as if it were standard practice in Gault Millau's February 1986 account of 'le vrai Sainte-Maure' in *La Nouvelle République du centre-ouest*. The report also assumed that the charcoal was premixed with salt, which leads to oversalting. The *pâte* should be fine and close-textured, the flavour rich, rather than sharp or salt.

The typical traditional cheese has a pronounced aroma and savour of goat cheese. The cheese when coated with *cendres* may develop surface mould but tends to stay white and mild inside (sweet if not oversalted) after its naturally crusted brother is well developed. *Cendré* or not, the most common fault in Sainte-Maure is oversalting. This is nothing new; Courtine complained of it in 1973, although he thought Sainte-Maure 'delicious' when well made.

*Sources of Sainte-Maure Fermier.* Anché: M. Bernard Ferrand Sainte-Maure and Pyramide (gold and silver medals Paris) 'Le Bichonnet', D760 (22km W) 64 **13**, bottom R); Bossée: M. Philippe Bennoin, La Benaudrie, Bossée, D760 (9km E), marked on roadside (S of road); Château de Beaurepaire (see lochois) (23km E); Bournan: M. Yann Gironnet (first prize 1985), D59 (11.5km SE); Braslou: M. Bacquiart (prize winner 1985, 1986), D760 N to Noyant, 4km; D58, D111 (22km SW); Chaveignes:

M. Denis Decésure, Aillou (tel. 47 58 22 73 for farm visits); markets: Beaujardin at Tours Wednesday and Saturday, D760–D58 (24km SW 68 **3/4**); Crouzilles: west of second level crossing, opposite big furniture (*meubles*) store, on north side of road: 'Ste-Maure Fermier', D760 (11km W 68 **4**, top); Drache: M. Édouard Fontaine, M. Martial Le Boeuf (third prize 1985), N10 (6.5km S 68 **4**); Grillemont: Élevage de Grillemont has made Sainte-Maure for nearly sixty years, *cendré*, and best at 20 days; comtesse de Saint-Seine, sampled happily 1980 (D760 E, turn SE on E side of Bossée 15km SE 68 **5**, high); Loir-et-Cher: M. et Mme Pierre François have won medals at regional and national shows for their Sainte-Maure (see AUTHON, which is within the *zone d'appellation*); Pussigny: M. Heribert, *affineur-expéditeur*, 37800 Ste-Maure-de-Touraine (N10 to Port-de-Piles, SW 3km 15km SW); La Roche-Clermault: *Éleveur-fromager* highly regarded in the trade (35km W 64 **13**, bottom C); Ste-Catherine: M. James Guéritault (Grand Prix D'Honneur 1985, first day); Mme Yvette Guéritault (Grand Prix D'Honneur 1985, second day) (N10 6km N) La Basse-Cour, Ste-Catherine-de-Fierbois, tel. 47 65 68 37 (64 **15**, near bottom); St-Épain: M. Claude Écherseau, L'Archerie; tel. 47 65 81 07 for farm visit; market Beaujardin at Tours Saturday 08.00–12.00; M. Durand, *affineur-expéditeur* St-Épain, 37800 Ste-Maure-de-Touraine; Ste-Maure: M. Leboeuf (D760, 5km E) Le Carroi des Louasses marked on roadside (N of road 68 **5**, top L); M. Tarte; N10 (4km N) La Vieille Poste; St-Senoch, Varennes: M. J. C. Moreau, D59 to Ligueil; D31 (29km ESE) near Varennes (see LOCHOIS); Sepmes: M. Jean-Pierre Proust (Prix d'Honneur 1985), M. Raguin (equal first 1985) D59 (6.5km SE); Villandry: Mme de Montferrier (second prize 1985), D760 (to W), D757 to Azay-le-Rideau (see p. 73) to D39 to (34km N) Villandry (64 **15**, E of C).

*Affineurs* of farm and *laitier* cheese (if ordering, specify farm cheese from the *zone d'appellation*); Courthial Père et Fils, Couturier, 36300 Pouligny-St-Pierre (see p. 85); Durand (see ST-ÉPAIN under sources above); Hardy, Meusnes (see p. 83); Héribert (see Pussigny above); Jacquin, La Vernelle (see p. 93).

STE-MAURE-DE-TOURAINE

**Fromages de Vache.** Cows'-milk cheeses and butter are made by Michel Écherseau at La Lande de Theille, Ste-Maure (tel. 47 26 52 80), where they also sell cereals, honey and milk.
*fermier; biologique; Nature & Progrès; vache cru.*
Indre-et-Loire; 68 **4/5**, top.

SAINTE-MAURE-AMY-BIQUE

200g *industriel* by a Besnier factory: *not* within Commanderie zone or quality standards.
*45% m.g.; industriel, chèvre pasteurisé.*
Anjou/Maine-et-Loire, Montreuil-Bellay.

SANCERRE

Tuesday market (Mar.–Nov.); Saturday. *Mairie* is seat of Syndicat de Défense du Crottin de Chavignol (see p. 77). Fête du Crottin de Chavignol early in May; Coopérative d'Élevage de Garennes: wine and cheese tasting. Leave Sancerre by N455 to SW; after about 3km, *after* D10 turning south for Vinon take next turn left. The goat cheese and wine combination is a feature of the region.
Berry/Cher; 65 **12**, R of C.

SANCERROIS

Name formerly used for 140g, about 5cm × 5.5cm deep; soft cheese newly emerged from Crottin mould; fluffy and out-swelling, light in texture; one of the most refreshing goat cheeses in France. M. Claude Crochet, Bué, told me in 1987 that the name was now illegal and that this delicious cheese had not been available for years.
*45% m.g.; fermier; artisanal; chèvre cru.*
Sancerrois; Bué: 5km S of Sancerre.

SANTRANGES

Chast et Voy (1984) reported this as 4 weeks ripened 'flattened bullet', Courtine (1973) merely as 'larger than Chavignol'. They were of the Crottin family at different ages, and are no longer legally sold under their old Commune name (see CROTTIN).
*45% m.g.; fermier; chèvre cru.*
Berry/Cher; 65 **12**, high R on N726.

**Fromage de Chèvre.** At western exit from Santranges on north side of N726.

*fermier; chèvre cru.*
Berry/Cher; 65 **12**, high R.

## Saumur

Wednesday, Thursday, Friday and Saturday market.
Anjou/Maine-et-Loire; 64 **12**.

## Le Select sur Feuille

190g round cheese, *frais* or *fleuri*, on leaf, by Jacquin (see LA VERNELLE).
*laitier; chèvre.*
Berry/Indre.

## Selles-sur-Cher

Thursday market; château. Syndicat de Défense du Véritable Fromage de Chèvre de Selles-sur-Cher, Hôtel de Ville (tel. 54 97 40 19). The region covers the north bank of the Cher from Montrichard (canton) to short of Vierzon to a depth of 12–25km; the south bank from Valençay to Lury-sur-Arnon, as far south as Vatan and north Issoudun.

**Selles-sur-Cher (AOC 1975).** 140–160g base of cone; about 10cm across base, about 4cm deep, 9.5cm across top; 1.25 l of milk per cheese, very lightly renneted at 18–20°C. *Caillage* takes 16–30 hours. Moulds (9.5cm base, 9.5cm high, 11cm across top) are filled with ladle by hand without breaking the curd. After 24 hours' drainage in moulds the cheeses are removed, coated with charcoal and salt, and placed in the *hâloir* for at least 8 days (10 days minimum *affinage* from day of making) at 12–15°C and about 75% humidity.
The finished cheese must have at least 55g of dry matter, of which fat must be at least 45%. The ten days' maximum *affinage* must take place in the defined region. Official leaflets say the cheese dates back to before 1887 but natives think it centuries older. The cheese was formerly made in large earthenware pots, and moulded and strained in earthenware moulds. The Syndicat recommends keeping the cheese at 53°F (12°C) or less in summer, room temperature in winter, and uncovered.
*Sources of Selles-sur-Cher*: apart from Selles-sur-Cher market, and the makers and *affineurs* listed below, the markets and three shops at Blois (see p. 74) are recommended.
North of the R. Cher, in Loir-et-Cher (*éleveurs-fromagers* unless otherwise stated): Billy: Éts Pierre Segré (64 **18**, R 5km S of Selles-sur-Cher); Châtillon-sur-Cher: Jean-Claude Rousseau (64 **17**, far R on river); Chémery: Michel Perrin (64 **17**, far R of C); Loreux: Charles Denur (64 **19**, NW of C); Pontlevoy: Patrice Moreau (64 **17**, NW of C on D764); Pruniers: Jacques Marier (64 **18**, R NE of Selles-sur-Cher); Sambin: Henri Bordas (President, 1986) (64 **17**, NW of C on D764).
South of Cher: Anjouin: Coopérative d'Anjouin (*fromagerie-laitière*) (64 **18/19**, low); Mareuil-sur-Cher: Frederic Bouland (64 **17**, NW of St-Aignan); Selles-sur-Cher: Raymond Dorlet (*affineur*) (64 **18**, L, on R. Cher); La Vernelle Éts Jacquin (*fromagerie/laitière/affineurs*) (64 **18**, R, 5km S of Selles-sur-Cher).
Groupement des Producteurs de la Vallée du Cher. SAAF handles the cheese at Rungis.
In 1984 and 1985 the independent producers listed above made 15 tonnes (about 100,000 cheeses). The three *fromageries* (with milk from 143 farms) made about 96 tonnes. The *affineurs* collected 9.6 tonnes of cheese from 67 farms, but production has been growing at 15% annually, and M. Jacquin estimated in 1987 that 200 farms were now making Selles-sur-Cher. In the 1960s production was principally farmhouse. There were no firm records before the AOC was granted in 1975. The first *syndicat* leaflet after that event must surely have overstated production by over ten times at 4 million cheeses, 700 tonnes, because only 63 tonnes of AOC cheese was made in 1978. Production rose to 100 tonnes in 1981 and 120 tonnes in 1982, after which it stayed steady for a year or two, and then took off again, increasing at a rate of 15% a year from 1985, as stated.

## Le Petit Silors, Cendré and au Foin

230g round, about 2cm deep, of Olivet type (see p. 83), made in Touraine, *affiné* by SILOR, 8 rue des Halles, 45000 Orléans.
45% m.g.; *artisanal; vache.*
Touraine, *affiné* Orléans.

## Sologne

**Chèvre.** On east side of D15, La Grande Motte, Fromage de Chèvre.
*fermier; chèvre cru.*

**Pavé de la Sologne.** See BLÉSOIS, PAVÉ DU. Orléanais/Loiret; 64 **8/9**, 2–3km N of Ligny-le-Ribault on D15.

SULLY-SUR-LOIRE

Monday market.
Orléanais/Loiret; 65 **1**, L.

THENAY

*Rond, croûte-fleurie* and notably soft, Camembert-like interior, found by Dr J. G. Davis in 1960s; Viard compared it with Olivet (1980).
*fermier; artisanal; vache cru.*
Sologne/Loir-et-Cher; 64 **17**, NW of C.

THIMERAIS

*Pays* north of Beauce including Drouais (see DREUX and BEAUCERON).
N Eure-et-Loir.

TOME BLANCHE

See LA VER.

TOMME DE CHÈVRE

2kg stout drum; *croûte-bleutée* with pinky-gold; smooth, firm, fat, white *pâte*, looking like brebis; pleasant consistency and flavour; made in Indre, *affiné* by Couturier at Pouligny-St-Pierre (see p. 85). See also AUTHON, TOMME DE CHÈVRE.
*artisanal; chèvre cru.*
Berry/Indre.

TOUR EIFFEL

See POULIGNY.

TOURAINE

See AMBOISE, AUTHON, AZAY, BICHONNET, BLÉSOIS, BOURGUEIL, CABRI, CHABI, CHAMP-COU, CHOUZE, CORMÉRY, FROMAGE FRAIS, LIGUEIL, LOCHES, LOCHOIS, MONTLOUIS, ROND, SAINTE-MAURE, VERNEUIL, VOUVRAY.

TOURNON, TOURNON-ST-MARTIN

Small *laiterie coopérative* (tel. 54 37 53 22) makes *lait-cru* Pouligny AOC and other cheeses, including Tournon, below.

**Le Tournon, le Tournon-Saint-Martin.** 200–300g half cone, taller than Crottin and wider at base, similar *pâte* and surface to those of Pouligny (1986); a flatter version was recorded by Courtine in 1973.
*45% m.g.; artisanal; chèvre cru.*
Berry/Indre; 68 **6**, low L.

**Le Tournon-Saint-Pierre.** 200–300g, similar cheese to Pouligny (see p. 85), ripened in about 3 weeks (Viard, 1980). In 1973 Courtine described it as like Le Tournon-Saint-Martin.
*45% m.g.; fermier; artisanal; chèvre cru.*
Indre-et-Loire; across R. Creuse from Tournon-Saint-Martin.

TOURS

Daily covered market with parking, Les Halles Centrales, 06.00–19.00, Sunday 06.00–13.00. Marché biologique: Beaujardin, Wednesday and Saturday 08.30–12.30. Cheese shops: France Fromages, La Montagne aux Fromages in Les Halles Centrales; Le Calendos, 1 rue Jules Favre; La Ferme Saint-Gilles, 107 avenue de Grammont; La Ferme Tourangelle, 2 Place Gaston Paillhou.
Farms near Tours (see also LOCHOIS, SAINTE-MAURE).
Indre-et-Loire; 64 **15**.

**Fromage de Chèvre.** Lucien Refour sells his chèvre, apples and apple juice at La Vieillerie, St-Aubin-le-Dépeint (tel. first, 47 29 25 31), and place de Beaujardin, Tours, Sat 08.00–12.00.
*fermier; biologique; chèvre cru.*
Indre-et-Loire; 64 **4**, low L on D10.

**Fromage de Vache.** See STE-MAURE-DE-TOURAINE.

**Fromages de Vache et de Chèvre.** See LOCHES.

**Fromage de Vache, Fromages de Chèvre.** Didier and Marie-Agnès Gandrille sell their cheeses, and cows' milk, vegetables and honey at Le Haut Aunai, 37330 Château-la-Vallière (tel. 47 24 02 25) on Friday afternoons; in morning markets at Château-du-Loir Saturday, and Le Mans Wednesday.
*fermier; biologique; Nature & Progrès; vache/chèvre cru.*
Indre-et-Loire; 64 **14**, top L.

TRÔO

Trôo is remarkable for its inhabited cave dwellings, church and medieval hospital, and La Butte, magnificent viewpoint.
Coopérative Laitière de la Région de Montoire, *zone industrielle*, route de Savigny, 41800 Montoire-sur-le-Loir. Originally

(from 1963) at Trôo, but lack of help against flooding drove it to Montoire; still collects milk from same farms, 1 million litres a year for cows'-milk cheeses below. Managing director, Jacky Charpentier (tel. 54 85 04 22).

**Le Petit Trôo.** 1. In 1985 one *paysanne* was still making this small flat drum of a cheese in the *commune*, mainly for herself and her family.
*fermier; chèvre cru.*
2. 130g, 160g flat drum with slightly rounded circumference; generous golden crust with *penicillium candidum* (sprayed on finished cheese); pale-cream, close-textured *pâte*. At 10 days medium flavour, on salt side; at 3 weeks harder, with good rich flavour. Made by M. Jacky Charpentier at the Coopérative at Montoire. Milk is collected every other day from the temperature-controlled tanks on the farms, pasteurised at 72°C for 4–5 seconds, renneted and left for 24 hours in vat (as for goats' milk); it is ladled into moulds for 24 hours' draining, and turned in the evening. The next day it is hand salted. *Cendré* cheese (see below) is coated with ready-mixed charcoal powder and salt. The dairy is kept at 15°C all year. During 6–7 days *desséchage* the cheese is turned every other day; after spraying with *penicillium candidum* the cheeses are matured for another 6–7 days at 12–13°C and 85% humidity. The *coopérative*'s other products are butter and the following cheeses: *fromage blanc battu* (whipped unsalted *fromage frais*); *fromage frais de campagne*; *fromage cendré*. Same size as Petit Trôo, but moister, and sold *frais*.
50% m.g.; *laitier; artisanal; vache pasteurisé.*
Orléanais/Vendômois/Loir-et-Cher; 64 **5**, R of C.

## Valençay

Tuesday market; impressive sixteenth-century château, park; local wine Valençay VDQS. Fromagerie des Forges, 36600 Valençay (see PETIT OLIVET, ROYAL PAILLAUD).

**Valençay; Valençay de l'Indre** (recent *label régional*). 250–330g truncated pyramid; 6–7cm at base, 4–5cm at top, 7–8cm height; coated with powdered charcoal; close-textured sweet white *pâte*, becoming ivory and sharper with age (tendency to oversalt, salt being bought ready-mixed with charcoal). Minimum eight days' *affinage*; average *affinage* is one month, before retail sale, of which 15 days are spent with the *affineur* in the Indre (Courtine gave 3–4 months 1973 but I was getting good farm cheese much younger then). Label régional Centre-Val de Loire-Berry (see ORLÉANS) has green top to label for *fermier*, red for *laitier*; the region for this label is the Indre (*département*), but many Valençay are made elsewhere (see LOCHOIS in Touraine); few big *laiteries* outside now label their charcoal-coated pyramides 'Valençay'.
Sources of Valençay (non-regional): Loches market and Lochois farms see LOCHES and LOCHOIS. Valençay de l'Indre: Jacquin, see LA VERNELLE, Fermier, Laitier Coopérative Fromagère d'Anjouin (see ANJOUIN) 220g *affiné*, 400g at 8 days.
It appears that the *label régional* has served the cheese well. A few years ago production was stable, but it has grown significantly in the last two to three years. M. Jacquin (*affineur* and *fromager*, see LA VERNELLE) estimated that 100 farms in the Indre were making Valençay in 1987. He was collecting 6–7000 cheeses (2 tonnes) a week himself; 90% of the cheeses are *cendrés*, the others being sold white, soon after the minimum eight days' *affinage* to meet special orders. For origin of cheese, see p. 67.
Berry/Indre; 64 **18**, bottom.

## Vatan

This pyramidal cheese, similar to Valençay in form, no longer appears under its own name; surviving local makers presumably sell their cheeses now to *affineurs* of Valençay de l'Indre.
*fermier; artisanal; chèvre cru.*
Berry/Indre; 68 **8/9**, high.

## Vendôme

Covered market all day Friday; and Sunday street market 'Aux Rottes'. Remarkable *abbaye* and old quarter, château; markets are rich in local cheeses (see VENDÔMOIS).

**Vendôme Bleu; Vendôme Cendré.** About 220–250g, flat round 11cm × 3.5cm deep; like thicker Olivet (see p. 83), or 'vaguely reminiscent of Coulommiers' (Courtine, 1973); 1 month ripened in

humid *tuffeau caves*, either to blue externally, or in wood-ash (preferably from *sarments de vigne*) to achieve a grey-brown, ashy crust, tending to make for a drier cheese than the *croûte-bleutée*. They were made for farm consumption originally, in a region not rich in meat, and *cendrés* for long conservation of flush-season cheeses, to meet harvest and winter needs. The traditional farm cheeses of cows' milk are now rarely seen. The Vendôme and Vendômois below (even the first, which *is* made of cows' milk) are really newer cheeses of the region, rather than of the old type.
50% m.g.; *fermier*; *vache cru*.
Orléanais/Loir-et-Cher; 64 **6**.

## Vendômois

**Le Petit Vendôme.** 160g round soft cheese; made in chèvre fashion, with slow coagulation over 24 hours; *croûte-fleurie-naturelle* (would formerly have been *bleutée*), white surface mould starting to take within a week. Admirably unsalt, loose-textured, creamy *pâte* when eaten within a fortnight of making, becoming a little more salty in maturity (*'demi-sec'* stage, as for a chèvre), but remaining very creamy. It has been compared with Chaource (see Chapter 10). Made by La Laiterie Taillard, Villiers-sur-Loir (see p. 94).
50% m.g.; *laitier*; *artisanal*; *vache thermisé*.
Vendômois; 64 **6**, 7km W of Vendôme on D5.
Montoire has market 11.30 p.m. Wednesday, Saturday a.m.

**Vendôme Fermier.** 1. A deep, neat drum, thickly charcoal-coated, with pleasing mousse-like consistency when young, but erring on the salt side (no doubt because salt ready-mixed with charcoal); sold in Montoire market.
2. Coulommiers-la-Tour. Guy Renvoise was making a Vendôme at Coulommiers-la-Tour in the 1970s, and certainly until 1982, which had a nutty flavour.
*fermier*; *chèvre cru*.
3. Les Morines. Mme Petit's Chèvre Fermier (not named but similar in form), eaten before the *demi-sec* stage is sweet and slightly winy; once *demi-sec*, the old trouble of ready-mixed charcoal and salt arises:

the lurking flavour is rather over-borne by the salt.
4. Saint-Rimay. A similar cheese, but more base of cone in shape, also salty, is sold at Montoire market by Mme Lefèvre; it is more Selles-sur-Cher in type (no farm visits).

## Le Vendômois

Base of cone, 10cm at base, 7cm top, 4cm deep; charcoal-coated, with sea salt mixed in; slightly flaky crust. At *demi-sec* stage the *pâte* is tacky, with a full flavour, just a little salty. Made by Mme Gillard at Naveil (see below). Over a litre of milk goes into each cheese; coagulation takes 24–36 hours, and the cheeses are drained for 24 hours in their moulds.
*fermier*; *biologique*; *chèvre cru*.
Orléanais/Loir-et-Cher; 64 **5, 6, 7**.

## Vendômois Farms

Farms and dairies around Vendôme, with distances from Vendôme:

**Bûche Cendrée.** Charcoal-coated log, admirably low-salted, sweet and mild, yet rich. Made by Laiterie d'Azé, 41000 Vendôme.
*laitier*; *chèvre cru*.
Orléanais; 64 **6**, 8km NW of Vendôme.

**Chèvre Fermier.** Cheese similar to Vendôme (chèvre); charcoal-coated; described under Vendôme Fermier (see above). Made by Mme Hubert Petit at Les Morines, on north side of road between Les Hayes and Houssay (see p. 62); two *chambres d'hôtes* and camping on the farm, and meals served for guests (Les Morines, Houssay, 41800 Montoire, tel. 54 77 19 64).
*fermier*; *chèvre cru*.
Orléanais; 64 **6**, SW of C from Vendôme; by D917 to Thoré Villiersfaux crossroads; there left (S) and first R (W); Les Morines 12km W of Vendôme.

**Fromages Fermiers.** See AUTHON.
Orléanais; 64 **5**, low far R on D9 and D71 Authon 23km SW.

**Fromages Fermiers.** Mme Lefèvre cannot receive visitors on her farm, but sells in markets: Montoire Wednesday from about 11 a.m. (well before the official opening) and Saturday mornings; Vendôme covered market all day Fridays; open market 'Aux Rottes', Vendôme Sundays. Her cheeses

include the following:
1. *Briques.* 250g, square *pavé* (150g *affiné* with grey or deep-golden crust), or 100g rectangular.
2. *Coeur.* 100g neat deep heart, natural grid-marked crust.
3. *Petite Bûche.* Log smaller than Sainte-Maure.
4. *Poivré.* 100–120g soft, round coated with coarse-milled black pepper.
5. *Pyramides.* Cheeses of smaller and larger Valençay proportions, according to age.
6. *Various.* 60g cheese of Crottin proportions, smaller fuller *affiné*; 60g of Chabichou appearance; 80g small drum; 110g flattened dome, striated sides, reminiscent of La Taupinière (see Chapter 3, p. 111).
7. *Vendômois Cendré* (see also VENDÔMOIS above). About 300g; 120g version, not *cendré*.
All *fermier; chèvre cru.*
Orléanais; 64 **6**, far L of C, St-Rimay 12km W of Vendôme.

**Petit Perche.** (See p. 84 for detail.) M. Michel Ponnet makes at Élevage Caprin de la Cohu.
45% m.g.; *fermier; chèvre cru.*
Orléanais; 64 **5**, upper R, Savigny-sur-Braye, 15km W of Vendôme.

**Le Petit Trôo.** 1. *Chevrière* making in Trôo (not for general sale).
*fermier; chèvre cru.*
Orléanais; 64 **5**, R of C, 25km W of Vendôme.
2. Coopérative Laitière making Le Petit Trôo at Montoire (see TRÔO).
*artisanal; vache pasteurisé.*
Orléanais; 64 **5**, far R, Montoire for market 19km W of Vendôme.

**Vendôme.** M. Guy Renvoise, *éleveur* at Coulommiers-la-Tour.
*fermier; chèvre cru.*
Orléanais; 64 **6**, R of C, 7km ESE.

**Le Vendômois.** (See p. 92 for detail.) Mme Yves Gillard makes this cheese at La Gennetière from the milk of her 50 Alpines; since 1970 she has adopted organic principles (see p. 63). Feed is mixture of wheat, barley and oats, and legumes on leys; hay and beet adds to winter feed. She mixes her sea salt and charcoal herself, and uses chemist's rennet. She sells at Vendôme markets.

*fermier; chèvre cru.*
Orléanais; 64 **6**, C, 2km NW.

LA VERNELLE

Fromagerie P. Jacquet La Vernelle, 3660 Valençay (tel. 54 97 57 08); *affineurs* of farmhouse *ronds*, Sainte-Maure, Selles-sur-Cher, Valençay; makers of Caprin, Chabis le Chabiquet, chèvres (*pyramide* and *super-pyramide, rond* and *rond super*), chèvre *blanc (faisselle* and in bucket), Cornilly, Crottin le Champignon, Grand Caprin, Pavé de Jadis, Pointe-de-Bique, Le Select sur Feuille, Tome Blanche; all *frais* or *cendrés* and *affinés.*
*Affineur/expéditeur:* Roger Piffet, farmhouse cheeses.
Berry/Indre; 64 **18**, 5km S of Selles-sur-Cher.

VERNEUIL

Laiterie Coopérative de Verneuil makes the following cheeses, *lait cru:* Sainte-Maure-size Bûche, Pyramide, Frais or Cendré; Chabi (tubby, larger than Crottin; Rond (Selles-sur-Cher type) Cendré. Also cutting Bûche and Lingot.
*laitier; chèvre cru.*

**La Belle Lochoise and l'Impérial.** Camembert types.
*laitier; vache pasteurisé.*
Dairy visits are restricted to parties of twelve, or purely professional (tel. 47 94 71 02 for appointments, Saturday excluded). Cheese is sold retail on premises daily 08.30–12.00, 16.30–17.00.
Touraine-Lochois/Indre-et-Loire; 68 **6**, high by N143 D41, 8km S of Loches.

VIERZON

Tuesday, Wednesday, Saturday market (old town).
Berry/Cher; 64 **19/20**.

VILLEBAROU

*Formerly:* 450g thin round soft cheese (made on farms of milk skimmed for butter-making, or of whole milk) matured 3 weeks with *croûte-bleutée*, deep gold or grey; presented on plane leaf; full flavour. M. Fichepin at Villiers-sur-Loir told me in 1986 that this had ceased to exist.
30–45% m.g.; *fermier; vache cru.*
400g plump cheese looking like a small young Brillat Savarin; extra mild; made by

Laiterie Fromagère d'Onzain, who also make Chaumont. The cheese was made at least until the 1960s at nearby Marolles (N of Blois) and St-Denis-sur-Loire (NE of Blois).
*52% m.g.; laitier; vache entier pasteurisé.*
Blésois; 64 **16**, high R N of Loire.

VILLIERS-SUR-LOIRE, LE VENDÔME-VILLIERS, ROND PUR CHÈVRE DE VILLIERS, LE PETIT VENDÔME

The cheeses made today under the last two names by La Laiterie Taillard at Villiers-sur-Loir are described under Rond and Vendôme. The *laiterie* collects its milk from 100 farms in the Loire Valley, mostly from *normandes* cows.

These cows'-milk cheeses were *affinés* in *cendres de sarments* in coffers, like so many cheeses in this region, when even cereal farms kept house cows to provide for family and hired labour.

*45% m.g.; fermier; artisanal; chèvre cru.*
Orléanais.

**Villiers, Rond pur Chèvre de.** See ROND and VENDÔME.

VOVES

Tuesday market (see DREUX).

**Voves, le Cendré de Voves, Voves au Foin.** On the scale of a Coulommiers, these cheeses were more of the farm protein-providers, made from milk which had already surrendered cream for butter. Soft in the Dreux style, ripened in humid *cave* 1 month to achieve *croûte-bleutée*, then 2–3 months in wood-ash, or occasionally in hay, if kept for harvest or winter. Ninette Lyon and Androuët lamented the passing of Voves in 1978 (see p. 61).
*low-fat; fermier; vache cru.*
Beauce/Eure-et-Loir; 60 **18**, N of C.

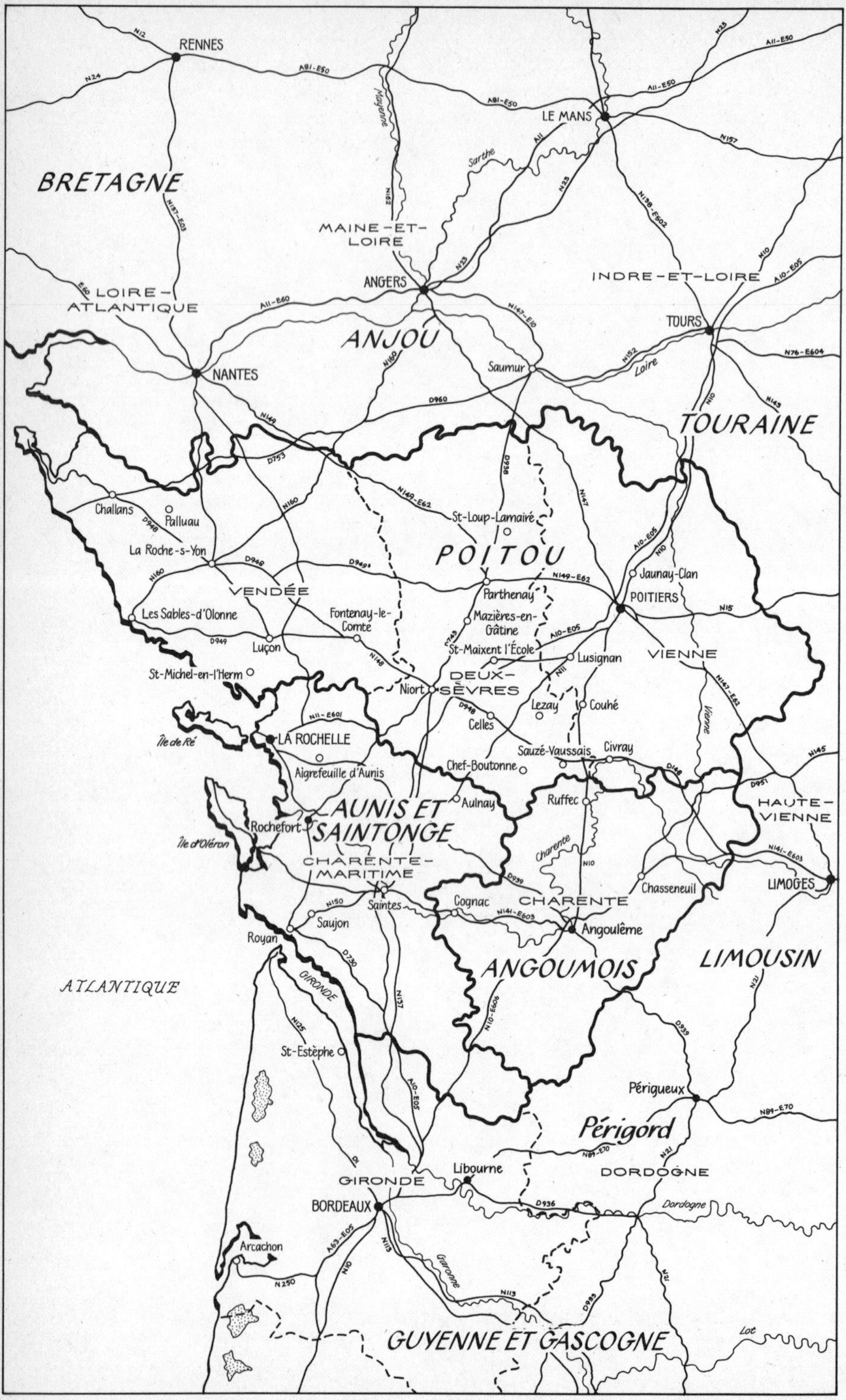

RENNES
LE MANS
BRETAGNE
MAINE-ET-LOIRE
ANGERS
INDRE-ET-LOIRE
LOIRE-ATLANTIQUE
TOURS
ANJOU
NANTES
Saumur
TOURAINE
Challans
Palluau
St-Loup-Lamairé
La Roche-s-Yon
POITOU
Jaunay-Clan
VENDÉE
Parthenay
POITIERS
Les Sables-d'Olonne
Fontenay-le-Comte
Mazières-en-Gâtine
Luçon
St-Maixent l'École
Lusignan
VIENNE
St-Michel-en-l'Herm
DEUX-SÈVRES
Niort
Lezay
Couhé
Celles
LA ROCHELLE
Île de Ré
Sauzé-Vaussais
Civray
Chef-Boutonne
Aigrefeuille d'Aunis
HAUTE-VIENNE
Aulnay
Ruffec
AUNIS ET SAINTONGE
Rochefort
Île d'Oléron
CHARENTE-MARITIME
Chasseneuil
LIMOGES
Cognac
CHARENTE
Saintes
Saujon
Angoulême
Royan
ANGOUMOIS
LIMOUSIN
ATLANTIQUE
GIRONDE
St-Estèphe
Périgueux
Périgord
Libourne
GIRONDE
DORDOGNE
BORDEAUX
Dordogne
Arcachon
Garonne
Lot
GUYENNE ET GASCOGNE

CHAPTER THREE

# *Poitou and Angoumois*

POITOU – AUNIS – SAINTONGE – ANGOUMOIS

Poitou, commonly spelt Poictou as late as the eighteenth century, is the flat dairy and marsh country south of Brittany, *pays* of the Pictons (Poitevins today). Their chief submitted to Roman rule in 56 BC; they were christianised in the third and fourth centuries (when Aquitaine was already a duché) and over-run by the Visigoths in the fifth century. The duché became part of the Frankish Kingdom when the Visigoths were defeated in 507. The last invaders from afar were the Saracens, expelled in 732; they bequeathed Poitou a multitude of goats, and Chabi, a cheese which derives its name from the Arabic *chebli*, goat: today's Chabichou.

In the eighth century Poitou became a comté, and in the ninth the comtes revived the great duché d'Aquitaine, to which Aliénor succeeded in 1137. She became Henry II of England's Queen Eleanor by her second, and only fruitful, marriage. Their eldest son and heir, Richard Cœur de Lion, pre-deceased her and on her death in 1204 Poitou and Aquitaine passed to their fifth son, John. Poitou then changed hands six times between the French and the English before the end of the Hundred Years' War. The Dauphin, Charles VII to be, reigning comte from 1417, made his capital at Poitiers until he regained Paris from England and Burgundy in 1436.

Drainage of the coastal marshes, started in the twelfth and thirteenth centuries, resumed after the Hundred Years' War ended in 1453 and was continued by Henri IV with the help of Dutch engineers. In the reign of his successor, Louis XIII, Colbert brought in Dutch cheesemakers to improve farm and dairy. Edam-style cheese persists here to this day (see list, p. 106), and it has long been used by Bordeaux-growers and *négociants* to accompany wine tastings.

## Chabichou

The most venerable cheese tradition in Aquitaine is obviously Chabichou. This I deal with at length under Périgord and Quercy, and the Rouergue (Chapters 4 and 6), where it survives in pedigree form: a small, round, *lait cru* chèvre, drying and acquiring a coat of mould naturally as it matures through its soft, *demi-sec* and *sec* stages to a final rich hardness, if it should live so long.

Pure-bred Chabichou *fermier* can be found in Poitou and the Angoumois, but it would not be recognised by inexperienced foreigners, because Chabichou is represented abroad almost entirely by a travesty: a powdery-white *croûte-fleurie* factory fiction written in pasteurised milk (in frozen curd or powdered milk in winter). It is mild and on the runny side of soft when young, shrinking and turning an ugly brown inside with keeping: unless it has been refrigerated into permanent dull, white-coated hardness from the start.

## Industrial chèvres

These characteristics regrettably apply to most Poitou goat cheeses familiar to foreigners and undiscriminating French *supermarché* shoppers. Sainte-Maure's logs from the Touraine and Valençay's *pyramides* from Berry (see Chapter 2) are copied in shape, given injections of white mould, or coated with often oversalted powdered charcoal. Rungis sells them to the world as the Sainte-Maure and Valençay they imitate, giving a libellous impression of the originals.

In earlier days farmers' co-operatives used raw milk and matured their cheeses naturally, achieving honest coats. Since the 1960s they have become factories, ever larger and more mechanised, drawing their milk from ever greater distances, so having to pasteurise all but a minute proportion of it. In the height of the season, surplus milk is frozen as curd or converted to powder for winter use, so that supermarkets can get round the truth that goat cheese is a seasonal joy. Their customers, led to expect the same unchanging products all year round, are, of course, deceived. Some factory cheeses are tolerable in season; some are even made of raw milk and good in their own right (*not* as Sainte-Maure or Valençay); but the cheeses customers buy in what should be the close season for chèvres have the wrong consistency and flavour and quickly deteriorate.

Since the 1960s the *laiteries* have been introducing large sizes of *bûches*, and *pyramides* broadened and lengthened for cutting in shops. They keep better than the small cheeses, and the less salt among them make pleasant eating in season. They are really new kinds of cheese. Those of the *laiterie* at Celles-sur-Belle have given me pleasure, and I have heard others speak well of them as not having suffered from the gigantism which has spoiled products bearing names I used to respect.

Let these words of warning provoke you into probing markets and good shops during your travels for the genuine articles which persist there. You will find splendid and unusual cheeses made by farmers and artisans, cheeses which owe their virtues to devotion to local tradition and high standards, with the natural use of raw milk. Saint-Maixent-l'École has an old reputation for rich farm cheeses, of which I have savoured and sold a few in my time. I can also recommend the succulent, rather flat *chèvres fermiers* de deux-Sèvres from three farms, to be found at Monsieur Jacques Guérin's treasure-house in Niort, and the lightly *cendrée* La Bonde de Gâtine, first on the list. I find that after we had eaten it I wrote in red across my note of its particulars: *'Parfait! Parfait! Parfait!'*

# Cheeses of the Vendée

Outside the Marais, the remaining marshland, the Vendée, is quiet. The north, with some heather, trees and hedgerows, is less desolate than southern Brittany, until it gives way to vast stretches of pasture where herds of Frisonnes, relieved by only an occasional Bretonne Pie-rouge, graze without windbreak, shade or water. Electrified wires alone stand higher than the grass.

Further south vines comfort the eye, but maize has created its own deserts towards Fontenay and Niort. A few trees and hedges survive, but the strong unifying factor in the landscape is wire: on the ground, to contain animals; overhead, to convey talk, light and heat. At last, as we leave the Vendée, near Niort, roadside trees have been replanted and there are even some spots for picnics. It seems like a national park compared with what we have come through. The *département* of the Vendée should take note, and take pity on man and beast.

Niort bestrides the River Sèvre-Niortaise where it divides the Deux-Sèvres part of Poitou from Bas-Poitou, most of which is in the Vendée. The Vendéens have always been fiercely independent and strongly Catholic. They caused the anti-clerical revolutionary regimes years of trouble, until the right to religious observances was conceded. Their local cheeses go in for odd shapes. Those I have known longest are La Taupinière (mole-hill) and Le Bicorne (two-pointed hat of the type formerly used in full dress by naval officers and army staff). They usually have a rough, mottled exterior, tending towards blue, and, if well *affinés*, a tasty melting interior. They are not always supported, or even looked for by local shopkeepers; two in Challans told me 'There isn't any cheese in the Vendée!' I found some in the market, and visited Monsieur Gérard Grondin 6 kilometres away at Le Garnachoix to hear about his Alpines and British black-and-white goats, and his cheese, a delightfully unsalt small chèvre, also made in a bigger, salter version for shops. He told me that there were forty to fifty *chevriers* making cheese in the Vendée, counting only those belonging to the departmental branch of the national goatkeepers' society.

The Vendée, with Niort and Parthenay to the west, also shares the Jonchée tradition with Aunis and Saintonge, whither I now turn.

# Cheeses of Aunis and Saintonge

The name Saintonge (and that of Saintes, its capital) is derived from its pre-Roman inhabitants, the Santones. Aunis (with its Parlement from the tenth century), and Saintonge (a fourteenth-century comté) were part of Poitou within Aquitaine, and have shared Poitou's history and changes of ruler.

The most prominent cheese tradition of Aunis and Saintonge centres on the presentation of *caillé*, fresh unsalted curd, on *bottes* (mats): whence the names Caillebotte, and Jonchée (meaning a scattering of reeds or rushes, materials from which mats were made). Both terms are used with various adjectives, geographical or descriptive, for the many variations developed locally, and in nearby Poitou. Poitou has its Caillebottes Niortaise, Parthenaise and Poitevine; and Bas-Poitou (the Vendée) has its triangular Trébèche or Tricorne of Sableau.

Ewes' milk was formerly widely used but survives now only in the Brebis d'Oléron (pronounced locally 'Ol'reun') and perhaps in some versions of the triangular Jonchée d'Aunis. The other Caillebottes and Jonchées are made of goats' or cows' milk, the latter becoming more common.

## Cheeses of the Angoumois

The south of the region covered in this chapter is the Angoumois, created by the Romans in the third century AD and made a comté by the Mérovingiens in the sixth. It came finally to the French crown in 1515 when the ruling comte succeeded as François I of France.

The Angoumois has a rich range of cheeses, some native, some acclimatised from neighbouring, or even distant provinces (as you can see from the Angoumois entry on the list). One of its most enterprising cheesemakers is Monsieur Gilles Jousseaume, *éleveur caprin* at Saint-Estèphe, President of the French Goatbreeders' Society. He makes and sells on his farm his own appetising, rustic-looking versions of half a dozen regional chèvres, including La Taupinière, Chabichou, and a gloriously rough-coated irregular cylinder called Le Braison, so named because it is recommended for serving hot on toast.

Between them, Angoulême, Niort, Rochefort, La Rochelle and Les Sables d'Olonne have shops and markets where you can find most of the cheeses listed for the *pays* of this chapter. If you take advantage of the smaller markets, particularly plentiful in coastal areas during the summer, you may well find the odd cheese (odd in every sense) of which no cheese-writer has ever heard.

## Cheeses of Poitou and Angoumois

### Abbé
See CLOS.

### Airvault, Pavé d'
About 350g, like a plump, deep Carré de l'Est *croûte-fleurie*; turns golden and looks and tastes like a *lait-cru* cheese.
*artisanal; vache.*
Poitou/Deux Sèvres; 68 **2**.

### Amalthée
125g, 200g soft 'Camembert de Chèvre' (name improper, but descriptive); very good; by Laiterie Coopérative de Chef-Boutonne. Amalthée was Jupiter's mother's Cretan goat, 'crowned by cornu-copia and weighed down by generous udders'.
45% m.g.; *laitier*; *chèvre*.
Poitou/Deux-Sèvres; 72 **3**.

### Angoulême
Tuesday to Sunday market.
Les Halles: MM. Grignoux and Machenaux, Crémerie des Charentes, local and regional cheeses, including Chèvres au Marc, Crottin Charentais and Chèvre Frais en Petit-Lait.
Charente; 72 **13**, R.

### Angoumois (Charente)
See ANGOULÊME, BRAISON, CABRO D'OR, CAMEMBERT, CHABICHOU, LA CHAPELLE, CHÂTEAU PUYREAUX, CHAVROUX, CHÈVRE BLANCHE, CHÈVRE FERMIER, COGNAC, CROT-

tin, grand'mémé, raclette, ruffec, st-estèphe, tante mignonne, taupinière.

## Aulnay de Saintonge

Unsalted Jonchée (see CAILLEBOTTE).
*artisanal; fermier; domestique; chèvre cru.*
Saintonge/Charente-Maritime; 72 **2**, L.

## Aunac

**Moulin d'Aunac.** 200g, split log, on flat base, made at Saint-Saviol (see p. 110).
45% m.g.; *laitier; mi-chèvre pasteurisé.*
Poitou/Vienne; upper L, W of Civray, 72 **4**, upper L.

## Aunay

About 200g, rectilinear, wider and longer at base, by Coopérative de la Mothe-Saint-Héray (see p. 108).
45% m.g.; *laitier; mi-chèvre pasteurisé.*
Poitou/Deux-Sèvres; 68 **12**, low.

## Aunis

300g, 10cm-sided, triangular; *frais* drained on reeds or rushes; rare; often eaten with sugar (and see BREBIS, CAILLEBOTTE, JONCHÉE).
*fermier; artisanal; domestique; vache/brebis.*
Aunis/Charente-Maritime; 71 **12**, Marans area.

## Auzay

*Mi-chèvre* reported as *'piquant'*.
*laitier; mi-chèvre.*
Bas-Poitou/Vendée.

## Bichounet

Small Chabichou of truncated cone form, natural crust.
*fermier; artisanal; chèvre cru.*
Poitou/Vienne.

## Bicorne

See LA CHAIZE.

## La Bonde de Gâtine

Short, upright cylinder; soft; lightly coated in powdered charcoal; very good cheese; by M. Barrault, GAEC de la Fragnel, Verruyes (see also FEUILLÉ).
*fermier; chèvre cru.*
Gâtine, Poitevine/Deux-Sèvres; 68 **11**, N of C.

## Le Petit Bondon

Small cylindrical chèvre.
*artisanal; chèvre.*
Poitou/Deux-Sèvres.

## Bordeaux

Daily market (except Sundays) – good for regional cheeses.

## Bougon

*Laiterie coopérative* making all standard forms and large cutting versions of chèvre from pasteurised milk; now tied with La Mothe-Saint-Héray (see p. 108) Bougon was formerly a 200g farm chèvre of Camembert appearance.
Poitou/Deux-Sèvres; 78 **12**, S of C.

## Bouin

M. Pascal Beillevaire, *fromager-affineur*, 52 route de Machecoul.
Bas-Poitou/Vendée; 67 **2** L.

## Le Braison Charentais

80g rustic-coated short cylinder by G. Jousseaume (see SAINT ESTÈPHE); good eaten hot on toast, accompanied by Pineau des Charentes.
45% m.g.; *fermier; chèvre cru.*
Angoumois/Charente; 72 **13**, SW of Angoulême, Roullet, St-Estèphe.

## Brebis d'Oléron (pronounced Ol'reun)

*Fromage frais* presented on reed or rush mat, in *faisselle*, or loose; eaten in late winter and spring, often with sugar, or salted and enlivened with garlic; reported as having disappeared in 1961, it has survived, to be reported in 1985 by Androuët as still disappearing; in 1978 he and Ninette Lyon found it also in Vendée (at Macens, which I have not been able to trace).
45–50% m.g.; *fermier; brebis cru.*
Aunis/Charente-Maritime; 71 **13 14**, Île d'Oléron/Poitou/Vendée.

## Bûche

Bûche means log, from the familiar Sainte-Maure to the modern larger Bûches de Chèvre for cutting, such as Lezay's, with *croûte-fleurie*, or *cendrée* or coated with *rocou* (annatto).

## Bûcheron

1.6kg log; soft; *croûte-fleurie* or *cendrée*; by Coopérative of Saint-Saviol (see p. 110) one of the better, richer cheeses in the large *laiterie* class.
*laitier; chèvre pasteurisé.*
Poitou/Vienne.

## Cabri des Versennes

Small, soft flat drum made at Versennes-aux-Genêts, Beaulieu-sous-Parthenay (see CHÈVRE FERMIER DU POITOU).
45% m.g.; *fermier; chèvre cru.*
Poitou/Deux-Sèvres, Gâtine Poitevine; 68 **11**, 8.5km S of Parthenay.

## Le Cabro d'Or

140g soft cheese by M. Chevrollier, Flamenac, Pranzac.
45% m.g.; *artisanal; chèvre.*
Angoumois/Charente; 72 **14**, C.

## Cafione

Chabichou (see p. 103) kept for winter in *coffins, couffins,* or *coffineaux* (baskets).
*fermier; artisanal; chèvre cru.*
Poitou.

## Caillebotte

Unsalted *caillé* drained on straw, reeds, rushes or osier (see also JONCHÉE) and eaten *frais*; the mats are called *bottes*, whence the name.
*fermier; artisanal; domestique; vache/ chèvre/brebis.*
Poitou/Aunis/Saintonge.

### Caillebotte d'Aunis.
*fermier; brebis cru.*
Aunis/Charente-Maritime.

### Caillebotte de Parthenay, Parthenaise.
On reed or rush mat; spring, summer (similar to Jonchée Niortaise, see p. 107).
45% m.g.; *fermier; domestique; vache/ chèvre cru.*
Poitou/Deux-Sèvres; 68 **11**, far R.

### Caillebotte Poitevine, Caillebotte à la Chardonette.
Milk is 'renneted' with flower of thistle or globe artichoke which has been soaked in a little water for 5–6 hours; curd is cut in large cubes, which are then brought gently to the boil, until the curd breaks up in the whey; when cool the whey is replaced by fresh milk, and cream and sugar may be added (sometimes *aromatisé* with cognac, Ninette Lyon has noted). *Larousse des Fromages* gives another quicker method.
*fermier; domestique; vache cru.*
Poitou/Deux-Sèvres; 68 **11**, Niort, 72 **2**, Thouars.

## Camembert type

The name Camembert de Normandie has had its AOC since 1983, but Camembert *tout simple* continues to be used all over France for round soft cheeses (some passable, some contemptible). M. Lescure matures a raw-milk cheese of Camembert type made in Angoumois (makers' code 16 D). Another is made at Chasseneuil (see p. 103). Big *laiteries* make pasteurised Camemberts in quantity, e.g. Lezay (see p. 107) under at least four names.
*laitier; vache cru/pasteurisé.*
Poitou/Angoumois.

**'Camembert' pur Chèvre.** Amalthée (see p. 100) is good, of this type; I have found another very good version with no *marque*, a true Camembert-type crust and very rich, satisfying interior; the use of the name 'Camembert' for a goat's cheese is, of course, stretching things beyond the limit of sense and good taste, let alone the law, which forbids it.
At Chasseneuil-sur-Bonnieure one of these is made of *lait cru* in season (extended by use of artificial insemination for breeding), but of frozen milk in mid-winter; so it is best bought within conventional goat season (see Glossary). See also MÉLUSINE: most big *laiteries* make something of this sort, but it is usually less deep and more quickly sunken and hard than the thicker cheeses; Bougon (p. 101) and Mothais (p. 102) *were* similar.
*laitier; chèvre cru.*
Poitou/Deux-Sèvres; Angoumois/Charente; 72 **14**, R.

## Capribeur

Name used by *laiterie* making cheese under label Saint-Loup (see p. 110) at Mazières.

## Carré de Saint-Cyr

Square soft cheese made by dairy at Dissay (which also makes Sainte-Maure-type logs and *pyramides*).
*laitier; chèvre.*
Poitou/Vienne; 68 **4 14**, off N4 on D15.

## CELLES-SUR-BELLE

Laiterie Coopérative Sèvre-et-Belle, one of the best, receives visitors (tel. 49 26 80 09); makes *lait cru* cheeses, including Le Chevrot (see p. 105).
Poitou/Deux-Sèvres; 72 **2**, top C.

## CHABICHOU, CHABI

100–180g, upstanding drum or truncated cone 7cm high, 6.5cm across; natural crust becoming *bleutée* or grey (farms); *croûte-fleurie* (*laitier*, sprayed on); spring to late autumn (see p. 98). Chaunay (72 **3/4**), Civray (72 **4**, upper L); Couhé (see p. 105), St-Maixent (see p. 110) are farm cheese centres; the ancient Chabichou area is Vouillé-Neuville-du-Poitou-Jaunay-Clan (68 **13**, high).
135g Chabichou M. Gilles Jousseaume, (gold medal Paris 1983, 1985) Saint-Estèphe (see p. 109).
*fermier; artisanal; laitier; chèvre.*
Angoumois/Charente; 72 **13**, SW of Angoulême.

**Chabis Fermiers de Deux-Sèvres.** Plain and *cendrés* drums and truncated cones, *bleutés* when mature. Bichounet means small truncated cone, form of Chabichou. Les Jumeaux, Coopérative du Centre-Ouest St-Loup-sur-Thouet (see p. 110).
*fermier; laitier; chèvre cru.*
Poitou/N Deux-Sèvres.

**Chabichou Lait d'Agneau.** A rare winter treat, when some of the suckling lamb's subsistence is taken from the ewe to make *Chabichou 'lait d'Agneau'*.
*fermier; brebis cru.*

**Chabichou Laitier.** About 100g; soft drum; *penicillium candidum* introduced for white crust; most of the large *laiteries coopératives* make Chabichou; keep to summer and autumn cheeses because early spring, late autumn and winter cheeses are likely to be made from frozen milk or curd reserved from the true season.
*45% m.g.; laitier; industriel; chèvre pasteurisé.*
Poitou/Angoumois.

## CHALLANS

Tuesday and Friday market with very good chèvres, particularly at *demi-sec* stage. 12km west, beyond Sallertaines, Rairé has a working windmill; 6km NE (turn N on to Chagnon road before La Garnache) farm for chèvres, see LE GARNACHOIX.
Bas-Poitou/Vendée; 67 **12.**

## CHAMBRILLE

180g; rectilinear oblong; *croûte-fleurie*; by *coopérative*, La Mothe-Saint-Héray (see p. 108).
*45% m.g.; laitier; vache/chèvre/mélange.*
Poitou/Deux-Sèvres; 68 **12**, low.

## CHAPELET-CHAPELAIS

90g of 2cm diameter chèvres, like large round beads, on a string; *affinage* by Société Anonyme Chèvréchard, La Chapelle-Saint-Laurent.
*45% m.g.; laitier; chèvre.*
Poitou/Deux-Sèvres.

## LA CHAPELLE

480g; big medallion; soft; *croûte-fleurie*; *affinage* one month dry *cave* (Stobbs, 1984, found it 'savoury').
*45% m.g.; fermier; vache cru.*
Angoumois/Charente.

## CHARDONETTE

See CAILLEBOTTE À LA CHARDONETTE.

## CHASSENEUIL-SUR-BONNIÈRE

Saturday market.

**Chasseneuil.** See 'CAMEMBERT' PUR CHÈVRE.
*laitier; artisanal; chèvre cru.*

**Chasseneuil Lait de Mélange.** 180g; beam-shaped, soft. From same source as 'Camembert' Pur Chèvre.
*laitier; vache/chèvre mélange.*
Angoumois/Charente; 72 **14**, top R.

## CHÂTEAU PUYREAUX

**Fromage de Chèvre Blanc.** 200g; rich soft cheese in red wax drum, made by Coopérative du Château Puyreaux; needs careful handling to keep wax intact. A very good Norman cheesemaker, M. Legoupil (*fils*) trained here (see MOYON, Chapter 1, p. 21).
*45% m.g.; laitier; chèvre.*
Angoumois/Charente; 72 **3 4**, bottom.

## CHAUMINE

Tomme Blanche; floury coat; pale smooth *pâte* with groups of little holes; mild.
*laitier; vache pasteurisé.*
Poitou.

### Chaunay

Monday market; a traditional centre for Chabichou. *Laiterie fromagerie coopérative* making pasteurised cheeses, including Le Rondin (see p. 109).
*laitier; vache pasteurisé.*
Poitou/Vienne; 72 **3/4**, high, on N10.

### Chavroux

150g *pyramide* (*frais* state); also 700g rounded *tomme*; white coat; semi-soft, close-textured, mild *pâte*; by Fromagerie Grand'ouche at Réparsac, part of Chaumes-Bongrain group.
60% m.g.; *laitier; industriel; mélange*: 90% *chèvre pasteurisé*, 5% *crème de vache pasteurisé.*
Angoumois/Charente; 72 **12**, N of C, NE of Cognac.

### La Chaize, Bicorne

Small crusted cheese in form of *bicorne* hat; imitated in Périgord (see Chapter 4, p. 119 under BICORNE).
*fermier; artisanal; chèvre cru.*
Bas-Poitou/Vendée.

### Chebli

See CHABICHOU.

### Chef Boutonne

Thursday market; centre for chèvres of district; Laiterie Coopérative de Chef-Boutonne (see AMALTHÉE), reported 1982 by Androuët as now pasteurising and using frozen curd for chèvres made in winter.
Poitou/Deux-Sèvres; 72 **3**, L of C.

### Chèvramour

110g; small flat drum; mould-ripened; by Saint-Loup, Mazières.
45% m.g.; *laitier; chèvre.*
Gâtine Poitevine/Deux-Sèvres; 68 **11**, N of C.

### Chèvres

Nearly all the cheeses of this region are chèvres. The farm and artisanal cheeses are *lait cru* and usually strictly seasonal (from spring to late autumn). Industrial cheeses are mostly pasteurised and available all the year round. This means that they use frozen milk or curd during the winter, or even milk powder. It is best to buy them only from late spring until mid-autumn, and so avoid the inferior flavours and textures of winter products.
At Chasseneuil (see p. 103) an *éléveur* is extending his season by use of artificial insemination.

**Chevre Blanc** see CHÂTEAU PUYREAUX.

**Chèvre Blanche.** 900g; log on straw or plastic straw; *croûte-fleurie* (or the *cendré* version) using also the name Ruffec (see p. 109), by the makers of Chavroux (see above). Given shelf life of 35 days.
45% m.g.; *laitier; industriel; chèvre pasteurisé.*
Angoumois/Charente.

**Chèvre Fermier.** 1. Small flat drum, natural crust; pleasant eating; by Paul Georgelet, Pays Plat, Villemain; sells on farm and Cognac market.
*fermier; chèvre cru.*
Poitou/Deux-Sèvres; 72 **3**, 12kms S of Chef-Boutonne.
2. Notice on roadside.
*fermier; chèvre cru.*
Angoumois/Charente; 75 **3**, D731 NW of Chalais, at top of rise near Brossac. Chalais has Monday market.

**Chèvre Fermier de Deux-Sèvres.** 150–200g cheeses from three farms sold by M. Guérin at Niort:
1. Neat thick medallion on plane leaf; melting under natural crust; moist but firmer white centre melts in mouth; rich aroma and flavour, not salty; succulent; surprisingly good keeping (we finished ours four or more days later).
2. Similar, but irregular, billowing surface, smaller.
3. Shallow mushroom top in form, lying on curved surface, reminiscent of Saint-Félicien (see p. 249).
*fermier; chèvre cru.*
Poitou/Deux-Sèvres; S and C.

**Chèvres Fermiers.** M. Jousseaume, Élevage Caprin de Couin, makes Le Braison (p. 101), Chabichou (p. 103), Grand'mémé (p. 106), Ruffec (p. 109), Saint-Henry (p. 110), Taupinière (p. 111).
*fermier; chèvre cru.*
Angoumois/Charente; 72 **13**, SW of Angoulême near N10 St-Estèphe.

**Chèvres Fermiers du Poitou, Frais and Affinés.** Made by M. C. and G. Ferjou, Les Versennes-aux-Genêts, Beaulieu-sous-Parthenay; retail and wholesale on farm

(except Sundays) 09.00–12.00 (tel. 49 64 51 63); and see CABRI DES VERSENNES.
*fermier; biologique; Nature & Progrès; chèvre cru.*
Poitou/Deux-Sèvres; 68 **11**, 8.5km S of Parthenay on D142.

**Chèvres Laitiers.** Most of these cheeses are pasteurised cheeses with added mould to produce *croûte-fleurie* (instead of natural crust development) or coated with a powdered charcoal and salt mixture, often too salt for the cheese. *Bûches* and *pyramides* abound, in imitation of the traditional Sainte-Maure of Touraine and Valençay of Berry. Since the 1970s these smaller imitations have begotten giant *bûches* and extended *pyramides*, sometimes better in flavour and texture than the original cheeses made by the same *laiteries*. Avoid chèvres made out of season.
For *laiteries* see CELLES-SUR-BELLE (where *lait cru* is used for some cheeses), CHEF-BOUTONNE, BOUGON, CHAVROUX (Grand'-ouche), LEZAY, LA MOTHE-ST-HÉRAY (make *lait cru* log), LOUDUN, LUÇON, ST-LOUP, ST-SAVIOL, SAUZÉ-VAUSSAIS.

### Chevrichons de Poitou; Des Deux Sèvres

Mentioned by Courtine (1973) without description.
*chèvre.*
Poitou/Deux-Sèvres.

### Chevrita

125g, round soft cheese by Saint-Saviol.
*45% m.g.; laitier; chèvre pasteurisé.*
Poitou/Vienne; 72 **4**, upper L.

### Le Chevrot

Small soft cheese '*moulé à la main*' by Coopérative Sèvre et Belle.
*laitier; chèvre cru.*
Poitou/Deux-Sèvres; 72 **2**, top C Celles-sur-Belle.

### Chevrotin

Bourbonnais-type truncated cone, with *croûte naturelle bleutée* and tasty interior; mine had acquired its thorough deep-coloured coat in *caves* in Savoie, after leaving *laiterie* of Saint-Loup (see p. 110).
*45% m.g.; laitier; chèvre.*
Gâtine Poitevine/Deux-Sèvres; 68 **11**, N of C Mazières.

### Le Chouan

Low dome (Taupinière type); mild.
*laitier; chèvre.*
Bas Poitou/Vendée.

### Cloche d'Or

*Laiterie* at Loudun.

### Clochette

250g; bell-shaped; natural, pale gold crust, becoming *croûte-bleutée* found by Viard (1980); M. Jousseaume makes a smaller cheese of this shape at St-Estèphe (Grand'-mémé), and St-Gelais (see p. 110) provides another version.
*artisanal; chèvre.*
Poitou.

### Clos de l'Abbé

4kg; semi-soft; washed-crust; mild imitation of monastic cheese by Union Coopérative de Vendée, Quai Est du Port, Luçon (which has Wednesday and Saturday market).
*50% m.g.; laitier; vache pasteurisé.*
Bas-Poitou/Vendée 71 **11**.

### Cœur du Poitou

Heart-shaped soft chèvre found by Philippe Olivier (who sells it at Boulogne, NORD, see p. 267).
*45% m.g.; artisanal; chèvre.*
Poitou.

### Cognac

Market with farm cheeses daily (Sat best); Les Halles include Maison des Fromages M. Christian Gayou, with good local farm cheeses. Cognac, three-star and VSOP, Pineau des Charentes, all organic, Brard-Blanchard, Chemin de Toutreau, Boutiers Cognac (tel. 45 32 19 58); *gîte rural*.
Angoumois/Charente; 72 **12**, L.

### Couhé-Vérac

220–250g; round and square, in chestnut leaves or on plane leaf; 9cm × 2.5cm; soft; natural crust *bleutée*; 3–4 weeks of *affinage* dry *cave*.
The town of Couhé-Vérac is one of the old centres for Chabichou (on map and in postal code it is Couhé).
*45% m.g.; fermier; chèvre cru.*
Poitou/Vienne; 68 **13**, bottom.

## Crottin Charentais

Small Camembert-type cheese of low acidity with unaccountable name, found in market at Angoulême (see p. 100).
*artisanal; vache entier.*
Angoumois/Charente.

## Edam Demi-Étuvé, La Micheline, Le Petit Vendéen

The name Edam is illegal (see HOLLANDE, p. 270). This must be a survival from Colbert's seventeenth-century introduction of Dutch cheesemaking to help the economy. Made by Union Sud Vendéenne Agricole Laitière, St-Michel-en-l'Herm (which has a Thursday market).
40% m.g.; *laitier; vache pasteurisé.*
Bas-Poitou/Vendée; 71 **11**.

## Extinct Cheeses

Ferté, Fleur de Poitou, Romagre were reported missing by Lindon in 1961; another he thought lost has survived, so look out for survivals or revivals.

## Faisselles

**Fromage Frais en Faisselles.** Unsalted *fromage frais* in plastic draining moulds is plentiful from the farms, M. Guérin told me, at Niort (see p. 108).
*fermier; vache cru.*
Poitou.

## Fermier, Le Bon

200g cheese of Saint-Marcellin thickness, but twice as wide; *croûte-bleutée*; seen in Paris in 1973. I do not expect a cheese of this sort of name to be *fermier*; but a very earthy-looking one, golden surface with pale blue mould, looking rather like a Saint-Félicien (see Chapter 7, p. 249), is illustrated in *Larousse des Fromages* (Courtine, 1973) p. 66, and the name does seem to be of old usage.
*artisanal; chèvre.*
Poitou/Deux-Sèvres.

## Feuille à la Chèvre

200–300g; round; in chestnut leaves by M. Barrault (see LA BONDE).
*fermier; chèvre cru.*
Gâtine Poitevine/Deux-Sèvres; 68 **11**, N of C, Verruyes.

## Chèvre à la Feuille

*Laitier* cheese, sometimes called Mélusine (see p. 107).
*laitier; chèvre pasteurisé.*
Poitou.

## Fromages Fermiers

I have seen medallion-shaped naturally crusted soft cheeses similar to La Chapelle (see p. 103) but usually smaller; cows' milk versions of the first cheese described under Chèvres Fermiers de Deux-Sèvres (see p. 104). See also CHÈVRES, p. 104.
*fermier; vache cru.*

## Frougnéa, Frougnée, Frougnes

Old names for Sableau (see p. 109).

## Le Garnachoix

150g tubby round; 1100g, 1500g Lingot (extended base of pyramid) *cendré*, for shops, much saltier than small cheese. M. Gérard Grondin has a herd of 80 Alpines crossed with British black-and-white goats, 66 in milk. He puts 12 drops of rennet in his 120l of mixed evening and morning milk, stirs it in with curved pierced spatula and leaves it for 24 hours in 8 × 15-l buckets; the curd is ladled into the moulds, turned after 24 hours and left for a further 24 hours before salting (0.5g for 150g cheese; three times that strength for large cheeses). The cheeses are sold on the farm, which is next door to a house called Fleur-de-Lys: on D32, 4km NE of Challans, 2km SW of La Garnache, turn N as for Chagnon; over level crossing, 1km after junction with road from right.
*fermier; chèvre cru.*
Bas-Poitou/Vendée; NE of Challans 67 **12**.

## Glorian

250g drum; soft, white exterior when young (met in market at Rouen).
*fermier; chèvre cru.*
Poitou/Deux-Sèvres.

## Grand-Mémé

170g; small soft chèvres, cylindrical with domed top; natural crust; by M. Jousseaume (see ST-ESTÈPHE). (Sometimes called Grand'mère.)
45% m.g.; *fermier; chèvre cru.*
Angoumois/Charente; SW of Angoulême.

## Halbran

3kg Tomme de Vendée by Union Sud-Vendéenne Agricole Laitière (see EDAM). Close-textured semi-soft cheese, bran-to-wheat coloured natural crust (*un halbran* is a young wild duck of the new season).
48% m.g.; *laitier*; *vache pasteurisé*.
Bas-Poitou/Vendée; 71 **11**.

## Jaunay-Clan

Friday market; an old, traditional centre for Chabichou.
Poitou/Vienne; 68 **14**.

## Jonchée

See CAILLEBOTTE; *jonchée* is a scattering of reeds or rushes, referring to the form of mat on which the cheeses are laid.

**Jonchée d'Aulnay.** See AULNAY DE SAINTONGE.

**Jonchée d'Aunis.** See AUNIS.

**Jonchée Niortaise.** Spring and summer *fromage frais* on reed or wicker mat, lactic flavour on acid side. As well as the Caillebottes, Sableau (Trois Cornes) (p. 109), Sable Nu (p. 109), and Les Sables (p. 109) are in the Jonchée family.
*chèvre/vache cru*.
Poitou/Deux-Sèvres.

**Jonchée d'Oléron.** See BREBIS D'OLÉRON.

**Jonchée de Saintonge.** Differing from other Jonchées in the optional introduction of bay leaves into the milk before renneting.
*fermier; domestique; vache cru*.
Saintonge/Charente-Maritime.

## Jumeaux

See CHABICHOU.

## Lezay

Tuesday market. Last Sunday in April Journée Gastronomique. Laiterie Fromagerie Coopérative de Lezay, one of the better large concerns; but, despite its emphasis on '*contrôle rigoureux*' of goats and 'control of salting' (so often lacking) it pasteurises milk and uses frozen curd for winter cheese. Makes every shape of goat cheese, *mi-chèvres*, and cows'-milk cheese (see Camembert) *pur chèvre*, square cheeses of the Saint-Maixent type (L'Étincelle and Les Trois As); also a Morbier type sent up to Franche-Comté for *affinage*, and sold as Le Noseroy (and see BÛCHE and MÉLUSINE).
Poitou/Deux-Sèvres; 72 **3**, top.

## Libourne

Listed in Chapter 4, p. 123, it is also a good centre for this region's chèvres: Tuesday, Friday and Sunday market.
Guyenne/Gironde.

## Limoges

Daily market.
Limousin/Haute-Vienne; 72 **17**.

## Lingot

See CAMEMBERT type and CAMEMBERT *pur chèvre*.

## Loudun

Laiterie Cloche d'Or makes pasteurised chèvres under name Purébique, in all the classic shapes.

## Lusignan

Wednesday market; source of Tourte-au-Fromage made of goat cheese and grapes; one maker has seven or eight different recipes.

**Lusignan, Rond de Lusignan.** 1. 200–250g *fromage frais*, round, 9–10cm × 3cm deep, usually eaten within 5 days (no crust); or *affiné* to become soft cheese, with *croûte-bleutée*; on strong side; farm cheese on straw or chestnut leaf.
2. 200g drum, soft, Laiterie Coopérative de la Mélusine (see MÉLUSINE).
3. Large cutting chèvre (*laitier*) in form of extended *pyramide* (*cendré*).
45% m.g.; *laitier; fermier; chèvre*.
Poitou/Vienne; 68 **13**, L on N11.

## Mélange, Lait de

Vache and chèvre milk mixed (*less* of chèvre but at least 25%; equal amounts are mi-chèvre, see p. 108); usually rectilinear in form rather than log-shaped; made by most big laiteries (and see CHAMBRILLE, CHASSENEUIL).

## Mélusine

Laiterie Coopérative de la Mélusine, Cloué, gives its name to a small Camembert-shaped chèvre.
45% m.g.; *laitier; chèvre*.
Poitou/Vienne; 68 **13**, .L, 5km NE of Lusignan.

**Mélusine Le Royal.** Sainte-Maure type wrapped in chestnut leaf.
45% m.g.; *laitier; chèvre.*
Poitou/Vienne, Cloué.

### LA MICHELINE

Name used by *laiterie* at St-Michel-en-l'Herm, Vendée (see EDAM).

### MI-CHÈVRE

Mixed milk with at least 50% chèvre, remainder vache; cheeses usually distinguished by shape (not log, not plain rectangular), see AUNAC, AUNAY.

### MIZOTTE DE VENDÉE

Mild cutting *tomme* by USVAL (see HALBRAN).
48% m.g.; *laitier; vache pasteurisé.*
Bas-Poitou/Vendée.

### MOTHAIS

Formerly a farm chèvre of thin Coulommiers shape, of rich goaty character, with a fine roseate crust, presented on leaf.
*fermier; chèvre cru.*

### LA-MOTHE-ST-HÉRAY

La Fromagerie Coopérative de La-Mothe-St-Héray (associated also with the *coopérative* at Bougon (see p. 101)) makes every shape and size of chèvre, Aunay and Chambrille (*lait de mélange*); it also makes:

**Sainte-Maure.** 250g log; *moulé à la main.*
*laitier; chèvre cru (lait sélectionné).*
Poitou/Deux-Sèvres; 68 **12**, L, SE of Saint-Maixent.

### MOULIN

See AUNAC

### NIORT

Astride the R. Sèvre Niortaise, which divides Deux-Sèvres and Vendée, Niort is good for cheeses from both sides.
Daily market (particularly active Thursday and Saturday).
Jacques Guérin, *maître-fromager* (Procureur-syndic de la Guilde des Fromagers), La Maison du Fromage, 19 rue Saint-Jean 'Fromages de chèvre fermiers de Tradition' (e.g. *lait cru* Ruffec Fermier twice weekly) and much more.

### NIORTAISE

See JONCHÉE.

### OLÉRON, ÎLE D'

See also BREBIS D'OLÉRON.
Wednesday to Sunday (best) market at Le Château d'Oléron.
Charente-Maritime; 71 **13/14**.

### PAMPROUX

Small local cheese on its way out (Viard 1980).
*fermier; chèvre cru.*
Poitou/Deux-Sèvres; 68 **12**, off N11.

### PARTHENAY

Wednesday market. See CAILLEBOTTE.

### LE PETIT POT DE POITIERS, OR FROMAGE FRAIS EN FAISSELLE

*artisanal; chèvre cru.*
Poitou; 68 **13 14**.

### LA PIGOUILLE, LA PIGOUILLE DU PAYS DU MARAN

*Pigouille* means punt pole, as needed in the marshes of Vendée, but the shape of the cheese was not related to its name. Formerly *fermier*, latterly 250g; round 11cm × 3cm deep; soft; natural, smooth, yellowish crust without mould; creamy white *pâte*; eaten young after a few days in the *hâloir* to dry out; or if kept longer, *croûte-fleurie* (thin); insipid made by a large *laiterie coopérative* de Marans in Aunis (*Marabout*, 1978) until about 1982.
traditionally 45% m.g.; *fermier; vache/chèvre* (formerly brebis) *cru*. Latterly 50% m.g.; *laitier; pasteurisé.*
traditionally Poitou/Vendée, now Aunis/Charente-Maritime; 71 **12**.

### POITIERS

Tuesday, Wednesday, Thursday, Saturday market.
Poitou/Vienne; 68 **13/14**.

### PURÉBIQUE

Name used by Laiterie Cloche d'Or (see LOUDUN) for pasteurised logs of 120g and Sainte-Maure (see p. 87) size.

### PYRAMIDE

The most famous and most imitated is the truncated pyramid, Valençay (see BERRY), traditional chèvre, *affiné* to achieve a *croûte-bleutée* (or, as is common today, coated with powdered wood ash or charcoal, the latter too often ready mixed with excessive salt). Most of the Valençays sold abroad now are imitations from *laiteries* in Poitou, made of pasteurised milk, or frozen milk or curd, even powdered milk, out of the goat season.

RACLETTE

1. Angoumois cheese *affiné* by Burgniard in La-Roche-sur-Foron, Haute-Savoie.
*laitier; vache.*
Angoumois/Charente.
2. 6kg cheese. Made by USVAL, St Michel-en-L'Herm (see EDAM).
45% m.g.; *laitier; vache.*
Poitou/Vendée.

LE RIVAUD

*Fromage frais* version of Ruffec by Laiterie Rivaud.
45% m.g.; *laitier; chèvre.*
Angoumois/Charente; 73 **3**, low R, Maine de Boixe.

ROCHEFORT

La Fromagerie, M. Frode, 15 avenue Lafayette and Crémerie des Halles; local cheeses, including Jonchées (see p. 107).
Aunis/Charente-Maritime; 71 **13**.

LA ROCHELLE

Daily market.
La Ferme Saint-Yon, M. Fouray, 46 rue Saint-Yon: shop specialising in mature farm cheese, chèvres, organic farm cheese (and cheeses of Auvergne and Corsica).
Aunis/Charente.

ROND DE LUSIGNAN

See LUSIGNAN.

ROND DES CHARENTES

150–200g, tubby drum; soft; *cendré.*
300–400g; similar shape; natural crust.
*artisanal; chèvre cru.*
Charente.

RONDIN

1kg; cutting chèvre, *croûte-fleurie*, by Fromagerie de Chaunay (Chaunay has Monday market).
45% m.g.; *laitier; chèvre pasteurisé.*
Poitou/Vienne; 72 **3/4.**

RUFFEC

Wednesday and Saturday market.

**Ruffec.** 250–300g; round 10cm × 4cm; eaten mostly in *fromage blanc* state or *frais*, or *affiné* in *cave humide* one month; presented on straw or chestnut leaf. Laiterie Rivaud make *fromage frais* version (see RIVAUD). M. Jousseaume makes Ruffec, and delivers it *frais* twice a week to Niort (see p. 108) where most of it is sold in this state (see ST-ESTÈPHE). The name is also used for a large pasteurised log made by the Fromagerie Grand'ouche (see CHAVROUX), and usually sold as Chèvre Blanche (see p. 104).
45% m.g.; *fermier; artisanal.*
Angoumois/Charente; 72 **4**, L.

SABLEAU, TRÉBÈCHE, TRI-CORNES

200–300g; sides 10–12cm, depth 2.5–3cm; triangular; soft; white natural crust, on aromatic reeds (called *acore*) or rush mat; drained for a week before consumption; acidulous flavour; spring to early autumn. It has been known as Frougnes (seventeenth century), Frougnéa and Frougnée. Fontenay-Le-Comte has a Saturday market. See also TRABÈCHE.
45% m.g.; *laitier; fermier; chèvre cru.*
Bas-Poitou/Vendée; Marais, 71 **1.**

LES SABLES D'OLONNE

Market daily except Wednesday; every day in summer.

**Sable Nu.** Similar to Sableau (see above).
**Les Sables d'Olonne.**
*fermier; domestique; chèvre cru.*
Bas-Poitou/Vendée; 67 **12.**

SAINT-CHEVRIER

1400g, *cendré*, rectangular, distributed by Triballat.
45% m.g.; *laitier; chèvre.*
Bas-Poitou/Vendée.

ST-ESTÈPHE

Élevage caprin de Couin; Gilles Jousseaume makes Le Braison, Chabichou, Grand'mémé, Ruffec, Saint-Henry and Taupinière (see p. 111) and sells on farm; he also grows vines.
Angoumois/Charente; 72 **13**, SW of Angoulême, N of N10.

### Saint-Étienne-du-Bois

All-year-round cheese reported without detail (1982).
*artisanal; vache.*
Bas-Poitou/Vendée; 67 **13**, Palluau.

### Saint-Gelais

280g; square; soft; natural crust; six weeks dry *cave*, developing *croûte-bleutée* with patches of red; presented on plane leaf; of Saint-Maixent family. St-Gelais is also the source of Chabichou (see p. 103), and a 300–350g cheese of Saint-Maure (see p. 87) type; and of a small Camembert-type farm cheese.
45% m.g.; *artisanal; chèvre.*
Poitou/Deux-Sèvres; 68 **11**, 10km NNE of Niort on D8.

### Saint-Henry

160g small pyramidal chèvre by M. Jousseaume (see ST-ESTÈPHE).
*fermier; chèvre.*

### Saint-Loup

110g round soft chèvre by Capribeur, Mazières.
*laitier; chèvre pasteurisé.*
Mazières-en-Gâtine; 68 **11**, N of C on D743.

### St-Loup-sur-Thouet

Coopérative Agricole du Centre-ouest makes the usual range of chèvres and a Chabichou *lait-cru*.
Poitou/Deux-Sèvres; 68 **2**, lower L.

### Saint-Maixent-l'École

Wednesday market.
Centre for farm cheeses including Sainte-Maure-type logs, plain and *cendrés* of rich flavour.
*fermier; chèvre cru.*

**Saint-Maixent.** Formerly square farmhouse cheeses of which examples may survive; square cheese now made by *laitiers* in Carré de l'Est moulds and ripened 5–6 weeks, *croûte-bleutée* with some red; on plane leaf.
*laitier/fermier; chèvre pasteurisé/cru.*
Poitou/Deux-Sèvres; 68 **12**, lower far L.

### Sainte-Maure (properly Touraine)

This name is still unprotected as I write (spring 1987), and much used in Poitou by the big *laiteries*; the best examples, though, are farm cheeses from around St-Maixent (see above); St-Saviol makes one of *lait cru, moulé-à-la-main*. See below.

### Saintes

Friday (smaller), Saturday and Sunday markets.
Saintonge/Charente-Maritime; 71 **4**.

### St-Saviol

Laiterie Coopérative de St-Saviol makes chèvres in Chabichou, 'Camembert de Chèvre', and plain and *cendré* Sainte-Maure forms (normal and Bûcheron sizes) of pasteurised milk (frozen curd in winter); a *mi-chèvre* (Aunac), a *lait cru* Sainte-Maure *moulé-à-la-main*, and the little Chevrita. I remember still with pleasure the first Sainte-Maure Cendré of theirs I tasted in the 1950s, before pasteurisation. St-Saviol now has the problems of much greater production, needing milk from distances (I believe it is now associated with Bougon).
Poitou/Vienne; 72 **4**, upper L W of Civray.

### St-Varent

Market third Sunday in month.

**Saint-Varent.** Small very local farm chèvre last mentioned by Viard in 1980; Stobbs mentions the name only as identifying dull *laitier* cheeses in 1984. I have not met it.
*formerly fermier; chèvre cru. Latterly laitier; chèvre pasteurisé.*
Poitou/Deux-Sèvres; 68 **2**, far L of C.

### Sauzé-Vaussais

Thursday market.

**Sauzé-Vaussais.** 200g medallion; soft; *croûte-bleutée* (Viard, 1980), but reported by Stobbs in 1984 as a *laiterie marque* for dull cheeses; Androuët noted in 1982 that the *laiterie* was pasteurising, and using frozen curd out of season.
*fermier; chèvre cru.*
Poitou/Deux-Sèvres; 72 **3**, R on D948.

### Semussac

Small, rich, creamy *fromage blanc* made around Semussac.
*fermier/artisanal vache cru.*
Saintonge/Charente-Maritime; 71 **5**, 10km S of Saujon, S of D730.

### Tante Mignonne

150g round cheese with hole in centre; seen young and creamy-greeny-coated in Charente and pinky-grey-white, more advanced, at Philippe Olivier's shop in Boulogne.

**Trou Tante Mignonne.** Tiny cylinder which quickly goes hard and brown – a cocktail bite for fingers or toothpick.
*artisanal; chèvre cru.*
Angoumois/Charente.

### Taupinière; La Taupinière Charentaise

270g low dome of a chèvre with rustic crust tending to bloom with blue; tasty interior, melting and rich if given long enough in moderate temperature; M. Jusseaume makes the Charentaise version at St-Estèphe (see p. 109), and took gold medals at Paris 1980–83 inclusive (he then ceased entering the Concours Agricole). I have seen these 'mole-hills' approaching the proportions of Gaperon d'Auvergne (see Chapter 7, p. 242), but always less deep.
Also 120g version, *croûte-bleutée* on chestnut-leaf, from Deux-Sèvres (and see CHOUAN).
45% m.g.; *fermier; chèvre cru.*
Poitou/Vendée/Deux-Sèvres/Angoumois/Charente.

### Tomme Grise de Chèvre

*Tomme affinée* in Haute-Savoie (see CHEVROTIN, same source); very good firm white *pâte* of melt-in-mouth quality; and see HALBRAN (Tomme de Vendée).
*laitier; chèvre.*
Poitou.

### Trabèche, Trébèche, Trois Cornes

Three-cornered cheese (see SABLEAU), formerly brebis, and thought by Chast and Voy to be so still (1984); Ninette Lyon has as chèvre (1978), and so does Léone Bérard (1982). I am told it is also made of cows' milk today.
45% m.g.; *laitier; fermier; domestique; brebis/chèvre/vache cru.*
Bas-Poitou/Vendée; Marais Vendéen.

### Vendée

Markets in Vendée are widespread and frequent in summer; Niort (see p. 108) on the southern boundary is also a good source of Vendéen cheese.
There are 40–50 *chevriers* in the Vendée belonging to le Comité de Défense du Fromage de chèvre fermier.

**Tomme de Vendée.** See HALBRAN.

### Vendéen

**Le Petit Vendéen.** Small cheese made at St-Michel (see EDAM).
*laitier; vache pasteurisé.*
Vendée.

### Verruyes

M. Barrault's GAEC La Fragnel makes the excellent La Bonde de Gâtine and Feuille à la Chèvre (see BONDE, FEUILLE).
Gâtine Poitevine/Deux-Sèvres; 68 **11**, N of C.

### Xaintray

Chèvres from farm and *laiterie* reported by Courtine (*Larousse*, 1973).
*fermier/laitier; chèvre cru/pasteurisé.*
Poitou/Deux-Sèvres; 68 **11**, L of C.

AUNIS ET SAINTONGE
LA ROCHELLE
Ile de Ré
Ile d'Oléron
ANGOUMOIS
CHARENTE
Angoulême
St-Junien
LIMOGES
HAUTE-VIENNE
LIMOUSIN
MARCHE
CREUSE
Guéret
Gouzon
Aubusson
Bourganeuf
Vienne
PUY-DE-DÔME
CLERMONT-FERRAND
AUVERGNE
CORRÈZE
Tulle
CANTAL
Lot
ATLANTIQUE
Gironde
Nontron
Brantôme
Périgord
DORDOGNE
Périgueux
Montignac
Les Eyzies
Sarlat-la-Canéda
Beynac
Belvès
Dordogne
Martel
Souillac
St-Céré
Rocamadour
Gramat
Gourdon
Livernon
LOT
Figeac
Libourne
BORDEAUX
Bergerac
GIRONDE
Cadillac
Arcachon
GUYENNE ET GASCOGNE
Cancon
Monflanquin
Prayssac
Fumel
Cahors
Quercy
Limogne
Villeneuve
Aubin
Rouergue
AVEYRON
Garonne
LOT-ET-GARONNE
Villeneuve-s-Lot
Agen
Agenais
Bas-Quercy
TARN-ET-GARONNE
Montauban
Tarn
LANDES
GERS
Armagnac

CHAPTER FOUR

# *Périgord and Quercy (Aquitaine) with Limousin and Marche*

## GUYENNE – PÉRIGORD – QUERCY – AGENAIS – LIMOUSIN – MARCHE

Aquitaine was a Roman province, embracing even more *pays* than are listed above. With the exception of the Marche, those I have brought together were all in the seventeenth-century Gouvernement-général de Guyenne et Gascogne, and had various other historic ties in common. Northern Aquitaine (Aunis, Saintonge and Angoumois) I have treated with Poitou (see Chapter 3), because their cheeses have more in common. Gascogne, a duché from AD 602, was independent from Roman times until its heiress, married to duc Eudes d'Aquitaine, succeeded in 1036, and the two duchés were joined together. Gascogne is discussed with the Pyrenees, alongside Navarre and Béarn (see Chapter 5), where its cheese traditions lie. From the early seventeenth century the Rouergue was within Guyenne and Gascogne, but its ancient and present association with the cheese of Roquefort demands a chapter to itself.

The name Guyenne, short for Aguienne (itself a corruption of Aquitaine), became attached to Aquitaine in the thirteenth century. On the Royal Cartographer's 1650 map it covers little more than today's *département* of the Gironde. Périgord's name comes from its pre-Roman population, the Petrocores; Limousin from its old tribe, the Lémovices; and Quercy from its oaks (oak in Latin is *quercus*). Marche means a frontier province, which is what it was for a thousand years.

Périgord, so beloved of the English, has a record of human occupation going back 400,000 years, the densest found in Europe from pre-historic evidence. The second human settlement (here from 38,000 BC) has left us a rich legacy of cave art. Roman occupation of the region gave way to the Visigoths, whom Clovis defeated in 507. The later Saracen invasion was stemmed in 732 by Charles Martel. Near the church he built in Haut-Quercy as a thanksgiving for victory arose the beautiful town of Martel.

Among its many attractive buildings is an elegant covered *halle* where local *fermiers* still sell their cheeses. The Saracens also left behind enough goats to found the tiny, yet great Cabécou.

By the late ninth century Aquitaine, briefly a Carolingian kingdom, had become a duché again, to which most of the *pays* in this chapter were subject. It was eventually a fief of the comtes de Poitiers. Limousin and Agenais became comtés in Carolingian times, the Marche and Périgord in the tenth century. (It is said that Hugues, the Capet from whom the hereditary monarchs descend, sent a herald to the comte de Périgord to ask: 'Who made you a count?' Périgord's retort was, 'Who made you a King?')

Through the marriage in 1152 of Eleanor (Aliénor) of Aquitaine with the future Henry II Plantagenet, the region enjoyed a union with England which lasted for 300 years. (One result was the still flourishing Bordeaux wine trade with England, and the withering of English vineyards, so recently revived.) Charles VII of France, inspired by Joan of Arc, finally drove out the English. His culminating victory came in 1453 at Castillon in Guyenne, over John Talbot, Earl of Shrewsbury, who died there. Castillon, recently renamed Castillon-la-Bataille, celebrates the battle with an annual pageant blissfully illustrating the peace of the English years, and brutally ending with the French invasion, against which the populace calls on the Earl of Shrewsbury for help from England. His defeat and solemn burial are followed by French reprisals (which actually went on for nine years). In 1983 Castillon's main street was renamed Talbot. There is a pleasing architectural heritage from those years of struggle: the *bastides*, the fortified, often arcaded towns and villages built by both sides during the thirteenth and fourteenth centuries (Monpazier is one of the best examples).

Périgord and Quercy descended to the ruling family of Navarre and Béarn, which inherited France in 1589.

## Cheese in Guyenne–Gironde

Guyenne–Gironde is so full of wine that there is not much room for cheese; but I must resist the temptation to linger liquefactiously, and be content to recommend Bordeaux market. The only local cheese farmer I have noted sells there (and at Cadillac), rather than on the farm. Winegrowers love cheese and expect it on their markets, though they have no space or time to produce it themselves. Chasteaux from Limousin used to be popular there.

## Cheeses of Limousin

Limousin is a land of broad plateaux and deep valleys. Except for the far eastern fringe (covered in Chapter 7), it raises cattle and sheep more for meat than for dairy (despite its Plateau de Millevaches). Robert Courtine (1973) alone among authors of cheese books I have read mentions Bleu de Bassignac, Chabricon and Chasteaux; the last is no doubt the Chasteaux chèvre found by Ninette Lyon for her *Tour de France Gourmand* in 1985. Otherwise, the only surviving traditional Limousin cheese seems to be Tomme de Brach. A rare ewes'-milk cheese of rustic appearance, smell and taste, in shape and size about one-third of a Fourme (which it is occasionally called), it originated at Brach in the canton of Tulle. It is also called Caillada de Vouillos, *caillada* meaning curd from loose or leftover milk. This suggests that on some farms it was a cheese made of whatever was available when other calls on the milk had been met, or perhaps of milk from ewes in non-dairy flocks taken after the lambs had been weaned.

## Cheeses of the Marche

The Marche is best known for its skimmed-milk Coupi and Guéret; a fatter modern dairy offshoot of these cheeses is made at Gouzon. Coupi is a very old farm and domestic product made from skimmed milk, and probably from whey or buttermilk too. Buttermilk suggests itself because the example Pierre Androuët found in La Souterraine in the 1980s was almost transparent, 'like raw casein', he told me. The curd is made in a ball of half a kilo or more, then flattened slightly or moulded to a generous Coulommiers shape. Local habits have been to harden the cheese and grate it into soup, or to dissolve it in *bouillon* prepared for soaking potatoes.

Guéret is of similar basic character, but normally of slightly smaller Coulommiers form; it is placed in pots while in its soft, sticky state, then left for up to six months to ripen. It has been found in La Souterraine in the 1980s. Apart from industrial cheeses, there are some cows'- and goats'-milk cheeses of interest in and around Bourganeuf (see p. 119).

## Cheeses of Périgord

We were captivated when we first set foot in Périgord in 1962. Excited by the Abbé Breuil's great book, we went there to see the prehistoric art galleries in the caves (before Lascaux had to be closed to the public to protect it from an excess of human breath). Yet we gloried as much in the countryside as we did in the caves: the rich, soft, rounded greenness of the chestnut-wooded hills, the small, unspoilt pastures alive with flowers and butterflies, the horses and Garonnais oxen drawing carts on the winding roads, the looking-glass rivers, reflecting cliffs, castles and graceful bridges. We were refreshed by river trout and *beignets de salsifis* at the Auberge at Le Moustier; and by mushroom-and-truffle omelettes and other *périgourdins* delights under the Hôtel Cro-Magnon's chestnut trees at Les Eyzies, with Purple Emperor butterflies descending on us to find out what was smelling so good. Across the little road and railway we bathed, or watched the butterflies over the flowerbeds, nearly every surviving English species and many more all in one garden in Périgord.

Périgord's walnuts and their oil stand out in those memories rather than her cheeses, but I was ignorant then of Cubjac, east of Périgueux. A source of good Périgord wine until the Phylloxera disaster of the 1870s removed four-fifths of the vineyards for ever, Cubjac was never replanted, and the abandoned slopes, overgrown with a grass called *palène*, became a nourishing haven for goats. The little Crottin-like cheeses, called Cubjac or Cujassous, thought to have died out before 1980, were found and declared '*délicieux*' by the Larousse-Sélection du Reader's Digest team preparing the Périgord section of their *Pays et Gens de France* in 1981.

At Bassillac, between Cubjac and Périgueux, originated the only blue cheese that I know of in Périgord. It has been described as similar to Bleu d'Auvergne; but Arthur Eperon compared it with Roquefort when he tasted it in 1984 at the Moulin de Montalétang, south-west of Bourganeuf in the Marche, influenced perhaps by its being served to him as a ewes'-milk cheese.

Among cheeses of Périgord which I met thirty years ago and can still find is the typical monastic *croûte-lavée* La Trappe, made by the Cistercian nuns of Échourgnac at the Monastère de Notre Dame de Bonne Espérance, a nineteenth-century foundation in the Forêt de la Double, north of Montpon. Another cheese that I remember from the late 1950s, but have not seen for many years, is Prince Noir, shaped like a deep shield and coated in truffle, very thinly sliced. Truffles, £10 a kilo then, must be beyond any cheesemaker's pocket now.*

In the last decade I have discovered the excellent range of interesting-looking and well-flavoured chèvres of the Fromagerie Artisanale Desport, south of Nontron at Saint-Martial-de-Valette, most of them labelled '*chèvrefeuille*'. Besace (a shepherd's bag, though the cheese is more like a dorothy bag) and Bicorne (two-pointed hat) are types borrowed from Vendée (see Chapter 3), where La Chaize (the name on the Bicorne) is to be found. Palet Périgourdin is slightly larger, in *pavé* form, and generously herb-coated; and the Lingot is a 1.5-kilo, oblong cutting cheese. Desport also makes a little chèvre of the Crottin type.

Two farm cheeses worth looking out for are L'Étoile and Pico. L'Étoile, a hand's breadth across, a finger's breadth deep, has a wrinkly natural crust. Ours turned pinky-gold and slightly blue in the four days we kept it safely in our car. It is a moist, creamy, cows'-milk cheese, quite delicious. The chèvre called Pico from GAEC Picaudine at Tocane-Saint-Apre on the Dronne (23 kilometres west of Périgueux by N710), is a neat 180-gram drum laid on a leaf inside a wooden box, so rich that I thought it must have been washed in wine or marc.

There have been big changes in Périgord since our first visit. Roads, straighter and wider, have altered the landscape in places, and I have not seen any oxen lately (though the Larousse-Sélection writers have). Cheeses on the factory scale have arrived too. Bongrain, who had been making Margotin for some time, recently started a passable, natural, soft, crustless cheese called Saint-Moret. The already well-established Chaumes from Béarn, whose name its makers adopted for their company (see Chapter 5), has been made since 1977 at Saint-Antoine-de-Breuilh, and the same company's new raw-milk Gourmelin was set up in a new dairy at Marsac in 1983. Their research, planning, and their supervision of milk production on the farms, which makes large-scale cheesemaking possible without pasteurisation, are praiseworthy examples for any British creameries which claim to be interested in something better than standardised mediocrity.

---

*In December 1987 a good harvest brought the price *down* to between £100 and £120 a kilo, or around £3 an ounce.

## CHEESES OF QUERCY

Quercy has its oaks, and, dependent on the smaller species of oak, its truffles, now expensively scarce (best snuffled out by a woman with a sow, but it probably takes exceptional talent to train a sow, so dogs are more common). Quercy also has its Causses, kinder in aspect than those of Rouergue (see Chapter 6), but still poor and depopulated. Sheep and goats graze their grasses and their various aromatic flora, including orchids and roadside honeysuckle.

Martel, capital of Turenne (the vicomté astride the Quercy–Limousin border) and capital of truffles (a title also claimed by Lalbenque), has its own Causse and is an enchanting place to stay. Local farm cheeses are brought to the venerable market hall on Wednesdays and Saturdays. To the south-east is Rocamadour and, beyond, the Causses de Gramat and Limogne, all conservers of Quercy's traditional Cabécous, of which more below.

Rocamadour's name on its own cheeses is properly hyphenated: Roc-Amadour. Amadour's intact body was dug up by chance in 1166 and exposed at the altar for veneration; in consequence of subsequent miracles witnessed there he was canonised. The typical Roc-Amadour cheese is a tiny, flat Cabécou-medal of a chèvre, with markings of the grid on which it was ripened. This is made at La Fromagerie Artisanale de Roc-Amadour 'Marcayon', at Les Bégourines in the *commune*. The same dairy makes a marc-washed and pepper-coated log, Lou Marcaillou, and the engaging Figalou. This, too, is a chèvre, weighing 35 grams (there is also a larger size) and shaped like a fig or a head of garlic. It is succulent inside, either plain or *cendré*. There is a visitable Cabécou farm north of Rocamadour about 2 kilometres along the Mayrignac-le-Francal road beyond Les Alix.

I know of only three ewes'-milk cheeses in Quercy, all made by the Roc-Amadour Fromagerie. Brebidoux (distinct from the Brebidou of Rouergue) is a small round cheese. Le Bourrian is a 45-gram oval, and Le Sénéchal is a 385-gram dome with striated sides, laid on a chestnut leaf.

## CABÉCOU

The goats'-milk Cabécou is the strongest feature, in any sense, of Quercy's dairy tradition. The name means 'little chèvre' in the *langue d'Oc*, and little it is. Fresh from the making (from a half-litre of milk on average), the biggest rarely weighs more than 40 grams and, after *affinage* to the *très sec* stage, the smallest can weigh as little as 20 grams. The milk is renneted still warm from the goats, and given a small dose of whey from the previous cheesemaking as starter, so the curd is quicker to form than with most chèvres. When ready, it is drained for a day. The curd is then kneaded by hand, giving it the close texture typical of the cheese. Some makers salt it and then hang it in bags for draining; others salt the moulded cheeses just before they are placed in the *cave* for *affinage*.

Cabécou can be eaten *frais* within forty-eight hours of making or matured with daily turnings for fifteen days to become *sec*, the normal practice of Madame Pégourié at Gramat. However, on her premises she can offer

Cabécou at the in-between stages of *crémeux* (at five to eight days), *moelleux* (soft and velvety) or *beurré* (buttery). She also has older cheeses, *très secs*: uncovered, or wrapped in chestnut leaves and ripened in marc inside glass jars. *Passé* is a term used for a Cabécou at the *très sec* stage, wrapped in oak or walnut leaves and fermented in pots for use on special occasions. Such cheeses may be served up in vine-leaves under the name Picadou. Pierre Androuët wrote, when he met some Cabécous at this culminating stage in 1982: 'They are scarcely to be found any more, but the rich savour of these rare treasures of the cellar is unforgettable.'

One other treatment of Cabécou is its maceration in *eau-de-vie-de-prune du pays*, the local plum brandy. It is then given the honourable title of Cabécou Truffé.

At whatever stage and under whatever name you eat your Cabécou, its basic flavour and individuality come from the exceptional natural qualities of the grazing and browsing available to the goats on the Causses of Quercy. From *beurré* onwards, it is an excellent cheese to nibble with your pre-meal drink. At the *crémeux* stage or slightly firmer, eat it with a salad, provided the dressing is not too vinegary.

Bleu du Quercy is now a pasteurised creamery cheese, rather like Bleu d'Auvergne and similarly packed in silver paper, but more intense in its blue and stronger in flavour. Tomme de Quercy usually comes from similar industrial sources, but I have met some good *lait cru* cheeses, outwardly indistinguishable from many a Tomme de Savoie (see Chapter 15).

Most of the other cheeses listed against Quercy (see p. 124) are either industrial products or local variants of Cabécou; but a group of organic farmers in Quercy and Bas-Quercy is given under the heading 'Chèvres'. One of them farms near Monpezat-en-Quercy, a *bastide* town of charm and interest in its own right. Its seigneurial family provided the Church with prelates of eminence, and filled the see of Montauban for most of the sixteenth century.

## Cheeses of Périgord and Quercy, Limousin and Marche

### Arago
See Dauphin d'Arago.

### Aubusson
Cheese Fair in July.
Saturday market.
Marche/Creuse; 73 **1**.

### Bassignac (le Haut), Bleu de
Listed in *Larousse*, 1973 (Courtine) without detail.
*vache*.
Limousin/Corrèze; 75 **10**, SE of C, S of Dordogne.

### Bassillac, Bleu de
As for Bassignac; also mentioned in Joy Law's *Dordogne* as like Bleu d'Auvergne; but reported 1984 as brebis by Arthur Eperon at Moulin de Montalétang, where it was served to him.
*vache*; *brebis*.
Périgord/Dordogne; Marche/Creuse; 75 **6**, lower L, E of Périgueux; 72 **9**, bottom L.

### Belvès
Saturday market; see chèvres, fromages de chèvres fermiers.
Périgord/Dordogne; 75 R, on D710.

### Bergerac
Markets: Wednesdays, Saturdays.
Crémerie Périgourdine, M. Blanchard, for

farmhouse Chèvres, local and regional, and Échourgnac.
Périgord/Dordogne; 75 **14/15**.

BESACE

**Besace du Berger, Le Chèvrefeuille.** 230g; shaped like closed dorothy bag (*besace* is such a bag, but usually less round); succulent within; by Fromagerie Desport (see also BICORNE, CROTTIN, LINGOT, PALET); Desport labels do not claim *lait cru*, but flavours suggest it.
*45% m.g.; artisanal; chèvre*
Périgord 'Vert'/Dordogne; 72 **15**, St-Martial-de-Valette, low, S of Nontron.

BICORNE, LE FROMAGE DE LA CHAIZE, LE CHÈVREFEUILLE

240g shaped like bicorne hat; similar in character to Besace (see above), same maker; rich white *pâte*; grey-blue coat. (La Chaize is in Vendée, where cheese originated.)
*45% m.g.; artisanal; chèvre.*

BLEU DES CAUSSES

See CAUSSES.

BLEU DE TULLE

See BRACH.

BLEU DE FIGEAC

See QUERCY.

BLEU DU QUERCY

See QUERCY.

BORDEAUX

Market daily except Sundays.
Marché des Grands-Hommes: No. 1, Frédéric Boktaric: wide range of regional chèvres and others, and of butter; Jean d'Alos, 4 rue Montesquieu: chèvres and others of region, and general range; market: Place St-Pierre Thursday: Chèvres, and Jersey milk and yoghurt from Le Petit-Jamin, Rimons, Gironde (not sold on farm).
Guyenne/Gironde; 71 **9**.

BRANTÔME

Friday market for regional cheeses.
Périgord/Dordogne; 75 **5**.

BOURGANEUF

Good cows'-milk cheeses reported in Wednesday market.

**Bourganeuf.** About 200g; long, triangular in section.
*chèvre; laitier.*
Marche/Creuse; 72 **9**.

LE BOURRIAN

See ROCAMADOUR.

BRACH

**Bleu, Fourme, Tome, Tomme de Brach, Caillada de Vouillos.** 600–800g cylinder 10cm × 8cm deep; 2–4 months *affinage*; smooth crust; *pâte* firm, yet giving; stable odour, taste of fleece fat is Pierre Androuët's description (*Livre d'Or*, 1984); Brach is the hamlet where it originated in the *commune* St-Priest-de-Gimel (10km NE of Tulle); usually recorded as a blue cheese; it is not necessarily so.
*50% m.g.; artisanal, fermier; brebis cru.*
Limousin/Corrèze; Tulle area.

LE BREBIDOUX

See ROCAMADOUR.

BREBIS

See BOURRIAN, BRACH and ROCAMADOUR.

CABÉCOU

By M. Minet, Bouscarrat, St-Denis-Catus (10km N of Cahors, 79 **8**, L) (also Prayssac market).
At Prayssac (79 **7**, S of C, N of R. Lot and D911) Friday market. (Further W are *tomes* and *fromages de chèvre frais* at Puy l'Évêque (see p. 121), Saint-Paulin Fermier and Comté-type at St-Aubin (see p. 122) and Villeneuve-sur-Lot with a Wednesday market.)

**Cabécou Truffé.** Cabécou du Quercy macerated in *eau-de-vie-de-prune du pays* (local plum brandy).
Cabécou Passé served up in vine leaves is called Picadou.

LOU CABÉCOU/DE CAHORS, DE GOURDON, DE GRAMAT, DE LIVERNON, DE LIMOGNE, DE MAYRINHAC, DE PÉRIGORD, DU QUERCY

30–40g *frais* (see CAILLADOU), 20–30g *affiné*; *galette*-type disc; 4–6cm across × 1cm deep, often from earthenware vats.
*45% m.g.; fermier; chèvre cru (Mar–Nov); laitier, chèvre (Dec–Feb).*

*Collection centres for Cabécou*: Cahors (including Saturday market (79 **8**, low L)); Figeac (79 **10**); Gourdon (79 **8**, 75 **18**, L); Gramat (79 **19**, high C); Issepts (79 **10**, far L, S of N140); Limogne-en-Quercy (79 **9**, bottom); Livernon (79 **9**, R of C; 75 **19**, low R); Mayrinhac-Lentour (75 **19**, R of C) with Monday and Wednesday markets; Rocamadour (79 **9**, top L or 75 **19**) (see p. 124); Souillac (75 **18**, N of C, above R. Dordogne). At Gramat seek Mme Pégourié (see pp. 117–18).

Cajassou, Cajassous, Cujassous are names for Cabécou, possibly derived from *cage à sous* because they are sometimes kept in close-meshed cages to dry out.

**Lou Cabron.** (See ROCAMADOUR.)

**Pur Chèvre Fermier du Causse.** By M. Laize, Mas de Laval, Salvagnac-Cajarc. At Salvagnac-Cajarc (79 **9**, S of Lot, just in Aveyron).
*45% m.g.; fermier, chèvre cru.*

### CADILLAC

Saturday market 8.00–12.00 includes chèvres (see BORDEAUX Place St-Pierre p. 119).
Guyenne/Gironde; 79 **2**, upper L.

### CAHORS

Rough, *'fruste'* (as Courtine says of it and the wine) and healthy local cheese.
Wednesday and Saturday markets.
*fermier; artisanal; chèvre cru.*
Quercy/Lot; 79 **8**.

### CAILLADOU, CABÉCOU FRAIS

50g medal-shaped, sold at Prayssac market (Friday a.m.).
*fermier; chèvre cru.*
Quercy/Lot.

### CAJASSOU, CAJASSOUS, CUJASSOUS

See CABÉCOU

### CANCON

**Tomme Blanche.** By Sylvain Mercier, Couret, St-Pastour (tel. 53 01 60 73).
*fermier; vache cru.*
Bas-Quercy/Lot-et-Garonne; 79 **5**, S of Cancon off N21 by D133.

### CAUSSES

**Bleu des Causses.** Within the Bleu des Causses AOC region (see ROUERGUE and also CABÉCOU, CUBJAC).
*laitier, vache.*
Eastern Quercy/Lot.

### CHABRICON

Local name for chèvre family found by Courtine (1973).
*fermier, chèvre cru.*
Limousin.

### LA CHAIZE

See BICORNE.

### CHARMILLES

**Fromage des Charmilles.** Salt-free, low-fat cheese (40mg sodium per 100g cheese). 20% m.g.; *artisanal; vache.*

### CHASTEAUX

Small cheese which Courtine found was much appreciated between Libourne and Bordeaux (1973; spelt Chasteau and thought to be vache. Ninette Lyon correctly reported it in her *Tour de France Gourmand* (1985) as chèvre from Chasteaux).
*fermier; chèvre cru.*
Limousin/Corrèze; 75 **8**.

### CHAUMES

2kg, semi-soft, *croûte-lavée* flat round cheese; pale cream-gold *pâte* with small apertures; pleasant flavour, including crust. First made at Jurançon in 1971 (see BÉARN, Chapter 5), it was such a success that the company became Fromageries des Chaumes, and started the dairy here just for this cheese in 1977 (for the name, see CHAUMES, Chapter 9). A good Franc-Comtois cheese of this kind, Champagnoles, seems to have died out since Chaumes appeared.
*50% m.g.; industriel; vache pasteurisé.*
Saint Antoine de Breuilh, Périgord; 75 **13**, on D936.

### CHÈVRES

See BESACE, BICORNE, BOURGANEUF, CABÉCOU, CROTTIN, LE FIGALOU, LE PALET PÉRIGOURDIN, PICO, ROCAMADOUR, and below.

**Chèvres.** J. Claude Talleux makes at Cazes-Mondenard.
*fermier; biologique; Nature & Progrès; chèvre cru.*
Bas-Quercy/Tarn et Garonne; 79 **17**, N of C.

**Chèvrefeuille.** See BESACE, BICORNE, LINGOT and PALET.

**Fromages de Chèvre Fermiers.** M. Laurent at Le Meynat, Carves 24170 Belvès; organic, will send by post (tel. 53 29 03 52); Belvès, through which you would probably travel, is worth lingering in and has a Saturday market. Les-Eyzies (Monday market), Beynac, Sarlat are not far off.
*fermier; biologique; chèvre cru.*
Périgord/Dordogne; 75 **16/17**, C 79 **6/7**, top.

**Tome de Chèvre.** Didier and Evelyne Baret at Salvagnac, Montpezat-de-Quercy. At Cahors market Saturday a.m.
*fermier; biologique; chèvre cru.*
Bas-Quercy/Tarn-et-Garonne; 79 **18**, high C.
There are cheeses, vegetables, yoghurt, butter and honey, all organic, at Vazérac, 27km to the west, at Odile and Jacky Lecointe's Domaine de Sol Vielh, visitable on Friday p.m. (or available at Montauban market on Saturday a.m.).
Bas-Quercy/Tarn-et-Garonne; 79 **17**, R of C.

**Tome de Chèvre, Fromage de Chèvre Frais.** Made by Monique and Jean-Paul Brouard (also *confitures*) all organic, at Les Vitarelles (tel. 65 36 65 87); daily except Wednesday and Friday a.m.; at market Wednesday at Villeneuve-sur-Lot, Friday at Prayssac (which is 5km E); 36km W, St-Aubin (see p. 122) offers cheeses, pâté, ham.
*fermier; biologique; Nature & Progrès; chèvre cru.*
Quercy/Lot; 79 **7**, lower L on R. Lot and D911 Puy l'Évêque.

COMTÉ-TYPE

See FROMAGES FERMIERS.

COUPI, CREUSAIN, CREUSOIS

This cheese has existed from time out of mind. Gouzon (73 **1**) and Jarnages (72 **10**) used to be sources of it in the shape of a flattened ball, or of Coulommiers, between 500 and 700g. It was usually dried and grated into soup or melted in *bouillon*, in which fried potatoes were to be soaked. Pierre Androuët found it in almost transparent form in La Souterraine (72 **8**) in the early 1980s, soft with *croûte-fleurie naturelle*. He found a smaller version made by a *laitier* at Gouzon (see p. 122). Guéret (see p. 122) is of the family.
*10% m.g.; fermier; domestique; vache cru écrémé (occasionally 20% m.g. chèvre cru).*
Marche/Creuse; Creusain, 72 **8 9 10**, Creusois, 73 **1**.

CROTTIN

70g cheese, a little flatter than Crottin de Chavignol, made by Fromagerie Desport (see BESACE).
*45% m.g.; artisanal, chèvre.*
Périgord/Dordogne; 72 **15**, low S of Nontron.

CUBJAC, CUJASSON, CUJASSOUS

Crottin-like cheese of about 40g made from the milk of goats on abandoned vineyard slopes of Causse de Cubjac; after it was thought to have disappeared, it was reported by Larousse-Sélection in December 1981. Viard (1980) said cows' milk was mixed in off-season (see end of CABÉCOU entry).
*fermier; chèvre (sometimes lait-de-mélange) cru.*
Périgord/Dordogne; 75 **6**, low.

DAUPHIN D'ARAGO

White-coated *tomme* distributed by Gilca-Orlac-Vivalp of Lyon; made in Bas-Quercy.
*50% m.g.; laitier; vache pasteurisé.*
Bas-Quercy/Lot-et-Garonne.

ÉCHOURGNAC, LA TRAPPE

300g (like small Reblochon), 10cm × 3cm; semi-soft; *croûte-lavée*; 3–4 weeks in *cave humide*, with washings and turning; mild but flowery, not dull; made by the Cisterciennes of Le Monastère de Notre-Dame de Bonne Espérance, near Échourgnac.
*45% m.g.; artisanal; vache cru.*
Périgord/Dordogne; 75 **3/4**, low.

L'ÉTOILE

10cm medallion, 1–1.5cm thick, with wrinkly white to pinky-gold crust, slightly blued; deliciously moist and creamy; kept well for 4 days in car (bought at Grillet in Aurillac (Auvergne).
*fermier; artisanal; vache cru entier.*
Périgord/Dordogne.

## Le Figalou

35g and larger (about 100g), shaped like a fig or a slightly flattened head of garlic; rich flavour; made by Fromagerie Artisanale de Rocamadour (see p. 124).
45% m.g.; artisanal; chèvre.
Quercy/Lot; 75 **18** 19, C Rocamadour.

## Figeac

Market: 4th Wednesday, 2nd Saturday in month.
Centre for Cabécou; name used in past for
**Bleu de Figeac.** One of the Bleus du Quercy (see p. 124).
Quercy/Lot; 79 **10**.

## Flormaigre

Semi-soft *tommes blanches* by Montauban (see p. 123).
20% m.g.; laitier; industriel; vache pasteurisé.
Bas-Quercy/Tarn-et-Garonne.

## Florneige

As Flormaigre.
50% m.g.; laitier, industriel; vache pasteurisé.
Bas-Quercy/Tarn-et-Garonne.

## Fromages Fermiers

See also CABÉCOU.

**Comté-type cheese, Saint-Paulin.** M. Gilbert Pozzer makes these, and Sarrasin flour, pâté and ham, 17km from Villeneuve (see above) at Gozefond, St-Aubin (79 **6** lower L) 47130 Monflanquin (tel. 53 36 42 41), which has a Thursday market; sales from farm Tuesday and Saturday evenings; market Villeneuve Wednesday 8.00–12.30, Fumel Thursday 9.00–12.30, Bordeaux (Dec–Mar only) Thursday 8.00–14.00.
fermier, biologique; vache cru.
Bas-Quercy/Lot-et-Garonne.

**Fromage Blanc, Fromages Frais.** M. Patrick George sells these, and butter and yoghurt, Wednesday a.m. at Villeneuve market (not on farm).
fermier; biologique; vache cru.
Agenais/Lot-et-Garonne; 79 **5**.

## Fromage Frais, Midi-Frais

220g soft, drum-shaped.
60% m.g.; laitier, vache.
Bas-Quercy/Lot-et-Garonne.

## Fromageou

Sometimes used for CABÉCOU (see p. 119).
fermier; chèvre cru.
Quercy.

## Fumel

Thursday market, 9.00–12.30.
Bas-Quercy/Lot-et-Garonne; 79 **6** low.

## Gourdon

Centre for Cabécou.
Quercy/Lot; 79 **8**, high L; 75 **18**, lower L.

## Gourmelin

1.9kg, flat, round; creamy, lightly washed crust with white mould, mild when young, but develops flavour; new enterprise by Fromagerie des Chaumes in 1983, made from selected farms' milk at a specially opened new dairy.
50% m.g.; laitier; industriel; vache cru.
Périgord/Dordogne; 75 **5**, Marsac.

## Gouzon

Tuesday market.

**Gouzon, le Petit Gouzon.** 250–300g, 11cm × 3.5cm; base of cone shape; *croûte-fleurie naturelle*; ripened 1 month; odour of mould and rustic flavour; a fatter version of the old Coupi (see p. 121) by a *laitier* in Gouzon.
30–40% m.g.; laitier; artisanal, vache cru semi-écrémé.
Marche/Creuse; 73 **1**, N of C.

## Gramat

See CABÉCOU.

## Grana

See PASS' L'AN SALIT.

## Guéret

Saturday market.

**Guéret.** 350–500g; 12–15cm × 3–5cm; skimmed milk cheese, soft and sticky; smooth, natural crust; ripened up to 6 months in closed earthenware pots in warm temperature; mainly found in La Souterraine; related to Coupi (see p. 121).
10% m.g.; fermier; domestique; artisanal; vache cru écrémé.
Marche/Creuse; 72 **9**, R, 72 **8**, high.

## Isserts

See CABÉCOU, for which it is a centre.

## Libourne

Tuesday, Friday, Sunday (morning) market. Alain Barbeyron, La Fromagerie, 53 rue Fonneuve (thirty varieties of chèvre, and much else).
Guyenne/Gironde; 75 **12**, high.

## Limogne

**Cabécou de Limogne.** See CABÉCOU.

## Limousin

See BASSIGNAC, BRACH (or CAILLADA DE VOUILLOS or BLEU DE TULLE), CHABRICON, CHASTEAUX, RACLETTE.

## Le Lingot

1.5kg *pavé* by Fromagerie Desport at St-Martial-de-Vallette (see also CHÈVREFEUILLE).
45% m.g.; *laitier; artisanal.*
Périgord Vert/Dordogne; 72 **15**, low S of Nontron.

## Livernon

**Cabécou de Livernon.** See CABÉCOU.

## Loubressac

200g soft, Saint-Marcellin-like, but larger (Stobbs/Olivier, 1984).
50% m.g.; *vache cru.*
Quercy/Lot; 75 **19.**

## Lou Marcaillou

85g, 100g, 10cm long, rolled in pepper; 1.5% marc within; by La Fromagerie de Rocamadour (see p. 124); rich.
45% m.g.; *artisanal; chèvre.*
Quercy/Lot; 75 **19**, far L of C.

## Marche

See BOURGANEUF, COUPI (CREUSAIN, CREUSOIS), GOUZON (PETIT GOUZON), GUÉRET, PAVÉ, PÉLERIN, SAINT-ELOI.

## Margotin

**Margotin Herbes de Provence, Margotin Poivré.** 100g, *banon*-shaped; described by Bongrain, the manufacturers, as 'produced by traditional techniques and made from a steamed cheese which is then coated with ground black pepper or with garlic and herbs'; it has the slightly artificial flavour you might expect from that, but many people like it.
58% m.g.; *industriel; vache pasteurisé.*
Périgord/Dordogne.

## Martel

Wednesday and Saturday a.m. markets; local *fermières* with own cheeses (see pp. 113–14).

## Mayrinhac-Lentour

Monday and Wednesday markets; a Cabécou centre (see p. 119).
Quercy/Lot; 75 **19**, R of C.

## Montauban

Saturday market.
**Mountalba.** Creamy coloured, closer-textured *pâte*, but outwardly typical factory-type black-coated, plump *tomme* of modern 'Pyrenean' style (Mountalba means Montauban) of which 4000 tonnes a year are made by Fromagerie Salit at Montauban, Italian-founded in 1925 (see also FLORMAIGRE, FLORNEIGE, PASSE' L'AN SALIT, TOMME DU QUERCY).
50% m.g.; *industriel; vache pasteurisé.*
Bas-Quercy/Tarn-et-Garonne; 79 **17/18**, low.

## Montignac

Wednesday (better) and Saturday markets. Close to Lascaux.
Périgord/Dordogne; 75 **19**, R of C.

## Nontron

Saturday market.
Fromagerie Artisanale La Chèvrefeuille Desport (see PALET).
Périgord/Dordogne; 72 **16**, L of C.

## Palet Périgourdin

300g chunky *pavé*-shaped cheese, herb coated.
45% m.g.; *artisanal; chèvre.*
Périgord/Dordogne; 72 **16**, L of C Nontron.

## Pass' l'an Salit

Grana-type hard grating cheese; oiled crust; matured over one year, made by Fromagerie Salit, Montauban (see p. 123); 1000 tonnes per year.
22–32% m.g.; *industriel; vache pasteurisé.*
Bas-Quercy.

## Pavé Frais mas Barronet

1.7kg *pavé* made by Michel Ponne at Masbaraud-Mérignat.
*45% m.g.; fermier; vache cru.*
Marche/Creuse; 72 **9**, N of Bourganeuf.

## Le Pèlerin

Large black *tomme* (Pyrenean type) in ring form, with striated sides; made by Éts Entremont in Creuse.
*industriel; vache pasteurisé.*
Marche/Creuse.

## Périgord

See BASSILLAC, BESACE, BICORNE, CHAUMES, CHÈVRES, CHÈVREFEUILLE, CROTTIN, CUBJAC, CUJASSON, DOUSCAR, ÉCHOURGNAC, L'ÉTOILE, GOURMELIN, LINGOT, MARGOTIN, PALET PÉRIGOURDIN, PICO, PRINCE NOIR, SAINTE-ALVÈRE, SAINT-MORET, TOMME DE VACHE, LE TOURTON.

## Périgueux

Wednesday and Saturday (special) market.
Périgord/Dordogne; 75 **5**.

## Le Picadou

A very rich and rare pot-ripened version of Cabécou (see p. 119) *passé* served in vine leaves.
*fermier; chèvre cru.*
Quercy/Lot.

## Pico

180g neat drum on leaf, in box; soft; pale, cream-coloured natural crust; by Gaec Picandine, Tocane-St-Âpre (see p. 116).
*45% m.g.; fermier; chèvre cru.*
Périgord/Dordogne; 75 **5**, L of C.

## Prayssac

Friday market.
Quercy/Lot; 79 **7**.

## Prince Noir

About 150g; half-oval, shield shape; soft cheese, natural crust coated in very thinly sliced truffle (see p. 116).
*laitier; vache.*
Périgord/Dordogne.

## Quercy

See BLEU DE FIGEAC, DU QUERCY, BOURRIAN, BREBIDOUX, CABÉCOU, CAHORS, TOMME BLANCHE (see CANCON), CHÈVRES, DAUPHIN D'ARAGO, LE FIGALOU, FIGEAC, FLORMAIGRE, FLORNEIGE, FROMAGES FERMIERS (COMTÉ-TYPE, SAINT-PAULIN), FROMAGEOU, LIMOGNE, LIVERNON, LOUBRESSAC, LOU MARCAILLOU, MOUNTALBA, PASS' L'AN, PICADOU, QUERCY (BLEU, TOMME DE), ROCAMADOUR (including SÉNÉCHAL), TOMME NOIRE (LE ROY).

**Bleu du Quercy.** 2–2.5kg, drum- or *fourme*-shaped (usually drum 18–20cm × 10cm); soft; natural crust now usually silver-paper-coated; *affinage* 3 months *cave humide*; fat-firm *pâte*; strong odour and flavour; regarded by Androuët as imitation of Roquefort with cows' milk. I have met 50% m.g. examples in Fourmes du Forez shape and proper crust, but with more intense blue (not like Roquefort or Bleu d'Auvergne). Eastern Quercy on the Rouergue/Aveyron border is within the Bleu des Causses AOC region (see ROUERGUE).
*45–50% m.g.; laitier; vache pasteurisé.*

**Tomme du Quercy.** Agreeable *tomme* (Savoie shape) with grey mould crust, sometimes enriched with other moulds; 9.5 and 25kg industrial version made by Salit, Montauban (see p. 123).
*45–50% m.g.; laitier; artisanal; vache cru.*
Quercy/Lot; Figeac, 73 **10**, Gourdon; 79 **8**.

## Raclette de Busseau

Pale-grey, mat surfaced, crusted cheese, neat exterior.
*laitier; vache pasteurisé.*
Limousin/Corrèze.

## Rocamadour

**Le Bourrian.** 45g oval; 7.5cm × 4cm × 1.5cm deep; soft; eaten young and sweet (before any crust has formed).
*50% m.g.; artisanal; brebis.*

**Le Brebidoux.** Small soft ewes'-milk cheese.
*50% m.g.; artisanal; brebis.*

**Le Roc-Amadour pur Chèvre.** Small soft cheese, shape of thick medal, gridded face.
*45% m.g.; artisanal; chèvre.*

**Le Sénéchal pur Brebis.** 385g dome-shaped, with striated sides, on chestnut leaf, semi-soft.
*50% m.g.; artisanal; brebis.*

All of the last four cheeses are made by the Fromagerie Artisanale de Roc-Amadour 'Marcayou', as is the little Figalou (see p. 122) and Lou Marcaillou (see p. 123).

**Lou Cabécou.** (See CABÉCOU.) Made by Mme Lacoste (second farm after Les Alix, just N of Rocamadour. Visits 09.00–19.00 except January, February (tel. 65 33 22 66). On Mayrignac-le-Francal road; 75 **19**, far L.

**Lou Cabron de Roc-Amadour.** Local name for Cabécou, which has been used for brebis version.
*fermier; chèvre cru.*
Quercy/Lot; 79 **9**, top L/75 **19**.

ROQUEGAUTIER

About 1.2kg *tomme*; lightly salted; pressed; supple and mild (*Marabout*, 1978).
*artisanal; vache.*
Agenais/Lot-et-Garonne; 79 **5**, S of Cancon.

SAINTE-ALVÈRE

Local chèvre, spring to late autumn; mi-chèvre or vache according to *Marabout*, 1978.
*fermier; chèvre cru.*
Périgord/Dordogne; 75 **16**, high L.

ST-CÉRÉ

Saturday market
Quercy/Lot; 75 **19, 20.**

SAINT-ÉLOY

Black Pyrenean-type *tomme* by Riches-Monts (saint and place, near Guéret: Éloi; cheese: Éloy).
*industriel; vache pasteurisé.*
Marche/Creuse.

ST-JUNIEN

Saturday morning market.
Limousin/Haute Vienne; 72 **6**, bottom.

ST-MARTIAL-DE-VALETTE

Fromagerie Artisanale Desport, maker of brebis (see ROCAMADOUR), CHÈVREFEUILLES (BESACE, BICORNE, PALET), CROTTIN and LINGOT.

SAINT-MORET

150g plastic-boxed soft cream cheese with added skimmed milk; no preservatives or additives; praised for 'taste and texture' above rival products of this class by BBC 2 *Food and Drink* programme; a Bongrain product (but see p. xxiii).
*industriel; vache pasteurisé.*
Périgord/Dordogne.

SAINT-PAULIN

See FROMAGES FERMIERS.

SARLAT

Wednesday a.m. market.
Périgord/Dordogne; 75 **17.**

LE SÉNÉCHAL

See ROCAMADOUR.

SOUILLAC

Centre for Cabécou (see p. 119), Monday, Wednesday, Friday markets.
Quercy/Lot; 75 **18.**

TARTARE

**Tartare Herb/Garlic, Green Peppercorn, Walnut.** 69g, 80g, 96g, 150g soft cream cheese by Bongrain.
*70% m.g.; industriel; vache pasteurisé.*
Périgord/Dordogne.

THIVIERS

See CUBJAC.

TOMMES

**Tomme Blanche.** See CANCON, FLORMAIGRE, FLORNEIGE.

**Tomme Noire le Roy, plain or black pepper.** Another black-coated, 4kg rounded Pyrenean imitation by Vivalp, boasting 21 days' minimum *affinage.*
*industriel; vache.*

**Tomme de Quercy.** See QUERCY.
Quercy/Lot

**Tomme de Vache.** Inviting cheese with blue-grey wrinkled crust found in Brantôme market (Fri).
*fermier; vache cru.*
Périgord/Dordogne; 75 **5.**

LE TOURTON

Fromageries des Chaumes invention of 1978 as 'local cheese', St-Antoine-de-Breuilh; semi-soft, brown crust.
*industriel; vache pasteurisé.*
Périgord/Dordogne.

LA TRAPPE

See ÉCHOURGNAC.

VILLENEUVE SUR LOT

Wednesday and Saturday a.m. market 8.00–12.30.
Agenais/Lot-et-Garonne; 79 **5.**

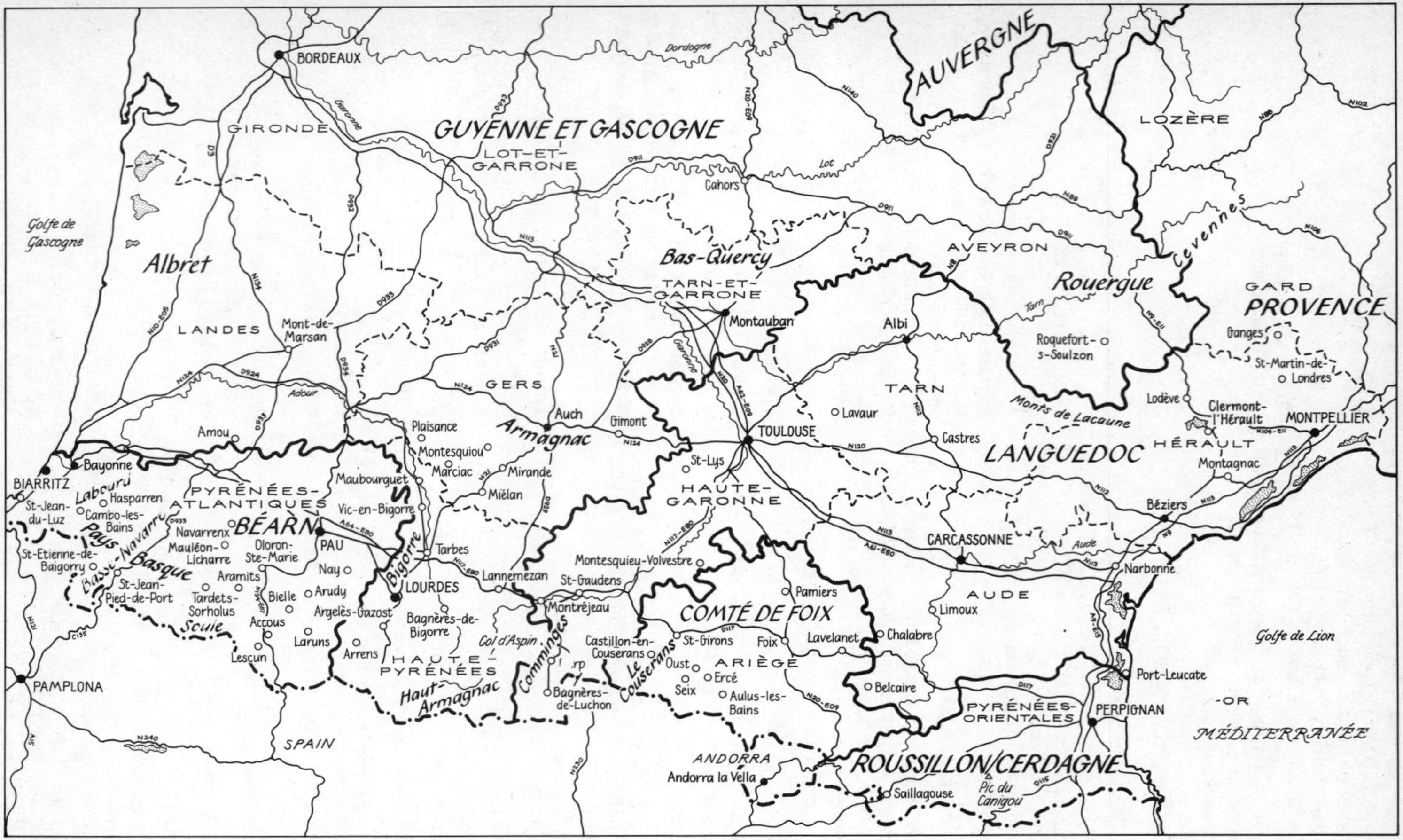

GUYENNE ET GASCOGNE
AUVERGNE
LOZÈRE
GARD
PROVENCE
Cevennes
Rouergue
AVEYRON
Bas-Quercy
TARN-ET-GARRONE
LOT-ET-GARRONE
GIRONDE
Albret
LANDES
GERS
Armagnac
TARN
LANGUEDOC
HÉRAULT
Monts de Lacaune
HAUTE-GARONNE
AUDE
COMTÉ DE FOIX
ARIÈGE
Le Couserans
Comminges
HAUTE-PYRÉNÉES
Haut-Armagnac
Bigorre
BÉARN
PYRÉNÉES-ATLANTIQUES
Labourd
Pays Basque
Basse-Navarre
Soule
PYRÉNÉES-ORIENTALES
ROUSSILLON/CERDAGNE
ANDORRA
SPAIN
Golfe de Gascogne
Golfe de Lion
MÉDITERRANÉE
BORDEAUX
Cahors
Montauban
Albi
Roquefort-s-Soulzon
Ganges
St-Martin-de-Londres
Lodève
Clermont-l'Hérault
MONTPELLIER
Montagnac
Béziers
Narbonne
CARCASSONNE
Castres
Lavaur
TOULOUSE
Gimont
Auch
Plaisance
Montesquiou
Marciac
Mirande
Miélan
Maubourguet
Vic-en-Bigorre
Tarbes
LOURDES
PAU
Nay
Arudy
Argelès-Gazost
Bagnères-de-Bigorre
Arrens
Laruns
Bielle
Oloron-Ste-Marie
Aramits
Accous
Lescun
Tardets-Sorholus
Mauléon-Licharre
Navarrenx
Mont-de-Marsan
Amou
Bayonne
BIARRITZ
St-Jean-du-Luz
Hasparren
Cambo-les-Bains
St-Etienne-de-Baigorry
St-Jean-Pied-de-Port
PAMPLONA
Lannemezan
Montréjeau
St-Gaudens
Montesquieu-Volvestre
St-Lys
Col d'Aspin
Bagnères-de-Luchon
Castillon-en-Couserans
St-Girons
Oust
Seix
Ercé
Aulus-les-Bains
Foix
Pamiers
Lavelanet
Chalabre
Limoux
Belcaire
Andorra la Vella
Saillagouse
Pic du Canigou
PERPIGNAN
Port-Leucate
Dordogne
Garonne
Lot
Tarn
Aude
Adour
N20-E09
N140
N88
N102
N106
D921
D911
N9-E11
N9
N113
N112
N120
N124
N21
D931
D928
D933
D932
D934
D924
N134
N10-E05
D3
N20
A62-E09
A61-E80
N117-E80
A64-E80
N134-E07
N121
C135
N240
A15
N230
D117
D115
A9-E15
N109-E11

CHAPTER FIVE

# *The Pyrenees and Western Languedoc*

The Pyrenees are rich in variety of landscape, animals, people and styles of living. I had grouped the *pays* of this region before finding my instincts justified by the Royal Cartographer's map of 1650. Everything south of the Poitou–Marche–Auvergne boundary except the Languedoc came under the Governor-General of Guyenne and Gascogne. The Guyenne has been dealt with alongside Périgord (Chapter 4); the rest, to the south, embracing Albret (the Landes), the Basque provinces, the Béarn, Armagnac and its surrounding Gascon *pays*, shares this section with Foix, Western Languedoc, and Cerdagne and Roussillon. Much of Western Languedoc formed the old comté de Toulouse, to which were added in the seventeenth century the Cerdagne and Roussillon from Spain.

The one feature common to all these old *pays* is their proximity to the very feature which divides them: the Pyrenees. The high watershed which became the French boundary with Spain in 1659 sends all its rivers northwards. The mountains through which they have to cut their way make serious east–west communications between the upper valleys impossible. Only below, among the rounded foothills and in the vales, can waters and traffic move laterally across country. There the central and western streams collect in the Atlantic-bound Adour and Garonne, while those of the Eastern Pyrenees join the Aude and the rivers of Roussillon to feed the Mediterranean.

This mountainous and watery heritage has resulted in longitudinal fragmentation of the region, with ethnic, linguistic and political divisions more complex than anywhere else in France. Eleven provinces divided between five modern *départements* exist on a frontage only 400 kilometres wide as the crow flies, from Saint-Jean-de-Luz on the Atlantic to Collioure on the Mediterranean (to walk the frontier would double the distance, but no crow would want to, and no man could).

Most of these provinces have spent far more time independent or under foreign rule than they have under effective French control. They spoke, and still cherish and preserve with varying degrees of success, five distinct non-French languages. Their styles of architecture, agriculture and cheese-making, as well as their customs, vary charmingly from valley to valley, with local patriotism much alive. French historians concede that when Edward II and Edward III of England were ducs de Guyenne, the majority of their Pyrenean subjects had no desire to become Frenchmen. Basques and Gascons felt no national sympathy with their neighbours of the north, and the towns especially were linked to England by close ties of commerce. As one historian put it, 'The English rule, if often weak, had never proved tyrannical, and they had a great dread of French taxes and French officialdom.'

The Basques, like the Bretons, still distance themselves: 'Oh, that's where you enter France,' a Basque cheesemaker said to me quite unselfconsciously of a village I mentioned to him. The Basques live where they have always lived, while temporary neighbours have come and gone in profusion for thousands of years. So let us turn first to them, the oldest inhabitants of the region.

## The Pays Basque
### VICOMTÉ DE LABOURD – BASSE-NAVARRE – VICOMTÉ DE LA SOULE

The term 'Basque' is of Gascon origin, but the Gascons are a different people. 'Euskadi' is the proper name of this timeless country, inhabited by the dark, sturdy Basques. They are not only the oldest inhabitants of the Pyrenees; they probably share with the original fair Illyrian race surviving in Albania the distinction of being the longest-settled peoples in Europe. In comparison with them, the rest of us Europeans are mere nomadic mongrels. The Basque language has been said to have grammatical echoes of Finno-Ugrian and to lie between the native American languages and Ugro-Altaï, but its roots defy attempts to ally them with any other known language.

At one time, Basque territory extended from the Ebro to the Gironde, but centuries of pressure from Celtibères in the south and Celts and Gauls in the north gradually confined them to their present heritage astride the Western Pyrénées. The succession of later invaders in Roman and post-Roman times seems to have bounced off this indestructible people, leaving its ancient blood remarkably undiluted, its language undefiled. After post-Roman chaos, the Basques emerged still together in the ninth-century kingdom of Navarre. This consisted of seven provinces: four (including Haute-Navarre) on the southern slopes of the Western Pyrenees, and three (including Basse-Navarre) on the northern slopes. These last are our concern here: Le Labourd, on the Atlantic coast, which became a vicomté in the eleventh century; Basse-Navarre; and, further inland, the ninth-century vicomté de la Soule. Their laws enshrined individual rights, which their monarch was sworn to preserve.

From the eleventh century until 1234 the kingdom owed suzerainty to Aragon, thereafter through Gascogne to Aquitaine. When Eleanor (Aliénor) of Aquitaine married Henry II Plantagenet of England in 1152, the lands came under the gentle suzerainty of the English. La Soule (although officially annexed to the French crown from 1306) and Le Labourd were so subject to the English for nearly 300 years, Navarre proper for a mere fifty. When the English were eventually despatched in 1453, France resumed possession of La Soule and annexed Le Labourd on the coast. Ferdinand of Castille had annexed the four southern provinces on marrying the Queen of Navarre's sister, so only the rump of the old Basque kingdom, Basse-Navarre, remained independent. However, thanks to family acquisitions by marriage, when Henri II succeeded his mother as sovereign of Navarre he was also vicomte de Béarn, comte de Foix, comte de Bigorre, and master of several other Gascon territories. Furthermore, as a descendant of Saint-Louis of France, he was in line for the French throne, heir to the childless Henri III of France from 1584. In 1589, when Henri III of Navarre succeeded his namesake as Henri IV of France, he claimed that he brought France to Navarre, not the other way round. His old domains now shared his sovereignty with France, but retained their Protestant faith. They lost their independent status only after Henri's death, and Béarn and Navarre were not absorbed into the French kingdom until 1620, eight centuries after their foundation. The kings of France continued to call themselves Kings of Navarre until the last direct-line Bourbon, Charles X, abdicated in 1830.

The new *départements* established in the 1790s officially wiped the old provinces off the map, with a prefectorial system keeping a strong rein in hand in Paris. Since then, the Basques have been subject to centralised government, but mercifully the excesses of republican education law have been recognised in the last few years, and the revival of the old languages is now officially encouraged.

The Basque language is given its most glorious showing in the churches, where the hymns are sung in Basque by congregations so fervent and vocally gifted, that they could challenge the best of professional choirs. The effect is enhanced by unaccompanied singing, and by the ancient tradition of sitting women and girls in the nave and men and boys in the galleries.

Traditionally, the Basques inside and outside the confines of their ultimate kingdom were tough mountain farmers, depending largely on sheep for their clothing, meat, milk and cheese. There were also, of course, the chickens, which Henri IV of France wanted to see in every peasant's pot. He must be satisfied, looking down from heaven today on the endless poultry running free with the grazing beasts. They feature on every Pyrenean menu, and the hens provide the eggs for *piperades* and *gâteaux Basques*. All the birds and beasts could retreat at night into the lowly regions of the vast matriarchal or patriarchal farmhouses to help keep the human element warm on the floor above. Many still do.

The wide, gently sloping roofs of the whitewashed houses of Labourd are usually tiled, and the upper parts often half-timbered, with generous wooden balconies. Inland and towards the mountains in Navarre and La Soule, tiles give way to slates, and roofs become steeper in the centre, splaying out at the sides lower down, where they sometimes almost reach the ground. These farms passed down from generation to generation, the eldest inheriting, often regardless of sex.

## Ardi-gasna

France has always cherished her varied regional dairy traditions. It was a rare piece of interference when the necessary but ineptly planned EEC milk quota was imposed in 1985. Fortunately, most traditional Basque *fromagers* could laugh, because the quota did not touch on ewes' milk, which is all that goes into their ancient local cheese: a golden, hard-crusted *fromage de brebis*, with an interior ranging from semi-soft to semi-hard, according to maker and age. It is sometimes sold hard as *brebis sec*, at over one year, for grating or strong eating.

The Basques call their cheese Ardi-gasna, which simply means *fromage du pays*, 'sheep cheese', to them. The name probably goes back to pre-Roman times, although its origins have been commonly attributed to more recent centuries. Three trustworthy recommendations from founts of knowledge in the cheese world led me up the hill south-west of Saint-Jean-Pied-de-Port in Navarre to a village cheese dairy. On the map, it is just short of Saint-Michel. The Basque name is Eiharalarre, meaning Land of the Windmill. In the Garazi dairy, where cheesemaking has gone on for 150 years, I found the *curé* of Saint-Jean-Pied-de-Port, Père Pierre Harymbat, and his colleague Monsieur Bengochea, who make Ardi-gasna from Christmas until mid-July. I touched on the timelessness of their cheese and the *curé* said, 'It's been the same cheese for at least four thousand years. The Romans knew it as an older cheese than Roquefort.'

In England we have the Gloucester cheese, until recently similar in its very hard gold crust and its rounded millwheel shape to the Basque cheese, with traditions also dating back to pre-Christian times. My growing certainty that Gloucester is a very ancient cheese indeed removes any scepticism I might have had about the history of Ardi-gasna, coming as it does from a settlement so much more unchanged through the ages than England.

Père Harymbat and Monsieur Bengochea make their 2.5-kilo cheese under the Appellation Contrôlee label 'Ossau-Iraty, Brebis Pyrénées'. A larger, 4-kilo cheese is made for one *maître fromager*, and the smaller Arradoy (named after a peak north of Saint-Jean-Pied-de-Port) for general distribution. They serve a group of twenty farmers in the Iraty region, whose 3500 ewes, on very rich pastures in a very soft climate, can be trusted to produce excellent milk for cheese; as the *curé* said, 'We are working with people we can trust.' Their ewes are of the old Manech *tête noire* breed (black-faced and horned), brought into the *bergerie* only in snow or tempest. This work for a group is like the *fruitière*, village dairy of Franche-Comté and Savoie (see Chapters 14 and 15). I sense that with their production at maximum, and with competition severe, twenty farms is almost as many as they would care to deal with. Pierre Harymbat explained that co-operatives can become too big, with the almost inevitable consequence of inadequate control over milk and cheesemaking standards. This could necessitate pasteurisation, at the cost of cheese texture, aroma and flavour, and the loss of the AOC, which demands use of raw milk.

The new milking and cheesemaking season begins when a lamb is carried in its shepherd's arms to the altar at the Midnight Mass heralding Christmas Day. The season ends in July, when the ram starts sowing his seed. Most of the ewes are in lamb before July, when by long local tradition milking ceases and cheesemaking ends. The ewe is five months in lamb, so lambing occurs in the first half of December, before the new season begins.

From June until September many flocks move up to the high mountain pastures rich in plant species and accessible only in summer. This is the *transhumance*, which rests the farmland from grazing and makes it easier to build up a reserve of winter forage. The trek is still made on foot over moderate distances, but multi-storey sheep waggons are now used for longer journeys.

Shepherds who make their own cheese during the *transhumance* live in a little *kaiolar*, Basque equivalent of the *chalet* of Savoie and rather smaller than the *buron* of Cantal and Salers (see Chapter 7). Ideally it should have a stream running underneath for essential water supply, and room to sleep and eat, to make cheese and to mature it, a little heaven of hard labour. The name of Arnéguy, a border village south of Saint-Jean, is used for some of the summer cheeses made in that area. Such cheeses are sold at Saint-Jean-Pied-de-Port in season just outside the old town gate leading to the Rue de l'Église in a little one-storey tiled shop under the sign *'Boucherie–Aguirre–Charcuterie et Fromage'*. This merchant told me that a number of flocks from the Esterençuby area (south of Saint-Michel) stayed up in the *transhumance* from early May until the end of October. At Saint-Jean's Monday market, on the way into the town from the north-west, I found a small stall selling *'Jambon et Fromage de Montagne'*. The smiling, broad-faced merchant had a variety of farm cheeses and told me with pleasure that the traditional cheese market is growing.

To the west of Saint-Jean-Pied-de-Port is Irouléguy, which provides red wine of strong enough character to stand up to the oldest of Basque cheeses. The Béarnais Madiran, perhaps more refined than Irouléguy, is another red wine of the *pays* which we found excellent with local food.

Between Saint-Jean-Pied-de-Port and Mauléon, by the Col d'Esquich, there is one of those endearing road signs: *'Zone de Patûrage'*. Careful driving leaves the unfenced roadside cows undisturbed, and likewise their pasture companions, more of Henri IV's chickens. We picnicked on the west side of the *col*, among chickens and deep-orange Clouded Yellow butterflies, looking out on two magnificent views. North, over the foothills and their rolling valleys, we could look down over the plain beyond; south we could look up to five lines of hills and mountain crests, ending with the highest Pyrenean horizon. In or near villages signs draw attention to sale of cheese by farm or *laiterie*: *'Vente sur Place'*. These are usually worth following up, and I list a number of them at the end of this section (see pages 135–8).

We established our Basque base in Abense-de-Haut, across the River Saison from Tardets in the Soule. The Hotel–Restaurant du Pont d'Abense is lively, and handy for Tardets market, where the interesting cheese stall comes only every other Monday. Its treasures included an aged Basque brebis *sec*, a Béarnais russet-lacquered brebis from the Vallée de l'Aspe, a *mixte* brebis–vache, another mixed-milk cheese from Arette, just over the Béarn border, a chèvre, marked Aysius (see list, p. 146) and two cows'-milk cheeses from the Béarn.

In Abense we would suddenly hear a mass of little feet padding quickly but lightly along the road under a harmony of bells. Looking up, we would see a flock of over fifty black-faced Manechs trotting down from the pasture to their *bergerie*, close-packed like a miniature mounted band behind their bell-wether bandmaster. They needed neither shepherd nor sheepdog to guide them, and later we saw *troupeaux* of up to 200 moving about like this. The custom is for every sheep to have a bell individually recognisable, yet attuned to the harmony of the whole. When an extra bell or a replacement is needed the shepherd selects one which, while not duplicating the sound of any other, will sound sweet with the rest. (There is more about these bells on page 145.)

At dinner our hotel served an excellent brebis made on the last farm up the valley at Etchebar. On our way there next day, we met a small flock of white Basco-Béarnaises with magnificently regal, almost right-angled bridges to their muzzles, and strong horns curled once round. Their shepherd told me that between mid-September and mid-June their milk is collected by the Chaumes cheese factory at Mauléon, to be used for the brebis called Étorki (see below). However, ewes whose lambs are weaned early give milk to the shepherd before the Étorki season, and at the end of the season there is always some milk from ewes not quite ready to be dried off. These surpluses enable him to make cheese for family consumption, its keeping quality such that cheeses from these two periods see them through the year.

Going on to the head of the valley, at the last house but one on the right at Etchebar, I found Monsieur Irigoyen, young, dark, smiling and rosy faced. It was early October, not long after he had trekked 30 kilometres with his 120 Basco-Béarnaises down from their summer *transhumance*. He was now going to have about six weeks' quiet preparation for the start of lambing in early November. He makes his golden-crusted cheeses weighing about 3.5 kilos from January until mid-May, and matures each cheese for at least three months, preferably longer. In his words, *'Plus il est vieux, meilleur il est'*. The hotel cheeses bore him out.

## ÉTORKI AND LOU PALOU

My next visit was to see cheesemaking on a different scale, in a factory built in 1979 by the Fromagerie des Chaumes at Mauléon (still in the Soule). In 1985 they used 6,800,000 litres of ewes' milk from the Iraty area, and from the Ossau valley in the Béarn, for their firm, hard crusted Étorki. Since 1986 all the milk is collected direct from sheep farms, most of which made and sold their own cheese in earlier days. Now, as we learned at Abense, there is always some uncollected milk before and after the factory season, so the *bergers* keep their hand in with this surplus, making at least enough cheese for themselves. Until 1984, 110 of these farms supplied milk for the Roquefort-makers (see Chapter 6), but their zone was ceded to Chaumes in 1985. Now Chaumes have 934 farms with 100,000 sheep. They are mostly Basco-Béarnaises in the Iraty region and in the valleys of the Aspe and Ossau, but there are some Manechs tête noire; and there are Manechs tête rousse (chestnut-faced and hornless) on the hills nearer the sea. Chaumes give technical help to encourage their suppliers to keep high standards of hygiene and quality.

The milk arrives at the creamery at 8–9°C and is pasteurised at 72°C for thirty seconds. It is then filtered and cooled to 4°C. They use starters of their own devising to help the ripening of the milk over a period of 12–15 hours. They used calves' rennet up to 1985, but are working on lambs' rennet and experimenting with an *aromagramme*, which aims at distinguishing the sources of flavour and aroma. The milk temperature at renneting is 36°C, whereas the general practice on farms and in small dairies is 30–32°C. The temperature in the dairy is 30°C. They told me that some farms still make their own rennet from skins in the old way, *'présure à l'ancienne'*.

Once formed, the curd is cut to wheat-grain size, put in plastic basin-shaped moulds which are stacked vertically for pressing. On the farm the curd is broken by hand or with a whip (*fouet*) then reheated and left in the whey for up to half an hour before being 'balled' and put in the mould. Traditional pressure is light, but Étorki, like its Navarrais factory cousins (owned by Société of Roquefort), Prince de Claverolle of Larceveau and Prince de Navarre of Saint-Palais, is closer textured and firmer than most farmhouse or artisanal cheese, so I suspect factory pressure is higher.

The finished cheese is immersed in brine for two hours, dried, and rubbed externally with salt several times over the following week. Pierre Harymbat leaves his cheeses in brine overnight for twelve hours, and brushes them regularly thereafter to avoid *le poil-de-chat* ('cat's hair', descriptive of an unwanted mould). Any excess of cheese mite (*les artisans*) is dealt with by further washing, but it is traditional to tolerate some degree of mite in the crust of farm cheese, just as it is in England's Stilton (most Stilton makers thought mite essential up into this century).

Thereafter treatment differs further between farm and factory. Étorki is vacuum-packed and kept at 4°C for between three and six months to arrest development. Weekly washing and rubbing continues for four weeks after the crust has fully developed. The cheese can be held for longer than six months to develop extra strength. Pierre Harymbat's cheeses are ripened at natural *cave* temperature and at 90 per cent humidity for at least three months. At four months they are rich in flavour and those that are left for six months achieve *onctuosité*. His stocks tend to run out in November and the new season's cheeses are not ready until mid-March. No doubt because of the nature of winter feed, February milk makes slow-developing cheese.

In the close season for ewes' milk, the Chaumes factory at Mauléon uses cows' milk from a limited Pyrenean zone to make Lou Palou (Béarnais for 'Le Palois', a citizen of Pau). The making is similar to that of the brebis until the cutting of the curd and the pressing. These are more lightly done to produce an almost white colour and a looser, softer texture with plenty of openings. Chaumes claim that this type was traditional on farms from the Béarn to Foix up to the middle 1960s; but cows'-milk cheeses made now on farms in the Béarn and the provinces further east are a very different matter. I have seen them, usually straw-coloured inside, with crusts of all colours, including some almost black. The latter were commoner in earlier days when more makers rested their new cheeses on slate shelves, which coloured the still moist and tender exterior of the cheese. Some, too, may have been coated with black paraffin wax or grape-pressings, which might be mixed with earth or olive oil or both. This I have not seen among today's cheeses. I shall mention this type of cheese again when we reach the Couserans, where interesting examples are made by artisanal methods (see pp. 158–60).

Lou Palou is made of pasteurised milk and ripened for twenty-one days. On the fourteenth day it is given its harmless black plastic coat, tarred, as it were, first on one side, then on the other, by machine, and hand finished on the sides. 'It has an aerated, firm, but soft texture, and a mild lactic taste': Chaumes' own description, with which I do not quarrel.

We discussed cows' milk at Mauléon. One of the senior staff deplored what he called the 'negative [state] system of payments for milk', which discourages quality in favour of quantity. He said that the virtues of the good old regional dairy breeds are now being remembered again. The EEC quota system which prevents expansion of milk production has had one good effect. Dairymen, particularly cheese producers, are thinking more about quality and less about quantity. The good traditional dairy breeds for cheesemaking provide the answer: milk not only with the quantity of fat and non-fat solids needed, but milk with the physical make-up and character in flavour and consistency which exploits the native local pastures to the full.

Breeds from in or near the Basque region which he mentioned as in need of revival included the Bazadoise or Bazace, originating in the Gironde and used in the Landes; the Blonde des Pyrénées, which have been bred towards beef in recent years, but which survive as dairy cows in three valleys; and the Rodez from the Rouergue, which once flourished in the Aude. Most of the cows' milk used by Chaumes comes now from Frisonnes (Friesians) and Holsteins, or Hollandaises as they are often called even when French-bred.

Pierre Harymbat had also criticised French milk policy of recent years for stressing crude quantity regardless of quality, which is often bad because of doubtful feeding stuffs. He deplored too the loss of pasture through 'road improvements' designed to help tourists. They are sometimes so crudely done that in addition to the loss of pasture to widenings and straightenings, surviving soil is sometimes washed away in storms and stones block new roads.

My final word about Basque cheese is of regret. It is splendid that the pure brebis of the Western Pyrenees should have been recognised with an AOC;

but the excellent Basque brebis should have stood in its own right as Iraty. It should not have been lumped together with the equally interesting but different cheese of the Vallée d'Ossau in the Béarn under the term Ossau-Iraty (between them they produce over 4000 tonnes of cheese a year).

It is true that the Basques and the Béarnais share one of the breeds of sheep notable for both milk and wool, the Basco-Béarnaise, which grazes alongside the flocks of Manech tête-rouge and the Manech tête-noire I have already mentioned. Nevertheless, Basque and Béarnais produce two distinct cheeses with interesting variations on their separate themes. To group them together because both are made of ewes' milk in the modern *département* of Pyrénées-Atlantiques is rather like lumping Chopin together with Tchaikovsky because both lived under Russian rule and both were composers. The Basques are at least as different from their Béarnais neighbours as the Poles are from the Russians. As for their cheese, it has been said that the Basques raise their milk to a higher temperature than the Béarnais, but in the Vallée de l'Aspe within the Béarnais Ossau region (the valley between Ossau and the Pays Basque) I found the opposite. It is also said that the Basques like their cheese more mature, but I have seen and tasted some well-aged Béarnais cheeses.

What matters is that cheeses are still made of raw ewes' milk on 500 farms* and in small *laiteries* by methods unchanged from ancient tradition. The tradition is the standard, and in some detail it may vary from valley to valley, from farm to farm. The AOC covers the nature of the raw material, its local provenance, and the minimum fat content of the resulting cheese (50 per cent). The rest of the specification is fortunately not tight enough to eliminate variations arising from local practices in the Basque provinces or in the Béarn. The Basques claim that their traditions are the oldest surviving in the world of cheese, and what parvenu Frank or Anglo-Saxon is in a position to contradict them?

## Cheeses of the Pays Basque

### Abbaye de Bellocq

### Abbaye de Notre-Dame de Bellocq (Ossau-Iraty AOC)

5kg cheese, washed golden crust; mild at normal selling age of 3 months; kept much longer it becomes pleasantly rich. This is an active Benedictine monastery, Urt 64240 Hasparren (tel. 59 29 65 55).
58% m.g.; *artisanal*; *brebis cru*.
W. Pyrénées-Atlantiques; 78 **18**, bottom, 85 **3**, top.

### Ainhice

**Fromage de Brebis.** 1km from centre turn SE towards Mongelos.
*fermier*; *brebis cru*.
W. Pyrénées-Atlantiques; 85 **4**, low L on D933, 8km NE of St-Jean.

**Vente de Brebis, Chèvre.** Sign on E of D933, 2km NE of Mongelos turning (see above), about Galzetaburu on map; 1km to travel.
*fermier*, *brebis/chèvre cru*.
W. Pyrénées-Atlantiques.

### Amou

See LANDES, CHALOSSE.

---

*In the Ossau-Iraty region: Pays Basque, Béarn and three *communes* in Bigorre (Hautes-Pyrénées), see p. 150.

## Araux

Crèmerie de la Navarre, Salomon, *route nationale*.
Local cheeses.
W. Pyrénées-Atlantiques; 85 **5**, NE of Navarrenx.

## Ardi-Gasna, Arradoy

**Ardi-Gasna Fromage de Zone de Montagne, Ossau-Iraty (AOC).** 2–2½kg (a few 4-kg bespoke) washed and brushed gold crust; 3–6 months (rich after 4 months, some *'onctueux'*); made end December–14 July.
*artisanal; brebis cru.*

**Arradoy Petit Ossau-Iraty.** Smaller version of Ardi-Gasna. Both cheeses available from April–mid-November; at Rungis: Tradition Fromagère, 1 avenue d'Auvergne, Bâtiment D4. NB Ardi-Gasna is Basque for sheep cheese.
Made by Société à Responsibilitaté Limitée, Garazi.
Père Pierre Harymbat, M. Bengochea, use milk of twenty local sheep farms to make the above cheeses (see p. 130).
W. Pyrénées-Atlantiques; 85 3, S on D301 from St-Jean, St-Michel or Eiharalarre.

## Arnéguy

Name used for local summer cheeses made during *transhumance*.
*kaiolar (chalet); brebis cru.*
W. Pyrénées-Atlantiques; 85 **3**, bottom C.

## Arradoy

See ARDI-GASNA.

## Bayonne

Monday to Saturday market (Thurs, Sat better).
W. Pyrénées-Atlantiques; 85 **3**, top L.

## Bellocq

See ABBAYE DE NOTRE-DAME BELLOCQ.

## Biarritz

Monday to Saturday (best) market; Sunday in summer. See GASTANBERRA.

## Le Capitoul

One of the black-coated industrial cheeses made in the Pays Basque.
63% m.g.; *laitier; vache/brebis pasteurisé.*
W. Pyrénées-Atlantiques.

## Chalosse

See LANDES.

## Chiberta

I sold this Basque cheese for years, but have not been able to buy it since the 1970s. It was 2–3kg pressed cheese of close texture and good flavour with a firm golden crust. Under this name Stobbs mentions a 450g soft cheese 12½cm across and 2½cm deep as 'rare'. I have not met it, but the smaller Régal Béarnais (see p. 148) seems to resemble it, at half size.

## Claverolle

See LARCEVEAU.

## Esterençuby

The St-Jean shop says that a number of *kaiolar* are active in this area in summer in the high pastures. Courtine has seen Ardi-Gasna and Arnéguy sold under this name.
*kaiolar; brebis cru.*
W. Pyrénées-Atlantiques; 85 **3**, S of St-Michel.

## Etchebar

**Ossau-Iraty (AOC).** 3½kg; at least 3 months; made January–mid-May; served at Hôtel du Pont d'Abense (see pp. 131–2).
*fermier; brebis cru.*
W. Pyrénées-Atlantiques; 85 **14**, top R, 4km S of Abense de Haut and Tardets.

## Etcheria

See LARCEVEAU.

## Étorki

4½kg; type same as cheeses above, but less hard and generally milder. Made since 1972 by Fromagerie des Chaumes, whose cheeses are sold here; but no view of cheesemaking (see pp. 132–4).
50% m.g.; *laitier; brebis cru.*

## Gastanberra

Basque brebis curd in earthenware pot, sold at 1000-et-un fromages, 8 avenue Victor Hugo, and at Les Halles in Biarritz (p. 136).

## Iholdy

See YOLO.

## Iraty

See OSSAU-IRATY.

## Jonchée du Pays Basque

*Fromage frais* drained on straw or reed mat.

## Landes

Sheep from the Béarn used to come down to the Landes between their mountain summers, but this has ceased, and with it the early-season brebis cheese formerly produced before they went up again.

## Landes Chalosse

**Amou.** Semi-hard, *non-cuite* cheese. Courtine says: 'vaguely reminiscent of Saint-Paulin'.
*fermier; brebis cru.*

**Chèvres.** Excellent Chalosse cheeses; some in market Niort (Deux-Sèvres). Mont-de-Marsan Jacques Darnade, *fromager*, 30 route de Sabre. Range of Basque and other Pyrenean cheeses.
*fermier; chèvre cru.*
W. Pyrénées-Atlantiques; 78 **8**, 82 **1, 2**.

## Larceveau

**Ossau-Iraty (AOC) Etchéria.** Made by Pyrénéfrom.
*laitier; brebis cru.*

**Prince de Claverolle, Fromage de Brebis Laitier.** 4–5kg hard, 4–6 months ripened, shiny golden-crusted brebis, close-textured, firm; good flavour if well aged. Made by Société of Roquefort. The name comes from Claveyrolles, a little river rising on the plateau de Cambalou, Société's home ground at Roquefort.
*50% m.g.; laitier; brebis pasteurisé.*
W. Pyrénées-Atlantiques; 85 **14**, 16m NE of St-Jean, E of D933 at road junction.

## Mauléon

Centre Régional d'Élevage Ovin (between Ordiap and Musculdy).
See ÉTORKI and LOU PALOU.
W. Pyrénées-Atlantiques; 5km to SW on D918 towards Col qd'Osquich, 85 **4**.

## Macaye

**Onetik.** Similar to Bellocq in type, made at Co-opérative Fromagère Berri, 64240 Macaye.
*45% m.g.; laitier; brebis.*
W. Pyrénées-Atlantiques; 85 **3**, SE of Cambo.

## Ossau-Iraty AOC (March 1980)

4–5kg (*fermier* up to 7kg); drum, slightly convex, about 26cm circumference; 12–14cm deep; sharp or rounded edges; lightly pressed *pâte* with small lateral apertures; natural gold to brown crust; salted, dried and rubbed during 3 months minimum of *affinage* at 12°C over 80% humidity. In maturity, *pâte* is firm but unctuous becoming harder with long *affinage*. Light aroma, full to sharp flavour.
Iraty is the name of place, forest and river in and beyond the mountainous frontier region of Navarre; Ossau is in Béarn (see p. 148). The AOC region covers all Pays de Basque and Béarn (Pyrénées-Atlantiques) and the Vallée de l'Ouzon is Bigorre (Haute-Pyrénées). See pp. 134–5 for my views on AOC and cheese reports.

## La Soule Mauléon-Licharre

**Lou Palou.** 3.9kg, black-coated, light, airy texture, mild, lactic flavour. Fromagerie des Chaumes.
*50% m.g.; laitier; vache pasteurisé.*
W. Pyrénées-Atlantiques; 85 **5**, L.

## Poustagnacq or Postagnac

A farmhouse and household confection of curd mixed with garlic or black pepper and sweet peppers, preserved in pots for from one month to one year. It originated among the shepherds of the Landes in the days of a working life on stilts, so Androuët stipulates ewes' milk; but a cows' milk version is served at the Hotel Arcé, St-Étienne-de-Baïgorry on D918 between Bayonne and St-Pierre-Pied-de-Port.
*fermier; domestique; brebis/vache.*

## Roquefort

The Pays Basque with Béarn has been within the legally defined outer radius for Roquefort during this century, and still is. However, after providing 13.5 per cent of Roquefort in the 1970s, and 11.5 per cent as recently as 1982, this region had retired from that scene by 1985, when Fromagerie des Chaumes took over the milk from the last 110 farms which had contributed, for Étorki. This cheese, and Société's Princes (see LARCEVEAU) account for most of the milk formerly going into Roquefort.
*laitier; brebis cru.*

## St-Jean-Pied-de-Port

Foire aux Fromages: one July Thursday, two Thursdays in August and in September.

Boucherie–Aguirre–Charcuterie et Fromages, for local Basque cheeses; Monday market had a rustic ham and cheese stall in 1985 (see p. 131, and ARDI-GASNA, ARRADOY and ESTERENÇUBY).

**Fromage de Vache Fermier.** Cheese of Reblochon (450g) size and appearance, except that crust is speckled. Made on farm near St-Jean (seen in Tardets markets, see below).
*fermier; vache cru.*
W. Pyrénées-Atlantiques; 85 **3**, low R.

## St-Michel

See ARDI-GASNA.

## St-Palais

Friday market.

**Prince de Navarre, Fromage des Pyrénées.** Cheese of consistent excellence; mild and melt-in-mouth at 3 months, attaining richness at 5–6 months. This *laiterie* is now owned by Société, the great Roquefort company.
*50% m.g.; laitier; brebis pasteurisé.*
W. Pyrénées-Atlantiques; 85 **4**, C.

## Tardets

Name used on some local brebis and mixed milk cheeses.

Market with cheese stall every other Monday (see p. 132).
*fermier; various laits crus.*
W. Pyrénées-Atlantiques; 85, **5**, bottom L corner.

## Urt

See ABBAYE DE BELLOCQ.

## Yolo Tomme de Brebis

Drum-shaped brebis, suggested for raclette. Made by Société of Roquefort.
*50% m.g; laitier; brebis pasteurisé.*
W. Pyrénées-Atlantiques; 85 **4**, far L C.

# Le Béarn
## PYRÉNÉES-ATLANTIQUES

We have just left the Basque country, where virtually all the traditional cheese is brebis. Le Béarn has a similar ancient tradition (protected under the name of Ossau-Iraty whose mongrel coinage I have already deplored). In addition, the milk of cows has so long been used by the Béarnais in its own right that the arms of Béarn proudly display two *'Vaches Passantes'* carrying bells at their necks. Some farms and *laiteries* make cows'-milk cheese throughout the season. Others top up ewes' milk with cows' milk towards the end of the *brebis* season as the ewes start drying off, and go on making cows'-milk cheeses thereafter until the cows are dry.

As elsewhere in the sheep world, goats have always featured as part of a *berger*'s establishment. They provide milk and cheese when ewes are dry, and nourish orphan lambs and lambs rejected by their dams. It is only in recent years that Béarn has seen the introduction of the herds of goats which now provide a few soft cheeses, and some traditional-looking hard cheeses with the difference detectable only inside.

Larousse embraces Gascon and Basque within the term 'Vascon', but the lack of any common base between the Basque and Gascon languages alone invalidates this. The Béarnais and their northern and eastern neighbours do share similar linguistic roots; but, perhaps because of a stronger pre-invasion stock, Béarnais developed into a distinct language with its own alphabet and grammar, admired by Montaigne. Its vocabulary exceeded 400,000 words, and Béarnais boasted its own literature.

Le Béarn is as big as the three Basque provinces in France put together. The Béarnais are not so long settled in this area as the Basques, but there is probably an element in their make-up more ancient than their Gascon provenance, which is itself respectably old. The Gascons (then Vascons) came in the seventh century AD from the Romans' most northern province in Spain, settling beyond the Pyrenean summits inland from the Basques. This was the beginning of Gascogne, later a suzerain of Aquitaine, of which the Béarn was a province of great individuality and a vicomté from AD 820. In the eleventh century it ceased to acknowledge any foreign suzerainty. The ruling houses of the Béarn and Foix were united by marriage in the thirteenth century and eventually the comtes de Foix came to rule the whole Pyrenean region westwards from Foix to Navarre and northwards from there to the Garonne.

Religious practices were similar to those of the Basques, and the Béarnais' peculiar eleventh-century political rights (*fors*) and their religious freedom were personally guaranteed by Henri IV, who had spoken nothing but Gascon in his childhood. The political independence of the Béarnais survived Henri's death by ten years, officially ending in 1620. Their religious freedom was extinguished only in 1685. Le Béarn's local customs and rights, including its own Parlement and Conseil d'État, persisted until the Revolution.

The freedom of Henri's chickens, until ready for the pot, survived him even longer, as we saw in the Pays Basque (see p. 129). In the Béarn too they are still to be seen in the fields and on the road, and to be tasted in *'la poule au pot de "nouste Henric"'*, stuffed with egg, breadcrumbs, and the liver and gizzard of the bird. The ancient cheesemaking habits of the Béarnais, 'of which the origin is lost in the night of time', survived too; the cheesemakers of the Vallée de l'Aspe say that it has gone on for ever there.

## CHEESES OF THE BARETOUS AND THE ASPE AND OSSAU VALLEYS

We crossed from the Basque Soule into the part of Le Béarn between Tardets and Aramits known as the Baretous. The name of Aramits is sometimes borne by cheeses of this locality, as is that of nearby Arette. In Tardets market I had met an excellent *fromage mixte d'Arette*, of cows' and ewes' milk, today called *'petit mixte'*. This description usually means about two parts cows' milk to one part ewes' milk. It is a large, rounded-edged, golden-brown-crusted cheese, not strong. North from Aramits, short of Ance, we found the Fromagerie de Baretous, selling brebis and *fromage de vache*. This dairy formerly made Roquefort *blancs* from the ewes' milk of neighbouring farms, cheeses which were sent to the *caves* of Cambalou for blueing and maturing.

A few miles to the north-west lies Oloron-Sainte-Marie, a cheese-market centre. This name is sometimes attached to the brebis made in the valley of the Gave d'Oloron, which collects the waters of the Béarn's two southern rivers, the Aspe and the Ossau (*gave* is Béarnais for river). South from Oloron, up the Gave de l'Aspe beyond Sarrance, the railway crosses under the road from the east and runs along the west side for half a mile to the first of two level-crossings in a short stretch. Just north of the first crossing and east of the road you will find *'Fromage du pays'*. South of the second level-crossing, 1 kilometre beyond Bedous, is another similar indication of cheesemaking.

Two kilometres further south we come to Accous. East of the road junction with the sign to Accous, in the angle of the road, are the *saloirs* and *caves d'affinage* of Les Fermiers Basco-Béarnais. They receive, for salting and maturing, brebis, *fromages de vache, mixtes* (vache–brebis) and some chèvres soon after they are made from farmers in the Aspe and Ossau valleys and the Baretous. The cheeses are sold retail and wholesale on the spot, or despatched to Rungis.

This establishment was having to enlarge its premises when I was there in 1985. It has thirty-two members in the Aspe co-operative and thirty-five in that of Ossau. In the Baretous (on the Basque–Béarn border around Aramits) membership is smaller. The valleys covered by this association are living illustrations of the historic *fors*. They were freed from any feudal duties and even from the Gabelle, the state salt-monopoly tax; and from the eleventh century, in return for promises of peaceful conduct, all their *communes* shared rights of winter pasturage in the Lande de Pont-Long north of Pau. These rights were legally confirmed and defined some 800 years later under

Charles X, in 1829. The farms in the Baretous also have pasturage during the *transhumance* in the Valle de Roncal in Navarra. This right goes back to 125 BC, they say, when the men of Roncal helped those of the Baretous to fight off invaders from the north. It is paid for by an annual tribute of three cows at La Pierre Saint-Martin on the frontier with Spain.

Most of their cheeses weigh about 5 kilos, but some are larger and some are of only 1200–1800 grams. They are made from January to August on each farm from the milk of its own *troupeau*, usually consisting of Basco-Béarnaises ewes. Many herds go up into the mountains for the *transhumance* from mid-May until September, when the cheeses are made in the *cabanes de bergers* or *cuyalas* (the Béarnais term). The co-operative takes them from as young as one day and continues to care for them until they are ready to sell.

The making on farm or *cuyala* begins when the fresh raw milk of its own herd is poured into the vat or *chaudron* and warmed to 30°C. It is then renneted and rested for one hour. In days gone by the milk might be warmed in the sun or in front of the open fire. The newly formed curd is broken by hand or by *fouet* before being raised to 38°C. After another twenty to thirty minutes' rest, the curd is collected at the bottom of the vat, rolled into a ball and hand-pressed into a perforated mould to shape the cheese and force out the whey. This drainage is assisted by piercing the curd with long needles (an old Cheshire custom too). The curd stays thus in the mould for twenty-four hours before being removed and taken to the salting room. This is the stage at which many cheeses arrive at Accous. Salting is done by hand-rubbing and turning of the cheese on as many successive days as the cheese weighs in kilos. Thereafter, every four or five days the cheese is rubbed with a brine-soaked cloth and turned again for the minimum four months given to maturing of *fromage de brebis*.

The new season's cheeses, when first eaten from the end of April until June, seem young and fresh. I tasted one from the cheese-iron between three and a half and four months old; it was firm, yet supple, and still mild and on the dry side on 1 October. The *fromages de montagne* from the *cuyalas* start coming on sale in October, fetching higher prices for their extra-rich flavour and longer-keeping quality.

Some farmers make cows'-milk cheeses after the brebis season is finished, some all the year round. The cows are predominantly Pie-noire Hollandaises, with some Blondes des Pyrénées and Blondes d'Aquitaine, especially during the *transhumance*. I sampled a two-and-a-half-month cheese full of agreeable character. A *mixte* (vache–brebis) was still only of medium flavour and fairly firm at three and a half months. Some farms start mixing the milk as the ewes' production begins to tail off in mid-June, and go on until the beginning of September. These tastings were a reminder that ewes' milk, with fats and other solids twice as dense as cows' milk, and spread right through the milk (forming no head of cream), makes for a slow-ripening cheese; but patience is rewarded with an eventual richness of character quite unlike that of cows'- or goats'-milk cheese. I bought some Vallée d'Aspe *pur brebis* later in Foix. This was a well-aged cheese, the *pâte* dark near the crust for nearly a centimetre. It was a smooth, close-textured, firm but not hard cheese, with a rich satisfying flavour on the sweet side, such as I love.

The cows'-milk cheeses are matured for at least two and a half months, and up to six months at the most, and the *mixtes* from three to seven months. *Pur brebis* get at least four months in the *cave*; but the summer *fromages de montagne* can be kept for between ten and twelve months. The chèvres from five farms are a comparatively recent introduction to this region. They are matured for three to seven months.

It was an old Pyrenean custom for each *fromager* to carve his own intricate design in his wooden cheese-moulds, for practical purposes of identification and not just for ornament. This has largely disappeared in the era of plastic moulds. However, the members of this co-operative keep up the tradition with initials and other motifs. Each is accompanied by an 'O' for *ovin* (sheep); a triangle in very free form for chèvre (in one case a trowel, in another case a heart); an 'I' or vertical rectangle for cows'-milk cheese; and an 'I' superimposed on an 'O', or an 'O' in a rectangle to show that the cheese is of mixed cows' and ewes' milk. Chèvre labels specify 45 per cent *matières grasses*, but the brebis, the vache and the *mixte* labels declare '*matières grasses non-précisées*'. You can take it that 45 per cent is the least they are likely to contain.

In 1985 the farms of the co-operatives had sold about 90 tonnes of cheese by October, and production and sales were on the increase. There are a further five or six small independent producers in the Vallée de l'Aspe, and others elsewhere who make enough cheese to sell to wholesalers. Beyond Accous to the south-west, on the Route du Col de Pau at Lescun, Monsieur Asserquet has his *saloir* and *caves d'affinage* for cheeses straight from the farm sold under the label '*Le Palangué*'.

We were now aiming for the Vallée d'Ossau and Laruns, where an annual cheese fair is held on the first Saturday in October for all the Ossau cheesemakers. The roads down the Aspe and Ossau Valleys are only about 8 miles apart at the Spanish frontier; but the nearest road between them (as opposed to mule-track) is over 40 miles away, so we had to return through Accous and take the road running east from Escot. On its north side are rich, red-brown-gold bracken slopes and the Forêt Domaniale d'Escot. Pastures on the south side are grazed by very mixed herds, including Blondes des Alpes and Blondes d'Aquitaine (horned and rather Jersey-coloured), a few Normandes, some brown-pied Monbeliardes, and Hollandaises. Some farm buildings round here have stone roofs and delicately pointed and curved tops to their little towers.

On the summit is the beautiful Forêt Domaniale de Bilhères, and then some open moorland. Slow driving is called for in this *zone de pâturage*. Cows have the freedom of the roads and, as they move, sound bells much more beautiful than those of bicycles. These cattle are Blondes, sharing the Plateau de Benou with horses from the nearby stud. There is a sign for '*Vente de Fromages*' on the north side of the road just before the bends where another road comes in from the west. If you are driving westwards to this point, watch out, because this road becomes a mere track leading to the Col de Marie Blanque where it rejoins the road to Escot.

Beyond the Col to the east, just west of the little chapel in this *zone de pâturage*, there is a sign for '*Élevage de Chevaux*' and another for '*Vente de Fromage*'. This is in the *commune* of Bilhères, which produced the winning and the fourth-prize cheeses at the 1985 Laruns Foire du Fromage. Downhill after the village of Bilhères, which has some notable houses, we joined the N934 at Bielle. In the centre of Bielle on the east side there is a sign for '*Vente de Fromage du Pays pur brebis*'.

We now travelled south through Gère, source of the fifth-prize cheese at Laruns. Five miles further on at Monplaisir a sign reads: '*Fromagerie Caves d'Affinage, Fromage d'Ossau-Vente-Dégustation*'. The Auberge de Monplaisir also advertises local cheese, but both establishments were closed on the day I passed through. On the other side of the Gave d'Ossau are Aste and Béon. Aste is the home of two *palmarès* (honourable mentions) of the cheese fair. Another local *berger*, Monsieur Bori, makes a good, rich, tingling *fromage de brebis* Laruns, with an agreeably light, crumbly texture. Just short of Laruns itself, across the river to the east, is Béost, village of another *palmarès* cheesemaker.

Laruns, which holds a notable folk-festival annually on 15 August, as well as the October cheese fair, is the centre of the Ossau cheese world. The annual Foire au Fromage (on the first Saturday of October) is not just a competitive cheese show; it is the market at which the new season's prices are settled between *bergers* and wholesalers. In 1985 1650 cheeses from the district, the canton de Laruns, were shown. A few of these were for competition only and not for sale, some were later sold elsewhere, and some remained unsold; but the nearly 5 tonnes of cheese was weighed for sale on the spot.

By general consent, the 1985 vintage was very good, but prices, at 56–62 francs a kilo, had scarcely risen above those of 1984. The judges' comments were compared by the local newspaper, *Béarn et Soule*, with those of winetasters. The reporter approved of this, writing of the cheese of the Vallée d'Ossau, '*C'est le Margaux du fromage*'. Judges' comments reveal the character old hands look for in this cheese: 'Very honest, but it lacks bouquet. Like a very pretty woman who lacks just a little something'; 'It holds well together, not brittle; I like its supple texture very much, but I regret somewhat a certain absence of bouquet'; 'I shall be very hard on that one, because I detect in it a flavour of factory cheese'. Appearance counts, and a good crust is needed for good keeping, but consistency, flavour and aroma are all more important than appearance.

In Laruns you can taste the cheeses of the region on the northern outskirts, where there is a sign: '*Fromage du Pays-Sandwichs*'. The town's cheese shop is up the hill on the south side of the square. It was closed on the day of our visit, but I found some good examples of local cheese at the little *épicerie* on the north-west side of the square, where D934 comes in. Monsieur Bori's cheese was one of these, and another was a well-aged, even stronger Laruns from Lys. The *commune* of Laruns supplied the second and third prizewinners at the fair, as well as two highly recommendeds. The names of the successful 1985 competitors are given against their villages in the cheese list (see pages 146–8), to help keen cheese-hunters trace them.

A good red wine to drink with such cheese is the Béarnais Madiran, of which we found the single-grape variety (*tannat*) particularly suitable.

A thousand tonnes of farm cheese is produced annually in the Ossau-Iraty region. One-third is the AOC brebis (this includes all the Basque cheese); half the rest, from Béarn and western Bigorre, is mixed cows' and ewes' milk. Twelve Béarnais and Basque *chevriers* continue a 300-year-old tradition producing about 20 tonnes of cheese a year.

## Saint-Albray and other cheeses of the Ouzon and Arrens valleys

The time came for continuing our journey east. There is a road from Laruns to the Ouzon and Arrens valleys, only about 16 miles as that old crow of mine flies, but 36 hard, high and convoluted miles on four wheels. We decided to turn back down the Ossau valley northwards along D934 beyond Bielle, where we had first joined it. At Louvie-Juzon local cheese is advertised for sale. Another 2 miles further on is Arudy, a name found on local Ossau cheeses, at which point we turned east. Five miles out of Arudy along D287 is Lys, where Monsieur Esturonne makes his excellent brebis *fermier*. I had already tasted good cheese from another Lys farm, that of Monsieur Ferdinand Pujalet, whose big 7-kilo, virtually unpressed cheese has an attractive light rind. Continuing east we came to Asson on the Ouzon, where brebis Ossau-Iraty is made under the name of Matocq.

While in Béarn we visited Jurançon where in 1961 a Dutch family built a *laiterie* under the name of Fromagerie Paloise to make cheese in the Edam style. The *laiterie* joined the Bongrain federation in 1966 and, after some unsuccessful trial products, came up in 1971 with its now famous cheese called Chaumes, the name since adopted by the company.

I have already described Chaumes, now made in the Dordogne (see pages 132–4). It was succeeded after two years at Jurançon by Belle-des-Champs (now made in the Thiérache: see Chapter 8). This was followed in 1974 by Doux de Montagne (or Boule du Béarn), a semi-soft, lighter-crusted cows'-milk version of a traditional form of local cheese, now also made elsewhere. The most recent arrival is Saint-Albray, the soft, roundly segmented cheese with a hole in the middle and a *croûte* the makers call '*demi-lavée*'. This cheese has been successful enough to take up the whole capacity of the Jurançon factory, being produced at the level of 7000 tonnes a year in 1985, compared with a total cheese production at Jurançon in 1965 of 1000 tonnes.

Each day 250,000 litres of milk are collected from 300 farms. All the milk of all the farms must be taken all year round, so the company has arrangements to store seasonal milk surpluses in Spain. Milk goes to the Étorki factory at Mauléon for the making of Lou Palou from mid-June to mid-December, while ewes' milk is not available there. Since 1983, the company has controlled the type and quality of milk from the 5000 Friesian and Holstein cows on the farms, and it pays different rates for the three grades of milk. The best is reserved for Saint-Albray.

Saint-Albray is made with pasteurised milk. The method is similar to that used for Chaumes, but the curd is cut less fine. This and the much deeper mould make for a softer, more airy texture. The cheese is not bathed in brine, but the rubbing of the crust with *rocou* (whence the term *demi-lavée*) forms a skin which attracts *penicillium candidum*, and turns golden and aromatic as the cheese ripens. After two days in the mould the cheese is left open on the shelf for six days, then wrapped in paper for its next twelve days of ripening.

The Chaumes company does considerable research into sources of flavour and aroma in cheese at Jurançon, in the effort to improve and vary these two factors in its own production. In 1985 cheeses at the experimental stage included a Brie (called Henri IV!) and a lightly-washed Saint-Thibaut, evolved from the Maroilles formula, now being made in the Thiérache. These and all the current range of Chaumes cheeses can be bought at the factory, east of N134 to the south of Jurançon; but cheesemaking is not on show to the public.

We finally said *au revoir* to the Béarn at Saint-Pé-de-Bigorre, where the Crémerie de Bigorre opposite the east end of the remarkable old church offered a 6-kilo brebis *fermier* Laruns de la Vallée d'Ossau, quite different from any I had seen before. It was millstone-shaped, not rounded, with a very rough golden-brown crust concealing a well-aged, rich interior. I was reminded of some of Pierre Harymbat's older and more mite-ridden Iraty cheeses, and of his telling me that some of the *fromagers* of Laruns achieve their russet crust with fifteen days of washing in brine. The *crémerie*'s other notable Béarnais cheese was a wonderful contrast, a shiny, golden and neatly rounded *fromage de vache fermier* with a smooth, succulent, slightly fissured pale-gold interior. This 2.5-kilo cheese came from Nay, 10 miles north-west of Saint-Pé, and was my last Béarnais cheese; for Saint-Pé, mentioned here for its good representation of the cheeses of the Béarn, is actually across the border in Bigorre.

Before passing on to Bigorre, however, I must recall that Nay is not only a source of good cheese, but of those delectable bells which adorn and identify so many of the sheep, cattle and goats throughout the Pyrenees (see also page 132). The family of Daban have been five generations in the bell-founding business. '*Ça fait du bruit, mais n'enrichit guère*', they say (it makes a noise but not much money). With methods unchanged for hundreds of years, this extraordinarily subtle craft, and *art*, produces *clarines* in almost unlimited variety of size and key and timbre. The bells made by the Dabans include the *pireneco* for sheep; the *esquillon* or *esquillard* less than 6 centimetres deep for lambs; the *esquire* with its bulbous crown for rams; the *trucou* or *metaü companè* of up to 40 centimetres for the leading cow of a herd; and the *platello* for goats. In 1985 they cost from £30 to £50 apiece according to size, so if you find one seek out the nearest shepherd or the nearest farm. It is a serious, life-saving object, as well as a joy to the eye and ear, and should not be regarded as a tourist trophy.

For many a *berger*, the bell identifies at a distance the size and sex of a straying beast, before he gets down to identifying the individual; some shepherds can detect the absence of a single sheep bell among a flock of a thousand. Nor is it only the shepherd, cow-herd or goat-herd and his dog (*labrit*) for whom the bell sounds. The herd has a sense of belonging which keeps the beasts together and the sound of the bells helps the occasional stray or laggard to rejoin the company. The animals are conscious of their own bells, and cows have been known to be so upset when their bells crack that they give no milk for forty-eight hours.

On what more sympathetic note could one leave Béarn?

## Cheeses of Le Béarn

### Accous

**Ossau-Iraty (AOC).** Salted and matured by Les Fermiers Basco-Béarnais, 64490 Accous (tel. 59 34 76 06); agents at Rungis: DPFC, Bâtiment D4, 63, avenue d'Auvergne, 94597 Rungis. Labelled: Pyrénées Fermier de la Vallée d'Aspe or d'Ossau pur brebis 2kg and 5kg cheeses (see p. 148).
*fermier; brebis cru.*
All *fermier; vache/brebis mixte, pur chèvre, pur vache, cru.*
E. Pyrénées-Atlantiques; 85 **16**, L.

### Ance

**Fromage de Brebis de Baretous.**
*laitier; brebis cru.*
**Fromage de Vache de Baretous.** Fromagerie de Baretous (see p. 140).
*laitier; vache cru.*
E. Pyrénées-Atlantiques; 85 **5**, low R.

### Aramits

Name used on some local cheeses.
*fermier.*
E. Pyrénées-Atlantiques; 85 **5**, low R.

### Arette, Fromage d'

Golden-brown crusted, rounded sides, large.
*fermier; vache/brebis cru.*
E. Pyrénées-Atlantiques; 85 **5**, bottom.

### Arudy

Name used on some local cheeses.
*fermier.*
E. Pyrénées-Atlantiques; 85 **6**, bottom.

### L'Aspe, Vallée de

**Vallée de l'Aspe Mixte.** (See also ACCOUS.) Large, rounded sides, crust 'lacquered, not washed' russet colour, made on four or five farms.
*fermier; vache/brebis cru.*

**Vallée de l'Aspe, Pur Brebis.** (See also ACCOUS.) I have tasted excellent examples; close, firm, smooth texture, darkened at edges in maturity; rich satisfying flavour, on sweet side (see pp. 141–2).
*fermier; brebis cru.*
E. Pyrénées-Atlantiques.

### Asson

**Matocq Vallée d'Ossau.**
*artisanal; brebis cru.*
E. Pyrénées-Atlantiques; 85 **7**, bottom.

### Aysius

**Fromage de Chèvre d'Aysius.** (*sic*, on label handwritten: possibly Aydius?) Aysius is untraced. Small, like young, therefore larger *crottin* met in Tardets market (see p. 132).
*fermier; chèvre cru.*
E. Pyrénées-Atlantiques; 85 **16**, NE of Accous.

### Aste/Béon

**Ossau (AOC)/Laruns.** Local cheesemakers include MM. Joseph Trésarieu, Jean Balesta (both *palmarès* (Laureates) Laruns, 1985, see p. 147); M. Bori (see pp. 143–4) makes Brebis de Laruns.
*fermier; brebis cru.*
E. Pyrénées-Atlantiques; 85 **16**, high R.

### Baretous

See ANCE, and pp. 140–2

### Béarnais

See RÉGAL BÉARNAIS.

### Bedous

Local cheesemaking advertised N and S of Bedous.

## Béost

**Ossau (AOC)/Laruns.** M. Bernard Sallanave (Palmarès Laruns, 1985).
*fermier; brebis cru.*
E. Pyrénées-Atlantiques; 85 **16**, NE of Laruns.

## Bielle

**Fromage du Pays Pur Brebis.** Made on E side of road and sold there.
*fermier; brebis cru.*
E. Pyrénées-Atlantiques; 85 **16**, top R.

## Bilhères

**Ossau (AOC)/Laruns.** MM. Raymond Arrateig (first prize Laruns, 1985) and Eugene Capdaspes (fourth prize) (see pp. 143–4).
*fermier; brebis cru.*
E. Pyrénées-Atlantiques; 85 **16**, top R.

## Gabas/Ossau type

Name sometimes used for local summer cheeses. Probably now sold as Ossau-Iraty AOC.
*fermier; cuyala; brebis cru.*

**Gabas Chèvre-Brebis Mixte.** Found by Viard locally; smaller cheese than Ossau. Cheeses of this type are *affinés* at Accous (see p. 146).
*fermier; brebis/chèvre cru.*
E. Pyrénées-Atlantiques; 85 **16**, C, S of Laruns.

## Gère

**Ossau (AOC)/Laruns.** M. Bonnemason (fifth prize Laruns, 1985).
*fermier; brebis cru.*

## Jonchée

As for Pays Basque, see p. 137.

**Fleuron des Côteaux.** Low-fat, open-textured, soft, white-coated, mild, 'stabilised'.
*20% m.g.; laitier; industriel; vache pasteurisé.*

## Jurançon

**Boule de Béarn or Doux de Montagne.** Large rounded shiny brown *tomme*, very mild, semi-soft *pâte* with many apertures. Invented at the above Fromagerie in 1974, now made at Beauzac in Velay.
*industriel; vache pasteurisé.*
E. Pyrénées-Atlantiques; 85 **6**, middle R, SW of Pau.

**Saint-Albray.** 1.8kg soft, rounded segments with hole in centre of cheese; crust rubbed with *rocou*; then acquires white mould (see p. 145). Invented here 1976; Fromagerie des Chaumes, RN134, E side, S of town. Other *chaumes* cheeses sold, but *laiterie* not visitable.
*50% m.g.; laitier; industriel; vache pasteurisé.*
E. Pyrénées-Atlantiques; 85 **6**, middle R, SW of Pau.

## Laruns

Name seen on many labels of local Vallée d'Ossau *cru* cheeses, brebis, vache and mixed. Marketing centre, with annual Foire du Fromage, first Saturday October. *Crémerie, Épicerie* in square. 'Fromage du Pays – Sandwichs' on N edge of town (see p. 143). Cheesemakers in commune include: MM. Etienne Géraut (second prize, 1985); Joël Cardet (third prize); J.-P. Haget and François Carrès (both *palmarès*).
*fermier; all types.*
E. Pyrénées-Atlantiques; 85 **16**.

## Lescun

**Le Palangué.** Name used on cheeses ripened by M. G. Asserguet, *affineur*, route du Col de Pau, Lescun, 64990 Bedous (tel. 59 34 78 37).
*fermier; brebis mixte, vache cru.*
E. Pyrénées-Atlantiques; 85 **15**, C R.

## Louvie-Juzon

**Fromage du Pays.** Advertised as for sale.
E. Pyrénées-Atlantiques; 85 **16**, top.

## Lys

**Brebis Fermier – Ossau (AOC).** M. Esturonnc and M. Ferdinand Pujalet make excellent cheeses (see p. 143).
*fermier; brebis cru.*
E. Pyrénées-Atlantiques; 85 **6/7**, N of Arudy on D287.

## Matocq

See asson.

## Monplaisir

**Ossau-Iraty (AOC).** *Fromagerie* gives *dégustation*; cheeses served at Auberge de Monplaisir.
*fermier; brebis cru.*
E. Pyrénées-Atlantiques; 85 **16**, N of Laruns.

## Nay

**Fromage de Vache.** 2½ kg; rounded, neat form; shiny golden crust; pale gold interior, slightly fissured, succulent; on sale at Crémerie St-Pé (see below).

## Oloron-Ste-Marie

Friday market.

**Oloron-Sainte-Marie.** Sometimes seen on local cheeses, including chèvres.
*various, lait cru.*
E. Pyrénées-Atlantiques; 85 **6**, low L.

## Ossau, Vallée d'

**Ossau-Iraty (AOC).** See p. 137.
*fermier; artisanal; cuyala; brebis cru.*

## Le Palangué

See LESCUN.

## Pau

Monday to Saturday market, Wednesday and Friday better.
Gabriel Bachelet, *fromager, affineur,* rue Joffre.

**Régal Béarnais.** 400g crust with golden-brown flecks; drum-shaped; 250g *frais,* yellowing exterior; flat disc. Sold in Tardets market in Soule (see p. 138).
*artisanal; vache cru.*

## Roquefort

Béarn is legally within the Roquefort region, but no longer makes it (see p. 137).
*laitier; brebis cru.*

## St-Pé

*Crémerie* opposite church sells good Béarnais cheeses (see p. 145).
On Bigorre side of Béarn border.

# Central Pyrenees (Gascogne)

Gascogne was part of Roman Aquitaine, afterwards conquered by the Visigoths. It became a duché in AD 602 and was reunited to Aquitaine in 1036 through the marriage of its ducal heiress with the duc d'Aquitaine. Their descendant, Aliénor (the English Queen Eleanor), brought it to the English crown, from 1154 until 1453. It was then conquered by France, where it has remained. Gascogne covers the far south-east of France below the Gironde, excluding the Pays Basque and the Béarn, down to the border with Foix and Languedoc.

In the Central Pyrenees, east of Béarn, four old Gascon *pays* line up at the frontier, all twice as long as they are wide. The *département* of Hautes-Pyrénées harbours Bigorre and Haut-Armagnac. A once-proposed Département des Pyrénées-Centrales should have mothered Comminges and the Couserans, each indisputably Gascon in tradition; but Pyrénées-Centrales never materialised, so these last two *pays* were fostered out, Comminges to the Haute-Garonne (Toulousain-Languedocien in spirit, with a Gascon tail), the Couserans to Ariège, which is dominated by Foix.

There are strong traditions of cow dairy in this region, which become more marked as we move east, where the Couserans boasts its notable Bethmale cheese. Ewes'-milk cheeses still feature as far east as Comminges, with Haut-Armagnac's Esbareich as the best-known standard-bearer; but the Couserans and Foix have almost lost the brebis for which they were renowned in Cathar times, and of which strong traces survived into the 1940s and 1950s.

Names such as Valcabrères (Valley of Goats) in Comminges remind us that goats are not new to the Central Pyrenees. They were there in Saracen times, yet Pierre Androuët could not find any in Valcabrères on his 1981 visit. The old tradition appeared to have been lost, but some goats no doubt survived, and in recent years more have started to return. As well as the spread of new farms making small soft cheeses, there are a number of farms and *laiteries* making larger chèvres and *mixtes* cheeses, outwardly similar to traditional Bethmale and Esbareich. In and around Foix, however, I found only small soft goat cheeses.

In all these *pays* there has been a reduction in farmhouse cheesemaking. The Bethmale area has abandoned the *transhumance* and lost the small co-operative village dairies, akin to the *fruitières* of Franche-Comté and Savoie (see Chapters 14 and 15). The *affineurs* and *fromagers artisanaux*, however, work hard to encourage the farms to produce good milk and to keep up cheesemaking traditions. They would like to see the sort of initiative taken here which has been so successful in Savoie in raising farmhouse and *fruitière* production: the encouragement of traditional breeds of cow; the local protection of cheese-names, in addition to the national Appellation Contrôlée; and combined information and publicity of a high standard for all the regional cheeses. It is a pity that two of the *départements* concerned, Haute-Garonne and Ariège, have centres of gravity well away from the old cheesemakers' valleys in the Pyrenees; but

Ariège is attractive to its neighbours on the Cerdagne side, *montagnards* of the Carol, who want to leave Pyrénées-Orientales to join it, so there must be some spirit there.

## *Bigorre–Armagnac*
### HAUTES-PYRÉNÉES – GERS

Bigorre and its capital, Tarbes, were known to Caesar, in whose time Tarbes was a market town and spa. The comté de Bigorre has much in common with neighbouring Béarn to the west: linguistic ties from shared Gascon roots; allegiance for centuries to the same ruling family; and eleventh-century individual and communal rights similar to those enjoyed by the Béarnais. The Bigourdans, unlike their Béarnais neighbours, were involved in the Hundred Years' War, during which they were occupied by the English from 1360 to 1406, and they suffered severely in the sixteenth-century wars of religion.

Armagnac was a Gascon comté, subject to Aquitaine after 1052. At the end of the fifteenth century Charles VII of France took it over, but François I returned it (with his daughter Marguerite in marriage) to the previous comte's nephew. The widowed Marguerite married Henri III of Foix, Béarn and Navarre, thus considerably tidying up the political shape of the Central Pyrenees. Armagnac, which retained its autonomy when Henri succeeded as Henri IV of France, was finally absorbed by the metropolitan kingdom, with Bigorre, on his death in 1607.

Armagnac consists of Bas- (or Black) Armagnac in the west, La Ténarèze in the centre, and Haut- (or White) Armagnac in the east. Bas-Armagnac, source of the brandy, is not rich in cheese, but produces some admirable small chèvres of Banon-shape. On the 1650 map the name Armaignac covers all these districts, extending south between Bigorre and Comminges beyond the *pays* called Rivière (which on that map cuts off its southern extremity) to the Spanish frontier.

Saint-Pé-de-Bigorre offers a remarkable introduction to the comté from Béarn. (I have already paid tribute to the earthy display of Béarnais cheeses in the Crémerie de Bigorre: see page 145.) In the valleys of the Ouzin and Arrens brebis are made on a number of farms around Arbéost, Ferrières and Arrens itself. This is the western Bigorre outpost of the Ossau-Iraty region, the only area outside the Pays Basque and the Béarn entitled to use that *appellation*. Bigorre has cheesemakers in other valleys, but the most familiar names of the comté are those of the main cheese markets: starting from the north, these are Maubourguet, Vic-en-Bigorre, Tarbes and Lourdes.

It is Haut-Armagnac, however, to which we turn for the most notable cheesemaking locality in this region: the Barousse.

## CHEESES OF THE BAROUSSE

As we travel eastwards out of Bigorre into Armagnac, the Gascon *gave* gives way as the word for river to *neste*, beginning with the Neste d'Aure. In this valley brebis cheeses, similar to those we shall meet and describe in the

Barousse, are found under the name of Esbareich. At the Col d'Aspin, the southernmost road crossing out of Bigorre, there is a good *fromage de chèvre*.

As the Barousse is unreachable by road from the west, we have to drive into Comminges and approach it from the south by way of Arreau, the Col de Peyresourde and Bagnères-de-Luchon. (If you choose to enter from the north you can visit the markets of Lannemezan and Montréjeau and then see Saint-Bertrand-de-Comminges on your way.) Our route, west along D618, touches some remote valleys, including the Val d'Oô. From Castillon a road leads up this valley along the Neste d'Oô to the village of Oô; thereafter becoming more of a track, it ascends to the Lac d'Oô beyond. This area helps French crossword-puzzle setters fill in awkward gaps, but I do not mention it just as a curiosity for crossword addicts: its countryside, village architecture and churches have charm and interest, on which Michelin offers some detailed guidance.

Further east, the valleys of the Pigue and the Garonne lead to the Barousse, which extends south and west from its *chef-lieu*, Mauléon-Barousse. Esbareich lies beyond Mauléon beside the eastern of the two upper courses of the Ourse, and is famous as the market source of the semi-hard brebis made in the local summer chalets. The rounded-edged crusts of these 3.5–6-kilo cheeses are washed and rubbed until smooth, and the cheeses are matured to achieve an attractive nutty flavour. Ourde, just north of Esbareich, and Sost, the next village to the south, have both boasted their own local brebis.

The Barousse is also the source of a much smaller cows'-milk cheese, which becomes hard and strong with age. Pierre Androuët says that it is made mainly for farm consumption but that surplus cheeses may be found on the markets at Lannemezan, Montréjeau and Saint-Gaudens. They are known both as Barousse, after the *pays*, and as Ramoun, the local name for this type of cheese.

We are now on the doorstep of Comminges.

## Cheeses of Bigorre–Armagnac

### Aoust

See ARGELÈS-GAZOST.

### Arbéost, Arrens

**Ossau-Iraty AOC.** Made on farms in the Vallée de l'Ouzon, eastern outpost of the AOC region.
*fermier; brebis cru.*
Bigorre/Hautes-Pyrénées; 85 **17**, NW of C.

### Argelès-Gazost

Tuesday market.

**Aoust.** Small cylindrical cheese reported by Courtine (1973) as made by *bergers* and eaten young. I have not met it.
*fermier; brebis cru.*
Bigorre/Hautes-Pyrénées; 85 **17**.

### Aspin, Col d'

**Chèvre.** Made by M. Poussin, who is also a cave explorer.
*fermier; chèvre cru.*
Bigorre-Haut-Armagnac boundary Hautes-Pyrénées; 85 **19**, L of C.

### Auch

Wednesday, Thursday, Saturday market (see MARCIAC).
Bas-Armagnac/Gers; 82 **5**.

## BAGNÈRES-DE-BIGORRE

Saturday market.
Hautes-Pyrénées; 85 **18**, high R.

## BAROUSSE, RAMOUN

Cheeses of the type Ramoun: 1800g–2kg; 18cm × 8cm; rounded sides, pressed, brushed; made in Barousse district, found in markets Lannemezan, Montréjeau, St-Gaudens (see p. 151).
40–50% m.g.; *fermier*; *cabane*; *vache cru*, or *mixte cru* (including *brebis-vache*).
Haut-Armagnac/Hautes-Pyrénées; 85 **20**, L of C.

## ESBAREICH

3.5–6kg; lightly pressed; supple *pâte* when young; washed-crust; up to 3 months' *affinage*; further aged can become sharp, and best grated. Made in and around Esbareich, in and above the two Ourse valleys; eating season April–October, but July and after for *transhumance* cheeses.
45% m.g.; *fermier*; *cabane*; *brebis cru*.
Haut-Armagnac/Hautes-Pyrénées; 85 **20**, in Barousse.

## FERRIÈRES

In Vallée de l'Ouzon (NE of Arbéost, p. 144), for Ossau-Iraty AOC.

## FONTINE FLEURANTINE

Larger version of Tomme de Lomagne (see LOMAGNE).

## FROMAGES BLANCS

See MARCIAC.

## FROMAGEON

See GASCON.

## GASCON, LE

Smaller version of Tomme de Lomagne (see LOMAGNE).

## GASCON

**Fromageon Gascon.** *Fromage frais* drained of whey, unsalted; add a little sugar or Armagnac, whipped; 1–2 hours; serve on chestnut leaf with fruit.
*fermier*; *domestique*; *vache/chèvre*.

## GIMONT

Wednesday market.
**Fromage de Brebis.** Local cheese served at Château de Larroque on N124, recommended by Éperon.
*fermier*; *brebis cru*.
Bas-Armagnac/Gers; 82 **6**.

## LANNEMEZAN

For local cheeses. Christian Casteran (Ramoun *fermier* since 1789; see BAROUSE).
Haut-Armagnac/Hautes-Pyrénées; 85 **9**, low R.

## LOMAGNE

**Tomme de Lomagne.** Semi-soft, pressed; light crust, milky-white; mild, pleasant (Ninette Lyon in *Marabout*, 1978); the larger size, fuller than Tomme de Savoie, is called: Fontine Fleurantine; the smaller tubby, round size is called: Le Gascon.
*laitier*; *vache*.
Bas-Armagnac/Gers, and Languedoc/Tarn-et-Garonne.

## LOURDES

For regional and local cheeses.
Bigorre/Hautes-Pyrénées; 85 **8/18**.

## MARCIAC

**Fromages, Fromages Blancs.** On sale daily with butter and vegetables, at GFA Le Béret, Louis Litges, near Marciac (tel. 62 64 91 59) and in markets: Monday Mirande, Thursday and Saturday Auch.
*fermier*; *biologique*; *Nature & Progrès*; *vache cru*.
Bigorre/Hautes-Pyrénées; 85, **8**, top R.

## MAUBOURGUET

Tuesday market.
As for Lourdes.

## MIÉLAN

Thursday market.
**Fromage de Chèvre.** Philippe Aladenise, Méliet, Laas (tel. 62 67 57 96) cheese, garlic, honey.
*fermier*; *biologique*; *Nature & Progrès*; *chèvre cru*.
Rivière/Gers; 85 **9**, high C.

## MIRANDE

Monday market (see MARCIAC); attractive *bastide* town.
Rivière/Gers; 85 **9**, top R.

## MONDEBAT AND GAEC D'ARLENS

See PLAISANCE.

### Ourde

*fermier; cabane; brebis cru.*
See ESBAREICH, for type.
Haut-Armagnac/Hautes-Pyrénées; 85 **20**, N of Esbareich.

### Plaisance

Thursday market. Foire aux Fromages de chèvre: 14 July.
**Fromage de Chèvre Gaec d'Arlens.** *Banon*-shape; pepper, herb, plain; latter tasted when crust pinky and melting, and interior rich and sweet.
*artisanal; biologique; chèvre cru.*
**Le Mondebat.** Plain; thicker than above, but less rich; made by Gaec d'Arlens.
*artisanal; biologique; vache cru.*
Bas-Armagnac/Gers; 82 **3**.

### Pondenas

**La Belle Gasconne.** Rich chèvre with Armagnac, now rare; Pondenas (on label) is mis-spelling of POUDENAS, where cheese is made, and marinated in Armagnac by Mme Gracia, whose restaurant it is named after.
*fermier; chèvre cru.*
Bas-Armagnac/Gers.

### Ramoun

See BAROUSSE.

### St-Pé-de-Bigorre

Wednesday market.
Crémerie de Bigorre opposite church has fine range of traditional local cheeses.
Bigorre/Hautes-Pyrénées; 85 **7/17**, on D937.

### Seissan

**Fromage de Vache.** Made by Jean-Jacques Delmas who sells cheese, lambs and cereals at La Favorite, Tachoires, 32360 Seissan (tel. 62 66 22 76) and Toulouse market Tuesday and Saturday a.m.
*fermier; biologique; vache cru.*
Bas-Armagnac/Gers.

### Sost

See ESBAREICH, for type; RAMOUN aged here.
*fermier; cabane; brebis cru.*
Haut-Armagnac/Hautes-Pyrénées; 85 **20**, S of Esbareich.

### Tachoires

See SEISSAN.

### Tarbes

Thursday market.
For local cheeses in shops and markets.
Bigorre/Hautes-Pyrénées; 85 **8**, capital of Bigorre.

### Vic-en-Bigorre

See TARBES above.
Hautes-Pyrénées; 85 **8**, C.

# *Comminges*
## HAUTE-GARONNE

The ancient comté de Comminges, together with Verdun to the north and the Couserans to the east, formed part of the Gascon complex which joined Aquitaine in 1052. They lie between Bigorre and Foix, long ruled by the same powerful family, and there were even Foix enclaves within their boundaries. (One such was the Nébouzan, centred on Saint-Gaudens, where you may now find local cheeses.) It was at the end of the Hundred Years' War that Comminges became part of France, with Muret as its capital and the seat of the *États* of the comté.

We have already met the famous brebis called Esbareich made close to Comminges. For centuries Cierp, south of Luchon, produced similar cheese. For years now it has been made of cows' milk, but cheeses similar to Esbareich are still said to be made in the high valleys of the Luchon and the Garonne, which I have not yet penetrated.

The boundary between Comminges and the Couserans was not defined by the King's Geographer on his 1650s' map, but I take it as running approximately along the present departmental boundary between Haute-Garonne and Ariège. The Couserans belonged to the comte de Toulouse up to the time of the Albigensian crusades. The two *pays* have tended to be territorially amalgamated under Comminges by modern writers, but the Couserans deserves better, as I will show.

## CHEESES OF COMMINGES

### BAGNÈRES-DE-LUCHON
Shop and market sources of regional cheeses.
Haute-Garonne; 86 **1**, bottom.

CIERP. Local brebis formerly for local consumption; often aged to great hardness and strength. *May* survive but not seen by me.
*fermier; brebis cru.*

**Cierp de Luchon.** Cows'-milk cheeses, semi-hard, small apertures; can be aged like old brebis above.
*fermier; artisanal; vache cru.*
Haute-Garonne; 86 **1**, SW of C.

### FROMAGE DE CHÈVRE, FROMAGE DE VACHE
Jean-Frédéric and Ursula Ducoteau (tel. 61 90 95 68) at Sarracatieux, Cazeneuve-Montaut.
*fermier; biologique; Nature & Progrès; chèvre/vache cru.*
Haute-Garonne; 82 **15**, bottom, 86 **2**, top L.

### MONTRÉJEAU
Monday market. Shop and market sources of regional cheeses.
Haute-Garonne; 86 **1**, high L.

### MONTESQUIEU-VOLVESTRE
Tuesday market.

**Fromage de Brebis.** Thought by Jean Faup of St-Girons in 1985 to be last surviving brebis *fermier* of the region but see Engomer and Caumont (both p. 162) for brebis laitier.
*fermier; biologique; brebis cru.*
Haute-Garonne; 82 **17**.

### ST-GAUDENS
Thursday market.
Shop and market sources of regional cheeses.
Haute-Garonne; 86 **1**, high R.

### TOULOUSE
Tuesday to Sunday market (Friday best).

# Le Couserans
## ARIÈGE

The eighteen valleys of the Couserans feeding the River Salat have a distinctive character of their own, apparent as soon as you talk to those who live and work there. Saint-Girons is the capital, not nearby Saint-Lizier, the old episcopal see. The soft green valleys interlacing the severe mountains have been rich in milk and cheese for centuries, but at the expense of human toil for too little reward. This is why there are now only 300 inhabitants in the most notable valley of them all, Bethmale.

## BETHMALE

As a base for our explorations we were attracted to Oust not just because of its association with local traditional cheese (and with a now extinct soft cheese of Camembert type) but also because of its architectural charm. Oust presents to the road a lofty bell-tower in the form of a simple, thick wall adorned by an over-hanging roofed balcony below the bell apertures. (This is almost duplicated across the road by the church of Vic d'Oust.) These distinctive bell-towers are called *clochers-murs toulousains*.

We settled at the Hôtel de la Poste, where the host is the fourth generation of the Andrieu family to run the hotel. As I expected, he knew his cheese, and encouraged me with introductions to three notable cheesemakers in the Couserans.

I turned first to Mademoiselle Sylvie Domenc at Castillon-en-Couserans, which guards the approach to the Vallée de Bethmale. There I found myself in the typical French situation of being in a *pays* within a *pays*. The people of this valley are a race apart, renowned for their splendid bearing and for a form of traditional dress more reminiscent in its details, down to the upturned, curling toes of the footwear, of the Balkans than of the Pyrenees. The local cheese claims the generic name of the village and valley of Bethmale, where it is made and sold by Monsieur Caux and a number of farms, and where Sylvie Domenc has a second outlet for her own cheese. Most of the cheesemakers in the other valleys use their village names for their cheeses, or the name of some nearby feature in the landscape.

Mention of Bethmale cheese goes back to the early twelfth century, when some was given to Louis VI of France during his visit to the *pays*. In the thirteenth century it was described as 'the fat cheese of Saint-Girons'. Its interior still glows with fatness when it is cut, however old the cheese, and is also striking for its multitude of tiny horizontal slits. Until the twentieth century it was made exclusively of ewes' milk; but cows, although comparatively recently introduced, have now almost entirely ousted ewes. Otherwise the methods of making, similar to those of the Basques, have passed down unchanged on farms and in the families of *laitiers* such as Sylvie Domenc, and Monsieur Caux of Bethmale itself. They are described by Sylvie Domenc as *'héritiers des traditions'*. On the hundred or so farms which were milking for cheesemaking in 1985, four out of five still milked by hand.

The golden-coated, open-textured cheeses are usually described as semi-hard. When aged some of them are indeed that, even very hard (and strong too); but I love best Bethmale in which succulence suggests youthfulness, while richness of savour shows maturity. Such a happy balance is achieved through a good, unbroken crust and an aerated interior. This allows the cheese to mature for many months and still emerge in a state better described as semi-soft than as semi-hard. An effective crust need not look neat, provided it is not cracked. I have seen some rough-looking coats still strong enough to protect their cheeses into melt-in-the-mouth maturity.

Sylvie Domenc is the fourth generation of her family to make Bethmale in Castillon. Her 'representative of the Bethmale family', as she calls it, is named *é Bamalou* (*é* is Gascon for 'the'). Her dairy collects 1500 litres a day, all used whole and raw. It comes from twenty-five farms milking Grises or Brunes Suisses, Hollandaises and a few surviving dairy Grises gasconnes. Despite new machinery, the methods are artisanal rather than factory. The result, after the minimum two months' ripening, is a natural pale-golden-crusted wheel of 50 per cent *matières grasses* weighing about 5 kilos. It is still refreshing and mild on first tasting, but already hints at the richer rewards of longer keeping which I have described above.

The *transhumance* survived in the Couserans into the 1970s. In 1974 my son Hugh found a number of *bergers* making their cheeses in *cuyalas* south-west of Castillon, between Seintein and the Étang d'Araing, and had the impression that there were two larger *cuyalas* where cheeses were collected. Sadly, so much of the younger family labour has deserted the farms that it has become uneconomic to keep up the *transhumance*. Farmers could not afford to hire outside workers to take the herds up into the mountains, look after them for the summer and make cheese up there. Eighty per cent of the local Grises gasconnes and Blondes d'Aquitaine are now beef cattle.

The traditional village co-operative dairies have also disappeared, unlike their prospering equivalents, the *fruitières* of Franche-Comté and Savoie (see Chapters 14 and 15). Most former members who have not gone over to beef now sell their milk to *laiteries* the size of Sylvie Domenc's or larger, which now make more cheese than the remaining farms. It is all *lait cru*, and the differences in tradition between one valley and the next, and in house style between the *laiteries*, continue to enrich the repertoire of the Couserans.

East of Comminges along Route Nationale 618 most villages have a dairy. At Saint-Lary, Alain and Gilberte Estarque name their *fromage de montagne* 'Le Pic de la Calabasse', after the 7000-foot peak at the head of their Vallée de la Bouigane. Alain Estarque took over the dairy from his father and made it into a *fromagerie* in 1960, after learning his trade from Monsieur Caux at Bethmale. He is not anxious to expand beyond his present capacity, being convinced that the maxim 'the smaller the better' is right for the real cheese world. I tasted one of their cheeses with a gloriously melting *pâte*, full flavoured and refreshingly unsalty, the softest I met in the Couserans.

The daily 1200 litres of milk comes from twenty farms in nine nearby villages and hamlets. More farms are lining up, so future supplies are assured. The milk is brought up to 30°C, renneted, and left for forty-five minutes before being mechanically stirred for ten minutes. The whey is then drained off, and the curd is hand-cut inside the copper vat while the whey is being put through the separator. The cut curd is carried in turn to each of the wooden hoops (lined with thick cloth and adjustable in size) which mould the cheese, and the first pressure is applied by hand. By the time the vat is empty of curd the earliest cheeses are ready to be turned for the first time, after which they are covered with a thick plank to expel more whey. In the evening the cloths are removed. The next day the cheeses will be salted on one side, the following day on the other. On the third day they go into the *caves* for at least four weeks, during which they are regularly brine washed. The finished cheese weighs about 3.7 kilos. Its grey-and-fawn crust can be almost Camembert-like in texture, its softness allowing the cheese to swell and round out its form. The cheeses are distributed in the Montréjeau district, Toulouse ('a little'), Muret and the Saint-Girons area.

At Engomer La Fromagerie du Moulin makes l'Estive in the local Bethmale style, and Jimmy Schubert makes an organic *fromage de brebis* (unluckily I heard about this rarity only after I had left the Pyrenees). In the next village, Luzenac, there is another *laiterie*; then at Moulis, Messieurs Guy Pujol and P. Coudray make Le Moulis, '*Fromage artisanal des Pyrénées ariégoises*'. The cheese I bought was younger and more upstanding than my Pic de la Calabasse from Saint-Lary. Its very pale golden-brown exterior retained marks of the cheesecloth, suggesting less rubbing of the crust. Inside the open texture was pleasantly refreshing on the tongue and melted in our mouths. It promised more tang with another month's keeping, but we enjoyed it as it was.

Le Rogallais is made by the *fromagerie artisanale* at Coumes, near Seix. Ours had a pink to rosy-gold crust, and the more rounded shape of our Saint-Lary cheese, which it also resembled in flavour, although it was slightly milder. Ercé and Aulus (with the tradition of a smaller cheese) in the Vallée du Garbet, and Ustou, Sérac and Saint-Lizier in the Vallée d'Ustou, all to the south-east of Oust and Seix, have old associations with the Bethmale tradition.

In addition, the *communes* of Oust and Seix harbour at least three *chevriers*. One makes Le P'tit Lisou, a pleasant, unsalty cheese, the size of Saint-Marcellin (see Chapter 6) but sharper in profile. It is usually available in *frais* or *demi-sec* state at the *crémerie* in Saint-Girons. A large chèvre Fermier des Pyrénées is made on the farm GIE Capriseix near Oust. It has a pinky-gold crust, and a *pâte* with apertures smaller and less numerous than those of Bethmale. The third goat farm near Seix is La Société Civile d'Exploitation de Saliens, where goats are raised and goat cheese is made on organic principles, under 'Nature & Progrès' tutelage.

## Cheeses of the Saint-Lizier–Saint-Girons area

In the rounded, wooded foothills of the Couserans the cows on the roadside, sometimes unconfined, are friendly reminders of the purpose behind our travels. They keep company with numerous black horses, and bays of the local Mérens breed. We were bound for Saint-Girons, where two notable *fromageries artisanales* were making unpasteurised cheeses from local farm milk, and the black *fromage des Pyrénées* from regional milk bought in bulk from further afield. Didier Lemasson's version of the latter is Montségur, very popular in the west of France, and the best in the market in my opinion. He is also the source of an admirable golden-crusted raw-milk brebis called Saint-Girons; but his *fromagerie* will have moved from Saint-Girons to larger, more modern premises in Caumont (north-west of Saint-Girons) by the time this book appears.

Jean Faup calls his version of the black cheese 'La Montagne Ariègeoise', but he told me about his more strictly traditional cheeses first, with a background of local dairy history. His great-grandfather made cheese at Saint-Girons before 1914. Around 1960 the family was making a Camembert type (like the one being made at Oust at the time, sold under that name). Jean took over the business in 1977 and turned to more traditional lines. He was particularly attracted by Les Orrhys (thus on the map, but sometimes spelt Horys). This cheese was still being made and matured in *cabanes* of stone, which he described as being 'like igloos'. They had originally been built as *bergeries* for sheep and shepherds to use during the *transhumance* on the high pastures of Orrhys de Carla and Orrhys de la Grouz, between Vicdessos and the north-western corner of Andorra. Despite the original purpose of the *cabanes*, Jean Faup insists that the cheese known as Les Orrhys had always been a cows'-milk cheese. Most of the herds up there while the *transhumance* was still practised came from the Saint-Girons district, especially from Oust and Seix, so one would expect a softer, richer version of the Bethmale type. It was, indeed, a golden-crusted, open-textured, unctuous mountain cheese, weighing 5–6 kilos. Latterly, the name Les Orrhys had not been restricted to cheeses made in that remote area of origin, but the most treasured always came from there, for good reason. They were rich in the savour and aroma of *mélisse* (balm), which abounds in those high *alpages*. *Mélisse* is Greek for bee, and the plant is called '*le piment des abeilles*', reputed for its digestive virtues and as a remedy for vertigo and fainting fits. These health-giving cheeses used to be brought down at the end of the *transhumance* and sold at the annual fair at Oust on 24 September.

By 1970 the *transhumance* had all but died out here and the cheese was thought to be extinct; but to Jean Faup's knowledge three or four farmers were still making Les Orrhys in the early 1980s. Now he and the regional agricultural authorities think that none survives. Jean Faup used a 'Les Orrhys' label for a time on cheeses of his own made to the recipe a few years ago. Then he used the basic formula for his originally brown-coated La

Montagne Ariègeoise, which has since followed the black-coat fashion, and to which I shall return.

Jean Faup's success in Saint-Girons has necessitated his investment in larger premises just outside the town. The pride and joy of his stable is rightly his 4-kilo Montagne de Bethmale. When first made, the cheese drains for twenty-four hours in its mould and is then hand-salted and placed on fir planks in the *salle d'affinage* at 12°C. It is washed twice a week in brine for at least six weeks, acquiring a natural pale-golden coat of rustic appearance, often with superficial *craquelures* (as opposed to cracks). Some cheeses are matured for eight weeks to suit more demanding palates. The *pâte* has the typical small apertures, tiny splits rather than holes. At its best it becomes unctuous in its combination of succulence and richness. The milk (3 million litres a year) comes from 116 carefully selected local farms where improvement of quality is constantly sought, and is used raw. The cows are Brunes des Alpes, Suisses (chestnut-brown), Grises gasconnes, and Montbéliardes, which were introduced a few years ago from Franche-Comté. More of the latter would certainly strengthen the character of milk produced for cheese in the Pyrenees, where the native cattle have been bred towards beef in modern times.

Jean Faup's second cheese is Le Labrit, which means herd-dog, not just sheepdog. I use the former term advisedly. The label shows an engaging white, hairy animal, a rather bent *berger* (herdsman here, not shepherd), his *cabane*, his goats and his cows, and not a sheep in sight. Le Labrit is a *mi-chèvre* of 45 per cent *matières grasses*. It has an attractive deep, golden-brown crust with radial and circular markings from a basket-type mould, and a smooth *pâte* with very small apertures. It has a smokey look, but is not a smoked cheese. Those I have tasted were of pleasing texture, but so mild that I would recommend at least another month of *affinage*.

Jean Faup's third cheese is the 4-kilo black, La Montagne Ariègeoise. This is his version of the Pyrenean (often pseudo-Pyrenean) cheese most familiar to the outside world in the form of a large, slightly flattened, shiny black ball. His making is based on his Les Orrhys formula, with its semi-soft open texture, and the cheese was at first brown crusted. Now all his follow the black-coated fashion. For this cheese he uses milk brought in from more distant Ariègeois farms, which he feels bound to pasteurise. The cheese caters for a wider, much less select market than his Bethmale type and his Labrit. His Montagne Ariègeoise fills a sixth of the total market for the black *fromage des Pyrénées*. This type of cheese claims traditional farm origins, but is generally a mere travesty of the Bethmale types common in the 1960s and still made on a number of farms. The milk is usually transported from a distance and pasteurised, and the cheeses are more open textured (without being succulent), bulkier, and have firmer crusts with black plastic coating.

A few of these modern *fromages des Pyrénées* are well-enough made to be treated as a different kind of cheese. If the best of them are given time to mature they can even become tasty and attractive. The raw-milk El

Torreros from further east and Montségur (made in plain or peppered form by Monsieur Lemasson) are the most acceptable of this class of cheese, followed by Jean Faup's Montagne Ariègeoise. Most cheeses sold as *fromages des Pyrénées* today are insipid creatures of poor consistency and revolting plastic surface, further from their claimed originals than almost any other French industrial cheeses I have met. Some are made so far away that to associate them with the Pyrenees is risible. The red label some are allowed to carry is meaningless, so far as discriminating cheese standards go. It means only that the milk and cheese come from the defined Pyrenean region of origin, and it would be equally appropriate and give more satisfaction to apply it to local soap.

The origins of black coats are various. One, still an active practice, though rare, is the resting and frequent turning of newly made cheeses on slate. Another, learned from shepherds in *cabanes* by Jean Faup's uncle, was the drying of new cheeses for three or four days in front of the fire. Some brown coats came from *brou de noix*, extracted from walnut shells at the green stage. *Terre de Sienne* (burnt Sienna) was also used up to ten or fifteen years ago. Black paraffin wax is a harmless coat which has long been used in England. Cheese surfaces in some regions benefited from mixtures of grape pressings, olive oil and, sometimes, good plain earth, which gave a sound natural protection during *affinage*, and did no harm to the stomach if some of it slipped down with the cheeses (though now one should be nervous of *Listeria* contamination). I dread to think of the black, glutinous twist in our guts if we swallowed the modern factory 'crust'. Its application reminds me of road-tarring by machine, but I prefer the smell of tar, and its look.

So my advice is to be selective and, as ever, taste before buying. El Torrero and Montségur stand out; Jean Faup's Ariègeoise, claiming only three weeks of ripening, is better than the rest of the field, but cheese shops, or better, cheesemakers, should hold it back for longer. It is time that the genuine native cheeses of the region, brown coated and rich, were properly protected, more widely distributed, and that we saw a revival of farmhouse cheeses. Above all we need those of the *transhumance*, especially in the Castillonnais and the *alpages* of Les Orrhys. Such cheeses would earn their keep.

## Brebis

From earliest times sheep have been milked for cheesemaking in the Couserans, but few are milked today, as we have seen in the case of Bethmale (see page 156). *Bergers*, relatives of Jean Faup, have told him that brebis and mixed brebis–vache cheeses were made here until the 1940s or 1950s, by methods similar to those used by the Basques. One farm at Engomer, Les Eygoutos, is making a brebis to be found in Saint-Girons market on Saturdays. Otherwise the nearest brebis *fermier* Jean Faup knows of is made near Montesquieu-Volvestre in the part of Comminges north of the Couserans. A few herds are milked for the brebis Saint-Girons *artisanal* already mentioned. Monsieur Pujol, the regional expert, thinks there are just one or two newcomers with perhaps twenty ewes making brebis now in the Couserans.

Apart from its almost abandoned sheep dairy, the Couserans shows a determination to keep cheese traditions alive and prospering. Few other areas of France outside the Saint-Nectaire region (see Chapter 7) can show such a concentration of producers loyal to ancient methods and standards, and unwilling to compromise them by pasteurising their milk. These *laiteries* produce about 350 tonnes of raw-milk cheese a year. There is another layer of more industrial-type production on top of this, catering mainly for a different market and not competing with the venerable Bethmale. What is more, it helps to keep more dairy farms alive, gives employment in the *laiterie*, and still produces cheese more worthy of the name than many factories away from the Pyrenees. Monsieur Pujol considers that the scale and equipment of production in the new establishments of Messieurs Faup and Lemasson have taken them out of the artisanal class of the smaller village dairies; but they still make some 350 tonnes of raw-milk cheeses a year, well worth eating when adequately matured.

We left the Couserans for Foix by way of Massat, with its striking octagonal church tower. There are a number of this style of *clocher* in the region, but the vast buttresses debouching at each corner from high up on the Massat tower gave it a monumental aspect I had never seen before. It left with us a memorable parting impression of the Couserans.

## Cheeses of Le Couserans

### Aulus
Like small Bethmale (see below). Courtine has brebis under this name, too, 'mostly eaten locally' (1973), but my informants doubted its survival.
*fermier; vache/brebis cru.*
Ariège; 86 **3/4**, bottom.

### Auzat
Local Bethmale type, perhaps closer to Les Orrhys (see p. 162).
*fermier; vache cru.*
Ariège; 86 **14**, top L.

### Bamalou
See below.

### Bethmale, Cau Bitalys
Also seen as Cau Vitalys.
M. Caux's cheese, see pp. 155–6.
*artisanal; vache cru.*
Ariège; 86 **2**, lower far R.

### Bethmale, Vallée de
**é Bamalou.** 5-kg cheese in old Bethmale tradition, made by Mlle Sylvie Domenc at Castillan-en-Couserans (see pp. 155–6). Also on sale at Bethmale.
*artisanal; vache cru.*
Ariège; 86 **2**, low R.

### Bethmale Fermier, Montagne de Bethmale Laitier.
See pp. 155–7. *Fromage laitier* made by Jean Faup, St-Girons (see pp. 158–60).
*fermier; laitier; vache cru.*
Ariège; 86 **2/3**, low.

### Samortein.
Irregular rounded drum, 500g pinkish coat with some white; semi-soft yellow *pâte*, tiny apertures, named after village adjoining Bethmale on NW.
*artisanal; vache cru.*
Ariège; 86 **2/3**, low.

### Bielle
See ustou, val d'.

### Bitalys
See bethmale.

### Brebis .
See aulus, caumont, engomer fromatjous, labrit (St-Girons, *mi-chèvre*), oust, saliens, seix.

### Cabécou
See saliens.

### Calabosse, Pic de la
See st-lary.

CASTILLON-EN-COUSERANS
See É BAMALOU.

CAU BITALYS, VITALYS
See BETHMALE.

CAUMONT
**Le Saint-Girons.** Large, brown-crusted, good close texture and flavour, made by Lemasson, see p. 158 and below.
*laitier; brebis cru.*
**Tomme de Montagne, Montségur.** Plain or with black pepper. Montségur is a 4-kg, black crusted, open-textured Pyrenean; the best of its class, in my opinion. These three cheeses are made by Didier Lemasson (who was formerly in St-Girons, whence the name of his *tomme de brebis*).
50% m.g.; *laitier; vache pasteurisé.*
Ariège; 86 **2/3**, on fold, middle.

COUMES
**Le Rogallais.** Cheese of the Bethmale family, pinkish to rose-gold crust, rounded sides; full flavour, not strong when tasted. Fromagerie artisanale, Coumes 09140 Seix.
*artisanal; vache cru.*
Ariège; 86 **3**, low C.

ERCÉ
Local Bethmale type.
*fermier; vache cru.*
Ariège; 86 **3**, low R.

ENGOMER
**L'Estive.** Bethmale type made by Fromagerie du Moulin.
*artisanal; vache cru.*
**Fromage de Brebis.** Organically produced brebis by Jimmy Schubert, Las Eygoutos, Engomer, 09800 Castillon-en-Couserans; St-Girons market Saturday.
*fermier; biologique; brebis cru.*

FROMATJOUS
Viard says this name is used for small chèvres (*frais* or *secs*). Androuët cites it as a potted cheese of the Ariège (see also p. 165).
*fermier; chèvre cru.*
Ariège; 86 **2**, far R.

HORYS
See ORRHYS.

LABRIT
See ST-GIRONS.

LUZENAC
**Fromage du Pays.** Unspecified on roadside notice.
Ariège; 86 **3**, mid-left.

MONTAGNE-TRADITION
1.5kg pale-gold crusted flat *tome* with loose texture, some Gruyère-size apertures.
50% m.g.; *artisanal; vache cru.*

MONTAGNE DE BETHMALE
See BETHMALE.

MONTSÉGUR
See CAUMONT.

MOULIS
**Le Moulis, Fromage Artisanal des Pyrénées Ariègeoises.** Bethmale family; very pale golden-brown crust (on fairly young cheese) with marks of cheesecloth. Melt-in-mouth open texture, refreshing flavour, promise of later tang; MM. G. Pujol and P. Coudray (tel. 61 66 09 64).
48% m.g.; *artisanal; vache cru.*
Ariège; 86 **3**, mid-L.

LES ORRHYS OR HORYS
5–6kg *transhumance* cheese; golden-crusted, succulent; aromatic interior, particularly owed to presence of *mélisse* (balm) in pastures; (the name was used for a cheese of this type made by Jean Faup at St-Girons some years back). Probably extinct (see p. 158).
*fermier; cabane; vache cru.*
Ariège; 86 **14**, C.

OUST
Oust fair 24 September used to feature *transhumance* cheeses, including Les Orrhys (see above).
**Chèvre Fermier des Pyrénées.** Smoky-looking gold-crusted with pinkish tones. Interior like Bethmale but firmer, fuller-flavoured and more salty. GIE Capriseix à la Ferme, Oust, 09140 Seix (tel. 61 66 82 15).
*fermier; chèvre cru.*
**Oust, Oustet.** Local cheeses of Bethmale type may be so named.

**Oust.** Extinct. Soft Camembert type made (into 1960s) here and sold under this name.
*artisanal; vache cru.*
Ariège; 86 **3**, low C.

P'TIT LISOU

See SEIX.

ROGALLAIS, ROGALLE

See COUMES.

ST-GIRONS

La Crémerie de St-Girons for local cheese.

**Le Labrit.** Golden-crusted *mi-chèvre*.
*artisanal; mi-chèvre/mi-vache cru.*

**La Montagne Ariègeoise.** 2½kg, 1kg drums; 1½kg rectangular. Black-coated deep slightly convex drums; open-textured; refreshing gentle flavour.
*laitier; vache pasteurisé.*

**La Montagne de Bethmale or Le Bethmale.** See p. 161.
*artisanal; vache cru.*
These three cheeses are made by Jean Faup at St-Girons; he has moved his *fromagerie* from 22 avenue St-Lizier to the outskirts (1985/1986). He also markets: Tomme de Brebis made in Pyrénées-Atlantiques.

**Saint-Girons.** A cheese of this name is made at Caumont (see p. 162).
*artisanal; brebis cru.*
Ariège; 86 **3**.

ST-LARY

**Le Pic de La Calabasse.** Wooden-moulded Bethmale type made by Alain and Gilberte Estarque, St-Lary (tel. 61 96 70 32) (see pp. 156–7).

*artisanal; vache cru.*
Ariège; 86 **2**.

ST-LIZIER

Local Bethmale cheeses.
*fermier; vache cru.*
Ariège; 86 **3**, bottom.

**Saint-Lizier.** A pleasant Bethmale type.
*artisanal; vache cru.*
Ariège; 86 **2**.

SALIENS

**Lou Cabécou, Fromage Fines-Herbes, Tomme de Montagne.** All chèvres. *Tomme* looks similar to Bethmale, but firmer, richer and more salty. Herbs are medicinal. Société Civile d'Exploitation Agricole de Saliens (tel. 61 66 92 06). Cabécou means small chèvre in Langue d'Oc.
*fermier; biologique; Nature & Progrès; chèvre cru.*
Ariège; 82 **3**, bottom by Seix.

SAMORTEIN

See BETHMALE.

SEIX

**Le P'tit Lisou.** Shallow drum, 100g *frais*, *demi-sec*; pleasant.
NB Coumes, Oust, Saliens (see p. 162 and above) are all near Seix.
*fermier; chèvre cru.*
Ariège; 86 **3**, bottom.

SÉRAC D'USTOU, USTOU, VAL DE

**Ustou.** A few farms still making 1985.
*fermier; vache cru.*
Ariège.

VITALYS

See BETHMALE.

# Foix
## ARIÈGE

Foix and the Couserans were part of the Roman Civitas Tolosatium, later occupied by Visigoths and Franks. Within Merovingian Aquitaine Foix was an independent principality, later attached to Toulouse, then to its vassal comté Carcassonne. Foix was hived off again under a cadet of the comtale house in 1002. In 1290 the ruling comte de Foix married the heiress to the Béarn and Bigorre, and later heirs and heiresses married into Navarre and Albret. Thus all the non-Spanish *pays* in the Pyrenees, and the Landes, came under one ruling house. The outstanding comtes were Gaston Phébus, who wrote the ravishingly illustrated *Livre de la Chasse* in 1387, after a life of international soldiering (fighting for and against the English), and the 'great Henri', Henri III de Navarre, IV de France.

There is admittedly more history than cheese in this part of France, but it is attractive country to travel through. From Massat we came into Foix by route D618 towards Tarascon (far removed from the Provençal home of Tartarin). On the lower slopes I saw almost every kind of native tree and much bracken. Above them stunted pines and birches withstood the elements. Strong bay horses abounded, but I missed the sturdy local black Mérens ponies. Their mountainous area of origin, south of Ax, was famous for good brebis in Cathar times. As we came to the Col de Four, *vaches grises* grazed on the north side and goats south of the road, with some cheese in the offing. The country opened out towards the Col du Port higher up into broad moor-topped ridges. In the nearer woods cattle roamed, Blondes at first, and then Pie-rouges. From the exposed Col de Port I distinguished seven or eight successive ridges to east and west.

At Prat Communal (a significant name in terms of Pyrenean grazing privileges) a *dame artisanale* makes a cows'-milk cheese of the Bethmale family. Further on east, just about Saurat, our hearts were lifted by the sight of a pair of oxen, Gascons gris, ploughing a steep slope which no tractor could have tackled. We headed for romantic Montségur on D9, where ravens and eagles hovered, and small birds wisely could only be heard, not seen. Thence we followed D16 to the east and found a goat farm near Les Coussats. It lies south of the road, down an avenue leading to a four-storeyed ochre *colonie de vacances* with dark-red shutters. The *chèvres*, lovely *alpines*, with horses and geese for company, were pastured nearby, and a pet sheep wandered loose. The family was out, but a friend told me that their cheese was soft and on the scale of Saint-Marcellin. He insisted that we were not in Foix, but in the Pays d'Olmes. I forebore to argue, but my old maps show the latter as part of the former.

Continuing east through Fougax we found another goat-cheese maker in the Hameau de Mijanes, south of the road. This was the last sign of cheesemaking that we met in our journey all the way to Perpignan.

Looking towards Languedoc, rather than Roussillon and Cerdagne, there are scattered goat farms, usually marked on the roadside, and masses of vineyards. One of my favourite wines is Fitou, which stands up to the richest of cheese with its warmth of character and is less well known than it deserves to be.

## Cheeses of Foix

### Belcaire

*Tomme de Montagne; vache.*
Strictly, over Foix border; see Western Languedoc, p.166.

### Chèvres

1. Ferdinand Ufkes, Ferme Soulère, Sieuras, 09310 Le Fossat
*fermier; biologique: chèvre cru.*
Ariège; 82 **16/17**, bottom; 85 **3/4**, top.
2. Small soft (Saint-Marcellin size) from *chèvres alpines.*
*fermier; chèvre cru.*
E of Col de l'Alauze S of road by Colonie de Vacances; 86 **5**, low R, W of Fougax-Les-Coussats.
3. *fermier; chèvre cru.*
E of Fougax, Hameau de Mijanes; 86 **6**, low L.
4. Chèvre Tourol
Made by M. Raulet at l'Élevage de Tourol; unsalted, 50g round, to eat *sec*, or wrap in herbs or serve in *brochettes*, which treatments are called: Tourolades, Touroules, or Tourouillettes.
Ninette Lyon (*Marabout*, 1978) recommends wrapping these cheeses in smoked flank of bacon and alternating them on the *brochette* with peppers and tomatoes or pimentos over the heat.
*fermier, chèvre cru.*
Bonnac-par-Escosse; Ariège; 86 **4**, top R.

**Caillé de Chèvre.** Whipped with sugar, or with salt, pepper and spring onions, of Pamiers origin (*Marabout*, 1978).
Ariège; 86 **4/5**.

### Foix

Wednesday and Friday market.
L; 86 **4/5**.

### Fromatjous

Small chèvres *secs* or *frais* reported by Viard in Ariège (1980).
*fermier; chèvre cru.*

### Lavelanet

Wednesday and Friday market.
Ariège; 86 **4/5**.

### Tourol, Tourolades, Tourouillettes

See chèvres, no. 4.

# Western Languedoc
## AUDE – HÉRAULT – TARN

Languedoc is the western half of the Gallic province called La Narbonnaise, set up by Rome in 118 BC, which included the large Civitas Tolosatium, forerunner of the great comté de Toulouse. When the Romans withdrew, Visigoths and Franks took turns in occupying the country before it was conquered as far east as Carcassonne by the Saracens. In the mid-eighth century it became part of Aquitaine, but in the feudal era reverted to the name of Toulouse, a comté embracing the duché de Narbonne, and larger than many a kingdom, ruled by a succession of Raymonds. Excluding Roussillon and Cerdagne, it covered all southern France east of Gascony to the Rhône. Agriculture was based on crop rotation. Laws were codified in the popular language, the *langue d'Oc*, in which literature bloomed from the eleventh century onwards and gave birth, with aristocratic encouragement, to the troubadours.

Religious heresies led to the miseries of the Albigensian crusade and brought the comté to the French crown in 1271 (the last heiress having married the King's brother). Lay customs, privileges and language were scarcely interfered with under the Ancien Régime; but republican suppression of the *langue d'Oc* was sadly too recently repealed for effective revival of a language which the first literary society in Europe was founded in Toulouse in 1323 to uphold.

I am omitting northern and eastern Languedoc from this chapter: Gévaudan (Lozère) is dealt with alongside Auvergne, with which its ancient cheese traditions are interlaced (see Chapter 7); and the Gard has so many links with Provence that I have treated them together (see Chapter 18). This leaves upland Tarn, Haute-Garonne, Fenouillèdes in the northern Pyrénées-Orientales, and the mountain-cum-coastal *départements* of Aude and Hérault, where wine and seafood are more prominent than cheese.

Nevertheless, there are excellent cheeses to be found, mainly chèvres, a number of which I have traced and list. Travellers will hit on many more during their mountain meanderings. Along these twisting roads with their breathtaking views and gradients a leisurely pace is advisable to ensure that you drive safely without missing scenery or a half-hidden cheese.

## Cheeses of Western Languedoc

### Albi
Markets on Saturdays and second and fourth Tuesdays of month.

### Belcaire, Tomme de Montagne
vache.
Aude; 86 **6**, low L (near Prades and Montaillou).

### Capritarn
200g, soft; made in Tarn, distributed by Ulpac of Toulouse.
45% m.g.; *laitier*; chèvre pasteurisé.
Tarn; 82 **10**.

### Castres
Market Monday (cattle), Thursday and Saturday.
Tarn; 83 **1**.

## Carcassonne

Daily market; shop: À la Bonne Cavée, Halles centrales, 51 rue Aimé Ramon (M. René Bousquet).
Aude; 83 **11**.

### Chèvres

1. Helen van Sweevelt, Domaine du Roulat, St-Benoît, 11230 Chalabre.
*fermier; biologique; chèvre cru.*
Aude; 86 **6**, C.
2. *Chevrière* (small stone farmhouse) with Alpines close to W side of A9, less than 1km on foot N from Shell petrol station (about 12km N of Salses, N of Leucate exit).
*fermier; chèvre cru.*
Corbières, Aude; 86 **9/10**, N of Leucate exit A9.
3. Farm at Labé-St-Étienne.
4. M. H. Postole, Mas de Clergue, opposite Prieuré St-Michel-de-Grandmont on D153 (8km); (tel. 67 44 19 58).
45% m.g.; *fermier; chèvre cru.*
Hérault; 83 **5**, NE of Lodève.
5. Montagnac has Friday market.
45% m.g.; *fermier; chèvre cru.*
Hérault; 83 **16**, Montagnac, 50m S off road to Mèze, E up farm track.
6. Eric Combes, Mas Rolland.
*fermier; biologique; chèvre cru.*
Hérault; 83 **5**, bottom L, Montesquieu.
7. Jean-Pierre and Nelly Boyer, En-Coulon-Fiac, 81500 Lavaur (tel. 63 41 31 94); wholesale, retail daily and at Lavaur market (Sat).
*fermier; biologique; Nature & Progrès.*
Tarn; 82 **9**.

**Fontjoncouse.** 70–100g drum, 5–6cm × 2–3cm deep; soft; natural crust; ripened 1–2 weeks; eaten *frais* or *demi-sec*; nutty flavour; spring and summer cheese.
45% m.g.; *fermier; chèvre cru.*
Corbières area; Aude.

**La Rove des Garrigues.** 100g; of Saint-Marcellin aspect; velvety-smooth ochre surface; close-textured; *pâte*: sweet, ripening to rich; keeps well; for Rove breed of goats, see p. 467; by Compagnons Bergers de Languedoc (tel. 67 96 13 98).
*fermier; chalet; chèvre cru de transhumance.*
Hérault; 83 **5**, lower R, SW of Clermont-l'Hérault.

**Tomme de Chèvre.** Chantal and Dragan Teotski, La Ginestarié, St-Antonin-de-Lacalm (tel. 63 45 53 48).
*fermier; biologique; Nature & Progrès; chèvre cru.*
Tarn; 83 **1**, R of C.

### Fromage Frais

Gérard Moreau, Le Carla, Rennes-Le-Château.
*fermier; biologique; Nature & Progrès; vache cru.*
Aude; 86 **7**, S of C, S of Couiza.

### Ganges

Market Tuesday and Friday.

**Ganges.** Pélardon-type cheese with rosemary, *sarriette* and marjoram found soaked in oil at St-Martin-de-Londres by Ninette Lyon (1978) and by Viard (1980) at Montpellier.
*fermier; chèvre cru.*
Hérault; 80 **16**.

### Hérault

See Chapter 6 for Bleu des Causses and Roquefort.

### Lavaur

Saturday market. Inhabitants are Vauréens (not *vauriens*, so watch pronunciation).
Tarn; 82 **9**.

### Maigrelet

2–5kg unsalted *tome* by Fabre Frères.
*laitier; vache pasteurisé.*
Viane; Tarn.

### Mazamet

**Petits Suisses.** For type of cheese, see p. 39. Made and distributed with other fresh milk products by Laiterie Sagne, and by Laiterie Boineau at nearby Lacalmilhe (spelt Lacalmille on map).
*laitier; artisanal; vache.*
83 **11/12**.

### Montauban

Saturday market (includes farm cheeses).
Tarn-et-Garonne.

### Montpellier

Tuesday market, wine featured.
M. Aimé Teyssier, *maître fromager*, Fromagerie du Buron, Le Polygone, Niveau-Bas.

Fromagerie et Crémerie Jean Puig et Tony Valero, Halles Laissac and Halles Castellanes.
Hérault; 83 **7**.

## MOUNTALBA

Patois for Montauban. Creamy-coloured *pâte* is closer-textured than most, with few and tiny apertures; crust is black, but less artificial-looking than most.
50% m.g.; *industriel; vache pasteurisé.*
Agenais/Tarn-et-Garonne.

## PÉLARDON

See GANGES, and ST-MARTIN-DE-LONDRES BELOW.

## PELOUDOU

Small cheese marinated in peppered *eau-de-vie* (Courtine, 1973, Chast and Voy, 1984).
*fermier; brebis cru.*
Hérault.

## LE PETIT BORNAND, TOMME

This has appearance of untidy Tomme d'Aligot (see Chapter 7) with a shiny brown smoked coat; I cannot explain Savoyard name.
55% m.g.; *laitier; artisanal; vache cru.*
Tarn.

## PETIT-SUISSE

See MAZAMET.

## REBARBE

*Chèvres du pays* kept six months in *marc* in earthenware pots (see also Chapter 6 for brebis version).
*fermier; artisanal; domestique; chèvre.*
Languedoc-Pyrénées.

## ROVE DES GARRIGUES

See CHÈVRES.

## ST-MARTIN-DE-LONDRES

Local cheeses, including Peloudou (see above) and Pélardon (noted by Androuët, 1982).
Hérault; 83 **6**, R on D986.

## TOMME

See CHÈVRES and PETIT BORNAND.

## EL TORRERO

A more solid cheese than most of its type; *pâte* good-looking and flavour reasonable (maker's code 47 E). About 4kg, rounded drum, standard-looking black exterior but good melting consistency and full flavour inside; a rare raw-milk example of modern Pyrenean *tomme*.
50% m.g.; *laitier; vache cru.*
Lot-et-Garonne.

# Eastern Pyrenees
CERDAGNE (CERDAÑA) – ROUSSILLON

This region was in the Narbonnaise under Roman occupation from 121 BC, with Ruscino (whence Roussillon) as its capital. In the eighth century the French claimed suzerainty over the counts of Roussillon, who became counts of Barcelona in 878 after the expulsion of the Moors from Aragon. The County of Barcelona extended along the coast to Perpignan and inland as far as Toulouse by 1117. In 1134 the last count left his fief to the Kingdom of Aragon.

During the thirteenth century Roussillon became an important source of cheeses, of which Varella was most noted. Perpignan had a special district for cheese merchants, who were as important as the candlemakers of the time (but never keep candles and cheese together). From 1276 to 1344 Perpignan was capital of the Kingdom of Mallorca (its Palais des Rois de Majorque still stands).

The history of Cerdagne (Cerdaña) is more obscure, because of its mountainous nature. That it is ancient is testified by the fact that the underground church at Saint-Martin-de-Canigou was built nearly 1000 years ago by the then Count of Cerdaña, already the tenth of his line.

After two exchanges between Spain and France in political deals in the late fifteenth century, Roussillon and Cerdagne went back to Spain. Finally they returned to France and prospered considerably after the Franco-Spanish frontier was settled along the Pyrenean watershed in 1678. They came under the Gouvernement-Général de Languedoc.

We travelled into this region due east from the Ariège, straying aside from our route to look for cheese. Our long and fruitless journey finished at Rivesaltes, outside Perpignan, where I asked the town's cheese-merchant for *fromages du pays*. He offered me one of those pasteurised black-coated *fromages des Pyrénées*. As I pointed out to him, it came from the western Ariège, and was very far from local. Under further probing he asserted that no cheese was made in Roussillon or Cerdagne.

It was early evening in October. I let his categorical denial excuse me from further search for food or lodging in an apparently cheeseless area, where hotels we had sought out or stumbled upon appeared to have no desire to serve the public (I was reminded of Pagnol's Cigalon), and we went as directly as whimsical roadsigning would allow from Rivesaltes to the *autoroute Catalane* in the direction of our home in Provence.

It is true that years of food- and travel-cuttings and endless books had failed to turn up a single cheese in this corner of France. Even Ninette Lyon, when exploring for her astonishingly comprehensive 1985 *Tour de France Gourmand des Spécialités Régionales*, scented no cheese here. Yet it was unheard of for me ever to give up the cheese chase and admit to a blank day, let alone to two blank provinces.

It seemed that cheese-lovers should travel to Cerdagne or Roussillon only for other compelling calls of love, such as the castles and fine Romanesque churches. Examples are the Benedictine Saint-Michel-de-Cuxa, where the old Prades music festival has gone on since Pablo Casals' death; and (for the footsure) Saint-Martin-de-Canigou's subterranean chapel, already mentioned. In that locality enquire after Rougeat du Canigou, a chèvre found by the Gault Millau team in Andorra in February 1986, some months after my Pyrenean exploration. Travellers to Spain can enjoy the curiosities of local history and the frontiers' eccentricities by taking the Sègres-Puigcerda route. The valley of Latour de Carol and thirty-three villages on the plateau of Cerdaña were specified for transfer to France in 1659, but part of the Carol Valley was forgotten until 1662; and Llivia, a town, not a village, was missed out altogether and remains a Spanish enclave in France to this day. Nearby is an oasis for the cheese-hunter, brought to my notice since my journey by the good offices of Nature & Progrès. Just east of the Llivia enclave and the Vallée du Carol (the Carol flows into the Sègre just over the frontier), Veronik and Gilles Flamant make chèvres on their organic farm. I hope keen-eyed readers will find other chèvres half-hidden in the remoter Eastern Pyrenees.

Pyrénées-Orientales, the *département* enclosing French Cerdagne and Roussillon, is dominated by the Roussillonnais, whose main concern is wine. They would like the *département* to be renamed Roussillon; but, as a Carol Valley dignitary protested: *'Nous sommes des Pyrénéens catalans, pas des Roussillonnais.'* It must be allowed in mitigation of the seeming insensitivity of the Roussillonnais that the vines of Roussillon and Languedoc cover 400,000 hectares, three times those of Provence and nearly a third of the total French *vignoble*. In contrast the same area produces 0.0024 per cent of French cheese.

It is probably because of neglect of upland agriculture that evidence of cheesemaking is so hard to find. I look forward to hearing that readers have succeeded where I have failed.

## Cheeses of the Eastern Pyreneees

### Andorra-La-Vella
Shop: Xavier, *maître fromager*, Place Victor Hugo with 250 varieties including Rougeat du Canigou (see CANIGOU).
Andorra; 86 **14** 15.

### Canigou
**Rougeat du Canigou.** Found by Gault Millau in Andorra-La-Vella (see above).
Cerdagne; 86 **17/18**.

### Engordany
Brebis of which I have no recent evidence of survival.
Engordany; 86 **6**, low L, at end of tortuous road running from S side of N2 just E of Andorra-la-Vella.

### Llo
**Chèvres.** Gilles and Veronik Flamant, Mas Patiras, Vallée du Sègre, 66800 Llo (tel. 68 30 14 55).
*fermier; biologique;* Nature & Progrès; chèvre cru.
Cerdagne; 86 **16**, lower C, S of Saillagouse.

### Perpignan
Daily market.
Roussillon; 86 **19**.

### Varella
Made in Roussillon in the thirteenth century (see p. 169).

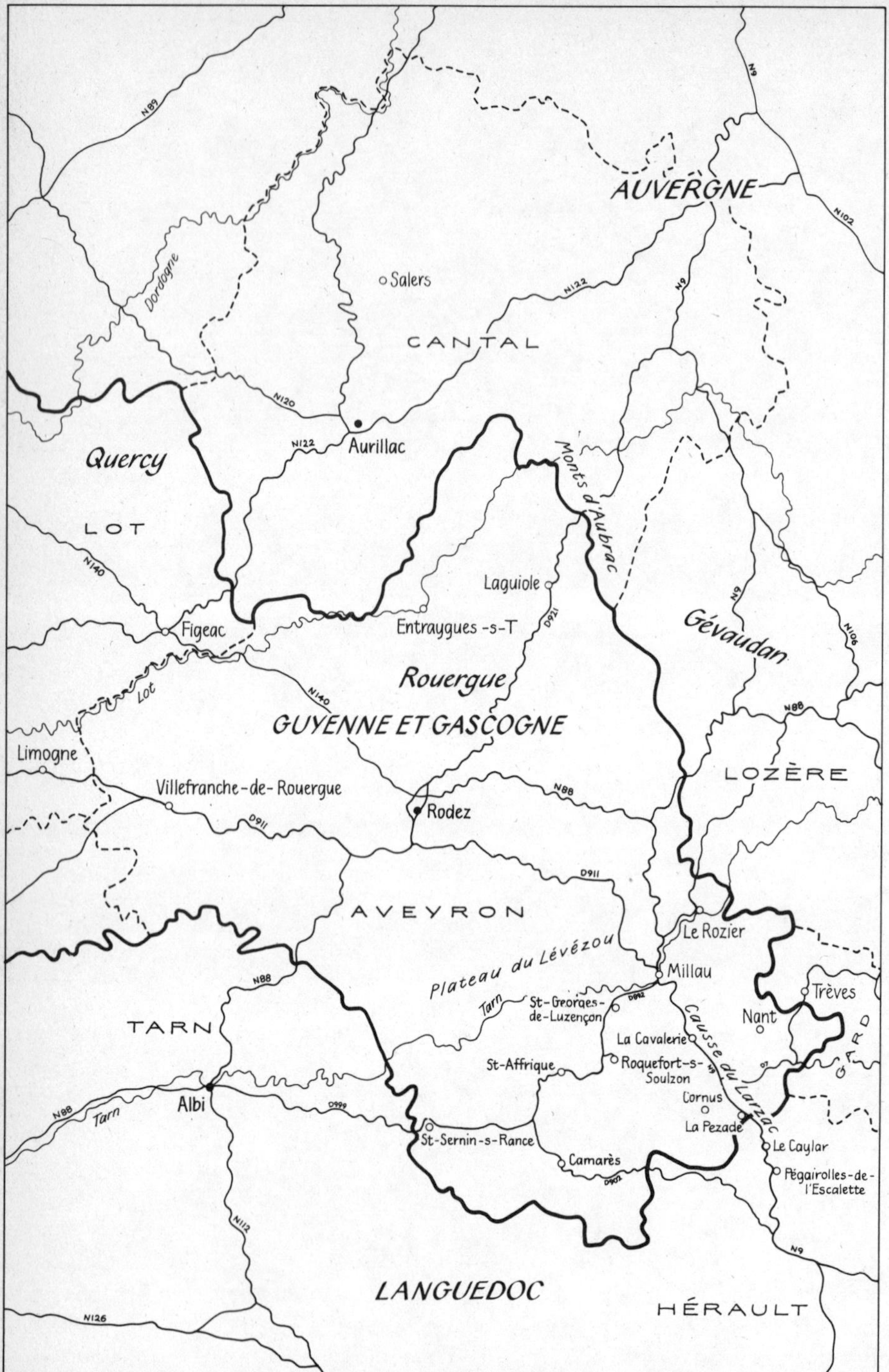

AUVERGNE
CANTAL
Salers
Aurillac
Dordogne
Quercy
LOT
Figeac
Lot
Limogne
Villefranche-de-Rouergue
Laguiole
Entraygues-s-T
Monts d'Aubrac
Rouergue
GUYENNE ET GASCOGNE
Gévaudan
LOZÈRE
Rodez
AVEYRON
Plateau du Lévézou
Le Rozier
Millau
Trèves
Nant
GARD
Causse du Larzac
St-Georges-de-Luzençon
La Cavalerie
Roquefort-s-Soulzon
St-Affrique
Cornus
La Pezade
Le Caylar
Pégairolles-de-l'Escalette
TARN
Tarn
Albi
St-Sernin-s-Rance
Camarès
LANGUEDOC
HÉRAULT
N89
N9
N102
N122
N120
N140
N106
N88
D921
D911
D992
D999
D902
D7
N112
N126

CHAPTER SIX

# *Rouergue and Roquefort*

## AVEYRON

Rouergue is an ancient comté, which came by marriage to the rulers of Navarre and Béarn, and to France with the accession of that line to the French throne in the person of Henri IV. It is at the heart of the Causses, primaeval sheep country, high, rocky plateaux, cliffs and gorges extending westwards into Quercy and eastwards into Gévaudan and the Cévenol tip of Languedoc. Entraygues, Le Fel and Montsalvy in the north-west are familiar names to lovers of Cabécou, that ancient and rich little goat cheese dealt with in some detail in Chapter 4. In the north the Rouergue includes Mont Aubrac and Laguiole, sources of the very old Laguiole cheese and the Aubrac breed of cattle. The regions for Laguiole, Salers and Cantal, shared with Auvergne and Gévaudan, are covered in Chapter 7, as is the region for Bleu d'Auvergne, which strays into Aveyron.

## BLEU DES CAUSSES

Apart from those cheeses shared with neighbouring provinces, Rouergue's one important non-ewes'-milk cheese is Bleu des Causses, which has become exclusively a cows'-milk cheese only since a decree of 1947. The preamble to a 1953 Millau Court judgment sums up its earlier history: 'From time immemorial there have been made in the region of the Causses *calcaires* and the region of the Aveyron cheeses of ewes' milk mixed with cows' or goats' milk, matured in natural caves called *"caves bâtardes"* [bastard, illegitimate caves] as opposed to those situated in Roquefort itself, these caves being nevertheless provided with *"fleurines"* [natural currents of air] ... set up thanks to the fissures existing in the chalk soils of the Causses.'

I am sorry that we have lost those varied mixed-milk cheeses, which faded out and gave way to cows'-milk Bleu d'Aveyron and Bleu des Causses as a result of a 1925 law on Roquefort. Previously some of them had been passed off as Roquefort. S. Baring-Gould, writing in the 1890s about his visit to cheesemakers in the Rouergue, presumed that they were Roquefort; but Roquefort had always been exclusively a ewes'-milk cheese and its *affinage* had been legally tied to the *caves* of Cambalou in the care of the people of Roquefort since 1407. Hence the use of the term *'caves bâtardes'* in the

Millau judgment. Such *caves* may not legally harbour any cheese to be called Roquefort, but have similar qualities to those of Cambalou, including the vital *fleurines*, which keep the *caves* at between 6° and 8°C and spread their spore-laden moisture to nourish and encourage the flowering of the mould in the cheeses. To most people in Roquefort the *fleurines* are the actual *failles* (cracks, fissures) in the rock through which the winds set up the air currents. (The word derives from *flouri*, Occitaine for blossom, which covers fungal as well as botanical flora.)

The 1947 regulations and AOC rules of 1979 and 1980 established Bleu des Causses as the name of a cows'-milk cheese made in the Rouergue and adjacent fringe communes of Quercy, Gévaudan and Languedoc. *Affinage* is confined to *caves* with natural *fleurines* in the Aveyron cantons of Campagnac, Peyreleau, Millau, Cornus and Saint-Afrique, Trèves in the Gard and Pégairolles-de-l'Escalette in Hérault. This aspect was the preoccupation of the Millau Court in 1953 when it convicted and fined a merchant who had sold as Bleu des Causses a cheese ripened in *caves* with no natural *fleurines*.

As the rules described in literature of the Association Nationale d'Appellations d'Origine des Fromages lay down *lait entier* (whole milk) but not *lait cru*, it is worth looking out for cheeses marked *lait cru*, mentioned on the list. The total annual production of Bleu des Causses is a little under 2500 tonnes, and there are only six makers.

The milk is renneted at 30°C in the vat. The curd is cut into large cubes and stirred several times before draining, and the mixing in of the *penicillium roquefortii*. It is then placed in moulds and kept in a draining room at 18°C for three or four days, with several turnings, before the cheeses are removed from the moulds for salting. This is done by rubbing dry salt on the circumference and on one face. Left on a grid for three days, they are then salted again on the outside, and newly on the other face. After three days' resting on its other face, the cheese is ready for the *caves*, where it lies on oak shelves, with regular turning, for at least seventy days (usually three to six months). When mature, and needed for sale, it has its crust scraped and is wrapped in silver foil with the AOC marking, provided it has passed its test. Failures cannot be sold as Bleu des Causses.

At its best the cheese has a creamy, ivory-coloured *pâte* (white in winter), and well-distributed blue mould, of similar strains to those of Roquefort. It melts on the palate, and the flavour is assertive but not harsh. In the *lait cru* cheeses the *pâte* is creamier, the flavour richer, without saltiness (superior to the *average* Roquefort in these respects), and the blue is part of the flavour without overwhelming the character of the delicious ivory *pâte*.

## Cheeses of the Causse du Larzac

Before we study Roquefort, one of the world's greatest cheeses, I want to spend a little time in the country visiting its birthplace on the Causse du Larzac and its fringes. Coming up from the south through Hérault on N9 we pass through Pégairolles-de-l'Escalette, one of the permitted cantons for *affinage* of Bleu des Causses. We enter Rouergue at La Pezade, no metropolis but right in the heart of Larzac, with farm chèvre, farm brebis and the museum of Larzac on its doorstep. More Bleu des Causses *caves bâtardes* lie 8 kilometres to the west at Cornus, and the Roquefort dairy of Fondamente is another 8 kilometres beyond. The Causse around is studded with both ancient and natural history. Sentier de Grande Randonnée GR71, part of the national network of long-distance footpaths, leads in various directions, including eastwards (as does road D185) to La Couvertoirade, an extraordinary fortified village built by the Templars. There is a beautiful *ferme* des Templiers de la Beaume with squat round towers, and you can see occasional dry-stone beehive-shaped shepherds' shelters, called *cazelles* on Larzac. GR71 continues north into the Parc National des Cévennes, less directly reached by road but still within 40 kilometres. Trèves in the west is the Gard outpost of *caves bâtardes* for Bleu des Causses.

In the last house on the right going north from La Pezade is a long-established *chevrier*, whose excellent soft cheese I first tasted years ago. On the opposite side, the last house on the left, at an angle to the road, is *La Mostra del Larzac*. I have never happened that way when this exhibition of local life has been open; but, retired soldier though I am, my sympathy has always lain with the people of Larzac in the campaign to save their bare but beloved country from being completely taken over by the army, which had long used part of it for battle training. The generals must have felt that they had struck their equivalent of gold in this wide, sparsely inhabited, rock-based and rock-strewn plâteau, *'où ne pousse ni pied de vigne, ni grain de blé'*,* as Charles VII's fifteenth-century charter had it. Few though the inhabitants might be, and stony their soil, however, many were their sheep, and older than history their traditions of sheep dairy and cheese. Their attachment to those traditions saw the Larzaciens through eleven seemingly hopeless years of struggle. Fortunately François Mitterrand had been conscious of their grievance. He kept his promise to halt army encroachment on Larzac as soon as he won the presidency in 1981, and considerably reduced the existing camp and training area.

In an abandoned camp 4 kilometres beyond our *chevrier* is La Ferme du Cun, signposted after l'Hospitalet du Larzac on the right of N9. It is a thousand metres along a track, with army buildings in evidence (including enough latrines for all the civil population of the Causses). Parisian-born Monsieur Digirolamo, of Italian parentage, has eighty-six Lacaune ewes now in milk. He remarked that the old Larzac breed had been much tougher than the Lacaunes, which were developed between the wars for increased meat value and milk yield. About 30 inches high, Lacaunes have a long tapering head with lop ears, and are given a working life of seven or eight years. In April the ewes were still inside the *bergerie* under the stone house (almost all sheep in the region are indoors from November to mid-April, but return to their *bergeries* every night, even in summer). Their limited fleece, which grows thick just on the back and part of the flanks, pays only for the cost of shearing; lamb and sheep skins, however, are important for the glove

---

*'where neither vine nor wheat can find root'.

and clothing industries of Millau. Vets learn to make injections in one spot to avoid spoiling the skins.

The Digirolamo cheeses are straightforward semi-soft *tommes*, 3 kilos when young, up to half a kilo lighter after six to eight weeks in his wet-floored *cave*. By then they have a good mould-coated protective crust and a firm but open-textured *pâte*, melt-in-the-mouth, and fresh but lively in flavour. Our half-cheese survived ten days of increasingly warm spring motoring, with enough left (in good, if slightly stronger order) to give pleasure to the family in Streatley on our return.

The ewes, milked on a machine six at a time, were giving about 1⅓ litres daily in mid-season. Cheese was made every three days, with 330 litres raw in the vat, using commercial rennet and a Corsican recipe. The *blancs* were salted by immersion in brine for thirty-six hours, then external salting on the third day. The cheese is well-balanced, with no intrusive saltiness.

## Pérails

Further up N9, beyond La Cavalerie, La Jasse (Occitaine for *bergerie*) is open in July and August for sale of farm produce and demonstrations of machine milking of ewes on a 'roto-lactor'. Not far to the east (within 20 kilometres of La Cavalerie, south of Nant) is Mas du Pré, where Fernand Mazel makes his Pérail de Brebis all the season; but most Pérails are late-summer cheeses.

Milk-collection for Roquefort-making lasts from December or January until the end of June or mid-July, but the ewes normally still have another two to three weeks of diminishing yield to offer. This aftermath shows up in a seasonal flush of Pérails from the farms whose Roquefort milk-collection has ceased. These cheeses are of medallion shape, 10–15 centimetres across and 1–2 centimetres deep, usually attractively irregular. They are refreshing when *frais*, but most delicious when their crusts have crinkled and their interiors have melted with a week's keeping, rather reminiscent of the best Saint-Félicien from Ardèche (see Chapter 7).

## Saint-Affrique and the by-products of Roquefort

A pleasant place to survey the full range of Larzac and other regional cheeses is Lou Péraillou, a shop on the Boulevard de la République at Saint-Affrique (which also has a Saturday market). The *fromagère*, Madame Laux, particularly expert on *fromages de brebis*, has an entertaining sideline in Roquefort's equivalent of *fromages forts*, an assortment of odd shapes and odours with such names as Rascala, Rascalata, Rascalou, Rasquelet and Rebarbe. There is a hamlet called Le Rascalat 40 kilometres away, to the north of Millau, on which the responsibility for the invention of these roof-of-the-mouth-raising (and removing) uses for Roquefort odds and ends and crust-scrapings might be pinned. Whether they are to your taste or not, such things are part of the fun of the cheese world, as well as part of its waste-not-want-not good housekeeping; and there are always some Tartarin-type *chasseurs de fromage* lurking for whom no cheese in the average shop is fiery enough. If Madame Laux catches them they will be hard put to it to find a liquor powerful enough to dowse the fire.

Before visiting Roquefort we made a little tour of the lower, softer countryside west of Saint-Affrique, to visit Patrick James's organic goat farm at La Maurelle. Driving as far as Bournac by D54 along the valley of the Dourdou in mid-April, we saw flocks of ewes already out with accompanying goats, but a prudent shepherd was still wearing his thick traditional cloak. We passed a *lavogne*, one of the dew-ponds scooped out of the rock, on which the animals depend for drinking water over most of the region. Buzzards were patrolling their stretches of territory overhead. After Bournac a hairpin bend precedes a sharp right turn off D54 (which continues to Broquiès). We took the turn and kept on bearing left on this pleasant road winding round the hills. The red soil and red sandstone houses were striking after all the grey of Larzac. The valleys were green and flowery, and beehives were in evidence, their occupants taking advantage of the first warmth and nectar of spring.

We found La Maurelle above the left of the road. A litre of Patrick James's Alpine and Saanen milk produces three or four slightly flattened Crottins, weighing about 80 grammes each (60 when *sec*). They make once a day, leave the curd to form naturally over twenty-four hours, ripen the cheeses for up to two weeks and sell them at the *fromage frais* stage (in *faisselles*), *jeune* or *sec*. We found that they keep very well, becoming slightly salty as they near the *très sec* stage.

You will find on the list other cheesemakers within reach of Larzac, Saint-Affrique and Saint-Sernin-sur-Rance, including Claude Boyer, who makes La Recuòcha (Occitaine for the familiar term 'ricotta' – *brousse* or *recuite* in French). This Brousse de Brebis is made from December to June at Martrin, above Saint-Sernin. Claude Boyer produces a card with ten recipes for the use of his Recuòcha (also usable in many other recipes instead of *fromage blanc*). It is refreshing to eat on its own, perhaps with pepper and olive oil, and, if you need it, a pinch of sea-salt.

# ROQUEFORT AND THE CAVES OF CAMBALOU

Just over 12 kilometres north-east of Saint-Affrique lies Roquefort, source for over two thousand years of the world's most famous blue cheese and never more prosperous than now. Yet not a cheese is made in the village itself.

As we have seen, the Rouergue has always harboured sheep, and it now seems safe to forecast that it always will. The ewes have been milked for cheesemaking from prehistoric times, and the legend passed down to account for the character of the ideal cheese is charming. A shepherd sheltering from the midday sun in the entrance to one of the *caves* of Roquefort (which means 'strong rock') caught sight of his love (a shepherdess, of course) as she passed by. He quickly put his bread and cream cheese down in a cleft in the rock and pursued her. Love appeased his hunger, and it was months before he happened again upon his long-forgotten *casse-croûte*. The cheese had changed in consistency and colour, but he was brave enough to try it, and relished the texture and flavour (mouldy bread would not have been a new experience for him, but later it would be appreciated as an agent for developing mould to accelerate the blueing of cheese). The shepherd started storing all his cheeses in this alchemistic haven and soon had to set up shelves and build a *cabane* at the entrance to keep up with demand, and to guard his *cave* and its contents. His example was followed by others until all the *caves* were occupied. (There were twenty-three natural *caves* in the 1890s, and another eleven with the character of cellars built into the rock. All the *caves* have this look today, except for the rock-face walls with their *fleurines*.)

That was the state of things when the Romans came in the first century BC. Caesar and his legions enjoyed the cheese at Saint-Affrique, and Pliny mentioned it in Book XI of his *Natural History* in AD 79, by which time it was well established on the Rome market.

The combined ephemeral chances of love, forgetfulness, survival of an abandoned lunch (why had no wolf devoured it?), and return of the shepherd to the same spot, lay behind the successful launch of this new cheese; but some far from ephemeral geological and fungal facts lay behind its blueing. The calcareous plateau of Cambalou* stands over the southern flank of Roquefort, above the River Soulzon. The northern section of its cliffs, eroded by seas in the Diluvian era, partly disintegrated and collapsed. Vertical and horizontal faults combined to create a 2-kilometre stretch of ventilated *caves* in the untidy rock between the surviving plateau and the scree along the Soulzon, 300 metres wide and 300 metres deep. The northern cliff-face at the old height perpetually shades from the sun the area between it and the collapsed rock with its newly formed *caves*. The *caves* breathe in the cool air and exhale the old through the *fleurines*. An annual 120 centimetres of rain keeps up the moisture, joining with the air-currents to form a micro-climate within the *caves* at 6–10°C and 95–98 per cent humidity.

Conditions are ideal for moulds, of which six or seven varieties have been identified. The favourable moisture in the atmosphere is helped by the use of oak for all the shelving and the massive beams, which become saturated, providing a constant reservoir of moisture. We saw axe-hewn timbers complete with bark, dating back 170 and 180 years. This indestructible oak is a general feature of the improved, more cellar-like *caves*, mostly constructed in the last century without effacing the natural rock walls or obstructing any of the *fleurines*. At their deepest the *caves* go down eleven storeys into the rock base. At the top are two or three storeys of offices and loading bays built against the exposed rock-face; formerly these upper floors included dormitory and dining accommodation for the workers and private quarters for some of the proprietors. There is little difference in the outward appearance of Roquefort's main street now from its aspect in nineteenth-century engravings. Expansion has gone on underground in fuller exploitation of the *caves* as production has increased. There is twice as much subterranean village as there is superficial. The basic source of the village's

---

*Often called Combalou, it is Cambalou on the map, derived from *campus bellum*; there are traces of a fortified camp on the plateau.

good fortune rests down there in the preservation of natural features first exploited probably hundreds of years before the Romans came.

The *caves* survived the Visigoths, and seduced some of them. Among the permanent settlers, no doubt, were the ancestors of the Alric family of twentieth-century Roquefort fame (see below), who have been farming south of Luzençon for 800 years (for well over half the period elapsed since Alaric II, King of the Visigoths, was defeated and killed by Clovis in 507). In 778 Charlemagne stopped and fed at the Abbaye de Vabre (4 kilometres west of Saint-Affrique) on his way back from fighting the Saracens in Spain. His secretary Eginhard (a monk from that guardian-house of learning, Sankt Gall) recorded that, because of Lenten fasting, cheese was the *plat du jour*: a mouldy old bit of cheese at that, in Charlemagne's eyes. He started picking at it to remove the mould until the Abbé explained that in this cheese the mould was the most prized part. Charlemagne was so won over that he asked the Abbé to send him a regular batch to Aix-la-Chapelle. The worried Abbé explained that he could never be sure that unopened cheeses would be of the same quality as the one he had tasted. Charlemagne told him to cut them in half before despatch to make sure, and then stick the good ones together again and hold them in with wooden hoops. That practice of halving is followed today by the Laur family with all their 'Gabriel Coulet' cheeses, to ensure no imperfectly ripened cheeses go out under their label.

Eleventh-century records of the Abbaye de Conques show that one donation it received included in the annual income a pair of cheeses from every *cave* in Roquefort, and that settlements, annuities and farm rents were commonly calculated in silver or Roquefort cheeses. Conques, 120 kilometres north of Roquefort by road and worth visiting, was a stage on the road to Santiago de Compostella.

In 1271 the comté de Toulouse, with suzerainty over the comté de Rouergue, came to the Royal House of France, which led later to Charles VI's interest in Roquefort. So little of France was left in his hands, so little even of Paris, that his successor was known as the King of Bourges, which Charles VI had made his capital. Roquefort must have been a comforting distraction for the poor monarch. In 1407 he recognised the people of Roquefort as having sole right to the *affinage* of the cheese in their *caves*, '*tel qu'il est pratiqué de temps immémorial dans les grottes du dit village*',* and gave the *commune* the privilege of electing magistrates to meet the needs of local trade. Four years later he reinforced this protection. The magistrates were given control of weights and measures, and seizure of cheeses in the *caves* by creditors was forbidden, unless a debtor had no other movable assets to set against his default.

In 1439 his son Charles VII gave the *commune* the right to demand in tax, for payment of communal expenses, one cheese from every consignment brought into the *caves* for ripening. Because their business was based on the *cabanes* built at the *cave* entrances, the *affineurs* and their workers had long been known as *les cabanières*, a term still in use.

*'such as has been the practice since time immemorial in the caves of the said village'.

In 1666 *la souveraine cour du Parlement de Toulouse* laid down that pastures producing milk for the cheeses should conform to the character of the Causses, confirmed existing royal privileges, warning all and sundry against buying cheeses which had not been through the *caves* and selling them as Roquefort. This could be called the first Appellation d'Origine Contrôlée. The Toulouse *Parlement* repeated this warning in 1785 to 'merchants, carters and others of whatever quality and condition they may be who may pick up and buy cheeses in the *cabanes* (not at the *caves*, but where cheeses were made) and other places in the neighbourhood of Roquefort against selling, delivering or invoicing them wholesale or retail as *véritables Fromages de Roquefort* on pain of 1000 livres fine' (about £40 sterling, over twice a contemporary English soldier's annual pay).

In 1842 the formation of the Société des Caves et des Producteurs Réunis de Roquefort marked the advent of bigger business, combining Roquefort merchants and *maîtres fromagers*, and leading to considerable modernisation inside the *caves*. By the 1890s our English traveller Baring-Gould was to remark: 'the manufacture of the cheeses has fallen into the hands of companies, and these, being impatient of so lengthy a process, and being eager for a rapid return, contrive to blow breadcrumbs into the curd, and the breadcrumbs become mildewed rapidly, and give to the cheese the appearance, if not the flavour, of old blue mould.' After describing the salting and the two consecutive fortnights of mould growth followed by scrapings, he wrote: 'Formerly it took from two to three months to ripen them; now they are ripened and sold off quicker.'

That all was not right with the Roquefort trade (except its annual 8 million Francs of takings, equivalent to £320,000, then a colossal sum) has already been indicated by Baring-Gould's impression that it was permissible to mix goat's milk with the ewes' milk. This could not have been explained by any failure to enquire. He poked his nose into a great many places, facts and figures. In the end Roquefort got the better of Baring-Gould's nose. Coming away he left Marvejols by the 3.10 p.m. overnight train for Paris, sharing a compartment with 'three little parties ... provided for the night (for supper, collation at midnight, early breakfast) with supplies of Roquefort cheese in an advanced state of ripeness, exhaling a very emphatic odour. I held out till shortly before midnight, and then fled to an hotel at Clermont, to continue my journey next day, *sans* Roquefort cheese.' It seems an age away from the suavity of today's cheeses.

From 1890 until 1921 numerous legal judgments defined the characteristics of Roquefort, culminating in the legislation of 1925 which finally assembled all the established laws in one statute for the AOC. Subsequent diplomatic negotiations won international recognition and the ruling-out of even such qualifications as 'type', 'in the manner', 'by the methods' of Roquefort, for imitations. In 1930 the Confédération Générale des Producteurs de Lait de Brebis et des Industriels de Roquefort was set up by the sheep-dairy farmers and the cheesemaking and maturing companies, and registered the red 'brebis' sign borne since on the wrappings of all Roquefort passing its test. In 1961 a Millau judgment defined the zone of *affinage*.

This and the 1925 rules, with the addition of provisions for pre-packing controls, were confirmed within the framework of the new national committee on Appellations Contrôlées for cheese by the AOC decree of 1979 and 1980.

The original Roquefort region was obviously the Causse du Larzac, with its immediate access to the *caves*. This Causse extends into Languedoc (western Gard and northern Hérault). Roman evidence attaches the Gévaudan to the cheese, so by that period cheeses must have been coming to the *caves* (or to similar *caves* in the Gorges du Tarn) from the Causses de Méjean and Sauveterre. Le Rayon (the radius), the region established since the seventeenth century, includes all Rouergue south of the Salers–Cantal–Laguiole region; what is now northern Hérault, west of Larzac to the Monts de l'Espinouse; les Monts de Lacaune, now in western Tarn; and, north of Lacaune, most of Tarn east of Albi, and the corner of what is now Tarn-et-Garonne nearest to Albi.

In the last century, and early in this, Aude, the Pays Basque, Béarn and Corsica, '*Hors Rayon*' ('outside the radius', or Outer Region), were allowed to contribute ewes'-milk cheeses after the salting stage, to become Roquefort in the *caves* of Cambalou. This helped to provide for extra sales made possible by the introduction of refrigerated *caves* in 1900: cheeses could now be stored for an extra six months to make Roquefort available all the year round. How much of a good thing this has proved I will examine when we come to *affinage*.

Roquefort continued to flourish, and production in the 1930s, when the last farmhouse dairies disappeared, rose to between 8000 and 9000 thousand tonnes. By 1970 it had almost reached 13,000 tonnes, made from the milk of 10,000 farms. From 1974 to 1982 production hovered around the 16,000-tonne mark. The hesitation was not because of shortage of demand, but because of shortage of milk. This difficulty was overcome in the 1980s to such an extent that by 1985 the last of the Roquefort contributions from *Hors Rayon* could be dispensed with. The Aude contribution had been only about one per cent, but the Pyrenees and Corsica had provided nearly a quarter of the 1972 total of 15 million tonnes, and a fifth of production right up into the early 1980s. Since 1985, Roquefort cheese has come once again from the traditional *Rayon* alone.

Corsica, Pays Basque and Béarn could still legally contribute cheeses to Roquefort, but it is much more satisfactory that their ewes' milk should now be going into local cheeses. For instance, La Fromagerie des Chaumes built its Etorki brebis factory at Mauléon in 1979. By 1985 it was using the milk of 100,000 ewes from 984 farms, of which 110 had been supplying a Roquefort dairy the year before (see Chapter 5). These changes mean that all Roquefort is now made from milk of the locally bred Lacaune sheep, whereas for most of the century a considerable amount had come from the Pyrenean Manechs (Tête Rouge and Tête Noire), Basco-Béarnaises, and Corsican long-haired sheep of black or white strains.

We have already met the Lacaunes (see p. 175), of which well over 1,200,000 are milked for the Roquefort manufacturers. There were 15,000 farms in the 1930s, producing half today's amount of milk, 10,000 in 1972, and 8000 in 1982, when Corsica and the Pyrenees were still making Roquefort. I was given estimates of 3000–5200 farms for 1985, but then found Société claiming 6200 for its own three companies. Papillon was using milk from 400 farms. The smallest *bergers* have a dozen or so ewes, the majority between 200 and 1200, I was told by Monsieur Pierre Laur.

With the aims of raising quality and quantity of milk yield, the Roquefort companies have paid close attention to breeding, feeding, equipment and hygiene. The Alric and Laur families set standards in their contracts with farms, excluding any industrial feed; permitted cereals (200 grams of oats a day), hay and *légumes* must be organically produced. A ewe's lactation of 180–230 days now ordinarily yields 120–160 litres (the record is 290), compared with 90 in the earlier days of the breed. Milk comes in at about 1.6 litres a day with lambing in December and starts to tail off in May.

Hand-milking continued on most farms into the 1970s, at a speed of twenty to twenty-five ewes an hour for an experienced milker. By 1985 it survived only among the smallest producers. Between 1929 and 1932 Monsieur Fleuri (a director of Société) devised a machine which could milk at the pulse-rate of a suckling lamb (faster than that of the calf) and allow necessary moments of repose during milking. One milker could now manage forty ewes in an hour. The Alric farms have machines with six, twelve, twenty-four, forty-eight and eighty stalls, according to the size of the flock, and this is the general rule now. The improved *Casse* system (named after the farm which developed it) achieves a rate of milking by one worker of 140 ewes an hour; and now the roto-lactor can bring the hourly rate up to 300. Ninety per cent of ewes were being machine-milked in 1985.

The season begins seriously when the first month-old lambs are weaned in December. Enough ewes lamb early for 500 tonnes of cheese to be made that month by *laiteries*, including those making Papillon and Gabriel Coulet. January production reaches about three times December's level, and April achieves the peak of about 2800 tonnes. The second half of June and the whole of July is the season of *la lutte*, when the rams (and, these days, the less exciting artificial-insemination teams) are busy; but there is enough end-of-season milk for 1600 tonnes of July cheese, on which Papillon *laiteries* work until mid-month. Normal gestation lasts five months, all but five days. This and a month of suckling bring us back to the start of another season.

The Lacaunes' milk is not as fat as that of the Friesland ewe, which has 9 per cent fat; but most Lacaunes live all the year round at 650–1100 metres above sea-level. Société's analysis of their ewes' milk compared with average French cows' milk shows a 50 per cent advantage in total solids (18 per cent), about 100 per cent advantage in fats (7 per cent), 73 per cent advantage in casein (4.5 per cent), virtual equality in lactose (4.8/4.7 per cent), and 50 per cent advantage in mineral salts (1.2 per cent). In 1985 the French producer's price for cows' milk was 1.65 Francs per litre, while Gabriel Coulet were paying 7 Francs a litre for their ewes' milk and Papillon

6.50 Francs (Monsieur Laur's and Monsieur Alric's figures). This amounted to between 78 and 84 Francs for each cheese, which weighs nearly 3 kilos when first made. A gallon of cows' milk makes a pound of hard cheese (one-tenth of the milk's weight); a gallon of Lacaune milk makes 2.35–2.44 pounds of Roquefort (nearly a quarter).

Most of the milk is piped straight from the ewes' teats on the machine to 40-litre *bidons* (churns), which are refrigerated until the lorry collection. Tankers are not used because they shake up the milk too much and break fat globules. Each *bidon* is identified as containing the morning or evening milking of the farm concerned, which is tested on arrival at the *laiterie*. It is then filtered into rectangular stainless-steel, water-jacketed *cuves*. Papillon's vats are of 500-litre capacity, Gabriel Coulet's of 1200. Pasteurisation, *thermisation*, standardisation and homogenisation are all forbidden by AOC rules (the fat in ewes' milk is in small globules evenly distributed throughout the milk, so it appears to be homogenised, having no head of cream).

The milk is brought to between 28° and 31°C for renneting (30°C at Papillon and Coulet, 31° at Société). Papillon use 10–15 grams of rennet per 100 litres of milk, Coulet 25 grams, and they stir it in very gently. I would have hoped to see lamb's rennet in general use, but Coulet use calves'. Société mixes in a solution of *penicillium glaucum roquefortii* spores before renneting, but most *laiteries* mix their powdered spores in at the last stage of the curd when it goes into the moulds. As is normal with any cheese, two or three acidity tests are carried out during cheesemaking.

After about two hours (shorter, Papillon say, for overnight milk or milk from a distance), the curd is ready to cut with a lyre-shaped curd-cutter into cubes the size of small sugar lumps (about 1.2 centimetres; Papillon cut late lactation milk to 1.5 centimetres). It is then stirred to encourage expulsions of whey from the curd. At Papillon, after about twenty-five minutes, when the surface of the whey is yellow, the ready curd is lifted by *puisets à caillé* (a sort of flat, round trowel, with a vertical guard in front of the hand-hold) and placed on cloths spread over wicker grids for twenty minutes of draining. The outside of the curd may be lifted from time to time with *l'escamadou* (old form of *écumoire*, skimmer) to assist drainage. Gabriel Coulet hand-stir the cut curd at the draining stage. Société stir the cut curd at varying speeds before transferring it to a perforated moving apron, which allows drainage while conveying the curd to the 'moulding unit'.

The drained *caillé* is hand-ladled into the moulds with *l'escamadou*. Some dairies put a layer of *penicillium glaucum roquefortii* in the mould first, then a layer of curd, another scatter of mould and a top layer of curd, hand-mixing each layer in turn. At Papillon a machine invented by Monsieur Albert Alric brushes the mould into the curd at a concentration of 4 grams to the kilo (about 100,000 million spores), and the curd is then moved and packed by compressed air into deep, double-size moulds in groups of eight. In most dairies the normal shallower moulds are put with their open faces together in pairs to make whole cheeses. Half-cheese-size moulds were designed to ease the mixing of *penicillium* and curd by hand, not possible in a mould deep enough for a whole cheese. Baring-Gould saw what he took to be breadcrumbs 'blown into the curd', and noted that 'they became mildewed rapidly, and give to the cheese the appearance, if not the flavour, of old blue mould.' He thought this was a new way of speeding things up, but bread, as we shall see, is a very old ally of Roquefort.

The cheeses in their doubled moulds are now moved to a draining room at 17–20°C and turned regularly: seven times a day for six days at 18° by Coulet; five times a day for four or five days at 17° by Papillon, and for three days at 18° by Société. Papillon also wash the cheeses daily in room-temperature water for four days. In the 1890s some dairies removed the cheese from the moulds after the first three hours, bound them in linen bandages, and then dried them, with regular turnings, for six to twelve days. This formed a crust which protected the cheese during its handling and cartage to the *cave* at Roquefort.

When the curd has settled down with the completion of whey-drainage, the cheeses are removed from the moulds and marked on one face with the date and vat number. Papillon cheeses weigh 2.9 kilos at this stage, having already lost 100 grams of original weight. They are stored at 10°C and 98 per cent humidity to await collection by lorry for the *caves*, which is done twice a week. Société and Gabriel Coulet cheeses go to *saloirs* at 10°C at the *laiteries*. They are salted round the circumference and on one face; left face-down for three days, then salted on the other face and again on the sides, and left for three days lying on the other face. When cheeses were made in Corsica and the Pyrenees they too were salted before despatch to Roquefort. Unabsorbed salt is brushed off the cheeses at the end of the week, often by *machine brosseuse*.

On arrival at Roquefort, Société cheeses are pierced by machine with thirty-eight 1.5-millimetre-diameter needles before being put in the *caves*. This releases carbon dioxide formed during fermentation and allows the spore- and moisture-laden air to enter the cheese and encourage mould development from the centre. The general practice elsewhere is to salt the cheeses on their arrival at the *caves* over a six-day period, as described for Société above. Papillon rest the cheese for four days after the first salting and two days after the second. Sea-salt, specially prepared for Roquefort in Narbonne, is used in a proportion of 3.5 to 4 per cent of curd weight. The cheeses at Papillon are brushed after salting and placed in perforated plastic containers under a machine with thirty-two 3-millimetre needles. In former days an individual needle with a wooden handle called a *birou* was used for pricking.

This is one of the stages of cheesemaking when the economically minded maker can collect scrapings for Rebarbe. The skin formed on the old cheeses and scraped off at the end of the salting week provided particularly strong material for this purpose (see p. 176). Baring-Gould saw it being rolled in 'boles' and 'rubarbes' in the 1890s ('rubarbe' was probably just his mis-hearing of *rebarbe*).

His scraped cheeses were covered within a fortnight by a white mould, which was removed before exposing them for a second fortnight, after which they were tested for ripeness, and, if ready, sold with under two months of *affinage*. Papillon cheeses are tested for salt six days after salting and again after *affinage*.

The salted and scraped cheeses now go down to the naturally ventilated *caves* to blue, lying on their sides on the moisture-saturated oak planks, '*gorgées d'humidité*', as Monsieur Alric put it; his *caves* are at 8°C and 98 per cent humidity. In the last century the shelves were covered with rye straw, now they are bare. Société allow their cheeses three to four weeks in this atmosphere. If the south wind is blowing, Monsieur Laur finds that his cheeses will start blueing within ten days and be ready for the final stage in fifteen rather than twenty. The Alrics try theirs after about three weeks. During these periods the internal mould development spreads, becoming a darker blue-green, the *pâte* softens, and the cheese starts to 'take on flavour'. The ability to judge the optimum state of the cheese at this stage is something you can learn only by looking, Pierre Alric told us. Experienced *maîtres affineurs* or *trieurs* bore sample cheeses of each batch from the same vat with their fine *sondes* (half the size of the English cheese-iron), using nose and eye, and tasting when still in doubt.

The ready cheeses are *plombés* (wrapped in stout tin-foil) by the *cabanières*, at a rate of up to a hundred an hour by old hands. This temporary coat has two advantages. Fitting closely against the surface, it prevents crust formation (never traditionally favoured, except for the shortlived travelling crust mentioned on p. 184). Being slightly porous it allows gas out and air in, not inhibiting mould development but slowing it down.

In the early part of the season, before the peak of milk production, cheeses may be left in the natural *caves* to complete their obligatory three months' *affinage* before sale. As production builds up the space is needed and the big companies send all the cheese into refrigeration, as described below. The foil (much more substantial than the final silver wrapping) is saved, melted down and recycled. Gabriel Coulet have used it since the 1880s.

The general practice, once the *trieurs* are satisfied that blueing is well established, is to isolate the cheeses from the natural *cave* temperature and humidity. The natural *caves* had formerly been maturing cheeses in two to three months without *ensemencement*, and even faster with it. Now the cheeses go into moisture- and temperature-controlled cold rooms within the *caves*. Papillon's spend at least 150 days, and up to nine months, at 0°C in 100 per cent humidity, which holds them in a state of '*momification*', as Monsieur Alric put it. The Laurs' Gabriel Coulet cheeses, kept from six to twelve months at −3°C in 98 per cent humidity, are pricked again after six months to release accumulated whey. Cheeses removed from the cold rooms to meet forward orders have time in the natural *caves* to complete development. They often release more whey, and some crumble on this change of surroundings. If the whey is excessive they are held back as sub-standard. I remember opening Roquefort cheeses in my apprenticeship days, getting soaked in whey and slipping in it on the shop floor. This taught me to open Société cheeses over a sink, and to wish all Roquefort companies would sacrifice that liquid profit (such waste and annoyance to the retailer) and copy the Laurs. They alone, I believe, follow the practice of pricking mature cheeses, and do it once more for any cheeses still in their *caves* at twelve months.

Pierre Laur defined a good Roquefort as blue to the edges, *blanc* in maturity, fat and *doux*. *Doux* is difficult to translate exactly, but I suggest 'sweetly gentle'. Monsieur Albert Alric emphasised the ivory colour of mature Roquefort, and mentioned the patois *gispre*, pejorative term for a cheese which tastes very 'sheepy'. The inhabitants of Roquefort believe in keeping their pieces of cheese with a little moistened salt inside bags or boxes in a cool place, so creating a miniature humid *cave* for it. I find a hanging cheese-cage in a dark cool corner best, with any *blue* cheese on a plate, the plate wrapped loosely in the paper the cheese is sold in. Buy little at a time, because it is so much better when fresh cut off the whole cheese.

This brings up the awkward question of when Roquefort is at its best. If enough cheeses were kept all their time in the natural *caves* to meet current demand during the making season, the answer would be simple. Assuming that the exaggerated Christmas sales leave enough of the old season's cheese to last until early April, we could hope to be buying new season's cheeses, three or four months old, from April until November or December. I would then expect cheeses held back by refrigeration to start flooding the market for Christmas trade, and to overlap with the new season's ripened cheeses in the April to come.

Unfortunately, as we have seen, in most *caves* cheeses go into cold storage to be held back from the moment their blueing is well established at five to six weeks, regardless of season. Almost all Roquefort is therefore eaten after a period of at least two months in conditions which to some extent de-nature any cheese. No one could now be driven from a train compartment by the smell of Roquefort; a blind man would not notice that a fellow passenger was eating away. All I can say is that, from May until November, in consultation with a competent *fromager* who looks at the dates on his cheeses (or better, insists on cheeses which have escaped, or have not been too long in the morgue, and turns them over quickly), you may buy Roquefort which has full refreshment in it. The rest of the year, unless your *fromager* buys young cheese and succeeds in keeping it in his own humid but unfrosted *caves*, you must subject the cheese to stern tasting before buying, and never plan a Roquefort course for an occasion too far ahead to be sure it will be worth eating. The inescapable problem is that cheeses go into cold storage after only the first stage (the first half at most) of their legal minimum of *affinage*, and that cold storage is not *affinage*. It can even neutralise what has started to develop in the *pâte*. Cheeses kept for so long at a temperature near or below freezing point will have their aromatic and textural development arrested and discouraged, and often come out tasting and smelling more of blue than of cheese. What is more, they deteriorate more quickly on returning to normal temperature than cheeses which have never known anything but natural *cave* conditions.

That few cheeses come through even the best of hands quickly enough to give real satisfaction after December was proved in January 1987 at a Gault Millau tasting of twelve Roqueforts.* Its timing was strange, as Gault Millau admitted, and unkind to Roquefort, but useful in showing up the weakness of the present *cave* system. The panel was made up of four *maîtres fromagers* of considerable reputation, three other *fromagers*, and a representative from Société des Caves de Roquefort. Without exception their judgments of cheeses which had come from their own shops were in line with the general verdict, even when very low marks were given (this suggests to me that one or two *fromagers* had not lately tasted their own Roqueforts, or they would surely not have submitted them to the panel). The Société member of the jury was much kinder than almost any of the others towards the bottom four cheeses, and not so kind, relatively speaking, to his own. The jury's integrity was unquestionable.

The clear winner, with 9 points out of 10 (9.4 on the vote of the *maîtres fromagers* alone) was a Constans-Crouzat cheese (from *maître fromager* Guy Genève's shop in Paris): 'a real Roquefort', 'very fat', *'fruité'*, 'forceful and subtle', 'excellent and refined'. This company uses the milk of sheep on the Monts de Lacaune in south-eastern Tarn and south-western Aveyron and makes 700 tonnes of cheese a year by artisan methods. It was founded before the First World War by the grandfather of the present head of family.

The runner-up, a Gabriel Coulet cheese (from Roland Barthélémy of Paris) with 7.4 points (8.75 on *maîtres'* verdict alone), was commended for beautiful appearance, even, well-spaced blueing, and fat *pâte*. It was criticised only for 'a slightly sharp after-taste'. Another Coulet cheese, entered by a different retailer, came seventh. 'Good-looking and of agreeable texture', it was found 'sharp, yet lacking in real flavour', illustrating my point that modern storage is not *affinage*. The Laur brothers make about 600 tonnes a year under the Gabriel Coulet label (see p. 179).

One Papillon cheese came third (from Gérard Lefèvre of Paris) with 7.3 (*maîtres* of the same opinion) and another equal fourth (from Guy Genève again) with 6.6 (*maîtres fromagers* alone giving 7.75, so ranking it third). The one placed third was 'a handsome cheese', 'a little salt, but very decent', with 'fat and supple *pâte*'. The fourth was praised for its blueing and criticised for its *pâte*: 'a little too young', 'a little dry'. This shows how effectively cold-storage mummifies cheese and inhibits ripening, for this cheese must have been at least six months old. The Alric family make 1000 tonnes of Papillon cheese a year in the Lévézou area (see p. 182).

Equal fourth was a Société cheese (from Guy Genève once more) of 'beautiful aspect, but firm', 'honest, but rather neutral', driving home the arrested development point (*maîtres fromagers* gave it 7). Société, with its subsidiaries Maria Grimal and Louis Rigal, make 80 per cent of all Roquefort, about 13,600 tonnes in 1985. All three *caves* use identical methods.

Next came a Maria Grimal with 6 (*maîtres* 5.5), 'beautiful, regular blueing, fat, supple but neutral'; a Gabriel Coulet (dealt with above); and

*Reported in *Gault Millau Magazine*, February 1986.

another Maria Grimal with 5.1, 'not very attractive appearance (lack of blue), faint taste of mould, rather neutral'.

The last four cheeses rated fewer than four points each. They had probably been over the top long before January, or long over-chilled, and then over-exposed, which could explain some of the faults. Cheeses listed as from Clément Laur and 'Laure et Daures' (Coulet?) both had a *'bel aspect'*, but were 'sharp and very disagreeable' and of 'bad taste, acid', respectively. The Bon Berger, by Maurice Bouet, who makes 150 tonnes a year, was 'sandy, strong and sharp', and a Carles cheese had 'very poorly distributed blue' and was 'sticky, with a taste of soap'. However, varying tastes have to be catered for. I noticed that Guy Genève, *maître fromager* of the remarkable Parisian stable whose four runners came first, third and equal fourth in this hard, unseasonable race, gave 5 to the Bon Berger, 6 to the 'Laure et Daures' and 4 even to the Carles cheese (which earned 5 from the Société juryman, but only 1 or 2 from the remaining six). Clément Laur (cousin of the Gabriel Coulet Laur family), Carles and the three smaller Roquefort producers not represented at the tasting (Combes, Vernières Frères and Coopérative Centre-Lait make about a 1000 tonnes a year between them, I deduced from 1985 figures).

I hope all the Roquefort sages and the Comité National des Appellations d'Origine des Fromages have studied this revealing test, from which only the Crouzat cheese emerged as beyond criticism. It would be stretching objective judgment into charity to say that more than three out of the twelve cheeses were good: 25 per cent against Henri Pourrat's 90 per cent of a generation ago.

I would like to see all the makers contribute, alongside cheeses which have followed the normal modern storage pattern, well-made six- or seven-month cheeses, never refrigerated but matured only in the natural *caves*, for blind testing to compare the results of old and new *affinage*. Some of the old-fashioned cheeses might prove too strong for most palates, but my guess is that almost all would come through with a good aroma and a better balance of blueing, texture and flavour: with strength in the sense of broad richness in maturity, as seems to have been the case with the winner, the *'fruité, puissant et subtil'* Crouzat, rather than through sharpness of blue in underdeveloped or deteriorated *pâte*. It is instructive that while aroma is suggested in the description of the winning cheese, there is no hint of any in the other eleven reports. Aroma is the quality on which any cheese should be judged before it is tasted, a quality more vital than appearance to the full enjoyment of cheese, as is true of wine. The novelist Henri Pourrat, for all his nostalgia for good old farm cheese, had to admit that nine-tenths of Roquefort post-1945 was good, compared with one-tenth before the 1930s, but I feel about it as I do about modern wine: what is passed as good is too often uninteresting, lacking in aroma. I would like to see more natural products at the risk of some roughness, with more satisfaction for both nose and palate.

Does this great cheese, so glorious at its best, need butter? It has been a deplorable but common custom in France to *mix* butter with Roquefort, making a spread of it. In my Breton guise (as if hailing from the banks of the great River Rance) I am used to eating butter under cheese (like the Normans), but mixing it, never. It spoils both. As a possible child of Rouergat ancestry (near Roquefort there is *'le tout petit ruisseau nommé Rance'*, as another Rouergat described it to me), I regard butter as quite unnecessary with any Roquefort I would choose to eat; but some demand it to take the edge off such cheeses as the sharper also-rans of the Gault Millau race.

As for wine, let any who have felt uneasy when accompanying Roquefort with red wine other than port try sweet or very fruity drier white wines. Château Yquem is the perfect but extravagant counsel of some great gourmets. Closer to hand, and more reasonable, are Périgord's Monbazillac, Banyuls and Rivesaltes rancis. In England a sweet old dark ale or barley wine would do well, especially out of doors.

I will end this chapter with facts and comments from two distinguished Roquefort characters, already considerably quoted, who were kind enough to give us much time and attention and to show us round their *caves*. Both have equal respect, typical of all who work at Roquefort, for ancient lore and modern science.

Monsieur Pierre Laur and his brother André (and their cousin Clément, who runs his own *cave*) are of a family built into the rock of Rouergue's traditions. Their family house dates back to Henri IV, last comte de Rouergue. Their great grandfather owned the *caves*, the oldest we visited, in the nineteenth century. Pierre Laur spoke much of the sheep, emphasising the great fragility of the Lacaunes: 'they never sleep out of doors'. In the course of work on improving the breed, 'invented in the 1930s', they pay great attention to artificial insemination, and even use *brebis porteuses*, the equivalent of surrogate mothers. All the sheep belong to the *paysans*, who are bound by contract to adhere to natural feeding (see p. 182) and organic practices of farming. No chemical products are used by the Laurs or the Alrics.

All the *laiteries* belong to the Roquefort *cave* proprietors. Weather conditions are charted daily, together with detailed timings of each stage of cheesemaking, and the amount of rennet and *penicillium* used. Even the wind direction is tested, by the wet-finger method, and recorded. A north wind is preferred for cheesemaking because it is cooling for the dairy; traditionally making might 'wait for the wind'. South wind from the sea is best for maturing, being the only one to penetrate the *fleurines* and create the necessary movement of moisture and spores throughout the *caves*. Monsieur Albert Alric told me that Papillon *laiteries* keep similar charts, and pointed out that if a customer complains and gives the date and vat of marking, it is possible to trace the conditions in which the particular cheese was made and all the details of its making to see whether the fault lay with the *laiterie* or the *caves*. Dairy workers are paid for the whole year, although they do not have to work in the period when no milk is being collected.

'There are eight storeys below us,' Monsieur Laur said as we left his office and started descending the steep old staircase down into the *caves*. The servants' staircase, it might be called, for people are only here to serve; the cheeses are the masters for whom the lift is reserved. It is salutary to think back to the days when they had to be carried up and down the stairs. Through the dimness, giving way to darkness away from the stair-shaft, only the cheeses seem to give off light against the deep, damp-saturated oaken uprights and shelves. Chill moisture is the constant factor, together with the invisible spores, the two combining to create and nourish a greasy floor-and-stair covering (take sensible, non-slip shoes and woolly clothing, and do not dig your heels in). On the south wall the naked rock is split by the irregular *fleurines*, great sinister cracks occasionally letting through the merest gleam from an upper, outer world.

The Laurs' *caves* are open only for professional visits, because they are too full of cheese for air to be spared for crowds; the temperature would be raised unacceptably by the bodies and their exudations. Monsieur Laur said that Société, with its all-year-round guided tours, Combes and Papillon were the only *caves* which had room for visitors.

We turned now to Papillon to visit Monsieur Albert Alric, tall Visigoth, more kind and courteous than the fierce Alarics of old, whose family has been on the Ferme de Linas, south of Millau, for 800 years. In 1906 his grandfather gave Albert's father 5 Francs, enough to pay for milk to make two cheeses. Forty-six years later Albert inherited the *cave*, over twenty small *laiteries* and about 40,000 cheeses. He has since concentrated cheesemaking, now a million kilos a year, in two *laiteries*. The one at Villefranche de Panat in the Lévézou makes four-fifths of the total. It must be encouraging for him to know that a Rouergat *fromager* of the inter-war years believed cheeses from Durenque were to be preferred to all others; for Durenque is very close to Villefranche, and they were probably from one of his father's *laiteries*. The Alric *laiteries* benefit from the most modern laboratory and dairy equipment, and every possible helpful test and process is used. Tests continue from the entry of the milk into the dairy in its *bidon* until six days after salting. This is apart from the periodic ironing of the cheese during *affinage*. The brush which pushes the *penicillium* into the curd is Monsieur Albert's own invention, making it possible to use the double-depth moulds, grouped so that the curd can be packed in by compressed air. The *piqueuse* with its thirty-two needles, twice the calibre of those used by Société, is another innovation. The raw milk of the ewes, lovingly fed only on the best, most natural food, is respected and cared for with all the aids that modern science can offer.

Monsieur Alric takes us back into pre-history with his 'Oak shelving is vital to the *caves*.' It helps to keep the temperature and moisture levels steady by acting as a tough reservoir capable of ingesting or exhaling humidity as the south wind blows or subsides. 'The oak must be cut at full moon in a North wind, and only from October to March, when no sap is rising.'

As for the moulds in the *caves*, they have long been domesticated to ensure the full blueing of the cheese. 'I'm the last to make my own *penicillium*,' Monsieur Alric told us, and went on to trace its history (his version ignores the lovelorn shepherd): 'In this poor country no wheat could grow. The number of beasts increased, and there was only natural manure. The soil was limed and they grew rye (*seigle*) and made bread from the stone-ground floor in 9-kilo loaves every two months. These were laid across two adjacent room beams. They *never* threw away bread, but ate it even if it was a bit mouldy. They warmed their ewes' milk in a *bain marie*, used rennet prepared from scraping *la caillette* [the vell, lining of the lamb's fourth stomach] to make cheese. They used to spread their cheese on bread, and found that when the bread was mouldy the cheese was better flavoured. That's how Roquefort was born, before Julius Caesar came here with his Roman legions and ate Roquefort. It's in his memoirs.

'I reckon I make the *real* Roquefort and it should be made only with real *penicillium*. I bring *seigle* from La Montagne du Lévézou and bake the bread in my oven, which weighs 135,000 kilos. It is made from bricks with 45 per cent of aluminium, to resist heat of up to 800°C. We make batches of thirty loaves, each of 9 kilos. We make yeast the night before and let it swell. The leavened dough is put in hand-made baskets to get its shape and baked at 800°C in *feu de bois* for two hours, acquiring a crust of several centimetres. The loaves are cooled in the bakery and then taken to the *cave*. They are given a quarter turn every week, standing upright on the oak shelves.

'After seventy days the loaf weighs only 3 kilos. They take off the crust and let the crumb dry at 35°C. In eight days it is desiccated. They break it up, sifting it through a very fine mesh so that the spores fall into two *bidons*. It's these spores that one puts in the *caillé*, two grams for each half kilo...

'I use the method I saw my father use when I was eight years old. I make four hundred loaves at the new moon in early September for the whole year, because that's when the *penicillium* grows best.'

## Cheeses of Rouergue and Roquefort

### Aligot
Potato, bacon, garlic and cheese dish, also called Patranque, for which Tomme Fraîche d'Aligot is used (see Chapter 7, p. 227), as is the next cheese below.
N. Rouergue; 76 **13 14**.

### Aubrac
**Tomme de Montagne d'Aubrac.** This is the unsalted curd of Laguiole or Salers (see AUVERGNE).
*fermier; coopérative; vache cru.*
N. Rouergue; 76 **14**, low L.

### Aurillac
Excellent market centre for Rouergue cheeses (see Chapter 7, p. 229).

### Aveyron, Bleu d'
Term used for some Bleu des Causses (see p. 192) before AOC of 1979/1980.
*laitier; artisanal; vache cru.*
Rouergue.

### Bassez
Small chèvre, 'classique' (Courtine, 1979); mentioned without detail by Viard (1980); I have not found Bassez's cheese.
*fermier; chèvre cru.*
N. Rouergue near Laguiole; 76 **13**, low on N921.

### La Bergère; Brousse de Brebis
500g in tub; Ricotta-type; Société Fromagère de St-Georges.
*20% m.g.; laitier; brebis cru recuite.*
Rouergue; 80 **14**, SW of Millau on D992, St-Georges-de-Luzençon.

## Berger

**Le Bon Berger:** *marque* of cheeses by Éts Bouet of Roquefort (see BLEU DE BREBIS, BLEU DES CAUSSES, ROQUEFORT, TOMME DE BREBIS).

## Le Bergerin Crème de Roquefort

In plastic *barque* for long-keeping; by Société de Roquefort (1987).
*industriel; brebis.*
Rouergue.

## Bleu

**Bleu d'Auvergne.** Northern Rouergue is within the AOC region for this cheese; see Chapter 7, p. 230.

**Bleu de Brebis du Rouergue.** Naturally crusted blue quite distinct from Roquefort; tasted in November, it had obviously never been in too restricted a low temperature, being of excellent smooth consistency and of gentler, less salt flavour than Roquefort. The provenance of this cheese was not known to my local *fromager*, but later I saw similar cheeses from Maurice Bouet of Roquefort (see p. 188); his Roquefort has been found too strong for some palates, but this could have been the result of too long keeping of late-season cheese (January).
*laitier; brebis cru.*
Rouergue.

**Bleu de Brebis le Dolmen.** Gabriel Coulet seconds, in half cheeses (Roquefort size), about 10% of production.
*laitier; brebis cru.*

**Bleu des Causses AOC 1979/80.** 2.3–3kg drum; about 20cm × 8–10cm; *penicillium Roquefortii* introduced into *caillé; affinage* in natural *caves* with *fleurines* (called *caves bâtardes*, as opposed to those of Roquefort) for at least 70 days, normally 3–6 months, within the cantons listed at the foot of this entry. The cheese is closer to Roquefort in character than to Bleu d'Auvergne. *Pâte:* yellow ivory, dewy; in winter whiter and drier, and stronger. (See pp. 173–4.)

Production in the earlier 1980s was between 2140 and 2357 tonnes. 94% of the cheese came from four private dairies, the other 6% from two co-operatives.

Cheeses of *lait cru* 50% m.g. are available from Fromagerie des Causses et d'Auvergne 21 rue de la Prade (N of Rodez, but postal code 12850, Onet-Le-Château); Quatre Saisons cheeses, matured in *caves* at Peyrelade on R. Tarn, W of Peyreleau, are particularly creamy and rich in texture and flavour (*pâte*, not just blue); Pujol, 12540 La Rivière-sur-Tarn, just W of Peyrelade 80 **4**, bottom R; Fromageries des Gorges du Tarn, Rodez, accept visitors (tel. 65 67 02 81); Caves Virazel, La Bastide (80 **12**, low R, E of D33); cheeses are creamy in colour, texture, and mould is greeny-grey.
*45% m.g.; laitier; vache entier cru.*
Rouergue and parts of Gévaudan/Lozère, Quercy/Lot, Languedoc/Gard, Hérault.
*Affinage: Aveyron:* Campagnac, 80 **4**, C; Cornus, 80 **14**, lower R; Millau, 80 **14**; Peyreleau, 84 **4**, low R; St-Affrique, 80 **13**. *Gard:* Trèves, 80 **15**, high. *Hérault:* Pégairolles-de-l'Escalette, 83 **5**, 80 **15**, on N9.

## Bole

Nineteenth-century version of Rebarbe (see p. 196), round cheese made of leftover scrapings after post-salting clean-up of Roquefort crusts.
*artisanal; laitier; brebis cru.*
Roquefort.

## Le Bon Villefranchois

100g soft cheese by Laiterie G. Soulié, Villefranche.
*45% m.g.; laitier; vache.*
Aveyron; 79 **20**.

## Braison

**Le Braison du Berger.** 125g potted Roquefort by Louis Rigal (since 1982).
*laitier; brebis cru.*
Aveyron.

**Le Braison d'Or.** 125g of potted Roquefort with sweet white grapes by Louis Rigal (since mid-1986).
*laitier; brebis cru.*

## Le Brebidou

About 400g, flattened dome, striated sides; semi-soft, close-textured; pleasant texture and flavour; by Société Fromagère de St-Georges, also makers of Le Pérail (see p. 195).
*50% m.g.; laitier; brebis.*
Aveyron; 80 **14**, SW of Millau on D992 St-Georges-de-Luzençon.

## Brebignole

4.5kg *tomme* by G. Soulié, Villefranche de Rouergue.
*laitier; brebis cru.*
Aveyron; 80 **20**, top.

## Bournac

**Fromages de Chèvre, Crottins.** Excellent small chèvres (60g *sec*) by Patrick James at La Maurelle (which is on map); between Banon (see p. 449) and Cabécou (see pp. 117–18 and 233) in size; sold at all stages; pleasing texture and flavour; a little salty when aged.
*fermier; biologique; Nature & Progrès; chèvre cru.*
Aveyron; 80 **13**, W of St-Affrique by D54; La Maurelle, N of Bournac.

## Brebis

Fromages de Brebis see: BERGÈRE, BERGER, BERGERIN, BLEU DE BREBIS, BRAISON DU BERGER, BRAISON D'OR, BREBIDOU, BREBIGNOLE, BROUSSE, CAILLÉ LISSE, CAILLOTE DE BREBIS, LE GRAND CAUSSE (La Cavalerie, La Jasse), CUN, LOU FANTOU (see CAUSSE), FERMIÈRE (TOMME DE BREBIS), FETA (see SALAKIS), FROMAGE FERMIER DE BREBIS DOMBRE-CASTANIER (see PÉRAIL), LA FROMAGÉE DU LARZAC, FROMIX, PÉRAIL DE BREBIS (LA PEZADE), RASCALA, LOU RASCALOU, LE RASQUELET, REBARBE, LA RECUÒCHA, ROQUEFORT, ST-AFFRIQUE (shop, *laiterie*), SALAKIS, TOMME DE BREBIS (FERMIÈRE, LAITIÈRE).

## Brillador (formerly Brillat-Savarin)

500g *triple-crème*; usually sold with crust still staring white (not the rich pinky-gold *croûte-fleurie* of the old Magnum); name change necessitated by right to original name having been bought by Besnier (it is used by the Fromagerie de Pansey in Champagne); Brillador is made by G. Soulié, who started pasteurising cows' milk in the 1980s.
75% m.g.; *laitier; vache pasteurisé.*
Aveyron; 79 **20**.

## Brousse de Brebis

400g cheese made by Société Fromagère de St-Georges; See ST-GEORGES-DE-LUZENÇON LA RECUÒCHA.
20% m.g.; *artisanal; petit lait de brebis.*
Aveyron; 80 **12**.

## Cabécou

See Chapter 7, p. 233, and Chapter 4, pp. 117–18.

**Cabécou de Montsalvy, d'Entraygues-sur-Truyère du Fel.** 40g, 4cm × 1cm (thick medal); *frais, mi-sec, sec*; similar to Cabécou, see Chapter 7, p. 233 (with which the above overlap) and Chapter 4, pp. 117–18; Montsalvy (just over Cantal border) and Entraygues are the important collection centres. The Entraygues cheeses have a particularly fruity reputation. Ninette Lyon has found Cabécou from this quarter made from milk of brebis and chèvre/vache *lait de mélange* as well as the proper *pur chèvre*. Le Fel (12km W of Entraygues) is a wine as well as a Cabécou appellation.
Mur de Barrez was mentioned by Lindon as source (1961).
*fermier; artisanal; chèvre cru.*
Aveyron; 76 **12, 13**, low.

## Cailladou

50g Cabécou or slightly larger; thick medal-shaped chèvre at *frais* stage.
*fermier; chèvre cru.*
Aveyron.

## Caillé Lisse de Brebis

Fresh brebis curd in smooth state.
40% m.g.; *fermier; brebis cru.*
Larzac; sold St-Affrique.

## Caillote de Brebis

Mixture of Brebis, mostly Roquefort 'unctuous and light', full flavour; in glazed earthenware pots with 150g of *pâte*; good keeping (indefinite if you like it strong); by two Société dependants: Fromagerie Maria Grimal, Roquefort and Armand Mialane, Le Mas, Roquefort; and see Le Petiot, by Gabriel Coulet.
50% m.g.; *laitier; brebis cru.*
Roquefort; 80 **14**, L.

## Cajassous, Cujassous

See CABÉCOU in Chapter 4, pp. 117–18.

## Camarès

**Fromage Pur Chèvre.** In rigotte/crottin form; soft to *sec*; made by E. Preisinger at Rigols; sold at Lou Péraillou in St-Affrique.
45% m.g.; *fermier; chèvre cru.*

Aveyron; 80 **13**, low R 4km S of Camarès by D51, D109 Rigols.

### Le Cambalou

In les Rochers du Cambalou are the natural *caves*, and cracks in the rocks which air them, in which all Roquefort cheeses must be ripened for at least three months; for visits see ROQUEFORT and pp. 189–90.
Aveyron; 80 **14**, L of C, S of Roquefort.

### Cantal

Northern Aveyron is within the AOC region for Cantal cheese (see Chapter 7, p. 234).

### Causse

**Causse, Pur Chèvre Fermier du.** Nearer crottin than Cabécou in shape; soft to *sec*; by M. Laize, Mas de Laval, Salvagnac-Cajarc.
45% m.g.; *fermier; chèvre cru.*
Causse de Limogne; 79 **9**, lower R, S of R. Lot.

**Le Grand Causse, Lou Fantou.** 1kg, 20cm × 3.5cm; soft, *croûte-fleurie* (Brie-style *pâte*). 125g small cheese called Le Fantou, Fromagerie Alric, Roquefort 1986.
*laitier; brebis cru.*
Causse du Larzac; 80 **14**, L of C.

### Causses

See BLEU DES CAUSSES.

### Chantichèvre

60g dome, 12cm across base; soft; succulent, tart interior; crust formed by strips of curd in curlicues turning down sides from top, forming intertwined petals.
*artisanal; chèvre cru.*
NE Rouergue.

### Chèvre

*Fromages de chèvre*: see BASSEZ, BOURNAC, CABÉCOU, CAJASSOUS, CUJASSOUS, CAMARÈS, CAUSSE, ENTRAYGUES, ÉTARLOU, LARZAC (including LA PEZADE), ST-AFFRIQUE, ST-SERNIN-SUR-RANCE.

### Cun

Ferme de Cun, see LARZAC.

### Le Dolmen

See BLEU DE BREBIS (Gabriel Coulet *marque*).

### Entraygues-sur-Truyère

See Cabécou.

### Étarlou

2kg and 4.5kg plump *tomme* by G. Soulié at Villefranche (see p. 198).
*laitier; chèvre cru (April–Sept).*
Aveyron; 79 **20**.

### Lou Fantou

See LE GRAND CAUSSE, of which it is the small size.

### La Fermière

See TOMME DE BREBIS (Bouet).

### Feta de Brebis

See SALAKIS.

### Fromagée du Larzac

100g in glass goblet, 160g in pot, 1kg cutting cheese (since 1979). Roquefort *pâte* by Maria Grimal (a Société company).
*laitier; brebis cru.*
Roquefort; 80 **14**, L.

### Fromages Fermiers

For brebis see CAILLÉ LISSE, LARZAC, PÉRAIL, ST-AFFRIQUE.
For chèvres see BASSEZ, BOURNAC, CABÉCOU, CAMARÈS, CAUSSE, LARZAC, PÉLARDON, ST-AFFRIQUE, ST-SERNIN-SUR-RANCE.

### Fromix

Range of *pur brebis* cooking cheeses, including Brousse (see p. 193) and Roquefort (see p. 196) by Maria Grimal (part of Société).

### La Jasse

Occitaine word for *bergerie*, mountain farmhouse for shepherd and flock, with dairy (*jasserie* in Forez, see Chapter 7, p. 243); one on the Causse du Larzac, la Maison du Larzac, is open July and August, 10.00–19.00; a rotolactor machine milks ewes, there is a cheese museum and farm products are on sale.
Aveyron; 80 **14**, Larzac, between Millau and La Cavalerie N9.

### Laguiole-Aubrac

(N Rouergue) See Chapter 7, pp. 203–5; part of AOC region is within Aveyron.

## Larzac

Plateau, Causse du Larzac, traditional stronghold and heartland of sheep dairy flocks providing milk for Roquefort (see LA JASSE).
Aveyron; 80 **14/15**.

**Tomme de Brebis.** 3kg (2.5kg after *affinage*); natural mould-enriched crust; 6–8 weeks *affinage* on farm in *cave humide*; firm, but open textured *pâte*; melt-in-mouth, good fresh, unsalty flavour; in our case, richer for a further ten days of travel which it withstood well (see also p. 176).
45% m.g.; *fermier*; *brebis cru*.
Aveyron; 80 **15**, N of l'Hospitalet du Larzac, R off N9, La Ferme du Cun.

**Fromage de Chèvre.** Small soft cheese, very good when I tasted it in 1970s; still good in 1985.
*fermier*; *chèvre cru*.
Larzac, south of above, first house in La Pezade, E of N9.

**Pélardon.** About 10cm × 2cm, natural crust melting into heart of cheese; moist, rich, white *pâte*; full flavour, no hint of saltiness.
*fermier*; *chèvre cru*.

## Le Pérail

Up to 250g; 10–15cm × 1.2–2cm. As well as farms and dairies which make all the season (Dec–July; see next four entries), numerous farms which supply Roquefort makers with ewes' milk from 1 December–30 June make Pérail from the end of season milk between the finish of Roquefort milk-collection and the drying-off of the ewes.
*fermier*; *brebis cru*.
Rouergue.

**Pérail Pur Brebis.** Fernand Mazel makes this disc of a cheese at Lou Mas del Prat, Mas-du-Pré (tel. 65 62 26 57).
50–55% m.g.; *fermier*; *brebis cru*.
Aveyron; 80 **15**, L of C, N of La Pezade by D185, D55, turn W 3km before Nant.

**Pérail Fromage Fermier de Brebis.** 100g; 10cm × 1.2cm medallion; by Le Gaec du Lumanson, Dombre-Castanier, Verrières; eaten at 10–14 days, agreeable rich sheepy flavour, not salty; firmish, close, smooth texture; kept well. At nearer 3 weeks crinkly natural crust, very rich melty interior (reminiscent in appearance and texture of good Saint-Félicien); after another week really strong, quite unlike any other cheese.
45% m.g.; *fermier*; *brebis cru*.
Aveyron; 80 **4**, bottom. 10km N of Millau by N9, W by D53 Verrières.

**Le Pérail Laitier.** La Fromagère Cigaloise. *laitier*; *brebis cru*, but if found Sept–Dec likely to be product of frozen milk.
Société Fromagère de Saint-Georges, makers of Brebidou and other cheeses.
Aveyron; 80 **14**, SW of Millau on D992 Saint-Georges-de-Luzençon.

A good range of Larzac cheese and by-products is on sale at St-Affrique (see p. 197).

**Roquefort.** M. and Mme Roc (who are biochemists) make cheese in 1000-litre vats for Crouzat of Roquefort.
*laitier*; *brebis cru*.
Aveyron; 80 **14**, lower SW of Cornus on D7 × D93 Fondamente.

## Mur-de-Barrez

Local cheese made of whey (*Larousse*, 1973). I have not met it.
*petit lait de chèvre cru*; *fermier*.
Aveyron; 76 **12**, far R.

## Pélardon

See LARZAC.

PÉRAIL, PÉRAL, PERRAIL (the first spelling is usual). See LARZAC.

## Lou Péraillou

By G. Soulié. See VILLEFRANCHE-DE-ROUERGUE.

## Le Petiot

Small plastic pot (100g?) of Roquefort *pâte* from Gabriel Coulet.
*laitier*; *brebis cru*.
Roquefort.

## Rascala, Le Rascalat, Lou Rascalou, Le Rasquelet, Le Rebarbe (Rubarbe)

All these names are, or have been, applied to preparations of *fromage fort* character in their everlasting and ever-strengthening qualities. They are made from the breakages, downgradings, and, literally, scrapings (off crusts) of the Roquefort dairies. I imagine that someone in Le Rascalat first had the idea.
Aveyron; 80 **14**, top, on N9.

**Rascala, Le Rasquelet de St-Affrique.**
Untidy roll of Roquefort *pâte*, kept for months; on sale at Lou Péraillou (see VILLEFRANCHE, p.198), St-Affrique (see p.197).
*laitier; brebis cru.*

**Rascala.** 250g drum of La Rebarbe type made by Société of Roquefort; strong, and getting slowly stronger; sold at Lou Péraillou, St-Affrique; and see LA TARTE AUX VIGNES.
*laitier; brebis cru.*
Aveyron.

**La Rebarbe** (Rubarbe): probably mishearing of Rebarbe by nineteenth-century traveller. 500g log of Roquefort *pâte* and trimmings, crustless; 'months of shelf-life', strong and getting stronger; by Maurice Bouet of Roquefort, who make Roquefort and Tomme de Brebis. See p. 198.

LA RECUITE, LA RECUÒCHA, BROUSSE DE BREBIS

What we know as *ricotta*; French *recuite* or *brousse*, in langue d'Oc *recuòcha*, 'La fleur de petit lait'; the whey is heated (hence, literally, recooked) and skimmed to produce this excellent form of *ricotta* (richer than that made from other milks and other whey cheeses, because ewes' milk is rich in fats and solids spread evenly through it); made by Claude Boyer, *fromager* of Martrin.
*artisanal; brebis whey, Dec–June.*
Aveyron; 80 **12**, N of St-Sernin-sur-Rance.

RODEZ

Good centre for regional cheese. Fromagerie des Gorges-du-Tarn (see BLEU DES CAUSSES) is visitable (tel. 65 67 02 81).
Aveyron; 80 **2**.

ROQUEFORT AOC (1979)

In prepacked portions, quarters, halves and the whole foil-wrapped 2.5–2.95kg drum; 19–20cm × 8.5–10.5cm deep; unpressed; gleaming clean white exterior; the palest of blue cheeses in its creamy-white basic *pâte*, with well-spread veining, smooth dewy, alabaster-like surface, some small, angular apertures; its aroma mild, but all its own, with a hint of the *penicillium roquefortii* (mixed either in the milk at renneting, or in the curd before it is packed into the moulds); on the tongue and palate: consistency firmer than cows'-milk cheese, especially when on younger side, flavour distinctly of ewes' milk with pronounced blue element. More melting and rich when fully matured, provided it has not been stored at very low temperature (0° to –3°C), which happens to most cheese made in the second half of the season (Apr–July), to keep it back for the late autumn and winter. With a minimum *affinage* of 3 months the first of the new season's cheeses can be expected on the market in April. The last unchilled cheeses are to be expected before the big release of reserves for Christmas trade. Makers claim that the salt is more obvious in young cheese, contrary to the usual experience of increasing salinity as a cheese loses weight with age. Roquefort should be only moderately salted.

The milk must be ewes' milk from Rouergue, Gévaudan (Lozère), Languedoc (Gard, Hérault, Tarn and Aude); and (since 1900, when refrigeration first made it possible to increase production and hold back stock for all-year-round distribution) the Pays Basque and Béarn (Pyrénées orientales) and Corsica. The *blancs* must be sent after salting and firming up (6–11 days) to mature in the moist, mould-rich (six or seven varieties of *penicillium roquefortii*) and *fleurine*-aired natural *caves* of Cambalou at Roquefort. (See p. 194). No cheese may be called Roquefort unless it has been made from whole ewes' milk from within the prescribed region and matured in the *caves* of Cambalou. By 1985 Roquefort had phased out its Corsican and Pyrenean regions where local cheeses have been taking up the milk. Société makes them in quantity in the Pays Basque, and in Corsica; Fromagerie des Chaumes' Étorki used nearly 7 million litres in 1985 (110 of the Chaumes farms had supplied Roquefort makers until 1984).

17,053,978 tonnes of Roquefort was made in 1985 (nearly 6 million cheeses) from milk of a million ewes. Roquefort makers and *affineurs* (as named by *fromagers* supplying cheeses) in the order of preference of a Gault Millau tasting panel in January 1986 (a bad month for a test): Éts Benjamin Crouzat (Constans-Crouzat), 700 tonnes, very clear leader with 9 out of 10 points; Gabriel Coulet (Pierre and André Laur), 600 tonnes, only professional visitors, tel. 65 59 90 21; Éts Albert Alric (Papillon

(Alric)), 1000 tonnes, all milk organic, *méthode agrobiologique* Lemaire-Boucher; Société des Caves (Société), about 13,600 tonnes, including Grimal and Rigal; Maria Grimal (Société company); Éts Gabriel Coulet, André Laur (so listed by Gault Millau: Pierre Laur administers, André Laur heads the practical side of the *affinage* and selection); Maurice Bouet, 150 tonnes, tel. 65 59 90 11, also makes Bleu de Brebis du Rouergue, Bleu des Causses, Tomme de Brebis; Clément Laur, 150 tonnes; cheese listed by Gault Millau as by 'Laure et Daures' (Coulet or Clément Laur); Carles. Not represented in the tasting: Éts Louis Rigal (Société company); Éts Yves Combes; Coopérative Centrelait; Éts Vernières Frères.

There are twelve makers now, seven fewer than in 1972. All their cheese is matured in Roquefort, but the cheese dairies are spread about the countryside near the sources of the milk (see LARZAC, ST-AFFRIQUE and VILLEFRANCHE DE PANAT).

*By-products*: 30% of production by Société and its offshoots is not Roquefort, but processed Crème de Roquefort and cheeses of Caillebotte, Rascala and Rebarbe types (see pp. 195–6) and LA TARTE AUX VIGNES, which use up damaged cheeses and other waste (see p. 176).

*Substandard cheese*: Cheeses made as Roquefort, but not up to AOC standard, are often sold as Bleu de Brebis (see p. 192). Some of them turn out as most agreeable, gentler cheeses. Others are broken up for strong-flavoured by-products such as Rascala and Rebarbe (see pp. 195–6).

*Caves visits*: Société runs well-conducted tours free, from 9.00–11.30 (last morning visit), and from 2.00–5.00; (every day except Christmas and New Year); they start at office on main street opposite the church; tel. 65 60 23 05 for frequency of visits, which varies with season (every 10 minutes in July and August), and if you need a tour with an English-speaking guide. Temperature is 43–46°F, humidity is high, floors are slippery, and there are many stairs to climb and descend, so dress accordingly. Papillon and Combes also accept some visitors.

Alric (Papillon) cheese is sold by French Dairy Farmers and the London Cheese Company wholesale in London; by Wells Stores, Streatley, Reading (0491 872367) by post or road. Gabriel Coulet cheese is available in Paris from Claude Anthes, 9 rue Langevin, 75004, for restaurants; from Alazard and Saff at Rungis.

Confédération Générale des Producteurs de Lait de Brebis et des Industriels de Roquefort, 36 avenue de la République, 12103 Millau tel. 65 60 46 32. The sign of genuine Roquefort Garanti d'Origine et de Qualité is a red ewe surrounded by these words in an oval, with the Confédération's full title within an outer margin.

52% m.g.; *laitier*; *artisanal*; *brebis cru*.
Roquefort; 80 **14**, L of C.

ROUERGUE, TOMME DE

Large low-fat *tomme*, semi-hard with natural crust.

20% m.g.; *laitier*; *vache*.
Rouergue.

RUBARBE

See REBARBE.

ST-AFFRIQUE

See BOURNAC and LARZAC for local cheesemakers and other features, and Société Roquefort *laiterie*.
Saturday market.
Lou Péraillou, *fromager*, 34 boulevard de la République (opposite Postes) open all day except Monday. Mme Laux is an expert in brebis, with a wide range of local and regional cheeses.
W of Larzac; 80 **13**, on D999.

SAINT-ANDRÉ; SAINT-ANDRÉ-POIVRE-VERT

1.8kg, plump drum, *triple-crème* made by G. Soulié at Villefranche-de-Rouergue (see p. 198).
*laitier*; *vache pasteurisé*.
Rouergue; 79 **20**.

ST-GEORGES-DE-LUZENÇON

Société Fromagère de St-Georges makes brebis: see BREBIDOU, BROUSSE, PÉRAIL (*laitier*).
Aveyron; 80 **14**, SW of Millau on D992.

ST-SERNIN-SUR-RANCE

See LA RECUÒCHA.

**Fromage Fermier de Chèvre.** Small cheese, base of cone shape, and log; soft, natural crust; on sale at Lou Péraillou,

St-Affrique; made by M. A. Hoarau, La Borie-de-Belly, St-Sernin, tel. 65 69 66 23.
45% m.g.; *fermier*; *chèvre cru*.
Aveyron; 80 **12**, far R on D999.

### Salakis

200g vacuum-packed slices of ewes'-milk Feta (Société, 1986). See also ROQUEFORT.
*laitier*; *brebis cru*.
Roquefort.

### Salers

Part of N. Aveyron is within the AOC region for Salers (see Chapter 7, pp. 251–2).

### La Tarte aux Vignes

250g and 500g square *pavé* of Rebarbe type (see p. 196) by Société of Roquefort. See also ROQUEFORT.
*laitier*; *brebis cru*.
Roquefort.

### Tomme

See BREBIGNOLE, LARZAC Ferme de CUN (brebis) and ROUERGUE (vache).

**Tomme de Brebis.** Made by Maurice Bouet (see ROQUEFORT), Le Bon Berger. Made by G. Soulié at Villefranche-de-Rouergue (see below). 3kg *rocou*-sprinkled cheese in scalloped-edged round, full flavour.

*laitier*; *brebis cru*.
Aveyron.

### Vache

In this predominantly brebis and chèvre region cows'-milk cheeses are the exceptions: see ALIGOT, AUBRAC, BLEU D'AVEYRON, BLEU DES CAUSSES, BRILLADOR, ROUERGUE (TOMMES) SAINT-ANDRÉ, SAINTE-ODILE, LE BON VILLEFRANCHOIS. AOC regions for BLEU D'AUVERGNE, CANTAL, LAGUIOLE, SALERS all include part of northern Aveyron.

### Vignes

See LA TARTE AUX VIGNES.

### Villefranche-de-Panat

Papillon/Alric *laiteries*.
Lévézou; 80 **13**, high L by lake.

### Villefranche-de-Rouergue

Shops: the late Madame Soulié's cheese shops (but no longer in the family). Her *laiterie* is continued by her son, M. G. Soulié, who makes Brebignole, Lou Péraillou, Tomme de Brebis, Étarlou (chèvre), Le Bon Villefranchois and Saint-André (vache), all listed above; 15 rue Marcelin Fabre in *zone industrielle*.

BERRY
Chalon-s-S
SAÔNE-ET-LOIRE
Saône
Cérilly
Allier
Bourbon-Lancy
Moulins
BOURGOGNE
ALLIER
BOURBONNAIS
Montluçon
Montmarault
St-Pourçain
Lapalisse
Bresse
Gouzon
MARCHE
CREUSE
St-Éloy-les-Mines
VICHY
Roanne
RHÔNE
Dombes
Limagne
Châtelguyon
Riom
Loire
Pontgibaud
CLERMONT-FERRAND
Thiers
Combraille
Noirétable
LYONNAIS
Rhône
Rochefort-Montagne
PUY-DE-DÔME
St-Dier-d'Auvergne
LOIRE
LYON
Laqueuille
St-Amant
Monts du Forez
Plaine du
Montbrison
Bourg-Lastic
La Bourboule
Murol
St-Nectaire
Cunlhat
Forez
Ussel
Tauves
Le Mont-Dore
Chambon-s-Lac
Ambert
St-Anthème
LIMOUSIN
CORRÈZE
St-Germain-Lembron
St-Bonnet-le-Château
ST-ÉTIENNE
Pélussin
DAUPHINÉ
Livradois
Ardes
Bourg-Argental
Condat
Limagne de Brioude
La Chaise-Dieu
Craponne
Velay
AUVERGNE
Brioude
Annonay
Vorey
Yssingeaux
Salers
St-Félicien
HAUTE-LOIRE
Tournon
Isère
CANTAL
St-Flour
le Puy
Fay-s-Lignon
St-Agrève
Lamastre
Thiézac
Vic-s-Cère
Vernoux-en-Vivarais
Valence
Aurillac
Mt Mézenc
Vivarais
La Voulte
Coucouron
Le Burzet
Montsalvy
Laguiole
ARDÈCHE
Entraygues-s-Truyères
Aubrac
Gévaudan
Largentière
Rouergue
Ruoms
LOZÈRE
Rodez
Le Pont-de-Montvert
AVEYRON
Alès
CTAT VENAISSIN
St-Jean-du-Gard
GARD
AVIGNON
Albi
NÎMES
MONTPELLIER
LANGUEDOC
PROVENCE

CHAPTER SEVEN

# Auvergne and other pays of the Massif Central

AUVERGNE – BOURBONNAIS – FOREZ –
GÉVAUDAN – EASTERN LIMOUSIN – LIVRADOIS –
VELAY – VIVARAIS

The *pays* covered in this chapter are geographically, and often historically, interlocked. None of them could be isolated without cutting across some shared or related traditions of cheesemaking. The destiny of Marche and Limousin on the west side of the Massif has usually lain with Aquitaine and Poitou (see Chapters 3 and 4), but the Combraille corner of Marche was part of the Bourbonnais for centuries; and the eastern finger of Limousin forms part of the Cantal–Salers *région d'origine*, as does the northern Rouergue, which is also associated with Laguiole on the plateau d'Aubrac.

Mountainous regions usually breed tough, independent people. The Arvernes, forebears of the Auvergnats in pre-Roman times, were no exception. Their civilised kingdom was a force to be reckoned with, noted for its mining and working of iron, bronze, silver and gold (whence Massif du Mont d'Or). There was well-established agriculture in the Limagnes, the fertile vales of the Allier, and flourishing dairy farming in the uplands. The Gabalès on the plateau d'Aubrac and their Arvernes neighbours were then already producing the ancestors of today's Laguiole,* Salers and Cantal, and the Arvernes and Vellaves (of Velay) were probably making the forebear of our blue *fourmes*.

Defeated by the Romans in 52 BC, the Arvernes and their neighbours prospered in Roman Aquitaine, establishing a military-cum-episcopal régime. (The bishops of the great diocese of Clermont remained powerful seigneurs until the Middle Ages, eventually losing temporal power in Clermont itself to Catherine de Medicis in 1551.) The Auvergne became part of Charlemagne's Kingdom of Aquitaine in the late eighth century, and a comté in the ninth; the final ruling house, de la Tour d'Auvergne, took on the title in 980. After family divisions in 1155, the usurping comte lost la

*pronounced 'la-yole'

Terre d'Auvergne to King Philippe Auguste. This became the duché in 1360, when it was granted to that revered patron of the arts, the duc de Berry, and later descended to the ducs de Bourbon. The reduced comté descended through Catherine de Medicis (who also seized the episcopal section of Clermont). The comte who had been displaced in 1155 kept Montferrand and the non-episcopal part of Clermont. This comté de Clermont, after a marriage with the Dauphin family (see Chapter 16), became the Dauphiné d'Auvergne. With the Forez, it descended to Charles III, ninth duc de Bourbon, and was forfeit in 1521 with the duché d'Auvergne and the Bourbonnais, when the duc sided with the Emperor against François Premier.

The Bourbonnais connects the Auvergne with Berry and Burgundy in the north, and its pre-Roman population was a mixture of Bituriges (today's Berrichons), Éduens (pre-Burgundians) and Arvernes. Aimard, or Adhémar, was the first seigneur in the early 900s. His family acquired the Château de Bourbon and adopted its name (from Borvo, Gallic god of waters). By later marriages the Bourbons acquired the Dauphiné d'Auvergne, the Forez and Beaujolais, and the duché d'Auvergne, but the Bourbonnais proper had reached its present boundaries by the twelfth century.

The Bourbonnais came through female descent to Louis IX's (Saint-Louis's) son Robert, whose heir was made first duc de Bourbon in 1327. In the sixteenth century Antoine de Bourbon of the cadet Vendôme line married the heiress to Navarre and most of south-west France and fathered France's first Bourbon king, Henri III de Navarre, IV de France.

In the north-west Bourbonnais, against Berry, is the Forêt de Tronçais, 'aquiver with springs', in René Barjavel's words. 'For perhaps a million years', he wrote, 'the forest has grown in this same spot.' Its oaks achieve enormous height and girth, and are said to make the finest cognac casks. The River Allier, which gives its name to the modern *département*, rises in the Gévaudan and flows through the Velay, before enriching Auvergne and Bourbonnais with its Limagnes and its salmon. The Bourbonnais insist that the Allier (already 410 kilometres long when it leaves them) runs to the Atlantic, not that mere tributary of the Allier, the Loire; but the Bourbonnais are themselves another ancient feature of their land: '*Gueux, Glorieux, Gourmands*', as the nineteenth-century Bonapartist Maréchal de Castellane described them ('rogue' is a fairly charitable translation of *gueux*).

Their oldest vineyards are those of Saint-Pourçain, which provided *réserves royales* in Louis XI's and Henri IV's reigns. The white has a particular fruity character and strength. They lie on the edge of the two main goat-cheese areas of the province, centred on Moulins (modern capital of the Bourbonnais) and Montmarault.

## CHEVROTON, MONTMARAULT AND OTHER FARM CHEESES

The characteristic cheese is the Chevroton, sometimes called Chevrotin (the *savoyard* spelling), a truncated cone or cylinder ranging from 100 to over 200 grams in weight. Similar to Burgundy's Charolais, around Moulins it is usually eaten within two weeks of making, *frais* or *demi-sec* rather than *sec*. Its mildness is enlivened by a touch of acidity. At the *demi-sec* stage some develop a pale pinkish-cream crust decorated with blue mould, and their firm yet delicate interior melts in the mouth with a refreshing flavour. I have kept some for a further week, during which they softened and achieved satisfying richness.

Montmarault cheeses, sometimes called Roumajou or Roumajoux, are more often eaten at this three-week stage and a version called Conne de Montmarault is ripened for up to six weeks. The terms Roujadou or Roujadoux are applied to Montmarault cheeses which have reddened through natural surface fermentation or through washing the crust.

I found excellent Chevrotons to the south-east, at Lapalisse, where they are modestly presented as chèvres *'du coin'*. The Hôtel Bourbonnais served some, after other agreeable food, and put me on to the Crémerie Nouvelle in rue Winston Churchill (the Dompierre Road, west of the bridge). As well as the Charolais-like chèvres *du coin*, made on several nearby farms, I found an appetising, fresh-flavoured cows'-milk *fromage du terroir*. Drum-shaped, and cream-coloured when young, it developed a *croûte-fleurie*, eventually looking rustically worthy of its name (the firm interior becomes crumbly with greater maturity).

Other Bourbonnais cows'-milk cheeses described on the list tend to be very local and to become ever thinner on the ground: Bessay from south of Moulins; Coulandon, a low-fat, Coulommiers-shaped cheese, also called Chaucetier or Chauceron (occasionally miscalled Chancelier and Chanceron, I believe), from west of Moulins; the newer Cérilly from further west; the bigger Chambérat from north-west of Montluçon; Gouzon and Coupi (also called Creusain and Creusois), curious skimmed-milk cheeses from a corner of the Bourbonnais cut out of the Marche, now in Creuse.

# LAGUIOLE

The earliest surviving mention of cheesemaking in the region is by Pliny the Elder (who died in AD 79), who in Book XI of his thirty-seven volume *Naturalis Historia* refers to cheeses made by the Gabalès of Gévaudan and the Arvernes, cheeses generally accepted as the forerunners of Laguiole from the plateau of Aubrac, and of Salers and Cantal from southern Auvergne. There is identifiable mention of Laguiole in the fourth century, and it was nursed by the twelfth-century monks of *la domerie* d'Aubrac on the route to Santiago de Compostela, so must have helped to feed the pilgrims. Cantal was praised by Saint Gregory of Tours in the sixth century, and its makers were given privileges by Charles VI in 1407. Some historians believe that the Fourme-makers of Livradois and Forez have been too modest in claiming seventh- to ninth-century origins for their cheese. Fourmes like theirs were probably well established in Arverne country before the Romans came.

Aubrac has its own ancient breed of cattle. Until recently no other was used for Laguiole, which has also been called Laguiole-Aubrac. *La race blonde d'Aubrac* is small, handsome and hardy, wheaten to fawn coloured, with curved, out-reaching horns and Alderney-like eyes. Its yield is low, but the quality of the milk is perfect for cheese. There were 50,000 of them in southern Auvergne in the late 1960s, but they no longer figured in the national milk records in 1986. These native beasts make plenty of fat and casein out of the unusual nourishment of the pastures on their basalt base, which include gentians, three-coloured violets, alpine fennel (*cistre*) and broom. Recent French research has reminded us of the inimitable qualities of the old breeds in exploiting their native soils and herbage, and measures have been taken to preserve these cattle (crossings with Charollais to improve the meat-quality of the beef calves had been affecting its purity).

Until recently all Laguiole was made in *burons*, the squat stone summer farmhouses on the plateau of Aubrac, occupied between late May and mid-October while the cattle are in *transhumance* on pastures between 800 and 1400 metres. The building has a room with a fireplace for the dairy, with beds for *le cantalou* (cheesemaker) and *le garde* (the herdsman), a separate, cooler room to store the cheeses, and often a *porcherie* for the pigs, which dispose of the whey. Rent for *buron* and pastures used to be paid partly in cheese. In 1900 there were 1000 *buronniers*. By 1960 only 250 remained, making 400 tonnes of Laguiole, while the only *laiterie co-opérative* made 20 tonnes. In 1975 the *burons* dropped below the hundred mark, and by 1984 only four survived, making just 10 tonnes of cheese against 550 made by the sole *co-opérative*. The rest are now abandoned, or used by their owners for occasional summer visits. In 1985 an experimental *buron* was set up to produce two cheeses a day between 5 June and 20 September, nearly doubling the *buron* production to about 450 cheeses.

The Co-opérative fermière Montagne at Laguiole makes 12,000 heavier cheeses a year now (getting on towards 600 tonnes), working all the year round. It is important, therefore, to look at the date on top of the cheese to see whether it is from *transhumance* milk or not. The *co-opérative* stores and distributes the *buron* cheeses, as well as its own, and can give directions to the *burons* still working.

The method of making has changed little over the centuries. The raw whole milk is brought fresh to the vat and raised to 37°C (this is the Syndicat's figure in 1985; La Crémerie française gave 35° in December 1983, Courtine 30–32° in Larousse in 1973). Rennet is introduced (35 millilitres per 100 litres of milk) and coagulation takes about one hour. Breaking, stirring and pressing of the curd inside the vat takes about forty-five minutes. It is then removed and placed in cloth on a slatted wooden base under the ladder-like *presses-tôme*. Pressure mounts during two hours (Syndicat's 1985 timing, which Pierre Androuët tells me is wrong; La Crémerie française 1983 gave six hours; Courtine 1973 'variable', which, strictly, must always be true). It is then left for eighteen hours of *maturation*. It may be sold in this fresh, unsalted, malleable state for cooking as Tomme fraîche de Laguiole, which is prized above the Tomme d'Aligot of Cantal, or even of Salers. (The recipe for the traditional Auvergnat Aligot is given on p. 227).

The next day, after the full eighteen hours, the curd is milled and salted very thoroughly by hand (about 25 grams per kilo of curd) before being placed in cloth-lined moulds and pressed for forty-eight hours. During this period the cheese is turned seven times. It is now ready for *affinage* in the *cave* at 12°C for at least four months, and up to six. The crust, which acquires mould naturally, is brushed regularly, and its initial white turns through shades of gold, bright at four months, amber and brown after further ageing. The top of the cheese is stamped 'LAGUIOLE' in relief, with a bull sign and the date of making. When passed by the grader it is given an aluminium 'CNAOF' tag on the side, bearing the code of the *buron* or *laiterie*. It may not be sold as Laguiole AOC without this seal of approval.

The *pâte* is straw coloured, smooth and firm, but melt-in-the-mouth. It has a noticeable bouquet with lactic overtones, and a clean, but slightly tart flavour, becoming richer with age. Laguiole's consistency when young can be reminiscent of Beaufort, but Beaufort is sweeter (see pp. 428–9). The *buron*'s cheeses have more tang. Because they average only one every other day, there usually has to be a mixture of two days' curd and the effect on the flavour recalls England's sharp Lancashire, with its close similarities in method but its more crumbly texture. Early in February 1987 I tasted a May 1986 *buron* Laguiole from Monsieur Gérard Paul (*maître fromager* of Aix and Salon-de-Provence); its colour was a warm, light gold, its consistency still supple and succulent, and its rich flavour had a sharp tang (killing red wine and going better with a *demi-sec* white). It was unlike any other cheese I have ever tasted.

# SALERS

Salers is an equally ancient cheese, similar to Laguiole, and the name is also given to the Auvergne's great dairy cattle, whose milk gave the lustre to this cheese, to Cantal *fermier* and to Saint-Nectaire. The Salers are deep chestnut and curly coated, bigger than the Aubracs and tougher in the face, with lyre-like horns. The breed was brought on in the last century, and up to 1914, through selective breeding by Monsieur Tissandier d'Escous of Salers. Sadly, numbers have decreased by two-thirds in the last twenty years, to fewer than 60,000 milkers in 1982, and have gone on diminishing disastrously.

In the Monts du Cantal and the Puys permanent pastures cover 80 per cent of the mountains, watered by 48 inches of rain at 800 feet and up to 78 inches on the heights. Never cut, they are reserved for the *transhumance* grazing season between 1 May and 31 October (lengthened by eight weeks in recent years). Long before AOCs were granted to these cheeses and to Cantal, a court judgment recognised that climate, altitude (cows giving milk for Salers graze at over 2600 feet) and the nature of the volcanic soils (strong in phosphates, potassium and magnesium) 'contribute to the rich herbage adorned with natural flora, varied and native, such as liquorice, gentian, anemone, arnica, myrtle, etcetera, obtaining for the cows who are nourished by it ... a *cru de lait* particularly appropriate for the making of *la fourme du Cantal*'.

Salers Haute-Montagne was the pre-AOC name for the local summer cheese of the *burons* around Salers in Cantal. The AOC of December 1979 extended the protected name Salers to Cantal made in *burons* throughout the Cantal region, covering all the *département* of Cantal, twenty-five *communes* in Puy-de-Dôme, one in Haute-Loire, eight in Aveyron and one in Corrèze (Limousin).

The cows graze freely by day, but are enclosed each night in a different place to spread the benefit of the manure. The *boutilier* or *cantalou* (plural: *cantalès*) is the master of his team of one or more *gardes* or *pastres*, who look after the cattle, milk them and help with cheesemaking and cleaning of equipment.

Salers production rose from 830 tonnes in 1980 to about 1200 tonnes in 1984, and the number of *burons* from 92 to 120 between 1983 and 1985 (one at Belles-Aygues, above Laveissière to the west of Murat, is now a museum, but you should try to visit one that is still working). Official production figures group Salers with Cantal, but Salers' total production has been estimated by dividing the gross AOC Cantal figure (19,000 tonnes plus) by fifteen; however, the proportion is probably becoming greater.

Herds have to be forty or more strong to provide the 350–500 litres of milk needed every day for an AOC cheese. In 1973 a young *buronnier* I talked to at Égliseneuve d'Entraigues market was making one 30–32-kilo cheese daily from the milk of twenty-seven cows. He worked his milk morning and evening, leaving none overnight. His cheeses would not be large enough now for Salers or Cantal AOC, but his milk would stretch to a Petit Cantal and a Cantalet.

The AOC does not specify the milk of the traditional breed; this should be rectified before it is too late for this noble name so long justified by cheese and cattle.

In some *burons* the milk is still carried in the *gerle* (a two-handled, barrel-like tub used as a vat) on a cart from hand-milked cows to the dairy, and heating to 32°C may still be done before an open fire. At that temperature the milk (whole and raw) is renneted. It takes from sixty to seventy-five minutes to form the curd, which the *boutilier* then breaks evenly by moving the *fréniale* (or *ménole*) up and down, steadily round the vat (this curd-breaker has a metal base of two concentric circles connected by radii, rather like a ski-stick). A surface too white with cream indicates that the breaking was started too soon, or done too fast; if the whey has greenish lights, it was started too late or done too slowly. If all is well, the *fréniale* will bring up clusters of curd knobs the size of hazelnuts. It is then ready to be stirred by the *attrassadou* (wooden rudder) or *ménadou* (wooden paddle) until it sinks to the bottom of the vat. The *attrassadou* is moved round the edge of the vat, gradually assembling the knobs into one mass of curd, called *la tome*. This may be followed by applying the mushroom-shaped *pouset* to press out more whey. The *boutilier* now removes the whey in bucketfuls, which his assistant puts through a cream-separator while he places the curd on to the sloping grid of the cloth-lined wooden *presse-tome*. The upper part of the press is like a ladder imprinting ridge and furrow in the curd as it is pressed. It is then cut, turned and pressed again six to eight times, until the dripping of whey has almost ceased, when it is left for fourteen to thirty-six hours' maturation at 15°C.

Next day, when the curd is ready, it is cut into slices and put through the *brise-tome* (curd-mill) to be ground into irregular grains, which should separate after being squeezed in the hand; if they stick together, more time is needed. The curd is salted (16–23 grams per kilo) by a succession of stirrings over two or three hours, then eased down into a wooden mould lined with fine cloth, 38–48 centimetres in diameter (the old Cantal farm custom was to line the mould or *facture* with beech-leaves), and put under pressure. Over a period of two days the curd is repeatedly removed, turned and re-pressed in a fresh cloth, until it is a firm, upstanding cheese. Now called a *fourme*, it is ready for the cool, humid *cave* (13°C), where it will be rubbed and turned every other day for a minimum of three months, at which stage the now golden cheese is graded.

The approved cheese bears a 'CNAOF–SALERS' rectangular red aluminium plaque, with the number of the *département* and the maker's code number. It must weigh between 35 and 55 kilos. At maturity the gold of the thick crust is mottled, almost marbled, with flecks of red and orange. The smooth yellow *pâte* is firm, yet giving. The flowery bouquet and flavour of the pastures and their soil grows with maturity. To see its beginnings and surroundings, enquire of the Syndicat d'Initiative at Vic-sur-Cère about *buron* visits (see list, p. 254).

## CANTAL

Cantal is basically the same as Salers, but the February 1980 AOC did not specify raw milk, and most of the remaining farmhouse cheesemakers now produce in the summer months under the Salers label; the methods laid down are similar to those for Salers and the defined region is identical. Unfortunately, tolerance of pasteurisation and the low minimum *affinage* of forty-five days, sops to the industrial *laiteries*, have made Cantal synonymous with dullness in many people's minds. Indeed, an American acquaintance was told by a French friend: 'If you prefer Cantal, you don't really like cheese.' This attitude is regrettable, and unfair to the raw-milk artisans, but it shows how a good name can be ruined by allowing it to be borne by substandard products. Luckily the use of raw milk is increasing, even among some of the large-scale makers such as Centre-lait Aurillac, and by 1985 was adopted for 70 per cent of all Cantal production.

About 18,000 tonnes of Cantal (excluding Salers) is made annually in fifty co-operatives and smaller *laiteries artisanales*. The number of farms decreased from 800 in 1960 to 150 in 1982. None was mentioned in La Crémerie française's survey of ANOC cheeses in December 1983, but I was told at Aurillac by the Comité Interprofessionnel des Fromages d'Auvergne in 1985 that, despite the larger number in the Salers scheme, there were still eighty-four farms making Cantal.

The finished cheeses have an aluminium plaque with the departmental and *laiterie* numbers, the day of making, and the letters CA for the 35–45-kilo cheese, CP for the 20–22-kilo Petit Cantal, and CT for the

8–10-kilo Cantalet (familiarly, *'tambourin'*, long drum). The crust is duller than that of Salers, on the greyer side up to three months, when it is called Cantal Jeune. It acquires some golden flecks between three and six months, when it is Cantal 'Entre-deux'; after six months it becomes Cantal Vieux. The *pâte* is smooth and ivory in colour, firm, vaguely lactic in aroma, and at the *vieux* stage should have a good nutty flavour. When cut it can show up to a centimetre of crust if it is really *vieux*. At its best, made with unpasteurised milk and matured for well over six months, Cantal is a warm, rich cheese not dissimilar to good Cheddar, except in its slightly metallic side-flavour, which betrays the volcanic soil (the best Cheddar has more sweetness, from its limestone base).

Laguiole, Salers and Cantal must contain a minimum of 45 per cent fat in solids, but AOC-graded cheeses do not have to state this. Pre-packing of Salers and Cantal is permitted, provided a quarterly return is rendered by the packer accounting for the source and quantity of cheese bought and the quantity and destination of all cheese sold. This should prevent industrial methods from being camouflaged in pre-pack form. I was assured that Cantal *laitier* was made in ways very close to *'méthodes ancestrales'*. The vat temperature is normally controlled by a water jacket, and brought to 30–32°C for renneting. The nature of the rennet is specified in the AOC. The old *presse-tome*, which persists in the small *laiteries*, may have a more mechanical substitute in larger dairies, but for AOC cheeses the basic methods are unchanged.

Three improvements are desirable for these cheeses: the restoration of the role of Salers cows (still boasted of in publicity); the fading out of pasteurisation; and the extension of *affinage* to a minimum three months for AOC cheeses. This would go a long way towards changing the rather static market for Cantal. Thirty *affineurs* concern themselves with Cantal. Most of them also deal with Salers, which, with its *transhumance* milk provenance, is obviously first choice for full flavour. A well-aged Laguiole, if you can find it, is an interesting alternative. Next comes Cantal Vieux, then Entre-deux. Whatever you see in front of you, insist on tasting before buying, because the pasteurised and unpasteurised, the mediocre and the good, the immature and the mature among these cheeses are as remote from one another as a nappy is from a Harris tweed.

## Fourme de Rochefort-Montagne, Bleu de Laqueuille

There is one more related cheese, equally ancient, but not given an AOC: Fourme de Rochefort-Montagne, or Cantalon. Similar in methods of making and in appearance of crust and *pâte* to Cantal, it is made of raw milk, by artisans or on farms within the *commune* and on the fringes of neighbouring *communes*. In 1969 production was still exclusively on farms from the milk of the red-pied Ferrandaises, and amounted to an annual 200 tonnes. The old breed is now unhappily near extinction (see p. 214). The cheese is marketed in Rochefort-Montagne itself, nearly 900 metres up in the west of the volcanic region.

Around 1840, Antoine Roussel of Villeviale, between Rochefort and Laqueuille, noticed that one of these cheeses, which he had put beside a mouldy rye loaf in the bread cupboard, had started to blue. He let it take its course, enjoyed the result, and so gave birth to the delicate Bleu de Laqueuille. This developed as an unpressed cheese, with a dry crust which stayed white on the sides, except for touches of red, but turned a ruddy ochre with flecks of red all over its two faces. Now rather industrialised, and generally sold as Bleu d'Auvergne (see pp. 210–11), its skin is usually kept moist and uninteresting by being wrapped in foil. Despite this, the cheese still has some worthy descendants, especially those from Laqueuille and from *artisans* elsewhere using raw milk, two of whom I visited. At Laqueuille one traditional practice thought to enrich the flavour is to warm the curd before salting. This is also done by the makers of Bleu de Thiézac, north-east of Vic-sur-Cère (see list, p. 254).

Aurillac, lying 19 kilometres south-west of Vic-sur-Cère, has an important covered market on Wednesdays and Saturdays, and you should also visit Monsieur Grillet's excellent Crémerie du Gravier on the Cours Monthyon. On the Promenade du Gravier nearby is the welcoming Grand Hôtel Saint-Pierre, offering at reasonable prices appetising regional dishes, plenty of vegetables, good Auvergne cheeses, and a tasty local red as *vin ordinaire*: a heartening headquarters from which to conduct cheese patrols in all directions.

For Cabécou, for which this south-eastern part of our region is famous, go west for Roumégoux, Glenat and Le Fel (and then 40 kilometres on for Gramat and Rocamadour, in Quercy, if you are still hungry). Go south on D920 for Montsalvy and Entraygues. For the further Gabilitain cheeses (see Gévaudan on the list, p. 242), such as Tomme d'Anceval, Fourme de Labro, the Pélardons and other chèvres, a visit is best planned from the south or east. You can approach from Alès (going north of the Gardon), or from Anduze (covering the area between the Gardon and the Gardon d'Anduze); or from the Picodon and Pélardon areas of the Vivarais in the east.

Further alternatives are the high, picturesque routes down D906 and N88, either via Brioude along N102 (taking in Lavadieu) or from Ambert over the Livradois, with a pause for La Chaise-Dieu. These give you the chance to investigate the survival of a chain of *bleus* and *fourmes* in the Velay (Loudes, Bains, Solignac, Cayres, Costaros and Coucouron) before you leave N88 at Langogne to go south up the Allier Valley into Gévaudan to la Bastide-Puylaurent. There the pleasant Fourme de Labro and the low-fat Sourire are made in a former *maison-rouge* (where the old-time host would have been a French Sweeney Todd). The road south (D906) is winding and beautiful, compensating for the slow speed with which you will penetrate the Parc National des Cévennes to find your Pélardons. A diversion westwards along D901 before continuing south through Villefort may disclose some Pélardons at Altier, a name long associated with that cheese;

but it is also the name of the river you are following, so look out for signs and investigate every *épicier*. I have had no recent experience of cheese made there, so you are on your own. Now I return to Aurillac to set off north up D922.

## BLEU D'AUVERGNE

North of Mauriac, which sits between two sainted volcanic puys, Marie and Thomas, we turned east at Le Vigean for Trizac. There Messieurs Reynal and Varagne make Cantal and Bleu d'Auvergne from *lait cru* in a dairy founded in 1875. Monsieur Varagne told me that they used the milk of fifty farms. The financial crisis, which has meant that more farmers' children have remained or returned to work on the farms, and the exemption of mountain farms from the EEC milk quota have no doubt contributed to the increase in farm cheesemaking in the Saint-Nectaire region, which begins 15 kilometres east of Trizac.

The Reynal and Varagne families have been making Bleu d'Auvergne at Trizac for over 110 years, during most of the life of the cheese, which is an offshoot of Bleu de Laqueuille (see p. 209). With one other old *laiterie* that I know of (Monsieur Col's at Saint-Anthème in the Forez) this must have been among the earliest places of manufacture off the farm, and it is suitable that they should be the rare upholders of the *lait cru* tradition.

In the farm days, and up to the 1960s, production was based on the dairy breeds of Aubrac, Salers and Ferrandaise, and was still all *lait cru*; but by 1969 farms survived only around Thiézac and *laiteries* were making most of the annual 4000 tonnes. Most of them have taken to pasteurisation and to the use of starters permitted in the AOC of March 1976, and of industrial powdered mould. This should be *penicillium glaucum*, the mould naturally acquired by most of Auvergne's blues (including the *fourmes*) if matured in natural caves. However, the booklet sponsored by the Association Nationale d'Appellations d'Origine Contrôlées (CNAOF), *Les fromages d'appellation d'origine*, disturbingly mentions *penicillium roquefortii* in its opening paragraph on Bleu d'Auvergne. This would alter the balance of the cheese, in which a creamy texture and flavour is adorned rather than killed by the rich but unsharp nature of the blue in the best cheeses. The milk is brought to 28–33°C (and starter is added by those who use it) before it is renneted. The *penicillium* may be introduced into the milk or (as I have seen it) into the curd before it goes into the moulds. Coagulation takes from thirty to seventy minutes (starter speeds things up). The curd is cut into cubes of about one centimetre and then stirred periodically until the grains are distinct. When sufficiently drained, in the vat or on a trolley or sieve, the curd is given its dose of *penicillium* (if the milk was not so treated) and placed in the 20-centimetre-diameter moulds. Makers upholding old traditions keep the cheeses for three or four days in a warm room at 18–28°C, with frequent turnings and daily washing (twenty-four to forty-eight hours only was specified in a recent account of AOC cheeses in La Crémerie française). Salting follows, either by hand over several days, with the cheese kept at between 10° and 20°C, or in a brine bath. (Pierre

Androuët considers 20°C too high.) Next comes pricking of the cheese to allow the aeration needed inside for the mould to develop. *Affinage en cave humide* at 8–10°C (6–12°C is permitted) lasts as little as fifteen days for 350- and 500-gram cheeses, two to three weeks for the kilo size, and at least one month for the full-size, 2.5-kilo cheese (the mould will usually have started showing within three weeks). At Trizac, and at Saint-Anthème, full-size, raw-milk cheeses are matured for at least forty days.

In the 1950s and 1960s Bleu d'Auvergne lost considerable trade to the new soft blues of Bresse (see pp. 382–3), with their highly industrialised methods and modern marketing techniques. However, the Auvergne has caught up on the marketing side (not quite, mercifully, on industrialisation), and production had risen to 6500 tonnes in 1982, of which 460 tonnes was exported. Subsequently the *lait cru* cheeses have been coming into the British market.

## Saint-Nectaire

To the east of Trizac lies Riom-ès-Montagnes, with a Cantal *co-opérative* and a Saturday market worth attention. Beyond begins the southern (Cantal) section of the Saint-Nectaire region. Here this richly rustic-looking cheese of indeterminable origin starts competing for milk with the ancient Salers and Cantal.

Saint-Nectaire has a fairly crisp, flat-Tomme shape, swelling a little round the side at its peak stage, and a stout coat of many colours: white, grey, red and mimosa-like yellow; sometimes a touch of jade green or of blue, which one romantic writer thought could arise from the presence of amethyst in Auvergne. It looks as old as man's use of *caves* for cheese purposes, the moulds from those *caves* providing the external colour and rich aroma of the crust. The esters from pasture plants of exceptional variety and sweetness give the interior a bouquet unrivalled by any other cheese I can think of. The words used for dairy equipment by the Monts Dore makers of Saint-Nectaire are of Celtic origin, and differ from the usages of Gévaudan and the Salers region.

Saint-Nectaire is ripened for two to four months. Thanks to its splendid crust, its interior succulence, owed to the rich milk of the Salers and Ferrandaises cows, will keep even longer if required, provided a cool, damp *cave* or undercroft is at hand. This and its moderate size (averaging 1.7 kilos before *affinage*) made it ideal for small, often isolated mountain farms at 800–1400 metres. They needed a cheese they could make independently morning and evening from the milk of a few cows; cheese of which the fair-weather surplus could be easily marketed, or, later in the season, kept to tide over the milkless months of cold and snow. Robert Courtine thinks this cheese has been made for over a thousand years, and only Pliny the Elder's failure to mention anything like it makes me doubtful that it was among the Arverne cheeses of Roman times. Perhaps it was one of the later monastic gifts. The powerful old ecclesiastical comté of Clermont covered the whole of the Saint-Nectaire region from the late Roman era until the fourteenth century. It is only surprising that we lack monastic documentary evidence, such as survives about cheeses in other provinces which have seen more changes than Auvergne.

Leaving Riom (ancient capital of the ducs d'Auvergne) on the south-east by D49 you come almost at once on the east side to the junction with D36. This road meanders up and down and in and out of successive river valleys through the southern Saint-Nectaire villages of the canton of Condat-en-Féniers: Marchastel, Lugarde, Saint-Bonnet-de-Condat, Marcenat, and (by D636) Montgreleix. Marcenat is remarkable in having twenty-eight Saint-Nectaire farms (in 1986), although it also harbours the Papon *laiterie* making Cantal: usually the existence of a *laiterie* has led to the disappearance of most local farm cheese.

Turning south at Saint-Bonnet you enter the canton of Allanches, with most of its Saint-Nectaire farms in Saint-Saturnin (seventeen in 1985) and Ségur-les-Villas (four). In Allanches itself two *laiteries* take most of the milk of the Canton, one of them, the Fromageries des Monts du Cézallier (Thuaire) making Cantal as well as Saint-Nectaire. In 1985 Landeyrat to the north was the only other village here to retain any Saint-Nectaire making, its two farms compensating for small numbers by record productivity: 24,000 cheeses between them in 1984, over twice the average for the whole region.

Allanches and Landeyrat, however, have another claim to notice: they have railway stations opened only twice a year, for herds ascending to and descending from the classic *transhumance* pastures of the Cézallier. To avoid crushing in the railway wagons, calves have to travel separately from their dams. Problems of family reunion after disentraining have been eased by rubbing salt on the calves' backs shortly before the date of travel; this encourages the cows to lick the backs of their own calves, making for quicker recognition by scent at journey's end.

If we turn north at Lugarde or Saint-Bonnet we get towards the heart of Saint-Nectaire country. I wish the ruins of the Abbaye de Féniers could speak to us of cheese; Les Essarts, west of Condat along the River Rhue, does suggest clearings of monastic origin. Condat-en-Féniers is a *commune* large enough to harbour Walchli's *laiterie*, making Saint-Nectaire and Cantal, and still keep twenty-five cheese farms busy (in 1985). In the northern part of the canton there were six more farms at Montboudif, and a further seventeen at Chanterelle. These *communes*, and the Canton of Champs-sur-Tarentaine further west (Trémouille, Marchal and Champs itself, with twenty farms between them, and Lanobre with the Laiterie du Plateau de l'Artense), complete Cantal's share of the region. This contributed nearly 800 tonnes of cheese, about a fifth of all the Saint-Nectaire made on farms in 1984.

Égliseneuve d'Entraigues on the Puy-de-Dôme side of the departmental boundary had seventy-one active farms in 1985. This *commune* produces half as much cheese again as any other in the region, and the canton de Besse-en-Chandesse, of which it forms part, produces over twice as much Saint-Nectaire as all three Cantal cantons put together (see Égliseneuve and Besse-en-Chandesse on list, pp. 239 and 230).

For farm visits in the Canton de la Tour d'Auvergne, on the beautiful high plateau de l'Artense, turn west 8 kilometres north of Égliseneuve. Picherande and Saint-Donat have eighty farms between them. The Charbonnel family is numerous in Saint-Donat, and two members, Marcel and Prosper, welcome visitors and sell Saint-Nectaire from the milk of Salers herds at their farms at Bertinet in that *commune*.

This country, although much higher than England's northern dales, nevertheless reminded me of them, with park-like pastures and streams and stone walls. In spring we were struck by the brilliance of the new dandelions, the delicacy of the miniature daffodils, the glowing terracotta of last year's beech leaves, and the rich red tufts of moss cresting stone walls and rocky outcrops. The Monts Dore reached up snow-topped behind Super-Besse, a modern skiing resort better not looked at too closely (at this point Michelin's *'pittoresque'* green line on the map is briefly inappropriate); look instead towards Lac Pavin on the opposite side of the road, source of the cheese-name found on some of the Petits Saint-Nectaire, 'Le Pavin'.

Before we settle in at Besse-en-Chandesse, to establish the current state of Saint-Nectaire at its headquarters and main market, I want to take you to the place which gave the cheese its name. Saint-Nectaire was the northernmost point reached by a neolithic community which followed the reindeer in a period of climatic change, and the dolmen in the park behind the baths is the best in Auvergne. The Romans made a spa of the lower town. Up above, the mediaeval seigneurs built a castle (lost without trace), and the Casadéenne community at La Chaise Dieu built the fine twelfth-century Romanesque church dedicated to Saint-Nectaire. It is to a seventeenth-century member of the leading local family, the warrior Henri de la Ferté-Sennecterre, duc and Maréchal, that we owe our gratitude for his peaceful contribution to gastronomy: he introduced his treasured local cheese to Louis XIV, and it was thenceforward known and sought after by the King and an ever-growing public under the name of the village from which the present had come, Saint-Nectaire, or Sennecterre (the family name had long been variably spelt). Père Audigier, a seventeenth-century canon of Clermont claimed (justifiably, I am sure) that 'these were cheeses as good as the most famous in Europe'; in the 1780s Legrand d'Aussy, keeper of manuscripts at the Bibliothèque Royale, said, 'In Limagne if they want to give you a treat it's Saint-Nectaire they'll serve.'

Much of today's cheese is still made and matured as it had been for many centuries before it came to Versailles. Since the arrival of the motor vehicle, the marketing, formerly dispersed, has increasingly centred on Besse and Égliseneuve, and the cheeses are no longer brought to market tied up in half-dozens, a practice suited to the former use of pack animals. The *grossistes–affineurs* collect cheeses in the *blanc* state (from three to fifteen days old) from their regular suppliers and keep an eye open for promising newcomers. They iron samples of each batch with slim cheese-irons, half the diameter of those we use in Britain. Honest criticism explaining rejections is important for the nineteen out of twenty farmers who have neither the space to mature all the cheeses they need to sell, nor the extra labour for the *affinage*. Space and labour are provided by the *grossistes*, in *caves* with all the natural attributes required: high humidity and inexhaustible reserves of natural moulds.

In the inter-war and immediate post-war years Saint-Nectaire suffered price competition from cheeses made outside the region (which was formally established by the tribunal at Issoire in 1955). Cheeses from other parts of France, even from Italy, assumed the robe and name of Saint-Nectaire in local *caves* (see Savaron, p. 252). The Ministry of Agriculture encouraged the formation of a *syndicat* of makers, which had the region defined, and, with the help of *affineurs* and distributors, evolved the oval green casein plaque with its identification of *département*, *commune* and farm, to which the Ministry gave legal effect in 1959. With changes of code for producers in 1984, this remains the mark of the Saint-Nectaire *fermier* today. (The *laiteries* have a square plaque.)

Until 1964 Saint-Nectaire was exclusively a farmhouse cheese produced from the unpasteurised milk of Salers and Ferrandaise breeds. The ancient unploughed pastures were naturally fertilised by the herds and by the litter of pigsty and winter cattle-shed. As late as 1968 there were 40,000 Salers in the Puy-de-Dôme, and 40,000 Ferrandaises (then exclusive providers of milk for Fourme de Rochefort-Montagne: see p. 248), but Montbéliardes had risen to an equal number and there were also 50,000 Frisonnes. These last have increased considerably since at the expense of the indigenous Salers and Ferrandaises; in 1982 the total number of Salers in the region was under 60,000 and Ferrandaises no longer featured on their own in the national figures.

The high-yielding Montbéliardes have a proven record of success in the Jura with Franche-Comté's *lait cru* cheeses, Comté, Emmental Grand Cru and winter Vacherin (see Chapter 14); but the old Auvergne breeds have a special talent for producing rich milk on their volcanic pastures, with a resulting cheese beyond compare. Frisonnes are quite unsuitable in such an environment and for such a cheese. Quantity is all they offer.

The desire for quantity has led to another crime against Saint-Nectaire: chemical fertilisation of pastures. As Britain's Cheshire farmers discovered too late, artificial fertilisers cloud the character both of the pastures and of the cheese which stems from them. In the Auvergne they eliminate the flowery aroma and flavour of Saint-Nectaire and cause the cheeses to swell, with the development of Gruyère-like holes. I was told this by Saint-Nectaire makers, including a notable family, some of whom had had this experience but had learned better quickly enough, and never abandoned their loyalty to the Salers breed.

The effect of Frisonnes and artificials has been severe enough to deter some old faithfuls from buying Saint-Nectaire in recent years. Noël Michelin, who during the war made it lovingly as a cover for his rôle in the Resistance, is one such, and knowledgeable enough to put his finger on what has happened. Now he proves his point about artificial fertilisation by making excellent wine from organically tended vines, and finishing in oak, at Terres Blanches in Provence; wine which draws custom and visitors from afar, including Masters of Wine from England. It stands out for interesting character above many more famous wines of western Provence, too many of which, by following modern fashions of fertilisation and vinification, have acquired an ordinary sameness, safe for supermarkets but so boring for wine-lovers who know better. This is the lesson for Saint-Nectaire makers. Their old breeds on their old, unadulterated permanent pastures still produce a *premier grand cru* unequalled for succulence, flavour and bouquet by any other combination of breed and pasture in France, or, indeed, in the world.

I started selling Saint-Nectaire in Streatley in the 1950s, and by the early 1970s my average sales were three cheeses a week. Late in 1972 I noticed quite suddenly that I was having to trim more off the cut cheeses than I was selling. A quick taste explained this: the cheese was dull; why should my customers, who taste before buying, have bought any? I supposed that it had been kept too cold on its way to me, and complained; but a subsequent batch, with the most inviting, glistening interior, patently innocent of refrigeration, still disappointed both nose and palate. I could only attribute the disappointment to pasteurisation, although this assorted ill with the rustic exterior of the cheese and with my experience of the Auvergne.

There was only one way to settle the matter. We went to Besse-en-Chandesse. Sure enough, in 1964 *laiteries* had started making Saint-Nectaire, and there in front of the little establishment at Besse was the sinister steam of a pasteurisation plant. There is an agricultural college with a dairy school at Besse, which I cannot forgive for letting such sacrilege be done under its nose to a noble name (but now, I am told, it gives cheesemaking courses which include the use of frozen goats' milk, so what else is surprising?).

The milk going to the *laiteries* comes from the same soil and pastures as that going into farm cheese, though more is likely to come from farms using chemicals and Frisonnes to boost their production. The biggest difference lies in the pasteurisation of the milk; but the *laiteries* were also leaving the curd longer in the vat and washing it (quite different from washing the *crust*) to make it softer: an industrial Saint-Paulin practice abhorred by monks. The cheese moulds used were metal or plastic, but these were becoming common on farms too, wooden moulds being more expensive and not everlasting (a pity, because they are kinder to the curd, which dislikes the sudden chill of metal or plastic). Naturally, the presses were of industrial type, and pressure could sometimes be overdone. The finished *blanc laitier*, however, would become Saint-Nectaire *affiné* in the same natural *caves* as the farmhouse cheese. The squareness of its green plaque (with the *laiterie*'s code letters and the number 63 for Puy-de-Dôme or 15 for Cantal) would be invisible under its multi-mould coat, indistinguishable externally from the oval-plaqued Saint-Nectaire *fermier* with its oh so different interior.

Thus it was that I, and many ignorant others, had been deceived by the familiar crust and the usual paper label and wrap proclaiming the cheese as Saint-Nectaire; as it still does, with the addition since 1979 of 'Appellation d'Origine Contrôlée CNAOF SAINT-NECTAIRE', the same for *ferme* and *laiterie*.

We were not to know that we must insist on *fermier*, which would now come under the same old *affineur*'s wrap and label with the addition of *'fabrication fermière'* (there was not then, nor has been since, on any of the many *affineurs* labels I have seen any mention of pasteurisation or *lait cru*).

I went into the markets, into the farmhouses and into the *caves*. We came back to England with as many farm cheeses as we had space for, the list of Saint-Nectaire *communes* and their codes, and firm instructions and addresses for our importers, so that they should never again have an excuse for accepting Saint-Nectaire *laitier* for us. Our sales, which had dropped to less than half a cheese a month, quickly rose to four or five a week.

I thought we were safe. We now cleared the mould from the oval plaques on the faces of the three cheeses in every case as it arrived, so that we could tell our customers from which *communes* they came: lovely names such as Saint-Anastaise, Saulzet-le-Froid, Le Vernet Sainte-Marguerite, Saint-Saturnin, Saint-Nectaire itself, and Saint-Genès-Champespe. I kept a record of the actual farms, too, until there was no more room on the list of *communes* to write them down. Then, suddenly, one evening, just back from a visit to English farms, I had a telephone call from Gregory Ward of the then famous Toastmaster's Inn in Kent, an old customer and devotee of Saint-Nectaire. 'Pat,' he said, 'first complaint in all these years: the Saint-Nectaires are dull.' Crestfallen, I consulted the shop and found that, as we had been without an uncut cheese when his order came, he had been sent two cheeses straight from the next new case to arrive, without their being unwrapped. We went down to the cellar and found the third cheese still in its case. We opened it up and scraped it: there was the tell-tale square plaque of a *laitier* cheese.

These true stories are convincing proof of the fatal and detectable effect of pasteurisation on the aromatic esters which give good cheeses their characteristic aroma and flavour, and are so regarded by prominent agricultural and dairy scientists.

It is no coincidence that my first experience of Saint-Nectaire *laitier* came in the year that *production laitière* first exceeded *fermière*. In the early 1960s there were nearly 2200 makers of farm cheese, which reached a peak of 3866 tonnes in 1963. The start of *fabrication laitière* in 1964 had surprisingly little effect on the quantity of farm cheese made, which only once dropped below 3300 tonnes; but it appealed to the less vocational and the least economical farm producers as a better source of income from milk with less labour (a half-filled vat takes nearly as long to make into cheese as a full one). By 1970 the *laiteries* had reduced the number of farms making cheese to just over a thousand, and there were only 629 in 1983 and 1984. In 1985 the tide turned: the number of farms jumped to 680, and they made as much cheese as 2200 had done in 1963. After rising almost without interruption, *laiterie* production reached its peak of 6172 tonnes in 1983, then dropped by 800 tonnes the following year.

I hope this is the first step in a lasting revival, which has not come before it was needed. Few cheese writers have drawn attention to the vital distinction between *fermier* and *laitier* Saint-Nectaire.* Noël Michelin and like-minded devotees, including some writers recently disappointed by Saint-Nectaire, have supposed that farmhouse cheese is virtually unobtainable. So have many retailers, who rely on *grossistes* outside Auvergne for their cheese. Customers who know better must educate their suppliers and encourage them to visit Besse-en-Chandesse to see and taste for themselves. They must understand that insistence on *fabrication fermière* is not only possible but essential to stimulate the resumption of cheesemaking on more farms. We did this in 1973 when checking up on pasteurisation, and again in 1985 when surveying the current state of affairs for this book.

Farmhouse cheese is made twice daily, after morning and evening milking. On our 1973 visit I arranged to watch Madame Féreyrol's morning cheesemaking at Chandèze, just outside Besse. At 6.30 a.m. between 100 and 115 litres (about 25 gallons) of milk came in straight from the thirty-seven Salers cows and was rennetted at once (about 30 cc per 100 litres, with milk at 31°C in summer, 33°C in winter). It usually coagulates in 50–60 minutes, and is ready when the finger can break the curd clearly, leaving the break oozing slightly. Madame Féreyrol's curd was ready in 45 minutes. She worked her *ménole* slowly up and down through the curd, moving it sufficiently after each vertical action to be sure of a uniform cut all round the vat. (The curd is reduced to maïs grain or *petit pois* size in summer, when the *décaillage* may be completed in as little as 10 minutes to avoid excessive development of acidity. In winter the grains may be as big as hazelnuts and *décaillage* can last up to 15 minutes, especially with a soft curd, to encourage acidity. The quantity of milk is another factor in timing.) The temperature of the curd needs keeping at least up to rennetting temperature (Madame Féreyrol brought hers to 35°C) by introducing water at 40–45°C (never warmer, or it will seal the surface of the curd and stop expulsion of whey).

The whey has a greenish tinge when the curd-grains are the right size, if the cheesemaker's judgment has been correct (too white means that breaking was started too soon or done too quickly; too green, started too late or done too slowly, just as we noted with Salers).

Madame Féreyrol then stirred with the *ménole* to firm up the grains of curd. After giving them a few minutes to settle at the bottom of the vat, she brought them together with the *ménadou* (also called *musadour* or *mouisadou*), to form the 'tome'. The implement is taken round the sides of the vat with a gentle turning movement to pile up the curd and encourage it to mass together, which usually takes 10 minutes. At this point the *pouse* or *puise-sérum*, an upside-down mushroom, is used to press down the curd and remove nine-tenths of the whey (which goes through a separator, the solids going to butter and the *babeurre*, buttermilk, to the pigs).

The curd is now cut into 10-centimetre cubes, distributed between shallow moulds (21 × 5 centimetres, the final cheese size) in which the curd

*One who did, Léone Bérard in an admirable study in *Le Livre des Fromages*, suffered an unfortunate printing error which gave the square plaque to the farm cheese and the oval to the *laitier*. The reverse is of course true.

is pressed down by hand, gently at first, gradually more firmly. Madame Féreyrol continued by putting the cheese into a much deeper mould under a tall lever-and-counter-weight press for one minute on each face, then applying the oval green casein plaque (then marked UO for Besse and 28, the farm number; it would now be 63 (for Puy-de-Dôme) UO, with B, the new farm letter, below) and salting on each face. Some makers salt one face and leave the other until the cheese is next turned. The Syndicat suggest 30 grams of No. 2 salt for each cheese; Madame Féreyrol, however, used 25 grams, and I am all for moderation.

The final pressing was done in a larger vertical press with a curved beam top taking six cheeses in each of its compartments. Madame Féreyrol turned hers after eight hours (they are usually left for twelve hours before turning, and for twenty-four hours altogether). The temperature during pressing should be 14–16°C. Draughts and winter cold are to be guarded against, because cheeses can turn bitter if chilled.

When taken from the press and removed from the moulds, the cheeses are usually washed and wiped and put to dry for between two and four days, according to the atmosphere and amount of whey, with daily turning. In summer drying is often done out of doors in a cage with shelves in a cool and shady corner, or in a room with controlled temperature. In winter an airy place between 9° and 12°C is desirable; over 14°C may encourage excessive acidification and 'blowing'. Several cheesemakers emphasised to us the importance of washing equipment in fresh spring water and of avoiding detergents, traces of which can taint cheese.

Most *affineurs' caves* are natural, dug out of the volcanic *tuf*, with a temperature between 9° and 11°C and 90–95 per cent humidity. After two or three days in the *cave*, the new cheese is washed in salt-saturated brine. Some *affineurs* include ochre in the brine to colour the crust, but patience and nature produce a more beautiful, less gritty result. After eight days, if the white or grey moulds have started to come on, the cheese is washed in unsalted water; if not, it is brine-washed a second time. Cheese destined for an old-fashioned length of *affinage* will get a third wash and be turned three or four times a week. After washings, the cheese is wiped with jute sacking. As with Bleu de Gex, where jute sacking lines the moulds, it was first used because it came free with the salt; but jute has a positively beneficial effect in forming crust. (In Britain Blue Cheshires are enclosed in jute, not ordinary cheesecloth.)

Within a fortnight the cheese gradually acquires its first, white-mould coat, *geotrichum candidum*, and often some grey *mucor*. The unwelcome black *mucor-aspergillus* is carefully removed by brine-washing and rubbing with the jute rag. The 1979/82 Appellation d'Origine Contrôlée rules allow cheese to be let out at twenty-one days (ridiculously inadequate for traditional crust development), but the custom upheld in respectable circles is to keep it for at least two months in the *cave*. It should by then have developed clusters of the charming yellow *petit mimosa* of *sporotrichium aureum*, and brilliant red patches of *oïdium auranticum*, without which two adornments no Saint-Nectaire *de bonne famille* is considered properly dressed. The tiny mimosa tends to get flattened when the cheese travels in its paper wrapping, but given the chance to rest from its journey in a sympathetically moist cellar it recovers and flourishes again in its fluffy yellow glory.

On my first visit to Besse for the Monday market, the whole place was jammed solid, a jigsaw puzzle of cheese-bearing vehicles from the farms. It surprised me that they ever got disentangled. My last visit, in the snowy March of 1985, was very different, and it was late morning before things got going at all. Our hotel of earlier years had deteriorated, and we were thankful for a friendly refuge at the Café de la Halle, where Marinette and Denis-Dominique Beauger and their dog Aldo provide smiles, and cheer of every other description. We made contact there with the most important man in Besse, Monsieur Verlaguet, *moniteur-laitier* of the Syndicat du fromage Saint-Nectaire. He was happy because more and more farms were registering, bringing the total to 680, fifty-one more than that for the previous two years, and the best since 1980. He gave me the complete list, the new code, and the AOC details, which had come into force since my previous visit.

Near the café and the Hôtel de Ville is the little shop of the Fromagerie Marcel Barbat et Fils, with its natural *caves d'affinage*, founded in 1900. Good Auvergne cheeses, including Saint-Nectaire *fermier*, are on sale there, retail and wholesale, under the present Monsieur Barbat. There are at least eight of the Barbat clan spread about the list of Saint-Nectaire farmers, and this is a feature of cheesemaking in the region. A dozen families or clans are represented on eight to twelve farms, and over half the other farms are run by families represented from two to seven times on the list.

## Murol, Vachard and Savaron

Before leaving this part of the Auvergne there are a few Saint-Nectaire relatives to meet. Murol, close to Saint-Nectaire, was perhaps the source of Saint-Nectaire cheeses bought in the inter-war years by the *affineur* Jules Bérioux, who gave them a hole in the middle and sold them as Grand Murols (why the final 's' was added I do not know; it has been deleted latterly, but persists in cheese lists). They have long been made now at Chaux Blanche, near Cournan, by the same firm, J. Bérioux; but through all the years I have known it, this cheese has been rather a decadent version of the original Saint-Nectaire: puny (450-gram Pavin-size) pasteurised, under-flavoured (but not improved by keeping), ochre-crusted, and frankly dull. The 'holes' brighten up cheese stalls in Murol, little cylinders coated in red wax sold as Trou de Murol or Trou du Curé. Since I was last there, however, Philippe Olivier has shown me his Murol in Boulogne, which he says is made of *lait cru* in Murol itself.

Vachard is a much older relation of Saint-Nectaire and outwardly similar, originally made on farms of milk part-skimmed for buttermaking. With less buttermaking and more factory collection of milk it has almost died out. In the Livradois until the end of the 1960s it was commonly reinforced with some goats' milk and could be *'de très bonne qualité'*. This mixed-milk cheese was usually rectangular. Roger Col of Saint-Anthème makes a lower-fat, cows'-milk cheese of this family, called La Genette, sometimes sold in shops as Vachard.

Savaron was a Saint-Paulin-type cheese (with washed crust), of similar appearance to Vachard, often made outside the Saint-Nectaire region but ripened at Saint-Nectaire in the ancient *caves* of the rue Savaron, whence its name. When it emerged its appearance made it an easy counterfeit for real Saint-Nectaire. It is still made, of pasteurised milk, by some dairies outside the region, and by the *laiterie* at Besse, which finishes it more in the golden Saint-Paulin style true to its type. I am told on highest authority that cheeses of this type are often put through *affinage* in *caves* and sold as Saint-Nectaire.

## GAPE AND GAPERON

Between Clermont-Ferrand and Thiers in the Limagne plain, from Saint-Amant-Tallende and Vic-le-Comte in the south to Randan in the north, lies the land of pink garlic, with Billom as its capital. It used also to be a buttermaking region. The local names for *babeurre* (buttermilk, proverbially of great digestive benefit) are *caillotte de beurre* or *gape*, from which was made the cheese known as Gaperon. The common custom was to precipitate its remaining solids by adding boiling water and leaving it for a few hours for the casein to settle. The colourless *sérum* was then gently decanted, and the white liquor and lees were bagged to drain for a day, to become a crumbly curd called *bara*. When salt and freshly crushed pepper and garlic had been added, it was moulded into rounded cones or domes held together with bass or raffia and allowed three months to mature, strung outside the house. The extent of these garlands of cheese indicated family wealth, and dowry prospects for any daughters.

Since the 1950s artisans in *laiteries* have taken over from farms. Initially their cheeses were still low in fat. Monsieur Allès, whom I visited in Saint-Amant-Tallende in the early 1970s, made the most delectable, almost smokey-flavoured 400–450-gram Gaperons of 30 per cent *matières grasses*. I remember the corner of his dairy redolent of the piles of garlic and pepper awaiting the next batch of cheese. The old buttermilk Gaperons were rennet-free, but today's cheeses (usually smaller) of 40 per cent *matières grasses* or more must be made of renneted, lightly skimmed milk, not the true *gape* of earlier days. La Perette, *marque* of Monsieur Allès, is carried on by A. Garmy et Cie at Pont-Astier, west of Thiers. They also make cutting versions of the cheese.

Pierre Androuët recalls that to test the readiness of a 'Gapron' (as it was often called) the farmer would lay it on the ground and drop a knife from eye-level. If it went right through the cheese, the cheese was ripe. If not, the cheese would be laid on a plank covered with very damp rye-straw to encourage fermentation. I have enjoyed old low-fat Gaperons which had gone well beyond this stage and hardened so thoroughly that I had to break them with a hammer. Their flavour was wonderfully rich, their consistency like fourteen-year-old Parmesan.

## Fourmes and other cheeses of the Forez

Now we go further east, into the Livradois and the Forez, for the blue Fourmes des Monts du Forez (d'Ambert et de Montbrison), and the Chevretons and related chèvres spreading as far as the Vivarais. Ambert is, not surprisingly, a good base from which to explore. Its unusual stone *mairie ronde* has an arcade all round it, under which a good variety of farm chèvres and mi-chèvres, including the beautifully crusted and succulent Briques du Forez, are to be found in season on the first and third Thursdays of the month. The market lasts till noon, but it is wise to be there before 9 a.m. Patrick Stein comes to the market from Craponne (see list, p. 239), a noted traditional centre for Fourmes and chèvres, offering a selection of farm and other regional cheeses, including his Cantal Vieux. I can also recommend the Fromagerie Michel Abonnenc (formerly Pontignat, at the junction of la Place de la Pompe and rue de la Salerie) for its admirable range of regional and local farm cheeses.

You will find within reach plenty of visitable farms, Monsieur Col's dairy near Saint-Anthème, the museum *jasserie* at Col des Supeyres, and the extraordinary working papermill dating from 1323 at Richard-de-Bas. The vital factor of the mill's siting is the chalk-free purity of the water, which also helps the local cheesemakers.

The most famous glory of the Forez, Livradois and Velay is the blue *fourme*, dating from the early feudal period. The famous seventeenth-century Maréchal de Turenne, Henri de la Tour d'Auvergne, said: 'God is on the side of the big battalions, especially when its soldiers have a bit of Fourme in their haversack and a well-filled *gourde*.' Monsieur Mazé, who investigated its making in 1927, asserted that this cheese existed alongside Cantal before the Roman conquest. He even dismissed Roquefort as 'probably nothing but a Fourme d'Ambert made of ewes' milk ... because in Auvergne the ewe's milk does not exist: it has never been seen; it remains a private affair between the ewe and her lamb.'

*Fourme*'s very long existence is attested in various legends and legal documents, as well as in ninth-century stone at La Chaulme, less than 10 kilometres south of Saint-Anthème (by D67 and D67E). Over the door of the seigneurial chapel, seven *pierres dîmales* (tithe stones) illustrate with carvings the tithes in kind to be rendered seasonally by the serfs: butter, ham, sausages, eggs, hay, corn, and an unmistakable *fourme*.

The AOC of 1976 restricted the use of the names Fourme d'Ambert and de Montbrison to cheeses made anywhere in the Loire and Puy-de-Dôme, and in five cantons around Saint-Flour in Cantal (of which Murat has been a source of particularly good cheese). The AOC excluded the southern extremities of the Massif du Livradois and the Monts du Forez within the Haute-Loire, and the main component of that *département*, the Velay.

The Velay (pays of the pre-Roman Vellavi and of today's Vellaves), a land of small farms, lace-workers and weavers, like the Livradois, was highly populated until factory production in both spheres damaged the competitive power of the small producers. Pastures have been reverting to forest; but sheep, lamb and wool fairs still feature in the calendar, and special measures have been taken to preserve the native black Velay sheep (a meat, not a dairy breed).

The Velay has nurtured blues of the *fourme* type for centuries, as far east as the bleakly beautiful plateau du Mézenc on the edge of the Vivarais. The general pattern in the southern Velay has been to use part-skimmed milk and to introduce mould cultivated on rye bread. These blues are usually crusted drums as wide as they are deep (about half the height of the 2-kilo Fourme d'Ambert). Fourme des Monts Yssingelais is of full *fourme* stature but not hard-crusted. Bûche d'Yssingeaux (Laiterie Gérentes) and Bûche du Velay Lys Bleu (Fromagerie des Chaumes) are just soft blue logs.

On page 209 above, I have suggested a route of discovery between Ambert and the Pélardon region. Craponne (see list, p. 239), where they were still drying their *fourmes*, called Fromages de Craponne, in the windows at the end of the 1960s, is off that route, but by less than 20 kilometres from La Chaise-Dieu. La Chaise-Dieu is richer in remarkable abbatial buildings than in the cheese, La Galette, which bears its name, but an organic farm chèvre can be found 10 kilometres to the west. None of the well-matured lifelong inhabitants I questioned, nor the Syndicat d'Initiative, had even heard of Galette de la Chaise-Dieu, and Abonnenc at Ambert had not seen it for years. (Bellevue-en-Montagne (see list, p. 229) offers the consolation of some other chèvres, by the way).

Another very different cheese of the region is Tomme Blanche du Velay, of mild, semi-soft *pâte* coated with *penicillium candidum*, and called by one maker in Auvergne Tomme des Neiges. It has been much copied elsewhere, to its cost; to most effect by Fromagerie des Chaumes with its Belle des Champs, now made in Thiérache.

Most of the *fourmes* which remain in the AOC fold were previously known by the local descriptions of Fourme d'Ambert (for Livradois and Monts du Forez), or Fourme de Montbrison (for the Plaine du Forez). The summer and autumn *transhumance* cheeses made in the *jasseries* between 15 May and All Saints' Day (1 November) were called Fourme de Pierre-sur-Haute. (Pierre-sur-Haute, on the departmental boundary between Puy-de-Dôme and Loire, rises 1634 metres in the heart of the Monts du Livradois.)

*Jasseries*, the Forez equivalent of the *burons*, were usually very simple low buildings with thatch down to the ground over their stone or cob walls. You will find seven of them still marked on the map north of D996 (Ambert–Saint Anthème) and south of Sauvain and Chalmazel.

The Fourmes de Pierre-sur-Haute, fruit of the unspoilt, organically manured mountain grasses and flora characteristic of this limited area, were, like all *transhumance* cheeses, the best and most sought after of their kind. The thought of so many cheesemakers at work up there makes me wish I had been born a century earlier. Some *jasseries* made as few as three cheeses a day (from a herd of eight to ten cows), but what cheese it was. The department of Eaux et Forêts caused alarm in 1902 by proposing reafforestation, but the council of Roche (west of Montbrison) protested that the land was indispensable to the proprietors as pasture for their beasts. Although the *jasseries* survived that crisis, the early 1900s saw the start of production in *fromageries* of what had hitherto been entirely a farm cheese. Methods were usually *artisanales*, based on farmhouse practices, but naturally resulted in more uniform cheese. Until the 1970s they were very acceptable, but inevitably, even on a humble scale, industrial practices and collection of milk subverted variety and continuity in farm production.

In June 1945 the Société d'Amélioration des Produits Laitiers de Pierre-sur-Haute had their definition of Fourmes legalised under that name and those of Ambert and Montbrison: *fourmes* were exclusively of cows' milk, with 'unpressed fermented *pâte*' lightly salted at the stage of packing the curd in the moulds; the blueing was to be natural, in the *cave*, without 'ensemencement' (introduction of mould into milk or curd); the crust was dry, naturally enriched by the white and red moulds of the *cave*. The minimum *matières grasses* after drying was 40 per cent, and minimum dry matter (after at least three months of *affinage*) 55 per cent.

Perhaps because of industrial pressure, this text was later revoked, and until the AOC of 1976 there was inadequate protection for honest *fourme*-makers. Nevertheless, there was plenty of good cheese to be had, characterised by the firm, but not dry consistency of the pale-gold *pâte*, with its small apertures encouraging development of the greenish-blue mould, and the thick, dry, grey-and-red crust. The flavour was gentle and nutty, becoming sweetly rich, with a slight touch of acidity, but not sharp. Stands of such Fourmes des Monts du Forez alongside Roannais and Forez wines were successful at the Paris Concours général agricole in 1963 and 1964. Genuine local production at that time was 600 tonnes a year. The widespread imitations from elsewhere were usually sold as Fourmes Bleues.

Unfortunately most *jasseries* were already abandoned and crumbling by the end of the 1960s, pastures having finally surrendered to reafforestation, sheep or even heather. At least the sheep come with shepherds, who put the *jasseries* to some use, and La Jasserie du Coq Noir remains near the Col des Supeyres as a museum. There you can see the old cheesemaker's equipment, buy Fourmes d'Ambert and de Montbrison, and eat a bowl of Brézoû. This can be cabbage and bacon soup or just rye bread in milk. Confusingly, Brézoû de Saint-Anthème (see list, p. 248) can be a *fromage fort*, and Brizou, another local concoction, is made from broken *fourmes*.

No *jasserie* was working in the middle 1980s, so Fourme de Pierre-sur-Haute is at best dormant. It could and should be resurrected, at least to the extent of making the Jasserie du Coq Noir a living dairy museum, surrounded in the *transhumance* season by a herd of Salers. We could then enjoy once more what I was not alone in thinking the most agreeable blue cheese in the world.

The AOC, far from saving the cheese, allows it to be made of pasteurised milk and cuts down the 1945 minimum *affinage* by more than half, to forty days. It allows the crust (when such a thing is given the time to develop properly) to be deprived of its dry, mould-rich charm by being enclosed in foil (instead of the old-style greaseproof paper, like Stilton). *Ensemencement* (introduction of mould) is now permitted, instead of the former insistence on natural blueing from the local mould.

The result is that many Fourmes can be confused with those upstart soft blue logs from Bresse (some of which have presumptuously adopted the name *fourme*). The crust has been officially described as *'fleurie de belles taches orangées'* spread in the white surface mould, and one leaflet writes of a grey velvet surface. The old *'taches rouges'* would need longer to develop than the meagre affinage required by the AOC, so they can no longer be promised; but the 'velvet' leaflet still offers them, as did the 1983 account in La Crémerie française, which promised *'le petit mimosa'* too. The old *fourmes* might have the mature velvet of moulds over their crusts, but the modern *'fourmes'* tend to miss out the crust and be content with dull young velvet. This quite changes the consistency of the cheese and its flavour, which is in most cases also untraditionally different because of the type of mould and the unnatural method of introducing it. There is no distinction between Ambert and Montbrison, names which can be borne by cheeses from the same dairy. The AOC Syndicat does have a little 'ANAOF' gold sticker to embellish the maker's label on approved cheeses, a very small mercy to be thankful for.

Three *fromageries* on the artisanal scale I have mentioned make their *fourmes* of unpasteurised milk: Viallon at Chalmazel, Tarit at Sauvain, and Roger Col outside Saint-Anthème (see list, p. 248), where the fifth generation of his family is now helping with the cheesemaking. These are three of the *fromageries* co-operating for sales and publicity in GIPRO-FOREZ, which runs the Maison de la Fourme at Sauvain and also exports (10 per cent of Fourmes go abroad).

Monsieur Col collects milk from eighty farms for his *lait cru fourmes* and Bleu d'Auvergne, and his *fromage de montagne* (La Genette, of Vachard type, and the low-fat Maigrette). His old-established *fromagerie* has five employees as well as three family members working for it, and can be visited daily after 2 p.m. It is approached by a track off the left side of D996, about 2 kilometres out of Saint-Anthème towards Ambert (it is easy to miss track and sign if travelling towards Saint-Anthème from Ambert).

The other two nearby *fromageries* make *fourmes* and cows'-milk Briques du Haut-Forez, of pale Pont-l'Évêque character. Pur-chèvres, Briques and Briquettes du Forez, historically known as Chevretons, are another notable feature of local cheesemaking in *laiteries* and on farms, as I mentioned when dealing with the market at Ambert. They are of Roman brick shape, sometimes slightly arched, sometimes hand-moulded and very irregular, with striated surfaces, and occasionally called Cabrions. They vary in weight from 150 to 400 grams, and in colour from white through pale blueish-grey to pinky gold. Briques du Livradois, de Viverols (south of Ambert, not in Vivarais), and d'Ambert, from west of the Forez, are similar.

Other chèvres of the Forez can be found with Patrick Stein at Craponne, at Ambert market on Thursday, and on Saturday in the market at Le Puy. These include the Rogerets from the Forez and the Cévennes (see list,

p. 235), a riot of tiny, but fierce, irregular discs, domes and drums, coloured from yellow to red ochre (whence Rougerin, Rogeret, their local names).

## Cheeses of Vivarais

This brings us to the Vivarais, a beautiful mountain *pays*. On its eastern flank crags and cliff-crested shale slopes tower over the *rivage* along the Rhône. The south-east, between the Ardèche and the Rhône, more like Provence, is called Ardèche à l'Huile. This was Helvie in Roman times, later ruled, like Velay, by sovereign-bishops, and came to the French crown in 1229. It was represented in the États du Languedoc from the fourteenth century, but I hope its modern inhabitants will excuse me for regarding it as a natural companion in its mountains and its cheeses to Velay, Forez and Auvergne.

This century has seen decline and depopulation, and latterly even the disappearance of the *transhumance*. The irregular charm of the old stone buildings has too often been hidden behind the dirty battledress of cement, or the hideous stark suburbanism of harl and rough-cast. What remains of Vivarais' past to delight the eye is the occasional handsome group of farm buildings, and nature itself, sometimes growing over the abandoned terraces of the mountain sides, where the exceptional tiny, high vineyard yet persists. Higher still, castles can be indistinguishable from crags, crags from castles. Far below are the working vineyards of today, producing wines which I have found pleasant with pasta and cheese. On the Rhône south of Valence, La Voulte-sur-Rhône on N86 offers a Friday market before you turn west on D20 for Saint-Laurent-du-Pape (see list, p. 254), where there is an organic goat farm. D120 provides one route up into Picodon country, with a farm at Gluiras by the way, before Pont de Chervil. Further north and west are a farm at Saint-Basile, and Lamastre, where all kinds of chèvres and some mi-chèvres are available.

On N86 north of Valence, Châteaubourg has a surviving castle, and above Tournon, Vion has a remarkable fortified church. Within 5 kilometres, at Lemps, the tiny Apérichèvres are made by Giralamo. Follow D532 and investigate Saint-Félicien for its tasty cheeses, especially those called *caillé doux* (sweet curd).

Rogerets, Rigottes (pur- and mi-chèvres), Brique d'Urfé, tiny hard *séchons* (any old, really hardened small chèvres) and other local chèvres from the Vivarais can be found at the pleasant Crémerie–Fromagerie Chomette-Gennesson at Bourg-Argental, on the Forez–Vivarais border. Here I also found examples of the flat, sometimes very irregular Saint-Félicien, which can be surprisingly rich and succulent inside when not too salt. Some of the best I have tasted were ripened by Monsieur Chauvin at Saint-Félicien itself.

The *pays* of Saint-Agrève, 21 rather wiggly kilometres west of Lamastre, was noted for Picodons and Fourmes, of which Marcel Bourette wrote in his *Contes et Fariboles du pays*: 'The location of cheeses . . . hides itself in vain at the foot of climbing alleys; its smell gives it away. There is the clan of the Picodons pur-chèvre and that, almost shamefaced, of the too white *"pidance"*. The opulent farmers' wives of the plateau line up their high cylindrical fourmes, ruddy of crust, blue and unctuous of *pâte*; they have no separators and their cheeses are at a premium' (none of your southern Velay skimming practices here).

The Picodon d'Ardèche shares its AOC with the Picodon de la Drôme, which I have written about more extensively in Chapter 16. Suffice it to say here that the AOC has regrettably allowed the under-ripe 'shamefaced Pidance' to share the name Picodon with its respectably ripened betters, and permits *thermisation* in the *laiteries*.

Curiosities of the Vivarais include its *fromages forts*, of which recipes are given in the list from Privas and Viviers for Foudjou, and from the Cévennes for Miramande de Pajels (see pp. 240 and 245). In such thoroughly chèvre country, some ferocity is to be expected. In the Viviers version the pot, into which chèvre, both fresh and piquant, salt, pepper, garlic, olive oil and marc have been piled up and matured, should never be emptied, so that some of the contents survive to provide an eternal ferment for future generations. Miramande has a similar tradition, and adds mustard for good measure. Monsieur Forot, author of *Odeurs et Fumets de Table*, had seen pots of which the bottoms had not been exposed to the eye for fifteen years.

Le Burzet is worth a visit on Good Friday for its 600-year-old traditional enactment of the Stations of the Cross up the rough path to its Calvary, 300 metres above the village. It is also the source of a Pélardon-style chèvre, delightfully named Gazimelle du Burzet.

The Vivarais also produces rivals for the Boutons de Culottes and Barattes of the Mâconnais: Chèvretines (and the Apérichèvres of Lemps), miniature drums of as little as 20 grams in bags or on half-toothpicks; and Bichoux. The Bichoux Cévénols are tiny truncated cones on a string, each a tasty nibble; the Bichoux de Cévennes from further south, in the Gard, are miniature hexagonal bells on half-toothpicks, almost unsalted, bright white inside, melting and delicious. I have recently met garlic-saturated examples of cows'-milk Chèvretines from the Ardèche, about 2 centimetres wide and deep, some coated thinly in *sarriette*, others thickly in pepper; these were particularly powerful.

Before leaving the Massif Central, I must mention an old Auvergnat friend for whom I have looked in vain for years: Bougnat (meaning coalman). This was a black-coated, firm *tomme* generously endowed with crushed black peppercorns, to the extent that its *pâte* appeared almost green when cut. The commonest example, made in a *laiterie* in 2-kilo and smaller sizes, with a fairly regular shiny coat, was very tasty; but the richest was a rough, mitey affair, reminiscent in form of the rope-bag-moulded Italian *pecorino*, but less regular, more dome shaped. In the early 1970s my orders for Bougnat were suddenly met by the comparatively upstart peppered versions of the black Fromage des Pyrénées (of which I already sold the best version, Montségur), mean in pepper, flabby in consistency. One lot even arrived with Bougnat labels, but gave themselves away in their *région d'origine* marked elsewhere. I complained to SOPEXA (in England now called Food from France), but I have never seen genuine Bougnat again. Perhaps it survives at La Bourboule, as Cajole, which Ninette Lyon found in 1979, but which has not yet come my way. I hope so, for no 'foreign' imitations have come near that lost old cheese of mine, so redolent of the Auvergne.

## Aligot

Purée enough potatoes (preferably old) for six people, and mix in pounded garlic, melted bacon fat and butter to taste. (Some devotees then soften the purée with *crème fraîche* and reheat; Pierre Androuët does *not* approve!)

Cut into thin strips 800 grams of *tomme fraîche* and add to the purée (while it is still very hot), mixing it in vigorously with a spatula.

When the whole is homogeneous, unctuous and runny without dripping, it should be eaten quickly, as it will go stringy if held too long over heat.

The *tomme fraîche* should be Cantal, Salers or, best of all (in Androuët's judgment), Laguiole.

A similar dish, the mountain 'Patranque' or 'Patrenque' (see below) uses bread in place of potatoes.

## Patranque

*For 4 people*
100g *tomme fraîche*
200g (8 slices) pain de campagne
2 litres milk
salt and pepper

Soak bread in milk and drain thoroughly.

Butter frying pan generously and add shredded cheese (Laguiole, Salers or Vieux Cantal). Stir continuously over a moderate heat.

Season the bread and put it in the pan.

When the cheese has melted, turn out on to hot plates.

An old Auvergnat authority, André Molle, says this dish is better reheated.

## Cheeses of Auvergne and other Pays of the Massif Central

### Aligot

**Tomme d'Aligot (Tomme Fraîche) la Fermière.** 7kg slabs of unsalted curd of Cantal, Salers or Laguiole (pronounced 'la yole') with corrugated top, cut from curd just pressed on draining ladder (hence corrugation) as it comes from vat. I have seen it made at Trizac (see p. 253) by M. Varagne (*lait cru*), and sold in good cheese shops (e.g. Abonnenc in Ambert, Grillet in Aurillac).
*artisanal; buron; vache cru.*
Auvergne/Gévaudan.

L'Altier, Pélardon de

80–120g, one of the Gévaudan names; see PÉLARDON.
45% m.g.; *fermier*; *chèvre cru*.
Lozère/Gévaudan; 80 **7**, N of C.

Ambert-en-Livradois

Market: first and third Thursdays of month until noon; round the striking Mairie Ronde; numerous farm cheeses (see CHÈVRES, CHEVRETONS). Patrick Stein among merchants (see CRAPONNE); get there by 8.30–9.00.
Michel Abonnenc (formerly Poutignat), *fromager*, 4 place de la Pompe/rue de la Salerie, 63600 Ambert (tel. 73 82 71 19 – does mail order; Tues–Sat 08.30–12.30, 14.30–19.00; Sun 09.00–12.00). Fine selection of regional and local farm cheeses.

**Col des Supeyres.** (D106) Musée Paysan de la Vallorgue, Jasserie du Coq Noir on D106 between Saint-Anthème (via D996 E from Ambert) and Valcivières (via D906, D66 N from Ambert). One of the *jasseries* (local name for *burons*, *chalets*) formerly used during *transhumance* season for making *fourmes* (see PIERRE-SUR-HAUTE, which is 8km N of Col des Supeyres on the ground). *Fourmes* and a bowl of Brézoû available. Fête de Jasseries: enquire about this August weekend occasion of the Syndicat d'Initiative, Chambre de commerce, 4 place de l'Hôtel de Ville (tel. 73 82 01 55). It was hoped that it would become an annual event.
See CHÈVRES for several local *chévriers*. Le Chevreton d'Ambert (local Brique pur Chèvre: see BRIQUES, CHEVRETON); Fourme d'Ambert (see FOURME).
Ambert is a convenient base for visiting M. Col's cheese dairy, where *lait cru* Fourme and Bleu d'Auvergne are made, together with a variety of other cheeses of local tradition (see ST-ANTHÈME, which has an annual Fête des Jonquilles on May Day).
The Comité Interprofessionnel de la Fourme d'Ambert et de Montbrison shares the address of the Chambre de Commerce (see Fête des Jasseries above).
Puy-de-Dôme; Livradois/Monts du Forez; 73 **16**, lower R, on R. Dore and D906.

Amigrette

Export name for low-fat blue Maigrette made at St-Anthème (see p. 248).

Anceval

**Tomme d'Anceval.** 300g flat drum and 500g deep drum semi-soft; natural white-mould crust; by Laiterie Sabadel, at Chambon-Le-Château, which is near source of R. Ance (whence Anceval, as name).
60% m.g.; *laitier*; *vache*.
Margeride N. Gévaudan/N. Lozère, near Haute-Loire border; 76 **16**, N of C.

Anduze

**Pélardon d'Anduze.** Also called Péraldou; Anduze is southern stronghold of Pélardon (see p. 245) in its main region of production.
*fermier*; *chèvre cru*.
Cévennes/Gard; 80 **17**, NE of C.

Annonay

**Bleu d'Annonay.** Cheese made in *burons* in eighteenth century, exported to Switzerland and sold in Paris for 24 sols *la livre* (1lb), only 1 sol less than the Roquefort of the day. Annonay market: Wednesdays and Saturdays (good for Picodons).
Vivarais/N. Ardèche; 77 **1**, NE of C.

Boulieu-Lès-Annonay

Fromagerie Ardèche (just within town coming from SE on the N82), advertises regional cheeses.
Ardèche.

Apéri-Chèvre

**Apéri-Chèvre di Giralamo.** Tiny drums about 1.5cm across on sticks, by Giralamo in style of Chevretines (see p. 236).
*artisanal*; *chèvre cru*.
Ardèche/Lemps near Vion; 76 **10**, NW of Tournon.

Araules

*Fromage frais* eaten with chives and garlic, made by Laiterie J. Gérantes (see YSSINGEAUX).
*laitier*; *vache*.
Velay, Haute-Loire; 76 **8**, low L, SSE of Yssingeaux.

Ardèche

See PICODON DE L'ARDÈCHE (AOC).

## Aubrac

Mountain and plateau region noted since Roman times for its cheese (see BASSEZ, CANTAL, LAGUIOLE, SALERS) and breed of cattle (see pp. 203–4).
Lozère, N. Aveyron, S. Cantal.

## Aurillac

Covered market: Wednesday, Saturday 08.00–12.00.
Comité Interprofessionnel des Fromages d'Auvergne Chambre d'Agriculture, avenue des Pupilles.
H. Grillet, *fromager*, Crémerie du Gravier, 22, Cours Monthyon, 15000 Aurillac (tel. 71 48 09 41; mail order in France). Fine range of local farm and regional cheeses and other *'bons produits d'Auvergne'*. Normally closed Sunday p.m., but open seven days a week July and August.
Cheesemaking: Centre-lait, HQ Boulevard du Vialenc (tel. 71 48 03 31), use name L'Auvergnat Gourmand for their Cantal and Cantalet (p. 234), Bleu d'Auvergne (p. 230), Diapason (p. 239) and Saint-Nectaire (pp. 249–51); and see AURILLAC, CARRÉ D'. They were establishing a *laiterie* for Cantal lait cru (AOC) in 1985. Their new soft bleu is Préférence (see p. 247). Fromageries Manhès; 14 boulevard de Paratou; similar range; also *affineurs* of Farm Saint-Nectaire (Coq d'Or label) (tel. 71 48 03 04). Alleyrangue (tel. 71 47 70 11) makes Cantal at Ytrac (76 **11**, far right, W of Aurillac).

## Aurillac, le Carré d'

1½kg square soft bleu by Centre-lait L'École Nationale d'Industrie Laitière d'Aurillac.
Grand Hôtel Saint-Pierre, place du Gravier, Aurillac, recommended for *bon accueil*, tasty food at reasonable prices, good *ordinaire rouge* (local), and good regional cheese (tel. 71 48 17 55).

## L'Auvergnat Gourmand

See AURILLAC, Centrelait, above.

## Baby Pan

½kg size Bleu d'Auvergne by Riches-Monts (*laiterie* at Besse, see p. 230).
*laitier; industriel; vache pasteurisé.*
Puy-de-Dôme/Haute-Loire/Ardèche.

## Bains, Bleu de

One of many small blue *fourmes* of earlier days.
*artisanal; vache cru.*
Haute-Loire, near Le Puy; 76 **16**, top R.

## Banon au Poivre d'Âne

Tasty cheese (of Provençal origin) made by M. Jacques, Dr Madeleine Brunier, *chévriers* at Darbres (tel. 75 94 25 41).
*fermier; chèvre cru.*
Vivarais/Ardèche; Darbres; 76 **19**, low C on R. Auzon D224.

## Bara, Gape or Caillotte de Beurre

Auvergnat for curd obtained from buttermilk (see FOUJOU, GAPERON, SARASSON and SARASSOU).

## Bassez

Small goat cheese described only as 'classic', coming from near Laguiole. (Courtine, 1973, Viard, 1980; but Androuët denies its 'classic' status and has never seen it.)
*fermier; chèvre cru.*
Aveyron/Haute-Loire/Ardèche.

## Bellevue-en-Montagne

**Brique.** 150–200g tasty small Briques; ask at village for M. Duffieux, who receives visitors.
*fermier; vache cru.*
Velay/Haute-Loire; 76 **7**, far L of C on D906.

**Chèvres.** Also honey, vegetables, strawberries in season, all organic; M. Gilbert Conord, Flaceleyres, 43800 Vorey (where there is a Sunday market).
*fermier; biologique; (Nature & Progrès); chèvre cru.*
Near Vorey, 12km SE of Bellevue.

## Bessay, Petit Bessay

200–230g; soft; natural crust; between Camembert and Coulommiers in texture. Formerly on market in Moulins except in spring. Viard says consumption very local (1984). Not to be confused with Burgundian Bessey-en-Chaume, often misspelt as Bessay.
*fermier; vache cru.*
Bourbonnais; 69 **14**, lower C, on R. Allier.

## Besse-en-Chandesse

'Capital' of Saint-Nectaire.
Monday market (10.00 a.m.) tends to jam up centre, so park outside Besse if you want to be able to get away during morning.
Marcel Barbat & fils, *fromager* (since 1900), beside Hôtel-de-Ville and near Café de la Halle. Matures farmhouse Cantal, and Saint-Nectaire under Le Super Besse label (tel. 73 79 50 06). Laiterie Saint-Nectaire: Coopérative Fromagère de Besse (Riches-Monts), July and August (tel. 73 79 51 29) D36 towards Le Mont-Dore, 200m Villetour, turn right.
*laitier; coopérative; vache pasteurisé.*

**Saint-Nectaire Fermier.** Visit farm daily except Saturday and Monday 08.00–10.00, 19.00–21.00, M. Fereyrol, Chandèze (2km) via D36 to SE; turn right on D149 for Chandèze.
For full details of cheese and other visitable farms, and villages worth exploring for farms, see SAINT-NECTAIRE. The Syndicat du Fromage Saint-Nectaire at Besse is looked after by its *moniteur laitier* (M. Verlaguet, see p. 219, has recently retired).
*fermier; vache cru.*
Puy-de-Dôme; 73 **13/14**, low.

## Bichou des Cévennes

Like miniature hexagonal bell, pierced by half toothpick; 2.5cm at base, 1.5cm at top, 1.5cm deep; bright white interior, melting, delicious, almost unsalted.
*artisanal; chèvre cru.*
Cévennes/Gard.

**Bichou Cévenol.** Tiny, neat, truncated cones on a string, each a tasty nibble.
*artisanal; chèvre cru.*
Cévennes/Ardèche.

## Bleu

Apart from cheeses immediately following below see ANNONAY, BABY PAN, CARRÉ D'AURILLAC, CODIBRI, CONQUÉRANT, COUCOURON PERSILLÉ, DEMI-FOURME, FOURMES, DIAPASON, LAQUEUILLE (including BLEU DES NEIGES), LE LISIEUX, MAIGRETTE, MAZET, LE PRÉFÉRENCE.

**Bleu d'Auvergne AOC (1975).** 350g, 500g (see for example BABY PAN, LE PETIT BLEU), 1kg; 2–3kg; latter 20cm × 8–10cm; *croûte-fleurie*, usually hidden by foil wrap; intense blueing in cream-coloured *pâte* produced by *penicillium roquefortii*, introduced into milk, or into curd at milling stage, assisted by later pricking of cheese and *affinage* in cool, humid, airy *caves*, in which the cheese should show blue in 3 weeks, and stay for 3 months (see also BLEU DE LAQUEUILLE). The zone for AOC is all Cantal and Puy-de-Dôme, *arrondissements* of Brioude (Haute-Loire), parts of *arrondissements* of Mende (Lozère, Gévaudan), Rodez (Aveyron, Rouergue), Brive-La-Gaillarde, Tulle, Ussel (Corrèze, Limousin), Figeac, Gourdon (Lot, Quercy). Total production of all makes of Bleu d'Auvergne mounted in the early 1980s to 6,500 tonnes in 1984. The best (apart from *lait cru* below) come from Laqueuille and Thiézac. Most of the cheese is industrial: reliably pleasant in its creamy consistency, and thorough in its blueing, but undistinguished.
50% m.g.; *industriel; vache pasteurisé.*

**Bleu d'Auvergne (AOC) au lait cru.** Two *laitiers* make cheeses lighter and more subtle than the previous one. 1. 1.3kg half-cheese; 2.5kg cheese; released to the trade with at least 40 days of *affinage*. Made by R. Col, Laiterie Ferme de La Genette, St-Anthème (see p. 248), Puy-de-Dôme, who makes several other regional cheeses. Wholesale marketing: Giproforez, Maison de la Fourme, Sauvain (see p. 252).
2. 50 tonnes of 2.5kg cheese (matured at least 40 days) made annually by SARL Raynal-Varagne, 15400 Trizac in Cantal (who also make *lait cru* Cantal and Tomme Fraîche), (tel. 71 78 60 76); *caves* open till 18.00 weekdays.
These cheeses have more character and charm than the factory product, being less dominated by the blue (which is common to so many other cheeses). Quinty of Clermont-Ferrand is *affineur* of *lait cru* Bleu d'Auvergne.

**Bleu des Causses AOC.** Part of this cheese's AOC region is here, but its heart is in the Rouergue (see Chapter 6, p. 192).
*laitier; vache.*
Cévaudan/Lozère.

**Bleu de Cayres.** Blued with mould cultivated on rye bread, of which crumbs are spread in curd; ripened in airy, damp *cave*; very local (latest confirmation Viard,

1980), similar to Costaros (below).
*low-fat; artisanal; vache cru.*
Velay/Haute-Loire; 76 **17**, high L.

**Bleu de Costaros.** Made of part-skimmed milk; 600g to 1kg; 12cm × 12cm drum; lightly pressed; rustic natural crust. May be sold as Bleu du Velay; the *bleus* of Cayres, Langeac, Loudes, and Solignac are related in type (Viard, 1980; Lyon, 1985).
*fermier; vache cru.*
Velay/Haute-Loire; 76 **17**, upper L on N88.

**Bleu de Langeac.** See COSTAROS above.
*fermier; vache cru.*
Velay/Haute-Loire; 76 **5**, low, far R.

**Bleu de Laqueuille.** See LAQUEUILLE.

**Bleu du Lisieux.** Drum-shaped mild blue, named because of Pic du Lisieux, 5km W of Mazet-Saint-Voy, where the cheese is made by the Laiterie Coopérative du Lisieux (for low-fat version see Le Lisieux).
*45% m.g.; laitier; vache.*
Velay/Haute-Loire; 76 **8**, bottom of C.

**Bleu de Loudes.** Two months' *affinage*; rustic, crumbly and hard (Chast et Voy, 1984); 'tasty' (Lyon, 1985).
*20–30% m.g.; fermier; vache cru.*
Velay/Haute-Loire; 76 **6**, low R.

**Bleu de Lozère, lou Meillou Bleu.** 500g drum; soft blue; *croûte-fleurie*, by Sabadel.
*50% m.g.; laitier; vache.*
Gévaudan/Lozère, Chambon-le-Château; 76 **16**, N of C.

**Bleu de Planèze.** Blue found in 1960s on Saturday market at St-Flour from local farms where milk was not skimmed. Courtine questioned its survival in 1973 (*Larousse*).
*fermier; vache cru entier.*
Cantal; 76 **4, 14**.

**Bleu de Pontgibaud.** Local blue in drum form (*Larousse*, 1973, Chast et Voy, regional list, 1984).
*artisanal; vache cru.*
Puy-de-Dôme/Pontgibaud; 73 **13**, high C.

**Bleu de Salers.** Variant of Bleu d'Auvergne found by Brangham (1972).
*vache.*
Cantal; 76 **2**, lower L.

**Bleu de Solignac.** See BLEU DE COSTAROS above.
*low-fat; fermier; vache cru.*
Haute-Loire/Velay; 76 **17**, high L.

**Bleu de Thiézac.** Soft blue, natural crust, salted when warm; of Bleu d'Auvergne size; Viard (1980) found this cheese in the upper valleys of the R. Cère and R. Jordanne. (The R. Jordanne runs parallel to the Cère about 5km NE.) The practice of salting when the curd is warm, followed also at Laqueuille, is thought to give a richer flavour.
*45% m.g.; fermier; vache cru.*
Cantal; 76 **12**, top far R, 76 **2/3**, low.

**Bleu du Velay.** Made of milk skimmed to varying degrees; 600–900g 12cm diameter × 12–15cm high; rustic, but neat and unfissured crust; firm *pâte*, strong flavour, but little odour. Androuët believes it to be an ancient regional cheese, probably introduced by monks. Cayres, Costaros, Langeac, Loudes, Mézenc and Solignac are all of this type. They are becoming harder to find. Le Conquérant (see p. 238) is more like Bleu des Causses. Lyon found Velay in 1985.
*20–30% m.g.; fermier; artisanal; vache cru.*
Velay.

BOUGNAT

*Bougnat* is Auvergnat for coalman, which explains its use for this black-skinned, generously black-peppered cheese formerly available in 450g, 1500g and 3kg sizes, from rustic to neat rounded *tommes* in presentation. Sadly, I have been unable to find it for years, and I suspect that its small manufacturers have been pushed out of the market by the industrial clout of the dull, meanly peppered black 'Fromage des Pyrénées'; not a patch on the mouth- and eye-watering and heart-warming Auvergnat original (but see CAJOLE, SAINT-ÉLOY).
*artisanal/laitier; vache cru/pasteurisé.*
Auvergne.

BOUQUET D'AUVERGNE

Washed-crust, soft or semi-soft cheese; russet surface with superficial white mould. Illustrated in *Larousse des Fromages* (1973), but without text; drum-shaped, equivalent to two Saint-Marcellins in volume.
*artisanal; vache.*

BOURBONNAIS

For Bourbonnais cheeses see BESSAY, CHAMBÉRAT, CHÈVRES, CHEVROTINS/CHEVROTONS,

COULANDON, COUPI, CREUSAIN, CREUSOIS, LAPALISSE, MONT CHALMOUX ROUJADOU, ROUMAJOUX, TERROIR.
Allier/Creuse.

## Bourg-Argental

Thursday and Sunday markets.
Crémerie-Fromagerie Chomette-Gennesson opposite PTT (tel. 73 39 13 78). Very good range of local farm cheeses, including Brique d'Urfé (see p. 233), Rigottes *pur chèvre* and *mi-chèvre*, Rogerets, Saint-Félicien, Séchons.
On Vivarais border with Forez/Loire; 76 **9**, NE of C on N82.

## Le Bourricot

500g flat drum, natural crust, semi-soft; made by Fromagerie Manhès at Aurillac (see p. 229). The label shows the small pack-saddled donkey, which gives the cheese its name.
30% m.g.; *laitier*; *vache pasteurisé*.
Cantal/Aurillac.

## Bouzac

Soft cheese by J. François-Poncet, Les Vallettes, Beauzac; sold daily on farm, Wednesday p.m. at St-Étienne market.
*fermier*; *chèvre cru*.
Beauzac/Haute-Loire; 76 **8**, far L of C.

## Brézoû de Saint-Anthème

Rennet-free *fromage fort* (in Molle's 1969 *Auvergne* list).
Puy-de-Dôme/Forez; 73 **17**.

## Brioude

Saturday market, including *chevrier* from near La Chaise-Dieu (see p. 235).
Limagne/Haute-Loire; 76 **5** C.

## Brique

The brick of this *sobriquet* for a widely spread class of cheese is the small, flat Roman one; sometimes the cheese is bent or otherwise irregular. From late spring to autumn most are *pur chèvre*, but cows' milk is added to some all year, and to others as goats' milk tails off. A few farmers and some *laitiers* make with cows' milk only. A rich succulent cheese if eaten *à point*; eat it soon after buying it.
45% m.g. minimum for chèvre; *fermier*; *chèvre/lait de mélange cru*; *laitier/artisanal*; *vache cru*.

Briques and Briquettes come from two local farms which have supplied Abonnenc in Ambert since the early 1950s, and others, of which two are listed below.
50% m.g.; *fermier*; *chèvre cru*.
M. Ménager, Moliachon near Col des Pradeaux (E of Col turn S off D996 on D57); sign 'Fromages, Gîte Rural'. The Gîte looks smart. He makes Petits Ronds as well as Briques.
*fermier*; *chèvre cru*.
Forez/Puy-de-Dôme; 73 **17**, lower, between Ambert and Saint-Anthème.
Farm at Pontempeyrat makes a rounded cheese from curd of the Brique type (Ambert market Patrick Stein).
*fermier*; *chèvre cru*.
Forez/Haute-Loire; 76 **7**, upper C on D498.
See also BELLEVUE-LA-MONTAGNE.

**Brique d'Ambert, de Viverols.** Briques of similar size or smaller made in Livradois or Forez near Ambert on a number of farms. It may be called Chevreton.
50% m.g.; *fermier*; *chèvre cru*.
Livradois/Forez; near Ambert, Puy-de-Dôme.

**Brique Ardèchoise.** 12–15cm × 3–4cm; rustic, golden crust; some made near Lamastre (see p. 243). It may be called Cabrion in the Cévennes (and see BRIQUE D'URFÉ).
45% m.g. minimum; *fermier*; *chèvre cru* (late March–Oct) or *mélange cru*.
Vivarais/Ardèche.

**Brique du Forez.** 250–400g, 12–15cm × 4–6cm × 2–3cm; white to grey, sometimes pinky-gold crust; sometimes fairly straight (or neatly sloping) sides, sometimes hand-moulded and very irregular, with arched upper surface, striated. It may be called Cabrion.
50% m.g.; *fermier*; *chèvre/mélange cru*.
Monts du Forez; N, E and S of Ambert, Puy-de-Dôme.

**Briquette du Forez.** 150–200g, neat sloping sides, rustically gridded top.

**Brique du Haut Forez.** 220g, regular shape like demi-Pont-L'Évêque, but paler. Fromagerie Tarit, Sauvain; Fromagerie Viallon, Chalmazel (see SAUVAIN). These cows'-milk Briques are sold by Giproforez of Sauvain.
50% m.g.; *laitier*; *artisanal*; *vache cru*.
Forez/Loire.

**Brique du Livradois.** 1. 150g neat, grid-marked top, sloping sides (also chèvre of Crottin size: *blanc* in *faisselle*; *frais*; *demi-sec* and *sec*) by Mme Bernert at Magnarot (Ambert, W of river, turn N on D65, which continues line of D906, as for Bertignat; take first turning left: 'Magnarot est à un km dans les bois'). Ambert Thursday market, also 2 and 3 below (under arcade of *mairie*).
*fermier; chèvre cru.*
2. Rustic Brique (or Chevreton d'Ambert; and 40–50g Crottin-type chèvres in all stages) by M. Besseyries at L'Anteyras (Ambert, but continue on D65 to within 1½km of Bertignat; L'Anteyras is on left).
3. Very rustic Brique (or Chevreton); and large, round, crusted, grid-marked *tomme* by farmer at St-Féréol-des-Côtes (S, 2km from Ambert on D906, W on wiggly D56, on which fork right within 2km).
*fermier; lait de mélange cru.*
Livradois/Puy-de-Dôme; 73 **16**, lower R near Ambert.

**Brique d'Urfé.** Small rustic Brique, 5cm × 4cm, 1cm deep (shop at Annonay, see p. 228); St-Romain-d'Urfé seems the most likely source.
*fermier; chèvre cru.*
Monts du Forez/Loire; 73 **7**, bottom L.

BRIZOU DE SAINT-ANTHÈME
Very local term for cheese put together from broken *fourmes* (*Larousse*, 1973).
*domestique; artisanal; vache cru.*
Puy-de-Dôme/Forez.

BÛCHE

**Bûche Forèzienne.** Industrial blue of 1960s and 1970s (*Larousse*, 1973).
*vache.*

**Bûche du Velay Lys Bleu.** 1.25kg and 2.5kg soft blue log from *Bongrain/Chaumes* stable, made at Beauzac.
*50% m.g.; industriel; vache pasteurisé.*

**Bûche Yssingeaux.** 10cm diameter 2kg log of soft blue by Laiterie J. Gérentes, 43200 Yssingeaux.
*50% m.g.; laitier; vache.*
Velay/Haute-Loire.

BURADO
See MIRAMANDE.

BURON
Simple summer farmhouse with dairy and cheese store (and beds) on high pastures used in *transhumance* by makers of Laguiole (see p. 243, five burons) Salers (see pp. 251–2, 120 burons), and Cantal (see p. 234). For visits, see VIC-SUR-CÈRE; or make friends with a farmer in a market (e.g. Besse, Mondays). Mountain walkers setting out from Lioran or Super-Lioran will find old *burons* on the high pastures. Brangham reported in 1977 (*Auvergne*) that the Buron de Belles-Aygues was fitted out as it would be for the traditional *berger* (enquire of Syndicat d'Initiative). This area (especially the slopes of Le Puy Mary) is notable for its Salers cheeses, all made in *burons*, and rich in the trefoil *réglisse*.
Auvergne/Gévaudan.

LE BURZET
Wednesday and Sunday markets.

**Gazimelle du Burzet.** Small rich goat cheese of Pélardon type (see p. 245).
*fermier; chèvre cru.*
Vivarais/Ardèche; 76 **18**, S of C, D215.

Ferme-auberge M. et Mme Chaneac, Les Grandes Sagnes, Sagnes et Goudoulet, 07450 Le Burzet (tel. 75 38 80 28 for reservation); local dishes, local cheeses, simple accommodation; meals bookable too, good value (*Larousse/Sélection* 1982). 7km N of Le Burzet.

CABÉCOU
This name for very small Chèvres (4cm across, 1cm deep on average) comes from W and S of the Auvergne (Quercy, Périgord, Rouergue, and beyond), and is in use on those fringes. They are usually about 40g when young and soft, about 30g *sec*, smooth-skinned, sometimes bluish; taste mild to nutty. Cheeses somewhat similar are made around Ambert on farms and sold there or on the market by several makers of Briques (see p. 232).
*about 45% m.g.; fermier; chèvre cru.*

**Cabécou d'Entraygues.** Entraygues-sur-Truyère (Aveyron) and Montsalvy (Cantal) are sources of Cabécou.
*fermier; chèvre cru.*
S Cantal/N Aveyron; 76 **12**, low.

**Cabécou du Fel.** Similar to the Glénat cheese, but smaller; Le Fel is a wine

*appellation* too, associated with Entraygues (see p. 239).
*fermier; chèvre cru.*
Rouergue/Auvergne border, Aveyron; 76 **12**, low, 10km W of Entraygues, N of R. Lot.

**Cabécou de Glénat.** I found 60–70g very lightly salted examples of this cheese (flatter than Crottin) made by P. and M. Roques at La Moissetie on D332 near the Cantal border. Sold in Aurillac (see p. 229).
*fermier; biologique; chèvre cru.*
W Cantal/N Aveyron; 76 **20**, upper R.

**Cabécou de Gramat.** Made outside Auvergne, near to Rocamadour, in Quercy, plentiful in Aurillac's shops and market.
*fermier; chèvre cru.*
Perigord/Lot; 75 **19**.

**Cabécou de Roumégoux.** Made by M. Ters, *éleveur* at Le Rouget (6km S of Glénat).
*fermier; chèvre cru.*
Cantal; 76 **11**, NW from C.

CABRION DU FOREZ

Term used for cheeses of *brique* form (see p. 232).
*fermier; artisanal; chèvre/lait de mélange cru.*
Forez.

CABRIOU

A variant of Cabrion (see above) used in Auvergne.

CAILLÉ

For unsalted Caillé see ALIGOT, p. 227 and TOMME.

**Caillé Doux.** Term used for 'sweet-curd' cheeses of St-Félicien (see p. 249).
*artisanal; vache cru.*

CAJOLE

Pressed semi-hard cheese with black pepper (*Marabout*, 1978) made at La Bourboule (in Bougnat tradition, see p. 231).
*industriel; vache pasteurisé.*
Puy-de-Dôme; 73 **13**, lower L.

CANTAL AOC 1980

Also known as Fourme de Cantal. This cheese was on the market in Rome, probably under the Republic, certainly in Imperial times (cf. Pliny the elder). The AOC allows pasteurised, and even *block* cheeses (made for pre-packing) if they conform to the central part of the recipe and are made within the prescribed region. Customers should insist on *lait cru* or nothing.
The *buron* cheeses of the *transhumance* are now sold as Salers (see pp. 251–2; AOC region identical with Cantal), and are like Laguiole (see p. 243; limited by AOC to the small Aubrac area), all unpasteurised, as are Fourmes de Rochefort (see p. 248), related cheeses from N of Mont-Dore. The region lies at 700–1000m (*burons* much higher) on fertile soil, well-watered and abundant and original in its flora. Size: about 45kg, 40cm diameter × 45cm high; hard, *non-cuit*; 45 days–3 months produces Cantal Jeune; 3–6 months Cantal Entre-Deux; 6 months Cantal Vieux, but it needs longer; silvery grey to golden crust (according to age); ivory *pâte*, firm, yet supple; nutty flavour when ready.

**Cantal, le Petit (AOC).** 20kg cheese.

**Le Cantalet (AOC).** 10kg cheese or smaller.

**Le Cantalon.** 4–6kg, sometimes used for Rochefort (see p. 248).

CANTAL (AOC) LAIT CRU

Of the 18,000 tonnes of Cantal (excluding Salers) produced annually towards the middle 1980s, 70% was *lait cru*, and the *laiteries* (as witness Centre-lait's 1985 initiative) were tending to turn increasingly to raw milk.
See SALIHÈS for farm visit.
*fermier; artisanal; vache cru.*
M. Varagne, whose dairy, la Fromagerie Reynal-Varagne at Trizac (see p. 253) dates back to 1875, uses *lait cru* from fifty mountain farms for his Cantal and his Bleu d'Auvergne (one of only two *lait cru* examples I found). Some of this Cantal curd goes out unsalted in 7kg slabs for culinary use (see p. 227 and ALIGOT).
*artisanal; vache cru.*
Trizac, Cantal; 76 **2**, C.

CANTAL, DÉPARTEMENT DE

For other local cheeses see AURILLAC; BLEU DE SALERS, DE THIÉZAC; BOURRICOT, CABÉCOU, CHÈVRES, FOURMES, SAINT-NECTAIRE, ST-FLOUR, SALERS, TRIZAC, VIC-SUR-CÈRE.
Auvergne/Gévaudan; *département* of Cantal adjacent *communes* in Aveyron (8),

Corrèze (8), Haute-Loire (1) and Puy-de-Dôme (27).

## Cantorel
Cheese *marque* of Centre-lait.

## Le Carré d'Aurillac
See AURILLAC.

## Causses, Bleu des
See ROUERGUE.

## Cayres
See BLEU DE CAYRES.

## Le Cerilly
220g; close-textured, moist; deep base of pyramid; develops pinkish skin; sweet, rich, lactic flavour; can be eaten *frais* to *sec*, keeps well. Made by M. Déret at Theneuille, 5km SE of Cerilly in the Bourbonnais/Allier, SE of the Forêt de Tronçais (69 **12/13**, D953).
45% m.g.; *vache; artisanal*.

## Cévennes
See DÉLICE, PÉLARDON, PICODON, ROGERETS.

## Cévenol
See BICHOU, PÉLARDON.

## Chabrilloux
Old term for small cylindrical chèvres made commercially in Auvergne.

## La Chaise-Dieu
**Galette de la Chaise-Dieu.** Described by Viard (1980) as a Brique (blue-coated when *pur chèvre*, grey when *mélange*); and by Courtine in *Larousse* (1973) as a very thin cheese of the Pélardon type, originating here, which seems to suit the term *galette* better. Makers and cheese must have emigrated. Abonnenc at Ambert had not seen it for years, and it was unknown to anyone I spoke to in the town in 1985, from young to very old (including Syndicat d'Initiative).
45% m.g.; *fermier; chèvre/lait-de-mélange cru*.
S Livradois/Haut-Velay/Haute-Loire; 76 **6**, N of C.
Geographically, but not in character, the nearest cheese I know of is Le Chevreton de Cistrières (of Crottin type), made by M. Gérard Bessac, to a recipe from Savoie for La Tome Tarentaise. He keeps chèvres at Feneyrolles 10km west of La Chaise-Dieu, S of D588 (organic) and sells from March to October on his farm, and at Brioude market on Saturday.
*fermier; biologique*.

## Chalmazel
**Briques du Haut Forez, Fourmes.** Fromagerie Viallon, tel. 77 24 80 11; sold by Giproforez (see p. 242).
*laitier; artisanal; vache/cru*.
Monts-du-Forez/Loire; 73 **17**, NW of C, far L.

## Chambérat
1–1.5kg, 16–20cm × 4–5cm flat, round, pressed cheese; *croûte-fleurie* (official list of Auvergne cheeses, 1969); Courtine thought it sad that it travelled no further than Montluçon (1973); Viard thought it was disappearing (1980), but Chast et Voy recorded it (1984). Traditionally sold at the Chambérat fair on the Sunday on or after 15 August (also a horse fair). *Guide Marabout* (1978) said it was made in Canton d'Huriel in *communes* near Montluçon, Archignat and Trignat, and was sold either *frais* or after 3 months' *affinage* in straw.
40–45% m.g.; *fermier; vache cru*.
Bourbonnais/Allier; 69 **11**, lower L on D71.

## Chambon-sur-Lac
Saint-Nectaire farms: M. Rigaud, de Berlaire; M. Roux, Le Cheix (not Mondays), see BESSE.
Puy-de-Dôme; 73 **13**, E of Le Mont-Dore.

## Chancelier, Chanceron, Chauceron, Chaucetier
See COULANDON.

## Chèvres, Fromages de
This section is for chèvres advertised by their makers without further description. See also BANON, BICHOU, BRIQUE, CABÉCOU, CABRION (see also BRIQUE DU FOREZ), CHEVRETON, CHEVROTIN, CHEVROTINE, CHEVROTON, DÉLICE, GALETTE, GAZIMELLE, PÉLARDON, PÉRALDOU, PICODON, RIGOTTE, ROGERET, ROUJADOU, SÉCHONS, TERROIR.
In 1969 Molle reported *chèvriers* at Apchat (76 **4**, high, SE of Ardes), Blanzat (73 **14**, NW of Clermont-Ferrand) and Cervières (73 **16**, high R, N of Noirétable).

Conquans and Lecaplain, MM. J. and J., La Maison Rouge, Route de Calvinet (D125), Sénézergue; 150g irregular tall drum; 40g Crottin type, *sec*; 60g neat drum; 60g flat disc, neat sides; *fromage blanc* in *faisselle*; Aurillac covered market (Wed, Sat).
45% m.g.; *fermier*; *chèvre cru*.
Cantal; 76 **12**, lower, far L Sénézergue.

Diemunsch, André, Les Chanaux, 43430 Fay-sur-Lignon, *fromages pur chèvre*, *fromages de vache*.
*fermier*; *biologique*; *chèvre/vache cru*.
Velay/Haute-Loire; 76 **18**, high, on D500.

François, M. Daniel, Castagnols, Vialas 48220 Le Pont de Montvert (tel. 66 61 00 87); wholesale and retail, mornings on farm; Vialas market, Saturday; also sells honey and pollen.
*fermier*; *biologique*; *chèvre cru*.
Gévaudan/Lozère; 80 **7**, S of C on D37 and D998.

Froidevaux, Jean-Paul, and Lehoux, Bernard, La Filature, 48330 St-Étienne-Vallée-Française (tel. 66 45 73 30).
*fermier*; *biologique*; *chèvre cru*.
Gévaudan/Cévennes/Lozère; 80 **7/17**, L.

Lafon, M. J., L'Hôpital, 15130 Giou-de-Mamou; 120g neat shallow drum; *fromage blanc* state, *frais* and *sec*; Aurillac covered market (Wed, Sat).
45% m.g.; *fermier*; *chèvre cru*.
Cantal; 76 **12** NW from Aurillac on N122; 6km L for Giou on D58; 3km to L'Hôpital.

Mondet, Michel, and Naudin, Gisèle, La Prunerette, St Martin d'Ollières, 63580 Vernet La Varenne.
*fermier*; *biologique*; *chèvre cru*.
Puy-de-Dôme; 73 **15**, low, on D999, Vernet.

Poncet, Jean-François, Les Valettes, 43210 Beauzac (tel. 71 59 20 69) sale at farm every day; St-Étienne-Vallée-Française market Wednesday p.m.
*fermier*; *biologique*; *chèvre cru*.
Haute-Loire; 76 **8**, far L of C.

Vergnol, M., at Avèze, near Limousin border of western Auvergne.
*fermier*; *chèvre cru*.
Puy-de-Dôme; 73 **12**, SE of C on D987 Avèze between Bourg-Lastic and Tauves.

Verron-Cœuignart, M., Boulon, St-Laurent-du-Pape 07800 La Voulte-sur-Rhône (tel. 75 85 16 52); all day on farm; market: Valence (Dragonne) Saturday; also sells wool, eggs.
*fermier*; *biologique*; *chèvre cru*.
Vivarais/Ardèche; 76 **20**, 77 **11**, C.

Villien, Michel, Ferme des Genêts, Les Fauries, 07410 Arlebosc, tel. 75 06 74 56 – *fromages de chèvre*, *fromages de vache*, on sale every day at farm.
*fermier*; *biologique*; *chèvre/vache cru*.
Vivarais/Ardèche; 77 **1**, low L.

Zerbib, Bernard and Monique, La Bruyère, St-Basile, 07270 Lamastre (tel. 75 58 00 57) daily on farm.
*fermier*; *chèvre cru*.
Vivarais/Ardèche; 76 **19**, top R, 77 **11**, top L.

CHEVRETINES

**Chevretines de l'Ardèche.** 200g packets of 10 small drums, *frais* (they can breathe in container).
35–50g irregular drums in bag of 10; *frais* (fluffy, lactic acid flavour) or *demi-sec*.
*laitier*; *chèvre cru*.
Vivarais/Ardèche.

I have also eaten powerfully garlic-saturated versions of cows'-milk Chevretines (2cm × 2cm drums,) with thick pepper or thin *sarriette* coating from the Ardèche, but do not know the maker (Valmont is not in the postal code). Both the plain cheeses above are distributed by Société des Monts du Lyonnais, St-Bricet (73 **19**).
*laitier*; *vache de montagne*.
Vivarais/Ardèche, Valmont.

There is yet another make of pleasant little white drum, slightly acid, minimally salt.
*artisanal*; *chèvre cru*.
Vivarais/Ardèche.

**Chevretines pur Chèvre de l'Ardèche.** Tiny drums on sticks, about 3cm across 2cm deep; see also APÉRI-CHÈVRE DI GIRALAMO.
*artisanal*; *chèvre cru*.
Vivarais/Ardèche; 76 **10**, low, NW of Tournon.

## Chevreton

**Chevreton d'Ambert.** 150–300g, up to 16cm × 8cm × 3cm deep, in form of *brique* (see p. 232); makers include M. Besseyries, L'Anteyras, 1½km S of Bertignat on D65, NW from Ambert, where he is in the market on Thursdays; he also makes a sort of Cabécou; Mme Bernert, Magnarot, N from Ambert W of river, D65 (Bertignat direction); take first turning left; Magnarot is 1km further on *'dans les bois'*; Ambert market, under arcade, Thursday.
See AMBERT for market and for Abonnenc (*fromager*).
45% m.g.; *fermier*; *chèvre cru*.
Livradois; Puy-de-Dôme; 73 **16**, SE of C.

**Chevreton du Bourbonnais.** See CHEVROTIN.

**Chevreton de Cistrières.** See LA CHAISE-DIEU.

**Chevreton de Cunlhat.** Noted for quality in 1960s. Cunlhat has a Wednesday market.
*fermier*; *chèvre cru*.
Livradois/Puy-de-Dôme; 73 **16**, far L of C.

**Le Chevreton Mi-chèvre; le Chevreton de Viverols.** 260–300g (350g Viverols); irregular *brique* forms, from a number of bigger farms around Ambert which keep both goats and cows; 2 l milk per *'demi-livre'* (about 225g) cheese (*pur chèvre* or *mi-chèvre*). Ripened for 15 days on rye-straw, some in straw between the beams of the cowsheds above the cow's heads. The *pâte* becomes unctuous, smooth and creamy, without apertures, and acquires a pronounced aroma of *chèvre*, especially the *pur chèvre* version; but this varies with the breed of goat and stage of lactation. One found at Ambert Thursday market is made at St-Ferréol-des-Côtes.
40–45% m.g.; *fermier*; *mi-chèvre cru*.
Livradois/Puy-de-Dôme; Saint Ferréol-des-Côtes; 73 **16**, 8km SW of Ambert by D906, D56 (fork R within 2km).

**Chèvre Fermier.** Small, dome-shaped soft cheese, bought young; nice, sweet acidity; keeps well; made at Les Verssades, Valcivières (sold by Abonnenc, Ambert, see p. 228).
*fermier*; *chèvre cru*.
Monts du Forez/Puy-de-Dôme; 76 **16**, from Ambert N by D906, D66, R on D67 E.

**Fromages pur Chèvre 'Sans Nom'.** 150–200g; neat-sized flat discs; truncated cones; neat miniature Camembert-shape; made on a number of farms around Ambert (see p. 228) and sold by Abonnenc.
*fermier*; *chèvre cru*.
Livradois/Monts du Forez/Puy-de-Dôme near Ambert.
Other makers from further afield are:

Bessac, M. Gérard, Feneyrolles (see LA CHAISE-DIEU).

Bouniol, M. Lucien, Rouires d'Oradour, 15260 Neuvéglise; 100g flat drum; Aurillac market (Wed, Sat).
45% m.g.; *fermier*; *chèvre cru*.
Cantal; 76 **13 14**, upper, W of Neuvéglise.

Chevrot, Colette, Colombières, 48330 St-Étienne-Vallée-Française (tel. 66 45 72 43).
*fermier*; *biologique*; *chèvre cru*.
Gévaudan/Cévennes; Lozère; 80 **7/17**, L.

The *communes* long renowned for Chevretons are Marat, Valcivières, St-Martin-des-Olmes, Ambert, Grandrif, St-Clement, St-Romain, and those in the *canton de* Viverols. In the 1960s many farms had just three or four goats alongside their cows, and the bulk of production was mi-chèvre. The *pur chèvres* from the *chevriers* were *'très recherchés'*.
Forez/Puy-de-Dôme/Viverols; 76 **7**, top L.

## Chevrotin de Thiers

500g thick square cheese, described as 'disappearing' by Viard (1980).
Thiers has a Sunday market.
*fermier*; *chèvre cru*.
Monts-du-Forez/Puy-de-Dôme; 73 **16**, top L.

## Chevroton

**Chevroton/Chevrotin du Bourbonnais.** 100–230g soft; truncated cone 6–8cm diameter × 5–6cm high; ripened 1–2 weeks; sold *frais*, *mi-sec*, or *sec*, when natural crust develops; when eaten young, mild with some acidity. They are not always labelled, and for examples of chèvres 'du coin', 'du terroir' see LAPALISSE. Below are local names sometimes used in the Bourbonnais with the generic term Chevroton (the version now preferred to Chevrotin by Androuët, also used in neighbouring south-

ern Burgundy (Mâconnais), in Saône-et-Loire). Many are dried in cages, hung in trees for shade.
Ygrande (69 **13**, NW of C) is a good source of Chevrotons.
40–45% m.g.; *fermier; chèvre/lait de mélange cru.*

**Chevroton de Cistrières.** See LA CHAISE-DIEU.

**Chevroton de Combraille.** (Plateau of SW Bourbonnais, E. Marche, N. Auvergne.)

**Chevroton de Cosne (Cosne d'Allier).** Ygrande; 69 **12**, R of C.

**Chevroton de Montmarault, Roumajou(x).** Called Roumajou, Roumajoux, to distinguish from cheeses of Moulins. (See also ROUJADOUX, for washed-crust version, and CONNE.) Montmarault cheeses are usually eaten more mature than those of Moulins.
Bourbonnais/Allier; 69 **13**, low L.

**Chevroton de Moulins.** Usually eaten young (see above). A pyramidal version of this cheese was found and appreciated by the *Larousse/Sélection* team (Feb 1982 No. 23 Allier).
Bourbonnais/Allier; 69 **14**, C.

**Chevroton de Souvigny.** This is the best in Viard's opinion (1980), and mentioned in Androuët's 1985 *Livre d'Or.*
Bourbonnais/Allier; 69 **14**, L of C.

CLERMONT FERRAND

Friday market. *Affinage* centre for Saint-Nectaire and other Auvergne cheeses. M. Michel Quinty, 185 rue de Blonzat (tel. 73 37 36 00) and Marché St-Pierre (tel. 73 37 57 12), specialises in farmhouse Saint-Nectaire and *lait cru* Bleu d'Auvergne.
Puy-de-Dôme; 73 **14**.

CODIBRI

Soft blue, from Centrelait, Aurillac.
*industriel; vache pasteurisé.*
Cantal.

CŒUR D'AUVERGNE

Industrial cheese of Saint-Nectaire-type *pâte* invented early 1970s (*Larousse*, 1973); never seen by me.

CONDAT-EN-FÉNIERS

See Saint-Nectaire for farms and *laiterie*; Auvergne cheesemakers and distributors:
Walchli (tel. 71 78 51 22).
Cantal; 76 **3**, N of C.

CONNE MONTMARAULT

200g; similar to Chevroton but ripened 6 weeks.
45% m.g.; *fermier; mi-chèvre cru.*
Bourbonnais/Allier; 69 **13**, bottom.

LE CONQUÉRANT

2.5kg, little Bleu des Causses, by CFVA, Beauzac; foil-wrapped.
*laitier; vache.*
Velay/Haute-Loire; 76 **8**, far L of C.

COSTAROS

Monday market.
See BLEU DE.
Haute-Loire; 76 **17**, upper L N86.

COUCOURON

Wednesday market.

**Coucouron, Fourme de.** 500g (average) blue cheese by Fromagerie Roche Albert, Coucouron (tel. 66 33 90 05).

**Le Coucouron.**
45% m.g.; *laitier; vache.*

**Le Coucouron Persillé.** 400g drums; natural crust; firm, smoothish *pâte; persillé* is very lightly blued, with horizontal apertures. Both cheeses made by Laiterie de Coucouron at altitude of 1213m.
25% m.g.; *laitier; vache.*

**Tomme Persillée de Coucouron.** Larger flatter cheese of similar character, let out when young and white, blueing within one month, rounding its sides as it matures; from Laiterie de Coucouron.
25% m.g.; *laitier; vache.*
Velay/Ardèche; 76 **17**, R of C.

COULANDON

Small, soft, skimmed-milk cheese (like a little Coulommiers in form), usually eaten at *frais* stage (May–Nov); also called Chaucetier, Chauceron (sometimes miscalled Chancelier, Chanceron).
*low-fat; fermier; artisanal; vache cru.*
Bourbonnais/Allier; 69 **14**, on D945, 5km W of Moulins.

COUPI, CREUSAIN, CREUSOIS

Ancient local cheese usually dried and grated for *soupe* or *bouillon* (see Chapter 4, p. 121).

10% m.g.; *fermier*; *domestique*; *vache cru écrémé*.
Bourbonnais-Marche/Creuse; 73 **1**, N of C.

## Craponne-sur-Arzon

Saturday market (including Patrick Stein). 'Rachat', Patrick Stein, 43500 Craponne-sur-Arzon (tel. 71 03 29 75). Good Vieux Cantal, fine selection of farmhouse cheese (see AMBERT). Craponne has been noted for its cheese since the Middle Ages.

**Fromage de Craponne.** This cheese, still in the 1969 edition of *Auvergne*, was of the pressed *fourme* family (see p. 240) with *croûte-fleurie*, used then to be dried in the windows.
*fermier*; *artisanal*; *vache cru*.
For farm visits within reach, see BELLEVUE-LA-MONTAGNE.
A *chevrier* makes round cheeses of *brique*-like curd at Pontempeyrat, 43500 Craponne.
Forez/Haute-Loire; 76 **7**, upper L.

## Creusain, Creusois

See COUPI.

## Cunlhat

Wednesday market. See CHEVRETON DE-CUNLHAT.

## Curé

**Trou du Curé.** Extracted from the 'hole' in Grand Murol, a tiny cheese in itself. (See also MUROL.) It is coated in red wax.
*laitier*; *vache pasteurisé*.
Murol.

## Darbres

M. Jacques Brunier makes farmhouse Picodon and sells on farm.
Vivarais/Ardèche; 76 **19**, low C.

## Délice des Cévennes

Truncated base of cone; soft; coated rather strongly with thyme, bay, red and/or green peppers, and black pepper; remove some of the coat to be able to enjoy the pleasant cheese.
*artisanal*; *chèvre cru*.
Cévennes.

## Demi-Fourme de Labro

See FOURMES.

## Diapason, Crème de Bleu

Mild, soft, deep, square blue; with 'white satin crust': Centre-lait's own description. They make it at Aurillac in their Cantorel range.
*laitier*; *industriel*; *vache pasteurisé*.
Cantal.

## Dompnac

2–3kg, natural crust, firm drum (like tubby *fourme*).
*artisanal*; *chèvre cru*.
Vivarais/Ardèche; 80 **8**, high L.

## Doux de Montagne (Boule de Béarn)

Rounded, shiny, brown-coated, large mild *tomme* invented by Fromagerie des Chaumes in Béarn in 1974 as an imitation Pyrenean cheese. The alternative name must surely have been surrendered since its making moved to Beauzac in the Velay.
*laitier*; *industriel*; *vache pasteurisé*.
Velay/Haute-Loire.

## Égliseneuve d'Entraigues

Wednesday market 10.00 a.m. (Cantal, Fourmes, Saint-Nectaire) Maison des Fromages d'Auvergne (1 June to mid-September). In 1985, seventy-one Saint-Nectaire farmers were registered in this *commune*.
Puy-de-Dôme; 76 **3**, high C.

## Entraygues-sur-Truyère

Centre for Cabécous.
Friday market.
N. Rouergue/Aveyron; 76 **12**, low R.

## Fairs and Fêtes

See BURZET, MONTBRISON, JASSERIE AU COQ NOIR, ST-ANTHÈME, ST-BONNET-LE-CHÂTEAU.

## Le Fel

See CABÉCOU DU FEL; Le Fel is also a local wine *appellation*.
Rouergue/Auvergne border, Aveyron; 76 **12**, 10km W of Entraygues, N of R. Lot.

## La Fermière

Trade name for a particular make of Tomme d'Aligot, etc. (see p. 227).

FOREZ

See AMBERT, BOURG-ARGENTAL, BRIQUE, CABRION, CHALMAZEL, CHÈVRES, CHEVRETON, FOURMES, MAIGRETTE, ROGERET, SAUVAIN.

**Tomme du Forez.** Large skimmed-milk cheese with yellow-brown crust and unevenly spread very small holes in its golden *pâte*; mild.
20% m.g.; *artisanal; vache cru.*

LE FOUDJOU

See also MIRAMANDE.
1. The Privas version, or Fromage Fort du Vivarais: piquant chèvre grated and mashed up with Tome Fraîche de Chèvre, pepper, salt, garlic and *eau-de-vie*, to serve with potatoes (and see LA TUMO).
2. The Viviers version: alternate layers of Tomme Fraîche de Chèvre and grated Tomme Piquante in an earthenware pot, covered with olive oil and *eau-de-vie*, seasoned with salt, pepper and garlic, and left until the surface is covered with a russet skin; prepared in autumn for end of winter consumption. The pot should never be emptied, as the lees help to ferment the next addition. C. Forot (*Odeurs de Fôret et Fumets de Table*, Editions Seill Aubenas, 1975) had seen pots whose bottoms had not been exposed for fifteen years.
*domestique; chèvre cru.*
3. Domestic production has diminished, but some *laitiers* make a 200g version in a plastic pot.
*laitier; chèvre.*
4. Curd from buttermilk (as for Gaperon, see p. 242, initially) diluted and whipped up with milk and a little cream, with added salt, pepper, garlic, especially a summer dish; rare now because little farm butter is made.
*fermier; domestique; babeurre.*
Vivarais/Ardèche.

FOURME

This is the old word for cheese, nearer to the Latin than *fromage*, derived from the form or mould, and still much used in and around Auvergne. A request for *fourme*, without any frills, would be met with an offer of Cantal (or Laguiole, Salers or Rochefort), just as an unadorned request for 'cheese' in England would be met with Cheddar. Here we are dealing with blue *fourmes*, thought to have almost as long a history as their plain compatriots, and almost certainly found by the Romans as an already long-established cheese made by the Arvernes.

**Fourme d'Ambert AOC (1976/1980), Fourme de Montbrison.** 2kg; 19cm tall × 13cm diameter; milk rennetted warm; curd salted and packed in moulds by hand (an extension doubles the height of the mould until the curd has settled); natural mould-enriched crust, grey-golden (wtih russet if matured in right caves) should be dry, almost Stilton-like. To save on weight-loss and increase profit, a deplorable modern habit has developed of foil-wrapping which makes the crust soggy and spoils the texture of the *pâte*, which should be creamy in colour, but firm, with well-spread green mould. The internal mould should be acquired in the *cave* naturally, not be injected into the curd and it should not dominate the flavour; but industrialisation and miswrapping have taken many cheeses nearer to a cross between Bleu d'Auvergne and Gorgonzola, even towards the character of the modern Bresse logs, some of which now call themselves 'fourmes'. The old nutty, subtle flavour, unique to Fourme d'Ambert has almost disappeared. The AOC allows pasteurisation and lays down a minimum of 40 days of *affinage*, sops to factory methods; poor cheese goes over quickly; good cheese takes 3 months in *caves*, with some brushings of the crust, and keeps well thereafter. If the dryness of the atmosphere makes wrapping desirable, this should be greaseproof (like Stilton's), never foil or plastic, and the AOC rules should specify this. Some recent, but pre-AOC history is given below under the earliest Appellation, Fourmes des Monts-du-Forez.
There are eight makers in Loire; mainly Montbrison label, seven in Puy-de-Dôme and two in Cantal mainly Ambert label.
The local equivalent of *burons*, the *jasseries*, have gone out of use except, in one case, as a museum–café–shop (see JASSERIE (au Coq d'Or) and FOURME DE PIERRE-SUR-HAUTE).
At St-Anthème (see p. 248) M. Col makes *lait cru* Fourme de Montbrison (or d'Ambert); sold by Giproforez and by Abonnenc (see AMBERT).
Made also by Laiterie Dauphin et Joandel,

Fromagerie Rizand at St-Bonnet-le-Courreau, Fromagerie Tarit at Sauvain (see p. 252), Fromagerie Viallon at Chalmazel (see p. 235).
*Distribution:* Maison de la Fourme (Giproforez) Sauvain; Rungis: Fromi-France (M. David), a German-owned firm. (See also LAQUEUILLE, where the *laiterie* makes Fourme d'Ambert.)
In the early 1980s total Fourme production (AOC) was steady at between 3200 and 3300 tonnes a year, but in 1985 it rose to 3400 tonnes.
50% m.g.; *artisanal/laitier; vache cru/pasteurisé.*
Livradois / Monts-du-Forez / Loire / Puy-de-Dôme/Cantal.

**Fourme de l'Ardèche.** See COUCOURON.
Velay/Ardèche.

**Fourme de Coucouron.** See COUCOURON.

**Fourme de Labro.** 550g crusted *'bleu fin'* made by Laiterie des Hauts Plateaux Cévenols at La Bastide Puy Laurent (Wednesday market), 48250 Rissoan Luc. They make the low-fat Sourire (see p. 252) and the Demi-Fourme de Labro, 400g, otherwise like the Fourme.
50% m.g.; *artisanal; vache cru.*
Gévaudan/Cévennes, Lozère; 76 **17**, bottom, 80 **7**, top C.

**Fourme de Laqueuille.** See LAQUEUILLE, related to nearby Rochefort (see p. 244).
*laitier; artisanal; vache.*
Puy-de-Dôme.

**Fourme de Mézenc.** See MÉZENC.
Velay/Virarais.

**Fourme des Monts du Forez.** This term covers the more familiar blue Fourmes, which La Société d'Amélioration des Produits Laitiers de Pierre-sur-Haute defined under that name and those of Ambert and Montbrison. The definitions were confirmed by a Government decree of 1945, later unfortunately abrogated. A new Comité Interprofessionnel was formed to resume the struggle and presented cheeses under the Monts du Forez title at the Concours générale agricole, Paris, in 1963 and 1964; 600 tonnes a year were produced locally by a dwindling number of makers, down to a dozen by 1969. It is sad that the AOC was not achieved until 1980 and that it was too loose in form to preserve the character of the old cheese (see AMBERT/MONTBRISON).

**Fourme de Pierre-sur-Haute.** With the final abandonment of the *jasseries*, the old *transhumance* mountain farm-dairies, this honourable name is now extinct (see JASSERIE).

**Fourme de Rochefort-Montagne.** See ROCHEFORT.

**Fourme des Monts Yssingelais.** See YSSINGELAIS.
*laitier; artisanal; fermier (jasserie); vache cru.*

**Fourme du Haut-Vivarais.** Local cheeses of fat and friable texture put to *bonner* (improve themselves) in cool damp *caves*, where they acquired rough, mite-rich, brown crusts and did not always blue (*Marabout*, 1978; I scent Lyon's trail here). St-Agrève (see p. 248) was formerly noted for rich-smelling *fourmes*.
*fermier; domestique; vache cru.*
Velay border of Haut-Vivarais around Tence, Haute-Loire; 76 **8**, lower R Saint-Agrève **9/19**.

FOURMETTE

450g thin cylindrical versions of blue *fourmes* made by some dairies; tending to be over soft.
50% m.g.; *laitier; vache.*

**Fourmette du Haut-Mont.** *Demi-fourme* size made by Benoît-Chapert at Aumont-Aubrac (where there is a Friday market in May). See also MAZET.
45% m.g.; *laitier; vache.*
Gévaudan/Lozère; 76 **15**, lower L.

FOURNOLS

About 2½kg flat, round, reddish-golden-crusted cheese of smooth consistency; very mild, needs taste of crust to register; by Société Fermière du Livradois, Fournols.
*laitier; vache pasteurisé.*
Livradois/Puy-de-Dôme; 73 **16**, low L on D37.

FROMAGÈRE

*Préparations fromagères*: term for rennet-free concoctions.

FROMAGE FORT

See LE FOUDJOU, MIRAMANDE, LA TUMO.

## Fromageon
Term used for very small cheeses of Cabécou-type chèvres with *croûte-bleutée*.

## Galette
See LA CHAISE-DIEU.

## Gaperon, Gapron; Gaperon d'Auvergne, Gaperon de Limagne (Auvergne list, 1969)
Five hundred years ago, according to local tradition, this formerly rennet-free cheese was developed in the pink-garlic-producing region, of which Billom (73 **15**, NW of C) is the capital (see p. 220). Household and *artisanals* cheeses were usually very low fat (unless cream had been added at the hanging stage), but had a pronounced character in their flavour (slightly smoky, as they are dried just above the wood fire), apart from generous garlic and pepper. The salt was just enough to heighten this flavour without proclaiming itself. Commercially made cheeses have all been fatter, and must have needed rennet. M. Allès in St-Amant-Tallende, S of Clermont-Ferrand, made cheeses labelled La Perrette of 30% m.g. This name survives, but his successors make a fatter cheese, and most Gaperons are now 40–50% m.g., and 350g or smaller (except for some new, cutting cheeses) compared with the 400–550g of earlier days. M. Allès started making when there were not enough Gaperons available for his shop, and invented the moulds for his cheesemaking. In the 1970s M. Marcel Gaydier also made Gaperons, at Château Gay, near Clermont-Ferrand.
30–45% m.g; *artisanal*; *vache écrémé*.
Limagne plain, Allier valley/Puy-de-Dôme, E of Clermont-Ferrand; 76 **14/15** and **5**.

**Gaperon la Perrette.** A. Garmy et Cie, Laiterie de La Vallée de la Dore (successor to Allès of St-Amant-Tallende), Pont-Astier, W of Thiers. A cutting version called Le P'ail is now made. Also a 350g Gaperon d'Auvergne and 250g Gaperonnet. *laitier*; *vache cru*.
Puy-de-Dôme; 73 **15**, top R.

**Gaperounet.** 150g and 200g. Cheese with fine bloom, very creamy, made at St-Germain-Lembron.
Puy-de-Dôme; 73 **14/15**, bottom.

**La Gaperonnette.** Ninette Lyon says this term is used for Gaperon *frais* (see above).

**Le P'ail.** Recently introduced cutting version in forms of ring and of hollow square, from Pont-Astier (A. Garmy et Cie).
40% m.g.; *laitier*; *vache*.

## Gazimelle de Burzet
See BURZET.

## La Genette, Tomme de Montagne
400g and 600g (*fromage de montagne*) and 1200g (Tomme); pressed, gold to white crust, matured 30 days minimum; see TOMME DE MONTAGNE for report on 18-week cheese, made by R. Col; and see SAINT-ANTHÈME.
30% m.g. (400g, 600g), 25% m.g. (1200g); *artisanal*; *vache cru*.
Puy-de-Dôme/Auvergne/Livradois.

## Gerbizon
About 350g, washed-crust; semi-soft; yellow; close texture; pleasant, keeps well; Fromagerie de Jussac, 43130 Retournac.
50% m.g.; *laitier*; *vache*.
Velay/Haute-Loire; 76 **7**, SE of C.

## Gévaudan
See ALIGOT, ALTIER, ANCEVAL, AUBRAC, BASSEZ, CANTAL, CHÈVRES (Daniel François, Vialas), FOURME DE LABRO, FOURMETTE DU HAUT MONT, LAGUIOLE, PÉLARDON, PICOLETTE, PISTOLE, SOURIRE.

## Giproforez
Sales and publicity association of *fromageries* making Fourmes and Bleu d'Auvergne, *fromages de montagne* and *briques*, with headquarters at Sauvain (see p. 252).

## Gluiras
M. Faivre makes Picodon at La Maisonette.
Vivarais/Ardèche; 76 **19**, NE of C.

## Gouzon
Tuesday market.

**Gouzon, le Petit Gouzon.** 250–300g, thick base of cone; *croûte-naturelle-fleurie*; rustic-looking, smelling and tasting, fatter version of old Coupi (see Chapter 4, p. 121); made by a *laitier* in Gouzon.

30–40% m.g.; *laitier; artisanal; vache cru demi-écrémé.*
Bourbonnais-Marche/Creuse; 73 **1**, N of C.

## Grand Murol

**Fromage Grand Murol\*.** (See also MUROL.) 450g pressed cheese in form of flat ring about 4cm deep, russet-colouring on crust; *pâte* of Saint-Nectaire type, but mild because pasteurised. The hole speeds up ripening and keeps cheese in shape when cut. The *rigotte*-like piece removed to make the hole is sold as Trou de Murol.
45% m.g.; *laitier; vache pasteurisé.*

**Trou de Murol\* or Trou du Curé.** A tiny, red-wax-coated drum; with its parent cheese it originated at Murol and is now made by M. J. Bérioux at Chaux Blanche, Cournon d'Auvergne.
*laitier; vache pasteurisé.*
Cournon, Puy-de-Dôme; 73 **14**, upper R, W of Clermont-Ferrand.

**Murol.** M. Philippe Olivier of Boulogne sells a *lait cru* version of the Grand Murol cheese, which he says is now being made in Murol again.
*artisanal; vache cru.*
Puy-de-Dôme; 73 **13**, lower R, D996.

## Gras

**Picodon de Gras.** See PICODON.

## Grionzola

Name used for imitation Gorgonzola made by a *laitier* in Auvergne until the 1960s. Other *laitiers* used the commoner Saingorlon.

## Haut-Vivarais

See FOURME DU HAUT-VIVARAIS.

## Jasserie

The Forez equivalent of the *buron*, the simple farm-dairy of the summer mountain pastures, formerly used for making Fourmes de Pierre-sur-Haute (see p. 241). La Jasserie au Coq Noir, Col des Supeyres, once so used, is now Le Musée Paysan de la Vallorgue, where all the furnishings and equipment are preserved. Brézoû (see p. 232), ham, *saucisson* d'Auvergne and

*Until the 1970s Grand Murols and Trou de Murols were spelt with the final 's', although Murol itself has never had an 's'.

Fourme d'Ambert can be eaten and bought to take away from 1 July to 15 September 10.00–12.00, 15.00–18.00. (Association Livradois-Monts du Forez-Ambert, tel. 73 82 03 11). There is a fair one weekend in August each year.
Forez, Col des Supeyres/Puy-de-Dôme; 73 **17**, off D106 SW of C.

## Labro

See FOURME, DEMI-FOURME DE LABRO.

## Lagorce

See PICODON DE LAGORCE.

## Laguiole

Saturday market in May and June.

**Le Laguiole AOC (1976).** Pronounced La-Yole; 30–50kg; 40cm across × 30–40cm; semi-hard *non-cuit*; thick, dry, golden rind; 4 months' *affinage*; marked on crust by a bull and 'Laguiole', plus aluminium plaque with maker's mark.
Region of Aubrac known for cheese in Roman times; *'fromage de garde'* (keeping cheese) made by monks of Aubrac (on pilgrimage route to Santiago de Compostela) from twelfth century, subsequently by *bergers* in summer *burons*. Present production must be approaching 600 tonnes made by 4 *burons* of long standing, 1 *buron expérimental* (1985), 1 *laiterie*: La Coopérative fermière, Montagne Laguiole, which markets almost all the cheese and can give information on *burons* and distributors handling the cheese. Androuët thinks that Laguiole's superiority is best demonstrated in *'la finesse, la délicatesse et l'onctuosité'* of its Tomme Fraîche, which makes prize quality Aligot and Patranque (see p. 227). At Laguiole: Coopérative Fromagère Jeune Montagne (tel. 65 44 35 54) for Laguiole, Laguiole Vieux, Tomme Fraîche.
45% m.g.; *buron; laitier; co-opérative; vache cru entier.*
Gévaudan/Rouergue/Plateau of Mont d'Aubrac/Lozère/Aveyron; 76 **13/14**, 80 **3/4**.

## Lamastre

Tuesday market.
Source of *chèvres*, including Brique and Picodon (see pp. 232 and 246–7) and Rogeret (see p. 248).

See BRIQUE ARDÈCHOISE for local cheeses; and CHÈVRES, Zerbib (organic).
Vivarais/Ardèche; 77 **11**, top L, 76 **19**, top R.

LANGEAC

See BLEU DE LANGEAC.

LAPALISSE

**Chevroton du Bourbonnais.** About 200g, regular drum; pale pinky-cream, later developing blue-mould coat; reminiscent of Charollais (see p. 362); firm but delicate *pâte*, melting in mouth; refreshing flavour (*demi-sec*); softens with further keeping; rich flavour after a week. Made by several farms round Lapalisse, where they are known as *chèvres du coin*; sold by R. Collange, Crémerie Nouvelle (opposite Casino) 8 rue Winston Churchill (first street W of bridge leading N to Dompierre-sur-Besbre); served at Hôtel Bourbonnais (very good food in 1985).
40–50% m.g.; *fermier; chèvre cru.*

**Fromage du Terroir.** About 300g flat drum (4cm deep); cream-coloured when young, developing *croûte-fleurie*, very much *du terroir* with age; firm *pâte*, becoming crumbly; pleasant fresh flavour. Also sold by Crémerie Nouvelle (see above).
*fermier; vache cru.*
Bourbonnais/Allier; 73 **6**, high L.

LAQUEUILLE

**Le Bleu de Laqueuille.** 2.25kg; 20cm × 8–10cm drum; unpressed (now of presentation similar to Bleu d'Auvergne, see p. 230). In the 1840s some fourme (Rochefort type) became blue by association with a mouldy rye loaf. The result was repeated to profitable effect. It was imitated around Laqueuille acquiring that name, and spread through the Auvergne into the Vivarais (even into Dauphiné and Savoie), becoming Bleu d'Auvergne. In the 1960s industrialisation spoilt the cheese and the market; the new *bleus* from Bresse took much of the trade. However, the local cheeses, whether under the Laqueuille label, or sold as Bleu d'Auvergne, are still reckoned to be a better bet than most *bleus*; but the crust should be dry, not kept in foil. The local practice of salting the curd warm is thought to give richness to the flavour and smoothness to the texture. At Laqueuille-Gare: Société Laitière de Laqueuille (tel. 73 22 00 31) Bleu des Neiges (Bleu d'Auvergne AOC); *fourmes*. Label *La Mémée*.
45% m.g.; *fermier/laitier; vache cru/pasteurisé.*
Puy-de-Dôme; 73 **13**, L of C.

LARGENTIÈRE-EN-VIVARAIS

Pélardon centre (see PÉLARDON); Tuesday market.
Vivarais/Ardèche; 80 **8**, high R.

LE LISIEUX

450g Laiterie Coopérative du Lisieux, Mazet-St-Voy; low-fat mild blue (see also BLEU DU LISIEUX, MAZET).
25% m.g.; *laitier coopérative; vache.*
Velay, Haute-Loire; 76 **8**, bottom R of C.

LIVRADOIS

See BRIQUE DU LIVRADOIS; see also AMBERT, BELLEVUE, BOURG-ARGENTAL, BRIQUE, CHÈVRES, CHEVRETON, FOURMES, FOURNOLS, TOMME, VACHARD.

LOUDES

See BLEU DE LOUDES.

LOZÈRE

See BLEU DE LOZÈRE.

LYS BLEU

See BÛCHE DU VELAY.

MAIGRE

**Fromage Maigre.** 5lb natural crust *tomme* by Fromagerie Bernard Gignat (sold also by Patrick Stein, see CRAPONNE).
10% m.g.; *laitier; vache.*
Puy-de-Dôme; 73 **14/15**, bottom, N of Saint-Germain-Lembron.

MAIGRETTE

**Maigrette du Forez.** (Amigrette label for export.) 500g and 900g low-fat; white to golden crusted blue; *affinage* 30 days minimum; mild; by Laiterie Dauphin-Joandel, St-Bonnet-le-Courreau.
25% m.g.; *laitier; vache.*
Forez.

MAZET

Thursday market.

**Tome du Mazet Bleu.** Like a Fourmette (see p. 241); blue made at Mazet-St-Voy.
*laitier; vache.*
Velay/Haute-Loire; 76 **8**, bottom R of C.

### Lou Meillou Bleu

See BLEU DE LOZÈRE.

### Mézenc

**Fourme du Mézenc.** Rustic blue of Haut-Velay (Viard, 1980), Bleu du Velay family (see p. 231), under which name it is sometimes found. Mézenc is a scenic volcanic feature.
*fermier; vache cru.*
Velay-Vivarais border, Haute-Loire/Ardèche; 76 **18**, high C.

### Miette

**Miette de Tauves, des Monts Dore.** Rennet-free *préparation fromagère* for *fromage fort.*
*vache cru.*
Puy-de-Dôme/Tauves/Monts Dore.

### Migno

Potato dish; see TOMME DU VIVARAIS.

### Miramande des Pajels

Made with buttermilk (*burado*), heated to extract remaining solids, which are then drained in cloth bag. After draining, the cheese is rolled into little balls which are dried and become hard and blue. They are then cut up and pounded with pepper and mustard, soaked in lukewarm boiled water (with butter or olive oil) and in marc, and left one or two months in a pot in a warm place. The pot, never emptied, serves as ferment for the next making; see also LE FOUDJOU (Viard, 1980).

### Montagne

See TOMME DE MONTAGNE.

### Montbrison

First weekend in October: Journées de la Fourme. See FOURME DE MONTBRISON.

### Mont Chalmoux

Small rustic chèvres from around Mont Chalmoux, on trans-Loire fringe of Bourbonnais (*Marabout*, 1978).
*fermier; chèvre cru.*
Bourbonnais; 69 **16** E of Bourbon-Lancy.

### Mont Dore

Local industrial *fourme*, now extinct (Viard 1980).

### Montmarault

See CHEVROTON DU BOURBONNAIS.

### Montsalvy

Collecting centre for Cabécous (see pp. 233–4; Androuët, 1982). 350g, 2.2kg rounded drum, soft to semi-soft, natural crust; by Centrelait, Aurillac.
50% m.g.; *industriel; vache pasteurisé.*
Cantal; 76 **12**, S of C.

### Moulins

See CHEVROTON DU BOURBONNAIS.

### Murol

Place of origin of Grand Murols (misspelt on label, now it is made elsewhere) (see p. 243) and now home of Murol *lait cru*, sold at Boulogne by M. Philippe Olivier.
*artisanal; vache cru.*
Puy-de-Dôme; 73 **13**, lower R.

### Neiges, Bleu des

See LAQUEUILLE, Société Laitière.

### P'ail

See GAPERON.

### Pavé d'Affinois

See PELUSSIN, where it is made.

### Le Pavin

Sometimes misspelt Pavan, small Saint-Nectaire (see p. 250) sold at Besse (see p. 230) and widely distributed.

### Pélardon

100–120g (reducing with age to as little as 60g); occasionally regular medal-shaped; usually rustic irregular disc; crust white (*frais*) to grey or blue; may be clothed or crowned with finely ground black pepper, herbs of *garrigue* or mountain (Cévennes are rich in *sarriette*); subtle to strong flavour.

Pélardon is said by *chevriers* to derive from *peluche*, the hairy-velvet skin it develops with mould. As shown above, the Pélardon region extends far SW of Auvergne. Local names are often attached.
45% m.g.; *fermier; chèvre cru.*

Vivarais, Cévennes, Gévaudan/Ardèche and Lozère; also Languedoc/Hèrault and Gard (see Chapter 18).

M. Christian Charton, Le Lauzas, St-Andéol-de-Clerguemort (48160 Le Collet de Dèze, tel. 66 61 02 68) sells daily on farm (also organic chestnuts, fruit, vegetables).
*fermier; biologique; chèvre cru.*
Gévaudan/Cévennes/Lozère; 80 **7**, low C.

M. Philippe Crausaz, Corbès, 48160 St-Martin-de-Boubaix (tel. 66 45 55 08) sells on farm 08.00–18.00 daily (also organic tomato conserves, vegetables; mail order in France).
*fermier; biologique; chèvre cru.*
as above, 80 **7**, bottom C.

Pélardons 70g; makers and *affineurs*: Coopérative de Pélardon les Cévennes, Moissac-Vallée-Française, 48110, Ste-Croix-Vallée-Française (tel. 66 45 72 35). Gévaudan-Lozère; 80 **17**, top L.

Coopérative fruitière Ste-Croix-Vallée-Française (visits in working hours).
*fruitier; biologique; chèvre cru.*
as above, 80 **6**, bottom R.

**Pélardon d'Altier.** An old district name and centre which could cover all the Pélardons above made in the Gévaudan.
Gévaudan/Cévennes/Lozère; 80 **7**, NW of C. (Place and river called Altier.)

**Pélardon d'Anduze or Péraldou.** This is a southern stronghold of Pélardon.
Cévennes/Gard; 80 **17**, NE of C.

**Pélardon de Burzet or Gazimelle.** See BURZET.

**Pélardon Cévenol, or des Cévennes.** Gévaudan/Cévennes/Lozère/Gard/Ardèche.

**Pélardon Fermier des Cévennes.**
*fermier; chèvre cru.*
1. F. and B. Michaud, Soret, 48 St-Martin-de-Lansuscle.
Gévaudan/Lozère; 80 **6**, Low R.
2. La Fromagerie Cigaloise 30170 St-Hippolyte-du-Fort.
Cévennes/Gard; 80 **17**, L of C.
3. *Chevrière modèle*, near St-Jean-du-Gard; sold as *St-Jeannais*. (If you are in this area, see also PICOLETTE.)
Cévennes/Gard; 80 **17**, high, on R. Gardon.

**Pélardon de Largentière, de Ruoms.** Other local centres of making and marketing, in the Vivarais. Largentière has Tuesday market.
Vivarais/Ardèche; 80 **8**, high R 80 **9**, upper L.

PÉLUSSIN

Saturday and Sunday markets.

**Rigotte de Pélussin.** 70–80g base of cone, eaten *frais, mi-sec* or *sec*; '*exquis*' (Lyon 1985), made round St-Etienne (Viard, 1980). 40–45% m.g.; *fermier; artisanal; chèvre/mi-chèvre cru.*
Haut-Forez/Loire; 76 **10**, top L.

**Pavé d'Affinois.** See Chapter 12, p. 378, made at Pélussin.

PÉRALDOU

See ANDUZE and PÉLARDON D'ANDUZE.

PÉRETTE

Marque of Gaperon (see p. 242).

PETIT BESSAY

See BESSAY.

PETIT-BEURRE

Another name for Sarassou (see p. 252).

LE PETIT BLEU, BABY PAN

Post-Second-World-War innovations: 500g sizes of Bleu d'Auvergne (see p. 230).
*industriel; vache pasteurisé.*

LE PETIT SAINT-NECTAIRE

See PAVIN and SAINT-NECTAIRE.

PICHERANDE

Market every other Friday (forty-eight Saint-Nectaire farms in commune 1985).
Puy-de-Dôme; 73 **13**, bottom L of C.

PICODON

**Picodon de l'Ardèche (AOC 1983).** 1. 60–150g rounded disc, 1–3cm thick; lightly rennetted; ripened on grid which marks cheese; natural *croûte-fleurie*, white to golden or powdery blue; flavour from sweet (minimum 12 days, to 3 weeks) to rich (at least 3 weeks) and strong (at least 1 month). See Chapter 16, pp. 447–8 for total AOC production and more details of making. This cheese has been made in the region 'for ever'. Many were prepared for winter use by washing in *eau-de-vie*, wrap-

ping in either clematis or vine leaf and storing in pots.
The EEC (*Règlementation du 1 janvier 1985*) is making bureaucratic difficulties for farms by insisting on expensive bacteriological and chemical analyses. This benefits the Coopératives of Crest (Dauphiné) and Caprilac, whose milk is *thermisé*, i.e. not strictly raw, and less severely tested.
45% m.g.; *fermier; artisanal/laitier; chèvre cru entier/thermisé*.
Vivarais/Ardèche, and Canton de Barjac; 80 **9**, lower L; N. Gard; Dauphiné/Drome, Valréas/Vaucluse.
2. M. Faivre makes Picodon at La Maisonnette, Gluiras.
*fermier; chèvre cru.*
76 **19**, NE of C.
M. Jacques Brunier makes Picodon and sells on his farm at Darbres.
*fermier; chèvre cru.*
76 **19**, low C.
M. Raymond Point, Serre Pointu, at Aubignas makes beautiful cheeses from Picodon recipe, but larger than AOC size. He has forty goats; sale on farm every day, tel. 75 90 52 20. N102 from Le Teil W, then first on right D363 to Aubignas.
*fermier; biologique; chèvre cru.*
Vivarais/Ardèche; 80 **19**, W of Le Teil top R, limit of map.

**Picodon de Barjac.**
Gard; 80 **9**, lower L.

**Picodon de Gras, de la Gorce.**
Vivarais/Ardèche; 80 **9**, NE–NW of C.

**Picodon de St-Agrève.** 120–150g, 8cm × 2cm, rounded; 3 weeks for *sec*; nutty flavour. St-Agrève and its surrounds was noted for its *fourmes* as well as its Picodons.
In *Contes et fariboles du pays de Saint-Agrève* Marcel Bourette wrote, 'the whereabouts of cheeses ... is hidden in rain at the bottom of climbing alleys; its aroma denounces it. There is the clan of Picodons, and that, almost shameful, of La Pidance *trop blanche*.' In 1969 there were isolated Picodon makers, *pur chèvre* (76 **4**, high SE of Ardes) at Apchat, Blanzat (N of Clermont-Ferrand, 73 **14**) and Nadaillet (Puy-de-Dôme) and at Cervières (near Noiretable, 73 **16**, and elsewhere in Loire.)
45% m.g.; *fermier; chèvre cru entier.*
Vivarais/Ardèche; 76 **9/19**, L.

PICOLETTE PUR CHÈVRE

Colombières, 48330 St-Étienne-Vallée-Française (not far from two Pélardon farms and the Coopérative *fruitière*, and two Cévennes makers (see p. 246 under Pélardon).
*fermier; biologique; chèvre cru.*
Gévaudan/Lozère; 80 **7/17**, L.

LA PIDANCE

Term used for young cheeses not fit to be called Picodon, which the AOC now accepts as such (see PICODON).

PIERRE-SUR-HAUTE

See FOURME DE PIERRE-SUR-HAUTE.

PISTOLE

2.5–3kg; 30–38cm × 5cm; ringed with tree bark; washed-crust with smooth surface; made to use up surplus curd from other cheese products in a big dairy (similar to Tourrée, see Chapter 16, p. 462).
60% m.g.; *laitier; vache.*
Gévaudan/Cévennes/Lozère.

PLANÈZE

**Bleu de Planèze.** Given by Viard (*Auvergne*, in index) as another name for Laqueuille (see p. 244 and BLEU DE PLANÈZE).

PONT-ASTIER

Centre of Gaperon-making. See GAPERON.

PONTGIBAUD

See BLEU DE PONTGIBAUD.

LA PRÉFÉRENCE

1½–2kg soft blue; flat, round, 24cm in diameter; made by Centrelait, Aurillac (see p. 229).
*industriel; vache pasteurisé.*
Cantal.

LE PUY

Wednesday, Friday and Saturday market (including Patrick Stein of Craponne).
Haute-Loire; 76 **7**.

PUY LAURENT

Wednesday market.

**La Bastide.** See FOURME LE LABRO.
Gévaudan/Lozère; 76 **17**, bottom; 80 **7**, top C.

### Raclette du Montvelay

A recent addition to French competitors with Swiss Raclette (sold in Fromagerie Coopérative du Beaufortin-Beaufort in Savoie, which probably matures it).
*laitier; vache.*
Monts du Velay.

### Rigotte de Pélussin

Other Rigottes I have seen on sale in the region (e.g. Bourg-Argental, see p. 232) are from S. Burgundy or Dauphiné.

### Riom

Saturday market.
Puy-de-Dôme; 73 **4**.

### Rochefort-Montagne

Sometimes known as Cantalon. As old as the related cheeses of Aubrac and Cantal (see pp. 229 and 234), but with a finesse surpassing most other cheeses of those types (Androuët, 1982); 3–10kg tubby cylinder, 15–20cm × 15–20cm; clean but granular-looking crust; firm pale *pâte* after 2–3 months in humid *cave*: slightly lactic flavour. See also BLEU DE LAQUEUILLE, originally developed from this cheese.
Auvergne/Puy-de-Dôme; 73 **13**, C.

### Rogeret; Rogeret des Cévennes; Rogeret de Lamastre; Rogeret Saint-Félicien (see p. 249 Saint-Félicien); Rougerin

Extremely varied 50g–150g; hand-moulded shallow domes, small discs (Pélardon (pp. 245–6) and Picodon (pp. 246–7) shapes), drums; *affinage* in natural *caves* in rock, sheds, barns, stables, kitchens, where they naturally ferment and become yellow to red ochre (whence Rougerin, Rogeret, local terms); tasty to fierce flavour. I have seen all these at Bourg-Argental (see p. 232), and some on sale by Patrick Stein, whose cheeses were *lait-de-mélange* (see CRAPONNE, LAMASTRE).
45% m.g.; *fermier; chèvre/vache/mélange cru.*
Forez, Cévennes/Vivarais/Ardèche.

### Roujadou, Roujadoux

Cheeses of Chevrotin de Montmarault family (see p. 238) with stronger crusts; washing or natural surface fermentation causes reddening (whence Roujadou, although Courtine considers it a corruption of *ronde-à-deux*). Found in 1982 at St-Pouçain-sur-Sioule by Androuët, *Guide Marabout* has Roujadoux as cows'-milk cheese from Montmarault, with crust as above, but the 1982 cheeses were of cow's, goats' and *lait-de-mélange*. St-Pourçain has a Saturday market.
*fermier; artisanal; chèvre/vache/mélange cru.*
Bourbonnais/Montmarault; Saint-Pourçain; 69 **14**, bottom.

### Roumajou, Roumajoux

Name given to Chevrotons of Montmarault, to distinguish them from Moulins cheeses.
*fermier; artisanal; chèvre cru.*
Bourbonnais/Montmarault.

### Ruoms

See PÉLARDON DE LARGENTIÈRE, DE RUOMS.
Vivarais/Ardèche.

### Saingorlon

At the end of the 1960s some Auvergne *laiteries* were still making this Gorgonzola substitute (see PAYS DE L'AIN). See GRIONZOLA.
*laitier; vache pasteurisé.*

### St-Agrève

See PICODON DE ST-AGRÈVE. Hôtel des Cévennes serves *gratin ardèchois* and *fromages du pays.*

### Le Saint-Amant

Name given to his Savarons (see p. 25. M. Allès, Gaperon maker of St-Amant-Tallende, commended by Androuët in 1982. When M. Allès retired, his La Pérette *marque* went to the Laiterie de la Vallée Dore, Pont-Astier (see GAPERON).
*artisanal; vache cru.*
Puy-de-Dôme; 73 **14**, C.

### St-Anthème

M. R. Col's *fromagerie* (see BRIZOU, BLEU D'AUVERGNE LAIT CRU, FOURME D'AMBERT and FOURME DE MONTBRISON LAIT CRU, LA GENETTE, MAIGRETTE; TOMME DE MONTAGNE); visits from 2 p.m., cheeses on sale. (See AMBERT.) Fromagerie Col is 1500m on Ambert side of St-Anthème, off south side of road along winding track past other farms. This was also a good area for *lait cru* farm cheese in 1985.
Puy-de-Dôme; 73 **17**, S of C.

## St-Bonnet-le-Château

Fête de la Fourme, July; Friday market.
Forez/Loire; 76 **7/8**, top.

## St-Diéry

Seventeen Saint-Nectaire farms in commune (1985).
Nearby at Moulin-Neuf, little Musée Auvergnat open 1 June–1 October, 09.00–12.00, 14.00–19.00.
Puy-de-Dôme; 73 **14**, lower L off D978.

## St-Donat

Market on alternate Saturdays.
Thirty-seven Saint-Nectaire farms; visits (not Mondays): M. Christian Charbonnel, Pommier; M. Marcel Charbonnel, Bertinet; Salers herds.
Puy-de-Dôme; 73 **13**, bottom L.

## Saint-Éloy

Large black-coated *tomme* made in Creuse, *affiné* by Riches-Monts, Clermont-Ferrand). No doubt there is a peppered version (see BOUGNAT).
*laitier; vache.*
Marche/Creuse.

## St-Étienne

Markets: Mondays and Fridays, and summer Saturdays. Heaviest cheese consumption per head in France, and, while mines were active, heaviest wine consumption too; so plenty of cheese in shops and market (especially *bleus* from Velay, *fourmes*, chèvres, Sarasson).
Forez/Monts du Lyonnais/Loire; W 73 **19**, 76 **9**.

## St-Félicien

Friday market.

**Saint-Félicien.** 60–120g; round, 8–10cm × 1.5–2cm deep; farm cheese usually wider than *laiterie* cheese; irregular (shapes reminiscent of Pérail) in the Rogeret or Pélardon style (see pp. 245–6). Some are too salt, but I have tasted excellent rich, melting farm cheeses collected and ripened by M. Chauvin, 07410 St-Félicien (tel. 75 06 00 99); I found a variety on sale at Bourg-Argental (see p. 232). M. Raymond Point's account: 'It should be 100–120g in weight (needing 0.9 l of milk). The cheese is obtained by a quick coagulation in 2–4 hours, renneted at 27–32°C. The curd is then cut and the *sérum* eliminated as it exudes. When the *sérum* becomes clear, the curd is put into moulds. One obtains a *pâte* called *caillé doux*. *Affinage* in a cupboard on straw or in a cool *cave* for 2–3 weeks. The crust is sometimes rubbed during *affinage*. The taste of this cheese is very characteristic.'
*fermier; artisanal coopérative; chèvre/mi-chèvre cru.*
Vivarais/Ardèche; 76 **10**, 77 **1**, lower L on D532, N from Tournon.
(The name Saint-Félicien has also been misappropriated by a cows'-milk cheese-maker in the Dauphiné, see p. 461, so watch out.)

## St-Flour

Saturday market.
Shop: Salvat-Truyol, rue du Lac.
Cantal; 76 **4/14**.

## St-Jean-Lachalm

See TOMME DE MONTAGNE and CHÈVRE.
Haute-Loire; 76 **16**, high R.

## Saint-Jeannais

Pélardon in rustic disc form, uncrusted; fine texture, aromatic; *chèvrerie modèle* (*Marabout*, 1978), near St-Jean-du-Gard, which has a Tuesday market.
*fermier; chèvre cru.*
Gard/Bas Cévennes; 80 **17**, or Gardon, high.

## St-Nectaire

Sunday market.
June–September: Exposition des Arts et Traditions d'Auvergne. July and August, 10.00–12.00, 14.00–19.00: Maison de Sailles nearby, all traditional features of farmhouse including box-beds.
Emile Bellonte makes Saint-Nectaire at Farges and accepts visitors (except Mondays). Syndicat du Fromage Saint-Nectaire, Besse, 63610 Besse-et-Saint-Anastaise (*moniteur-laitier*).
Puy-de-Dôme; 73 **14**, far L.

**Saint-Nectaire (AOC 1979/1982).** 1.5–1.7kg, 21cm × 5cm; semi-soft, lightly pressed; *affinage*: minimum 3 weeks, in natural *caves* (95% humidity); but traditionally 2–4 months are needed to achieve the full *croûte-fleurie*: white-grey, '*le petit mimosa*', and russet moulds; *pâte* should be ready to swell out when cut (with *small* apertures here and there), and melt in the mouth. Little aroma or flavour (except from crust) in *laiterie* cheeses, because of pasteurisation. Avoid outer wraps or paper surface labels with *no* mention of *'fermier'* or *'fabrication fermière'*; or, failing labels, avoid cheese with square green casein plaque set into one face: these indicate pasteurised *laitier* cheese.

45% m.g. (minimum); *fermier; laitier; vache cru/pasteurisé.*

**Saint-Nectaire Laitier.** The *laiteries* started in 1964, production rising from 386 to 6172 tonnes in twenty years. In 1984 it dropped by 845 tonnes.

The *laiterie* pasteurises the milk, thus killing the vital bacteria and aromatic esters which give the cheese its internal character. *Laiteries* also use commercial starters, and stir the curd longer in the vat, making for a drier consistency. Then 'the *caillé* is more or less washed, which limits acidification and allows the development of a more supple *pâte*'. This last practice is in the industrial Saint-Paulin class, and deplored by monks and other artisans. These cheaper, *laitiers* cheeses acquired a big market, and reduced the number of farms making cheese by over two-thirds. (There had been 2000 in 1960.) But the dissatisfaction of old Saint-Nectaire lovers, and the education of others, has led to a revival of farm cheese. In 1985 nearly 4000 tonnes a year was being made on 680 farms. See p. 212.

**Le Petit Saint-Nectaire.** Smaller cheeses originally made to use up last curd in vat; 500g 13cm × 3.5–4cm.

(Le Pavin (see p. 245) is a *laitière* cheese of similar size made at Besse-en-Chandesse but not sold as Petit Saint-Nectaire.)
*usually laitier; vache pasteurisé.*

**Saint-Nectaire (AOC) Fermier.** The difference in this cheese is marked by *'fermier'* or *'fabrication fermière'* on wraps and paper labels, and by an oval green plaque on the face of the cheese. This is obvious on the *blancs* (young cheese as sold to *affineurs*), but it will be covered by white *geotrichum candidum*, perhaps grey *Mucer et Aspergillus*, and given the right time, yellow *sporotrichum aureum* ('*le petit Mimosa*'), and finally the red *oïdium aurantiacum*. So, if the cheese has been properly matured, these three or four surface moulds will conceal the plaque's detail, and it will be necessary to scrape it gently to be sure of its shape and to identify the cheese's provenance. Farm and *laiterie* cheeses are matured in similar conditions and the plaque alone distinguishes their crust. The difference lies inside. The flowery aroma and flavour of the *fermier* cheese arises from these factors: the farm where cheese is made is less likely to have used chemical fertiliser (some have tried them; the resulting loss of flavour in the cheese and puffy texture taught them a lesson); and it is more likely to have kept to Salers or Ferrandaises cows. The cheese is made morning and evening, unpasteurised, as the milk comes fresh from the cows; the whey feeds pigs, which in turn enrich the pastures naturally, as do the cows. Vessels and equipment are washed in boiled water from fresh springs or wells, with no detergents (which can contaminate milk and spoil cheese). For the history of Saint-Nectaire, see pp. 211–12.

Below are the communes where Saint-Nectaire was being made in 1985, with the number of farms then active. The letter code for each commune is given, as placed on the bottom of the oval plaque. (Avoid visiting Puy-de-Dôme farms on Mondays, unless the farm has a sign, because of Besse market.)

*Département de Puy-de-Dôme (63); Canton d'Ardes sur Couze* (76 **4**, high): Ardes (Z)2, market second and fourth Monday in month); La Mayrand (AE)3; Mazoires (AG)4; Saint-Alyse-ès-Montagne (AH)12; (76 **3**, high R): La Godivelle (AJ)12; (73 **14**, low): Chassagne (AA)3, Roche Charles (AC)4.

*Canton de Besse-en-Chandesse* (76 **3**, high): Espinchal (Q)7; Égliseneuve (see p. 239) (P)71; Compains (R)37; (73 **14**, lower L): Le Valbeleix (S)20; Sainte-Anastaise (T)18; St Pierre Colamine (U)9; St-Diéry (V)17; (73 **13**, lower R): Besse (see p. 230) (N)45; St-Victor La Rivière (W)16; Chambon-sur-Lac, see p. 235 (Y)26; Murol (X)10, including farms at Beaune-le-Froid (where there are also *affineurs*).

*Canton de Champeix* (73 **14**, S and SE of C): Creste on D26 (AM)2; Montaigut le Blanc (AL)2; Saint-Nectaire (AS)8.

*Canton de St Amant-Tallende* (73 **14**, L of C 13 R of C): Aydat (AV)3; Saulzet-le-Froid (AW)9; Le Vernet-Sainte-Marguerite (AX)18.

*Canton de Rochefort-Montagne* (see p. 248) (73 **13**, C and below C): Orcival (AY)2; La Bourboule (BB)1, Saturday market (summer daily)1; Le Mont-Dore (BC)1.
*Canton de Tauves.* Tauves (A) SW of La Bourboule, 3.
*Canton de Latour* (73 **13**, low L): La Tour d'Auvergne (F)9; Chastreix (5)33; Picherande, see p. 246 (K)48; St-Donat (see p. 249) (H)37; (73 **12**, SW of La Tour): Bagnols (G)7; Cros (E)1; (76 **3**, high L): St-Genès-Champespe (L Thursday market)30.
*Département de Cantal* (15), *Canton de Champs-sur-Tarentaine* (76 **2**, high R, **3**, upper L): Champs (BZ)5; Marchal (BF)5; Tremouille (BE)10.
*Canton de Condat-en-Féniers* (see p. 238) (76 **3**, C and higher): Montboudif (BJ)8; Chanterelle (BR)18; Condat (BS)25; Montgreleix E of Condat (BQ)9; Marcenat (BP)30; St-Bonnet-de-Condat (BN)5; Lugarde (BL)9; Marchastel (BM)3.
*Canton d'Allanche* (76 **3**, C): Landeyrat (BV)2; St-Saturnin (BY)17; Ségur-Les-Villas (BX)4.
Syndicat du Fromage Saint-Nectaire (covering farmers and *laitiers*), Besse-en-Chandesse (tel. 73 79 52 57) *moniteur-laitier*. Laiteries and plaque code: Puy-de-Dôme: (73 **13**, lower L) La Bourboule (Saturday market, summer daily) Société Subirana et ses enfants (63 U); (73 **12**, lower R) Tauves: Coopérative (63 BH); 73 **14**, L of C Aydat (NE of lac Aydat): Société Laitière de la Montagne (Toury), Rouillas Bas (63 Z); (73 **13/14**, low) Besse: Coopérative (Riches-Monts) (63 BA) Cantal (76 **3/4**) Allanche (Tuesday market): Société Marque Lucien (sold to Fromageries des Causses et d'Auvergne) (15 BF); Fromageries des Monts du Cézallier (15 EZ) (76 **2**, top C) Lanobre (76 **2**, top): Société Laitière du Plateau de l'Artense (Centrelait) (15 DT) (76 **3**, NW of C), Condat en Féniers (Tuesday market): Walchli (15 AR) also *affineurs* of farm cheese.
*For trade buyers*
*Affineurs/grossistes.* Attend the Monday market at Besse (see p. 230), making your base the Café de la Halle, where you may well be able to make a rendezvous with the *moniteur-laitier* and get some tips on current form. You can then watch the *grossistes* at work with their cheese irons and make contacts where you feel drawn (with *affineur/grossiste* or farmer). Many farms keep back some cheeses in the tourist season for direct sale, but most of their cheese is matured in the mould-rich, humid caves (usually natural) of the *affineurs*.

There are *caves d'affinage* at Clermont-Ferrand, including Aubière in SE quarter of Clermont-Ferrand in Soron's old wine *caves*; at Beaumont (southern Clermont), R. Babut; at Beaune-Le-Froid (N of Murol); at Besse (see p. 230), M. Barbat et fils; at Saint-Julien (63320 Champeix, 2km to W) J. J. Roche, of whose cheese I had excellent reports in 1987 from my son Hugh and found them better than any I had recently been able to buy retail in France. At Champeix *Le Figaro* reported some years back: 'good *affinage* (by Sagnelonge-Pathon) with weekly brine-washings and brushing with red clay; after two months the beautiful crust is adorned with fluorescent patches of mould, and the flesh of the cheese is melting; not acid, but just *à point* in its rich savour'. At Compains, Maison Verdier (Le Brion); St-Haon-Le-Chatel, where they prefer lightly crusted cheeses 'from the colour of pale wine lees to the violet side of pink' (Androuët, 1982); at Ytrac, where the Allayrangue *caves* give a perfect aroma to crusts of cheeses left there long enough, and the farm selection is exceptional, 76 **11**, far R, W of Aurillac. La Fromagerie Manhès sells at Aurillac (see p. 229), but has *caves* in the Saint-Nectaire region 60km away.

## St-Pourçain-sur-Sioule

Saturday market; ancient wine centre.

## Saint-Rieu

300g with grey crust, shaped like a smaller Reblochon (see p. 435); made and *affiné* by Union Coopérative des Fermiers Cantalais, Riom (where there is a Saturday market). Cantal-Riom; 76 **2**, far R of C.

## Salers

Important Thursday market, 1 May–31 October.

**Salers AOC, 1979/1980.** 35–55kg squat cylinder 38–48cm across 30–40cm high, hard (pressed as *caillé* and as cheese); dry natural rind achieved by 3–6 months of *affinage* with washing and brushing; 8 months is preferable; golden surface, patches of red and orange; *pâte* is firm and

has an edge to its flavour when aged. The cheese has a red metal plaque on its side.
The name Salers has been extended since 1980 to cover Cantal made in *burons* all through the Cantal AOC cheese region. Production is on the increase. See pp. 205–7. For *buron* visits (May–Oct) consult Syndicat d'Initiative at Vic-sur-Cère (see p. 254) or Salers (tel. 71 40 70 68).
45% m.g.; *buron*; *vache cru entier*.

## Salihès

**Cantal Fermier.** François and Catherine Verdier (tel. 71 47 52 16).
*fermier; vache cru (Salers)*.
Cantal NE of Vic-sur-Cère; 3km off N22 76 **12**, high R.

## Sarasson, Sarassou, Sarassoun

*Fromage fort* based on curd skimmed or precipitated from buttermilk, potted, and enlivened with *fines-herbes*, garlic, salt and pepper to taste. The name comes from Saracen. In the Vivarais, for Sarassou, fresh milk is beaten in and its acidity goes well with potatoes. It is potted and sealed up for long keeping (authority: Androuët, who found some fresh Sarasson in St-Étienne market in 1982). Petit-Beurre is another name in use.
Forez/Vivarais.

## Saulzet-le-Froid

Saint-Nectaire farm: Ernest Pélissier, Saulzet.
Puy-de-Dôme; 73 **13**, SE from C.

## Sauvain

Maison de la Fourme (Giproforez, tel. 77 76 80 09, see ST-ANTHÈME) and Fromagerie Tarn (see FOURME D'AMBERT, FOURME DE MONTBRISON, BRIQUES DU HAUT FOREZ, MAIGRETTE, LE GENETTE); *musée* (M. Didier).
Président Société Interprofessionnel Fourmes d'Ambert et de Montbrison (1985) M. Grilot, Dizangues (W of Sauvain), tel. 77 76 81 20.
Chalmazel (see p. 235) is 8km W.
Forez/Loire; 73 **17**, L of C.

## Savaron

1.5–2kg semi-soft pinky-gold washed-crust cheese; more rounded at edges than SAFR's *laitier* Port-Salut. Made by Besse *coopérative* and ripened by Soron at Aubière (see Saint-Nectaire *affineurs*); but the cheese got its name from rue Savaron in St-Nectaire, where there are ancient *caves*, to which cheeses of this sort were sent from the Midi and Normandie up to the early 1970s. *They* came out looking like Saint-Nectaire, causing some (intentional?) confusion.
*laitier; vache pasteurisé*.
Puy-de-Dôme.

## Séchons

This term is used for ultra-*sec* small chèvres, but some are good for eating, not just for making *fromage fort*. I found some lovely *bleutés* examples at Bourg-Argental (see p. 232). They need not be very old; rather, perhaps, very small cheeses or the last few cheeses made from a big batch of curd, which tend to dry out more quickly, because the curd dries as cheesemaking proceeds.
*fermier; chèvre cru*.
Vivarais/Forez/Ardèche.

## Solignac-sur-Loire

Tuesday market. (See also BLEU DE COSTAROS.)

**Fromage Fermier.** Also milk and meat, all organic; Pierre Vallette, Eycenac, St-Christophe-sur-Dolaison.
*fermier; biologique*.
St-Christophe-sur-Dolaison, Velay/Haute-Loire; 76 **17**, high L, NW of Solignac.

## Sourire

385g slimmer's cheese, Camembert shape; *fromage blanc* state; made by Fromagerie Rissoan, Luc.
25% m.g.; *laitier; vache pasteurisé*.
Gévaudan/Lozère; 76 **17**, 80 **7**, low on D806 N of La-Bastide-Puy-Laurent.

## Terroir

**Fromage du Terroir.** See LAPALISSE.

## Thiers

Sunday market. See CHEVROTIN DE THIERS.

## Thiézac

Centre for Bleu d'Auvergne and Cantal (see p. 234) including distributors, e.g. Chautard (tel. 71 47 01 08).
Cantal; 76 **12/13**, top on N22.

## TOME, TOMME

Often used of small young soft cheeses; see also MAZET.

## TOMMES

See also ANCEVAL, FOREZ.

**Tomme de Ferme.** See ALIGOT.

**Tomme Lait-de-Mélange.** Substantial grid-crossed, regular, round *tomme*; Ambert Thursday market.
*fermier; lait-de-mélange cru.*
Livradois.

**Tomme de Montagne.** 250–300g, 500g heavily moulded grey-crusted, like rustic round patties (smaller) or pies (larger); found at Abonnenc in Ambert (see p. 228) and Barbut in Besse-en-Chandesse (see p. 230). Abonnenc had some with mite-rich crusts. The mites (familiarly called *arterons, artisans,* or *cirons*, scientifically the *lacarien Tyroglyphus ciro*) are encouraged by some makers to dry the cheese: '*ça bonifie le fromage*'. One such mitey cheese, Reblochon size (see p. 435), is made at St-Jean-Lachalm, Haute-Loire (76 **16**, high R).
*fermier; vache cru.*
Auvergne.

**Tomme de Montagne la Genette.** *Croûte-fleurie* including *le petit mimosa* and russet mould (which varies with the season). I tasted one ripened for 18 weeks; despite low fat, it had good flavour, and beautiful, close, but semi-soft texture; sold by Abonnenc, Ambert and Fromagerie Col (see ST-ANTHÈME and LA GENETTE), where it is made.
*25% m.g.; laitier; artisanal; vache cru.*
Puy-de-Dôme.

**Tome Blanche; Tomme du Velay.** Patrick Stein (see CRAPONNE) sells this 2kg white crust turning golden; soft open texture, melting; made by Coopérative Le Lisieux (see p. 244). A number of *laitiers* make a white-crusted soft Tomme de Velay, one of them called Tomme des Neiges, an unripened, white-skinned mild cheese.
*laitier; vache cru/pasteurisé.*

**Tomme Persillée du Velay.** See COUCOURON.

**Tomme du Vivarais, Toummo.** Small, soft. Used for Sarassou, Sarassou (see p. 252) and for Migno (boiled potatoes with cream and seasoning roasted in oven or on open fire). Eaten as young as four hours old in summer; best demi-sec or 'Toummo chalustro' (*Odeurs de Forêts et Fumets de Table*) in May. In Bas-Vivarais (Vallon-Pont-D'Arc and Saint-Mortant notably, according to Charles Foron, the best provenance), there was competition to sell off January kids quickest and produce the first Toummo of the year. The curd had to be coaxed to form in the warmth of the kitchen, with snow outside.
*fermier; chèvre/vache (in winter) cru.*
Velay/Haute-Loire; 76 **8**, bottom R; Velay in general.

## TOURNON

Saturday market. M. Robert Bourgeat, *maître fromager*, Fromagerie, 59 Grande-Rue.
Vivarais/Ardèche on Rhône.

## TRIZAC

SARL Reynal-Varagne (D678 towards Vallette) makes *lait cru* Cantal, Tomme-Fraîche and Bleu d'Auvergne; *caves* open until 18.00 on weekdays; tel. 71 78 60 76.
Cantal; 76 **2**, C.

## TROU DU CURÉ, TROU DE MUROLS

See MUROL.

## LA TUMO

An alternative to Pélardon for straight use; or (when freshly drained) crushed with a fork, flavoured with garlic, olive oil, vinegar, pepper and pimento, and served with hot potatoes (found by team from *Larousse/Sélection*, September 1982); La Tumo is a *langue d'Oc* term).
*fermier; chèvre/mi-chèvre/mi-brebis cru.*
Vivarais/Ardèche.

## URFÉ

See BRIQUE.

## VACHARD

**Vachard-Mélange.** 500–600g up to 1.5kg *fromage de pays* of the brushed-crust Tomme de Montagne (see above) type formerly made on farms; often milk had been part-skimmed for butter-making. Reduction of domestic butter-making and more collection of milk by *laiteries* has made Vachard rare. Fromage de Montagne la Genette by

M. Col is of the family, and is sometimes sold as Vachard. His cheeses have fat, creamy texture despite part-skimming. At least up to the end of the 1960s, it was common for farms to add some goat's milk. Such cheeses were of *'très bonne qualité'*, according to the 1969 *Auvergne* cheese guide. Outward appearance resembled Saint-Nectaire (of which Androuët thinks Vachard is the ancestor).
30–40% m.g.; *fermier; vache/lait-de-mélange cru.*
Forez/Livradois; Ambert area.

## Valence

Market daily except Sundays.

## Velay

See BLEU DU, TOMME DU. See also BELLEVUE, BAINS, BLEU DE CAYRE, COSTAROS, COUCOURON, DU LISIEUX, LANGEAC, LOUDES; BÛCHES; LA CHAISE-DIEU, CONQUÉRANT; FOURMES DE MÉZENC, LAVAUDIEU, LISIEUX, DU MAZET, GERBIZON, RACLETTE, SOLIGNAC, TOMMES, LA TUMO, YSSINGEAUX, YSSINGELAIS; also ST-ÉTIENNE.

## Vernoux

Thursday market.
Vivarais/Ardèche; 76 **20**, upper L.

## Vialas

Sunday a.m. market (including in early 1980s a chevrier who had been Directeur of Le Théâtre Quotidien of Marseille: *banon*-type in chestnut leaves).
Gévaudan/Lozère; 80 **7**, S of C.

## Vic-sur-Cère

Tuesday and Friday markets.
Visits to *burons*: Syndicat d'Initiative (tel. 71 47 50 68); on foot or by cable car including Belles-Aygues and Paillerol, mid-June–end Aug. Syndicat makes up groups, maximum of twenty-five in party (and see nearby Salihès(p. 252) for Cantal farm visit).
Cantal; 76 **12**, high R.

**Fromage Fermier de Vache.** 100g neat-edged, medal-shaped soft cheese made in same way as chèvre on a few farms; remarkably rich and creamy without being sharp, even after three days in car; beautiful flavour, melting consistency. Mine was made by M. Fresquet, La Garrigue, St-Clément, 15800 Vic-sur-Cère.
*m.g. non précisée; fermier; vache cru.*
Cantal; 76 **12**, E of R. Cère.

## Vivarais

See ANNONAY, APÉRI CHÈVRE, ARAULES, BANON, BICHOU, BOURG-ARGENTAL, BRIQUES, BÛCHES, BURZET, CHÈVRES, CHEVRETINES, CHEVROTONS, DARBRES, LE FOUDJOU, FOURMES, LAMASTRE, PÉLARDON, PICODON, PIDANCE, ROGERET, ST-FÉLICIEN, SARASSOU, SÉCHONS, TOMME, VERNOUX, LA TUMO, LA VOULTE.

## La Voulte-sur-Rhône

Friday market; and see CHÈVRES, farm St-Laurent-du-Pape.
Vivarais/Ardèche; 76 **20**, C.

## Yssingeaux

Thursday market.
*Laiterie* J. Gerentes (see BÛCHE).
Velay/Haute-Loire.

## Yssingelais

**Fourme des Monts Yssingelais.** 2kg high cylindrical blue with skin rather than crust.
50% m.g.; *laitier; vache.*
Velay/Haute-Loire; 76 **8**, lower L.

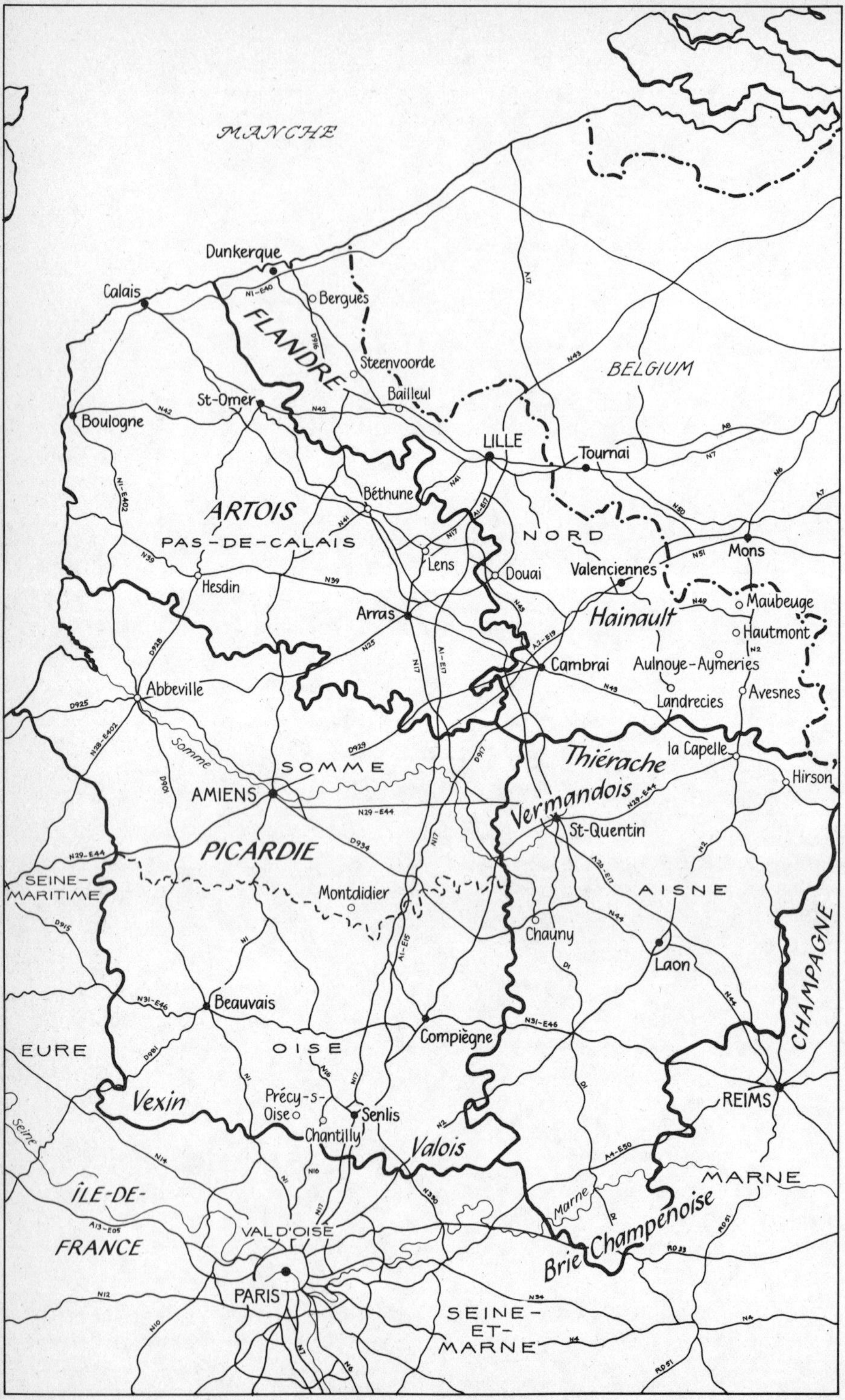

MANCHE
Dunkerque
Calais
Bergues
FLANDRE
Steenvoorde
Bailleul
BELGIUM
St-Omer
Boulogne
LILLE
Tournai
Béthune
ARTOIS
PAS-DE-CALAIS
NORD
Lens
Douai
Valenciennes
Mons
Hesdin
Arras
Hainault
Maubeuge
Hautmont
Cambrai
Aulnoye-Aymeries
Abbeville
Landrecies
Avesnes
Thiérache
la Capelle
Somme
SOMME
AMIENS
Hirson
Vermandois
St-Quentin
PICARDIE
SEINE-
MARITIME
Montdidier
AISNE
Chauny
Laon
CHAMPAGNE
Beauvais
Compiègne
EURE
OISE
Vexin
Précy-s-
Oise
Senlis
Chantilly
REIMS
Valois
Seine
ÎLE-DE-
FRANCE
MARNE
Marne
Champenoise
Brie
VAL D'OISE
PARIS
SEINE-
ET-
MARNE

CHAPTER EIGHT

# The North

## FLANDRE – HAINAUT – THIÉRACHE/AVESNOIS – CALAISIS – BOULONNAIS – ARTOIS – PICARDIE

The Northern *pays* of France have a subtly different feel from those of neighbouring Normandy, Champagne and the Île de France. Their air, light, landscape, arts and architecture are those of the Low Countries, and that is where they belonged from pre-Roman times until the reign of Louis XIV. After various post-Roman invasions in the early fifth century, the Franks came through to assimilate with the southern population and evolve the Picard language and province, while the northerners remained in the sphere of culture and trade which was eventually to develop into the distinctive Pays Bas.

From the sixth century the Church began to exercise its power, of which the profusion of *abbayes* and the cheese of the region, Maroilles, are surviving evidence. From 843, the comté de Flandre became the lay power; the comtés of Hainaut and Artois were later offshoots. In the post-Charlemagne divisions Flandre stayed with the Empire, associated with Lorraine. Artois, cut out of Flandre, went in dowry to Philippe II Auguste in 1180 when he married Isabelle de Flandre-Hainaut. Philippe made Artois a free comté.

The twelfth century saw the advent of municipal power. With Flemish immigration, trade, especially through the cloth industry, brought a growth in bourgeois wealth. Cities were fortified and adorned with trade halls and belfries, many of which survive. This prosperity, so much due to trade with England, was interrupted in the fourteenth century by the Anglo-French struggle for the right to the French throne, which became the Hundred Years War. Calais was English from 1377 to 1558, Dunkerque as late as the 1660s, and the English gave the Somme cities of Picardie to their ally Burgundy. Artois, Flandre and Hainaut went by marriage to Burgundy towards the end of this period, and, with Picardie, shared in the golden age of the arts and trade of one of the most powerful and glorious states Europe has ever seen. It disintegrated in 1477 on the death of Charles le Téméraire, who had made enemies all around him.

France seized the duché of Burgundy and Picardie. (Burgundy is dealt with in Chapter 11.) Picardie boasted a round cheese called Rollot, from its original source near Montdidier, which was to please Louis XIV later.

Latterly more often heart-shaped, it has almost disappeared from its native soil (see list, p. 273), as has the local peculiarity called Clovis (see list, p. 268), so sadly I shall have no reason to linger in the province.

Flandre, Hainaut and Artois passed by marriage to the Habsburgs; these provinces stayed in the Empire for nearly two centuries, barring intervals of French invasion. Because the senior line of the House of Habsburg married on to the Spanish throne, the Pays Bas, with Flandre and Hainaut, became known as the Spanish Netherlands.

In 1659 Artois and part of Hainaut were ceded to France. Four years later Louis XIV married Marie Thérèse of Austria and Spain, who claimed to inherit the Pays Bas through her mother. Her inheritance was disputed, so Louis went to war. His gains filled in most of the gaps in the North, bringing him close to the present frontier when peace was made by the treaty of Nimwegen in 1678. The Treaty of Utrecht in 1713 settled the boundaries of France and the Low Countries as they now exist, giving France part of Flandre and some more of Hainaut; the rest of Flandre and Hainaut are Belgian provinces today.

Historically speaking, therefore, the North is comparatively new to French rule. This explains its conservative attitude towards the Revolution, its welcome for the restoration of the monarchy and the resumption of international trade in 1815, and the persistence of the Pays Bas atmosphere in the region.

# MAROILLES

What could not be restored with the monarchy was the North's national and international cheese trade. This had had as its fount the ancient Abbaye de Maroilles, from which the region's basic cheese stemmed some time between the *abbaye*'s foundation by Saint-Humbert in 652 and the year 960, when the first specific mention of the cheese appears in documents surviving the *abbaye*'s destruction in the Revolution. Then called Craquegnon, it was the result of achieving for an essentially soft cheese a crust which would conserve it through the winter months when little milk was available.

Humbert had been given a *seigneurie* in the well-watered and woody Thiérache, the region of marl and chalk at the western end of the Ardennes massif. Forest was cleared for the new *abbaye*, and from an early date dairy farming was active. Craquegnon was probably first made in the monastic dairy from the milk of its own farm, and, as demand grew, from that of tenant farms as well. By a charter of 1010 the privilege of making the cheese was extended to the whole *abbaye* estate, 'La terre de Saint-Humbert', on the payment of a cheese-tithe in kind. On St John the Baptist's Day, 24 June, every cow-owning tenant and peasant was required to devote all the evening milk of his beasts to making cheese, which was to be carried or sent next day to the church in the town of Saint-Humbert (as Maroilles seems to have been called), or to *commis* or deputies of the *abbaye* at appointed places elsewhere. The same procedure was called for on the evening of Saint-Remy's Day, 1 October, and on the day following. This *escripte des pâturages* was confirmed in the eleventh century and again in 1245. My source is a 1345 version made on behalf of the peasants, usually interpreted as requiring one lot of cheese made on St John's Day to be delivered on Saint-Remy's; but I read it as two distinct payments in kind. This would keep the monks and their trade going through the winter, three to four months being the normal time for *affinage*, while the best cheeses would keep for longer in their admirable *caves*.

By the twelfth century the basic cheese had the form, weight and measurements of today's Maroilles Gros. This needs 8 litres of milk, which is within the daily capacity of a good cow on adequate pasture but not attainable at a single milking. Owners of single cows must therefore have met their obligations with smaller cheeses, which obviously became customary around Sorbais and Monceau: both village names are still attached to the three-quarter size of cheese and Sorbais is the Appellation Contrôlée description. The widespread use of Saint-Remy's name for smaller, square, washed-crust cheeses almost certainly derives from this early association of such cheeses with his name-day. (The cheese, Saint-Rémy, is usually given an accent, not the saint, Remi or Remy.)

Of other names found in twelfth-century documents, Dauphin is said to have been used for the whole-milk cheese. At that time this term would have had no glamorous royal significance, as it had when it was applied in the seventeenth century to flavoured Maroilles cheeses (see p. 263). I have seen no suggestion that the dolphin-shaped moulds characteristic of the later Dauphin were in use (although that cannot be ruled out) as a means of distinguishing the good cheese from debased versions made from part-skimmed or fully-skimmed milk. These were apparently called, respectively, Angelot and Larron. Angelot, the ancient coin depicting an angel (presumably the Archangel Michael) disposing of a dragon, is a strange name to attach to a square cheese.* Larron is much more apt, as it means a robber, and many an almost fat-free Larron was probably sold without qualification to customers who supposed it to be good cheese. Fortunately, no doubt because the *abbaye*'s servants were knowledgeable and alert, these lesser versions of Maroilles died out.

Meanwhile, the *abbaye* was feeding its cheese not only to the community but also to distinguished visitors, who for over 600 years carried it away from Maroilles with them and gave it its name and fame abroad. They included King Philippe Auguste, Louis IX (Saint-Louis), Charles VI, François I, Charles Quint (King of Spain and Emperor) and Philippe II of Spain, Henri IV and Louis XIV. *Le Gazetin de Comestible* in 1780 noted that customers could have their coats of arms impressed on the crust of Maroilles. Cheeses were despatched commercially to customers after their first visit to Maroilles (except to Henri IV, whose cheeses were bought from a merchant on the Quai de Bercy). They were sent to other monasteries, to the episcopal and archi-episcopal palaces at Cambrai, Cologne, Laon, Liège, Maestricht

---

*It has also been claimed as an ancient name for Pont-l'Évêque, but this cheese is thought by some authorities originally to have been round (see Chapter 1); the name is understandable for early Camembert and Brie.

and Mainz, and to the Holy See in Rome. The channels for this important trade were lost with the dispersal of the Maroilles community and the destruction of most of the monastic buildings during the Revolution.

Nevertheless, by 1804 the new *département du Nord* was producing six times as much Maroilles as it consumed. The rest went to neighbouring *départements*, Burgundy, eastern France, and the Bordeaux region, by the horsedrawn wagons of the *rouliers*, whose associations dated back to the sixteenth century, when, for example, the *cœuilleurs*, or collectors, of Etrœungt carried cheeses between Avesnes and La Capelle. The *rouliers* were supplanted by the railways in the mid-nineteenth century, but otherwise the pattern of distribution was sustained throughout the nineteenth century, with the additional trade of new port and industrial areas, some agricultural regions (especially the Massif Central) and wine-growing districts. The strength of the cheese made it economical: small cuts on large hunks of bread satisfied the palate of the manual worker and helped fill his capacious stomach without doing too much damage to his purse.

As late as the inter-war period, many farms still made the cheese. On some, milk was brought from the fields to the dairy in little carts drawn by dogs. Local distribution was often still in the one-horse, canvas-topped carts remembered by the Révérend Père Lelong, who preached the millennium celebration sermon at Maroilles in 1960. He recalled 'Père Octave' (not a *révérend père*), who had several kinds of Maroilles: one for the rich and for feast days, which was cut in thin slices to make it last; and the 'popular model', with its thick crust for small purses, which came honestly by its name of *'Puant'* (stinker). 'The mahogany surface', Lelong wrote, 'was encrusted with bits of rye-straw bearing witness to long and wise periods of contemplation in *hâloirs* and *caves*, for ripening!'

The market for Maroilles among industrial workers has been shrinking severely since the Second World War. Production, having long lost its profitable Court and ecclesiastical high-table trade and found no substitute, has shrunk too. In 1960 seventeen farms and fourteen dairies produced 3000 tonnes of Maroilles, *au lait cru*. By 1986 there were only three farms left making under 70 tonnes of *lait cru* cheese and four dairies making just over 2000 tonnes with *lait thermisé*. Maroilles needs to penetrate the quality market and the export trade again if it is to survive.

One old quality factor which cannot be restored was the use of the Maroilles breed of cattle, described by Messieurs Dion and Verhaeghe of Lille University as 'the result of patient crossings of the Flamande with local breeds'. The First World War stopped production from 1914 to 1918, and the breed soon disappeared; one of the last surviving cows was photographed in Belgium in 1920. The gap was filled by the Frisonne française pie-noire, copious in quantity of yield but indifferent in the qualities required for a distinguished cheese. One reason given for the demise of the Maroilles is that they flourished in the more marshy conditions, relishing the reeds and rushes which other breeds could not cope with. As drainage improved, Frisonnes moved in.

The old Flamandes survive at Boulogne-sur-Helpe on Monsieur François Comtès' farm, where he makes Maroilles Sorbais in the old wooden moulds. His cheeses can be sampled at the *abbaye caves* at Maroilles, where Monsieur Michel Mathieu ripens and sells them. They speak for themselves.

Dion and Verhaeghe have found that the pastures, too, have deteriorated, with the disappearance of many local plant species and the consequent loss of the old natural character in the flavour of the cheese. Rye-grass, as pasture or hay, and maize can offer no real flavour;* furthermore, maize makes for poor cheese milk, and rye-grass as silage introduces unwanted ferments.

The Comité Nationale des Appellations Contrôlées might well look to restoration of traditional qualities as a way of arresting the decline of Maroilles. It should follow the example of Syndicats in Franche-Comté and Savoie (see Chapters 14 and 15) by paying attention to the nature of the pastures and of the winter feed of the cattle indoors, and to the breed producing the milk; and it should insist on the use of raw milk for the AOC cheese. *Thermisation* is not as bad as pasteurisation, but it is not as good as the real thing, and the introduction of calcium chloride during manufacture is not something a traditional cheese appellation should tolerate.

Breeds of cattle change quickly these days. At the Artificial Insemination Centre at Gunsbach in Alsace in August 1986 there was not a Frison among the bulls. Monsieur Clouet, the Director, told me that they were out of date, and that the backbone of the Pie-noire française was now the Holstein. He did, however, have a splendid young Vosgien bull, which would soon be helping to revive the Vosgienne race for Munster. Let the same be done with the Flamande, with suitable crosses, to aim at resurrecting the *race de Maroilles*, and let it and its *lait cru* be advertised proudly on the label of the cheese.

Another point to be considered has nothing to do with the quality of the cheese, but a lot to do with its chances of extended marketing, and with its state on arrival at the retail shop: the size of the case. The smaller retailer with a good range of cheese will not want more than six Maroilles of the same age, of whatever size. Wholesalers and importers in other countries, coping with a cheese known by few people outside the North of France, are unwilling to pass on less than a whole case because they suffer loss through pilfering, damage or unsold cheese when they break cases. For years in England I could very rarely get hold of Maroilles. When I did, they might turn out to be the sad fag-end of an old part-sold case; or I would have to take twice as many as my customers wanted, or even more. Maroilles stayed on my list only for sentiment's sake. Cheeses seeking new markets must present themselves in small quantities in perfect condition to give the retailer a chance to introduce them successfully enough to be asked for more.

A current recipe for Maroilles is given on p. 264.

---

*This explains why farm trout, often maize-fed, are so dull.

Before moving on to other cheeses of the North, let us look at a strong variant of Maroilles. Lille, great centre of the industrial North, with its workaday preference for beers and spirits rather than wine, has long cherished that literal stinker of a cheese: Le Puant de Lille (more politely Gris de Lille). It develops from prolonged *affinage* of Maroilles and similar cheeses (from three to seven months), sometimes with washings in beer or long immersions in salted water. These methods result in a strong, usually salty interior, giving but not soft, inside a muddy, viscous crust. Richard Boston discovered a Lille bye-law forbidding the carriage of these stinking, sometimes designedly ammoniacal cheeses in public-service vehicles. Ninette Lyon considers them a menace in the house (p. 273). They are cherished, nonetheless, by the strong palates of the region, and appreciated by miners, dockers and other industrial workers far afield in France. Their peculiarities are covered in the list under Fromage Fort de Béthune, Le Puant Macéré, Le Puant du Cambrésis, Gris de Lille, Puant de Lille, Vieux Lille, Le Vieux Gris and Le Vieux Puant.

## BELVAL, MONT-DES-CATS, BERGUES

The other two surviving monastic cheeses of the North, Belval and Mont-des-Cats, are nineteenth- and twentieth-century innovations. Belval, and its smaller version, Fromage d'Hesdin, are made by the Cisterciennes at Belval, 5 kilometres north of Saint-Pol-sur-Ternoise, whose community, an offshoot of Laval (see Chapter 1), dates from 1892. Eaten young, Belval is mild; the Fromage d'Hesdin, however, is ripened for up to eight weeks (at least one *fromager* does this in white wine) and has a strong flavour. Mont-des-Cats has been made by monks at the Abbaye du Mont-des-Cats at Godewaersvelde, near Bailleul, since 1880, and 200 tonnes a year are now produced. The cheese was a favourite of the crews of sailing ships. In modern times local tastes have turned more to Maroilles, but Pierre Androuët found Bergues still surviving in traditional form in 1982. He thought its origins to be associated with the old Abbaye de Saint-Winocq. With the exception of Bergues (see list, p. 266), all the hard cheeses, based on Dutch types, are immigrants, most of them established for under sixty years.

## DAUPHIN

All the other cheeses of the North with any length of tradition stem from Maroilles. Where they are of the same texture and crust, they owe their names to villages where different sizes became customary, and, as we have seen, Sorbais has become the official AOC description of the three-quarter-size Maroilles. Other local names are likely to disappear because of the prestige of the AOC appellation, unless there is something irregular in their make-up or they come from outside the defined AOC zone.

The present-day Dauphin is a variation on the shape and a spicing up with tarragon of the interior of Maroilles going back at least three hundred years. It is not unlikely that cheese of the sort was made even earlier from broken Maroilles, as a more elegant form of re-using and presenting cheese leftovers than Boulettes (see list, p. 267). The first evidence of its existence in *abbaye* records, however, is after 1670. It also figures in the account of Louis XIV's visit to Flandre and Hainaut with the Dauphin in 1678 after the Treaty of Nimwegen. Raymond Lindon says that the royal visitors were offered a Maroilles cheese flavoured with tarragon, parsley, cloves and pepper for the occasion, and that their approval led to its being called 'Le Dauphin', but Pierre Androuët maintains that cloves and pepper have been used only in Boulettes. Robert Courtine is sceptical about this *légende* and attributes the name to the earlier exemption of Maroilles carters from the levy at Cambrai of one denier on every wagon from Hainaut, part of *les droits du dauphin*; but in fact Cambrésis came to France only in 1678. Perhaps the two events were part of the same visit and the exemption was practical royal acknowledgement of the enjoyment Maroilles had afforded King and Dauphin, with the consequent adoption of Dauphin as the name of the cheese.

It was logical to devise a different mould for the flavoured cheese, to avoid confusion, but I do not know when the practice began. The most attractive existing ones are dolphin- or fish-like. Others take the form of crescents, *baguettes* (elongated, rectilinear), curved *parallélépipèdes*, hearts or shields.

Nowadays most Dauphins are made from Maroilles curd in *laiteries*, whereas until the early 1970s they were largely a farmhouse product, and rare, according to Robert Courtine. Monsieur Largillière makes them in curved dolphin moulds alongside his Maroilles and Boulettes at his Ferme Verger-Pilote beside the Landrecies road outside Maroilles.

Monsieur Michel Mathieu makes Dauphins from farmhouse Maroilles bought as *blancs* from Marbaix. He ripens them for one month in the old *abbaye caves* at Maroilles before breaking them up, adding the traditional herbs and spices, moulding them in an enchanting scaly-fish mould, and ripening them for a further fifteen to twenty-one days. Their farmhouse-cheese base and their herbs and spices (Monsieur Mathieu has a chef's flair for quality and freshness) make them outstanding.

# BOULETTES

Boulettes, like so many *fromages forts*, evolved as an economical household way of avoiding waste. On farms they were usually made from the last solids remaining in *babeurre* in butter-making households, or, where only cheese was made, from whey supplemented with a little fresh curd if necessary. The resulting curd was mixed with pepper, cloves and herbs, usually the locally favoured tarragon and parsley. The hand-moulded result was a round or conical Boulette. In the Cambrésis, if not eaten fresh, it was matured for two or three months with brine, sometimes with beer-washings. In the Thiérache, households making Boulettes fixed shelves above their windows to take advantage of such sunshine as might come their way to dry their Boulettes.

In modern times *laiteries* making Maroilles have used up broken or defective cheeses for Boulettes, which are consequently full-fat cheeses. A range of Boulettes is covered in the list (see p. 267), but the most attractive are made from farmhouse Maroilles *blancs* by Monsieur Michel Mathieu in the *abbaye caves* at Maroilles, alongside his Dauphins.

It is heartening that Maroilles now has a showcase in one of the few remaining *abbaye* buildings and that farm Maroilles Gros from Marbaix, and Sorbais from Boulogne-sur-Helpe, are matured there in the cellars. From the upstairs windows you can look down on the old mill and see the nearby *abbaye* tithe barn, beautifully restored. As well as the Maroilles, Dauphins and Boulettes, you will find a refreshing local-farm soft cheese, half the size of a Camembert, local chèvres, *fromages blancs* from a local dairy, and butter. There are also Monsieur Mathieu's own pastry Flamiches, made with his Maroilles, and a number of good foods made up within 30 kilometres of Maroilles. They can be tasted on the premises, accompanied by local ciders (including one made from the Brabant pear of Thiérache), or bought to take away. There are old *équinons* (wooden cheese-moulds, as still used by Monsieur Comtès), butter churns and various pieces of traditional dairy equipment around the room; but the crowning glory is an eighteenth-century architectural maquette, to scale and in colour, of the entire *abbaye* complex as it was before the Revolution. There is no better place to drink in the historic past and the still appetising present of the cheese of Maroilles.

## Maroilles

The milk for Maroilles must come from farms within the defined region of origin (see list, p. 271), the Thiérache, comprising 102 *communes* of the Nord and eighty-seven in the Aisne.

The milk is rennetted (14g to 100 litres of milk) at a moderate level of acidity, and coagulates in about 1½ hours (*laitiers* use calcium chloride to help). The curd is cut and lifted in a cloth on to a *mignaut*,* where it is shaken to assist drainage of whey. After it has drained for 20 minutes the curd is packed into the *quinons* (or *équinons*), which are turned several times over a period of one or two days (shorter in summer) before being removed from the moulds and hand-rubbed with *semi-fin* salt. They are salted a second time, next day, by brine bath at 15–20°C to give the *pâte* 'souplesse et homogénéité'. The *fromages blancs* should now weigh 800g, of which at least 350g are of solids ('dry matter'). They are now ready for the first stage of *affinage* in the *hâloir* or *séchoir*. The cheeses should be taken there straight from the brine bath and laid on reed mats or metal grids, either flat or on their sides, well spaced.

*The blueing phase.* The first fermentation in the cheese helps to develop surface moulds, giving the crust a blue–green colour while it is drying in the

---

*The *mignaut* is a sloping table with raised borders and two gutters at the lower end to channel the whey into the buckets (now for the pigs, in former days for making whey butter or Boulettes). A *mignaut* can be seen at Maroilles at the *abbaye caves*.

*hâloir* at 12–14°C and 80 per cent humidity; when this is completed (in 48 hours) the cheese undergoes *débleuissage* by being brushed with weak brine in a temperature of 8–12°C to remove the blue mould before the final stage of *affinage*.

*The red phase.* This takes place in vaulted brick cellars, at least half underground, at 10–12°C and 85–95 per cent humidity. The cheeses are laid on wicker trays, well spaced, held by nickel wires to a scrupulously clean frame. At least once a week they are turned out and brushed delicately on each face with brine (enriched by some makers with the red ferments of the mature cheese). They soon take on a pale, natural colour, and at this stage are called *Blondins*. In about four weeks the crust has formed but two to four months, according to size, are required for completion of *affinage*.

The mature cheese has a natural red crust, and a pale yellow *pâte*, unctuous, but neither bitter nor ammoniacal.

## Cheeses of the North

### Abbaye de Belval

**Abbaye Notre Dame de Belval or Trappistine de Belval.** About 450g, 2kg; 20cm across; 6cm deep; pale golden to pink *croûte-lavée*; semi-soft; mild when young, but Philippe Olivier matures them fully at Boulogne.

**Fromage d'Hesdin.** See HESDIN.
*40–42% m.g.; artisanal; vache cru.*
Saint Pol; Artois/Pas-de-Calais; 51 **13**/53 **1**
(Fromage d'Hesdin 51 **12**/**13**), L; D 87, N9.

### Abbaye du Mont-des-Cats

**Abbaye Sainte-Marie du Mont, Trappe de Bailleul, Mont-des-Cats, Trappe de Sainte-Marie du Mont.** 2kg (and smaller); golden washed-crust; semi-soft, of original Port-du-Salut type; ripened up to 3, 4 or 5 weeks in humid *cave*.
*40–45% m.g.; laitier; fermier; vache.*
Abbaye du Mont-des-Cats, Godewaersvelde, near Bailleul (tel. 28 42 52 50); Flandre/Nord; 51 **5**.

### Abbaye de Saint-Winocq

See SAINT WINOCQ (the *abbaye* is not active).

### Angelot

Name used from ancient times for round cheeses from Brie and Camembert country, presumably to relate their shape to that of the old coin (see p. 259). More recently Angelot was used for a *fromage fort*, which had virtually disappeared by 1973; probably a straightforward cheese similar to Fromage Fort de Lens (see p. 270).
*formerly vache mi-écrémé.*
Flandre.

### Arras

Thursday, Saturday and Sunday a.m. market: M. Foucart-Baudrin from Beuvry (see p. 266) specialises in Northern cheeses and matures Mimolette and its relations (some in port). Inhabitants of Arras are Arrageois or Artésiens.
*Fromagers:* Christian Leclercq, Aux Fromages, Place Courbet; Jean-Claude Leclercq, 39 Place des Héros (at the corner with the street connecting this notable square with the splendid Grand Place) (tel. 21 71 47 85); *artisan affineur,* excellent *cave,* fine range of cheeses (many from farms), local dishes cooked with cheese, wines, closed on Mondays.
See also CŒUR D'ARRAS.
Artois/Pas-de-Calais; 53 **2**, C.

### Artois

*Comté* formed in twelfth century in Western Flandre so attributions Artois and Flandre overlap. See ABBAYE DE BELVAL, ANGELOT, ARRAS, BETHUNE, BEUVRY, BOULOGNE, CHÈVRES, CŒUR D'ARRAS, FROMAGE FORT, HESDIN, LENS, LE MONCHELET.

### Aulnoye-Aymeries

Tuesday market.
Thiérache/Nord; 53 **6**, lower L.

### Avesnes-sur-Helpe

Friday market.
See BOULETTE D'AVESNES, CŒUR D'AVESNES, SAINT-AUBIN, CARRÉ D'AVESNES and PAVÉ D'AVESNES.
East of Avesnes, at Avesnelles, M. Fauquet's dairy makes Boulettes, Cœurs, Dauphins and Maroilles.
Thiérache/Nord; 53 **6**, low L.

### Baguette

Three 500g elongated versions of Maroilles (post-1945 industrial innovations); 250g *demi-baguette*.

**Baguette Avesnoise.**
*50% m.g.; industriel; vache pasteurisé.*
Thiérache/Nord.

**Baguette de Thiérache.**
*45% m.g.; industriel; vache pasteurisé.*
Thiérache/Nord.

**Baguette Laonnaise.**
*45% m.g.; industriel; vache pasteurisé.*
Picardie/Aisne.

### Barzy-en-Thiérache

See LA BOULE DU PAYS.
Aisne; 53 **15**, high R.

### Belle-des-Champs

**Belle-des-Champs.** 2kg white, mould-crusted, rounded, soft cheese invented by the Fromageries des Chaumes at Jurançon in the Pyrénées; made for several years now at Le Nouvion (see also SAINT-THIBAUT).
*50% m.g.; industriel; vache pasteurisé.*
Thiérache/Nord.

### Belval

See ABBAYE DE BELVAL.

### Bergues

**Bergues.** Up to 2kg; 20–25cm diameter flattened *boule*; from milk of Flamandes; 3 weeks–2 or more months of daily washing in beer (classic) or brine; semi-hard *pâte*, strong smell; or (*frais*) like soft chalk. *Affinage* is done in *hoofsteads*, ancient *caves* in tumulus form. Sold (autumn 1986) by Mme Fauconnier, Crémerie Voltaire, rue Albert Camus, Dunkerque.
*10–20% m.g.; fermier; artisanal; domestique; vache écrémé/sérum/babeurre.*
Near Dunkerque; Flandre/Nord; 51 **4**.

### Béthune

Monday and Friday market.
**Le Fort de Béthune, Fromage Fort de Flandre.** Noted for its cheese in the Middle Ages, Béthune has latterly given its name to a Fromage Fort de Flandre: Maroilles fermented in airless conditions and consequently becoming ruddy in hue and stinking ammoniacally; equivalent to an extreme stage of Le Puant de Lille (see p. 273), but sold potted (no doubt because it could not otherwise be tolerated *en passage*). Androuët cites use of remains of Maroilles mixed in terrine with pepper, parsley, tarragon and beer, left for 2–3 weeks covered, then remixed to become smooth in texture, turned into a pot and left for as long as suits one's taste.
*artisanal; domestique; vache.*
Artois/Pas-de-Calais.

### Beuvry

M. Foucart-Baudrin, À la Petite Ferme, Place R. Salengro (tel. 21 57 29 76); wide stock; specialist in *affinage* of Mimolette (including *au porto*). His motto: 'Dégustez, jugez, appréciez.'
Near Béthune; Artois/Pas-de-Calais.

### Blaincourt

**Fromage de Chèvre.** M. Éric Mazincant, Mme Évelyne Viguié, 4 rue Leleu Robert, 60460 Blaincourt; organic, under *Nature & Progrès* banner. Sold at Chantilly market.
*fermier; biologique; chèvre cru.*
Near Précy-sur-Oise; Picardie/Oise.

### Blondin

Maroilles at early stage of *affinage*, when its crust has a pale natural colour.

### Boule

**La Boule du Pays.** 900g, small, well-crusted Mimolette; keeps well and eats well; sold at Maroilles.
*laitier; vache.*

**Boules Fraîches.** Domes rather than *boules*; 250g and 500g *fromage blanc*; plain or with pepper, garlic, *fines-herbes*. Laiterie de Barzy-en-Thiérache; sold at Maroilles.
*laitier; 0% and 40% m.g., respectively; vache pasteurisé.*
Thiérache/Aisne; 53 **15**.

**Boule de Lille.** See MIMOLETTE.

## Boulettes

**La Boulette d'Avesnes.** 1. Traditional farm: red-gold, conical or round, hand-moulded cheese; 150–250g; low-fat; enriched with tarragon, parsley, crushed cloves, salt and pepper, and ripened for up to 4 months, part of which may be spent on windowsills or on special shelves nailed in above windows, *if the sun shines*; they are coloured with *rocou* and may be washed in beer. Ferme Verger-Pilote, Maroilles: M. Largillières makes round Boulette from same curd as Maroilles, washed weekly in brine during *affinage*. 2. *Laiterie* made from *blancs* of Maroilles, mixed with the same flavourings as the farm cheese, covered with *rocou* or paprika and ripened for a few weeks. Fauquet makes at Avesnelles.
*formerly fermier; very low-fat babeurre or sérum, cru; now artisanal or laitier; 45% m.g.; vache pasteurisé.*
Thiérache/Avesnes/Nord.

**Boulette Avesnoise.** M. Mathieu makes with farmhouse Maroilles *blanc* from Marbaix and tarragon (*no* salt), hand-moulded, uncoloured, at the old *abbaye caves*, Maroilles. Sold at *frais* stage.
*45% m.g.; artisanal, fermier; vache cru (Maroilles curd).*
Thiérache/Avesnes/Nord.

**La Boulette de Cambrai.** About 300g, hand-moulded, mixed with pepper, tarragon, chives and parsley, and usually eaten *frais* (surface not coloured, but greenish appearance, naturally). May be in cone or ball shape. (See also CAFFUTS.)
*45% m.g.; fermier, domestique; vache cru.*
Cambrésis/Nord; 53 **3/4**, low.

**La Boulette de Papleux.** M. Philippe Olivier says this is the strongest of all Boulettes.
*vache.*
Papleux, NW of La Chapelle; Thiérache/Aisne; 53 **16**, upper L.

**La Boulette de Prémont.** Fatter and slightly milder than the Boulette d'Avesnes (M. Philippe Olivier, 1986).
*vache.*
Prémont, Vermandois/Aisne; 53 **14**, upper R.

**La Boulette de Thiérache.** Similar to or identical with the Boulette d'Avesnes in appearance, with pepper, tarragon and parsley. Known in Flandre and Hainaut as *'le suppositoire du diable'.*
*45% m.g.; vache.*
Thiérache/Aisne.
See also CAFFUTS.

**La Boulette du Nord à l'Estragon.** Flattened ball, or dome 10cm × 5–6cm deep; made from fat-free whey *fromage blanc*, with salt, pepper and tarragon; air-dried with three washings in beer or in hot water over a ripening period of 15 days; it is then potted for a further 6 weeks; by M. Mathieu at the old *abbaye caves* at Maroilles using *fromages blancs* from Barzy.
*0% m.g.; artisanal; from sérum pasteurisé.*
Boulogne-sur-Mer; Boulonnais/Pas-de-Calais.

## Boulogne

Wednesday and Saturday market.
M. Philippe Olivier, 43–45 rue Thiers (tel. 21 31 94 74), (Tues–Sat 8.30–12.30, 14.30–19.30) *maître fromager, artisan-affineur, marchand de fromages.* M. Olivier is an enthusiast who seeks out farmers and artisans, and cares for their cheeses in his *caves*, to which customers were to be invited after reconstruction of the shop in 1987. He has twenty traditional cheeses of Flandre, Hainaut, Calaisis and the Boulonnais, and many rareties from further afield. Pas-de-Calais.

## Bouquet de Thiérache

Rectilinear version of Dauphin (see p. 269).
*laitier; vache pasteurisé.*
Thiérache/Nord/Aisne.

## Caffuts

Cambrai term for unsaleable, damaged, gone-over cheeses, pounded with herbs and moulded into *boulettes*; distinct from Boulette de Cambrai (see above).
*vache.*
Nord.

## Caisse

**Fromage de Caisse.** Fat cheese with marbled *pâte*, stacked for *affinage* in chests lined with walnut-leaves in cool *cave*. Viard said (1980): 'Eaten young, it is like a gentle Munster; fully matured, it equals a strong Vieux-Lille' (see Le Puant, p. 273).
*full-fat; artisanal; vache.*
Flandre.

## Calais

Wednesday, Thursday, Saturday (best) and Sunday market. Jacques Guislain, 1 rue Andre, Gerschel, Calais Nord and Au Fin Bec, Boulevard Lafayette, Calais Sud ('worth hiking for' in the opinion (mid-1980s) of Robin Young of *The Times*).
Pas de Calais.

## Cambrésis

**Le Puant de Cambrésis.** Defective Maroilles cheeses diced and soaked for 12 hours, or overnight, in strong beer with fresh-chopped onions (*Marabout*, 1978). Other Cambrésis cheeses: see LA BOULETTE DE CAMBRAI, CAFFUTS, LE LARRON D'ORS.
*artisanal; vache; thermisé.*
Nord; 53 **3/4**.

## La Capelle

La Foire aux Fromages de la Capelle (the twentieth was held in 1987) is an annual event of early September (on a Saturday, Sunday and Monday). *Laiterie* on N2 makes Maroilles and can be visited.
Thiérache/Nord; 53 **16**.

## Carré d'Avesnes

Term used for Maroilles type, probably for cheeses not meeting AOC measurements.
*laitier; vache.*

## Chantilly

Wednesday and Saturday market. (See BLAINCOURT.)
Île-de-France/southern Oise.

## Chauny

Tuesday and Friday market.

**Chauny.** This long-lost cheese, renowned up to the sixteenth century at least, has been associated with the Île-de-France, but seems properly to have belonged to Picardie. Manicamp (see p. 271) is near Chauny. Both cheeses probably resembled the Maroilles Quart (200g *blanc*, 180g *affiné*).
*fermier; vache cru.*
Picardie/Aisne; 56 **3/4**, high.

## Fromages de Chèvre Fermier

Chèvres are not thought of as traditional in the North. However, EEC Quota prevents expansion of cows'-milk products so newcomers to cheese dairy with goats are well placed. The herd at the Ferme Davoine (below) includes some of the local race, so there must have been a few goats around ('the poor man's cow') for many years. The Davoine-Duteriez know of at least seven other *chèvriers* in the Nord and the Pas-de-Calais.
Farms include the following:

**Chèvres Fermiers.** St-Wulmer, W of N1 on S edge of Samer.

**Chèvre Frais d'Hucqueliers.** M. Leduc makes 150g soft, rounded drum, sold plain or coated with red juniper berries at Ergny near Hucqueliers. Sold by Philippe Olivier, Boulogne; Leclercq, Arras.
Boulonnais/Pas-de-Calais.

**Fromage de Chèvre Cendré; au Paprika; au Poivre.** 150g round, sold *frais;* similar but 220g is Fromage de Chèvre à l'Estragon; also Crottin 80g flat form sold young; and Pyramide à l'Ail et aux Fines-Herbes, 320g *frais*. Sold daily by M. et Mme Davoine-Duteriez at La Ferme Davoine, rue Cerfmont (tel. 27 84 76 24) (S of D9 59 Landrecies-Maroilles 53 **5**, bottom) and at markets: Aulnoye-Aymeries (53 **6**, low L) Tuesday; Hautmont (53 **6**, SW of Maubeuge) Friday.
*fermier; chèvre cru.*

**Fromages de Chèvre.** M. Albert Viatour makes at Le Favril SW of Landrecies (53 **5**, bottom).
*fermier; chèvre cru.*

**Fromage de Chèvre; aux Herbes; au Poivre.** 150g cheeses usually *frais*, made by M. Philippe Gravez, 14 voie de Sars, Felleries (tel. 27 59 08 12) (53 **6**, low, S of Sars-Poteries); visits to farm Sunday only 14.00–17.00. Sold at Maroilles, Caves de l'Abbaye (see p. 272) by M. Michel Mathieu.
*fermier; chèvre cru.*
Thiérache/Nord.

**Fromages de Chèvre.** See BLAINCOURT.

## Clovis

Bean-pod shaped or oval, soft cheese; Courtine found cheeses of this name in Soissons before 1973 in the form of *haricots*, which, he said, was their sole merit. Philippe Olivier (see BOULOGNE) deemed it extinct in 1986. (It has to be said that the *haricots* of Soissons are not like other *haricots*. They are grown to a considerable size, whether containing just four large white beans, or more numerous fat green ones.)

*artisanal; vache cru.*
Picardie; Soissonais/Aisne.

## Coeurs

**Cœur d'Arras.** Washed-crust; described by Courtine in 1973 as 'strong and of powerful scent, redolent of Maroilles'.
*artisanal; vache.*
Artois/Pas-de-Calais.

**Cœur d'Avesnes.** About 200g, washed-crust red-golden cheese of Maroilles curd. Made by Fauquet, Avesnelles, east of Avesnes.
*45–50% m.g.; laitier; vache thermisé.*
Thiérache/Avesnes/Nord/Aisne.

**Cœur Rollot.** About 200g, washed-crust, much paler than Cœur d'Avesnes; similar *pâte* but milder. Rollot (see p. 273) survives on at least one farm in round form. It has been made in Thiérache under the label Cœur d'Avesnes – Rollot. One of the best was made at La-Chapelle-aux-Pots (see ÉTOILE).
*40–50% m.g.; laitier; vache pasteurisé.*
Picardie/Somme, near Montdidier, in origin; latterly made at Lillebonne in Normandie.

## Le Dauphin

1. 150–500g; Maroilles cheese, flavoured; *croûte-lavée*; in form of rectangle, heart, shield, crescent or dolphin; *pâte* of Maroilles curd, with tarragon, parsley, cloves and pepper added. See pp. 262–3.
*45% m.g.; laitier; vache thermisé.*
2. 200g; washed-crust, in form of curved dolphin; the curd is the same as for Maroilles also made by M. Largillière (see MAROILLES, p. 272).
3. Similar cheese, 15cm long, 4cm deep, made in a particularly fine mould (though more of a scaly fish than a dolphin) by M. Mathieu from one-month-old farmhouse Maroilles (bought as *blancs* from Marbaix) and ripened for a further 15–21 days in the old *abbaye caves* at Maroilles (see p. 272).
*artisanal; vache cru.*
4. Dauphin Laitier is made at Avesnelles, Hirson (e.g. 150g, 50% m.g. by Les Fromagers de Thiérache), Mondrepuis.
*laitier; vache thermisé.*

**Bouquet de Thiérache** is a rectangular version of Dauphin.
*laitier; vache pasteurisé.*
Thiérache/Avesnois/Nord/Aisne.

## Douai

Daily market; ancient capital of Flandre.
M. Etienne Gourlin, 112 rue de Paris, *maître fromager.*
Flandre/Nord; 51 **16.**

## Doullens

Thursday market.
Picardie/Somme; 52 **8.**
Gérard Quentin, 10 avenue du Maréchal Foch, *maître fromager.*

## Dunkerque

*Fromagers:* Mme Fauconnier, Crémerie Voltaire, rue Albert Camus; 8.30–12.00 Tuesday–Sunday, 15.00–19.30 Sunday–Friday; many *lait cru* 'farm cheeses', including Bergues (see p. 266); M. et Mme Obert, Le Manoir, 19 rue du Président Poincaré, 8.30–12.30, 14.00–19.30 Monday–Saturday; seasonal cheeses; every kind of butter.
Flandre/Nord; 51 **3/4.**

## Edam Français

1.5kg, 12cm diameter ball, ripened 3 months. See Chapter 3, p. 106. (See also MIMOLETTE and HOLLANDE.) Steenvorde is the regional centre of manufacture.
*40% m.g.; industriel; vache pasteurisé.*
Flandres/Nord and elsewhere.

## Étoile

About 200g, drum-shaped *triple-crème* soft cheese; *croûte-fleurie*, made by Fromagerie de l'Étoile, La-Chapelle-aux-Pots, which also made an oval 60% m.g. Île-de-France (much better than Caprice, see p. 328) and a 45% m.g. Rollot Cœur; all fine cheeses but I suspect the dairy was bought up and closed in the 1970s.
*75% m.g.; vache.*
Picardie/Oise.

## Flandre

La Flandre or Les Flandres; see also ARTOIS: ABBAYE DU MONT-DES-CATS, BERGUES, CAISSE, DOUAI, EDAM, GOUDA FRANÇAIS, LILLE, MIMOLETTE, SAINT-PAULIN, SAINT-WINOCQ, STEENVORDE.

## Fromage Blanc Frais

MM. Marlier Frères, 42 rue Louis Hellin, 59199 Hergnies; farm (*not* Wed., Sun.) 8.00–9.00, 18.00–19.00, but telephone first (27 40 00 43).

M. Mathieu at the *abbaye caves* at Maroilles (see p. 272) has Fromage Blanc from a *laiterie* at Barzy.
*fermier; biologique; Nature & Progrès; vache cru entier.*
Hainaut/Nord; 53 **4**, high R, N bank of the Escaut.

### Fromage Fort

**Flandres, Fromage Fort des.** See ANGELOT.

**Lens, Fromage Fort de.** Golden-crusted cheese, very local (*Larousse* 1973).
*fermier; vache.*
Artois; Piandre/Pas-de-Calais.

### Gouda Français

Imitation of Dutch cheese, usually sold at 3 months (see HOLLANDE, below).
*industriel; vache pasteurisé.*
Flandre and elsewhere.

### Goyère

La Goyère Valenciennoise is a tart of *fromage blanc* and eggs strengthened with Maroilles, similar to flamiche on short or puff pastry. Courtine relates that it was originally made with *fromage blanc* and eggs, sweetened with brown sugar or honey and scented with orange flower, and gave rise to a variant with bacon, perhaps the ancestor of flamiche and quiche. He thinks the name came from *goguer* (to enjoy oneself), whence *goguette* (alcoholically merry). Froissart, François Villon (who put it in verse) and François I all enjoyed it in their time.
Androuët says the cheese should be half *fromage blanc*, half *fromage affiné* and disagrees about the connection with flamiche.
Hainaut/Nord.

### Gris de Lille

See LE PUANT.

### Maroilles gros

See MAROILLES.

### Guerbigny

Round or heart-shaped, *croûte-lavée*, style of Rollot (see p. 273). Guerbigny is near Montdidier, Rollot country (*Viard*, 1980), but Androuët did not find such cheese in the area in 1982 (listed in *Larousse Gastronomique* 1961).
*laitier; vache.*

### Hainaut

Ninth-century *comté*, to France with Burgundy 1678. See FROMAGE BLANC, GOYÈRE, HAUTMONT, STOFFET.

### Hautmont

Tuesday and Friday market.
Hainaut/Nord; 53 **6**, C, S of Maubeuge.

### Hesdin

Thursday market.

**Fromage d'Hesdin.** Small, 450g, version of the Trappistines cheese of Belval (see ABBAYE, p. 265), which some *affineurs* keep 2 months with washings in white wine, an initiative originally designed for the market at Hesdin, where strong cheese is favoured. Sold by Philippe Olivier at Boulogne. (See also p. 267.)
*artisanal; vache cru.*
Artois/Pas-de-Calais; 51 **12/13**.

### Hirson

Monday and Thursday market. *Affineurs* of Maroilles: MM. Fonne-Goubaule.
Thiérache; 53 **16**, R of C.

### Hollande

**Vieux Hollande.** This term is sometimes used for French-made Mimolette (see pp. 272–3), and is equivalent to one of the meanings of Vieux Lille. It should not be used, nor should Gouda or Edam, even with *français* as qualifying adjective: such terms were outlawed by a 1935 treaty between France and Holland but little notice seems to have been taken of it.
*laitier; vache pasteurisé.*
Nord.

### Hucqueliers

See CHÈVRES FERMIERS.

### Île-de-France

Succulent oval double-cream cheese formerly made in the Oise (see ÉTOILE).
60% m.g.

### Landrecies

Saturday market.
The restaurant 'Au Père Mathieu' at the Hôtel Dupleix (west side of bridge) serves local cheeses of the Maroilles family (see pp. 271–2). One of M. Mathieu's sons, Michel, ripens farm and *laiterie* Maroilles

in the old *abbaye caves* at Maroilles (see p. 272) 5½km E of Landrecies, and makes Dauphin (see p. 269) and Boulettes (see p. 267) there. Two goat farms make cheese near by (see CHÈVRES, p. 268).
Thiérache/Nord; 53 **5**, bottom.

LAON

See BAGUETTE LAONNAISE. Tuesday, Wednesday morning, Thursday and Saturday (afternoon) market.
Picardie/Aisne; 56 **5**.

LE LARRON D'ORS, FROMAGE D'ORS

Robert Courtine in 1973 and MM. Chast et Voy in 1984 reported this low-fat square cheese of the Maroilles family made in Ors locality and ripened 6–7 weeks (Philippe Olivier thinks it is no more, 1986). See p. 259.
30% m.g.; *artisanal; vache cru mi-écrémé.*
Cambrésis/Nord; Ors 53 **15**, **5**, at top on Canal de Sambre 6km E of Le Cateau.

LENS

Tuesday and Friday market; and see FROMAGE FORT.
Pas-de-Calais; 51 **15**.

LILLE

Tuesday to Sunday market, Saturday and Sunday more interesting. Schouteeten, Le Relais du Fromage, 212 rue Gambetta.
See PUANT (p. 273) and MIMOLETTE (p. 272).
Flandre/Nord.

LONGUET

**Longuet d'Hirson; Longuet de Thiérache.** 200g rectilinear cheese of Maroilles-type curd.
*laitier; vache.*
Thiérache/Aisne; 53 **16**, R of centre.

LOSANGE

**Losange de Thiérache.** Diamond-shaped version of Maroilles. Fromageries Alexandre, Chigny (Aisne) were a source of this cheese.
45% m.g.; *vache thermisé.*
Thiérache.

LE MAGNON

Maroilles washed in *eau-de-vie* of juniper.
*laitier; artisanal; affinage; vache pasteurisé.*

MANICAMP

Like a Quart de Maroilles formerly made in this locality, and mentioned with approval in Raoul Ponchon's *La Symphonie des Fromages;* extinct by 1973 (Courtine).
*fermier; artisanal; vache cru.*
Picardie/Aisne; 56 **3/4**, high.

MAROILLES

The first specific mention of their cheese in documents surviving the Revolution was dated 960. See also pp. 258–61.

MAROILLES OR MAROLLES

The AOC of 1976 includes the old, now rarely seen corruption Marolles. It defines the region, of which the boundaries (including the places named and all within) run: North side: Locquignol (53 **5**, S of centre in Forêt de Mormal), Berlaimont, Bachant (N of Aulnoye), Limont-Fontaine, Beaufort, Damousies, Obrechies, Quiévelon; East side: Quiévelon SSW to Sars-Poteries, Rainsars (53 **16**, high); thence SE to Fourmies, S to Hirson (all *communes*); thence ESE 13km to Any and S to Aubenton (all *communes*); thence S to Les Autels, Résigny, SW to Rozoy-sur-Serre; South side: Rozoy NW to Nampcelles-la-Cour; Vervins (all *communes*); thence E to Voulpaix, Lemé; NW to Le Sourd, Beaurain, Flavigny, Guise; West side: Guise N to Étreux, La Groise, Oisy; NW to Rejet-de-Beaulieu, Câtillon, Bazuel-Pommereuil; thence NE to Robertsart, Hecq, Locquignol.
Minimum sizes and *affinage* as laid down by AOC:
Gros: 720g (800g *blanc*), 12.5–13cm sides, 6cm deep, 5 weeks.
Sorbais: 540g (600g *blanc*), 12–12.5cm sides, 4–5cm deep, 4 weeks.
Mignon: 360g (400g *blanc*), 11–11.5cm sides, 4cm deep, 3 weeks.
Quart: 180g (200g *blanc*), 8–8.5cm sides, 3.5–4cm deep, 15 days.
The AOC rules stipulate that Maroilles is a soft cheese of whole cows' milk (but a summary of methods suspiciously mentions 'standardisation' of milk at the start). It is unpressed, with cut curd, lightly salted and fermented, ripened with washings of crust for at least 5 weeks from the day of making. This short minimum time for *affinage* within the *région* must have been at the demand of the bigger *affineurs*

outside it, and of the *laiteries*; literature distributed by the Syndicat, referring to the 100 days allowed in the twelfth century *escript*, says: 'Thus it needed at that time, as it does nowadays, three to four months to perfect the *affinage* of le Maroilles.' The finished cheese should be russet in colour, with yellow *pâte*, close in texture, unctuous and without bitterness. For stronger versions, see PUANT (see p. 273) and BÉTHUNE (see p. 266).

AOC; 45% m.g.; *fermier, lait cru; laitier, lait thermisé.*

For production details, see p. 260.

**Maroilles Fermier AOC.** At Boulogne-sur-Helpe, M. François Comtès makes 60 Maroilles Sorbais *blancs* a week (600g cheeses) in *équinons* from the raw milk of Flamandes and Frisonne-Flamande crosses, which M. Mathieu ripens for 3 months at the *abbaye caves* in Maroilles. A farm at Marbaix between Maroilles and Avesnes makes *lait cru* Maroilles Gros cheeses which M. Mathieu buys as *blancs*. He fully ripens some and uses the rest for his Boulettes (see p. 267) made from *blancs*, and for his Dauphins (see p. 269), made from cheeses kept for a month before conversion.

At La Ferme Verger-Pilote N of D969 outside Maroilles, towards Landrecies, M. Largillière makes from milk of his large herd of Frisonnes: Maroilles Gros (720g), Mignon (360g), Quart (180g) and a few Sorbais (540g); Dauphin in a curved dolphin mould; Boulettes (round). The Maroilles Gros receives 5–6 brushings during its two months' *affinage*, and benefits from natural mould spores. Some calcium chloride added. He has a shop and a spacious *salle de dégustation* close to the road. His milk is all from his own herd. La Tradition Fromagère, Rungis, handles M. Largillières' cheeses.

*45% m.g.; fermier; lait cru.*

Note: M. Roseleur of Ferme du Château Courbet, Boulogne-sur-Helpe is listed in a Maroilles leaflet, but I was told he was not making cheese in 1986.

**Maroilles Laitier AOC.** *Laiteries* include Fauquet et Avesnelles; Fonne-Leduc at Sommeron (53 **16**, S of La Capelle); Goubault at Le Petit Dorengt N of Lavaqueresse (53 **15**, N of centre); Lesire et Roger at Mondrepuis (53 **16**, N of Hirson)

(see also PUANT: Vieux Lille, p. 273). Cheeses must be ripened in the defined region by law, but the derisory 5 weeks leaves plenty of work for *affineurs* to do before the cheeses are ready to eat: *Affineurs*: M. Robert Henouille at Erloy (53 **15**, R of centre); M. Ducornet at Fontenelle (53 **16**, L high); MM. Fonne-Goubault at Hirson (53 **16**, R of C) gold medal, Paris, 1983; M. Oudart at Marbaix (53 **5**, low R).

M. Dubois at Homblières (53 **14**, E of St-Quentin) and M. Idée-Bourgeois at Prémont (53 **14**, N of C above Bohain) are outside the region, so presumably finish cheeses bought at 5 weeks.

Syndicat des Fabricants de Maroilles, 1 avenue des Champs Elysées, 02500 Hirson (tel. 23 58 37 77).

*45% m.g.; laitier; lait thermisé.*

Thiérache/Avesnois/Nord Aisne.

LA MERVEILLE DE MAROILLES

An old and appreciative name for Maroilles.

Thiérache.

MIGNON

**Maroilles Mignon AOC.** The half-size Maroilles (see MAROILLES).

MIMOLETTE

**Mimolette Française, Boule de Lille.** Mimolette (from *mi-molle* for the *pâte*) became the name for Dutch exports of Commissie-Kaas to France, fine cheese with an orange-coloured *pâte* and plain rind. Official French 1966 description: 2.5 to 4kg ball slightly flattened (like a wood in bowls); pressed; deep orange to red interior, hard with minimum of apertures; crust dry, grey to brown.

This cheese is at its best a straight imitation of the Dutch original. (See also HOLLANDE, p. 270.) It is often released much too young in an almost semi-soft state, like a dull Edam, with only colour to distinguish it. Apart from Steenvorde, Flandre, much is made at Lillebonne and Isigny.

Properly made and matured 6–9 months it earns the titles *Demi-Vieux, Demi-Étuvé.*

**Vieux Lille; Vieille Mimolette; Vieux Hollande.** See HOLLANDE. Mimolette over 9 months and preferably 12–18 months old. Although the crust is brushed it often remains a prey to mite; a well-aged full-flavoured cheese can look like a rust-bitten cannon-ball. Regard such an exterior as an invitation to break and enter that will reward you well. Maison Losfeld, rue du Luxembourg, Roubaix (51 **6/16**) matures cheeses 18–20 months.

**Mimolette au Porto.** M. Foucard-Baudrin of Beuvry (see p. 266) and Arras market (Saturdays) matures cheeses up to a year and more, and treats some with liquor. I have eaten a very agreeable Isigny *coopérative* cheese matured in port: firm, clear red, not crumbly (at around 6 months), full-flavoured, not strong, and excellent with an apéritif.

**Vieux Gras; Vieux Cassant.** Terms distinguishing fat Mimolette with the texture described immediately above, and hard, dry Mimolette at the limit of maturity, which cannot be cut but must be broken apart with a strong weapon.
*40% m.g.; industriel; vache pasteurisé.*
Flandre.

LE MONCEAU

Another name for the Maroilles Sorbais (¾-size cheese). See MAROILLES.

LE MONCHELET

This name has been borne by a cheese related in type to Le Rollot (see below). My guess is that it derived from Monchel-sur-Canche (51 **12**).

MONT-DES-CATS

See ABBAYE SAINTE-MARIE DU MONT.

PAVÉ D'AVESNES

Term used for Maroilles-type cheese, probably not made in AOC mould, or not fully ripened.
*vache.*
Thiérache/Nord.

PICARDIE

Lindon wrote of Picardie in 1961, 'there is scarcely anything to be found but Le Rollot'; but when Androuët searched in 1982 he could not find that. Le Rollot, see below, is now made on one farm not located. However, see BAGUETTE, BLAINCOURT, DOULLENS and THIÉRACHE. The old favourites, Chauny, Clovis and Guerbigny and Manicamp (see pp. 268, 270 and 271) seem to have died.

PUANT

**Le Puant de Lille; Le Puant Macéré; Fromage Fort de Béthune; Gris de Lille; Le Vieux Gris; Le Vieux Puant.** These terms, varying from 'Stinker of Lille', through 'soaked stinker', 'strong cheese of Béthune' (see BÉTHUNE), 'Toper (literally half-drunk) of Lille', 'Old Toper' to 'the old stinker', are used for Maroilles subjected to a second salting and matured in a special way for 6 to 7 months. See p. 262.
*45% m.g.; artisanal, laitier; vache thermisé.*
Lille/Flandre/Nord.

**Le Puant du Cambrésis.** See CAMBRÉSIS.

**Vieux Lille.** 700g (note loss of weight), ripened 6 months with beer, to red-gold; melting from outside inwards; surprisingly mild, and not excessively salty; made by MM. Lesire and Roger, Laiterie de Mondrepuis.
*45% m.g.; laitier; vache thermisé.*
Thiérache/Aisne; 53 **16**, R, N of Hirson.

QUART, MAROILLES, AOC

The smallest quarter-size Maroilles. See MAROILLES.

LE ROLLOT

160–200g; flat round, or thicker heart-shaped; golden *croûte-lavée*, softer than Maroilles and the Cœurs from further north. It originated at Rollot near Montdidier, but Androuët could find no sign of it then in 1982. Philippe Olivier (see BOULOGNE) has a round, attractive golden cheese from a farm in that area, perhaps the only native product surviving. It used to be made in Picardie (Oise) at La-Chapelle-aux-Pots by the respected Fromagerie de l'Étoile and outside the region in the Thiérache at Avesnes. My most recent cheeses came from Lillebonne in Normandie (Seine-Maritime).
Louis XIV was served Le Rollot by M. Debourges, whom, in his flush of pleasure with the cheese, he nominated *fromager royal*. 'Douzaines de Rollots' were sometimes specified as part of rent up to the eighteenth century. Guerbigny (see p. 270) and Monthelet (see above), described as varieties of Le Rollot, have not been seen lately.
*45% m.g.; fermier; vache cru.*
Picardie/Santerre/Somme; 52 **19**.

### Saint-Aubin

150g flat drum, soft, natural white-mould crust; refreshing light flavour; made by M. Delavacque from the milk of his Frisonnes at Dompierre. His production of 10–15 per day goes to M. Mathieu at the *abbaye caves*. See MAROILLES.
*fermier; vache cru.*
Thiérache/Avesnois/Nord.

### Saint-Kilien

400g; shape of small Reblochon; washed-crust; low-fat.
*20% m.g.*
Artois/Pas-de-Calais.

### Saint-Paulin

Steenvorde is the regional centre of making for this unregional French cheese.
*industriel; vache pasteurisé.*
Flandre.

### Saint-Rémy

Square washed-crust cheeses made in the north and east of France (see pp. 258–9).

### Saint-Thibaut

A rectangular, lightly washed-crust cheese derived from Maroilles by Fromageries des Chaumes. I tasted it at Jurançon at the experimental stage, but it was too cold, too young and too firm for me. The name celebrates the comte de Champagne who acceded to the throne of Navarre in 1234, drawing North and Pyrenees together (he is usually spelt Thibaud).
*industriel; vache pasteurisé.*
Le Nouvion; Thiérache/Nord; 53 **15**, high R.

### Saint-Winocq

Washed-crust cheese described as between a small Munster and Livarot, and *'pratiquement abandonné'* in 1961, by Lindon. It originated at the *abbaye*, but continued to be made on farms. It has also been likened to Bergues (see p. 266), so may have been made in various sizes and shapes.
*fermier; vache cru.*
Flandre/Nord; Esquelbecq near Dunkerque 51 **3/4.**

### Sorbais

**Maroilles Sorbais AOC.** Sorbais has long given its name to the ¾-size Maroilles. See MAROILLES.

### Steenvorde

Centre of industrial manufacture of Saint-Paulin, *boules* of Edam/Mimolette types and Gouda Français.
Flandre/Nord; 51 **4.**

### Stoffet

Curd, obtained from slowly heating whey or buttermilk, strained, drained, salted and pressed; crumbled to cover the bottom of a pot, enriched with chopped *fines-herbes* and pepper, crushed until smooth and served without further ado (Mostoffe of Lorraine and La Maquée liégeoise are similar; Ninette Lyon, 1978).
*fermier; domestique; vache cru sérum.*
Hainaut/Nord.

### Le Suppositoire du Diable

See BOULETTE, La Boulette de Thiérache.

### Thiérache

Ancient *pays*, part of Picardie, now in Nord and northern Aisne; see AULNOYE-AYMERIES, AVESNES-SUR-HELPE, BAGUETTE, BELLE-DES-CHAMPS, LA BOULE DU PAYS, BOULETTES, BOUQUET, LA CAPELLE, CHÈVRES, CŒUR D'AVESNES, LE DAUPHIN, LANDRECIES, LONGUET, LOSANGE, MAROILLES, MERVEILLE, MIGNON, LE MONCEAU, PAVÉ D'AVESNES, PUANT (VIEUX LILLE), QUART, SAINT-AUBIN, SAINT-THIBAUT, SORBAIS.

### Vieux Lille

See MIMOLETTE and LE PUANT DE LILLE.

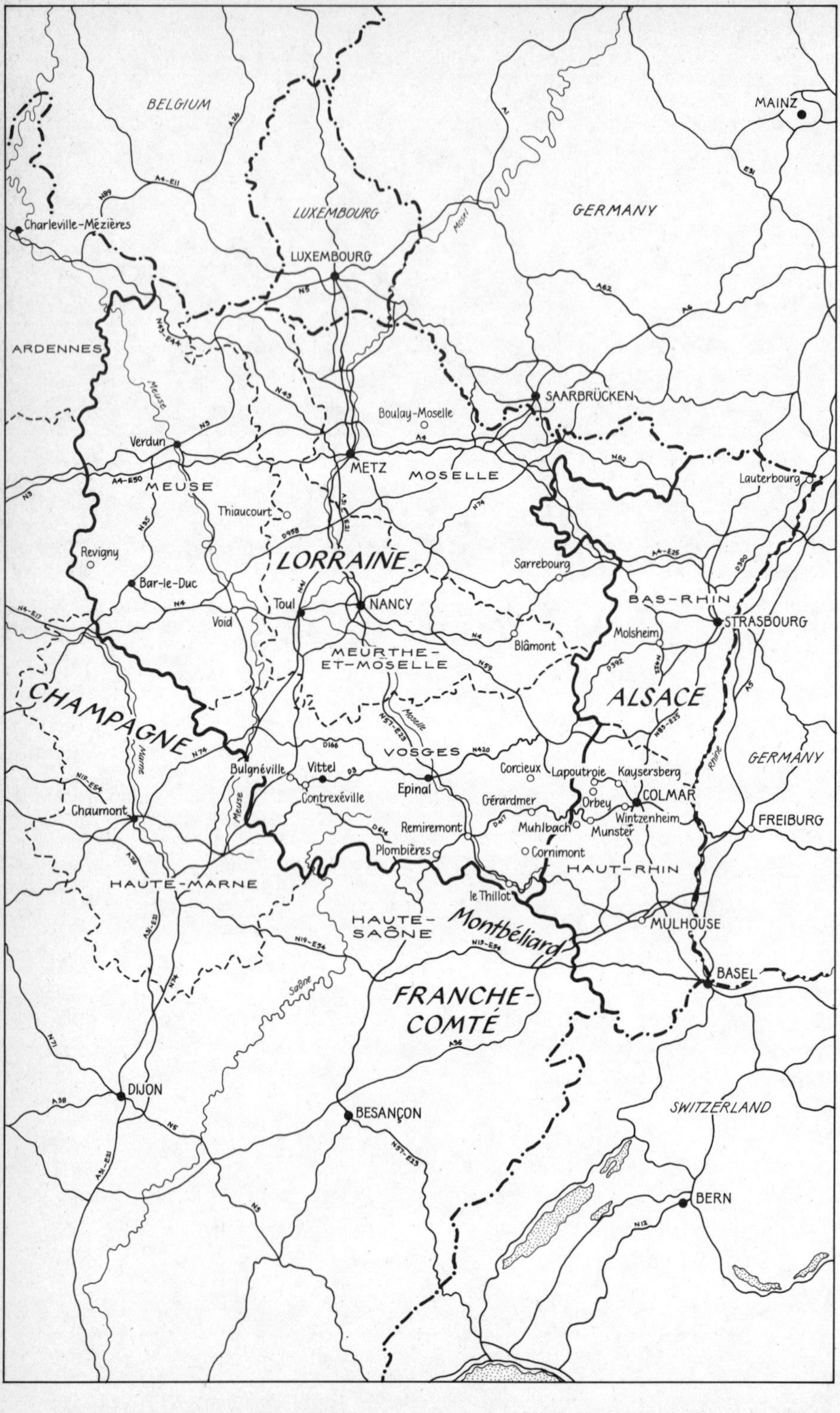
BELGIUM
LUXEMBOURG
GERMANY
MAINZ
Charleville-Mézières
LUXEMBOURG
ARDENNES
SAARBRÜCKEN
Boulay-Moselle
Verdun
METZ
MOSELLE
MEUSE
Lauterbourg
Thiaucourt
Revigny
LORRAINE
Sarrebourg
Bar-le-Duc
Toul
NANCY
BAS-RHIN
Void
STRASBOURG
Molsheim
Blâmont
MEURTHE-ET-MOSELLE
CHAMPAGNE
ALSACE
GERMANY
VOSGES
Bulgnéville
Vittel
Corcieux
Lapoutroie
Kaysersberg
Epinal
Orbey
COLMAR
Contrexéville
Gérardmer
Wintzenheim
FREIBURG
Chaumont
Remiremont
Muhlbach
Munster
Plombières
Cornimont
HAUT-RHIN
HAUTE-MARNE
le Thillot
HAUTE-SAÔNE
Montbéliard
MULHOUSE
BASEL
FRANCHE-COMTÉ
DIJON
BESANÇON
SWITZERLAND
BERN
Meuse
Marne
Moselle
Mosel
Rhine
Saône

CHAPTER NINE

# *Alsace, Bar and Lorraine*

HAUT-RHIN – BAS-RHIN – MEUSE – HAUTE-MARNE –
ARDENNES – MEURTHE-ET-MOSELLE – MOSELLE – VOSGES

In Celtic and Roman times Alsace and Lorraine were already provinces whose northern parts were populated by the same Celtic tribe. Post-Roman invasions from the German side of the Rhine in the fifth century were said to have left a racial imprint, although André Beneler, in a portrait of the two provinces, asserts that it was not until three centuries after Charlemagne's conquest of Germany that the Alsatians accepted 'the Alemannian and Teutonic dialects' as their way of speaking.

The history of Alsace and Lorraine is closely bound with both France and Germany. In the ninth century they became part of the German Empire;* but in the tenth the House of Lorraine established virtual independence, and the Middle Ages saw Alsace divided into a chaotic mixture of self-ruling seigneuries, bishoprics and city–states. Religious conflict added to the confusion, of which France took advantage, and in 1648 the Habsburgs eventually abandoned their claims to Alsace. In 1736 Alsace and Lorraine (with the duché de Bar) were ceded by the reigning duc to Louis XV's father-in-law, Stanislaw Leszczynski, in exchange for Bourbon-ruled Tuscany. When Stanislaw died (after beautifying Nancy) all Alsace and Lorraine became French, except Mulhouse, an independent city–state until 1798.

Cheesemaking in Alsace and Lorraine goes back to the late sixth and the seventh centuries, when many monasteries were founded. The most important of these for dairy farming was Saint-Grégoire, which gave its name to the place and the valley in which Munster cheese began. Munster, derived from the early word for monastery, eventually supplanted the saint's name in popular usage.

One account of the first monks described them as Benedictines from Italy who received Irish reinforcements (*colons*, or colonists) to help in the task of clearing forest for pasture on the eastern slopes of the Vosges mountains.

---

*Lorraine derives from Lothaire, who in 843 created *Lotharii regnum*; it became Lothringen in German. The name Alsace was recorded as early as the sixth century, becoming a duché in the seventh.

There is, however, a stronger tradition that the first preaching of the Gospel here was by Irish monks from the following of Colomban. This Irish saint had founded the monastery (now a seminary) at Luxeuil-les-Bains, close to the southern border of Lorraine and only 30 kilometres west of Haute-Alsace, in the sixth century, and lived on well into the seventh.

Pressure from the east left one beneficial trace in Alsace, of lasting importance. The Burgondes, retreating from the Huns, passed through to found their new kingdom in what later became Franche-Comté (previously tied to Alsace) and Burgundy. On the way they shed some of their cattle, probably the foundation of the Vosgienne breed, on which the monks were able to base their cheese-dairy success. On the new pastures the Vosgiennes could feed and multiply. The lower farms and the *chaumes*, as the high pastures became known, were let to farmers or *marcaires* who paid at least part of their rent in the cheese the monks had taught them to make. The cows were brought to the *chaumes* (as they still are) on Saint-Urbin's Day, 25 May, until Michaelmas, 25 September. The *marcaires* looked after the herds in *transhumance* in the summer, living and making and storing their cheese under one roof in the *marcairerie* (equivalent of the chalet in Savoie or the *buron* in the Auvergne), the simple two-compartment stone structure set in the high pastures. For the first few centuries the cheese had a natural mould-covered crust and was heavier and deeper than modern Munster, closer to the Géromé still made on some Lorraine farms.

Lorraine's cheese is indeed closely related to that of Alsace. It may have been the result of monastic teaching missions or of *marcaires* from Alsace who came over the mountains on to the western, Lorraine, slopes of the Vosges in the earliest seasons of the *transhumance*. However it started, Lorraine's Géromé has retained more of the form of the original Munster. The crust of Géromé and Munster in its present washed form and golden colour, free of surface moulds, developed between 1000 and 1200.

Alsace (except for Belfort) and north-eastern Lorraine were taken by Germany in 1871 after the Franco-Prussian War and returned to France in 1918. Hitler repeated the annexation from 1940–4.

Bar-le-Duc was distinguished in the nineteenth-century cheese world because it had the first *gare fromagère** in France. Unfortunately, the older cheeses of the Barrois have tended to disappear. Noyers-le-Val and Le Thionville (attributed to Bar, although the town is in Lorraine) survived into the 1960s, but have certainly not come my way; and no one need travel to the Barrois to meet the ubiquitous factory Port-Salut now made there. Bar's contribution towards Brie production is dealt with under that region (see Chapter 10 and also p. 280).

The Vosges mountains, however, have preserved the heritage of the monks of Munster on the Alsatian and Lorraine slopes, as over 400 farms can show. Furthermore, their cheese and that of the *laiteries* within the region (mainly on the Lorraine side) is recognised and 'protected' by an Appellation d'Origine Contrôlée.

*cheese railway station

My satisfaction over this 'protection' is unfortunately qualified by severe reservations. First, it lumps together Munster and its bigger, deeper Lorraine cousin, Géromé. The permitted measurements allow for each tradition, but Munster, so much the better-known name, is used more and more at the expense of Géromé.* Speaking of his unmistakably genuine Géromé (far closer to the ancient original Munster in its 12-centimetre depth and 1.5-kilo weight than the flat, much smaller Munster of today), a Lorraine farmer told me: 'We *used* to call it Géromé.' I fear that with the dropping of the name, the dimensions themselves will gradually be abandoned. That will mean the loss of the interestingly different texture and flavour of the more substantial Géromé.

My second reservation is the AOC's flabby concession to factory cheese, permitting pasteurisation of milk. Why should dairy products thus robbed of most of their bacterial interest, and of all the aromatic esters from the Vosges pastures so vaunted in official publicity, be allowed equal standing with the pure, full-blooded cheese of the farm?

A third regret is that official publicity also errs in vaunting the virtues of Munster made 'exclusively' from milk of the old Vosgienne breed. These cattle have black ears, muzzle, udders and eye-surrounds, and black or blue-roan flanks; but their dominant characteristic is the generous but ragged-edged white stripe which starts at the collar and runs the length of the back and under the belly. The tail is all white. (They probably originated in Scandinavia, the possible source of one of Britain's oldest breeds, the Gloucesters, which also have a characteristic white back marking, thinner and more regular than that of the Vosgiennes.) At over 400 metres these attractive, tough, disease- and cold-resistant beasts thrive, producing better milk for the native cheese than any other, milk particularly rich in casein. However, not only have I *seen* the cheese being made from milk of Frisonnes (and I know that milk of Pie-rouge de l'Est is used too), but there are not nearly enough Vosgiennes surviving in Alsace and Lorraine to cater for all the 8000 tonnes of Munster AOC declared in official statistics. In 1986 there were only 300 Vosgiennes in all Lorraine, perhaps 4000 in Alsace, of which well over half serve farms making their own cheese. Fortunately, the breed is in course of revival (see p. 283), but it will take some time and much pushing to bring the herd-book to the necessary strength, and I hope measures are taken to see that milk is not wasted. Pasteurisation should be phased out over a limited number of years; and within that period active encouragement of the native breed should enable the boast about the exclusively Vosgienne source of milk for Munster to be made good.

Another traditional regional distinction in practice exists between the once-a-day cheesemaking in most of Alsace and the morning-and-evening making in the district round Lapoutroie and Orbey and on Lorraine farms. Robert Courtine wrote of this as still current in 1973, but I think morning cheesemaking is more general now.

*Géromé is one of the local pronunciations of Gérardmer (the other is Gérarmé), which has long been used as the name of the cheese made in that area and further afield in Lorraine. Chapin became Chopin here too, before the composer's family emigrated to Poland.

Most Lorraine and Alsace milk goes into industrial-scale manufacture from pasteurised milk of French Emmental, and of shiny white cheeses of many shapes, most of them bearing the name of Brie. Parts of the region west of the Meuse, including part of Verdun and the Barrois (notably Le Vallage), are legally inside the Brie region, as defined in its AOC; but even within the region, cheeses qualify as Brie de Meaux only if they are made of raw local milk, hand-ladled into the moulds and ripened for a minimum of four weeks. So I find it astonishing that 1986 publicity for Lorraine-Lait's factory at Vigneulles-lès-Hattonchâtel, well east of the Meuse and of the Brie boundary, can talk of its producing 'essentially Brie de Meaux (*Appellation d'Origine Contrôlée*)', even if it does get away with '*également des Coulommiers*', and disposes of 72 per cent of its production in exports. The factory uses 'ultrafiltration' of milk, treating 40,000 litres (enough for nearly 5 tonnes of cheese) in one hour. The system rolls out 54 metres of continuous curd, turns automatically '*piles complètes de Brie*',* and wraps them by machine. '*Compte tenu d'un repos de huit jours dans un hâloir, il faut dix jours pour faire un Brie*'.† Production was expected to absorb 320,000 litres of milk a day by December 1986, 500,000 litres or 50 tonnes of cheese a day during 1987. If any of that qualifies for Brie de Meaux AOC, I will give an AOC to my hat.

This is the kind of product in which most Lorraine and Alsatian milk ends up. Lorraine-Lait, started as a co-operative with 1850 members in 1970, is part of an industrial group embracing the appetisingly named SODIMA (including Yoplait, Candia), with Est-Lait, Alsace-Lait, Calas and l'Union laitière de la Meuse thrown in. Chapter 10 deals with the acceptable and unacceptable faces of Bar's and Lorraine's claims to Brie status, but I cover this much here to give an idea of the degree and the nature of factory domination of the provinces' cheesemaking. Many smaller private and co-operative dairies, once making recognisable cheese, have been closed to achieve the sort of soulless mass product dear to ambitious industrialists, who cannot surely eat such stuff themselves.

L'Union laitière Vittelloise is another large concern, developed from the Coopérative de l'Ermitage at Bulgnéville in the Vosges, which started with 211 members in 1931. It has modern dairy machinery and now makes over 12,000 tonnes of cheese a year; but, while its soft white cheeses of assorted shapes (including Brie types) are unexciting, it still manages to make acceptable pasteurised versions of Munster and Géromé, of which I prefer the latter. It has also developed a successful hard cheese combining the mountain traditions of the Vosges, the Jura and Savoie, called La Brouère. Bargkass, a surviving local hard cheese made on a dozen Alsatian Munster farms, and on at least one farm in Lorraine, has no doubt contributed; but the crust of Bargkass is that of a good Beaufort, with an imitation of its concave circumference, whereas that of La Brouère is distinguished by bas-relief figures of capercailzies and fir trees, carved out of the wooden

---

*'whole piles of Brie'.
†'Allowing for the eight days it spends in the drying room, it takes ten days to make a Brie'.

circlets which form the moulds. The texture is nearer Beaufort than Comté, the flavour between the two, and we found both texture and flavour most satisfying. It must be excellent for Raclette. Matured up to seven months (as I can witness), it keeps well as a cut cheese.

From Bulgnéville we went to Remiremont, curious to discover any modern trace of the cheeses paid to its *chanoinesses* in the fourteenth century, or of the type appreciated by the Swiss in the eighteenth. There was none, so far as we could see through the window of the closed *crémerie*, but we did find local cheese, including chèvre, at La Vie Verte in the corner of the stone-built *halle*. The kind man who sold them, and other attractive organic foods, sent us off towards Le Thillot to visit a pocket of farmhouses where Munster and Géromé were still being made.

The upper Moselle and Moselotte Valleys, between their tree-covered higher slopes, were deliciously green after a very wet start to the autumn, with streams winding through the pastures and overflowing their banks. The cows were Pie-rouges and Pie-noires interspersed with assorted beef cattle and a number of *noires*. The red-and-white were the familiar Pie-rouge (or Tachetée) de l'Est and the larger Montbéliarde. The Pie-noires, as I was to discover, were not Frisonnes (though still so called) but were predominantly of American Holstein blood, this having been the prime strain in French Pie-noire breeding since 1975 (the familiar initials FFPN, for Frisonne française pie-noire, no longer make sense). The blacks are mostly the result of wartime importations through Germany, variously attributed to Flemish and Scandinavian roots (one does not exclude the other) and now well established both in this region and further north. There is also an element of the Swiss Herens, another black breed.

Le Thillot is 23 kilometres up the Moselle Valley, south-east of Miremont. Rupt, about halfway, has some cheese farms, one of them close to the road, where it bends south of La Roche. Our destination was Le Prey, off the Gérardmer road north from Le Thillot, up the first turning to the right (before Le Ménil). A climb of some 2 kilometres brought us to La Colline, where Messieurs Rollet and Fêtet were making their cheese in 1986. In 1987 they were to move their dairy and *affinage* up to the Ferme-Auberge de la Tête du Loup, because the family owning La Colline was returning. (I hope the dairy and *cave* are kept in use by this family, which made cheese there for years in the past.)

'Ferme-auberge' was a term sometimes applied to the *marcaireries* which served their cheese and associated dishes to wanderers in the high *chaumes*. Now it covers a number of normal mixed farms offering regional dishes made from their home-raised stock and produce. (I have listed seven from the 1986 Vosges leaflet which make cheese: see p. 288.) Accommodation, dormitory, *chambre d'hôte* or *gîte*, is provided on some of these farms.

La Tête du Loup serves not only its own Munster, and *la tarte au Munster*, but also the old Lorraine Géromé, and Bargkass, a cheese now almost lost to Lorraine. This is a 10-kilo, pressed cheese ripened for three months or more, traditionally a keeping cheese made in addition to Munster or Géromé in the *marcairerie* in summer, also known as Gros Lorraine. In Alsace a dozen farms still keep up the tradition with a 15-kilo cheese, making 600–1000 kilos each in a season in May–June during the milk flush. It was on one of those that our cheesemaker at La Tête du Loup learned about its making, so that he could revive it in Lorraine. It is agreeable to eat straight and, in the makers' estimation, good for Raclette, but Pierre Androuët says it does not melt easily enough. It is also used on this farm in a Tête du Loup dish called *porc au Bargkass*. (The name was originally *Berg-käse*, 'mountain cheese' in standard German.)

The Géromé is sold as *fromage frais* on Saturdays in Épinal market, but the unsold cheeses are ripened on the farm with brine-washings in the normal way. It was formerly the custom for many large Géromés (up to 6 kilos or more) to be sold *frais*, usually as Lorraine; I found that this was unknown to some younger men in the modern Lorraine cheese world.

These cheeses are made from the milk of a dozen native Vosgiennes (see p. 279). Still at Le Prey, above La Tête du Loup, Monsieur Marchal makes Munster from his herd of twenty; and down on the main road towards Gérardmer another Munster farm lies to the right of the road before Le Col du Ménil. Further on at Cornimont you may like to consult the *épicière*, after buying one of her local cheeses, and find your way to the only brebis cheesemaker I have heard of in all this region, Monsieur Rémy.

At La Bresse, where you turn towards the summits of the Vosges, with Munster beyond, there is a Ferme-Auberge La Retelière, with its own pigs, sheep and goats, *fromages de chèvre*, *rillettes*, and leek and myrtle tarts.

The Alsatian side of the Vosges is more craggy than the Lorraine until you descend to the lower slopes, which are rich in vineyards for 120 kilometres and where every town and village name is redolent of wines drunk over the years. Alsace saw its first vineyards planted in AD 222. My own memories go back to the 1930s, when I was lucky enough to have my attention drawn to the inimitably aromatic yet comparatively inexpensive luxury accessible in those slim green bottles. They contain the natural, unsugared virtues of the grape named on the label and the benefit of a degree of sunshine surprising in a northern province.

Only the Pinot Noir disappoints. At first tasting Pinot Noir Rouge struck me as just another murkier rosé, to the extent that I re-read the label to be sure it was supposed to be a red. I have no reservations about Alsace white wines, which have such depth and penetration among the Tokays and the Gewürtztraminers that the stronger meats and cheeses need no reds. There is astonishing range within one grape variety, according to vineyard, time of picking the grapes (*vendanges tardives* of great years), and ageing. After enjoying a Meyer Tokay with sole and cheese on several occasions, a *restaurateur* found me a little card revealing that the vineyard is organically managed under the auspices of the Syndicat d'agriculture bio-dynamique. The difference does tell, as it does in the cheese world; and in Alsace that world, so far as farms go, is almost entirely free of chemical fertilisers.

Munster itself is still a good setting-off point for La Route des Fromages (see list, p. 293); but, a congress having taken over Colmar and captured most surrounding hotels as well, we were forced (happily, as it turned out) to take refuge at Le Grand Faudé, 700 metres above Lapoutroie, in a beautifully converted farmhouse hotel called Les Alisiers. In mid-September the surrounding pastures were still multicoloured with flora, for which the generously flowered pink and red and occasional white clovers, and other *légumes*, were providing nature's nitrogen. There were luminous blue patches of harebells, some big and rounded, others slim and fluted. The woods below, of pine, beech, chestnut, acacia and fir, were carpeted with mosses and fantastic fungi of every size, shape, texture and colour. The hotel proprietors, the Degouy family, or one of their guests made a discriminating daily collection for the kitchen, and we enjoyed a visual and aromatic treat as they were prepared in the hotel sitting room.

I visited one of the six farms in the *commune* making Munster and watched a process differing from the classic recipe (see list, p. 291, under Lapoutroie). The whey is lifted before the moulds are filled, and the cheeses are turned immediately after moulding is complete, inside the moulds, a deft operation with the fingers, repeated at intervals of two hours until evening (similar to *laiterie* practice). The maturing cheeses are washed in fresh spring water, not in brine. The cheese is made once a day, rather than every morning and evening from milk straight from the cows. Another break with the past is that Vosgiennes have been displaced here by Pie-noires.

Jacques Degouy, patron of Les Alisiers, introduced me to Monsieur Clouet, who not only runs the important Artificial Insemination Centre at Gunsbach, but is something of a godfather to farmhouse Munster. He has steeped himself in this and his cattle-breeding cares since he arrived from Burgundy in 1954. His happy, glowing face shows that he has long found his vocation, and suggests unfairly that he is almost never indoors and never under pressure.

The picture he painted of Munster today is encouraging. There are 450 farms, compared with just over 250 in official figures given out in 1983. They make about 600 tonnes of Munster a year and production is 'gently growing'. He confirmed that farming practices are almost entirely organic. Many farms, like the one I visited at Lapoutroie, are now using only part of their milk and making cheese part time. This means that there is great potential for expanding farm production without milk-quota difficulties, as they can apply to retain more milk and send less to the *laiterie*, and they can benefit from being treated as mountain farms. It is a case of vine-growing up to 400 metres and Vosgienne-raising above.

Monsieur Clouet said there were 2800 cows on the Munster farms, most of them Vosgiennes, and 8000 cows altogether producing milk for cheese in Alsace, of which half were Vosgiennes. (Nearly all the *laiteries* are in Lorraine.) He took me to meet his bulls, with whom he is on affectionate terms. All but one were enormous Holsteins; the exception was a sturdy eight-month-old Vosgien. I look forward to his success in restoring the all-Vosgien character of the Munster dairy herd.

I asked Monsieur Clouet to run through the classic Munster recipe, which is summarised in the list (see p. 292). He laid emphasis on the importance of moving the curd out of the whey into the moulds as quickly as possible, and leaving it there undisturbed until evening. Even then the cheeses should be removed only for a very light salting on top and should not be turned until salted on the other side next day. Next, he stressed the gentle nature of *le lissage*, which starts on the third day. For this action of smoothing the surface and helping the crust to form, the hands are dipped in a bowl of lightly salted warm water and 'caress the cheese'. The golden colour, often becoming pink (but it must be even) is enriched by the *Bacterium linens* present in the *cave*, on the stone and in the wood of the shelves.

'The farmer lives with this life of the cheese; observation and elements of touch are as important to him as they are to the *pâtissier*,' To these words of Monsieur Clouet's, himself *éleveur*, breeder, on a grand scale, I need add only that there is a diploma of Le Syndicat Interprofessionnel de Munster, so far earned by no more than thirty cheesemakers. It is reserved for *'le parfait éleveur de fromage'*.

## Recipe for Munster

This is Monsieur Clouet's farm recipe.

Evening milk put to ripen naturally in cool *cave* in copper, zinc or wood. (Vosgien milk being so fat, a little cream might be taken for butter-making next day.)

Morning milk mixed in, brought to 36–38°C and renneted; curd forms in 30 minutes.

Curd cut with flat-bottomed scoop or *harpe* to ½cm cubes.

Curd then trawled from *chaudron* without removing whey and ladled with colander into moulds set out on draining table (*égouttoir*) as quickly as possible, and left in 17–20°C until evening. It is then lifted out, *not* turned, and very lightly salted on one side.

Next day cheeses turned, salted on other side, and taken to *cave* (7–12°C).

On the third day, *lissage* begins: smoothing of cheese by wetting hands in lightly salted warm water and caressing cheese. This and turning of cheese happens every other day for 10 days.

Cheeses are then turned daily on their wooden shelves for 21–30 days according to the temperature (or season, if the *caves* are not deep enough for constant temperature) to acquire the *bacterium linens* naturally present in the *caves* and on their shelving.

Some *fromagers* give one final *lissage* gently with just two or three fingers. Some Lorraine farms dry their cheeses in the sun after salting and give another *lissage* before putting them in the *cave*, where they get a month of washing. Their *caves* are 10–14°C and 80–85% humid.

## VARIATIONS

**Farm.** This differs from the Lapoutroie practice, but that area with Orbey had the tradition of making morning and evening, so some speeding up of *égouttage* would be understandable. Monsieur Clouet thinks that it makes for more variable cheese, confirming experience of a restaurateur. Variability also arises from not making cheese every day.

**Industrial.** Industrial *laiteries* use starters as well as rennet on their pasteurised milk, which coagulates in ten minutes; they cut curd to walnut-sized knobs, and speed up drainage of whey; they turn the newly moulded cheeses five times in the first 10 hours, and add Tyrothrix (to inhibit unwanted bacteria) and *bacterium linens* ('to make sure') to the brine in which the cheeses are washed.

## CHEESES OF ALSACE, BAR AND LORRAINE

### ABBAYE DE NOTRE DAME D'OELENBERG

**Trappiste d'Oelenberg.** 1200–1400g, 22cm × 4cm round; *croûte-lavée*, pale golden; semi-soft; 2 months in *cave humide*; similar to original monastic Port-du-Salut (not the industrial Barrois cheese) made at Entrammes; made by monks of l'Abbaye de Notre Dame d'Oelenberg, 68950 Reiningue.
45% m.g.; *artisanal*; *vache cru*.
S. Alsace/Haut-Rhin; 66 **9**, N of C and A36 marked *couvent*.

### AMMERSCHWIHR

Pierre Gaertner, aux Armes de France, 1 Grand'rue, recommended by Gault Millau (Feb 1986) for superb *plateau de fromages*, good advice and right wines (wine festival: Apr).
Alsace/Haut-Rhin; 62 **18/19**.

### L'ARTISAN DU BRIE

A very tolerable full-size raw-milk cheese by Jean Hutin, Bovée-sur-Baboure, 11km SW of Void (see p. 296).
45% m.g.; *artisanal*; *vache cru*.
Lorraine/Meuse; 62 **2**, on R. Baboure ENE of C.

### BARGKASS, BERGKÄSE, VACHELIN

10kg (up to 15kg in Alsace); *pâte demi-cuite*, pressed (Gruyère-type); brushed crust; ripened for 3 or more months in 97% humidity; MM. Roger Rollot and Nicolas Fêtet, having learned in Alsace, have revived this old traditional summer hard cheese of the *marcaireries* on the *chaumes*. It can be used like Raclette. They won a silver medal at the Concours d'Étival (Jura) in October 1985. Lorraine (S. Vosges): *ferme-auberge* La Tête du Loup, Le Prey (sign on right of road from Le Thillot to Gérardmer) where they also make Géromé Munster from the milk of their traditional Vosgiennes (see LE THILLOT for this and other nearby farms).
*fermier*; *vache cru*.
Lorraine/Vosges/Alsace/Haut-Rhin/Bas-Rhin; Lorraine: Le Menil 66 **8**, top L.

### BIBBELSKÄSE, BIBELAKAS

*Fromage frais* (from farm or bought milk) salted, flavoured with *raifort* (horseradish) and *fines-herbes*. Scarcely, if at all, on market, it is eaten with *sautées* potatoes.
45% m.g.; whole milk; *fermier*; *vache cru*; if bought retail: *domestique*; *vache pasteurisé*.
Alsace.

### BLÂMONT

Friday market.

**Fromages Fermiers** (and other dairy produce). Ferme de la Meix, Reillon 12km W of Blâmont.
*fermier*; *biologique*; *vache cru*.
Lorraine/Meurthe et Mosel; 62 **19**, upper far R.

### BLANC

See FROMAGE BLANC.

### BOOTZHEIM

**Fromages Frais, Tome.** Ferme Durr, Am Allach 67230 Bootzheim daily (tel. 88 74

60 20 camping possibilities); markets Colmar, Mulhouse, Strasbourg.
*fermier; biologique; Nature & Progrès; vache cru.*
Alsace/Bas-Rhin; 62 **19**, upper far R.

## Bracq

Local name for slowly drained curd, mixed when drained with fresh milk; bread would be soaked in it for hours, and afterwards enjoyed as *'mérande'* or *'goûter'* (snack). Known as Broca around Metz, Brockel E of Metz around Bonday-Moselle; and Brocq is the more general name in Lorraine.
*fermier; domestique; vache cru.*
N. Lorraine/Moselle around Thionville.

## Brebis

Lorraine, see CORNIMENT.

## La Bresse

**Fromages de Chèvre.** Ferme-auberge La Retelère, M. Michel and Mme Sylviane Bruneau (tel. 29 25 52 10) 5km by D486 towards Col de la Grosse Pierre; open all week in holiday seasons, weekends rest of year.
*fermier; chèvre cru.*
Lorraine/Vosges; 62 **17**, lower R.

## Brie

Many cheeses are made in Lorraine under this name by industrial methods of pasteurised milk, but Brie properly comes from the Brie region (see Chapter 10); I have noted one *lait cru* cheese (l'Artisan) and two named Coulommiers of *lait cru.*

## Broca, Brockel

See BRACQ.

## Brocotte

Solids left in *petit-lait* from Munster-making, from which a *recuite* (ricotta) is made in the high *chaumes* of the Vosges (the mountain pastures of summer) by the *marcaires* in their *marcaireries*, or summer chalets; it is called Chigre or Schigre, and eaten with boiled potatoes. Known as Brokott in E Lorraine, W Alsace, Vosges, Haut- and Bas-Rhin.
*low-fat; fermier en marcairerie; sérum vache cru.*
Vosges mountains.

## Brocq

See BRACQ.

## Brokott

See BROCOTTE.

## La Brouère

Made from milk specially gathered from nearby farms. About 12kg, 43cm × 11cm with concave sides figuring capercailzies and pine trees (hand-carved inside the wooden moulds); matured 4–7 months; brown-golden crust; *pâte* firm, between Comté and Beaufort in character, agreeable in texture and rich in flavour. Started in 1984 (trials); launched in 1985 by Fromagerie de l'Ermitage, Bulgnéville and going well in USA. The name is a version of Bruyère (heather).
*52% m.g.; laitier; vache.*
Lorraine/Vosges; 62 **14**, NW of C.

## Bûche

150g soft, *croûte-fleurie*, same *pâte* as Fol Amour (see p. 289); has won silver medal Paris.
*50% m.g.; industriel; vache pasteurisé.*
Lorraine/Meuse.

## Bulgnéville

La Fromagerie de l'Ermitage (Union Laitière Vitelloise) was founded by 211 Vosges farmers in 1931; 1200 farmers belonged by 1985, when it made 12,600 tonnes of cheese, now all from pasteurised milk. Products include Munster, Munster Géromé (larger and thicker), Carré de l'Est, Emmental Français (Ermitage Est-Central), Le Marcaire (thicker crust milder than Munster), the new La Brouère (see above), the large soft white Fleur de l'Ermitage, rectangular Troubadour, 60% m.g. Vosges Crème, and various soft cheeses of Camembert and Brie shapes (Frère Jacques, Le Père André and Ermitage are names used).
Lorraine/Vosges; 62 **14**, NW of C.

## Caprice des Dieux

135g oval, soft, very white cheese, made by BG Sarl, subsidiary of Bongrain. Its Lorraine dairies at Darney and Le Tholy in Vosges and Vatimont in Moselle produce about 12,500 tonnes of cheese a year from 110 million litres of milk from about 1300

farms (see ROUMILLAT, LE THOLY). Caprice is now made at Bourmont (near Chaumont) in Bassigny, part of the Barrois.
60% m.g.; *industriel*; *vache pasteurisé*.
Barrois/Haut-Marne.

## Carré

**Carré de l'Est** (*croûte-fleurie*). The mould-coated version of this cheese (from 125g, usually 200g), produced in vast quantities over an area much wider than Lorraine, is usually a staring white square, with the dull interior which its crust leads any cheese-lover to expect. I have not seen an unpasteurised one for many years and cannot bring myself to single out any make for special mention. It is now a supermarket, not a *fromager*'s, item (and see below, various CARRÉ and RÉCOLLET).
45–50% m.g.; *industriel*; *vache pasteurisé*.

**Carré de l'Est** (*croûte-lavée*). This may be worth eating, e.g. as made by Schertenleib, who also makes good Langres at Saulxures. See Chapter 10, p. 328.
*laitier*; *vache cru*.
Haute-Marne; 62 **13**, bottom.

**Carré de Lorraine.** 230g, *croûte-fleurie*, square; under Le Révérend *marque* but with *Label Rouge* a silver-medal winner in Paris for Carrés *lait cru*; 15% larger, and justifiably 45% dearer, than the same maker's Carré de l'Est. Saint-Hubert *industriel laitière* (at Ludres on label, but at Vézelise 62 **4**, far R on a Concours list) obviously think that discriminating buyers will not touch a cheese called plain Carré de l'Est. Coulommiers Le Révérend *lait cru* is made here (the same company makes pasteurised cheeses, also called Le Révérend, at Magnières).
50% m.g.; *laitier*; *artisanal*; *vache cru*.

**Carré Vosgien.** Just another Carré de l'Est.
45% m.g.; *laitier*; *vache pasteurisé*.
Lorraine/Meurthe-et-Moselle.

## Carvi de Hollande

(*Kümmel* in German, caraway in English), although disapproved of by some purists, is traditionally mixed in or scattered over Munster (to taste, of course); but it is often called Cumin (or Cumin is substituted). Cumin (French or English), *Kreutz* or *Kümmel* (German) is quite distinct. I have also seen it called *cumin d'Alsace*, *cumin des prés*, *faux-cumin* or *cumin hollandais*. Used in Dutch Leiden cheese.

## Chaumes

Regional term for the high mountain pastures cleared of trees, or above the tree-line, often only free of snow in the summer. The cows go here Saint-Urbin's day, 25 May, until Saint-Michel (Michaelmas), 29 September. See p. 278. These are the *chaumes* which gave their name to the cheese of the name invented in Jurançon, and to the Fromageries des Chaumes, who make it in Périgord.
Alsace/E. Lorraine.

## Chèvre, Fromages de

These provinces are not traditional goat country, but since the 1970s a number of *chévriers* have established themselves. (See also LAPOUTROIE and WITTENHEIM.)

**Fromages pur Chèvre Fermiers.** M. Eriksen-Gérum makes these *banon*-shaped cheeses, sold *frais* or *affinés*, at Val d'Ajol.
*m.g. non précisée*; *fermier*; *chèvre cru*.
Lorraine/Vosges; 62 **16**, bottom.

**Petits Fromages de Chèvre.** At Ribeaugoutte (ask there) M. Giovanni Bambou makes these little cheeses, many of which are sold *frais* to Colmar restaurants.
*fermier*; *chèvre cru*.
Alsace/Haut-Rhin; 62 **18**, N of C off N415 above Lapoutroie.

## Chèvre, Fromages de, at fermes-auberges

1. M. Michel and Mme Sylviane Bruneau, Ferme-auberge La Retelière (see La Bresse above).
Lorraine/Vosges; 62 **17**, lower R.
2. 'Brigitte et Joël', Ferme-Auberge de Liézey, near Gérardmer, at 750m; local specialities and goat cheese; open except Mondays in holiday periods, weekends out of season; bedrooms, dormitory (tel. 29 63 09 51).
Lorraine/Vosges; 62 **17**, C.
3. M. and Mme Francis Papelier, Ferme-auberge Les Grands Près, Plainfaing, at 670m; chickens, sheep, goats, raspberries, special local pâtés and meat dishes (tel. 29 50 41 66).
Lorraine/Vosges; 62 **18**, L on N415.

4. M. Georges Ruaux, Ferme-auberge Les Chevrettes, Frain; goat cheeses, lamb dishes (his 400 sheep go up for *transhumance*); open all year, but preferably reserve (tel. 29 09 72 02).
Lorraine/Vosges; 62 **14**, SW of C D25.

### Chigre, Schigre

See BROCOTTE.

### Colmar

Thursday and Saturday market.
M. Pierre Michel, *fromager*, 75 route de Neuf-Brisach (which is the direction for a *'petit train'* and Rhine excursion between Breisach and Marckolsheim in season). Wine festival week in mid-August. Syndicat Interprofessionnel du Fromage de Munster, 1 place de la Gare (tel. 89 23 99 40) Centre d'Études Technologiques Agricoles, Chambre d'agriculture.
Alsace/Haut-Rhin; 62 **19**.

### Corniment

**Fromage de Brebis.** Unique in the region? I was too late to find the farm, but the cheese is made by M. Rémy at Ferme Perrin, Gaec de la Chaume, beyond the Saulxures turn, 'on the left behind an orchard'. (Buy something at the *épicerie* on the left [W] coming in from Le Thillot, and ask for clearer directions from there.)
*fermier; brebis cru.*
Lorraine/Vosges; 62 **17**, low.

### Coulommiers Lait Cru

Le Révérend made at Ludres (see Carré de Lorraine) Meurthe-et-Moselle. Fromagerie Renard-Gillard make one (gold medal, Paris) Biencourt-sur-Orge, Meuse.
*industriel; laitier; vache cru.*
Lorraine.

### Délice des Vosges

Good-looking cheese of Munster family made at Corcieux with milk brought down from the Alsace side of the high Vosges.
*laitier; vache pasteurisé.*
Lorraine/Vosges; 62 **17**, N of C.

### Emmental

**Emmental Français Ermitage Vosges.** Made at Bulgnéville and matured for at least 10 weeks at not over 22°C.
*45% m.g.; industriel; vache pasteurisé.*

**Emmental Français Est-Central.** Approximately 75kg cheeses made of pasteurised milk to a regional standard, and much used for prepacking (see Chapters 14 and 15, pp. 406 and 432). Most Munster factories make some, or ripen it for a rather limited period. Ermitage (see BULGNÉVILLE) is one of the *marques*.
*45% m.g.; industriel; vache pasteurisé.*

**Emmental Français Grand Cru.** This raw-milk cheese of good quality and flavour is made in Franche-Comté and Savoie from milk of farms with controlled pastures and winter feed (see Chapter 14, p. 406), at least 10 weeks ripened. The cheeses may bear labels of Lorraine dairies, such as Ermitage, but are only stored, cut and prepacked there.
*45% m.g.; laitier; fruitière; vache cru.*
Lorraine/Vosges and Franche-Comté.

### Épinal

Wednesday, Thursday and Saturday market, including *fermiers*.
Lorraine/Vosges; 62 **16**, L.

### Faurupt

**Munster Fermier.** West of Lapoutroie at 900m Mme Gérard Claudepierre makes Munster, matured for 7 weeks, from milk of her husband's 20 Vosgiennes on their flower-rich pastures. In off-season moments they make their own cheesemoulds, baskets, churns, rakes, etc., which can be bought on the farm, as can the cheese, daily 18.00–21.00 (tel. 89 47 55 04).
*fermier; vache cru.*
Alsace/Haut-Rhin; Le Bonhomme; 62 **18**.

### Fermes-Auberges with own cheese

All serve this and other local dishes. Some offer accommodation, from dormitory style to *gîte*. See LA BRESSE, FRAIN, GÉRARDMER, GRANGES-DE-PLOMBIÈRES, PLAINFAING, LE THILLOT, UZEMAIN.
N.B. *Ferme-auberge* is another term for *marcairerie* (see p. 278). For a list write to l'Association des Fermes-Auberges des Vosges, Chambre d'Agriculture, rue André Vitu, 88025 Épinal.

### Fleur de l'Ermitage

About 1400g, plump *tome, croûte-fleurie*, sold white; semi-soft to soft; made by Fromageries de l'Ermitage.

52% m.g.; industriel; vache pasteurisé.
Lorraine/Vosges; Bulgnéville (see p. 286).

## Fol Amour

2kg oval croûte-fleurie soft cheese by H. Hutin, La Croix sur Meuse (gold medal Paris) (and see bûche).
62% m.g.; industriel; vache pasteurisé.
Lorraine/Meuse.

## Frain

See chèvre, fromages de, at fermes-auberges.

## Fremgeye

Fromage frais broken up and sieved into a pot, highly seasoned with salt and milled pepper, well stirred to make smooth, and sealed in with a weight over the cheese; left 2 months in coolest part of cellar, it should emerge pink (Auricoste de Lazarque, La Cuisine Messine). Androuët says it smells putrid, is viscous and has a powerful taste. It can be eaten straight or on bread with chopped shallots or onions; fremgeye is a dialect word for cheese, as is fromgi.
domestique; vache.
Lorraine/Moselle/Metz region.

## Fromage aux Fines-Herbes

1kg round, soft, croûte-fleurie, by Lorraine-Lait (gold medal Paris).
50% m.g.; industriel; vache pasteurisé.
Lorraine/Metz.

## Fromage Frais aux Fines-Herbes

150g fresh cheese, no crust, by Unicolait.
70% m.g.; industriel; vache pasteurisé.
Lorraine/Moselle; 62 **8**, Sarrebourg.

## Fromage Blanc

Sarrebourg (Moselle) holds a Fête du Fromage Blanc on the first Sunday in July. Much is used in household preparations such as fremgeye. La Ferme-Auberge La Chènevière at Granges-de-Plombières (see p. 290) serves its own and makes a Crémet.
laitier, vache pasteurisé; fermier, domestique, vache cru.

**Fromage Blanc de la Messine.** Made from milk with cream taken off before coagulation and returned after cheese is drained; served with chopped shallots, onions, spring onions, and with salt and pepper (Marabout).

## Fromage Cuit Lorrain

Recipes start with fremgeye (see above), which, if not used all at once, should be stirred every time it is opened up; 1kg is turned into a casserole with 250g of butter and 1.5 l of milk mixed in, and melted slowly over the heat until it is runny, peppered, and poured into a pot with pork crackling, to be used on bread or toast.
Another recipe involves heating fromage blanc until the whey is expelled, hanging it in cheese cloth or butter muslin for 4–5 days, then treating as fremgeye and leaving in cave 1 week (testing maturity and stirring every other day); when soft, it is turned into a casserole with milk and seasoning to taste, and kept moving as it melts over the heat; when it is liquid it is taken from the heat and 2 egg yolks added; it is returned to the heat and stirred continuously until it coheres, then poured into a cool pot, and left for 1 week before serving (Marabout, 1978).

## Fromage en Pot

Similar to latter recipe for Fromage Cuit, but draining the curd 4–5 days in pot, not cloth, 3cm deep with fine salt, pepper and fennel seeds; this is repeated until the pot is filled, at which point it is sealed and left in the cool for 6 weeks; the surface mould is then removed, the cheese stirred again, and kept where insects cannot get at it (Viard, 1980).
domestique; vache cru.
Lorraine/Moselle/Metz area.

## Fromage Fort

See gueyin.

## Fromage Frais

See bootzheim and fines-herbes.

## Fromagère, Fromagie

Lorraine version of Cancoillotte (see Chapter 14, p. 396). Spécialité Fromagère (see p. 295) is no relation.
Lorraine.

## From'gi

Old popular word for cheese.

## Géramont

215g, oval, soft, white-coated cheese made by BG Sarl (Bongrain) at Illoud, in Bassigny,

not strictly within the region, but bearing a name which might be confused with derivations from Gérardmer.
56% m.g.; *industriel*; *vache pasteurisé*.
Bassigny/Haute-Marne; Chaumont.

### Gérardmer
Thursday and Saturday market.

**Gérardmer.** Pronounced Gérar'mé. Up to 6kg, 30cm × 8cm deep, round, in box; sometimes *croûte-lavée*, sometimes uncrusted like Géromé *frais*; quite long established, to cater for mild palates and children of the region. Gérardmer is at the heart of the cheesemaking area of Lorraine on the western slopes of the Vosges mountains, with a tradition of methods similar to those of Alsace and its Munster, but producing larger, thicker cheeses (see GÉROMÉ).
40–45% m.g.; *industriel*; *vache pasteurisé*.
See also CHÈVRES, Ferme-auberge de Liézey (near Gérardmer), and MUNSTER, Ferme-auberge Firstmiss (near Gérardmer) and LE THILLOT (farms, several cheeses).
Lorraine/Vosges; 62 **17**.

### Géromé, Munster Géromé, AOC 1978
The name is a corruption of the common pronunciation of Gérardmer, Gérar'mé, and is believed to be contemporary with Munster in its origins, which were similarly eighth-century monastic. Géromé comes from the western slopes of the Vosges mountains, Munster from the eastern. Methods of making are related because monasteries shared knowledge; but it has been suggested that cheesemaking was brought across the Vosges by the *marcaires* with their herds in *transhumance* from Alsace farms. See p. 278.
The larger, much deeper form of Géromé makes it a different cheese, which should never have come under one AOC with Munster. The unfortunate result is loss of identity and rare use of its own honoured name.

**Munster Géromé AOC.** 1.25kg, soft; washed-crust, gold becoming pink; boxed; very good succulent cheese (if not chilled) by Fromagerie de l'Ermitage, Bulgnéville (see p. 286).
50% m.g.; *laitier*; *industriel*; *vache pasteurisé*.

**Géromé Fermier.** 1.5kg cheese, 12cm deep; some sold *frais* in Épinal market (Saturdays), some ripened where made: Ferme-auberge La Tête du Loup (see LE THILLOT). Unlike the Munster practice, Géromé milk was not traditionally reheated.
Courtine, writing in 1973, mentioned very large cheeses sold fresh as Lorraine (see p. 292) or Gros Lorraine; 750–1000g cheeses ripened 3–4 months and attaining great strength; but Androuët insists that 'good Lorraine' is properly a 5–6kg cheese, either sold *blanc* or matured for 6 months at least. Some have, or had, *carvi* (see p. 287) in curd, some *anis*.

**Géromé Anisé.**
*vache*.

**Géromé au Cumin** (des Près). This was made on the Alsace side of the Vosges, but could not be called Munster, according to Courtine.
*fermier*; *vache cru*.
Alsace/slopes of Vosges.

**Géromé au Fenouil** is mentioned in Michelin's *Green Guide*, but neither Androuët nor I have ever seen it.

**Géromé de Bruyères.** Courtine mentions this without description. It could have been normal Géromé made around Bruyères (62 **16/17**); or, as one of my Lorraine informants thought, a keeping cheese of the Bargkass or La Brouère type; its name derived from heather in the mountains. It is made in *marcaireries*. (See BARGKASS, BROUÈRE.)
*fermier*; *vache*.
Lorraine/Vosges.

### Le Graingeaud
Farm cheese made at Granges-sur-Vologne (see p. 291).

### Granges-de-Plombières
**Fromage Blanc: Le Crémet de la Chenevière.** Émile, Clémence and Bernard Cornu offer these, and their farm pork, poultry and veal, quiches, *tourtes vosgiennes* and seasonal vegetables and fruit at their *ferme-auberge* La Chenevière, 3km NW of Granges. Open for reservations weekends, public holidays, *jours de fête* (tel. 29 66 01 25 or 29 67 03 25).

*fermier; vache cru.*
Lorraine/Vosges; 62 **16**, low L.

**Le Graingeaud.** 1800g farm speciality (undescribed in the Paris price list where I found it) made by Pierre François at Les Chappes, Granges-sur-Vologne.
*fermier; vache cru.*
Lorraine/Vosges; 62 **17**, L of C.

GUEYIN, GUEYUN, FROMAGE FORT DE LORRAINE

Made from Trang'nat (see p. 295) in very dry condition, either potted after *affinage* until ripe, or put into pot with other pounded cheeses already in course of fermentation, placing each new layer on a bed of straw; the closed pot should be placed in the warm for a month or two before use, either as it is (yellow, creamy and strong), or cooked over heat or in the oven. It is very rarely seen in shops.
*domestique; vache cru.*
Lorraine.

HABSHEIM

Le Moulin du Kaegy, recommended by Gault Millau (Feb 1986) for cheese including four Munsters; Steinbrunn-Le-Bas, Habsheim (tel. 89 81 30 34).
Alsace/Haut-Rhin; S of Mulhouse.

KAYSERSBERG

Monday market; charming old town near vineyards and cheese farms (see LAPOUTROIE, MUNSTER).
Alsace/Haut-Rhin; 62 **18**, R of C.

LANDERSHEIM

Auberge du Kochersberg renowned for its fine show of cheeses, and for a *sommelier* who knows how to suit wines to them; Route de Saessolsheim (tel. 88 69 91 58).
Alsace/Bas-Rhin; 62 **9**, high N of C.

LAPOUTROIE

Friday market.
Hotel Les Alisiers, off a winding road 700m above Lapoutroie (find it in daylight), was a delightful headquarters for cheese exploration, with usefully knowledgeable Jacques and Ella Degouy and their local dishes and cheeses (tel. 89 47 52 82). Orbey (see p. 293) is not far off, likewise Plainfaing (see p. 293). There are five or six farms, mostly *biologique*, making Munster in the commune of Lapoutroie, an increase in recent years.

**Munster Fermier.** At this farm, on the right off the lane up to Les Alisiers GAEC Pierrevelcin, cheese was made for many years until 1952, and again from 1977. They make four 240-litre vats a week, the rest of their milk going to the Laiterie Marcillat (quota regulations allow them to retain more milk for cheese on application). Their 500–550g and half-size Petit Munster is sold on the farm and in markets (Kaysersberg Mon, Winzenheim Fri).
Their milk is not *vosgien* and methods differ slightly from the classic recipe given under Munster: rennetting is done at a dairy temperature of 23°C and the curd, once formed, broken once with a vertical cut. Two hours after rennetting the whey is removed in buckets from the top of the *cuve* for the calves, and the pierced moulds (15cm diameter, 15cm deep for full-size) are filled by ladle to the top. As soon as the last is filled (55–65 cheeses) the first cheese is turned within the mould by hand. This turning is repeated every 2 hours on the first day (temperature is kept up by electric fire; the first turning sometimes has to wait up to 30 minutes if dairy-temperature has dropped). Cheeses are salted after 2–3 days, then washed with water every other day during 4 weeks of *affinage* in the *cave*.
*fermier; biologique; vache cru.*
Alsace/Haut-Rhin; 62 **18**, N of C.

**Fromage de Chèvre.** Chevrerie du Bambois, M. Fr. Giovanni.
*fermier; biologique; chèvre cru.*
Lapoutroie.

LAUTERBOURG

Tuesday and Friday market.
La Poêle d'Or, recommended by Gault Millau for cheeses and their labelling (Feb 1986); 35, rue du Général Mittelhauser (tel. 88 94 84 16).
Far NE Alsace/Bas-Rhin; 57 **20**, upper R.

LINGOT D'OR

About 1800g, 13cm × 25cm × 6cm; washed-crust; soft, mild, similar in curd and crust to Marcaire (see p. 292), but much thicker. It won silver medals at Paris in 1980 and 1981.
*50% m.g.; industriel; vache pasteurisé.*
Lorraine/Vosges.

## Lorraine

Up to 6kg, boxed cutting cheese, *frais*, uncrusted (see GÉRARDMER).
40–45% m.g.; *industriel; vache pasteurisé*.
W slopes of Vosges.

## Marcaire, Marcairerie, Marcairie

See p. 278 and Glossary.

## Le Marcaire

200g, 10cm; 1300g, 20cm; 4000g, 33cm; round, flat; washed-crust of strong gold (the big cheese won a gold medal at Paris in 1981, silver 1982); softer, but thicker crust, and milder when young, than Munster; has been made for many years by Fromagerie de l'Ermitage, Bulgnéville (see p. 286).
50% m.g.; *industriel; vache pasteurisé*.
Lorraine/Vosges.

## Matton

*Recuite* similar to Metton of Franche-Comté (see Chapter 14, p. 396) used for equivalent of Cancoillotte (see also p. 396 and see BROCOTTE and CHIGRE for Alsace variants).
*domestique; vache whey*.
Alsace.

## Metz

Market daily except Sundays.
Éts Théophile Conrad, La Fromagerie, 3 allée des Murs, Centre Commercial Saint-Jacques; a fine national range of cheeses, as well as those of Alsace and Lorraine.
Lorraine/Moselle; 57 **14**.

## Molsheim

Wine festival 1 May; and see SAINTE-ODILE.
Alsace/Bas-Rhin; 62 **9**.

## Mostoffait, Mostoffé

Like Stoffet Hainaut (see Chapter 8, p. 274); or just a fluffy *fromage frais* made by whipping *fromage blanc* before much whey has been drained from it.
*domestique, vache sérum/entier*.
Lorraine.

## Mulhouse

Tuesday, Wednesday, Thursday and Saturday market.
*Maître fromagers*: M. Gilbert Ladouce, 10 Passage de l'Hôtel de Ville; Le Moulin du Kaegy-Habsheim (see p. 291); M. François Schmitlin, 45 rue du Runtz. Recommended by Gault Millau, Feb 1986: Crémerie du Bouton d'Or, 5 place de la Réunion (a number of Munsters, and of chèvres, some local); Le Globe, 27–31 rue du Sauvage (including lesser-known good cheeses).
Alsace/Haut-Rhin; 66 **9/10**.
Muhlhausen; 66 **9/10**.

## Munster

Tuesday and Saturday market.

**Munster, Munster Géromé AOC 1978.**
Alsace/Eastern Vosges.
AOC Region of Origin. Alsace: almost all cantons, including part of Territoire de Belfort. Lorraine: Vosges mountains, whole *département des* Vosges; parts of Haute-Saone, Meurthe-et-Moselle and Moselle bordering on Vosges.
AOC Sizes. Le Munster: Minimum 450g, 13–19cm × 2.4–8cm (this degree of latitude caters for larger, deeper Géromé (see p. 290). Le Petit Munster: 'about 125g'; 7–12cm × 2–6cm.
AOC *Affinage*. '3 to 6 weeks', with turning and washing of crust every other day. Crust is smoothed and developed by rubbings and other wet treatments. The orange-yellow colour, sometimes tending towards red, is essentially owed to ferment of *bacterium linens*.
The Munster Syndicat's points for cheese judges add that it should be regular in form, uniform in colour and free of mould over the surface of the *bacterium linens* (up to 5 points). The *pâte* should be free of splits, have few apertures, be homogeneous, not granular, not hard, not runny (up to 5 points). The flavour and aroma should be straightforward, agreeable and *'typique'* (only experience can explain *'typique'*), but it should not be too acid, too strong, or too salt; nor should it be bitter. (Up to 10 points; deductions of up to 4 for acidity, bitterness, abnormality in taste or aroma; up to 3 for excessive strength.) For production figures, see p. 283. See recipe, p. 284.

**Munster Fermier AOC.** Faurupt (see p. 288) has farm with Vosgiennes, Lapoutroie (see p. 291) 5–6 farms. Orbey (see p. 293) has a Syndicat des Producteurs of its own. M. Ancel makes at nearby Tannach and is an *affineur* of farm cheese in Orbey. Ask there for guidance on the Route du Fromage de la

Vallée de Munster, embracing an area strong in farm cheese. Elsewhere there are signs of Munster cheese on roadsides, but if you strike unlucky, ask at the next *mairie* or *Syndicat d'Initiative* (in small places, often the same building).
*fermier; mainly biologique; vache cru.*
Alsace/Haut-Rhin; 62 **18**, N of C.
La Route du Fromage de la Vallée de Munster, starting W from Munster (62 **18**) turns N off D417 on to D48 at Soultzeren to Tannach (see ORBEY and above); turn W on D48; S after Col du Calvaire on D148 and follow La Route des Crêtes 34km nearly to Le Markstein (62 **18**, bottom L), turning N on D17 to Sondernach; thence sharp S, following *Route Forestière* (RF on map) to Soultzbach, over R. Fecht, and W for Gunsbach Munster.

**Munster Géromé, Munster au Cumin.**
Farms making: at Vagney (62 **17**, lower L) Ferme Gegout: Munster; Le Menil near Le Thillot: Ferme-auberge La Tête du Loup making Munster, Munster au Cumin, Gérome and Bargkass (see pp. 281-2); see Le Thillot for details. There are a number of other farms in this area. See recipe, p. 284.
*fermier; mostly biologique; vache cru.*
Lorraine/Vosges.

**Munster (Laitier) AOC.** 125g, 200g, 250g, 500g, 700g, 1500g boxed; *all* these sizes at Bulgnéville (see p. 286), Vosges (l'Ermitage); the Syndicat Interprofessionnel map shows *laiteries* also at Benestroff, Moselle (Lorraine-Lait); Corcieux, Vosges (Marcillat); Éloyes, Vosges (Grandemange); Herbevillier, Meurthe-et-Moselle (Co-op de Blamong); Molsheim, Bas-Rhin (Union Mon Lait); Neufchâteau, Vosges (Avid), where there is a Saturday market; Riedseltz, Bas-Rhin (Co-op); Rochesson, Vosges (Coop Hautes-Vosges); Rupt-sur-Moselle (Coop Haute-Moselle); St-Louis, Haut-Rhin (Co-op); Ville-sur-Illon, Vosges (Leclerc); Xertigny, Vosges (Sté-Fromagère-de-l'Est); not listed, Saulxures-sur-Moselotte, Vosges, where Remy-Rudler used to make a succulent cheese. Some make Munster au Cumin 750g (including Bulgnéville, see p. 286); some make Munster Géromé; e.g. 1250g from Bulgnéville, boxed in wood, under a most attractive pictorial label. They say there that the tradition is milder than Munster. *Affinage* is 6 weeks for this large cheese and the larger Munsters. Paris prefers less mature cheese, and so does the Midi.

*Affineurs* listed by the Syndicat: Huttenheim, Bas-Rhin (Frech); Lapoutroie, Haut-Rhin (Hubert Pierrat); Muhlbach sur Munster, Haut-Rhin (Sengèle); Orbey, Haut-Rhin (Primalait for farm cheese); Ostheim, Haut-Rhin (Sté-Fromagère-de l'Est, see also as makers, at Xertigny); Rosheim, Bas-Rhin (Siffert), where there are Tuesday and Friday markets; Ste-Croix-aux-Mines, Haut-Rhin (Kurtzemann); Ste-Marie-aux-Mines, Haut-Rhin (Laurent), where there is a Saturday market.

NOYERS-LE-VAL

Low-fat small cheese, usually *cendré*, reported by Courtine in 1973 as on its way out (ducs de Lorraine were latterly also ducs de Bar).
30–35% m.g.; *fermier; vache cru.*
Barrois/Haute Marne/Chaumont area.

OELENBERG

See ABBAYE.

ORBEY

Centre of Munster farms: Affineur Primalait, 78 rue Général de Gaulle (tel. 89 71 20 02); farms near by include M. Ancel at Tannach, S of Orbey; enquire for route du Munster (see MUNSTER FERMIER).
Alsace/Haut-Rhin; 62 **18**, R of C.

PLAINFAING

See CHÉVRE FROMAGES PUR CHÈVRE FERMIERS (M. Papelier).

POIL DE CAROTTE

205g oval soft cheese by Marcillat at Corcieux (a Munster dairy).
60% m.g.; *laitier; vache pasteurisé.*
Lorraine/Vosges.

POIVRE, FROMAGE AU

1kg cheeses (*croûte-fleurie*) made by Marcillat at Corcieux, Lorraine-Lait at Metz. *laitier; vache pasteurisé.*
Lorraine.

## Port-Salut

220g, and about 1800g; this semi-soft white cheese in its artificially orange, dry crust owes its name (but not its present recipe) to the monks of Entrammes, Mayenne (see p. 43). The monks sold the name to the Fermiers Réunis dairy when the anti-monastic laws interrupted their activities. When the monks resumed, the making of the *laiterie* cheese was moved to Révigny-sur-Ornain.
50% m.g.; *laitier*; *industriel*; *vache pasteurisé*.
Barrois/Meuse; 56 **19**, bottom R.

## P'Teux

Broken or overripe cheeses, trimmed, cut up, potted and stirred into one amalgam; as occasion arises another cheese or fragment is added and stirred in, the pot being sealed after each addition. Before serving, resalt if necessary and add pepper.
*fermier*; *domestique*; *vache cru*.
Lorraine/Vosges; Géromé/Munster valleys.

## Récollet

Lightly salted, old Carré de l'Est was probably once made by reformed Franciscans, who were known as Récollets. More recently made by Gérard at Le Tholy (see p. 295), and described by Courtine as giving an initial taste of Munster, then veering towards strongish Camembert. If it had survived it could not have been so interesting under today's industrial régime (Bongrain), but Ninette Lyon established that it had finished by 1978.
*artisanal*; *industriel*; *vache cru/pasteurisé*.
Lorraine/Vosges.

## Remiremont

Tuesday and Friday market.
Market hall with permanent health-food shop *La Vie Claire* in one corner which sells farmhouse cheeses, including chèvres.
Lorraine/Vosges; 62 **16**, lower R.

## Revidoux

250g hexagonal, soft, *croûte-fleurie* by Saint-Hubert Industrie Laitière, Magnières.
50% m.g.; *industriel*; *vache pasteurisé*.
Lorraine/Meurthe-et-Moselle.

## Roumillat

200–215g, 'semi-washed rind' (Bongrain's words), 'very soft texture', 'mellow flavour'; rounded drum in cardboard collar.
50% m.g.; *industriel*; *vache pasteurisé*.
Lorraine/Vosges.

## Le Rondfaing

250g soft, *croûte-fleurie* by Union Fromagère des Hautes-Vosges, Dommartin, near Remiremont.
50% m.g.; *laitier*; *vache pasteurisé*.
Lorraine/Vosges.

## Saint-Benoît

Made by SICA Fromagerie at Thiaucourt; the name properly relates to an Orléanais cheese; this company also makes pasteurised versions, equally misplaced geographically, of Brie and Camembert.
60% m.g.; *laitier*; *vache pasteurisé*.
Lorraine/Meurthe-et-Moselle.

## Saint-Hélian

200g soft round boxed cheese of half-skimmed milk from 'Les Vosges'; halfway between Belle-des-Champs and Camembert Laitier; as described to me: 'a bit dull'. The Saint is new to me and is not in the *code postal* nor in my gazetteer.
30% m.g.; *laitier*; *vache pasteurisé, demi-écrémé*.
Lorraine/Vosges.

## Sainte-Odile

With *carvi*; in 1973 Courtine exploded at the *carvi* engraving on the label 'to make people think it comes from Alsace'; ... '*non sans quelque effronterie*', he said of Paris *fromagers* selling it; but it might have been made by Union Mon Lait at Molsheim (62 **9**); 15km SSW of Molsheim is the Mont, named after this saint (daughter of nasty Adalric or Étichon, seventh-century *duc d'*Alsace) who founded a convent at her family home, the *Château de Hohenbourg*, and another on the slopes of Mont Sainte-Odile at Niedermunster. There is a modern successor convent there now, and her eighth-century sarcophagus and remains are in the twelfth-century Chapelle Sainte-Odile (see Michelin Green Guide).
Alsace/Bas-Rhin.

## Saint-Rémy

200–300g, square, boxed, *croûte-lavée* to pale gold or brick colour; although pasteurised, some flavour from crust (see Chapter 8, pp. 258–9 for my theory on origin of name, and correct spelling; the name has also been used in Franche-Comté).
*45–50% m.g.; laitier; vache pasteurisé.*
Lorraine.

## Sarrebourg

Fête du Fromage Blanc, first Sunday in July.
Lorraine/Moselle.

## Schigre

See BROCOTTE.

## Spécialité Fromagère

200g, oval, *croûte-fleurie* soft cheese by Saint-Hubert; this sort of thing comes in all shapes (see REVIDOUX); nothing to do with Fromagère, Fromagie (see p. 289), which are Lorraine versions of Cancoillotte (see pp. 396, and NB warning).
*62% m.g.; industriel; vache pasteurisé.*
Lorraine/Meurthe-et-Moselle.

## Strasbourg

Markets on Tuesdays, Wednesdays, Thursdays, Fridays and Saturdays.
Shops and restaurants recommended by Gault Millau (Feb 1986): Au Bec Fin, 8 rue des Orfèvres; Crémerie René Bréard, 33 Grand'rue; Centre Commercial Esplanade; Centre Commercial des Halles; M. Klein, 28 boulevard d'Anvers and rue des Sept-Hommes; Crémerie Perrin, 20 rue d'Austerlitz; Zimmer-Sengel, 8 rue du Temple-Neuf, for fish, *fruits-de-mer* and fine cheeses.

## Le Thillot

Saturday market.

**Munster.** Ferme-auberge (see p. 281) La Tête du Loup, Le Prey (look for first right turn, with sign, off D486 after Le Thillot and persist 2–3km before Le Ménil); Munster from traditional milk of Vosgiennes (see p. 279) once a day: rennetting; curd in 30 minutes; vertical cut; 30 minutes later horizontal cut, to cubes of 1–2cm; after 30 minutes into moulds, otherwise see pp. 283–4; *affinage* 3 weeks summer, 4–6 weeks in winter. They also make Munster au Cumin (p. 293), Géromé (p. 290) and Bargkass (p. 285) or Vachelin (p. 296). Their cows are in the revived breeds herd-book.
M. Roger Rollot and M. Nicolas Fêtet serve the cheeses they make and la tarte au Munster, le porc au Bargkass; and, to order, porcelet rôti à la brôche (young pig on spit) (tel. 29 25 20 94 or 29 25 18 24 for reservations preferably; daily except Monday lunch).
*Other farms in locality:* M. Marchal at Le Prey, uphill from La Tête du Loup; Ferme des Clarines, Le Ménil (66 **8**, top L); farm on right of D486 beyond Le Ménil before Col du Ménil (66 **7**); farm NW of Le Thillot by La Roche, N of N66, 2km before Rupt (62 **16/17**, bottom).

## Le Thionville

Mentioned without description by Lindon (1961), and Courtine, who said it was locally consumed (1973).
*low-fat; artisanal; vache cru.*
Bar/Lorraine/Moselle.

## Le Tholy

**Mignon Tholy, Le Petit Tholy.** I remember this little cheese (about 120g) of Camembert texture and crust from the 1960s as being most acceptable, and sold it for years. Éts Gérard at Le Tholy (established 1898) now form part of the great Bongrain complex (mentioned in Viard, 1980).
*industriel; vache pasteurisé.*
Lorraine/Vosges.

## Tome

See BOOTZHEIM.

## Torte

3–3.5kg soft cheese, ringed with tree-bark, brown-coated, creamy colour and texture inside; made at Sarreguemines.
*laitier; vache.*
Lorraine/Moselle; 57 **17**, top L.

## Trang'nat, Trang'natt

Ninette Lyon's recipe for this small soft household cheese: 4 l milk rennetted at 28–30°C; when curd formed, bag it in muslin, place in 13–14cm diameter circlet of wood, and drain 24 hours at 20°C; then turn (still in muslin) and drain another 24

hours. If firm, extract curd, mould into cylinder, salt all faces, cover surface with black pepper and leave in cellar on reed mat until needed for Gueyin (see p. 291). Alternatively, it may be hung in muslin from the ceiling for 3–4 weeks, then potted, to become Gueyin.
*domestique; vache.*
Lorraine (rural).

### Trappiste
See ABBAYE D'OELENBERG.

### Troubadour de l'Ermitage
1.5kg, 13cm × 25cm rectilinear; *croûte-fleurie*; soft, creamy, from Bulgnéville (see p. 286) (silver medals, Paris, 1981, 1982).
60% m.g.; *industriel; vache pasteurisé.*
Lorraine/Vosges.

### Uzemain
**Fromage Blanc.** Ferme-auberge Méloménil, M. Bernard, Mmes Cécile and Marie-Line Houillon, in heart of Vosges, near Canal de l'Est (fishing); own cattle, pigs, poultry; *gîte*, or *chambres d'hôtes* with full *pension*; restaurant (tel. 29 67 70 79).
*fermier; vache cru.*
Lorraine/Vosges; 62 **15**, SE of C.

### Vachelin
See BARGKASS, hard farm cheese.

### Valmeuse
1kg soft white-crusted cheese of familiar industrial design by H. Hutin; Dieue-sur-Meuse.
50% m.g.; *industriel; vache pasteurisé.*
Lorraine/Meuse.

### Vigneulles-Lès-Hattonchâtel
Promotion centre for local wines, spirits, cheeses and other produce, Parc Régional de Lorraine (1 July–15 Sept daily *except* Mon; Easter to Christmas weekends).
Lorraine/Meuse; 57 **12**, C.

### Void, Le Fromage dans la Cendre
Thought to be one of the oldest cheeses, related to Maroilles, Munster, Belgian Herve; *washed-crust*; excellent, but disappearing already in 1973 (Courtine). A *cendré* version has been mentioned.
40–45% m.g.; *fermier; vache cru.*
Lorraine/Meuse; 62 **3**, at N4 × D964.

### Vosges-Crème
200g rounded-cornered rectilinear, small version of Troubadour (see above).
Lorraine/Vosges.

### Winzenheim
Friday market.
Alsace/Haut-Rhin; 62 **18/19**, W of Colmar.

### Wittenheim
Friday market.
**Fromage de Chèvre.** Hugues Zettel, rue du Hanean, Schoenensteinbach.
*fermier; biologique; chèvre.*
Alsace/Haut-Rhin; 66 **9**, high R on D430, 5km NW of Mulhouse Schoenensteinbach.

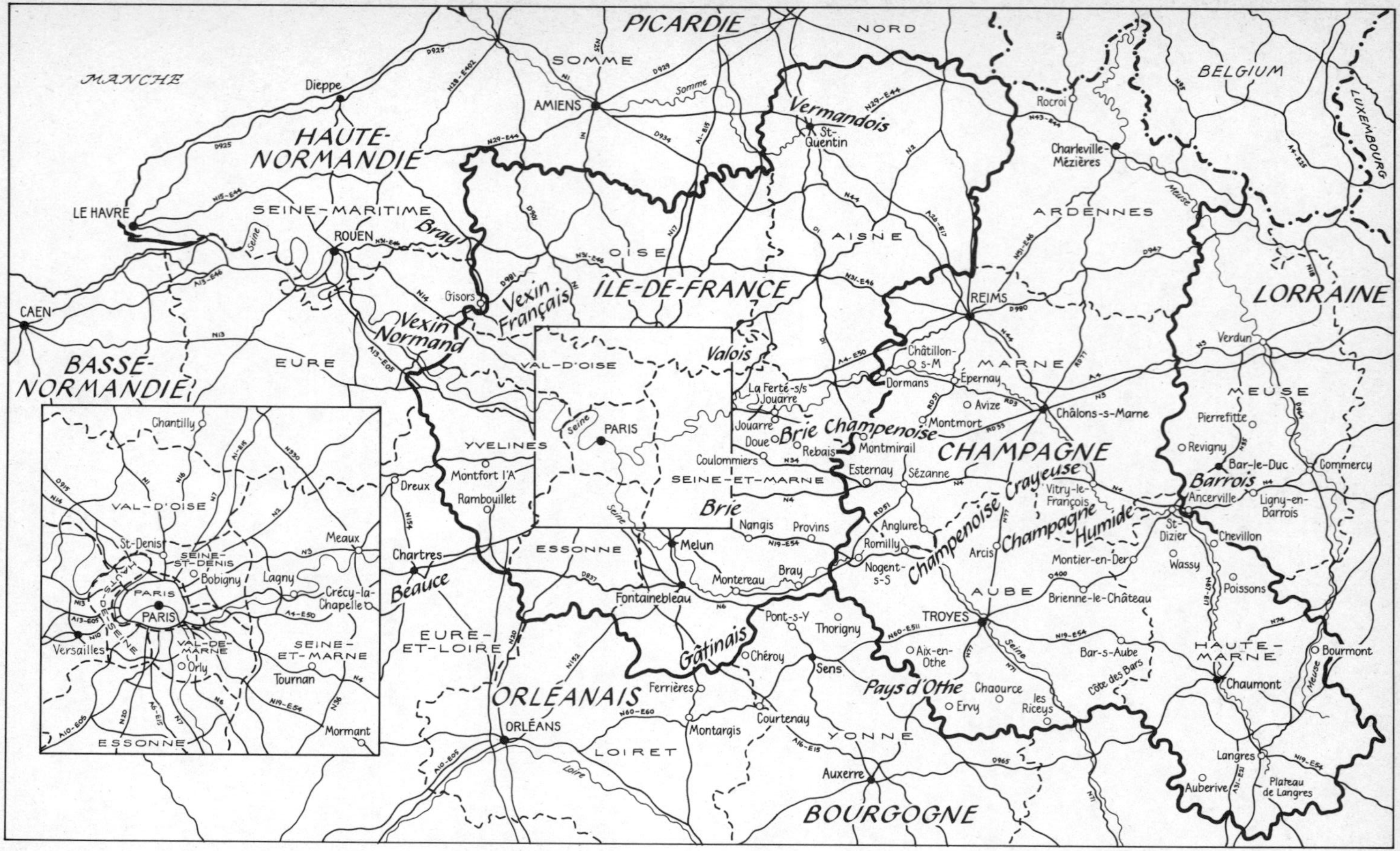
MANCHE
PICARDIE
NORD
SOMME
BELGIUM
LUXEMBOURG
HAUTE-NORMANDIE
BASSE-NORMANDIE
LORRAINE
ÎLE-DE-FRANCE
CHAMPAGNE
ORLÉANAIS
BOURGOGNE
Vermandois
Bray
Vexin Français
Vexin Normand
Valois
Brie Champenoise
Brie
Champenoise Crayeuse
Champagne Humide
Barrois
Beauce
Gâtinais
Pays d'Othe
Côte des Bars
Plateau de Langres
SEINE-MARITIME
EURE
OISE
AISNE
ARDENNES
MARNE
MEUSE
VAL-D'OISE
YVELINES
SEINE-ET-MARNE
ESSONNE
EURE-ET-LOIRE
LOIRET
YONNE
AUBE
HAUTE-MARNE
Dieppe
LE HAVRE
ROUEN
CAEN
AMIENS
Gisors
Dreux
Chartres
ORLÉANS
St-Quentin
Rocroi
Charleville-Mézières
REIMS
Verdun
PARIS
Montfort l'A
Rambouillet
Châtillon-s-M
Dormans
Épernay
Avize
Châlons-s-Marne
Montmort
Montmirail
La Ferté-s/s Jouarre
Jouarre
Doue
Rebais
Coulommiers
Esternay
Sézanne
Vitry-le-François
Pierrefitte
Revigny
Bar-le-Duc
Commercy
Ancerville
Ligny-en-Barrois
St-Dizier
Chevillon
Wassy
Poissons
Montier-en-Der
Nangis
Provins
Melun
Anglure
Romilly
Arcis
Nogent-s-S
Bray
Montereau
Fontainebleau
Brienne-le-Château
TROYES
Pont-s-Y
Thorigny
Chéroy
Sens
Aix-en-Othe
Chaource
Ervy
les Riceys
Bar-s-Aube
Chaumont
Bourmont
Langres
Auberive
Ferrières
Montargis
Courtenay
Auxerre
Chantilly
St-Denis
SEINE-ST-DENIS
HAUTS-DE-SEINE
Bobigny
Lagny
Meaux
Crécy-la-Chapelle
Versailles
VAL-DE-MARNE
Orly
Tournan
Mormant
Seine
Somme
Meuse
Loire

CHAPTER TEN

# Brie, Champagne and the Île de France

## ÎLE DE FRANCE – BRIE – CHAMPAGNE AND BARROIS*

### THE EARLY HISTORY OF BRIE

Legend tells us that the earliest Frankish king was Pharamond, elected in AD 420 at Heinsburg, north of Aix-la-Chapelle. Among the edible gifts brought for this celebration were cheeses made by the tribe of the Meldes. Inhabitants of Meaux, and of the country north of it, between Ourcq and the Marne called the Multien, are cheesemaking Meldes to this day. The plateau to the south of Meaux, which became known as Briga and Bria (meaning an eminence), eventually passed with Multien into the comté de Brie. The celebratory cheese, of course, was Brie.

The Romans recorded their appreciation of a number of Gallic cheeses, but Brie was not among them. Pierre Androuët and Yves Chabot suggest in their delightful book *Le Brie*† (1985) that in the time of the Romans it was a poorly drained, black-coated affair, and developed its full glory only after their departure. There is a gut feeling in the cheese world, unconfirmable by hard evidence, that the earliest Bries were of middling size, in the style of Melun, the probable ancestor of them all.

In the mid-fifth century the first authenticated Frankish king, Merowig (Merovée in French), having defeated Attila at Châlons-sur-Marne in Brie, tried the defeated Huns' mares'-milk curd. He is said not to have taken to it, indeed, to have called it a food for Barbarians, and to have stuck to his Meldien cheese.

In Merovingian times Dux Campania (the late Roman geographical term for Champagne) and France (what we know as the Île de France around Paris), sharing the pays de Brie between them, were of great importance. The bishops helped Clovis to unite the Franks, and he was christened by Saint-Remi at Reims, which was to become the mystic fount of monarchial consecration. Disunity followed Clovis's death. Both Paris and Orléans were

---

*The Barrois has also been dealt with in Chapter 9, Alsace and Lorraine, as the two were formerly ruled together. However, as parts of it are in the modern *zone d'origine* for Brie-de-Meaux, it must be touched on here too.
†le Brie = the cheese; la Brie = the *pays*.

individual kingdoms for a time, but in the Carolingian period Aix-la-Chapelle became the focal point of power. It was on his way back there in 774, after defeating the Lombards, that Charlemagne first met Brie.

The King's assiduous monastic secretary, Eginhard (Einhard in English books), gives us an eye-witness account of this occasion, the first clear historical mention of the cheese. The royal party halted for refreshment 20 kilometres east of Meaux at the Prieuré of Reuil-en-Brie. The prior, apologetic at not having much to offer, meat and game not being on his Order's menu, brought up some of his staple *fromages du pays* from the cellar. As soon as the King had tasted Brie he exclaimed that he had been vain in supposing that he already knew all there was to know about good food: '*Je viens de trouver un des mets les plus délicieux* [I've just discovered one of the most delicious of all dishes].' He immediately ordered two batches a year to be sent to him at Aix.

The monks noticed that he was removing the crust, and put him right. He enjoyed it so much that he instructed his servants to leave the crust on the cheese. It delights me to cite ecclesiastical and royal precedent for insisting on enjoying the whole cheese, the modern French having the shamefully wasteful habit of cutting crusts away. Provided your cheese is in prime condition, eat it all up, scorning any frowns from ignorant, non-Briard natives.

During the next two centuries the Capet family were building up domaines and influence. Their first great leader was Robert le Fort, who died in 866. As well as his comté de Paris and duché de France, he was comte d'Anjou, and beat off Breton and Norman attacks on the centre. Two of his sons were elected kings of the Franks; but his grandson Hugues, comte de Paris and duc de France, could still walk round *France*, his duché, in the course of a day. Hugues's son, another Hugues, France's last elected king, established the hereditary monarchy by having his son Robert anointed during his lifetime. All subsequent kings of France (as opposed to emperors) have been his descendants, and the millennium of Hugues Capet's accession in 987 was celebrated in 1987 as the millennium of modern France. There is still a comte de Paris descended from Hugues, the most generally recognised claimant to the vacant French throne.

Champagne had been put in the charge of the Archbishop of Reims in 940, but most of the temporal power fell in subsequent centuries to the comtes de Troyes. They acquired Multien, too, the comté de Meaux, and merged it with Brie Champenoise in the comté de Brie, calling themselves *comes campaniae et Briae*. They also became comtes de Barrois, later the duché de Bar.

Brie, put on its mettle by Charlemagne, kept up its standards. The eleventh-century monk Foulcoie wrote poetry comparing Meaux with Elysium: 'There is nothing you cannot come by in Meaux: plums, apples, pears, dogberries ... and cheeses born of the rich pastures of the Vallée du Grand Morin.' This, with the addition of fresh milk, eggs and wine (and, selectively, fish) was the monastic diet; and let modern anti-cholesterol fanatics take note that in times when the average human lifespan was very short, most monks lived to a great age.

Robert succeeded his father Hugues in 996 and earned the cognomen 'Le Pieux', partly by feeding 300–500 poor daily in his palace. Their fare was bread, occasional bacon, and commonly a gruel with *fromage en pot*, earliest evidence of a long-lasting Brie tradition. *Fromage frais* was put in covered earthenware pots to ferment and expel more whey in the dark. The whey was removed with a wooden spoon. When the cheese ceased to exude any, it was ready. This is the recipe for the Meaux speciality, Brie-en-pot, still considered correct by purists today. (Other recipes resemble the *fromages forts* of other regions, usually made with old cheese.) Tradition has it that Brie-en-pot started with goats' cheese before the spread of cattle through the region. There were many *chevriers* in those early times and many sheep too, so *fromage de brebis* may have featured in this *fromage en pot*. Sheep persisted in important numbers for meat and wool into the nineteenth century (there are still 15,000 in Brie).

Philippe Auguste, who ruled in the late twelfth century and well into the thirteenth, found Brie *escuelent*, and made it a feature of his presents to visitors and rewards to courtiers. In 1217, on the instructions of the comtesse de Champagne, Blanche de Navarre, the *receveur* for the *foires de Provins* in southern Brie (named Gervais, first of his clan recorded in cheese annals) sent 200 cheeses to the King, costing 12 *sols*. At this rate Brie de Provins today, weighing 1500 grams, would cost 60 Francs a kilo, not an unlikely price at wholesale level.

The Navarre heiress having married into the House of Champagne, Thibaud IV of Champagne succeeded as roi de Navarre in 1234, and the family interests were concentrated more in the south. Later in the century Philippe IV le Bel of France married Jeanne II of Navarre and Champagne; thenceforth, although Navarre stayed independent, Champagne, apart from the vicissitudes of the Hundred Years' War, stayed with France. With the thirteenth-century growth of Paris, more and more agricultural produce, including cheese, went to markets in the city or on its fringes by barge on Seine and Marne. This direct trade cut out the *grandes foires* of Provins and Lagny, where most Paris merchants or their agents had previously bought.

Farm leases in Brie in those times and up to the end of the farmhouse-cheese era, well after the Second World War, included dozens of full-cream milk cheeses ready for the *cave*, and sometimes 'cheeses of large mould to be delivered at Martinmas' (11 November). The latter would be full-sized summer and autumn Bries to see the landlord through the early winter and the festive season.

In the fourteenth century the poet Eustache Déchamps declared le Brie to be the only good thing that came out of the *pays* (he should have read Foulcoie). The much younger Charles d'Orléans, father of King Louis XII, was seigneur of Brie-Comte-Robert (where Monsieur Rouzaire produces a cheese of that name today), a lover of Brie and women, and a considerable poet. His *concièrge* signed a receipt on 6 December 1407, when Charles was only sixteen, for twenty dozen cheeses *'de pais de Brye'* ordered by the young seigneur to be given as presents at the coming New Year. Ladies of the court were among the beneficiaries of his largesse, and one of them found this message with her Brie:

> Mon doux cœur, je vous envoie
> Soigneusement choisi par moi
> Le Brie de Meaux délicieux
> Qui vous dira que, malheureux
> Par votre absence, je languis
> Au point d'en perdre l'appétit.

This professed loss of appetite rather undermined the force of his final couplet:

> Et c'est pourquoi je vous l'envoie.
> Quel sacrifice c'est pour moi.*

Brie remained a royal favourite, Charles VIII preferring it 'above all other cheeses'. With France and Champagne united, the kings were able to take advantage of the proximity of Brie and maintained several *châteaux* in the comté. In the sixteenth century François I's *intendant* at Nantouillet, 20 kilometres west of Meaux, took a personal interest in the making of cheeses for his king. This was the century of Rabelais, whose Gargantua, removing the bells of Paris from the church towers to 'ring them harmoniously', conceived the idea of attaching them to the collar of his mare, which he was getting ready to send laden with *'fourmaiges de Brye'* and fresh herrings to his son Pantagruel. Parisian street-cries of the time included *'Fourmaige de Brye, fourmaige à la livre'* (by the pound). Pierre Androuët thinks this cheese by the pound was *fromage blanc*, but it could also include large Bries cut for the customer. The cry went on: *'Angelots de Byre, de grands et petits, d'acheter vous prie, ils sont d'appétit.'* These Angelots were little flat rounds and balls of *pâte de Brie*, sold as *fromage frais*.

In the 1590s Queen Marguerite's expertise in selecting Brie is said to have kept Henri IV faithful for at least one night at their Château de Coulommiers, when he might otherwise have been two hours' ride away with his mistress, Gabrielle d'Estrées, at Monceaux-lès-Meaux. The king made sure that Gabrielle's *château* was well supplied too. Even Louis XIII, Henri's son by his second wife, Marie de Médicis, much less of a man for feasting, found the Brie at Coulommiers delectable in 1631.

In 1643 the Condé heir, the duc d'Enghien, later *'le Grand Condé'*, having beaten the Spanish invaders from The Netherlands at Rocroi (beyond Brie's borders, but famous for *fromage cendré*), demanded Brie at his evening meal

---

*Sweetheart mine I send to you
Selected with all care that's due
A Brie de Meaux to make you sigh,
To let you know that, saddened by
Your absence, languishing, I'm quite
Deprived of all my appetite.
And that is why I send this Brie;
What sacrifice it is for me.

after the victory. The cheese came from the Multien, the old comté de Meaux, from which his home at Chantilly was normally supplied.

In 1690 Liger's *Dictionnaire* described Brie as we know it today: 'The cheese of Brie, which is so common in Paris, is very fat and made in *grandes éclisses* [the low, adjustable circlets used in the later stage of *moulage*], flat and broad. It is excellent and much esteemed.'

## The eighteenth and nineteenth centuries

In Louis XIV's reign cheese was in eclipse at Court, and likewise at fashionable tables. It would be seen by society only at picnics for the hunt or shoot. After his death, during the regency for the infant Louis XV (Louis XIV's great-grandson), Brie reappeared at Court and fifty wagons of the cheese a week left Meaux for the capital under armed escort against highwaymen. When the King was old enough to marry, his representatives went out from Fontainebleau to greet his bride Marie Leszcynska of Poland at Donnemarie, between Paris and Montereau. The meal they provided for her included '*tartes de Brie*', a common local term for the familiar flat round cheeses. They may well have been the smaller cheeses of this southern part of the region, and were written down as '*gâteaux de Brie*'. This gave rise to the supposition that they were the original '*bouchées à la reine Marie*', but these were devised later by the Queen and her chefs, whose version has not survived. Modern recipes are a variety of guesses.

In *La vie privée des Français*, the eighteenth-century writer Legrand d'Aussy distinguished between Bries for the table, of which 'the best are those of Nangis', and 'those which, being liquid, arrive in pots ... known as *fromages de Meaux*.' They are likely to have been small Bries *secs*, put in stone or earthenware at twenty to twenty-five days and covered, so that they would gradually soften and keep indefinitely. Such by name, and probably by nature, were the cheeses sent to Frederick the Great by the postmaster at Meaux, Monsieur Petit, whose *fromages de la poste aux chevaux de Meaux* were renowned. These cheeses 'of extreme delicacy', which often kept for more than a year, were still available in 1858, according to an encyclopædia published that year. Pierre Androuët, to whose research with Yves Chabot I am indebted, regrets their passing.

Eighteenth-century Paris did not depend only on the classic Bries, whose savour and reputation made up for the notoriously poor wine of the region. Villages circling the capital (long since absorbed in modern suburbs) were actively making cheese, especially *fromage frais à la crème*. Vanves had been known for this for many years (cited by a seventeenth-century abbé de Maroilles); Clamart and Viry-Châtillon likewise gave their names to cheeses, and those of Montreuil and Grosbois also won mention. It was said in the nineteenth century that a grand dessert course was never complete without Fromage de Viry.

Cheesemaking at Clamart continued into modern times, as Léone Bérard revealed in her *Livre des Fromages* (1978). In 1927 Lorenzo Cugusi arrived from Sardinia at Petit Clamart, near the beautiful valley of the Bièvre, and set up his sheep and goat farm and a dairy. He made about 200 cheeses a week to sell in the Sunday market of Le Plessis-Robinson under the name of Cabri de Paris. Every day he held up the traffic on D2 to cross over his mixed flock, guided by his two *bergers*, to graze the pastures between the woods of Meudon and the cemetery of Clamart, where goats had browsed since Henri IV's time. This rustic interruption of Parisian traffic lasted until 1973, when Cugusi retired to Sardinia at the age of seventy; but it was the advance of urban development and traffic pollution, rather than the burden of his years, which drove Lorenzo Cugusi into retirement and ended the four-centuries-old tradition of goats in Clamart.

To return to the eighteenth century, Louis XVI's predilection for Brie proved fatal. On 20 June 1791, in the course of his intended flight abroad, he stopped at Varennes-en-Argonne to enjoy the hospitality of an old retainer. Despite the impatience of his entourage, he insisted on finishing the Brie de Meaux before leaving. The King having been recognised at Sainte-Ménéhould on the way, this prolonging of his break for refreshment gave his enemies time to catch up with him. A retired grocer myself, I am ashamed to say that it was an *épicier*, Monsieur Sauce, who arrested his monarch. Forced to return to Paris, Louis was soon confined for the remaining eighteen months of his life to the tower of the Temple, a twelfth-century monastery fortified by the Templars, which was demolished in 1811.

Napoleon was not really a gastronome so I have no story connecting him with Brie; but his defeat did Brie some good. It led to the enthronement not only of the restored Bourbons in the person of Louis XVIII (the ten-year-old Louis XVII having died in the Temple in 1795), but of Brie as monarch of all cheeses at the Congress of Vienna, according to a story told by the secretary to the French delegation, the comte de Vielcastel. While the European nations were busy trying to untie the bonds of Napoleon's rapacious family takeover business, his Empire, their representatives found time to eat well. The French were led by the duc de Talleyrand. Priest and bishop under the *ancien régime*, member of the *constituente* and a conformist prelate during the Revolution, lay foreign minister to *directoire*, *consulat* and Empire (Napoleon made him a prince\*), and now to the restored kingdom, he was constant only in his devotion to Brie. The Austrian delegate, Prince Metternich, having disputed Talleyrand's claim for the supremacy of Brie, it was agreed that every delegation should present the cheese of its choice and put the matter to the vote. At the appointed banquet sixty cheeses arrived at the head of the dessert course. The jury's verdict, reported as unanimous, was expressed in Metternich's words, proclaiming Brie *'Prince des fromages et premier des desserts'*. (Metternich was consoled when his Sachertorte won the day for sweet desserts.)

The French soon raised Brie from prince to king, and said of Talleyrand that Brie was certainly the only monarch that he would never betray. The congress cheese came from a farm owned by Monsieur Ogier de Baulny at Estouville in the *commune* of Villeroy, just south-east of Meaux (this farm

---

\*Princes (other than the extinct Condé line) were and are inferior to ducs in France, especially *imperial* creations.

served Talleyrand for forty years), and there is no reason to suppose that it was anything but Brie de Meaux of the classic proportions preserved in today's cheese. The smaller Melun is believed to be the oldest, but I do not know on what evidence the usually much smaller Coulommiers is supposed to have evolved in the tenth or eleventh century. Montereau, Provins and Nangis may be local variations on Melun and Coulommiers. The earliest specific mention of any of them is Legrand d'Aussy's praise of Nangis in the eighteenth century and this does not indicate its size.

In the nineteenth century the plains of Brie north and south of Meaux were all dairy country, with 100,000 Flamandes, Normandes and Picardes to provide the milk. In addition to the farm herds, the wife of every rural employee or artisan owned a cow, for which she cut roadside grass during the week. On Sunday she did the housework and the children looked after the cow in the *pré*, or *prat, communal*. Everyone loved Brie, up to Victor Hugo, who said 'the most beautiful Alexandrines are not equal in the mouth to a morsel of Brie'. The marketing centres for cheese were Meaux (where 3000 tonnes of cheese were sold annually), Lagny and Brie-Comte-Robert in the west, and Melun, Nangis and Provins in the south. Nearly every farm in the Melun district was making cheese.

The Franco-Prussian War of 1870 caused great damage in the region, from which the dairy herd never completely recovered. As the century wore on, ownership of farms fell increasingly into the hands of professional and industrial investors, while women became better educated and less inclined to take on the burden of cheesemaking, which farmers and farmers' sons had previously demanded in the marriage contract. The result was a gradual move towards beef-raising in place of dairying.

Yet on the average Saturday in 1895, Androuët and Chabot tell us, 20,000 Bries were sold in Meaux market, fetching 100,000 Francs: again, not wildly different from the equivalent wholesale price at today's values. The cheeses came from Chambry (noted up to 1914), Lizy and Vareddes in the old Multien north of Meaux; from Sammeron and La Ferté-sous-Jouarre to the east; from Dampmart near Lagny to the south-west (noted up to 1914, and home of six makers of *clayettes* for the cheesemakers and *affineurs*); and from Nanteuil-lès-Meaux, Quincy and Crécy-en-Brie (not the battlefield) south of Meaux. Coulommiers and Brie-Comte-Robert remained the other major markets for farm cheese. In 1895 Brie was still making 6000 tonnes of cheese a year (more than the total of Brie de Melun and Brie de Meaux produced in 1984), but by 1914 the total herd was little more than half what it had been fifty years before.

## THE TWENTIETH CENTURY

In the twentieth century the region has suffered from continuing incursions of beef-raising, with consequent widening of the maize-belt, and the new blight of sugar beet. Much of this once green *pays*, with proper shelter for beasts in hedgerows and trees, has become a land of desolation. It made me feel that *la chasse* there could now provide as game nothing but a line of automotive tractors pursued by *chasseurs* in Land-Rovers.

By 1929 the herd had recovered from the effects of the First World War to reach almost the 1914 figure. About 24 million litres of milk were going annually into cheese, but this was only enough to provide a little over 3000 tonnes, half the figure of the 1890s. The average cow yielded 2250 litres, a sufficient increase to make one extra Brie de Meaux a year per cow over the figure for 1900; but farming was still primarily organic, the cows were of traditional breeds and farm cheese was still abundant and rich.

The Second World War was not so destructive in material and human terms in the Brie region. The herd was almost back to 1929 figures by 1953, and milk yield was up by nearly 30 per cent, with cows now averaging 2920 litres per lactation, enough for 146 full-size Bries de Meaux. The Bries of Meaux, Melun, Montereau, Provins, Nangis, and *façon* Coulommiers were still being made on farms and in small *laiteries artisanales*. Cheeses were generally made from curd slowly coagulated without cutting; even *malaxage* (stirring) was forbidden in the practices laid down in 1955 restrictions on the use of the name Brie de Meaux.

From the 1950s until the early 1970s I was able to buy Bries de Melun varying in size and tidiness, but always authentic in thickness and in crust. Almost without exception they were satisfying in consistency and flavour, glorious to eat from the moment they started to ooze close under their rosy-golden coats. At this stage the close-textured *pâte* between, although still nearer white than gold, was appetisingly moist and rich, setting off its more gooey and colourful surround.

Brie de Meaux *fermiers* came in weighing around 3 kilos, swelling out to make their deep sides irregularly convex. They were often as thick as Melun, with never a sharp edge. Their golden crusts, starting to redden, enclosed a rich, clotted, straw-coloured *pâte*. Like the *pâte* of Brie de Melun, it was ready to eat the moment it oozed beneath the surface, with never a suggestion of chalkiness.

The smaller Brie de Montereau used to be sold at a weight of about 600 grams, but in the 1970s mine arrived very young, weighing 900 grams or more, with the crust still white. They were much thinner than their Meaux brothers, both in form and in texture. The lighter *pâte* liquefied faster, before the crust had fully coloured up. In contrast, when I visited the market at Montereau in the late 1960s I saw untemptingly brown and flattened Bries de Montereau piled on barrows, much too high for their good. Ten years later supplies of Montereau at the international market at Rungis dried up. I thought the cheese must have expired, until Pierre Androuët reported an artisan maker of a smaller Montereau at Saint-Julien-du-Sault in the southern (Gâtinais français) fringe of the Brie region in 1982. When I went to find him in 1985, however, he had gone. The big *laitier* Senoble had bought him up for his milk supplies, closed the dairy and killed the cheese. Mercifully, Montereau survives at the *fromagerie* of Bonnet-Petit at Grisy-sur-Seine, where the bigger activity is the making of Brie de Melun. Supplies are so limited that the century-old family firm of *affineurs*, Goussin, gets only sixty cheeses a week.

The 1970s saw the end of farmhouse and small-scale artisan cheesemaking so far as the great Bries were concerned. Apart from the advance of industrial farming, unpaid cheesemakers were no longer to be had on the farms. Women refused to sign marriage contracts committing them to this toil, so milk went to *laiteries*. Between 1968 and 1975 agricultural employment in the region went down by nearly a third. There are now about a dozen *laiteries* making Brie de Meaux AOC. On the smaller scale, Madame Klein makes the last Brie de Meaux *fermier* at Les Glandons de Glandelu.\* There was an excellent *laiterie* making Meaux and Coulommiers at Doue, but it closed in 1987.

Two *laiteries* now make Melun, and I must be frank: their cheeses are not so reliably pleasurable as the general run of cheeses a decade ago. A tendency to over-salt, defying the AOC term 'lightly salted', not only spoils the flavour but leads to hardening of the crust, insufficient drainage, and often results in an untypically loose texture which runs at a stage when the crust should still be developing.

I have met Bries de Melun in recent years which I should not have recognised at a blind tasting, and one or two which did not even look like Melun. It is hard to believe that all these cheeses are made from *caillé* which has been given the minimum 18 hours to form laid down by the AOC. Pierre Androuët told me in 1988 that Melun was dying. Only 100 tonnes were made in 1986, against 400 in 1983.

There are still many adequate Bries de Meaux, but they tend to be too rigid and angular in the crust round their circumferences. They lack that old lively impression of spontaneous expansiveness, and few attain the richness of clotted consistency characteristic of the cheeses from farms with traditional breeds of cattle. What is more, the old thick-textured cheeses were better keepers, with a longer period of enjoyable climax. Modern cheeses suffer from too much milk of a breed so inferior from the cheese-lover's point of view, the Frisonne-Holstein, and from the loss of permanent pastures; and the common use of artificial additives in the cheese and chemical fertilisers in the pasture diminish their aromatic character.

## Brie de Meaux and Brie de Melun in the 1980s

In 1969 the Syndicat for Brie de Meaux instituted an annual Concours du Brie d'Or, and by 1980 production was reported to have reached the nineteenth-century figure of 6000 tonnes again. On 18 August that year, Appellations d'Origine Contrôlée were decreed for Brie de Meaux and Brie de Melun. The ANAOF booklet of 1984 claims that 'Brie de Meaux has known how to conserve the farmhouse traditions of its manufacture, *caillage* obtained by renneting'. The rules lay down that the *caillé* shall not be cut (*divisé*).

Official figures since 1980 have been wildly contradictory, even in the

---

\*In a hamlet not far from Jouasse. Pierre Androuët agrees with me that it is kinder if only professional buyers seek her out.

national annual of *L'économie laitière en chiffres*, varying according to which page you read. The Syndicats for Meaux and Melun deepened the mystery by keeping their records of production figures secret in 1981 and 1982. One set of figures had the combined production of Meaux and Melun dropping from 6256 tonnes in 1980 to 5019 in 1981. Some reduction was to be expected because of the AOC rules just instituted, but the defined region, extending east to the Meuse, was wider than it might have been. Another factor could have been that the quantity of cheese setting out to become Brie de Meaux or Brie de Melun was reported in one set of figures, while the amount actually getting there after grading was reported in the set for AOC cheeses. Between 10 and 30 per cent of Bries fail the test at the pre-*affinage* stage, and another 3–5 per cent on examination before leaving the *caves*. Whatever the reasons, the page in *L'Économie laitière* devoted to cheeses with national *appellations contrôlées* showed only 4905 tonnes (not the 6256 quoted above) of Meaux and Melun for 1980, 18 per cent below 1895 production, dropping to 4360 tonnes (against 5109 above) in 1981. In 1984 the twelve *laiteries* making Brie de Meaux took 36 million litres of milk from 450 farms with an average herd of 25, and produced 5180 tonnes of AOC cheese (p. 63; 5542 on p. 52), a ratio of roughly 1:7 weight of milk to weight of cheese, against the 1:8 Androuët and Chabot consider normal. This cannot be explained by improvement in milk solids, which reached a peak of 8.05 per cent in 1979, when the national average lactation yield was 4455 litres. Yield has gone up steadily year by year to 5202 litres in 1985, but the solids have reached 8 per cent again only once since 1979, and the better producers of solids-not-fats, Normandes and Flamandes, have been giving way to the Frisonnes, bottom of the class for solids-not-fats. The other explanations are the use of short-cuts in cheesemaking to speed up the work and standardise curd. I am told that cutting the curd is now tolerated, and commonly practised although this is against the AOC methods as originally laid down.* It has been excused as achieving 'greater regularity of *pâte*'. One permitted cut has become three or four, with the connivance of the departmental authorities deputed to enforce AOC rules. *Affinage* may be skimped, too, to sell a moister cheese. These changes would account for deterioration in texture, and for higher ratio of cheese-weight to milk used, to the makers' profit. They mock the AOC rules and the official booklet issued by the National Association for Appellations Contrôlées de Fromage (ANAOF). It is not surprising that Brie de Meaux has deteriorated.

Page 63 of the 1987 *Économie laitière* gives the figures for 1985, the latest available before this book went to print: 6176 tonnes of Meaux AOC (7009 on p. 52) and 100 tonnes of Melun AOC (200 on p. 52). Brie de Melun seems to be in a volatile state in more senses than one, and I hope the long-established *affineurs* will make its proper revival the subject of their close attention. In 1981 396 tonnes was made, and it was of steadier quality.

*My enquiry on this subject, and on *Listeria* in Brie, made through the section of SOPEXA specialising in AOC cheeses (at the recommendation of the Guide de Fromagers), has elicited no explanation or further enlightenment on either subject.

I hope that both the *affineurs* and the ruling bodies of the AOC Syndicats will also press the makers of Brie de Melun and Brie de Meaux to pay more attention to the farming methods and breeds of cattle of their milk producers, as is done by the Syndicats in Franche-Comté and Savoie (see Chapters 14 and 15). AOC rules insist on *lait cru*, and *thermisation* is excluded, but the basic sources of an authentic flavour and consistency need to be restored. This requires organic management of permanent pastures to pass on the aromatic esters unhindered by chemicals, and the traditional breeds of the region to convert those pastures into milk of the right make-up to achieve rich texture in the cheese.

Chemicals in farming and the 'ubiquitous Frisonne-Holstein', both foreign and inimical to the sacred *terre de Brie*, have increased milk yield but lowered standards and removed traditional character from the cheese. Numbers of Normandes have been dropping, but the breed is still near the top of the national table. Flamandes have almost disappeared, surviving in farms making Bergues and one farm making Maroilles; yet their yield is third highest in France (after Frisonnes and Montbéliardes), at over 5000 litres a lactation, and their levels of fats and solids-not-fats come fourth (after Normandes and well ahead of Frisonnes), with admirable balance for cheesemaking.

The revival of traditional breeds can do much for Brie, as opposed to the mass-production Frisonne, with its milk a more suitable raw material for standardised industrial cheese, and intervention butter and milk powder. Friesians came 17th out of 17 for solids-not-fats in my list of breeds recorded in France in 1986, with only 3.06 per cent against an average of 3.22 for all breeds. Jerseys head the list with 3.71, Normandes have 3.31, and Flamandes come next with 3.26. English readers will understand the difference if I compare it with the contrast between white Friesian doorstep milk and the golden Channel Island liquid.[*] Skimmed to provide a 100-gram or more head of cream, Channel Island milk can still be richer than shaken-up, whole, Friesian milk, partly because Friesian milk is so poor in solids-not-fats. Milk of Normandes and Flamandes is not as rich as Jersey, but it has a similar effect on the texture of soft cheese. Brown Flamandes were the foundation of Maroilles' past greatness (see Chapter 8).

My sad doubt is whether the Syndicats[†] want to face up to the need for full control and improvement. They seem interested only in making things easier for industrial cheesemakers. On 18 October 1985 I thanked them for the cyclostyled information they sent me when I first wrote to say I was preparing a book on French cheese. Most of this was the text of the AOC decrees of 1980 for Meaux and Melun, defining the zones of origin but otherwise scantly informative. On Melun there were no historical facts at

---

[*]But it should be said that French Friesians' fresh liquid milk, unskimmed, is far below the standard of our silver-topped doorstep milk. It has no head of cream; and it does not arrive on the doorstep, either.
[†]Syndicats for Meaux and Melun are nominally separate, but share the same address and telephone.

all. With my thanks, I repeated unanswered questions on production figures, asked for names of producers and *affineurs*, and enquired whether Brie de Nangis and Saint-Jacques survived. I also related an odd experience my shop in Streatley had just had, which I thought should concern them: in response to an order to Rungis for Brie de Montereau we had received two round 'demi-Bries' of Meaux style (which I am fairly certain originated in Baye). These were labelled 'Coulommiers' by the *affineurs*, Société Fromagère de Brie in Saint-Siméon, but invoiced as Brie de Montereau. I should have been happy to regard this as an odd but isolated mix-up, were it not that nearly two years have elapsed without the raising of a metaphorical eyebrow, let alone the passing on of any further information to me, by the Société Interprofessionnelle de Défense du Brie de Meaux; *Interprofessionnelle*, maybe, but *professionnelle, non*. Fortunately many of my questions have since been answered by friendly *affineurs* or by Pierre Androuët and Yves Chabot in their timely book. I learned, for instance, that Brie de Nangis and Brie le Provins do survive. The authors could not, however, ease my discomfort about the present and future state of Brie, and their book showed the degree to which my anxiety is shared.

## Brie façon Coulommiers

Brie façon Coulommiers is the neglected member of the Brie family. This ancient cheese is still without an AOC, and, ridiculously, is no longer allowed to call itself Brie, even if made in the region. We have no means of knowing how much of the 17,120 tonnes produced in 1985 (nearly 22 per cent up on 1984) is *lait cru* and authentic. Historical evidence distinguishing Bries from one another is rare. It has been suggested that smaller cheeses were developed in the eleventh century for safer carriage, and that those were the first Coulommiers. The name has been applied to almost all Bries of any size smaller than Meaux not identified as Melun, Montereau, Nangis or Provins. Many people have thought that the addition of extra cream to the curd distinguished Coulommiers, but this is not true. The milk was often so rich that Coulommiers could be up to 60 per cent *matières grasses*. Lincet produced a 350-gram Coulommiers of 60 per cent *matières grasses* at the Moulin de Gaye, which was admirable until excessive refrigeration along the line, or some other fault, too frequently resulted in white, hard-crusted cheeses which came to nothing.

As far as exports to England are concerned, Goussin distribute a 325-gram raw-milk *laitier* cheese; and Les Fromagers de Saint-Jacques at La Boissière in Yvelines distribute an excellent Coulommiers *fermier* of 380 or 400 grams, which we sell in Streatley, and which I can buy from our market *fromager* in Fontvieille. Information from *affineurs* in the heart of Brie in 1987 indicates that the only source of Coulommiers *fermier* now is Madame Storme-Naret at Les Pleux, Saint-Denis-les-Rebais. I have mentioned the 1400-gram *lait cru* version labelled as Coulommiers by the Société Fermière. If, as I suspect, this is identical with the demi-Meaux I know, it is made in exactly the same way as the same maker's full-size Brie de Meaux

AOC. For this cheese, unconventionally, half the curd is cut in 5-centimetre cubes; the other, uncut, half of the curd is laid over it with the *pelle à Brie* when the cut curd has settled down one-third of the way up the mould. The same makers cut their Coulommiers curd to 3-centimetre cubes.

Monsieur Claude Lauxerrois, described by Yves Chabot as *'the maître-fromager du secteur'*, is *affineur* at La Ferme Jehan de Brie in the Place du Marché in Coulommiers; and Madame Burin fills the same rôle just outside Coulommiers at La Ferme des Bleus, Boissy-le-Châtel.

Madame Paulette Lauxerrois, mother of Claude, is quoted in *Le Brie* as demanding milk rich in cream, renneted immediately after milking. She lays down that the first filling of the mould should rest until evening and then be covered to fill the mould again with a second batch of curd (there is no mention of any curd-cutting). The rest of the procedure is similar to that of Brie de Meaux, including the use of *éclisses*, but the cheeses need only four weeks to mature. 'Affinage in cool (not cold) rooms needs the greatest care and the job of *affineur* is unending (no holidays, no Sundays off). Our dairies, established along the River Grand Morin, send off by the hundred to the rest of France and the whole world these cheeses which have demanded so much care.'

There are a lot of loose ends to tie up in Coulommiers. Perhaps that is why there is no AOC. I should be sorry to see all the variety of methods standardised, so it might be possible to dictate use of *lait cru* from a recognisable region, and to permit several established traditional methods with the condition that they should be distinguished on the label.

## INDUSTRIAL BRIE

In 1985, 78,179 tonnes of cheese called Brie were produced in France, of which perhaps 10,000 tonnes (including Coulommiers) were made in the Brie region of unpasteurised milk. Allowing that some unpasteurised cheese is quite well made in large *laiteries* outside the AOC region, it is still a reasonable estimate that 60,000 tonnes of this production is related to Brie in its shape alone, and that a considerable proportion of it can be termed cheese only by a stretch of industrial imagination. The AOCs for Brie should be both broadened and strengthened by becoming subsections of an overall AOC for the cheeses of Brie. This should recognise the legitimacy of honoured traditional cheeses, such as Brie de Montereau, Brie de Nangis, Brie le Provins, Ville-Saint-Jacques, and Coulommiers, prescribing to each its respective zone of making within the region. In the interests of better flavour and texture it should encourage the resumption of traditional pasture-management and use of traditional breeds, as I have already suggested.

It should also set a term of years for the abandonment of the name Brie by all cheesemakers outside the region, and by all those within it who do not conform to one of the traditional methods and do not use raw milk. Some makers of tolerable cheese will find it profitable to invest the money, time and trouble needed to assume effective control of their milk supplies (eliminating the need for pasteurisation), and to adjust equipment and train staff to make AOC cheese. Others will have time to familiarise their customers with the name that their cheese will eventually bear when it may no longer be called Brie. Some of these cheeses may well earn more respect under their own name than they earn now as pseudo-Brie. My own practice has always been to eliminate 'Brie' from the labels of any cheeses from outside the region which I kept for their own sakes: for example, 'Brie' du Château de Vallières from the Pays de Bresse which I used to stock years ago, before the factory was quite so mechanised as it is now.

To give force to my plea for the restriction of the use of the name of Brie, I will demonstrate below, entirely from a Lorraine-Lait publicity handout, just how far industrial imagination stretches the realm of Brie. I ask the French Ministry of Agriculture, SOPEXA and the ANAOF to consider the harm this blatant disregard of authentic quality must do to the reputation of Brie abroad, where 72 per cent of Lorraine-Lait's 'Brie' is destined to be eaten.

This company was born in 1970 as a co-operative with 1850 milk-producing members outside the Brie Region in Moselle, Meurthe-et-Moselle and Meuse. It is now grouped with Yoplait and Candia (under SODIMA), Alsace-Lait, Calas and Union Laitière de la Meuse. In 1987 it opened a monster *fromagerie* at Vigneulles-lès-Hattonchâtel, 17 kilometres east of Saint-Mihiel on the right bank of the Meuse. Here the river's left bank forms the eastern boundary of the AOC zone for Brie. The right bank is in outer darkness. Even Saint-Mihiel, *chef-lieu de canton*, is not within the AOC zone, only the *communes* of the *canton* lying on the opposite bank. Yet the publicity reads:

> With an investment of 120 million Francs Lorraine-Lait has played the card of the future. Vigneulles will make essentially Brie de Meaux.
>
> Brie is a soft cheese on which Lorraine-Lait is counting heavily to develop its exports.... they are making 2.5 kilogram cheeses for cutting into *pointes* [portions]. Allowing for eight days repose in the *hâloir*, it needs ten days to make a Brie.
>
> Vigneulles-lès-Hattonchâtel will make essentially Brie de Meaux (AOC) [*sic*] and Coulommiers. The factory planned to be using 500,000 litres *per diem* by 1987.
>
> The new technique of ultra-filtration for the treatment of the milk has been instituted, which can cope with 40,000 litres an hour. Taking account of the extremely varied sources of milk in such a concern, the milk must be brought up to a consistent quality. Furthermore, Lorraine-Lait is going for a world record. The factory has a continuous assembly line of coagulation 54 metres long. Lorraine-Lait is innovatory, too, with its automatic turning of *piles complètes de Brie* in the course of treatment and in assuring machine-wrapping of the cheeses.
>
> This will put Lorraine-Lait in second place in the Brie market, with 13 per cent, of which 72 per cent will be exported.

The decision to build this factory was taken in 1982, two years after the AOC had made it quite clear that the product described above in Lorraine-Lait's own publicity would never, on either geographical or technical grounds, qualify as Brie de Meaux; but whether or not Lorraine-Lait goes to the length of so describing it, this is a horrifying example of the impression most foreigners are given of the noble name of Brie.

In 1986 the United States, Austria and Germany detected *Listeria monocytogenes* in imported French pasteurised, factory cheeses, including 'Brie'. In 1987 Switzerland reported it in twenty-four cheeses (none of them farmhouse), including 'Brie' Le Président, made by the biggest, most mechanised factory giant of them all (see Besnier, p. 46). These countries deserve bad cheese, because they exclude the well-tested, legal representative of the species, Brie de Meaux, by reason of its being unpasteurised. Four *marques* of French industrial Brie were then withdrawn from the market (including cheese from the enormous Fromageries Bel), and all French soft cheeses were excluded from Mexico and from the state of Massachusetts. In 1985, thirty-nine Californians had died from infection by the same bacteria present in a 'Mexican-style' cheese eaten in California. So when Dr Jean Auclair of the French Dairy Research Institute was questioned by Britain's foremost cheese authority, Dr J. G. Davis (to whom I had sent a French report of the 1986 incidents), Dr Auclair blamed Mexico for the 1986 occurrence. This was a far-fetched excuse, Germany and America having had the same trouble at the same time. It is worth recording here that the British Government's Central Public Health Laboratory in London (responsible for national statistics on infectious diseases) has gone three decades without hearing of any cases of infection from raw cows'- or goats'-milk cheeses. Against that there were cases of multiple infection from pasteurised creamery cheeses made by the most modern methods in Australia and New Zealand in the earlier part of that period. Other industrial Brie (including Le Président) was listed as infested with *Listeria monocytogenes* in late 1987, but raw-milk cheeses have been notably resistant to this trouble.

# Fromages cendrés and Chaource

On a recent visit to the Brie region, I went to Brie Champenoise in the Marne. I wanted to bring myself up to date about local Brie practices, and to see whether the old *fromages cendrés* of the region were still around. From Rocroi in the Ardennes through Heiltz-le-Maurupt in the Marne to Les Riceys in the Aube (and, beyond Champagne, to Aisy in Burgundy), there was a traditional farm practice similar to that of the Orléanais: in the flush season, cheeses were stored in wood ash to be available for extra demand in harvest and *vendange*, and for the cheeseless days of winter. The farm economy usually required at least the top of the cream to be taken off the milk for other purposes before it went into the cheese; so 30–40 per cent was the normal level of *matières grasses* in the surplus which found its way to market, and in *artisanal* cheese which imitated the farm cheese to meet unsatisfied demand.

Another source of *cendré* cheeses now, I find, is the *laiterie* making other types (for example, Brie here, Époisses in Burgundy). There is a considerable saving of milk during spring, when it is so rich that less is needed to attain the standard weight of cheese. There is milk enough left over to make other local specialities, including the *cendré*.

We approached Brie on this occasion from Burgundy through the Aube. As we drove north, the woods became fewer and fewer, and on that late spring day scarcely a cow was to be seen over a stretch of 30 kilometres. In some of the denuded areas strip-cultivation was the pattern, so why had farmers gone to the expense of removing all the trees and natural field-boundaries?

Suddenly we were into the *vignoble* of Champagne, faced with slopes defended by an army of vines in slim, straight lines, perfectly dressed, almost oppressively so; but, in the spaces between the vineyards, countryside survived, with substantial and handsome villages. Their tidiness, apart from a few crumbling barns, had none of the industrial-cum-suburban desolation of those villages which should have been oases in the desert we had just crossed. Buildings were full of colour and decorative touches: stone-faced brick had lattice-work patterns; some shutters painted with diagonal zebra stripes meeting to make squares within squares resting on corners when the shutters were closed; blue shutters weathering to pale Wedgwood setting off rose-coloured brick; brick-and-stone surrounded façades of old mortar and stucco, which wore so much more happily than shabby concrete. A delectable variation is to be found at Possesse, where timber is still predominant on many house-fronts.

We stopped at the Lion d'Or at Montmort-Lucy and finished an agreeable dinner with three cheeses. The fine, fat Maroilles, was *à point* right through. A rather salty young Chaource was only too typical of the pasteurised *laitier* cheese which is allowed by its 1977 AOC.

Chaource* is a cheese of the Champagne Humide, close to the Burgundy border. The local cattle are Brunes des Alpes, Frisonne françaises and Tachetées de l'Est. Pierre Androuët thinks the cheese may have originated at the *abbaye* of Pontigny. Its roots certainly go a long way back in history, as it was the favourite cheese of Louis X's queen, Marguerite de Bourgogne, whose mother was the comtesse Jeanne Première de Champagne. Unfortunately for the Chaource trade, Marguerite's indiscretions with Enguerrand de Marigny at the Tour de Nesle, the Bourgogne ducal town house in Paris, led to her execution in 1315 at the age of twenty-five, and that of Enguerrand. The cheese was presented not long after at Chaource to Charles le Bel, the last of the Capet direct line to rule over France (he died in 1328).

In making Chaource, the milk is allowed to ripen naturally before renneting, after which the *caillage* takes about twenty-four hours. After draining slowly in perforated wooden hoops, it should be removed and lightly salted, dried on wooden shelving in the *hâloir*, then matured for at least fourteen days on rye straw. A thoroughly and evenly ripened Chaource is a rarity: it is a difficult cheese to bring to full fruition because of its deep

*Chaource is also covered on pp. 346–7.

coat and broad, drum-like shape. It ripens from under the mould-coat inwards, and the ripening process has a long way to go to reach the centre.

There are some good *lait cru* cheeses made by Hugerot and distributed by Rouzaire, and some made on the farm in the *commune* of Chaource (obtainable from Monsieur Millet of Ervy-le-Châtel). Be patient with your *lait cru* cheese. Keep it in damp cellar conditions and turn it at least every other day. You will be rewarded when it ripens to perfection; it has a light-hearted richness and texture like no other cheese in the world.

The third of our dinner cheeses at Montmort was the local *cendré*, on the dry side with its bare 30 per cent of *matières grasses*, but pleasant. Some people remove the *cendres*, but I find them as essential as the crust on bread.

## CHEESEMAKING AT BAYE

The next morning we drove 10 kilometres south to Baye, to find the Fromagerie Pichelin et Genou, where our *cendré* was made. The dairy is not marked on the highway, but you cannot miss the *château* and the Tour de Charité, east of the road towards Sézanne. Opposite, up a slope, is the Place Berthelot de Baye, with car-parking. Penetrate to the far, southern end, through a courtyard or two as far as you can go, and you will find the *fromagerie* on the left, with an office up five steps. Local people were coming and going with their milk cans, among them some nuns, Sœurs de Jésus Crucifié from the Prieuré Notre Dame. The dairy sells its unpasteurised milk and cheese retail to *les gens du pays*.

Between 15,000 and 16,000 litres of milk come daily from 'Hollandaises, Normandes and about every breed there is' from nearly forty reliable local farms, much of it earning bonus payments for high quality. The grazing is mainly three-to-four-year leys, but some pastures are left unploughed for as long as twelve years. Only two farms now hand over their milk in *bidons*.

Baye is in the comté de Brie, well within the AOC region, and the *fromagerie*'s main cheese is Brie de Meaux. This required only 22 litres of fat spring milk at the time of our visit (23 litres at other times of the year), so there was plenty to spare for seasonal production of their 300-gram *cendré*, which needs 3–4 litres. It is only sold locally. They were also making Coulommiers, which takes 3–5 litres.

The dairy was kept at a sweltering 28°C and 90–95 per cent humidity. The milk arrived in the early morning, was renneted, and left for twenty-four hours to coagulate. The previous day's curd was cut to 3-centimetre cubes for Coulommiers and to 2 centimetres for the *cendré*. For Brie de Meaux (including the half-size cheese already referred to), about half the curd needed was cut to 5-centimetre cubes and some of the whey was ladled out before *moulage*. At 8 a.m. the moulds with *éclisses* around their base were filled with the cut curd in one operation. When this curd had sunk to a third of the mould's depth, it was completely topped up with the uncut curd. By noon the curd had settled enough for the moulds to be removed and the *éclisses* to be tightened round the newly formed cheeses. These, with straw mats under and over them, would now be turned three times at hourly intervals.

The cheeses removed from their moulds the previous day were salted by hand all over, with the one necessary turn to expose the lower face, and left to rest on metal grids in the *saloir* for three days. Brie de Meaux and Coulommiers from Baye go to the société Fromagère at Saint-Siméon. A Brie weighs 3 kilos at this stage and is 2.5 centimetres deep. It will undergo five weeks of *affinage*, with turning every four or five days. Demi-Bries, identical in curd to the Meaux, are of the same depth, smaller in diameter and half the weight. The Coulommiers weigh 400–650 grams and are 4–5 centimetres deep. The *cendré* is 12–13 centimetres across and 2 deep.

## Other cheeses of Champagne

On our way back from Baye we called in on a young *chevrière*, who trades as Micheline at the last farm on the west of the Montmort road in La Caure. Her fifty goats were two-thirds Alpines, one-third Saanens. She was making a Chabichou 6 centimetres wide and deep, a Crottin under half that size, and a cheese the size and shape of a Champagne cork. When I asked its name she answered: 'On ne donne pas de nom parce qu'il n'y a pas d'appellation.' I was saddened by this result of unnecessarily oppressive bureaucracy. French officialdom, so *laïque* in tradition, has paradoxically put into citizens of France the fear of God (Christian and classical) over permitted baptismal names. This tyranny has been carried over into the realm of AOCs for cheese, where many innocent *fromagers* suppose that only names handed down from above are legitimate. (In Berry worse has happened, honoured names being suppressed by the Syndicat for Crottin de Chavignol, even when denoting a different type or stage of cheese. It is ridiculous that Micheline should feel inhibited from calling her own original chèvre, of such appropriately local significance, Bouchon de Champagne.

Some of her curd she rolls as *fromage blanc* in garlic and *herbes de Provence*. They sell well, both on the farm and in the markets of Montmirail, Vertus, Avize and Dormans through the week. She sells alongside her friend Jacqueline of La Ferme de la Daye-en-Brie, who makes *pyramides* and logs. There are male *chevriers* too in this lively group, where organic farming practices prevail. At Bannay, 3 kilometres west of Baye, you ask for Antoine. At Bannes on D43, north-west of Fère Champenois, you look for Monsieur Pérot. Finally, at La Veuve, 11 kilometres north-west of Châlons-sur-Marne, Jean-Louis is not only *chevrier* but miller of his own flour and baker of his own bread.

Before summing up the state of Brie and Champagne, I must touch on a cheese of curious form which originated on, and was named after, the Plateau de Langres. It is still made there, on the Champagne rather than the Burgundy side of the plateau, and in Le Bassigny, north-east of Langres. The cheese is shaped like a drum with a rounded top, and the top is depressed in the centre, forming a bowl from 1–2 centimetres deep. It can be bought in the white, *fromage frais* state, or *affiné* with washings of brine and *rocou* over a period of six weeks to three months. The curd, which is cut before moulding, is very close textured and initially resembles a firm Époisses (see pp. 347–52). It may well be an offshoot of that cheese, possibly from some cheesemaker's observing the way a defectively moulded cheese with a sunken top pooled the brine, which then sank slowly into the curd. This is what makes the consistency of Langres du Plateau unique in its richness.

The mature cheese is golden and rather spread-out if made by Schertenleib at Saulxures in Bassigny; deep orange, firmer and more upstanding if it comes from Henri Germain on the plateau (or from the Marcillat *laiterie* in Lorraine, not strictly a Langres). These cheeses weigh 180 grams. Henri Germain also makes a 300-gram Langres des Grands Clos, nearer in character to Schertenleib's. Both these cheeses are *'moulés à la louche'* and of 50 per cent *matières grasses*, but the smaller Germain and the Marcillat cheeses are 52 per cent. During the 1980s production has hovered around the 200-tonne mark, reaching 224 tonnes in 1985, the last published figure before this goes to press. This cheese of great character and attractive and unusual appearance should qualify for an AOC.

The cheering side of Brie and Champagne in the 1980s has been the growth of *chevriers*, the invention of new cheeses appropriate to the region's traditions, and the revival of Montereau, Nangis and Provins. In the 1950s the old Tournan family of *affineurs* Rouzaire started a tangy cheese of rather Nord-ish character: Gratte-Paille. It is named after a lane in Tournan so narrow that straw-waggons used to leave some of their burden stuck to the walls of the houses on either side. More recently, Monsieur Rouzaire has created his Pierre-Robert, a *triple-crème* with added cream. This is in my view the cheese which would have been most worthy, in its full ripeness, to carry on the tradition of the lost Magnum, and to be called Brillat-Savarin (not legally possible: see p. 32).

The most refreshing of added-cream cheeses is Boursault, invented in 1953 by Henri Boursault at Le Perreux-sur-Marne. (No family or parish records exist to prove when this family left Boursault near Épinay.) Increasing demand necessitated the move from Le Perreux to a bigger dairy at Saint-Cyr-sur-Morin, where the cheese is still made. The firm of Boursin bought the dairy, where the *lait cru* gold-label Boursault is still produced,[*] but not the larger Délice de Saint-Cyr, which the inventor had developed before he sold up. I recommend removing the cheese from its too ingenious box (which squeezes it out of shape) and from its internal wrap as soon as it reaches you. Place it on straw in a humid cellar and turn it daily. If the atmosphere is too dry, cover it loosely with a thin, slightly dampened cloth. It should be turned daily until it has acquired its pink coat, a matter of twenty to thirty days from the date of wrapping on the box (which you should keep beside the cheese). The golden glory of the interior and the beauty of its coat give a promise of flavour which will not disappoint.

The length of the region's existing list of cheeses bears witness to enterprise (sadly cut by the 1987 closure of the SICA de Doue); but I would like to see more of our modern *fromagers–adventuriers* go back into farmhouse making of both greater and lesser Bries. It needs doing while there are still

---

[*] A silver-labelled version is pasteurised and uninteresting.

some good farm cheesemakers alive to show them the way. Perhaps the aborted nineteenth-century idea of a school for *fromagers* in Meaux could be revived in the form of a living and fruitful museum of the traditional cheesemaking arts and equipment of Brie.

The market for French cheese is becoming more and more receptive to farm products of great tradition, loyal to old farming methods and indigenous breeds of cattle. Revival must be basic, starting with soil, pastures, Flamandes and Normandes. Are there are Picardes left? They get no mention on my 1986 list of milk recordings of seventeen breeds (the seventeenth, Ferrandaises, added to the official list at my request), but some devotee of old breeds and traditional cheese might try to rescue them.

The *affineurs* have done much for Brie in the past. One or two of the old family firms should look out for suitable farms, *fromagers–fermiers*, and cows, so that we can again be excited by the sight of cheese bearing the label Brie de Meaux *fermier*, and even more excited by the rich texture, aroma and flavour it offers, recalling the glorious pre-1980 standards of genuine Brie de Meaux.

## Cheeses of Brie, Champagne and the Île de France

### Abbaye d'Igny, Trappiste d'Igny
1200–1300g; rounded sides; 20cm × 4cm deep; semi-soft; pressed; *croûte-lavée*; rac-lée (scraped) 1 month; lactic aroma, mild, slightly acid flavour; made by Cistercian monks of the Abbaye de Notre Dame d'Igny, about 15km W of Reims.
*40% m.g.; artisanal; vache cru.*
Champagne/Marne; 56 **15**, top middle, Arcis-le-Ponsart.

### Aisy
Aisy (see p. 361) is in Burgundy, but the name is sometimes assumed by *cendrés* made further north, where a similar tradition is kept up (see CENDRÉS).

### Aix-en-Othe
Wednesday and Saturday market.
Auberge de la Scierie, strongly recommended by Eperon, serves local Crottin d'Othe (see CROTTIN) grilled, and selection of fifteen other cheeses including Troyes (Barberey) (see p. 319), a creamy, rich Chaource (p. 329), and Autun (see Chapter 11, pp. 356–7).
Champagne/Pays d'Othe/Aube; 61 **15**, R of C, S of N60.

### Angelot
Ancient name meaning little angel, attached to a medieval coin, three Norman cheeses, and small rounds and larger balls of *pâte de* Brie at the *fromage frais* stage; sold in Paris in sixteenth century (see pp. 2–3).

### Ardennes
See CENDRÉS.

### Argonne
See CENDRÉS.

### Arrigny
Square, soft, *croûte-fleurie* cheese, probably known as Carré de l'Est since 1973.
*artisanal; vache.*
Champagne/Marne; 61 **8/9**, C line, NW of lake.

### Avize
Thursday market including local chèvres.
Brie Champenoise/Marne; 56 **16**, SE of C.

### Baby Brie
See GÉRAMONT.

### Bannay, Bannes
See CHÈVRES.

### Bar le Duc
Tuesday, Thursday and Saturday market.
Bar/Meuse; 61 **10**, top.

## Bar-sur-Aube
Saturday market.
Champagne Côte des Bars/Aube; 61 **19**, upper L.

## Barberey, Cendré de Troyes, Troyes or Troyen
250g; round 11cm × 2.5cm deep; semi-soft on firm side; *affinage*: 1 month in *cendres de bois*; little aroma, flavour can grow interesting; the name is that of the place outside Troyes where the *affineurs* had their *caves* (for origins of type and variations, see CENDRÉS and p. 313). Some local cheeses of Camembert type are *cendrés*, and softer than Barberey proper. The village of Barberey has been swallowed up by Troyes.
20–30% m.g.; *industriel*; *vache écrémé*.
Champagne/Aube, 61 **16**, Troyes NW corner, Barberey-St-Sulpice.

## Bar
The old duché de Bar, or the Barrois, lies between Lorraine and Champagne on the left bank of the Meuse, within the AOC *région de* Brie. See Chapter 9, p. 278.

## Barrois
**Cendré du Barrois.** Original name of Éclance (see p. 332).

## Baye
At south end of Place Berthelot-de-Baye, the Fromagerie Pichelin et Genou makes Brie de Meaux (AOC), Demi-Brie, Coulommiers and Cendré (see pp. 321, 326 and 328–9), sold, with lait cru, at the dairy.
Brie Champenoise/Marne; 56 **15**, low R.

## Beauvoir
When Bries were commonly conserved for winter use in chests of *cendres de bois*, Beauvoir, accessible to Melun and Nangis, was reputed for its skill in this practice (see BRIE BLEU).
Brie/Seine-et-Marne; 61 **2**, far R of C.

## Le Bellifontain
*Fromage blanc* from skimmed milk (0% m.g.) enriched with emulsified cream, invented by M. Marcel Marmet at Thorigny (see p. 338).
40% m.g.; *artisanal, vache écrémé enrichi de crème*.
Brie/Seine-et-Marne; 56 **12**, low, N bank of Marne.

## Biquet-des-Hersents (Vexin)
See VILLIERS-SUR-TRIE.

## Blennes, Cendré de Blennes
Local cheese kept in wood-ash for eating after hunt or shoot and during wine harvest.
*low-fat; fermier; vache cru.*
Brie/Seine-et-Marne; 61 **13**, 18km SSE of Montereau on *département* boundary.

## Bleu
See BLEU DE MEAUX, BRIE À LA CHIFFE, BRIE À LA LOQUE, BRIE DE MELUN BLEU, FONTAINE-BLEUE, MONTEREAU BLEU, MORMANT, NOIR DE NANTEUIL.

## Le Bleu de Meaux
*Fromage frais (caillé de Brie)* in 8–10cm balls rolled in powdered charcoal and dried on wood; sold either *frais* or *sec* and crumbly for farm workers and journeymen; they used to be sold on les barrières de Clichy, and at the various *portes de Paris*.
45% m.g. min.; *laitier; vache cru*.
Brie/Seine-et-Marne/Clichy (NNW Paris).

## La Boissière École
260g, soft cheese; *croûte-fleurie* (maker rightly recommends eating the *croûte*); gentle but not dull, very pleasant when eaten in the Midi in mid-summer. Made at la Ferme de la Jouvence. (Les Fromagers de Saint-Jacques, *affineurs* of Coulommiers Fermier, Rambouillet (see p. 337), are only 17km away to W, through or round the S of the forest.)
*m.g. non précisée; fermier, vache cru*.
Île-de-France/Yvelines; 60 **9**.

## Boissy-le-Châtel
Mme Burin at La Ferme des Bleus is *affineur* of many local cheeses including Brie: e.g. Melun, and Coulommiers Fermier from Storme-Naret.
Brie/Seine-et-Marne; 61 **3**, high, NE of Coulommiers.

## Boursault
225g, drum-shaped; soft triple crème; thin *croûte-fleurie*; melting; rich golden interior. The cheese gains from immediate unwrapping on arrival in shop or house,

placing on straw (with dated box beside it), and keeping until 20–30 days from date of wrapping. It should be kept in fairly moist cellar atmosphere, and turned daily; crust should turn pinky-gold. Invented 1953 by Henry Boursault; now owned by Boursin, but Gold Label cheese is still good (see p. 317). Silver label is a pasteurised shadow of the gold. Grand Vatel and Délice-de-Saint-Cyr were names for a double size, abandoned by Boursin. Grand Vatel has been passed on by Androuët, its originator, to the *fromagerie* at St-Jean-de-Losne (see Chapter 11, p. 366. See also p. 317).
75% m.g.; *laitier; vache; entier cru (Gold Label)/pasteurisé (silver label), both with added cream.*
Brie/Seine-et-Marne; 56 **13**, 9km SE of La-Ferté-Sous-Jouarre, St-Cyr-sur-Morin.

## Boutons de Capote

Tiny *fromage frais* on sticks, flavoured with diverse spices by Marcel and Michèle Marmet (see THORIGNY).
*artisanal.*
Brie/Seine-et-Marne.

## Le Bréard

*Triple-crème*, of the type labelled Brillat-Savarin in recent years; maker deciphered as Charrol (?), Asnières.
75% m.g.; *laitier, vache enrichi de crème.*
Île-de-France/Hauts-de-Seine.

## Brie

For the history of Brie, see pp. 299–305. 1985: Twelve *laiteries* making Meaux (AOC 6,176); two *laiteries* making Melun (260 tonnes? conflicting figures); two *laiteries* making Montereau; one *laiterie* making Nangis; one *laiterie* making Provins; one farm making Brie de Meaux; one farm making small (non-AOC) Melun.
NB: to make it easy to find all the different variants of Brie, after Brie à la Chiffe or à la Loque, Brie au Poivre, Brie Bleu, I have listed them alphabetically under Brie de ... and Brie ..., although in some cases the cheese might commonly be named simply (e.g.), Macquin, Macquelines, Montfort (not Brie de ...), Le Noir de Nanteuil (not Brie Noir).

**Brie à la Chiffe, Brie à la Loque.** Late spring cheese washed with a *chiffon, chiffe,* or *loque* (rag) soaked in *cidre-raide* (made of apples and Carési pears) during *affinage*

in the farm cellar. The crust becomes almost black, the *pâte* brown, and the cheese may be kept 2–5 months (2 years has been known): a fierce affair, to be accompanied with *pain de campagne* and *cidre bouché*. It is still being made on certain farms between Crécy-La-Chapelle (56 **13**, bottom L) in the Vallée des Morins and Coulommiers (61 **3**, top R); might be found on the market in Meaux (56 **12 13**), Crécy-La-Chapelle, Rebais (56 **14**, bottom L), Coulommiers (Foire, too), La Ferté Gaucher (61 **4**, high) and at a few retail *fromagers* (*Le Brie*, 1985).
45% m.g. min; *fermier; vache cru.*
Brie/Seine-et-Marne; 56 **13/14**, 61 **3/4**.

**Brie au Poivre.** 1kg, 20–25cm diameter; *croûte-fleurie* coated with black peppercorns (one made by Martin Collet, Raival).
50% m.g.; *laitier; vache pasteurisé.*
Bar/Meuse.

**Brie Bleu.** See BRIE À LA CHIFFE, À LA LOQUE, BLENNES, BRIE DE MEAUX, BRIE DE MELUN, BRIE DE MONTEREAU, NOIRE DE NANTEUIL. Beauvoir (61 **2**, far R of C) was reputed in earlier days (before refrigeration) for conservation of Brie in chests of *cendres de bois*; it is equidistant from Melun and Nangis, no doubt treating cheeses from both districts.

To combat competition from German Cambazola, some *laiteries* make a half-size Brie with internal mould, not very good.
50% m.g.; *laitier; vache pasteurisé.*

**Brie d'Amateur.** Overripe cheese, appealing to very strong palates; perhaps subjected to treatments of Brie à la Chiffe, à la Loque (see above) or Noire de Nanteuil.

**Brie de la Poste aux Chevaux de Meaux.** Brie-en-Pot sold by postmaster of Meaux, 1770s, and still going in 1858 (see p. 303 and below).

**Brie de Macquelines, Macquelines.** Local cheese originating at Rouvres (Oise, *not* Seine-et-Marne, according to Courtine and Androuët–Lyon). It is of small Brie or Coulommiers size, more resembling Camembert in Courtine's opinion; already rare in 1973 (*Larousse*) and more rare 1978 (*Marabout*); perhaps gone by 1985 (no mention in Androuët's *Le Brie*).

**Brie de Macquin.** Brie bearing name of noted nineteenth century maker from

Nangis; purely a period piece of his lifetime.
*fermier; vache cru.*

**Brie de Meaux (AOC 18 August 1980).** 20–23 l of raw milk is needed for one cheese (about 1 l less in spring flush); weight 2.4–2.8kg at 4 weeks, the minimum legal *affinage*. Unless extra *affinage* method (AAA) is asked for, a shop should receive a cheese weighing at least 2½kg, preferably nearer 3kg, or even more, because heavier cheeses naturally tend to be thicker and steadier. If the cheese is thinner on one side, start cutting it on that side, which must ripen more quickly.

35–37cm diameter × 2.5–3.5cm deep. Milk should be as fresh from the cow as possible (a factor favouring the farm cheeses, now no longer made for the general trade). Some farm milk was so clean and fresh that a starter of part-ripened skimmed milk was added to get it moving, and to reduce slightly on excessive level of fat; 3.3–3.5% fat-in-solids is easiest for the cheesemaker, but this is not a reason for using milk of Frisonnes, which have almost the lowest level of solids-not-fats (sixteen of seventeen breeds in a list of 1986 tests; this is unsuitable for good cheese).

Milk (acidity 18° Dornic) is renneted at 28–31°C (according to season and dosage; it must never be raised above 37°C), with dairy at same temperature. Any change in temperature must be gently achieved. It rests in stoneware or steel containers of 60–80 l capacity, or in large copper vats, covered during coagulation. Calves' rennet at 1:10,000 is given, usually at 15–18g per 100 l of milk, aiming at coagulation within 2½–3 hours.

*Caillé* should retain enough moisture to allow for greater evaporation than in most cheeses, because of great extent of exposed surface. Too little rennet means excess of whey and a runny cheese; too much makes whey drain too fast, leaving a dry and hardening cheese. *Caillé* is ready when it can be pressed with the back of the finger without attaching to it, the finger only being wet from whey. The whey in the depression should be clear.

Despite farmhouse tradition, supposed to be conserved: instead of the *caillé* being left unstirred and uncut until removed in the *pelle à Brie*, it is now cut not just once, but three or four times in most *laiteries* (to 5cm cubes, where I have observed). Some makers reserve uncut *caillé* to top up the mould when the cut curd has sunk a third of the way down. *La pelle à Brie* (or *saucerette* or *pelle à caillé*) is a flat round cutting-edged shovel, with a handle curved up and over from the back. It is 20cm or more in diameter.

AOC *moules* are open-ended hoops 35–37cm in diameter, 10cm deep. Each mould rests on a *clayette* (straw, reed or wicker mat) on a board, and has an *éclisse*, a girdle, slightly deeper than the final cheese, with an *agrafe* (a clip); or an *éclisse* will be fitted round it when the *caillé* has sunk to the eventual thickness of the cheese. In most *laiteries* the *moule* also has a springy interior extension, '*la hausse*', to double its height and enable the *caillé* for the whole cheese to be shovelled in at once. If the *moule* were made rigid to the full height, the first shovelfuls, *pelletées*, of uncut *caillé* could not be so carefully eased into the mould, and would break. (With cut *caillé* this is not such a problem.) The *hausse* is inserted when the basic *moule* is nearly full; it is held in place by its springiness, and by the pressure of the *caillé* as it is eased into place from the *pelle* in great horizontal slices. (In contrast, *caillé* for Camembert is ladled into the mould in four or five doses at hourly intervals.) After about 12 hours, the *caillé* having sunk to basic mould level, the *hausse* is extracted.

The cheeses are piled in their *moules* four or five high on gently sloping tiled stone shelving (or on level shelving with wedges under), to assist drainage.

After 24 hours, with the *éclisse* in place circling it, ready to be tightened, the *moule* is sharply twisted to left and right to free it from the cheese, lifted, and removed; the *éclisse* is immediately adjusted to the diameter of the cheese, to avoid any spreading out, and any break in its perimeter; 12 hours later the cheese inside the *éclisse* is covered with a fresh dry *clayette* covered by a light board and turned, bringing the base *clayette* and board to the top. The old *clayette* is changed. After 12 hours the operation is repeated. If the cheese is well drained, with the two faces evenly moist, the *éclisse* is removed and the cheese is salted (*salage*) on the outside and on the exposed face and returned to its *éclisse* (some *fromagers* salt both faces in quick succession). Twelve hours later the cheese is turned again, released and salted on the other face, and replaced in the *éclisse*. Fine salt of 8% humidity is applied with a special hand dispenser to spread it widely and evenly, starting with the perimeter and working inwards concentrically over the faces; 3g salt to 125g of cheese is standard, 66g suffices for a cheese weighing 2.75kg at this stage. Cold weather or slow drainage delays salting. Hot weather, speedier drainage, bring it forward, and may call for slightly more salt. Undersalting, or salting of an under-drained cheese (where whey continues to drain and takes salt with it), attracts oïdium, leading to a greasy, ruddy crust. Excessive salt dries the cheese to a crumbly state unfit for *affinage*. A dried-up, hardened crust can also result, further inhibiting normal expulsion of whey, thus producing a cheese which runs internally before the *pâte* is ripe. Only dry-salting is allowed: brine-washing, common in industrial cheese, is excluded by AOC rules.

The salted cheeses, fitted back in their *éclisses* with straw *clayettes* and boards, are placed on shelving in the dairy for 48 hours, with four turnings. They are then placed on fresh individual straw mats in the *séchoir* (Brie's term for *hâloir*) at 12–15°C and 70–75% humidity. Too high a temperature makes cheese run, too low frustrates it. With the cheeses still in *éclisles* and ranged on close gridded shelving, the spaces between the straw are the only means of access for air and the spores of *penicillium candidum*. The straw is replaced whenever it becomes moist during the week normally needed for *séchage*.

When the cheese has thoroughly drained and is *moussé* (has acquired its white mould coat), it is steady enough to travel to the *affineur* within the AOC region (extended to the whole Île-de-France for *affinage*).

*Caves* are kept at 10–12°C and moderate humidity. Cheeses are sold after at least 3 weeks *en cave* (totalling the minimum of 4 weeks from day of renneting); often after 4–6 weeks, according to orders from *grossistes* at Rungis and elsewhere, usually in one of these three stages: 1. A – minimum *affinage*: surface still white, faintly rippled; *pâte* still firm; requiring 10 days or more for full fruition (the cheese needs to continue in correct cellar conditions, with straw under and over, and regular turning); 2. AA – Surface rippled, well filled out, and showing signs of colour; *pâte* moist on outside, *âme* (heart) moistening, but still wide and ivory in colour; requiring another week for full ripening, but ready for those with less strong preferences; 3. AAA – Ideally, appearance should suggest that the cheese wants to burst out of its crust, but that the crust is rich and supple enough to hold it in; surface golden with roseate tinges; interior straw-golden all round under crust, with ivory *âme* moist and slim, almost gone; ready to eat for most tastes. My own preference is for the stage just before the *âme* disappears, and the cheese should be cut in thick enough slices to give the full joy of the mixed textures of crust, melting interior, and surviving *âme*. If eaten on crusty bread, it should be laid on the bread in slices, never spread, so that the texture, aroma and flavour come open from the cheese, and are not lost by pressing down. The knife should be sharp and slim enough to go cleanly through without squeezing the cheese, and long and wide enough to carry the cut slice whole to the plate.

*Faults*: hard crust, angular edges, excessive whiteness of exterior do not hold out hope of any joy, nor does a dry, firm white interior.

Blue or black moulds or greasy oïdium on the crust, inhibiting the *penicillium candidum*; *caves* harbouring these moulds should be used for other cheeses, or experimenting with the old blue surface moulds for soft cheeses; otherwise the *caves* will need treating with chlorinated water, and the walls should be limewashed.

AOC test: to be sold as Brie de Meaux, cheeses are liable to spot checks with marks from 0–20:5 for form and appearance, 5 for *pâte* including texture; 10 for flavour and aroma. Pass marks are 12, including at least 6 for flavour and aroma.

45% m.g. (min. 44% of mature cheese must be solids including fats); *laitier*; *vache cru*.

*AOC zone d'origine*

| départements | arrondissements | cantons |
|---|---|---|
| Seine-et-Marne (77) | all | all |
| Loiret (45) | Montargis | Courtenay, Ferrières |
| Yonne (89) | Sens | Chéroy, Pont-sur-Yonne |
| Marne (51) | Épernay | Anglure, Dormans, Épernay (commune St-Martin-d'Ablois only), Esternay, Montmirail, Sézanne |
| | Reims | Châtillon-sur-Marne |
| | Vitry-Le-François | St-Rémy-en-Bouzémont, St-Genest-et-Isson, Sompuis (communes Bréban, Chapelain, Corbeil, Humbauville, St-Ouen-Domprot, St-Utin, Sompuis, Somsois). |
| Aube (10) | Bar-sur-Aube | Chayaudes, Brienne-Le-Château (communes Bétignicourt, Blignicourt, Courcelles, Lassicourt, Lesmont, Molins-sur-Aube, Rances, Rosnay-L'Hôpital, St-Christophe-Dodimcourt, Yèvre-Le-Petit) |
| | Nogent-sur-Seine | All cantons and communes |
| | Troyes | Arcis-sur-Aube, Ramerupt. |
| Haute-Marne (52) | St-Dizier | Chevillon, Éclaron-Braucourt, St-Livière, Montier-en-Der, Poissons, St-Dizier, Wassy. |
| Meuse (55) | Bar-Le-Duc | Ancerville, Bar-le-Duc, Ligny-en-Barrois, Montiers-sur-Saulx, Révigny-sur-Ornain (only old communes of Bussy-la-Côte, Varney), Vaubécourt. |
| | Commercy, Verdun | Communes on left (W) bank of Meuse only; none on right (E) bank. |

*AOC zone d'affinage*
Affinage may take place in the zones above and in the Île-de-France *départements*: Hauts-de-Seine (92), Seine-St-Denis (93), Val-de-Marne (94) and Ville-de-Paris (75); this area has harboured *affineurs* of Brie for centuries.

Sources of Brie de Meaux AOC *lait cru*.
Makers of *Brie de Meaux Fermier*: Mme Klein, Les Glandons de Glandelu near Jouarre.
Makers of *Brie de Meaux Laitier* (*affineurs* in brackets after name of *laiterie*) or 'transformateurs' (part of AOC organisation).

*Haute-Marne*
Fromagerie de Pansey, 52230 Pancey (canton de Poissons) (62 **2**, lower L on D960 and R. Saulx).

*Loiret*
Coopérative de la Vallée de la Cléris (Goussin) 45320 Courtenay (61 **13**, low 4km W of A6–N60 interchange).

*Marne*
Fromagerie Pichelin et Genou. (Goussin), Baye 51270 Montmort. Also make 1400g cheese (not AOC), Coulommiers; and Cendré in spring (56 **15**, low R).
Société Pain-Jesson, St-Martin-d'Ablois 51200 Épernay (Goussin) (56 **16**, 8km SW of Épernay on D11).

*Meuse*
Fromagerie Barthélémy et Fils (Goussin) Ménil-sur-Saulx, 55500 Ligny-en-Barrois (61 **10**, far R of C, D9 × D129A).
Fromagerie Donge (Goussin) Triconville, 55500 Ligny-en-Barrois, gold medallists (62 **2**, high 8km NE of Ligny).
Laiterie Martin-Collet, Raival, 55260 Pierrefitte-sur-Aire 57 **11**, lower L.
Fromagerie Renard-Collett, Estab. 1886 (Goussin) Biencourt-sur-Orge, 55290 Montiers-sur-Saulx. They also make Coulommiers and are *affineurs* (62 **2**, 18km S of Ligny by D966 and D127).

*Seine-et-Marne*
'Fromagerie A.L. (*affiné* by Société Fromagère de la Brie).' In August 1987 cheeses so marked were sinking in middle and running, while too-thick crust was still white; salt killed rest of flavour: an appalling demonstration of inept making and *affinage*, and lack of quality control.
Loiseau, Achères-La-Forêt, 77760 La Chapelle-la-Reine, which also makes Melun (61 **11**, high R).
Laiterie Nouvelle Bonnet-Petit, Grisy-sur-Seine 77480 Bray-sur-Seine, which also makes Melun and Montereau (61 **4**, low).
Laiterie du Pré-Forêt, 77610 Fontenay-Trésigny, which also makes Nangis (61 **2**, upper R).
Sica du Véritable Fromage de Brie, Doue, 77510 Rebais highly praised by Androuët (see Doue for other cheeses) but, regrettably, closed 1987 (56 **13**, low far R).

Brie de Meaux AOC production in 1985 was 6,176 tonnes (last published figures before spring 1988).

*Affineurs of Brie de Meaux AOC Lait Cru* (Syndicat, 1 rue des Alouettes, 94320 Thiais). The Collège des Affineurs is part of the AOC organisation.

*Bar Meuse*
Fromagerie Renard-Gillard, Biencourt-sur-Orge, 55290 Montiers-sur-Saulx.

*Brie Seine-et-Marne*
Berton/Yoplait, 77100 Nanteuil-lès-Meaux; Mme Burin, La Ferme des Bleus, 77169 Boissy-Le-Châtel; Sté Fermière Rouzaire, 10 rue de la Madeleine, 77220 Tournan-en-Brie and Rungis D5; Sté Fromagère de la Brie, St-Siméon, 77169 Boissy Le Châtel; Mme Ganot, *Affineur des fromages de* Seine et Marne, 77640 Jouarre; (SICA du Véritable Fromage de Brie, Doue, 77510 Rebais closed 1987).

*Hauts-de-Seine*
Gratiot (marque: Le Suzerain) 122 bis, boulevard Voltaire, 92600 Asnières.

*Île-de-France, Seine-St-Denis*
Berton, A. et Fils, 13 ter, rue Garibaldi, 93400 St-Ouen (and La Grande Madeleine 77100 Mareuil-Les-Meaux, Seine-et-Marne); Collet, Michel, 37 rue H. Martin, 93310 Pré-St-Gervais; Duchosal, 26 Allée Emile-Zola, 93320 Pavillons-sous-Bois; Gallois, Pierre, 9 rue Simonnot, 93310 Pré-St-Gervais; Gallois, Raymond, 50 rue Rouget-de-l'Isle, 93500 Pantin; Martin, 93500 Pantin; Roland, Pierre, 9 rue des Noyers, 93300 Aubervilliers; Société Rey-Rolland, 93300 Aubervilliers (55 **20**/56 **10**).

*Val-de-Marne*
Collet André, Ets. Goussin, SA Nugier, P. 1 rue des Alouettes, 94320 Thiais/Rungis.

*Ville de Paris*
Lepienne, André, 83 rue de Reuilly, 75012 Paris.

**Brie de Melun AOC 18 August 1980.** 13 l of milk is needed for one cheese, usually lightly skimmed; 1.5–1.8kg (after 4 weeks' *affinage*; 7 weeks normal; 10 weeks traditional); cheese should weigh at least 1½kg on arrival in shop, with two weeks to go; 27–28cm diameter, 3.5–4.5cm deep; *Method*: Renneting. *Lait cru* heated once only to not over 30°C (37° is permitted for Meaux, but normal is 28–31°C). *Caillage* (coagulation) must take at least 18 hours; subsequent operations similar to those for

Meaux; *moulage*: curd ladled into moulds (*à la louche*); *salage*: only light salting (cf. Meaux; 'light' is often disregarded, leaving cheese over-salt after full *affinage*).
*Affinage*: Minimum 4 weeks in AOC zone.
*Finished cheese.* I recommend ordering Melun at the A stage (see p. 322), allowing two weeks of development if necessary provided you have good humid cellar conditions, because to some palates the cheese is delightful before full maturity. The crust is usually more developed in relation to ripeness of *pâte* than is the case with Meaux. At the AA stage the cheese is starting to move under the crust, and my own favourite stage is when it has ripened to about a centimetre all round, with the *âme* still whitish, but moist (and melt-in-the-mouth), and the crust rosy-gold. The AAA stage is when the *âme* has virtually disappeared and the *pâte* is dewy-golden right through.
The flavour should be rich but not salt. That over-salting is common today makes the fully ripened Melun less attractive, salt becoming more obtrusive as the cheese shrinks with evaporation. The Hostellerie du Moulin at Flagy (see p. 333) serves Melun.
45% m.g. *(40% min. of mature cheese must be solids including fats); laitier; vache cru.*

*AOC zone for milk production, making and affinage:*

Seine-et-Marne: (77) whole *département*. Aube (10): Cantons de Nogent-sur-Seine, Marcilly-Le-Hayer. Yonne (89): Cantons de Chéroy, Pont-sur-Yonne, Sergines.
*Makers of Brie de Melun (AOC)*: Bonnet-Petit, La Ferme de la Quinotte, Grisy-sur-Seine 77480 Bray-sur-Seine (61 **4**, bottom L); Loiseau, Achères-La-Forêt 77760 La-Chapelle-La-Reine (61 **11**, high R) (the only two makers known of in 1987 producing 1.5kg (minimum) cheeses).
*Petit Brie du Genre Melun*: 1300g (too small for AOC); 24cm diameter, 3–4cm deep; 10 weeks' *affinage*. I have seen a 1300g Melun under the Société Fromagère de la Brie label with AOC sign, despite non-AOC weight and diameter (it *could* have lost 200g after its first 4 weeks of *affinage*, but that is a high proportion for a cheese that had not the look of anything like 10 weeks' *affinage*).

Brie de Melun AOC production dropped from 425 tonnes in 1983 to 260 tonnes or less in 1985 (last published figures).

*Affineurs of Brie de Melun in AOC zone, all in Seine-et-Marne*:
Société Fermière Rouzaire (Bonnet-Petit and Loiseau cheeses), 10 rue de la Madeleine, 77220 Tournan-en-Brie and Rungis D5 (61 **2**, N of C); Société Fromagère de la Brie, St-Siméon, 77169 Boissy-Le-Châtel (see PETIT BRIE) (61 **3**, top R NE of Coulommiers); Burin, La Ferme des Bleus, 77169 Boissy-Le-Châtel (see PETIT BRIE).

*Other* affineurs *(either using premises not at these addresses or taking cheeses at 4 weeks):*

Hauts-de-Seine: Gratiot, 122bis boulevard Voltaire, 92600 Asnières (whose cheeses I have found on the salt side, and not of traditional substantial Melun character in the *pâte*);

Val-de-Marne: Goussin, Nugier, 1 rue des Alouettes, 94320 Thiais.

**Brie de Melun Bleu.** Melun coated at *frais* stage with powdered charcoal, usually sold still *frais*; but originally done in chests of *cendres de bois* to conserve cheeses for out of season eating. Only done to order now, and my own orders have never been fulfilled.
45% m.g.; *laitier; vache cru.*

**Brie de Melun Frais, Melun Frais.** 2.2–2.5kg; 26cm diameter, 4cm deep. Before AOC of 1980 which prescribes minimum 4 weeks' *affinage* for Brie de Melun it was possible to get this cheese in the *frais* stage for immediate consumption; it must now be called Melun Frais; beware of saltiness; see also GRISY BLANC.
45% m.g.; *laitier, vache cru.*

**Brie de Montereau, Ville Saint Jacques.** 800–1000g; 18–25cm diameter, 2–2.5cm deep; methods originally similar to those of Melun; 5–6 weeks *affinage*; *croûte-fleurie*. In the recent past a cheese of 400g was made at St-Julien-du-Sault (*fromagerie* closed). Earlier I had known Montereau as wide as 30cm, but usually much slimmer than Melun (see p. 306 for recent history). Served by Hostellerie du Moulin, Flagy (see p. 333).
40% m.g.; *laitier; vache cru.*

*Makers.* Seine-et-Marne: Bonnet-Petit, La Ferme de la Quinotte, Grisy-sur-Seine,

77480 Bray-sur-Seine (77) and see BRIE DE MELUN.
*Affineurs*. Seine-et-Marne: Mme Ganot, *affineur des fromages de* Seine-et-Marne, 77640 Jouarre; Goussin, 1 rue des Alouettes, 94320 Thiais (only sixty cheeses a week available in 1987) (56 **13**, lower R).

**Brie de Montereau Bleu.** Brie conserved in chests of *cendres de bois* for winter use in the past (before refrigeration with temperature control).
40% m.g.; *vache cru*.

**Brie de Montfort.** See MONTFORT (not usually described as Brie, but of the type).

**Brie de Nangis.** Brie of similar proportions and character to Melun, reputed in eighteenth century, but thought to be lost in 1970s with diminution of dairy farming in district. Revived on initiative of Rouzaire, *affineurs*, 10 rue de la Madeleine, 77220 Tournan-en-Brie, and reported by Androuët and Chabot as 'de belle qualité' (1985). A 1kg cheese is now made by Laiterie du Pré-Foret, Fontigny-Cresigny (61 **2**, R) which M. Rouzaire says is very similar to Montereau. Formerly some Nangis cheeses were probably conserved in wood-ash for harvest and winter use (see MORMANT).
45% m.g.; *laitier*; *vache cru*.
Brie/Seine-et-Marne; 61 **3**, S of C.

**Brie-en-pot, Fromage-en-pot.** (Originally chèvre or brebis cru.) *Fromage-en-pot* started in early days of *chèvre* and *brebis*, before prevalence of cattle as dairy beasts of Brie.
1. 8–10cm cheeses, 3–4cm thick were dried for 23–25 days to become hard, brittle and strong; they were placed in stone or earthenware pots in cellar or *cave* and with indefinite keeping (perhaps years), could recover softness of consistency and taste of nut or apple. They were brought out for special celebrations, and best eaten with strong cider or champagne.
2. Purists point to the recipe used by M. Petit, postmaster of Meaux in the 1770s (see p. 303). This was sometimes covered in cider, locally called '*Goutte de pomme*' (drop of apple).
*Vache cru*.

**Brie de Provins Brie le Provins** (present label). Well reputed in this and last century, lost in recent years, and now revived: 1.5kg 27cm diameter, about 4cm deep; made from local milk (14 l for one cheese); hand-made, *moulage à la pelle*; 30–35 days *affinage* on straw, turned every three days. Revival resulted from shared feeling for tradition and initiative of M. Guy Alip (suitably president of the local Syndicat d'Initiative) and a native *Fromager*.
*Source*. Société Brie Le Provins, 77160 Provins; *fromager*: La Ferme, in Provins.
45% m.g.; *laitier*; *artisanal*; *vache cru*.
Brie/Seine-et-Marne; 61 **4**, lower L.

**Brie de Valois, Brie du Valois.** Name once current for cheese similar to Meaux from neighbouring Valois, north of Brie (see MACQUELINES, which would have qualified).
*vache cru*.
Valois/Aisne/Oise.

BRIE FAÇON COULOMMIERS

**Coulommiers; Brie Façon Coulommiers; Brie Petit Moule; Fromage à la Pie (Coulommiers Frais).** Since the 1980 AOCs for Meaux and Melun, it seems that the ancient and honourable family of Bries called Coulommiers has been arbitrarily disinherited, relegated to the rôle of a waste-basket for any cheeses made in the region not conforming to the AOCs in size, and not claiming other names such as Montereau, Nangis and Provins. I have seen the name Coulommiers attached to cheeses varying from 250g to 1400g, the former too small to warrant the name, the latter a palpable *demi* Brie de Meaux.
Authorities in the region disclaim the theory that Coulommiers differed from other Bries in being enriched with added cream, but they do claim that the natural richness of local milk could make it seem so (which is why I have put the upper limit of m.g. as high as 60%).
Dairies making Coulommiers alongside other Brie, and following the newly tolerated practice of cutting the curd, cut it smaller (e.g. Baye: 5cm cube for Meaux, 3cm cube for Coulommiers); but I should have thought the nature of the cheese would be best preserved in uncut curd.
*Sizes*: 350–500g; 13–15cm diameter, 2.5–3.5cm deep. First day: 650–1,000g; 21–24cm diameter (*moule fermier*). Caillage, renneting: immediately milk comes from cows, natural *caillage*. Égouttage in *moules* on straw until evening, when moule is topped up. Second day *éclisse*

replaces *moule*, and is tightened round new cheese. When drainage is complete cheese is very lightly salted and placed in *séchoir* for several days to acquire coat of *penicillium candidum*.
*Cave*: 'salle fraîche (et non froide)': cool, not cold room; daily attention to cheese with turnings and changes of straw. Finished cheese: velvety white crust, touched with red (and turning golden when past the stage considered *à point* by purists). *Pâte*: straw-coloured right through (no *âme*). Flavour, aroma: no saltiness, nor butteriness in consistency or aroma; fresh light nutty richness, not as strong as Meaux or Melun.
45–60% m.g.; *fermier, laitier artisanal, vache cru*.

**Fromage à la Pie.** Coulommiers eaten *frais* immediately after salting.
*Sources*:
Mme Burin, La Ferme des Bleus, specialist in *affinage* Coulommiers *fermier* (cheese from Mme Storme-Naret).
Brie/Seine-et-Marne; 61 **3**, high R, E of Coulommiers, Boissy-Le-Châtel.
Most, if not all, *affineurs de Brie* (see BRIE DE MEAUX). Les Fromagers de Saint-Jacques, 78120 La Boissière.
Île-de-France/Yvelines.
Mme Storme-Naret, Les Pleux-de-St-Denis-Les-Rebais, believed to be the last maker of Coulommiers on the farm.
*Grossistes and affineurs*:
M. Claude and Mme Paulette Lauxerrois (whose advice is quoted on p. 311), La Ferme Jehan de Brie, Place du Marché, Coulommiers; with makers in the valley of the River Morin.
Mme Ganot, *affineur* des Fromages de Seine-et-Marne, 77640 Jouarre.
Brie/Seine-et-Marne; 56 **13**, lower R on D402.
La Sica du Veritable Brie used to make 450g and larger Coulommiers at Doue, but closed in 1987.
Brie/Seine-et-Marne; 56 **13**, low R.
Chevru (see below, e.g. Le Fougéru), has sometimes been classed with Coulommiers.
Le Rambouillet (see below), is of Coulommiers type.

**Brie Fermier.** Old-fashioned 800g cheese of Meaux type *affiné* by M. Lepienne, rue de Reuilly, Paris 12.
45% m.g.; *fermier, vache cru*.

**Brie Laitier.** Seen in lists of medallists at Paris as Bries *crus* (not Brie de Meaux). Some of these are quite tolerable *lait cru* cheeses (but not to be compared with authentic, rich-textured Brie de Meaux) made by large dairy concerns, whose methods or location may not conform to AOC regulations.
45% m.g.; *laitier industriel; vache cru*.
Fromageries Jules Hutin, Blaise-sous-Arzillières; 75% of the firm's shares sold to Britain's Express Dairies in 1973; 20% of its then 8000 tonnes annual production (of all kinds) was being exported. Outside AOC zone.
Champagne/Marne; 61 **8**, N of C 6km S of Vitry-le-Francois.
Fromagerie Jean Hutin, Bovée-sur-Barboure; in AOC zone.
Bar/Meuse; 62 **2**, ENE of C, far R.
Fromageries Martin-Collet, Raival (not on map) 55260 Pierrefitte-sur-Aire (in AOC zone). This firm makes pasteurised cheese at Asfeld (Ardennes) and St-Maurice-sous-Côtes (Meuse).
Bar/Meuse; 57 **11**, lower.
Fromageries Jean Lincet, Gaye, 51220 Sézanne in AOC zone and 51260 Anglure in AOC zone (where they formerly made only pasteurised cheese), including Brie of 53% m.g.
Brie Champenoise/Marne; 61 **6**, far L of C.

Some Bries which set out to be Meaux but fail their AOC examination (before or after *affinage*) are sold as Brie Laitier or Fromage de Meaux.

**Brie Industriel.** There is a class of *industriel* cheese made from *lait pasteurisé, standardisé* which the cheesemaker virtually never sets eyes on. Pages 311–13 explain why it is only of interest to Brie lovers as a curiosity, or a candidate for the Chamber of Horrors.

**Le Noir de Nanteuil, Brie d'Amateur.** About 1kg or less; Coulommiers or Meaux diameter; 1cm deep. Cheeses subjected to *affinage* before completion of *égouttage*, for up to 2½ months: surface mould turns black, and may throw out new spores, becoming grey; interior stays moist, but turns brown or darker. Reckoned to test the strongest wines. Still sometimes found on markets at Meaux and Coulommiers (see p. 331) (and see FOIRE).

45% m.g.; *vache cru*.
Brie/Seine-et-Marne; 56 **13**, far L, S bank of Marne, S of Meaux.

**Brie Truffé.** Mm Cénéri, Père et Fils of Cannes (see Chapter 18, p. 510) and M. Paul Corcellat of Paris will prepare this cheese to order.
45% m.g.; *prepared by retail fromagers; vache cru*.

BRIENNE-LE-CHÂTEAU

Thursday market.
Champagne/Aube; 61 **8 18**.

BRILLAT D'ARMANÇON

Cheese of type described below under Brillat-Savarin, by Fromagerie d'Auxon.
70% m.g.; *laitier, vache cru*.
Champagne/Aube; Auxon.

BRILLAT-SAVARIN

500g; about 15cm diameter, 45cm deep; usually sold *frais*, although tradition was to apply name to fully *affiné triple-crème* (see Chapter 1). Made by Fromagerie de Pansey (sic), 52230 Pancey.
75% m.g.; *laitier, vache cru*.
Champagne/Haute-Marne; 62 **2**, low L N of D960 on R. Saulx.

LA BUTTE

300g; rectangular *Pavé; croûte-fleurie*; rich in autumn, stronger in late winter; made by Sica du Véritable Fromage de Brie at Doue (bronze medal 1979 Paris), which closed in 1987; the nearest substitute would be Gratte-Paille (see p. 334).
70% m.g.; *laitier; vache cru*.
Brie/Seine-et-Marne; 56 **13**, low far R.

CABRI DE PARIS

Cheese made at Clamart 1927–73 by Lorenzo Cugusi from Sardinia (see pp. 303–4).
45% m.g.; *fermier, chèvre cru*.
Île-de-France/Hauts-de-Seine; SW of Paris.

CALVADOS

See CHÈVRE FRAIS AU CALVADOS.

CANNOC

Chèvre *cendré*; the name is not in postal code or gazetteer.
45% m.g.; *fermier, chèvre cru*.

CAPRICE DES DIEUX

Originally 62% m.g.; marked then 'following the tradition of the monks of Courupt'; 125g oval; 900g hollow oval; soft, white-mould-coated. Now made by 'very modern, and nearly fully automated' methods by Bongrain at Illoud; started there in 1956 as Bongrain's first cheese, it passed the 1000 million mark in 1986, when the new, larger version was introduced. Illoud collects 240,000 l of milk a day, enough for 30 tonnes of soft cheese.
60% m.g.; *industriel, vache pasteurisé*.
Barrois-Bassigny/Haute Marne; 62 **13**, L of C, NW of Bourmont.

CARRÉ D'ARGONNE

One of many Carrés de l'est (see below).

CARRÉ DE L'EST

125g–250g square; *croûte-fleurie* (usually thick and irremediably white); or washed-crust; exception to industrial bores: washed-crust cheeses by Schertenleib of Saulxures, Haute-Marne (see LANGRES).
See SAINT-REMY (Chapter 8, pp. 258–9) for possible origin of *carrés*.
50% m.g.; *vache pasteurisé/industriel; laitier, artisanal*
Champagne/Barrois/Lorraine.

CENDRÉS

*History*: From Rocroi in the far N of the Ardennes, across Champagne to northern Burgundy (Aisy), there has been an immemorial practical custom of preserving surplus flush-season cheeses. Round and flattish, these were made from partly skimmed milk, in chests of wood-ash. A few farms still keep up the practice; but most of today's cheeses are made by *laiteries*.
Bries were also so treated (see BRIE BLEU); Mormant will have been in this class.
*Character*: Because they are low in fat, cendré cheeses often seem on the dry side in texture on first impact, but soften pleasantly in the mouth. Few are kept long enough these days to be strong, so the wood-ash coat makes good seasoning, to my taste, and should not be scraped off, as is sometimes recommended (e.g. CENDRÉ DE CHAMPAGNE). The pleasantest *cendrés* are from *sarments*. See CENDRÉ DE CHÂLONS, CENDRÉ DE CHAMPAGNE for special traditions.

**Cendré des Ardennes or Rocroi.**
*20–30% m.g.; vache cru.*

**Cendré d'Argonne.** Now rarely found (*Marabout*, 1978) but surviving on farms (*Le Brie*, 1985).
*35% m.g.; vache cru.*
Champagne/Marne; 61 **9**, high, Heiltz-le-Maurupt; Barrois/Meuse; 59 **19**, low R Noyers-Le-Val.

**Cendré de Barberey or de Troyes.** See BARBEREY.

**Cendré du Barrois or Éclance.** See ÉCLANCE.

**Cendré de Blennes.** See BLENNES.

**Cendré de Cannoc.** A goat version.
*45% m.g.; chèvre cru.*

**Cendré de Châlons-sur-Marne or Fromage de Cul** (13th C). Soft; ripened under ashes of beechwood in earthenware 2 months, very local (Viard, 1980). Said to have been conserved in women's urine in thirteenth century, and called Fromage de Cul (not polite).
*30% m.g.; vache cru.*
Champagne/Marne; 56 **17**.

**Cendré de Champagne, Cendré Champenois, les Riceys, Cendré des Riceys.** 250g, 11–15cm × 3cm deep; kept 6–8 weeks in wood-ash (traditionally from fire in which pigs' trotters had been cooked). Ninette Lyon found bits of ash got between her teeth.
*20–40% m.g.; vache cru.*
Champagne/Aube; 61 **17**, bottom R.

**Cendré de Heiltz-le-Maurupt.** See HEILTZ-LE-MAURUPT.

**Cendré de Mormant.** Probably Brie from Nangis area, *cendré* at Mormant.
Brie/Seine-et-Marne; 61 **2 3**, 15km NW of Nangis.

**Cendré de Noyers-le-Val.** See NOYERS-LE-VAL.

**Cendré de Rocroi.** See ROCROI.

**Cendré de Troyes, Troyen.** See BARBEREY.

**Fromages Frais Cendrés.** A different class of cheese from the *cendrés* listed above. Bleu de Meaux and Brie de Melun Bleu come into this category. So do Cesson and Savigny.

**Véritable Cendré.** 300g cheese by Pichelin et Genou, Baye, 51270 Montmort; texture on dry side; pleasing to palate, but salty. See BAYE.
*30% m.g.; laitier; vache cru.*
Brie/Champenoise/Marne.

CESSON

Fat cheese formerly made to eat *frais*, plain or *cendré*; or for keeping to eat *affiné* (see BLEU DE MEAUX, SAVIGNY).
*full-fat.*
Brie/Seine-et-Marne; 61 **2**, NW of Melun.

CHANTELOUP

Marcel and Michèle Marmet's cheese shop, with original local specialities (see THORIGNY, where the main shop is).
Brie/Seine-et-Marne; 56 **12**, low, SE of Lagny.

CHANTILLY

Wednesday and Saturday market (the latter more interesting). Paris.

CHAOURCE

Daily market (including Sunday); in even-numbered years Foire au Fromage third Sunday in October.
Champagne/Aube; 61 **17**, low L.

**Chaource (AOC 1987).** AOC region: Champagne/Aube; N. Burgundy/Yonne. 200–280g; 8 × 5–6cm deep; 450–500g, 11 × 6–7cm deep; drum-shaped. Soft, close-textured *pâte*, slightly nutty and sharp; thick, white-mould coat, with faint red sometimes appearing when ripe. Milk comes from Brunes des Alpes, Tachetées de l'Est (red-pied) and the inevitable Frisonnes françaises.
*Method.* Renneting: milk is ripened before renneting and given a starter. *Caillage*: 24 hours from renneting (AOC book); or 12 hours (Dec 1983 issue of *La Crémerie Française*). *Moulage: caillé* is put by ladle or *pelle à Brie* into perforated hoops rested on wood. *Égouttage*: natural and slow; there should be no artificial encouragement. *Salage, Séchage*: when fully drained, cheeses are salted lightly (usually not lightly enough in most *laiteries*) and dried on rye-straw mats. *Affinage*: 2–3 weeks for *mi-affiné*, 1–2 months *affiné* (dry *cave*); but AOC only demands 15 days from time of renneting.
A cheese of this solid shape made by the traditional methods, including slow *cail-*

*lage*, slow *égouttage* (not speeded up by cutting or pressing of curd) cannot ripen in the time prescribed by the AOC as minimum. Professor Juillard of the dairy school at La Roche-sur-Foron (see Chapter 15, pp. 435–6) considers Chaource a difficult cheese to ripen right through from the crust, because of its shape; and it is uncommon to find one in a completely satisfying, evenly ripe state, and sadly rare to find one unsalty.

A temperature of 6–8°C (43–46°F) is recommended for keeping, which I think too low if the poor cheese is ever to show life.

50% m.g.; *vache cru/pasteurisé*; *fermier*; *laitier*; *industriel*.

**Chaource Fermier.** *Sources*: One farm in commune of Chaource makes cheeses, including a 1kg drum at least 8cm deep (slightly convex sides), which François Millet washes with *rocou*. The interior is cream-coloured, and I have only tasted it in winter, when it was far from ripe, though pleasant (see Chapter 11, pp. 346–7). The farm also makes a wider-diameter cutting cheese, 5–6cm deep, which is sold with its normal crust.

*Affineur-fromager*: François Millet, Charrey, 10130 Ervy-Le-Châtel (tel. 25 70 57 28).
Aube.

**Chaource AOC Laitier.** *Sources*: 200g and 450g; Fromagerie de l'Auxon, 10130 Auxon.
Champagne/Aube; 61 **16**, S of C on N77.
200g and 450g approx.; Fromagerie de Champagne, Vaudes, 10260 St-Parres-lès-Vaudes.
*laitier*; *vache thermisé*.
Champagne/Aube; 61 **17**, 12km SE of Troyes.
200g and 450g; G. Hugerot, Maisons-lès-Chaource; also available from Rouzaire, *affineur* Tournan-en-Brie (see p. 338) and labelled *au lait cru*.
50% m.g.; *laitier*; *vache cru*.
6km SSE of Chaource.
Fromageries Lincet, whose cheeses I find too salt.
Arthur Eperon reported a rich creamy Chaource served at Aix-en-Othe (see p. 318), which does sound right.

*Production*
(AOC figures) 1980 1720 tonnes, 1981 1480 tonnes, 1982–3 about 1220 tonnes, 1984–5 about 1090 tonnes. I attribute drop in demand to disappointing cheese, so much of it pasteurised, stodgy and too salt; at its best Chaource is irresistible.

### Châtillon-sur-Marne
Wednesday market.
Champagne/Marne; 56 **15**, upper R.

### Chaumont
Monday and Sunday markets.
See chèvres (la veuve).
Barrois-Bassigny/Haute-Marne; 61 **20**, and 62 **11**.

**Chaumont.** 200g soft cheese in shape of steep dome; *croûte-lavée*; nearest cheese in character: Langres du Plateau (see p. 335). A local invention made at Neuilly-sur-Suize; Philippe Olivier stocks at Boulogne.
45% m.g.; *artisanal*; *vache cru*.
5km S of Chaumont.

### Chauny
Cheese much appreciated in Paris and praised by sixteenth-century writer on cuisine, Platine, as 'the best of all' in his *De honesta voluptate et valetudine*.
*vache cru*.
Picardie.

### Chèvres

**Fromage Frais de Chèvre au Calvados et aux Raisins Secs.** Ball of fresh goat cheese enriched with Calvados and raisins, sold at Marcel and Michèle Marmet's shops (see thorigny).
*chèvre cru*.
Brie/Seine-et-Marne; 56 **12**, low Chanteloup, SE of Lagny.

### Fromages de Chèvre
A group of *chevriers*, with a varied repertoire, make cheese in this area and sell at markets in Avize, Dormans, Montmirail, Vertus (and see baye for Brie, Coulommiers and Cendré).
Bannay: ask for Antoine *le chevrier*.
*fermier*; *chèvre cru*.
Brie-Champenoise/Marne; 56 **15**, low W of Baye.
M. Pérot, *chevrier*, is on the road to Fère-Champenoise from Bannes.
*fermier*; *chèvre cru*.
Brie-Champenoise/Marne; 61 **6**, far N of C Bannes.

*La chevrière* Micheline makes Chabichou, Crottins and her special champagne-cork-shaped cheeses, and *fromages blancs* rolled in garlic and *herbes-de-Provence*; her house is last in La Caure, east side of road before Montmort (tel. 26 59 14 26); see pp. 335.
*fermier*; *chèvre cru*.
Brie-Champenoise/Marne; 56 **15**, low far R S of Montmort.
*La chevrière* Jacqueline makes cheeses including *pyramides* and *bûches* at La Ferme de la Daye en Brie (tel. 26 59 11 89).
*fermier*; *chèvre cru*.
Brie-Champenoise/Marne; 56 **15**, low R 6km NW of Montmort Mareuil-en-Brie.
*Le chevrier* Jean-Louis makes cheese and grinds his own flour and bakes his *pain à l'ancienne* at La Veuve.
*fermier*, *biologique*, *chèvre cru*.
Brie-Champenoise/Marne; 56 **17**, 11km NW of Châlons.
All these *chevriers* are mainly, if not entirely organic in their methods.

CHÈVRES, OTHER

**Chèvre Fermier.** Small drum-shaped cheese, *frais* or *sec* liked by Androuët, made by M. B. Picard at Bois-Lamboust, near Dagny, on the banks of the R. Aubertin.
45% m.g.; *fermier*; *chèvre cru*.
Seine-et-Marne; 61 **3**, far R 15km SE of Coulommiers D15 × D215.

**Le Clos Josse.** Small cheese like slightly flattened Crottin, sold *frais* and up to *sec* (hard); also enjoyed by Androuët. Made by Michel Ludwig of Saincy, Bellot.
Seine-et-Marne; 56 **14**, bottom 7km E of Rebanson Bellot).

**Crottin d'Othe.** Cheese admired by Eperon, served at l'Auberge de la Scierie, La Vove, just SE of Aix-en-Othe (see p. 318).
*fermier*; *chèvre cru*.
Champagne/Pays d'Othe/Aube; 61 **15**, R of C.

**Villiers-sur-Trie,   Biquet-des-Hersents.**
See VILLIERS-SUR-TRIE.

CHEVRU

500g of small Coulommiers diameter, but much thicker; soft, Brie-type curd but usually sold *demi-frais*, in bracken. The cheese has existed for most of this century, originating in farms round Chevru, and featured in *Larousse des Fromages* (1973). It was made until 1987 by la Sica de Doue (see p. 332) now closed; and is made for *affinage* in larger form by Rouzaire at Tournan-et-Brie, as Le Fougéru.
45% m.g.; *laitier*; *vache cru*.
Brie/Seine-et-Marne; 61 **3/4**, N of N4.

**Le Fougéru.** 600g boxed (new); 700g 16cm diameter, 4–5cm deep; the *caillé* is cut early to speed up *égouttage*; *affinage* 5–6 weeks at 8°C and 95% humidity by Rouzaire; wrapped in bracken (*fougères*, whence *fougéru*). Just before it has ripened right through the *pâte*, and during its few days of being *à point*, the cheese is rich and delicious, an excellent centrepiece for the cheese course. Demand *lait cru* version.
45% m.g.; *laitier*; *vache cru* or *pasteurisé*.
As Chevru.

CLAMART

Tuesday, Wednesday, Saturday, Sunday markets; old-time source of fresh cheeses, and Brie market for Paris; and see CABRI DE PARIS.
Île-de-France; SW of Paris N306.

LE CLOS JOSSE

See CHÈVRES.

COEUR À LA CRÈME, COEUR DE CHAMBRY

Heart-shaped *fromage blanc*, often accompanied with *crème de Chantilly*; type Fontainebleau (see p. 333).
*vache cru*.

COEUR DE MAURUPT

See MAURUPT.

COMMERCY

Monday and Friday market.
Bar/Meuse; 62 **3**, top L.

COULOMMIERS

Wednesday (notable), Saturday, Sunday markets. Foire Internationale aux Vins et aux Fromages on Palm Sunday (week before Easter). For cheeses see BRIE FAÇON COULOMMIERS. For *affineurs* see: Mme Burin, Ferme des Bleus, Boissy-Le-Châtel (just NE of Coulommiers); M. Claude Lauxerrois, La Ferme Jehan de Brie, Place du Marché, Coulommiers.
Brie/Seine-et-Marne; 61 **3**, high R.

CRÉCY-LA-CHAPELLE

Thursday, Saturday and Sunday market.
Brie/Seine-et-Marne; 15km S of Meaux on Grand Morin.

CROTTIN

See CHÈVRES

CROTTIN DE L'OTHE

See CHÈVRES

LE CROUPET

400g *triple-crème*, drum-shaped; eaten at a few days old; soft and creamy; named after a hamlet SE of Doue, where it was made by la Sica de Doue until its closure in 1987.
75% m.g.; *laitier*; *vache cru*.
Brie/Seine-et-Marne; 56 **13**, low far R.

FROMAGE DE CUL

See CENDRÉ DE CHÂLONS.

DÉLICE DE SAINT CYR

500g version of Boursault started and named by M. Boursault, inventor of Boursault (see p. 317). When the dairy was bought by Boursin this larger cheese was given up.
75% m.g.; *laitier*; *vache cru*.
Brie/Seine-et-Marne.

DÉLICE DU MESNIL

Pleasant drum-shaped *triple-crème* from Burgundy *affiné* at 78121 Crespières, Yvelines by SCAF.
75% m.g.; *laitier*; *vache cru*.
Burgundy/Île-de-France.

DÉLICET

Diamond-shaped soft cheese, *croûte-fleurie*.
*laitier*; *vache pasteurisé*.
Champagne.

DORMANS

Saturday market, including chèvres.
Brie Champenoise/Marne; 56 **15**, on R. Marne.

DOUE

Until its closure in 1987 the firm called la Sica du Véritable Fromage de Brie, of the 'first rank in quality' in the opinion of Androuët and Chabot, made Brie de Meaux, La Butte, Chevru, Coulommiers,

Le Croupet, Le Jehan de Brie.
Brie/Seine-et-Marne; 56 **13**, low R.

DUQUESNE

**Le Triple-Crème Duquesne.** Small, deep drum-shaped cheese, sold young and delicate in texture, made by la Fromagerie du Petit Morin at La Trétoire (see EXPLORATEUR).
75% m.g.; *laitier*; *vache cru*.
Brie/Seine-et-Marne; 56 **14**, low L 3km N of Rebais.

**Le Triple-Crème Duquesne aux Raisins de Corinthe.** The cheese above coated with raisins from Corinthe, reviving old memories of cheese as part of sweet dessert; prepared by M. Claude Lauxerrois, Ferme Jehan de Brie, Coulommiers. He also prepares Duquesne with pepper.
75% m.g.; *laitier/affineur*; *vache cru*.
Brie/Seine-et-Marne; 51 **3**, high R.

ÉCLANCE, CENDRÉ DU BARROIS

One of the regional *cendrés*, which originated at Éclance as a way of keeping cheese for harvest and winter needs by storing in wood-ash.
*low-fat*; *fermier*; *artisanal*; *vache écrémé*.
Barrois/Aube; 61 **18**; upper R 10km NW of Bar-sur-Aube.

L'ÉCUME

Very rich *triple-crème* sold by Carmes (see PARIS 17).

EMMENTAL FRANÇAIS GRAND CRU

Made by Coopérative de Champigny-sous-Varennes (this cheese is covered in Chapter 14, p. 396).
45% m.g.; *laitier*, *vache cru*.
Champagne/Haute-Marne 66 **4**, upper L.

ÉPERNAY

Saturday market.
Champagne/Marne; 56 **16**.

ERVY-LE-CHÂTEL

Friday market.
*Fromager–affineur*: François Millet at Charrey, 10130 Ervy-Le-Châtel (tel. 25 70 57 28); *affinage* of farm Chaource, Soumaintrain (see Chapter 11, pp. 362 and 369).

**Ervy-Le-Chatel.** 450–550g; 12 cm diameter base, smaller top, 4.5cm deep; *pâte* similar to Chaource (see p. 329); *croûte*

*fleurie* on generous side; 1–2 months in *cave humide*.
45–50% m.g.; *fermier; artisanal; vache cru*.
Champagne/Aube; 61 **16**, low.

## Explorateur

250g, 400g, 1800g, round flat, 5–6cm deep; rich texture; *croûte-fleurie*; eaten when creamy right through. Invented in 1960s by M. Duquesne of La Fromagerie du Petit Morin, La Trétoire, and named to honour the explorer Bertrand Flornoy, then *Député* and *Maire de* Coulommiers. He was a great encourager of cheese and helped to launch the Coulommiers *Foire aux Fromages* in 1969. The *fromagerie* makes Duquesne, Friandise (see p. 332 and below).
75% m.g.; *laitier; vache/vache cru enrichi de crème*.
Brie/Seine-et-Marne; 56 **14**, low L, 3km N of Rebais.

## La Ferté-sous-Jouarre

Tuesday and Friday market.
Brie/Seine-et-Marne; 56 **13**.

## Flagy

Eperon found the Hostellerie du Moulin serving six cheeses of Brie region, including Meaux, Montereau ('sharp'), Melun ('sweeter, stronger-smelling'), Coulommiers, Le Fougéru and Gratte-Paille.
Brie/Seine-et-Marne; 61 **13**, upper L 7km S of Montereau.

## Fleur de Decauville

Cheese of Coulommiers type, made by a M. Decauville, and thought to have died with him before 1960.
*vache cru*.
Île-de-France.

## Fontainebleau

Tuesday, Friday and Sunday market.
**Fontainebleau.** Presented in plastic containers or sold loose, as soft *fromage blanc* enriched with cream; lactic-creamy aroma; creamy flavour. Method: 1. (*Livre d'Or*, 1984): 350g full-fat *fromage blanc*, 150g single cream; beat *fromage blanc* until smooth; whip cream to aerate it; mix the two, lifting as you mix; chill; serve straight or with sugar, or with fresh fruit or compôtes. 2. *Fromage blanc* should be coagulated with rennet and starter, and resulting *caillé* should be drained very slowly (naturally); mix 250g *caillé* with 1000g *crème fraîche*; it is wrapped in muslin and sold in waxed pots.
m.g. non-précisée to 60% m.g.; *industriel; vache pasteurisé enrichi de crème delayée [thinned] or crème fraîche*.
Île-de-France/Brie/Seine-et-Marne.

## Le Fontainebleue

Fontainebleau-type recipe by M. Marcel Marmet of Thorigny (see p. 338) using *crème fraîche*; slightly sweetened and flavoured with vanilla.
50% m.g.; *artisanal; vache enrichi de crème fraîche*.
Brie/Seine-et-Marne.

## Le Fougéru

See CHEVRU.

## Une Friandise

About 250g; like small Explorateur, but *double-* not *triple-crème*; more nutty in flavour; sold with dark collar almost surrounding cheese; made at La Trétoire (see EXPLORATEUR).
60% m.g.; *laitier; vache cru*.
Brie/Seine-et-Marne; 56 **14**, low L.

## Fromage à la Crème

See COEUR; FONTAINEBLEAU, FONTAINEBLEUE, PARIS 4ÈME, VANVES, VIRY.

## Fromage à la Pie

See BRIE FAÇON COULOMMIERS

## Fromage Blanc

See FONTAINEBLEAU, FONTAINEBLEUE

## Fromage de Monsieur Fromage

M. Philippe Olivier sells a version 75% m.g. (against the traditional 60%) made in Île-de-France, but I cannot concede that it earns the name (see BASSE NORMANDIE).

## Fromage Frais

See BOUTONS DE CAPOTE, CHÈVRES, DUQUESNE, GRISY, JAMBON, MELUN, LE GRAND MOGOL TRIPLE CRÈME.

## Géramont

215g, oval with flattened ends; soft; white crust; by the Bongrain factory at Illoud; which also makes Baby Brie.
56% m.g.; *industriel, vache pasteurisé*.

**Baby Brie.** In plain, herb, onion, mushroom versions.
50% m.g.; *industriel*; *vache pasteurisé*.
Barrois-Bassigny/Haute-Marne; 61 **13**, L of C NW of Bourmont.

## Gisors

Monday, Friday and Sunday market; and see VILLIERS-SUR-TRIE (BIQUET-DES-HERSENTS). Île-de-France-Vexin Français/Oise; 55 **9 10**, bottom.

## Le Grand Mogol

Small round *triple-crème*, 'melt-in-mouth' (Androuët); gentle; made by Rouzaire (see TOURNAN).
75% m.g.; *laitier*; *vache cru/pasteurisé enrichi de crème pasteurisé*.
Brie/Seine-et-Marne.

## Grand Vatel

Name invented by Androuët for former 500g *triple-crème* of this region; given by him in 1982 to M. Coudor of St-Jean-de-Losne (see Chapter 11, p. 336) when Besnier stopped him from using name Brillat-Savarin.

## Le Gratte-Paille

350g; deep, rectangular *pavé*; soft, *caillé* produced at raised temperature (see JEAN GROGNE), enriched with cream, and hand moulded. Now described as *croûte-fleurie* (with straw markings), but gave impression of *croûte-lavée* in earlier years. Rich flavour, ageing to strength. See TOURNAN, p. 338.
70% m.g.; *laitier*, *vache cru enrichi*.
Brie/Seine-et-Marne.

## Grisy-sur-Seine

**Le Grisy Blanc.** 2.2–2.5kg; 26cm diameter, 4cm deep; like a Melun (see p. 324); Androuët says (1985): 'mild, and a little stodgy, sometimes a little salt, but not devoid of character'; sold under *marque* 'Le petit Briard'.

Fromagerie Bonnet-Petit makes Bries de Melun and Bries de Montereau here, and may be a source of this cheese.
45% m.g.; *laitier*; *vache cru*.
Brie/Seine-et-Marne; 61 **4**, low, S bank of Seine.

## Heiltz-le-Maurupt

Quite distinct from Maurupt (see p. 335). Round cheese made on farms, of which many are kept in chests of wood-ash for harvest and winter use; not commonly on sale.
*low-fat*; *fermier*; *vache cru écrémé*.
Champagne/Marne; 61 **9**, top.

## Hersents, Biquet des

See VILLIERS-SUR-TRIE.

## Jambon Fumé, Fromage Frais au

One of the cheeses prepared by Marcel and Michèle Marmet at Thorigny (see p. 338).
Brie/Seine-et-Marne.

## Le Jean-Grogne

500g, round, soft *triple-crème*; *caillé* produced at raised temperature (see GRATTE-PAILLE), mixed with *crème fraîche*; by Rouzaire (see TOURNAN).
75% m.g.; *laitier*; *vache cru/pasteurisé enrichi*.
Brie/Seine-et-Marne.

## Le Jehan de Brie

Made at DOUE until 1987 when dairy closed.
250g *triple-crème* eaten *frais* or *croûte-fleurie affiné* to its heart.
75% m.g.; *laitier*; *vache cru enrichi*.
Brie/Seine-et-Marne; 56 **13**, low R.

## Langres

Friday market.
*Affineur* (including Emmental Grand Cru): Champlait-Udcal, on route de Montigny at 52200 Peigney, NE across Marne from Langres. Langres gives its name to the plateau on the border with Burgundy.

## Le Langres

180g deep drum with depressed top, leaving rounded edges and a crater: as Langres this cheese is sold *frais* (available from Henri Germain, see LANGRES DES GRANDS CLOS).
50–52% *laitier*; *vache*.

**Langres des Grands Clos.** 300g cheese. Fromagerie Henri Germain makes these cheeses at Chalancey, 52160 Auberive. Neatly moulded bright-orange-coloured versions, which keep well, if not chilled

(when they harden instead of softening).
50% m.g.
Plateau de Langres/Haute-Marne; 65 **10**, lower R on *département* border.

**Le Langres du Plateau.** 180g cheese; *caillé* broken to speed drainage and thicken final texture; *croûte-lavée* (with *rocou* now to colour the brine, whereas *bacterium linens* used to do the job naturally. The pooling of the brine in the crater after twice-weekly washings (traditionally for 2–3 months) allows it to seep slowly into the *pâte*. This gives it a richer consistency and flavour than most *croûte-lavée* cheeses, except those washed in marc (as Langres used to be) or in wine (eg. Époisses and some Saint-Marcellins). Available from Henri Germain (see LANGRES DES GRANDS CLOS).

**Fromage de Langres.** 180g cheese of similar appearance to the above made by Marcillat in the 'tradition Haute-Marnaise', but in Lorraine at Courcieux (not traced in post-code booklet or gazetteer).
52% m.g.; *laitier, vache*.
Lorraine.

**Véritable Fromage de Langres.** 180g cheese of succulent *pâte*, tending to spread somewhat, laterally; of golden colour (helped by *rocou*, but less ruddy than the cheese above); hand-made by Schertenleib at Saulxures, where he also makes the only interesting Carré de L'Est I know of.
50% m.g.; *laitier; artisanal; vache cru*.
Bassigny/Haute-Marne; 62 **13**, bottom.

LUCULLUS

Name given by retail *fromagers* to *triple-crème* cheese from this region; Philippe Olivier sells one made in the Brie region, much flatter and broader than Boursault, but of that type.
75% m.g.; *laitier; vache cru*.
Île-de-France/Brie.

LUNE ROUSSE

250g paprika (or *rocou*?) coated cheese sold *frais* (Stobbs, 1984).
*laitier; vache*.
Brie/Seine-et-Marne.

MACQUELINES

See BRIE DE

MACQUIN

See BRIE DE

MARLY-LE-ROI

Tuesday, Friday and Sunday market; near Malmaison (good Rueil Malmaison markets, Mon, Sat) and Versailles (see p. 339).

MAURUPT

Cheese in heart shape, made and eaten *frais* during winter, quite distinct from Heiltz-Le-Maurupt (see p. 334) (Courtine 1973).
*fermier; vache cru*.
Champagne/Marne; 61 **9**, N of C.

MEAUX

Tuesday, Thursday and Saturday market (Sat notable); see BRIE DE MEAUX.

**Fromage de Meaux.** Cheese of full Brie size *affiné* by Rouzaire (see TOURNAN).
50% m.g.; *laitier; vache pasteurisé*.
Brie/Seine-et-Marne; 56 **12/13**.

MELUN

Wednesday, Thursday and Saturday market; see BRIE DE MELUN. Early May: Grande Foire Régionale. *Fromager*: M. Boussion, 9 rue Carnot (see BRIE DE MELUN).
Brie/Seine-et-Marne; 61 **2**, L.

MONTEREAU

Wednesday and Saturday market; see BRIE DE MONTEREAU.
Brie/Seine-et-Marne; 61 **13**, top L, Fault-Yonne.

MONTFORT

Brie-style cheese made in very small quantity in Île-de-France (Courtine, 1973, Lindon, 1961); presumably at Montfort L'Amaury, W of Versailles, N of Forêt de Rambouillet.
*vache cru*.
Île-de-France/Yvelines.

MONTMIRAIL

Daily market including Sunday (farm chèvres on Mondays from La Caure and Mareuil, see CHÈVRES).
Champagne/Marne; 56 **15**, low L.

MONTMORT

Lion d'Or serves local chèvres (see p. 314);

group of *chevriers* in locality (see CHÈVRES), and *laiterie* making BRIE DE MEAUX, COULOMMIERS, VÉRITABLE CENDRÉ (see BAYE and p. 319).

### MORMANT
Mormant formerly noted for its treatment of cheeses in wood-ash; it is convenient for Nangis (11km) and Melun (20km; see BRIE DE MELUN BLEU).
Brie/Seine-et-Marne; 61 **2/3**.

### NANGIS
Wednesday (special) and Saturday market; see BRIE DE NANGIS and MORMANT.
Brie/Seine-et-Marne; 61 **3**, low.

### NANTEUIL-LÈS-MEAUX
See BRIE NOIR DE NANTEUIL, and nearby MEAUX for markets.
Brie/Seine-et-Marne; 56 **13**, far L, S of Meaux.

### NEUILLY-SUR-SEINE
*Fromager*: Pierre Faia, Le Petit Fromager, 108 avenue du Général de Gaulle, 92200 Neuilly-sur-Seine.
Île-de-France/Hauts-de-Seine.

### NOGENT-SUR-SEINE
Wednesday and Saturday market.
Brie/Seine-et-Marne; 61 **4/5**, low.

### NOYERS LE VAL, CENDRÉ DE NOYERS DE VAL
One of regional cheeses usually *cendré* (see pp. 328–9) for harvest and winter eating, like Heiltz-Le-Maurupt; 'disappearing' (*Larousse des Fromages*, 1973).
30–35% m.g.; *fermier; vache*.
Barrois/Meuse; 56 **19**, lower R.

### PANCEY
Site of Fromageries de Pansey (different spelling insisted on by dairy), which has made tolerable Brie de Meaux (within AOC area, Canton de Poissons) and the only Brillat-Savarin legally so called; see also VIGNOTTE, VIGNERONS, and LE PETIT PANSEY; pasteurisation adopted in 1986 for non-Brie cheeses, so may not be making Brie de Meaux now.

### LE PETIT PANSEY
250g deep drum; soft; *croûte-fleurie*; presented in high black, waxed box; first seen in 1987; by Fromageries de Pansey (see PANCEY).
70% m.g.; *laitier; vache pasteurisé*.
Pancey; Champagne/Haute-Marne; 62 **2**, lower L.

### PARIS
*Spring*: annual Concours Général Agricole. Open to the public; ask Mairie (see below) for details.
*Markets*: La Mairie de Paris, Hôtel de Ville, 75196 Paris Cedex 4 (tel. 42 76 49 61), publishes a list of markets.
*Visits* (e.g. to Rungis, the central wholesale cheese market): Robert Noah, Paris-en-Cuisine, 78 rue de la Croix Nivert, 75015 (tel. 42 50 04 23).
The following are *fromagers* recommended by respected authorities:

**1er arrondissement.** Jean-Claude Benoît, Tachon, 38 rue de Richelieu, *maître fromager* (informative labelling); Tuesday to Saturday 09.30–13.30, 16.00–19.30; Ferme Saint-Roche, 203 rue Saint-Honoré; Willi's Bar (Restaurant) 77, rue des Petits-Champs, 75001 Paris for notable *assiette de fromage*; English spoken.

**2ème arrondissement.** Durand, 147 rue Saint-Martin: tiled and marbled épicerie of character, with goat cheeses, and bread from Poilâne; Lair, 98 rue de Montorgueil: *Auvergnat* food, including Cantal, Laguiole and other cheeses (bakery next door).

**4ème arrondissement.** Raymond Lecomte, 76 rue Saint-Louis-en-l'Île, specialises in Parisian *fromages à la crème*, including Fontainebleau, and Brie; Lefranc, 38 rue Saint-Louis-en-l'Île for Brie and other regional cheeses; Pierre Lucien, Marché de la Bastille (Thurs, Sun, a.m.) for traditional *fromages à la crème*; Les Fils Peuvrier, 43 rue Saint-Antoine; tiled crèmerie, good chèvres.

**5ème arrondissement.** Crémerie des Carmes, 47ter Bvd Saint-Germain, Marcel Charbonnet, *maître fromager*, and Claude Limousin; La Ferme Sainte-Suzanne, 4 rue des Fossés Saint-Jacques: good selection, mainly *lait cru*, Monday to Friday 08.00–13.00, 16.30–19.30; restaurant for *Dégustation* attached, Monday–Friday, 12.00–14.30 (19.00–21.30 Thurs); both closed Aug; Maison du Fromage, 62 rue de Sèvres; Monsieur Kraemer, 60 rue Monge;

marble counters and the aroma of *lait cru* cheese.

**6ème arrondissement.** Ferme Sainte-Hélène, 18 rue Mabillon; *épicerie* and *fromagerie*; Maison du Fromage, 62 rue de Sèvres (6è, 7è borderline).

**7ème arrondissement.** Roland Barthélémy *maître fromager*, 51 rue de Grenelle; an Auvergnat, a Roquefort selector, and master of much besides; Marie-Anne Cantin and her husband Antoine Dias; she is daughter of Christian Cantin (see 15ème) and 3rd generation *fromager*; 2 rue de Lourmel; 08.30–13.30, 15.30–19.30 (except Mon, Sun p.m. and Aug); *cave humide* and drier *cave* for chèvres; *croûte-lavée* cheeses are appropriately washed until brought up into shop (their Camembert from Moulin de Carel won Gault Millau Feb 1986 test).

**8ème arrondissement.** Androuët, 41 rue d'Amsterdam, 08.30–18.30 except Sundays; founded 1909 by Henri Androuët, whose son Pierre instituted the upstairs restaurant in 1962 to give more space to *dégustation*. His retirement in 1986 ended an epoch, but the shop and restaurant (modernised by his successor Patrick Arena (Michel Bonnet is now manager for corporate owners of Androuët)) continue; Créplet-Brussol, 17 Place de la Madeleine 09.00–19.00 Tues–Sat; look inside, not at packets in window; La Ferme Saint-Hubert, 21 rue Vignon (11.00–19.00 Tues–Fri, 08.30–19.00 Sat). Henry Voy, *maître fromager*; his cheeses are fully matured; Maroilles is beer-washed. Restaurant next to shop for *dégustation* (12.00–14.30 Mon–Fri; 19.00–21.30 Thurs; closed Aug).

**9ème arrondissement.** Jean Molard, *maître fromager*, 48 rue des Martyrs; attractive shop; his Pont-l'Évêque (Lepeudry, Veuve Rigaud, Lanquetot) came equal first in Gault Millau February 1986 tasting: good chèvres.

**15ème arrondissement.** Christian Cantin *maître fromager*, second generation and father of third generation Marie-Anne in 7ème), 2 rue de Lourmel.

**16ème arrondissement.** Genève, Genève et Fils (Guy Genève *maître fromager*), 16 rue Dufresnoy; J.-C. Lillo, 35 rue des Belles-Feuilles (08.00–13.00, 16.00–19.30, except Mon closed, and Sat 09.00–13.00); his Pont-l'Évêque (as for Molard, 9ème) was equal first in Gault Millau test; Dominique Sellier, Fromagerie de Courcelles, 11 rue de la Grande Armée.

**17ème arrondissement.** Jean Carmes et Fils (Patrick), 24 rue de Levis; Alain Dubois, 80 rue de Tocqueville, where he converted old family *crémerie* to excellent *fromagerie* in 1970s; M. and Mme Dubois travel to find their cheeses; Guy Genève, *maître fromager*, 11 rue Lebon.

**18ème arrondissement.** Jean Barthélémy, 72 rue Duhesme; La Boutique au Fromages, 48 rue des Abbesses; La Ferme Poitevine, 64 rue Lamarck; Maurice Grousset, Fromagerie de Montmartre, 9 rue du Poteau.

LE PAVÉ DU PRÉ

800g deep; rectangular *pavé*; *pâte* compared by Androuët with Pierre-Robert from Rouzaire.
75% m.g.; *laitier*; *vache cru*.
Brie/Seine-et-Marne.

PIE

Fromage à la Pie.
See BRIE FAÇON COULOMMIERS.

POIVRE

See also BOURSIN AU POIVRE, BRIE AU POIVRE.

**Fromage Aromatisé au Poivre.** About 200g, deep drum *fromage frais* coated with crushed pepper.
75/50% m.g.; *laitier/artisanal*; *vache cru/pasteurisé*.
See also BRIE LAITIER and DUQUESNE.

PROVINS

Thursday and Saturday market; see BRIE DE PROVINS (Brie Le Provins).
Brie/Seine-et-Marne; 61 **4**, lower L.

RAMBOUILLET

Wednesday, Thursday and Saturday (especially good) markets.

**Le Rambouillet.** Flat, round, soft Coulommiers-style cheese (stocked at Boulogne by Philippe Olivier, 1986).
50% m.g.; *laitier*; *vache*.
Île-de-France/Yvelines; 60 **9**, 96 **23/24**.

REIMS

Daily market.
Champagne/Marne; 56 **6, 16**.

## Les Riceys

Market second and fourth Thursdays of month.

**Les Riceys, les Riceys Cendré, le Champenois.** 250–300g, round; 11–15cm × 3cm deep; soft, traditionally *cendré* in ashes of vine roots or prunings (*sarments*) after *affinage*, but now usually *affiné* 1–2 months in *cendres* in *cave humide*; formerly common in region, and named Les Riceys because local cheeses surplus to farm requirements and *artisanales* imitations were marketed there; usually firm, on strong side, and with tendency towards ammoniac if aged (see CENDRÉS for general background).
40–45% m.g.; *fermier*; *artisanal*; *vache cru*.
Champagne/Aube; 61 **17**, bottom.

## Rocroi

Saturday and Tuesday market (excluding first Tues of month unless it falls on first day). Foire du Fromage: end of June. Rocroi is strictly outside Champagne, but is the source of the northernmost of the family of *cendrés* (see p. 328 for general background).

**Rocroi or Rocroi Cendré.** 200–400g; round 12–14cm diameter 3cm deep, formerly also square; semi-soft, *affinage* 1–2 months in wood-ash in *cave humide*; on strong side, watch out for ammoniac element.
20–30% m.g.; *fermier*; *vache cru écrémé*.
Argonne/Ardennes; 53 **18**.

## Romilly-sur-Seine

Monday, Thursday and Saturday market.
Brie/Seine-et-Marne; 61 **5**, lower, well S of river.

## St-Dizier

Good Saturday market.
Champagne/Haute-Marne; 61 **9**, R of C.

## Saint-Foin

Camembert-size, soft, *croûte-fleurie*; with one chestnut leaf folded around one side of cheese; label claims farm-made, but only gives *département* of origin, Seine-et-Marne.
*fermier*; *vache cru*.
Brie/Seine-et-Marne.

## Saint-Paulin

The future of the small *laiteries* Moreau making this cheese in Margut and Rouvray-sur-Audry was in question in late 1985. Larger industrial concerns continue to churn it out elsewhere (see Chapter 1, pp. 26 and 48).
40–50% m.g.; *laitier*; *vache pastuerisé*.
Champagne/Ardennes.

## Saint-Remi, Saint-Remy

The name of this saint (properly *not* accented), fifth-century archbishop of Reims, has been appropriated by numerous square *croûte-lavée* cheeses, for which I give a possible explanation in Chapter 8, pp. 258–9.

## St-Siméon

Société fromagère de la Brie, makers and *affineurs* of Brie.
Brie/Seine-et-Marne; 61 **3/4**, high, N of N34.

## Savigny le Temple

Fat cheese for eating *frais* (plain or *cendré*) or *affiné*.
Brie/Seine-et-Marne; 61 **1/2**, NW of Melun.

## Sézanne

Saturday market.
Brie/Seine-et-Marne; 61 **5**, upper R.

## Thorigny

*Maître fromager*: M. Marcel and Mme Michèle Marmet, present alongside traditional cheeses their own Boutons de Capote, Chèvre au Calvados et aux Raisins de Corinthe, Fromage Frais au Jambon Fumé (see pp. 320, 330 and 334) at Thorigny and at Chanteloup.
Brie/Seine-et-Marne; 56 **12**, low.

## Tournan-en-Brie

*Fromager–affineur*: Société Fermière Rouzaire, 10 rue de la Madeleine, 77220 Tournan-en-Brie (tel. Paris 407 00 92, or au Rungis 686 84 37); *Collecteur-affineur* of Brie de Meaux (AOC), de Melun (AOC), Coulommiers, and of Chaource (Hugerot) *lait cru*; originator of Gratte-Paille, Le Fougéru, Le Jean-Grogne, Pierre Robert, Villentrois (see pp. 334, 333 and 339). Rouzaire now make *lait cru* and pasteurised versions of all their non-AOC cheeses, so be careful to specify *lait cru*

when ordering. They also make a pasteurised Fromage de Meaux of Brie size.
Brie/Seine-et-Marne; 61 **2**, N of C.

Le Triple-Crème Duquesne, le Triple-Crème Duquesne aux Raisins de Corinthe

See DUQUESNE.

Le Troyen, Troyes, Cendré de Troyes

See BARBEREY.

Troyes

Daily market, Saturday best.
Capital of Champagne/Aube; 61 **16 17**.

Vanves

Old market for Paris, and former sources of:

**Vanves à la Crème.** An Abbé de Maroilles in the seventeenth century cited this as his favourite cheese; 'also a little community there makes *beurre de l'Enfant Jésus*'.
Île-de-France/Hauts-de-Seine.

Verdun

Tuesday, Wednesday and Friday market.
Argonne/Meuse; 57 **11**.

Versailles

Daily market.
Île-de-France.

Vertus

Tuesday market (with farm chèvres, see p. 331) for *chevriers* in district).
Brie Champenoise/Marne; 56 **16**, low R, on D9.

La Veuve

Tuesday market (chèvres, as for Vertus).
Brie Champenoise/Marne; 56 **17**, C 11km N of Chalons.

Le Vignelait

400g drum; *triple-crème* eaten *frais* or *affiné* to *croûte-fleurie*; by Société fromagére de la Brie, St-Siméon (see p. 338); label is shape of vine leaf, and Philippe Bobin, *maître affineur* in Paris presents the cheese in real vine leaves.
75% m.g.; *laitier, vache cru enrichi.*
Brie/Seine-et-Marne; 61 **3/4**, high.

Vignerons

**Véritable Fromage des Vignerons.** 150g tall cylinder; soft uncrusted; by Fromageries de Pansey (see PANCEY); small version of Vignotte (see below) which is now pasteurised, so this cheese has probably changed since I bought it.
72% m.g.; *laitier, vache cru.*
Champagne.

Vignotte

2kg drum-shaped soft cheese of mousse-like texture, *croûte-fleurie;* until the middle 1980s made of *lait cru* but now pasteurised; see PANCEY.
72% m.g.; *laitier; vache pasteurisé.*
Champagne/Haute-Marne; 62 **2**, lower L.

Le Villentrois

230g round, deep drum, *croûte-fleurie*, made for Rouzaire and *affiné* at Tournan, see p. 338.
75% m.g.; *laitier; vache cru enrichi.*
Brie/Seine-et-Marne; 61 **2**, N of C.

Ville-St-Jacques

Close to Montereau, see p. 335 for markets. The *affineurs* of farm Coulommiers: Les Fromagers de St-Jacques are at La Boissière-École (see p. 319).

**Ville-Saint-Jacques.** Respected old cheese of Brie family, similar to its close neighbour, Brie de Monterereau (see p. 325).
40% m.g.; *laitier; vache cru.*
Brie/Seine-et-Marne; 61 upper far L, S of N6.

Villiers-sur-Trie, Biquet-des-Hersents

Soft chèvre; long established, local, mild and sweet (*Marabout*, 1978). Gisors has Monday, Friday and Sunday markets.
*fermier; chèvre cru.*
Île-de-France/Vexin Français/Oise; 55 **9**, low L 5km NE of Gisors.

Viry-Châtillon

Daily market (except Sat p.m., Mon), old market for Paris.

**Fromage à la Crème de Viry.** This delicacy was sold in pots in the eighteenth century at 2½ times the price of Roquefort, and bought for the Queen. In 1806, 'the very best cheeses of Viry-Châtillon' were

sold by M. Delaine, *épicier* at 7 rue de la Monnaie in Paris.
*vache cru.*
Île-de-France/Essonne; 61 **1**, 96 **27**, S of Orly, W of Seine.

### Vitry-le-François

Thursday market.
Some of the *arrondissement* of Vitry is within the Brie AOC region (see p. 323).
Champagne-Perthois/Marne; 61 **8**, N of C.

### Void

Made around Void, N to Commercy and S to Vaucouleurs; 700–850g, rectangular 15–20cm × 6cm × 6cm deep; soft; washed-crust 2 months in *cave humide*; similar to Maroilles (see Chapter 8, pp. 258–61); marked rustic aroma and flavour (still recorded in Chast et Voy, 1984, but long reported as disappearing).
*40–45% m.g.; fermier; vache cru.*
Bar/Meuse; 62 **3**, 9km S of Commercy on Marne.

### Voves

See ORLÉANAIS.

Brie
SEINE-ET-MARNE
CHAMPAGNE
AUBE
HAUTE-MARNE
TROYES
Chaumont
Gâtinais
Sens
Courtenay
St-Julien-du-Sault
St-Florentin
Joigny
Ervy
Chaource
Flogny
Tonnerre
Châtillon
ORLÉANAIS
LOIRET
Auxerre
Toucy
Chablis
YONNE
Puysaye
Vermenton
Montbard
Venarey-les-Laumes
Alise Ste-Reine
Époisses
Semur-en-Auxois
CÔTE-D'OR
HAUTE-SAÔNE
Vézelay
Avallon
Clamecy
Cosne-Cours-s-Loire
Vitteaux
Précy-s/s-Thil
DIJON
Varcy
Pouilly-s-Loire
Lormes
Saulieu
Corbigny
Morvan
Pouilly-en-Auxois
Gevrey-Chambertin
Montsauche
Liernais
Vougeot
Nuits-St-Georges
La Charité
NIVERNAIS
BERRY
CHER
St-Saulge
Beaune
FRANCHE-COMTÉ
NIÈVRE
Autun
Loire
BOURGOGNE
Decize
Chalon-s-S
Buxy
SAÔNE-ET-LOIRE
St-Gengoux-le-National
Tournus
Moulins
Brancion
Charollais
Cluny
JURA
BOURBONNAIS
Saligny
Charolles
Bresse
ALLIER
Mâconnais
Mâcon
La Clavette
VICHY
LYONNAIS
Beaujolais
Ain
AIN
RHÔNE
AUVERGNE
Dombes
PUY-DE-DÔME
Saône
LOIRE
CLERMONT-FERRAND
LYON
ISÈRE
Rhône
Marne
N4
N19-E54
N77
D400
N67-E17
N74
N60-E511
D905
N71
A26
A31-E21
N6
A6-E15
D965
D980
N74-E21
N151
A38
N5
A36
N73
D978
N76
N7
D973
D994
N70-E607
N80
N79-E62
N83
N9
N144-E11
N82
A72-E70
A43-E70

CHAPTER ELEVEN

# *Burgundy*

YONNE – CÔTES d'OR – NIÈVRE – SAÔNE-ET-LOIRE

Burgundy is known everywhere as the source of the world's most famous red wine. It is also the home of a people little changed from the years when their land was one of the most brilliant and powerful in Europe. The year 1987 marked the 1550th anniversary of the kingdom named by the Burgondes, a Baltic race driven out of their Rhineland home by the Huns. The Romans encouraged them to settle in the territory of the Eduens, thus bringing brave new blood to an indigenous people with an already illustrious history of independence, industry and culture going back at least 1300 years. The Burgondes were described by the Latin poet Caius Sollius (who was also the Arverne-born Bishop Sidoine Apollinaire): 'Tall, fair, loud of speech, big eaters', as ready with plane and plough as they were with lance and hunting knife.

From 534 Burgundy was ruled by Merovingians until the Carolingians supplanted them. After Charlemagne came fratricidal conflict and fissiparous feudalism. In 843 the mountainous lands east of the Saône (already renowned for cheese and shortly to become the comté de Bourgogne) were allotted to the Emperor Lothaire. His brother, Charles the Bald, King of the Franks, remained King of Burgundy. After his death and that of his son Louis II, Charles's brother-in-law Boson reigned in the comté, and Boson's brother Robert ruled the duché, as it became.

The King of France claimed the duché in 1016, and bequeathed it to a younger son, another Robert. The period which followed was notable for monastic achievements in building and agriculture. The foundations of Cîteaux and Clairvaux were particularly important; and the now dormant monasteries of Fontenay and Pontigny bequeathed Époisses and Chaource to the cheese world, in which the Abbayes de Cîteaux and La Pierre-Qui-Vire are prominent today.

In the fourteenth century Philippe II le Hardi, given the duché at the age of twelve for bravery during the Battle of Poitiers, married into Flanders, Artois, Rethel (in the Ardennes), the comté de Bourgogne and Nevers. There followed a glorious cross-fertilisation of Flemish and Burgundian talents in art, music and architecture.

The next duc, Philippe le Bon, inherited Luxembourg, Namur and Hainaut, making Burgundy one of the most powerful states in Europe, extending from Mâcon to the North Sea. Sadly, Philippe's son, Charles le Téméraire, perversely unsatisfied with his vast power and possessions, harassed France and other neighbours with self-destructive excess. In 1477 he was killed in front of Nancy, capital of Lorraine, whose duc he had dispossessed; his folly made him the last duc de Bourgogne.

Charles's heiress, Marie, paid for her father's aggressions. They had been too much even for Louis le Patient, who seized for France the duché, and also the comté d'Artois. The rest of the Pays Bas (most of today's Belgium and Holland) and Franche-Comté were ruled by the Habsburgs until 1678.

The sturdy independence in life and temper of the Burgundians has kept the region distinct in character through the centuries of its official submission to France. Warmth of heart combined with generous hospitality gives Burgundians a magnetism which has had a surprising effect in the north. The Yonne includes parts of the original French kingdom, the Île de France, of the Orléanais and of Champagne, and the Senonais. When Larousse and the *Readers' Digest* were doing research for their *Pays et Gens de France* in 1981 they discovered an interesting tendency among the people of these borderline fragments of other ancient *pays*: they had come to feel closer to their Burgundian neighbours than to the rest of their ancestral provinces.

Through the centuries the Burgundians have maintained a reputation for gourmandise and gastronomic flair. Colette reckoned that Bourguignons eat as much garlic as Provençaux, if not more: a vital aid, along with the native wine, to the digestion of such a rich heritage.

## CHEESES OF THE PUISAYE

Before entering Burgundy from the north-west by RN6 on a recent visit, we passed through the Gâtinais. The Gâtinais orléanais on the west includes the Burgundian *pays* de La Puisaye, delectable cradle of Colette (whose house you can see at Saint-Sauveur-en-Puisaye), who wrote of 'its little valleys, sometimes mere ravines, with woodland invading all'. Its inhabitants are Poyaudins, and Ninette Lyon found a chèvre called le Poyaudin at Perreux in the 1970s. Colette recalled: 'Not far from my village they made Soumaintrains, the red Saint-Florentins, which came on to our market dressed in beet-leaves. I remember that the butter reserved for itself the long, elegant chestnut leaf with its serrated edges.'

Toucy de l'Yonne is at home in Puisaye, an engaging bell-shaped, blue mould-coated chèvre. Another chèvre, similarly coated, a rounded-off cone, is called Pourly. This is the name of a hamlet in the *commune* of Essert, where the cheese has been made since the 1950s by Monsieur Allard at his Chevrerie des Chapoutins. He also perpetuates the Vermenton cheese. I found that nearby village almost unaware of its own tradition, but finally an Englishwoman running a wine-tasting at the Syndicat d'Initiative put me on its track, saying 'Tell Monsieur Allard that Angela sent you.' (This was helpful, as it proved to be outside his hours, which are 8–12 noon daily, except Sundays.) The cheese is a sweet, rich, *cendré* base-of-cone, looking like a Selles-sur-Cher. Earlier versions of Vermenton, not now to be found, were smaller, round-topped, with a naturally blued rather than a *cendré* coat.

## Cheeses of the Morvan

Travelling from La Puisaye to the south-east through Clamecy, where you should find local goat's cheese on sale, you will come to Dornecy and Vézelay, which have both given their names to good chèvres. (This area can also be reached via Avallon.) Pierre Androuët found *'chevriers de talent'* here in 1982, but I think they must have come from outside the *commune*, perhaps from Corbigny. In 1986 the locals at Dornecy said that all the local cheeses had been cows' milk since 1975. They are sold in a creamy state or *sec*, with natural unwashed crust, and come from the Avallon side of the village. One elderly *fromagère* was living in a *pavillon* in the village itself.

Vézelay is still crowned by its remarkable, fragile-looking Basilica of Sainte-Madeleine, but the *commune* seems to have lost its cheese. A knowledgeable character in the local farming world told me that all the traditional local cheese (a truncated-cone chèvre) comes now from other *communes*, such as Fontenay-près-Vézelay to the south. He also mentioned Beaufort, a village or hamlet I have failed to trace.

South from Vézelay in the Morvan is Lormes, where I found in the village shop some tasty, naturally crusted cylindrical cheeses. This was in early 1986 out of the goat season, so they were cows'-milk cheeses made by the Fromagerie Lormoise, under the names of Le Fin Morvan and Mont-Saint-Alban. In 1982 Pierre Androuët found some good *chevriers* here too, in the goat season. Their cheeses were usually truncated cones or cylinders, such as used to be found near Varzy.

Further south, beyond the Forêt des Minimes, is the island town of Decize, once topped by the *château* of the comtes de Nevers. This junction of waterways used to boast its own cows'-milk cheese, but this disappeared in 1942 or 1943.

## Factory Époisses, Soumaintrain, Chaource and Saint-Florentin

Going back north to follow a more easterly line down through Burgundy, we are in the Gâtinais français, part of the original French kingdom. It lies north-east of RN6 at the edge of the Yonne, bordered to the south by Sens and the Senonais. The Senonais is an old ecclesiastical *pays* now rich in large-scale cheesemaking, and it includes southern outposts of the AOC Région de Brie.

At Saligny, near Sens, the big Lincet *laiterie* makes the golden *rocou*-coated Saligny d'Or (long described as *'spécialité Époisse'*) (*sic;* the local usage in Époisses is *'Espicéen'*). It is not like the Époisses of the Côte d'Or. Similar cheese in the same golden dressing is labelled Soumaintrain de l'Yonne when presented in other forms: a fragile, 350-gram thin circle with rounded edges, or a better-keeping 700-gram version made of two such cheeses ripened together, looking like a golden-hearted sandwich when cut.

There is also a 2-kilo version, more interesting and melting in character.

The cheeses above are closer to Soumaintrain (see below) than to Époisses, but different from the farmhouse originals. When young, with their staring, white, mousse-like interiors, the best of the *laiterie* cheeses under either name can be pleasantly refreshing to eat. As they age, however, their darkening appearance comes closer to that of the washed-crust originals, but tends to relapse into slimy, unpleasant sharpness. Other *laiteries* in the Senonais and nearby Pays d'Othe make similar cheeses.

Four *laiteries*, including Lincet, make a recognisable Chaource as well, but with a tendency towards over-saltiness (AOC cheeses should be *lightly* salted). In addition its own *triple-crème*, Lincet has Délice de Saligny, subtitled '*Specialité de Bourgogne*' (where Burgundy begins is an arguable point). Still in the Senonais, but some way up the Armançon, near Joigny, is Saint-Julien-du-Sault, where Pierre Androuët found a small version of the rare Brie de Montereau. Alas, the little dairy had been sold to the local dairy giant, Senoble, which had closed it before I arrived in early 1986.

The Pays d'Othe, really part of Champagne, is north of the Armançon, on which lies Saint-Florentin. This is a name familiar to cheese *cognoscenti* and usually associated with Burgundy. Unfortunately the big *laiteries*, especially one at Flogny, buy up most of the local milk. The old farmhouse Saint-Florentins, with their reddish-brown washed crusts, have been almost, if not entirely supplanted in the 1980s by factory cheese. The *rocou*-coated industrial versions vary in consistency from mousse to blancmange. Total production of Saint-Florentin was 368 tonnes in 1980, but the figures have since been hidden in shameful secrecy. The cheeses tend to be sold very young, sometimes virtually *en faisselle*, like one presented in plastic by Senoble at Joigny.

## Farmhouse Soumaintrain and Chaource

Between Saint-Florentin and Ervy-le-Châtel lies the village of Soumaintrain, which harbours two genuine farmhouse makers of that cheese among the fifty or so inhabitants. They wash their 250-gram Soumaintrain in brine every other day for between six and eight weeks. The crust develops in the last few weeks from a crinkly greyish-yellow to a ruddier hue. The flavour becomes 'pretty strong', according to François Millet of Ervy, who was apologetic for offering me only three-quarter-ripe cheeses in the market at Semur-en-Auxois.

Monsieur Millet also sells the only farmhouse Chaource, made in the village of that name in Champagne (28 kilometres north-east of Tonnerre). As well as the normal deep drum-shaped cheese of 200 or 450 grams, this farm also makes cutting versions. One is the size of a deep Brie de Melun, the other a one-kilo, tub-shaped cheese, which Monsieur Millet coats with *rocou* before he ripens it himself. The flavour was pleasant, and the interior kept for over two weeks; but it was more like a good *sec* goat cheese, although creamier in colour: it had not the melting, slightly clotted quality of the plain *croûte-fleurie* cheese at its best. True, this was in mid-winter, not the ideal time for Chaource; but it illustrates the force of criticism I heard from Professor Juillard at the Laroche-sur-Foron Dairy School: the centre of the *pâte* is too remote from the crust for the cheese to ripen evenly throughout. Nevertheless, it is this very bulk of soft interior that gives the successful Chaource its unique texture and flavour; it has a lactic quality remote from Brie and Camembert, slightly reminiscent of the cheeses in the Vallée de Bray but, when authentic, much less salty.

The probable origin of Chaource in Pierre Androuët's opinion is the Abbaye de Pontigny, offshoot of Cîteaux, which was founded in 1114 on a site where three episcopal sees and three comtés meet. It was said that if the three bishops and the three counts dined on the bridge, they were all on their own land; the monastery benefited from their combined patronage. The *abbaye* was later a refuge for Thomas à Becket, Stephen Langton and Saint Edmund. The monks cleared land for agriculture and viticulture, establishing the great wines of Chablis, as well as the more modest cheese now enjoying its AOC as Chaource. (The Chablis label appeared after the war on impossible quantities of fraudulent, mediocre and poor white wines. The best now shines with integrity; but keep to the Premiers Crus or the brilliant Grands Crus – some lesser Chablis are over-priced.)

Resuming our journey south-east along the Armançon through Tonnerre, we get glimpses of the beautiful Canal de Bourgogne, no longer commercially active north of Dijon. Do not miss the remarkable Renaissance *châteaux* of Tanlay and Ancy-le-Château. Ancy, France's first Renaissance classic, was still lived in until 1986 by Mérode descendants of the Clermont-Tonnerre, who commissioned it from Serlio in 1546. The new owner, Monsieur de Menton, means to establish opera there with Glyndebourne as his model.

## Cendré d'Aisy and real Époisses

Between Ancy and Fulvey there have been some regrettable clearances of hedgerows and trees, but continuing towards Aisy you will see a lovely *ferme-manoir* in more kindly treated surroundings. The local cheese here, Cendré d'Aisy, is matured in ashes of *sarments* (vine prunings) to keep it over the summer months before it emerges as sustenance for workers in the harvest and the *vendange*. Pierre Androuët suspects that most of it is still reserved for this purpose, but Monsieur Robert Berthaut, whom we shall meet below (see pp. 349–50), is one maker who sells the cheese at Époisses. It is firmer, closer-textured, deeper and rounder-edged than orléanais cheeses ripened in wood ash, or the similarly coated Les Riceys in Champagne.

Gravitating towards Époisses, we were happily advised to make our base in walled and turreted Semur-en-Auxois, one of the most engaging and least-spoiled towns in France. At the rightly named Hôtel-Restaurant des Gourmets, where Patrick Recrouvreur is *chef-patron*, we ate and drank Burgundian, finishing one night with Époisses from Époisses and a red Irancy, the next with L'Amour des Nuits from Nuits-Saint-Georges accompanied by Marsannay. The marc-washed, deep-gold crust of Époisses enriches the melting, creamy, gold interior but does not over-sharpen its flavour. The cheese from Nuits is considerably paler, and lighter in consistency, but is given an edge to its flavour by the marc in which it is washed.

If you are at Semur for cheese-hunting, do not neglect the town's own great charms, nor those of the sixth-century BC treasure of Vix in the Renaissance Maison Philandrier at Châtillon-sur-Seine. On the way to Châtillon lies the Abbaye de Fontenay, Saint-Bernard's second Cistercian foundation and possibly the first home of the cheese we know as Époisses. There is a story that the cheese was used in one of the once-customary forms of trial by ordeal (was it supposed that only the guilty could not stomach its honest power?). Fontenay is monkless now, and the farm buildings and dairy are long gone; but the rest of the *abbaye* has been lovingly restored, presenting a complex of monastic buildings almost unrivalled in extent. (English visitors can enjoy the generosity of the refugee Bishop of Norwich, contemporary of Saint-Bernard, who built the church in 1147.)

Époisses, active lay capital of the cheese passed on by the monks and only ten minutes west of Semur, is an ancient village with a fairy-tale *château*, where the great Condé lived as Gouverneur-Général de Bourgogne. Our objective, the *fromagerie* in Le Champ de Foire, or Place des Perrières, is an irregular space reached by way of several alleys from the main street. There Monsieur Robert Berthaut and his uncle, Monsieur Arbaut, gave me the story of the cheese named after their village.

Towards the end of the Middle Ages, the Cistercians, having found the local soil and pastures good for dairy farming, evolved a cheese recipe which they passed on to the *paysannes* around Époisses. According to tradition it was made at the *château* in the fourteenth century. From the sixteenth, cheesemaking spread to most good dairy farms within a radius of 50 kilometres. In Louis XIV's reign it was introduced to the Court by a gentleman-of-the-wardrobe, the comte de Guitaut, whose descendants still live in the *château*. From that time, the name Époisses was generally associated with the cheese. A 1775 study of the duché by Courtepée asserted that 'the cheeses of Époisses are superior to those of Brie'; Napoleon, a later devotee, no doubt accompanied his Époisses with his favourite Burgundy, Chambertin; and Brillat-Savarin called it *'le roi des fromages'*.

Most local dairy farmers were also *vignerons* until the nineteenth-century phylloxera disaster. Their wine had no great reputation, but they were licensed to distil marc and many continued to exploit this right in a variety of styles after abandoning commercial wine growing, some making *eau-de-vie* of the plums which flourished among the vines. The one factor their liquor had in common was strength. Proverbially it takes four Bourguignons to drink a glass of marc: one to hold the bottle, one to hold the glass, and two to hold up the Bourguignon with the glass while he drinks it.

Until the 1930s there were hundreds of Époisses-makers. Some of them enriched their rennet with fennel, black pepper and cloves. They washed their cheeses in white Burgundy, in their own *marc* or in a mixture of both. It was eaten young in summer and increasingly mature in winter, leading to Michel de Saint-Pierre to describe it through one of his characters as *'une espèce aimée, plus molle, onctueuse et pestilentielle que tous les autres.'* Robert Courtine wrote in 1973 that some Bourguignons marinated Époisses in a mixture of white Burgundy and marc de Bourgogne. When the whole thing became one soft mess, they called it *confit*. Pierre Androuët asserts that *either* wine or marc was used, not the two together.

The quality of the cheese, however, lay decisively in the *terres* with the *charmoutien inférieur* subsoil. The same farmlands provided pastures and milk for prizewinning cheeses year after year, generation after generation. Then, under the impact of war, cheesemaking here virtually ceased.

Up to about 1930 *la grande blanche*, the original white Burgundy dairy breed, was still converting these pastures into good milk for the cheese. In the 1930s breeders started putting Simmental bulls to selected Burgundy dams to raise milk yield and produce more side-profit from beefier bull calves. Thus evolved the Tachetée de l'Est, a brown-flecked cow, paler, deeper-bodied and stouter in the leg than the famous Montbéliarde. More like a beef animal to look at, this is the modern dairy breed of Burgundy; but the pastures are dominated by the white of the Charollais, the beef offshoot of the old Burgundian breed. Sadly, today there are more Frisonnes to be seen than natives; this has lowered the standard of the regrettably small quantity of milk now devoted to cheese. Nevertheless, if you avert your eyes from the black-and-white intruders, much of this Burgundy landscape retains the character of the glorious illustrations in the duc de Berry's *Très Riches Heures*.

Robert Berthaut's family have been farming at Époisses for generations. He took over the farm in 1955, determined to revive the almost defunct local cheese. For three or four years he increased his herd to cope with demand and then, as he put it, 'the cheese took over'. The comte de Guitaut had small dairy premises 100 metres from the *château* in the Champ de Foire, where an excellent Gruyère had been made up to 1939. ('If only they had milk like that in Switzerland', was the local comment at the time.) Once installed here, Berthaut could expand production to meet the unsatisfied demand for genuine Époisses, of which he was for some years the only significant producer. In 1985 he was converting larger premises in the same unchanged quarter of Époisses to meet the need for still higher output.

Before the new dairy was ready he was using 5000 litres of milk a day from over forty farms, reliable enough in their standards for him to collect by tanker and still have no need to pasteurise. Like so many *laitiers*, the Berthauts pay attention to the source of their milk and discourage chemical fertilisers.

The milk arrives at 6.30 a.m. and is allowed about six hours to reach naturally the appropriate degree of acidity, at which point a few drops of rennet are added. The milk is then left to coagulate slowly for twenty to twenty-four hours before the curd is hand-moulded, further drained, and salted by hand (brine is less suitable at this point). Each cheese needs 2 litres of milk.

The cheeses are weighed for excess humidity and left until the third day before spending twenty-four hours in the *séchoir*. From here they are taken to the *caves*, where they are wiped and washed twice a week with *very* lightly salted water. After three weeks they begin to turn yellow. *Bacterium linens* is attracted to the surface of the cheese and encouraged by the washing, reddening the crust. In the final stages the cheeses are washed two or three times a week in marc. They are too fragile for any machine treatment.

The Berthaut dairy also makes a larger version of the cheese, using 6 litres of milk, called Perrière d'Époisses, which can be ordered in a less-ripened state as Perrière d'Époisses Export. Sealed in a wooden case with a cardboard sleeve as it leaves the *cave*, this cheese has enough air to allow its full ripening during the period of travel and storage before sale.

Five to six weeks after making, the standard 250-gram Époisses are wrapped in imitation vine leaves and boxed individually for despatch. They should be kept in the box and turned two or three times a week (daily in unavoidably warm circumstances) until they are ready to eat at two months. Too often, because it is kept too cold, or because of the desire for quicker profit, or through heedless impatience or sheer ignorance, Époisses is sold and cut when unready. There are then complaints that 'the Époisses aren't ripening properly at the moment', an injustice to a cheese of great integrity and merit. Those who buy and sell in the trade should know their stock well enough not to chill it, and to hold it back when cold weather slows down its development. The Berthauts set an example at Époisses by inviting customers with special celebrations ahead to order three weeks in advance, so that they can have an *'affinage personnalisé'* and thus enjoy it in its perfect state.

The future of Époisses now seems assured. The Berthauts, father and son, and a handful of others, farmers and artisans, have arrested the tendency towards extinction; and the export market has opened up, towards which I have done my bit in England. Production increased by 17 per cent in 1982 (the last national figures available to me) to over 1000 tonnes. Monsieur Arbaut, living in his beautiful old family house in Époisses after years overseas, is looking forward two generations. He has held on to the pastures of his family farms in the hope that they will be a source of milk for Époisses when his grandson is old enough to take them on.

It would be a service to French gastronomy if the ancient and noble name of Époisses were legally protected. Its use should be confined to cheeses within the traditional range of sizes, made from raw whole milk from farms within a prescribed area around Époisses. Rules should specify traditional methods, including washing in marc de Bourgogne, other local *eau-de-vie*, or white Burgundy; and a minimum period of *affinage* should be established.

We were recommended to the Hôtel du Lac, near Semur, run by the Laurençons, in whose blood run farming and Époisses-making. Monsieur Laurençon's mother used to make Époisses, and Madame Laurençon's family farmed the same land near Dijon for three centuries. Like the Berthauts, Madame Laurençon regrets that this fine dairy country is not fulfilling its best role, while less suitable parts of France produce indifferent milk and cheese in plenty. The Époisses we ate at the hotel, a little deeper and narrower than Berthaut's, is made by Monsieur Boix at nearby Précy-sous-Thil. We liked it (it is now stocked at Streatley), but Madame Laurençon considered it nearer to Langres du Plateau in taste. We drank with it a beautiful 1983 Bourgogne Aligoté from Henri-Naudin-Ferrand at Magny-lès-Villiers, Nuits-Saint-Georges. It had a broad rich flavour with none of the hardness which spoils some Aligotés.

In Semur market the next morning we found an excellent small, upright cylindrical chèvre ripened for one week in summer and a little longer in cooler weather. Neither sharp nor salty, it had an encouraging flavour, owing some of its richness to an eminently edible pinky-gold crust. Madame Muel made this cheese by hand from the milk of her Alpine goats, and also a fresh goat curd presented *en faisselle*, at La Ferme de Barain at Vitteaux. Her market neighbour, Madame Jadot, from Marcilly-lès-Vitteaux, was selling a refreshing one-month-matured *fromage de vache fermier*, Époisses-shaped but larger, using 4–4½ litres of milk, and washed only in brine once a week. Both these makers sell on their farms and at other markets (see list, p. 364).

Beside them was Madame Jacob of Souhey, with her beautiful rich but not sharp farmhouse Époisses. Its consistency was moist and slightly flaky, its crust melting. Probably made more quickly than Berthaut's, it is marc-washed only in its last week of ripening. Madame Jacob is at Semur market on Thursdays and Saturdays.

Other Époisses-makers include J. Delin at Gilly-lès-Citeaux, Henry Germain at Chalancey (recommended by Henry Viard) and Jean Gaugry at Brochon, outside Gevry-Chambertin. Jean Gaugry pasteurises his milk, and makes the marc-ripened Ami du Chambertin. The Paris *maître fromager* Jacques Vernier admires this cheese, but we have found it unpalatably salt and stodgy, although our tastings included a cheese bought at the Gaugry dairy itself. Jean Millet, the *affineur* of Burgundy and Champagne cheeses, told me later that he likes Gaugry's Époisses, but I am not clear from the same maker's description of L'Ami du Chambertin whether there is any distinction between the cheeses sold under the two labels. One account of L'Ami credits it with being washed in Chambertin, but this is not claimed on any of the labels I have seen and is not the case.

The colour of the powdery, gold-coated factory cheeses called Époisses, made further north, comes from *rocou*, not from traditional methods of washing in brine and *marc*, and their consistency in youth is that of a fluffy white mousse. Very refreshing in this state, they sometimes acquire a runny surface and an interesting richness with age or in hot weather; but generally their advanced state is stodgy, not appetising. The connoisseurs of the Époisses world do not regard them as worthy of the name.

Cheeses related to Époisses in methods of making, but usually larger, have been made in the Auxois under local names such as Alésia, Alise-Sainte-Reine, Les Laumes, and Sainte-Marie. Les Laumes, the best known, weighing up to a kilo, is sold *frais* in summer, or matured for up to three months with crust washed sometimes in wine. Alise-Sainte-Reine is similar. Sainte-Marie (not to be confused with the small chèvre related to Sainte-Saulge in the Nièvre) is in the form of base of cone less than half the weight of Les Laumes, and sold fresh; it has been made around Alésia and Venarey-lès-Laumes. All these cheeses have been reported as 'disappearing' in the 1980s, but Les Laumes, Alise-Sainte-Reine and Sainte-Marie survived on the Burgundy list issued by the Guilde des Fromagers for the 1987 Foire Internationale et Gastronomique de Dijon.

My last word on Époisses is a true story with a horrible warning, told me by someone born into the farming and cheese traditions of this region and still actively in touch with it. To avoid opening any wounds or prejudicing an impeccable present product, I name no names. Years back, a very successful farmhouse cheesemaker was bought up by some hard-headed investors, who saw a great future for his Époisses in an under-supplied market. Unfortunately for them, they did not understand the dependence of the genuine, palatable article on absolute patience with natural development of the curd, and on its delicate treatment by hand in the later stages of making. The cheeses, when made on a large scale by factory methods, were described as 'awful' and 'bitter', and were rejected by the customers. So the industrial business failed. The happy ending is that the original cheesemaker, licking his financial wounds, resumed his craft in its traditional form and scale, and has fully justified the first rosy forecast of success. My informant summed it up: 'You cannot make Époisses *en gros.*'

## La-Pierre-Qui-Vire

Between Époisses and Saint-Lèger-Vauban, where I had a monastic rendezvous in prospect, the well-wooded countryside harbours abundant wild flowers, birds and butterflies. I revelled in this evidence of natural farming with particular satisfaction after hearing from Frère Jean-Noël the history of farming and dairying at the Abbaye de Sainte-Marie de la Pierre-Qui-Vire.

In 1938, anticipating the approaching war, the monastery bought the nearby hillside mixed farm, L'Huis Saint-Benoît. The 60 hectares were to provide milk and cheese for the monks. A dairy was set up by the late Père Ansschaire, who invented the cheese called La Pierre-Qui-Vire ('the stone that turns', a local megalith), like an innocent version of Époisses. (When I asked Frère Jean-Noël whether they ever washed their cheeses in alcohol, he answered simply: 'No, we prefer to drink that separately.')

Ten years after the war it was decided to expand the dairy side of the farm, and by the 1960s the fashion for intensive dairy farming had reached the *abbaye*, which naturally wanted to make the most of its limited pastures. Experts prescribed chemical spraying, massive applications of chemical fertilisers, to achieve higher milk yields. On the same advice, most of the original Brunes des Alpes of 1962 were replaced by Frisonnes before 1967. Modern cow-houses were built in 1964 in order to save greatly on space and straw.

By 1969, Père Jean-Noël said, the effects were catastrophic. The whole dairy herd was sick, and the milk was not only unusable for cheese, but undrinkable. Veterinary advice was to put down the herd, rest the land, and start again later from scratch. This was more than the Community could afford, but they at once had daily veterinary visits to the animals, and completely abandoned the use of chemicals on the farm. Within six months they saw a remarkable improvement in cattle and milk, from which they have never looked back. The Frisonnes had needed twice as much veterinary attention as the tougher, more local Brunes des Alpes, which became once more the only breed at La Pierre-Qui-Vire. By 1978 their yield was 10 per cent higher than the best pre-crisis yield of the mixed herd and almost twice the yield of the crisis years.

The leaflet distributed by the *abbaye* with its cheeses reads: 'Cheese guaranteed to be from unpasteurised whole milk solely from the herd of the Abbaye de la Pierre-Qui-Vire, managed since 1969 on organic lines without chemical fertilisers or pesticides.' The *abbaye* emphasises that it farms organically now for essentially practical, not religious reasons. When I was there, the thirty cows of their herd of eighty in milk were averaging a daily 23 litres per cow.

The curd is drained over a period of forty-eight hours, indicating patience and integrity. The basic cheese, of small Époisses size, coloured with *rocou* and brine-washed, is sold either *frais* or *affiné*, as La Pierre-Qui-Vire. A larger, cutting version of 1200 grams is called Le Trinquelin (a local place-name). Some of the fresh curd is rolled with *fines-herbes* into a ball of 150–200 grams and labelled La Boule des Moines (usually listed by shops and books as La Boulette de La Pierre-Qui-Vire). All these cheeses are marketed as *fromages fermiers* with the level of *matières grasses* unspecified. They are sold in shops and markets at Accolay, Auxerre, Avallon, Looze, Vermenton and Joigny, and distributed from Rungis (see pp. 360–1). They provide half the *abbaye*'s income, which should make the abbots and abbesses of cheeseless communities sit up and take notice.

## Triples-crèmes at Saint-Jean-de-Losne

South-west of Dijon on the Saône and the Canal de Bourgogne (with connections to north-east and south-east) is the important canal port of Saint-Jean-de-Losne, the smallest *commune* in the Côte d'Or. We went there in search of the well-hidden dairy of André Coudor, tucked away up a little lane behind the red-brick and stone sixteenth-century church, on rue Fénélon. Coudor Père had made Camembert and Carré de l'Est there since the 1920s, and in 1973 his son André started making a 500-gram *triple-crème* soft cheese which won awards at several Concours Généraux Agricoles in Paris, and in 1978 the silver medal for Burgundian exporters. He called it Brillat-Savarin, a name first applied to such cheese by Henri Androuët between the wars. The name was finally absorbed by the large concern of Besnier, who exerted their exclusive right to its use in the late 1970s. (Brillat-Savarin is now made of *lait cru* at Pancey in Champagne; see Chapter 10.)* The Fromagerie Overney of Saulieu devised the name Brivarin for their *triple-crème*, and André Coudor was rescued in 1982 by Pierre Androuët's suggestion that he use the name Vatel, which he (Androuët) had

---

*Pasteurisation has now taken over.

applied before 1939 to similar cheeses he sold from various makers. (Vatel was the great chef who took his own life after gravely under-ordering the raw materials for a banquet given by the Prince de Condé for Louis XIV. Coudor's Brillat-Savarin-sized cheese is called Grand Vatel, his half-size is Prestige de Bourgogne, and his miniature of 125 grams is Petit Vatel. He has recently added Le Super Grand Vatel of 1500 grams as a cutting cheese.

In 1985 the *laiterie* was receiving 1500 litres of milk and 300 litres of extra cream daily, supplies not threatened by the EEC milk quota. The milk is pasteurised on arrival, but not renneted until 5 p.m. At 8 a.m. the next day, the curd is ladled into the moulds. Le Petit Vatel is ripened for four weeks, and has been likened to the nineteenth-century Norman Fromage de Monsieur Fromage; but that cheese was only 60 per cent *matières grasses*, not 75 per cent, was unpasteurised, and had a closer texture and more Camembert-like crust (see Chapter 1). Le Grand Vatel is ripened for up to six weeks, except for those distributed as *fromage frais* at two to three weeks old. Some cheese is sold at the dairy, but most goes to Rungis for resale to specialist cheese shops. These cheeses have a substantial, smooth white crust, a meal in itself, which finally develops a golden surface. The interior attains some richness, despite pasteurisation.

Close to Saint-Jean-de-Losne is Maison Dieu, where *maître fromager* Geneviève Berger makes her beautiful Pavé de Chèvre Cendré. She also makes plain Crottins, flatter but heavier than the familiar Crottins of Berry. She now sells them from as young as three days, because of changed public demand. This she attributes to distaste for the sort of strength given to some Crottins in recent times by a practice she deplores, that of feeding goats with silage, often imperfectly made. The rue de Paradis lies appropriately on the way to Madame Berger's treasures. You should check your directions with the tiny épicerie-café, and I would advise telephoning first (see list, p. 366).

## Cîteaux

L'Abbaye de Notre Dame de Cîteaux is only a few miles from Losne. This is the Benedictine foundation of 1098 where that well-born Bourguignon who was to become Saint-Bernard was professed fifteen years later and where he instituted the great reformed order to which Cîteaux gave its name, the Cistercians. Eighteenth-century reforms introduced the term 'Trappist' to the order (often applied to monastic cheeses elsewhere). Cheese featured early in Benedictine work and diet. William the Conqueror asked his abbot uncle for Benedictines (who later adopted the Cistercian rule) to settle the border area of the North Yorkshire Dales. There they sustained the Norman troops with a blue ewes'-milk cheese, softer than modern Roquefort. The cheese now made at Cîteaux, however, is a comparatively modern, wider, deeper and slightly drier-crusted version of the Savoyard Reblochon (see Chapter 15).

The *abbaye* soil is poor: 'terre blanche'. They would prefer to leave their old pastures unploughed, but the land is too full of chemicals. This has led to an invasion of Butyrique in recent years, and to their policy of periodic ploughing and re-seeding. Their red-pied Montbéliardes are on the pastures for only six months of the year, but the *abbaye* claims to have achieved a reliable technique of silage-making. (The true technique has recently been rediscovered in Britain, where centuries-old rules, especially the exclusion of air, had long been neglected; but it must be said that the rules for several respected AOC cheeses exclude silage feeding.) The herd is 200 strong, including calves. Its eighty milkers, of which a dozen are usually dry, produce an average of 1200 litres a day.

Three monks under Frère Fromager Cyrille make the cheese and instruct the next generation of cheesemakers. The recipe is broadly that of Reblochon, but the soil and pastures, and in consequence the resulting cheeses, are completely different. The *abbaye*'s bursar, Frère Frédéric, emphasised that the cheese had no relationship to the modern pseudo-monastic Saint-Paulin, of which the curd is washed in the middle of the cheesemaking process.

Cîteaux has a delicious, melt-in-the-mouth, refreshing character all its own, set off by its fine crust, more even in patina than that of Reblochon. Like the crust of the good bread with which it deserves to be paired, it is an important part of the cheese's savour and consistency against the palate, and should never be cut away and wasted. (A recipe for Cîteaux is given on p. 360.)

Cîteaux production can never meet demand on present pastures, and the EEC milk quota has restricted it from 1985; but the *abbaye* has declined an offer of milk from outside, because it is determined to keep to the milk of its own farm which can be used raw without risk. Two-thirds of the cheese is sold to visitors, the rest to cheese shops in the region. It is not available at Rungis. If you are visiting Cîteaux for cheese, avoid July and August, when there is less likely to be any available which is mature.

As our serious business was coming to an end, Frère Frédéric brought in one of his kilo-sized cheeses and an encouraging bottle of rich red hue. The Burgundy was excellent, though not now from the Clos de Vougeot, lost to the *abbaye*'s domaines during the Revolution. That *vignoble*, source of Stendhal's favourite wine, was highly revered as the result of the monks' conscientious care over many centuries.

Not far away is Gilly-lès-Cîteaux, source of Monsieur Delin's Époisses, and of his similar but larger Véritable Fromage des Gillotins; and along the Côtes d'Or are Nuits-Saint-Georges where Monsieur Chiciak makes L'Amour des Nuits, and Brochon by Gevrey Chambertin where Monsieur Gaugry makes L'Ami du Chambertin (see p. 362).

# BESSEY-EN-CHAUME

Some years back, at the Col de Bessey on the Montagne de Beaune, a *chevrier* making a small bluish-coated cylindrical cheese called it by the name of the *commune*, Bessey-en-Chaume, because the goats browsed in the *chaume* (stubble) on the mountain. La Bâche is a name applied to Bessey after it has been made into a *fromage fort* by steeping in marc or white wine, and potting. (It is attributed by some writers to the Lyonnais.) Here in the

Côte d'Or the name Claque-bitou is given to the fresh local goat cheese when it is mixed with garlic, *fines-herbes* and parsley in summer and autumn. Henry Viard says that versions of the cheese called Autun are to be found on the Arrières-Côtes-de-Beaune. Perhaps this is the same as Bessey, so far as the goat cheese is concerned; I do not know of a cows'-milk cheese up there, but Pierre Androuët found some makers of the soft, white log chèvre, called Montrachet, in the Beaune area.

There have been twenty centuries of wine here, and my experience of Burgundy is limited to one-fortieth of that time; but I do find that the too-refined modern methods of making have removed the magic from a number of wines: that indefinable enchantment of the first impact on the nose and the lift to the palate which used to precede my every swallow of a respectable Burgundy at its peak. 'What they allow in Montrachet I have never done here in Mâcon,' said the *vigneron* of Pierre-Clos in 1986. He proved his point with his Mâcons, which *The Times* wine expert Jane MacQuitty found to outclass many similarly priced Côte d'Or whites and reds. Pierre-Clos is made from grapes of low-yielding, organically treated old vines, picked in two stages. There is no filtering, pumping or sulphuring of the wines, and the grapes are pressed in a seventeenth-century handpress.

## CHAROLLAIS

So this is the moment to turn south-west for Autun and the Charollais. The town of Autun is too full of treasures for me to let myself loose on them, so I will settle for the cheese of cylindrical Charollais appearance which bears Autun's name. Courtine and Viard put it at between 35 and 40 per cent *matières grasses*, and as a summer cheese of cows' milk, with *mi-chèvre* later. I would have expected *pur chèvre* in full season (but this would have to be 45 per cent *matières grasses*), with cows' milk added in autumn and early winter as the goats dry off; but further south, as Pierre Androuët deplored, there are mixed-milk versions of Charollais in full season.

Southwards from the Morvan we enter the comté of Charollais, forming a large proportion of the Saône-et-Loire *département*. Here we are in rolling uplands and hills, with soft valleys, shining streams, the greenest of fields and good hedgerows. The farm buildings are well settled in the landscape and adorn it. Their surface colourings are warm, their roof outlines clear-cut, but never hard. The romantic scattering of feudal castles and the fairly brief stretch of mines and iron-workings around Le Creusot and Montceau-les-Mines are two older aspects of Burgundy.

There are a few of the greyish Brunes-des-Alpes in the fields, and distant patches of white which appear to be sheep. They are not. The dominating living features of the landscape from now on are the considerable herds of the modern white Charollais as far as the eye can see (the only truly French breed that exceeds them in number is that of the north's champion milker for cheese, the Normande).

South-east of Montceau-les-Mines is the centre of marketing and competition for Charollais cheesemakers, Gênelard. It is on the way to Charolles, where the castle of the comtes de Charolles stands high, and its more modern apartments now house the Hôtel de Ville. The Charollais cheese owes its name to the comté, not to the Charollais cows. In its much older, pure form it is a white or bluish-mould-coated cylinder, 5 centimetres across and 8 centimetres deep, of 200 grams, made from pure goats' milk. Eaten at two to three weeks, it is goaty, nutty and firm, but not hard: it hardens only if aged for four weeks or more in airy, dry conditions. Throughout the comté, however, cheeses with variations in size, shape and milk content are sold as Charollais. There are some excellent small, truncated cones in the *pur chèvre* range. There are also cheeses of the standard form, and in other shapes, made of mixed cows' and goats' milk all through the season. Some authorities accept them as Charollais.

Pierre Androuët remarked, during a tour through the Charollais in 1982, on the free-ranging goats in hedged fields, able to feed on lower branches and shoots, and on the striking difference between cheese made from their milk and that made from the milk of goats kept indoors. Our tastings confirmed their 'gently nutty taste'. Those in search of Charollais *en gros* can press on further south to Ozolles, on D168 south-east of Charolles. There Monsieur Thevenet matures his Charollais *fermiers*.

We turned east now to continue our route south on N981 through Givry and Buxy. The country was still lit up by endless herds of Charollais and dignified by towered farms and the occasional castle. Cermolles behind its glassy water, near Givry, and Sercy, with its particularly attractive warm, mediaeval appearance in the autumn sunshine, are memorable. Sercy is a good place to pause and look; then turn west to nearby Saint-Gengoux-le-National, where Montrachet is made by the local *laiterie*. This soft, white to bluish goat log is comparatively modern. It is drained for a few days, then kept for one week in an airy cellar before being wrapped in chestnut or vine leaf. I like it best in its youth. There is a Mâconnais farm 5 kilometres to the north on N481, after Saint-Boil, at the edge of Les Filletières.

Now we set off to find a goat farm at Hurigny, just north-west of Mâcon, where Louis Chevenet and his son Thierry draw together the threads of the Charollais chèvres of south-west Burgundy and the smaller, harder chèvres of the Mâconnais in the south-east. These connect naturally with those of the Beaujolais and the Lyonnais to the south. Here they make the tiniest of chèvres, the straw-pierced Baratte of their own devising, and a cheese of proper Charollais proportions. I must warn readers that, while their cheeses are quite widely sold in good shops, the Chevenets cannot cope with visitors to the farm, other than members of the trade.

Cheesemaking in the Mâconnais is a traditional complement to the more important wine growing. Most *vignerons* kept a few cows and goats for their personal satisfaction, and matured their cheeses at home to a very dry, strong state, against which they tasted and tested their wines. This still goes on, and some of the very dry cheeses are matured further in marc for out-of-season enjoyment in mid- and late winter. In addition there have always been some *chevriers* with bigger herds making cheeses for the market. A particular Mâconnaise tradition is the Bouton-de-Culotte (trouser button), something tiny to munch as a single mouthful between tastings of wine.

Years ago, one of these *chevriers paysans* kept his Alpine goats on the hilltop site of a burned-down farmhouse behind the Chevenets at Hurigny. Louis Chevenet used to be taken for a walk up there as a child, and fell in love with a kid; so much in love that it was bought for him, which is how his present enterprise began. The goats are still Alpines, not the highest in milk yield, but tough and healthy. Only natural reproduction is practised, and the herd now numbers 400, of which half are milkers in season. When not ranging free they live in an enormous barn, which is always open on one side to a great yard, allowing them to come and go as they wish. 'It doesn't do to coerce a goat,' Louis told us. 'That's where we get the word "capricious".' They need and relish their freedom, but are still full of friendliness and curiosity. Louis is proud of their jauntiness and shining healthy coats. Swallows were flying in and out of the barn: 'Very important to catch the flies,' he reminded us.

Though so independent, goats are gregarious and like to feed in clans. When indoors they are fed only on the fresh pasture cuttings and hay of the farm, never on silage or cake. Even so, seasonal changes in the herbage, both in species and in richness, make it necessary to watch the coagulation of the milk at regular intervals during cheesemaking. Nature is the master of the timetable, and Monsieur Chevenet's curd is sometimes ladled into the moulds at 3 a.m.

Blessed with natural wisdom and a healthy herd, Louis can afford to be reserved about veterinary services. 'Vets can be very dangerous people. I would never let one near one of my animals if I weren't sure that he liked cheese. Ideally a vet should be a friend who drops in to buy cheese from you.' These views are not as eccentric or old-fashioned as they sound; they are shared by one of the most scientific and successful goat-keepers and cheesemakers in England, George Lovering of Skomer in Oxfordshire. The result of these beliefs and of the Chevenets' organic farming is that their herd has the best record of production in the large and goat-rich *département* of Saône-et-Loire.

One of the local traditions arising from living in goat country is that the children take cheese to school with them. They also take chocolate, the custom being to warm pieces of chocolate near the stove (unless it has been naturally warmed in a trouser pocket) and then dip the cheese into the chocolate before biting at it. The Chevenets' standard cheese was the Charollais, turned daily and ready in one month. In the 1960s Louis' son Thierry thought up a tiny *bonne-bouche* of a cheese with a straw through it. They say now that the idea of the straw was to bring the cheese to the height of its taller neighbours on shop shelves and so draw attention to it. This it certainly does, but I also reflect how much easier it must make the handling and chocolate-dipping of the cheese at school break. These cylindrical miniatures (less than 2 centimetres across) are salted after moulding and given two days in the open air before the straws are inserted. The straws, from their own organically grown corn, are cut and sterilised before use. The cheeses then spend a further thirteen days in the *cave*.

This *cave* is out of the ordinary. It is a deep, wide well with 90 per cent humidity, and plenty of natural mould in its lower reaches. This led the Chevenets to experiment with their cylindrical Charollais by piercing the ends of the cheese, which they found well blued after ten days. After a month it emerged with a weight of between 150 and 200 grams. The first delivery was made on 8 July 1985 to Messieurs Cénéri at Cannes, but in 1986 the Chevenets decided that the experiment would have to be interrupted until their next expansion of herd and dairy. They found themselves unable to meet demand for their traditional cheeses and could not afford the extra time and material required by the blue. They had several possible names for this cheese, the nicest of which was Chèvre Persillé du Mâconnais, and I look forward to their being able to resume the production of such a rarity.

Another experiment I should like to see followed up at Hurigny is a succulent cheese they made using the Reblochon recipe. Made with their goats' milk, it could be called a Chevrotin du Mâconnais.

## BOUTONS DE CULOTTE AND OTHER CHÈVRES

Before leaving Burgundy proper, we found an enchanting *pays* 15 kilometres south-west of Tournus between Brancion and Cruzille, rich in *châteaux*, *manoirs*, sheep and goats. We approached it along D14 from Tournus, finding our first farm, La Chevrerie de Beaufer, on the *col* of that name. Three kilometres further south, Ozonay has an 1180 church and a handsome *château-ferme* with a barn on the south-east corner welcomingly marked *'Fromages de Chèvre'*. Still continuing south we came to Cruzille, which used to have a name for Boutons de Culottes. The village itself disappointed us, having no *épicier* to consult, and no locals on the street who knew of the cheese; but we found it surviving in the countryside.

We took the Route des Buis, which turns sharp right from Cruzille, and found chèvre signs on the road towards Champliaud, one kilometre further north. There on the west side of the road at La Ferme d'Ouxy, Chevrotin is made of Alpine's milk under the farm name from mid-March to mid-December. The 1985 season was weeks behind because of hard weather; we saw many lambs, but could sample no cheese. However, Madame la Fromagère at Ouxy was very informative, telling us that the term Bouton de Culotte was now often applied to ordinary Mâconnais, especially those ripened at Cenves. She thought the term Bouchon would be fairer, because most Mâconnais are not as small as Boutons. She mentioned the Chevenet cheeses, Les Barattes, as the best examples of the genuine article.

We went north from La Ferme Ouxy towards Nobles and Mont-Saint-Romain, keeping right for Bourg de Brancion, and found another *château-manoir* chèvre near the D14 junction.

Further north at the enchanting mediaeval *bourg* of Briancon, we stayed in the charming *auberge*, between castle and market hall. It provided among its agreeable refreshments a little Mâconnais from Fleurville and a moderately priced Mâcon Supérieur Blanc of great character from Les Vignerons de Mancey, just north of Brancion. It had an iron-like element, but a broad, full flavour, not hard.

As we went on our way the next morning, just outside Brancion, a fox calmly crossed our path, although we found a pack of hounds meeting in the next village (the fox must have known they were staghounds). There were as many pairs of buzzards along the route as the extent of the territories they need for sustenance would allow. The misty March morning acquired enough warmth to tempt out the first brimstone butterfly, although there was still snow in the woods and on north-facing slopes and banks. Gradually the sun's glow made the rolling landscape with its castles and great farms as rich as any ancient illuminator could have wished it. We could not have had a more beautiful goodbye from the duché de Bourgogne.

## Recipe for Cîteaux

Unpasteurised milk stored at 10°C brought up to 33°C, or a little lower if acidity is above normal.

Granday rennet added (diluted 1/10,000): 19c.c. per 100 litres, or a little less if acidity is above normal.

Curd forms in 35–45 minutes, according to degree of acidity, and is then cut: 6–10 minutes.

Curd stirred at a temperature of 32–34°C for 20–25 minutes.

Curds and whey placed on a rising, moving belt long enough for most of the whey to drain by the time it reaches the top.

Curd packed as quickly as possible into moulds by a machine with four vertical tubes (400 cheeses per half-hour). Cheeses immediately put under pressure of 400 grams to the cubic centimetre, where they stay for 18 hours.

Removal of cheeses from moulds into brine of 16° salt-density for 4–5 hours according to season.

Cheeses are placed in a cellar at 15°C and are turned and washed on *one face only* daily for 2 weeks. *Affinage* lasts 3 weeks in summer, 6 weeks in winter, when the cellar temperature is allowed to drop because sales are slower.

## Cheeses of Burgundy

### Abbaye de Notre Dame de Cîteaux

**Cîteaux.** Semi-soft cheese of Reblochon recipe, but made in form of 1kg *tomme*, ripened for 2 months; (see above). Sold at *abbaye*, but liable to run out in July and August. *Not* available through Rungis.
45% m.g.; *artisanal; vache cru.*
Nuits-St-George/Côte d'Or; 65 **20**.

### Abbaye de Sainte-Marie de la Pierre-Qui-Vire

**La Boule-des-Moines.** Often called *La Boulette-des-Moines*. Curd in *fromage frais* state rolled into ball with *fines-herbes*.
m.g. non-précisée; *fermier; biologique; vache cru.*

**La Pierre-Qui-Vire.** Soft, brine-washed, 200g (Époisses-shape).

*m.g. non-précisée; fermier; biologique; vache cru.*

**Le Trinquelin, Fromage Fermier du Morvan.** Large, cutting version (with vegetable colouring) of La Pierre-Qui-Vire.
*m.g. non-précisée; fermier; biologique; vache cru.*
These three cheeses are produced at the Abbaye's *ferme* and Fromagerie de l'Huis St-Benoît, at St-Léger-Vauban. The milk comes from the herd of Brunes des Alpes on pastures free of chemical fertilisers and pesticides since 1969 (see pp. 352–3). On sale at the *abbaye* and in shops and markets in Accolay, Auxerre, Avallon, Looze; markets at Joigny, Vermenton. Rungis: Saff, Dischamps, Bonneterre.
Yonne; 65 **17**, L of C via St Léger-Vauban.

### Aisy Cendré

200g soft cheese of Montbard district ripened in wood-ash (preferably from *sarments*, vine strippings) after brine-washing of crust, giving pale-grey-on-golden appearance, and succulent interior; made by R. Berthaut & Fils (see ÉPOISSES). M. Berthaut recommends scraping surface; I do not.
*50% m.g.; artisanal; vache cru entier.*
Côte d'Or, around Montbard; 65 **7**, low; 65 **17**, high.

### Alésia, Alise-Sainte-Reine

Names formerly found on cheeses of the Époisses type (see p. 364), but larger, up to 1kg. (See LES LAUMES and SAINTE-MARIE.)
Côte d'Or; 65 **18**, top.

### Ami du Chambertin

See CHAMBERTIN.

### Amour

See NUITS ST GEORGES.

### Anost

Local cheese similar to Charollais (see p. 362).
*fermier; chèvre/chèvre–vache cru.*
Saône-et-Loire; 69 **7**, high L.

### Autun

Local cheese similar to Charollais (see p. 362). Courtine said cows' milk in summer, mixed milk in autumn, and that the name attaches to *pur chèvre* made on Arrières Côtes de Beaune (1973).

*fermier; vache/chèvre–vache cru.*
Saône-et-Loire; 69 **7**.

### Avallon

Thursday and Saturday market (including M. Millet's stand on Saturday, see ERVY-LE-CHÂTEL).

### La Bâche

Name used by one maker of Bessey-en-Chaume (see below) when *macéré* in pots with marc or *vin blanc*.
*artisanal; chèvre cru.*
Côte d'Or; 69 **9**.

### Baratte

Miniature cylindrical chèvre with name flag on straw. Louis (*père*) and Thierry (*fils*) Chevenet, Les Mars, 71870 Hurigny near Mâcon. No farm visits, except professional; cheeses widely distributed; tel. 85 39 84 78. (See pp. 357–9.)
*fermier; biologique (even straw); chèvre cru.*
Mâconnais.

### Beaune

Thursday and Saturday market; great wine centre.
Côte d'Or.

### Bessey-en-Chaume

120g small soft cylindrical chèvre produced on stubble of Montagne de Beaune; *frais* or *mi-sec* May–Nov; winter, see LA BÂCHE (the name has usually been spelt Bessay by cheese writers).
*45% m.g.; artisanal; chèvre cru.*
Côte d'Or; 69 **9**, high L of A6.

### Bleu le Bois Soret

140g, mild soft cheese, from Montchanin (Saône-et-Loire).
*45% m.g.; artisanal; vache.*
Mâconnais.

### Bouchon

Used for Mâconnais (see p. 366), small, but larger than Bouton (see p. 362). Some are bottled in olive oil.
*fermier; artisanal; chèvre cru.*
Mâconnais.

### Boule/Boulette des Moines

See ABBAYE DE LA PIERRE-QUI-VIRE.

BOURGOGNE, FROMAGE DE

280g soft, white, flat-sided oval; soft white-mould coat. Maître Colas, Flogny.
*laitier; vache pasteurisé.*

BOUTON DE CULOTTE

30–40g soft cheese made in Mâconnais. When hard, used for grating or for *fromage fort* (see p. 365). Hardened for up to 2 months after making season (May–Oct). *Affinage* (see MÂCONNAIS) Cenves, Gênelard, Ozolles. (See p. 359.)
*fermier; chèvre/chèvre-vache cru.*
Mâconnais/Saône-et-Loire; 69 **17 18**, 73 **7 8**.

BRILLAT D'ARMANÇON

500g slightly salty version of next cheese; by the Fromagerie d'Auxon near Ervy-Le-Châtel (see p. 365).
70% m.g.; *artisanal; vache cru.*
Aube; 61 **16**, on N77 Auxon.

BRILLAT-SAVARIN

This name was used by Burgundy makers of *triple-crème* cows'-milk cheeses until it was claimed as registered by Pansey (Champagne). See BRILLAT, BRIVARIN, SAULIEU and VATEL.

BRIVARIN

450g soft cheese, lightly washed, made at SAULIEU (see p. 365).
75% m.g.; *artisanal; vache.*
Côte d'Or.

CABRION

Similar to Bouton de Culotte (see above), made in Charollais.
*fermier; artisanal; chèvre cru.*
Charollais/Saône-et-Loire.

CENVES

*Affinage* of Mâconnais (see Chapter 12, p. 376).
Juliénas/Beaujolais.

CHABLIS

Sunday market (including M. Millet, see ERVY-LE-CHÂTEL).
Yonne; 65 **5**, **6**.

CHAMBERTIN, L'AMI DU

Époisses-sized cheese washed in marc de Bourgogne made by Jean Gaugry, Laiterie de la Côte, rue de la Malardière, Gevrey-Chambertin, 21220 Brochon, 1½km after Gevrey on left of Dijon road. Jacques Vernier (*maître fromager* in Paris) and others like it. I find it much too salt (I have bought it at the dairy and eaten it in restaurants).
*artisanal; vache pasteurisé.*
Côte d'Or; 65 **20**, lower L.

CHAOURCE

Monday market. Cheese fair third Sunday in October; lilies of the valley (*muguets*) on May Day.

**Chaource.** One farm in the *commune* makes this deep 200g or 450g drum-shaped cheese; a 1½kg cutting version (size of Brie de Melun); and a tub-shaped version of 1kg which the *affineur* François Millet (see ERVY-LE-CHÂTEL) coats with *rocou* before ripening (see pp. 346–7).
50% m.g.; *fermier; vache cru.*

**Chaource Laitier.** 200g and 450g cheeses are made in the Aube and the Yonne by the Fromagerie de l'Armançon, Auxon (Aube); by the Fromageries Paul-Renard in the Aube (but distributed from Flogny (Yonne)); by Lincet, in the Aube; I usually find these industrial cheeses too salty to enjoy (see pp. 345–6). The history of the cheese is covered in Chapter 10, pp. 314–15).
50% m.g.; *laitier; vache pasteurisé.*
Yonne/Pays d'Othe/Burgundy/Champagne.

CHAROLLAIS

120g truncated cone, chèvre; vache and *lait-de-mélange* cheeses are cylindrical, 150g sold *frais* (when quite large), *demi-sec* and *sec*. If too dry they crumble (see p. 357). *Affineurs* at Gênelard and Ozolles, Dijon and La Clayette (see pp. 365, 364, and 363). Crusts can be pale blue, grey and white or blue and gold.
40–45% m.g.; *fermier; artisanal; chèvre/ lait-de-mélange cru.*
Saône-et-Loire/Charolles.

CHAROLLES

Wednesday market.
This name is sometimes used for Charollais, but has also been used on a soft Camembert-type cheese.

## Chèvres Fermiers

See pp. 357–8 and 359, and LES FILLETIÈRES, LOSNE, MANLAY, MONTSAUCHE, OUXY, OZENAY, VITTEAUX for farms; DIJON, GÊNELARD, OZOLLES for *affineurs*.

## Chevreton, Chevrotin, Chevrot, Chevroton

All these terms, and Cabrion, have been used for small soft chèvres in the Charollais and Mâconnais range of sizes, (although Chevreton in Auvergne and Chevrotin in Savoie mean quite different cheeses (see OUXY)); but many farms just use the term 'chèvre'. The Union Syndicale Interprofessionelle Laitière de la Côte d'Or listed 'Mâconnais ou Chevreton de Mâcon' at the 1987 Dijon fair. Viard says that Chevrotons are often ripened in marc, then wrapped in plane leaves, or grated when dry for use in *fromages forts*.
*fermier; chèvre cru.*

## Cîteaux

See ABBAYE DE CÎTEAUX.

## Claque-Bitou

Sold *frais* with garlic, *fines-herbes*, parsley in summer and autumn, in the Montagne-de-Beaune area (see pp. 355–6).
45% m.g.; *fermier; chèvre cru.*
Côte d'Or.

## La Clayette

Monday market; *affineurs* of farm cheese: Loris Lassara.
Charollais/Saône-et-Loire; 69 **17/18**, bottom.

## Cluny

Saturday market. Alice Bénat at Blanot near Cluny was recommended as *fromager* by Gault Millau in February 1986 (see p. xvii).
Saône-et-Loire.

## Confit

A mixture of Époisses, wine and marc (see pp. 348–9).

## Corbigny

See DORNECY.

## Crottin de Chavignol AOC 1976

The AOC for this Berrichon cheese includes an area E of the Loire covering from the N the *communes* of Arquian and St-Vérain in the Canton St-Amand-en-Puisaye, all those of the Canton de Cosnes-sur-Loire, Donzy, ten *communes* of the Canton de Pouilly-sur-Loire and Narcy, Varennes-Lès-Narcy, Raveau and La-Charité-sur-Loire in the Canton La Charité. (See Berry, p. 73.)
45% m.g.; *fermier; laitier; chèvre cru.*
Nivernais/Nièvre; 65 **13**.

## Decize

Friday market; cows'-milk cheese thought by Viard to be extinct by 1980. Recorded in *Larousse Gastronomique* (1961) as Brie-like. All year round.
Nièvre.

## Délice de Bourgogne

Soft *triple-crème* made by Maître Colas at Flogny (Yonne); and (1½–2kg 72% version) made at Laiterie de Vougeot.
75% m.g.; *artisanal; vache/vache cru.*
Côte d'Or.

## Le Délice de Mesnil

Good, rich *triple-crème* ripened in Île-de-France by SCAE, Yvelines.
75% m.g.; *laitier; vache.*
Yonne.

## Délice de Saligny

200g soft *triple-crème* made by Lincet at Saligny.
75% m.g.; *laitier; vache pasteurisé.*
Yonne.

## Dijon

Daily morning market, Halles Centrales. *Maîtres fromagers*: M. Robert Perrot, 28 rue Musette; Mme Simone Porcheret, 18 rue Bannelier; Le Palais du Fromage, 12 rue Bannelier (stocks Barattes); Halles: Brenner: unusual farm cheeses; Mlle Greenbaum, Fromagerie au Gas Normand; La Baratte.
N.B. Cîteaux cheeses are delivered to Dijon on Wednesday.
Côte d'Or; 65 **20**.

## Dornecy

Formerly made on a number of farms, chèvres and *mi-chèvres* of this name were not being made in the commune in 1986. Similar cheese to the old chèvre may be found as Corbigny (Nièvre 65 **15**, low C). In

1986 Mme Pageot was making cows'-milk cheese (ask at *épicerie*; and see Vézelay p. 369).
*fermier; chèvre/mi-chèvre cru. fermier; vache cru.*
Morvan/Nièvre; 65 **16**, on N151.

## Ducs

225g, soft, white-coated cheese, oval; unexciting; made at La-Chapelle-Vieille-Fôret (see also SUPRÈME DES DUCS and PRAIRIE).
50% m.g.; *laitier; vache pasteurisé.*
Flogny-la-Chapelle/Yonne; 65 **6**, top L.

**Suprème des Ducs.** 300g, fatter cheese than Ducs made by Paul-Renard at Flogny-la-Chapelle.
62% m.g.; *laitier; vache pasteurisé.*
Yonne.

## Emmental Français

Some Burgundian milk goes into the factory product, some into the *grand cru* version dealt with in Chapter 14 (see p. 406) and in chapter 15 (see p. 432).
*laitier; vache pasteurisé/cru.*

## Éperon à Boire

Term sometimes used for a cheese like Aisy Cendré (see p. 361), probably a version washed in marc before its ripening in wood-ash.
*fruitière; vache cru.*

## Époisses

**Époisses Artisanal.** 1. 250g, Camembert-shaped, succulent, soft cheese in paper vine leaf in wooden box, decorated with turret of the château at Époisses, in which village it is made. Three weeks of mild brine-washing (twice a week) followed by frequent handwashings in marc. It won two golds and one silver medal at Concours Agricole, Paris 1985. Made by Robert and Jean Berthaut, Fromagerie de la Perrière, Champ-de-Foire, 21460 Époisses, who also make a 50g version called Le Trou du Cru Aisy Cendré (p. 361), La Perrière d'Époisses (p. 365) and La Perrière d'Époisses Export (p. 365). All these cheeses are available from SAFF, avenue de Lille, Rungis.
50% m.g.; *artisanal; vache cru.*
Côte d'Or; 65 **17**, top C.
2. Drum 3.5–4cm wide, 2.5–3cm deep.
(Narrower, deeper than Berthaut's Époisses.) Golden crust, marc-washed; made by M. Boix at Précy-sous-Thil.
*artisanal; vache cru.*
Côte d'Or; 65 **17**, 25km SE of Semur.

**Époisses Chiciak.** Made at Nuits-St-Georges (see p. 367).
*laitier; vache pasteurisé.*
Côte d'Or.

**Époisses Fermier.** 300g rich, not sharp cheese, delicious; moist, slightly flaky consistency under melting crust; marc-washed in last week of ripening. Made by Mme Jacob of Souhey, sold at Thursday and Saturday markets at Semur-en-Auxois, *not* on farm.
*fermier; vache cru.*
Côte d'Or; 65 **18**, high L.

**Époisses (Laitier).** This cheese is usually a *rocou*-coated, white mousse-like inside, not marc- or wine-washed, far removed from the farm cheeses. Makers and distributors include: Fromageries Henry Germain, 52160 Chalancey (in Brie country); Fromagerie Le Fol, 21500 Fain Les Montbard (which also makes a *demi*); Fromagerie de l'Armançon, Auxon (makes a *demi*); Fromageries Paul-Renard, Flogny (includes a *demi* of 200g made by Hersteller); Éts Lincet at Saligny, 89110 Sens, which calls its cheese: Saligny d'Or Spécialité d'Époisses (see p. 345).
*laitier; vache pasteurisé.*
Haute-Marne; Côte d'Or; Aube; Yonne.

**Époisses au Marc.** 250g conventional Époisses shape, marc-washed, more salty than others; made by M. Jean Gaugry outside Gevrey-Chambertin (see AMI DU CHAMBERTIN, and p. 351). François Millet likes this Epoisses (see ERVY-LE-CHÂTEL) but I find too much salt and too little marc.
*laitier; vache pasteurisé.*
Côte d'Or.

**Époisses au Marc de Bourgogne.** 250g.
*artisanal; vache.*
Côte d'Or.

**Époisses des Vignerons.** 250g cheese made by Fromagerie J. Delin, Gilly-Les-Cîteaux sometimes wine-washed (see Chapter 13, PONT-DE-VAUX p. 390) 21640 Vougeot (see also GILLOTINS).
45% m.g.; *laitier; vache pasteurisé.*
Côte d'Or.

**Époisses de Villaines les Prévôtes au Marc.** About 7cm × 6cm deep drum; made by Les Fromagers de l'Armançon; succulent.
*vache cru.*
Yonne; 65 **7/17**, R on D103.

**Fromage de Vache Fermier.** 400–450g cheese (4–4.5 litres of milk, twice Époisses size) of Époisses type but washed weekly in brine not marc, for one month. Made by M. and Mme Jadot of Marcilly-Lès-Vitteaux; sold there and at Saturday market in Semur-en-Auxois.
*fermier; vache cru.*
Côte d'Or; 65 **18**, high C.

**La Perrière d'Époisses.** 750g cutting version of Époisses. (See ÉPOISSES ARTISANAL 1.)

**La Perrière d'Époisses Export.** Specially packed on straw in wooden tray with cardboard sleeve. (See ÉPOISSES ARTISANAL 1.)
Côte d'Or.

### ERVY-LE-CHÂTEL

Friday market. *Affinage* of farmhouse Chaource and Soumaintrain, François Millet, Charrey, 10130 Ervy-le-Châtel. Attends markets at Avallon (Sat) Chablis (Sun) Semur-en-Auxois (Thur).
Aube; 61 **16**, 5km from Soumaintrain.

**Ervy-le-Châtel.** Related to Chaource. See Chapter 10, pp. 332–3.

### LES FILLETIÈRES

**Chèvre.** On D481, south side of village, sign 'Fromage de Chèvre' (between Saint-Bol (S) and Buxy (N)).
*fermier; chèvre cru.*
Mâconnais; 70 **11**, high L.

### FIN MORVAN

See LORMES.

### FLEUR DE MORVAN

450g soft white cheese made by Overney (see SAULIEU).
Côte d'Or.

### FONTENAY

1118 foundation by St Bernard; *abbaye* where Époisses may have originated; astonishing range of buildings survives but, alas, not the dairy.
Côte d'Or; 65 **8**, low L.

### FROMAGE FORT

See CHEVROTON and Chapter 12, p. 376.

### GÊNELARD

*Affinage* of chèvres of Charollais and Mâconnais. Mme Devillard, rue de Laugère.
Saône-et-Loire.

### GEVREY

See CHAMBERTIN, AMI DU, and ÉPOISSES ARTISANAL (Gaugry).

### GILLOTIN, GILLEY-LES-CÎTEAU

**Fromage des Gillotins.** 400g, related to Époisses des Vignerons (see p. 364) (not marc- or wine-washed); Soumaintrain (see p. 369) is also made here by Fromagerie J. Delin, Gilly-Les-Cîteaux, 21460 Vougeot.
*50% m.g.; artisanal; vache.*
Côte d'Or; 65 **20**, low L above Nuits-St-George.

### GLUX

Name of chèvre made at Glux-en-Glenne until maker died (*Larousse*, 1973).
*fermier; chèvre cru.*
Nièvre.

### GRUYÈRE FRANÇAIS

Some milk from eastern Burgundy goes into this cheese, which at its best, and matured for over 4 months, can be very good (see SAVOIE Chapter 15, p. 433).

### LANGRES DU PLATEAU

Plateau (and cheese) now strictly champenois (see Chapter 10, pp. 334–5), although in ancient Burgundy.
*artisanal; vache cru.*
Champagne.

### LES LAUMES

Wednesday market.

**Les Laumes.** 800g–1kg, soft (like large version of Époisses), at least 12cm square × 6–8cm deep in form of *pavé*. Crust washed in brine, sometimes in wine. Courtine even remembers *fermières* who put coffee in the water for the washing of the crust. Now not known locally; only an industrial version (M. Allard of Pourly (see p. 367) told me in 1986).
*industriel; vache.*
Côte d'Or; near Alésia, Alise-Ste-Reine.

## Lormes

Thursday market; La Fromagerie Lormoise, shop with local cheeses (see VÉZELAY, p. 369).
65 **16**, SW of C.

**Lormes – le Fin Morvan.** 270g pleasant small soft cheese; natural crust: Laiterie de Lormes (label Mont-St-Alban).
*50% m.g.; artisanal; vache cru.*

## Losne, St-Jean-de-

Saturday market.
1. Le Grand Vatel. 500g.
2. Le Petit Vatel. 125g.
3. Le Super Grand Vatel. 1500g.
4. Le Prestige de Bourgogne. 200g.

These cheeses, rich and pleasant, are of the type commonly called Brillat-Savarin (name now restricted to Pansey, see p. 362), and the Grand Vatel was sold as such for years. The curd is hand-ladled into the moulds. Petit Vatel is ripened for 4 weeks, Grand Vatel up to 6. Made and sold by André Coudor and his cheesemaker M. Daloz behind the church at 21170 St-Jean-de-Losne. At Rungis from SAFF (M. Pompon), 70 avenue de Flandre Bât. E4 94587 Rungis (cheeses can be ordered at 2–3 weeks, at *fromage frais* stage).
*75% m.g.; artisanal; vache pasteurisé with added cream.*
Côte d'Or; 70 **3**.

**Chèvre Fermier; Crottins; Lingot Cendré.** Crottins, 70–80g, larger but flatter than Berry cheeses, are sold as young as 3 days old. The rectangular 500g Lingot (for cutting) has a beautiful staring-white *pâte*. The *maître fromager* is Mme Geneviève Berger, La Corvée aux Moines, rue de la Croix-Girard, 21170 Losne (tel. 80 29 01 86; reached by rue du Paradis; ask at little *café-épicerie*).
*fermier; chèvre cru.*
Côte d'Or; 70 **3**.

## Mâcon

Saturday market.
Christiane Polo, fromager, 118 rue Carnot.

## Mâconnais, Chevreton de Mâcon

Small soft goat cheese, bigger than Crottin, often aged, and used in *fromages forts* (see Chapter 12, p. 376). For cheese farms see LES FILLETIÈRES, OZENAY, OUXY; *affineurs*, see BOUTONS DE CULOTTE, and CHEVRETIN.
*fermier; artisanal; chèvre cru.*

**Petit Mâconnais.** Cows'-milk cheese made all year round at Laiterie de Fleurville, *frais, à la crème, demi-sec, sec, âgé*, (*âgé* is like miniature Tomme de Montagne, but more brittle).
but more brittle).
*laitier; vache.*
Mâconnais; 69 **19/20**; 70 **11**, centre far R.

## Manlay

**Chèvre.** 120g soft half cone (truncated), Mme Nicole Barmay, Bois-du-Chaume, Manlay, 21430 Liernay.
*45% m.g.; fermier; chèvre cru.*
Côte d'Or; 65 **17/18**, bottom.

## Marcilly-les-Vitteaux

**Fromage de Vache Fermier.** 400–450g cheese, soft, refreshing; proportions of Époisses, but larger, with slightly convex sides; brine-washed for 4 weeks. Made by M. and Mme Jadot; sold on farm and Semur (see p. 368) Saturday market.
*fermier; vache cru.*
Vitteaux, SE of Semur; 65 **18**, high C.

## Montrachet

Comparatively modern; log in chestnut leaf or vine leaf, 200g or 90g; 1–2 weeks' ripening; or as cream cheese in plastic pot. Makers: Laiterie Saint-Gengoux-Le-National (Saône-et-Loire) (70 **11**, high L); Laiterie Savigny-sur-Grosne (Saône-et-Loire) (*Larousse*, 1973).
*45% m.g.; artisanal; chèvre.*
Saône-et-Loire.

## Montréal

Version of Époisses reported by Mitchell-Beazley (1987) as made on small scale in valley of the Serein. Montréal is 15km WNW of Époisses.
Yonne; 65 **16**, top R.

## Mont-Saint-Alban

110g; name used for local cheeses, survives in cheese made at Lormes (see p. 366) by La Fromagerie Lormoise. Crinkly natural crust, tacky consistency, but lively character, good to eat; flavour as though wine-washed.
*50% m.g.; artisanal; vache cru.*
Morvan/Nièvre.

## Montsauche

**Chèvre.** Signs at road junction W of Montsauche.
*fermier; chèvre cru.*
Nièvre; 65 **16**, lower R.

## Morvan

See FLEUR DU MORVAN, CORBIGNY, DORNECY, LORMES, MONT-ST-ALBAN.

## Nuits-St-Georges

Monday and Friday markets.

**L'Amour de Nuits.** 400g soft cheese of rich flavour, presented under green paper vine leaf, related to Époisses (see p. 364). Fromagerie Chiciak, 21700 Nuits-St-Georges.

**Le Nuits d'Or.** Golden version of L'Amour de Nuits. Époisses type; same maker.
*laitier; vache pasteurisé.*
Côte d'Or; 65 **20**, low L.

## Ouxy

**Chevrotin de la Ferme d'Ouxy.** Handmade from Alpine goats' milk (Mâconnais type) at the farm, Champliaud, 71260 Cruzille (see p. 359), mid-March to mid-December. D14 to 1½km W of Brancion, turn S (at this junction a *château-manoir* offers chèvres).
*fermier; chèvre cru.*
Mâconnais/Saône-et-Loire; 69 **19**, 70 **11**.

## Overney

See SAULIEU.

## Ozenay

**Chèvres Fermiers.** 1. Notice on barn at corner of château farm, Ozenay; 2. Notice 3km N of Ozenay on D14 towards Tournus, at Col de Beaufer for Chèvrerie de Beaufer.
*fermier; chèvre cru.*
Mâconnais; 69 **19**, 70 **11**, on D14 6km SW of Tournus.

## Ozolles

*Affinage* of chèvres.
Saône-et-Loire; 69 **18**, lower L, 9km SE of Charolles.

## Perrière

See LOSNES.

## Petit Mâconnais

See MÂCONNAIS.

## Pierre-Qui-Vire, La

See ABBAYE DE SAINTE-MARIE DE LA PIERRE-QUI-VIRE.

## Pourly

300g, 6–7cm diameter, 7–8cm high (narrowing to rounded top); ripened in airy *cave*; crinkly crust at 5 days, nutty flavour sweet and mild. Made by M. Allard at model Chevrerie des Chapoutins, Essert (of which *commune* Pourly is a hamlet). Available April to November. At the farm 8.00–12.00 daily except Sunday.
*50% m.g.; fermier; chèvre cru.*
Auxerrois; 65 **6**, low L.

## Prairie

Coulommiers-type from La Chapelle-Vielle-Forêt (home of Ducs (see p. 364)).
*50% m.g.; laitier; vache pasteurisé.*
Flogny-La-Chapelle; Yonne.

## Prestige de Bourgogne

See LOSNE.

## Régal de Bourgogne

Deep, drum-shaped soft cutting cheese coated with marc and pepper.
*maison fromager; vache.*

## Le Rouy

Small square washed-crust invented in Dijon by Rouy early in twentieth century, bought by Fermiers Réunis. Made for years in Champagne, but in 1980s at their Entrammes *laiterie* in Mayenne, next door to the *abbaye*.
*laitier; industriel; vache pasteurisé.*
Côte d'Or, now Mayenne.

## St-Alban

See MONT-ST-ALBAN and LORMES.

## St-Florentin

Monday market.

**Saint-Florentin Fermier.** 450–500g, soft, washed-crust 2 months-ripened cheese of brown to red appearance. A more melting cousin of Soumaintrain (see p. 369) from the Armançon valley. Farm cheeses rare by 1980 (see p. 346); can be strong; but in *fromage blanc* stage good for salad.
*45% m.g.; fermier; vache cru.*

**Saint-Florentin Laitier.** The big *laiteries* in this corner of the Yonne and the nearby Aube use most of the milk that once went into farmhouse Saint-Florentin (above), Soumaintrain (p. 369) and Chaource (p. 362). The industrial cheeses are *rocou*-coated, rather than repeatedly washed, to give a bright russet-gold colour, and usually sold young and innocent. Their pasteurised milk leaves little of the savour and bouquet which used to be exciting in even young farm cheese (see p. 362); *laiteries*, see ÉPOISSES LAITIER).
A 300g version in plastic dish is made by A. Senoble at Jouy, sold at *fromage blanc* stage.
50% m.g.; *laitier, industriel; vache pasteurisé*.
Yonne/Senonais/Pays d'Othe; 65 **5**, top R 61 **15**, bottom.

### ST-GENGOUX

See MONTRACHET. Markets first and third Tuesday each month.
Saône-et-Loire/Charollais.

### ST-JEAN-DE-LOSNE

See LOSNE.

### SAINTE-MARIE

This name has been used for soft cheese sold in *faisselles* by makers over much of Burgundy. 1. 400g truncated cone, sold young. A late spring–early summer cheese already rare in 1980. *Pâte* similar to that of Alésia, Les Laumes (see pp. 361 and 365), where (especially at Venarey-Les-Laumes) the cheese was once most likely to be found and is still recorded (late 1987) by the Union Syndicale Interprofessionelle Laitière de la Côte d'Or. Androuët attributes the name to the season of making, rather than locality.
45% m.g.; *fermier; vache cru*.
Côte d'Or; 65 **18**, high L.
2. 45% m.g.; *fermier; chèvre cru*.
Morvan/Nièvre; near St-Saulge.

### ST-SAULGE

Friday market.
Small local chèvres, usually truncated cones, originating in these communes (and found in nearby Prémery in the 1970s). They eluded me in 1986.
Morvan/Nièvre; 69 **5**.

### SALIGNY

Site of Lincet industrial *laiterie* (see ÉPOISSES, CHAOURCE, SAINT-FLORENTIN, SOUMAINTRAIN, DÉLICE DE SALIGNY).
Senonais/Yonne; 61 **14**, Sens.

### SAULIEU

Saturday market.
**Époisses au Marc de Bourgogne, Saulieu-Brillat-Savarin, Brivarin.** These cheeses are made at Saulieu, 6 rue du Four, by the Fromagerie Overney.
50% m.g. or 75% m.g.; *artisanal, vache*.
Côte d'Or; 65 **17**.

### SEMUR-EN-AUXOIS

Tuesday, Thursday and Saturday markets for farm and *artisanal* cheeses.
Hôtel-Restaurant des Gourmets and Hôtel du Lac (the latter outside town, which is beautiful) serve Burgundian cheeses and know about them (see pp. 347–8 and 350–1).
Côte d'Or; 65 **18**, high L.

### SOUMAINTRAIN

**Soumaintrain Fermier Artisanal.** 250g, soft, cheese brine-washed every other day for 6–8 weeks; crust develops in last weeks from crinkly greyish-yellow to russet. Medium flavour at 6 weeks, strong at 8. Two farms in village make it. An *artisanal rocou*-coated version is made at Gilly-Lès-Cîteaux (see p. 365).
*fermier; artisanal; vache/vache cru*.

**Soumaintrain de l'Yonne.** 350g (thin circle), 700g (double depth) and 1500g, *rocou*-coated cheeses made by Lincet at Saligny (see pp. 345–6). Other industrial *laiteries* produce these mild versions. The largest Lincet cheese is the best bet.
*laitier; industriel; vache pasteurisé*.
Yonne/Pays d'Othe; 6km ENE of Saint-Florentin on D51; 61 **16**, low L.

### SUPRÊME DES DUCS

See DUCS.

### TEIGNY

Marie-Louise Le Treust, *Fromagère*, commended by Gault Millau, February 1986.
Nièvre; 65 **15**, E of C.

## Le Toucy de l'Yonne

Bell-shaped, blue-mould-coated cheese of engaging character.
*fermier; artisanal; chèvre cru.*
Puisaye, 20km WSW of Auxerre; 65 **4**, SW of C.

## Tournus

Saturday market.
Saône-et-Loire.

## Trinquelin

See ABBAYE DE SAINTE-MARIE DE LA-PIERRE-QUI-VIRE.

## Varzy

Thursday market.

**Le Trou de Cru.** Succulent 50g cylinder of Époisses (new 1987) made by Berthaut et Fils at Époisses (see p. 364).
Côte d'Or.

**Varzy.** Name sometimes attached to local chèvres.
*fermier; chèvre cru.*
Morvan; SW of Clamecy; 65 **14**, C.

## Vatel

See LOSNE.

## Vermenton

Tuesday and Friday market.

**Vermenton.** Almost unheard of in village, formerly reported on farms of Val de Puits as 50g, soft, truncated cone, 2 weeks dry cone, natural blue crust, spring, summer and autumn cheese, small production. Now 200g base of cone (10cm base, 8cm top diameter, 4–5cm deep), *cendré*; rich, sweet, not salty (at 1 week); made by M. Allard at Essert within the *commune* (see POURLY).
*m.g. non-précisée; fermier; chèvre cru.*
Yonne; SE of Auxerre, 65 **5**, low R.

## Vézelay

200g, truncated cone, similar to Vermenton (see above) but larger; no longer made (early 1986) in Vézelay itself, but similar cheeses made in neighbouring communes. My Vézelay informant said they were made by *chevriers* in Fontenay-près-Vézelay (65 **15**, 5km S of Vézelay) and nearby Beaufort (not on my map); Dornecy and Lormes were given as sources by the Union Syndicale Interprofessionnelle Laitière de la Côte d'Or in 1987, but I did not see them in either village in 1986.
*fermier; chèvre cru.*
Morvan/Nièvre; 65 **15**, upper R.

## Le Vougeot

*Fromage blanc salé.*
*artisanal; vache cru.*

**Le Petit Vougeot.** Fresh cheese of about 150g.
*artisanal; vache cru.*
These two cheeses are made at the Laiterie at Vougeot (see also DÉLICE DE BOURGOGNE).
Côte d'Or; 65 **20**, low L.

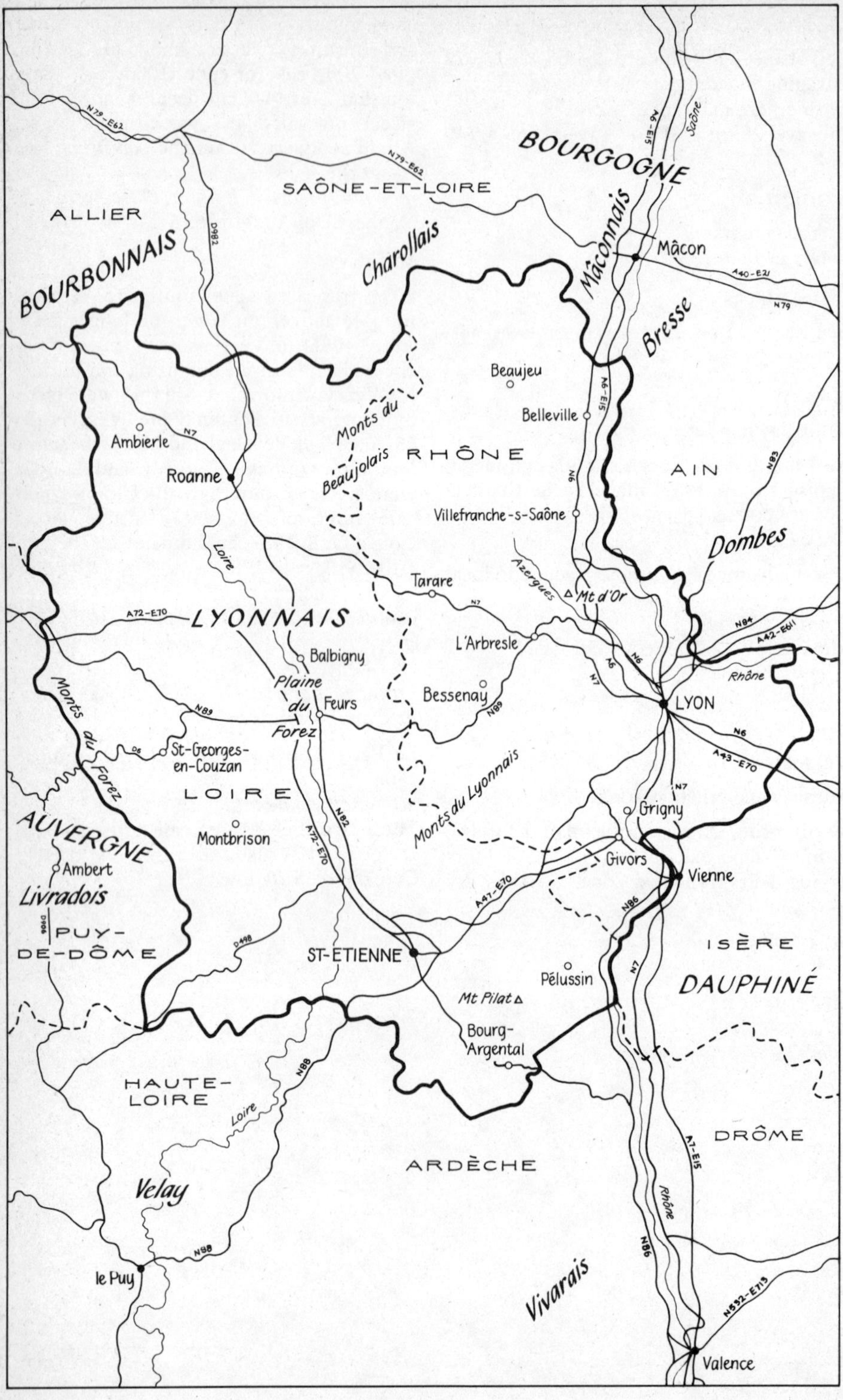

BOURGOGNE
SAÔNE-ET-LOIRE
ALLIER
BOURBONNAIS
Charollais
Mâconnais
Mâcon
Bresse
Saône
N79-E62
A6-E15
A40-E21
N79
D982
Beaujeu
Belleville
Ambierle
N7
Roanne
Monts du Beaujolais
RHÔNE
AIN
N83
Villefranche-s-Saône
N6
Dombes
Loire
Tarare
Azergues
Mt d'Or
A72-E70
LYONNAIS
L'Arbresle
N84
A42-E611
Balbigny
Rhône
Plaine du Forez
Feurs
Bessenay
N89
LYON
Monts du Forez
D5
St-Georges-en-Couzan
N6
A43-E70
LOIRE
Monts du Lyonnais
Grigny
AUVERGNE
Montbrison
N82
A72-E70
Givors
Vienne
Ambert
Livradois
D906
PUY-DE-DÔME
D498
A47-E70
N86
ISÈRE
ST-ETIENNE
Pélussin
DAUPHINÉ
Mt Pilat
Bourg-Argental
HAUTE-LOIRE
N88
ARDÈCHE
DRÔME
Velay
A7-E15
N88
le Puy
Vivarais
N86
N532-E713
Valence

CHAPTER TWELVE

# *Lyonnais*

## RHÔNE – LOIRE

The Lyonnais has not seriously changed its name for 2000 years. The Romans started colonising the country of the Segusiavi in the first century BC, making their capital Lugdunum (Lyon), at the junction of the Saône and the Rhône, the confluence of roads and waterways from every part of Gaul and beyond. The Roman province called the Lyonnaise stretched from the Saône to the Atlantic, from the mouth of the Loire to the Bresle, later the eastern boundary of Normandy.

After Roman times the heart of the Lyonnais around the capital was ruled by Burgundians and Franks in turn until it became a suzerain comté of the Holy Roman Empire in 1032 (finally ruled by the archbishops). It came under the French Crown in 1312, but the city of Lyon was granted the charter of free government which led to its economic rise. Lyon attracted German printers and Italian bankers in the fifteenth century and Genoan weavers in the sixteenth. Its four annual fairs then attracted trade from all over Europe, and its population was greater than that of Paris. Arts, crafts and literature flourished, and the city became known as 'the capital of silk'. The provincial boundaries were extended in the 1500s by the addition (at the expense of the duc de Bourbon) of the comtés of Beaujolais and the Forez. The Revolution caused tragic damage, as the *Directoire* violently repressed Lyonnais and Beaujolais resistance to the act which cut the clergy off from Rome. Napoleon restored reason, order and economic progress, benefiting especially the luxury trades.

The number of *'canuts'*, as Lyonnais silk workers are called, dropped from 30,000 early in the nineteenth century to 5000 in 1914. Now a mere twelve workshops employ thirty survivors in the great traditional craft; a further 400 workshops produce other materials or carry out related processes. *Canut* is more familiar today in the name of the cheese Cervelle de Canut (see pp. 375–6).

Lyon was a centre of *la Résistance* during the Second World War, and suffered in consequence. The Lyonnais are great respecters of tradition as well as of industry and progress. Old quarters of the city have been lovingly preserved and restored, rather than altered: Saint-Jean, for instance, retains mediaeval, Gothic and Renaissance buildings, some of them used as practical and attractive tenements with passageways through them at different floor levels called *traboules*.

## Cheeses of Lyon

Like Burgundy, the Lyonnais has a great gastronomic reputation, typified by the innovative chef Paul Bocuse, whose family has been in *restauration* here for 250 years. At Lyon itself, in the new market, can be found two of France's most notable *maîtres fromagers*, *fromagères* Madame Maréchal, and Mère Richard (with her daughter), famous for her Saint-Marcellins ripened into melting dreams. The suburbs of Lyon and Les Monts d'Or Lyonnais are full of cheesemakers who draw on the traditions of the Vivarais and of the Saint-Marcellin region of the Dauphiné (see list). There are also *affineurs* who collect farm and artisanal cheese from the surrounding regions, as well as that of their own home ground. Some improve on Saint-Marcellin by washing it in wine during its *affinage*.

Les Arômes de Lyon are small local goats'-milk, cows'-milk or mixed-milk cheeses, dried out then ripened in vats of white wine for a month. They are left for another month in a dry *cave*, then wrapped in chestnut or plane leaves for further keeping or sale. Les Arômes à la Gênede de Marc are similar cheeses left for varying periods, according to taste, in fermenting marc, where they develop a smelly crust. They are left unwrapped when taken out of the marc.

Local cuisine offers Cervelle de Canut, or Claqueret Lyonnais. The first name means 'silk-weaver's brain', the second is that of the wooden spoon used to beat the pepper, salt, shallots, *fines-herbes* and garlic into the curd. Ninette Lyon recommends keeping the finished Claqueret in the terrine for two days before immersing it in vinegar, white wine and a little olive oil; she says that it can be served after a few days' ripening in a cool cellar.

## Cheeses of the Beaujolais

As we leave Burgundy from the Mâconnais, the comté du Beaujolais greets us. There are no impressive heights, but the hillside vineyards and golden-stone villages have great charm. The typical *vigneron*'s house has an arched entrance to its ground-level *cave*, over which steps from either side lead up to a first-floor gallery, giving access to the living quarters. The forward extension of the roof provides the *êtra*, an awning supported by pillars which protects the gallery passage.

The young wines are familiar to English-speaking readers, many of whom will have joined in the annual winter scramble for Beaujolais Nouveau, leading to premature exhaustion of stocks. At their best these are refreshing accompaniments to the little chèvres of the *pays*, and to the *triple-crème* cows'-milk Tarare, formerly made locally. This rich-textured, soft cheese with a flowery mould crust, usually sold *frais*, is well worth keeping to develop its full flavour. Then, perhaps, it should be eaten with a Morgon, or one of the other select wines of the Beaujolais, which can stand comparison with good Burgundies.

Amid the chèvres in private houses and farms we may find a Fromage Fort du Beaujolais. One recipe for this preparation mixes equal amounts of *pur* or *mi-chèvre*, preferably *boutons-de-culotte* (see Chapter 11) too hard to bite, and old Gruyère (both grated). These are moistened with butter or olive oil, dry white wine and an old local marc, all potted and sealed up, and kept in the cellar for two or three weeks. Traditionally, the pot is never emptied; new ingredients are just mixed in with the old as space allows, to maintain a speedy rate of fermentation. Another version uses two small chèvres of Mâconnais proportions (5 centimetres across and 1.5–2 deep), dried out, grated, and mixed over heat with 225 grams of finely grated Gruyère, a tablespoonful of walnut or olive oil and 225 grams of butter, given a shot of marc, and kept for three or four weeks. The result has been described as 'dynamite'.

If you enter the Beaujolais from Charolles, N985 brings you to Belleroche. To the south, under the western slopes of the Monts du Beaujolais, the valley of the Azergues is a fruitful source of chèvres in season, explored by Pierre Androuët in 1982. Many farms follow the old *chevriers'* practice of drying their cheeses of all shapes and sizes in outdoor cages, like meat-safes or fine-meshed rabbit hutches. The cheeses come from pure goats' milk in full season, or from various strengths of mixed goats' and cows' milk as the goats dry off. Pure cows'-milk cheeses follow in the mid-winter months. The Azergues Valley can also be approached from the Rhône via Beaujeu and up the Ardières Valley near Beaujeu there is an organic goat farm at Malleval (see list, p. 377). Close to l'Arbresle a little road takes you the 2 kilometres to Savigny, where you should ask the way to Trente-Côtes. There Monsieur Jouvray conducts his *affinage* of Saint-Marcellin in white wine: not an everyday find.

From the southern end of the Bois d'Oingt, at Les Ponts-Tarrets, you can follow D35 south-west to the valley of the Tardine. Join N7, which passes through Tarare on the way to Roanne. There are some larger-scale *laiteries* here, but 3 kilometres north on the right of D482 near Vougy, Les Charmilles, organically farmed, sells its own chèvres *frais* and *secs* daily between 6 and 7 p.m.

## Cheeses of the Forez

Driving north to Pouilly you can cross the Loire on D4 and follow it west and south-west 4 kilometres beyond Saint-Germain-Lespinasse, then turn right for Ambierle. In impressive countryside, after a bit of a climb, you will find the Berthelet family's goats and their caged cheeses, invitingly called 'Goûtez-moi'; they are, to quote Ninette Lyon, '*un élevage et des fermiers bien sympathiques*'.

We are now in the Forez, comté under one line from the tenth century until 1372, when it descended to the duc de Bourbon. The western and southern Monts du Forez lie in the Auvergne (in the Puy-de-Dôme), while the eastern Monts and the Plaine du Forez are in the Loire *département* of the Lyonnais. The oldest traditional cheese of the Forez is the blue *fourme* with which I have dealt under the Auvergne, where most of the surviving makers operate (see Chapter 7). Montbrison, capital of the Forez, is one of the old names attached to that cheese; sadly 'Fourme de Montbrison' is now found on the labels of cheese made around Ambert, and is identical with the same makers' Fourme d'Ambert. Except for a few still used by shepherds, the old *jasseries*, the simple summer farmhouse-cheese dairies of the Monts du Forez, have been abandoned or have become secondary homes or cafés. One in the Auvergne (see 'Jasserie' on the Auvergne list, p. 343) is set up as a museum and sells cheese, but I know of none where *fourme* is still made.

The Plaine du Forez, east of Montbrison, is part of the broad upper Loire Valley, full of ponds, small lakes and water-courses, which might suit buffalo better than local breeds of cattle. The French have imitated Gorgonzola in similar country east of Lyon, so why not Mozzarella here?* Perhaps the buffalo would find it too cold ... The old capital, Feurs, sits in the middle (on N82), and 9 kilometres north of it is Balbigny. Here Monsieur l'Essor's *laiterie* makes Le Palet de Balbigny, an attractive small oval cheese of cows' milk, soft and creamy-coloured when young. It can get firmer and darker if kept, becoming more like a chèvre, with the superficial appearance of a light smoking. I saw it on sale elsewhere, in Aurillac (Auvergne) and at Crémieu (see the Dauphiné list, p. 453).

On the map, the rest of the southern Lyonnais, close to the Rhône, seems nothing but towns and roads; cheesemaking survives, however, with results to be found in local markets, shops and restaurants. South-west of Givors,† at Échalas, Monsieur Bourdin's *laiterie* makes, among a range of raw-milk cheeses, Le Chatenay, a white, softish *rigotte*, sold *frais* or *mi-sec*. At Isigny, 7 kilometres north of Givors, Monsieur Edmond Reynard makes a *pur chèvre* on the edge of the Lyon refinery district.

The most famous of Lyonnais cheeses, the little drum-shaped Rigotte de Condrieu, comes from south of Vienne, though its *rocou*-coloured form is widely imitated by industrial products as far afield as the alps of the Dauphiné. Pierre Androuët thinks that *rigottes* may go back to the Roman era. The name probably derives from *ricotta*, to which its spelling is much closer than the modern French *recuite*. Ricotta originated with ewes'-milk cheesemakers, whose whey cheese is richer than any other, and richer than much part-skimmed-milk cheese from cow or goat. The average *rigotte* in the Lyonnais is 40 per cent *matières grasses*. Made mostly in factories or *laiteries*, and almost always of cows' milk, it is normally given a week to drain, and is sometimes pierced with a straw. *Rigottes* are usually eaten while firm to the touch but soft inside and slightly sharp-edged in flavour. South-west of Condrieu in the Parc du Pilat, Pierre Androuët has found a maker of *pur chèvre rigottes* at Pélussin.

Pélussin is also the source of the Fromagerie Guilloteau's little Pavé d'Affinois. This small, soft, white, rectangular cheese of whole cows' milk originated at Crémieu in the Dauphiné, and had a rustic look on its simulated straw mat. In 1986 it started to appear smooth and square, almost a cube, on plastic trays instead of mats; not an improvement. The label boasts that the maker dispenses with rennet by using centrifugal force to

---

*Since writing these words I have found La Mozzarella *à pâte-filée* made at Brignais, south-west of Lyon (73 **20**, L of centre).
†If you are in Givors on the first Sunday in July, there is water-jousting dating back to Roman, possibly Greek, times.

separate its solids from the whey. This innovation has also separated the cheese from its original character, which saddens Crémieu (see pp. xxiii–iv).

The small chèvres and *rigottes* of the Lyonnais contribute in their hardened state to the richness of the Fromages Forts du Lyonnais, sometimes called Fromfort (for which I have also seen Chevretons du Mâconnais specified). Chèvres, *mi-chèvres* and *fromages de vache* (including Saint-Marcellins *demi-secs* from the Dauphiné) are mixed with leek stock, a little marc, and thyme, tarragon, salt and pepper to taste. After two or three weeks in closed pots the mixture is given a lengthy stir, then sealed up again for another month. Pierre Androuët, who gives a full recipe for this and for the Beaujolais version in his *Livre d'Or du Fromage*, says you must wait three months to eat the result if your cellar is cold.

This seems a suitably savoury note on which to leave the Lyonnais and turn east into that mongrel of a *département*, the Ain.

## Cheeses of the Lyonnais

### Affinois
See pavé.

### Ambierle
Thursday market.

**Goûtez-Moi.** Berthelet family at Pierrefitte, 42820 Ambierle (tel. 77 04 52 22 for appointment and directions).
*fermier; chèvre cru.*
Loire/Forez; 73 **7**, middle L.

### Arômes
**Arômes à la Gêne, Pélardon, Picodon, Rigotte, Saint-Marcellin.** Cheeses ripened in *marc* and coated in wine-pressings; sold in Les Halles at Lyon (see p. 377).
Rhône.

### Azergues valley
**Chèvres Fermiers (various).** This valley, from SW foot of Mont St-Rigaud down to Bois d'Oingt and L'Arbresle, is recommended by Androuët; and see Chambost-Allières (in the valley) for Fête du Fromages (see p. 373).
*fermier; chèvre cru.*
Rhône; 73 **9**, N of C, along R. Azergues/ D485 to 73 **19**, top R.

### Balbigny
**Palet de Balbigny.** Small oval cheese, 5cm long, firmish; creamy-coloured crust, darkening with age, when cheese more like a chèvre *sec.* Made by l'Essor, laitier, 42510 Balbigny.
52% m.g; laitier; artisanal; vache cru.
Loire/Forez; 73 **18**, top L, on N82 N of Feurs.

### Belleville-sur-Saône
Tuesday market.
Rhône; 73 **10**.

### Le Bougredin
100g, soft, smooth, white (Saint-Marcellin shape) eaten within first 4 weeks. Made by Bourdin, see échalas.
*40% m.g.; laitier; vache.*

### Bourg Argental
Thursday and Sunday market.
Crèmerie-Fromagerie Chomette-Gennesson for uncommon farm cheeses.
Vivarais–Forez border/Loire; 76 **9**.

### Brillat
500g; type Brillat-Savarin made by Bourdin. See échalas.
*72% m.g.; laitier; vache.*
Rhône.

### Brise Arôme au Poivre
1kg cheese, made by Bourdin, Échalas (see p. 376), Rhône.
*58% m.g.*

### Bûche
See pavé.

### Canut or La Cervelle de Canut
*Fromage blanc* with shallots, chives, *fines-herbes*. The name is the Lyonnais term for

a silk-weaver, or his brain (see CLAQUERET, and p. 372).
*domestique; vache cru.*
Lyon.

## CENVES

*Affinage* of Mâconnais including smaller ones called familiarly Boutons-de-Culotte (see p. 362).
Rhône/Juliénas; 69 **19**, bottom L, follow D23 on river P't'te Grosne for another 2km, keeping R at T-junction.

## CERVELLE

See CANUT.

## CHAMBOST-ALLIÈRES

Third Sunday in May: Fête du Fromages.

## CHATENAY

62.5g, soft white *rigotte* made by Bourdin, Échalas (see below), Rhône (NE of St-Étienne, W of Givors); *frais* or *demi-sec*.
50% m.g.; *laitier; vache cru*.
Rhône; 74 **11**.

## CLAQUERET LYONNAIS

Another cheese from Canut world (see p. 375). *Claqueret* is a wooden spoon, used to beat the curd (in domestic making), after which pepper, salt, shallots and *fines-herbes* are added, and the cheese is *'piqué d'ail'* (garlic inserted). My authority is Ninette Lyon (who is *not*, however, a Lyonnaise). Courtine, who adds onions and specifies chives among the herbs, says that Claqueret is the proper name. (See p. 372.)
50% m.g.; *domestique; vache cru*.
Rhône.

## CONDRIEU

See RIGOTTE.

## DOUSCAR

About 200g; drum shaped; soft; *croûte-fleurie;* pleasant, rich cheese, which I have not seen for a few years, exact provenance unknown; *affiné* and marketed by Gilca-Orlap Vivalp of Lyon.
75% m.g.; *laitier; vache*.
Lyonnais.

## ÉCHALAS

Washed-crust *rigotte*, golden; Laiterie St-Étienne, Échalas. Bourdin makes Bougredin, Brise Arôme, Chatenay, Tomme de la Drôme and other cheeses there.
*laitier; vache*.
Rhône; 74 **11**, 8.5km W of Givors on D103.

## FOURMES

**Fourme de Montbrison.** This name is now used only by makers nearer to Ambert, and it is included among Auvergne cheeses (see p. 240).
*laitier; vache cru*.
Forez.

**Fourme Lyonnaise.** Smoothish golden-brown-over-white crusted, 2kg cylinder (upright), with mild blue interior. One make is called La Reine du Passe-Loup.
*laitier: vache*.

## FROMAGES FORTS

**Fromage Fort du Beaujolais.** See pp. 372–3.
*domestique; artisanal; laitier; chèvre; mi-chèvre et vache*.
Beaujolais.

**Fromage Fort de la Croix Rousse.** Strong blue cheese (without crust) steeped in dry white wine in earthenware pot. Later add grated chèvre (very dry) and yeast. After serving fill up with wine, and add butter if too dry. Stir daily.
*domestique; vache; chèvre*.
Lyon.

**Fromage Fort du Lyonnais.** See p. 372.
*domestique; artisanal; laitier; chèvre; mi-chèvre; vache*.

**Fromfort.** See above and p. 375.
Forez.

## GALETTE DES MONTS D'OR LYONNAIS

100g disc, gold crust, rich clotted texture, rich creamy flavour; by Jouvray, Savigny, 69210 L'Arbresle.
45% m.g.; *artisanal; vache cru*.
Monts du Lyonnais; 73 **19**, high R.

## GÈNE

See ARÔMES.

## GIVORS

Tuesday, Wednesday, Friday and Sunday market. See footnote, p. 374.
Rhône; 74 **11**.

## GOÛTEZ-MOI

See AMBIERLE.

## La Grignette

180g flat-bottomed half-log; soft, *croûte-fleurie*, made for Bourdin (as is Saint-Valentin, see p. 379) by Fromagerie Duernoise, Duerne 69850 St-Martin-en-Haut.
50% m.g.; *laitier*; *artisanal*; *vache cru*.
Rhône; 73 **19**, N of C, Duerne D34 and D489.

## Grigny

See TOMME.

## Irigny

Thursday a.m., Wednesday and Saturday p.m. market.
**Chèvres Artisanaux.** Made by Edmond Reynaud, La Cavalerie, 34 rue de la Visina, 69540 Irigny (tel. 78 46 39 80).
*artisanal*; *chèvre cru*.
Rhône; 74 **11**, S of Lyon refineries W of D15.

## Lyon

Daily market.
*Maîtres fromagers:* Maison Beninca, La Vacherie, 9 rue Claude-Joseph Bonnet, 69004 Lyon; M. Lucien Colombet, chemin de la Chapelle, 69140 Rillieux-La-Pape (NE outskirts Lyon); M. Maurice Janier, Fromages de France, 27 rue Seguin, 69002 Lyon (*grossiste-affineur* specialising in farm cheeses); Mme Eléonore Maréchal, Fromagerie Maréchal, Halle de Lyon-Part-Dieu, 102 Cours Lafayette 69428 Lyon; M. Paul Pechoux, Champagne-au-Mont-d'Or; Mme Renée Richard, Mlle Renée Richard, 'Mère Richard', 102 Cours La Fayette, Halles de Lyon, 69003 Lyon. One of the most famous and respected *maîtres fromagers* in all France. Especially noted for fully ripened Saint-Marcellin *coulant*.
Some other shops: La Bergerie, 108 rue Bossuet, 69006 Lyon; Colombet, 6 place de la Croix-Rousse and 10 Boulevard des Brotteaux, 69004 Lyon; Fauret, 116 rue de Sèze, 69006 Lyon; Fromagerie Tête d'Or, 51 rue Tête d'Or, 69006 Lyon; Gentelet, 18 rue de Marseille, 69007 Lyon; La Jasserie, 9 quai des Célestins, 69002 Lyon.
Lyon; 74 **11/12**.

## Malleval

**Chèvres Fermiers.** Organic cheeses made by Suzanne Michon and Alain Pinard, Gaec de la Tour Malleval, 69430 Beaujeu (tel. 74 04 82 10).
*fermier*; *biologique*; *chèvre cru*.
Not on map, near Beaujeu in Forez; 73 **9**.

## Le Mi-Sel

See VAULX-EN-VELIN.

## Monpila

Cheese of unknown character but thought worth importing by a Swiss *fromager* in the eighteenth century (Mont Pilat, now in national park).
Loire; 77 **1**, top L; 76 **9**, top R.

## Montbrison

Saturday and Tuesday June–October market.
Journée de la Fourme du Forez, first week in October (and see FOURME).
Forez/Loire; 73 **17**.

## Mont d'Or

200g–250g Camembert-shape, soft, *croûte-fleurie*; two days in controlled temperature to start crust, 2 weeks' *affinage*; made until mid-1980s by Marc Vial at Brullioles (see also POTHU and VIAL D'OR), but production had stopped by 1988.
*fermier*; *vache/chèvre cru*.
Rhône/Brullioles; 73 **19**, high, N of N89–D101 junction.

## Monts d'Or

**Fromages des Monts d'Or du Lyonnais, de Lyon.** Soft, flat discs of about 120g, 1-week-old *frais*; 2 weeks, natural crust, *bleutée*, nutty flavour; can be runny; local; for other *artisanal* and farmhouse versions see cow's-milk GALETTE.
about 45% m.g.; *artisanal*; *fermier*; *chèvre/mi-chèvre cru*.
Lyon; not to be confused with Franc-Comtois-Swiss Mont d'Or or Montdore of Auvergne.

## Le Mourrachu

60g, pinkish crust, firm, yet moist, rich, sweet interior; made at Élevage du Bate, 69850 Saint-Martin-en-Haut.
*fermier*; *chèvre cru*.
Rhône/Monts du Lyonnais; 73 **19**, C.

## Palet

See BALBIGNY.

Passe-Loup
**La Reine du Passe-Loup.** See FOURME LYONNAISE.

Pavé
**Pavé d'Affinois.** 160g almost cube, soft; interior melts to anonymous sort of runny curd, shiny-white, thick coat; in plastic tray; (I understand that this cheese is now made without rennet and is being separated from whey by centrifuge). Originally made at Crémieu in Dauphiné. Until early 1986 it was a pleasant, more rustic-looking, straw-marked rectangle on a little mat. Fromagerie Guilloteau, Parc National du Pilat 42410 Pelussin; Bûche d'Affinois *lingot* version of this. See pp. xxiii–xxiv.
45% m.g.; *laitier; vache entier pasteurisé.*
Loire; 77 **1**, top L.

**Pavé Dauphinois.** 300g (approx), soft, round, close-textured, pale with golden edges near crust; crust golden with bluish mould, straw-marked; from Vaulx-en-Velin, Rhône (see p. 379).
*artisanal; vache cru.*
Lyon; ENE suburb.

**Pavé d'Or.** 60g, flat disc, ridged underside; succulent, from St Étienne.
*artisanal; vache.*
Saint-Étienne; 73 **19**.

Pélussin
See PAVÉ and RIGOTTE.
Saturday and Sunday market.
Loire; Parc National du Pilat; 77 **1**, top L.

La Pierre Dorée du Beaujolais
110g truncated cone, lightly washed golden crust; Bourdin at Échalas (see p. 376).
60% m.g.; *laitier; vache cru.*
Rhône.

Pothu
100–120g with protruding angular waist; little rennet; 48 hours in beaker-shaped *faisselle*, turned at half-time, hence shape; made until mid-1980s by M. Vial at Brullioles (see also MONT D'OR) but production had stopped by 1988.
*fermier; vache/chèvre cru.*
Rhône; 73 **19**, high N of N89–D101 junction.

Rigotte
**Rigotte de Condrieu.** 40–50g cylinder, soft, thin natural crust, usually *rocou*-coated and kept 1 week before sale. Kept longer it hardens for grating and use in *fromages forts* (see p. 376). It should have a dairy odour, be firm and taste slightly acid.
40% m.g. *(min); laitier (industriel/coopérative); vache.*

**Rigotte de Pélussin.** Rare *pur chèvre* rigotte found by Androuët, who believes rigottes originated in Roman times.
*fermier; chèvre/vache cru, in season.*
Rhône; 73 **20**, far S of C.

Roanne
Tuesday, Friday, Sunday market.
Loire; 73 **7**.

Romans
A version of this Dauphinois cheese is made at Vaulx-en-Velin (see p. 379); I'm told it is good (but see ST-FÉLICIEN).
*laitier; vache.*
Lyon; ENE suburb.

Rontalon
Bergerie-restaurant (weekends only), cheese shop, 69510 Thurins; run by Rive family.
Rhône; 73 **19**, S of Thurins off D11 by D75.

Saingorlon
See AIN.

St-Étienne
Market (recommended by Androuët) held on Mondays, Fridays, and summer Saturdays.
Loire; 76 **9**, 73 **19**.

St-Félicien (Vaulx-en-Velin)
Strictly speaking geographically St-Félicien is in Ardèche, in the Vivarais, and its cheese is *pur chèvre*, but a cows'-milk version is made at Vaulx-en-Velin (see also PAVÉ DAUPHINOIS, TRABOULIN). This 150g gold, white and blue crusted cheese, with a straw-lined, rustic look of great beauty, I bought on the young side, in perfect condition, except for excessive salt, which destroyed flavour.
At Villeurbanne (E side of Lyon) another is made by Cellerier: 160g with blue-mould-coated crust, good consistency and flavour.
40% m.g.; *laitier; vache.*
Vivarais/Ardèche/Lyon ENE; 76 **9/10**, lower.

## St-Georges-en-Couzan

Wednesday market.
From the 1985 *French Farm Holiday Guide*: M. Lucien Charles at La Chanale, 42990 St-Georges-en-Couzan (tel. 77 24 85 12) offers farm holidays, with his cheeses, poultry, rabbits and eggs.
Forez/Loire; 73 **17**, 17km NW of Montbrison on map; 10km longer by road.

## St-Marcellin

**Saint-Marcellin Surfin.** Fromagerie du Dauphiné, St Christophe. Deep gold crust, rich *pâte*, as though washed in liquor; by Rogemond, 59 rue de la Libération, 69780 Mions (SE of Lyon).
60% *m.g.*; *artisanal*; *vache*.
Mions; 74 **12**, L of C.

**Saint-Marcellin Affiné au Vin Blanc.**

## Saint-Valentin

180g deep Saint-Marcellin shape, by Fromagerie Duernoise for Bourdin (see LA GRIGNETTE).
50% *m.g.*; *laitier*; *vache*.
Rhône.

## Savigny

*Affinage* of Saint-Marcellin in white wine by M. Jouvray at Trente-Côtes.
Rhône; 73 **19**.

## Tara Crème

170g soft, striated drum (distributor Scoff, see TOMME GRISE).
60% *m.g.*; *laitier*; *vache*.
Rhône; Grigny, 74 **11**, SE of C.

## Tararcrème Frais

Small, creamy, white-coated cheese, drum-shaped, made by Coopérative de Tarare, but Androuët tells me (autumn 1987) that production has ceased.
Lyonnais; 73 **9**, low.

## Tarare

Rich, tasty, soft *triple-crème*; small circular, about 2cm deep. I have memories of a larger version eaten N of Villefranche among *vignerons*.
75% *m.g.*; *fermier*; *vache cru*.
Rhône/Lyonnais; 73 **9**.

## Tomme Grise des Monts

400g drum; semi-hard; rustic, mould-rich crust; by Bourdin; formerly distributed by Scoff, avenue Marcellin-Berthelot, which is no longer in business. Grigny.
*vache cru*.
Rhône; 74 **11**, SE of C.

## Tourette du Père Joseph

This 1kg low-fat, crinkly grey-crusted cheese, slightly domed, is made in the Lyonnais, but ripened in Chambéry by Bouquet-de-Savoie. I have seen other rustic, low-fat Tommes Lyonnaises made in the Rhône, but ripened and sold in Savoie.
30% *m.g.*; *vache cru*.
Rhône.

## Le Traboulin

180–200g rich white-and-gold-crusted soft cheese made at Vaulx-en-Velin.
70% *m.g.*; *artisanal*; *vache*.
Rhône; ENE Lyon.

## Vaulx-en-Velin

Source of a Romans (p. 378), Saint-Félicien (cows' milk, p. 378), Le Mi-Sel, Pavé (p. 378) and Le Traboulin (see above). They are usually available at Pont-de-Vaux (see Chapter 13, p. 390).
Laiterie Fuster, 8 rue Jean Marie Merle.
Rhône; ENE Lyon.

## Vial d'Or

100g Mont d'Or cheese made until mid-1980s by M. Marc Vial, Le Pitaval, Brullioles, 69690 Bessenay, but production had stopped by 1988; Concours Agricole medallist. (See also MONT D'OR, POTHU.)
45% *m.g.*; *fermier*; *chèvre cru*.
Lyonnais; 73 **19**, upper centre SW of Bessenay.

## Vignolas

500g soft cheese in Coulommiers style (formerly distributed by Scoff, avenue Marcellin-Berthelot, Grigny; see TOMME GRISE).
30% *m.g.*; *laitier*; *vache*.
Rhône.

## Villefranche-en-Beaujolais

About 1½km SW of Villefranche on N6, sign reads *vente de fromages*.
Rhône; 71 **1**.

## Vougy

**Fromages Frais Secs.** Sold daily 6–7 p.m. on farm, Les Charmilles, 42720 Vougy.
*fermier*; *biologique*; *chèvre cru*.
Rhône; 73 **8**, far L C.

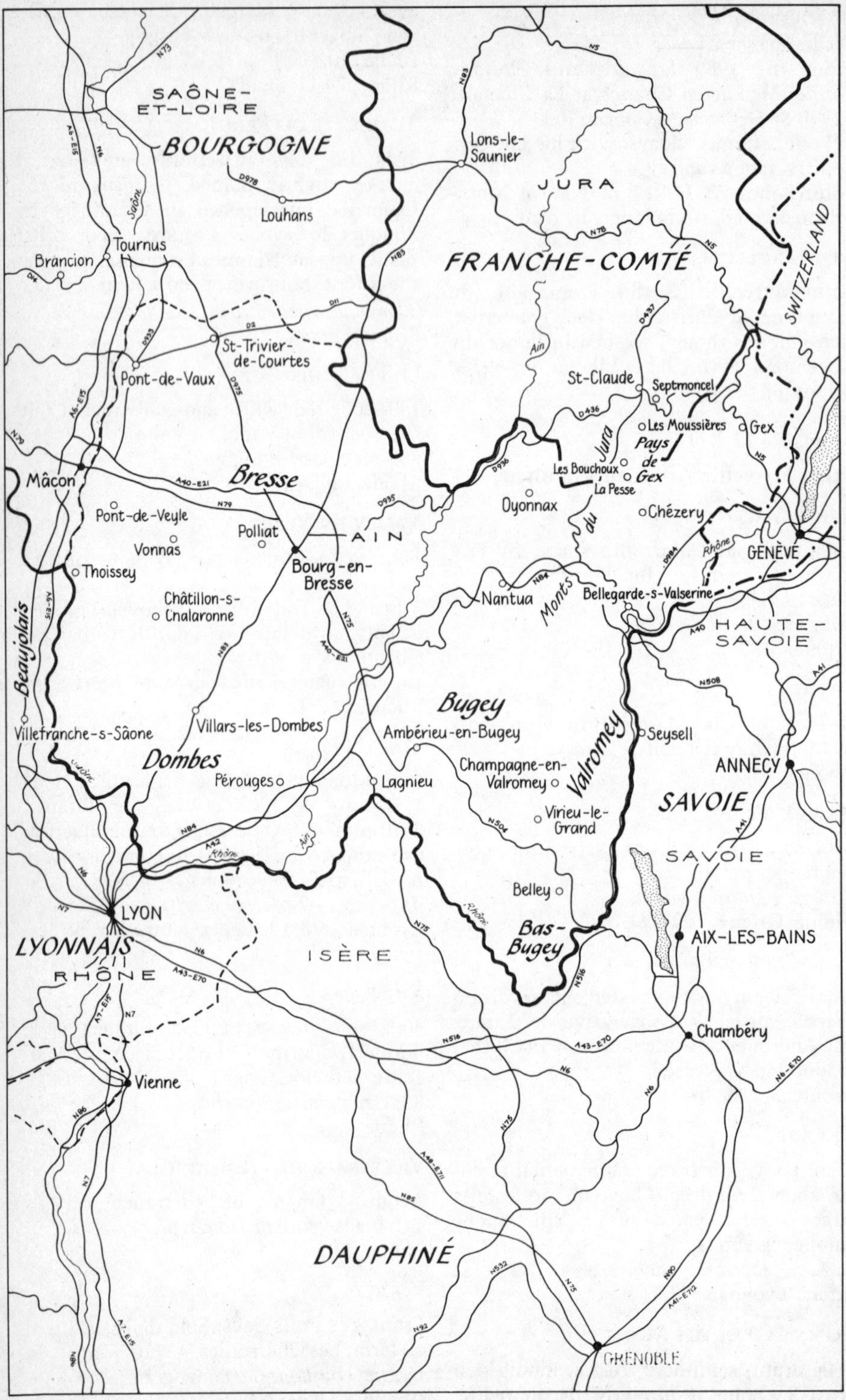

SAÔNE-ET-LOIRE
BOURGOGNE
Lons-le-Saunier
JURA
Louhans
Tournus
Brancion
FRANCHE-COMTÉ
SWITZERLAND
St-Trivier-de-Courtes
Pont-de-Vaux
St-Claude
Septmoncel
Les Moussières
Gex
Pays de Gex
Les Bouchoux
La Pesse
Mâcon
Bresse
Oyonnax
Chézery
Pont-de-Veyle
Polliat
AIN
GENÈVE
Vonnas
Bourg-en-Bresse
Thoissey
Nantua
Monts du Jura
Bellegarde-s-Valserine
Châtillon-s-Chalaronne
HAUTE-SAVOIE
Beaujolais
Bugey
Villefranche-s-Saône
Villars-les-Dombes
Ambérieu-en-Bugey
Seysell
Valromey
Dombes
ANNECY
Pérouges
Lagnieu
Champagne-en-Valromey
SAVOIE
Virieu-le-Grand
Belley
LYON
Bas-Bugey
AIX-LES-BAINS
LYONNAIS
ISÈRE
RHÔNE
Chambéry
Vienne
DAUPHINÉ
GRENOBLE
Saône
Rhône
Ain

CHAPTER THIRTEEN

# The Pays of the Ain

BRESSE* – GEX† – BUGEY – VALROMEY – DOMBES

Bresse, Gex, Bugey, Valromey and Dombes came into Burgundy after it had become a *Gouvernement-général* under the kings of France. All except Dombes were acquired in 1601 from the duc de Savoie in exchange for the least convenient of Henri IV's many inheritances, the Marquisate of Saluzzo, or Saluces, in Piedmont. These lands owed much to the Church in the way their watery areas had been adapted for controlled fishing and grazing, and their mountain pastures for dairy purposes. The pastures provide milk for Comté and Bleu du Haut Jura today.

The principality of Dombes became an independent enclave within French territory in 1601, an anomaly tolerated for another 160 years, no doubt because this strange, rather desolate and watery *pays* was too poor to attract predators in search of gold or glory. St Vincent de Paul, a domestic chaplain in Dombes in 1617, described it as a *'région effroyable'*. The only notable feature, after game, fish and marsh fever, was a native race of horses for which the reigning prince, François de Bourbon-Montpensier, established an annual fair in 1605. The reigning family ceded the principality to the French crown in 1762.

The horse fair is still held on the nearest Saturday to 8 September at Montmerle-sur-Saône, but other things have changed, generally for the better. The country is less watery, and more healthy and smiling than it was. It now caters for ornithologists as well as horse-lovers, with a rich bird-sanctuary at Villars-lès-Dombes. Pérouges is worth a visit. You can take tea between two and six in season at the Ostellerie Vieux Pérouges (or stay there, if you are rich); it is a museum in itself, in a *bourg* restored to life as a *monument historique*.

Gex, and Valromey (the valley running south through Haut-Bugey on the Savoie side), had been in the ancient Kingdom of Burgundy, and were later ruled by the comtes de Genève before joining Savoie. The inhabitants, especially in the Manche (the north-eastern extremity of Gex, reached through the Collonges gap beside the Rhône), retained habits of dress,

---

*The northern part of Bresse-Louhannaise is in the *département* of Saône-et-Loire.
†Part of Gex is with Franche-Comté in Jura.

speech and trade more related to Switzerland than to Savoie or France. Eastwards from the crests of the Monts Jura to the Swiss border, the Manche has long formed a special custom-free zone. Right on the border is Ferney (now Ferney-Voltaire), where Voltaire spent his last twenty years.

Bugey has a respectable pedigree in the cheese world, with Comté and the smaller native goats'- and cows'-milk cheeses. (A fifth of all France's Comté and Emmental Français is produced in the Ain, but these two cheeses are covered in detail under Franche-Comté and Savoie (Chapters 14 and 15).) Another feather in the region's gastronomic cap is its fathering of Brillat-Savarin, a loyal son of Belley. In the Val de Bugey and Seyssel, Bugey grows agreeable light wines to accompany its cheeses. (Two Seyssels face each other across the Rhône, sharing the Appellation d'Origine Contrôlée name between Bugey and Savoie.)

## Saingorlon and the soft blue cheeses of Bresse

Bresse is famed for its red-crested, blue-legged, white-feathered chickens, happily free range for five out of the six months of their lives, and then more confined for finishing. Bresse, Dombes and Bugey are all notable for their game, freshwater fish, eels and *écrevisses*; and for that extraordinarily laborious transformation of the fibrous flesh of the pike into edible form, *quenelles de brochet* (*quenelles* is derived from *Knödel*, the German noodle). These simple, light, refreshing *gnocchi* (the Italian seems nearer to *Knödel*) are a wonderful excuse for indulging in rich sauces, such as Nantua (of which there should always be a generous reserve on the table to top up with).

Outside the gourmet world, however, Bresse is now more widely known abroad for its modern, industrial blue cheeses. These pasteurised products in their blue-and-silver foil uniforms owe their existence to fascist folly. When Italy entered the war against France in 1940, the Midi's many devotees of Gorgonzola were cut off from their favourite cheese. To console them, *laitiers* of Bresse turned profitably to making an imitation of Gorgonzola which they called Saingorlon. When Gorgonzola production and export were eventually re-established in the late 1940s, the Bresse cheesemakers, while not abandoning Saingorlon (2000 tonnes were made in 1982), turned their minds and resources to quite a different sort of soft blue. Bresse Bleu was typical of such cheeses, and their pioneer in the export trade. At their best these blues are melting in texture and mildly interesting in flavour. They are quite unlike Gorgonzola in flavour and colour, being white and blue while Gorgonzola is pale cream and green.

Thoroughly industrialised, the new cheeses suffer three serious disadvantages: pasteurisation of the milk, artificial speeding up or skimping of the ripening process, and the general tendency of those who handle them all along the line to keep them too cold. When these faults combine, the result is stodgy dullness. Typical of the modern pattern in Bresse is the Laiterie Coopérative de Grièges. Formed by forty-eight farmers in 1934, it now has 1800 members. Its annual production, with the most modern factory machines, amounts to 6800 tonnes, consisting mainly of Bleu de Bresse-

France-Bresse, Pipo Crem and Saingorlon. The *laiterie* makes 1200 tonnes of white soft cheeses: Bibress (a small log) and the quite good Vallières range, in Brie and Coulommiers style.

In a Burgundy market I found small Bresse Bleu marked *'fermier'*, soft with a beautiful *croûte-fleurie*, not looking at all like the factory cheese; however, the merchant was unable (or unwilling?) to tell me where it came from, so, as Bresse Bleu is not traditional, it must have been a case of factory cheese given extra, rustic *affinage*.

In the Bresse Louhannaise (of which the northern part lies in Saône-et-Loire) there is an unusual cheese shop at Pont-de-Vaux run by Monsieur J.-J. Desroches, a young *fromager* and *affineur*. Showing refreshing enterprise, he not only presents cheese of Bresse and neighbouring Lyonnais; he converts a local *fromage blanc* into traditional Vieux Bressan, and into *tartes Bressanes* of six kinds. He also makes other appetising cheese products of local tradition, or of his own devising, from curds and *fromages frais* of nearby farms (see Pont-de-Vaux in list, p. 390).

## Chèvres

On either side of Pont-de-Vaux lie Simandre and Sermoyer, old sources of goat cheese which Pierre Androuët visited in 1982. I confirmed in 1986 that good drum-shaped goat cheeses, much bigger than Mâconnais, are still made on farms around Sermoyer. I also enjoyed a young chèvre of Charollais format, made on a farm at Chavannes-sur-Reyssouze and bought from Monsieur Desroches. We ate it picnicking on the west bank of the Saône among the barge moorings below the bridge. The backdrop included cruising swans, and herons on their beat above the high poplars lining the opposite bank. Afterwards we crossed the Saône again, and drove through heath and stream country scattered with ponds, and oak and birch woods, all typical of lower-lying Bresse.

## Bleu de Gex and Bleu de Septmoncel

After Bresse, it seemed appropriate to contrast with those industrial and most modern of blues one of France's oldest, and least changed cheeses, Bleu de Gex. (A current recipe for Bleu de Gex is given on p. 386.)

For over six centuries Bleu de Gex has been made in *fruitières* from the milk of beasts grazing these timeless mountain pastures, or wintering on hay made from the same plants and grasses. The cheese is usually more gentle, yet more interesting in flavour, than any other blue. In the early 1970s my wife discovered why. She was in Gex to write an article on the craftsmen who turn and carve boxwood chessmen at Oyonnax; but she knew that I would want to hear about traditional local products of a more edible nature. At a small Oyonnax *crémerie* she found a farmhouse Bleu de Gex made at over 1000 metres and ripened for nearly three months in the natural *caves* of Saint-Germain-de-Joux. With it she was given a story not included in any account of the cheese that I have read.

The official leaflet of the National Committee for Appellations d'Origine Contrôlées de Fromage attributes the typical aroma and flavour of Bleu de

Gex to the extremely varied and scented flora of the highest pastures in the Jura, but they miss out the secret of natural blueing known to the farmhouse cheesemakers (now, alas, all gone). The flowers are not all that matters, but two of them do make a special contribution. The leaves and stems of *Grande pimprenelle* (burnet or bloodwort) and *Alchémille* (Alpine Lady's-mantle) are hosts to a fermenting fungal bloom; so the red-pied cows, all Montbéliardes, ingest the mould with the plants while grazing, and some of it goes with the plant oils into their mammary glands. The blue of that Gex was in the milk before the cheesemaker went to work on it. The resulting cheese survived a long journey to be relished, along with its story, by a favoured few in Streatley.

Bleu de Gex is made entirely from the milk of Montbéliardes. (This fine breed has also long shared with the Pie-rouge de l'Est, and the splendid high pastures, the credit for putting the backbone into Comté.) May to October is the season in the higher pastures, and the maximum period of ripening is three months, so late July to January is the best season for eating. It is not by chance that I have eaten perfect Bleu de Gex at the end of January and a rather dull cheese in early February.

The pedigree of the cheese goes back to the knowledge and skill of those Dauphinois *fromagers* who came to Gex when their native Dauphiné was handed over to France in 1343 (see Chapter 16). They were welcomed by a compatriot, the Abbé Jean de Roussillon at the ancient Abbaye de Saint-Claude. The *abbaye* had started keeping goats for goat-hair drugget manufacture in the thirteenth century, and a dairy by-product of this enterprise was their goats'-milk *chevret* (the local term for a usually rectangular chèvre). They had also started to make cows'-milk *tommes grises* in dairies at Les Bouchoux and at Les Moussières, where an active *fruitière* survives to this day. The Dauphinois *immigrés* introduced to the dairies their own native recipe for Bleu de Sassenage, which became known in their new *pays* as Bleu de Gex and Bleu de Septmoncel. They probably used a mixture of goats' and cows' milk. (More than a century later the best Dauphinois cheesemakers around Sassenage were mixing goats', cows' and ewes' milk for their cheese.*)

The *coopérative fruitière* system, already active in Comté cheesemaking, is likely to have co-existed with the monks' cheese dairy for the early making of Gex and Septmoncel; but the *abbaye*'s strict strict rule of work and worship was already on its way out, so *fruitières* and, later, farms became the sole sources of the cheese. Five farms were still making Bleu de Gex in 1960, of which the Perriers', near La Pesse, was still active when I started researching this book in 1984. Unhappily, two generations of the Perrier family suffered severe illness and death within two years and, when I revisited the neighbourhood in 1986, making had ceased and I was told that it was unlikely to resume. All production is now in *fruitières*, and the names Gex and Septmoncel are interchangeable for the same cheese under the umbrella AOC, Bleu du Haut Jura.

*Olivier de Serres, *Théâtre de l'Agriculture et Ménagier des Champs*, 1600.

The five *fruitières* of the Pays de Gex making this cheese are at Lajoux, Les Moussières and La Pesse in the Jura, and at Giron and Chézery in the Ain. In 1985 they were collecting 600,000 litres of milk a month from 250 farms, enough for 550 tonnes of cheese. This was a 10 per cent increase since 1960, when the number of farms had been 500. The annual rate of production levelled out at about 650 tonnes in 1986, by which time it was being affected by the EEC milk quota, so I was told at Les Moussières, despite its being a full-blooded mountain cheese.

Until recently the cheese was made morning and evening, the milk being renneted at milking temperature (with rennet prepared on the farm from the vell (see Glossary) or *caillette*). The practice is now to mix the overnight milk with the morning milk and to raise the temperature for renneting to between 28° and 30°C (at least at Les Moussières). Industrial rennet is in general use and a light dose of *penicillium roquefortii* is injected at this stage, two sad factors diminishing the local character of the cheese. As is the common fashion, the cheesemaking timetable has been speeded up, but in detail the methods show little change. Vats are bigger, and rectangular, but the design and scale of implements suits artisanal rather than factory practices. The *fruitières* have an average daily total of only 250 cheeses between them.

In 1935 an AOC was created for Bleu de Gex and Bleu de Septmoncel, confirmed in a 1977 decree of Appellation Contrôlée (which added the collective term 'Bleu de Haut Jura'). Milk production for the cheese is confined to its fourteenth-century area of origin, the cantons of Gex in the Ain and of Saint-Claude and Les Bouchoux in the Jura. The milk must come only from Montbéliardes pastured at over 1000 metres, and when the cows are not out in their traditional permanent pastures their main sustenance must come from the local hay. Silage is ruled out, together with any other feedstuffs which could interfere with the truly native character of the milk.

These safeguards are some comfort. So many blues of respectable ancestry have been allowed through pasteurisation, factory methods and the indiscriminate use of factory *penicillium roquefortii* to grow more and more like each other and less and less like their admirably eccentric ancestors. It disturbs me that, although the Comité National des Appellations Contrôlées properly lays down that Bleu du Haut Jura should develop its internal mould naturally in the *cave*, the practice has crept in of injecting at the renneting stage a version of the common *penicillium roquefortii*. This is designed 'to inhibit or pre-empt foreign moulds', I was told at Les Moussières; but I wonder whether that fungal gift of the alpine flowers survives this treatment, for no mould could be more native or more desirable than that.

Gex and Septmoncel have at least preserved their traditional crust, a factor of enormous importance in maintaining proper texture and flavour within a cheese. One element contributing to this is the use of jute sacks to line the moulds. They were first used to save money, as they came free with the salt (and are, of course, impregnated with it). Now they are known to absorb whey and to encourage crust formation.*

The Pays de Gex has suffered from partition, but I have treated her as one *pays*, disregarding the Ain–Jura boundary. Now we can return to the north to study the main part of Franche-Comté beyond.

## Recipe for Bleu de Gex

Evening and morning milk renneted (9c.c. industrial rennet to 80 litres = one cheese). Temperature 23–26°C in spring and summer, 26–29°C in autumn and winter.

*Day of making*

| | |
|---|---|
| 40–60 minutes after start: | milk sets. |
| 80–110 minutes after start: | skimming of cream (fat level too high). |
| 120–140 minutes after start: | coagulation completed. |
| 140–155 minutes after start: | curd turned and cut to between pea and small walnut size. |
| 160–205 minutes after start: | curd left to continue expulsion of whey. |
| 205–250 minutes after start: | curd very slowly piled with *poche percée* (something like a colander) on one side of the vat, making for more loss of whey through pressure of piled-up curd. |
| 215–280 minutes after start: | whey released from vat and curd left to harden (10 minutes in summer, 20–30 minutes in winter). |
| | curd packed by hand or *poche* into moulds lined with 90cm square cloth, being broken up by fingers in the process and packed against sides of moulds. Enough curd is packed to make cheeses of 7–9 kilos. |
| 5 minutes after moulding: | cheeses turned. |
| 3–4 hours later: | cheeses turned again (according to effectiveness of whey drainage) and sometimes a third time. Moulds placed in circular wooden *baquets* (not pierced) slightly bigger than the moulds themselves. One handful of salt applied to top of each cheese and moulds are piled in *salles d'égouttage* at 17–20°C. |

*Jute is used instead of traditional cheesecloth for wrapping Blue Cheshire in England, an innovation by Mrs Hutchinson-Smith at Whitchurch, Shropshire, in the cause of producing a better crust.

*1st day after making*
Cheeses turned again; brine removed and other face salted.

*2nd day (morning)*
Repeat of above (the volume of brine, *saumure*, is diminishing). More salt applied to well-drained cheeses, less to those still too moist, which could take in too much.

*3rd day (morning)*
Repeat with less salt (*fromage affiné* has 2.5–3% salt).

*4th to between 10th and 13th days*
Cheese turned without salting until whey has ceased to drain.

*Out of salle d'égouttage into séchoir*
Cheeses placed on high shelves of spaced planks for circulation of air; ventilated from 8–12°C, 75–85% humidity.

*After 2 days (10 days in a few fruitières)*
Cheeses turned and pricked; sometimes repricked after 3 weeks if blue has not developed. *Affinage en cave* 45–60 days. Moist soft cheeses blue more quickly, but have a more pronounced bitterness in their flavour.

(See page 385 on the natural development of mould.)

## Cheeses of the Pays of the Ain

### Ambérieu
50g truncated cone, very local (and see RAMEQUIN).
*fermier; chèvre/mi-chèvre cru.*
Bugey; 74 **3**, lower R.

### Belle Bressane
2kg soft blue ring. If not chilled to stodginess, one of the best of the Bresse *bleus*, and practical for cutting in its naturally crusted ring; from Coopérative de Grièges. 50% m.g.; *industriel; vache pasteurisé.*
Grièges; 73 **1**, top R.

### Belley
Saturday market.
Bugey; 74 **14**, top R.

### Belley, Chevret or Tomme de Belley.
150g chèvre April to November, natural crust. Square, 2cm deep, or round, flat. Natural *croute-bleutée*, sometimes with red patches.

40–45% m.g.; *fermier; chèvre/mi-chèvre cru.*
Bugey; 74 **14**, top R.

### Bibress
Small soft white log, Coopérative de Grièges.
*industriel.*
Grièges.

### Bleu
See BRESSE and GEX.

### Boules Aromatiques
See PONT-DE-VAUX.

### Bourg-en-Bresse
Fine Wednesday and Saturday markets; Grande Foire first Wed. of the month.
Bresse; 74 **3**, top L.

### Bressan or Petit Bressan
60–100g truncated cone, soft when young, but dries quickly; sometimes kept until

very hard. Sold from one week old. Crust becomes soft golden, then blues as it hardens in many cases. Thoissey (see p. 390) is similar. See also VIEUX BRESSAN.
40–45% m.g.; *fermier; chèvre/mi-chèvre cru.*
Bresse-Louhannaise/Valromey.

BRESSE

**Bleu de Bresse.** Similar in sizes and character to the below, but the large cheese is in drum form, not cylindrical. I have found them usually less melting than Bresse Bleu. Bleu de Bresse comes from Coopérative de Grièges (Ain), which makes the pleasant log, Pipo Crem (see p. 390). *Note:* I am told that accelerated *affinage* sends some industrial cheeses out into the world little more than a week old.
*industriel; vache pasteurisé.*

**Bresse Bleu.** 125g, 250g and 500g soft, mould-coated blue cheeses of Saingorlon type. Smaller cheeses are given cardboard collar; all are foil-wrapped. Pleasant, if not stodgy through overkeeping or overchilling. Made by Laiterie Coopérative Servas (Ain), which also makes a 2.5kg foil-wrapped log, called by the maker *'fourme'*.
*industriel; vache pasteurisé.*

**Bresse Bleu Fermier.** I have once seen a cheese so labelled, about 250g size, in a market, but have my doubts.
*fermier; vache cru.*
Servas/Grièges; 74 **2**, mid R/74 **1**, top R.

BÛCHE AUX NOIX

200g soft curd rolled with walnuts made by *fromager* at Pont-de-Vaux (see p. 390).
*shop product; vache.*
Bresse.

BUGEY

**Bugey, Petit Bugey.** Crottin-like, smooth, bluish coat; Laiterie St Benoît, 01300 Belley.
*laitier; vache.*
Ain; 70 **14**.

**Rigoton de Bugey.** 50g golden, hardening fairly quickly (see also FROMAGE FORT and RAMEQUIN).
*fermier; artisanal; vache cru.*

**Tomme or Tomme de Bugey.** See BELLEY.

CHAMPAGNE-EN-VALROMEY

Thursday market.
Valromey; 74 **4**, lower R.

CHAVANNES-SUR-REYSSOUZE

**Chèvre Frais.** 100g truncated cone, soft; sold at Pont-de-Vaux (see p. 390).
*fermier; chèvre cru.*
Bresse; 70 **12**.

CHÈVRES

See BRESSAN, CHAVANNES, DOMBERGÈRE, FAREINS, PONT-DE-VAUX, SAINT ANDRÉ, SERMOYER.

CHEVRET

See BELLEY and Chapter 14, p. 405.

CHÉZERY-FORENS

**Bleu de Gex.** Fromagerie de l'Abbaye; André and Suzanne Gros; 30 years' experience; make 45 cheeses a day, 07.00–12.00 and 19–20.00. Tel. 50 56 91 67.
Gex; 74 **5**, top.

COMTÉ

Parts of Gex, Bresse and Bugey are within the AOC region for Comté and make large quantities.
*fruitière; vache cru.*
Comté.

COEUR DE BRESSE

One of the big Bresse *laiteries* now makes a heart-shaped version.
*industriel; vache pasteurisé.*
Bresse.

CRÈME DE BLEU AUX NOIX, CRÈME DE BLEU CHÈVRE

See PONT-DE-VAUX.

DOMBERGÈRE

Small chèvre recommended (with Pouilly to drink) by MM. Cénéri, the *maîtres fromagers* of Cannes.
*fermier; chèvre cru.*
Dombes.

DÔME AU POÎVRE

See PONT-DE-VAUX.

ÉTOILE

See REVERMONT.

FAREINS

**Chèvre Fermier.** M. M. Vapillon runs a *ferme-auberge* (closed on Thursday evenings), serving his own cheese and Poulet de Bresse *à la crème*, at La Bicheronne, Fareins, 01480 Jassans-Riottier (across

Saône from Villefranche). Tel. 74 61 81 01.
*fermier; chèvre cru.*
Bresse; 74 **1**, NE of Villefranche.

FOURME

See SAINT-BRICEL and BRESSE BLEU.

FROMAGE BLANC

By Reybier at Lie-St-Trivier-de-Courtes; sold at Pont-de-Vaux and commended.
*laitier; vache pasteurisé.*
Bresse, 70 **12**, C.

FROMAGE FORT

Remnants of various cheeses mixed with white wine and put on slices of bread in the oven.

**Fromage Fort de Bresse au Vin Blanc.**

**Fromage Fort du Bugey or du Petit Bugey.** Ramequins (see p. 391) kept long and strong, melted and eaten or potted with suitable additives. I have heard of but not tasted this potted and enriched version of this cheese. I would expect rigotons to be used too. (And see TRACLE, FROMAGE FORT DE SAINT-RAMBERT-EN-BUGEY.)
*domestique; vache cru.*
Bugey.

GEX MARKET

Mon, Thur.

**Bleu de Gex, Bleu du Haut Jura.** (Both AOC.) 7–9kg round-edged wheel 36cm × 10cm; salted in wooden vat during drainage of curd; brushed crust achieving dry, floury, pale-gold, slightly rough surface with GEX stamped on face. The *pâte* is creamy yellow, close-veined with greeny blue unctuous: *'fromages à pâte femelle'*. If *too* yellow, it will be too bitter (inadequate drainage of whey); if white, too hard, underripe and little blue: *'fromages noués'*. The cheese is ripened for a minimum of 70 days (usually 3–6 months). Blueing of a special natural character (see pp. 383–4).
*50% m.g.; haute-montagne chalet over 1000m; vache (Montbéliarde only) cru.*
Fruitières. Ain: Giron W of St-Germain-de-Joux (74 **5**, top L, 70 **15**, bottom L). Chézery-Forens (see p. 388); Forens, N of Bellegarde (74 **5**, top). Jura: La Pesse (70 **15**, low L, S of St-Claude, between N43 and N84); Fromagerie Coopérative du Plateau des Moussières (successors to Roger Vuaillat), Lajoux (E of Septmoncel 70 **15**, on N436 towards La Valsérine, tel. 84 42

60 38). Sales at dairies usually between 08.00 and 12.00, 14.30 and 19.00 (but see CHÉZERY-FORENS and I found no one at Lajoux on a September Monday afternoon).
Rungis agents: Reybier, Arnaud.
Local markets: Gex (Ain), St-Claude (Jura), 70 **15**, SE from C.
*Note:* Mature cheeses have only 40–42% humidity.

**Bleu de Gex Fermier.** There were five farms in 1960, but the last ceased production in 1985 (see p. 384).
*chalet; fermier; vache cru.*

GÊNES

See PONT-DE-VAUX.

GRIÈGES

**Bleu de Bresse.** Laiterie Coopérative de Grièges makes Belle Bressane, Pipo Crem, Saingorlon (6800 tonnes a year) and Vallières (Brie-, Coulommiers-types) and Bibress (1200 tonnes of soft white a year).
Bresse; 74 **1**, top R.

GRUYÈRE FRANÇAIS

This region contributes milk to the large-scale manufacture of the Gruyère type (distinct from Comté, see p. 382).

LAGNIEU

Monday market.

**Lagnieu.** 50g soft truncated cone (*rigotte*-type), ripened up to 3 weeks (thereafter see RAMEQUIN DE LAGNIEU).
*30–50% m.g.; fermier; chèvre/mi-chèvre cru.*
Bugey; 74 **3**, top R.

LATINICIEN

See RAMEQUINS.

LIE-ST-TRIVIER-DE-COURTES

Laiterie Reybier (see FROMAGE BLANC, LES SARRAZINS).
Bresse; 70 **12**, C.

LOUHANS

Gilles Guyon, *fromager*, 4 Grand'rue.
Bresse; 70 **13**, top L.

MONTMERLE-SUR-SAÔNE

**Montmerle.** Small soft cheese (see p. 381 on Montmerle.)
*artisanal; vache cru.*
Dombes 12km N of Villefranche; 74 **1**.

### Morbier
Golden-crusted, semi-soft cheese with dark vegetable layer (see SARRAZINS for makers and Chapter 14, pp. 398–9).
*laitier; industriel; vache pasteurisé.*
Bresse.

### Nantua
Saturday market.
Gex; 74 **4**.

### Ordonnaz
**Soft Cheese** (unspecified). Made and served by M. R. Laracine (with his raw ham and *roulette de Bugey*) at his *ferme-auberge*, Vieille Ville, Ordonnaz, 01510 Virieu (open weekends; closed Dec; telephone in advance about weekdays: 74 36 42 38).
*fermier.*
Bugey; 74 **4**, bottom.

### Oyonnax
Markets: Mon, Thur, Sat.
Gex; 74 **4**, top.

### Parbressan
Industrial imitation of Parmesan from Bresse.
*laitier; vache.*

### Pass'ain
Grana-type made at Châtillon-sur-Chalaronne.
Passe l'an, similar, is made in Quercy.
*low-fat; laitier; vache.*
Dombes; 74 **2**, L.

### Petit Bugey
See BUGEY.

### Pipo crem
2kg cylindrical soft blue, natural white crust. One of the pleasanter modern blues of the region made by Coopérative de Grièges.
*laitier; industriel; vache pasteurisé.*
Bresse; 74 **1**, top R.

### Polliat
Local spring to early winter chèvre.
*fermier; artisanal; chèvre.*
Bresse; 74 **2**, top R on N79.

### Pont-de-Vaux
Wednesday market.

*Crémerie*: Apart from a selection of local cheeses from Bresse and the Lyonnais, and from further afield, M. J. J. Desroches, *fromager* and *affineur*, prepares the cheeses below from local curd (cows' and *chèvres'*) and from local *fromage blanc*.
Bresse; 70 **12**, mid-left.

**Boules Aromatisées.** *Fromage frais* rolled into balls flavoured with cumin, *fines-herbes, herbes-de-Provence*, walnuts, paprika or pepper (6 kinds in 1986).
*made on premises; lait de mélange cru.*

**Bûche aux Noix.** 200g *fromage frais* rolled with crushed walnuts into log.
*made on premises; vache cru.*

**Chèvre aux Gênes.** 150g chèvre (from Chavannes, see p. 388) coated with *gênes de grappe de raisin* (grape pressings before they have gone into the *alambic* [still] for making of marc). M. Desroches sprinkles marc on to the cheese surface at the moment of sale (if desired). Only available in February.
*fermier, enriched on premises; chèvre cru.*

**Crème de Bleu aux Noix.** Rectangular layered cheese, alternating white curd and blue with walnuts, coated with butter.
*made on premises; vache cru.*
Bresse; 70 **12**, mid L.

**Crème de Bleu Chèvre.** Cheese similar in appearance, but without walnuts, and made of goats' curd.
*made on premises; chèvre cru.*

### Pourri or Vieux Bressan
Almost fat-free *fromage blanc* treated with 'good white wine' and yeast. Farms used to ferment Pourri in fireplaces. Spoon to eat. (Pont-de-Vaux shop.)
*made on premises; vache pasteurisé.*
Bresse.

### Ramequins

**Amberieu, Ramequin d'; Lagrieu, Ramequin d'.**
*30–50% m.g.; fermier; domestique; chèvre/mi-chèvre cru.*

**Bugey, Ramequin de; Latinicien, Ramequin.**
*30–35% m.g.; fermier; domestique; chèvre/mi-chèvre cru.*

The above four cheeses are small and often kept until very strong for fondue and local version of *fromage fort*.

### Revermont

**L'Étoile de Revermont.** 200g soft round cheese made by Sica, Mns, 01240 Servas.
55% m.g.; *laitier; vache.*
Bresse.

### Rigoton
See BUGEY.

### Saingorlon

Gentle blue cheese made by Éts Rousset (8A) 16 Bvd J. Curie 69631 Vénissieux (Lyon) and Laiterie Coopérative de Grièges.
50% m.g.; *laitier; industriel; vache pasteurisé.*
Bresse.

### St-André-d'Huiriat

**Chèvres.** Made by M. Georges Lebon, at La Mare Caillat, St-André-d'Huiriat, 01290 Pont-de-Veyle, his organic farm.
*fermier; biologique; chèvre cru.*

**Tomme de Vache.**
*fermier; biologique; vache cru.*
Bresse; 74 **2**, high L, 5km SE of Pont-de-Veyle.

### St-Bricel

**Fourme Saint-Bricel.** Log-shaped, soft-crusted blue.
*laitier; vache pasteurisé.*

### St-Rambert-en-Bugey, Fromage Fort de
See TRACLE.

### Sarrazins

**Fromage des Sarrazins.** Agreeable 1kg semi-soft, washed-crust cheese; deeper than Chaumes (and senior to it), becoming quite rich in its golden crust. This is thin when young, stouter when aged. Made by Reybier, Lie-St-Trivier-des-Courtes, where they also produce *fromage blanc* and a version of Morbier (see Chapter 14).
*laitier; industriel; vache pasteurisé.*
Bresse; 70 **12**, C.

### Sermoyer

**Chèvres.** Several farms round this village were still making chèvres rather bigger than Maconnais, sold *frais* and *demi-sec* in 1986. Androuët praised them in 1982.
*fermier; chèvre cru.*
Bresse; N of Pont-de-Vaux on Tournus road 70 **12**, left C.

### Tartes Bressanes
See PONT-DE-VAUX.

### Thoissey

Cheese like Bressan (see p. 388).
*fermier; chèvre/mi-chèvre cru.*

**Fromage Frais.** Made in Thoissey.
*laitier; vache.*
Bresse; 6km from Mâcon, 29km from Villefranche; 74 **1**, NE of C.

### Tome, Tomme
See BELLEY.

### Tracle

**Fromage Fort de Saint-Rambert-en-Bugey.** Made with local cheeses and wines, similar to other Bugey preparations (Ninette Lyon, 1978).
*laitier; vache.*
Bugey; 74 **3/4**.

### Vallières
See GRIÈGES.

**Château de Vallières.** Name of approximately 1kg Brie-type and smaller Coulommiers-type soft cheese, well made and agreeable; the crust turns a good golden colour if properly kept; made by Coopérative de Grièges.
50% m.g.; *industriel; vache.*

### Vieux Bressan

Another name for Pourri (see p. 390).

### Villars-les-Dombes

Tuesday market.
Caves d'Affinage des Dombes (tel. 74 98 06 54).
Dombes/Ain; 74 **2**, S of C.

### Vonnas

Thursday market.
*Maître fromager et affineur,* specialising in cheeses which are *'sains'* (healthy), organic, authentic. He will not sell Roquefort Société, but only Roquefort Papillon, 'because Société adds factory *penicillium roquefortii,* while Papillon collects it in the caves.'
Bresse/Ain; 74 **2**, high L.

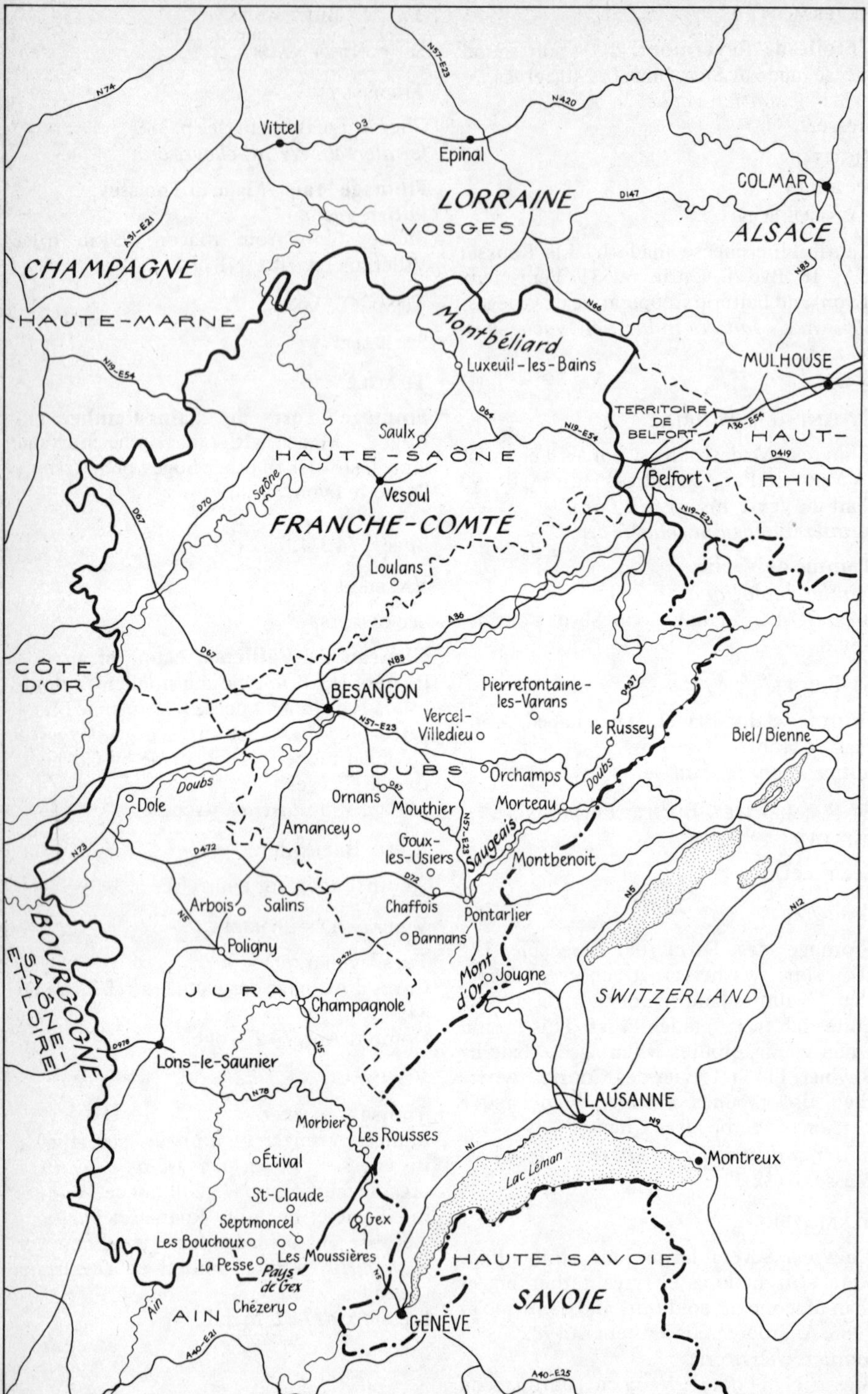

N74
Vittel
D3
N57-E23
Epinal
N420
COLMAR
LORRAINE
VOSGES
D147
ALSACE
A31-E21
CHAMPAGNE
N83
HAUTE-MARNE
Montbéliard
N66
Luxeuil-les-Bains
MULHOUSE
N19-E54
D64
TERRITOIRE DE BELFORT
A36-E54
HAUT-RHIN
Saulx
HAUTE-SAÔNE
D419
Belfort
Vesoul
Saône
D70
D67
FRANCHE-COMTÉ
N19-E27
Loulans
A36
CÔTE D'OR
N83
BESANÇON
Pierrefontaine-les-Varans
D437
Vercel-Villedieu
N57-E23
le Russey
Biel/Bienne
DOUBS
Orchamps
Doubs
Ornans
Mouthier
Morteau
Dole
Amancey
Goux-les-Usiers
Saugeais
Montbenoit
N73
D472
D72
Chaffois
N5
Arbois
Salins
Pontarlier
N12
BOURGOGNE
SAÔNE-ET-LOIRE
Bannans
Poligny
D471
Mont d'Or
Jougne
SWITZERLAND
JURA
Champagnole
D978
Lons-le-Saunier
N78
LAUSANNE
Morbier
Les Rousses
N9
N1
Montreux
Étival
Lac Léman
St-Claude
Gex
Septmoncel
Les Bouchoux
Les Moussières
La Pesse
Pays de Gex
HAUTE-SAVOIE
SAVOIE
Chézery
AIN
Ain
GENÈVE
A40-E21
A40-E25

CHAPTER FOURTEEN

# La Franche-Comté

DOUBS – HAUTE-SAÔNE – JURA – AIN* – CÔTE D'OR – HAUTE-MARNE – VOSGES

This land between the Saône and the summits of the Jura has been known for the independence of its people and character since pre-Roman times. Then called Séquanie, its capital was Vesontio (still the capital today, but now spelled Besançon). Its shepherds and cowherds were already noted for their cheeses. In 1366 La Franche-Comté was first mentioned as such in an official document. This comté was notable not only for its implicit self-rule but also for its gender. Franche-Comté is unique in its femininity among all the comtés of France.

The comté went by marriage to Burgundy and later to the Habsburgs. Under the Emperor Charles V, whom you can see in his final moments of golden glory in a tapestry at the Palais Granvelle in Besançon, it enjoyed its greatest period of prosperity. The Francs-Comtois were always jealous of their self-rule, and it was not until 1678 that Louis XIV finally acquired the comté by treaty.

## Gruyère de Comté

The Séquanes had welcomed the Burgondes in AD 457 and become part of their shortlived new kingdom, conquered in 534 by the Franks. When the greatest of Frankish kings, Charlemagne, established the Holy Roman Empire (all modern France and Switzerland, and much of Germany), he created a corps of *officiers gruyers* to manage the *grueries* or *gruyeries*, as his forests were called. Cheesemakers used large quantities of fuel in the course of their work, cheese being made twice a day as each milking came fresh from the cows. They had to buy the fuel from the local *gruyer*, and this term became attached to the resulting cheeses, some of which were collected by the *gruyers* as payment for fuel.

Hence the name became geographically attached to the great Swiss centre of cheesemaking: Gruyère, or Greyertal. The word is also found in place-names in Savoie. Because the geographical Gruyère went finally to Switzerland, the Swiss have come to regard the term as strictly theirs; but historically there was no monopoly of the technical term. Gruyère de

*Some *communes* of Ain fall into the Franche-Comté region, as defined in 1952.

Comté is perfectly proper, and the term Gruyère has been agreed upon as the co-property of France and Switzerland.

The use of wood fuel in dairies has almost ceased, but the modern successors of the *gruyers* now supply the bark of *épicéa* (spruce) to encircle Vacherin.

Franche-Comté gained an appendage after the Revolution with the annexation in 1801 of the principality of Montbéliard. Formerly ruled by the House of Württemberg, this *pays* was the source of the great mountain breed of white-headed, red-and-white cattle which bears its name. There are now about 800,000 Montbéliarde cows in milk, a number exceeded only by Frisonnes français and Normandes; they are second only to the Frisonnes in yield, and on their home pastures are certainly superior. The quality of their milk is incomparably better. Milk of Montbéliardes, or of the Pie-rouges de l'Est is legally specified by the Appellation d'Origine Contrôlée for the making of Gruyère de Comté; and milk of Montbéliardes alone is demanded for Bleu de Gex and Bleu de Septmoncel (see pp. 383–6).

From the twelfth century the monasteries were pioneers in dairy farming for cheese, although the ancestors of the cheese we know as Comté existed before the great days of the monks. The twelfth and thirteenth centuries saw advances in agriculture and dairy, with the clearance of the high plateaux of the Jura, creating *alpages* above the tree-line to provide the necessary rich pastures for the summer *transhumance*. The importance of using to the full, or 'fructifying', the brief summer access to the high pastures had already been recognised. Large, hard-crusted cheeses had proved a safe means of storing surplus production for sustenance through the long, hard winters. As many as 530 litres of milk go into the average Gruyère de Comté, which is the yield of thirty cows. Most Comté farms have fifteen or fewer, and even that is far more than most of their predecessors. The problem was overcome by the co-operative system of delivering milk to a jointly owned village dairy, or *fructerie*. The farms were rewarded in proportion to their milk contributions, after paying for the cheesemaker, the dairy and its equipment. Over the years the name became *fruitière*, the adjective *fruitier*. The *fruitière* and its method of working can be traced in documents of 1264, 1267 and 1278 concerning the *communes* of Levier and Desservillers (near Amancey), now in the Doubs.

Over 300 *fruitières* operate today in the original region, but just after the Second World War the making of Comté spread well beyond its old confines. This led to decrees in 1958 restricting the area qualifying for the cheese's name; in April 1976 Comté won its AOC. This further restricted the area in which the cheese could be made and matured, allowing ten years for the removal or closing of enterprises outside the newly defined region. It still extends to Belfort (pronounced Béfort), the Côte-d'Or, and the Ain.

The AOCs for Gruyère de Comté and Bleu du Haut-Jura (covering Gex and Septmoncel, see Chapter 13) specify not only the breed of cow, but safeguards about their feeding. To preserve the local character derived from the natural pastures, and the high standard of texture of the cheese, the cows must 'be nourished according to the customs codified in the rules of the *fruitière*'. When they are in for the winter, their feed must be local hay and must exclude silage and 'any other fermented elements'. The AOC is therefore firmly based on the traditional practices maintained by the co-operatives for centuries. The only concession to an easier life is that cheese now need be made only once a day, not morning and evening as was the rule until recently. Some *fruitières* have installed controlled-temperature storage tanks on the farms and collect the milk once a day; but the law lays down that the milk must still be collected within twenty-four hours of milking time, except in severe winter conditions when thirty-six hours is permitted. The milk must only be used raw: 'Any system or installation capable of heating the milk before renneting to a temperature above 40°C is forbidden'.

Correct *affinage* is vital. The notice given to *affineurs* outside the region expired in April 1986, so all Comté now available has been locally matured. Grading is severe, and only cheeses given fourteen points out of twenty are stamped round their circumference with the green bell and the name 'COMTÉ'. If the cheese is pre-packed for sale, every piece must prove its traditional provenance by presenting 'one crusted, grainy surface characteristic of the Appellation'. French supermarkets could not get away with a Comté equivalent of the pre-packed 'farmhouse' rindless block Cheddar sold by their English counterparts; but they do not need to. The 40,000 tonnes of traditional raw-milk Comté produced annually is five times the 1986 production of all the British farms making any cheese in traditional ways.

In 1984 270 *fruitières* and 59 *laiteries artisanales* were producing mainly or entirely Gruyère de Comté. Their milk came from 5500 farms with an average yield of about 60 gallons a day. Most *fruitières* make seven or fewer cheeses a day, and there is no such thing as a Comté factory.

L'Institut National de la Recherche Agronomique at Poligny prepares starters related to local flora, and will tailor one individually suited to any cheesemaker. Many cheesemakers still guard their own secrets about preparing their *aizy* for starting and renneting, and about the ideal temperature for their different operations. On farms visited by Pierre Androuët in 1982, he described 'cows cared for like human beings with every sort of consideration, and tenderness too'. These factors, and the natural feeding of native breeds, are the foundation of the character and virtue of the cheeses of Franche-Comté.

Twenty *affineurs*, most of them Comté specialists, each take from 600 to 1700 tonnes of the cheese a year. By law it must be matured for at least ninety days, but four to five months is the time considered respectable and six months to a year is demanded by many devotees: the Swiss were looked on askance by the comtois in the 1970s for letting Gruyère out at only three months. Half the total production is sold by traditional *fromagers*, in shop and market, the other half in supermarkets and hypermarkets. Research has shown that over 40 per cent of the French eat Comté.

## Emmental Grand Cru

Of the remaining 50,000 tonnes of cheese produced annually in Franche-Comté, a large proportion is Emmental Grand Cru. This is made in great swelling wheels of up to 100 kilos, needing 1200 to 1300 litres of milk. Regional regulations for this raw-milk cheese are similar in strictness to those for Comté. They are backed by funds enabling sub-standard cheese to be withdrawn from the market, and in larger dairies allowing production to be switched between Comté and Emmental, according to demand. Emmental, which is matured for at least three months, is widely produced in the lower-lying *fruitières*. There is co-operation between the national and the regional professional bodies for French Gruyère, Comté, Beaufort and Emmental Grand Cru in studying production problems and market needs, and in exploiting their cheeses to the full.

Emmental has interesting by-products. Metton, or Meton, is coagulated milk or Ricotta made from whey. It is used to make Cancoillotte, or Fromagère. Metton was originally a domestic recipe for using up leftover milk or whey after cheesemaking, and Pierre Androuët thinks the use of whey for Metton goes back to the early nineteenth century, when whey was first treated to extract its remaining fat and other solids instead of being fed entire to pigs or calves. Mettons is a popular dish with the comtois, featuring even on the breakfast table.

To make Cancoillotte, the metton, once drained, is left to dry and then to ferment until golden-yellow with greenish lights (*pourrir* is the local term; see 'Pourri' in the list for the Ain, p. 390). In the country this fermenting used to be done in a little wooden bowl under the eiderdown next to the bedwarmer in the bed, or else in a warm *cave*.

> *Chaque femme de la Canton*
> *Vous dira que le metton*
> *Doit mûrir sous l'édredon.*\*

When it is a greeny-yellow with no trace of white it is melted in a *cocotte* or casserole over a gentle fire, with a few spoonfuls of salt water. As it starts to melt, ready-heated salt water and butter are gradually stirred in (30 grams of each for each 100 grams of Cancoillotte). After adding pepper and salt to taste, garlic or white wine too if required, and stirring until it is liquid, it is poured into pots holding 200 or 400 grams. There it can be kept cold for a few days. Superficial greying betrays fermentation, necessitating remelting and the addition of another spoonful of water or wine. That is Pierre Androuët's advice. Léone Bérard says that if greying is allowed to advance too far, this 'vigorous spread' is no longer edible. Ninette Lyon advises eating Cancoillotte warm, but keeping it cold until you are preparing to serve it. It can be eaten as a straight cheese, or used for Croque Monsieur or

---

\*Every woman in the Canton
Will tell you that the metton
Should ripen under the eiderdown.

to enrobe roast potatoes or poached eggs. There are claims that Cancoillotte goes back to pre-Roman times in Séquanie. It is certainly older than the sixteenth century, and is so deeply established as an essential tradition of Franche-Comté that there was a special ration card for it from 1940 to 1945.

The making of Comté is something the early-rising traveller should arrange to see. Most Syndicats d'Initiative will be able to direct you to a neighbouring *fruitière*, or to the École Nationale d'Industrie Laitière at Poligny.

The first event of the day is the arrival of the morning milk, which is closely inspected by the *fromager* before it is added to the overnight milk. On one of my visits to a *fruitière* I was told that the embarrassed farmer waiting outside was in deep trouble for bringing in milk contaminated by blood. The acceptable milk was already in the copper-lined vats, like enormous kettle-drums without skins. Below, gas jets heat the milk. Above runs a gantry leading to the bench where the cheese moulds are waiting. The moulds look like sections cut from a barrel, with toggled ropes around them.

Monsieur Thalmann showed me his way with Comté a few years ago at Les Grangettes. He had one vat large enough to provide for two cheeses, and one single-cheese vat. He put in his starter at 7 a.m. and his rennet at 7.10, by which time his milk temperature was up to 33°C (32° is now usual, 40° the legal maximum). He stirred in the rennet gently, a few droplets at a time. By 7.50 the whey was yellow and the curds seemed ready to cut (if whey is still white it is too soon to cut, if it is green it is too late). He relit the gas under the vat and started cutting the curd with his fifty-year-old, 6-foot *harpe* (ten wires with a spread of 6 inches on either side of the central column, and driven round the vat by electric power). If the curd is satisfactory, Monsieur Thalmann said, it need not be cut too fine, but if at all doubtful it should be cut much smaller. The usual standard is the size of a grain of wheat or rice. By 8.35 the temperature was 53°. At 8.50 he prepared the moulds, those unfixed circles of wood with overlapping ends held in place by the ropes (these run through slots in two wooden protuberances and can be loosened or tightened according to the amount of curd). They were lying on round spruce boards of much bigger circumference. From the sunlit wall outside he fetched in his *toiles*: cheesecloths which will do six months' service 'if looked after'.

At 9.07 the feel of a handful of curd told Monsieur Thalmann that it was ready to come out of the whey. The curd held together, but the grains were still separable and slightly hardening. He removed the cutter, pumped out the whey, and prepared the first cheesecloth. On one side he knotted the two corners of the cloth together and held the knots between his teeth. The edge of the opposite side of the cloth he dampened in the whey and curled round a whippy strip of metal (like one of those coiled-spring steel measures). Holding the two ends stretched out in his widespread hands, he suddenly took off, apparently on a dive into the vat. As he lunged, he shaped the metal-lined side of the cloth to fit the curve on the far side of the vat. Just in time, with his thighs already over the near side of the vat, he steadied himself by kicking his feet back against the wall behind, and began to trawl the curd out of the vat with the net-like cloth. The metal-lined edge closely caressed the rounded base of the vat, the cloth billowing as it collected the curd, until the *fromager* hauled it out up against his apron. He brought the steel-lined edge under his jaws, which still firmly held the other corners of the cloth. Dextrously flipping away the metal strip, he knotted the other two corners of the cloth together, and hung them and the knot from his mouth on the gantry hook overhead.

The enormous dripping sack must have weighed well over 50 kilos when still suspended from his teeth, which suggests an unexpected physical requirement for a cheesemaker: strong incisors, and all his own (most dairies now dispense with this circus-style feat of strength and legerdemain by using suction to extract the curd into two cloches suspended over the vat, each of which holds enough curd for one cheese).

Monsieur Thalmann then shunted the cloth to a point over the waiting mould and let it down inside. He loosened the ties and hand-pressed the curd down to fill the circlet and expel more whey. When the surface was flattened, he tightened the ropes. After filling his second mould, he took a small cloth to collect the little curd remaining in the vat and, lifting up one side of the big cheesecloth, pressed this curd into the side of the cheese. He placed his *fruitière*'s oval green casein plaque on the surface at this point and covered the cheese again. The cheesecloth would mark the surface of the cheese for the rest of its life.

At 9.20 he placed a heavy follower on the first cheese without applying pressure. By 9.30 the second cheese was ready and he put weights on the first. At 9.45 he applied an old vertical screw-press. Two hours later the first cheese was turned and pressure reapplied: the last operation before its removal to the *cave* for maturing.

## Morbier

My *fromager* made an interesting point about that last bit of curd rescued from the vat. He did not approve in principle of adding any curd to the complete cheese with its crust already beginning to form; but as the green plaque would alter the character of that section of the surface and the cheese behind it, he regarded this avoidance of waste as acceptable. However, as he reminded me, the purist view of an early nineteenth-century farmhouse Comté-maker in Morbier had led to the invention of a new cheese, long before green casein labels were thought of.

This man of Morbier did not like wasting the odd bit of curd; but his skill was such that the leftover was never big enough to make a respectable cheese. So he decided that, by covering its exposed surface with soot rubbed on to his hand from the base of the *chaudron*, he would inhibit crust from forming on top of the surplus curd from the morning Comté, and would also protect it from fly. In due course he would crown it with the leftover curd from the evening cheese. The result, brine-washed and rubbed to give it a good crust, was matured for two months, producing a cheese which had a refreshing, ivory-coloured, semi-soft interior with tiny apertures, and a thin horizontal layer of charcoal running not too tidily across the middle.

Other farms and *fruitières* copied this practical way of using up leftover curd insufficient for a full-sized Comté, or of exploiting their limited winter milk. Demand rose, and a growing number of dairies now devote part of their milk and labour to Morbier. They have formed a Syndicat des Fabricants du Véritable Morbier au Lait Cru de Franche-Comté to keep up the standards of this cheese as it grows in popularity.

The present-day Morbier is made from curd with a character between that of Comté and Vacherin. The milk is heated to 37–38°C and cut into one-inch cubes. The cheese is halved horizontally when removed from the press, given its layer of *noir végétal*, and re-pressed. The old layer of soot, or sometimes wood ash, is rarely available, but Patricia Wells found two farms at Chapelle-des-Bois (see list, p. 405) making it in the traditional way in 1987. Most filling for today's Morbier sandwich is a harmless and characterless vegetable product. The finished cheese is given two surface saltings, and rubbed twice a week in pure water for two months.

Monsieur Philippe, who makes Morbier from time to time at Chauffois, told me another story of its origin. A *fromagère*, having too little curd for a cheese one evening, left it near the hearth to wait for the morning. During the night a fall of soot sprayed the top of the cheese. In the morning she prepared the next day's curd and noticed, too late to arrest her act of topping up the previous night's cheese, that the soot had intervened. When she had cut the resulting cheese she exclaimed: *'C'est joli!'* and decided to make it again on purpose, using the soot from the base of her *chaudron*.

When buying Morbier, insist on the Véritable Lait Cru version. There are factories making it of pasteurised milk well outside the region, who try to cover their tracks by having it matured in Franche-Comté. In 1975 Monsieur Thalmann recommended the cheese made by Messieurs Graffe & Gerbier at Entre-les-Fourgs in La Chaumière à Potence, east of Jougne.

## VACHERIN DU MONT D'OR

Another happy by-product of the Comté dairy is Vacherin du Mont d'Or. This succulent seasonal cheese is of such glory that it has become the solace of our winter months. Cheese of this name has long been made in Franche-Comté and in the Vaud, a star of gastronomy whose light transcends frontiers. The Francs-Comtois never questioned Swiss use of the name, but always believed that it originated on their own side of the border in the eighteenth century. Most of the Mont d'Or, including its peak, lies well inside Franche-Comté, but the Swiss had nonetheless started to claim the name as their own before I visited Franche-Comté in 1973. I thought the French claim unassailable, but in the event the Swiss purloined the exclusive legal right to the name Vacherin Mont d'Or, previously shared with the Francs-Comtois for so many peaceful years.

In those times, if the maker's name and village of origin were not on the box, the almost infallible clue to the cheese's nationality was grammatical: Vacherin Mont d'Or *tout court* was probably Swiss; the more pedantic Vacherin *du* Mont d'Or was almost certainly French. Now both are Swiss, and the Francs-Comtois have to be content with 'Le Mont d'Or' or 'Vacherin du Haut-Doubs', a nonsense if ever there was one. Vacherin was invented before the *département* called Haut-Doubs was ever thought of. However, these are the names given to the cheese by their new AOC.

In the 1980s the Swiss have added injury to insult by pasteurising the milk for their Vacherin. This has not saved their cheeses from disastrous infections with *Listeria monocytogenes*, finally publicised in the winter of 1987–8 as having caused at least thirty-seven fatal cases of Listeriosis since 1983. This would have been bad enough if its effects had been confined to Switzerland; but the name Vacherin was blackened likewise through ignorant reporting about 'unpasteurised cheese'. Raw-milk cheese, on the contrary, has proved remarkably resistant to *Listeria monocytogenes*, though winter Vacherin-makers in France had to destroy their glorious, unsullied cheese because of undiscriminating sales-resistance. Some reports even suggested that Swiss Vacherin was the sought-after cheese and French the poor relation. This was ignorant *snobisme* at its most ridiculous. No experienced or informed cheese-lover would hesitate to prefer French Mont d'Or (or Vacherin du Haut-Doubs).

As we have seen, the mainstay of the dairy in Franche-Comté is the very big cheese requiring the daily milk of two or more farms, whence the practical value of the *fruitières*. In winter this region is often the coldest in France; early in 1987 the temperature dropped to −30°C. In the old days, when the milk of the smaller farms could no longer be brought into the *fruitières*, either they could mix several days' milk to make a Comté, which is undesirable for this sort of cheese, or they could make something smaller every day.

In my mind's eye I have often put myself in the place of a snowbound cheese-loving comtois farmer, collecting logs from the neat stack under the snow-heavy eaves. I have pictured his being suddenly struck by the warm beauty of the cut spruce and its resinous bark, which can glow like mahogany and smell like heaven. A cheese could look like this, he might well have felt. So, on a base cut across the log, with a ring of *épicéa* bark around it to contain its enthusiasm, a new soft cheese was born.

Bathing in brine helps seal bark and cheese together, and the resinous flavour and aroma spread into the cheese as it ripens. My nose tells me when the first cases of the new season's Vacherin have arrived in my shop in Streatley. Year after year, I find this seasonal joy as exciting as ever.

The surface of the mature cheese varies from pale yellow to pinkish gold, and is billowy. If cut before it runs, the interior is moist, pale creamy-white with a delicate scatter of tiny holes. A saw-edged knife is usually necessary to deal with the bark. When you pull or carefully cut away your portion of Vacherin from its bark, the outside edge of the cheese can be bright orange, and its odour magnificent. To enjoy the texture and savour to the full, slice the cheese in strips up to a quarter of an inch thick, and lay it, do not spread it, on thick crisp-crusted bread. Make sure you have your share of the bark, and scrape it to sprinkle the tasty remains of cheese adhering to it over your slice. If you are not in stuffy company, lick your bark after each mouthful of cheese, and do not waste what is left; put it on the fire to die in a scent of glory. I am writing this in front of our wood fire in Provence, with the euphoric aftertaste still in my mouth of the most succulent Vacherin this winter has yet produced. I bless the Badoz family at Pontarlier for making this February day worth a red letter in the calendar, despite a temperature well below zero. How satisfying it is that the box can boast a gold medal at the Paris Concours Agricole of 1985. My palate has been giving Badoz cheeses gold medals ever since the early 1970s when I first brought them into the United Kingdom.

Apart from Swiss purloining and sullying of the name, the recent French history of Vacherin has been a happy one. The number of farms contributing winter milk to making the cheese has risen from 150 in 1960, with a total production of 200 tonnes, to nearly 400 farms and approaching 700 tonnes of cheese in 1986. I like to think that I have contributed personally to this rise in prosperity by introducing Vacherin for the first time to countless private customers (including many Americans), and to restaurateurs and fellow cheese merchants in Britain.

Making begins for a few *fromagers* on 15 August, the earliest permissible date, and ends on 31 March. Late in the season few makers produce it daily; the quantity tails off sharply, little being made after mid-March. Every drop of milk for Vacherin comes from Montbéliardes or Pie-rouges de l'Est on their winter diet of natural hay, and must be used unpasteurised. The standard of cheeses is very high, but it is vital that they should not be sold too young and firm for the market, however strongly retail demand may tempt *affineurs* to release them. Paradoxically, the smaller cheeses take longer to ripen; let out too young and kept too cold, they will be lost forever. At their best, usually deeper than the big cheeses, they are superb, and are ideal for a household or small restaurant. Buyers just need to test for softness with great care.

Vacherin perpetuates the old relationship between the forester, the *gruyer* of ancient times, and the *fromager*. I was told in 1973 that three or four specialist *bûcherons* go round the forests inspecting spruces (locally called *fuve* rather than *épicéa*) after they have been marked for felling, to select and buy the best barks. These are stripped from the trunks and cut horizontally into circlets an inch or more wide, for sale to the makers of Vacherin. They are called *sangles* and the sellers are sometimes nicknamed *sangliers*, which means wild boars. Vacherin production has more than trebled since 1973, so there must now be more of these bark-strippers, dealing with hundreds of trees in the course of a season.

I revisited Franche-Comté in mid-September 1986, coming down from Alsace through Belfort and Montbéliard, late enough in the season to see Vacherin being made. In slightly misty autumn sunshine, the comté was at its beautiful green best: dairy country *par excellence*. We drove 60 miles between flowery pastures with not a black-and-white cow in sight: nothing but the rich red and white of sturdy Montbéliardes and Pie-rouges de l'Est. On either side of the road the valleys are enclosed by wood-topped hills and ridges up to 1100 metres high. The farm buildings, more beautiful than barracks and more modest than mansions, are yet on that sort of scale. They embrace one or more houses, a dairy, and extensive barns for forage, farm implements and winter housing for the beasts. Some are in chalet form, with one widespread gable reaching almost to the ground. Most are in the shape of an English Queen Anne house, but with smaller, square, wide-bordered windows.

We stopped north-east of Pontarlier at Montbenoît, in the heart of the little valley called the Saugeais. With its eleven villages, this *pays* was given by the Sire de Joux in 1127 for the founding of a monastery. The first Augustinian monks were Saugets from the Valais, who called in lay compatriots to help clear the lower-lying forest, and to establish pasture and dairy. A sixteenth-century abbot, Cardinal de Granvelle, was Charles V's confidant; this, no doubt, helped to keep Charles supplied with his much-cherished Comté cheese. There are still seventeen centuries-old *fruitières* in this delectable little region. (The abbey at its centre has remarkable cloisters, statues and choir stalls; do not miss La Loi d'Aristote and the attractive Delilah wielding sheep-shears on her slumbering Samson's locks.)

We stayed the night above Montbenoît at the well-named Bon Repos (the nearby railway line has only two trains a day). The Poulet au Vin Jaune et aux Morilles was excellent. As the remarkable Vin Jaune is very expensive, we contented ourselves with the generous amount of it in the chicken, and drank an acceptable Blanc du Pays en pichet at about a tenth of the price.

Next day we visited Monsieur Bernard Philippe's *fromagerie* at Chaffois, just west of Pontarlier. He himself has retired from cheesemaking, which is now done by his son Claude and two assistants. They were fully occupied with the new season's Vacherin every day except Sunday, when they resumed Comté-making to allow them a shorter working day. Even this limited relaxation would be sacrificed in November, to prepare for the enormous Christmas demand for Vacherin.

The 2.5-centimetre-wide strips of bark, the *sangles*, are bought in bunches of about twenty-five. Enough for one day's cheeses are soaked overnight in salt water, and brought to the boil in the morning to bring out the aroma and flavour (this also eliminates any foreign bodies, insect or fungal, which might affect the cheese).

When the morning milk arrives from the farms it is added raw to the naturally ripened overnight milk, already in the copper-lined *chaudrons*. In each of these in turn 1000–1200 litres are brought up to 35°C. Renneting is done half an hour later, and within another half hour the curd has usually formed. After being rested for half an hour it is cut into cubes of about 5 centimetres and stirred about six times at ten- to fifteen-minute intervals with the *pelle* (a dustpan-shaped scoop). When the curd is right the whey is pumped out, ready for collection by the pig farm next door.

Meanwhile the pierced moulds are prepared. For the larger cheese these measure 25 centimetres across and are nearly as deep. They are filled straight from the vat. The small moulds are about half that diameter but deeper. They are ranged in a mobile trough. A vertical-sided tray with holes fits over the ten or so moulds; the curd is poured on by the bucketful, and eased by hand into the moulds below. These are removed to a bench when full and replaced by empties until the curd is exhausted (the trough can be swung on its cradle for cleaning and turned over for draining).

Inside the full moulds the curd is turned once before it has drained enough to be turned out on to the bench where it is encircled in the spruce bark. Inevitably, the big moulds hold slightly varying quantities of curd, and on release from the mould it must be gently pressed to a proper depth: too deep a cheese overfills its box; its crust sticks to the lid and may be pulled away when the lid is removed. The curd may spread slightly before the cheesemaker secures it in the *sangle* by pinning the overlapping ends together with a pair of sharp wooden dowels. Forty or so new cheeses are ranged on a fine-meshed sheet over the wide, plastic-covered shelf of a trolley. They are then covered with another meshed sheet, another plain sheet, and a very light but strong hardboard. On top of this the whole process is repeated until all the cheeses have been dealt with.

The curd for the small cheeses is turned out of the moulds as though it were going to be a *fourme* of the Forez type (see Chapter 7), but the content of each cylinder is cut to produce six to eight small cheeses. These are ringed with shorter strips of bark, secured with elastic bands, and then shelved like their bigger brothers.

In the evening the cheeses have an hour-long salt bath, and the next day they go for ripening into the *caves* of Monsieur Philippe at Bannans, the next village to the west. Vacherins are kept separate from Comté and Morbier in a humid *cave* of their own. They are turned and rubbed with lightly-salted water daily, except Sundays, for at least three weeks. Because, paradoxically, they are deeper, the smaller cheeses need longer. The maximum temperature in this *cave* is 14°C; at just 1° higher the cheese ferments and overfills its box, with the damaging results we have described and the further disaster of spoiled flavour. As Monsieur Claude Philippe said, 'Vacherin is either very good or it is hopeless. There is no in-between.'

His father took me to watch the boxing of the matured cheeses, glowing with their gold to pinkish, supple, undulating surfaces. The larger boxes are between 25 and 30 centimetres across, to allow for inevitable variations in such thoroughly hand-made cheeses. The charming girl on the job removed the dowels from the bark overlap in the big cheeses (or the elastic bands from the smaller), and gently persuaded cheese after cheese into the matching box that she selected with an unerring eye from the many ranged at the back of her table against the wall. Every now and then no box was big enough. She then gauged how much of a tuck she must take in the cheese to make it fit, nicked a tiny triangle from the edge, and closed the wound as she eased the cheese into its box, where the cut edges of bark made a perfect join. I caused her and Monsieur Philippe some satisfaction and amusement by begging a few of the resinous triangular trimmings and relishing them as I watched.

Over the years I have handled many of these skilfully trimmed Vacherins, and can testify that they quickly heal without any deterioration of the cheese. The surgery is betrayed to a knowledgeable eye only by a more pronounced fold in the crust, and by the line of the join in the bark, which makes a better starting point for cutting the cheese before selling or serving than the double thickness of the overlap.

After each cheese is tucked down, the mark made by the brown bark is wiped from the upper inside of the box and the lid is put on. The Philippe cheeses usually bear the imprint of Messieurs Arnaud of Poligny, the final *affineurs* and distributors, and the number PS25 identifies their Chaffois provenance. The boxes are piled four high (another reason for being careful not to overfill them) and are kept at a temperature of 11°C until they are sold.

We left Franche-Comté carrying with us the aroma and flavour of one of France's most luscious cheeses, which dates back 200–300 years. Travelling along route N437 hearing cow bells on either side of the road, we came across the foundry at Labergement Sainte-Marie, where Obertino et Cie make every imaginable size of bell, set off with magnificent collars. Along this route there are frequent sawmills, and enormous horses are still used for the most difficult extractions of timber from the forests. The road through Mouthe and Saint-Laurent is called, with good reason, 'La Route du Comté', but one of its prizes is the rare chance to eat fresh *truite de source* with local *vin blanc* in the sunshine in front of the Hôtel de la Truite at Foncine-le-Haute; enough said.

## Cheeses of La Franche-Comté

### Amancey

*Affineur:* Perrin Vermot at Cléron (N of Amancey).
Coopérative: Fromagerie d'Amondans (N of Amancey).
Milk, butter, cream and cheese from organically managed farms.
*fruitier; biologique; vache cru.*
Doubs; 70 **5**, high R.

### Arbois

Coopérative Laitière et Fromagère, rue des Fossés 07.00–12.00; 17.30–21.00 watch cheesemaking, buy cheese (tel. 84 66 09 71). Port Lesney, Grange-de-Vaivre: visitable Société de Fromagerie (tel. 84 73 84 81) making Comté, Mettons, Morbier.
Jura; 70 **4**, R of C.

### Arc-et-Senans

Annual *fête du fromage*, towards end of June.
Doubs; 70 **4**, high R.

### Belfort

Usually pronounced Béfort. Wednesday to Sunday market.
*Maître fromagers:* M. Jacques Poirel, 1 rue Michelet; M. Bernard Maillot, A la Renommée du Bon Fromage, 40 Faubourg de Montbéliard.
Jura; 66 **8**.

### Besançon

Daily market except Sunday.
*Affineurs:* UCCFC.
Headquarters of Emmental Français Grand Cru (see p. 406).
Doubs.

### Bleu du Haut-Jura, AOC

See SEPTMONCEL, and this chapter, pp. 394–5, and Chapter 13, pp. 383–6.
Gex/Jura/Ain.

### Cancoillotte

See p. 396 for composition and use.
**Cancoillotte au Beurre et à l'Ail.**
Coopérative Laitière 70190 Rioz, Haute-Saône. There is a Confrérie des Taste-

Cancoillotte, and the cheese has a *label régional Franche-Comté*. See pp. 396–7.

**Cancoillotte Franche-Comtoise au Beurre.** 50% lactic curd, 50% renneted curd (3.4% of this is water and butter) 'Produit Landel-Marcillat', Loulans-Les-Forges, Haute-Saône (see LOULANS).
*laitier; vache.*

**Cancoillotte Raguin.** In sterilised 200g and 400g tins or 200g plastic pots; made and posted within France by Raguin, 25110 Baumes-Les-Dames, Haute-Saône, who won gold medals at Paris in 1979, 1980, 1982.
*laitier; vache.*

CHAFFOIS

Fromagerie Bernard Philippe; Comté, Morbier, Vacherin; ripened at nearby Bannans to the W (number on labels: PS25) see pp. 402–4.
Doubs; 70 **6**, R of C on N72.

CHAMPAGNOLE

This golden washed-crust cheese of pleasantly rustic appearance and rich flavour was made at Champagnole before Chaumes, so widely known today, was thought of. Perhaps Chaumes killed it, as people in the Franc-Comtois cheese world tell me it is no longer made (certainly it is many years since I was able to order it from Rungis). I hope this entry may prove to be wrong, or that it will provoke some local cheesemaker into reviving an excellent cheese.
*laitier; artisanal; vache cru.*
Jura; 70 **5**, low.

CHAPELLE-DES-BOIS

**Coopérative.** Milk, butter, cream and cheeses made from organically produced raw milk.
*fruitière; biologique; vache cru.*
Doubs; 70 **16**, top L on D46.

**Morbier Fermier.** Two farms in Combe-des-Cives just N of Chapelle-des-Bois were making Morbier in the traditional way over the open fire in 1987 from milk of Montbéliardes. 5kg cheeses, natural ash layers, turned and lightly washed; salt-rubbed daily for 3 months.
*lait cru; fermier.*

CHARCENNE

**Mon Charcennay.** 160g soft white-mould-coated cheese of *carré de l'est* type made by Établissements Milleret, a *laiterie* recommended by Gault Millau in February 1986. 55% *m.g.*; *laitier*; *vache.*
Haute-Saône; 66 **14**, on D12, NE of C.

CHAUX-DES-CROTENAYS

*Fruitière* cheesemaker: Gilbert Banderier (tel. 84 51 51 75) – Comté, Morbier, Raclette, Vacherin (Oct–Mar) 07.00–12.30 daily, 14.00–20.00 except Sunday.
Jura; 70 **15**, top E of N5.

CHÈVRES

**Chèvre, Fromages de.** Made from organically produced raw milk by Emile-Bernard Bourdier, Le Rondeau, Lavans-Vuillafans, 25580 Nods (tel. 81 59 21 31).
*fermier; biologique; chèvre cru.*
Doubs; 66 **16**, D392/D27 bottom R.

CHEVRET

Historically made by Abbaye de St Claude before introduction of Bleu de Gex, Septmoncel (see p. 409). Cheese of square or oblong *pavé* type, rarely round; 150–200g, with thin bluish crust. The *chèvres* were with the herds of cows in *transhumance*. Dates from thirteenth century if not earlier. Gault Millau reported in February 1986 that it was being revived as a cows'-milk cheese by a *laitier* at Les Rousses (see also BELLEY, Chapter 13, p. 387).
45–50% *m.g.*; *fermier*; *chalet*; *chèvre/mi-chèvre cru. laitier; vache.*
Les Rousses; 70 **15/16**, N5 SE of Morez.

LE COMTÉ (OR GRUYÈRE DE COMTÉ) AOC

'Grand Fromage d'Appellation Contrôlée'. For full account of cheese see pp. 394–5; there is *no* factory Comté, yet annual production from 330 *fruitières* (82%) and *laiteries* (18%) totals about 40,000 tonnes. Average size 45kg, 40–70cm in diameter, 10–11cm deep. Raw milk, cooked curd, ivory *pâte*, few and small holes, if any, sometimes cracks (*lainures*), increasing with age; texture gains in smoothness with age. Inimitable nutty flavour, distinct from and richer than all but the rarest old Swiss Gruyère. Granular gold to brown crust with marks of cheesecloth, green oval casein plaque on side, identifying maker;

best cheeses have green design of bells and the name Comté on crust. Do not buy any other.
Some salt-free Comté is made – enquire of Marcel Petite (see PONTARLIER).
Comité Interprofessionnelle du Gruyère de Comté BP 26, 39800 Poligny, Jura (tel. 84 37 23 51); Musée de Comté, Poligny.
Makers and *affineurs:* see AMANCEY, ARBOIS, BELFORT, CHAFFOIS, CHAPELLE-DES-BOIS, CHAUX-DES-CROTENAY, ÉPENOUSE, FRAROS, GOUX-LES-USIERS, JOUGNE, LIÈVRE-MONT-VILLAGE, LONS-LE-SAUNIER, METABIEF, MONTBENOÎT, MORTEAU, ORCHAMPS, ORNANS, PIERREFONTAINE, PLASNE, POLIGNY, PONTARLIER, RECOLOGNE, LE RUSSEY, LES ROUSSES, SALINS-LES-BAINS, SAULX, VERCEL, VERS-EN-MONTAGNE.
You can visit small *fruitières*, in nearly every village S of Pontarlier, and in the Saugeais, around Montbenoît (see p. 407) NE of Pontarlier.
*minimum 50% m.g.; fruitier; laitier; artisanal; vache cru.*

### Croix d'Or

Chèvre known to Raymond Lindon in the 1961 editions of *Le livre de l'amateur de fromage* (Laffont) and repeated by Chast and Voy in the 1984 edition (Laffont-Archimbaud).

### Dole

Tuesday, Thursday and Saturday market. Emile Morel, 3 rue d'Enfer (recommended February 1986 by Gault Millau).
Jura; 70 **3**, top R.

### Domblans

*Affineur:* Pianet.
Jura; 70 **4**, 10km N of Lons-le-Saunier, low L.

### Doubs

See PONTARLIER, PETITE.

### Edelweiss

Trade name of 220g boxed Vacherin by Fromagerie S.A. Perrin, Vermot, 25330 Cleron; the batch I examined had been plastic-wrapped too young for any crust to form on open faces, sad fault.

### Emmental

**Emmental Français Grand Cru, Emmental Français Est-Central** *(marque chaud-ron hanging on potence).* This regionally protected *lait cru* version of Emmentaler has been made in many *fruitières* and *laiteries* from the Vosges, through Franche-Comté to Savoie, from the thirteenth century. Milk must come from cows on pastures, or naturally fed (excluding silage and fermented feeds). Minimum *affinage* 8 weeks; 80–100kg, 80cm–1m in diameter. Syndicat des fabricants et affineurs d'Emmentals Traditionnels 'Grand Cru', 26 rue Proudhon, 25000 Bescançon (tel. 81 83 46 13).
Buy only Emmental Grand Cru (marked on cheese, with red oval plaque on side). Never buy prepack. Vesoul, capital of Haute-Saône, is the old French Emmental capital too, and the cheese is made in *fruitières* in almost every surrounding village (see ÉPENOUSE). UCAFCO, 1 quai René Veil 70002 Vesoul is *affineur.* Much of the whey goes into Metton (see p. 407) for Cancoillotte (see p. 432 under Savoie for further comment on Emmental français).
*min. 45% m.g.; fruitier; laitier; artisanal; vache cru.*
Haute-Saône; 66 **5/6**.

### Entre-les-Fourgs

See MORBIER.

### Épenouse

Fruitière making Comté, Emmental/Grand Cru, butter.
Doubs; 66 **16, 17**, off D19 N of Vercel-Villedian.

### Étival

*Concours* for cheesemakers in Oct.
Jura; 70 **14**.

### Fleurey

Gilber Granderrin, *fromager*, noted by Gault Millau, February 1986.
Haute-Saône; 66 **6**, top C on D84.

### Fondue

Melted Comté (or Bleu du Haut-Jura) with white wine in wooden bowl (latter first rubbed with garlic). Before serving add small glass of kirsch from Mouthier or Fougerolles. Fondue Nantuatienne uses 500g rich Comté and 150g of Bleu de Gex.

## Goux-Les-Usiers

**Comté.** Making and *affinage*: Napiot, 25520 Goux-Les-Usiers.
*laitier; vache cru.*
Doubs; 70 **6**, upper C.

## Les Grangettes

**Comté, Vacherin.** *Fruitiére* (see pp. 405 and 409–10).
*vache cru.*
Doubs; 70 **6**, centre R, Lac de Saint Point.

## Haut Jura

**Bleu du Haut Jura.** Syndicat Interprofessionnel du Bleu de Gex-Haut-Jura-Septmoncel (see Bleu de Gex p. 389); Septmoncel (see p. 409) Route Royale, 39220 Les Rousses (tel. 84 60 01 59).

## Jougne

See VACHERIN.

## Joux, Forêt de

See VACHERIN.

## Lajoux, La Pesse

*Fruitières* for Septmoncel (see p. 409; *not* the Lajoux near Chésery in the Ain).
Jura.

## Lavans-Vuillafans

See CHÈVRES.

## Longevilles

**Comté, Vacherin.** M. Roger Pourchet, middle of village, near Poste.
Doubs; 70 **6**, lower R.

## Lons-le-Saunier

Thursday, Saturday market.

**Comté, Gruyère.** *Affineurs*: Jacquemin Rivoire, Montmorot 39000 Lons-Le-Saunier for Jura Gruyère, Jura Comté. Michel Brocard for Comté; mention in Gault Millau, February 1986.
Jura; 70 **4/14**.

## Loulans

Third Sunday in August: Fête de la Cancoillotte.
Haute-Saône; 66 **16**, high L on D15.

## Luxeuil-les-Bains

*Maître fromager*: M. Paul Figard.
Haute-Saône; 66 **6**.

## Mamirolle

500–600g rectangular, washed-crust (2 months' brine), related to Limburg or Gratte-Paille (see Chapter 10, p. 334), made by Fromagerie which is part of a national industrial dairy school.
40% m.g.; *laitier; vache.*
Doubs; 66 **16**, lower L, N57 E of Besançon.

## Métabief

Fromagerie Sancey (Richard) makes Comté, Morbier and (Oct–Mar) Vacherin. 10.00–12.00, 16.00–18.00, not Sunday.
Doubs; 70 **6**, lower far R, W of N67 near Jougne.

## Le Metton/Meton

Whey recooked (*ricotta, recuite*), drained, broken up, until hard, grainy and smelly. Fermented in warm conditions to provide cheese ingredient of Cancoillotte (see pp. 404 and 396–7). Largely a by-product of Emmental *fruitières.*
*domestique; laitier; fruitier; vache.*
Haute-Saône.

## Montbenoît

**Comté.** Société Coopérative Les Maîtrets, La Longeville, 25650 Montbenoît (tel. 81 38 11 39); milk, butter, cream, Comté from organically produced milk. There are *fruitiéres* around Montbenoît in the Saugeais. NW: Arc-sous-Cicon, La Chaux, Les Granges Brûlées, Largillat, La Montagne de Gilley; NE (or D131): Les Auberges, Gilley, La Longeville (see above), Les Maîtrets; NE (off N437) and E: Combe St-Benoit, Les Jarrons, Remonot; S and SE (off N437): Les Allies (D320/D47), Arçon, La Brune, Hauterive (D320), Lièvremont.
*fruitier; biologique; vache cru.*
Les Saugeais (see p. 402)/Doubs; 70 **7**, high L.

## Mont d'Or

See VACHERIN.
Not to be confused with Mont d'Or in the Lyonnais, or Montdore in the Auvergne.

## Morbier au Lait Cru de Franche-Comté

See pp. 398–9. 3–9kg pale beige to gold, rubbed crust, 30–40cm diameter, 6–8cm deep. Pale ivory *pâte* with very small openings, and a layer of bluish vegetable extract across the centre. Mild, refreshing

after 2 months in *cave* (humid, 12–14°C), can develop rich flavour with longer keeping. Do not bother with stodgy factory substitutes, some of which (e.g. Le Nozeroy, made by Coopérative Lezay, Deux-Sèvres, see Poitou, p. 107), though ripened in Comté, are made far afield.
*fermier; fruitier; artisanal; vache cru.*
Association des fabricants de Véritable Morbier au lait cru de Franche-Comté, 2 place Payot, 25000 Besançon (tel. 81 80 81 11).
Makers include: Mme Burris (with *chaudron* over fire and black layer in cheese) at Chapelle-des-Bois (see p. 405); MM. Graffe and Gerber, La Chaumière à Potence, Entre-Les-Fourgs, E of Jougne (70 **7**, lower left). See also CHAFFOIS, CHAUX-DES-CROTENAY and MÉTABIEF.

### Morteau

Tuesday and Saturday markets.
Second Sunday in August: Journée des Produits Regionaux.
Guy Rième, *affineur* and seller La Fruitière (08.00–12.00 (except Sun, Mon), 14.00–1900 (except Sun)), 30 Grande Rue, 25500 Morteau (tel. 81 67 07 05); Morbier, Comté, Vacherin. Seventy other French cheeses are matured by M. Rième.
Doubs; 70 **7**, top R.

### Les Moussières

**Bleu du Haut-Jura.** See SEPTMONCEL. Fromagerie du Plateau des Moussières.
Jura; 70 **15**, low, D25 S from N436.

### Orchamps-Vennes

*Affineur*: C. A. D. Loray (Comté).
Doubs; 66 **17**, low middle.

### Ornans

*Affineur*: Grillot (good mature Comté throughout the year).
Doubs; 66 **16**, bottom L.

### La Pesse

*Fruitière* for Bleu du Haut Jura (see SEPTMONCEL).
Jura; 70 **15**, low L on D25.

### Pierre Fontaine

*Affineur:* Joly
Doubs; 66 **17**, lower middle.

### Plasne

Fromagerie de Plasne, is farm co-operative *fruitière* for Comté, made by M. et Mme Guyot (1987) 06.00–12.00 daily (tel. 84 37 14 03 if you want to watch).
Jura; 70 **4**, S of C, 4km S of Poligny.

### Poligny

Monday and Friday market. Last weekend in July: Fête du Comté.
École Nationale d'Industrie Laitière (its Vacherin won a gold medal at the 1980 Concours Agricole, Paris).
*Affineurs*: Arnaud Frères, (Luxe = fully matured and *fruité*, Rouge = mild, lighter flavour). Label Juraflore (tel. 84 37 14 23). Among their cheeses are those of MM. Philippe of Chaffois (see p. 405 and pp. 402–4) shop at 15 place Nationale, 08.30–12.30, 14.30–19.00 (except Tues p.m. and Sunday); *affinage* and wholesale: avenue de la Gare, 07.00–12.00, 13.00–18.30 (except Sat), tel. 84 37 14 23, for appointment to view; Brun; Grillot; Juramonts Comté; Vagne.
Musée du Comté, avenue de la Résistance: history of cheese and dairy equipment; slide shows, visits to *fruitières*; 09.00–12.00, 14.00–18.00 July to 15 August (out of season, tel. 84 37 23 51). Institut National de la Recherche Agronomique (research into *présure* and local flora; individual recipes for each cheesemaker).
Comité Interprofessionnel du Comté, avenue de la Résistance, 39800 Poligny (tel. 84 37 23 51).
Jura; 70 **4**, lower R.

### Pontarlier

*Laitier/affineur*: Éts Badoz (office) 23 rue de la Paix, Comté and Vacherin (tel. 81 39 02 31)
*Fromageries*: Marcel Petite, Doubs 25300 Pontarlier, for Comté, Morbier, Vacherin (tel. 81 39 07 54). Roger Martin, 7 rue Sainte-Anne; both recommended by Gault Millau February 1986. François Petite, 22 chemin de Saint-Loup. M. François Petite is president of the Syndicat for Vacherin (see pp. 409–10). Pourchet Frères, Place des Bernadines, for Comté, Vacherin.
Doubs; 70 **6**, R.

### Raclette

This cheese for melting and scraping is made in numerous places including

Chaux-des-Crotenays and Les Rousses (see p. 405 and below).
50% m.g.; *fruitière; vache cru.*

### Recherchon

Small hard cheese made from leftover Comté and Gruyère curd in vat by cheesemakers who do not stick it on the side of the cheese before pressing nor use it for Morbier (see pp. 407–8).

### Recologne

*Laitier/affineur:* Jouffroy, Lavernay, 25170 Recologne (on D13, D415).
Doubs; 66 **14/15**, lower middle at join.

### Les Rousses

Syndicat Interprofessionnel du Bleu de Gex-Haut-Jura-Septmoncel, route Royale, 39220 Les Rousses (tel. 84 60 01 59).
Co-operative Fromagère des Rousses, 137 rue Pasteur (tel. 84 60 02 73) 08.00–12.00 daily, 15.00–19.30 (except Sun), for Morbier, Comté, Raclette, *fromage blanc, beurre lait cru,* from milk of ten local farms; telephone to see cheesemaking (very early morning).
Jura; 70 **16**, centre L.

### Le Russey

**Comté.** *Coopératives* selling organically farmed milk, also butter, cream and cheese made from it are: Société Coopérative les Cerneux-Monnots (tel. 81 43 76 18) which also makes Vacherin in season (NE of Le Russey D414/D457); Société Coopérative Narbief-Le Bizot (SW of Le Russey D437/D329 (tel. 81 67 02 29)).
*fruitier; biologique; vache cru.*
Doubs; 66 **18**, low L on N437.

### St-Claude

Best source of Septmoncel (see below).
**Saint-Claude.** 100–200g square monastic cheese (see CHEVRET, and BELLEY, Chapter 13, p. 387); disappearing (*Larousse*, 1973, Viard, 1980, Chast et voy, 1984). Surviving perhaps in Bugey.
45% m.g.; *fermier; chèvre.*
Jura; 70 **15**, lower L.

### Le Saint-Rémy

200g cheese of Carré de l'Est type but washed-crust. Courtine compares it with Gérómé in mild state and mentions a round as well as a square version.
45–50% m.g.; *laitier; vache pasteurisé.*
There is a Saint-Rémy in Haute-Saône (66 **5**, upper R), the only one in Franche-Comté, which shares the credit for the cheese's origin among writers with Lorraine, which also has a Saint-Rémy in the Vosges. However, the name could go back to the saint's day rather than to place names. See Chapter 8, pp. 358–9.

### Salin les Bains

*Affineur:* Nicole, 4 rue Gambetta.
Jura.

### Saulx

M. Paul Figard, *maître fromager,* Mailleroncourt-Charette, has a shop at Luxeuil (see p. 407) mentioned by Gault Millau, February 1986.
Haute-Saône; 66 **6**, on N57, NE of Vesoul.

### Septmoncel AOC, Bleu de Gex, Bleu du Haut-Jura

This fourteenth-century transplant from Dauphiné into the monastic dairies of the Pays de Gex thrives today in the area near St-Claude which first offered its makers abbatial hospitality (see p. 384; for Syndicat see LES ROUSSES).
*fruitier; vache cru.*
*Fruitières* in Jura: Giron and Chézery (in Ain; see p. 388); Lajoux (70 **15**, on N436 E of Septmoncel); La Pesse (70 **15**, low L); Les Moussières (70 **15**, low L). All the *fruitières* make AOC cheeses which are labelled Bleu de Gex or Bleu de Septmoncel according to the wishes of the merchant to whom they are being sent.
Local market and shop sources: St-Claude (70 **15**, lower L).
Agents at Rungis: Reybier, Arnaud.

### Traque

Local method of using broken or leftover Septmoncel by crushing it, soaking it in white wine and flavouring it with garlic for as long as it suits the family's taste.
*fermier; domestique; vache cru.*
Pays de Gex/Jura/Ain.

### Vacherin

**Vacherin du Haut-Doubs: Fromage Mont d'Or AOC.** For history and making, see pp. 399–404. Small cheeses, 500–800g; large, 1.8–3kg. All are ringed with spruce bark, in which they are placed when removed from the mould, and rubbed with brine for three weeks. The bark becomes attached to the outside of the cheese and its resinous savour and aroma gradually penetrate inside the white *pâte*, which becomes meltingly soft as it comes to full maturity. The crust is yellow to pinkish gold, and billowy, marked with the cloth that lined the mould when the curd was first ladled in. Some farm makers wash their cheeses in white wine for family consumption.

*50% m.g.; fruitier; artisanal; vache cru.*
*Sources*: There are makers at Cerneux-Monnots, Chaffois, Chaux-des-Crotenays, Le Russey, Longevilles, Métabief, Morteau (Guy Rième), Pontarlier (see entries above) and Jougne; Les Hôpitaux-Neufs, Les Hôpitaux-Vieux Supt are good areas for small makers (70 **7**, lower left).

The Syndicat Interprofessionnel de Défense du Fromage Mont d'Or ou Vacherin du Haut-Doubs, 2 place Payot, Besançon (tel. 81 80 81 11).
Rungis: DPFC (Distribution des Produits Francs-Comtois) Bâtiment D4–63, avenue d'Auvergne, PLA 159/94597 Rungis.

VERCEL

*Laitier–affineur*: Liniger (Comté).
Doubs; 70 **6**, top, on D32/D19, NNE of Mouthiers.

VERS-EN-MONTAGNE

**Comté.** Made by M. Vertamboz *à l'ancienne*, unchanged for over fifty years at Domaine du Parc, Vers-en-Montagne, 39300 Champagnole (tel. 84 51 43 62).
*artisanal; vache cru.*
Jura; 70 **5**, low C, D467.

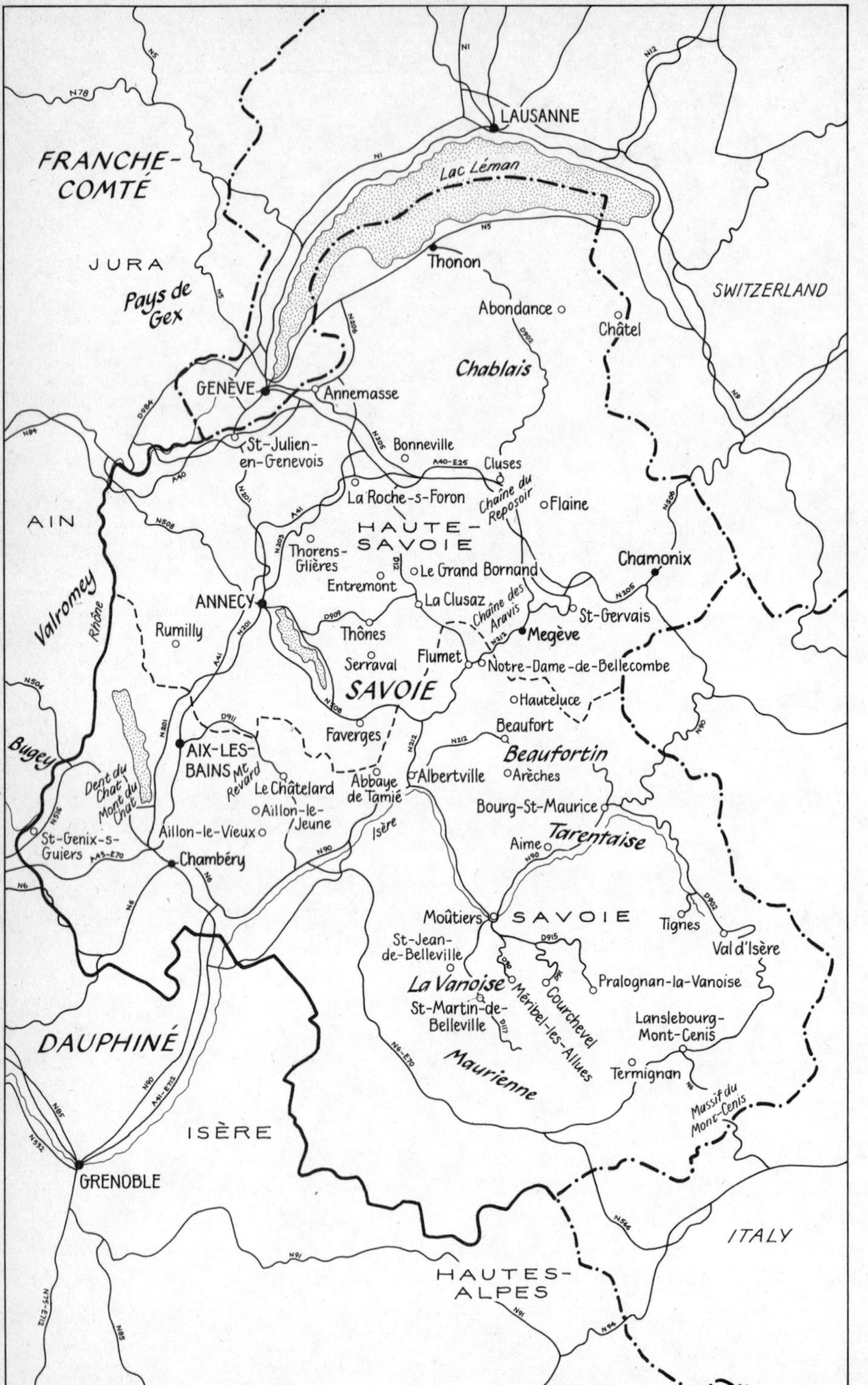

FRANCHE-COMTÉ
JURA
Pays de Gex
LAUSANNE
Lac Léman
Thonon
SWITZERLAND
Abondance
Châtel
Chablais
GENÈVE
Annemasse
St-Julien-en-Genevois
Bonneville
Cluses
La Roche-s-Foron
Chaîne du Reposoir
Flaine
AIN
HAUTE-SAVOIE
Thorens-Glières
Le Grand Bornand
Chamonix
Entremont
ANNECY
La Clusaz
Chaîne des Aravis
St-Gervais
Valromey
Rhône
Rumilly
Thônes
Megève
Serraval
Flumet
Notre-Dame-de-Bellecombe
SAVOIE
Hauteluce
Beaufort
Faverges
Bugey
AIX-LES-BAINS
Mt Revard
Beaufortin
Dent du Chat
Mont du Chat
Le Châtelard
Abbaye de Tamié
Albertville
Arèches
Aillon-le-Jeune
Bourg-St-Maurice
St-Genix-s-Guiers
Aillon-le-Vieux
Isère
Tarentaise
Aime
Chambéry
Moûtiers
SAVOIE
Tignes
St-Jean-de-Belleville
Val d'Isère
La Vanoise
Courchevel
Pralognan-la-Vanoise
St-Martin-de-Belleville
Méribel-les-Allues
Lanslebourg-Mont-Cenis
DAUPHINÉ
Maurienne
Termignan
Massif du Mont-Cenis
ISÈRE
GRENOBLE
ITALY
HAUTES-ALPES
N5
N78
N1
N12
N206
N9
N84
D984
A40
N201
N205
A40-E25
A41
N508
N203
D12
N506
D909
N504
N508
D911
N212
N90
N516
A43-E70
N6
D902
D915
D90
D91
D117
N6-E70
N85
N532
A41-E712
N566
N91
N94
N75-E712

CHAPTER FIFTEEN

# *Savoie and Bas Bugey*

SAVOIE – HAUTE-SAVOIE

Two-thirds of this beautiful region are mountain.

In the fourth century the name Sapaudia ('between the waters') was used by the historian Marcellinus to describe what is now essentially Savoie and Le Bugey. Within a century it had become Saboia. The province was important from Roman times because of its control of the passes of Mont Cenis and St Bernard, and it maintained its status as an independent duché for many centuries. Ruled by the House of Savoie from the early ninth century, its possessions included lands on both the Swiss and Italian sides of the French border, and from 1559 it made its capital Turin. Annexed by Republican France in 1792, Savoie was however restored to its ducal House in 1815, and it was not until 1860 that the Savoyards finally became French, in return for Napoleon III's help to the House of Savoie in uniting Italy.

Today Savoie's two *départements* harbour 10,000 dairy farmers making cheese themselves or supplying milk to 1300 cheesemaking *fruitières*. There are sixty *affineurs* of farm and *fruitière* cheese. Some of Savoie's cheese traditions, admirably preserved, go back to pre-Roman times, when the Centrons of the Tarentaise were making their version of what we now call Beaufort. (Their memory lives on in the village of La Cuvette de Centron in the Beaufortin, south-west of Aime.) One of the results of the change was the introduction of Swiss cheesemakers to raise the quantity of Emmental-type cheese made in Savoie. The outcome is today's excellent Emmental Grand Cru.

## Abondance

Abondance, however, is the word with which to start our survey of Savoie, for more solid reasons than its alphabetical precedence. Just south of Lac Léman, and now in Haute-Savoie, the twelfth-century Abbaye d'Abondance was, as likely as not, the originator of the cheese bearing its name, because it is similar to a cheese made around Sion, the Swiss mother-house of the Abbaye d'Abondance. The name is also borne by a splendid breed of cattle, mahogany with brown-patched eyes set in a white head, lightly curved horns emerging from a curly white crown, white belly and white points. These cows provide the excellent milk used for Abondance cheese; they also share with the Tarines the credit for the great Beaufort, and provide almost all the milk for Savoie's internationally known and distributed star, the succulent Reblochon. There are 220,000 head of Abondance, mainly in the Alps and the Massif Central, where they are ideally suited to altitude and climate.

There are fears for the survival of Abondance as a cheese, but in 1986 Professor Juillard of the National Dairy School (ENIL) at La Roche-sur-Foron assured me that production continued in the valleys of the Dranses d'Abondance and de Morzine and was still essentially farmhouse (except for the co-operative at Vacheresse). This *artisanale* dairy of a *fruitière* character makes from 150 to 200 tonnes of cheese a year, all the milk coming from Abondance cows. Negotiations have been going on for an Appellation d'Origine Contrôlée, but such matters proceed slowly. The cheese deserves this recognition and should prosper.

The traditional 7–10-kilo cheese, with its concave circumference and salt-rubbed, pale-golden crust, looks like a very small Beaufort. Six months of washing and rubbing leave the crust still thin and the golden creamy *pâte*, with its spread of tiny holes, firm but refreshing in consistency. Some cheeses, not moulded to give the concave surround, have a deeper-golden, softer look. Others, formed in a *marmite*-shaped mould, are called *toupins*, the local name for *marmites*. Even the younger cheeses have a pleasing edge to their aftertaste. Abondance is ideal in consistency and flavour for Raclette.

In late autumn and winter Vacherin d'Abondance, with its wine-washed crust, is made on a small scale around Châtel and across the Swiss border, in firmer and smaller form than the Mont d'Or cheese. Professor Juillard described its production in Savoie as marginal. The curd is raised to a higher temperature than that of the other Vacherins, resulting in a firmer *pâte*. Some farms wash their cheeses in a stone bath hollowed out to conform to the shape of the cheese. The liquor is white wine mixed with *morge*, which is brine enriched with scrapings from old cheeses and sometimes with whey. It contains at least 480 species of bacteria, Professor Juillard told me. A flat stone is placed across the bath and the cheese is removed two or three times a week during *affinage* to be rubbed with the wine-and-*morge* mixture and turned.

# Reblochon

The most famous cheese of Savoie is Reblochon, with its national AOC. The legal zone for its making covers most of Haute-Savoie (excluding only parts west of Annecy and on the shores of Lac Léman). In the Savoie *département* it includes the eastern slopes of the Aravis to the Val d'Arly and the southern communes of Lanslebourg and Lanslevillard. The *vallées* most noted for cheese are those of Chinaillon, La Pierre Percée and La Colombière. The heart of this region is the Chaîne des Aravis with its northern continuation, the Chaîne du Reposoir. La Combe du Reposoir was cleared for pasturage by the Carthusians of the Chartreuse du Reposoir in the Middle Ages, and is described by Robert Courtine as the 'cradle of

Reblochon'. Every year the *paysans* asked the monks for a blessing on their chalets in the new *alpages* and offered them their cheeses, which became known as *fromages de Dévotion*. As time went on *alpages* proprietors were paid a percentage of the value of the milk produced, which was measured by periodic inspections. For these occasions the farmers developed the practice of only partially emptying the udders, so reducing their rental obligations; the inspection over, the beasts would be milked a second time (or *reblochées*, which means rather more than the English term 'stripped'). This practice had the advantage not only of economy but also of preserving the richest part of the milking for the farmer. The especially rich cheeses resulting from this bonus milk were called Reblochon. They were kept discreetly for home consumption and for centuries were never sold on the market. The old verb *rablassâ*, meaning to maraud (and from which comes the noun *reblâche*), is probably the root of *reblocher*, indicating that something was being filched from the landlord.

By the 1700s Reblochon had become the accepted name for the local cheese, which had itself become an accepted part of rent, as witnessed by an agreement dated 12 March 1704 between Canon Gaspard Ducrest and the brothers Périllat-Collomb of Le Grand Bornand, granting a six-year lease of the mountains of Châtillon and Le Chat. The rent was 260 Florins, 25 Reblochons (*'un quarteron'*) and 12 lb of fresh butter.

After the Revolution Reblochon was marketed openly. However, its unterritorial name frustrated the attempt to protect the cheese at Annecy in 1938. This has been put right by the decrees of 1976, which defined the zone, specified whole milk from the race of Abondance in its raw state, and recorded the traditional recipe to be followed.

Production rose by 700 tonnes between 1980 and 1982. By the middle 1980s some 305 farms were producing about 1500 tonnes of Reblochon, and 55 *fruitières* 4500 tonnes. They are backed up by about 30 *affineurs* (at least the first fifteen days of *affinage must* be completed within the zone of origin). At the height of the season some of the biggest *fruitières* (such as Thônes) may have a surplus of milk, which they have recently started to put into *lait cru Raclette* to compete with the much dearer Swiss cheese. Travellers will find little difficulty in arranging with farm or *fruitière* to see the cheese made, but I advise them not to try the La Clusaz area on summer weekends or in the height of the holiday season.

I went to a little *fruitière* on a farm just north of Entremont, under the Grand Bornand. Between 6.30 and 7 in the morning and 6 and 6.30 in the evening, 250 litres of milk come from the Abondance cows of four farms, so this is true farmhouse-scale cheesemaking. (It takes 5 litres of milk (well over a gallon) to produce a cheese which reaches the shop weighing between 450 and 500 grams (1 lb–1 lb 2 oz.) The cheesemaker, who has lived here for thirty years, is Maurice Périllat. His father made Reblochon for sixty years in the Grand Bornand, where many farms still make Reblochon and a few make Chevrotins. It was Périllat forebears who were making those Reblochons to help pay the rent of the *alpages* on Châtillon and Le Chat in the first decade of the eighteenth century.

The cheese dairy, in a shady corner of the farmhouse, has one ancient *chaudron* of copper-lined iron and one modern vat. At about 6.30 p.m., as soon as the evening milk had been brought in it was renneted (this is done at between 30° and 35°C). After thirty to forty minutes Monsieur Périllat cut the curd briefly across the vat with the *harpe* and then moved the surface with a dustpan-shaped scoop. After ten minutes he cut and stirred again in the same way, then round and round with the *harpe* for fifteen minutes. He then heated the curd for five minutes to bring it to 32°C. As the level of acidity was low, he raised the temperature to 35° during a further five minutes' continuous stirring, after which he pressed a cheesecloth down over the curd in the vat and lifted whey off the top in buckets (the whey went into the butter churn and the eventual buttermilk to the pigs).

Cloth-lined Reblochon moulds lay ready in serried ranks on a sloping table, shaped at the lower end to channel the remaining whey into a bucket. The curd was trawled out of the vat in the big cheesecloth, then spread and delicately hand-pressed into the moulds, a stage where the children helped (there was no waste curd left in the vat). Within ten minutes the cheeses could be turned in the cloth, smooth faces uppermost, to be covered by wooden followers with 1300-gram weights on top, and left for four to eight hours (according to the speed of *égouttage*). The cheeses would be turned again twice, the cloths being removed on the second occasion. At the end of pressing they would spend two hours in a brine bath (some makers dry-salt by hand).

Monsieur Périllat's cheeses would have seven days of brine-washing and rubbing to form the crust, and one day to dry before going to the *caves* of Monsieur Pochat et Fils at Thônes. There, at 16°C or just below, they would be turned daily for three weeks, under the care of a family which has been doing the job for many years (this stage usually happens in the *caves* of such specialist *affineurs*).

Warmth and humidity (nearly 100 per cent) are of great importance to the cheeses; and the traditional method of providing them, still practised on some farms and by some of the most successful *affineurs*, is to have three compartments in the *cave*. The outer one takes the strain of the cold in winter (its doors are always being reworked to fit tightly); the second harbours one or more sheep (according to the space to be conditioned), as their presence increases the warmth and humidity of the *cave*; the third, furthest from the elements, contains the Reblochons. An experienced senior member of the staff at the Reblochon-makers' co-operative in Thônes told me that there was a big difference between the character of cheeses so treated and that of cheeses of equally good making matured in more modern and clinical conditions.

In some smaller *caves*, used mainly for winter when it may be impossible to take cheeses to the *affineur*, one sheep is kept in the middle in a sunken pen, providing exactly the right degree of warmth and humidity for the Reblochons on the shelves around it. By the end of its dark winter's duty, the sheep is likely to have gone blind, so it is killed and eaten before it becomes conscious of its lost sight.

The finished cheese should have an unbroken, fine-grained crust and a golden to pinkish colour under a white surface mould. Its interior is pale cream with tiny apertures, and ripens meltingly from the crust inwards. For this reason the tubby Petit Reblochon, or Reblochonnet, of 250 grams does not ripen so effectively, and I agree with Professor Juillard, who regards it as virtually a different cheese.

Before despatching the cheese, the *affineur* protects the crust of Reblochon inside its paper wrap with two chipboard discs, which are of great importance in preventing the surface from becoming soggy. If there is any sign of the crust's adhering to these wooden protectors, they should be peeled off carefully with the help of a very fine knife and scraped, and the crust should be mopped with absorbent paper or muslin. The dry side of the wood should then be placed against the cheese, and it should be rewrapped loosely overall in its original wrap, if this is still in fair condition, or in muslin. Too much care cannot be given to this superb product of the Abondance cow, the rich *alpages*, and the ancient traditional skills of maker and *affineur*.

The *alpages* and lower pastures, and the hay meadows of Savoie, are a joy to the eye and the nose. Among many other species, long-stemmed, heavy-headed clover and other *légumes* enrich the meadows with nitrogen below ground and provide gourmet-cows' delights above. Dairy farming here is mercifully organic, with delectable and profitable results. I found as many as fifty-six different plant species in a 1½-acre field between road and stream near Serraval, where we settled for a few nights at the welcoming La Tournette.

## CHÈVRE AND BREBIS

Above La Sauffaz (the *-az* is silent), visible from our bedroom window across the valley to the south, a *chevrier*, Monsieur Jean-Claude Bosc, keeps alive the local traditions of Chevrotin and Persillé des Aravis. Chevrotin is the raw goats'-milk equivalent of Reblochon in zone of production and outward appearance. Full-bodied but not strong in flavour, its texture liquefies on the tongue. The Persillé (sometimes mixed milk) is normally deeper and tubbier or even cylindrical in shape. Though the blueing is often not obvious these days, it is quite unlike any other cheese.

Monsieur Bosc adds a small soft chèvre of Picodon derivation to his repertoire. He uses no heating, but sets to with his milk at the temperature it leaves his fifty goats, local blacks, and chestnut Alpines-chamoisées. The curd is given twelve hours to form. He dries his cheese in the open, according to the wind: from three hours if it is strong to two days in still, humid weather. Monsieur Bosc is one of forty *chevriers fermiers* in Haute-Savoie. A very few make a large Chevrotin (35 or so centimetres across) of almost Gruyère-like interior, thick crust and excellent refined flavour. Monsieur Gérard Paul, *maître fromager* of Aix and Salon, finds them from time to time.

Higher still over La Sauffaz, Monsieur Patrick Barder farms sheep at Les Frasses and makes his delicious Saint-Marcellin-like Pras d'Zeures.

## Abbaye de Tamié

The road leaving Serraval (uphill from D12 opposite the hotel) forks after Le Bouchet, the right fork leading to La Savataz (-*az* silent again). There Monsieur Blanchin makes cheese from the milk of cows whose bells sounded round the hill to our bedroom, intermittently as they grazed and in orchestral *tutti* as the herd went in and came out at milking times.

While staying at Serraval, we spent the Feast of the Assumption on a visit to Tamié. The *abbaye* lies at the head of the beautiful Val de Tamié, running north from the *col* which also bears the name. Before attending 11 o'clock Mass with hundreds of other visitors, we gave ourselves time to see the *fromager*. Frère Philippe, who heads a team of twelve monks in the cheese dairy, does not know for certain when it started, but thinks it likely that cheese has been made for the refectory ever since the monastery was established in 1132. The recipe is the ancient one for Reblochon, but the cheese has always been marketed outside as Abbaye de Tamié. The *abbaye* lies south of the Haute-Savoie boundary, just outside the southern limit for the Appellation Reblochon.

On my previous visit to Tamié, the cheese, then still made from milk of the monastic herd, could scarcely be found outside the community. For the last few years, however, they have been expanding production by buying in milk, and have given up their herd. Milk now comes from the Abondances and Tachetées de l'Est of thirty reliable farms nearby, none of which has itself made cheese in recent years. Their 3000 unpasteurised litres a day provide for 300 kilos of cheese. Tamié's change in policy was timely, as it forestalled EEC quota worries. In 1985 production was up 30 per cent on the year before, as much as present or foreseeable dairy and labour resources can cope with. They have installed a modern Dutch vat to ease temperature control, drainage of whey and cleaning, but their methods of making are still completely traditional. Of the weekly 2.1 tonnes of cheese produced, half is sold on the spot, 750 kilos goes to local shops and markets, and 300 kilos to Société Anonyme des Fromagers Fermier (SAFF) at Rungis.

The cheeses weigh half a kilo and 1.3 kilos. Much deeper than Reblochon, they are also more regular and angular in their crust, but they manage to escape the uneven ripening risks of the tubby Reblochonet. When young they have a pale-golden to pink crust, and an even, firm but creamy texture with a refreshing flavour all their own. When allowed to mature fully (or brought on willy-nilly by exposure to hot weather) their crust takes on the most beautiful, rich pink hue and the interior softens right through into superb unctuosity. The uncut cheese, insulated from cold or heat by thickly folded newspaper or a 'cool bag', without close-sealing, travels remarkably well.

## Beulet and Tavaillon

When the *abbaye* was affected by France's anti-monastic legislation, the Tamié recipe was passed on to the family of Girod, who started making cheese just outside Geneva in 1881. Their Beaumont, from the village of that name, where it is still made of raw milk, is similar to Tamié, but thinner crusted and more rounded. It goes all over the world, except to the local market area of Tamié, where it would not wish to compete with its godfather.

The Girod family also produces large quantities of Reblochon under the Beulet label, and in 1984 devised Le Tavaillon, a Tamié-recipe cheese of which Frère Philippe thinks well. It is of the Vacherin type, but made all the year round. Firmer than any of the French Vacherins, it is also different in flavour from any I have tasted, perhaps because of the larch bark with which it is ringed.

The Girods are pioneers in the use of unpasteurised milk on a large scale for cheesemaking. Their success, like that of the Reblochon-makers, stems originally from their attention to the provenance, quality and cleanness of the milk they use.

The Reblochon-makers recommend eating their cheeses with Savoie white wines, *'secs et fruités'*, at 8–10°C, and with light and fruity reds at 12–14°C; but it has to be remembered that the French drink most of their red wine much colder than the English do, and south of Burgundy positively chill them. Such wines can accompany most Savoyard cheese.

# Tommes

Tomme de Savoie, probably the most familiar cheese name connected with the duché outside the world of connoisseurs, is the ancient mountain cheese made when winter conditions confine family to house and cows to byre. Yield is limited, and milk cannot be taken to the *fruitière* to contribute towards the making of big cheeses; nor can the cheeses made from it on the farm be collected or taken regularly to market. So a cheese is needed which will keep until marketing is possible, to tide the household over the cheeseless period during calving. Household milk is often skimmed for other domestic needs, which means that it is not usually a whole-milk cheese. (A recipe for Tomme de Savoie is given on pp. 425–6.)

The two *départements* of the duché have combined to give regional protection to the name Tomme de Savoie. An oval red casein plaque, numbered 73 for Savoie, 74 for Haute-Savoie, identifies the source of the cheese and its *matières grasses* (at least 40 per cent). This plaque, and the outer wrap with a mark of four hearts framed on four sides by the name Savoie, can be borne only by cheeses made of raw milk matured by approved *affineurs* within the duché. These and a *lait cru* label are the signs for which the customer buying elsewhere should look. Locally, some small-scale makers still sell good cheeses direct to shops and market-merchants without plaque or wrap, but the obligatory tasting will soon lay any doubts to rest. In 1981, 530 tonnes of Tomme de Savoie were registered; in 1982, 800 tonnes; and growth has continued.

A tasting of *tomme fermière* reminds us of what we usually miss in Britain. Too many trade buyers accept any old grey drum as representative of the cheese, making retail customers write this off as dull. Those are pasteurised, factory-made substitutes, often produced outside Savoie. They are sometimes ripened in good *savoyardes caves*, however, and acquire red and mimosa-mould patches which delude us into thinking that the real *pâte* may be found inside. Where the interior *does* live up to its robe, it is melt-in-the-mouth, unsalt, gently pleasing, not dull.

I am sorry to say that *'tomme'* is used by Savoyards as a term of contempt equivalent to *'nigaud'* ('fat-head' or 'simpleton'; they also use *'chèvre'* in this sense, as we use 'goat'). Nevertheless, it has its honoured associations, not just with the familiar Savoie, but with the Bauges and Colombier, west of Tamié; Belleville (Doron de Belleville, Saint-Jean- and Saint-Martin-de-Belleville, south of Moûtiers); Les Allues (Doron des Allues, next valley to the east, under Courchevel); Courchevel itself (the *commune*); and Praslin and Pralognan, further east. This area is known as Les Trois Vallées. Some makers and *affineurs* stick to the local names; others are content to market their cheeses as Tomme de Savoie.

The Bauges have their distinctive tiny Gruyères, succulent *tommes* (Bauges and Colombiers), *chevrettes* and winter Vacherins (sometimes in birch bark). The Doron de Belleville cheeses are small, of lower-fat cows' milk, while those of Allues are of goats', cows' or mixed milk, larger, and closer to Gruyère. The small Courchevel, Pralognan and Praslin cheeses are now chèvres in summer and cows' milk out of holiday season, and are noted for their sweet aroma. (Most of these cheeses are dealt with in more detail in the cheese list to this chapter.) *Tommes* go well with an apéritif of Apremont, Abymes, or other white Savoyard wine, served cold. At the end of a meal, Mondeuse or Gamay de Chautagne are recommended.

## Emmental Français

A document dated 1575 shows that Emmental was being made in Savoie at that time under the name Vachelin (which was also used for Vacherin when it first developed about two centuries later). Larger-scale making of Emmental started with the arrival of Swiss cheesemakers in the mid-nineteenth century, but many of today's *fruitières* are still producing only one cheese a day, which requires 900 litres of milk.

Savoie contributes to the raw-milk Emmental Français Grand Cru, and also has its own regional red-label Emmental de Savoie. This may be made of raw milk or of milk *thermisé* at below 65°C for under a minute; pasteurisation is specifically forbidden. Quality is controlled by the Institut Technique du Gruyère (ITG), whose inspectors examine between a quarter and a third of all the production. As many as 100 *laiteries–fruitières* shared in the 3500 tonnes of cheese given the red label in 1982. An inadequate minimum period of ten weeks is laid down for *affinage*. When matured for at least four months these cheeses are of supple but un-rubbery consistency, and their flavour has a lift to the palate peculiar to the larger-holed alpine cheeses. The holes should be well spaced and no bigger than walnuts. Do not touch pre-packed Emmental from any source, and, as ever, taste before you buy to avoid immature cheese or pasteurised cheese of non-alpine provenance.

## Gruyère de Savoie

Savoie produces some excellent raw-milk Gruyères, usually halfway between Swiss Gruyère and Comté in character. Some of them come from areas on the Comté border within the Comté AOC zone, but are not within the prescribed size limits of AOC cheese. Some of the little Bauges cheeses are also called Gruyères, and Tommes des Allues can have Gruyère character. As we have seen with Comté (see Chapter 14), the name Gruyère, used in France for the whole family of large alpine cheeses, is not of geographical origin but relates to the ancient imperial management of forests in a region not defined by modern political frontiers.

## Beaufort

Now we come to the star cheese of southern Savoie: Beaufort. It is made entirely of whole, raw milk collected in *bidons,* so that the cheese dairy can identify each farm and each milking for tests of quality, and can reward producers accordingly. Beaufort has had its AOC since the spring of 1976, but its pedigree was established a little earlier. It was being made by the Centrons before the first Romans entered the Tarentaise over 2100 years ago; Pliny the Younger commented on the presence of the cheese of the Centrons in Rome and recorded its source as the market at Venthon, which is on the Doron de Beaufort, 2 kilometres north of present-day Albertville. During the French Revolution, the cheese was so noted for its keeping quality that the Committee of Public Safety commandeered 10,000 *quintals\** of *'grévire de Beaufort'* to feed Paris.

The heart of the zone of production is still the Tarentaise, with the Beaufortin to the north and the Maurienne to the south. It covers all the *département* of Savoie west of Albertville and south from La Chambre. In the north it takes in one *commune,* Praz-sur-Arly, in Haute-Savoie. Straightforward Beaufort (with a blue, oval casein plaque) is made in twenty *fruitières* in the valleys, of which some have grown into fairly large *coopératives.* Some, like that at Beaufort itself with its 270 farmer members, make it all the year round, others only outside the summer chalet season. Total Beaufort production has grown recently to about 2000 tonnes a year, a quarter of which comes from the Beaufort *coopérative*, which in summer keeps its Haute-Montagne milk separate from the rest because it makes better cheeses. Members are paid according to the fat, protein and bacterial quality of their milk, and the *fromager* prepares his own *aisy* (home-cultured starter) and *présure* to suit the milk he is using. Thirty chalets operate during the *transhumance* from mid-June to mid-September, producing Beaufort Haute-Montagne (marked with a green oval plaque), one of the most succulent cheeses in the world. The cows are on *alpages* of rich aromatic value, most of them at over 2000 metres.

---

\*10,000 *quintals* = 1000 tonnes, or 2,240,000 lb – more than a year's production in recent times.

Starting from Aime on D86, it took an hour to climb by car to the Chalet d'Aval, a distance of under 8 kilometres on the map point to point but over 2 kilometres above Aime in height. We meandered uphill through three separate hamlets marked Côte d'Aime,* turning left beyond them off D86 for La Bergerie and Gitte. Beyond Gitte the footpath GR5 comes in on the right from Valezan. Where the cart-track ends we found the chalet of the Aime *coopérative*, a broad-eaved stone building on Mont Rousset, 2640 metres above sea-level. Two kilometres further on, GR5 threads between Pierre Menta (2711 metres) and Le Roignais (2999 metres) towards the Cormet de Roselend.

Up above the tree-line in the mid-August sunshine, 110 cows were enjoying the unfenced *alpages*. I counted thirty-six plant species in flower within a few square yards near the road, in a carpet bordered with brash pink willow herb and starred with deep, almost purple, yet luminous harebells. More species flowered higher up where the cattle were grazing. The cows are the herds of the farmers belonging to the *coopérative* of Aime, brought together to exploit the *'grande montagne'* as *'fruits communs'*, the ancient common grazing rights. A few individually owned *alpages* are grazed by the proprietor's herd and by animals hired by him for the summer, from whose yield he profits. Some of the remote chalets still use wood fires.

Tarines, here in their native Tarentaise commonly called by the full regional name, have appealing black eyelashes and nostrils. Their wheaten to chestnut coats are lighter, and their moderate-length horns more angled than those of the white-crowned, mahogany Abondances with whom they share the pastures. There are also some *noires rustiques*, blacks produced by local cross-breeding. In the Beaufortin and Tarentaise, the Tarentaises cows provide 80 per cent of the milk.

Monsieur Dédé Thomas heads *les bergers de la commune d'Aime*, a team of six tanned, weathered men who share the duties of herding, milking, cheesemaking and *affinage*. One of them has been milking and making cheese since he was twelve. Their day starts with hand-milking on the *alpages* at 3 a.m. and each milks seven or eight cows an hour. Their hand-carved stools, seats with a single piano-leg-like support, are decorated with initials in tacks or studs, and lines and circles of brass stars. Chains or ropes serve to carry the stools or to hang them on the wall of the chalet between milkings. On one side of each stool, under the seat, the soap for washing the cows' teats is held in a pocket formed by the toe of an old boot or *sabot*.

One of the marks of a veteran milking hand is the humped callous developed by the final milking motion of the thumb-joint against the teat, in the case of Monsieur Thomas almost doubling its thickness.

The milk is brought down to the dairy in 40-litre (9-gallon) *bidons* by an old truck which can manage the carpet-like surface and the gentler slopes of the high pastures. In more broken-up *alpages* this can still be done by mule

---

*Misleadingly, only the middle one, La Côte d'Aime, is on the standard map. Below it is La Côte d'Aime (Villard) and above it La Côte d'Aime (Prébarand).

or on the milking-hand's back. Yield at this season is about 1450 litres (about 3 gallons, or 13.5 litres, per cow) a day, filling thirty-five or so 40-litre *bidons*: enough for three or four average cheeses of 40–50 kilos.

The dairy takes up the north-facing half of the chalet, which cuts into the mountainside. Outside are free-ranging pink pigs and a long trough with pumped water for washing the utensils. *Bidons* (including back-cans), milking stools and cheesecloths adorn the wall. Inside are two old *chaudrons*: black-coated cauldron-type vats, of bright reddish-pink copper, their handles of shining brass. One of them is over 200 years old. Inside them, at between 32° and 35°C, the whole, raw milk is given its *présure* (80 to 100 centilitres per 1000 litres of milk), prepared by the cheesemaker from *caillette* (the vell, or calf's stomach) macerated in *aisy*. After twenty to thirty minutes the curd-cutting *harpe* is used and then the wheat-sized grains of curd are slowly stirred for ten to fifteen minutes before the *cuisson* (scald) to not more than 56°C. I must emphasise that 65°C is the normal temperature for a French *pâte cuite*, and Monsieur Thomas and other Beaufort-makers do not consider their cheese *pâte-cuite*. Its melt-in-the-mouth quality, completely different from the impact of Emmental and other cheeses in the Gruyère category, bears them out. Nevertheless, Robert Courtine puts *cuisson* temperatures at 53–57°C; and officially, as well as in its own leaflets, Beaufort is classed with the *pâtes-cuites*. Indeed, it was declared *'le Prince des gruyères'* by Brillat-Savarin.

During the heating of the curd, stirring is speeded up until the temperature reaches 45°C, and continues during the last phase of intensified heating to 55° or 56°C, long enough to expel more whey from the grains but not to remove so much that they cannot stick together. When the cheesemaker judges that *'le fromage est fait'*, the curd is trawled out in the cloth and deposited in a beechwood *cercle*. This is outwardly like the Comté hoop, but has a markedly convex lining which gives the Beaufort its almost unique concave circumference and sharp edges. In the modernised dairies the 4000-litre *chaudrons* are still of copper, inside a water jacket electrically controlled. The cloth-lined *cercles* have metal *cloches* fitted over them, into which the curds and whey are sucked by vacuum. The curd settles in the *cercle* the whey is then released and the *cloche* removed.

The chalet cheese is left in its cloth and mould under pressure for twenty hours (in the Beaufort dairy this pressure is of one ton applied vertically on four cheeses for twenty-four hours with several turnings). When the cheese is first turned, the cloth is opened up on one side to allow the distinctive green oval 'BEAUFORT HAUTE-MONTAGNE' plaque to be pressed in. The cheese is stamped with an 'x', the old Beaufort sign, and with the month of making. After several turnings, it spends twenty-four hours in a cool *cave* before submersion for a day in brine. Thereafter the cheese is turned and hand-salted on one side every morning and rubbed every afternoon, resting on spruce-wood shelving.

This process goes on for between one and two months. When the crust is satisfactory, the routine changes to a twice-weekly turning and application of mixed salt and *morge* (see p. 414), producing a slightly granular, russet crust. *Affinage* needs at least 90 per cent humidity, but the temperature may be between 8° and 15°C (47–58°F; constant, of course, not variable; I regard 50°F as low for the sensitive quality of this cheese). *Affinage* also must continue for at least six months altogether, of which at least four must be in the legal zone of production. This is long enough to make the Haute-Montagne cheese rich and pleasurable, but most valley and all winter cheeses benefit from longer. However, as demand is much greater than production, this is like asking for the moon; a moon which a few devoted *affineurs* are patient enough to reserve for their customers: those made at Beaufort, for example, average seven months before sale. The resulting cheese can weigh from 20 to 70 kilos legally, but is usually between 40 and 50 kilos, taking around 450 litres of milk. The maximum diameter is 75 centimetres and height 18 (30 inches by about 7). Its maximum moisture content is 38 per cent; its minimum *matières grasses* is 48 per cent, though chalet cheese is usually 50 per cent. When cheeses are graded at four months, only those awarded 14 points or more out of 20 are granted the AOC and allowed out of the region.

The firm, but not hard, interior of the finished cheese is on the straw side of ivory in colour, the *alpage* cheese naturally being more golden. It may have a few tiny holes called *'yeux de perdrix'* (partridge eyes), and a few horizontal cracks, *'lainures'*, provoked by the lateral pressure of the convex *cercle*. The Haute-Montagne cheeses are *'biologiquement purs'*, strictly organic; their pasturelands would qualify for the British Soil Association Certificate. Even after eight months they melt in the mouth, and their flavour has an aromatic richness all its own. They set off most wines beautifully, and my only reservation would be that too dry a wine could conflict with the natural sweetness of the cheese.

Sérac is the Ricotta-type by-product of many Beaufort dairies, but at our chalet remaining solids separated from the whey are churned for butter. The morning's work finishes at about 11.45: it has been an eight-hour day from the time of setting off to milk. This welcome break for lunch and rest ends at whatever time it is necessary to start climbing up to the cows again for the 2 p.m. milking, the beginning of the second eight-hour day in the twenty-four hours.

Check with the parent co-operative to find out which chalet is in current use and how to reach it, as *remues* of the herd between different sets of *alpages* during the season may necessitate a move from one chalet to another (sometimes with the *chaudrons* upside down on the backs of strong mules). You might time your arrival to see the last hour of the morning cheesemaking; then find out where the herd is pastured and picnic nearby so that you can watch the afternoon milking. Follow the first lot of milk down to the chalet, and you will be able to see the earlier stages of cheesemaking (of course, you should hold back until you see someone between jobs from whom you can ask permission to watch).

Before we left, Monsieur Thomas found time to show us the *caves* in the southern half of the premises, where he spends non-milking hours seeing to the turning and *affinage* of his cherished cheeses. Here and there in the chalet, beds lurk in corners, rather under-used during these intensively active three months. I noticed only two modern elements in today's Savoyard *transhumance* which were incompatible with the life of two centuries ago, when that older *chaudron* was new, or of two millennia ago, when the Centrons were making their cheese. One was the substitution of a motor vehicle for mules (still not the case everywhere). The second was the absence of cow-bells, the *potets* and lighter *campanes*, as they call them in Savoie. That is a recent change, sadly imposed on this herd by the thieving behaviour of selfish tourists. When you come across herds or flocks still happily belled, bear in mind the importance of those bells to animals in the mountains, and their cost to the farmer who owns them (see Chapter 5).

Monsieur Thomas is of cheesemaking stock, and told us of relations and friends making cheese in Les Allues and in the Courchevel–Pralognan area, where he spends his winters maintaining ski-lifts. Most of us would be worn out by three months of sixteen-hour days without time for relaxation, but he and his splendid team are proud of their work and of its results, as they have every right to be. For all the superficially primitive conditions I have described, the milk, ideal for cheese, comes from cows bred for these altitudes and for the climatic contrasts, pastured in perfect natural and chemical-free conditions. Part of their contentment is attributed to the continued employment of local bulls; Tarines are not fond of artificial insemination. They are milked with care and attention to hygiene, and their milk goes straight to the cheesemaker. Equipment is old but efficient and shiningly clean. Beaufort is a perfectly bred and nurtured aristocrat, flourishing on tradition.

I will leave Savoie on that happy note, and with a useful tip to those of you who court a Savoyarde: you will know that your claim has been accepted for the hand of the daughter of the house if you find yourself seated in the place of honour by the fireside and given a bowl of soup with a great deal of cheese.*

## Recipe for Tomme de Savoie

15 litres milk for 1.5 kilos of cheese. A 1.2–2-kilo cheese is about 18cm in diameter, 5–8cm high. The crust should be grey with a spread of red and of yellow (mimosa-like) moulds. *Pâte* should be semi-hard, white to yellow, and may have tiny holes called 'trous de moulage'. 40 per cent m.g. minimum. Flavour should be full and slightly salt.

*Lait cru* renneted at 30–33°C

After 25–30 minutes harping and stirring (temperature may be raised to 33–36°C) curd is reduced to grain of maize size by further harping or by hand-breaking of curd.

---

*Estella Canziani, *Costumes, Mœurs et Légendes de Savoie*, trs. A. van Gennep, Chambéry, 1920.

*Artificial introduction of bacteria or moulds and washing of curd is forbidden.*

After the curd is placed in moulds lined with very fine muslin, it is pressed for several hours to release remaining whey. It is then salted in a brine bath or by hand-rubbing.

After four or five days' drying it goes into a dry *cave*. *Affinage* in *caves* within the duché must last at least six weeks. The moulds develop on the coat and are rubbed in by hand every time the cheese is turned. For the first week they may also be rubbed with salt, rubbing then being daily. Rubbing gradually drops in frequency thereafter. *'La fleur'* develops naturally.

## *Fondue Savoyarde*

*Equipment*
Earthenware or iron casserole, wooden spatula, pepper mill, spirit stove or other table heater suitable for fondue (set in centre of table)

*Ingredients (for six)*
600g Emmental de Savoie
500g Beaufort
6 glasses dry white Savoie wine (approx. 1 bottle)
½ glass kirsch (approx. 6cl)
1 clove garlic
black peppercorns (in mill)
pain de campagne

*Wine to accompany*
Dry white Savoie wine, served cold

*To prepare (15 minutes)*
Cut bread into single-mouthful cubes. Cut cheese into thin flakes. Cut garlic clove in two and rub open surfaces all over sides of casserole.

*To cook*
Pour wine into casserole and place over medium heat. When wine bubbles, add cheese and stir slowly with spatula. Before cheese has quite melted, place casserole on fondue heater, continuing to stir. Pepper the fondue and pour in kirsch, still stirring. When cheese is fully melted, turn down heat.

*To eat*
Impale bread cube on fork and plunge it in fondue with stirring motion, turning the fork to coat the bread with cheese. The fondue must be kept moving, but losing the bread in it costs a forfeit to the offender.

# Cheeses of Savoie and Bas Bugey

## Abondance

7–10kg, 35–45cm × 8–9cm; semi-hard, *pâte-cuite*, washed and rubbed pale-golden crust (6 months); creamy golden *pâte* with spread of very small holes; pleasing edge to flavour (in aftertaste of even young cheese); from farms in valleys of Dranse d'Abondance and Dranse de Morzine, and round La Chapelle d'Abondance, and from the Coopérative de Vacheresse (like a *fruitière*; *artisanal*, see p. 414). (For Abondance cattle see pp. 413–14).
45–48% m.g.; *fermier; laitier; artisanal; vache cru*.
Haute-Savoie; 70 **18**, low centre.

**Le Vacherin d'Abondance; le Vacherin des Dranses.** ½–1½kg cheeses, rubbed with white wine to give extra character (done in Comté too, only for the family), and sometimes enclosed in a stone bath of wine and *morge* (see p. 414). The cheese is encircled with spruce, pine or wild-cherry bark. A firmer Vacherin than those of Les Aillons, Les Bauges and Le Mont d'Or. (See also Chapter 14, pp. 409–10.)
40% m.g.; *fermier; artisanal; vache cru*.
Haute-Savoie; 70 **18**, low right Châtel.

## Les Aillons

**Vacherin des Aillons.** (See also Bauges for general details.) Androuët, on a fairly recent (1980s) tour, found the cheese moister than Mont d'Or, liquefying more quickly, and keeping a lactic, acidic flavour. Made in late autumn and winter.
Savoie; 74 **16**, upper middle; Aillon le Jeune and Aillon le Vieux are in the Aillon valley south of Lescheraines; École and Châtelard are the market centres.

## Aime

Thursday market.
Local cheeses also from *crémerie* beside post office and Lion-Codec S of N90 on Moûtiers side.

**Beaufort; Beaufort Haute-Montagne.** La Coopérative Laitière d'Aime (Fromagerie in back street, makes cheese in non-*alpage* season); *cave d'affinage* (Caves Coopératives du Beaufort de Haute Montagne) and shop (on N side of Moûtiers road beyond ancient Basilique St-Martin) 10.00–12.00, 16.00–18.00 weekdays, Sunday a.m. in season; all the classic local cheeses, chèvres and Sérac (*vache* and *chèvre*) including those of Aime; for directions to reach the Beaufort chalet and small cheesemakers, see pp. 421–5 and 428–9. Rungis: Beaufort Haute-Montagne from Aime sold by La Crémerie de la Neige.
*Chalet d'Aval (Jun–Sept); Fromagerie Coop Fruitière (winter); biologique; vache cru*.

**Tomme de Chèvre and Sérac (summer only).** 250g dark-coated drum made by M. Barral, above Les Côtes d'Aime towards Chalet d'Aval (when metalled road gives way to track turn right, get firm directions in Aime).
*fermier; chèvre cru*.

**Tomme de Savoie.** Grey *tomme* with lovely patches of red and mimosa moulds made by M. Usannaz at Valezan, E of La Côte d'Aime.
*fermier; vache cru*.
Tarentaise/Savoie; 74 **18**, on N90, L of C.

## Albertville

Thursday market.
Savoie; 74 **17**, upper middle.

## Les Allues

**Tomme des Allues.** 3–4kg, some smaller (see below); 25cm × 6–8cm; *pâte-cuite*; washed-crust, grey to pale yellow; 2 months' *affinage* centred on Méribel. One maker has 40 cows and 150 goats and makes his '*petites* Tommes de Savoie' of goats', cows' or mixed milk according to season (*Les Allues*, 1985). Androuët (1984) described cheeses he tasted, with Abymes wine from La Combe de Savoie, as like little gruyères, with firm, fine white *pâte*.
45% m.g.; *fermier; chalet; chèvre/vache/ mélange cru*.
Savoie; 74 **18**, low L.

## Alpages, Tomme des

See TOMME AND MOÛTIERS.

## Annecy

Tuesday (best), Wednesday, Saturday, Sunday markets.
Haute-Savoie; 74 **6**.

## Annemasse

Gilbert Bouvard, 24 avenue de la Gare (tel. 50 38 04 59) *fromagers-affineurs* since 1878.
Haute-Savoie; 74 **6**, top R.

## Aravis

**Chevrotin des Aravis.** Occasionally 200g; 400–700g, 13 cm × 4cm or smaller; natural crust, 2 months' *affinage*; appearance like a firm Reblochon, but usually plumper; *pâte à point*: white, darkening and opening up and melting at edges, melt-in-mouth; flavour rich, flowery, goaty in aroma; makers M. Bosc (see Serraval, p. 437); Coopérative, Thônes (Le Petit Fermier: *à point*, darkening and opening up slightly as it melts under the crust towards a moist white centre; liquefies on the tongue; flavour full-bodied but not strong); *fermiers* of Le Grand Bornand. I have found young white, natural-crusted 500g cheeses at the Timy shop in arcade by town hall, Thônes. Exceptional: 35–40cm × 7cm deep; thick grey crust, smooth, almost Gruyère texture; fine flavour.
45% m.g.; *fermier*; *chalet*; *chèvre et mi-chèvre cru*.

**Persillé des Aravis.** 500g–1kg, cylindrical, or half-cone, rounded top; pressed; blue, though blue is scarcely perceptible in many, brushed crust becoming rough grey to blue; sometimes almost black, with white mould over; rich, firm yet flaky *pâte*. To be found in Thônes, La Clusaz; made by M. Bosc (see Serraval, p. 437). A very individual cheese. Some are made like Reblochon, others of curd broken in the evening (see Chiguet, p. 431), left in whey, and mixed with next day's curd.
45% m.g.; *fermier*; *chalet*; *chèvre cru*.
Haute-Savoie; 74 **7**, lower R.

## Arêches

**Grataron d'Arêches.** 200–300g average, 7½cm × 6cm; washed-crust 1 month; smooth and brown; not too strong, but good goaty flavour; melting interior; Doron de Beaufort, Roselend, Plateau du Cormet de Roselend (74 **18**, high, off D217); and at Granier (N of Aime, see p. 427, Le Groupement Pastoral du Cormet d'Arêches (74 **18**, L of C). M. F. Gachet makes a rustic Grataron with grey and brown overtones on its roughish gold coat (150–250g),

white, moist interior melting from the outside in; rich, towards strong; at Queige (74 **17**, high centre, off D925 6½km W of Beaufort).
45% m.g.; *fermier*; *chalet transhumance*; *chèvre cru*.
Beaufortin; 74 **17**, upper far R, S of Beaufort
Savoie.

## Bauges

**Chevrette des Bauges.** 800g, 12–1500g, 18cm × 5cm; pressed, washed-crust, 2–3 months; thin, smooth, light rosy crust; light, goaty taste. Still made around Châtelard.
45% m.g.; *chèvre cru*.

**Gruyère des Bauges, Gruyère des Savoies** (*not* under AOC). Old tradition: 'Little Tommes now *rarissimes*' (Androuët on his 1984 tour). Very good; softer, more melting than Swiss Gruyère or most Beaufort, slight sting in aftertaste; quite distinct from Swiss Gruyère or Beaufort.
*fermier*; *fruitier (very little)*; *vache cru*.

**Tomme des Bauges.** 5–15kg, 35–45cm × 8–10cm; rustic grey, natural, brushed crust; 3 months or over in drier *caves*; medium strength, pleasant flavour; creamy white, melt-in-mouth texture. Made at Massif des Bauges (74 **16**, upper half) southwards to Le Châtelard, École; Vallée des Aillons (see p. 427). I found them mild, even after 3 months, never dull. See Thônes.
45% m.g.; *fermier*; *fruitier*; *coopérative*.

**Vacherin des Bauges.** Winter cheese; spruce or birch bark placed round it halfway through *affinage*; about 2kg, 20–25cm × 4–6cm; pale pinky-gold crust. More melting than Mont d'Or, needs eating quickly. Different fermentations give it a more acid, slightly bitter flavour. Raymond Lindon (1960) found it especially among makers of Colombier (see p. 431). Some are washed in white wine. Originally named 'Vachelin'.
45% m.g.; *vache cru*.
Savoie; 74 **16**, upper C around Le Châtelard.

## Beaufort

Wednesday market; Laiterie Coopérative du Beaufortin: 9.00–12.00, 19.00–22.00 every day May–September (9.00–12.00 October–April) to see Beaufort making with audiovisual of old and modern styles; buy cheese (shop, except Sundays, *fêtes*, 8.00–12.30; 14.00–19.30 July, August; 8.00–12.00, 14.30–18.00 rest of year). (This *coopérative* also sells at its Crémerie des Saisies (74 **17**, D218 N of Beaufort) and its Chalet d'Arêches (74 **17**, 4km S of Beaufort). Times are not forecastable. Enquire for postal service of Sica Sarl Le Beaufort des Montagnes Beaufortaines, Service de vente par correspondance, BP5, 73270 Beaufort-sur-Doron (Savoie).

M. Vialet on D218 (Arêches road) makes and matures superb Beaufort, and I have tasted a very rich September 1985 Haute-Montagne of his in June 1986 (long after most suppliers have exhausted previous summer's mountain cheeses, and before new season's are a quarter ready).

M. Gonigaze, *affineur* (*premier adjoint du maire*, 1985).

**Le Beaufort.** AOC.
48% *m.g.; fermier; fruitier; laitier; coopérative; vache cru entier.*

**Le Beaufort Haute-Montagne.** 20–70kg cheese, 35–75cm × 11–16cm; usually classed as *pâte-cuite*, but chalet makers dissent (see p. 423); moulded in ring of beechwood with convex interior, which gives Beaufort its almost unique concave circumference; the *pâte* is on the creamy side of pale gold, without holes, but sometimes, particularly in old cheeses, with *lainures*: cracks which open up and thereby speed the rate of ripening. Beaufort is still mild after the minimum of 4 months' *affinage*, but Haute-Montagne cheeses even then have a sweet, nutty richness. This is the characteristic flavour which strengthens with age but is never harsh and lingers on the palate. Texture remains supple and at the firmest only semi-hard, and melt-in-mouth. I had never known any cheese as good as the summer 1985 vintage until I tasted June 1987 as early as the end of August that year. The cheese keeps well, even in poor conditions (heat, travel), if it is wrapped with Kleenex, then surrounded with more Kleenex and rewrapped overall in its original wrap (until this needs renewal). This advice follows for all hard cheeses in summer conditions.

Sources: Aime (see p. 427); Beaufort-sur-Doron (see above); Col des Saisies (Beaufortin/Tarentaise); Moûtiers*; Bourg-St-Maurice*, La Chambre*, St Sorlin d'Arves* (W Maurienne); Lanslebourg (Laiterie du Val Cenis (se Vanoise); all have *fromageries* with direct sales*. Asterisked places have *'circuit de visite'*. For chalet visits consult the *fromagerie*, even if you know of chalets, because the herds move from one *alpage* to another during the summer and you might make an arduous climb in vain. (For breed of cattle (Tarentaises/Tarines), see p. 422.)

Rungis: Beaufort cannot meet demand, especially Haute-Montagne, but chances are best in autumn and early winter. M. Audimet sells a Beaufort from the foot of Mont Blanc, a gold medal winner at Paris a few years back.

55% *m.g.; chalet; vache cru entier; biologiquement pur.*
Beaufortin/Maurienne/Tarentaise/Savoie/Vanoise.

BEAUFORTIN

**Tomme du Beaufortin..**
30–48% *m.g.; chalet; vache cru.*

**Tomme de(s) Belleville(s).** 1½–3kg, 18–22cm × 4–6cm; natural, brushed crust.
Tarentaise/Savoie; 74 **17**, low right St Jean- and St-Martin-de-Belleville.

**Coopérative Laitière du Beaufortin.** See BEAUFORT.

BEAUMONT

500g and 1500g, 20cm × 5cm; lightly washed crust, pinky gold; refreshing flavour, melting consistency, almost a large Reblochon, but smoother. Made at Beaumont, 74160 St Julien-en-Génévois (within the custom-free zone S of Geneva) by the Girod family's *fromageries* since 1881 (see also Tamié (p. 437) and Tavaillon (p. 437)).
50% *m.g.; laitier; vache cru.*
Haute Savoie; 74 **6**, upper left C.

BELLEVILLE, TOMME DE
See BEAUFORTIN.

BERGERS

**Tomme des Bergers.** This dark mould-coated cheese, shaped like a deep truncated cone is matured by La Baratte in Dijon.
*m.g. non-précisée; fermier; brebis cru.*

## Bessans

**Bleu de Bessans.** 2–2½kg rustic blue (like Tignes, see TIGNARD, p.438), thought to be extinct but in 1984 Androuët was told to 'ask the curé'. In 1985 I was told that the Bleu and the Tomme de Bessans were still to be found on 'le Sommet de la Maurienne' and the Col d'Iseran (74 **19**, low right).
40–45% m.g.; *fermier; chalet; vache cru*.

**Tomme de Bessans.** See Bleu de Bessans, above.
*fermier; chalet; vache cru*.
Savoie/Vanoise/Tarentaise near Maurienne.

## Beulet

450g. Name used by Fromageries Girod (see Beaumont, p. 429) for their Reblochon *(lait de montagne)*.
48% m.g.; *laitier; vache cru*.
Haute Savoie.

## Bleu or Persillé

See ARAVIS, BESSANS, GRAND-BORNAND, MONT-CENIS, STE-FOY, TERMIGNON, TIGNARD/TIGNES.

## Boudane/Boudanne

**Tomme de Boudane or Boudanne.** These terms (I have not traced any territorial association) are used for chalet and farm-made *tommes* of part-skimmed milk for domestic consumption. They are pressed and have natural crusts. I have seen 4–5kg cheeses under these names in markets. Ninette Lyon reported them (1985) in *fruitières* of the Beaufortin and Les Bellevilles, and said they were sometimes found below Courchevel.
20–30% m.g.; *fermier; domestique; fruitier; chalet; vache cru*.
Savoie.

## Bourg-Saint-Maurice

Saturday market.
*Coopérative* collecting milk all year round for Beaufort-making.
M. Arpin, *chevrier*, see Le Tarentais (p. 437); M. Villeod, *chevrier*, see Sérac (p. 436).
Savoie; 74 **18**, NE of C.

## Brebis

See also BERGERS (p. 429).

**Fromage de Brebis, le Pras d'Yeures.** See PRAS D'YEURES.

## Brisco, Brisego, Brisegoût

3–5kg, 20–22cm × 18–20cm; rough but clean crust, 4–6 months *en cave*; hard, strong aroma and flavour. Can be used *frais* as ricotta. By-product of Beaufort cheese-making (Androuët, Livre d'Or 1985; Viard has m.g. as 10–25%, 1984).
*low-fat variable*, 10% m.g. maximum likely; *chalet; vache cru écrémé* and ricotta with whey.
Haute-Tarentaise, Montagne de Beaufort/Savoie.

## Caillette

Madame Jorcin, who was born and bred in Lanslebourg, was brought up very strictly; her 'leisure' time was spent spinning very fine thread of the wool of her family's sheep; talking about cheesemaking to Simone Guet (see acknowledgements) she gave her the recipe used for making rennet when she was a girl in the early 1920s. The lamb, kid or calf providing *caillette* (fourth, last stomach of ruminant) must be a suckling, which has never tasted solid food. The fourth stomach, with its contents, must be hung like a sausage to dry for 15 days–1 month. When it is really dry it should be sealed in a jar, where it can keep dry for a year. To make *présure* (rennet) 1 litre of water is needed to soak a half-vell of lamb or goat, 4 litres are needed for a calf's vell. One soupspoonful of *présure* serves for 10 litres of milk. See Glossary.

## Cérat, Cevrin

See SÉRAC.

## Le Chalet

2kg, semi-soft, soft; washed-crust, orange to pink. Very pungent, ranking with ripe Munster.
*laitier; vache cru*.

## Chambéry

Daily market.
Syndicat de défense du Fromage de Beaufort, 1 rue du Château, 73000 Chambéry (tel. 79 33 17 36).
Savoie.

## Le Chamois des Alpes

1200g; *affineur*: Pierre Pochat et fils, 74230 Thônes (see p. 437).
40% m.g.; *artisanal; vache cru*.
Haute-Savoie.

## Châtel

La Fête des Alpages, La Belle Dimanche (about third Sunday in August) celebrating descent from *transhumance*; assembly around La Chapelle de l'Abondance. The beauty queen of the cows is chosen.
Haute-Savoie; 70 **18**, low R.

## Châtelard

See AILLONS, BAUGES, VACHERIN des.

## Chèvre, Fromages de

See AIME, LES ALLUES, ARAVIS, ARÊCHES (GRATARON), BAUGES (CHEVRETTE), BEAUFORTIN (COURCHEVEL, PRALIN/PRASLIN), CHEVRETON, COLOMBIER DES BAUGES, ENTREMONT, FLAINE, FROMAGE FERMIER DE MONTAGNE, FROMAGE FORT SAVOYARD, LENTA (CHEVRINE), PETIT BORNAND, SERRAVAL. There are forty farmhouse *chevriers* in Haute-Savoie.

**Chèvre, Tomme de.** 2–3kg, 25–30cm × 4cm; good grey crust; light, crumbly, white *pâte*, good flavour (sold in Épicerie La Plagne (74 **18**, low C D221, D224 from Aime).
*artisanal; chèvre cru.*

**Chevreton.** *Brique; affineur:* R. Picault, Broys 74800 La Roche-sur-Foron.
*fermier; artisanal; chèvre cru.*
Haute-Savoie.

**Chevrette des Bauges.** See BAUGES.

**Chevrine de Lenta.** See LENTA.

**Chevrotin.** 500g almost black-crusted irregular drums, with white mould over. Firm white *pâtes*, full flavour.
*fermier; mi-chèvre.*

**Chevrotin des Aravis.** See ARAVIS.

**Chevrotin du Grand Bornand.** See ARAVIS.

## Chiguet

Skimmed, part-skimmed milk cheese mixed with garlic and potted (*Chiguet*: earthenware pot); eaten at 7–10 days.
*domestique, Dec–Jul; vache cru écrémé.*
Haute-Savoie; 74 **7/17**.

## La Clusaz

Monday market; Tuesday market; centre for Reblochon. La Fête du Reblochon (end of August).

**Persillé de la Clusaz.** Viard mentions this, as being like Persillé du Grand Bornand (1980).
Haute-Savoie; 74 **7**, low C.

## Colombier

About 1½kg, 20cm × 2½cm; grey, cloth-marked crust, on thick side; *pâte* soft, melt-in-mouth, spread of tiny holes; rich, *not* salty (tasted in August, *lait de mélange*).
*fermier; vache cru/chèvre cru, lait de mélange varying with season.*
Savoie; 74 **16**, just N of C, L of École in the Bauges.

## Colombière

600–750g in form and character of extra-large Reblochon; ripened 6–8 weeks. Pierre Androuët noted in 1982 that only one maker of this traditional cheese survived.
*50% m.g.; fermier en chalet; vache cru.*
Massif in Chaîne des Aravis, Haute-Savoie; 74 **7**, L C.

## La Combe de Savoie

*Tomme* preserved in fermented grape-must (*moût*), the original version of Tomme au Raisin, of which the modern travesty is painted dried grape pips stuck on to a processed drum; or even, in one case, on to the plastic wrapping round the 'cheese'. Androuët recorded the real thing as surviving in 1984. It may be ripened in pots in Mondeuse or *eau-de-vie-de-gentiane*. It was made for *vignerons*, and no doubt treated with their own liquor.
*fermier; domestique; vache cru.*
The valley of the Isère SW from Albertville (74 **17** to Montmélian 74 **16** lower L, which is in the wine-growing area including Chignin and Apremont).

## Courchevel

**Tomme de Courchevel.**
*45% m.g.; chalet; fermier; chèvre cru.*
Savoie; 74 **18**, low L.

**Tomme de Pralognan, Tomme de Praslin (or Pralin).** 1½–2kg, 20–25cm × 4cm; pressed; washed-crust, ochre-rosy. Ninette Lyon found them in Courchevel and 'the wild deep valleys below' in 1985. Androuët described them as sweet and aromatic in 1984. M. Thomas (*fromager* of Beaufort Haute-Montagne above Aime in summer), a native of Courchevel, told me in 1985 that the cows' milk of this locality all goes to Beaufort-making for the holiday resorts in summer, so the cows' milk *tommes* are only made out of *transhumance* season. He recommended Pralognan (La Montagne des

Avals, enquire locally), where his brother-in-law M. Christian Rolland makes 1–1½ kg *tommes* (marketed usually as Tomme de Savoie) and Beaufort. Most of his cheese goes to local hotels.
*vache cru.*
Savoie; E from Courchevel over the mountains, from the Doron de Belleville and the Doron de Allues.

## La Dent du Chat

**Le Petit Montagnard de la Dent du Chat.** 350g, 6–7cm × 3cm; double cream, white mould-crusted, by Société Coopérative Laitière d'Yenne (Yenne has a Tuesday market).
*60% m.g.; laitier coopérative; vache cru.*

**Tommette de la Dent du Chat.** Small Tomme de Savoie, recommended by MM. Cénéri of Cannes; Société Coopérative Laitière d'Yenne.
*laitièr coopérative; vache cru.*
Savoie; N end of Mont du Chat, W of Lac du Bourget, 74 **15** near Yenne.

## L'Emmental de Savoie; Emmental Français Grand Cru

60–80kg, 80–85cm × 25cm (at centre) domed; *pâte-cuite* (to 55°C); pressed 24 hours, then 24–48 hours in brine bath; crust brushed and greased, yellow to light brown, with date of making and stamp of regional name. Minimum *affinage* is 10 weeks; longer is better, but these *lait cru* cheeses have a good consistency and refreshing alpine flavour even on the young side. The *pâte* should be on the yellow side of ivory with holes never bigger than a walnut and not close together. The cheese was recorded in Savoie in 1575 under its old name Vachelin (see p. 420).
*Source*: Fromageries Perrin, rue de Méral, 74270 Seyssel whose mark is Le Perce-Neige de Savoie, which won a silver medal at the Concours Agricole 1980 when I was there.
*45% m.g. (label rouge); fruitier; vache cru ou thermisé, under 60°C (pasteurisation forbidden).*
Haute-Savoie.

## Entremont

**Fromages de Chèvre.** Small soft *fromage des* Alpes, like young Saint-Marcellin. Tubby small Rigotte like young Crottin: enquire in village or at *fruitière* (see below) for directions to the high pastures – in Maurice Périllat's words *'deux ans de marche à pied'*.
*fermier; chèvre cru.*

**Reblochon** (see p. 435). N of Entremont sign *'Lait, beurre, reblochon'* at roadside; turn E and cross little bridge over the Borne to farm with small *fruitière*; cheesemaker Maurice Périllat (see pp. 415–16).
*fruitier; vache cru.*
Haute-Savoie; Les Étroits, N of La Clusaz on D12, 74 **7**, SE of C.

## Fenouil, Tomme de

Fennel-enriched *tommes* are traditional, but have been disappearing. I found no makers, and the only cheeses I saw in the markets came from Dauphiné (see p. 454).
*fermier; vache cru.*
Savoie.

## Fermier de Montagne

About 70g when ripe; irregular flattened discs marked by the wide grille on which first laid (reminiscent of most rustic Saint-Félicien). Glorious pinky-gold crust, deepening with age; rich creamy interior. *Affineur*: Fromagerie Pochat et Fils, avenue de Mandallaz, BP 12 Annecy.
*m.g. non-précisée; fermier; chalet; chèvre cru.*
Savoie.

**Le Petit Fermier.** See aravis (chevrotin).

## Flaine

**Chèvre.** Soft 100g vertical cylinder made from milk of the few goats accompanying 600–700 sheep in *transhumance*.
*chalet; chèvre cru.*
Haute-Savoie; 74 **8** just L of C, which is Tête Pelouse, N of Désert de Platé.

## Flumet

Tuesday market.
(This is the Savoie *enclave* in the otherwise Haute-Savoie country of Reblochon.)
Savoie; 74 **7**, low R.

## Fromage Fort Savoyard

Androuët describes this recipe 'as weeks of work', producing 'long life in the pot': 500g old grey *tomme*, 500g chèvres *secs*, 500g *fromage blanc well pressed*, 25cl white wine (Abymes); 50cl of leek stock, lightly salted, salt; crushed peppercorns; finally

5cl *eau-de-vie de marc du pays*. In general, local cheeses are used in the home according to waste or generosity of supply, and the result keeps from 3 weeks to 3 months.
*domestique; vache/chèvre cru.*

### Glières

La Maison du Reblochon: Pédat Frères (from father to sons since 1870).
Glière-lès-Petit-Bornand; 74 **7**, L of C.

**Fromage de Glières.** Reblochon-shape but larger; creamy-gold coloured crust; smooth *pâte* with tiny holes and clean, creamy look, semi-soft, melt-in-mouth; full flavour on tongue though eaten young. Made by E. Delmont, La Balme de Thuy, (W of Thônes on D216). On sale in Thônes at Coopérative de Reblochon and at Timy in the Arcade.
*45% m.g.; vache cru.*
Haute-Savoie; 74 **6/7**, low.

### Le Grand Bornand

Fête Champêtre de Lormay (last Sunday in July); Fête de l'Alpage au Chinaillon (early August). Tuesday market.

**Chevrotin du Grand Bornand.**
*fermier; chèvre cru.*

**Persillé du Grand Bornand.** Similar to cheeses of Les Aravis (see p. 428). This mountain is surrounded by Reblochon makers, some of whom make the Persillé.
*fermier; vache cru.*
Haute-Savoie; 74 **7**, lower C.

### Grataron des Arêches

See p. 428.

### Grataron de Hauteluce

See below.

### Graviers du Guiers

Soft to firm miniature drums (5 in a bag weigh 35g), made by Fromagerie de Saint-Colombe, 73240 Saint-Génix-sur-Guiers.
*laitier; artisanal; vache cru.*
Savoie; 74 **14**, R of C.

### Gruyère de Savoie

20–30kg, 55–60cm × 10cm; *croûte morgée*, *raclée*; at least 3 months' *affinage*. This *lait cru* cheese well matured can stand up to comparison with its Swiss namesake in correct consistency, full flavour and aftertaste. Some are from the Comté region on the Savoie border, but too small for Comté AOC. See also BAUGES.
*laitier; artisanal; vache cru.*
Savoie.

### Hauteluce

**Grataron de Hauteluce.** In 1985 I was unable to confirm the survival of this cheese in the village (including enquiry at *épiceries*) which sells *tommes* made locally but not in commune of Hauteluce. *Guide Marabout* reported it as scarce, but available in Albertville market.
*fermier; chèvre cru.*
Savoie; 74 **17/18**.

### Lenta

**Chevrine de Lenta.** 450–600g, 12cm × 8cm; moulded in wooden hoops; pressed; rustic crust; crumbly. Made by 'the most archaic methods' (Androuët) during the *transhumance* (June to September) from the milk of the goats accompanying the cows in the high pastures. It is basically the family cheese of the *bergers*, but some may be found in season at Bonneval-sur-Arc.
*45% m.g.; chalet; chèvre cru.*
Bonneval, Vanoise/Haute-Maurienne, Savoie; 74 **19** foot

### Marc

**Tomme au Marc de Raisin.** See LA COMBE DE SAVOIE

### Marques

Naming of cheeses: Association Marque Collectif Savoie, Maison de l'Agriculture, 52 avenue des Îles, BP 327, 74037 Annecy.

### Maurienne

See TOMME DE MAURIENNE.

### Montagnard, le Petit

See LA DENT DU CHAT.

### Montagne

See FERMIER DE MONTAGNE and TOMME DES ALPAGES.

**Fromage de Montagne du Val de Thônes.** Sold by the Coopérative de la Vallée de Thônes, Les Pérasses, Route d'Annecy, Thônes (8.00–12.30, 14.00–19.00 hours).
*vache cru.*

**Petit Fromage de Montagne.** 5kg regular big-drum shaped; bright yellow-gold crust; smooth creamy interior, like Glières (see p. 433) but a little firmer; sold at Coopérative de Reblochon, Thônes.
*fermier; vache cru.*

**Tomme de Montagne.** Term used for cheeses from high farms (not so much *transhumance*; see TOMME DES ALPAGES). I bought a winter cheese in Codec at Aime (see p. 427) with a thick grey/red/yellow crust, good pale-cream *pâte*; semi-hard but not too close-textured; medium, pleasant flavour, not salt.
*40% m.g.; fermier; vache cru.*
Haute-Savoie; 74 **7**.

## Mont-Cenis

**Persillé du Mont-Cenis.** 3–8kg, natural crust, 3–4 months *affinage*, kept by *montagnards* for winter; similar to Aravis of the friable kind, good aroma, but not strong; rare.
*fermier; chalet; vache ou vache/chèvre mélange cru.*

**Tomme du Mont-Cenis.** 2–3 and 5–6kg, sometimes shaped like flat-topped dome, as though moulded in striated bowl or in basket; thick, rough, mottled light brown crust; close-textured, firm to softish golden-cream *pâte* with spread groups of small holes; brownish near edges when mature (when crust gets powdery with cheese mite); gentle flavour with slight sting in aftertaste.
*fermier; vache cru.*
Maurienne, Savoie; 77 **9**.

## Mont-Tournier

**Le Régal de Mont-Tournier.** Reblochon-sized cheese of Munster-like character.
*laitier; vache.*
Savoie.

## Moûtiers

Tuesday market.
Noted for *affinage* and marketing of Tommes d'Alpages (see p. 438) and all-year-round coopérative for Beaufort.
Foire de Moûtiers 11 September: cattle fair, important for Tarentaises/Tarines.
Tarentaise, Savoie; 74 **17**, lower R.

## Paladru, Palendru

In *The Provinces of France* (1951) Samivel, the artist-author of the Savoie-Dauphiné chapter, mentions Palendru alongside Reblochon, Vacherin, Chevrotin and the Tommes as one of 'the predominating cheeses'; it must have been from Paladru (74 **14**, L, N end of lake) in Isère, Dauphiné, a Sassenage-like cheese, finished by 1973 according to Robert Courtine.
*artisanal; vache cru.*

## Le Pédat

250g size of cheese, otherwise of Reblochon formula (see Glières, p. 433).

## Persillé

See ARAVIS, GRAND-BORNAND, LA CLUSAZ, MONT-CENIS.

## Petit Reblochon

See REBLOCHONNET.

## La Poivrette

A Raclette (see below) with black peppercorns, reminiscent of the old Bougnat ('the coalman') of Auvergne.
*laitier; vache.*

## Pralin/Praslin, Pralognan

See COURCHEVEL.

## Pras d'Yeures

Soft, rounded *banon*-like brebis, pleasing consistency, sweet, rich flavour (not too strong). Made by M. Patrick Bardin above La Sauffaz (pronounced Sauffe), S of Serraval (see p. 437). Available on farm or in Thônes (see p. 437) at Saturday market.
*m.g. non-précisée; fermier; brebis cru.*
Haute-Savoie; 74 **7/17**, L.

## Le Pressy-Moye

M. Bernard Brissaud, *maître fromager*, good selection of cheese. Markets: Rumilly Thur, Thônes (see p. 437).
Haute-Savoie; 74 **5**.

## Raclette, Fromage à Raclette

Cheese of Abondance (or small Gruyère) size and appearance for heating and scraping. Made by Coopérative at Thônes with milk surplus to Reblochon needs at peak of milk production. These cheeses are 5.3kg; salt-rubbed three times a week over 3–4 months. No doubt other *coopératives* do likewise, as there is more and more French Raclette on the market. Abondance (see p. 427) is excellent for the purpose.

Before use the cheese is cleaned and slightly dampened on the surface and cut in two. The two cut surfaces are presented towards the fire (or special raclette table-stove) and as they melt to a depth of a quarter centimetre or so, are scraped onto plates and eaten with baked potatoes (in skins), gherkins, small onions in vinegar, and pepper, accompanied by a Savoie white wine with an edge to its flavour. The recipe is centuries old, from the *bergers* in the mountains.

*fruitier; vache cru.*

## Reblochon AOC 1976, 1980

250g, 10cm × 3cm (*demi*); 450g (minimum)–550g, 14cm × 3½cm; soft, washed-crust (gold to pink); 3–5 weeks *affinage* (at least 15 days of which in zone of origin); unctuous *pâte* with flavour peculiar to this cheese, enhanced by eating the beautiful crust, unless hot weather or over-enclosure of cheese has made crust soggy and bitter (see pp. 414–17).

Reblochon Syndicat Interprofessionnel and AOC signs in black or red on the wrapping, show *laitier* or *fruitier* cheese; from 1987, a green casein circle on the crust of about 2cm diameter, marked '*fermier*', and green signs on the wrapping have denoted farmhouse cheese made with milk straight from cows, morning and evening; all Reblochon comes from the milk of cows on natural pastures, or on winter feed derived from them (no silage); no antibiotics or detergents may come into contact with milking or cheese-dairy equipment. No cheese without the signs may be sold as Reblochon. The Aravis region – Thônes, La Clusaz, Grand Bornand, Chinaillon – is the historic centre and many farms are indicated on the roads, but avoid La Clusaz and Le Col des Aravis at the height of the holiday season or at weekends. Lieu-Dit is a farm in the *alpages* at Prat Riand near Manigod (74 **7**, low, half L, SE of Thônes). Entremont (see p. 432) has a *fruitière* easy to find.

GAEC Vercot makes farm cheese, which I noted as 'best ever' in October 1987 (Haute-Savoie, *Commune* of Pers and Jussy, 74 **6**, NW of La Roche Foron, off D2). A number of *coopératives* and *fruitières* offer visits. La Coopérative Agricole des Producteurs de Reblochon, ½km outside Thônes (see p. 437) on the right of the Annecy road show actual making of the cheese and audiovisual accounts of it. Regional cheeses are on sale.

M. Daniel Bessan, prominent in agricultural and Reblochon circles, has a high *alpage* farm. Above Manigod take D16 to Col de la Crois Fry, turn right towards Pointe de Merdassier for 1½km, and at the end of a wood turn left along a rocky road, and ask for M. Bessan at the farm (74 **7**, low half, L and C). Total Reblochon production: 1980 5000 tonnes; 1982 5700 tonnes.

*45% m.g.; fermier; chalet; fruitier; coopérative; vache cru entier.*

**Reblochonnet.** 250g; Petit Reblochon not generally ripening as lusciously as the conventional cheese, because it is more tubby; it may therefore suit those for whom Reblochon ripens too quickly and richly in summer conditions.

*laitier; vache cru.*

Chaine des Aravis W of Annecy, Abondance, Mont Blanc in Haute-Savoie; adjacent part of Savoie, area Ugine-Flumet; 74 **6/7** and top of **16/17** within Haute-Savoie.

## Rennet

See CAILLETTE.

## Revard

**Tomme du Revard.** 1½–2kg, 20cm × 6–8cm; typical Tomme de Savoie (see p. 436).

*30–40% m.g.; fermier; vache cru.*

Haute-Savoie; 74 **15**, upper R, E of Aix-Les-Bains.

## Les Rigottes de Sainte-Colombe

60g, cream-coloured, *sec*; made at St-Genix-sur-Guiers.

*laitier; vache.*

Savoie; 74 **14**, middle R.

## Rochebrune

Trade name on cheeses such as Emmental (p. 432), Tommes de Savoie (p. 436), and Reblochon (see above), distributed by Schoepfer of Avignon (Est. 1798).

## La Roche-sur-Foron

Dairy School: École Nationale des Industries du Lait et des Viandes, Étaux, 74800

La Roche-sur-Foron (tel. 50 03 01 03; visits for groups can be arranged).
Haute-Savoie; 74 **6/7**, middle H.

RUMILLY

Thursday market (including Bernard Brissaud).
Haute-Savoie; 74 **5**.

SAINTE-FOY-TARENTAISE

**Bleu de Sainte-Foy.** 5–6kg, 30cm × 8.5cm (approx.); naturally rough-crusted upright cylinder; interior like Persillé des Aravis (see p. 428) firm *pâte*, slightly bitter. Needs strong wine.
45% m.g.; *fermier; chalet; artisanal; vache/chèvre/mélange cru.*
Savoie; 74 **19**, middle L.

ST-FELIX

Monday market.
SW of Alby-sur-Cheran, Haute-Savoie; 74 **15**, top R.

ST-GÉNIX-SUR-GUIERS

Wednesday market.

**Saint Génix.** 250g thick round white cheese; white uncrusted; close texture on acid side, but not salty. (58% m.g.)
360g deeper, tubby-shaped; light creamy-gold crust; moist, white, crumbly texture; eaten young, slightly salty and refreshing (salt might obtrude with keeping). Fromagerie de Ste-Colombe, St-Génix-sur-Guiers, which also makes Graviers (see p. 433).
60% m.g.; *laitier; vache cru.*

**Saint-Génix Fermier.** 200g flattish and 400g tubby; similar cheese, rustic looking.
*fermier; vache cru*
Savoie; 74 **14**, middle R.

ST-JULIEN-EN-GENEVOISE

Friday market.
WSW of Geneva, Haute-Savoie; 74 **6**, upper L.

SAVOIE

**Tomme de Savoie.** (Regionally protected.) 1–3kg, 18–30cm × 5–8cm (occasionally much larger); natural crusts grey, white moulds enriched with red and mimosa-like yellow; firm texture, good on tongue and often melt-in-mouth; varying flavours, mould-rich, earthy, mild, but never dull if the genuine unpasteurised article. M. Paccard at Thônes assured me that the protected cheeses are *never* pasteurised, although this condition is not laid down.
*Various tastings*: La Tournette (hôtel at Serraval) serves cheeses all very well crusted, pleasant firm interiors; one aged cheese extra-thickly crusted and hard white inside, like ewes' milk cheese. *Tommes fermières* from Épicerie at Serraval have wonderful red and mimosa on grey *croûte*, gentle pleasant flavour, melt-in-mouth (see also THÔNES). See also Rochebrune (p. 435).
With the exception of some cheeses made and ripened on farms and not sold through *affineurs*, cheeses should have a red oval casein plaque on the side with departmental number (73 or 74), four hearts ringed with Savoie on the wrapping and 'au lait cru'. Many cheeses made elsewhere are sent to Savoie for *affinage*, and may acquire a rich coat. Pierre Androuët warns us to 'watch out for cloth marks, and for *too* smooth a *pâte*'. Taste and be safe.
*fermier; chalet; artisanal; fruitier; laitier; coopérative; vache cru.*

See also ALLUES, BAUGES, BEAUFORTIN, LA COMBE, COURCHEVEL, FENOUIL, MONTAGNE, MONT-CENIS (PRALOGNAN, PRALIN, PRASLIN, with COURCHEVEL), REVARD, THÔNES, TOMMES.

SÉRAC, CÉRAT OR CEVRIN

1. *Cows' milk*: 2kg, 20cm × 5cm white, irregular surface (uncrusted) close-textured; made from *recuite* of Beaufort cheesemaking in chalets in summer (e.g. above Aime, see p. 427) where it can be bought.
*low-fat; chalet; fermier; vache* (whey) *cru.*
2. *Goats' milk* (summer only): 300g, 400g, 600g standing cylinder, made by M. Villeod, Peisey above Landry, E of N90 between Aime and Bourg-St-Maurice (74 **18**, R of C).
*fermier; chèvre* (whey) *cru.*
3. 300g flat drum-shaped made by M. Borral above Les Côtes d'Aime on way to Mont Rosset and the Beaufort chalet; track to right where road ends. (74 **18**, left of centre; get firm directions in Aime (see p. 427).)
*fermier; chèvre* (whey) *cru.*
Beaufortin/Savoie.

## Serraval

An agreeable centre for cheese visits; local *épicerie* opposite church sells good local *tommes*. For visits see BREBIS (Pras d'Yeures above La Sauffaz), REBLOCHON (Lieu-Dit and M. Bessan), TAMIÉ, THÔNES and FROMAGES DE CHÈVRE, CHEVROTIN DES ARAVIS and PERSILLÉ DES ARAVIS.
Haute-Savoie; 74 **7/17**, L.

## Sixt

See TOMME DE SIXT.

## Tamié

**Abbaye de Tamié.** Made from milk of thirty local farms to Reblochon recipe, just outside the région; ½kg and 1.3kg, 12cm × 4cm, 20cm × 5cm; washed-crust, attaining glorious pink at peak of ripeness with melting white *pâte*, rich flavour. *Fromager*: Frère Philippe. Cheeses on sale 10.00–12.00, 14.00–18.00 hours. Visitors are welcome in the Abbey church (mass at 11.00) and in the *hostellerie* restaurant. SAFF at Rungis get 300kg of Tamié every week.
45% m.g.; *artisanal monastique; vache cru.*
Savoie; 74 **17**, left, S of Chaine des Aravis, below Faverges.

## Le Tarentais

200–300g, standing cylinder 5cm × 7.5cm; light rough crust; moist white *pâte*, yellowing from edges as it ripens; very tasty. Made by *chevriers* of the Beaufortin/Tarentaise including M. J. M. Arpin, Seez, NE of Bourg-St-Maurice, who goes up to the Vallée des Chapieux in summer (tel. 79 07 38 37). Sold also in Thônes (see below), Timy, and Aime (see p. 427) in the Beaufort *coopérative*. (For Tarentaise/Tarine breed of cattle, see p. 422.)
45% m.g.; *fermier; chalet; chèvre cru.*
Beaufortin/Tarentaise/Savoie; 74 **18**, C.

## Le Tavaillon

1½kg cheese ringed in bark of *mélèze* (larch); washed-crust; creamy-golden *pâte* with a slightly Gruyère look, but softer impact. Distinctive flavour (from larch?), rich earthy. Made since 1984 by Girod at Beaumont (see p. 429). Unlike Vacherin it is available most of the year.
48% m.g.; *laitier; vache cru.*
Beaumont, Haute-Savoie.

## Termignon, Bleu de

Jacques Vernier found two producers of this cheese a few years ago in the Parc de la Vanoise.
*fermier; vache cru.*
Parc de la Vanoise, Savoie; 77 **8**, Modane area.

## Thoiry

Sunday market.
St-Alban-Leysse, Savoie.

## Thônes

*Musée du pays* with room upstairs on Reblochon making (end June–end August, 10.00–12.00, 14.00–18.00). Vieille Fête savoyarde second fortnight in June. Headquarters of Reblochon. Syndicat Interprofessionnel du Reblochon, Les Villards 74230, Thônes.
*Affineurs*: including old firm of Pochat et Fils, 33 rue Saulne (tel. 50 02 11 98) Pointe Percée and Coopérative des producteurs de la Vallée de Thônes 'La Bergère' Reblochons Fermiers (Reblochon Fermier, Le Val du Fier, 'Impérial Savoy').
Saturday market: Véronique Charmot and Bernard Brissaud for local cheeses.
*Shops*: Timy in Arcades; La Coopérative Agricole des Producteurs de Reblochons de la Vallée Thônes ('La Bergère', Reblochons Fermiers) Les Perrasses–Route d'Annecy, Thônes (for Abondance, Beaufort, farmhouse butter, Chevrotin, Emmental de Savoie, Fromage de Montagne du Val de Thônes, Persillé des Aravis, Raclette and Reblochon (both made there), Reblochon Fermier, Tomme de Savoie Fermière (and Fruitière of their own making). Daily 8.00–12.30, 14.00–19.00; tasting, visits to *fromagerie* for making, and to *caves*.

**Persillé de Thônes.** Like Persillé des Aravis (see p. 428).
*fermier; chèvre/vache cru.*

**Tomme de Savoie.** 1000–1200g upright tubby cylinder, irregular; richly coated crust with plenty of yellow (mimosa-style); (on sale at Fromagerie Coopérative in Thônes) 1kg rather dome-shaped *fruitière* cheese: grey crust, very good semi-soft, slightly pitted, cream-coloured *pâte*; good, broad, sweet flavour.
*fermier; coopérative; fruitière; vache cru.*

**Tomme de Thônes.** Sometimes irregular in shape (like overturned wash-tub); thick crust; smooth firm-looking *pâte* with even spread of small holes, melt-in-mouth; at 1½ months achieves good full cheesy flavour, not salt, not strong. Made on several local farms, and available at Saturday market.
*fermier; vache cru.*
Haute-Savoie; 74 **7**, lower L.

### Thonon les Bains

Androuët found a *maître fromager* here in 1981 who knew the 'lacis des routes' in the Dranses d'Abondance and de Morzine where the cheese makes are to be found.
Haute-Savoie; 70 **17**, on L. Leman.

### Tignard

**Bleu Tignard; Bleu de Tignes.** 2–3kg rustic blue. Unfortunately old Tignes was submerged when the water level of the lake was raised for a barrage, and cheese notables I talked to thought the cheese was drowned with the village. Androuët and Ninette Lyon reported it (*Marabout*) as surviving in 1979, and one of my regional informants thought it might still be made 'very locally', but I did not find it in 1985.
40–45% m.g.; *fermier; chalet; vache cru.*
S. Tarentaise; on L. de Tignes at head of Val d'Isère, E of Vanoise/Savoie; 74 **19**.

### Tomme au Raisin

See la combe.

### Tomme d'Alpages

Name for *tommes* made during transhumance; École and Moûtiers are known for *affinage* and marketing.
*chalet; vache cru.*
Tarentaise; 74 **17**, low R.

### Tomme de Chèvre

See chèvres.

### Tomme de Fenouil

See châtelard.

### Tomme de Maurienne, Savoie Grosse

8–12kg pressed *tomme* made around St-Jean-de-Maurienne; the biggest are said to be November cheeses.
Savoie; 77 **7**, upper L.

### Tomme de Montagne

See montagne.

### Tomme de Savoie

See savoie.

### Tomme de Sixt

*Tomme* kept for years and said by Curnonsky to need an axe; last mention *Larousse*, 1973.
Sixt-Fer-A-Cheval; Haute-Savoie; 74 **8**, N of C on D907.

### Tommette

See la dent du chat.

I have met the following cheeses in markets without detailed provenance.

**Tommette au Cerron (Ciron) ou aux Artisans.** About 220g; base of cone; grey mould on mite-rich crust; *pâte* tending towards hard, sharp.

**Tommette de Savoie (affinage moyen).** About 300g; slightly domed; blue-grey mould on crust, colour so deep on some cheeses that it gives illusion of *cendres*; pleasant rich interior; white, close texture, but not hard.

### Toupin

6kg, 20cm × 15cm *marmite*-shaped cheeses of Abondance type (see p. 427). (Toupin is the local name for a *marmite*.)

### Ugine

Wednesday market.
Savoie; 74 **17**, top.

### Vacherin

See abondance, bauges, tavaillon.

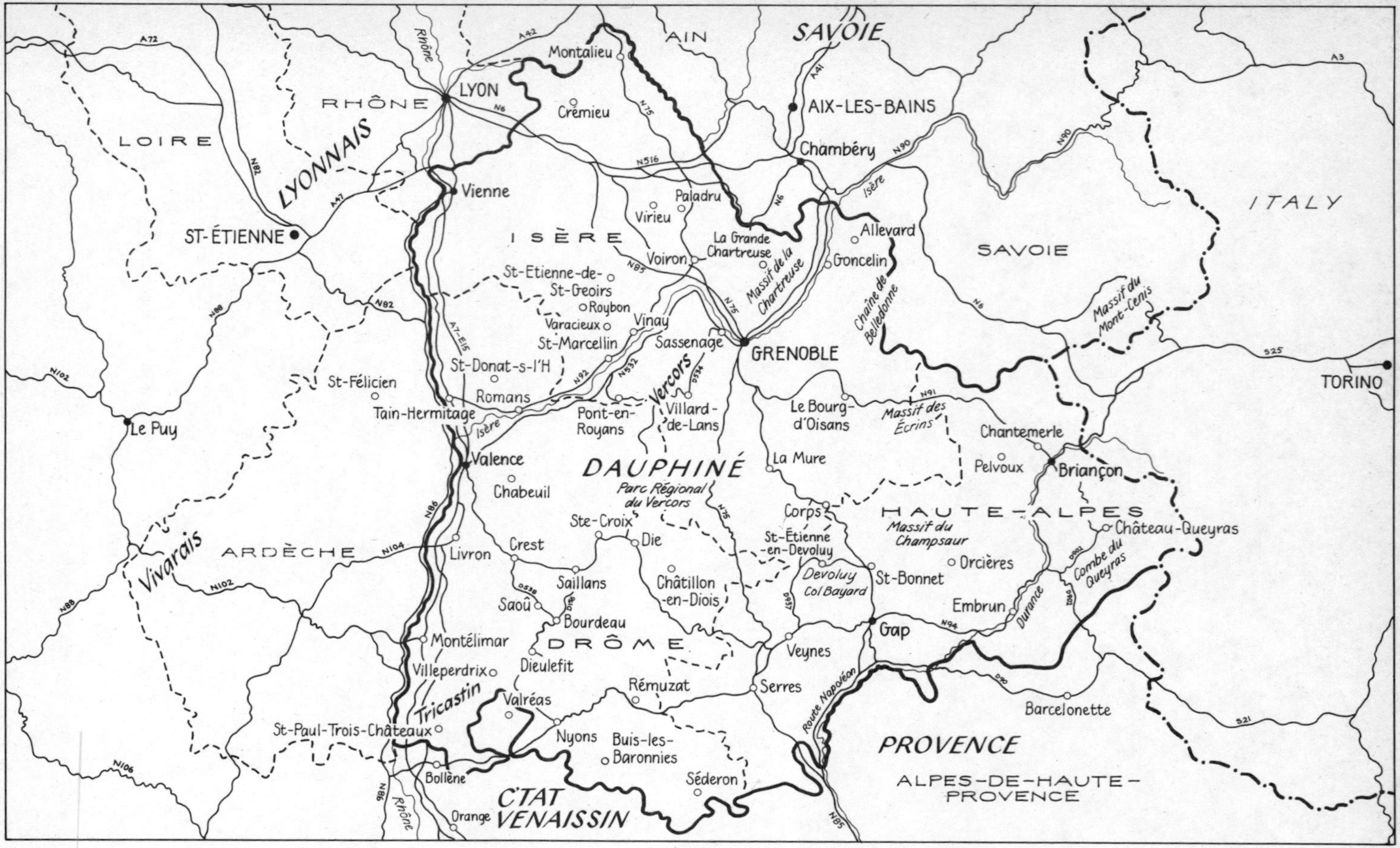

SAVOIE
AIN
ITALY
LYON
RHÔNE
LOIRE
LYONNAIS
ST-ÉTIENNE
Montalieu
Crémieu
AIX-LES-BAINS
Chambéry
Vienne
Paladru
Virieu
ISÈRE
La Grande Chartreuse
Massif de la Chartreuse
Allevard
Goncelin
Chaîne de Belledonne
SAVOIE
Massif du Mont-Cenis
Voiron
St-Etienne-de-St-Geoirs
Roybon
Varacieux
Vinay
St-Marcellin
Sassenage
GRENOBLE
TORINO
St-Donat-s-l'H
St-Félicien
Romans
Tain-Hermitage
Vercors
Pont-en-Royans
Villard-de-Lans
Le Bourg-d'Oisans
Massif des Écrins
Chantemerle
Le Puy
Valence
Chabeuil
DAUPHINÉ
Parc Régional du Vercors
La Mure
Pelvoux
Briançon
Corps
HAUTE-ALPES
Massif du Champsaur
Château-Queyras
Ste-Croix
Die
Crest
Livron
ARDÈCHE
Vivarais
St-Étienne-en-Devoluy
Devoluy
Col Bayard
Orcières
Combe du Queyras
Saillans
Saoû
Bourdeau
Châtillon-en-Diois
St-Bonnet
Embrun
Durance
Gap
Montélimar
DRÔME
Veynes
Villeperdrix
Dieulefit
Rémuzat
Serres
Route Napoléon
Barcelonette
Tricastin
Valréas
St-Paul-Trois-Châteaux
Nyons
Buis-les-Baronnies
PROVENCE
Bollène
Séderon
ALPES-DE-HAUTE-PROVENCE
Orange
C'TAT VENAISSIN
Rhône
Isère
A72
A42
A41
A47
A3
A7-E15
N6
N75
N516
N90
N82
N85
N88
N102
N92
N532
D534
N91
S25
N86
N104
N106
D538
D902
N94
D937
D90
S21
N85

CHAPTER SIXTEEN

# *Dauphiné*

HAUTES-ALPES – DRÔME – ISÈRE

The immense Dauphiné stretches eastwards from the Rhône Valley to Italy. North to south, from Savoie to the Gapençais, a succession of mountain chains inhibits contact between east and west, the great zigzag of the Isère Valley and the lesser one of the Romanche gorges carrying the only serious east–west route; but they carry it so indirectly that crows' distances are almost doubled. We have to go as far south as Gap to find the Durance, the Luye and the Buech shaping a recognisable east–west path on the map, which is still quite a meander on the ground. This fragmentation is reminiscent of the Pyrénées, but the surprising difference is that Dauphiné has so long been politically undivided by its geography.

The pre-Roman peoples were the Vocontii (Voconces) with their capital at Die, and the Allobroges, who also populated part of Savoie. After the Roman occupation they experienced the descent of the Burgondes and, except for the Mérovingian–Carolingian interval, formed part of several Burgundian states. Finally the region was absorbed in the Jurassian Kingdom which went to the Emperor in the ninth century. Neither Empire nor Kingdom, however, exercised effective control over cities, bishops and feudal lords and in 1029 the most successful of these last, the comtes d'Albon who ruled the Viennois, took over the whole province. Gigues V adopted the title of Dauphin du Viennois and included the dolphin in his arms in 1120. In 1349 Humbert II, having lost his only son, handed his dominions over to Charles, grandson of King Philippe VI of France. In return the King paid 200,000 Florins and undertook that Charles and all future heirs to France would hold the title of Dauphin until they acceded to the throne, and would maintain the people's privileges. Humbert, then only thirty-six, became a Dominican monk; he died six years later.

In the course of the years there were some tidyings-up of the frontier, the most important being the acquisition of the Diois in the south and the Valentinois (capital Valence) and Montélimar in the west. In 1560 the Dauphiné formally became part of France, and after the Revolution it was divided into the three *départements* of Isère, Hautes-Alpes (which also includes a fringe of Provence) and Drôme.

The old *dauphinois* word *toma* has become the *tome* or *tomme* used for small round cheeses or for crusted drums in south-eastern, central and southern France today.

## SASSENAGE AND OTHER CHEESES OF THE VERCORS

The great mountain region of the Vercors, stretching north from the Diois to the loop of the Isère west of Grenoble, became a by-word for the *Résistance* during the Second World War. The old *quinze-neuf*, the 159me Régiment d'Infanterie Alpine based on Briançon, was nobly reconstituted from the fighters in the Maquis. In September 1945 in Vienna I had the privilege and pleasure of arranging for their entertainment by the British 3rd of Foot, the Buffs. Their magnificent band and *cors-de-chasse* marched into Schönbrunn and played before the palace (then British headquarters) for the first time since the childhood of Napoleon's son, roi de Rome, duc de Reichstadt. The enormous *béret* of the Chasseurs Alpins is a reminder of the harsh mountain climate it was designed to withstand. It can be pulled in every direction as a shield against wind-borne cold, can act as a sun-visor, or envelop the whole head if need be.

The Vercors has ancient cheese traditions and is proud of its *ravioles dauphinoises*. These are of crisp, thin pastry stuffed with chèvre, gruyère and parsley. Remote now from ravioli, they are thought to have originated with immigrant Italian charcoal-burners who could no longer find meat to put into their pasta.

In the north-eastern Vercors lay the ancient Seigneurie de Sassenage, which extended its authority over the valley of the Furon with Villard-de-Lans at its head. Monks of the region developed a blue cheese which came to provide the livelihood of numerous cheesemakers and merchants in Villard-de-Lans. Its importance was recognised by the Seigneur, Baron Albert de Sassenage, in a charter of 28 June 1338. This established the right to sell their cheeses unhindered for the inhabitants of Villard-de-Lans, which has its own breed of cattle, producing high-protein milk and is still the source of Bleu de Sassenage today. Eleven years later, when the Dauphiné was ceded to the first French Dauphin, a number of these cheesemakers emigrated to the pays de Gex, where, with monastic encouragement, they instituted Bleu de Gex and Bleu de Septmoncel (see Chapter 14). These two cheeses, still produced entirely on the artisanal *fruitier* scale, have upstaged their Sassenage ancestral line by earning a national Appellation d'Origine Contrôlée under their own names and the joint description 'Bleu du Haut Jura'. The Dauphinois cheese was for centuries made of mixed milks; Olivier de Serres, the agricultural writer of the Tricastin on the southern border of Dauphiné, wrote in 1600 that the best Sassenage included the milk of cows, goats and ewes. The cheese continued to be widely known and respected through the seventeenth and eighteenth centuries.

In modern times writers and others who have eaten only the pasteurised version of Sassenage have supposed that the cheese was entirely industrialised. However, in 1982 Pierre Androuët found the old traditions still kept up by the smaller *laiteries* of Villard, though he noted that trials with the old mixture of milks had proved 'inconclusive'. It seems, nevertheless, that at least one *laiterie* does use mixed cows' and goats' milk. This was reported by the Larousse-Sélection team in *Les Pays et Gens de France* in September 1982 and confirmed by Arthur Eperon in 1984, after he had sampled the cheese at the Hôtel Castel Anne near Voiron (which presents other good Dauphinois and Savoyard cheeses).

The Bleu de Sassenage usually available weighs between 3 and 4 kilos; it is smaller than Gex, and its otherwise similar rounded, golden exterior is smoother. The well-spread, greeny-blue-on-cream interior looks like Gex, and has a mild flavour, with some bitterness in the aftertaste. It would be of service to the community and to gastronomy if steps were taken to protect the true traditional cheese, with no compromises about pasteurisation. The enterprises of Savoie and Haute-Savoie, and the success of Comté and Bleu du Haut Jura, have set good examples for neighbouring Isère to follow.

Voiron is noted for the local *fromage fort* Pétafine. It also offers its visitors a monastic distillery outpost of the Grande Chartreuse, which keeps forty monks busy. I regret that the 900-year-old monastery, 26 kilometres north of Grenoble, offers no cheese to tourists, although it was noted for a mixed-milk cheese (brebis-vache) in the 1780s, and in the 1860s its cows, bred and milked by the *frères*, won prizes at dauphinois cattle shows. At Mont-Saint-Martin, within 20 kilometres of Voiron towards Grenoble, you can visit an organic goat farm (see list, p. 464).

## SAINT-MARCELLIN

If you enter or leave Dauphiné by the north-east, use D523 and look into the cheese shop at Froges and into cheesemaking at Brignoud and near Concelin. In the north-west, 20 kilometres by road along the right bank of the Isère from Voiron, lies Saint-Marcellin country. From Villard it is the same 20 kilometres by pigeon, but 39 kilometres by road along the Gorges de la Bourne. As Saint-Marcellin is the best-known cheese of the Dauphiné, the Isère would give its reputation and that of the cheese a great lift by applying some control to the use of the name. What reaches most corners of the outside world is a stodgy, white pasteurised misrepresentation of the real thing.

Small, rounded goats' cheeses with the outward appearance of Saint-Marcellin are found throughout the southern half of France, and any household with a litre of milk to spare can produce one; but when you find the *lait cru* Saint-Marcellin which has been brought to perfection by a good *affineur*, even if it is a cows'-milk cheese (let alone one of the few goats'-milk survivals), you will experience something unique to the Dauphiné. Eaten *frais* it is good, but not all that different. The interest comes with the *affinage*: dry *caves* produce blue coats on a firmish cheese; damp *caves* turn the skin orange to russet and keep the cheese soft. It can run inside, and sometimes slip its coat, as used to happen with an old English cheese called 'Slipcote'. I have eaten such Saint-Marcellin brought straight from la Mère Richard in Lyon (see Chapter 12), a sumptuous revelation of what can be achieved from so small a beginning.

No one knows Saint-Marcellin's real origins, but a story of 1445 attests to its being already an accepted part of life in the Vercors. The energetic Dauphin Louis was on a wolf-hunt when he found himself in thick undergrowth face to face with an enormous bear. His cry for help was answered by two woodcutters, who scared off the bear and took the Dauphin into their hut. There they comforted him with the small amount of Saint-Marcellin which was all they had, before setting him off on his road to Saint-Laurent-en-Royans. In gratitude, Louis set up a still-existing charity and the cheese was good enough to retain his custom for life. As Louis XI of France he had Saint-Marcellin served at the Louvre and at Plessis-lez-Tours.

It was not until 1870 that the cheeses started being collected by *affineurs* for distribution in cities, such as Grenoble, Lyon and Avignon. The railways helped them to Paris, where Sacha Guitry was moved to say '*Saint Marcellin, comme je comprends qu'on t'ait canonisé!*' (a liquid tribute to that saint is paid annually by the Provençaux winemakers and drinkers of Boulbon, near Tarascon (see Chapter 18)).

At Saint-Marcellin itself, Monsieur and Madame Ray-Piefert have made their shop, La Petite Ferme, a chapel-of-ease for Saint-Marcellin-lovers. Five or six farms bring in *pur chèvre* versions on Mondays in season. These may all be sold before the week is out, so time your visit with forethought, or telephone an order; but there are always pleasing *mi-chèvre* or *vache lait cru* cheeses to be had. The list at the end of this chapter includes numerous makers of Saint-Marcellin and several *affineurs*, including one in the Lyonnais who matures the cheese in wine.

Halfway down the Isère to the Rhône from Saint-Marcellin is Romans, source of a cows'-milk cheese deserving special mention. It has been described as a double-size Saint-Marcellin, but this does its individual character an injustice. Properly ripened, its crust ripples invitingly, a little more creamily than that of a Camembert, and its interior has a rich, close-clotted texture reminiscent of a young Melun or of the Saint-Martin which used to be made near Bayeux. The flavour, however, is quite different from either of them, and from Saint-Marcellin. I like the cheese cut across in slices about a centimetre thick, laid on good crusty rye bread, and I find it hard to stop before I have eaten more than my ageing appetite can do justice to. I have never seen the old chèvre version of Romans, but Le Gaudre (Monsieur Nicole's Fontvieille cheese, see Chapter 18), must be something like it.

## Chambarand

Before leaving the Saint-Marcellin region we visited the Cistercian nuns in the Forêt de Chambaran. For some reason this convent, the Monastère de Notre Dame de Chambarand, adds a final 'd' not used by geographers (the site is marked on the map as Abbaye de la Trappe de Chambaran). The nuns were established there in the 1860s, but expelled with all the other religious communities at the beginning of this century, and the buildings were sold in 1901. In 1932 the community returned and started making butter and cheese. Pierre Androuët's father, Henri, named their cheese Beaupré de

Roybon. They collect the milk of twenty farms, between 2000 and 2500 litres a day, which, to my regret, they pasteurise. They follow the Reblochon method (see Chapter 15), and allow twelve to fifteen days for *affinage*. The resulting cheese looks neat, but has little flavour. Most of their cheese is 45 per cent *matières grasses*, but since 1978 they have catered for dieters with some of 25 per cent.

Whatever my reservations about their cheese, I have none about the voices of the nuns. You should make a point of visiting when there is a sung office, as provision is made for visitors to hear the services.

Numerous other cheeses are made between the Vercors and the Rhône, so look up the list before you leave the area.*

## Queyras and the transhumance country

We went south from Grenoble by the Route Napoléon, N85. In some of the city outskirts and nearby villages many plain but unexceptionable stone or rubble-walled houses are rendered with sad cement that has weathered dirtily, providing an aspect of gloom instead of gold. Further along the route, forested hills to the west contrast with the light, grassy slopes, sometimes terraced, leading up to the bare moorland heights to the east. Between them are valleys which widen as we go south, and behind these eastern hills are the great mountains of the Écrins stretching towards Briançon, Mont Dauphin and Embrun, divided by the upper valley of the Durance from the Queyras. The Queyras, much of it now a regional park, used to be a source of an interesting blue cheese of that name, especially around Saint-Véran; but since before 1914 most survivors of the name have been made by *laitiers* in Briançon. Many of the chalets where they and the Tommes du Queyras were once made can now send their milk down the mountain by *téléphérique* to the road, where the lorry collects it for the *laitier*. The local race of sheep, the Savournon, is still bred, but the renowned fat lambs are sent down to the Provençal market of Sisteron.

Like the Vercors, all these ranges are rich in *alpages*, which welcome countless flocks of sheep for the *transhumance* during their brief snow-free period. Some less distant shepherds still go on foot with their flocks and their goats, as Marie Mauron describes so fully and so feelingly in her book *La Transhumance*, and most have to do the last stretch on foot from the nearest road; but most of the distance is now covered in long, three-storeyed lorries. I was surprised to see one Provençal shepherd still down in Fontvieille after mid-June, and asked him whether he now managed without the *transhumance*. He was expecting his lorry within a few days. Formerly he had needed a month to make the passage to Grenoble which now takes one day. His bright, chestnut-coloured goats were cross-breeds, but had the appearance of the *chamoisées* of the Dauphiné with their great flattened, twisted horns. In the evening sun they were shafts of rich gold in the grey cloud of sheep.

*See Cailloux, Eydoche, Geyssans, Meylan, Pont-en-Royans (particularly attractive), Roissard, Roc-du-Toulaux, Saint-Bardoux, Saint-Donat-sur-l'Herbasse, Saint-Just-de-Claix, Saint-Michel-sur-Savasse, Tèche, Varacieux, Virieu-sur-Bourbre.

On a Monday morning the market at La Mure is worth a pause; and in 1985 there was a *chevrier* on the north-west side of the town.* Monday shop closures were a disadvantage at Corps, but a knowledgeable local reassured me about the survival of Tomme de Corps.

Further south, Laye, too, was dormant, but up at the *fromagerie* on the Col Bayard the cheeses of Champsaur proved to be alive and impressive in their variety. The shop attached to the dairy was deservedly crowded; so, although I could sample the cheeses and buy, I dared not hold up the queue to ask questions of the amiable girl who was serving. Exploring outside, I found what looked like a small pasteurisation plant, but no staff. My follow-up letter has not been answered, so I am not sure how much this enterprise pasteurises, nor whether it ripens some cheeses made elsewhere; the variety seemed wide for a single dairy, but their range of fat content fitted in with a balanced use of milk (see Col du Bayard on list). Bleu des Hauts Pâturages was a pleasantly flavoured un-bitter cheese, otherwise similar to Sassenage. A 1.5-kilo *fromage de chèvre* (in Savoie it would have been called a *tomme*) had flavour, texture and rich external moulds up to good Savoie standards. There were *faisselles des pâturages* and several young white cheeses of cows' milk or *lait de mélange*. Finally, I lingered over their Tommes de Champsaur: not the soft chèvres from the upper Drac Valley mentioned by Robert Courtine, but pressed cows'-milk cheeses. They were of 450 grams with 25 per cent or 40 per cent *matières grasses* and of 2 kilos with 40 per cent *matières grasses*. The latter, in various stages of *affinage*, from pale cream to grey in crust, were all on the gentle side, but with an agreeable edge in the aftertaste.

After Gap we followed the Petit Buech westwards and found some good local produce in the cheese shop at Veynes, and in the Codec supermarket. One of them was a brebis made at Saint-Julien-en-Beauchêne, 17 kilometres to the north on N75. Our road was D994, which joins N75 north of Serres to cross the Buech and then turns west again along the Eygues through the Baronnies towards Picodon country.

The scenery is full of contrasts: the big *bassin de Gap*; prolonged crests of sheer cliff above the treeline; extraordinary shale slopes shaped by descending waters to rounded ridge and furrow; and beyond them the rocky peaks of the Préalpes and the distant glory of the Alps themselves. For miles most riverbeds were dry, but we were refreshed by a constant smell of lavender, even when the source was out of sight. We passed through gorges and looked up, if we dared, to enchanting perched villages, such as Saint-May, between Rémuzat and Villeperdrix. There are cheeses and wine along this route and on some of its byways, so it is worth studying the list and marking the map before setting off.†

---

*After La Mure it is possible to turn south-west along D526, taking in St Jean d'Hérans (see Montagne on list), north-west by D34 to Roissard and N75, south by D7 to Chichiliane (see list).
†See Chanousse, Éourres, Eygliers, Nyons, Villefranche-le-Château, Villeperdrix

# Picodon

Now we move out of the Hautes-Alpes and into the southern part of the Drôme, old Picodon country. Picodon de la Drôme and Picodon de l'Ardèche have boasted a joint AOC since July 1983. It covers goat cheeses with certain specifications made in either *département*, or in the cantons of Barjac, in the Gard, and in Valréas, which is part of Vaucluse and the Comtat Venaissin but which forms a Provençale enclave within the Drôme. There was a time when almost every farm had its goat, *'la vache du pauvre'*, and made and washed in wine or in *gnaule* (or *gnôle*, the local *eau-de-vie*; I have also seen it as *gniaule*) the cheese which won the name Picodon because of its piquancy (from the verb *piquer*, to prick, bite or sting).

This ancient cheese satisfied the need in a rather poor mountainous region for a small goat cheese fit for prolonged keeping during the off-season of three to four months. There is a written record of the arrest and fining of several *fromagers* with their donkey-loads of such cheeses in 1361 by their Seigneur, because they had not passed through the *péage* (toll) of Montboucher, just east of Montélimar. In 1893 their trade was eased by the institution of a railway connection between Dieulefit and Montélimar, which lasted until 1935. The *affineurs* used it to such effect that the odour left in the carriage-stock caused the little train itself to be named *Le Picodon*.

As the milk for Picodon comes from the goats it is cooled to 22°C between mid-May to mid-September, and to 25°C during the rest of the year. Two hours later it is given combined kid's rennet and starter: 0.8 c.c. of rennet (at 1:10,000) and 25 centilitres of the best whey from the previous day for every 20 litres of milk. Dairy temperature should be between 17° and 22°C, and the milk is left there to ripen for twenty to thirty hours. When the curd is ready, it is hand-ladled into 6-centimetre-deep draining moulds (7.6 centimetres across at the bottom, 8.5 at the top). There it stays for six to eight hours before being turned and rubbed on the newly upturned face with 0.5 grams of salt. After another twelve to fifteen hours the cheese is removed from the mould, turned, and salted on the other face. The cheeses are placed on grids, of which they bear the mark thereafter. They should be kept in a well-aired room (with artificial ventilation if need be) out of reach of sunlight.

*Affinage* must last for at least twelve days from the time of renneting, but this minimum is regarded by old hands as a sad compromise with the hasty habits of modern *laitiers* and with the lighter palates of Valréas. Picodon must earn its name, they reasonably claim, and a cheese only twelve days old cannot be *piquant*.

*Affiné méthode Dieulefit* is their creed (Dieulefit, in the south of the region, has long given its name to the most venerated examples of Picodon), and it is provided for in the AOC rules as a refinement and extra *appellation* for cheeses matured with periodic washings of their crust in white wine for at least a month. This produces a golden crust and a vinous odour. In the old days, to provide cheeses during the dry and kidding seasons, many Picodons had to survive for three months or more. They were kept, wrapped in cabbage, vine, walnut or chestnut leaves, inside *biches en terre*, local earthenware pots. All cheeses were sold in the leaves tied up with raffia. Cheese mite (*tyroglyphus ciro*, called *artisans* or *cirons* in French, *artisons* in patois), often attacked the cheeses, choosing the best, in the opinion of connoisseurs. Today's less interesting, but agreeable, unwashed cheeses are usually ripened at about 18°C in 85–95 per cent humidity, and the development of a blue coat from *penicillium album* is looked for; most, however, are sold while still white or pale cream.

Two-thirds of the Picodon goats are golden *chamoisées*, the rest more or less pure Saanen. Total production of Picodon in the whole AOC region in 1984 was 2900 tonnes. The AOC standards were met by 2000 tonnes, of which 1740 tonnes was farmhouse cheese. In 1985 there were fifty-five Picodon farms using *lait cru*, and five dairies using *lait thermisé*, milk given heat treatment some way below that of pasteurisation, but not strictly *lait cru*. Some ridiculous EEC rule is interfering with Picodon exports. The care taken with French AOC cheeses is more than adequate to give them a clean bill of health for any sane country.

Although Picodon may be made legally anywhere in the Drôme, its heart is in the south: Montélimar, the Diois, the Tricastin and the Baronnies. Much of this region has the look and smell of Provence, with its stone and rounded tiles, its lavender and herbs. Montélimar is now most famous for nougat, a by-product of Olivier de Serre's introduction of the almond tree in the sixteenth century. The Diois has a notable forest, and an ancient *vignoble*, of which the *cave coopérative* alone supports a quarter of its population. It also inherits a charming legacy of troubadour music from the gifted comtesse de Die of the early fifteenth century. At Sainte-Croix (see Die on the list) an organic vineyard makes the traditional *crémeuse* Clairette de Die (and a dry version), and Noix Franquette; and not far away is an organic goat farm at Vachères-en-Quint. At Saoû, between Crest and Bourdeaux, the annual Fête du Picodon is held in late July; and nearby are two Picodon farms, one of them with the added interest of a *fromage fort*, Madame Janot's own Roquefort-laced Pétafine. Bourdeaux itself has been notable for Picodon, and to the south of it lies Dieulefit, so famous for *affinage*.

Further south lies the Tricastin (three Castles, capital Saint-Paul-Trois Châteaux), of which one part is in Valréas. This outpost of the comtat Venaissin (papal province from 1274 to 1791) offers mainly the unpiquant Picodons, newly legitimised by the 1983 AOC. Now we are in Vaucluse, but there is a Dauphinois corridor to cross in the south between this *'enclave des papes'*, the main Comtat border and the rest of the *département*. This border runs along a river named simply 'Waters': Eygues while it is in the Dauphiné, it becomes Aigues as it turns south into Provence; but before we finally get settled into Provence, now my second home country, we shall use her in her ancient role of gateway to Corsica, through Marseille.

# Cheeses of the Dauphiné

## Banon, Banon d'Or, Banon au Poivre d'Âne

A Banon is a small, fat, rounded disc which originated on farms around the place of that name in Haute-Provence, where the brebis form has disappeared but the chèvre survives (see p. 505). In modern times it has been taken up by large producers in the Dauphiné, who now use usually pasteurised cows' milk. They serve it in chestnut leaf as *banon d'or*, in rosemary (instead of *sarriette*) as *poivre d'âne*, very occasionally in *sarriette*; in *herbes-de-provence*, *fines-herbes*; in black pepper as *banon au poivre*, in cumin, paprika, and even in curry powder: *au curry*. No doubt I have forgotten a few variations, but however pleasant some versions may be to eat in their *frais* or *demi-sec* state, they are *not* Banons proper.

Most of them travel in sealed plastic, from which they should be released at once. In cellar conditions they develop a mould coating which improves their prospects of ripening to the *sec* state, if you wish them to. If they have already started to melt from the outside they are best treated as eccentric versions of Saint-Marcellin (which they are nearer to in any case) and eaten at whatever stage of melt you most relish them. For an excellent goats'-milk Banon, see below, Banon *fermier*.

Here are some tolerable Dauphinois Banons:

**Banon du Coteau du Camp de César.** 80g chestnut-leaf wrapped, Fromagerie Martin, Plan, 38590 St-Étienne-de-St-Geoirs.
*50% m.g.; laitier; vache (not declared as cru).*
Isère; 77 **3**, upper far R, 7.5km SE of St-Étienne.

**Banons de Cumin, Herbes, Paprika.** Made by Terrier at Virieu-sur-Bourbre and Eydoche (see p. 454).
*vache.*
Isère.

**Banon d'Or Royal Ventoux.** Dauphinois cheeses ripened by R. Ricard (successor to G. Dorgall, Eygaliers 26170 Buis-les-Baronnies.
*50% m.g.; artisanal/fermier; vache/vache cru.*
Drôme; 81 **3**, lower R, S of Buis.

**Banon Fermier.** Jacky Tourre, Bellecombe, Drôme (20km S of Remuzat) see PRÉALPES DRÔMOISES.
*fermier; vache cru.*
Drôme; 81 **3**, far R of C.

**Banon Fromage Fermier.** Collected and ripened by F. Bannouin, Montbrun-Les-Bains (see p. 457). If bought before *sec* stage, ripens, meltingly from outside; rich flavour.
*m.g. non-précisée; fermier; vache cru.*
Drôme; 77 **4**, half L.

**Banon Géant.** 750g in chestnut leaves; Fromagerie Royannaise, Tèche (see p. 460). Similar cheese by another banon *laiterie* is called Bruleur de Loup (see p. 451)
*50% m.g.; laitier; vache pasteurisé.*
Isère.

**Le Gournier.** See p. 455.

**Le Banon de Saint-Justin.** 80g distributed by La Coopérative Laitière de Crest (see p. 455).
*45% m.g.; laitier; vache pasteurisé.*
Drôme.

**Banon sous Feuille.** Banon d'Or type; Coopérative de Montélimar (see p. 457) Saint-Géry label.
*laitier; vache pasteurisé.*
Drôme; 81 **1**.

## Le Barbriquet

Rectangular, white crustless, straw-markings; made by Terrier of Eydoche.
*laitier; mi-chèvre.*
Isère; 74 **13**, low R.

## La Bâtie-Divisin

**Crottin.** Made by M. Yvon Prouchet, La Charrière, La Batie-Divisin (Concours Agricole medallist).
*45% m.g.; fermier; chèvre.*
Isère; 74 **14**, lower C on N75 S of Les Abrets.

## Bayard, Col du

Laiterie du Col Bayard, Laye, 05500 St-Bonnet-en-Champsaur makes, and/or matures and sells an astonishing range of cheeses, keeping a number of local traditions alive, listed below (as seen in 1985). The single-handed shop was too busy to cope with questions, and I found no one in office or dairy, so some details are lacking and a letter evoked no response.

**Bleu des Hauts Pâturages.** About 2kg, 20 × 10cm, convex sides, golden crust; *pâte* of Sassenage type (see p. 462), gentle blue, with pleasant aftertaste (less bitter than Sassenage).
45% m.g.; artisanal; vache cru.

**Fromage de Chèvre du Champsaur.** 1.5kg, 20 × 4cm straight side, rich crust (moulds: petit mimosa, some white, some red); pleasing texture and flavour (also on sale at Froges, see p. 455).
45% m.g.; artisanal; chèvre cru.

**Pâte Molle.** (Unlabelled) 10 × 2½–4cm straw-marked; soft; white crust, greying, not softening further with keeping.

**Le Petit Bayard.** About 450g 12–13 × 5cm, straw-marked natural crust, off-white on gold, with some external blue. Similar to Bleu des Hauts Pâturages.
45% m.g.; artisanal; vache cru.

**Spécialité de Champsaur, Faisselle des Pâturages.** Unsalted *fromage blanc*.
laitier; vache.

**La Tomme aux deux Traites.** 250g, 12 × 2½cm, neat wheel; white; silver medal at Concours International de Fromages de Montagne, Dijon 1984.
45% m.g.; artisanal; 75% vache, 25% chèvre.

**Tomme de Mélange du Champsaur.** 180g, 8 × 4–5cm, drum; white, firmish, giving slightly.
45% m.g.; artisanal; 50% chèvre, 50% vache.

**Tomme du Champsaur.** 450g, neat drum, low-fat; 450g, 10 × 7cm neat drum and 2g, 20 × 5cm neat wheel.
25%/40% m.g.; vache.

All these *tommes* had crusts varying with age from pale cream to grey, and gentle flavours with pleasing edge to aftertaste.
Hautes-Alpes; 77 **16**, on Route Napoléon, N85, 8km N of Gap.

LE PETIT BAYARD
See BAYARD, COL DU.

BEAUPRÉ DE ROYBON
See CHAMBARAN.

BELLEDONNE, CHAÎNE DE
**Fromage de Montagne (Belledonne).** About 2kg, and 25 × 5cm; when first made and removed from its cloth-lined adjustable wooden hoop, it looks like a young monastic Port-du-Salut. Made in copper *chaudron* (over fire), curd broken with solid long stick still preserving first few side branches on bottom 35cm. The milk, rennetted at milking temperature, is left for an hour and a half. The curd's temperature is raised again (*not cuit*) and it is broken with the stick described. When ready it is removed in cheesecloth and placed in its *cercle*, which can be tightened by cord attached to the open end and adjustable as a wooden ratchet. The cheese is pressed and matured in the *cave* for 2 months. (Larousse-Sélection's *Pays et Gens de France*, No. 47, 16 September 1982.)
m.g.; non-précisée; fermier; vache cru.
Isère; 77 **6**/74 **16**, upper L lower L.

BESANÇON
Markets daily except Sunday.

BIZONNES
**Chèvre Fermier.** 90g cheese; M. Ferdinand Moyroud, Bizonnes (Concours Agricole medallist).
45% m.g.; fermier; chèvre cru.
Isère; 77 **13**, low R.

BLEU (PERSILLÉS)
See BAYARD, COL DU (BLEU DES HAUTS PÂTURAGES, LE PETIT BAYARD), BLEUDOUX, BOURG D'OISANS, BÛCHE CARRÉE, COL VERT, PELVOUX, PIC-DE-BURE, QUEYRAS, SASSENAGE (MABER BLEU (see p. 456) is not *persillé*, but blue-*coated*).

BLEUDOUX
Mild, soft blue by Château de Marlieu, Virieu (see p. 464).
laitier; vache pasteurisé.
Isère.

BODONSECS
**Petits Bodonsecs.** Tiny Rigottes sold in bags of 12–16 weighing 500g; thin golden crust, firm, agreeable flavour, good keeping. Made by B. Cardot, Fromagerie du Domaine de Bodon, Geyssans, 26750 Romans-sur-Isère.
50% m.g.; laitier; vache.

Drôme; 77 **2**, lower R, on D52, 6km N of Romans.

## Bourdeaux, Picodons de
Commended by Larousse-Sélection's *Pays et Gens de France, La Drôme* (No. 46, 9 Sept 1982), see PICODON.
*fermier; artisanal; chèvre cru.*
Drôme; 77 **13**, low L.

## Bourg d'Oisans
Saturday market.

**Bleu de Bourg d'Osians.** Found by Larousse-Sélections *Pays et Gens de France, Isère* (16 Sept 1982).
*vache cru.*
Isère; 77 **6**, lower L.

## Brebis

**Brebis Fermier.** 200g drum; golden crust; soft open texture; refreshing. Made at St-Julien-en-Beauchêne (05140 Aspres-sur-Buech, which is 15km south of St-Julien). Sold at Veynes (see p. 463) (81 **5**, top) by Codec.
*fermier; brebis cru.*
Hautes-Alpes; 77 **15**, lower L, W of N75.

**Brebis Fermier and Chèvres Biologiques.** Laurence and Jean-Noël Noll make at Les Granges, Chanousse (05700 Serres, tel. 92 66 25 66) and sell eggs, culinary and medicinal plants. On farm, afternoons *except* Saturdays and Sundays. Markets: Nyons (see p. 457) Thursday a.m.; *NB transhumance* to Super Dévoluy in holiday season (77 **15**, lower, far R).
*fermier; biologique; brebis/chèvre cru.*
Hautes-Alpes; 81 **5**, far L of C.

## Briançon
Wednesday and Thursday markets.

## Brignoud
Tuesday and Saturday markets. Fromagerie closed at the time I went that way, but I was told that they make *tomme de Chèvre, Tomme de Vache.*
Isère; 77 **5**, NE of C on D523, E of river Isère.

## Brique

**Brique de L'Argentière.** Rectangular, pure goat cheese from L'Argentière la Bessée, 15km from Briançon.
*fermier; chèvre.*
Hautes-Alpes; 77 **18**.

**Brique mi-Chèvre.** Brick-shaped, white-mould coated; soft; by Cardot, Geyssans (see p. 455).
*laitier; vache/chèvre pasteurisé.*
Drôme.

## Broussin
Dauphinois term for Brousse (see Chapter 18, pp. 507–8).

## Brûleur de Loup
Ancient Dauphinois expression for the Isérois, whose practice when wolf-hunting was to burn the wolves in their lair. Name of 750g banon d'or.
*laitier.*
Isère.

## Bûche Carrée des Sources de la Bourbre
Square blue cheese by Château de Marlieu, Virieu (see p. 464).
*laitier; vache pasteurisé.*
Isère.

## Bûche Florine
Soft blue log in the Bresse style made by Prédor.
*industriel; vache pasteurisé.*
Isère.

## Buis-les-Baronnies
Wednesday and Saturday market; local Pélardons.
Drôme; 81 **3**.

## Cailloux

**Cailloux des Provinières.** In 300g bags of 12: tiny, firm pleasant Rigottes from Mme Reboud, 38470 Vinay. On sale at Froges (see p. 455).
*artisanal; vache cru.*
Isère; 77 **3**, middle, far R.

**Cailloux du Vézy.** In 300g bags of 7: cylindrical, firm, clean young crust from Téche, 38470 Vinay. On sale at Veynes, (see p. 463) (Codec).
*artisanal; mi-chèvre.*
Isère; on N92, 4km S of Vinay.

## Cancoillotte
See CHAMPOLÉON.

### Capra, Tomme de
50g made by *maître tommier* François Pozin, St-Bardoux, 26260 St-Donat-sur-L'Herbasse, Drôme.
45% m.g.; *fermier; chèvre cru.*
Drôme; 77 **2**, low C.

### Carré du Trièves, Le Trièves
175g, square, soft. Tastes between Carré de l'Est (see p. 287) and Saint-Marcellin (see p. 461). Sold by Fauret, 116 rue de Sèze, Lyon (Gault Millau, Feb 1986; Le Trièves mentioned by Larousse- Sélection, *Pays et Gens de France, L'Isère,* 19 Sept 1982): made by Laiterie du Mont Aiguille, Roissard.
50% m.g.; *artisanal, vache.*
Isère; 77 **14**, upper R, E of N75 on D34.

### Cellier du Dauphin
See Saint-Marcellin Affiné au Vin Blanc (see p. 461).

### Chabeuil
Recorded by Androuët in December 1982 as having long been a collecting centre for a tasty range of rustic *tommes* including Crest.
Drôme; 77 **12**, D68, 11km E of Valence.

**Picodon Fermier.** Mme Géry, Les Gariots, Montelier, 26120 Chabeuil.
*fermier; chèvre cru.*
Drôme; 5km N of Chabeuil.

### Chambaran
**Chambarand (or Beaupré de Roybon).** 160g, 300g, 2kg; washed-crust; Reblochon recipe; 12–15 days' *affinage* – mild. 160g size is also made in low-fat form. Made by Cistercian nuns of Monastère Notre-Dame-de-Chambarand, La Trappe, 38940 Roybon, on map Abbaye de La Trappe de Chambaran (see pp. 444–5); geographically there is no *D* in Chambaran (tel. 76 36 22 68).
45% m.g.; *artisanal; vache pasteurisé.*
Forêt and Massif de Chambaran, Isère; 77 **3**, C. From St-Marcellin D71k–D71 to Roydon; there double back left on D20 along lake and follow signs for La Trappe.

### Champoléon
**Champoléon les Borels.** Sort of Cancoillotte (see p. 396) made of *fromage fondu, herbes* and *savoyard* white wine at the village of this name. Reported 1973 by Courtine, 1980 by Viard.
*vache cru.*
Hautes-Alpes; 77 **17**, L of C on R. Drac Blanc.

**Champoléon, Bleu de.** Said by Courtine to have 'pratiquement disparu' by 1973.
*vache cru.*

### Le Champsaur
**Fromage de Chèvre du Champsaur; Spécialité du Champsaur: Tomme des deux Traites du Champsaur, Tomme de Mélange du Champsaur, Tomme du Champsaur.** See BAYARD (Laiterie du Col du Bayard).

**Tomme du Champsaur.** Small soft goat cheeses (Courtine 1973). See BAYARD for current Champsaur chèvres.
*fermier; chèvre cru.*
Hautes-Alpes; upper Drac valley (Blanc et Noir); 77 **17**, mid L, N of Orcières.

### Chanousse
**Brebis and Chèvres Biologiques.** See BREBIS FERMIER.

### Chantemerle-les-Blés
**Chantemerle.** Picodon-type, like Dieulefit (Viard, 1980).
*artisanal; chèvre cru.*
Drôme; 77 **2**, lower L, 4km NE of Tain l'Hermitage.

### Chartreuse
See SOLITAIRE DE CHARTREUSE. La Grande Chartreuse was known in the eighteenth century for its cheese of mixed milk, brebis/vache (*Le Gazetin du Comestible,* 1780). See p. 443.

### Chasseur, Tomme du
60g, neat drum; golden/white; made by René Chilliard at Varacieux (see also LE GOURMAND).
*artisanal; vache cru.*
Isère; 77 **3**, R of C.

### Châtillon-en-Diois
Friday market.
Drôme; 77 **14**, SW of C on D539/D120.

### Chèvres
**Chèvres.** Farms, artisans, *laitiers, non-biologique,* to be found under LA BÂTIE-DIVISIN, BIZONNES (or BAYARD), (see CAPRA),

BOURDEAUX, BRIGNOUD, CHANTEMERLE (Viard, 1980), CHEVRETTE, COMBOVIN, CONCHARBIN, CORPS, CREST, DIEULEFIT, LE GÉRY, GEYSSANS, GONCELIN, LIVRON, MARGUERITE, MINISTRE, LA MURE, PELVOUX, PICODON, PONT-EN-ROYANS, QUATRE VENTS, RÉMUZAT, ROC-DU-TOULAUX, SAILLANS, SAINT BARDOUX, ST-DONAT-SUR-L'HERBASSE, VACHÈRES-EN-QUINT, VESC.

**Fromages de Chèvre Biologiques.** See BREBIS FERMIER (CHANOUSSE), DIE, ÉOURRES, MONT-SAINT-MARTIN, SAINTE-CROIX, VILLEFRANCHE-LE-CHÂTEAU, VILLE-PERDRIX, all organic farmers under *Nature & Progrès* banner.

## Chevrette

**Chevrette des Neiges.** 100g, white soft, garlic and *fines-herbes*, Fromagerie Alpine, Romans.
70% m.g.; *laitier; chèvre.*
Drôme; 77 **2**, bottom.

**Picodon Chevrette.** See PICODON.

## Chichiliane

**La Maison de la Transhumance.** Information at *mairie* (tel. 76 34 40 13).
Hautes-Alpes; 77 **14**, NE of C.

## Le Cigalon aux Herbes du Maquis

Rather larger than Banon, sold from jars of olive oil (35 to jar).
46% m.g.; *laitier; vache.*
Isère.

## Col du Bayard

See BAYARD, COL DU.

## Col Vert, Fourme de

1½kg cylindrical, and half-size, drum; blue, natural dry crust; by Fromalp, Villard de Lans (who made Valchourin).
*laitier; vache.*
Isère; 77 **14**.

## Combovin, Tomme de

250g, round, soft; natural crust, ripened 4 weeks in dry, ventilated *cave*, made end of spring to autumn inclusive. (Chast et Voy 1984.)
45% m.g.; *laitier; vache.*
Drôme; 77 **12**, far R, above middle.

## Concharbin

Found by Viard 'in small quantities' on 'Élevage de la Pessière' (1980). Mentioned as Dauphinois cheese by Chast et Voy (1984) with no detail.
*fermier; chèvre cru.*
Dauphiné.

## Corps, Tomme de

450g; 75 × 10cm high; lightly pressed *tomme*; ripened in cool dry *cave*. I was assured in Corps that it was 'flourishing' (autumn 1985).
45% m.g.; *fermier/artisanal; vache cru/chèvre cru.*
Isère; 77 **15/16**, above middle.

## Le Crémeux

250g soft, golden exterior; Mme Reboud, Vinay.
60% m.g.; *artisanal; vache cru.*
Isère; 77 **3**, far R of C.

## Crémieu

Wednesday market.
Crémieu, ancient city of the Dauphin, with his château, a fine priory, and fourteenth century covered market still in active use on Wednesdays, with plenty of local cheeses. These can be found in other days at La Cave aux Fromages (Mme Giles), opposite market; Aux Petites Halles by the fountain opposite the Augustine church also keeps farm cheese. La Petite Auberge is a very old building, and serves farm cheeses.
Isère; 74 **13**, NNW of C.

## Crest

Coopérative Laitière de Crest (see BANON, PICODON and ST-JUSTIN).
Wednesday and Saturday market; Picodon makers in market. Crest customers like them creamy (1985).

**Tomme de Crest.** 100g, 6cm × 2cm soft; thin bluish crust; 2 weeks in dry *cave*; like a young Picodon (available in Chabeuil, see p. 452, and see LIVRON).
La Coopérative Laitière de Crest makes Saint-Marcellin (p. 461) and Picodon (p. 458).
45% m.g.; *fermier; chèvre cru.*
Drôme; 77 **12**, lower R.

## Crévoux

Cheese which probably disappeared earlier this century when milk collection by road became easier.

*fermier; vache cru.*
Hautes-Alpes; 77 **18**, bottom, E of Embrun.

### Cumin, Tomme au

Rounded, firm-crusted large *tomme*; *pâte* firm with spread apertures; made by Bernard at Eydoche who also makes Tomme au Fenouil.
*laitier; artisanal; vache cru.*
Isère; 74 **13**, on D51 low R, E of D85.

### Le Délice du Chevrier

60g drum, white, light yet cohesive *pâte*, agreeable consistency and flavour, with edge to it; yet neither sharp nor salt. Made by Royannais (p. 460), Tèche.
45% *m.g.; laitier; chèvre.*
Isère; 77 **3**, far R of C on N92.

### Dévoluy, Tomme de

'Production faible,' reported years ago, but I was assured in Corps in 1985 that it survives.
*fermier; vache cru.*
Gapençais, Hautes-Alpes; 77 **15/16**.

### Die

Wednesday and Saturday market.
Local *chevrier*, see VACHÈRES.
Diois, Drôme; 77 **13**, far R of C.

### Dieulefit

Friday market.
**Picodon de Dieulefit AOC.** Old centre for Picodon (*mairie* was headquarters for makers' association); *méthode* Dieulefit is classic for making and *affinage* (see PICODON).
Drôme; 81 **2**, high R.

### Le Dromadaire

About 250g, like Ministère (see p. 456) but larger; by B. Cardot, Geyssans.
45% *m.g.; laitier; vache.*
Drôme; 77 **2**, lower R.

### Drôme, Tomme de la

Entered for its name, but made by Bourdin at Échalas in the Rhône, Lyonnais (see Chapter 12, p. 376).
*laitier; vache.*

### Éourres

**Fromage de Chèvre.** SCI Fermière du Jas; Gilles Roi and Robert Yasée, Éourres (26560 Séderon); wholesale and retail, daily 08.00–18.00 on farm, also medicinal plants, tel. 92 65 10 95.
*fermier; biologique; Nature & Progrès; chèvre cru.*
Baronnies; from Séderon 81 **4**, low, R of C. By D542 E to D201 over Hautes-Alpes border; D24 to Éourres, 81 **5**, lower L.

### Étoile du Vercors – Saint-Marcellin

80g soft cheese, tasty; by l'Étoile du Vercors, St Just (see p. 461), which dairy makes Picodon (*lait-de-mélange*), Saint-Félicien, Saint-Marcellin, Fromage de Maber, Maber Bleu, all *lait cru.*
40% *m.g.; laitier; artisanal; vache cru entier.*
Saint-Just-de-Claix, Isère; 77 **3**, lower C, on N532.

### Eydoche – Picodon Fines Herbes

100g, herb-coated; by Terrier at Eydoche (see also BARBRIQUET and LE LIERS).
*laitier; vache.*
Fromagerie Bernard, source of raw milk Tomme au Cumin (see above) and Tomme au Fenouil.
Isère; on D51 low R.

### Eygaliers

*Affineur:* R. Ricard (successor to G. Dorgal), Dauphinois cheeses including Banon d'Or.
Drôme/Baronnies; 81 **3**, lower R; from Buis-Les-Baronnies by D5, D72.

### Faisselles

**Faisselles de Pâturages.** Unsalted *fromage blanc* from Col Bayard (see pp. 449–50).
**Royan Frais.** Sold in *faisselles;* from Fromagerie de l'Étoile de Vercors (see above).
*laitier; vache.*

### Fenouil, Tomme au

See CUMIN, TOMME AU.

### Fine-Forme

2kg, *croûte-lavée;* like vast, pale Pont-L'Evêque; bought at Froges (see p. 455); possibly from Virieu-sur-Bourbre (see p. 464).
*vache.*

### Finliers le Liers

Pure goat cheese, Saint-Marcellin appearance; by Terrier, Virieu-sur-Bourbre.

40% m.g.; *laitier; chèvre.*
Isère; 74 **14**, lower L.

## Le Finvel

300g soft round drum by Terrier (see FINLIERS).
*laitier; vache.*

## Florine

See BÛCHE.

## Le Foudjou

Old Picodon (*pur chèvre*) or other goat, mixed with *fromage blanc*, hot peppers and Gnole (marc dauphinois), and remains of last Foudjou from bottom of pot. Mme Tariot mixes in Roquefort too. Dauphinois versions of Vivarais *fromage fort*. Guy and Michelle Tariot, Saou (see p. 462) (go E 1km on D538; Ferme de Floréal is on left; they make Picodon Floréal).
*domestique; artisanal; chèvre; vache.*
Dauphinois.

## Froges

*Fromagerie* on W of D523 with good range of Dauphinois cheeses, including local, e.g. and see CAPRA, MI-CHÈVRE FERMIER, MABER, MABER BLEU, CHÈVRE DE CHAMPSAUR: Jean Arnaud-Goddet, Froges, 38190 Brignoud (tel. 76 89 45 11).
Isère; 77 **5**, NE of Grenoble along D523.

## Fromage Blanc

See FAISSELLES, ROYAN FRAIS.

## Fromages Forts

LE FOUDJOU (see above), FROMAGE FORT DU DAUPHINÉ, FROMAGE FORT VIENNOIS, PÉTAFINE (see pp. 457–8), RAMEQUIN DE MONTALIEU (see p. 457)

## Gap

Wednesday, Thursday and Saturday markets.

## Gardian

Misuse of the name of the Provençal *brebis frais* made in and near the Camargue (see Chapter 18, p. 492). About 200g, Saint-Marcellin-shaped but larger; stodgy–soft with garlic and *herbes-de-Provence*; unrelated in *any* respect to the real Gardian; from Veyrey-Veilleux, near St-Marcellin.
*laitier; vache pasteurisé.*
Isère; 77 **3**.

## Le Géry, Picodon

60g, 110g, 160g Picodon type, by Coopérative Laitière de Montélimar who do a potted version (see PÉTAFINE). *Not* to be confused with farmhouse cheese by Mme Géry (see CHABEUIL).
50% m.g.; *laitier; coopérative; chèvre thermisé.*
Drôme.

## Geyssans

Bernard Cardot produces Bodonsec (p. 451), Dromadaire (p. 454), Brique Mi-Chèvre (p. 451), Ministre (p. 456), Picodon Drômois (p. 458), etc., Rosée des Prés (p. 460), at Fromagerie du Domaine de Bodon, Geyssans.
Drôme; 77 **2**, lower R, NNE of Romans.

## Goncelin

**Tomme de Chèvre Fermière.** Take D525 NE towards Allevard; this cheese is advertised on the road, beside a bridge (shops in Goncelin did not know of any local cheese).
*fermier; chèvre cru.*
Isère; 77 **5/6**, D525 high.

## Le Gourmand

150g soft, by René Chilliard, Varacieux.
60% m.g.; *laitier; vache entier.*
Isère; 77 **3**, R of C.

## Le Gournier

65g soft cheese of Picodon shape; Coopérative de Montélimar.
45% m.g.; *laitier coopérative; vache.*
Drôme.

## Grenoble

Markets on Tuesday, Thursday, Friday (good), Saturday (good) and Sunday (good).
Isère; 62 **8, 9**.

## Jacquemart

See RIGOTTES.

## Laboureur

**Fromage Sec du Laboureur.** 40g, natural coat; from St-Just-de-Claix.
50% m.g.; *laitier; vache.*
Isère; 77 **3**, lower C on N532.

## Lavaldens, Bleu de

Credited by Viard (1980) as the ancestor of Bleu de Sassenage, Bleu de Champoléon,

and Bleu de Pelvoux 'all practically extinct or in course of extinction [*disparition*]'; see SASSENAGE which survives.
*fermier; vache cru.*
Isère; 77 **5**, bottom.

### LAYE, TOMME DE

Laye is on the fringe of Champsaur. See COL DU BAYARD – TOMME DU CHAMPSAUR.
*fermier; artisanal; vache/chèvre cru.*
Hautes-Alpes; 77 **16**, lower C, N85.

### LE LIERS

250g white drum made by Terrier at Eydoche 77 **13** low R. This name is also included in labels of most cheeses made by Terrier, Le Liers, Virieu-sur-Bourbre (see p. 464).
*laitier; vache.*
Isère; 77 **13**, lower R, 77 **14**, lower L.

### LES LIES

Soft-crusted cheese, certainly tasting as though marc-washed, but not so claimed on label; by Terrier, Virieu-sur-Bourbre (see above).
*laitier; vache.*

### LIVRON, TOMME DE

100g or larger. Similar to Tomme de Crest (which is 15km to the E), under which name it may be sold (Viard, 1980).
45% *m.g.; fermier; laitier; chèvre cru.*
Drôme on river; 77 **12**, far L from C.

### LYON

For good Dauphinois cheese, especially Saint-Marcellin: Fauret, La Ferme Dauphinoise, Renée Richard, La Vacherie (Mère Richard is famous for melting Saint-Marcellin: see Chapter 12, p. 372).

### MABER

**Fromage de Maber.** 200g, white to golden coated, Saint-Marcellin type, '*moulé à la louche*'.
*artisanal; vache cru.*

**Maber Bleu** (blue-coated). These two cheeses, distinguished by humid and dry *affinage* respectively, are made by Fromagerie l'Étoile de Vercors, St-Just-de-Claix; both sold at Froges (see p. 455).
*artisanal; vache cru.*
Isère; 77 **3**, below C, on N532.

### LE MARCELLINOIS

100g Banon-shaped, pepper-coated; not salty but a little acid.
40% *m.g.; laitier; vache.*
Isère.

### MARGUERITE

1½kg white mould-crusted soft cheese '*moulé à la louche*' in form of flower with round-ended petals: mild flavour while still white; by Fromagerie Ageron, St-Michel (see p. 462).
45% *m.g.; artisanal; chèvre cru entier.*
St-Michel-sur-Savasse; 77 **2**, far R, lower, on D52, NNE of Romans.

### LE MÉAUDRET

1500g semi-soft *fromage de montagne*, rounded sides; gold crust with white mould; tacky *pâte*, open textured, medium flavour, but I advise cutting away very bitter crust. Its bitterness and gritty consistency suggest that the gold is sprayed on in powdered form, not genuine *morge* (see Chapter 15, pp. 414). Made by Fromalp, Villard-de-Lans.
50% *m.g.; industriel; vache pasteurisé.*
Isère; 77 **4**.

### MEYLAN

Wednesday p.m. market.
(For Tomme de Chèvre see MONT-ST-MARTIN.)
Isère, NE outskirt of Grenoble; 77 **5**, L C.

### MI-CHÈVRE FERMIER

150g drum; natural golden crust, ripening from edges; pleasant full flavour. Bought at Froges (see p. 455).
50% *m.g.; fermier; mi-chèvre cru.*
Isère; 77 **5**.

### MINISTRE, LE DÉLICE DU

80g rounded drum: *demi-sec* stage: good, natural coat; very good close texture, white; rich flavour. 160g flatter shape: good natural crust; good firm, close texture; rich, not too salt, nor too dry when eaten *demi-sec*; also enjoyed young. By Bernard Cardot, Geyssans (see p. 455).
45% *m.g.; chèvre.*
Drôme; 77 **2**.

### MOILLES, FROMAGE DES

1½kg, soft, white natural crust; eaten young, mild, refreshing; by Terrier, Le

Liers, Virieu-sur-Bourbre (see p. 464).
60% m.g.; *laitier; vache.*
Isère; 74 **14**, lower L.

### Montalieu

50g truncated cone, soft; or used as *fromage fort* in Ramequin.
*fermier; chèvre/mi-chèvre cru.*
Isère; 74 **13**, high R.

### Montagne, Tomme de

200–250g, grey-crusted, neatly moulded; from St-Jean-d'Hérans; bought in market at La Mure (see below).
50% m.g.; *fermier; vache cru.*
Isère; 77 **15**, SW of La Mure.

### Montélimar

Wednesday to Saturday, a.m. market (good for Picodon (see p. 458)); *affineur* (also Picodon Chevrette): Fromagerie Geslin, rue du Moulin.
Drôme.

### Montbrun-les-Bains

*Affineur* (including Banons *fermiers*): F. Bannouin.
Drôme; 77 **4**, low, half L.

### Mont-St-Martin

**Tommes de Chèvre.** Organically produced by Marie-Claire Ducrocq, Charbottier, Mont-St-Martin, 38120 St-Égrève (whence take N75 3km to Fontanil Cornillon, and turn right at crossroads. Telephone first (76 75 68 52); market at Meylan Wednesday p.m. (NE edge of Grenoble).
*fermier; biologique; Nature & Progrès; chèvre cru.*
Isère; 77 **4**, far R, above middle, N of St-Égrève.

### La Mure

Monday market: Tommes, Saint-Marcellin, Sassenage and knowledge of local cheeses, stall on south side of market near narrow lane leading back to N85.

**Fromage de Chèvre.** Approaching La Mure from N by N85; after Shell garages, turn sharp back right on road which then bends westward round hill; take earth track off left of road (confirm at garage).
*fermier; chèvre cru.*
Isère; 77 **15**, high, on N85.

### Neiges

See **chevrette des neiges.**

### Nyons

Daily market, including Brebis (see p. 451) and chèvres.

**Tomme de Nyons.** This term has probably been swamped by the advent of Picodon AOC in 1983.
*fermier; chèvre cru.*
Drôme; 81 **3**, L of C.

### Paladru

Source of cheese of Sassenage-type blue still known in Savoie in 1940s and 1950s (see Chapter 15, p. 434) but finished by 1973 (Courtine, *Larousse*).
*artisanal; vache cru.*
Isère; 74 **14**, low, N of lake.

### Pélardon pur Chèvre

Made at Malataverne. Found at market in Buis-les-Baronnies (see p. 451). For detail of Pélardons, see Chapter 7, pp. 245–6 and Chapter 18, p. 516.
Drôme; 80 **10**, N of C on N7.

### Pelvoux

**Bleu de Pelvoux.** Small local blue, thought by Viard to be based on Lavaldens. Believed to have died out some years ago with the last maker. Courtine says it was formerly made by Gravier Fils et Cie in Briançon (see **queyras**).
*artisanal; vache/vache-chèvre mélange cru.*

**Tomme du Pelvoux.** Similar to Tomme de Savoie (Viard 1980).
*fermier; chèvre/vache/mélange cru.*
Hautes-Alpes; 77 **17**, upper R.

### Pennes le Sec

**Pennes.** 250g flat round, soft; natural crust, 1 month; full flavour (Stobbs/Philippe Olivier, 1985).
20–30% m.g.; *artisanal; vache.*
Drôme; near Saillons; 77 **13**, low, half R.

### Père Selme

250g soft, rounded, *mi-frais;* Terrier, Virieu-sur-Bourbre (see p. 464).

### La Pétafine

Fromage Fort du Dauphiné: *tommes de*

*chèvre* and *de vache* in white wine with vinegar and clove of garlic. Larousse Sélection (1982) were told: *tommes* with water, salt, white wine, pepper, vinegar, garlic and *eau-de-vie*.
Ninette Lyon favours spices, raisins, and olive oil rather than vinegar. She also adds that the pots of Pétafine were kept under the low stools on which peasants sat to do kitchen tasks, their skirts making a warm protective tent round the maturing *fromage fort*.
*domestique; chèvre/vache cru.*
Voiron; 77 **4**, top and Vercors 77 **4**, S of R. Isère into **14**.

### Le Pic-de-Bure

Drum-shaped *bleu* of Sassenage type (see p. 462; blueing well spread; gentle; by Fromagerie Clerc, 4 place du Rereilly, 05000 Gap; sold by Codec at Veynes (see p. 463).
*45% m.g.; artisanal; vache.*
Gapençais; 77 **15/16**; Gap, 77 **16**, bottom, 81 **6**, top.

### Picaudon

*Picaudon* is an old spelling of Picodon.

**Le Picodon de la Drôme** (AOC 1983). The *appellation* is shared with Ardèche and the Canton of Barjac in the Gard (which are grouped with Auvergne, see Chapter 7). The joint Association de Défense et de Promotion du Picodon de la Drôme et du Picodon de l'Ardèche is at 11, avenue de Romans, 26000 Valence (tel. 75 56 26 06), where farm visits can be arranged.
NB See SAOÛ for La Fête du Picodon and farm addresses. The Picodon mould (pierced all round and below) measures 76mm across at narrowest, 85mm at widest; its height must be at least 60mm. The use of frozen curd is forbidden. 100g (young) down to 40g (*sec*); *banon* shape, but firmer; *affinage*: 12 days minimum; *méthode* Dieulefit 1 month, with *lavages*. For more detail, including some history, see pp. 447-8.
*45% m.g.; fermier; artisanal/laitier; chèvre cru entier/thermisé.*

**Picodon de la Drôme.** 70g 12 days cheese, light consistency (W of the Rhône would have been scorned as Pidance in the old days) by Cavet Frères at Dieulefit (see also PICODON DE DIEULEFIT).
*artisanal; chèvre thermisé.*

**Picodon Dieulefit/affiné méthode Dieulefit** (AOC cheeses subjected to this *affinage* may, and *should*, be so marked). Picodon ripened for at least a month, with periodic washing in brine and wine, giving a sweet richness and sharp edge to flavour in the traditional way (hence the name Picodon, from *piquer, piquant*) and golden crust. Some are given longer *affinage* in earthenware pots with white wine, and are the best type for Foudjou (see p. 455).
*fermier; chèvre cru.*
Valréas; Drôme.

### Picodon de Dieulefit

50g average; 1 month old; by Cavet Frères at Dieulefit.
*min. 45% m.g.; artisanal; chèvre thermisé.*
Drôme; 81 **2**.

**Picodon Fermier** (only used for cheeses made from raw milk, of the farm, and ripened in the AOC region).
*min. 45% m.g.; fermier; chèvre.*
Drôme; 81 **2**.
See CHABEUIL and SAOÛ (Floréal and Rochecolombe).

*Names used by various makers or affineurs:*

**Le Géry** (see p. 455). Coopérative laitière de Montélimar.
*laitier coopérative; chèvre thermisé.*

**Picodon d'Arles.** Now an irregular name. See Chapter 18, p. 516.

**Picodon de Bourdeaux.** See p. 451.

**Picodon Chevrette.** Affineurs Fromagerie Geslin, rue du Moulin, 26200 Montélimar.
*50% m.g.; fermier; chèvre cru.*

**Picodon de la Drôme.** 40g.
*artisanal; chèvre; entier.*

**Picodon Drômois.** 60g, Fromagerie Cardot, Domaine de Bodon, Geyssans (see p. 455).
*45% m.g.; artisanal; chèvre cru.*

**Picodon Fines-Herbes** (not AOC). See EYDOCHE.
Drôme; Valréas.

**Picodon Floréal.** See SAOÛ.

**Picodon au Lait de Mélange** (not AOC). Laiterie L'Étoile du Vercors, St-Just-de-

Claix (see p. 461).
*laitier; lait-de-mélange (vache et chèvre) cru.*

**Picodon de Roche Colombe.** See SAOÛ.

**Picodon de Valréas.** Normally sold *frais* or soon after the minimum 12 days' *affinage* if bearing AOC.

M. Point gave us his definition and recipe for Picodon: Region of Drôme, Ardèche, Vaucluse. Two varieties particularly renowned: Picodon of Dieulefit (Drôme); Picodon of Valréas (Pope's enclave in Vaucluse). Made from goats' milk; a little round flat cheese, 5–7cm in diameter, and 2–2.5cm thick, weighing 80–100g; 0.7 litres of milk per cheese; *pâte molle; caillage lent*; once formed, the curd is ladled into the moulds without pre-draining. Salt with dry salt. *Affinage* (used to be in *panières*, cages with metallic netting protection) during 2–10 days according to season. Nowadays the *affinage* takes place in the *fromagerie* in a locale maintained at 12°C with ventilation and regulation of hygrometry, or in a *cave* for about 1 month. White and blue moulds develop. Red moulds/ferments appear after more than 3 weeks' *affinage* when the *cave* is humid. Dry Picodons are sometimes placed in stoneware where they ferment for 2–3 months, acquiring a very strong taste, often pungent. The *affinage* of Dieulefit Picodon is interspersed with washings in water which modify the *affinage* flora and give a more supple *pâte* with a slightly piquant flavour, but with no bitterness. The Picodon of Valréas is eaten *demi-sec*.
Valréas (Vaucluse); Drôme; 80 **10**, top R, 76 **20**, bottom R.

PoIvre d'Âne

See BANON and PRÉALPES DRÔMOISES.

Pont-en-Royans

**Fromage de Chèvre.** This maker has sign on D54 (1985) below this spectacular rock-perched village, skirted by the tumultuous river Bourne. M. Béruguier makes Saint-Marcellin (see p. 461) here; St-Just-de-Claix (see p. 461) is not far W of here (the seat of l'Étoile de Vercors dairy, see p. 454).
*fermier; chèvre cru.*
Isère; 77 **3**, low R.

Préalpes

**Tomme des Préalpes.** Laiterie du Château de Marlieu, Virieu-sur-Bourbre.
*50% m.g.; laitier; vache pasteurisé.*
Isère; 74 **14**, lower L.

Préalpes Drômoises

**Banon Chèvre Fromage Fermier des Préalpes Drômoises.** Delicious cheese of light-moussey texture when young, made by Jacky Tourré at Bellecombe; sold by Fromagerie Ranc in Avignon who coat some of these *banons* generously in *sarriette* to sell as Poivre d'Âne.
*m.g.; non-précisée; fermier; chèvre cru.*
Drôme; 81 **13**, far R of C.

La Préalpine sur Marc

Soft marc-washed cheese from Fromagerie Alpine, 26100 Romans (see also RIGOTTE LEROI).
*laitier; artisanal; vache cru.*
Drôme.

Quatre Vents

Cheese from farm of this name praised and sold by Mme Renée Richard (see LYON).
*fermier; chèvre cru.*
Isère.

Queyras

**Bleu de Queyras.** 3–5kg, drum, natural crust foil-wrapped; *affinage*: 6–8 weeks in damp *cave*. Androuët (1985) attributes origin to *montagnards* who had studied blue cheese in the Pays de Gex. A number of farms round St-Véran made cheese in the early 1900s, but making was concentrated in Briançon by the *laitier* Jules Gravier. In 1936 Nestlé's competition in the milk market had a severe effect on production of the cheese (see PELVOUX).
*45–50% m.g.; industriel; vache.*

**Tomme de Queyras.** The original mountain cheese of this area, reduced by industrial take-up of milk. It is to be noted that the range of mountains west of St-Véran (77 **19**, mid-L) runs from Col des Fromages above Le Villard to Col des Près de Fromage in the N above Molines-en-Queyras.
*fermier; vache cru.*
Hautes-Alpes; 77 **18/19**.

Raclette-Préalpes

Standard Raclette-type made at Virieu-sur-

Bourbre.
*laitier; vache.*
Isère; 74 **14**, lower L.

### RAMEQUIN DE MONTALIEU
See MONTALIEU.

### RÉGAL DU LIERS
400g, firm, white crust turning gold; Terrier, Virieu.
60% m.g.; *laitier; vache.*
Isère.

### RÉMUZAT
**Fromage pur Chèvre.** D94 just S of turning N to Rémuzat and Die (20km S of Rémuzat farm at Bellecombe, see PRÉALPES DRÔMOISES).
*fermier; chèvre cru.*
Drôme; 81 **3**, far R of C.

### RIGOTTES
**Rigottes, Petites Rigottes, Rigottes des Alpes.** Mass-produced from cows' milk by large *laiteries*, sometimes plain white; also orange-coloured with *rocou*, peppercoated.
*industriel; vache pasteurisé.*

**Rigotte Jacquemart.** 50g; 7½cm tall × 5cm diameter; soft, close-texture; pale gold crust (not *rocou*, slightly washed?); slightly acid and salt flavour; by Cardot, Domaine de Bodon, Geyssans.
50% m.g.; *laitier; artisanal; vache.*

**Rigotte du Mont Sauvage.** Isère cheese sold by Cénéri, Cannes.
*artisanal; vache cru.*

**Rigotte le Roi des Préalpes.** 200g, looking more like large Banon; from Fromagerie Alpine, 26100 Romans, Drôme (see also LA PRÉALPINE SUR MARC).
60% m.g.; *laitier; artisanal; vache cru.*

**Les Provençales.** Petites *rigottes* in *herbes-de-Provence* and olive oil from Royannais, Tèche, Vinay.
*laitier; vache pasteurisé.*
Drôme; 77 **2**, 6km N of Romans.

### LE-ROC-DU-TOULAUX
200g, irregular Banon-shape, by Louis Boucher fils, Izeron, Isère.
45% m.g.; *artisanal; chèvre cru.*
Isère, Izeron, across the river from St-Marcellin, 77 **3**, lower far right.

### ROMANS-SUR-ISÈRE
Tuesday, Wednesday, Friday, Saturday and Sunday market.

**Le Romans or Tome de Romans.** 350g; soft; natural, rippled golden crust; ripened 3 weeks in airy *cave*; close *pâte* of clotted texture, reminding me of young Brie de Melun; *pâte* melts in mouth, with rich flavour, as cheese ripens from outside. A few Romans *vache cru fermier* are to be found.
50% m.g.; *laitier; vache.*

**Le Bon Romans.** Version of Le Romans made by Cardot at Geyssans (see p. 455) in the Drôme.
*laitier; vache entier.*

**Le Romans Maber.** 200g version by Berruyer. St-Just-de-Claix (see p. 461).
*laitier; vache cru.*

**Le Romans Poivre, or Ail et Fines-Herbes.** 150g cheeses, not characteristic of Le Romans, made by Fromagerie Royannais, Tèche, Isère. Most *affineurs* of Saint-Marcellin (see p. 461) also ripen Le Romans.
*laitier; vache pasteurisé.*
Drôme; 77 **2**, bottom.

### ROSÉE DES PRÉS
80g; small, irregular drum; soft, light texture; curly crust when ripe; by Bernard Cardot (see GEYSSANS).
40% m.g.; *laitier; vache.*
Drôme; 77 **2**, lower R NNE of Romans.

### ROYAL VENTOUX
See BANONS.

### ROYANNAIS
Fromagerie in Tèche making large-scale Banons, Picodon (not AOC), Rigottes, Romans, all with various coats, and Banon Géant (see p. 449).
Isère; NE of Saint-Marcellin on N92; 77 **3**, lower R of C.

### ROYANS
**Fromage du Royans.** Declared 160g (nearer 220g *frais*); 10cm diameter, 2½cm deep; drained or hexagonal pattern grid; 'fromage du Royans au lait cru entier'; made by Barret-Gemard, La Motte-Fanjas.
50% m.g.; *vache cru.*
Drôme; 77 **3**, low on D76.

### Saillans
Sunday a.m. market for Picodons (locals like them old).
Diois, Drôme; 77 **13**, lower L, on river and D93.

### Le Saint-Blandin (Tommes des Alpes)
Made by Château Marlieu, Virieu-sur-Bourbres (see p. 464).
*laitier, vache pasteurisé.*
Isère.

### St-Bonnet-en-Champsaur
Monday market (see COL BAYARD).

### St-Donat-sur-l'Herbasse
**Fromage de Chèvre.** 50g neat, vertical-sided disc; sold at Froges (see p. 455). See CAPRA.
*artisanal; chèvre cru.*
Drôme; 77 **2**, lower, NW of Romans.

### Sainte-Croix
**Fromages de Chèvre.** Gaec Touret, Vachères-en-Quint (D129, D740 up Sure valley from D93 near Sainte Croix). Cheeses and aromatic and medicinal plants sold on farm and at markets: Die (7kms to E) Wednesdays, Châtillon Fridays.
Postal: Vachères-en-Quint, 26150 Die; tel. 75 22 12 07.
*fermier; biologique; Nature & Progrès; chèvre cru.*
Diois, Drôme; 77 **13**, C.

### Saint-Félicien
150g, *'moulé à la louche'*; flat disc; rich flavour; from l'Étoile (see p. 454) St-Just-de-Claix. Saint-Félicien originates from the place of that name in the Vivarais (see Chapter 7, p. 254).
60% m.g.; *laitier; artisanal; vache cru.*
Drôme.

### St-Just-de-Claix
L'Étoile du Vercors dairy (see p. 454) and *laiterie coopérative.*
Isère; 77 **3**, lower C.

### St-Marcellin
Tuesday, Friday and Saturday market.
La Petite Ferme, 6 rue Jean-Baillet, 38160 St-Marcellin (tel. 76 38 18 89); M. and Mme Rey-Piefert stock a good range of local cheese, including Saint-Marcellin *pur chèvre*. On Monday they receive from five or six farms (in season).

**Le Chartrousin (Le Tout Gras).** Laiterie Louis Boucher Fils, Izeron, near St-Marcellin.
*artisanal; vache cru.*
La Colombaise, Entre-Deux-Guiers; 74 **15**, low L.

**Saint-Marcellin.** Makers other than those mentioned below include l'Étoile du Vercors (see p. 454); Béruguier, Pont-en-Royans (see p. 459). Good examples are ripened by M. Gérard, rue des Marseillais, Aix-en-Provence; and by the great *fromagers* of Lyon (see p. 377).
*fermier; vache cru*

**Saint-Marcellin Affiné au Vin Blanc.** Affinage by Rabatel et Cie (Isère); M. Jouvray, Trente-Cotes 69210 Savigny in the Lyonnais (see Chapter 12, p. 379) under Saint-Marcellin, Savigny. This cheese has been called 'Cellier du Dauphin'.
48% m.g.; *vache.*

**Saint-Marcellin le Crémeux.** 180g, from Fromagerie Reboud, Vinay (see LE CRÉMEUX).
50% m.g.; *artisanal; vache entier.*

**Saint-Marcellin Lait Cru.** Fromagerie Berruyer, St-Just-de-Claix (77 **3**, lower C).
50% m.g.; *laitier; vache cru.*

**Saint-Marcellin Lait de Mélange.** Stocked at La Petite Ferme (see above).
*fermier; mélange chèvre/vache cru.*

**Saint-Marcellin Poivré.** I was told that this came from St-Sernin in the Isère, which I cannot trace (under Sernin or Cernin).

**Saint-Marcellin-pur-Chèvre.** This is now a rarity, and it is wise to buy early in the week at La Petite Ferme.
*fermier; chèvre cru.*

**Saint-Marcellin-sec-en-Feuille.** Some makers or *affineurs* wrap cheeses in *feuilles de blette* (blette: spinach beet or Swiss chard).
*fermier; artisanal; vache cru.*

**Saint-Marcellin, Tome à L'Huile de Tournesol.** Tomes (young Saint-Marcellin) have been kept from 3–12 months in

sunflower seed oil.
*fermier/artisanal; vache/chèvre.*
Isère; 77 **3**, SE of C.

ST-MICHEL-SUR-SAVASSE

**Saint-Michel.** Saint-Marcellin type made by Fromagerie Ageron, St-Michel-sur-Savasse, which also makes Marguerite (see p. 456).
50% m.g.; *artisanal; vache cru entier.*
Drôme; 77 **2**, far R, lower; on D52 NNE of Romans.

ST-SERNIN

See SAINT-MARCELLIN POIVRÉ.

SAINT-VERAND, FROMAGE DE

100g, soft, round cheese of Saint-Marcellin type by Fromagerie Jullin.
Isère; 77 **3**, SE of C, above St-Marcellin.

SAOÛ

La Fête du Picodon around 21 July annually. For information on this and on addresses of Picodon makers, tel. 75 76 01 72, Syndicat d'Initiative.
Two farms near Saoû (pronounced 'Sou') follow.
Drôme; 77 **12**, low R.

**Picodon de Floréal.** Guy and Michelle Tariot, Ferme de Floréal, 1km E of Saoû on D538 on left (NE). They also make Foudjou (see p. 455).
*fermier; chèvre cru.*

**Picodon de Roche Colombe.** Emile and Solange Magnet; D538 W from Saoû until D136, where turn left (SW) for 300m to farm.
*fermier; chèvre cru.*
Drôme; 77 **12**, low R.

SASSENAGE

Friday market.

**Sassenage, Bleu de.** 3½–6kg convex circumference; 24–30cm × 6–9cm; smooth crust; smooth *pâte*, greeny blue, spread; mild; bitter aftertaste. Originally of mixed milks; at least one such appears to survive (Larousse-Sélection, *Pays et Gens de France*, Isère No. 47 (16 Sept 1982); Eperon, *The French Selection* (1984), served at Hotel Castellane near Voiron (see p. 464). Androuët noted in 1982 that several *laiteries* in Villard-de-Lans 'were continuing the making of this cheese following ancient, traditional principles', but the recent use of mixed milk is not mentioned in any cheese literature that I have seen, except experimentally. Makers at Villard-de-Lans include Fromalp (see COL VERT); Mestraller, Zone de Fénat; best cheeses from milk of local cattle (see p. 442).
45% min. m.g.; *laitier/artisanal; vache pasteurisé/mi-vache cru/mi-chèvre cru.*
Montagne-de-Lans, Isère; 77 **4**, eastern Vercors; Villard-de-Lans original centre of making.

SOLITAIRE DE CHARTREUSE

300g soft, natural crust, rich flavour; by Robert Berruyer, Entre-Deux-Guiers.
60% m.g.; *artisanal; vache cru.*
Isère; 74 **15**, bottom L.

TOMMES, TOMES

As for example in Tomme de Chèvre for 1–2-day-old cheese, Tomme Fraîche for 8–10-day-old cheese, in Dauphiné these terms are more often used for small young soft cheeses than for the mould-encrusted semi-soft or semi-hard types of Tomme de Montagne. The latter are represented by: Fromage de Chèvre du Champsaur, Tomme du Champsaur (see COL BAYARD); Fromage de Montagne (see BELLEDONNE); Tomme de Corps (see CORPS); Tomme de Cumin (see CUMIN, TOMME DE); Tomme Daubée (Tomme Blanche with vinegar, olive oil, garlic, *fines-herbes* from Vienne); Tomme de Dévoluy (see DÉVOLUY); Tomme de Fenouil (see CUMIN, TOMME DE); Tomme de Laye (see LAYE); Tomme de Montagne (see MONTAGNE); Tomme du Pelvoux (see PELVOUX); Tomme de Queyras (see QUEYRAS). See also CUMIN, FENOUIL, PRÉALPES, ST-BLANDIN.

TOURNESOL

See SAINT-MARCELLIN, TOME À L'HUILE DE TOURNESOL.

TOULAUX

See LE ROC-DE-TOULAUX.

TOURRÉE DE L'AUBIER

2kg. Imitation of Vacherin made throughout the year; ringed with inner bark (*aubier*) of conifer family; made by Prédor in the Isère, distributed by Gilca, 4 quai des Etroits, 69005 Lyon. Pleasant, but not as aromatic or succulent as the seasonal *lait*

*cru* vacherins of Franche-Comté and Savoie (see Chapters 14 and 15).
60% m.g.; *laitier*; *vache*.
Isère.

## Transhumance

Maison de la Transhumance: information from *mairie* at Chichilianne, tel. 76 34 40 13.
Isère; 4km SE of Clelles, by D7 and D79, 77 **14**, high C R.

## Le Trièves

See CARRÉ.

## Vachères-en-Quint

Chèvre, see SAINTE-CROIX

## Valchourin au Poivre

Banon-type pepper-coated cheese by Fromalp, Villard-de-Lans (who make Col Vert, see p. 453).
*laitier*; *vache pasteurisé*.
Isère.

## Valence

Daily market, except Sunday. Tuesday, Place St-Jean; Thursday, Saturday, Place des Clercs.

## Valréas

Market: Wednesday and Saturday.

**Le Petit Valréas.** *Fromage frais* by Ch. Lafont.
58% m.g.; *laitier*; *vache pasteurisé*.
Condorcet, Drôme; 81 **3**, high C.

**Picodon** (AOC). Sold younger than traditional Dauphinois cheeses (see PICODON).

**Valréas.** Very soft, virtually *frais* state of Picodon; almost unsalted; soufflé-like texture.
*artisanal*; *chèvre cru*.
Vaucluse; Drôme; 81 **2**, C.

## Varacieux

René Chilliard's *fromagerie* (Le Gourmand, Le Marcellinois, Tomme du Chasseur, Vercorin, etc.).
Isère; 77 **3**, R of C.

## Ventoux

**Royal Ventoux.** See BANONS.

## Le Vercorin

300g small *croûte-lavée* cheese, on salt side; by René Chilliard, Varacieux.
50% m.g.; *laitier*; *vache entier cru*.
Isère; 77 **3**, R of C.

## Vercors, Tomme du

Round, small, soft cheese, natural crust; *vache* version labelled Vercors Royannais.
45% m.g.; *laitier*; *chèvre/vache*.

## Vercors

See L'ÉTOILE DE VERCORS.

## Vesc

**Fromage de Chèvre.** 120g soft; eaten almost at *fromage blanc* stage; mousse-like; yet already rich, slightly smoky flavour; by M. Simond, Col d'Espréaux, Vesc, 26220 Dieulefit.
45% m.g.; *fermier*; *chèvre cru*.
Drôme; 81 **3**, high L.

## Veynes

Thursday market.
Cheese shop with local range, and good Codec cheese counter (including Brebis *fermier* (see p. 451) made 17km to the N).
Hautes-Alpes; 81 **5**, top C.

## Vienne

Saturday market. Famous restaurant, Pyramide (Mme Point).
Isère; 74 **11 12**.

## Le Vigneron

60g flat soft cheese by Fromagerie Alpine, Romans.
40% m.g.; *vache*.
Romans-sur-Isère; Drôme; 77 **2**, bottom.

## Villard-de-Lans

Sunday market. For local breed see p. 442. Where Bleu de Sassenage was first recognised and where surviving Sassenage is made (and COL VERT, see p. 453). See also LE MÉAUDRET (Fromalp).
Isère; 77 **4**.

## Villefranche-le-Château

**Fromage de Chèvre.** Michel and Claude Mathieu sell cheese and medicinal plants daily on farm (tel. 75 28 51 02).
*fermier*; *biologique*; Nature & Progrès; *chèvre cru*.
Drôme; 81 **4**, low C, NW of Séderon.

### Villeperdrix

**Fromages de Chèvre.** Jean-Pierre Guérand sells chèvres, *épeautre* (ancient wheat) and mint leaves at Léoux de Villeperdrix (tel. 75 26 13 50).
Drôme; 81 **3**, NE of C, off D94 and R. Eygues.

### Virieu-sur-Bourbre

Friday market.
Terrier's *fromagerie*: Le Liers (p. 456), Les Lies (p. 456), Moille (p. 456), Régal (p. 460), etc. Laiterie du Château de Marlieu: Bleudoux (p. 450), Sassenage (p. 462), Bûche Carrée (p. 451), Tomme des Préalpes (p. 459), Saint-Blandin (p. 461).
Isère; 74 **14**, lower L.

### Voiron

Wednesday market.
Good for Sassenage (including Hôtel Castel Anne, 3km along N92 to W), Tommes de Chèvres (p. 462), Saint-Marcellin (p. 461). Distillery for Grande Chartreuse is here, worked by forty monks.
Isère; 77 **4**, top.

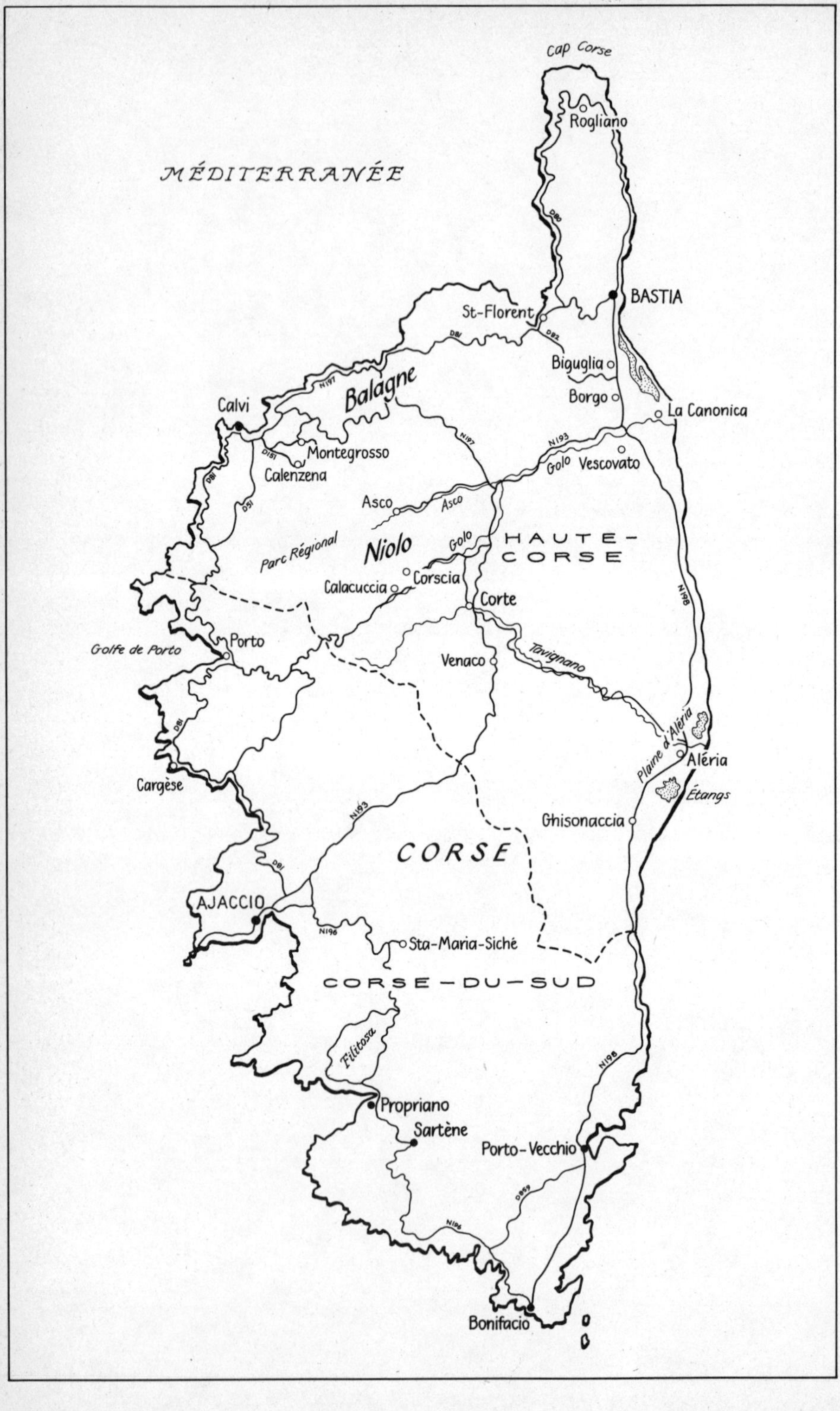
Cap Corse
Rogliano
MÉDITERRANÉE
D80
BASTIA
St-Florent
D81
D82
Biguglia
Borgo
La Canonica
Balagne
N197
Calvi
N193
Montegrosso
Golo
Vescovato
D151
Calenzena
D81
D51
Asco
Asco
Parc Régional
Niolo
Golo
HAUTE-
CORSE
Corscia
Calacuccia
Corte
N198
Golfe de Porto
Porto
Venaco
Tavignano
D81
Plaine d'Aléria
Aléria
Cargèse
Étangs
Ghisonaccia
N193
CORSE
D81
AJACCIO
N196
Sta-Maria-Siché
CORSE-DU-SUD
Filitosa
N198
Propriano
Sartène
Porto-Vecchio
D859
N196
Bonifacio

CHAPTER SEVENTEEN

# *Corsica*

HAUTE-CORSE – CORSE DU SUD

Corsica is mostly mountain and *maquis*, inhospitable to inquisitive strangers and law-enforcers alike. Villages perch high, and individual houses are built high too, typically strongholds of unmortared granite or porphyry with windows so deep-set that shutters have to be inside. The old living pattern placed animals at ground level and the family on the first floor. Human beings benefited from the warmth generated below, and from the insulation provided above by crops and forage stored in the loft.

By the start of the first millennium BC the original inhabitants had been joined by Torréens, to be followed in turn by Ligurians (still the basic stock of Haute-Provence) and Iberians. The island was called Kyrnos. I suspect that in the high interior the human mix has changed little since.

Greeks established Alalia on the east coast in the sixth century BC, and are credited with the introduction of vine and olive. Alalia became Aléria, standing today for red and white wines of character, and for that rare find anywhere in the modern wine world, a pleasing non-acid rosé.* The Greeks may well have introduced in addition their methods of sheep-rearing, and cheesemaking customs such as the use of basket moulds and the rubbing of crusts with olive oil (which survive so strongly in Sicily).

After the Greeks, the Etruscans and Carthaginians in their prime touched the Corsican coast, followed in the third century BC by the inevitable Romans, who needed over 120 years to subdue the island. I find that Seneca, of whom I had always thought kindly, took it on himself a century and a half later to record 'the dislikable customs' of the inhabitants, *méchants* in his eyes, no doubt, because they had had the impertinence to defend themselves so long and so bitterly against his Roman countrymen. *Vendetta* came first on his list: so what else is new?† Roman ways with cheese are witnessed today in Cacavelli and Sarteno (see list, pp. 475 and 478).

With the fading of the Western Empire, Corsica came first under Byzantine rule and then, in the ninth century, under Papal protection,

---
*Visitors to Corsica should also seek out the AOC Vin de Corse, Côteaux d'Ajaccio, pleasing red and white wines, and rosé. Domaine Martini, made and bottled by GAEC de Biso-Martini frères et Ledentu, at Eccica-Suarella, 21 kilometres east of Ajaccio. The vineyard is organically managed (Nature & Progrès).
†Homicides averaged 900 a year from 1715 to 1863.

which brought her little joy. When the respected Conte Arrigo, founder of the defensive bastion called Bastia, died in AD 1000, the native inhabitants said that things would go 'from bad to worse', a forecast of sad accuracy, mitigated only by the brief Pisan interlude. This was a period of repeated Saracen incursions on the coast, from which the only possible benefit could come from their leaving some goats behind them. Peace came after papal delegation of power to the Archbishop of Pisa in 1077. Church-building was accompanied by a movement towards unity and independence.

Unfortunately the greedier Genovese began to nibble at Pisan power in the twelfth century and had entirely supplanted it by the fourteenth. North and south were divided, there were intrusions from Aragon, France and Milan, and feudal *signori* made for further fragmentation. Furthermore, the negligent Genovese administration allowed the resumption of raids by Barbary pirates.

'All those *signori* are bastards. The only noblesse lies in the *familles caporales.*' Thus spoke Prosper Mérimée's Corsican heroine, Colomba.* Into one of these *familles caporales*, the Buonaparte, Napoleon was born in 1769 (whence his army nickname, *'Le Petit Caporal'*). The Genovese rulers controlled the coast, or tried to, but the inaccessible interior, divided into *pièves* (now *cantons à la française*) knew only the law of vendetta. *Banditti* were considered as Robin Hoods and *Résistants*, not as terrorists. *Bandit* meant *banni* (outlawed, by the foreign oppressor), and anyone subject to banning was said to be *'alla campagna'* (in the country).

France, which had ruled Corsica for six years in the sixteenth century, finally took over from Genoa in 1768. The interior had been controlled for thirteen years by Pascal Paoli, a genuine Corsican Capo. He now resisted the French, but their more penetrating enforcement of the law drove him to emigrate to England in 1769.

Corsica retained a degree of autonomy under the kings of France, but none under the Revolutionary régime. Revolution was all right for the French, but not for subject peoples, such as Basques and Corsicans. With British support Paoli returned for three years in the 1790s to fight for home rule, until finally defeated by Le Petit Caporal himself, traitor to his native soil and rank. Corsica came under military rule and was denaturalised by being made part of metropolitan France.

Economic crisis and heavy emigration marked the next 150 years. At last in 1970 Corsica became a region in her own right, achieving her own assembly in 1982.

Until the American forces brought DDT to bear on the anophiline mosquitoes in 1943, the lower-lying coastlands were malarial. The average lifespan in Biguglia in the early 1800s was twenty-two, while that of *montagnards* was forty. Coastal pastures were used by shepherds only in winter, during lambing and the beginning of the cheesemaking season. In

---

*Colomba, 1840. Mérimée had spent two months in Corsica in autumn 1839. The book features a likeable English father and daughter as friends of the *famille caporale* through Colomba's brother.

spring they took their flocks to pastures round villages halfway up the mountains towards the final stage of *transhumance*, pastures they would graze again on their way down at the end of summer.

The summer *bergeries* at 1600–2000 metres are of simple stone. The vats are copper cauldrons, called *paghuli*. A wooden ladle, a *cocchja*, is used for skimming and transferring curd to moulds called *cajadhia* or *fatoghie*. *Fatoghie* were formerly in wicker-basket form but are now usually plastic. This is aesthetically sad, as the flat impressions of the plastic lack the beauty of those made by true basketwork.

The intermediate stages of the *transhumance* have largely disappeared now that almost all the journey to and from the high pastures can be done by lorry within a day. The highly flavoured herbage and lower brush of the *maquis* (including juniper and honeysuckle) no longer earn those halfway villages a useful income; their flavours no longer enrich the spring cheeses in their special way. The system of farming and *élevage* has also been changed and cut down by loss of coastal pastures to tourist activity, as well as by the lack of young entrants willing to take over from the retiring shepherds.

Corsica's wine regions suffered in the eighteenth century from the change to French rule, losing their Genovese trade without gaining a significant substitute in the well-supplied French market. The nineteenth century dealt another blow with Phylloxera, especially in the north; by the 1970s the vineyards of Cap Corse covered no more than one-fifth of their pre-Phylloxera area.

The only region to enjoy agricultural revival and growth in recent years has been the east coast. *Pieds-noirs*[*] from Algeria started settling there in the 1950s, building anew, and concentrating on wine and fruit production (enriching the Midi's diet with their '*chinois*', smallest and most delectable of the family of miniature pipless oranges called Clémentines).

Ghisonaccia does have some cheese to show, but dairying is unfortunately seldom part of *pied-noir* experience. Old Corsica looks on askance and comments: '*Corse, tu ne seras jamais heureuse*'. Depopulation has become the general rule. Mountain cantons have lost two-thirds of their inhabitants, and many hamlets are deserted. There are more than 6 million Corsicans scattered throughout the world, ten times as many abroad as there are at home. Inevitably there are fewer sheep and, according to one estimate,[†] only one-tenth of the goats of sixty years ago.

As well as the abandoned pastures and vineyards, the *chataigneraies* have become neglected. These chestnut woods formerly provided staples of Corsican animal and human diet. Free-ranging, chestnut-eating pigs used to give Corsican pork and *charcuterie* an inimitable flavour and consistency, now seldom found outside limited mountain districts. Relatively characterless French pigs are now imported by industrial *charcutiers*, a sad

---

[*] French colonists who left North Africa during the period leading up to independence from France, and after.
[†] See page 470.

gastronomic come-down. A less plentiful supply of chestnuts also affects Corsican cuisine more directly. Many old Corsican recipes have a chestnut or chestnut-flour base, from which twenty-two different dishes are prepared for a strictly traditional wedding feast. A more simple dish is customarily offered to the Corsican bride by her mother-in-law on the threshold of her new home: a bowl of freshly curdled milk, called *caghiatu*.

In the late nineteenth century Corsica became part of the legal region for ewes'-milk cheeses entitled to be called Roquefort after *affinage* in the *caves* of Cambalou in the Rouergue (see Chapter 6). This occurred when the advent of artificial temperature control made it possible for Roquefort to be stored longer and sold all year round, nearly doubling the amount of cheese which could be sold annually. Roquefort companies, predominantly the vast Société, set up *laiteries* and collected milk from the *bergers*. In modern times most of the ewes' milk produced in Corsica has been so used.

By the early 1980s, however, the original Roquefort region was becoming self-sufficient in ewes' milk, and the outer regions, including Corsica, were being phased out. The *laiteries* have remained under the same ownership, but cheeses of Roquefort dimensions are now blued in Corsica and sold as Bleu de Corse. More milk now goes into smaller cheeses of local character, such as the neat little Corsica made at Borgo by Société (see p. 472), and larger, hard-crusted cheeses of the Basque type.

French national and regional dairy statistics published annually allow no cows to Corsica, and do not show her share of dairy sheep and goats. A Reader's Digest–Larousse study of 1976 gave 100,000 sheep and 40,000 goats (the latter one-tenth of the 1929 figure), and put the number of *bergers* at 1000. That number of sheep would have needed to be all in-milk ewes to suffice for the 2000 tonnes of Blancs de Roquefort being made in Corsica at the time; and even putting the proportion of Roquefort to other *fromage de brebis* at the highest estimate (four to one), another 25,000 ewes would have been needed for the other cheese. In 1982 Pierre Androuët was told officially that there were 200,000 sheep (CNIEL figures), which seems nearer the mark. As for present figures, it is hard to believe that all the milk used for Roquefort has been absorbed in Bleu de Corse and the expansion of other local types.

The common factors in most Corsican cheesemaking (chèvre or brebis) are the use of round and square basket-moulds and the production of Brocciu. Brocciu is the equivalent of Ricotta in Italy and of Brousse in Provence (see Chapter 18), but more varied than the spellings of its name. Mérimée described it as 'a sort of *fromage à la crème cuit* ... a national dish in Corsica ... very appetising'.

Mérimée's description does not fit in with the usual idea of Ricotta or Brousse. This is represented most nearly in Corsica by Brocciu made of the whey resulting from normal cheesemaking, enriched by about 10 per cent of wholemilk in its content, and eaten within four days of making (I give the recipe of Monsieur Joseph Giudicelli of Ghisonaccia in the list, p. 476). Of course, milk or cream can always be added to a fresh, whey-based Brocciu with pleasant effect, especially if it is eaten within twenty-four hours of birth, as its makers recommend. The *fromage à la crème* type of Brocciu, however, is basically a wholemilk cheese, diluted only by the addition of a generous amount of whey from the previous day's cheesemaking to act as starter. The milk should be warm from the ewe or goat. After addition of the whey, it is brought up to 85–90°C to precipitate the solids, which are skimmed off with the *cocchja* into the *fatoghie* to drain for three days. At the unsalted *frais* stage it has the appearance of basket-moulded Ricotta, but is naturally much richer (though it must be remembered that Ricotta and Brocciu from ewes' milk contain up to 30 per cent fat, because many of the tiny, evenly distributed fat globules escape into the whey while heating). Unsalted fresh Brocciu may be served on its own, with fruit, in pastries, or sweetened.

Where this fatter Brocciu differs more strongly from Ricotta and Brousse is that it may be salted at three days and kept to eat after weeks or even months of *affinage*. With longer keeping and various treatments of the crust, Brocciu can emerge from *affinage* as semi-soft mild, semi-hard semi-strong, or hard strong and sharp cheese. The imprints of the basket-moulds usually survive, though less obviously now than when they were made of wicker. Words meaning 'basket' even feature in the names of Canistrelli and Furagliu in Corbella, the former a crunchy *gâteau* from Corte as well as a rather elusive cheese.

The washed crusts of some Brocciu become a rich gold. I know of one farm *chèvre* of this type, rather sour and dry on the palate at one week (in September), but preferred by the maker at several months of age, when it is hard and strong. At intermediate stages it has the appearance of Époisses (see Chapter 11), or, when the top has sunk into concavity, of an expansive Langres du Plateau (see Chapter 10).

Apart from Brocciu, there is a Corsican recipe for Ricotta aux galets which must surely date back to the Stone Age. Pebbles are brought to a great heat and then thrown into goats' milk, making it boil vigorously. As it cools to 35°C, kids' rennet is added and Robert Courtine describes the result as '*crème gélatineuse*'. I was assured by Corsican friends that the recipe was still in circulation in 1987.

The standard recipe for *fromage* (as opposed to Brocciu) favoured by Monsieur Giudicelli is given in simple terms in the list under Fromage de Brebis (see p. 476). It refers to ewes' milk, but could apply with variations in timing to goats' milk. Both milks are used separately for Venaco, Asco and Niulincu (the preferred Corsican spelling of the more familiar Niolo, the central plateau). Asco and Niulincu may also be made of the two milks mixed. Asco is round, but Niulincu and Venaco are formed in the commoner Corsican square basket-mould with rounded corners. Niulincu covers the whole mountain region of Niolo in north and north-west Corsica. Asco is in its heart, Venaco on its south-eastern fringe, near the centre of the island. La Balagne, between Asco and the north coast, is the district most famed for Niulincu.

In the *fromage frais* state these cheeses can seem like a creamy Brocciu, but most of them undergo prolonged *affinage* with washing and scraping of the crust (reminiscent in nature and result of another square cheese: Le Puant de Lille, from the far north of France (see Chapter 8)). They become straw-coloured, then white to rosy-grey according to age, and are fierce at three to four months, with a firm, buttery interior. Niulincu is fiercer than Venaco (a claim, sometimes questioned, but confirmed by my Corsican acquaintance), and the chèvre versions become fierce sooner than the brebis. Juniper and honeysuckle are among the *maquis* plants given credit for the distinctive flavour in cheeses made during the *transhumance*.

This sort of character is also typical of the best Calenzana and its longer-matured version, Corsevieux, which are chèvres. The small cheese is a round base-of-cone; the larger is square. Crusts are washed or salt-rubbed. They are usually matured for five or six months, but larger ones kept to become Corsevieux may be given up to a year's *affinage*. Their makers say that the milk is redolent of the *maquis*. One unwashed round version is made, and sold in a mild, white state, by the Domaine de Blotali at Montemaggiore on the slopes of Montegrosso, north of Calenzana.

To the south-west, on the coast, *chevriers* near Cargèse produce another square cheese of similar type with a grey crust which becomes roseate after six months in a damp *cave*. The town, perched up on a rock overlooking its fishing port, has a seventeenth-century Greek colony, still hundreds strong with its own active church (Orthodox, become Uniate).

More rustic cheeses, brebis and chèvres, are made in *bergeries* and *cabanes*. Some *bergers* inherit a tradition asserting that cheese is not ready to eat until it is infested with maggots. A young English customer of mine had one with her when she came to my shop on her way home from Corsica in the 1970s. She had just tracked it down for her father, an *aficionado* of what might be called not so much a moveable as a moving feast. There are still Englishmen who like their game and their Stilton in that state (in the eighteenth century they were given spoons to deal with their fancy). The custom still generally known throughout Corsica is to put a freshly made cheese in a *pignato* (marmite), either exposed to fly or with maggots introduced into the feast. The result is sometimes called Appignato.

This is a striking contrast to the tubby little striated brebis most widely representing Corsica in the cheese-shops of Europe and actually named Corsica. Tidy, mild, and quite agreeably melt-in-the-mouth, they are made by Société at the old rock-set village of Borgo in the north-east of the island. Borgo as a cheese-name, however, attaches more anciently to rich, creamy brebis and chèvres made by *bergers* and *chevriers* in the mountains to the west and seldom found far from their place of making.

Another of Société's brebis products from the north-east is Golo, a hard, golden-crusted cheese, more in the Pyrenean hard-cheese style (such as Chiberta, Prince de Claverolles: see Chapter 5). This *laitier* element is counterbalanced in the export market by younger, softer versions of Asco, Niolo and Venaco, thickly coated in herbs of the *maquis*: round U Macchione made by the *veuve* Dolcerocca at Casatorra near Bastia, and the long cheese, triangular in section, called Fleur du Maquis, are examples. Fleur du Maquis, sold *blanc* or, in the family's words, *'un peu fait'* (a little 'done') is made by Antoine Ottavi at Ghisonaccia in the east. Similar cheeses, brebis, chèvres and mixed milk, square and rectangular, are sold as Brin d'Amour. All these herb-coated cheeses can be most appetising, and the brebis are usually the sweetest.

Corsica's range of cheeses has been dictated by its reliance on sheep and goats, with limited seasons, and the need to extend the life of the seasonal produce to cover the winter. The result is a treatment strangely like that used for most of the cows'-milk cheeses made in Flanders, Hainault, Artois and Picardy (see Chapter 8), in climate and landscape as remote as can be from Corsica. Those with a taste for the sharp and rich can be most easily satisfied in Corsica, but the more fragile palate may still find seasonal delight in the youngest states of these cheeses, and in their herb-coated cousins. Above all, though, the tenderly inclined should relish that national dish of Corsica, the young Brocciu.

## Cheeses of Corsica

### Appignato

*Fromage de brebis* made anywhere in Corsica, put before *affinage* in a *pignato* (earthenware *marmite*); some devotees will not eat it until it is crawling with maggots (confirmed as custom persisting in late 1987; see BLEU DE CORSE).
*berger; domestique; en cabane; brebis.*

### Asco

Round cheese similar, except in shape, to Niulincu (see p. 477). Eaten April–November after 3–4 months' *affinage* with washing and scraping of crust, confirmed as both brebis and chèvre in late 1987.
*fermier; brebis/chèvre/mélange cru.*
Haute-Corse; 90 **14**, in heart of Niolo/Niulincu region.

### Bastelicaccia

Brebis *frais*, coated with herbs, made by a *berger-propriétaire* well known locally for his cheeses; enjoyed by Androuët, with *'un excellent vin ajaccien'* in 1982 (the last evidence I have).
*fermier; brebis cru.*
Corse-du-Sud; 90 **17**.

### Bastia

Monday market.
Haute-Corse; 90 **3**.

### Bleu de Corse

1. 2500g cheeses of Roquefort dimensions blued in Corsica. From the late nineteenth century until the early 1980s most of them went as freshly salted *fourmes blanches* to graduate as Roquefort (see Chapter 6, pp. 196–7) in the *caves* of Cambalou. The original more local Roquefort region is now self-sufficient in ewes' milk, so this trade (still legal) has ended, at least for the time being. Most Corsican ewes' milk continues to be used for cheese of this type, sold as Bleu de Corse and, for smaller cheeses, by the *laiteries* largely owned by Société Anonyme des Caves de Roquefort (see BORGO and GOLO).
2. Cheeses made in the central region in the villages at the start of the season, in the *bergeries* or *cabanes* in the summer, eaten in autumn and winter after six or more months of *affinage*. Cheeses made by *bergers* in their *cabanes* in the remoter pastures during the *transhumance* may be less tidy.
3. There is a quite widespread and persistent tradition that such cheeses are not ready to eat until they are fly-infested and crawling; but my Corsican intelligence tells me that cheeses of this type are placed as *fromage frais* in a *pignato* (earthenware *marmite*) to mature (see APPIGNATO), into which the bluebottle can get to lay its eggs, or into which the maggots are introduced.

45% m.g.; *laitier*; *brebis cru*.
Haute-Corse; 90 **5**, C, around Corte.

## Borgo

1. Soft, creamy cheese made in *cabane* during the *transhumance* in the mountains.
2. Neat round, mild, gently crusted, basket-moulded, semi-soft cheeses made in *laiteries* (see CORSICA, which is made in Borgo).
*fermier*; *laitier*; *brebis cru/brebis pasteurisé*.

**Corsica.** 375g, 500g; slightly domed with striated sides (basket-moulding); semi-soft; natural mould-coated crust; matured one month; melt-in-mouth, pleasantly mild, unsalt; made by Fromagerie du Pont de Golo, Borgo, owned by Société Anonyme des Caves de Roquefort. These cheeses may blue in time.
*laitier*; *brebis*.
Haute-Corse; 90 **3**, from Bastia S 20km, 8km W of airport.
See also CORSE (brebis and chèvre).

## Brebis

See APPIGNATO, ASCO, BASTELICACCIA, BLEU DE CORSE, BORGO, BRIN D'AMOUR, BROCCIO, BROCCIU, BRUCCIO, CORSE, CORTE, FLEUR DU MAQUIS, FROMAGE DE BREBIS, FURAGLIU, GHISONACCIA, GOLO, U MACCHIONE, MUNTANACCIU, MUVRONE, NIOLIN, NIOLO, NIULINCU, PECORINO, POLETTA, ROQUEFORT, SANTA MARIA-SICHÉ, SARI D'ORCINO, SARTENAIS, SARTÈNE, SARTENO, TUMO, VENACO, VENAÇAIS.

## Brin d'Amour

600–800g; 12–14cm square, 4cm deep, with rounded corners, or rectangular, or log with round triangular section; firm *pâte*, softens in mouth; pale crust under coating of *sarriette* or rosemary; 'scent of mint or hay'; best in summer, and not usually strong, except in aroma; all the cheeses I have met have been brebis (see also FLEUR DU MAQUIS, MACCHIONE). The basic cheese is like a young Asco, Niolo or Venaco, and these cheeses have been reported from all the mountainous areas. *Brin d'Amour* means a 'bit of love'; *brin* also means 'sprig', referring to the herbs of the *marquis* which coat the cheese.
*laitier*; *brebis*; *chèvre*; *mélange*.

## Broccio, Brocciu (preferred spelling), or Bruccio

1. 200–300g, 500g, 1kg, 2kg; *frais*: (earliest November, latest mid-August for brebis); *petit-lait* from previous making (up to 20% of whole milk in volume) is mixed in with new milk still warm from ewe or goat in copper cauldrons (*i paghuli*) and stirred continually while it is being brought up to 85–90°C; solids in the milk are precipitated and rise to the surface; they are skimmed off, with a ladle (traditionally wooden: *a cocchja*), strained, then ladled into basket-moulds (originally wicker *fatoghie*, now often plastic); they are sold unsalted after three days' draining; Brocciu can be served sweetened, or used in pastries or with fruit.
2. *Affiné* (all year round); the curd is salted when taken out of the moulds and the cheeses are matured in *caves* for weeks or months; in humid conditions they can acquire a golden surface; the smaller ones (disregarding the marks of the mould) can appear in shape and colour like an Époisses (see Chapter 11, p. 364), or, when the top has sunk, like an expansive Langres du Plateau (see Chapter 10, p. 335). September chèvres from one maker seemed a little dry and sour on the palate after a week; but be prepared to keep them for months, to become hard and strong.
Brebis, softer and gentler, are made in *cabanes* or *bergeries* at 1600–2000m in summer *transhumance*, the rest of the year in farms nearer the coast while the sheep are on the lower pastures, the *impaghia*.
*fermier*; *artisanal*; *lait entier de brebis cru/mélange cru with petit-lait*.
3. This is more the conventional Ricotta-type cheese, made from the whey resulting from a standard *fromage de brebis*. The whey is placed into a 20-litre *chaudron* leaving room for 2 l of whole milk to be added after putting a little salt in the whey. Over a period of 30 mins stir two or three times, skim the foam and '*les petits grains de lait*'; when the Brocciu separates from the whey turn off the heat, or remove *chaudron* from heat immediately, and ladle the Brocciu into a mould.
M. Joseph Giudicelli of Ghisonaccia, who gave me this recipe, says that the best time to eat the cheese is the day after making, but that it can be kept for three or four days.

30% m.g.; *fermier; artisanal;* 90% *petit-lait de brebis,* 10% *lait de brebis entier.*

## Cacavelli

Chèvre mentioned only as made in Corsica and eaten *frais, demi-sec* or *sec* (*Marabout,* 1978). The name sounds like a corruption of Cacciocavalli: Italian cheese made from curd which is first drained, then rested under a covering of warm whey for up to 20 hours before being drained again, cut, and worked by hand in very hot water until it becomes elastic. (See SARTENO for a cheese in this tradition, thought to go back to Roman times.) I have not met it, and my Corsican friends do not know it.
*chèvre cru.*

## Caghiatu (Lait Caillé)

Freshly curdled milk in bowl handed to a Corsican bride on the threshold of her new home by her mother-in-law.
*domestique; chèvre cru.*

## Calenzana

150g (8–9cm diameter) base-of-cone, 450g square; both have basket-mould marks on top and surround. Firm but supple *pâte;* white to grey washed or salt-rubbed crust, according to age (5–6 months normal, but up to a year for a larger cheese); *piquant.* (See CORSEVIEUX (strong), MONTEGROSSO (mild).) Traditionally the methods of making this cheese have been passed down through the female line from generation to generation.
*fermier; artisanal; chèvre cru.*
Haute-Corse; 90 **13**, 11.5km SE of Calvi.

## Canistrelli

Cheese made in basket-mould in which it is drained. It stays in the basket if sold *frais* (see FURAGLIU IN CORBELLA). Otherwise it is decanted and sold *demi-sec* or *sec.* It is sometimes kept to harden for grating (as is its Sicilian ewes'-milk counterpart Canestrato). The name Canistrelli, derived from the word for basket, is also used for a crunchy *brique*-shaped *gâteau* made at Corte.
*fermier; chèvre cru.*
Haute-Corse; 90 **5**, Corte.

## Cargèse

See p. 472. 350–500g; about 12cm square, 4–5cm deep with rounded corners; soft;

Crust grey, becoming roseate with age, after up to 6 months in humid *cave.* A full 6 months is thought best in Piana, Androuët and Ninette Lyon tell us (in *Marabout,* 1978).
m.g. *non-précisée; fermier; chèvre cru.*
Corse-du-Sud; 90 **16**, 51km N of Ajaccio; 90 **15**, 31km N of Cargèse.

## Casamaccioli

Animal Fair 7–9 September.
Haute-Corse; 90 **15**, 5km SW of Calacuccia.

## Chèvres

See BRIN D'AMOUR, BROCCIO, BROCCIU, BRUCCIO, CACAVELLI, CAGHIATU, CALENZANA, CANISTRELLI, CARGÈSE, CORSE, CORSEVIEUX, FURAGLIU, MONTE GROSSO, MUVRONE, NIOLO, NIOLIN, NIULINCU, RICOTTA AUX GALETS, SARI D'ORCINO, SARTENAIS, SARTNE, SARTENO, VENACO, VENAÇAIS.

## Corscia

Village perched on rock and rich in animals; a place where Niolo (see p. 477) might be found.
Haute-Corse; 90 **15**, N of Calacuccia.

## Corse

1. Whole milk is rennetted with *caillettes* from unweaned kids. Curd is broken and placed in round-cornered square moulds, or wooden moulds 15cm in diameter and of equal depth, then pressed down by hand and left to drain. When drained it is dry-salted or bathed in brine, then dried on straw mats in a room protected from fly by fumigation. Eaten *frais:* soft, of agreeable flavour. *Sec:* strong, to local taste; crust may be rubbed with olive oil or brine.
2. The label Corse is now seen everywhere in Corsica on brebis and chèvres, which are presumably the same as Corsica (see BORGO).
*fermier; artisanal; chèvre cru.*
Haute-Corse; W of C Niolo region.

## Corsevieux

About 450g; irregular square with rounded corners; soft: '*au lait de chèvres de l'odorant maquis corse*'; made and *affiné* at Calenzana (see above).
45% m.g.; *fermier; artisanal, chèvre cru.*
Haute-Corse; 90 **13**, 11.5km SE of Calvi.

## Corsica

See BORGO.

## Corte

Brebis made in central Corsica, presumably to eat young, as its availability was said to be March–July. My Corsican intelligence service cannot add to that (1987). (See also CANISTRELLI.)
*fermier; brebis cru.*
Haute-Corse; Central 90 **5**.

## Fleur du Maquis

Sold *'blanc'* and *'un peu plus fait'*. Long cheese of rounded-triangular section, coated thickly with herbs (see also BRIN D'AMOUR); made by Antoine Ottavi, 20240 Ghisonaccia (tel. 95 56 13 03).
50% *m.g.; artisanal; brebis cru.*
Haute-Corse; E Coast 90 **6**, SE corner of plain astride Tavignano delta.

## Fromage de Brebis

Recipe from M. Joseph Giudicelli of Ghisonaccia: milk from brebis (7 a.m. and 6 p.m. milkings) collected in a wooden tub is poured into an aluminium vat, and a soup-spoonful of rennet is added. The milk is warmed and rested for 2 hours. When the curd has partly formed it is given *'petites incisions'* with a skimmer. It is then deposited in small moulds (*cajadhia*). As the whey separates it is removed to a 20-litre *chaudron*. When the separation is complete the curd is placed in a larger *cajadhia* on an *égouttoir*. When drained it is turned by hand several times and left in the mould. Three hours later it is lightly salted on the sides. After 3 more hours it is turned and salted again. The next day the cheese is removed from the mould, lightly salted once more, and placed on a shelf. For 5–6 days, so long as it is soft to the touch, it is turned morning and evening. When firm it is dried in an airy place, and then matured in the *cave*.

## Furagliu in Corbella

*Fromage frais* drained in basket mould, from which it is turned out when ready (*Corbella = corbeille* = basket); not known to my Corsican informants in December 1987.
*fermier; brebis/chèvre cru.*
Haute-Corse; NW Niolo region.

## Ghisonaccia

See FLEUR DU MAQUIS, FROMAGE DE BREBIS.

## Golo, Tomme Corse

In *Larousse des Fromages* (1973) this cheese is listed just as 'Golo (brebis)' (but see PECORINO). Hard cheese of the Golo valley is now represented by a *tomme* rather in the style of a golden hard-crusted Basque *tomme laitière*, such as PRINCE DE CLAVEROLLES. This is not surprising, as Société des Caves de Roquefort makes both. Their Golo is made at Fromagerie du Pont de Golo, Borgo (see p. 474), and aged for 3 months (still only semi-hard and mild), or for 6 months and more (hard and *piquant* to very hard and strong for grating).
50% *m.g.; laitier; brebis.*
Haute-Corse; 90 **3**.

## U Macchione

**Fromage de Brebis aux Herbes.** 400–500g, round, soft; thickly coated with rosemary, *sarriette* and thyme which flavour and scent the cheese agreeably. Made by Mme Veuve Dolcerocca, Fromagerie de Casatorra, 20200 Bastia (tel. 95 31 35 57/95 33 18 87).
45% *m.g.; laitier; brebis.*
Haute-Corse; 90 **3**.

## Maquis

Bushy, herby, rocky landscape (see FLEUR DU MAQUIS), nourishing goats, sheep and pigs in a way that enriches the flavour of their meat, and enhances the aroma and flavour of *lait de chèvre* and *lait de brebis*, and thus of the cheeses made from those milks.

## Montegrosso

150g, about 8cm diameter, and 500g; cheese of Calenzana type (see p. 475), but the crust not washed. Shape is base-of-cone, basket-mould-marked; the larger cheese is much deeper. White; firm, yet supple, not strong; made by Domaine de Blotali, Montemaggiore, on slopes of Montegrosso.
*fermier; chèvre cru.*
Haute-Corse; 90 **13**, Montemaggiore 14km ESE of Calvi, N of Calenzana.

## Muntanacciu (Montagnard)

Brebis reported by Courtine (without description) as made in late summer and eaten in October. This suggests late-season cheese, made on those farms which supply milk to *laiteries* until midsummer. Until the early 1980s, these Corsican *laiteries* used to make *blancs* which were then *affinés* in Roquefort *caves*. Nowadays the *laiteries* make Bleu de Corse or Corsica cheese.

The corresponding cheese in the Rouergue on Roquefort's doorstep is Perail, which is eaten young. Such cheese uses up the milk of ewes still in milk after the *laiteries* have stopped collecting, until the ewes have dried out.
*fermier; brebis cru.*
Haute-Corse; 90 **5**, Venaco area, S of Corte.

### Muvrone

I have heard only that a cheese of this name is available March–December, but cannot find Corsican confirmation (Dec 1987).
*brebis/chèvre cru.*

### Niolin, Niolo or Niulincu (last is preferred Corsican spelling)

450g (*affiné*) to 700g (*frais*); 12–14cm square, 4–6cm deep; all with rounded corners; soft to firm, close texture, but melts in the mouth. The crust, washed and scraped, retains marks of basket-mould. 1–2 weeks *séchage* are followed by brine bath and 3–4 months in *cave humide*, with periodic washing and scraping. The resulting surface is smooth and grey to yellow in colour; the *pâte* is firm and buttery, the flavour is spicy from juniper, honeysuckle and the other riches of the *maquis*, and powerful because of the nature and length of its *affinage*. Le Puant de Lille (see Chapter 8, p. 273) comes to mind, but Niolo's emphasis is on the *maquis*, that of Le Puant on beer. Venaco is similar. When *frais* the cheese is like a creamy, soft Brocciu (see p. 474). In 1982 Androuët found a few cheeses around Corscia and wrote that the locals preferred them hard and very sharp. In 1987 Corsicans say the best come from La Balagne, further north, between Asco and the coast.
*fermier; brebis cru (transhumance chèvre cru/mélange cru).*
Haute-Corse; Niolo; 90 **15**, N of Calacuccia; 90 **13**, E and NE of Calenzana.

### Patrimonio

Syndicat Interprofessionnel de Défense et Promotion des Produits Corses, Casa Paesana, 20253 Patrimonio (tel. 95 37 03 78); write for up-to-date information about wine and cheese, and possible visits, before travelling to Corsica.
Haute-Corse; 90 **3**, from Bastia W 18km by D81.

### Pecorino Corse

Basket-moulded *fromage de montagne* mentioned by Lindon in 1961 as available May to December, and made at La Bergerie du Col de Manganeto. (I have sought this in vain on my map; it may be in the area of Capo al Mangano NW of Calacuccia, where some other *bergeries* are mapped.) The availability suggests long enough *affinage* for a semi-hard or hard *tomme*, Golo-style perhaps, as the river Golo runs S of Capo at Mangano. Not known to Corsicans I have consulted (1987).
*fermier; brebis cru.*

### Poletta

This is another briefly noted, undescribed cheese which some Corsican reader may be able to locate and define; my friends cannot (1987).
*brebis.*

### La Restonica

River with gorges running NE down to Corte; its valley has been noted for *bergeries* making Venaco (see p. 478).
Haute-Corse; 90 **5**.

### Ricotta aux Galets

Described by Courtine (1973) as '*crème gélatineuse*' made by throwing very hot pebbles into the milk, which boils vigorously; when it has dropped to 35°C, kids' rennet is added. Season March–July. The recipe is confirmed by my informants, but not its provenance or survival (1987).
*fermier; chèvre cru.*
Corse-du-Sud; 90 **18**, Sartène.

### Roquefort

Corsica is still legally part of the permitted region for ewes' milk to be made into Roquefort, but has not sent *blancs* to Roquefort for *affinage* in the *caves* since the early 1980s (see BLEU DE CORSE, and ROQUEFORT in Chapter 6, pp. 196–7).

### Santa-Maria-Siché, Sainte-Marie-Sicché

As for Poletta, see p. 477.
*brebis*.
Corse-du-Sud; 90 **17**.

### Sari d'Orcino

Mentioned as worth visiting for its cheeses by Androuët (1982). There are said to be in season June–December, so they must be semi-hard if making begins with the *brebis* season in the New Year.
*chèvre/brebis cru*.
Corse-du-Sud; 90 **17**, 30km N of Ajaccio by N193, D1, D301.

### Sartenais, Sartène, Sarteno

Sometimes *fumé*. 1–1.5kg; flattened ball, 12–13cm diameter, 9–10cm deep; pressed, semi-hard *pâte filée* (see CACAVELLI); smooth, thin crust, washed and rubbed, sometimes coloured brown by smoking, sometimes oiled or polished; ripened 3 months, so season for eating is mid-spring to late autumn; close-textured, firm but not hard; flavour rich to sharp. Its origin and Italian way of making are thought to go back to Roman times.
*fermier; brebis/chèvre/mélange cru*.
Corse-du-Sud; 90 **18**.

### Le Tavignano

River, with gorges running ENE down to and around the S of Corte; its valley has been reputed for *bergeries* making Venaco, see below.
Haute-Corse; 90 **5**.

### Tumo de Corse

Name applied to *tomme* sold *fraîche*. (In Sicily, the name Tuma is used for some Pecorino sold before the hardened stage, and the word is also current in Sardinia.)

### Venaçais

See VENACO.

### Venaco, Venaçais

500–700g; 12–14cm square, 4–6cm deep. Brebis softer, and milder in earlier stages than chèvre. Natural crust, scraped during 3–4 months *affinage* in humid natural *caves*. Ninette Lyon recommended eating it grated mixed with olive oil, herbs and garlic, spreading the result thinly on toast, and drinking the strongest available Corsican wine with it (Côteaux d'Ajaccio, Aléria). Androuët classes this cheese with Niolo, but my Corsican sources say Venaco is milder.
*fermier; berger; brebis/chèvre cru*.
Haute-Corse; 90 **5**, 12.5km S of Corte, Venaco, and Restonica and Tavignano valleys SW from Corte.

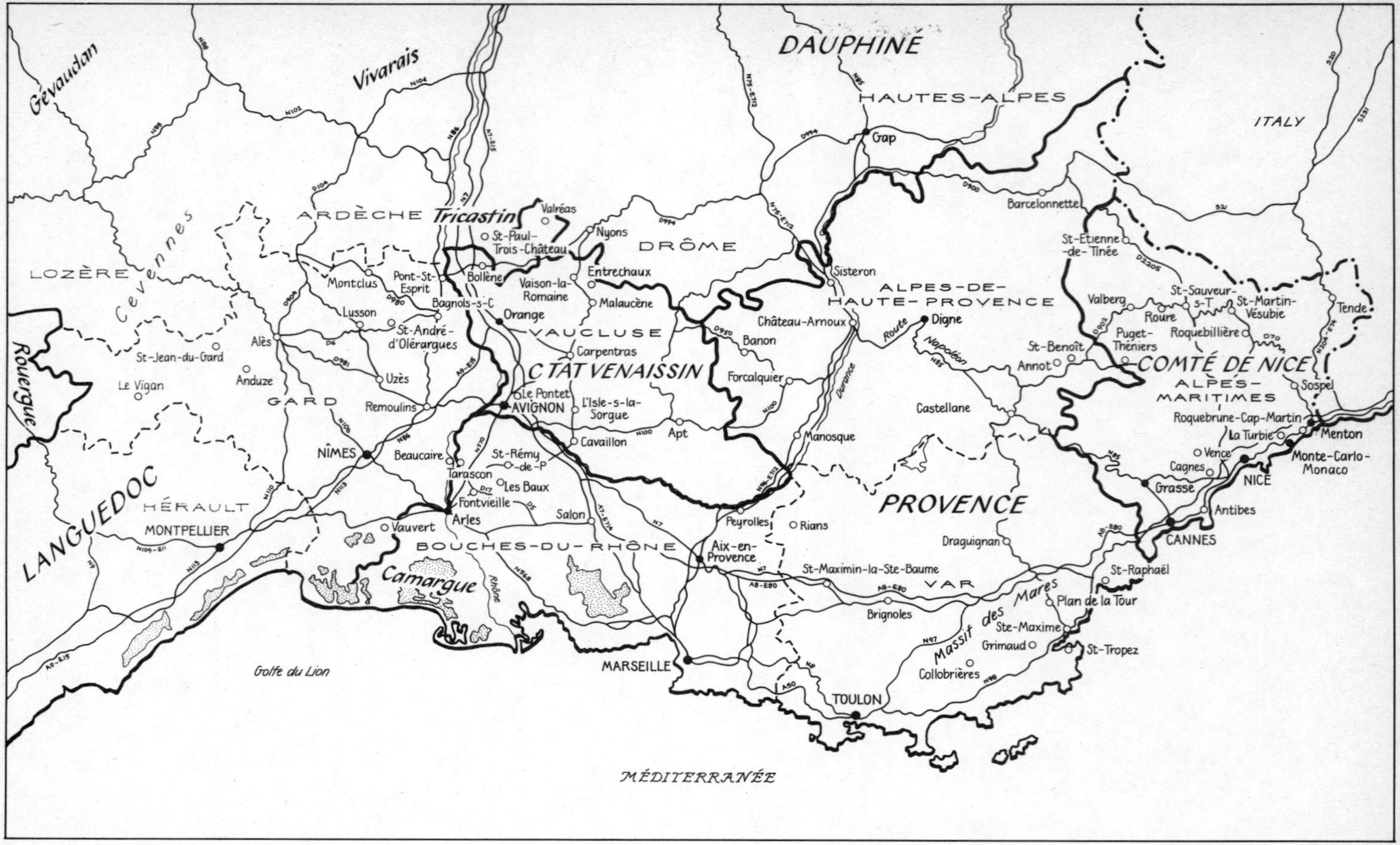
DAUPHINÉ
HAUTES-ALPES
ITALY
Gévaudan
Vivarais
Gap
Barcelonnette
St-Etienne -de-Tinée
ARDÈCHE
Tricastin
Valréas
St-Paul-Trois-Château
Nyons
DRÔME
LOZÈRE
Cevennes
Montclus
Pont-St-Esprit
Bollène
Entrechaux
Vaison-la-Romaine
Malaucène
Sisteron
ALPES-DE-HAUTE-PROVENCE
Digne
Valberg
Roure
St-Sauveur-s-T
St-Martin-Vésubie
Tende
Bagnols-s-C
Orange
Lusson
St-André-d'Olérargues
VAUCLUSE
Château-Arnoux
Banon
Route Napoléon
Puget-Théniers
Roquebillière
Rouergue
Alès
St-Jean-du-Gard
Anduze
Uzès
Carpentras
C TAT VENAISSIN
Forcalquier
St-Benoît
Annot
COMTÉ DE NICE
ALPES-MARITIMES
Sospel
Le Vigan
GARD
Remoulins
Le Pontet
AVIGNON
L'Isle-s-la-Sorgue
Durance
Castellane
Roquebrune-Cap-Martin
La Turbie
Menton
Monte-Carlo-Monaco
Apt
Manosque
NÎMES
Beaucaire
Cavaillon
St-Rémy-de-P
Tarascon
Vence
Cagnes
NICE
LANGUEDOC
Les Baux
Fontvieille
PROVENCE
Grasse
HÉRAULT
Salon
Antibes
MONTPELLIER
Vauvert
Arles
Peyrolles
Rians
Draguignan
CANNES
BOUCHES-DU-RHÔNE
Aix-en-Provence
St-Maximin-la-Ste-Baume
St-Raphaël
Camargue
Rhône
VAR
Massif des Mares
Plan de la Tour
Brignoles
Ste-Maxime
Grimaud
St-Tropez
Golfe du Lion
MARSEILLE
Collobrières
TOULON
MÉDITERRANÉE

CHAPTER EIGHTEEN

# *Provence and Eastern Languedoc*

EASTERN LANGUEDOC – AVIGNON WITH COMTAT VENAISSIN, ORANGE, VALRÉAS, TRICASTIN – WESTERN PROVENCE – CENTRAL PROVENCE – EASTERN PROVENCE AND COMTÉ DE NICE – HAUTE-PROVENCE

Provence lives up to the promise of the road that leads to her, *l'Autoroute du Soleil*. Even in winter it is rare for us to go more than a few days without being able to lunch out on our south-facing balcony, with a butterfly and a dragonfly to cheer us, even into December. Native *provençaux*, of course, would not think of doing so. Our neighbours show a mixture of amusement and concern as we expose ourselves to the dangers of overheating on still days and catching cold on all the others. A pocket handkerchief of cloud or a breath of wind brings the plaint: *'Fait pas beau aujourd'hui!'*

Paradoxically, that periodic driving force from the north, the Mistral, so much more than a mere breath of wind, is responsible for clearing our sky of clouds. It might be expected that Provence would be burnt-sienna in summer. So it once was, and in the higher *garrigue* and the mountains rain may still be anxiously awaited; but in the lower river valleys and the coastal plains the superb, ever-extending irrigation canals keep the land eternally green and nurture every fruit and vegetable in season. In the mountainous interior life is hard, against a picturesque, but stony and inaccessible landscape. Depopulation is severe and many villages have been abandoned.

The Mistral is providential for the *chevrier*. He can put his new cheeses in cages in the open and save days of waiting when *'le grand sécheur des fromages'* is blowing. Houses turn their backs on the blast, fortresses to windward with few and minimal openings. Thick stone walls and wood fires in wide fireplaces keep in the warmth and expel the damp in winter, and preserve an airy coolth in summer. Rubble walls were traditionally covered with lime-based plaster which can breathe, a sound practice being retaught to local craftsmen today. Modern wall-coatings are not only hideous, both in pristine brightness and in weathered squalor, but cause stuffiness and condensation. Ancient walls are preferable to modern walls in houses, just as traditional crusts are preferable to plastic crusts on cheeses: both for aesthetic reasons, and for their stifling effect on life within.

Out of doors, crops and soil are shielded from the Mistral by windbreaks of poplar, cypress, yew and bamboo. Roads, squares and *boules* grounds are beautifully shaded by plane trees. The *provençaux* seek the shade, but look as if they spent all their waking hours in sun and wind. Their looks and their laughs do not belie them. They are incomparably warm, generous and amusing neighbours.

The *provençaux* are bred from millennia of interchanges stimulated by art, craft, and commerce between people from all sides: Iberians from the west, Ligurians from east of Marseille, inland peoples from up the Rhône to the north, and Greeks and all the other traders and raiders from the sea. The Greeks, who were buying iron from the Eduen kingdom (today's Burgundy) and exporting pottery at least as early as the seventh century BC, founded the ports of Massalia (Marseille)* at the end of the seventh century, and Nice and Antipolis (Antibes) in the sixth. They brought with them vine, olive, nut, cherry and fig. The Greeks cherished the fig tree for more than just its fruit. It had been their immemorial custom to guard every shrine with a fig tree, from which the shepherd could tear a branch to stir his ewes' milk for cheesemaking. The curdling properties of its sap reinforced the work of the lamb's rennet, an element of divine insurance against failure. The olive came in useful for cheese too. Its oil was (and is) rubbed into the crust of hard cheeses to improve their keeping quality. It is probable that the long predominance of sheep-raising and sheep-dairying in Provence owed something to Greek influence.

In the second century BC the Massaliotes called in the Romans to protect them against the inland Salyens, a Celtic–Ligurian league defeated in 122 (the tough Ligurian strain survives in mountainous Haute-Provence). With its eastern boundary on the Var and its new capital at Aquae Sextiae (Aix), the new Provincia Transalpina was formed: Provence, largely in the shape and name it has today. (Nice, beyond the Var in Italia, joined Provence from the tenth century until 1388, and again in 1860 for good).

Rich monuments of Provincia remain in use, such as the arenas at Arles and Nîmes (noted for cheese in Roman times), and the theatres at Arles and Orange are still used. On a humbler scale, the typical garden tables and benches are still cut from stone to Roman patterns, and another, living monument of classical times is the *provençal* profile, particularly striking in the women when they put up their hair in the traditional coiffure. It seems distinct from North Italian and Spanish looks, although the inflow from both sides has continued into modern times, particularly of Italian foresters and Spanish stone-cutters and masons. The great film-maker Marcel Pagnol's first ancestor to settle in Provence had been known on arrival as *'l'Espagnol'*, and his grandfather Pagnol was a master-mason. Within two or three generations, as we have witnessed, the female

---

*Massilia for English classicists; Marsilya for the present-day inhabitants of Foça near Smyrna from which its founders sailed 2600 years ago: *les Phocéens* still alluded to in Marseille's nickname. A recent traveller found Foça like the *vieux port* de Marseille; the locals seemed conscious of another surviving Italian offshoot but not aware that the great Marsilya was in Provence.

descendants of Spanish immigrants acquire those distinctive *provençaux* features.

After the collapse of the Roman Empire, Provence was incorporated in the new kingdom of the Franks in AD 536, but retained most of her independence. She even sided with the invading Saracens in the eighth century. The Saracens were to return in 884, to occupy the mountains now commemorating them as Le Massif des Maures, and harried the land for a century. Moorish influence may have led to the permanent presence of goats and goat cheese here, the cheese usually of small *tome* or *banon*-shape, like the *labna* of the Middle East.

In the ninth century the kingdom of Burgundy and Provence was formed, in which Provence remained a comté, subject to imperial suzerainty. Comtés within the comté were formed, such as Arles (a kingdom in name by 1178), Avignon, Les Baux, Forcalquier and Venaissin (still called Le Comtat), and Marseille. Grasse (with Cannes as trading port) and Nice were virtually city-states in the old Greek pattern.

In 1125 two heiresses inherited Provence. One was married to the comte de Toulouse (Raimond, like all his line), who took the Marquisat (the marches or borderland, facing his great Languedoc possessions across the Rhône), comprising much of what is now Vaucluse and Hautes-Alpes. In the next century this ruling family, having defended religious freedom and having been defeated by the forces of the Pope and the French king, surrendered independence and finally all its domains to the French crown. In 1309 the Popes were invited by the King of France to take refuge from their Roman troubles in the Comtat de Venaissin and later bought Avignon from the comtesse de Provence. They were only dispossessed in 1793. The neighbouring principality of Orange descended from a general of Charlemagne's to the House of Nassau (whence the Dutch royal house, Orange-Nassau), coming to France in the seventeenth century.

The other *provençale* heiress in 1125 was married to the count of Barcelona (named Raimond-Bérenger, as usual in *his* line). The family established authority over the feudal seigneurs, gradually acquiring comtés, including Forcalquier and Les Baux (see p. 495).

In the thirteenth century the rulers of Provence became royal once more. The heiress to Provence married Charles d'Anjou, brother of Louis IX (Saint-Louis). Charles became comte de Provence in 1246, briefly King of Sicily (reduced to Naples after the anti-French revolt, the Sicilian Vespers of 1282), and transiently King of Albania (1271) and Jerusalem (1274). This ambitious, much-travelled ducal house even provided kings of Hungary in the next century. One of the family was the first husband of Jeanne de Provence, who succeeded to the throne of Naples and Provence in 1343. He was murdered before she was crowned, but she at once married Louis d'Anjou, King of Hungary and other realms. (Hungary has stores of old Provençale music.)

The last effective independent comte de Provence was René, duc d'Anjou, titular but frustrated King of Naples and Sicily and dispossessed duc de Bar et Lorraine. He retired to Provence for peace and enjoyment of the arts, and he and his second wife, Jeanne de Laval, were widely popular. René bequeathed Provence to his nephew Charles, duc du Maine, from whom Louis XI inherited Provence and Maine in 1481. The kings of France were comtes de Provence thereafter.

From 1539 northern French, the *langue d'oïl*,* was imposed on officialdom in Provence, inevitably undermining the use of Provençal in educated circles, although there was a literary revival in the 1820s after the Bourbon restoration (accompanied by care for architectural heritage; the Roman arena in Arles was cleared of 200 houses). In 1854 the Félibrige, a group of seven poets, took up the cause under Joseph Roumanille and Frédéric Mistral, but Jules Ferry's republican education act forcibly closed schools with clerical associations and outlawed the speaking of anything but French in class, even in the playground; and it was discouraged at home by materialistic bourgeois and intellectual snobs. In the 1980s the old provincial languages of France were officially encouraged again, but too late: it needs two Provençal-speaking parents for children to grow up with it as a living language, which becomes ever rarer.

The language is kept up in some churches, such as that of Raphèle, in La Crau near Arles, and at Notre Dame des Vignes at Visan. The traditional music of the *galoubet* (pipe) and *tambourin* (deep, narrow drum), played simultaneously by the *tambourinaires*, the dances, and the becoming *arlésiennes* fashions of dress and coiffure are maintained by active local societies. They are to be seen and heard on many festival occasions, together with the gardians armed with *lou ferre* (trident-topped chestnut stave) held like a lance on their white Camarguais horses. The gardians and their mounts work in and near the Camargue with the *manados*: the herds of horses† and black *camarguais* cattle kept by the *manadier* (owner and breeder), which run free for the first few years of their lives.

All the *camarguais* milk goes into the calves (the whole of Provence makes only one-thousandth of all France's cows'-milk cheese) and butchers do not even recommend the beef. These animals are bred for sport. Spanish and Portuguese bullfights are still popular in the bigger towns, and Portuguese teams occasionally come to demonstrate the most ancient art, that of taking the bull by the horns, the sport of Minoan times going back 3000–4000 years and more. The commonest spectacle in local arenas, however, is Provence's own, an uncontroversial entertainment. About a dozen *raseteurs* in white shirts and trousers face a succession of single long and sharp-horned black bulls, called *cocardiers*. The only weapon is a cross between a knuckle-duster and a curry-comb, not used to assault the bull but to detach the *cocarde* and the two *ficelles*, strings tying the *cocarde* to the horns. The greater part of the entertainment lies in watching the bull chasing the *raseteurs* as they try to snatch the trophies from its horns on the run.

*The *langue d'oïl* is the language of the north, where *oïl* = yes; the *langue d'oc* is the language of the south, where *oc* = yes. Provençal is a language within the *oc* group.

†The breed is thought to stem from the prehistoric race of Solutré (in Burgundy) and to have changed very little over the millennia.

Sheep, for many centuries the main dairy animal, play a less combative rôle in the life and lore of Provence. At midnight on Christmas Eve (and on some other festivals) in many a church the shepherd leads in a ram pulling a lamb in a little cage-chariot, or carries the lamb in over his shoulder. The lamb is blessed and adds a live note to the figures in the Christmas crib. The sheep of western Provence are indoors only in severe winter weather, otherwise staying out on the Camargue, the Garrigue or the Crau from late autumn until early summer. Except for one flock on the edge of the Camargue, which stays to supply seasonal cheese to the surrounding district, their summers are spent in the mountain pastures of Dauphiné and Savoie, and *alpages* such as the Vallée d'Ubaye high up in the Niçois. This is *La Transhumance*, the title of a moving book by Marie Mauron, who had taken part in the traditional trek on foot and reveals the rich traditions, and the satisfactions and desperate hardships of the journeys. The shepherd's life is now eased in part by the use of motor transport for all but the highest part of the migratory journey, reducing it from a matter of weeks to one of hours.

In the mountainous comté de Nice and Haute-Provence most of the bigger mountain cheeses were brebis until the middle of this century. A few survive, but many have become *tomes de chèvre*, or *tommes de vache*, with some mixing of milks between seasons. Their by-product is the Brousse (like Ricotta), sold in its young whiteness all over Provence.

In the centre and west, the sheep are *mérinos*, famous for wool, but first bred in France almost entirely for meat (attention has been paid latterly to improving their wool again). The exceptions are the Lacaune sheep in the Gard (mostly milked for Roquefort) and some early-lambing *mérinos* in or near the Camargue from which come young cheeses commonly called Gardians (we return to these and the Camargue later in the chapter).

The natural barriers presented by the mountains and gorges of Provence and the Niçois make it necessary to tour these *pays* in stages, so I have noted against each *département* the relevant places and cheeses within it. I shall now cover the country from east to west, taking wing first to the Côte d'Azur.

# Cheeses of the Niçois

Let us parachute straight into the Niçois hinterland. Le Mercantour in the far north-east came to France only after the Second World War. A favourite hunting ground of the House of Savoie, it had been held back when the rest of 'Nizza' was ceded to France in 1860. It has enriched France with two pockets of farmhouse cheesemaking and a man-decorated mountain landscape of unique character, La Vallée des Merveilles. The quickest approach from the coast is up the Valley of the Roya (Roia in Italy), which flows into the Mediterranean at Ventimiglia. Our road north is S20, becoming N204 as it crosses the frontier. About 40–50 kilometres from the coast, several farms around Tende produce a semi-hard square brebis (with echos of Corsica) about 1 kilo in weight, Brousse, and unsalted Caillé de brebis from mid-November until July, when the ewes dry off cheeses sold at Grasse. Ten kilometres further north on the Col de Tende, Ninette

Lyon found a *chevrier* making Brousse in the 1970s. Except in Corsica, this usually indicates that another cheese is made as well.

Picturesquely perched, Tende and La Brigue, to the south-east, have vestiges of castles of the seigneurs who ruled them until the eighteenth century, the Lascadis. Between Tende and La Brigue D91 leads west up the more open Minière Valley from Saint-Dalmas-de-Tende. It gives easier access than the old six-hour walk or mule-ride to the approaches to La Vallée des Merveilles. The lighter rocks of the multicoloured mountain-faces above this valley are carved with tens of thousands of stylised human figures and other signs of uncertain date and meaning, thought to be the work of early Ligurians. In this and nearby valleys, several farms make a broad, round *tomme* of about 6 kilos from cows' milk. Until the mid-1940s this was Italy, and the cheeses are Italian in character.

Working towards the next cheese valleys to the west, we descend the Roya again to 15 kilometres below Saint-Dalmas for the turning to Sospel. The scenery is a foretaste of the astonishing giant's-playground scale of geology apparent throughout the Alps of the Niçois and Provence. Rock strata are prominent above the treeline and where forest has been cleared, and above the shale crumble in the sheer cliff-face, unless masked by glacial remains. The strata have by turns been moulded into graceful curves, forced suddenly into hairpin bends, negligently pushed aside, and violently knocked down by a giant hand. Sometimes it is hard to believe that there can be any place for dairy animals. Yet there are saucers of green high up in these rugged surroundings; and grassy slopes on the gentler curves, and rounded breasts of mountains which appear to have settled down and rested on one elbow to recover from the shocks of subterranean disturbance. There is a suggestion of the morning after the night before: night of a prodigious, unruly geological party over 100 million years ago. Man has sought safety in beautiful villages up on rocky eminences, and has tamed the less fierce mountainsides by terracing; but the population has dwindled, terracing has gone back to the wild, and fewer animals mean less cheese. The old colour-washed plaster on Nizza's houses has crumbled to reveal stone walls, often of rubble.

Sospel, with its Thursday market, used to be a source of *tomme de brebis* and its natural by-product, Brousse. Later, similar cheeses were made with goats' milk. In 1971 the first edition of Pierre Androuët's *Guide du Fromage* still had the two existing together, but by 1973 only a *tomme de vache* seemed to survive. It was described that year by Robert Courtine as 'like a large Tome de Savoie', locally called 'Froumai gras', *patois nissard* for fat cheese.

Coastwards from Sospel lies Roquebrune-Cap-Martin around its tenth-century castle. Behind it at nearby Gorbio, another hilltop village, a *chevrier* makes cheeses which can be bought in season at the Fromagerie de l'Édelweiss in Nice. A few kilometres south-west, between N7 and the *autoroute*, La Turbie harbours a *chevrier* making a small pressed *tomme*.

From the Nice bank of the Var, N202 leads upriver 15 kilometres to the Gorges de la Vésubie, and on a further 7 to the Gorges de la Tinée, with

Bairols beyond. These two valleys are connected about 20 kilometres further north by a road meandering westwards from Saint-Martin-Vésubie through the Valdeblore to the Tinée. Another 4 kilometres north, near Saint-Sauveur-sur-Tinée and Roure, the valley of the Vionène leads west to Valberg. All these valleys were long renowned for *tommes* and Brousses de brebis, usually called Vésubie, Valdeblore and Valberg. Since the Second World War the number of sheep has diminished, and these names have been increasingly represented first by *tommes* and Brousses de chèvre, and latterly by cows'-milk cheeses. On his 1982 tour, Androuët found one *berger–chevrier* at Bairols who continued to make a brebis in season, overlapping with seasonal chèvres in early and midsummer before lambing, and taking over from the chèvres again in late autumn. They were flat *tommes*, varying in size, and kept long enough to attain a certain sharpness of flavour. Valberg was cited just as chèvre by *Larousse des Fromages* in 1973; otherwise only *tommes de vache* appear to be made in the Tinée and Vésubie under the old names. At Roure, *vache* is traditional. The Tuesday market at nearby Saint-Sauveur-sur-Tinée should provide some evidence of what survives locally, but not all these cheeses reach market or merchant.

The *tommes* range from 4–12 kilos in weight. Their fine *pâte* is compared by Pierre Androuët with that of the not-so-distant Italian Val d'Aosta's Fontina, much used in fondue. Fontina has become a rather tidy golden cheese, though, while the *niçois* cheeses tend to stay more rustic and moist externally, becoming an attractive pink with long keeping. Their flavours, too, are distinct from Fontina and more pronounced. In Androuët's *Livre d'Or* of 1984, groups of *vacheries* were reported along the Vésubie and around Roquebillière at 2000 feet, and near Saint-Martin-Vésubie at over 3000 feet; along the Valdeblore, from 3000 to well over 5000 feet; and around Valberg at nearly 6000. Inevitably at such altitudes the cattle spend much of the year indoors, so summer cheeses made when the high pastures are usable (whether the grass is cut and carried to the stables, or grazed) are worth seeking out from August onwards.

Descending the River Tinée again we can rejoin the Var, going upstream with N202 alongside. This road goes west through Puget-Théniers and turns south at Les Scaffarels, 2 kilometres short of Annot. There are *chevriers* at Les Scaffarels and at Saint-Benoît (north up D460 from the main road 4 kilometres back); but their chèvres are different from the semi-hard, pleasant (but not strong) Tomme d'Annot. This I remember eating at Annot in June in the 1960s, when we reached that charming old village by the Chemin-de-Fer de Haute-Provence from Nice. It was too early in the season to sample the already rare brebis version, a *transhumance* cheese which needed at least two months to achieve maturity. In 1973 Robert Courtine listed only the *tomme de chèvre* under Annot, and in more recent years even this has not been in evidence in Annot itself, once the collecting centre for these cheeses of the upper Var Valley. Puget-Théniers is the nearest source of Tomme d'Annot I can find today. In 1987 some people in Annot (including one hotelier) had not even heard of their namesake cheese until I questioned them about it.

Before continuing west, I should mention the rather far-removed Vallée de l'Ubaye, 80 kilometres to the north, with its own pressed *tomme de chèvre*. Barcelonnette is the district's centre, with markets on Wednesdays and Saturdays. The local *laiterie coopérative* unfortunately pasteurises the milk it puts into its Brousse-style *tommes fraîches*.

## CHEESES OF THE VAR

Now we must wing back to the coastal region, briefly touching on the Var before we work upcountry again by another route. Grasse and a considerable area of Eastern Provence, including the lower Var Valley, were embraced by the Alpes-Maritimes when that *département* was created on the acquisition of Nizza in 1860 (bureaucracy would not have thought of calling it Nice, and was quite content that the Var should continue to name the truncated *département* through which it no longer flowed).

Grasse is most famous for its flowers and the natural scents directly distilled from most of them. To extract the scent from some of the more reserved species, such as jasmine, another method is needed, which demonstrates a scientific fact vital to cheesemakers. The flowers are laid out on trays of fat until the fat is saturated with their aroma, which is then distilled from the fat. Plant oils and animal fats are conductors of the aromas and flavours contained in aromatic esters. In the world of cheese these aromas and flavours are attracted to the body fat and mammary glands of the grazing animals. They emerge in the milk, and, provided they are not neutralised by pasteurisation, survive to enrich cheeses and give them the character which varies with local soil and pasture.

Grasse has markets every weekday except Monday and is blessed with La Fromagerie in the old town. There Mesdames François Gérace and Yvonne Morgante show their flair, and that most important characteristic of the best *fromagers*, lively interest in and knowledge of their own region. They should be visited on a reconnaissance before you set out for the mountains in any direction. If you have too little time for such exploration, at least you can sample most of the cheeses here, including some of the rarest. Another place of pilgrimage for the serious cheese-worshipper is the remarkable establishment in Cannes of the *maîtres fromagers* Cénéri *père et fils*. Theirs is one of the great cheese shops of France, backed up by superb cellars; the willingness to travel to find good cheese is typical of this hard-working father, son and daughter.

The Var has a scattering of *chevriers*, but is not great cheese country. Fortunately the markets attract cheesemakers from a distance. For instance, in the quite small market at Plan de la Tour in the Massif des Maures we found several cheeses we had never seen before, including those of Castellane and Séranon, to which we are coming now.

Our next road into the hinterland is N85, La Route Napoléon. Napoleon took it when he landed on this coast in March 1815, to disturb Europe's peace again for the Hundred Days, culminating in the Battle of Waterloo. Today's architectural horrors on the Côte d'Azur would probably have repelled him before he set foot on land, and sent him fleeing back to Elba (but if he had landed now he would never have been able to cross the line of traffic on the coastal road). My advice is to keep to the *autoroute* during Riviera visits for as long as possible, thus avoiding the endless traffic jams, hoardings and concrete ziggurats along the coast. Patches of this blight do reappear from time to time on the Route Napoléon, such as snack advertisements defacing the *garrigue* fifty feet above the road. Traditional architecture crumbles, while new breeze-block, concrete, shocking pink tiles, even corrugated iron, stand out across the valleys.

However, further up the Var Valley the extraordinary stratified geology asserts itself. The soil is increasingly red and traditional buildings blend into the landscape with their bare stone, or plaster weathered to pale gold, and their aged, yet ageless tiles. A semi-soft cows'-milk cheese called Tomme de Ferme de Castellane, weighing just under a kilo, is made at La Roque-Esclapon, 24 kilometres short of Castellane, off the Route Napoléon to the south. A few kilometres east of there, north of the *route*, Séranon gives its name to a cows'-milk cheese in the same natural-crusted class. In this stretch of country, and towards Castellane, there are hives in the *garrigue* and invitations to buy honey, royal jelly and *parfums*. There is a *chevrier* 2 kilometres east of old Castellane itself, and local cheeses sell in the Wednesday and Saturday markets. South-west of Castellane, the upper Verdon Valley leads through the Canyon du Verdon beneath the Corniche Sublime, where one or two *chevriers* or *chevrières* lurk.

We pass through Moustiers-Sainte-Marie, famous for the charm of its decorated glazed pottery (which is said to have been introduced by a monk from Faenza, whence the French term *faïence*). Our route continues west over the lavender-growing Plateau de Valensole: in this countryside I have known the scent so strong that a breeze can waft it into one's nostrils when the lavender fields are out of sight over a crest.

We revert now to the Route Napoléon, on its increasingly beautiful way to Digne. Digne has a Wednesday, Thursday and a more interesting Saturday market, and a *fête* for *lavandes* on the first Sunday in August. Twenty-five kilometres on, La Bonne Étape at Château-Arnoux makes a feature in its cooking of fresh, locally grown ingredients, and serves Banons from a nearby *chevrier*. Some of them, wrapped in chestnut leaves, are treated with brandy and kept for months. Sisteron, 14 kilometres further north, clings to the mountainside under its rocky citadel on the west bank of the Durance. Across the river La Baume, rising out of the water, is a striking example of the vertical strata I have mentioned. Sisteron has Wednesday and Saturday markets, where you can expect Dauphinois cheeses. Chanousse, Éourres and Villefranche le Château (see Chapter 16, pp. 452, 454 and 463) are within visitable distance.

## Cheeses of the Alpes de Haute-Provence

Returning 6 kilometres south of Sisteron, we leave the Route Napoléon and follow D951, D13 and D950 to Forcalquier, once capital and stronghold of a feudal comté. The Monday market there has plenty of organic produce, and needs exploring for the various farm chèvres, which are spread about the town, not herded together. You can travel south and west by D100 from Forcalquier to Apt in the Vaucluse, which has a Saturday market and, in its Maison de l'Agriculture on the Avenue des Druides, the headquarters of the Société Coopérative Agriclole des Monts de Vaucluse. This *coopérative* does *affinage* of small farmhouse chèvres, including *tomes*, *briques*, and the Banon-type Chevrachu. My samples were a bit on the ripe side and rather salty.

From Apt, D22 (becoming D51 across the departmental border in Alpes de Haute-Provence) leads north-east to Banon, passing the remarkable hilltop Simiane-la-Rotonde. The twelfth-century *rotonde* is in fact a hexagonal tower with sloping sides above a fortified village, where the outside houses form part of the walls. The hillsides have sandy rock faces with patches of orange, yellow and pink, interspersed with various shades of green. Vineyards are starting to reappear.

The other way to Banon is by D950 from Forcalquier. We passed Le Rocher des Ongles (the rock of claws), and within 2 kilometres, on the right of the road, found a *chevrier*. After the charming village of Le Largue, off the road to the right, we went through extensive oakwoods beyond which a large herd of Alpine goats was browsing. There was no roadside cheese sign, so their milk is probably collected by Monsieur Ripert, who makes Banon 6 kilometres away. We went through the small rock-perched fortified town of Banon, coming out on D51 and, after crossing a little bridge, took the second turning on the left, marked 'Fromage de Chèvre', and found the farm buildings enlivened by a peacock on the roof.

Monsieur Romain Ripert settled here in the mid-1960s, after making cows'-milk cheese in Morocco. Here he adopted the dairy animal and the cheese of the *pays*: the goat and the Banon. He sounded old *paysans* on the secrets of the traditional cheese and set out to revive it. Banon is the only internationally known cheese associated with Provence, but few foreigners have ever tasted the original. They have been fobbed off for years with the mass-produced pasteurised cows'-milk versions made in the Dauphiné, mainly in distant Isère (see Chapter 16).

The small flat, rounded cheeses of this district, marketed at Banon and so named, were for centuries made from ewes' milk in season, and from goats' milk in the late summer and autumn. In nearly nine years of living for much of the year in Provence, I have never seen a ewes'-milk Banon on sale. The few local cheeses bearing the name have all been chèvres.

Monsieur Ripert uses about 1500 litres of milk a day, most of which he collects himself from neighbouring *chevreries* (his own herd was only sixty strong in 1986). Among the traditional cheesemaking families, the young generation is disinclined to take on twice-daily milking and the old is tiring of it, so the larger herds have been decreasing in number. According to Monsieur Ripert the surviving *chevriers* (mostly ecologically minded newcomers of the 1960s and 1970s) like the local cross-bred goats. Their herds are smaller than was traditional; and their cheeses are often looser-textured *tomes fraîches* rather than Banons, most of them sold within four days of making.

These young cheeses are in demand in the Marseille region and on the Côte d'Azur and constitute nearly nine-tenths of Monsieur Ripert's own sales. He produces 1000 hand-made cheeses a day, including 100 Banons, well-renneted and firm in consistency when *affinés*. First they undergo *séchage*. In periods of the Mistral they dry quickly to a golden colour, in calmer weather more slowly, attracting a blue surface mould before drying out. Almost all non-wrapped Banons, and the little hand-moulded logs called Bûchettes de Banon, Monsieur Ripert's innovation of the last few years, are decorated with the herb the *provençaux* call *pebre d'aï*: donkey's pepper (*poivre d'âne* or *sariette* in French; the term *pebre d'aï* is seldom found on labels). Related to our savory, the herb grows wild everywhere in Provence and is widely used; you don't have to be a donkey to enjoy it. Sometimes just a sprig is added to the Banons; sometimes the cheese is coated with it. Also local are the chestnut leaves in which most of the Banons are wrapped two or three weeks after the start of their *affinage*. This is a very old and effective practice: chestnut leaves are porous, yet resistant to the acid which continues to drain from the cheese with the whey. The traditional preparatory treatment for the leaves is a bath in vinegar, wine or *eau-de-vie*. Monsieur Ripert prefers *eau-de-vie*, giving the leaves a quick dip before folding them round the Banons and tying them with raffia. These cheeses are sold as Banons à la Feuille (or sometimes as Banon d'Or). After another three or four weeks the cheeses are at the *crémeux* stage and ready. In the farm shop you can taste before you buy, served with interest and pride by a charming lady from another cheesemaking family.

## Cheeses of the Comtat Venaissin

West of Banon lies the Plateau de Vaucluse in the Comtat Venaissin (with Apt as a market town), bordered in the north by Mont Ventoux, noted for its *fromages forts*: Cachat, Cacheia, Cacheille, and Fromage Fort du Mont Ventoux.

The modern capital of the Comtat, Avignon, was owned by the Popes until under two centuries ago. Prosper Mérimée's first impression was: '*En arrivant à Avignon il me sembla que je venais de quitter la France*' ('On arriving in Avignon I felt that I had left France behind me'). As Inspecteur des Monuments under the July monarchy from 1834 he was concerned with the preservation and part-restoration of the walls of the city by Viollet-le-Duc. Avignon is too full of architectural and other treasures for me to select favourites. Monsieur Pierre Hiély will feed you well in his notable Restaurant Hiély overlooking the rue de la République, and serve you excellent local cheeses. He buys them from La Fromagerie Ranc, a welcoming shop in the rue Bonneterie. Monsieur Ranc (no relation) was received into the Guilde des Fromagers on the same occasion that I was. Not far from his shop is the covered market, and there are various street markets listed at the end of this chapter where local cheeses appear.

North of Avignon, beyond Orange, is the curious enclave of the Vaucluse within the Drôme, centred on Valréas, bought by the Popes from the Dauphiné. It forms part of the AOC region for Picodon de la Drôme and

Picodon de l'Ardèche, fully dealt with in Chapters 7 and 16. Picodons de Valréas should have been excluded from the AOC since they cannot be truthfully called 'Picodons de la Drôme'. The more accurate name Picodon de Valréas is now illegal under AOC regulations. Picodons here used to be eaten at about one week, much younger than allowed by the traditions of Picodon. (Such youth was dismissed scornfully under the term *Pidance* over the Rhône in the Vivarais: See Chapter 6.) They must now be kept for twelve days before sale, still not long enough in the opinion of Picodon-makers elsewhere.

Between Valréas and the Rhône lies the ancient tribal territory of the Tricastin, part in Drôme (with its capital Saint-Paul-Trois-Châteaux), and part in Vaucluse, around Bollène (with its daily vegetable market). There are some *chevriers* and *chevrières* in this district, including Madame Brunier, who may be found with her plain and *sarriette*-coated *tomes* on Saturday mornings in the market across the Rhône at Pont Saint-Esprit.

## CHEESES OF THE GARD AND EASTERN LANGUEDOC

This brings us into the Gard and Eastern Languedoc, such a crossroads of long-distance land and water trade routes that Beaucaire had the greatest fair in Europe from mediaeval times until the railways came. Not surprisingly, many of the Gard cheeses are related to those of neighbouring *pays*. Of these, Picodon and Pelardon are covered in the Auvergne (Chapter 7), Bleu des Causses, Pérail de Brebis and Roquefort in the Rouerge (Chapter 6).

At Saint-Hippolyte-du-Fort the Fromagerie Cigaloise sells the outstandingly delicious brebis Pérail du Mas Pinel, and a number of chèvres. Other distinctive contributions from the Gard are typified in the appetising range made by Monsieur Van den Haute in his Fromagerie Fermière at La Chafranière, at Saint-André d'Olérargues. This includes small Pérail-like brebis, chèvres with herbs, and larger, well-crusted, cutting *tommes*, both chèvre and mi-chèvre. Some small cheeses made there and some from another farm may be eaten in season at Le Mûrier at Montclus, near the Gorges de la Cèze: an intimate restaurant within ancient walls, featuring local produce and wines. Twenty kilometres south of Montclus, Le P'tit Cohidon is made by the Cohidon family as Lussan. (Within fifteen minutes lies the remarkable duché d'Uzès: see p. 521.) We tasted this little cheese served in the superb olive oil of Maussane, at Le Bistrot des Alpilles in Saint-Rémy-de-Provence. Its succulence and savour took me back to my first experience of eating Mozzarella in this way in Lucania.

The south-eastern corner of Languedoc is part of another world, the Camargue. This extends from the salt pans near Aigues-Mortes (built as a port for Saint-Louis' crusades, the Seventh and Eighth) eastwards over the Petit Rhône into Provence and across the delta to the Grand Rhône, and more salt pans at Salins de Giraud. We have already looked at the ancient breeds of horses and cattle and their *gardians*; but nearly half La Camargo is marsh, pond and lake, teeming with smaller wildlife. Boar (*sanglier*) I have heard, but not seen, in the reedy undergrowth by a bridge where we have often picnicked; but I read in a November 1987 copy of *Le Provençal* of a boar's joining in a football match at Mas Thibert. The boys abandoned the ball and (unsuccessfully) chased the boar.

Vauvert lies north of Aigues-Mortes, by the inland road to Saint-Gilles, on the edge of the Camargue. There, in the bathroom of a flat, René and Josiane Bouet started making their Tomme d'Arles, Le Trident, some years ago, from the milk of their few ewes, using the bath itself as the vat. The walls were covered with waxed cloth, and the windows were sealed: not to exclude the draughts, but to contain the dairy odours which might disturb the neighbours. Monsieur Bouet remarked that his bathroom had become the most modern in the building by the time they left for their present villa, where a big ground-floor room has been made into a well-lit dairy.

His brother was a shepherd with 60 sheep of his own, to which René added 200. In the 1985–6 season they had a hundred merino ewes in milk, yielding in all about 75 litres a day. Their yield is much smaller than that of the Lacaune breed of Central Languedoc and Rouergue (see Chapter 6); but the Bouet family prefer the *mérinos camarguais*, established here for nearly 200 years, which pay for themselves in fat lambs, plus something for the wool.

René Bouet had a brief period of alliance with a large *laiterie* in the Rouergue, when in exchange for the use of his recipe they supplied him with the extra milk he needed. Neither their mass-produced cheeses, nor his own made from the mixed milks, pleased the public. He had to resume his original methods, producing less, but all from his own milk, to win back lost customers. Obviously this experience made him cautious: he pasteurises his milk, which I can only think a pity, and unnecessary in view of the high dairy standards he and his brother set themselves. As he has said himself of his beloved ewes, pastured on the winter herbage of the vine-rich Costières du Gard, their milk is *'superbe, riche, et avec du parfum'*.

The milk is brought to just short of 30°C in winter, raised as the weather warms up to a maximum of nearly 32°C in summer, and given a tiny dose of rennet. Even fractionally higher temperatures would spoil the cheese. As soon as the *caillé* is formed it is placed in the moulds to drain. By early afternoon, so lightly salted that you would not know, it is ready to receive a light powdering of very finely ground thyme and half a bay leaf, and to travel to Fromages d'Arles and other distributors on the northern fringe of the Camargue.

This delicate cheese, the size and proportions of a substantial medal (it weighs 80 grams), has a junket-like consistency. If eaten at once it is wonderfully refreshing but almost tasteless. I think it justifiable to treat it like Mozzarella and add oil and coarsely milled pepper, and sometimes, for variety, the mixture of five different peppers commonly sold now in Provence. If the cheese is kept moist and cool for a few days in its original wrap (to prevent its drying out), it gains in flavour, like Mozzarella. I enjoy it at all its stages, with and without the suggested additions.

South of historic Saint-Gilles at L'Albaron on the Petit Rhône, Madame Galleron makes a raw-milk brebis, Le Gardian, similar to Le Trident in consistency but more substantial and tasty at the *caillé* stage, and becoming rich within a week of making. She also makes a delicious chèvre of Banon size. I tasted these for the first time late in 1987 at Le Mas Teulière at Maussane, near Les Baux, an impressive small restaurant with delightful pictures (the *chef-propriétaire* is also a sculptor).*

Continuing south, but bearing left before Méjanes, we can skirt the Étang de Vaccarès and turn south again for Sambuc.† There La Commanderie has been a *chevrerie* for fifty years, notable for making cheese from the milk of the old long-horned, red-haired breed of Le Rove. (The area of Le Rove, where the goats originated, is an hour away to the east, overlooking the sea near the Marseille end of the Chaîne de l'Estaque.) The sole source of Brousse du Rove is the one surviving *chèvrerie* there, which has unfortunately replaced the native breed with Alpines Chamoisées.

Twelve kilometres north of Sambuc, on a little side-road to Gageron, Monsieur Bernard Cardot makes his Gardian, a brebis of Banon proportions, which starts appearing in November. It is much more substantial in size than Le Trident, salter (but not excessively), with a light, moussey, yet close texture in its first week, tasting both sweet and acid under its topping of chopped *sarriette* and bay leaf. One I had already started in late November kept for another ten days in a hanging cheese-cage. It ripened right through, richly creamy, yet not running away, and glorious in flavour, without sharpness or saltiness. These cheeses bear no individual labels, but are sold in the markets in season as Gardians (for instance by Maison Bleuze at Arles on Saturdays). The season ends with the *transhumance* in early June.

There is one cheese of similar shape, with a printed 'Gardian' label, to be avoided at any price: a pasteurised cows'-milk factory cheese of stodgy consistency and poor flavour from the Dauphiné. I am writing in 1987, and more sophisticated labelling might be adopted for the genuine article before you read this, so be sure to inspect labels carefully before deciding to buy or reject what you are offered.

A similar cheese to the Gageron Gardian, made in several different sizes, is recorded on the list under Arles as Le Camarguais. It is slightly firmer, more like a Banon, and less acid. A mixed brebis–chèvre version is produced towards the end of the brebis season. We have not pinned down its source for certain, but believe it may be a farm in the eastern Camargue whose suspicious *patronne* disapproves of curious visitors, as we discovered while enquiring at her stall in Arles market. (This experience was unique among all our hundreds of exchanges with *fromagers* on their farms and in markets. Some could not cope with visitors on the farm, as I have made clear in those few cases, but all save this one were happy to talk to us about their cheeses.)

Arles market is attended by a number of farmers from the Gard and the Bouches du Rhône, of whom some sell their chèvres alongside honey or other fresh produce. In addition, especially in the enormous Saturday

---

*Mas*, meaning farm, is in general use in the Midi.
†The edge of the Vaccarès beyond Méjanes should be the object of a sunset visit in summer, to watch the bedtime descent of flights of flamingoes on the waters. Vaccarès derives from the Latin (and Italian) *vacca* for cow. The black *camarguais* cattle have always grazed around its edges.

market, there are merchants with a range of national cheeses, usually accompanied by a generous sprinkling of really local chèvres.

Just east of Arles, to the right of the little road from Pont-de-Crau to Fontvieille via Barbegal, Madame Souchal makes Banon-shaped cheeses from the milk of forty-five Saanens, Alpines and 'Communes' (a local crossbreed). She also makes a smaller Cachat, placed in olive oil at the *faisselle* stage with *sarriette*, thyme and pepper. These cheeses are of melting texture, becoming rich at the *demi-sec* stage, with a pink-to-gold crust, and a little salty when *très sec*. This farm is on the edge of La Crau, famous for its abundant and aromatic hay, so the flavour of the cheese is not surprising, nor that of the honey also sold here.

Beyond La Crau, to the east, Aix and Salon-de-Provence are blessed with cheese shops run by the eminent *maître fromager* Gérard Paul and his charming and knowledgeable wife. North of Salon, Monsieur Gérard Nicolino makes a varied range of pleasing chèvres at Alleins, where another *chevrier* makes small *pyramides* with *croûtes-bleutées*. South-east of Salon at Grans, the Vanneyre family make a *brique*, and a chèvre called Le Granouillen, pleasing at the unsalted *caillé* stage and at its later naturally crusted stage of development. At Le Jas des Vaches at Grans, Monsieur Jacques Graillon makes a *tomme* (of cows' milk, naturally).

From Orgon, on the Durance north of Salon, La Chaîne des Alpilles runs west towards Tarascon, finishing at the little chapel of Saint-Gabriel with its naive façade and resonant interior. Under 30 kilometres in length, and only once reaching our conventional mountain height of 1000 feet, the Alpilles earn their name with a rugged alpine appearance and many an unscalable rock-face. Yet this relatively minor range of hills seems to protect the country that lies between its southern slopes and the sea against at least some of the storms from the north. We can sometimes watch them raging beyond the Alpilles around Saint-Rémy, while basking in our sun-favoured micro-climate to the south.

Les Baux makes a fairytale centre for this fairytale landscape. In the twelfth century troubadours flourished here, and romantic tradition insisted that the ruling family of the comté des Baux was descended from the biblical wise man Balthazar. (The family emblem, the Star of Bethlehem, can still be seen on stonework in Les Baux.) It also attracted Dante Alighieri, who is thought to have based his idea of the Inferno on the strange, solid rock landscape of Les Baux. Its appearance has been rendered even more sinister and severe by the seventeenth-century destruction of town and castle as Protestant strongholds, and by the extraction of bauxite for aluminium (discovered and named here in the nineteenth century). Despite its infertile aspect, 'Les-baux [sic] en Provence' was mentioned by Olivier de Serres for the delicacy of its little fourmageons in the sixteenth century.

On the northern slopes of the Alpilles, above Saint-Rémy-de-Provence, lie the partly excavated, Greek-style third century BC remains of Gallo-Roman Glanum and the high-standing mausoleum and triumphal arch from the reign of Augustus. On the same level is the old monastery of Saint-Paul de Mauséole, the hospital where Vincent Van Gogh found comparative calm and a productive painting streak in 1889. (His famous painting *Irises* was done here, and the irises still flourish in the hospital garden.) On their farm, Les Cabanes de Draguignan, Georges and Marie-Paule Ruéda make a close-textured and tasty chèvre of Picodon shape called Le Saint-Remois, and, from the milk of their six cows, La Bûchette Saint-Remoise. I have seen this little cylinder become a succulent dome after being stood on end for a few days. They are on sale in Saint-Rémy at the *fromagerie* in rue Carnot which also sells fresh pasta. (The non-accented Remois is correct for the old northern Saint-Remi or Remy and for these cheeses.)

There are a number of organically managed vineyards around the Alpilles producing wines of notably natural character, admirable as accompaniments for equally natural local cheeses. Le Mas de Gourgonnier near Le Destet, east of Maussane, is one of these. In season it sells a very pleasing young *tome de chèvre* made by Monsieur Basset of Le Jour Blanc at Mouriès, whose goats browse part of the year on the *garrigue* above the vineyard. Across the Alpilles at Terres Blanches, Monsieur Noël Michelin makes his red and white wines of medal-winning quality, aged in oak vats fashioned in the Pyrenees and re-erected in his *caves*. Monsieur Michelin is also a *fromager*. He made Saint-Nectaire *fermier* as cover when a *résistant* during the war. His witness of the deterioration of so much Saint-Nectaire since, because of the adoption of chemical fertilisers and the abandonment of the old Salers breed (see Chapter 7), has reinforced his belief in organic methods (and in traditional breeds of cattle for cheese).

At Mollégès, 5 kilometres away, Monsieur Masson makes an extraordinary range of chèvres shaped as *briques*, *crottins*, *rigottes*, *chapelets* (strings of prayer-beads), cherries, apricots, figs, and birettas (called Cardinals).

A few miles west is Tarascon, renowned for a castle not to be missed, and for two more frivolous reasons: the mythical beast, the Tarasque, tamed by Sainte-Marthe, which parades the town annually; and for Alphonse Daudet's hero, Tartarin de Tarascon. North from Tarascon runs La Montagnette, a *garrigue*-covered mountain, little indeed (it scarcely exceeds 500 feet), and much less rugged than the Alpilles. Tucked into its south-eastern face, the Abbaye de Saint-Michel de Frigolet started in the eleventh century as an airy convalescent retreat for ailing monks from the fever-ridden marshes then surrounding the Abbaye de Montmajour. The white-robed order of Prémontrés acquired the buildings and established a school which became, under Joseph Roumanille, the greatest force in the revival of Provence's language and literature, until suppressed by Jules Ferry's anti-clerical legislation. In 1986 the shop at Frigolet started selling cheese, made from the milk of the *abbaye*'s own herd: small, low-salt chèvres of mousse-like consistency slightly dry on the palate. It is available from late spring to late autumn in two sizes at stages from *frais* and uncrusted to *sec* with *croûte-bleutée*. The *abbaye*'s shop also sells the monastic liqueur called Frigolet, distilled from the flowers of plants on the *garrigue*. This 'élixir' is now made elsewhere for the *abbaye*, but it was first distilled here (see Daudet's imaginative, thirst-making and heart-warming story in *Lettres de Mon Moulin*).

The windmill called Le Moulin de Daudet is the only one in this part of the region to have been restored and given back its sails (though it no longer grinds corn): it is a memorial and museum devoted to Alphonse Daudet. On the solid rock summit of a southern outpost of the Alpilles overlooking Fontvieille, it benefits from thirty-two winds, each with a *provençal* name, most famous among them the Mistral and the Tramountano.

# FONTVIEILLE

As much home for me now as my dear Streatley in Berkshire, Fontvieille is where this book has been shaped and written. Inevitably we finish up here, which is no bad thing.

Fontvieille is a microcosm of traditional Provence; and Provence has long tugged at the heart of so many French from further north, who have sought and found there very much more than just the warmth of the sun. So I shall dwell fondly on Fontvieille to leave you with the final taste of France through a *pays* beloved of French and English, and much older than France herself.

Vincent van Gogh visited Fontvieille in the summer of 1888 and painted a gardener called Patience Escalier, whose boots are probably those in another of his famous works. The painter wrote of Fontvieille to his brother that July: 'The natives are like Zola's poor *paysans*, innocent and gentle beings....' We saw the great 'Van Gogh In Arles' exhibition of the 1980s in New York; not only the pictures, but a film juxtaposing pictures and places. So on our return to Fontvieille we were able to astound our close neighbour and friend Joseph Roumanille (namesake and 'tenth cousin' of the founder-*félibrige*) with the news that in New York we had watched him playing *boules* under the plane trees of Fontvieille.

Joseph is a noted fisherman, and mushroom-hunter in damper weather. His sister is married into the Téna family, well rooted in the local soil and generous with fruit and vegetables in season. Our house once belonged to her brother-in-law who was a *puisatier* at a time when well-diggers were still of vital importance. Madame Téna told us of the customary advice given to any young man looking for his first job on a farm: 'Walk all round the *mas* and inspect *la merde*. If you find great big turds go and work there. If there are only tiny *crottins* don't take the job; it means they won't feed you properly.' 'On va dans les champs' was the brush-off still given to me and many another innocent traveller enquiring for a *toilette* in the country in the 1950s, when little had changed here since Van Gogh's time.

Motors and mopeds have now replaced mules and Shanks's pony, mechanisation has reduced the prospects for employment on the farm. Few of the remaining labourers live in, except in the remoter uplands. Living in such remote conditions (many hamlets lie miles beyond and above the nearest road) is now only for the other-worldly; and for those native survivors of that other world who are still loyal to their inheritance, or have nowhere else to escape to, or no assets on which they can raise the money needed to escape with.

Life in places like Fontvieille has been transformed, but part of the human change has only been the mixture as before. I have already mentioned friends and neighbours of Spanish–Provençal descent in this context. Other friends, of Berrychon, Bourbonnais and Corsican ancestry, have been proud and delighted to share with us their knowledge of, and even the actual cheeses and wines of their *pays d'origine*. Provence goes on attracting, mixing and retaining migrants from all over.

To our west, the Rhône Valley is cultivated from the river to the *garrigue*-covered slopes of the Alpilles, guarded by the eleventh-century chapel of Saint-Gabriel. This lofty little edifice, of a solidity even more indestructible in its look than the rock it stands on, has the most shamefaced Adam and Eve you ever saw on its front, and an astonishing resonance within. Further up is the clean-cut silver masonry of an earlier fortress quarried on the spot. Round the corner from Saint-Gabriel towards Arles, a *mas* with cows and goats makes a refreshing small Brousse de vache and a chèvre. The chèvre is a cylindrical Charollais-like cheese of excellent close consistency, fine interior whiteness and rich flavour. I found both cheeses in the *boucherie* opposite the church in Fontvieille.

Two kilometres down D33, running south-east from Saint-Gabriel along the foot of the Alpilles, on the road to the right called Route Saint-Jean, is the eleventh-century chapel of Saint-Jean du Grès. This was Fontvieille's parish church until the first part of the present church was built in 1695. The parish comes to the old chapel on Saint John's day, 24 June. The Route Saint-Jean and the main road both lead to and cross La Grand' Draille, the timeless, wide sheep-droving route for flocks going up to or descending from the *transhumance*.

On the left of D33, between the Route Saint-Jean and the Grand' Draille, is a section of old carriageway from which a track leads up into the Alpilles between Mont Valence and the flat-topped rock and ruined fort of Mont Paon (*paon* is not peacock here, but Pan). After one kilometre, another rough track leads off into the Vallon des Cabrières on the right, where Monsieur and Madame Jean-Denis Maingé's *élevage caprin* is hidden in a *pinède*. Their first milking begins at 5.30 a.m., so we chose to visit in the late afternoon. In the morning Monsieur Maingé takes his goats, Alpines and a few crossbreds, horned and hornless, up into the *garrigue*, staying with them for half an hour if they are new to the area. Ten to eleven hours later they come down of their own accord to enjoy the hay put out ready for them, and to line up, young ones first, for the evening milking. They spend the day out of doors during eleven months of the year.

It took us nearly a quarter of an hour to drive the 2½ kilometres from the road. Maingé children and other animals were playing in front of the stone house and the goats were at their hay in the *bergerie*. Their *chevrier* is a smiling man in his thirties with copious curly brown hair and beard. As soon as he had put a fistful of barley at the heads of the four stalls on the high milking platform, up jumped the youthful Diana, Barbara, Flora and Léa. With their udders now at his eye-level, he washed their teats with an antiseptic solution, and put the first four or five pulls from each teat in a special pail reserved for the cat. The rest of the milk was strained, given a minimal dose of rennet (at 1/10,000 strength) and a little of the previous day's whey as starter, and left in a cool controlled temperature for twenty-four hours. Young goats yield about 1½ litres each (more than enough for two cheeses), the adults about 2 litres.

The *caillé* from the previous day's milk was then ladled into the moulds. After *démoulage* in the afternoon the new cheeses would be salted very lightly (2 grams per cheese), and left in airy conditions to dry for two days before going into the *cave*. During up to three weeks of *affinage* they would be tasted from time to time for readiness.

Monsieur Maingé tops some of his cheeses with *sarriette* gathered in the *garrigue*, and coats a few in powdered charcoal. The latter are interesting at the *sec* stage when they have acquired a natural coat of blue-mould over their *cendres*. Others, as *tomes fraîches*, he puts in olive oil with *sarriette*, rosemary and bay leaves, to sell at three to four weeks as Le Garrigou. La Calèche, the fish restaurant at Saint-Rémy, serves this version (alternating it with a *chevrotine* from the Vivarais), as Le Cigalon. These cheeses are delicious, in the *tome fraîche, demi-sec, sec*, and 'Garrigou' states, as is the fresh Brousse made with some of the whey.

Over the brow of the hill from Le Vallon des Cabrières at the foot of the Alpilles lie the vineyards of the Château d'Estoublon, source of a substantial red wine and, until 1979, of an excellent full-flavoured dry white, which kept for years. With wise friends I have been spinning out the last bottles of that fine year to accompany especially worthy fish well into 1987, and praying that it may not after all be the last white made at Estoublon. A deplorable southern fashion of drinking red or rosé with everything has swept away this and other good whites of the Midi. I find myself wanting a sole *meunière* more than anything else in a restaurant, but am deprived because there is nothing fit to drink with it. *Soupe de poisson*, which I love, and some other Mediterranean seafood and fish dishes go well with red wine; but the best and simplest ways of serving the finest fish cry out for a good white wine.

Between Estoublon and Fontvieille grow all the fruits in season, including the locally owned olives from which Monsieur Henri Bellon, our *Maire* for many years, makes part of his superbly aromatic medal-winning *huile d'olive extra-vièrge*. In this section of Fontvieille, on La Grand' Draille near its crossing with the Route Saint-Jean, are the farms of another family of *chevriers*, Nicolle *père et fils*, Mas de Musareigne and La Mourredonne. Two of their cheeses are much larger than Monsieur Maingé's. Le Gaudre, a striated inverted tub of 220 grams (made in small Brousse basket-moulds) reminds me of Romans (see Chapter 16) in its close texture and rich flavour, though a Romans *pur chèvre* is a rarity these days. It is matured for only two weeks on wood, but its character comes from its size and slow *égouttage*; two *faisselles* of curd are combined after seventy-two hours of drainage. Le Moka is a kilo version kept for a month. Le Gaudriole is a small cheese sold *en faisselle*, good for keeping and eating in olive oil.

Ancient and modern lines of communication run parallel here: the old sheep-droving route, La Grand' Draille, and the railway from Arles. The railway used to serve villages beyond Fontvieille as far as Salon, but was cut after the Second World War. It features in Van Gogh's *Landscape near Montmajour with Train*. *Le petit train* was kept up between Arles and Fontvieille by amateur enthusiasts until about 1980, but the line now serves only the Ministry of Defence depot on the edge of Fontvieille, and the local *berger* who uses it as another *draille*. I was surprised to meet him and his canine *bergers* moving along the railway with their sheep and their dramatically long- and twirling-horned golden goats one June evening; when I asked why he had not left for the *transhumance* he said he would be gone in a few days. A road-transporter was booked to take his flock all the way except the last few rough kilometres of the journey, saving all but a day of the three weeks that used to be needed on foot. Unfortunately, any cheese he makes is reserved for himself and his team.

If you want to be sure of enjoying the spectacle of flocks ready for the *transhumance*, go to Saint-Rémy on a Whit Monday. Hundreds of sheep with shepherds of all ages (down to proud eleven- and fifteen-year-olds when I last watched) parade with their *bergers* dogs, their handsome chestnut goats with enormous curly horns, and their donkeys, pack-saddled and drawing a cart. The most eye-catching animals are the *tintinajos*, the magnificent bell-wethers, leaders of the flocks, with wonderfully tailored woollen tussocks on their backs to mark their regal rank.

South of the railway and the road to Maussane and Les Baux are the modern quarries. They are sadly under-used now that breeze-block and artificial stone come so far and so cheap. The ancient quarries were in Fontvieille itself, so ancient that they provided stone for the Pont du Gard and the arenas at Arles and Nîmes. The houses on the old, winding, now rather backstreet Grand' Rue, and in our little impasse called rue de Maître Cornille, were built in the worked-out sections. Houses on the north side of these roads often have the quarry-face as their back walls, or are cut right into the rock, genuine *maisons troglodytes*. Above them tower the houses atop the rock-face, on the street called Corniche des Blocs, which speaks for itself.

To the south-west, near the still-used public wash-house and now rather crowded by a new housing development, is the old spring, *la vieille font*, which gave Fontvieille its name. Closer to the Avenue de Montmajour is the fourteenth-century Tour Pierre de Canilhac, built by the abbot of that name as an outpost of Montmajour, to which a later abbot added the *château*. Across the main road to Arles from the avenue is the rue Saint-Victor with ruins of the Saint-Victor chapel, centre of a peasant and fishing community before the marshes between there and Arles were drained by the monks.

Nearer Montmajour are five neolithic *hypogées*, tumuli up to 50 metres long in the Waylands' Smithy style, but larger. One is on the rocky eminence north-west of the road, where Le Castellet stands. This was the heart of an ancient *baronnie* rich in quarries, with a *château* and chapel largely destroyed in the fourteenth century when most of the quarrying moved to Fontvieille. In those days the Abbaye de Montmajour, on its own bigger eminence beyond, was surrounded by marsh and water, communicating with Arles by punt (and with La Tour at Fontvieille by tunnel, it is said).

Subsequent drainage and controlled irrigation notwithstanding, heavy rains can restore that mediaeval look of the landscape, and in normal conditions rice flourishes beside the road to Arles, and trout are farmed on the edge of La Crau to the south.

Turning back on the Crau side of the road, rocky outcrops increase in size towards the extensive hill above Fontvieille. The road south of the hill is crossed by a Roman aqueduct, which leads to another ridge, where the aqueduct forks. One channel veers off to the right (originally to supply Arles with water); the other leads straight on, cutting through the solid rock crest of the ridge. Its water used to cascade down the slope on the far side in a steep, stepped mill stream to turn a succession of water-wheels powering a series of hillside mills grinding corn. This Meunerie de Barbegal is recorded as the largest water-powered factory in the Roman Empire.

Coming back over the big hill towards Fontvieille, you can see great distances over La Crau, the Camargue and the Rhône Valley from the top. Below Daudet's windmill stand the bare stone towers of three other mills, and to the right the well-wooded grounds of the Château de Montauban. Before they were tidied up by the *commune*, we twice saw a lizard well over a metre long descending the outer park wall. This was where Alphonse Daudet stayed with friends and absorbed the local lore and names from which he compiled his *Lettres de Mon Moulin*. Cornille and Seguin (and his goat), for instance, were real characters, not just names on tombstones (or, now, on street corners). Their families live in Fontvieille today.

Daudet liked rough local wine that rasped his tongue, and with it cheese on the ripe side, *'un peu fait'*, in his words. This was the understatement of a lifetime, put right in the description that followed: *'"une horreur"*, as the ladies say, when it is brought in *"odorant et terrible"'*. He would have appreciated the deeply rich and succulent Pélardons from Anduze in the Gard, served today in Fontvieille at L'Amistodouso. He would have loved their fresh herbs gathered in the *garrigue*, their superb *soupe au pistou*, and their lively local wines too.

The local chèvres on sale in the Friday market would need longer keeping to suit Daudet, but they stand up to being aged to taste in a *garde-manger* hung in the shade. Monsieur Maingé sells his own cheeses there (and sometimes in Fontvieille's Monday market too), and the Nicolle cheeses are sold on Fridays by the charming and knowledgeable Philippe and Dany from Salon. They have other regional *chèvres*, and make periodic journeys to collect Saint-Nectaire *fermier*, Beaufort Haute-Montagne and other treasures for their well-judged national range of French cheeses. (Occasionally, when we happen to have returned from Streatley by ferry and road, they are able to offer a twelve- to eighteen-month Somerset farmhouse Cheddar.)

There is a good *pâté* and sausage stall, and a fish stall run in partnership with the fishermen themselves. Several large fruit and vegetable stalls offer almost everything imaginable; but we treasure a small smiling *paysan* of Italian extraction whose own produce includes delectable old-fashioned tomatoes, tiny potatoes, and purple figs in their respective seasons.

Apart from its markets, Fontvieille has five bakers, two *pâtissiers*, and three *bouchers–charcutiers*. Of the latter, it is Monsieur René Aumède who sells the Saint-Gabriel chèvre and Brousse, and also the brebis *gardian* called Le Trident.

Fontvieille has its own arena and four cafés. On a normal, sunny day, after you have bought your local chèvres and brebis, and any further cheeses or other food that smells good, take them to the Café du Cours opposite the Poste, where they offer that public service once (but no longer) common in France: *'Ici on reçoit avec ses provisions.'* So you can sit down with your food at an outside table, under the plane trees, near the *boules* ground, and order whatever you want to drink. On summer days and holidays you may sniff a savoury breeze from the kebab and pizza wagon a few yards off. If this tempts you to an extra unplanned course, you will not be disappointed. It may come home to you, as you enjoy your picnic in this agreeable old French fashion, that Fontvieille is indeed an amalgam of so much that is best in Provence and in the old royaume de France beyond.

## Cheeses of Provence and Eastern Languedoc

### Abbaye de Frigolet
See FRIGOLET.

### Aix-en-Provence
Tuesday, Thursday and Saturday market. Gérard Paul, *Maître fromager*, 9 rue des Marseillais, tel. 42 23 16 84; fine national range; expert on Haute-Provence; also has shop in Salon (see p. 519).
Coteaux d'Aix Commanderie de la Bargemone: red and white wines of character and substance.
Bouches-du-Rhône; 84 **3**, 93 **13**.

### L'Albaron
**Chèvre.** Banon-sized cheese with sprig of *sarriette*; *frais*: loose texture yet substantial cheese with attractive sweet-rich flavour (see ARLES, LE GARDIAN).
*fermier; chèvre cru.*
Camargue/Bouches-du-Rhône; 83 **9**, on D570 and Petit Rhône.

### Alleins
**Les Amours de la Tambarlette (round, plain and au Poivre); Bûche; Brique; Cœur.** Round is size and shape of Banon; *frais*: soft, white, rich, pleasing not sharp; *demi-sec* to *sec*: crust towards golden; melt-in-mouth; flavour rich, slightly bitter edge. Plain or pepper-coated.
*Bûche* is about 100g; *frais*: very soft, but not runny, pleasant and admirably low salt level.
*Brique*: small double-cube (about 4cm square section); white mould-coat.
*Cœur*: succulent; beautiful blue-mould coat. All made by Gérard Nicolino, 13980 Alleins, who was given his first recipes by a local shepherd; all refreshing with admirably low salt level, from milk of his *Alpines chamoisées*.
45% m.g.; *fermier; chèvre cru.*

**Pyramides Cendrées, Bleutées.** 150g cheeses made on another farm near Alleins.
*fermier; chèvre cru.*
Bouches-du-Rhône; 84 **2**, L of C on D17D, S of R. Durance.
See also Lamanon (6km W) for another good *chèvre fermière*.

### Alpes de Haute-Provence
See ANNOT, BANON, BARCELONNETTE, LA BRÉOLE, CACHEIA, CACHEILLE, CASTELLANE (with SÉRANON), LE CHAFFAUT, ST-VINCENT-SUR-JABRON, CHÂTEAU ARNOUX, LOU CROUSTIGNOU, DIGNE, FORCALQUIER, MANOSQUE, SISTERON, UBAYE.

### Alpes, Hautes-
See GAP, and Chapter 16.

### Alpes-Maritimes
See ANTIBES, BAIROLS, BROU, BROUS, BROUSSE, CAGNES, CAILLÉ, CANNES, CLAQUERET CANNOIX, GORBIO, GRASSE, ISOLA, MERVEILLES,

NICE, PEYMEINADE, ROURE, ST-ÉTIENNE-DE-TINÉE, ST-JEANNET, ST-MARTIN-VÉSUBIE, ST-SAUVEUR-SUR-TINÉE, SOSPEL, TENDE, LA TINÉE, LA TURBIE, VALBERG, VALDEBLORE, VALBONNE, VENCE.

Amours de la Tambarlette

See ALLEINS.

Anduze

**Pélardons pur Chèvre.** Plain, peppered and herb-coated, made by M. Postolle in nearby village; and see PÉLARDON and FONT-VIEILLE.
*fermier; chèvre cru.*
Gard; 80 **17**.

Annot or Tomme d'Annot

600–1000g; 16–22cm × 4–5cm deep; semi-soft, pressed; natural brushed crust; at its best comparable with Beaufort (see Chapter 15, pp. 428–9) in consistency; gentle flavour, but not dull. I enjoyed the Chèvre version in the 1960s at Annot. Androuët failed to find any on his 1982 tour and lately I have not heard of anything nearer than Puget-Théniers (see p. 487). Near-by St-Benoît, 4km to E on N202, has Tuesday market, with an American *chevrier* (autumn 1987).
45–55% m.g.; *fermier; brebis/chèvre/mélange cru.*
Alpes-de-Haute-Provence; 81 **18**, upper R.

**Fromage de Chèvre.** Ingrid and Bernard de Brabanter make cheese at Les Gastres, Les Scaffarels, 04240 Annot, tel. 92 83 27 86.
*fermier; chèvre cru.*
SE of Annot, junction of D908 and N202.

Antibes

Greek Antipolis at least as far back as the fifth century BC. Market Tuesday (best) to Sunday inclusive. L'Étable, *fromagerie*, 1 rue Sade (attention to regional chèvres and brebis from Corsica).
Alpes-Maritimes; 84 **9**.

Apt

Saturday market.

**Brique Cendrée, Chevrachu, Tomes de Chèvre Fermières.** 180g brique; 250g (deep Banon-shape) Chevrachu; 100g flat *tomes; affinées* by Société Coopérative Agricole des Monts-de-Vaucluse, c/o Maison de l'Agriculture, avenue des Druides, Apt; I found medium-ripe specimens rather salty.
45% m.g.; *fermier; chèvre cru.*
Vaucluse; 81 **14**, lower L.

Arles

Fifth-century Roman capital; tenth-century kingdom of Arles.
Wednesday market, with some farm *chevriers*, remarkable for vegetables and herbs; Saturday market bigger. Look for cheese stall run by the two brothers Bleuze. Arles Fromages, 40 rue des Porcelets (closed Monday).

**Arles, Tomme d', Tomme Arlésienne, Camargue, Tomme de, Le Gardian.** All these names have been used over the years for small brebis (round, or log with triangular section) made in or around the Camargue (see p. 492). They are usually eaten in the salted *fromage blanc* stage. They often have a fine powdering of thyme or sariette and a bay leaf (*laurier*) on top. The surviving or recently current examples I know follow.
*artisanal; brebis.*

**Le Camarguais pur Brebis.** 125g, 250g, 500g round (Banon-shape) deep, with slightly scalloped edge round the top, which is covered with *sariette* (savory) and *laurier*; these cheeses are soft and sweet, eaten at the *fromage frais* stage. Source in Camargue not identified.
*artisanal; brebis.*
Bouches-du-Rhône.

**Le Camarguais Mélange Brebis-Chèvre.** 250g, 10cm × 2.5cm deep; 500g, 15cm × 6cm deep; topped with *sariette* and *laurier; fromage frais*: source as for *pur brebis* above.
*artisanal; brebis/chèvre/mélange.*
Bouches-du-Rhône, 83 **10**.

**Chèvre (L'Albaron).** Mme Galleron at L'Albaron in Camargue makes a fine chèvre of *banon* size with a sprig of *sariette*; at *frais* stage, loose texture, yet substantial cheese.
*chèvre fermier; cru.*

**Le Gardian (L'Albaron).** Thick medallion; in almost unsalted *caillé* state (junket-like); topped with finely chopped rosemary, *sariette*, thyme, and a whole small bay leaf; refreshing and tasty. After

3-4 days, the cheese has drained to ⅔ size and is rich (both tasted December 1987). Also made by Mme Galleron at L'Albaron.
*fermier; brebis cru.*
Camargue/Bouches-du-Rhône; 83 **9**, on D570 and Petit Rhône.

## Camargue

**Le Gardian.** Banon form, 7cm × 2cm deep; *fromage frais;* topped with *sarriette* and a bay leaf; close texture; sweet and acid flavour; made by Bernard Cardot, near Gageron in Camargue (see p. 494). Season: November–May; sheep in *transhumance* June–September. Sold in Arles Saturday market by Maison Bleuze (tasted November 1987); the cheese's name has been misappropriated by a *laiterie* in the Dauphiné, for an undistinguished cows'-milk cheese, so look for the brebis label.
*fermier; artisanal; brebis cru.*
Bouches-du-Rhône; 83 **10**, 7km S of Arles by D36, D36B.

**Le Trident.** About 80g; round, flat, medallion; lightly renneted, almost unsalted *fromage blanc* (almost junket-like at first); topped with finely powdered thyme and a half-leaf of *laurier;* refreshing consistency, but almost flavourless at youngest stage; (they are delivered to *fromagers* on the afternoon of their day of making); natives may eat them with anchovy and olive oil. Extra herbs, crushed pepper, or the five assorted peppers of Provence make an agreeable accompaniment if more strength is wanted. The cheese acquires more richness within a few days, but (like Mozzarella) it needs to be kept cool and moist, or in olive oil. Made by René and Josiane Bouet on the edge of the Camargue at Vauvert in the Gard. René's brother is *berger.* Limited production starts after the first lambs have been weaned in early October, with only enough for local consumption until the end of that month, and continues until early summer.
The sheep are of the old Merinos d'Arles or Camarguais breed, good for wool and meat. They only produce ¾ litre of milk a day, but it is very rich, and redolent of their natural herb-strewn grazing.
*fermier; brebis pasteurisé.*
Gard; 83 **8**, far R off N572.
This is sometimes sold as Tomme de Camargue.

## Avignon

City of Popes 1309 to 1376 (and in papal possession until 1793). Pope John XXII established the vineyards at Châteauneuf-du-Pape. A city to wander in, not drive through; park against *Remparts* near Pont St-Bénézet (*Le* Pont d'Avignon).
Markets: covered Halles Centrales, place Pie 7.00–12.00 daily except Friday (17.00–19.00) and Monday (closed). Outdoor: Tuesday, Wednesday (La Rocade), Thursday (St-Jean), Friday (Monclar), Saturday and Sunday (Remparts).
*Fromagers*: Fromagerie Ranc, 50 rue Bonneterie (closed 12.30–16.00) and Halles Centrales (good national range and local farm cheeses, including Brebis, Pérail Fermier). Mme Jacqueline Hortail, Halles Centrales and street markets has *cave* near Rhône, and matures her Roquefort there in natural conditions for extra months.
Wholesale distributor: Schoepfer, SA, since 1798, label Rochebrune (includes good Tomme de Savoie (*lait cru*), *zone industrielle* (tel. 90 88 19 53).
Restaurant: Hiély, 5 rue de la République (first floor); impeccable service and food, including cheese from Ranc (see above); M. Hiély manages to be a fine chef and a warm host.
Local cheesemakers: see LE PONTET, PUJAUT.
Vaucluse; 81 **11/12**.

## Bagnols-sur-Cèze

Wednesday market including farm chèvres; good restaurant with knowledge of (and serving) local cheese at Monclus, 20km to NW, S off D980 (including cheeses below).

**Chèvre au Poivre et au Thym.** About 200g upstanding cylinder; soft, white interior, coat of pepper and thyme over crust developing blue-black mould; delicious, and not over-strong.
See also ISSIRAC, PONT-ST-ESPRIT, ST-ANDRÉ-D'OLÉRARGUES (where above cheeses are made), and ST-CHRISTOL.
*artisanal; chèvre cru.*

**Le Magnum.** 200g flat drum; made like Pélardon (see p. 516); coated with rosemary and *sarriette*, under which the crust becomes golden (appearing to be washed, but not so); rich.
*artisanal; chèvre cru.*
Gard; 80 **10**.

## Bairols, Tomme de Bairols

Variably sized, flat, round; pressed; natural, clean crust; 2–3 months in cool, humid *cave*; semi-soft to hard, according to age; light aroma of chèvre or brebis; flavour tending towards sharpness (*Livre d'Or*, Sept 1984); chèvre April–November, brebis winter to early summer (see TINÉE).
m.g. non-précisée; artisanal; chèvre/brebis cru.
Comté-de-Nice/Alpes-Maritime; 81 **20**, N of C, by D56, N of D2205.

## Banon

Tuesday (special) and Saturday markets, with local chèvres; traditional market which gave its name to the cheese described below, made now in the area Haute-Provence, Comtat, Tricastin and southern Dauphiné.
Alpes-de-Haute-Provence; 81 **14/15**, high.

**Banon.** About 100g; made by Jacky Tourré at Bellecombe (labelled Fromage Fermier des Préalpes Drômoises); light consistency for a Banon, but delicious; sold by Ranc (see AVIGNON), who coat some in *sarriette* (*pèbre d'aï*).
m.g. non-précisée; fermier; chèvre cru.
Dauphiné/Drôme; 81 **3**, far R of C on D162.

**Banon, Banon à la Feuille, Banon d'Or.** Ancient cheese of the region, originally a brebis; 60–120g (according to age); plump with rounded edges, about 7.5cm diameter, 2.5cm deep; soft; but firmer than most chèvres of Midi; wrapped, after 2–3 weeks' cool, dry *affinage*, in chestnut leaves (made supple by soaking in vinegar, wine or *eau-de-vie*) kept in place by raffia; goldening and natural blueing of crust will occur in time; plastic wraps applied by some *laiteries* should be removed at once.
45% m.g. min.; fermier; laitier; industriel; chèvre cru; vache/chèvre pasteurisé.

**Banon de Banon (Banon à la Feuille).** Made with rennet; 60g when wrapped, after 2–3 weeks in *salle d'affinage*, in chestnut leaves dipped in *eau-de-vie*; M. Romain Ripert explains the choice of leaf (common to many parts of France for wrapping chèvres): chestnut leaves resist the acid in the residue of whey exuded by any cheese. Banons form only 10% of his daily production (from about 1500 litres of milk, most of it collected from local chevriers, the rest from his own 60 *chèvres*); his other cheeses are:
1. Bûchette de Banon. Small, slim log, hand-rolled on straw mat; invented here in 1980s; *affinée* like Banon, but uncovered, except for a tiny sprig of *sarriette*.
45% m.g.; artisanal; chèvre cru.
2. Tome de Chèvre Fraîche. Small soft lactic cheese with a sprig of *sarriette* (but distinct from Banon au Poivre d'Âne or Pèbre d'Aï, see below), dispatched to the trade after 3 days.
45% m.g.; artisanal; chèvre cru.
M. Ripert made cows'-milk cheese in Morocco, near Fez before settling in this chèvre region in the middle 1960s in his early thirties. His cheeses are well made, but a little on the salt side for my taste. His farm shop (8.30–12.30, 15.00–19.00 1 Apr–30 Nov) gives tastes before you buy. When the *mistral* blows cheeses dry quickly and turn golden; at other times slowing drying-out encourages a blue surface.
New: 1989 MASCARÉ (*chevre-brebis*); 1990 LA FÉDO (*brebis*).
Alpes-de-Haute-Provence; 81 **14/15**, high; from Banon, S by D51, after crossing small bridge, second turn to left.

**Banon à l'Ancienne.** 1. As formerly kept for winter use in *eau-de-vie* with pepper, thyme, cloves, and bay leaves in sealed jars. Olive oil is more often used today and the five peppers may be included in the jar to good effect; the cheeses so treated in shops now are usually Rigottes (cows' milk), but some *chevriers* have taken to preserving their *tomes* in this way (see BOSSONS MACÉRÉS, FONTVIEILLE).
2. Washed in *eau-de-vie* or marc after drying, then wrapped in chestnut leaves soaked in the same liquor, tied with raffia and placed in pots to ferment, taking 10–15 days to start softening again.
artisanal; chèvre/vache cru.

**Banon Mi-Chèvre, Vache.** About 100g, wrapped in golden chestnut leaves; *vache*: generous size; perfect consistency, rich smoky-leafy flavour; *mi-chèvre*: agreeable flavour; labelled 'S.P.F.'
artisanal; chèvre/vache or vache cru.
Vaucluse; 61 **12**, R, 6km S of Carpentras.

**Banon au Poivre d'Âne or Pèbre D'Aï.** *Poivre d'âne*, donkey's pepper, is the translation of *pèbre d'aï*, the Provençal name for *sarriette* (English savory, Latin *satureia*). This herb is abundant in the *garrigue*, the typical wild Provençal landscape, and has probably been used for coating or decorating banons (before *affinage*) and *tomes fraîches* for nearly as long as cheese has been made there. It is applied to the banon after the cheese has been drained and dried. With longer keeping a blue mould will envelop crust and herb, but the interior of the cheese will remain white until it is near the hard stage.

The term *poivre d'âne* has also been used for *romarin* (which derives from rosmarinus, *rosée de la mer*, dew from the sea), but this is incorrect. It should only be used for *sarriette*, and most *chevriers* in Provence use the native term, *pèbre d'aï* for the herb.

*fermier; artisanal; chèvre cru.*

**Banons pur Chèvre.** Made on farm serving La Bonne Étape (see CHÂTEAU-ARNOUX).
*fermier; chèvre cru.*
Alpes-de-Haute-Provence; 81 **16**.

**Banons au Cumin, au Curry, au Paprika, au Poivre, au Romarin, aux Fines Herbes, aux Herbes Provençales.** Nearly all the cheeses so coated are made by *laitiers*, not in Provence but in the Dauphiné, from cows' milk; sometimes pleasant, but not true banons.
*laitier; vache pasteurisé.*

### BARBENTANE

Charming place; shop 'Fruits, Légumes, Fromages, Oeufs, Boissons' with chèvres, including Cœur from Drôme (see Chapter 16, pp. 452–3).
Bouches-du-Rhône; 80 **20**, S of Rhône-Durance junction.

### BARCELONNETTE

Town founded 1231 by the Count of Barcelona, Raimond Béranger, who was *Comte* de Provence. Wednesday and Saturday market, including farm cheesemakers: the pressed Tomme de l'Ubaye comes from the river valley near here (see UBAYE).

**Tomes Fraîches.** Made by La Coopérative Laitière de la Vallée de Barcelonnette and compared by them with Brousse du Rove (see p. 508).
*laitier; vache pasteurisé.*

**Raclette.** Started in 1986 with investment of 1.5m FF in new dairy and *salle d'affinage* by same *coopérative*.

*laitier; vache pasteurisé.*
Alpes-de-Haute-Provence; 81 **8**.

### LES BAUX

Semi-troglodyte town crowning Alpilles; visit in evening or out of season. See p. 495. Noted for the delicacy of its little *fourmageons* (see FONTVIEILLE, SAINT-RÉMY).
Bouches-du-Rhône; 80 **20**, bottom R, 81 **11/12**, bottom, 83 **10**, R of C.

### BEAUCAIRE

Thursday and Sunday market; within reach are Remoulins, Tarascon, Fontvieille.

**Le Petit Sixtois.** Tome de Chèvre made by M. A. Monory, route de la Brasserie (tel. 90 59 27 33).
45% m.g.; *artisanal; chèvre cru.*
Languedoc/Gard; 81 **11**, low L.

### BEAUMES-DE-VENISE

Source of remarkable dessert wine; and of the chèvre, Li Cabro des Dentelles (see CABRO).
Vaucluse; 81 **12**, top R.

### BERGÈRE

See BROUSSE DE BREBIS.

### LE BICHOU DES CÉVENNES

Tiny bell-shaped cheese, 2.5cm across 'mouth', 1.5cm at top, with six slightly scalloped sides, impaled on end of toothpick; bright white interior, delicious, almost unsalted, of melting texture; made in the Gard (variants are made in the Vivarais, so this cheese is also mentioned in Chapter 7, p. 230).
*artisanal; chèvre cru.*
E. Languedoc/Gard.

### BLEU DES CAUSSES

See Chapter 6, p. 194. The part of the Gard bordering Aveyron is within the AOC region for this cheese.

### BODON, DOMAINE DE

Drôme, see Chapter 16, pp. 452–3. *Fromages de chèvre et de vache* are deservedly on widespread sale in Provence. Their source is near Romans in the Drôme.

### BOLLÈNE

Monday market, cheese, and daily market

for *primeurs* (fruit and veg.) (Pont-St-Esprit is 9km to W). Monday: classic market day.
Vaucluse; 81 **1**.

BOSSONS

Courtine records attributions of origin of name to a hamlet on the edges of Chamonix (not in my gazetteer or post code) but places the cheese now in the Alpilles. He thinks the result 'abominable' but has been unlucky. Basic cheese is freshly strained curd (chèvre) still in ball in its cloth; it is sometimes termed Cachat (see PONT DE CRAU), but Cachat is more commonly used to mean the *fromage fort*.

**Bossons Macérés.** Chèvres kept sometimes for months, in pots or jars of white wine, spirits or olive oil, with aromatic herbs and spices (e.g. today, five different kinds of peppercorn); see BANON À L'ANCIENNE, FROMAGE FORT DU MONT VENTOUX.
*chèvre cru.*
Alpilles/Bouches-du-Rhône.

BOUCHES-DU-RHÔNE

See AIX, ALLEINS, ARLES (including GARDIAN, CAMARGUAIS, TRIDENT), BARBENTANE, LES BAUX, BOSSONS, BROUSSE DU ROVE, CAMARGUE, LA CRAU, FONTVIEILLE (including GARRIGOU, GAUDE, GAUDRIOLE), GRANOUILLEN, JOUQUES, MARSEILLE, MÉRILAIT, MOLLÉGÈS, MOURIÈS, NOVES, LA PALETTE, LE PARADOU, PÉLISSANE, PEYROLLES, PONT-DE-CRAU, RAPHÈLE, ROVE, ST-RÉMY, SALON, LE SAMBUC, TARASCON.

BREBIS

See ANNOT, ARLES (TOMME D'ARLES, ARLÉSIENNE, CAMARGUAISE, GARDIAN, TRIDENT), AVIGNON (Ranc), BAIROLS, BANON, LA CHAFRANIÈRE, GRASSE (La Fromagère), PÉRAIL (including CIGALOIS, ST HIPPOLYTE-DU-FORT), PEYROLLES, PLAN-DE-LA-TOUR, TENDE, VALBERG.

LA BRÉOLE

**Fromages de Vache, de Chèvre.** Made by Richard and Nicole Pigelet at Le Forest, 04560 La Bréole, and sold there (tel. 92 85 52 89 before visiting), and on markets at Barcelonette (Wed), Gap (Sat).
*fermier; biologique; Nature & Progrès; vache/chèvre cru.*
Alpes-de-Haute-Provence; 81 **7**, S of lac, on D900B.

BRIGNOLES

Wednesday and Saturday (better) market.
Early April *foire aux vins*.
Var; 84 **15**.

**Fromage de Chèvre.** 1. Approx 100g; chubby log; soft; no crust; made at Fromagerie du Cazamy, Domaine St-Christophe, 83176 Brignoles.
*45% m.g.; fermier; chèvre cru.*
Var; 84 **15**.
2. Made by M. Priori on Domaine de Combecure, Cabasse; sold on farm and at market Plan-de-la-Tour (see p. 517).
*fermier; chèvre cru.*
Var; 84 **15**, 14km E from Brignoles by N7 and D79.

BRIQUE

See ALLEINS, GRANS, ISSIRAC and MOLLÉGÈS.

**Brique.** Small, thick rectangular *brique*, topped with herbs made by small dairy near Valréas.
*laitier; artisanal; lait de mélange (vache/chèvre).*
Valréas/Vaucluse; 81 **2**.

LOU BROUS, OR BROU DE MONTAGNE

Described by Jacques Médecin (eternal *Maire de Nice*) as an explosive mixture: any handy *caillés* (brebis, chèvre, vache) in layers of a covered terrine interspersed with layers of chopped garlic, pepper and local *eau-de-vie*. It is (or was) eaten 'when the maggots started to enliven it', grilled on toast (grilling dispersed the maggots). The upper Vallée de la Tinée was still a stronghold in the 1970s. Known in Piedmont. See also BROUSSIN.
*domestique; brebis/chèvre/vache.*
Comté de Nice/Alpes-Maritimes; 84 **19 20**.

BROUSSE

Traditionally made after cheesemaking from Petit-lait (whey) or from skimmed milk, the remaining fats, casein and other solids being separated by raising the temperature (whence *recuite*, *ricotta*, meaning recooked), sometimes with the help of a minute quantity of vinegar: as coagulation occurs the whey is lightly beaten or brushed (*broussé*, whence Brousse) to bring the solids to the surface to be skimmed off (it is not salted). Brousse (today mostly made from cows' milk) often includes a large proportion of whole milk (e.g. Brousse Fraîche, see below, of 50% m.g.). Brousse made of *petit lait de brebis* (which has no head of cream, but evenly distributed fine fat globules) could have as much as 30% m.g., Brousse de Chèvre rather less, but, as can be seen below, the Provençal way has been to include enough whole milk to raise the percentage of fat to 45% m.g. or more. Brousse de Brebis appears in late winter and spring, Brousse de Chèvre in late spring and summer, Brousse de Vache all year round.

The old farmhouse method placed the first skimming of solids in muslin to drain in a glazed earthenware strainer with three feet. It was then beaten again and placed in muslin-lined baskets or pierced iron moulds to drain a second time. These recipients gave it its final form (Italian Ricotta has always been moulded in baskets). Baskets are usually plastic now making a less satisfying mark and shape.

Brousse may be eaten with sugar, sprinkled with orange flower water. It was reputed to make children sleep and be good. It was also eaten at midday with oil, vinegar, garlic, herbs and onion.

**La Bergère.** 500g and larger cutting cheese made by Société Fromagère de Saint-Georges-de-Luzencon (see Chapter 6, p. 197).
20–30% m.g.; *laitier; artisanal; brebis cru*.

**Brousse de Brebis.** See GRASSE, La Fromagerie, for whom a local *berger* makes it.

**Brousse de Chèvre Fermier.** See FONT-VIEILLE (Lé Vallon des Cabrières).

**Brousse Fraîche.** 350g, tub-shaped, sold by Fromagerie Tortora of Aix; sold under the name Tortora, but I am told that most of their cheeses are imported from Italy.
50% m.g.; *laitier; vache*.
Aix-en-Provence; Bouches-du-Rhône; 84 **3**, 93 **13**.

**Le Brousse du Rove.** 60g thin cone, *faisselle* stage, one maker. The arrival of Brousse du Rove used to be the subject of street cries and trumpet calls in Marseille, 'Lei Brousse dé Rové' still heard up to Second World War. Source: Gilbert Gouivan et Fils (André), avenue du Logis Neuf, Le Rove. (Gilbert's father was one of the street-criers). The traditional breed (La Rove) has sadly given way to Alpines Chamoisées (but see RAPHÈLE, SAMBUC).

**Brousse de Sospel.** By-product of Tomme de Sospel.
*fermier; vache cru*.
Comté-de-Nice/Alpes-Maritimes; 84 **19 20**, C.

**Brousse de Tende.** 500–700g, stocked by La Fromagerie, Grasse (see p. 513) which sells Caillé and Brebis de Tende from the same farm, November to July (Nov 1987). A Brousse made by a *chevrier* was found by Ninette Lyon above the Col de Tende in the 1970s.
*fermier; chèvre/brebis cru*.
Comté-de-Nice/Alpes-Maritimes; 84 **10**, bottom on N204.

**Brousse de Vache.** 2–2.5kg rectangular block made in Provence.
*laitier; vache pasteurisé*.

**Brousse de Valberg.** No longer in evidence.
*fermier; brebis cru*.
Alpes-Maritimes; 81 **9 19**, C.

**Brousse de Valdeblore.** By-product of local Tomme.
*fermier; vache*.
Comté-de-Nice/Alpes-Maritimes; 84 **18 19**, top.

**Brousse de la Vésubie.** This Brousse was sometimes preserved in terrines with garlic, pepper and salt. I am told that it is no longer made, but Tommes de Vache survived in the 1980s (see ST-MARTIN-VÉSUBIE).
45% m.g.; *fermier; artisanal; brebis/chèvre cru*.
Comté-de-Nice/Alpes-Maritimes; 84 **19**, top.

LE BROUSSIN DU VAR

Made from cheese leftovers soaked in gnaule (*eau-de-vie*) in sealed pots. Ninette Lyon says that to keep off fly and discourage maggots *paysans* use foul-smelling '*feuilles d'une espèce de noyer*' (hickory?). They press it on toast, grill this over the fire: 'It makes a man of you.' (and see BROU).

BÛCHE SAINT REMOISE (VACHE)

See SAINT REMOIS.

BÛCHETTE DE BANON (CHÈVRE)

See BANON.

## Buis-les-Baronnies

In Dauphiné but near Comtat border N of Mont Ventoux; Wednesday and Saturday market, reports of local Pélardons (see p. 516); daily market in cherry and apricot seasons.
Dauphiné; 81 **3**, SE of C.

## Le Cabremaures

Tome de Chèvre made by Loic de Saleneuve, Collobrières, in the Massif des Maures; found on St-Tropez Tuesday market.
*m.g. non-précisée; fermier; chèvre cru.*
Var; 84 **16**, R of C.

## Le Cabro des Dentelles

Tome de Chèvre made by Bouniol, Lafare 4km N of Beaumes-de-Venise (tel. 90 62 95 33). Named after spiky mountain ridge.
*45% m.g.; fermier; chèvre cru.*
Comtat Venaissin/Vaucluse; Mont Ventoux; 81 **12**, top R.

## Cachat, Lou Cachat, Froumagi Cussinous, Fromage Fort du Mont Ventoux

Cachat has sometimes been used to denote the freshly drained ball of curd, still in its cloth, e.g. at Pont-du-Crau (see p. 517).

Old Provençal family *recette* quoted by C. Chanot-Bullier: put 1 teaspoonful rennet in litre of *lait de brebis* or *chèvre* warm from the animal; place resulting curd in a hoop-mould and leave 2 days; remove cheese and salt all over; after 2 days wash in lukewarm water (thus removing surplus salt) and leave to ferment for at least 1 week in an earthenware vessel, turning twice a day with wooden spoon; when fully fermented pour over it a small glass of *eau-de-vie* and knead it in.

Ninette Lyon, to whom I owe the above, says that olive oil or unfermented new sweet white wine may be used in place of *eau-de-vie*, and that aromatic herbs and spices may be added. Madame *la Patronne* of the restaurant Le Moulin à Huile, on the old town side of the Roman bridge at Vaison-la-Romaine is Lyonnaise-born, so understands this type of nourishment. She uses all her leftover pieces of cheese, prefers brandy to marc, and keeps her Cachat for a month in winter, serving it a little longer in summer. The result is generally pleasantly smooth-cum-sticky in consistency, but with some solids still to bite on, a pale golden-beige in colour, very rich on the palate with some basic sweetness.

Lou Croustignou (see p. 511) is of this type. Other makers use local chèvres, Tomes du Mont Ventoux (there are no longer brebis there), such as Le Cabro des Dentelles (see above).

Entrechaux and Malaucène are long-known sources of Cachat. Ninette Lyon and Androuët add Gavoie, not big enough to rate entry in postcode or Michelin's gazetteer. Naturally Côtes de Ventoux is drunk with Cachat.
*fermier; domestique; chèvre cru.*
Comtat/Venaissin/Vaucluse; 81 **2/3**, **12/13**.

## Cacheia, Cacheille

Mme Waton de Ferry's recipe, originally expressed in verse form in Provençal: 'If you wish to make la cacheia, take a *toupin* (Savoyard, haut-provençal type of *marmite*) half full of good milk which has fully coagulated. Knead in some *crème de lait* (cream of top of the milk), put it over the fire, add a little *eau-de-vie*, two grains of pepper, and finally a tablespoonful of whey. Take the *toupin* down to the cellar and leave it there all winter, not forgetting to cover it well. When spring comes, uncover it and you will smell the wild aroma of the Vallée de l'Ubaye.' *fermier; domestique; chèvre cru.*
Alpes-de-Haute-Provence; 81 **8**.

## Cagnes-sur-Mer

Vieux- or Haut-de-Cagnes on hill topped by Grimaldi château; daily market. Pierre Venzac, La Fermière, fromager, 10 rue Giacosa, near covered market, pedestrian street; well-kept cheeses, good range of chèvres.
Comté-de-Nice/Alpes-Maritime; 84 **9**, N of C.

## Caillé

I was brought some delicious Caillé from La Fromagerie in Grasse (see p. 513). Had I not been assured that it came from Valbonne I should have guessed its provenance as Laguiole or Salers.
*artisanal; vache cru.*
Comté-de-Nice/Alpes-Maritime; 84 **9**.

**Caillé de Brebis.** From same sources as

Brousse and Brebis de Tende sold at La Fromagerie, Grasse (see p. 513).
*fermier; brebis cru.*
Comté-de-Nice/Alpes-Maritime; 84 **10**, bottom.

## Camarguais, Camargue

For cheeses, see ARLES. See also, p. 494.

## Cannes

Markets: Tuesday to Sunday inclusive (Sat, Sun best). *Maîtres fromagers*: MM. Cénéri Père et Fils, La Ferme Savoyarde, 22 rue Meynadier (tel. 93 39 63 68), with three different *caves d'affinage*, all superb, and wines. One of France's great cheese shops. *Fromager Chevalier Taste-Fromage*: M. Adrien Agnese, 114 rue d'Antibes; Mme Marguerite Agnese, who makes the *fromages blancs* (tel. 93 38 53 66), specialist in brebis, chèvre; home delivery of *plateaux de fromages* (family business established 1914).
Côte d'Azur/Alpes-Maritime; 84 **9**.

## Carpentras

Important Friday market all year (very large, round much of town); daily market April–November. Pernes les Fontaines is 6km to S (see BANON MI-CHÈVRE/VACHE).
Comtat-Venaissin/Vaucluse; 81 **12 13**.

## Castellane

Wednesday and Saturday market; within 25km to SE.
Alpes-de-Haute-Provence; 81 **18**, 84 **7**.

**Chèvre.** Farm on N85 2km towards Grasse.
*fermier; chèvre cru.*

**Tome de Vache de Séranon.** About 400g; made locally; sold by La Fromagerie, Grasse (see p. 513).
Alpes-de-Haute-Provence; 24km SE by N85, then D81 to NE.

**Tomme de Ferme de Castellane.** 900g; round; semi-soft; natural crust; made at La Roque Esclapon.
42% m.g.; *fermier; vache cru.*
Var; 84 **7**, from Castellane SE 25km by N85 and D21.

## Cavaillon

Daily market (not exciting for cheeses).
Michel et Michèle Rostand, *fromagers*, 67 rue Raspail Regional chèvres, brebis, including chèvres *affinés, crémeux* for grilling; good Corsican collection.
Comtat-Venaissin/Vaucluse; 81 **12**.

**Pur Chèvre Fermier.** Small sharply defined thick medallion; soft, white; made by Raymond Sylvestre at Cheval Blanc.
*fermier; chèvre cru.*
As above; SE from Cavaillon 4.5km on D973.

## La Chafranière

*Fromagerie fermière* making a brebis and a range of chèvres (see ST-ANDRÉ-D'OLERARGUES).
Gard.

## Château-Arnoux

Tuesday, Wednesday, Friday, Sunday market; locally made *banons* (see hôtel below). Hôtel-restaurant: La Bonne Étape, Gleize *père et fils et famille* serve food based predominantly on fresh local produce; their banons are from a local *chevrier*, some treated with brandy and kept for months.
Alpes-de-Haute-Provence; 81 **16**, high L.

## Chevrachu

See APT, fermiers des Monts de Vaucluse.

## Chèvres

The regional Fédération des Éleveurs Caprins has about twenty members, and over thirty *chevriers* compete in the annual regional *concours*, held in a different town every year to coincide with its *foire*.
For chèvres see ALLEINS (LES AMOURS DE LA TAMBARETTE), ANDUZE, ANNOT, APT, ARLES (LE GARDIAN, L'ALBARON), BAGNOLS, BAIROLS, BANON, BICHOU, LA BRÉOLE, BRIGNOLES, BRIQUE CENDRÉE, BROUSSE, CABREMAURES, CABRO DES DENTELLES, CACHAT, CACHEIA, CACHEILLE, CHÂTEAU-ARNOUX, CHEVRACHU, COARAZE, CŒUR, LOU CROUSTIGNOU, DIGNE, DRAGUIGNAN, FONTVIEILLE (BROUSSE, GARRIGOU, GAUDRE, GAUDRIOLE, MOKA, VALLON DES CABRIÈRES GENRE TOMME), FRIGOLET, GRANOUILLEN, GRANS, LAMANON, LUSSAN, MEYNES, MOLLÉGÈS, MONTVENTOUX, MOURIÈS, NOVES, PÉLARDON, PÉLISSANE, PEYMEINADE PICODON (D'ARLES, DE VALRÉAS), PLAN-DE-LA-TOUR, PONT-DE-CRAU, PONTÉSIENNE, PONT-ST-ESPRIT, PORT GRIMAUD, PUJAUT, RAPHÈLE, ROVE (see BROUSSE), ST-ANDRÉ-D'OLÉRARGUES, ST-CHRISTOL, ST-HIPPOLYTE-DU-FORT (CIGALOISE) ST-JEAN-DU-

GARD, ST-RÉMY (ST-REMOIS), ST-VINCENT-SUR-JABRON, SALON, SAMBUC, SOSPEL, TENDE, LA TURBIE, UBAYE, UZÈS, VENTOUX, VIDAUBAN.

CIGALON DES ALPILLES

Smallest of M. Maingé's cheeses (see FONT-VIEILLE) marinated in olive oil from Mouriès with rosemary, *sarriette* and thyme, served at la Calèche, a good fish restaurant at St-Rémy (see p. 519).
*fermier; chèvre cru.*

CLAQUERET CANNOIX

*Fromage fort à la* Lyonnaise made by Cénéri Père et Fils, Cannes (see p. 510).

COARAZE

Beautiful hill-top village. Gault Millau (1986) found M. Dehinin's chèvres at Le Par, 5km off (not mapped, so enquire). Comté-de-Nice/Alpes-Maritime; 84 **19**, C.

CŒUR DE RIANS À LA CRÈME; CŒUR DE VALRÉAS, FROMAGE À LA CRÈME

Fromages Blancs in plastic *faisselle*. See also BARBENTANE, RAPHÈLE.
*artisanal; chèvre.*
Var; 84 **4**, Rians; Vaucluse; 81 **2**, Valréas.

LA CRAU

Plain E and SE of Arles, S of Alpilles; noted for quality and quantity, with three hay harvests (*fenaisons*). Crops produced when sheep are away in *transhumance*; sheep winter there (fewer than formerly).
Rouches-du-Rhône; 83 **10/20**, 84 **1**.

LOU CROUSTIGNOU

Every kind of leftover cheese grated into earthenware pot and pounded with garlic, marc and vinegar. 'It is allowed to mature until it is infested with maggots' (as told to Ninette Lyon by Ange Bastiani, from *Le Tour de France Gourmand*, 1985). Other Provençaux types of *fromage fort* appear under Cachat (see p. 509).
*domestique.*
Haute-Provence.

DIGNE

Wednesday, Thursday, Saturday (best) market.
Alpes-de-Haute-Provence; 81 **17**, top L.

DRAGUIGNAN

Wednesday, Saturday market.
Var; 84 **7**, lower L.

**Fromages de Chèvre.** *Tomes* made by M. Michel Carrio, at Les Bastides, Taradeau; sold on farm, and at markets, Draguignan, Plan-de-la-Tour (see p. 517), Saint-Maximin (see p. 519).
*fermier; chèvre cru.*
As above; 12km SSW of Draguignan.

ENTRECHAUX

See CACHAT and MONT VENTOUX.

FONTVIEILLE

See p. 497–502. Market: Monday (small), in summer usually *chevrier* from Vallon des Cabrières); Friday: same *chevrier*.
At Friday market look for stall of Philippe et Dany Condamine, travelled and knowledgeable, with excellent range of *lait cru* regional and national cheeses; local cheeses include le Gaudre (see below); Dany also coats little *boules de chèvre* from Charente in paprika, pepper and curry powder.
Restaurants: L'Amistadouso, 14 route Nord (tel. 90 97 73 17) has mature Pélardons pur Chèvre from M. Pistolle (see ANDUZE); a moderately priced selection of really local wines of character, and a marvellous *soupe au pistou*.
Regalido, route du Nord, serves local farm chèvres (see LE VALLON DES CABRIÈRES below); good restaurant, partly in garden in summer.
Outstanding, prize-winning olive oil *(extra-vierge)*: M. Henri Bellon, Mas Bédarrides, E side of route de Tarascon, D33, immediately after level crossing and bridge, leaving Fontvieille (8.00–12.00 daily, 14.00–18.00 except (Sunday).
Olives in tins, retail, wholesale: M. et Mme Arnaud, opposite Bédarrides. See also MAUSSANE.

**Le Gaudre.** 200g; inverted tub with striated sides; soft, but very close-textured (reminiscent of good Romans, see Chapter 16, p. 460; coat turns pinky-gold with *affinage*, eventually taking blue surface mould; melt-in-mouth rich flavour, with maturity.
*Method*: milk filtered before put into vat and given rennet and starter; after 24 hours *caillé* into *faisselles*, where drainage and salting takes another 72 hours; two *faisselles* of curd go into one 'double-thickness

cheese', named Le Gaudre; *affinage* 2 weeks in cool room on wood.
m.g. *non-précisée; fermier; chèvre cru.*

**Le Gaudriole.** Small cheese (one *faisselle*); good for keeping in olive oil.

**Le Moka.** 1kg cutting cheese matured one month (otherwise as for Gaudre).
All by MM. Didier and Jean Nicolle, La Mourredonne (tel. 90 97 75 14) and Mas de la Musaraigne (tel. 90 54 64 76), on road running E, N of cemetery and railway; sign on road: *Produits de la Ferme*; there are about 140 goats, including billygoats (*Alpines*, some *Saanens*).

**Le Vallon des Cabrières (Genre Tomme) and Pèbre d'Aï.** 80–100g; *tomme*; soft; natural coat sometimes *cendré*, or matured to natural blue, or *sariette*-coated); delicious sweet cheese, gaining richness with keeping, but never too salt; most are sold *frais* or *demi-sec*; sarriette for the Pèbre d'Aï (see BANON) is gathered from the rocky slopes of the Alpilles, where the goats browse, behind the rewarding vineyards of Château d'Estoublon (take D17 E of Fontvieille towards Maussane; turn left on to D33A towards Tarascon; pass vineyard on right; fork right on to stretch of abandoned road and take track to right off it; up to 15 minutes slow, stony drive *uphill* to stone farmhouse in *pinède* (pine grove).
*Method*: filtered milk is rennetted lightly (1:10,000 rennet), given a little of the previous day's whey as starter, and left for 24 hours, before being placed in moulds (70cl milk needed per cheese) to drain for a day. After *démoulage*, salting 2g per cheese (very light); 48 hours *séchage*, then to *cave* for up to 3 weeks' *affinage*. Some are *cendrés*, some naturally *bleutés*. Le Garrigou is the same cheese kept 3–4 weeks in olive oil with *sarriette, romarin* and *laurier*.
Brousse (see pp. 507–8) is made from the whey.
M. et Mme Jean-Denis Maingé, Le Vallon des Cabrières, 13990 Fontvieille (tel. 90 97 78 30); their cheeses have won prizes for several years at the Concours Régional (see CHÈVRES).
m.g. *non-précisée; fermier; biologique; chèvre cru.*
Bouches-du-Rhône; 83 **10**, C, 11km SE of Tarascon, 8km NE of Arles, 9km SW of Les Baux.

FORCALQUIER

Monday market, spread through town; plenty of farm chèvres (not all together), some Brousse, plenty of organic produce (Banon is 25km to NW, Château-Arnoux 30km to NE, Manosque 18km to S).
Alpes-de-Haute-Provence; 81 **15**, C.

FOURMAI GRAS

See SOSPEL.

FRIGOLET

See p. 496. Cheesemakers since the monks acquired a herd of goats in the mid-1980s.

**L'Abbaye de Frigolet pur Chèvre.** About 110g; drum 5cm diameter × 2.5cm deep; about 200g: 8cm diameter × 3.5 cm deep; sold *frais* and at many different stages of *affinage* in season, acquiring *croûte bleutée* when *sec*; when *frais* the consistency is moussey with slightly dry impact on palate. Sold in monastery shop which also offers the fabled liqueur, see p. 496.
*artisanal; monastique; chèvre cru.*
La Montagnette, Bouches-du-Rhône; 83 **10**, N of C in fork D79A, going S with N570 SW to Tarascon.

FROMAGE FORT

See also BOSSONS, CACHAT, CACHEIA, CACHEILLE.

**Fromage Fort du Mont-Ventoux.** 1. Put 'Cachat' (here denoting Tomme de Chèvre just drained) in *toupin* (Provençal *marmite* of local type); add salt and pepper, cover; during fermentation pink skin forms, which needs regularly reincorporating in body of cheese; keep from one to several months; vinegar, wine, marc may be added to taste just before serving. 2. Put freshly drained *tomme*, with salt and pepper into earthenware pot and cover; add cream from top of milk. Viard tells us it is left to become very strong and sharp, and is eaten in hollowed-out onions from spring to autumn (Viard, *Fromages de France*, 1980).
*domestique; brebis/chèvre cru.*
Vaucluse; 81 **2/3**, **12/13**.

FROMAGE FRAIS

Most chèvres and some brebis are sold *frais* as well as *affinés*; and see BARCELONETTE,

BROUSSE, CAILLÉ, CŒUR, MÉRILAIT, NÎMES, PONT-DE-CRAU, ST-HIPPOLYTE.

## Froumay Gras
See SOSPEL.

## Gap
Saturday market for farm cheese.
Hautes-Alpes; 77 **16**, bottom, 81 **6**, top.

## Gard
See ANDUZE, BEAUCAIRE, BICHOU, BLEU DES CAUSSES, LA CHAFRANIÈRE, ISSIRAC, LUSSAN, MEYNES, MONTCLUS, NÎMES, PÉLARDON, PÉRAIL (PÉRAL, PERRAIL), PONT-ST-ESPRIT, PUJAUT, RAURET, REMOULINS, ST-ANDRÉ-D'OLÉRARGUES (for good brebis, Magnum, Pélardons, *tommes*), ST-CHRISTOL, ST-JEAN-DU-GARD (LE SAINT-JEANNAIS), UZÈS, LE VIGAN.

## Gardian
See ARLES for the genuine article; beware cows'-milk factory cheeses from Dauphiné miscalled Gardian on labels.

## Garrigou, Gaude, Gaudriole
See FONTVIEILLE.

## Gorbio, Chèvre de
Available at Fromagerie l'Édelweiss in Nice (see p. 515).
*fermier; chèvre cru.*
Comté-de-Nice/Alpes-Maritime; 84 **19 20**, NW of Roquebrune.

## Granouillen
**Brique.** Flat rectangular cheese of classic shape.
*fermier; chèvre cru.*

**Le Granouillen.** About 80g *frais*, 60g *sec*; base of cone, soft, *fromage blanc* to *Sec*. *Fromage blanc* stage: unsalted, in aerated plastic *faisselle*, almost junket consistency, but pleasing edge of flavour on point of tongue. *Sec* stage: good, close texture still slightly moist and clinging; good natural mould crust; flavour pleasant, broad, not too salt. Made by *famille* Vanneyre, *Éleveurs* at Grans, who also make a small drum-shaped cheese and the *brique* above.

**Fromage de Vache.** Tommes de Vache made by M. Jacques Graillon, Le Jas des Vaches, Grans (*jas* is Provençal for *bergerie* or bird's nest).

*fermier; vache cru.*
Bouches-du-Rhônes; 84 **1/2**, SW of Salon.

## Grasse
Market: Tuesday to Saturday inclusive.
Françoise Gérace and Yvonne Morgante, *fromagers*, La Fromagerie, 5 rue de l'Oratoire, Vieux Grasse; brebis (p. 507), Brousse (pp. 507–8) and Caillé de Tende (pp. 509–10), Caillé (see pp. 509–10) from Valbonne, Chèvre Frais de Peymeinade (6km to SW of Grasse) and other regional mountain cheeses; range of national classics; wines.
Alpes-Maritimes; 84 **8**.

## L'Isle-sur-la-Sorgue
Sunday market.
Vaucluse; 81 **12 13**.

## Isola
20–25kg wheels of hard cheese resembling Comté (*Larousse*, 1973).
*artisanal; vache cru.*
Comté-de-Nice/Alpes-Maritimes; 81 **10**, lower L on D2205 and R. Tinée.

## Issirac
**Pélardon.** (See p. 516.) About 80g plain; also with thyme, garlic; all made by Annick and Jean-Yves Rollot, second house entering Issirac from N (tel. 66 82 15 85); see BAGNOLS for district.
*fermier; chèvre cru.*
Gard; 80 **9**, S of C D3015 for D901.

## Jouques
Sunday a.m. market, including Jan Stéphan, *chevrier*.
Bouches-du-Rhônes; 84 **4**, L of C, S of Durance and Canal.

## Lamanon
**Fromage de Chèvre Fermier.** Small *tomme fraiche* maturing to *croute-bleutée* and *buche cendrée* (Saint-Maure size) succulent *pâte*. Made by F. Vuillermet.
*45% m.g.; fermier; chèvre.*
Bouches-du-Rhône; 84 **2**, far L of C.

## Lussan
A locality rich in *chèvres fermiers* of which some are served at the Hôtel Marie d'Agoult, Château d'Arpaillargues, 4.5km W of Uzès (see p. 521).

**Le P'tit Cohidon.** Small chèvre, *affiné*, by the makers at M. et Mme Cohidon's

Élevage, La Lèque near Lussan. I have eaten it when its crust was melting succulently round a still compact *pâte*, served in *huile d'olive extra-vierge* at Le Bistrot des Alpilles, St-Rémy; its richness reminded me of the finest Mozzarella similarly served after a few days of keeping.
*fermier; chevre cru.*
Gard; 80 **19**, top L.

## Magnum, Le Chèvre

Served at Le Mûrier, Montclus (see BAGNOLS) and made at St-André-d'Olérargues (see p. 518).

## Malaucène

Known for Cachat(see p. 509).
Mont-Ventoux/Vaucluse; 81 **3**, 9km SE of Vaison.

## Manosque

Saturday market.
Alpes-de-Haute-Provence; 81 **15**.

## Marseille

Daily market; for cheese-lovers the object of pilgrimage is: La Fromagerie des Alpes, 18 rue Fontange, 6é (tel. 91 47 06 23) where *maître fromager* Georges Bataille (aided by his son and son-in-law) offers a superb coverage of Provence and of the cheeses of Corsica, apart from those of neighbouring France. Chèvres are on show at every stage of innocence and sophistication. Gault Millau have searched Marseille for a rival *fromager* without success; no other comes near.

## Maussane-les-Alpilles

Thursday market. M. Maingé sells his goat cheese there in season; see FONTVIEILLE. Les Baux is close, and Paradou(see p. 515) for restaurant with local cheeses) adjoins it to W. Splendid olive oil: Coopérative oléicole, rue Charloun Rieu.
Restaurant: Le Mas Theulière, on road to St-Rémy, N from crossroads on E side of village. Excellent *accueil* and food, including cheeseboard with fine brebis and chèvre from Albaron in Camargue (see ARLES, LE GARDIAN and L'ALBARON).
Bouches-du-Rhône; 84 **1**, far L of C, 83 **10**, far R.

## Mélange de Lait, and Mi-Chèvre

See ARLES (CAMARGUAIS brebis–chèvre, BANON MI-CHEVRE, BRIQUE).

## Mérilait

**Ricotta Mérilait.** Cows'-milk Ricotta made by M. Giacomo Pellegrino since 1959, Chemin Véranne, Velaux: available from Philippe and Dany in market Fontvielle (see p. 511), and elsewhere; but 90% of production is exported to Italy (tel. 42 87 43 62).
15% m.g. min.; *laitier; vache/petit lait.*
Bouches-du-Rhônes; 84 **2**, N of Rognac on D55.

## Merveilles, Vallée des

See p. 486.

**Fromages de la Vallée des Merveilles.** La Fromagère at Grasse (see p. 513) sells cheeses from this remote and strange retreat of earlier mankind; 6kg Tommes de Vaches, made on several farms there. La Vallée des Merveilles is approached by D91 W from Saint Dalmas-de-Tende (S of Tende on N204).
*fermier; vache cru.*
Alpes-Maritimes; 84 **9/10** and **19/20**.

## Meynes

**Fromage de Chèvre Fermier.** Banon Pèbre d'Aï type; soft, but close-texture; *sarriette*-coated; sweet, gentle flavour; made by M. Poletti at Meynes.
45% m.g.; *fermier; chèvre cru.*
Gard; 80 **19/20**, 5km S of Remoulins, W of D986.

## Mi-Chèvre

See MÉLANGE DE LAIT.

## Mollégès

**Fromages de Chèvre.** Abricot and Figue: larger, shaped like fruit; Bouton de Culotte: smaller than Crottin; Calisson: boat-shaped cheese with diagonal gridmarks (Calisson is an almond *petit-four*, named after Calissoun, Provençal for a pâtissier's drying-mat of that shape); Cardinal: biretta-shaped cheese with Cumin; Cerise: tiny rounded cheese; Chapelet: tiny cheeses, strung together; Crottin; Crottin Glacé: neat tub-shape, smooth crust for keeping; Lingot: small, stout *brique*; Rigotte. All made by M. Masson, 3 avenue du Lauron, Mollégès (tel. 90 95 19 81).
*artisanal; chèvre cru.*
Bouches-du-Rhônes; 81 **12**, low, W of N7 and D99.

## Montclus

Restaurant: Le Mûrier; Tim Broadbent and Fiona Gibson offer good food based on fine regional ingredients, including local chèvres (see BAGNOLS and ST-ANDRÉ-D'OLÉRARGUES) and interesting local wines (including very local red St Anne cuvée Notre Dame).
Gard; 80 **9**, low L, S off D901, D980.

## Monts de Vaucluse

Société Coopérative Agricole Chèvres Fermiers des Monts de Vaucluse, see APT.

## Mont-Ventoux

See CACHAT, FROMAGE FORT and VENTOUX.

**Tomme de Mont Ventoux; Cachat d'Entrechaux.** *Tomme fraîche*, with added *herbes*, unless to be used in FROMAGE FORT (see p. 512) from milk of animals on slopes of Mont Ventoux.
45% m.g.; *fermier*; *chèvre cru*.
Comtat-Venaissin/Vaucluse; 81 **2/3** and **12/13**, Entrechaux is 6km ESE of Vaison.

## Mouriès

**Chèvre.** *Frais*: about 100g, regular drum; about 6cm × 2.5cm deep; no crust, sprig of *sarriette* on face; a few days' old, soft, not yet melting; sweet, with hint of agreeable acidity. Made by M. Basset at Le Jour Blanc, Mouriès; his goats spend part of their time on the *garrigue* above the vineyards of le Mas de Gourgonnier, which sells the cheese in season (source of full-blooded, earthy-rich organic reds and a rosé), 2–3km N, off D78 between Maussane (see p. 514) and Le Destet.
*fermier*; *biologique*; *chèvre cru*.
Bouches-du-Rhônes; 84 **1**, W of C, S of Alpilles.

## Nice

Tuesday (best)–Sunday market.
*Fromagers*: Gilbert Braet, La Ferme Fromagère, 13 rue Assalit; farm cheeses, traditionally churned butter. Paul Chervet, l'Édelweiss, 55 rue de France; good range, including local chèvres, one from Gorbio, NE of Menton.
Baker: André Espuno, 22 rue Vernier and 35 rue Droite, who suits different breads to different cheeses.
Alpes-Maritimes; 81 **19**.

## Nîmes

Tuesday and Friday market; Tuesday, Chemin Bas d'Avignon, Friday, Boulevard Jean Jaurès.

**Fromage Frais; Tome de Vache.** M. Henri Ferté, Mas de Mayan, Nîmes (tel. 66 38 23 28); on farm and Tuesday and Friday markets, as above.
*fermier*; *biologique*; *Nature & Progrès*; *vache cru*.
Gard; 80 **19**.

## Noves

**Chèvres.** 150–250g; base of cone; soft; natural *croûte-bleutée* when *sec*, made by M. et Mme Fleury, Chemin de l'Eau, Noves.
*fermier*; *chèvre cru*.
Bouches-du-Rhônes; 81 **12**, SW of A7, N7 junction at Durance crossings.

## Orange

Thursday a.m. market (large); daily market 15 May–15 October.
Fromagerie La Populaire (Alain Parant, member of Guilde des Fromagers), 4 rue Stassart.
Vaucluse; 81 **11/12**.

## Le Paradou

Le Bistro du Paradou (chez Jean-Louis), closed Sundays. Serves a set-menu lunch, and in July and August a set dinner too; food, including cheese and wine are *du pays*; cheeses include a Banon d'Or (literally golden in leaf), Le Gaudre (see FONTVIEILLE), and chèvre *frais* in beautiful olive oil from next-door Maussane (see p. 514).

## Pèbre d'Aï

*Pèbre d'Aï*, or donkey's pepper, is the wild provençal herb which flourishes on the rocky slopes of hills and mountains, and in the *garrigue*. Our nearest equivalent is savory. The Latin is *satureia hortensis*, the French *poivre d'âne* from the Provençal, or *sarriette des montagnes* from the Latin (there is a more fragile *sarriette des jardins*). It is strong-smelling and peppery, whence its local name, and in Provence comes in useful in almost everything (rather as Oregano is used in Italy). Banons (see BANON AU POIVRE D'ÂNE, PÈBRE D'AÏ) coated in it are called Pèbre d'Aï. Makers of small Tomes de Brebis or Chèvre commonly put a sprig on top of their cheeses, as does M. Ripert of Banon (see BANON DE BANON) on his Bûchette, too.

### PÉLARDON D'ANDUZE, PÉLARDON FERMIER, PÉLARDON DES CÉVENNES

See also Chapter 5, p. 168 and Chapter 7, pp. 245–6.

80–120g (sometimes aged to 60g or less); thick medallion or more rounded *banon*-shape, sometimes irregular, sometimes thinner; soft when young; natural crust, either scraped to preserve whiteness, or allowed to acquire grey-blue mould surface (*pélard* means timber from which the bark has been removed, which suggests that the scraped crust is the traditional practice); normal *affinage* lasts 2–3 weeks, but some are certainly given longer, and some are sprinkled with powdered pepper or *sarriette* (see ANDUZE and FONTVIEILLE, Restaurant d'Amistadouso).
*45% m.g.; fermier; chèvre cru.*
Cévennes/Gard; 80 **19**, top L, St-André-d'Olérargues; 80 **17**, NE of C, Anduze; 80 **9**, S of C, Issirac; 80 **19**, top L, Lussan; 80 **17**, high L, Saint Jean-du-Gard.

### PÉLISSANE

Sunday a.m. market (where cheeses below are sold).

**Fromages de Chèvre.** Made by Guy and Mireille Constant, chemin des Aspres, Pélissane (tel. 90 55 12 07) (organic vegetables too).
*fermier; biologique; Nature & Progrès, chèvre cru.*
Bouches-du-Rhônes; 84 **2**, 4km E of Salon.

### PÉRAIL DU MAS PINEL

Pérail, primarily from the Rouergue rather than Provence, is an irregular flat cheese weighing from 60–100g, measuring 6–15cm in diameter, 1.2–2cm in depth. It is kept to dry for 1–2 weeks, and this example weighs 80g when wrapped (more typical than larger sizes). Firm, close texture, yet delicate in mouth: 'lovely consistency' I wrote after eating it. Flavour: gentle, yet fully satisfying, with no hint of saltiness. Made by Fromagerie Cigaloise, 30170 St-Hippolyte-du-Fort, in the part of the Gard which merges in character with Rouergue as you travel north-west. Courtine (1973) mentions Péral, which I have not seen used, as alternative spelling (nor have I met another variation, Perrail). He mentions cows as an alternative source of milk, which I have not met either. There is a flush of Pérail in July and August from *bergers* within the adjacent Roquefort region after the Roquefort makers have ceased to collect milk, but before many ewes have dried off. The name is of local origin, not geographical so far as I can trace (see Chapter 6, p. 176).
A similar cheese is made at St-André-d'Olérargues (see p. 00).
Gard; 80 **17**, L of C.

### PERNES-LES-FONTAINES

Banon Mi-Chèvre and Banon Vache made by 'S.P.F.' found here (see BANONS).
Comtat-Venaissin/Vaucluse; 81 **12/13**.

### PEYMEINADE

**Chèvre de Peymeinade.** 100–130g, cylindrical, *chabis*-type chèvres sold *frais*, or conserved in very good olive oil; 'délicieux' in either case according to Gault Millau (May 1987), who tried them at La Fromagerie in Grasse (see p. 513).
*fermier; chèvre cru.*
Alpes-Maritimes; 84 **8**, 6km SW of Grasse.

### PEYROLLES-EN-PROVENCE

Wednesday market; daily April–June.

**Fromage de Brebis Fermier.** Small flat drum with green label; met in *frais* state, pleasant.
*fermier; brebis cru.*
Bouches-du-Rhônes; 84 **3**, far R of C on N96.

### PICODON D'ARLES

Chèvres (presumably originally from Valréas or the Drôme) soaked in vinegar, wrapped in walnut leaves and stacked in earthenware pots. As Picodons now have an AOC (de l'Ardèche, de la Drôme) this name must be in legal trouble; 'à l'Arlésienne' might be more acceptable.
*45% m.g.; artisanal; chèvre cru.*

**Picodon de Valréas, (Picodon de la Drôme).** This cheese now comes within the AOC Picodon de la Drôme, although Valréas is within Provence, as part of the Comtat. The tradition here is for cheeses to be released much younger than traditional Picodon (what the Vivarais would call, with scorn, Pidances); see PICODON,

Chapter 7, pp. 246–7, and Chapter 16, pp. 458–9.
45% m.g.; *fermier; artisanal; laitier; chèvre cru/thermisé.*
Comtat-Venaissin/Vaucluse; 81 **2**, C.

## Plan-de-la-Tour

Thursday market; good variety of farm and artisanal cheeses, including those below.

**Fromage de Ferme Brebis.** 200g *tome* from Haut Var.
*fermier; brebis cru.*

**Tome Blanche Père Ségador.** 2kg white cheese, mild, selling at 51F per kg in 1986.
50% m.g.; *artisanal; vache.*

See also CASTELLANE, DRAGUIGNAN for cheeses on sale here.
Var; 84 **17**, 9.5km NW of Sainte-Maxime.

## Poivre d'Âne

See BANON and PÈBRE D'AÏ.

## Pont-de-Crau

**Cachat.** Small cheeses placed in olive oil at *faisselle* stage with *sarriette*, thyme and pepper.
*fermier; chèvre cru.*

**Fromages pur Chèvre.** *Tommes fraîches*, 400g, 6–7cm × 2.5cm deep; melting consistency; sweet, pleasant flavour, very light acidity. *Demi-sec:* 5cm × 2cm; pinky-gold crust; excellent rich flavour, not salty. *Sec:* 4cm × 1cm; gold with some white spots; salt starting to obtrude.
*fermier; chèvre cru.*

**Le Petit Bonement.** Smaller *fourme* coated with mixed herbs (*sarriette*, sage, thyme, not rosemary because too dominating); kept in olive oil, the local Clavenco of the Chau.
All the above are made by Mme Souchal at Mas Bonement, Coste Basse, Pont-de-Crau (tel. 90 96 30 70) and sold retail (and semi-wholesale to restaurants and shops) daily 14.00–19.30.
The Crau is famous for its grass and hay, and the aromatic local honey, also sold here; there factors lead to expectations of good cheese.
Bouches-du-Rhônes; 83 **10**, SE edge of Arles, farm on E of D33B within 2km of Pont-de-Crau.

## Le Pontet

Thursday market.

**La Pontesienne.** Made by Daniel Carré, Domaine de l'Ortolan, Le Pontet (tel. 90 32 18 96).
45% m.g.; *chèvre.*

**Ventoux, Ventoux Poivré, Le Ventoux Frais.** 100g. Made by Fromagerie le Ventoux, Domaine Cassagne (marked on map above words Le Pontet; tel. 90 31 01 68).
50%/30% m.g.; *laitier; vache.*
Vaucluse; 81 **12**, L of C, NE outskirt of Avignon.

## Pont-St-Esprit

Saturday Market. Reachable from Pont-St-Esprit: Issirac, and St-Christol (20km W), Monclus (23km W).

**Chèvres.** With and without *sarriette*, made by M. Jacques Brunier.
*fermier; chèvre cru.*
Gard; E border with Vaucluse; 80 **10**, low L.

## Port Grimaud

I am told that there is good food, including a chèvre made on the spot, at La Fontaine (not mapped), within 4km of Port Grimaud.
Var; 81 **17**, W shore of Golfe de St-Tropez.

## Pujaut

**Fromage de Chèvre.** *tomes* made by M. Soto at Élevage des Molles, in country about 2km N of Pujaut, W of Sauveterre.
*fermier; chèvre cru.*
Gard; 80 **20**, NE of C near airport.

## Raclette

See BARCELONNETTE.

## Raphèle-les-Arles

**Chèvres Cœur, Pyramide, Tome.** Made at Mas de la Safranière, *quartier* Balarin, Raphèle (tel. 90 93 23 65) from milk of Alpines, Saanens, Roves; second generation *chevrier.*
*fermier; chèvre cru.*
83 **10**, low 8km E of Arles on N453 N side.

## Rauret

**Fromage de Chèvre.** 40g neat thick medal, made by M. Bianciotti; he sells in Arles Saturday market, opposite Grand Café de la Bourse.
45% m.g.; *fermier; chèvre cru.*
Gard; 80 **17**, on D999 near Sardan.

### Remoulins

**Fromage de Chèvre.** Made at farm 5.5km W of Remoulins on N side of D981 after D112 to Vers, just before D192 to Vers.
*fermier; chèvre cru.*
Gard; 80 **19**, R of C.

### Ricotta

See MÉRILAIT.

### La Roque Esclapon

See CASTELLANE.

### Roquebillière

Reported by Androuët (*Livre d'Or*, 1984) as one of the centres for Tommes de Vésubie (see ST-MARTIN).
Comté-de-Nice; 84 **19**, high.

### Roure

Sometimes mistakenly called Rouvres.
**Tome de Roure.** Tome de Montagne made in very small quantities for many years at Roure, overlooking the Gorges de Valabres on the R. Tinée; some full-milk cheese already rare in 1973 (*Larousse*), but found in 1985 by Ninette Lyon (*Le Tour de France Gourmand*).
*artisanal; vache entier cru.*
Alpes-Maritimes; 81 **10**, bottom L.

### Rove

See BROUSSE DU ROVE.

### St-André-d'Olérargues

Produits fermiers de la Chafranière follow:
**Fromage de Brebis.** About 80g, small flat drum, similar to Pérail (see p. 516).
*fermier; brebis cru.*
**Fromage de Chèvre au Poivre et au Thym.** About 200g, dome-topped drum, soft, coated in pepper and thyme; crust develops blue surface under herbs; delicious, not too strong, served at Montclus (see p. 515).
*fermier; chèvre cru.*
**Fromage Frais.** Sold at 48 hours in big bowl of herbs.
*fermier; vache cru.*
**Le Magnum aux Herbes.** 200g drum made as Pérail, but thicker, and coated in rosemary and *sarriette*; golden crust under herbs; looks as though washed, but is not; rich flavour; served at Montclus (see p. 515).

**Pélardon Fermier.** About 80g, medallion-shaped; eaten young, when close-textured, melt-in-mouth, with good flavour; pale creamy-gold crust, melting from edge.
45% m.g. max.; *fermier; chèvre cru.*
**Tommes de Chèvre.** 1850g; rounded-edged wheel; firm, fat, white interior, attractive, crisp, grey crust; melting texture, good flavour, not sharp. 3kg: at 3 months, neat sharp-edged wheel; brebis-like texture; very good flavour. 5kg: golden crust, lined on face of wheel in spoke fashion.
**Tomme Mi-Chèvre.** 1600g neat-edged drum, grey-crusted.
All the above made by M. Van Den Haute, Fromagerie Fermière de la Chafranière, Mas de Christol, St-André-d'Olérargues 30330 Connaux (tel. 66 79 01 89).
*fermier; chèvre/vache cru.*

### St-Christol-de-Rodières

**Fromage pur Chèvre Fermier.** Pleasant 80g medallion of Pélardon appearance; distributor: R. Ferrero, St-Christol-de-Rodières, 30760 St-Julien-de-Peyrolas (tel. 66 82 19 47).
45% m.g.; *fermier; chèvre cru.*
Gard; 80 **9**, SW of C D1805 from D901; D141 N from D980.

### St-Étienne-de-Tinée

Friday and Sunday market (Brousse and *tomme* country).
Alpes-Maritimes; 81 **9**.

### St-Hippolyte-du-Fort

See PÉRAIL DU MAS PINEL.
Fromagerie Cigaloise makes and matures cheese, including the following:
**Fromage Frais.** 150g; loose, moist texture; on acid side, improved by addition of mixed peppercorns fresh-milled.
45% m.g.; *artisanal; chèvre.*

### St-Jean-du-Gard

Androuët remarked on the Pélardons Pur Chèvre of this *commune* in 1982.
Tuesday market; Saturdays in summer.
**Le Saint-Jeannais.** Described by Viard as 'little irregular disc, scented with the herbs of the Garrigue on which the goats browse'; made by Élevage de Chèvre Saint-Jeannais.

*fermier; chèvre cru.*
Other sources of local cheese: Coopérative Laitière de La Cévénole (tel. 66 85 31 73); Bernard et Dominique Amar make chèvres (and produce honey) at La Bigorre, 30270 St-Jean-du-Gard (tel. 66 85 37 89), which they sell daily on farm 12.00–15.00, and in St-Jean market on Tuesday. Fromagerie (chèvre), Mas de la Combe, St-Jean-du-Gard (tel. 66 85 31 98).
Gard; 80 **17**, high, on D260 and R. Gardon.

## St-Jeannet

Thursday market.
Comté-de-Nice/Alpes-Maritimes; 84 **9**, high, NE of Vence.

## St-Martin-Vésubie

This is the centre of a district renowned for its pastures, but in his 1982 tour Androuët only came on one of these *tommes* ('*excellente*') by pure chance, so persistence is needed to find them (see VÉSUBIE).
Comté-de-Nice/Alpes-Maritimes; 84 **19**, top.

## Ste-Maxime

Covered market (mornings), including Crémerie des Burons (owned by member of Guilde) with excellent selection in good condition.
Var; 84 **17**, N of C.

## St-Maximin-la-Ste-Baume

Friday market with farm cheeses.
Var; 84 **4**, bottom R.

## St-Raphaël

Daily market. Fromagerie: Jean de Brie, 183 avenue du XVè Corps.
Var; 84 **8**.

## St-Remois

**La Bûche Saint-Remoise.** About 4cm high, 3cm diameter; natural crust; crust may melt, *bûche* becoming a succulent dome if left on its end, vertical.
*fermier; vache cru.*

**Le Saint-Remois.** Cheese of Picodon size and shape; close texture; tasted *demi-sec*, pleasing character, not salty; made by Georges and Marie-Paule Rueda, La Fromagerie des Alpilles, 13210 St-Rémy-de-Provence. They also make a vache.
45% m.g.; *fermier; chèvre cru.*
Bouches-du-Rhônes.

## St-Rémy-de-Provence

Market: Wednesday (for cheese) and Saturday (small). Shop: Beurres, Fromages, Pâtés fraîches: Gondrand et Ferrero, 27 rue Carnot; local cheeses (see ST-REMOIS).
Annual parade of sheep ready for *La Transhumance* with shepherds, goats and donkeys on Whit Monday (Pentecôte).
Le Bistrot des Alpilles, 15 Boulevard Mirabeau, M. et Mme Raff, and charming staff (tel. 90 92 09 17); serves good Provençal food cheerfully and generously at moderate prices; their *réserve maison* is Mas de la Dame (on Saint-Rémy–Maussane road) and they list one of the Domaine de Trévallon wines (1985 vintage in late 1987; see below). They serve a succulent chèvre (see LUSSAN) in superb olive oil from Maussane (the impact on my palate equalled that of the best Mozzarella in Italy).
Bouches-du-Rhônes; 81 **12**.

## St-Sauveur-sur-Tinée

Tuesday market.
Comté-de-Nice/Alpes Maritimes; 81 **10/20**.

## St-Tropez

Tuesday and Saturday market, not exciting for local cheese (better at STE-MAXIME, PLAN-DE-LA-TOUR).
Var; 84 **17**.

## St-Vincent-sur-Jabron

**Fromages de chèvre; Pâte Pressée Croute-Lavées.** 100 chèvres per day made by Isabelle Doneaud from milk of Alpines and crosses at Paressons.
Alpes-de-Haute-Provence; 81 **5**, low on D946.

## Salon de Provence

Wednesday market.
M. Gérard Paul and Mme Danièle Paul, *maître fromager* (also in Aix, see p. 502; his *caves* are here).
The shop is 35 Boulevard Clémenceau (tel. 90 56 29 41), and was founded by M. Paul's father. Cheesemakers: see ALLEINS (12km NE), GRANS (5.5km SW) and PÉLISSANE (4km E), which has Sunday a.m. market.
Bouches-du-Rhônes; 84 **2**.

## Le Sambuc

**Fromages de Chèvre.** Made by Sophie Berton, Joëlle d'Arve, and sold with their honey at La Commanderie, Le Sambuc, where they keep the now rare Rove breed (large-horned red goats). This *chèvrerie* has been going for fifty years.
*fermier; chèvre cru.*
Camargue/Bouches-du-Rhônes; 83 **10**, bottom.

## Séranon (Brebis)

See CASTELLANE.

## Sisteron

Wednesday and Saturday market.
Alpes-de-Haute-Provence; 81 **5/6**.

## Sixtois

See BEAUCAIRE.

## Solliès-Toucas

**Chèvre.** Local cheese mentioned in *Larousse des Fromages*, 1973.
*fermier; artisanal; chèvre cru.*
Var; 84 **15**, C.

## Sospel

Thursday market.

**Brousse de Sospel.** See BROUSSE.

**Tomme de Sospel or Froumai Gras.** 6–9kg pressed *tomme* with natural crust similar to Valdeblore and Vésubie (see ST-MARTIN-VÉSUBIE); Courtine gave only as *vache* (*Larousse*, 1973), 'now rare', and compared it more with Tomme de Savoie made very large (which I have seen and enjoyed).
*fermier; artisanal; brebis/chèvre cru; vache cru.*
Comté-de-Nice/Alpes Maritimes; 84 **19/20**.

## Tende

Wednesday market. To W of Tende Mont Bégo and la Vallée des Merveilles (see p. 486).

**Brousse.** Ninette Lyon found a *chevrier* above the Col de Tende (*Marabout*, 1978).
*fermier; chèvre cru.*

**Tomme de Tende.** Local pressed Tomme de Brebis; stocked by La Fromagerie at Grasse (see p. 513), which also sells *transhumance* cheese from La Vallée des Merveilles in season.
*fermier; chèvre cru.*
Alpes-Maritimes; 84 **10**, bottom on N204.

## La Tinée

River and Valley of Haute-Provence formerly noted for its pressed Tommes de Brebis and de Chèvre, now often made of cows' milk. In danger of disappearing because of increased fresh milk consumption on the Côte d'Azur. For cheeses of this area see BAIROLS, LE CROUSTIGNOU, ROURE, ST-ÉTIENNE-SUR-TINÉE, ST-SAUVEUR-SUR-TINÉE).
Comté-de-Nice/Alpes-Maritimes; 81 **9/10, 20**, joining R. Var.

## Tome/Tomme

The term is used, more often spelt *tome*, by *chevriers* for their small round cheeses when young; and, usually as *tomme*, by *fromagers* using all kinds of milk for their larger pressed cheeses.
See BAIROLS, CASTELLANE, MERVEILLES, PLAN-DE-LA-TOUR, ROURE, ST-ANDRÉ-D'OLÉRARGUES, SÉRANON, SOSPEL, LA TINÉE, LA TURBIE, UBAYE, VALBERG, VALDEBLORE, VÉSUBIE; and TOMMES DE VACHE.
Comté-de-Nice/Alpes-Maritimes; 81 **9, 10, 20**, joining R. Var.

## Tommes de Vache

*Tommes fraîches* made at Saint-Auban and Caillé. About 400g *tommes* made at Séranon; see also MERVEILLES for 6kg *tommes fermières*; all sold at La Fromagerie, Grasse (see p. 513)
*fermier; vache cru.*
Comté-de-Nice/Alpes-Maritimes; 81 **18/19**.

## Tortora

See BROUSSE FRAÎCHE.

## Toulon

Daily market (except Monday 15 Sept–15 March), best on Saturdays.
M. Jacques et Mme Claudette Gonnet, *fromagers*, 8 bis, rue des Bouchones.
Var; 84 **15**.

## Le Trident (brebis)

See ARLES.

## Turbie, Tomme de la

2kg pressed *tomme*, natural crust.
45% m.g.; *artisanal; chèvre cru.*

Comté-de-Nice/Alpes-Maritimes; 84 **10**, 10km E of Nice by A8, 18km by D2564.

UBAYE, TOMME DE L'

Pressed *tomme* made near BARCELONNETTE. *artisanal; chèvre cru*.
Alpes-de-Haute-Provence; 81 **8**.

UZÈS

Saturday market. Le Buron à Uzés, *fromager* (tel. 66 22 59 40). M. et Mme Cohidon, *chevriers*, La Lèque, near Lussan (see p. 513).
Gard; 80 **19**, NW of C.

VAISON-LA-ROMAINE

Tuesday market.
Lou Canestou, *fromagerie*, 10 rue Raspail (local and regional cheeses and wines). Restaurants: Au Coin Gourmand (Mme Nicole Dejoux), 14 rue du Maquis: Patricia Wells reports good food, including locally gathered truffles, and local cows' and goats' cheeses; Le Moulin à Huile, Quai Maréchal Foch, near Roman bridge, at the foot of the *Haute-Ville*; local cheeses and wines; own Cachat (see p. 509).
Comtat-Venaissin/Vaucluse; 81 **2/3**, low.

VALBERG, TOMME DE VALBERG

1971 (Guide): brebis, similar to Valdeblore (9–12kg); natural crust; gentle or pronouncedly fruity. 1973 (*Larousse*): chèvre 4–5kg; thin assiduously washed crust; 1978/1984 (*Marabout, Livre d'Or*): vache (one of Tommes du Pays Niçois).
*fermier; brebis/chèvre cru*.
Comté-de-Nice/Alpes-Maritimes; 81 **9 19**.

VALBONNE

Friday market; and see CAILLÉ.
Comté-de-Nice/Alpes-Maritimes; 84 **9**, 9km ESE of Grasse.

VALDEBLORE, TOMME DE VALDEBLORE

1971 (Guide): brebis, 9–12kg, 30–35cm diameter, 6–8cm deep; pressed; natural crust, light washing and brushing over 3–6 months, becoming pinkish grey. Semi-soft, lactic flavour, mild and creamy when young; semi-hard, pronounced sheepy aroma and strong flavour at full maturity. Already becoming rare. 1973 (*Larousse*): brebis, 4–5kg, thin, well-washed crust; 1978 (*Marabout*): listed under Tommes de Chèvre: 'resembles Vacherin without its bark-surround; 5–7kg; kept in large earthenware containers on straw over a bed of twigs; becomes blue and roseate in patches; it is soft and velvety.' 1984 (*Livre d'Or*): Grouped under Tommes of Pays Niçois made in *vacheries* (see VÉSUBIE, Androuët's description of Tomme found during his visit of 1982).
*fermier; vache cru*.
Comté-de-Nice/Alpes-Maritimes; 81 **18/19**, top.

VALRÉAS

Wednesday market all year. April–June: Monday, Wednesday, Friday and afternoon on Saturday; local cheeses: see BRIQUE, PICODON.

**Valréas.** Name used on very soft chèvre (pre-*affinage* Picodon?) at unsalted *frais* stage; *soufflé* light in texture (1987). From same source, Poivre d'Âne version at same stage.
*artisanal; chèvre cru*.
Comtat-Venaissin/Vaucluse; 81 **2**.

VAR

See BANDOL, BRIGNOLES, BROUSSIN, DRAGUIGNAN, PLAN-DE-LA-TOUR, PORT GRIMAUD, STE-MAXIME, ST-RAPHAËL, ST-TROPEZ, SOLLIÈS-TOUCAS, TOULON, VIDAUBAN.

VAUCLUSE

See APT, AVIGNON, BANON (MI-CHÈVRE), BEAUMES-DE-VENISE, (BUIS-LES-BARONNIES), CABRO, CACHAT (including ENTRECHAUX, MALAUCÈNE), CARPENTRAS, CAVAILLON, FROMAGE-FORT-DU-MONT-VENTOUX, L'ISLE-SUR-LA-SORGUE, MONTS-DE-VAUCLUSE, MONT VENTOUX, ORANGE, PERNES-LES-FONTAINES, PICODON, LA PONTÈSIENNE, LE PONTET, VAISON, VALRÉAS, VENTOUX.

**Chèvre des Monts-de-Vaucluse.** See APT, CHÈVRE FERMIER.

VELAUX

See RICOTTA.

VENCE

Friday market (good); Danièle et Jean-Louis Barbier, *fromagers*, 12 rue du Marché (small restaurant in season).
Comté-de-Nice/Alpes-Maritimes; 84 **9**.

VENTOUX

See FROMAGE FORT, MONT-VENTOUX, LE PONTET.

### Vésubie

See BROUSSE and TOMME DE VÉSUBIE. 9–12kg; pressed; fine textured *pâte*; pink crust, on moist side. They are of the Italian heritage of Nizza, compared by Androuët with Fontina in their type, but not their flavour. He said in 1982 that they were produced on a number of farms in near-by valleys, from the milk of cattle kept indoors; but seldom seen in shops, even locally. He later mentioned Roquebillière (see p. 518).
*fermier; vache cru.*

### Vidauban

**Fromage de Chèvre.** Made by M. Legros: 'Surgout'; sold in market Sainte-Maxime. Var; 84 7, bottom L.

### Le Vigan

**Fromage Fermier de Chèvre.** Made by M. Grenouillet, Les Molières, Arphy, 7km N of Le Vigan (*not* to be confused with near-by Molières Cavaillac). Like a small, plump Picodon; *sec, demi-sec*, good texture, tasty.
45% m.g.; *fermier; chèvre cru.*
Gard; 80 **16**, C.

# Appendix 1

# *Listeria monocytogenes* and *Listeria*

During the winter of 1987–8 Switzerland took off the market and destroyed all stocks of Vacherin Mont d'Or (made in the canton of Vaud from *pasteurised* milk in late autumn and winter), and stopped its production. Seven deaths from Listeriosis had been traced to the presence of *Listeria monocytogenes* in the new season's cheese. It was further revealed that a total of thirty earlier fatal cases in the Vaud had been similarly caused since 1983. (The earlier cases received attention in Swiss scientific reports published in French, but none in the international press.)

The Swiss Health Ministry later published a list of twenty-four other Swiss, French and Italian soft cheeses in which *L. monocytogenes* had been found. None was made of raw milk, and, excepting three made by the Swiss Dairy School at Rutli/Rüti, all were of *laitier* origin, mostly industrial.

Inadequate official information and uninvestigative, slovenly reporting led to press attacks on *un*pasteurised cheese (typified by a pontifical warning against buying it from Dr Thomas Stuttaford, medical wiseacre of *The Times*). The unfortunate French makers of the impeccable Franc-Comtois raw-milk cheese Le Mont d'Or (or Vacherin du Haut-Doubs) were hit by the scare. (Its true name, Vacherin du Mont d'Or, had been inexplicably appropriated exclusively to Swiss use in the 1970s.) The name of Vacherin was blackened, and they had to destroy tens of tonnes of good cheese which a misled public would not buy (see Chapter 14).

I summarise below the nature of this disease, and enough of its history to help consumer, farmer and cheesemaker to avoid trouble, so far as present knowledge will allow. One clear lesson can be learned from the evidence: pasteurised cheese is most at risk. Pasteurisation, far from being the remedy, leaves an open field for *Listeria monocytogenes* to invade and conquer. In all the international investigations, no raw-milk cheese has been impugned.*

## *Listeria monocytogenes*

Up to April 1988, thirteen serotypes of *L. monocytogenes* had been accepted by the Central Public Health Laboratory for England and Wales at Colindale, London, all associated with one or other case of Listeriosis. Serotypes 4b (59 per cent of cases) and 1/2a (18 per cent) and 1/2b (14 per cent) are the main villains in Britain. The bacteria are present in soil and water and carried by birds and fauna. This is one of eight species of *Listeria*, and 'with the exception of very few rare cases' (Dr McLauchlin), the only one to cause infection. Rosenow and Marth found that 100–1000 cells could be a

---

*BMJ, Vol. 297, 24 September 1988, p. 54, Dr N. S. Galbraith, 'Listeriosis', cites two cases from 'unpasteurised cheese' as the only cases of foodborne *Listeria* recorded in Britain. The first case (Bannister *Journal of Infection*, 15, 1987, pp. 165–8) was traced to a French soft cheese for which 'the manufacturing process . . . includes pasteurisation of the milk from which it is made.' In the second case (Hampshire goat cheese made from several farms) I was told that milk had been heat-treated, though not to pasteurisation level.

hazardous quantity for ingestion, a low count (a quart of milk kept at 4°C could reach this in a few days, if only lightly contaminated originally.*

I am grateful to Dr J. McLauchlin, Senior Microbiologist at Colindale, for answering earlier questions and for commenting, as quoted in the text, on this Appendix, and for sending me copies of relevant papers.

## Listeriosis

Listeriosis is the disease caused by *L. monocytogenes*. It does not attack people in a normal physical state; 13–14 per cent of the French population, for example, are healthy carriers.† Those whose immunity has been weakened (*les immuno-déprivés*) or suppressed are at risk. Of 214 English and Welsh cases in 1987, 146 were immuno-compromised adults, 68 foeto-maternal, resulting in twelve abortions, four stillbirths and twelve infant deaths, born ill or cross-infected in hospital. (It is thought that Queen Anne's seventeen miscarriages may have been caused by Listeriosis.) Listeriosis can bring on septicaemia, meningitis and encephalitis, with a fatality rate of 30 per cent; 70 per cent of French infant meningitis is so caused, according to a French ministerial report.

Listeriosis can cause mastitis in dairy animals, an easy way for the disease to spread unless scrupulous attention is paid to the state of udders, to disinfection of udders, hands and equipment, and safe disposal of mastitis milk.

## History of Listeriosis

**1926–1950** Listeriosis was first identified and described in rabbits in 1926, and the few human cases identified up to 1950 were attributed to animal infection. The earthy nature of rabbit life was to prove significant.

**1960s** Palsson noticed coincidence of cases in Greenland with the silage season (fed to beasts in winter and early spring). The original rules for silage-making and storage had been long neglected (as I note in my *Great British Cheese Book*). Instead of clean, airtight, controlled fermentation, there was commonly putrefaction. This nourished unsolicited bacteria, including *L. monocytogenes*, picked up with soil at various stages: during cutting of crop (mower set too low, or ground uneven); during shovelling and packing of crop into pit or silo; during removal of silage and its stacking for use near mangers. Any such infestation could result in infected meat or milk.

The Finnish Nobel Prize winner A. I. Virtanen made Finland, Norway and Sweden take note of Palsson's research, eliminating foeto-maternal Listeriosis by rigid adherence to the original basic rules for silage making, and attention to the need to avoid contact of crop and of silage with soil.

The rest of the world paid little attention, and in 1988 I found that scientists engaged in combating Listeriosis had not even heard of Palsson or Virtanen. 1967 and following years: Dr McLauchlin reported in February

---

*'Growth of Listeria monocytogenes, etc.' *Journal of Food Protection*, Vol. 50, No. 6, June 1987, pp. 452–9.

†Le Service d'Hygiène Alimentaire du Ministre de l'Agriculture, reported in *Le Provençal* of Marseille, 1 January 1988. In Britain, however, despite official 1987 figures given above, Dr McLauchlin tells me that 15 per cent of Listeriosis patients were previously healthy.

1987 (*Journal of Applied Bacteriology*, 63, pp. 1–11): 'it has long been realised that there is a relationship between the feeding of silage and Listeriosis in animals.'

**1970** Growth of silage in France. Claude Bourgignon* wrote in spring 1988: 'Most of our livestock farms developed silage in the 1970s, usually without respect for rules of hygiene, and have thus become homes for Listeria, that bacterium finding them a choice environment in which to multiply. The numerous traces of *L. monocytogenes* isolated in dairy and meat products, likewise in the surroundings of *laiteries* and livestock farms, bear witness to this.' Dr McLauchlin comments: ' . . . the fact that many wild animals and birds also contain *Listeria monocytogenes* suggests that this [presence in many meat products] has little to do with silage.' To me it reinforces the Scandinavian view that earth contacts are the common factor.

**1979** *Boston, Massachusetts, USA:* pasteurised milk used for cheese possible source of Listeriosis in twenty-three hospital patients.

**1981** *Cumbria, UK:* outbreak traced to pasteurised cream.

Outside Scandinavia meat products have continued to harbour *L. monocytogenes*, including 50 per cent of raw chickens (up to over 65 per cent in late summer and autumn). Salad vegetables, growing close to the soil or in it, have also been a source of Listeriosis. Dairy products have lately come into prominence as sources of trouble in the cases listed below.

**1983** *Massachusetts, USA:* 49 neo-natal or immuno-suppressive cases from serotype 4b in pasteurised milk traced to storage tanks and cows on four farms.

*Vaud, Switzerland:* first troubles, including fatal cases, attributed to the local Vacherin, but not internationally publicised until 1987 (see below).

**1985** *California, USA:* 86 cases (29 fatal between 1 January and June) traced to serotype 4b in one make of Mexican-style fresh cheese. '*It was said* [my italics] that pasteurisation had been inadequate or that small quantities of raw milk were present in the product' (Ian Leighton, Department of Microbiology, Hull Royal Infirmary in Oxoid's *Culture*, 2 September 1985, where 4b was misprinted as 5b). Dr McLauchlin tells me in December 1988 that the case has at last been published (Linan *et al., New England Journal of Medicine*, 1988); but this, while increasing the cases to 140, has not elucidated the cause. Dr McLauchlin can still offer only the uncertainty: 'This outbreak was certainly due either to raw milk being added to the processed cheese, or to contamination of the plant.'†

**1986** *USA:* in February the Food and Drugs Administration detected 'noxious strain of Listeria' in pasteurised factory Bries from France; taken off the market before trouble arose.

*Austria, Germany:* in June pasteurised industrial cheeses Bonbel and Le Gracel (made by the French industrial giant Fromageries Bel) found to be Listeria-infected and dangerous; withdrawn before causing trouble; public warned of these *marques* 'until further notice'. (Enigma: the Austrian minister concerned absolved producer, importer and retailer from blame. In

*\*Ingénieur-agronome*, specialist in soil microbiology, article in *Les Quatre Saisons du Jardinage*, No. 49, 1988.

†Circumstantial evidence exists of milk supply surplus to pasteurisation capacity, but in later tests raw milk of all supplying herds was found clear of *Listeria* and the herds were clean; so plant contamination is indicated. Incidentally, only one farm used silage.

February 1988, on the advice of the Guilde des Fromagers, to which I belong, I wrote to a named authority in SOPEXA in Paris about the 1986 (and 1987) Brie cases, but have had no response.)

**1987** *Vaud, Switzerland:** in early winter seven deaths were attributed to *L. monocytogenes* 4b in Swiss pasteurised Vacherin Mont d'Or. All stocks were withdrawn and destroyed, and production was stopped. There followed the first international publicity about the hundred cases since 1983 in the Vaud (leading to thirty deaths) attributed to the same source. (I was told by Colindale that Swiss scientific papers published earlier had received no attention because they were in French,† a frightening indictment of scientists' lack of curiosity and failure to communicate and warn of danger across frontiers.) The British and French press were entirely unprepared. It has been reported that bacteria concentrate in the crust.

*France:* on 4 December the Centre Interprofessionel de Documentation et d'Information Laitière, Paris (CIDIL), quoted the Professor of Microbiology, Université de Tours, and the Chef de Travaux, Laboratoire Nationale de la Santé, as affirming: 'There has never been any proof of a connection between Listeriosis and the consumption of French cheese, either in France or abroad.' CIDIL also quoted from a joint *communiqué* by the French Ministries of Agriculture and Health: 'In France cases [of Listeriosis] registered in the course of a number of years have never been traced to any origin in food' (French Listeriosis cases run at about 1000 per annum). In France, Denmark, Germany and Switzerland 120 analyses had been made from stocks totalling 500 Franc-Comtois Vacherins (Mont d'Or/Vacherin du Haut-Doubs), all negative for *L. monocytogenes*. Unfortunately, the undiscriminating publicity for the Swiss disaster had already blackened the name of Vacherin and killed demand. Ironically, the only suspicion cast on a French Vacherin resulted from a tasting given in Paris on 10 December to publicise its clean bill of health and counter its association with the distinct, condemned Swiss cheese. *Science et Vie* reporters stole one of the cheeses and later claimed that it was infected with serotype 1/2a (declared harmless by the French Minister of Agriculture, yet responsible for 18 per cent of British Listeriosis). The irregular multiple-handling of this cheese and the lack of impartial control of the test must cast doubt on the validity of the declared result.

*Switzerland:* on 18 December the *Bundesamt* for Health listed twenty-four Swiss, German, French and (one) Italian cheeses found to harbour *L. monocytogenes*. None was farm-made, none made of raw milk (one, a *marque* of the giant Pont-l'Évêque type, I had thought to be *lait cru, artisanal*, but it had come under new ownership and was now made on a larger scale of heat-treated milk). Three were pasteurised cheeses from the

---

*This canton adjoins the Doubs *département* in Franche-Comté. The Mont d'Or bestrides the frontier.

†In November 1988 Dr McLauchlin contradicted my firm record of this answer. He stated that it did not become clear that cheese was the Swiss culprit until 1987. He said other scientists' attention was drawn 'after 1984', and he published papers in the *Journal of Medical Microbiology* in 1986, and in the *Journal of Applied Bacteriology* in 1987. I do not think any cheesemakers, let alone consumers, outside Switzerland knew of these cases until late in 1987.

Swiss Dairy School at Rutli/Rüti. The rest were pasteurised *laitier* cheeses. They included some from two enormous industrial concerns in the Région de Bresse and two so-called Bries, one from a factory in the Vosges and 'Brie Président' from the industrial giant Besnier (centred on Maine) by the ultimate in mechanised, untouched-by-human-hand methods, using not only pasteurised but almost de-natured, standardised milk.

*England and Wales:* of all the cases of Listeriosis (mostly in late summer and autumn), one was traced to a cheese (from serotype 4b) made from heat-treated goats' milk, and one to a standard French soft cheese.

**1988** *England:* in spring Colindale tested fifty imported factory soft cheeses, bought retail, and found *L. monocytogenes* present in strength in nine (18 per cent).

## Opinions on pasteurisation

**1988** *Geneva:* on 15–19 February the World Health Organization Symposium declared pasteurisation 'a safe process which reduces the number of *L. monocytogenes* in cheese to levels that do not pose an appreciable risk to human health'.

*London:* on 4 March the Deputy Director of CPHL, Colindale, quoted this in a letter to the *Sunday Times*, but also affirmed that 'the presence of *L. monocytogenes* in cheeses prepared from pasteurised milk is due to recontamination after heat-treatment of the milk'. The same letter had already allowed that 'Some studies have shown that when large numbers (1000–10,000 cells per ml) of *L. monocytogenes* present within leucocytes of milk were pasteurised, occasional survivors were detected after extensive testing. . . . This is an extreme condition since less than 5 per cent of raw milk has been shown to be contaminated with *L. monocytogenes* and the numbers present are 100 cells per ml. In other studies surviving *L. monocytogenes* were not detected.'

Ian Leighton (see p. 525) said it had been shown that *L. monocytogenes* can survive pasteurisation if present in numbers exceeding $5 \times 10^4/cc^3$ (50,000 to the ml).

Paul Gibbs of British Food Manufacturing Industries Research Association told Egon Ronay in February 1988: 'After pasteurisation damaged bacteria [*L. monocytogenes*] can revive in milk when it is chilled.' (See p. 529 below on long shelf-lives of industrial cheeses and growth of *L. monocytogenes*.)

## Advantages of raw-milk cheese over pasteurised

Gray and Killing (*Bacteriological Review*, 30, 1966, pp. 309–82) found *L. monocytogenes* 'relatively acid intolerant' and stated that it would not grow in environments below pH5.5.

In April 1988 Dr McLauchlin told me that he knew of no case involving raw-milk cheese, and attributed this immunity to the low pH, usually under 4 (pH of good silage is 3), i.e. lower alkalinity, higher acidity of traditionally made raw-milk cheese. He found *L. monocytogenes* flourishing in the higher pH6 or more of pasteurised cheeses of similar types (pH7 is reached in poor silage).

Dr McLauchlin has since emphasised to me that there is much debate on post-pasteurisation survival, but that he considers 'post-process contamination as more important'. He adds, 'I am not aware of any evidence that cheese produced from pasteurised milk is any more susceptible to contamination by *Listeria monocytogenes* than cheese produced from unpasteurised milk.' This conflicts with his answers in April (see above) to my questions on the subject, and with the absence up to December 1988 of any cast-iron case of contamination of raw-milk cheese. It also conflicts with the strong argument in the paragraph below.

Faith in pasteurisation as a cure for all ills in milk seems to be a barrier to the pursuit of lines of research which could point to the reason for and sources of infection and how to combat them. (There is similar resistance in agricultural research to recognition of the benefits of organic farming.)

I would add these further factors as explanatory of the comparative immunity of raw-milk cheese, and as reasons for preferring it.

The practices of milking parlours where milk is going straight to the cheese dairy for raw use are generally far stricter in hygiene, as are the subsequent cheese-dairy practices, than where it is known that milk will be pasteurised. In the latter case trouble is spread by bulk tanking and storage of milk before it reaches the cheesemaker (sometimes several days after milking and before pasteurisation).

Roots and silage, easily infected with *L. monocytogenes* through soil contact, are abhorred by good cheesemakers because of flavour taints. They are specifically excluded by AOC rules, which insist on local hay, for French Vacherin, Comté, Beaufort and Reblochon (national AOC), and Emmental Grand Cru and Gruyère de Savoie (regional *appellations*). *Lait cru* is insisted on in all these *appellations*.

Lower salt levels in raw-milk cheese encourage bacterial activity hostile to *L. monocytogenes*.

## Vulnerability of pasteurised milk and cheese

Dr J. G. Davis has pointed out that pasteurisation kills 99.9 per cent of beneficial bacteria in milk (it also kills the aromatic esters), while not 100 per cent effective against harmful bacteria. This lays the milk open to the latter, including *L. monocytogenes*, which can flourish unhindered. Cheese made from such milk, whether it contains *L. monocytogenes* or not initially, is similarly vulnerable to cross-infection, or to invasion from earthy contacts or dirty shelving in *caves*, as happened in some of the Swiss cases (Arenenberger cheese was withdrawn, its *cave* closed, and a new one opened with clean results).

Maurice Janier (co-founder of the Guilde des Fromagers), legal arbitrator in cheese matters in the Lyonnais and *affineur* of *lait cru* farmhouse and *artisanal* cheese, put it to me in this way in May 1988: 'Pasteurisation kills the antibodies which can discourage Listeria.' As a consequence, he said, the Swiss are now turning from pasteurisation to *thermisation* as a less destructive level of heat treatment. There is a parallel line of thought in work done at the Institute of Food Research in Bristol against Salmonella in chickens. On 30 November 1988 the *Guardian* reported: 'Dr Mead hopes to beat Salmonella with a method called "competitive exclusion", whereby harmless bacteria from Salmonella-free chickens are cultured and fed to the young hens in the rest of the flock. The bacteria take hold and in field trials have greatly reduced the levels of Salmonella they compete with.'

The Janier theory gains further credibility from this finding by Linnan *et al.*\* 'Soft cheeses may be an especially effective vehicle for *Listeria*, a halo-tolerant organism, because they are often treated with brine [for salting] which leads to high sodium chloride concentrations that inhibit competing organisms'. What applies to salting applies to pasteurisation (only more so, because pasteurisation kills); and higher levels of salting occur in pasteurised factory cheese.

Linnan *et al.* found: 'dairy products with longer shelf-lives provide an effective vehicle for transmission of *Listeria* ... allow extended periods of cold enrichment and subsequent multiplication of *L. monocytogenes*'.

N. S. Galbraith† has written of *L. monocytogenes*: 'it grows at the temperatures [*sic*] of refrigeration (4°C): indeed "cold enrichment" is used to culture the organism in the laboratory. A small inoculum on foods may proliferate, during prolonged refrigeration, outgrowing competing organisms and producing infection and illness in susceptible people'.

Ryser and Marth found that '*Listeria* counts increased most rapidly in surface [i.e. crust] and wedge [cut] samples. ... A minimum increase of at least tenfold in numbers ... was observed between seventeen and thirty days of ripening ...'. As we have seen, modern industrial cheeses tend to have thick crusts and low acidity, and boast storage lives of forty-two to seventy days (at 4°C *L. monocytogenes* doubles every forty hours). Some strains of *L. monocytogenes* did not grow in their Camembert test (inoculating with the bacterium) but were 'readily detected using "cold enrichment"'. In unripened cheese at pH4 all but one strain decreased to low level after four days of storage at 6°C. *L. monocytogenes* failed to show in partially ripened Camembert at pH5.5. 'All four *Listeria* strains tested increased at least tenfold between twenty-five and thirty days of storage'. What the WHO considers an acceptable level of surviving bacteria after pasteurisation is not going to stay so if it is given weeks to multiply.

## Possible sources of infection for Swiss Vacherin

Silage is made in the Vaud; has it been used by some makers of this winter cheese? It is excluded in Franche-Comté (where the level of healthy Listeriosis carriers is only 9 per cent against the 13–14 per cent of France as a whole).

Spruce trees, the bark of which is used to ring Vacherin cheeses, could be a source of infection, especially if bark is taken after felling (though I would not expect this practice). In Franche-Comté the strips of spruce-bark are simmered overnight before use on the next day's cheese, which would seem to eliminate any chance of bacterial survival.

\*'Epidemic Listeriosis, etc.', *New England Journal of Medicine*, Vol. 319, No. 13, 1988, p. 828.
†'A review, Listeria monocytogenes, etc.', *Journal of Applied Bacteriology*, 63, 1987, pp. 1–11.

The use of pasteurised milk seems, from what is recorded above, to make it more vulnerable than the raw-milk Franc-Comtois cheese, although pasteurisation could have been introduced only with the contrary intention.

## Conclusions

I am reminded of what Dr N. S. Galbraith (Director of Colindale) wrote to me in 1981: 'I am inclined to agree with you that we can certainly interfere excessively with nature, but this is rarely in the cause of safety, and usually in the cause of mass-production of foodstuffs.' His colleague N. D. Noah had written in the *British Medical Journal* in 1974: 'Even those with palates for very ripe cheese do not apparently risk their health in eating it.'

Dr Galbraith still regarded pasteurisation as right for safety, but the Listeriosis cases in the dairy world have thrown a new light on safety since 1981. Though reluctant to recognise it, Dr McLauchlin's findings suggest that the combination of pasteurised milk, factory cheesemaking methods and prolonged refrigeration provides a happy environment for *Listeria monocytogenes*, whereas raw-milk cheese is repellent to it.

Healthy cheese-lovers are apparently not at risk, but raw-milk cheese of good acidity is certainly safer, as well as far better in texture and flavour (pH under 5.5 has been reported safe; raw-milk cheese is usually under pH4). It is apparent that the destruction of the natural, healthy bacteria in milk heightens the danger from rogue bacteria such as *L. monocytogenes*. This danger is further heightened by factory methods of salting.

Immuno-suppressives and pregnant women should avoid soft and semi-soft cheeses and prepacked salads, and should take enormous care in washing any vegetables to be eaten raw.

Cheesemakers should check that the milk they use comes from:

1. Animals fed on hay (preferably from local sources, to preserve the character of the cheese) when not pastured. Roots, cattle-cake and silage are all to be avoided for flavour reasons, apart from the risk of contamination by *L. monocytogenes* (and, in the case of cattle cake and other synthetic foods, from Salmonella).

2. Milking parlours with uncompromising standards of dairy practice, with special attention to elimination of soil contacts, immediate safe disposal of mastitis milk (as *L. monocytogenes* causes mastitis, with heavy infection of milk), and extreme care to avoid cross-infection through hands, machines or any other equipment used.

They must avoid introduction of soil into the cheese dairy, and ensure that their water supplies are pure.

They should also use the minimum level of salt (a rule prescribed by most AsOC, but not observed by many larger *laiteries*).

Dairy and livestock farmers who insist on using silage should keep their meadows smooth and not set their mowers too close to the ground. They must go to great trouble to avoid the introduction of Listeria through soil contamination, including the use of clean planks over crops or silage where man or machine has to encroach. Scientists have warned against the use of plastic sheeting for covering pits or baling silage, because it is too liable to rip.

# Appendix 2

## Cheese and Human Health

Animal fats, which include the fats in milk, derive from the plant oils in the pastures which nourish the grazing animal. They make meat and milk (and thence cheese) more pleasurable to the palate through the aromatic esters carried in them. The animal digestive system converts them into the poly-saturated fats contained in dairy foods and meat fat, of which an excess, called cholesterol, may adhere to human artery walls. This harm can be averted by consumption of essential poly-*un*saturated fats and other natural digestive aids, such as olive oil, fish, garlic and wine.

In January 1987 Michael Oliver, Professor of Cardiology at the University of Edinburgh, wrote in the *Lancet*: 'Until now, the evidence has appeared to suggest that heart disease is caused by eating too much saturated fat. Our research suggests it is a deficiency of poly-*un*saturated fat which is important.' This study of over 6000 people showed a lower level of essential (*un*saturated) fatty acids in body fats in those with heart attacks than in the rest of the sample.

The Edinburgh study could help to explain the failure of the drastic anti-cholesterol campaign in America to get to grips with the problem. In twenty years (up to 1985) it reduced fat intake in the USA by 25 per cent and smoking by 40 per cent. Yet in 1985, 32 per cent of American invalids were still cardiac cases, against 16 per cent of French and 12 per cent of an Italian sample. Yet French and Italian cheese consumption per head (12–14 oz per week) had been rising steadily during that period to about three times the American level. A similar disparity between the levels of British and Latin cholesterol problems and cheese consumption had struck a research team at St Mary's Hospital, Paddington, in the 1970s. Their findings attributed the low incidence of cardiac trouble in Latins to their addiction to wine and garlic.

In May 1988 the British Medical Research Council's environmental epidemiology unit published research on fats and heart troubles conducted in three towns. Significantly, the town with the lowest fat consumption had the highest rate of heart disease. This adds weight to Professor Oliver's contention that more trouble comes from unhealthy imbalance of fats than from the amount of polysaturated fat (such as that in cheese) which is consumed.

A vital new inference, however, was drawn from the three-town survey. Susceptibility to heart trouble was attributed to the poor diet of expectant and nursing mothers. It is in the womb and at the breast that the weak or sound foundations of future adult health are laid.

Cheese is a healthy and nourishing, calcium- and protein-rich food. Those who have symptoms of digestive or heart trouble will of course consult their doctors about diet. The rest of us can eat, drink and be merry, provided we insist on ample variety in our diet, with special respect for wine, garlic and olive oil.

# Appendix 3

# Buying, Keeping and Serving Cheese

## Buying cheese

Buy little and often. Cheese is usually better kept in quantity by the *fromager*. Use a shop or market stall where the cheeses are obviously well chosen and looked after. A certificate on the wall from the Guilde des Fromagers should guarantee a knowledgeable *patron* or *patronne*. With small whole cheeses, look for a healthy, outswelling crust and good aroma. Seek out the words *'Fermier'* or *'Lait Cru'* on labels, and with Saint-Nectaire check for the (*fermier*) *oval* green plaque on the face of the cheese.

Broadly speaking, cows'-milk cheeses are now made all the year round, although production on small farms will be very low in the calving season in early spring. The first spring cheeses are usually some of the best of the year. Goats'-milk cheeses have traditionally been made from April to October, but the start of the new season may be delayed by weather conditions. You may still find some good goat cheeses as late as November, but beware of midwinter cheeses which cannot be made from fresh milk, as that is the kidding season.

Lambing is earlier in France than in Britain, so many lambs have already been weaned to free milk for cheesemaking by December. The ewes dry out in July and August. The small, softer ewes'-milk cheeses (brebis) are available therefore from early December: very young Gardians in Provence, fresh Brocciu in Corsica. Towards the end of the season, in the Rouergue, Pérail cheeses become available in larger numbers because they are made on farms which have up till then been providing milk for Roquefort. I have met Pérail still too young to eat in mid-September.

Roquefort, and the larger hard-crusted Pyrenean cheeses mature for months before they are released, so they are available throughout the year from skilful *fromagers*. The time to enjoy Roquefort at its best, though, comes between March and September when a good *fromager* may be able to serve you cheese that has been through natural *affinage* only and has escaped the very low-temperature longer-term storage.

If you read that a cheese is made in a certain season, bear in mind that it will not be available until the first cheeses have been matured; and that the last cheeses will be on the market after the cheesemaking season has finished. Vacherin, a winter cheese, is a good example of this. Look from October to early April for Le Mont d'Or, or Vacherin du Haut-Doubs, unpasteurised cheeses from Franche-Comté, avoiding *Swiss* Vacherin du Mont d'Or, which is pasteurised.

## Keeping cheese

Keep your cheese in cellar conditions, or the nearest you can achieve to this. They should be kept in a temperature of 50–60°F, cool but not cold. (See table of recommended temperatures and humidity for various classes of cheese: p. 534.) Kitchens are usually too warm, and refrigerators *far* too cold and airless; so try to find a cool, dark spot, perhaps in a garage if you have no cellar or larder. We have found a suspended, wooden cheese-cage (like a miniature meat-safe) keeps most cheeses happy for a few days, even in a warm climate.

Once a soft or semi-soft cheese is cut, the exposed surfaces will need airtight wrapping. This needs to be firmly applied, but should not be allowed to overlap too much of the crust. The crust should be at most loosely covered, so that it retains its natural character, its moulds having air-space in which to develop. Keeping soft cheese on a slight slope, with the cut surface uppermost, helps to control the flow if it is on the ripe side. Little marble bars help to hold a soft cheese surface in place.

In hot weather, or when travelling, hard cheeses and the firmer semi-soft cheeses sweat, and the cut surfaces tend to go leathery. A layer or two of white absorbent kitchen paper or tissue held against the cut surface by the usual wrap helps to contain the sweat and reduce the leathering.

Rest firm cheese on its biggest cut surface; after use it should be rested on a different face. Whole cheeses, and pieces too soft or too thin to be laid on a cut surface, should be turned over every other day, or daily if the temperature rises much above 60°F.

The slightly waxed papers used by most French cheese merchants are re-usable unless they become mouldy or sticky. Clingfilm or Polyvinyl (PVC) is not recommended because its chemical content can transfer into the cheese (it has been passed only for use at room temperature by the USA Food and Drugs Administration). Perforated wraps such as Saran Wrap (Polyvinyledene) and GladWrap (Polyethylene) are more acceptable. These have the advantage that cheese can breathe through them.

Foil has the characteristic of inhibiting the formation of natural crust. In very dry conditions muslin or other thin cloth, moistened in slightly salted water, may be laid loosely over the cheese and tucked in under the mat or board. This keeps the cheese moist and excludes flies. Humidity over an area of shelving can be achieved by hanging wet cloths, either kept with the bottom edge trailing in water, or re-wetted daily.

The harm done by airtight wrapping should be enough to warn people off buying pre-packed cheese. It can be illustrated by a tasting conducted by Gault Millau in February 1986. They began the test by giving the panel a taste of fresh-cut, Swiss raw-milk Emmental, properly matured. (It was then sold by Marie-Anne Cantin in Paris at 47.60 Francs per kilo.) Christian Millau gave this nine out of ten. The panel then set out to test the pre-packs against this good standard. The best mark among the pre-packs was given to its 64.90 Francs a kilo Swiss cousin; Millau gave this six out of ten, the rest of the panel averaging 5.2. All but one of the pre-packs cost more per kilo than the fresh cheese. The test proved that, whatever their provenance, it is exceptional for pre-packs to be anything but poor, immature and expensive alternatives to fresh cuts from whole cheeses; and *these* you can taste before you buy them.

## Table of temperature and humidity for storing cheeses

| Type of cheese | | Temperature | Humidity (for trade) |
|---|---|---|---|
| Soft | croûte-fleurie | 10–15°C (50–57°F) | 80–85% |
| | croûte-lavée | 10–15°C (50–57°F) | 90% |
| | chèvres croûte-fleurie or cendrés | 10–15°C (50–57°F) | 85% |
| Semi-soft (e.g. Saint-Nectaire) | | 10–15°C (50–57°F) | 85% |
| Blue | | 10–12°C (50–53°F) | 95% |
| Hard | | 10–15°C (50–57°F) | 80–85% |

1. The lower temperatures are only for whole cheeses stored by the trade. The upper temperatures are suitable for households, and may be stretched safely to 60–65°F for short-term storage.

2. Do not stack uncased cheeses on top of one another.

3. Cases of cheese may be stacked; but if the cheeses arrive on the moist side, or if the storage area is over-moist, they should be spread out.

4. Soft cheeses should have straw on top and bottom so that they can be turned every other day, and should be in airy but draught-free conditions.

## Presentation of cheeses

Curnonsky deplored the crowding together of cheeses with conflicting aromas. He liked to present each cheese separately on its own dish. This separation is ideal if space permits, and a knife for each cheese is essential.

Some compromise on the degree of separation is reasonable, however, and more practical. Wickerwork trays with loose straw or reed mats are kindest for all but the messiest of cheeses because the air can get all round them. Messy cheeses are better laid on leaves over earthenware or wood. Separate the sheep from the goats, and both from the cows; isolate blues, washed-crust cheeses and cheeses with herbs or spices. A harmonious group of three or four uncrowded cheeses on one tray is acceptable and more convenient than individual dishes. But each cheese should still have its own knife. One simple tray of good cheeses in prime condition is preferable to a bigger assortment of less perfect examples, no matter how rare.

At a big party cheeses are ideally laid out separately on a buffet, each with its own knife, for guests to help themselves. It should be a *sine qua non* that no cheese be presented without its name and provenance (this advice also applies to shops and restaurants). Good cheeses deserve the same respect as good wines. Even if wines are decanted, they are specified on formal menus, and always talked about as they are served, in houses where gastronomy matters. It follows that, as there are usually more cheeses than wines, they should be listed helpfully on the menu and identified by cards on the table. We never use spiked labels in our shop or home, as spikes damage the crust.

The Belgian Maurice des Ombiaux, called 'Le Cardinal de la Gastronomie', had over-fussy ideas about garnishing his cheese-tray with breads, biscuits, radishes, celery, fennel, salt and cumin. These items, if served at all, should be kept well away from the cheese. The beauty and aroma of good cheese need no enhancement, no other flavour to set them off. Their bed of leaves or matting provides the only background to be wished.

Small soft brebis such as Le Gardian from the Camargue in Provence and some goat cheeses at the *crémeux* stage can be served like Mozzarella, with olive oil *(extra-vierge)* and black pepper from a not too finely set mill.

Most cheeses should be cut like a cake, taking a fair share of crust, and never cutting across the nose of a triangular piece. It is a sad mistake to spread good cheese. Spreading destroys the impact on the palate, tongue and nose of the full flavour and aroma and subtle texture. The cheese should be sliced as thick or as thin as you choose and laid on the bread. If you are serving yourself from a small goat cheese, to eat it on bread, take a half-cheese and slice it laterally across the face in strips.

At table, the French attack cheese with knife and fork, taking their bread on the side. Butter is rarely served with it, except in Normandy, where so much butter is made that it is taken as much for granted as it is in England. Salt butter is an insult to the cheesemaker. The use of unsalted butter, while largely a matter of taste, has its practical side. Butter attaches hard or crumbly cheese to the bread, if it is eaten in the English way or away from the table without plates and forks.

Butter is recommended, even in France, to set off the richness of Roquefort and other blue cheeses of strong character, but I deplore the custom of mixing butter and cheese into a paste.

With *triples-crèmes*, ripe Camembert and Brie, and soft chèvres, butter is unnecessary; but I like it, as it prevents runny cheese from sinking into the bread. Savour and texture are lost if the cheese is mixed up with dough.

Bread should be a good, crusty platform or accompaniment for the star of the show. Better serve no bread than limp dough with a cardboard or brown-paper skin. If the bread is not still crusty and warm from the baker, it should be crisped up quickly in the oven shortly before serving. The flavour and consistency of crust and dough in good breads are a joy in themselves. I ring the changes with *pain de seigle* (rye), *son* (bran), *complet* (wholemeal) and *pain de campagne* (country bread with thick crust for keeping).

'French bread', as the English think of it, the long white *baguette*, is rarely the pleasure it used to be because of the general change from wood-fired ovens to steam-baking. In summer *baguette* bread tends to dry up at the table, before the cheese comes round. The other breads are rich in crust and flavour, and keep better, standing up well to re-heating. When travelling by road, we have found that *pain de campagne* will stay crisp if exposed to the sun in the rear window.

## Wine and cheese

When you travel, seek out traditional local wines to accompany local cheeses. You will experience refreshment and pleasure not available elsewhere. These wines are seldom made on a big enough scale for the general market. They include a number made from rare and ancient indigenous species of grape. Some raise heart and palate on the spot, but, inexplicably, taste flat and sad in exile. In general, I look out for organic wines, and others matured in wood. I find them richer in flavour and texture than the run of wines made by modern methods of vinification.

The excess of additives in wines made by fashionable modern methods adds to their unhealthy inheritance from chemically treated soil and vines. Ammonium sulphate and potassium cyanide treatment are allowed, but need not be declared (as would have to happen with foodstuffs). It is common for such wines to cause sneezing (my wife suffers), and headaches, as *The Times* wine correspondent Jane MacQuitty has reported. Chemicals also affect bouquet, tending to suppress its natural aroma (as in cheese). They may make it positively malodorous on occasion, as Château Phélan-Segur found out in 1987. This noted Bordeaux vineyard had to withdraw from sale its 1983, 1984 and 1985 vintages on that account, and sued the American chemical company which had supplied its 'faulty systemic insecticide'.

A contrast to this misfortune is provided by an account of 1985 wines produced by the Belgian grower and vintner Jean-Marie Guffens: Mâcon-Pierreclos AC Blanc and Cuvée Vieilles Vignes (red), and Pouilly-Fuissé AC Les Crays. All were produced from old vines; but the secret of ultimate success came from their organic exploitation, and vinification without filtering, pumping and sulphuring. Jane MacQuitty found the Pouilly-Fuissé the star, with its 'wonderful pale, greeny-gold colour and elegant smokey taste'. The Pierreclos Blanc's colour and fine bouquet outclassed many a Côte d'Or white at the same price known to her. The red stood up similarly to comparison with the Côte d'Or. Jane MacQuitty's verdict was: 'They are the finest Mâconnais wines I have ever tasted.'

The matching of wine and cheese by Pierre Androuët in his *Guide du Fromage* is exhaustive and unrivalled. My advice is confined to broad counsel on match and mismatch, based on the reactions of my own palate over half a century.

Blue cheeses, washed-crust cheeses of any strength, and tangy Laguiole cut across the impact of subtle red wines. With such cheeses try fruity, even sweet white wines. With strong washed-crust cheeses, try Alsatian wines, strong beer or marc. If you insist on red wine with these cheeses, keep to something strong and rough, such as a good old-fashioned Cahors, rather than one of the over-refined modern versions.

With brebis and chèvre local wines are usually best. Sancerre and Pouilly Fumé with Berrichon chèvre show how glorious white wines can be. In Provence there are few white wines of such quality, but many reds to choose from. Here again, avoid the over-smooth and seek out those with a more rustic, Provençal character. There are some notable organic (*biologique*) red wines with plenty of character and more suitable for anyone suffering from allergies than the more common chemically doctored wines. Our own favourite *biologiques* wines are Terre Blanches and Mas de Gourgonnier (both Coteaux d'Aix en Provence, AOC, Les Baux).

I hope my readers will find as much satisfaction as I have in hunting and matching the local wines and cheeses of France.

# Glossary

**Abondances** Breed of dairy cattle (Savoie).
**Affinage** Maturing of cheeses.
**Affiné** Cheese that has been matured.
**Affineur** Specialist in the maturing of cheeses.
**Agrafe** Clip used to secure *Éclisse* (q.v.) round Brie.
**Aizy** Home-cultured starter, sometimes combining starter and rennet (q.v.).
**Alpages** High mountain pastures used for summer grazing.
**Alpines** Breed of goat.
**Âme** The heart of the cheese; used of the visible whiter centre of Brie or Camembert before it has ripened right through.
**AOC** See *Appellation*.
**À point** 'Just right' – cheese neither under- nor over-ripe.
**Appellation Nationale d'Origine Contrôlée** Legal definition of how cheeses are made and the limits of their area of origin. There are twenty-seven ANOC cheeses. There are also some regionally controlled *appellations*, e.g. Emmental Grand Cru.
**Ardi-gasna** Basque word for sheep cheese.
**Aromatic esters** Flavour- and aroma-carrying fatty acids and glycerides in plants, transmitted from pastures to milk and thus to cheese.
**Artisanal** Cheese made by hand rather than by machine.
**Artisons** Patois term for cheese mites (*cirons*).
**Attrassadou** Wooden rudder for stirring curd (Auvergne).
**Babeurre** Buttermilk (q.v.).
**Bacterium linens** See *Linens*.
**Bannette** Draining-frame laid across vat to drain large cheeses.
**Bara** Auvergne word for well-dried curd used in making Gaperon.
**Basco-béarnaises** Breed of horned sheep (Pyrénées).
**Baste** Two-handled tub used to carry milk to the *buron* (q.v.) (Auvergne).
**Battoir** Straw-covered grid.
**Berger** 1. Shepherd; cattle herdsman. 2. Sheepdog; dog used to herd cattle.
**Bergerie** Building used to shelter sheep.
**Beurré** Buttery.
**Bidon** Milk churn.
**Biologique** Organic farming – i.e. using natural fertilisers and avoiding chemical fertilisers and pesticides.
**Blancs** Unsalted whole fresh cheeses before any *affinage* (q.v.). N.B. not the same as *fromage blanc* (q.v.).
**Bleuté** Cheese with blue or blue-grey surface mould acquired naturally in the *cave* (q.v.).
**Blondes d'Aquitaine** Breed of dairy cattle.
**Blondes d'Aubrac** Breed of dairy cattle of the Rouergue and southern Auvergne.
**Blondes des Pyrénées** Breed of dairy cattle.
**Bottes** Mats on which cheeses are drained and sometimes sold.
**Boutilier** Cheesemaker in mountain *buron* (q.v.) (Auvergne).
**Brebis** 1. *La brebis:* ewe. 2. *Le brebis:* cheese made of ewes' milk.
**Brine** Very salt water.
**Brine-washing** See *croûte-lavée*.
**Brique** Cheese shape, usually rectangular and on the thin side.
**Brousse** Cheese made from whey or skimmed milk (Provence).
**Brunes des Alpes** Breed of dairy cattle.
**Bûche** Log-shaped cheese.
**Buron** Simple mountain dairy and cheese-store with sleeping space (Auvergne).
**Buttermilk** Liquid remaining after butter-making.
**Cabane** Mountain chalet where cheese is made in summer (Pyrénées, Corsica).
**Cabanières** Workers in the Roquefort *caves* (q.v.).
**Caghiatu** Freshly curdled milk (Corsica).
**Caillage** Coagulation of milk to form curd.
**Caillé** Curd.
**Caillette** Vell, lining of the fourth stomach of a calf used in making rennet (q.v.).
**Caillotte de beurre** Buttermilk (q.v.).
**Cajadhia** Basket-like mould (now usually plastic) used in Corsican cheesemaking.
**Cantalou** Cheesemaker in mountain *buron* (q.v.) (Auvergne).
**Canton** French district containing several *communes* (q.v.).
**Carré** Cheese shape, square.
**Casein** Milk's chief protein, precipitated into curd by use of rennet (q.v.). It is used to make some cheese labels embedded in the crust. *Caséine* in French.
**Causses** Limestone plateaux of the Massif Central.
**Cave** Natural cave or cellar in which cheeses are ripened and stored.

**Cave humide**  Cheese storage cellar with high humidity.
**Cazelles**  Drystone shepherds' shelters on the Plateau of Larzac, Rouergue.
**Cendré**  Cheese coated, ideally, with ashes of *sarments* (q.v.), but today usually with industrially powdered charcoal ready-mixed with salt.
**Cendres de bois**  Wood-ashes; see *cendré*.
**Chalet**  Simple mountain dairy and cheese-store with sleeping space.
**Charollais (or Charolais)**  The beef branch of the old Burgundian cattle breed. The Charollais cheese is named for the Charollais region and should be made of goats' milk.
**Châtaignier**  Chestnut tree, the leaves of which are used to wrap some cheeses.
**Chaudron**  Cauldron used for cheese-making.
**Chaumes**  High pastures. Also stubble (Vosges).
**Cheese-iron**  Small metal corer for removing a plug from the interior of a cheese to test aroma, flavour and texture (*sonde*).
**Cheptel**  Herd.
**Chèvre**  1. *La chèvre*: nanny goat. 2. *Le chèvre (fromage de chèvre)*: goats'-milk cheese.
**Chevrerie**  Goat farm.
**Chevrier, chevrière**  Goatkeeper.
**Claquerette**  Wooden spoon used to beat curd in domestic cheesemaking.
**Clayette**  Straw, reed or wicker mat on which moulded cheeses are set to drain.
**CNAOF**  Comité Nationale d'Appellations d'Origines de Fromage. See *Appellation*.
**Coagulation**  The clotting of milk, usually by rennet (q.v.).
**Cocchja**  Wooden ladle used in cheesemaking (Corsica).
**Commune**  Smallest unit of French local government, equivalent to English parish but with more powers.
**Communes**  Provençal term for cross-bred goats.
**Concours**  Competition.
**Couche**  Layer (of mould).
**Coulant**  Runny.
**Crémerie**  Cheese shop.
**Crémeux**  Creamy stage in development of some cheeses.
**Croûte-bleutée**  Cheese with blue or blue-grey surface mould naturally acquired in the *cave* (q.v.).

**Croûte-brossée**  Brushed crust.
**Croûte-fleurie**  Cheese with mould-ripened crust.
**Croûte-lavée**  Cheese salted by washing crust in brine (q.v.). Wine, beer or *eau-de-vie* (q.v.) are sometimes used.
**Cru**  Raw, e.g. *lait cru* (unpasteurised milk).
**Cru de lait**  Term sometimes used of extra-good quality milk, as with wine.
**Curd**  The coagulated fats and other solids produced from milk by natural ripening and renneting (see *rennet*).
**Curd mill**  Mill for grinding curd into pieces, the size of the pieces varying according to the type of cheese.
**Cuve**  Large-scale vat.
**Cuyala**  Béarnaise term for mountain chalet where cheese is made in summer (Pyrénées).
**Dégustation**  Tasting.
**Demi-écrémé**  Half-skimmed.
**Demi-étuvé**  Medium ripe.
**Demi-sec**  Halfway stage of ripening of a small goat cheese.
**Demi-sel**  Fresh cream cheese made from pasteurised milk and salted, at least 40 per cent *matières grasses* (q.v.) and 2 per cent salt.
**Démoulage**  Turning out cheeses from moulds.
**Département**  Modern administrative division of France, often disregarding old provincial boundaries.
**Dessalage**  De-salting.
**Desséchage**  Drying.
**Domestique**  Domestic scale of cheese production, usually just for the cheesemaker's own household.
**Double-crème**  Double-cream cheese – i.e. having not less than 60 per cent *matières grasses* (q.v.).
**Draille**  Broad sheep-drovers' path used for *transhumance* (q.v.) (Provence).
**Eau-de-vie**  Spirit usually made from wine-pressings (e.g. *marc* (q.v.)).
**Éclisse**  Low, adjustable circlet used to retain shape in the later stages of cheesemaking.
**Écrémé**  Skimmed.
**Égouttage**  Draining of cheeses.
**Égouttoir**  Draining table for new-made cheeses.
**Élevage**  Breeding.
**Éleveur**  Breeder (normally of cattle, sheep or goats, but see p. 284).

**Ensemencement**  Introduction of mould into milk or curd.
**Ensilage**  Silage (q.v.).
**Épicéa**  Spruce, the bark of which is used to encircle Vacherin.
**Épicerie**  Grocery and provision-merchant's store.
**Équinon**  Wooden cheese-mould (Nord).
**Escamadou**  Skimmer to assist drainage of curd (Auvergne).
**Esters**  See *aromatic esters*.
**Étuvé**  Mature (see Edam, p. 17).
**Faisselle**  Perforated draining-mould used for soft cheeses. Also, unsalted soft curd sometimes sold in the *faisselle*.
**Faisselier**  Large perforated tub in which cheese is placed to drain (Normandy).
**Fatoghie**  Basket-like mould (now usually plastic) used in Corsican cheesemaking.
**Fats-in-solids**  See *matières grasses*.
**Fenaison**  Haymaking.
**Ferme-auberge**  Farm offering regional dishes from home-raised produce.
**Fermier**  1. Farmer. 2. Farm-made cheese.
**Ferrandaises**  Disappearing breed of dairy cattle found in the Auvergne.
**Feuille**  Leaf. Cheeses *à la feuille* are leaf-wrapped.
**Fines-herbes**  A mixture of parsley, chives, tarragon and chervil.
**Flamandes**  Breed of dairy cattle (Nord).
**Fleurines**  Spore-laden draughts in storage *caves* (q.v.) which aid the maturing of Roquefort (Rouergue).
**Flush**  Spring and autumn seasons of rich pasture giving extra milk yield.
**Foin**  Hay. Cheeses *au foin* were traditionally bedded in hay during *affinage* (q.v.).
**Follower**  Circular lid used within hoop or mould to press down curd.
**Fourme**  The old word for cheese derived from the form or mould it was made in; still used in the Auvergne.
**Frais, fraîche**  Fresh.
**Fréniale**  Curd-breaking implement (Auvergne).
**Frísonnes, Frisonnes françaises**  Originally Friesian breed of black-and-white dairy cattle, now predominantly of Holstein blood (q.v.).
**Fromage**  Cheese (from Latin *forma*, shape).
**Fromage blanc**  Fresh cream cheese either unsalted or with salt content so low that it can be eaten for dessert with sugar or salt.

**Fromage cuit**  Hard cheese of which the curd has been brought to 65°C during making (e.g. Emmentaler).
**Fromage du terroir**  Cheese getting its character from the local soil and pastures.
**Fromage fort**  Strong preparation usually made from cheese leftovers with liquor and herbs added; usually potted.
**Fromage frais**  Cheese which has been salted but sold unripened.
**Fromager**  1. Cheesemaker. 2. Wholesaler or retailer of cheese.
**Fromagerie**  Cheese-dairy; cheesemaking enterprise. Also used by some cheese shops, though *crémerie* is more common.
**Frotté**  Rubbed.
**Fruité**  Fruity flavoured.
**Fruitière**  Co-operative village cheese-dairy using members' raw milk.
**Gape**  Buttermilk (q.v.) (Auvergne).
**Garde-manger**  Wooden cage with fine-mesh sides hung as airy larder; excellent for keeping cheeses at home.
**Gare fromagère**  Railway station specially provided for loading of cheeses.
**Garrigue**  Wild, rocky Provençal landscape rich in the herbs used to garnish local cheeses.
**Geotrichium candidum**  White mould at early stages of Saint-Nectaire making.
**Gerle, gerlou**  Two-handled tub used to carry milk to the *buron* (q.v.) (Auvergne).
**Gispre**  Pejorative patois term for a cheese tasting very 'sheepy' (Rouergue).
**Grises gasconnes**  Breed of cattle now mostly used for beef.
**Grossiste**  Wholesaler, selling *en gros* as opposed to *en detail* (retail).
**Gruerie**  Carolingian word for forests, whence Gruyère (Franche-Comté).
**Gruyer**  Forester who sold fuel for making Gruyère (Franche-Comté).
**Halle**  Covered market.
**Halles: Les Halles**  Formerly France's great central market; its successor is at Rungis (q.v.).
**Hâloir**  Place where cheeses are laid out to dry and where some cheeses receive their *croûte-fleurie* (q.v.) from mould naturally formed on the walls. See also *séchoir*.
**Harpe**  Stringed implement for cutting curd during cheesemaking.
**Hausse**  High, moveable extension to cheese-mould used in early stages of cheesemaking (Brie).
**Hollandaises**  Breed of dairy cattle (*pie-*

*noir* and occasionally *pie-rouge* (q.q.v.)).
**Holstein** Breed of black-and-white cattle. Holstein bulls now dominate the breeding of French dairy cattle (see *Frisonnes françaises*).
**Humide** Moist, humid.
**Impaghia** Low-lying pastures (Corsica).
**Industriel** Indicates a large-scale, factory-style creamery with mechanised cheesemaking.
**Iron** See *cheese-iron*.
**Jasserie, jasse, jas** Shepherd's hut in the mountains for summer cheesemaking (Auvergne and Rouergue).
**Jonchée** A scattering of reeds or rushes from which cheese-mats were made.
**Kaiolar** Basque term for mountain *cabane* or chalet where cheese is made in summer (Pyrenées).
**Lacaune** Breed of sheep milked for Roquefort.
**Laîches** Strips of raffia bound round the circumference of a Livarot cheese.
**Lainures** Cracks in cheese.
**Lait cru** Milk neither pasteurised nor given other heat treatment such as *thermisation* (q.v.).
**Lait de mélange** Cheese made from a mixture of milks, with cows' milk usually predominant.
**Lait entier** Whole milk as it comes from the dairy animal, completely unskimmed.
**Laiterie** Dairy, from artisan to industrial in scale.
**Laitier** 1. Dairyman. 2. Dairy-made cheese.
**Lait thermisé** Milk which has been heat-treated but to a lower temperature than pasteurised milk.
**Laurier** Bay (not to be confused with *laurier rose*, oleander).
**Lavage** Washing (as in *croûte-lavée* (q.v.)).
**Lavogne** Dew pond used by grazing animals (Rouergue).
**Légumes** Class of pasture plants which collect nitrogen.
**Limousins** Breed of cattle, today used mainly for beef.
**Linens** *Bacterium linens* is a slime-type bacterium attracted to *croûte-lavée* cheeses (q.v.) in particular, imparting a russet colour.
**Lissage** Smoothing the crust of cheeses by hand.
**Listeria monocytogenes** Bacteria (of which thirteen serotypes have been published) present in 5 per cent of new milk, probably through soil contamination, which may start with contamination of silage (q.v.). Listeriosis can result (see Appendix 1).
**Louche** Ladle used to put curd into moulds.
**Lutte** Mating season of the Lacaune sheep (q.v.). General meaning: struggle.
**Maître fromager** Master cheesemaker, or cheese expert. Fewer than 100 are listed by the Guilde des Fromagers.
**Malaxage** Mixing of curd at early stage of cheesemaking.
**Malessui** Cheese going runny between crust and interior (Touraine). Slip-coat.
**Manechs** Breed of sheep, either *tête-noir* (blackfaced with horns) or *tête-rouge* (redfaced with horns) (Pyrenées).
**Marc** Spirit made from wine pressings.
**Marcaire** 1. Tenant farmer in Alsace-Lorraine. 2. Cauldron.
**Marcairerie** Stone farm building in high pastures of Alsace-Lorraine, used for summer cheesemaking.
**Matières grasses** Degree of fatness of cheese, expressed as a percentage of fat in total 'dry matter' (i.e. fats plus solids-not-fats). This percentage is constant throughout the life of the cheese, whereas the percentage of fat in the whole cheese increases as moisture evaporates with the ageing of the cheese and so cannot be precisely defined for the buyer.
**Menadou** Wooden paddle for stirring curd (Auvergne).
**Menole** Curd-breaking implement (Auvergne).
**Menove** Curd-breaking implement (Auvergne).
**Mergue** Whey (Auvergne).
**Mérinos** Breed of sheep mostly used for wool but which give milk for Gardian cheeses (Provence).
**Meton, metton** Re-cooked whey used to make Cancoillotte (Franche-Comté).
**Mezadou** Curd-breaking implement (Auvergne).
**m.g.** See *matières grasses*.
**Mi-chèvre** Cheese made with at least 50 per cent goats' milk, usually mixed with cows' milk.
**Mignaut** Sloping table for draining whey from curd (Nord).
**Mimosa** See *petit mimosa*.
**Mi-sec** See *demi-sec*.

## GLOSSARY

**Moelleux**  Soft and velvety.
**Moisissure**  Mould in or on a cheese.
**Moisson**  Harvest.
**Monilium candidum**  Mould sometimes found on Pont-l'Évêque but disapproved of by purists.
**Montbéliardes**  Breed of dairy cattle, the backbone of Franc-Comtois cheese and now spreading.
**Morge**  Brine (q.v.) enriched with scrapings from old cheeses, used to rub surface of Gruyère and other cheeses.
**Mou, molle**  Soft.
**Moulage**  Moulding.
**Mould**  1. Wood, metal or plastic container used in cheesemaking which dictates the shape of the cheese. 2. Fungal species enriching crust of cheeses or blueing their interiors, preferably acquired from the surroundings in which the cheeses are matured, but often artificially introduced.
**Moulé à la louche**  Cheese whose curd has been hand-ladled into the moulds.
**Moulé à la main**  1. Cheese whose shape has been hand-moulded. 2. Cheese whose curd has been hand-ladled into moulds.
**Moulinet**  Curd mill (q.v.).
**Moussé**  Cheese which has acquired its first, white coat of mould.
**Mucor aspergillus**  Unwelcome black surface mould removed by Saint-Nectaire makers.
**Muzadour**  Wooden paddle for stirring curd (Auvergne).
**Nature & Progrès**  An organisation advising organic farmers (see *Biologique*).
**Normandes**  Breed of dairy cattle (Normandy).
**Oïdium**  Mould which forms a greasy surface on cheese.
**Oïdium auranticum**  Sought-after brilliant red surface mould on Saint-Nectaire.
**Organic farming**  See *Biologique*.
**Paghuli**  Copper cauldron used in Corsica for cheesemaking.
**Palmarès**  Prizewinner.
**Passé**  Very over-ripe cheese, often used to make *fromage fort* (q.v.).
**Pasteurisation**  Heat treatment to destroy harmful micro-organisms in milk, which also destroys most flavour-enriching micro-organisms. Lower degrees of heat treatment include *thermisation* (q.v.).
**Pâte**  Interior of finished cheese.
**Pavé**  Cheese shape, usually square and thick.

**Pays**  One's native soil, used of village, district or province. Also used of one's fellow-native: *pays* or *payse* (f.).
**Pebre d'aï**  'Asses' pepper': Provençal name for *sarriette* (q.v.). See also *poivre d'âne*.
**Pelle**  Round cutting-edged shovel used to handle curd (Brie).
**Penicillium**  Mould family *mycellium*, of which the common types influencing cheese-development are listed below.
  **Penicillium album**  White mould, but developing into blue on surface (particularly goat cheeses).
  **Penicillium candidum**  White mould commonly used on the crust of soft cheeses.
  **Penicillium glaucum**  Mould producing internal and exterior blueing in cheeses (see *croûte-bleutée*).
  **Penicillium roquefortii**  Mould deriving from the Caves de Cambalou where Roquefort is blued, and in general use for blueing other types of cheese.
**Permanent pasture**  Multi-species natural pasture left unploughed.
**Persillé**  Blue cheese.
**Petit lait**  Whey (q.v.).
**Petit mimosa**  Sought-after yellow surface mould found on properly matured Saint-Nectaire cheeses.
**Picardes**  Breed of dairy cattle (Nord).
**Pies-noires**  The more common of the two types of Hollandaise dairy cattle; black and white, as opposed to the few red-pied.
**Pies-rouges de l'Est**  Red-pied cattle of eastern France, also called Tachetées de l'Est (q.v.).
**Pignato**  Small earthenware pot (Corsica).
**Piquant**  Sharp-tasting.
**Plomber**  To wrap cheese in foil coat (Rouergue).
**Poivre d'âne**  'Asses' pepper': from Provençal name for *sarriette* (q.v.), *Pebre d'aï*.
**Pouset**  Mushroom-shaped implement for pressing out whey (Auvergne).
**Prat communal**  Communally shared grazing land.
**Pré**  Grazing land.
**Presse-tôme**  Ladder-like grid for pressing and draining curd.
**Présure**  Rennet (q.v.).
**Puiset à caillé**  Flat, round trowel for lifting curd (Provence).
**Pur chèvre**  Cheese made only with goats' milk. See *mi-chèvre* and *lait de mélange*.

**Quinon** Wooden cheese-mould (Nord).
**Raclette** Dish made from melted cheese (literally 'scraper'). See pp. 434–5.
**Recuite** Literally 're-cooked'. Cheese made from the solids precipitated in reheated whey.
**Rennet** Distilled extract of the abomasum (fourth stomach of the ruminant) containing enzymes which break down the solids in milk into digestible form, helping coagulation. Some plants (e.g. fig, thistle) can have the same effect as rennet (q.v.).
**Repassé** Very over-ripe cheese, often used to make *fromage fort* (q.v.).
**Rocou** Ruddy vegetable colouring matter.
**Romarin** Rosemary.
**Rove** Breed of goat particularly known for its use in Brousse de Rove (Provence).
**Rungis** France's most important wholesale food market, south-east of Paris; successor to Les Halles (q.v.).
**Saanens** Breed of goat.
**Salage** Dry-salting, either of the curd or of the exterior of the cheese.
**Salers** Breed of dairy cattle native to the Auvergne and northern Rouergue.
**Saloir** Salting room.
**Sangle** Spruce-bark circlet put round Vacherin cheese.
**Sarments** Vine roots or prunings traditionally used to make wood-ash for *cendrés* cheeses (q.v.).
**Sarriette** Herb related to savory, often used to top goat cheeses in Provence. See also *Pebre d'aï* and *Poivre d'âne*.
**Saumure** Brine (q.v.).
**Sec** Term used for fully ripened goat cheese when the surface is firm and usually mould-coated.
**Séchage** Drying.
**Séchoir** Place where young cheeses are put to dry (Brie). See also *hâloir*.
**Seigle** Rye, rye bread.
**Sérum** Whey (q.v.).
**Silage** Green fodder fermented and stored free of air for winter feed. May taint cheese flavour, so excluded by some AOC regulations (see *Appellation*).
**Sonde** Cheese-iron (q.v.).
**Starter** Lactic bacterial culture used to start transformation of solids in milk into cheese.
**Syndicat** French trade or professional association.
**Syndicat d'Initiative** Chamber of Commerce, often found at the *mairie* (town hall).

**Taches rouges** Desirable red patches on surface of *fourmes* and Saint-Nectaire cheeses.
**Tachetées de l'Est** Breed of dairy cattle, same as *Pies-rouges* (q.v.).
**Tarentaises** Breed of dairy cattle from the region of that name, usually called *Tarines*.
**Tarines** See *Tarentaises*.
**Tendre** Mild (referring to Edam cheese; see p. 17).
**Thermisation** Heat treatment of milk at a lower temperature than pasteurisation (q.v.), held at temperature below 65°C for under one minute.
**Tintinajo** Belled leader of flock of sheep, or of herd of cows or goats.
**Toile** Cheesecloth.
**Tôme, tomme** 1. Small round goat cheeses when young. 2. Larger pressed cheeses from all types of milk.
**Tonne** Metric ton, 1000 kilos.
**Transhumance** The movement of flocks or herds from winter pasture or stabling to high mountain pastures in summer.
**Trappiste** Term often applied to monastically made cheeses.
**Trieur** Experienced *affineur* (q.v.) who irons a sample of cheese to test its maturity.
**Triple-crème** Cheese made from full-cream milk with added cream, attaining 75 per cent *matières grasses* (q.v.).
**Troupeau** Flock or herd of sheep, goats or cows.
**Tuffeau** Porous cliff, in the caves of which mushrooms are grown and cheeses matured (Touraine).
**Ultrafiltration** Separation of milk solids by a filter of 99.9 per cent fineness. Used in industrial cheesemaking.
**Vache** 1. Cow. 2. Cows'-milk cheese.
**Vacherie** Stabling for cows; may include milking parlour.
**Vell** Skin of the abomasum (fourth stomach of the ruminant) from which rennet (q.v.) is distilled.
**Vendange** Wine harvest.
**Vigneron** Wine grower.
**Vignobles** Vineyards.
**Vosgiennes** Traditional cattle of Alsace and Vosges regions.
**Washed crust** See *croûte-lavée*.
**Whey** Residue of milk after most of the fats and other solids have been coagulated into the curd (q.v.).
**Whole milk** Milk as it comes from the dairy animal – i.e. completely unskimmed.

# Bibliography

## A note about maps

Map references in this book are taken from the Michelin yellow map series 1:200,000, 1cm:2km, with *pli* (fold) numbers 1 to 20, available in both England and France. France is also covered by Michelin maps in one-volume editions, both hardback and paperback (*Motoring Atlas of France*, Paul Hamlyn, 1987). Most of the places mentioned in the book can be found in the index of the *hardback* version of the Michelin *Motoring Atlas of France*, but not the *pli* numbers.

## Books about cheese

Androuët, Pierre, *Guide du Fromage*, Stock, 1971 (in French). English translation, Aidan Ellis, 1973; 2nd edition, Aidan Ellis, 1977; revised 1983).
——, *Le Livre d'Or du Fromage*, Atlas, 1984.
——, 'Le Tour de France des Fromages', in *Touring Magazine*, No. 952, December 1982.
——, and Chabot, Yves, *Le Brie*, Presses du Village, Etrepillat, 1985.
——, and Lyon, Ninette, *Le Guide Marabout des Fromages de France et du Monde Entier*, Marabout, 1978.
Bérard, Léone, *Le Livre des Fromages*, La Courtille, 1978, and Temps Actuel, 1982.
Centre National Interprofessionel de l'Économie Laitière, *L'Économie Laitière en Chiffres*, annual.
Chast, Michel, and Voy, Henry, *Le Livre de l'Amateur de Fromages*, Robert Laffont, 1984 (1st edition 1961 by Raymond Lindon).
Courtine, Robert J., *Larousse des Fromages*, Librairie Larousse, 1973.
Davis, John Gilbert, *Cheese*, 4 vols, Churchill Livingstone, 1965–76.
*Gault Millau Magazine*, special cheese issue, February 1986 (including regional editions).
Graham, Peter, *New Classic Cheese Cookery*, Penguin, 1988.
Lacroix, Danièle, *Les Fromages d'Appellation d'Origine*, La Nouvelle Librairie, 1984.
Lindon, Raymond, *Le Livre de l'Amateur de Fromages*, 1st edn, Robot Laffont, 1961.
Lyon, Ninette: see Androuët and Lyon; and see below.
Mackiewicz, François, *Fromages et Fromagers de Normandie*, Vive les Traditions, 1983.
Marabout: see Androuët and Lyon.
Marquis, Vivienne, and Haskell, Patricia, *The Cheese Book*, Simon and Schuster, 1964.
Milk Marketing Board, *EEC Dairy Facts and Figures*, annual.
Molle, André, *Fromages d'Auvergne*, G. de Bussac, 1969.
Rance, Patrick, *The Great British Cheese Book*, Macmillan, 1982, Papermac, 1983; revised edition, 1988.
Stobbs, William, *Guide to the Cheeses of France*, Apple Press, 1984.
Viard, Henry, *Fromages de France*, Dargaud, 1980.
Voy, Henry: see Chast and Voy.

## Books about food

These books all offer good regional cheese guidance.

Christian, Glynn, *Edible France*, Ebury Press, 1986.
Lyon, Ninette, *Le Tour de France Gourmand des Spécialités Régionales*, Marabout, 1985.
Nature & Progrès, *Guide de la Vente Directe des Produits de l'Agriculture Biologique*, Services Librairie, 1985.
——, *Les Bonnes Adresses de la Bio*, Services Librairie, 1985.
Wells, Patricia, *The Food Lover's Guide to France*, Methuen, 1988.
——, *The Food Lover's Guide to Paris*, Methuen, 1984.

## Books about France

Ardagh, John, *Rural France*, Century, 1983.
Brangham, A. N., *The Naturalist's Riviera*, Phoenix House, 1962.
——*Auvergne*, Spurbooks, 1977.
Binns, Richard, *French Leave 3*, Corgi, 1983.
Canziani, Estella, *Costumes, Mœurs et Legendes de Savoie*, French translation by A. van Gennep, Chambery, 1920.
Eperon, Arthur, *The French Selection*, Pan Books/BBC, 1984, 1988.
*French Farm and Village Holiday Guide*, Farm Holiday Guides Publications, annual.

Hennequin, Bernard, *Guide des Loisirs et des Vacances en France*, Bordas, 1985.

Lands, Neil, *Beyond the Dordogne*, Spurbooks, 1978.

——, *The French Pyrenees*, Spurbooks, 1980.

Larousse/Sélection du Reader's Digest, *Pays et Gens de France*, Larousse, 1982.

Law, Joy, *Dordogne*, Macdonald, 1981.

Mauron, Marie, *La Transhumance*, Librairie Académique Perrin, 1959.

Michelin, *Green Guides to France*, Michelin, 1970s and 1980s.

Ogrizek, Doré (ed.), *The Provinces of France*, McGraw-Hill, 1951.

de Serres, Olivier, *Théâtre d'Agriculture et Mesnage des Champs*, 1600.

*Note:* For an understanding of the light and the dark of the Provençal character and landscape, read d'Arbaud, Audouard, Bosco, Giono, Marie Mauron and Pagnol.

# Index

Abbaye de Belval, 265
Abbaye de Bricquebec, 12, 14, 43
Abbaye de Campenac Trappiste, 52
L'Abbaye de Frigolet Pur Chèvre, 512
Abbaye d'Igny, 318
Abbaye de la Coudre, 41, 44, 45, 51
Abbaye de Melleray, 52
Abbaye de Notre Dame de Bellocq, 135
Abbaye de Notre Dame de Belval, 265
Abbaye de Notre Dame de Cîteaux, 354, 360
Abbaye de Notre Dame d'Oelenberg, 285
Abbaye de Notre Dame du Port-du-Salut, 46
Abbaye de St-Winocq, 262, 265
Abbaye de Ste-Anne-d'Auray, 52
Abbaye de Ste-Marie de la Pierre-Qui-Vire, 352, 360
Abbaye de Ste-Marie du Mont, 265
Abbaye de Tamié, 418, 437
Abbaye de Timadeuc Trappiste, 52
Abbaye du Mont-des-Cats, 262, 265
Abbaye en Frigolet, 502
Abbé, 100
Abondance, 412–13, 417, 427
Accous, 140, 141, 142, 146
Affinois, 375
Agenais, 113–25
L'Aigle, 12
Ail et Fines-Herbes, 460
Aillons, Les, 427
Aime, 422, 427
Ain, 375, 385, 394
Ainhice, 135
d'Airvault, Pavé, 100
Aisy, 313, 318
Aisy Cendré, 361
Aix-en-Othe, 318
Aix-en-Provence, 502
L'Albaron, 493, 502, 503
Albertville, 421, 427
Albi, 166
Alençon, 12
Alesia, 351, 352, 361
Aligot, 191, 227
Alise-Ste-Reine, 351, 352, 361

Alleins, 502
Allues, Les, 420, 425, 427
Alpages, Tommes des, 427
Alpes de Haute-Provence, 489–91, 502
Alpes, Tommes des, 461
Alpes-Maritimes, 502
Alsace, 277–96, 401
l'Altier, Pélardon de, 228
Amalthée, 100
Amancey, 394, 404
Ambérieu, 387
d'Ambérieu, Ramequin, 391
Ambert-en-Livradois, 228
Ambierle, 373, 375
Amboise, 71
L'Ami du Chambertin, 351, 355, 361, 362
Amigrette, 228
Ammerschwihr, 285
Amou, 135, 137
Amour, 361
L'Amour de Nuits, 347, 355, 367
Amours de la Tambarlette, Les, 502, 503
Ance, 140, 146
Anceval, 228
Andorra-la-Vella, 170
Anduze, 209, 228, 501, 503
Angelon, 2, 12
Angelot, 4, 12, 259, 265, 318
Angers, 71
Angoulême, 100
Angoumois, 97–111, 100
Anjou, 9, 71
Anjouin, 72
Annebault, 12
Annecy, 51, 415, 427
Annemasse, 428
Annonay, 228
Annot, 487, 503
Anost, 361
Antibes, 503
Aoust, 151
Apéri, 72
Apéri-Chèvre, 225, 226, 228 di Giralamo, 228
Appignato, 473
Apt, 490, 503
Aquitaine, 113–25
Arago, 118
Aramits, 140, 146
Araules, 228
Araux, 136
Aravis, 414, 428
Arbéost, 150, 151
Arbois, 404
Arc-en-Senans, 404
Ardèche, 228

Ardennes, 258, 277–96, 313, 318
Ardi-Gasna, 130–2, 136
Fromage de Zone de Montagne, 136
Arêches, 428
d'Arette, Fromage, 140, 146
Argelès-Gazost, 151
Argonne, 318
Ariège, 154, 155–63, 164–5, 169
Arles, 494, 495, 500, 501, 503
d'Arles, Tomme, 503
Armagnac, 150–3
Arnéguy, 131, 136
Arômes, 375
à la Gêne, 375
à la Gênede de Marc, 372
de Lyon, 372
Arradoy Petit Ossau-Iraty, 136
Arras, 265
Arrens, 144–6, 150, 151
Arrigny, 318
L'Artisan du Brie, 285
Artois, 257–74, 265
Arudy, 144, 146
Asco, 471, 472, 473
Aspe valley, 132, 133, 135, 140–4, 146
d'Aspin, Col, 151
Asson, 144, 146
Aste, 143, 146
Aubrac, 191, 203, 204, 215, 210, 229
Aubusson, 118
Auch, 151
Aude, 134, 164, 166–8, 181
Auge, 5, 8, 9, 12
Augelot, 12
Aulnay de Saintonge, 101
Aulnoye-Aymeries, 265
Aulus, 157, 161
Aunac, 101
Aunay, 101
Aunis, 99–100, 101
Auray, 52
Aurillac, 191, 207, 209, 210, 229, 374
d'Aurillac, Le Carré, 229
Authon, 72
Autun, 356
L'Auvergnat Gourmand, 229
Auvergne, 164, 201–54, 373, 374
l'Auvergne, Gaperon de, 242
Avesnois, 257–74
Aveyron, 173–98, 206
Avignon, 491
Avranches, 12

**546** INDEX

Auzat, 161
Auzay, 101
Avallon, 361
Avesnes-sur-Helpe, 266
d'Aveyron, Bleu, 173, 191
Avignon, 504
Avize, 318
Aydes Bleu, Les, 72
Aydes Cendrè, Les, 72
Aysius, 132, 146
Azay-le-Rideau, 73
Azergues valley, 373, 375

Babon Vache, 505
Baby Brie, 318, 334
Baby Pan, 229, 246
Bache, La, 355, 361
Bagnères-de-Bigorre, 152
Bagnères-de-Luchon, 151, 154
Bagnoles de l'Orne, 13
Bagnols-sur-Cèze, 504
Baguette, 266
   Avesnoise, 266
   de Thiérache, 266
   Laonnaise, 266
Baies Roses, 73
Bains, Bleu de, 229
Bairols, 505
Balbigny, 375
Bamalou, 161
Bannay, 316, 318
Bannes, 316, 318
Banon, 150, 449, 490, 491, 505
   à l'Ancienne, 505
   à la Feuille, 491, 505
   au Cumin, 506
   au Curry, 506
   au Paprika, 506
   au Poivre, 506
   au Poivre d'Âne, 229, 449, 505
   au Romarin, 506
   aux Fines Herbes, 506
   aux Herbes Provençales, 506
   Chèvre Fromage Fermier des Préalpes Drômoises, 45
   de Banon, 505
   de Cumin, 449
   d'Or, 449, 491, 505
   d'Or Royal Ventoux, 449
   de Paprika, 449
   de Saint-Justin, 449
   des Herbes, 449
   du Côteau du Camp de César, 449
   Fermier, 449
   Fromage Fermier, 449
   Géant, 449
   Mi-Chèvre, 505
   Pur Chèvre, 506
   sous Feuille, 449
Banvou, 13
Bar, 277–96, 319
Bar de Luc, 318
Bar-sur-Aube, 319
Bara, 229

Baratte, 357, 361
Barbentane, 506
Barberey, 319
Barbriquet, Le, 449
Barcelonnette, 506
Baretous, 140–4, 146
Bargkass, 280, 281, 282, 285
Barousse, 150–1, 152
Barrois, 44, 278, 280, 299–340, 319
Barzy-en-Thiérache, 266
Bas Bugey, 413–38
Bas-Rhin, 277–96
Basque, 128–38, 150, 181
Basse-Navarre, 128–38
Basse-Normandie, 2–27
Bassez, 191, 229
Bassignac, (Le Haut) Bleu de, 118
Bassillac, Bleu de, 118
Bastelicaccia, 473
Bastia, 473
Bastide, La, 247
Batie-Divisin, La, 449
Battu, 18
Bauges, 420, 428
Baule, La, 52
Baux, Les, 494, 495, 500, 506
Bayard, Col du, 449
Bayard, Le Petit, 450
Baye, 315–16, 319
Bayeux, 8
Bayonne, 136
Béarn, Le, 116, 132, 134, 135, 139–48, 150, 181
Béarnais, 132, 146
Beaucaire, 506
Beauce, 57–94
   Petite, 59–60, 61, 73
Beauceron, 61, 73
Beaufort, Le, 205, 280, 281, 345, 414, 421–5, 427, 428, 429
   Haute-Montagne, 427, 429, 501
Beaufortin, 421, 429
Beaugency, 73
Beaujolais, 357, 372–3
Beaumes-de-Venise, 506
Beaumont, 418, 429
Beaune, 361
Beaupré de Roybon, 444–5, 450, 452
Beaussault, 33
Beauvoir, 319
Bedous, 146
Bel, 46
Belcaire, 165, 166
Belfort, 278, 394, 401, 404
Belle Bressane, 387
Belle-des-Champs, 144, 222, 266
Belle Gasconne, La, 153
Belle Lochoise, La, 93
Bellebonne, 450
Belledonne, Chaîne de, 450
Belleville, Tome de, 429
Belleville-sur-Saône, 375
Bellevue-la-Montagne, 229
Belley, 387

Bellifontain, Le, 319
Bellocq, 136
Belval, 262, 266
Belvès, 118
Bény-Bocage, Le, 11, 13
Béon, 143, 146
Béost, 143, 147
Berger, 192
Bergerac, 118
Bergère, 507
Bergère, La, 191, 508
Bergerin Crème de Roquefort, Le, 192
Bergers, 429
Bergkäse, 285
Bergues, 262, 266, 309
Bernières, 13
Berry, 64, 69, 73, 316
Berrychon, Le, 73
Besace, 119
Besace du Berger, 119
Besançon, 404, 450
Besnier, 46
Bessans, 430
Bessay, 203, 229
   Petit, 229
Besse-en-Chandesse, 212, 213, 215, 217, 218, 219, 220, 230
Bessey-en-Chaume, 355–6, 361
Bethmale, Le, 155–7, 158, 160, 161, 163
Bethmale, Vallée de, 155, 161
Bethmale Fermier, 161
Béthune, 266
Béthune, Fromage Fort de, 273
Beulet, 418–19, 430
Beuvron-en-Auge, 13
Beuvry, 266
Biarritz, 136
Bibbelskase, 285
Bibelakas, 285
Bibress, 383, 387
Bichonnet, Le, 73
Bichou Cévenol, 226, 230
Bichou des Cévennes, Le, 226, 230, 507
Bichounet, 101
Bicorne, 101, 104, 116, 119
Bielle, 143, 147, 161
Bigorre, 144, 145, 150–3
Bigoton, 72, 73
Bilhères, 143, 147
Billy, Le Petit, 73
Bique, La Pointe de 73
Biquet-des-Hersents, 319, 331, 334, 339
Biqueton, Le, 71, 73
Bitalys, 161
Bizonnes, 450
Blaincourt, 266
Blamont, 285
Blanc, 285
Blennes, 319
Blésois, 59, 61, 62–3, 73
Bleu, 74, 119, 192, 230, 319, 387, 430
   d'Annonay, 228
   d'Auvergne, 116, 118, 192,

209, 210–11, 224, 230
  au Lait Cru, 230
d'Aveyron, 173, 191
de Bains, 229
de Bassignac, 114, 118
de Bassillac, 118
de Bessans, 430
de Bourg d'Oisans, 451
de Brebis de Dolmen, 192
de Brebis du Rouergue, 192
de Bresse, 383, 388, 389
de Cayres, 230
de Champoléon, 452
de Corse, 470, 473
de Costaros, 231
de Figeac, 119, 122
de Gex, 218, 383–7, 388, 389, 394, 409, 442, 443
  Fermier, 389
de Langeac, 231
de Laqueuille, 208–10, 231, 244
de Lavaldens, 455
de Loudes, 231
de Lozère, 231
de Meaux, 319
de Pelvoux, 457
de Planèze, 231, 247
de Pontgibaud, 231
de Quercy, 124
de Queyras, 459
de Sainte-Foy, 436
de Salers, 231
de Sassenage, 442, 443, 462
de Septmoncel, 383–6, 394, 442
de Solignac, 231
de Termignon, 437
de Thiézac, 209, 231
de Tignes, 438
de Tulle, 119
des Causses, 119, 120, 173–4, 175, 192, 230, 235, 492, 506
des Hauts-Pâturages, 446, 450
des Neiges, 245
du Haut-Jura, 384, 385, 389, 394, 404, 407, 408, 409, 442, 443
du Lisieux, 231
du Quercy, 118, 119
du Velay, 231
le Bois Soret, 361
Tignard, 438
Bleudoux, 450
Blois, 63, 74
Blondin, 266
Bodon, Domaine de, 506
Bodonsecs, 450
Boisgency, 73, 74
Boismorand, 60, 74
Boissey, 7, 8, 13
Boissière École, La, 319
Boissy-le-Châtel, 311, 319
Bole, 192
Bollène, 492, 506
Bolottée, La, 46
Bon Fermier, Le, 106
Bon Romans, le, 460

Bon Villefranchois, Le, 192
Bondard, 13, 29, 33
Bondaroy au Foin, 60, 74
Bonde de Gâtine, La, 98, 101
Bonde Neufchâtel, 33
Bonde-Platte, 33, 36
Bondon, 13, 29, 33
  Petit, 101
Bonneville, Carré de, 13
Bonneville, Curé de, 14
Bonneville-la-Louvet, 13
Bootzheim, 285
Bordeaux, 66, 101, 114, 119
Borgo, 472, 474
Bossons, 507
Bossons Macérés, 507
Bouches-du-Rhône, 494, 507
Bouchon, 361
Boudane, 430
Boudanne, 430
Bouelles, 33
Bougnat, 226–7, 231
Bougon, 101
Bougredin, Le, 375
Bouille, La, 13, 33
Bouin, 101
Bouine, La, 46
Boule, 266
  Aromatique, 387
  Aromatisée, 390
  de Béarn, 144, 147, 239
  de Lille, 266, 272
  du Pays, 266
  Fraîche, 266
Boule-des-Moines, La, 353, 360, 361
Boulette, 263–4, 267
  Avesnoise, 267
  d'Avesnes, 267
  Cambrai, 267
  de Papleux, 267
  de Prémont, 267
  de Thiérache, 267
  des Moines, 361
  du Nord à l'Estragon, 267
Boulieu-les-Annonay, 228
Boulogne, 219, 267
Boulonnais, 257–74
Bouquet d'Auvergne, 231
Bouquet de Thiérache, 267, 269
Bourbonnais, 203, 231
Bourdeaux, Picodons de, 451
Bourg Argental, 225, 232, 375
Bourg d'Oisans, 451
Bourg-en-Bresse, 387
Bourg-St-Maurice, 430
Bourganeuf, 115, 116, 119
Bourges, 74
Bourgogne, Fromage de, 362
Bourgueil, 74
Bournac, 177, 193
Bourrian, Le, 117, 119, 124
Bourricault, Le, 232
Boursault, 317, 319
Boursin, 28, 33
Boursin-à-l'Ail-et-aux-Fines-Herbes, 33
Boursin au Poivre, 33
Bouton de Culotte, 226, 358,

359–60, 362
Boutons de Capote, 320
Bouzac, 232
Brach, 115, 119
Bracq, 286
Braison, 192
  Charentais, 101
  d'Or, 192
  du Berger, 192
Brantôme, 119
Bréard, Le, 320
Brebidou, Le, 192
Brebidoux, Le, 117, 119, 124
Brebignole, 193
Brebis, xviii, 119, 161, 193, 286, 417, 430, 451, 474, 507, 520
  Biologique, 452
  d'Oleron, 100, 101
  Fermier, 147, 451
  Le Couserans, 160–1
  see also Fromage de Brebis
Bréole, La, 507
Bressan, 387–8
  Petit, 387–8
Bresse, 211, 224, 282, 312, 381–91, 382–3, 388
Bresse, La, 286
Bresse Bleu, 383, 388
  Fermier, 388
Brest, 52
Bretagne, 50–5
Bretteville-sur-Dives, 4, 14
Brézoû de Saint-Anthème, 223, 232
Briançon, 359, 442, 445, 451
Bricquebec, see Abbaye de Bricquebec
Bridelcrem, 52
Brie, 2, 6, 74, 278, 280, 286, 299–340, 347
  à la Chiffe, 320
  à la Loque, 320
  au Poivre, 320
  Baby, 334
  Bleu, 320
  d'Amateur, 320, 327
  de la Poste aux Chevaux de Meaux, 320
  de Macquelines, 320
  de Macquin, 320
  de Meaux, 3, 32, 305, 306, 307, 307–10, 311, 313, 315, 316, 321–4
  de Melun, 10, 305, 306, 307–10, 324, 346, 444
    Bleu, 325
    Frais, 325
  de Montereau, 306, 311, 317, 325, 346
    Bleu, 326
  de Montfort, 326
  de Nangis, 306, 311, 317, 326, 346
  de Provins, 311, 317, 326
  de Valois, 326
  du Valois, 326
  Façon Coulommiers, 310–11, 326
  Fermier, 327

Industriel, 311–13, 327
Laitier, 327
le Provins, 326
Petit Moule, 326
Truffé, 328
Brie-en-Pot, 326
Brienne-le-Château, 328
Brignoles, 507
Brignoud, 443, 451
Brillador, 193
Brillat, 375
Brillat d'Armançon, 328, 362
Brillat-Savarin, 14, 34, 63, 193, 328, 353, 362
Brin d'Amour, 473, 474
Brioude, 209, 232
Briouze, 14
Brique, 14, 229, 232, 451, 502, 507, 513
  Ardèchoise, 232
  Cendrée, 503
  d'Ambert, 224, 232
  de L'Argentière, 451
  d'Urfé, 225, 233
  de Viverols, 224, 232
  du Forez, 221, 224, 232
  du Haut Forez, 224, 232, 235
  du Livradois, 224, 233
  Mi-Chèvre, 451
Briquette
  du Forez, 224, 232
  Neufchâtel, 34
Brisco, 430
Brise Arôme au Poivre, 375
Brisego, 430
Brisegoût, 430
Brittany, see Bretagne
Brivarin, 362, 368
Brizou de Saint-Anthème, 223, 233
Broca, 286
Broccio, 474
Brocciu, 474
Brockel, 286
Brocotte, 286
Brocq, 286
Brokott, 286
Brou de Montagne, 507
Brouère, La, 280, 286
Brousse, 470, 471, 485, 486, 502, 507, 520
  de Brebis, 177, 191, 193, 196, 485, 508
  de Chèvre Fermier, 487, 508
  de la Vésubie, 508
  de Sospel, 508, 520
  de Tende, 508
  de Vache, 508
  de Valberg, 508
  de Valdeblore, 508
  du Rove, 494, 508
  Fraîche, 508
Broussin, 451
Broussin du Var, Le, 508
Bruccio, 474
Bruère Allichamps, 74
Bruleur de Loup, 451
Buchail, 34
Bûche, 53, 74, 81, 101, 233,
286, 375, 502
au Noix, 388, 390
Carrée des Sources de la Bourbre, 451
Cendrée, 92
du Velay Lys Bleu, 222, 233
Florine, 451
Forèzienne, 233
Mi-Chèvre, 74
Paillée, 75
St-Remoise, 508, 519
Yssingeaux, 222, 233
Bucheron, 102
Bûchette d'Anjou, 71
Bûchette de Banon, 491, 508
Bûchette Saint-Remoise, La, 4
Buchy, 34
Bugey, 381–91, 388
  Petit, 388
  Ramequin de, 391
  Rigoton de, 388
  Tomme de, 388
Buis-les-Baronnies, 451, 509
Bulgnéville, 280, 281, 286
Burado, 233
Burgundy, 65, 66, 313, 314, 316, 343–69
Buron, 233
Burzet, Le, 226, 233
Butte, La, 328

Cabécou, 117–18, 119, 161, 193, 209, 233
  d'Entraygues, 233
  d'Entraygues-sur-Truyère du Fel, 193
  de Glénat, 234
  de Gramat, 234
  de Limogne, 123
  de Livernon, 123
  de Montsalvy, 193
  de Roumégoux, 234
  du Fel, 233
  Frais, 120
  Truffé, 118, 119
Cabic, 75
Cabic du Berry, 75
Cabourg, 14
Cabremaures, Le, 509
Cabrette, La, 75
Cabri, 75
  Blanc, 75
  de Paris, 328
  des Versennes, 102
Cabrion, 224, 362
  du Forez, 234
Cabriou, 234
Cabro d'Or, Le, 102
Cabro des Dentelles, Le, 509
Cacavelli, 475
Cachat, 491, 509, 517
  d'Entrechaux, 515
Cacheia, 491, 509
Cacheille, 491, 509
Cadillac, 114, 120
Caen, 14
Caffuts, 267
Cafione, 102
Caghiatu, 475

Cagnes-sur-Mer, 509
Cahors, 120
Caillada de Vouillos, 115, 119
Caillado, 193
Cailladou, 120
Caillé, 234, 509
  Campagnard, 14
  de Brebis, 509
  de Chèvre, 165
  Doux, 234
  Lisse de Brebis, 193
  Rennaise, 52
Caillebotte, 51, 99, 100, 102
  à la Chardonette, 102
  Bretonne, 52
  d'Aunis, 102
  de Parthenay, 102
  de Rennes Jonchées, 52
  Parthenais, 102
  Poitevine, 102
Caillette, 430
Caillotte
  de Brebis, 193
  de Beurre, 229
Cailloux, 451
  des Provinières, 451
  du Vézy, 451
Caisse, 267
Cajassou, 120
Cajassous, 120, 193
Cajole, 227, 234
Calabosse, Pic de la, 161
Calais, 268
Calaisis, 257–74
Calenzana, 472, 475
Calvados, 2–27, 328
Camarès, 193
Camarguais, 494, 510
  Mélange Brebis-Chèvre, 503
  Pur Brebis, 503
Camargue, 503
Camargue, Tomme de, 503, 504, 510
Cambalou, Le, 140, 173, 174, 181, 194, 470
Camembert, 2, 3–7, 13, 14, 45, 52, 347, 353
  de Normandie, 13, 14
  Fermier, 14
  Lait Cru Périers d'Isigny, 19
  Pur Chèvre, 102
Cambrésis, 262, 268
  Puant du, 262
Campagnard, 18
Campénéac, 44, 51, 53, 174
Cancoillotte, 396, 397, 404, 451
  au Beurre et à l'Ail, 404
  Franche-Comtoise au Beurre, 405
  Raguin, 405
Cancon, 120
Canigou, 170
Caniquet, Le, 45
Canistrelli, 471, 475
Cannes, 510
Cannoc, 328
Cantal, 131, 181, 194, 203,

204, 205, 206, 207–8, 210, 211, 215, 221, 234
'Entre-deux', 208
Fermier, 252
Jeune, 208
Lait Cru, 234
Petit, 206, 207, 234
Vieux, 208, 221
Cantale, Département de, 234
Cantalet, Le, 206, 208, 234
Cantalon, Le, 208–10, 234
Cantorel, 235
Canut, 375
Capelle, La, 260, 268
Capitoul, Le, 136
Capra, Tomme de, 452
Capribeur, 102
Caprice des Dieux, 286, 328
Caprin, Le, 75
Capritarn, 166
Carcassonne, 167
Carentan, 16
Cargèse, 472, 475
Carpentras, 510
Carré, 16, 22, 287
  Breton, 53
  Choisy, 16
  d'Argonne, 328
  d'Aurillac, 229, 235
  d'Avesnes, 268
  de Bonneville, 22
  de Bray, 16, 34
  de l'Est, 41, 42, 58, 287, 328, 353
  de Lorraine, 287
  de Moyaux, 22
  de Rouez-en-Champagne, 41–2, 46
  de Saint-Cyr, 102
  du Plessis (Launay), 23
  du Trièves, 452
  Goût du Jour, 75
  Neufchâtel, 29, 34
  Vosgien, 287
Carvi de Hollande, 287
Casamaccioli, 475
Caserette, 34
Castel, 16
Castellane, 488, 489, 510
Castillon-en-Couserans, 155, 162
Castres, 166
Cau Bitalys, 161, 162
Caudiau, 34
Caumont, 158, 162
Causse, Pur Chèvre Fermier du, 194
Causse du Larzac, 174–6, 181
Causses, 120, 173
Causses, Bleu de, 235
Cavaillon, 510
Cayres, 209, 235
Celles-sur-Belle, 98, 103
Cellier du Dauphin, 452
Cendré, 75, 328
  Champenois, 329
  d'Aisy, 347–52
  d'Argonne, 329

de Barberey, 329
de Blennes, 319, 329
de Cannoc, 329
de Châlons-sur-Marne, 329
de Champagne, 329
de Heiltz-le-Maurupt, 329
de l'Éclance, 329
de Mormant, 329
de Noyers-le-Val, 329, 336
de Rocroi, 329
de Troyes, 319, 329, 339
de Voves, Le, 94
des Ardennes, 329
des Riceys, 329
du Barrois, 319, 329, 332
Normand de Grand Papa, 16
Véritable, 329
Cenves, 359, 362, 376
Cérat, 430, 436
Cerdagne (Cerdaña), 164, 169–70
Cérilly, Le, 203, 235
Cervelle, 376
Cervelle de Canut, La, 372, 375
Cesson, 329
Cévennes, 224, 226, 235
Cévenol, 235
Cevrin, 430, 436
Chabeuil, 452
Chabi, Le, 75, 103
  Fermier, 75
Chabichou, 68, 72, 75, 97–8, 100, 103, 316
  Lait d'Agneau, 103
  Laitier, 103
Chabiquet, Le, 75
Chabis, 75
  Blanc, 72
  Fermier, 75
  Fermier de Deux-Sèvres, 103
Chablis, 362
Chabricon, 114, 120
Chabrilloux, 235
Chabris, 76
Chaffois, 402, 405
Chafranière, La, 510
Chaîne de Belledonne, 450
Chaise-Dieu, La, 209, 211, 222, 224, 235
Chaize, La, 104, 116, 120
Chalet, Le, 430
Challans, 99, 103
Chalmazel, 222, 224, 235
Chalosse, 136
Chambaran, 452
Chambarand, 44, 444–5, 452
Chamberat, 203, 235
Chambéry, 430
Chambon-sur-Lac, 235
Chambost-Allières, 376
Chambrille, 103
Chamois d'Or, 46
Chamois des Alpes, Le, 430
Champagne, 313, 314, 316–18, 346, 353
Champagne-en-Valromey, 388

Champagnole, 405
Champcou, Le, 76
Champenois, Le, 338
Champoléon, 452
  Bleu de, 452
  les Borels, 452
Champsaur, Le, 446, 452
Chancelier, 235
Chanceron, 235
Chanousse, 452, 489
Chanteloup, 329
Chantemerle, 452
Chantemerle-les-Bles, 452
Chantichèvre, 194
Chantilly, 268, 329
Chaource, 63, 313–15, 329, 345–6, 362
  AOC, 329
  AOC Laitier, 330
  Factory, 345–6
  Farmhouse, 346–7
  Fermier, 330
  Laitier, 362
Chapelet-Chapelais, 103
Chapelle, Le, 103
Chapelle-des-Bois, 399, 405
Charcenne, 405
Chardonette, 103
Charente, 100
Charmilles, 120
Charollais, 203, 356–9, 362, 383
Charolles, 357, 362, 373
Chartres, 59, 60, 64, 76
Chartreuse, 452
Chartrousin, Le, 461
Chasseneuil, 76
  Lait de Mélange, 103
Chasseneuil-sur-Bonnière, 103
Chasseur, Tomme du, 452
Chasteaux, 114, 120
Château-Arnoux, 489, 510
Château de Vallières, 391
Château du Loir, 76
Château Gontier, 42, 43, 46
Château Puyreaux, 103
Châteaubriant, 53
Châteaudun, 76
Châteauroux, 76
Châtel, 414, 430
Châtelard, 430
Chatenay, 374, 376
Châtillon-Coligny, 76
Châtillon-en-Diois, 452
Châtillon-sur-Indre, 76
Châtillon-sur-Marne, 330
Chaucetier, 203, 235
Chaumes, 120, 287
Chaumine, 103
Chaumont, 76, 330
Chaumont-sur-Loire, 76
Chaunay, 104
Chauny, 268, 330
Chaux-des-Crotenays, 405
Chavannes-sur-Reyssouze, 383, 388
Chavignol, 64–6, 76
Chavroux, 104
Chebli, 104

Chécy, 76
Chef Boutonne, 104
Chevrachu, 490, 502, 510
Chevramour, 104
Chèvre, xviii, 13, 16, 53, 76, 89, 104, 120, 135, 137, 151, 165, 170, 194, 229, 287, 330, 331, 359–60, 363, 364, 366, 383, 388, 391, 405, 417, 432, 452, 475, 503, 508, 510, 515, 517, 520
  à la Feuille, 106
  au Poivre et au Thym, 504
  aux Gênes, 390
  Artisanal, 377
  Basse-Normandie, 10–11
  Blanc, 104
  Blanche, 104
  Biologique, 451, 452
  Cœur, 517
  de Gorbio, 513
  de Peymeinade, 516
  des Monts-de-Vaucluse, 521
  Fermier, 92, 104, 237, 268, 331, 363, 364, 367, 375, 377, 389, 450
  Fermier de Deux-Sèvres, 98, 104
  Fermier des Pyrénées, 162
  Fermier du Poitou, Frais and Affiné, 104
  Frais, 388
  Frais d'Hucqueliers, 268
  Industriel, 98
  Laitier, 105
  Magnum, 514
  Pyramide, 82
  Tome, 517
  Tomme de, 431
  see also Fromage de Chèvre
Chèvrefeuille, Le, 119, 121
Chevret, 387, 388, 405
  de Billy, 387
Chevretines, 226, 236
  de l'Ardèche, 236
  Pur Chèvre de l'Ardèche, 236
Chevreton, 237, 363, 431
  d'Ambert, 237
  de Cistrières, 237
  de Cunlhat, 237
  de Mâcon, 366
  de Thiers, 237
  de Viverols, 237
  du Bourbonnais, 237, 255
  Mi-Chèvre, 237
Chevrette, 16, 453
  des Bauges, 428, 431
  des Neiges, 453
  Fromagerie des Neiges, 34
Chevrichon de Poitou, 105
Chevrine de Lenta, 431, 433
Chevrita, 105
Chevrot, 363
Chevrot, Le, 105
Chevrotin, 16, 105, 224, 363, 415, 417, 431
  de la Ferme d'Ouxy, 367
  des Aravis, 428, 431
  du Bourbonnais, 237
  du Grand Bornand, 431, 433
  du Reculey, 13
Chevroton, 202–3, 237, 363
  de Cistrières, 238
  de Combraille, 238
  de Cosne (Cosne d'Allier), 238
  de Montmarault, 238
  de Moulins, 238
  de Souvigny, 238
  du Bourbonnais, 244
Chevru, 331
Chézery-Forens, 388
Chiberta, 136, 472
Chichiliane, 453
Chigre, 288
Chiguet, 431
Chinon, 76
Chouan, Le, 105
Chouzé, 76
Chouzé-sur-Loire, 76
Ciboulette Neufchâtel, 34
Cierp, 154
  de Luchon, 154
Cigalon aux Herbes du Maquis, Le, 453
Cigalon des Alpilles, 511
Cîteaux, 347, 354–5, 360, 363
Clamart, 331
Claque-Bitou, 356, 363
Claqueret
  Cannoix, 511
  Lyonnais, 372, 376
Claverolle, 136
Clayette, La, 363
Clécy, 16
Clermont Ferrand, 220, 238
Cloche d'Or, 105
Clochette, 105
Clos de l'Abbé, 105
Clos Josse, Le, 331
Clovis, 268
Cluny, 363
Clusaz, La, 415, 431
Coaraze, 511
Codibri, 238
Cœur, 16, 30, 31, 269, 502
  Cendré, 72
  d'Arras, 269
  d'Auvergne, 238
  d'Avesnes, 269
  de Bray, 35
  de Bresse, 388
  de Camembert au Calvados, 16
  de Chambry, 331
  de la Crème, 331
  de Maurupt, 331
  de Poitou, 105
  de Rians à la Crème, 77, 511
  de Valréas, 511
  Neufchâtel, 29, 35
  Rollot, 269
Cœurmandie, 16, 41–2, 47

Cognac, 105
Col d'Aspin, 151
Col des Supeyres, 221, 223, 228
Col du Bayard, 446, 449
Col Vert, Fourme de, 453
Colmar, 282, 288
Colombier, 420, 431
Colombière, 414, 431
Combe de Savoie, La, 431
Combovin, Tomme de, 453
Commercy, 331
Comminges, 150, 151, 154, 156, 160
Comtat Venaissin, 447, 481–522, 491–2
Comté, 214, 281, 388, 399, 407, 409, 410, 443
  AOC, 405
  de Nice, 481–522
Condat-en-Féniers, 212, 238
Condé-sur-Sarthe, 16
Condrieu, 374, 376
Confit, 363
Conne Montmarault, 238
Connerre, 47
Conquérant, Le, 238
Contres, 64, 77
Coopérative, 405
Coopérative Laitière du Beaufortin, 429
Corbigny, 345, 363
Cormery, 77
Corne d'Or, 77
Cornilly, 77
Corniment, 282, 288
Corps, Tomme de, 446, 453
Corscia, 475
Corse, 475
Corse du Sud, 467–78
Corsevieux, 472, 475
Corsica, 181, 184, 467–78, 486
Corte, 476
Costaros, 209, 238
Côte d'Or, 343–69, 393–410
Cotentin, 17
Cotentinette, 17
Côte-du-Nord, 50–5
Coucouron, Le, 209, 238
  Fourme de, 238
  Tomme Persillée de, 238
Coucouron Persillé, Le, 238
Couhé-Vérac, 105
Coulandon, 203, 238
Coulommiers, 203, 305, 306, 307, 311, 315, 316, 326, 331
  Frais, 326
  Lait Cru, 288
Coumes, 157, 162
Coupi, 115, 121, 203, 238
Courchevel, 431
Courtonne-la-Meudrac, 5
Courtonne-les-Deux-Églises, 5
Couserans, Le, 154, 155–63, 164
Coutançais, Le, 16
Coutances, 17
Craponne-sur-Arzon, 239

Crau, La, 495, 501, 511
Crécy-la-Chapelle, 332
Crème de Bleu, 239, 388
　aux Noix, 388, 390
　Chèvre, 390
Crémet, 51, 52
　Breton, 53
　d'Angers, 47
　d'Anjou, 58, 71, 77
　de la Chenevière, 290
　de Nantes, 53
　Nantais, 53
Crémeux, Le, 453
Crémieu, 374, 375, 453
Crest, 448, 453
Creusain, 121, 203, 238
Creusois, 121, 203, 238
Crevoux, 453
Crézancy-en-Sancerre, 77
Croix d'Or, 406
Croque Chèvre, 77
　Frais, 72
　Mirabel, 72
Crottin, 72, 77, 82, 121, 177, 193, 332, 354, 366, 449
　Charentais, 106
　de Chavignol, 58, 64–6, 70, 77, 316, 363
　de l'Othe, 331, 332
　Non AOC, 78
Croupet, Le, 332
Croûte Cendré, 82
Croûte-Naturelle, 82
Cubjac, 115, 116, 121
Cujasson, 121
Cujassous, 115, 120, 121, 193
Cumin, Tomme au, 454
Cun, 194
Cunlhat, 239
Curé, 239
　de Nantes, 53
　Nantais, 53
Curieuse, La, 42–3

Dampierre St-Nicholas, 35
Darbres, 239
Dauphin, Le, 259, 262–3, 264, 269
Dauphin d'Arago, 121
Dauphiné, 44, 374, 375, 441–64, 485, 490, 491
Deauville, 17
Decize, 345, 363
Délice
　de Bourgogne, 363
　de Mesnil, 363
　de Saint-Cyr, 317, 332
　de Saligny, 346, 363
　des Cévennes, 239
　des Vosges, 288
　du Chevrier, 454
　du Mesnil, 332
　du Ministre, 456
Délicet, 332
Demi-Fourme de Labro, 239
Demi-Pont-l'Évêque, 23
Demi-Sel, 29, 35
Demi-Suisse, 35
Dent du Chat, La, 432
Deux Sèvres, Des, 105

Devoluy, Tomme de, 454
Diablotin, 47
Diapason, 239
Die, 448, 454
Dieppe, 35
Dieulefit, 447, 448, 454
Digne, 489, 511
Dijon, 347, 350, 353, 363
Dit du Curé, 53
Dole, 406
Dolmen, Le, 194
Domaine de Bodon, 506
Dombergère, 388
Dombes, 381–91
Domblans, 406
Dôme, 17, 79
Dôme au Poivre, 388
Domfront, 17
Dompnac, 239
Dormans, 316, 332
Dornecy, 345, 363
Douai, 269
Double-Bonde, 29, 30, 31, 33, 35
Double-Cœur, 35
Doubs, 393–410, 406
Doue, 307, 332
Doullens, 269
Douscar, 376
Doux de Montagne, 144, 147, 239
Draguignan, 511
Dreux, 59, 60, 61, 79
Dromadaire, Le, 454
Drôme, 447, 448, 491
Drôme, Tomme de la, 454
Drouais, see Dreux
Ducs, 364
Dunkerque, 269
Duquesne, 332

é Bamalou, 161
Échalas, 374, 376
Échourgnac, 43, 116, 121
Éclance, 329, 332
Écouché, 17
L'Écume, 332
Edam Demi-Étuve, 106
Edam Français, 17, 269
Edelweiss, 406
Égliseneuve d'Entraigues, 206, 212, 213, 239
Eiffel, La Tour, 79
El Torrero, 168
Elbeuf, 35
Emmental Français, 51, 280, 288, 364, 406
　de Savoie, 420, 432
　Ermitage Vosges, 288
　Est-Central, 288, 406
　Grand Cru, 214, 288, 332, 396–8, 406, 420, 432
Engomer, 157, 160, 162
Engordany, 170
Entrammes, 41, 43, 44, 45, 47, 51
Entraygues-sur-Truyère, 194, 209, 239
Entre-les-Fourgs, 406
Entrechaux, 511

Entremont, 415, 432
Éourres, 454, 489
Épenouse, 406
Épernay, 332
Éperon à Boire, 364
Épinal, 282, 288
Époisses, 314, 364
　Artisanal, 364
　au Marc, 364
　au Marc de Bourgogne, 364, 368
　Chiciak, 364
　de Villaines les Prévôtes au Marc, 365
　des Vignerons, 364
　Factory, 345–6
　Fermier, 364
　Laitier, 364
　Real, 347–52
Ercé, 157, 162
Ervy-le-Châtel, 315, 332, 345, 365
Esbareich, 151, 152, 154
Esclavelles, 35
Esterençuby, 131, 136
L'Estive, 157, 162
Étarlou, 194
Etchebar, 132, 136
Etcheria, 136
Étival, 406
Étoile, 269, 333, 388–9
L'Étoile, 116, 121
L'Étoile de Revermont, 391
Étoile du Vercors-Saint-Marcellin, 454
Étorki, 132–4, 136, 144, 181
Eure, 28–40
ewes'-milk cheese, see brebis
Excelsior, 17, 32
　Dormant, 35
Explorateur, 333
Eydoche-Picodon Fines Herbes, 454
Eygaliers, 454

Faisselle, 106, 454
　de Rians, 79
　de Pâturages, 450, 454
Falaise, 17
Fareins, 388–9
Faurupt, 288
Fécamp, 35
Fel, Le, 209, 239
Fenouil, Tomme au, 454
Fenouil, Tomme de, 432
Fermes-Auberges, 17, 287, 288
Fermier, Le, 17
Fermier, Le Bon, 106
Fermier de Montagne, 432
Fermière, La, 194, 239
Ferrières, 29, 152
Ferté, La, 79
Ferté Bernard, La, 47, 79
Ferté Macé, Le, 17
Ferté-sous-Jouarre, La, 305, 333
Fervaques, 17
Feta de Brebis, 194
Feuille à la Chèvre, 106

Figalou, Le, 122
Figeac, 122
Filletières, Les, 357, 365
Fin-de-Siècle, 17
   Dormant, 35
Fin Morvan, 345, 365
Fine des Prés, 47
Fine-Forme, 454
Finistère, 50–5
Finliers le Liers, 454
Finvel, Le, 455
Flagy, 333
Flaine, 432
Flandre, 257–74, 269
Flandres, Fromage Fort des, 270
Flèche, La, 47
Flers, 17
Fleur de Decauville, 333
Fleur de l'Ermitage, 288
Fleur de Maquis, 472–3, 476
Fleur de Morvan, 365
Fleurette, 17
Fleurey, 406
Fleuron des Côteaux, 147
Florine, 455
Flormaigre, 122
Florneige, 122
Flumet, 432
Foin, 17
Foix, 134, 141, 161, 163, 164–5
Fol Amour, 289
Fondue, 406
   Creusoise, 122
   Savoyarde, 426
Fontainebleau, 333
Fontainebleue, Le, 333
Fontenay, 99, 365
Fontevraud, L'Abbaye, 79
Fontgombault, Le, 79
Fontine Fleurantine, 152
Fontjoncouse, 167
Fontvieille, 445, 495, 497–502, 511
Forcalquier, 489, 490, 512
Forêt de Joux, 407
Forez, 203, 210, 221–5, 240, 373–5
Forges-les-Eaux, 32, 35
Fort de Béthune, Le, 266
Fosse, Le, 29, 35
Foudjou, Le, 226, 240, 455
Fougères, 44, 53
Fougerolles-Duplessis, 47
Fougeru, Le, 331, 333
Fourmai Gras, 512
Fourme, 119, 221–5, 235, 240, 376, 389
   d'Ambert, 221, 222, 223, 240, 373
   de Col Vert, 453
   de Coucouron, 238
   de Labro, 209, 241
   de Laqueuille, 241
   de l'Ardèche, 241
   de Mézenc, 241, 245
   de Montbrison, 221, 223, 240, 373, 376
   de Pierre-sur-Haute, 222, 223, 241
   de Rochefort-Montagne, 208–10, 214, 241
   des Monts du Forez, 223, 241
   des Monts Yssingelais, 222, 241, 254
   du Haut-Vivarais, 241
   Lyonnaise, 376
   Saint-Bricel, 391
Fourmette, 241
   du Haut-Mont, 241
Fournols, 241
Frain, 289
Franche-Comté, 11, 130, 156, 214, 261, 309, 393–410
Fremgeye, 289
Frère Alexandre, 41–2, 47
Friandise, Une, 333
Frigolet, 512
Frinault, 61, 76, 79
Frinot, 79
Froges, 455
Fromage à la Crème, 333, 511
   Viry, 339
Fromage à la Pie, 326, 327, 333
Fromage à Raclette, 434
Fromage Affiné, 71
Fromage Allégé de Bretagne, 54
Fromage Aromatisé au Poivre, 337
Fromage Artisanal des Pyrénées Ariègeoises, 162
Fromage au Foin Grand Papa, 17
Fromage au Poivre, 293
Fromage aux Fines-Herbes, 289
Fromage Blanc, 13, 18, 47, 71, 80, 82, 122, 152, 289, 290, 296, 333, 389, 455
   à la Crème, 18
   à la Pie, 53
   Battu, 80
   Caillé, 18
   de la Messine, 289
   Frais, 269
   Pyramide, 82
Fromage Cendré, 62, 80, 313–15
Fromage Cuit Lorrain, 289
Fromage dans la Cendré, Le, 296
Fromage d'Arette, 146
Fromage de Bourgogne, 362
Fromage de Brebis, 135, 152, 154, 162, 430, 471, 476, 518
   aux Herbes, 476
   de Baretous, 146
   Fermier, 516
   Laitier, 137
Fromage de Caisse, 267
Fromage de Chèvre, 13, 19, 21, 22, 53, 71, 80, 82, 85, 88, 90, 152, 154, 193, 195, 235, 266, 268, 286, 287, 291, 296, 330, 405, 431, 432, 454, 457, 459, 461, 463, 464, 503, 507, 511, 514, 516, 517, 518, 519, 520, 526
   au Paprika, 268
   au Poivre, 268
   au Poivre et au Thym, 518
   aux Herbes, 268
   Biologique, 453
   Blanc, 103
   Cendré, 82, 268
   d'Aysius, 146
   du Champsaur, 450, 452
   Fermier, 53, 121, 268, 513, 514
   Frais, 121
   Gaec d'Arlens, 153
   Petit, 287
Fromage de Craponne, 222, 239
Fromage de Cul, 329, 332
Fromage de Ferme Brebis, 517
Fromage de Glières, 433
Fromage d'Hesdin, 262, 265, 270
Fromage de l'Abbaye, 44, 46
Fromage de l'Abbaye de Melleray, 54
Fromage de la Chaize, Le, 119
Fromage de la Vallée des Merveilles, 514
Fromage de Langres, 335
Fromage de Lyon, 377
Fromage de Maber, 456
Fromage de Meaux, 335
Fromage de Monsieur Fromage, 10, 18, 333, 354
Fromage de Montagne, 450
Fromage de Montagne du Val de Thônes, 433
Fromage de Neufchâtel, 37
Fromage d'Ors, 271
Fromage de Saint-Verand, 462
Fromage de Vache, xviii, 22, 53, 72, 88, 90, 148, 153, 154, 507, 513
   de Baretous, 146
   et de Chèvre, 90
   Fermier, 138, 366, 367
Fromage des Charmilles, 120
Fromage des Gillotins, 368
Fromage des Moilles, 456
Fromage des Monts d'Or, 377
Fromage des Pyrénées, 138, 226
Fromage des Sarrazins, 391
Fromage du Lyonnais, 377
Fromage du Pays, 147, 162
Fromage du Pays Nantais, 53
Fromage du Royans, 460
Fromage du Terroir, 244, 252
Fromage Fermier, 18, 54, 80, 92, 106, 122, 194, 252, 285
   Bûche, 53
   de Chèvre, 197, 522
   de Vache, 254
   du Morvan, 361
Fromage Fines-Herbes, 163
Fromage Fort, 241, 270, 289, 365, 376, 389, 455, 512

de Béthune, 262, 273
de Bresse au Vin Blanc, 389
de Flandres, 266, 270
de la Croix Rousse, 376
de Lens, 270
de Lorraine, 291
de Mont Ventoux, 509
de St-Rambert-en-Bugey, 391
de Trôo, 80
du Beaujolais, 372, 376
du Berry, 80
du Bugey, 389
du Lyonnais, 375, 376
du Mont-Ventoux, 491, 512
du Petit Bugey, 389
Savoyard, 432
Fromage Frais, 18, 54, 72, 80, 82, 122, 167, 285, 289, 333, 391, 512, 515, 518
au Jambon Fumé, 334
aux Fines-Herbes, 289
Campagne, 80
Cendré, 329
de Chèvre au Calvados et aux Raisins, 330
en Faisselle, 106, 109
Isigny-Ste-Mère, 18
Pur Chèvre, 80
Rians Plumé, 80
Salé, 80
Sec, 379
Fromage Grand Murol, 243
Fromage Maigre, 244
Fromage Midi-Frais, 122
Fromage Mont d'Or, 409
Fromage Pur Chèvre, 82, 193, 460, 517
Fermier, 287, 518
'Sans Nom', 237
Fromage Sec du Laboureur, 455
Fromage-en-Pot, 289, 326
Fromagée, 80
Fromagée, La, 47
Fromagée du Larzac, 194
Fromagée Salée, La, 47
Fromageon, 152, 242
Gascon, 152
Fromageou, 122
Fromagère, 241, 289, 396
Fromagie, 289
Fromatjous, 162, 165
Frometon, 28–9, 36
Fromfort, 376
From'gi, 289
Fromix, 194
Frougnéa, 106
Frougnée, 106
Frougnes, 106
Froumaget, 36
Foumagi Cussinous, 509
Froumai Gras, 486, 520
Froumay Gras, 513
Fumel, 122
Furagliu in Corbella, 471, 476

Gabas, 147
Gabas Chèvre-Brebis Mixte, 147
Gaec d'Arlens, 152
Galette, 222, 242
de la Chaise-Dieu, 235
des Monts d'Or Lyonnais, 376
Ganges, 167
Gap, 446, 455, 513
Gape, 220, 229
Gaperon, 220, 242
d'Auvergne, 242
de Limagne, 242
la Perrette, 242
Gaperonnette, La, 242
Gaperounet, 242
Gapron, 242
Gard, 164, 174, 175, 181, 226, 485, 492–7, 501
Gardian, Le, 455, 493, 494, 503, 504, 513
Garnachoix, Le, 99, 106
Garrigou, 499, 513
Gascon, 7
Gascon, Le, 152
Gastanberra, 136
Gâtinais-orléanais, 58, 59, 60, 80, 344
Gaude, 513
Gaudre, Le, 444, 511
Gaudriole, Le, 499, 512, 513
Gauville, 18
Gazimelle, 246
du Burzet, 226, 233, 242
Géant, 80
Gêne, 376
Gênelard, 357, 365
Gênes, 389
Genette, La, 220, 224, 242
Géramont, 289, 333
Gérardmer, 281, 282, 290
Gerbizon, 242
Gère, 147
Géromé, 278, 279, 280, 281, 282, 290
Anisé, 290
au Cumin, 290
au Fenouil, 290
de Bruyères, 290
Fermier, 290
Géry, Le, 455, 458
Gevaudan, 166, 174, 181, 201–54, 242
Gevrey, 365
Gex, 381–91
Geyssans, 455
Ghisonaccia, 469, 470, 473, 476
Gien, Le, 80
Giennois, Le, 80
Gilley-les-Cîteaux, 351, 355, 365
Gillotin, 365
Gimont, 152
Giproforez, 242
Gisors, 36, 334
Givors, 374, 376
Glières, 432
Glorian, 106
Gluiras, 225, 242
Glux, 365

goats'-milk cheese, see chèvre
Golo, 472, 476
Goncelin, 455
Gorbio, Chèvre de, 486, 513
Gouda Français, 18, 270
Gourdon, 122
Gourmand, Le, 455
Gourmelin, 116, 122
Gournay, 18, 28–9, 36
Gournay-en-Brie, 36
Gournier, Le, 449, 455
Goûtez-Moi, 375, 376
Goutu, 18
Goux-les-Usiers, 407
Gouzon, 115, 122, 203, 242
Petit, 122, 242
Goyère, 270
Gracay, 64, 80
Graingeaud, Le, 290, 291
Gramat, 117, 122, 209
Grana, 122
Grand Béron, Le, 18
Grand Bornand, Le, 415, 433
Grand Caprin, 75
Grand Causse, Le, 194
Grand-mémé, 106
Grand Mogol, Le, 334
Grand Murol, 243
Grand Papa, 18
Grand Rouy, Le, 48
Grand Rustique, 19
Grand Sainte-Mère, 19
Grand Siècle, 47
Grand Vatel, 334, 354
Grand Veneur, 42, 47
Grande Clotte, 18
Granges-de-Plombières, 290
Grangettes, Les, 407
Granouillen, Le, 495, 513
Gras, 18, 243
Grasse, 488, 513
Grataron
de Hauteluce, 433
des Arêches, 428, 433
Gratte-Paille, Le, 317, 334
Graviers du Guiers, 433
Green Peppercorn, 125
Grenoble, 445, 455
Grièges, 389
Grignette, La, 377
Grigny, 377
Gris de Lille, 270, 273
Grisy Blanc, Le, 334
Grisy-sur-Seine, 306, 334
Gros Bondard, 36, 40
Gros Lait, 51, 52, 54
Gruyère, 349, 373, 407, 420
de Comté, 393–5, 405
des Bauges, 428
des Savoies, 421, 428, 433
Français, 365, 389
Guerbigny, 270
Gueret, 115, 122
Gueyin, 291
Gueyun, 291
Guingamp, 54

554  INDEX

Guyenne, 113–25
Guyenne–Gironde, 114

Habsheim, 291
Hainaut, 257–74, 270
Halbran, 107
Haut Bleu de Bassignac, Le, 118
Haut Jura, 407
Haut-Rhin, 277–96
Haut-Vivarais, 243
Haute-Alpes, 441–64, 502
Haute-Corse, 467–78
Haute-Garonne, 154, 164
Haute-Marne, 277–96, 393–410
Haute-Mont, Fourmette de, 241
Haute-Vivarais, Fourme du, 241
Haute-Normandie, 28–40
Haute-Provence, 481–522
Haute-Saône, 393–410
Haute-Savoie, 413–38
Hauteluce, 433
Hautmont, 270
Havre, Le, 36
Hayons, Les, 19, 36
Heiltz-le-Maurupt, 313, 334
Héloup, 19
Henri IV, 145
Hérault, 164, 166–8, 167, 174, 181
Hersent, Biquet des, 319, 334, 339
Hesdin, 270
Hirson, 270
Hollande, 270
Honfleur, 19
Horys, 162
Houssaye, La, 19
Hucqueliers, 270
Huppemeau, 81

Iholdy, 136
Île-de-France, 59, 270, 299–340
Île d'Oléron, 108
Ille-et-Vilaine, 50–5
Illiers-Combray, 81
L'Impérial, 93
Incheville, 36
Industrial Brie, 311–13
Industrial Chèvre, 98
Iraty, see Ossau-Iraty
Irigny, 377
Isère, 441–64
Isi Blanche, 19
Isi d'Or, 19
Isidoux, 19
Isigny-sur-Mer, 19
L'Isle-sur-la-Sorgue, 513
Isola, 513
Isserts, 123
Issirac, 513

Jacquemart, 455
Jambon Fumé, Fromage Frais au, 334
Janville, 19

Jasse, La, 194
Jasserie, 243
Jaunay-Clan, 107
Jean-Grogne, Le, 334
Jehan de Brie, Le, 334
Jonchée, 51, 54, 99, 107, 147
  d'Aulnay, 107
  d'Aunis, 100, 107
  d'Oléron, 107
  de Saintonge, 107
  du Pays Basque, 137
  Niortaise, 107
  Rennaise, 54
Jonchère, La, 81
Josselin, 54
Jougne, 399, 407
Jouques, 513
Joux, Forêt de, 407
Jumeaux, 107
Jura, 214, 280, 385, 393–410
Jurançon, 144, 145, 147

Kaysersberg, 291

Laboureur, 455
Labrit, Le, 159, 162, 163
Labro, 243
Lagnieu, 389
Lagorce, 243
Lagrieu, Ramequin de, 391
Laguiole, 181, 203–5, 208, 243
Laguiole-Aubrac, 194
Lait à Madame, 54
Lait Caillé, 475
Lait Cuit, 54
Lait de Mélange, 74, 107
Lait Marri, 54
Lait Ribot, 51, 54
Lajoux, 385, 407
Lamanon, 513
Lamastre, 225, 243
Landersheim, 291
Landes, 134, 137
Landes Chalosse, 137
Landrecies, 270
Langeac, 244
Langres, 334
Langres, Le, 334
Langres des Grands Clos, 317, 334
Langres du Plateau, Le, 317, 339, 365
Languedoc, 164, 174, 181
  Eastern, 481–522, 492–7
  Western, 127–70, 166–8
Lannemezan, 151, 153
Lannion, 54
Laon, 271
Lapalisse, 203, 244
Lapoutroie, 279, 283, 291
Laqueuille, 209, 244
  Fourme de, 241
Larceveau, 133, 137
Largentière-en-Vivarais, 244
Larron d'Ors, Le, 271
Laruns, 142, 143, 144, 146, 147
Larzac, 174–6, 177, 181, 195
Latinicien, 389

Ramequin de, 391
Laumes, Les, 351, 352, 365
Lauterbourg, 291
Laval, 41, 43, 44, 45, 48, 51, 262
Lavandens, Bleu de, 455
Lavans-Vuillafans, 407
Lavaur, 167
Lavelanet, 165
Laye, Tomme de, 446, 456
Lens, 271
Lens, Fromage Fort de, 270
Lenta, 433
Lescun, 142, 147
Levroux, 67, 81
Lezay, 107
Libourne, 107, 123
Lie-St-Trivier-de-Courtes, 389
Liers, Le, 456
Lies, Les, 456
Lieury, 19
Ligueil, 81
  Bleu, 81
Lille, 262, 271
  Gris de, 262, 270
  Puant de, 262, 472
  Vieux, 262, 274
Lillebonne, 28, 36
Limagne, Gaperon de, 242
Limoges, 107
Limogne, 117, 123
Limousin, 113–25, 114–15, 123, 201–54
Lingot, 107, 116
Lingot, Le, 123
  Cendré, 366
  d'Or, 291
Liniez, 67, 81
Lisieux, 19, 244
  Petit, 19
Lisse, 18
Listeria, 523–30
Listeria monocytogenes, xx–xxii, xxvii–xxviii, 523–30, et passim
Listeriosis, 523–30
Livarot, 7–9, 11, 19, 20
  de la Perrelle, 23
  Petit, 20
  Quart, 20
  Trois-Quarts, 20
Livernon, 123
Livradois, 203, 209, 219, 221, 244
Livron, Tomme de, 456
Lize, Tomme de, 54
Llo, 170
Loches, 69, 81, 82
Loire, 207, 209, 219, 221, 371–9
Loire-Atlantique, 50–5
Loivarot, 22
Lomagne, 153
Longevilles, 407
Longny-au-Perche, 82
Longuet, 271
  d'Hirson, 271
  de Thiérache, 271
Lons-le-Saunier, 407

# INDEX 555

Lormes, 345, 366
Lormes – le Fin Morvan, 366
Lorraine, 277–96, 292
Losange, 271
   Thiérache, 271
Losne, St-Jean-de-, 366
Lou Brous, 507
Lou Cabécou, 119, 125, 163
Lou Cabron, 120
   de Roc-Amadour, 125
Lou Cachat, 509
Lou Croustignou, 511
Lou Fantou, 194
Lou Marcaillou, 117, 123
Lou Meillou Bleu, 144, 231, 245
Lou Palou, 132–4, 137
Lou Péraillou, 195
Loubressac, 123
Loudes, 221, 222, 244
Loudun, 107
Louhans, 389
Loulans, 407
Lourdes, 150, 153
Louvie-Juzon, 144, 147
Lozère, 166, 244
Lucullus, 21, 335
Lune Rousse, 335
Lusignan, 107
Lussan, 513
Luxeuil-les-Bains, 407
Luzenac, 157, 162
Lyon, 372, 377, 456
Lyonnais, 355, 357, 371–9
Lys, 143, 144, 147
   Bleu, 244

Maber, 456
   Bleu, 456
Macaye, 137
Macéré, Le Puant, 262
Macquelines, 320, 335
Mâcon, 366
Mâconnais, 226, 357–9, 366, 373, 375, 383
Macquin, 335
Magnon, Le, 271
Magnum, Le, 32, 504
   aux Herbes, 518
   'Brillat-Savarin', 32, 317
   Chèvre, 514
   Dormant, 36
Maigre, 18, 244
Maigrelet, 167
Maigrette, 224, 244
   du Forez, 244
Maine, Le, 41–9, 51, 52
Maingaux, 51, 52, 54
Maingeaux Rennais, 54
Maison de la Transhumance, La, 453
Malakoff, 29, 36
Malaucène, 514
Malessui, 82
Malleval, 373, 377
Mamirolle, 407
Manche, 9
Manicamp, 271
Manlay, 366
Manosque, 514

Mans, Le, 48
Maquis, 476
Marbray, Le, 21
Marc, 433
Marcaire, Le, 292
Marcairerie, 292
Marcairie, 292
Marcellinois, Le, 456
Marche, 115, 116, 123, 203, 212
Marciac, 152
Marcilly-les-Vitteaux, 351, 366
Margotin, 116, 123
   Herbes de Provence, 122
   Poivré, 123
Marguerite, 456
Marly-le-Roi, 335
Maroilles, 145, 258–62, 263, 264–5, 271, 309, 314
   Fermier, 272
   Gros, 259, 264, 270
   Laitier, 272
   Merveille de, 272
   Mignon, 272
   Quart, 273
   Sorbais, 261, 274
Marolles, 63, 271
Maromme, 21, 36
Marques, 433
Marsauceux, 60, 83
Marseille, 491, 514
Martel, 117, 123
Massif Central, 201–54
Matignon, 54
Matocq, 144, 147
Matocq Vallée d'Ossau, 146
Matton, 292
Maubourguet, 150, 152
Mauléon, 131, 132, 133, 134, 137, 144, 181
Maurienne, 421, 433
Maurupt, 335
Maussane-les-Alpilles, 514
Mayenne, 9, 41–9
Mayrinhac-Lentour, 123
Mazamet, 33, 167
Mazet, 244
Meaudret, Le, 456
Meaux, 335
Meilleraye-de-Bretagne, La, 54
Mélange, Lait de, 107
Mélange de Lait, 514
Mélange Mi-Chèvre, 514
Melleray, 51, 54
Melleray, Fromage de l'Abbaye de, 54
Melun, 335
Melun Frais, 321
Melusine, 107
Melusine Le Royal, 108
Mérilait, 514
Merveille de Maroilles, La, 272
Merveilles, vallee des, 514
Merzer, 54
Mesnil, 21
Mesnil-Mauger, 29, 30, 36
Metabief, 407

Meton, Le, 407
Metton, Le, 396, 407
Metz, 292
Meurthe-et-Moselle, 277–96
Meuse, 277–96
Meusnes, 83
Meusnois, Le, 83
Meyland, 456
Meynes, 514
Mézenc, 222, 245
   Fourme de, 241
Mézières en Brenne, 83
Mi-Chèvre, 108, 514
   Fermier, 456
Mi-Sel, Le, 377
Micheline, La, 106, 108
Miélan, 152
Miette, 245
   de Tauves, 245
   des Monts Dore, 245
Migno, 245
Mignon, 272
   Tholy, 296
Mignot Blanc, 21
Mignot Passe, 21
Mimolette, 28, 272
   au Porto, 273
   Française, 21, 272
Mingaux, 54
Mingots, 54
Mini-Pavé d'Auge Fermier, 22
Ministre, Le Délice du, 456
Mirabel, 83
Miramande de Pajels, 226, 245
Mirande, 152
Mizotte de Vendée, 108
Moilles, Fromage des, 456
Moka, Le, 499, 512
Mollégès, 514
Molsheim, 292
Mon Charcennay, 405
Monbenoît, 407
Monceau, Le, 259, 273
Monchelet, Le, 273
Mondebat, Le, 152, 153
Monpila, 377
Monplaisir, 143, 147
Monsieur, 21
Mont-Cenis, 434
Mont Chalmoux, 245
Mont d'Or, 377, 399, 400, 407, 414
Mont-des-Cats, 262, 265, 273
Mont Dore, 245
Mont-St-Alban, 345, 366
Mont-St-Martin, 443, 457
Mont-Tournier, 434
Mont Ventoux, 491, 515
Mont Ventoux, Fromage Fort du, 509
Montagnard, 476
   Petit, 433
Montagne, 245, 433
   Tomme de, 457
Montagne Ariègeoise, La, 158, 159, 160, 163
Montagne de Bethmale, La, 159, 162, 163

Laitier, 161
Montagne-Tradition, 162
Montalbanais, Le, 54
Montalieu, 457
Montargis, 60, 83
Montauban, 118, 123, 167
Montauban de Bretagne, 54
Montbrison, 222, 223, 224, 245, 373, 374, 377
  Fourme, 376
Montbrun-les-Bains, 457
Montclus, 492, 515
Montegrosso, 476
Montélimar, 448, 457
Montereau, 305, 335
Montesquieu-Volvestre, 154, 160
Montfort, 335
Montignac, 123
Montlouis-sur-Loire, 83
Montmarault, 202–3, 245
Montmerle, 389
Montmerle-sur-Saône, 389
Montmirail, 316, 335
Montmort, 315, 335
Montoire, 58, 62, 63, 83
Montoire-sur-le-Loir, 83
Montpellier, 167
Montrachet, 356, 357, 366
Montréal, 366
Montrejeau, 151, 154, 157
Montrichard, 64, 83
Monts d'Or, 211, 213, 372, 377
Monts de Vaucluse, 515
Monts du Forez, 221, 373, 374
  Fourmes de, 241
Monts Yssingelais, Fourme des, 241
Montsalvy, 209, 245
Montsauché, 367
Montségur, 158, 160, 162, 164, 226
Montviette, 7
Morbier, 55, 390, 398–9
  au Lait Cru de Franche-Comté, 407
  Fermier, 405
Morbihan, 50–5
Mormant, 336
Mortagne-au-Perche, 83
Morteau, 408
Morvan, 345, 356, 367
Moselle, 277–96
Mostoffait, 292
Mostoffe, 292
Mothais, 108
La-Mothe-St-Heray, 108
Moulin d'Aunac, 101
Moulin, 108
Moulins, 202–3, 245
Moulis, Le, 157, 162
Mountalba, 123, 168
Mouriès, 515
Mourrachu, Le, 377
Moussières, Les, 385, 408
Moutiers, 420, 434
Moyaux, 21
Moyon, 21

Mulhouse, 292
Munster, 278, 279, 280, 281, 282, 283, 284–5, 292, 295
  au Cumin, 293
  Fermier, 288, 291, 292
  Géromé, 290, 292, 293
  Laitier, 293
Muntanacciu, 476
Mur-de-Barrez, 195
Mure, La, 446, 457
Murol, 219–20, 243, 245
Muvrone, 477

Nangis, 305, 306, 336
Nantais, 55
Nantais Dit du Curé, 53
Nantes, 51, 55
Nanteuil-les-Meaux, 305, 336
Nantua, 390
Nay, 145, 148
Nesle-Hodeng, 36
Neufchâtel, 29–32, 37
  Fermier, 39
Neufchâtel-en-Bray, 37
Neuilly-sur-Seine, 336
Neuville-Ferrières, 39
Nice, 485, 515
Nicois, 485–8
Nièvre, 351
Nîmes, 500, 515
Niolin, 477
Niolo, 472, 477
Niort, 98, 99, 100, 108
Niortaise, 100, 108
Niulincu, 472, 477
Nogent-sur-Seine, 336
Noir de Nanteuil, Le, 327
Noirville, 21
Nontron, 116, 123
Normandie, 1–55
Notre-Dame-de-Courson, 22
Notre-Dame-de Fresnay, 8, 22
Noves, 515
Noyal-sur-Vilaine, 55
Noyers-Le-Val, 278, 293, 336
Nuits d'Or, Le, 367
Nuits-St-Georges, 347, 351, 355, 367
Nyons, 457

Oelenberg, 293
Oic-de-Bure, Le, 458
Olivet, 59, 61
  au Foin, 61, 83
  Bleu, 61, 83
  Cendré, 61, 83
  Petit, 61
d'Oléron, Île, 108
Oloron-Ste-Marie, 140, 148
Onetik, 137
Onzain, 62, 84
Orange, 481–522, 515
Orbec, 22
Orbey, 279, 293
Orbiquet, 22
Orchamps-Vennes, 408
Ordonnaz, 390
Oré, 22

Orléanais, 57–94, 84, 313
Orléans, 60, 61, 67, 84
Ornans, 408
Orne, 2–27
Orrys, Les, 158, 159, 162
Ossau, 146, 147
d'Ossau, Vallée, 132, 133, 135, 140–4, 148
Ossau-Iraty, 130, 133, 135, 136, 137, 139, 144, 146, 147, 150, 151
  Etcheria, 137
Ossau-type, 147
Ourde, 151, 153
Oust, 155, 157, 158, 162, 163
Oustet, 162
Ouxy, 367
Ouzon valley, 144–6, 150
Overney, 367
Oyonnax, 383, 390
Ozenay, 367
Ozolles, 357, 367

P'ail, Le, 242, 245
Paillaud, 84
Paladru, 434, 457
Palangué, Le, 147, 148
Palendru, 434
Palet, 377
  de Balbigny, 374, 375
  Perigourdin, 116, 123
Palluau-sur-Indres, 84
Pamproux, 108
Pancey, 336, 353
Pannes, 84
  Cendré, 84
Pansey, Le Petit, 336
Paradou, Le, 515
Parallélépipède – Neufchâtel AOC, 39
Parbressan, 390
Parfait, 22
Paris, 336
Parthenay, 99, 108
Pass'ain, 390
Pass l'an Salit, 123
Passe-Loup, 378
Patay, 61, 84
Pâte Molle, 450
Pâte Pressée Croute Lavées, 519
Patranque, 227
Patrimonio, 477
Pau, 140, 148
Pavé, 19, 84, 378
  Dauphinois, 378
  d'Affinois, 245, 247, 374, 378
  d'Airvault, 100
  d'Auge, 9–10, 11, 22
    Fermier, 22
    Mini Fermier, 22
  d'Avesnes, 273
  de Chèvre Cendré, 354
  d'Isigny, 22
  de Jadis, 84
  de la Sologne, 73, 90
  de Moyaux, 22
  d'Or, 378
  de Pont-l'Évêque, 23

du Blésois, 73
du Plessis (Launay), 23
du Pré, 337
Frais Mas Barronet, 124
Normand, 22
Pavin, Le, 245
Pays Basque, *see* Basque
Pays d'Auge, *see* Auge
Pèbre d'Aï, 505, 512, 515
Pecorino Corse, 477
Pédat, Le, 434
Pélardon, 168, 195, 209, 222, 245, 375, 492, 501, 513
  Cévenol, 246
  d'Altier, 228, 246
  d'Anduze, 228, 246, 516
  d'Annonay, 228
  de Burzet, 246
  de Largentière, 246
  de Ruoms, 246
  des Cévennes, 246, 516
  Fermier, 516, 518
  Fermier des Cévennes, 246
  Pur Chèvre, 457, 503
Pèlerin, Le, 124
Pélissane, 516
Peloudou, 168
Pélussin, 246, 374, 378
Pelvoux, 457
Pennes, 84, 457
  Cendré, 84
  le Sec, 457
Pepper, Plain, or Black, 125
Pérail, Le, 176, 195
  du Mas Pinel, 516
  Fromage Fermier de Brebis, 195
  Laitier, Le, 195
  Pur Brebis, 195
Péral, 195
Péraldou, 246
Perche, Le, 57–94
Père Selme, 457
Perette, 246
Périgord, 97, 113–25, 115–16, 124, 189
Périgueux, 115, 116, 124
Pernes-les-Fontaines, 516
Perpignan, 164, 169, 170
Perrail, 195
Perrelle, La, 23
Perrière, 367
Perrière d'Époisses, La, 350, 365
  Export, 365
Perle du Berry, La, 84
Persillé, 430, 434, 450
  de la Clusaz, 431
  de Thônes, 437
  des Aravis, 417, 428
  du Grand Bornand, 433
  du Mont-Cenis, 434
Pesse, La, 384, 385, 407, 408
Pétafine, La, 448, 457
Petiot, Le, 195
Petit, 85
Petit Bayard, Le, 450
Petit Bessay, 229, 246
Petit-Beurre, 246
Petit Billy, Le, 73

Petit Bleu, Le, 246
Petit Bondon, Le, 101
Petit Bonement, Le, 517
Petit Bornand, Le, 168
Petit Bressan, 388
Petit Bugey, 388, 390
Petit Cantal, Le, 234
P'tit Cohidon, Le, 492, 513
Petit Fermier, Le, 432
Petit Fromage de Chèvre, 287
Petit Fromage de Montagne, 434
Petit Gouzon, Le, 122, 242
Petit Lisieux, Le, 19
P'tit Lisou, Le, 157, 163
Petit Livarot, Le, 20
Petit Mâconnais, 366, 367
Petit Mitagnard de la Dent du Chat, Le, 432
Petit Montagnard, Le, 433
Petit Moyonnais, Le, 21
Petit Olivet au Foin, 85
Petit Pansey, Le, 336
Petit Perche, Le, 59, 62, 72, 84, 93
Petit Pont-l'Évêque, 23
Petit Pot de Poitiers, Le, 108
Petit Reblochon, 417, 434
Petit Saint-Nectaire, Le, 246, 250
Petit Silors, Le, 89
Petit Silors au Foin, Le, 89
Petit Silors Cendré, Le, 89
Petit Sixtois, Le, 506
Petit-Suisse, 23, 28, 29, 32–3, 39, 85, 167, 168
Petit Tholy, Le, 295
Petit Trôo, Le, 62, 85, 91, 93
Petit Valréas, Le, 463
Petit Vendéen, Le, 106, 111
Petit Vendôme, Le, 63, 92, 94
Petit Vougeot, Le, 369
Petite Beauce, La, 73
Petites Rigottes, 460
Petits Bodonsecs, 450
Peymeinade, 516
Peyrolles-en-Provence, 516
Pic de La Calabasse, Le, 163
Picadou, Le, 118, 124
Picardie, 257–74, 273
Picaudon, 458
Picherande, 213, 246
Pico, 116, 124
Picodon, 209, 225, 226, 246, 375, 447–8, 455, 463, 492
  Affiné Méthode Dieulefit, 458
  au Lait de Mélange, 458
  Chevrette, 453, 458
  d'Arles, 458, 516
  de Barjac, 247
  de Bourdeaux, 451, 458
  de Dieulefit, 454, 458
  de Floréal, 458, 462
  de Gras, 243, 247
  de l'Ardèche, 226, 246, 447, 492
  de la Drôme, 226, 447, 458, 491, 492, 516
  de la Gorce, 247

de Roche Colombe, 459, 462
de St-Agrève, 247
de Valréas, 459, 492–3, 516
Drômois, 458
Fermier, 452, 458
Fines-Herbes, 458
Picolette Pur Chèvre, 247
Pidance, La, 247
Pie, 337
Pierre Dorée du Beaujolais, La, 378
Pierre Fontaine, 408
Pierre-Qui-Vire, La, 352–3, 360, 367
Pierre-sur-Haute, 247
  Fourme de, 241
Pigouille, La, 108
Pigouille du Pays du Maran, La, 108
Pipette-Neufchâtel (non-AOC), 40
Pipo Crem 383, 390
Piquette de l'Avranchin, 23
Pistole, 247
Pithiviers au Foin, 63, 85
Plainfaing, 293
Plaisance, 153
Plan-de-la-Tour, 517
Planèze, 247
Plasne, 408
Ploermel, 55
Poids Plumé Normand, 23
Poil de Carotte, 293
Pointe de Bique, La, 73
Poitiers, 108
Poitou, 97–111
Poivre, 337
Poivre, Fromage au, 293
Poivre d'Âne, 459, 517
Poivrette, La, 434
Poletta, 477
Poligny, 408
Polliat, 390
Pondenas, 153
Pont-Astier, 220, 247
Pont Audemer, 23
Pont d'Auge, 23
Pont-de-Crau, 517
Pont-de-Vaux, 390
Pont-en-Royans, 459
Pont l'Évêque, 2, 3, 8, 9–10, 11, 13, 17, 19, 22, 23, 24, 42, 59, 224
  Demi, 23
  Doux Trois Amis, 48
  Fermier, 24
  la Varinière, 25
  Laitier Artisanal, 25
  Launay, 25
  les Écussons Normands, 24
  Petit, 23
Pont-St-Esprit, 492, 517
Pontarlier, 402, 408
Pontet, Le, 517
Pontgibaud, 247
Port-du-Salut, 43–4, 46, 48, 51
Port Grimaud, 517
Port-Salut, 278, 294

## 558    INDEX

Pontesienne, La, 517
Postagnac, 137
Pothu, 378
Pouligny-Notre-Dame, 85
Pouligny-St-Pierre, 66–7, 81, 85
Pourly, 367
Pourri, 390
Poustagnacq, 137
Prairie, 367
Pralin, 434
Pralognan, 420, 425, 434
Pras d'Yeures, Le, 427, 430, 434
Praslin, 420, 434
Prayssac, 124
Préalpes, 459
Préalpes Drômoises, 459
Préalpine sur Marc, La, 459
Préclos, 42–3, 48
Préférence, La, 247
Président, 16, 25, 58
Pressy-Moye, Le, 434
Prestige de Bourgogne, 354, 367
Prince de Claverolle, 133, 137, 472
Prince de Navarre, 133, 138
Prince Noir, 116, 124
Provençales, Les, 460
Provence, 164, 169, 481–522
Providence, 12, 25
Provins, 305, 306, 337
P'Teux, 294
Puant, 273
Puant de Cambrésis, Le, 262, 268
Puant de Lille, Le, 262, 273, 472
Puant du Cambrésis, Le, 273
Puant Macéré, Le, 262, 273
Puisaye, 344–5
Pujaut, 517
Pur Brebis, 146
Pur Chèvre Fermier, 510
 de Forez, 224
 du Causse, 120, 194
Purebique, 85, 108
Putanges, 25
Puy, Le, 224, 247
Puy Laurent, 247
Pyramide, 67, 72, 86, 108, 517
 Bleutée, 502
 Cendrée, 503
Pyrénées, 127–70, 181, 184
Pyrénées-Atlantiques, 135, 139–48

Quart Livarot, Le, 20
Quatre Vents, 459
Quercy, 97, 113–25, 117, 124, 174, 209
Queton d'Isigny, Le, 25
Queyras, 445–6, 459
Quimper, 55

Raclette, 25, 109, 281, 282, 408, 434, 506, 517
 de Busseau, 124
 du Montvelay, 248
 Valco, 25
Raclette-Préalpes, 459
Rambouillet, Le, 337
Ramequin, 390
 d'Ambérieu, 390
 de Bugey, 390
 de Lagrieu, 391
 de Montalieu, 460
 Latinicien, 391
Ramoun, 151, 152, 153
Ranchy, Le, 10, 25
Raphèle-les-Arles, 517
Rascala, 176, 195, 196
Rascalat, Le, 177, 195
Rascalata, 176
Rascalou, 176
Rasquelet, Le, 195
Rasquelet de St-Affrique, Le, 196
Rauret, 517
Rauville-la-Bigot, 25
Rebarbe, Le, 168, 176, 184, 195, 196
Reblochon, 354, 355, 359, 414–17, 418, 419, 432, 435, 445
 Petit, 417, 434
Reblochonnet, 417, 418, 435
Recherchon, 409
Recollet, 294
Recologne, 409
Recuite, La, 196
Recuocha, La, 177, 196
Régal
 Béarnais, 148
 de Bourgogne, 367
 de Mont-Tournier, 434
 du Liers, 460
Régitome, 42, 48
Reims, 337
Reine du Passe-Loup, La, 378
Remiremont, 281, 294
Remoulins, 518
Rémuzat, 446, 460
Rennes, 55
Rennet, see Caillette
Restonica, La, 477
Revard, 435
Revermont, 391
Revidoux, 294
Rhône, 371–9, 501
Rians, 86
Ribotte, 26
Riceys, Le, 313, 329, 338, 347
 Cendré, 338
Ricotta, 374, 396, 424, 470, 471, 485, 518
 aux Galets, 477
 Mérilait, 514
Rigoton, 391
 de Bugey, 388
Rigotte, 225, 375, 378, 460
 de Condrieu, 374, 378
 de Pelussin, 246, 248, 378
 de Ste-Colombe, 435
 des Alpes, 460
 du Mont Sauvage, 460
 Jacquemart, 460
 le Roi des Préalpes, 460
 Petite, 460
Riom, 212, 248
Rivaud, Le, 109
Le-Roc-du-Toulaux, 460
Roanne, 373, 378
Rocamadour, 117, 124, 209
Roc-Amadour Pur Chèvre, Le, 124
Roche-sur-Foron, La, 435
Rochebrune, 435
Rochefort, 100, 109
Rochefort-Montagne, 208–10, 248
 Fourme de, 241
Rochelle, La, 100, 109
Rocroi, 313, 329, 338
 Cendré, 338
Rodez, 196
Rogallais, Le, 157, 162, 163
Rogalle, 163
Roger Bernard, 26
Rogeret, 224, 225, 248
 de Lamastre, 248
 des Cevennes, 248
 St-Félicien, 248
Rollot, Le, 273
Romans, 378, 444, 460, 499
 Bon, 460
 Maber, 460
 Poivre, 460
Romans-sur-Isère, 460
Romilly-sur-Seine, 338
Romorantin-Lanthenay, 86
Rond, Le, 82, 86
 Bleu, Le, 82, 86
 de Chèvre Fermier de Ste-Maure, 86
 de Lusignan, 107, 109
 de Romorantin, 86
 des Charentes, 109
 Pur Chèvre de Villiers, 63, 86, 94
 Super, 86
Rondfaing, Le, 294
Rondin, 109
Rontalon, 378
Roque Esclapon, La, 518
Roquebillière, 518
Roquefort, 116, 133, 137, 140, 148, 195, 354, 470, 477, 485, 492
Roquegautier, 125
Rosée des Prés, 460
Rouen, 40
Rouennaise, 40
Rouergue, 173–98
 Tomme de, 197
Rougeat du Canigou, 170
Rougerin, 248
Roujadou(x), 203, 248
Roule, 86
Rouleau, 82, 86
Roumahoux, 248
Roumajou(x), 203, 238, 248
Roumillat, 294
Roure, 487, 518
Rousses, Le, 409
Roussillon, 169–70
Route du Fromage, La, 12
Rouy, Le, 48, 367

Rove, 518
Rove des Garrigues, La, 167, 168
Royal, 84
Royal Ventoux, 460, 463
Royan Frais, 454
Royannais, 460
Royans, 460
Rubarbe, 195
Ruffec, 109
Rumilly, 436
Ruoms, 248
Russey, Le, 409

Sable Nu, 109
Sable-Solesmes, 48
Sableau, 100, 109
Sables d'Olonne, Les, 100, 109
Saillans, 461
Saingorlon, 248, 378, 382–3, 391
St-Affrique, 174, 176–7, 197
St-Agathon, 55
St-Agrève, 225, 248
St-Alban, 367
St-Albray, 144–6, 147
St-Amand, 86
St-Amand-Montrond, 86
St-Amant, Le, 248
St-André, 197
St-André d'Huirat, 391
St-André-d'Olerargues, 492, 518
St-André-Poivre-Vert, 197
St-Anthème, 210, 211, 220, 221, 222, 224, 248
St-Aubin, 274
St-Benoist, Le, 86
St-Benoît, 86, 294, 487
St-Blandin, Le, 461
St-Bonnet-en-Champsaur, 461
St-Bonnet-le-Château, 249
St-Bricel, 391
St-Brieuc, 55
St-Céré, 125
St-Chevrier, 87, 109
St-Christol-de-Rodières, 518
St-Christophe, Le, 87
St-Claude, 385, 409
St-Denis-de-l'Hôtel, 87
St-Diéry, 249
St-Dizier, 338
St-Donat, 213, 249
St-Donat-sur-l'Herbasse, 461
St-Éloy, 125, 249
St-Estephe, 109
St-Étienne, 249, 378
St-Étienne-de-Tinée, 518
St-Étienne-du-Bois, 110
St-Félicien, 225, 249, 378, 461
St-Felix, 436
St-Florentin, 344, 346, 367
  Factory, 345–6
  Fermier, 367
  Laitier, 368
St-Flour, 221, 249
St-Foin, 338

St-Gaudens, 151, 154
St-Gelais, 110
St-Gengoux, 368
St-Génix, 436
  Fermier, 436
St-Génix-sur-Guiers, 436
St-Georges-de-Luzençon, 197
St-Georges-en-Couzan, 379
St-Germain-de-Montgommery, 5
St-Gildas, 55
St-Gildas-des-Bois, 55
St-Girondins, 158–60
St-Girons, Le, 155, 157, 160, 162, 163
St-Hélian, 294
St-Henry, 110
St-Hippolyte-du-Fort, 392, 518
St-Jean-de-Losne, 353–4, 368
St-Jean-du-Gard, 518
St-Jean-Lachalm, 249
St-Jean-Pied-de-Port, 130, 131, 138
St-Jeannais, Le, 249, 518
St-Jeannet, 519
St-Jouvin, 26
St-Julien-en-Genevoise, 436
St-Junien, 125
St-Just-de-Claix, 461
St-Kilien, 274
St-Lary, 156, 157, 163
St-Laurian, 87
St-Lizier, 155, 157, 158–60, 163
St-Lo, 26
St-Loup, 110
St-Loup-sur-Thouet, 110
St-Lubin-de-la-Haye, 61, 87
St-Lunaire, 55
St-Maclou, 4, 26
Saint-Maixent, 110
St-Maixent-l'École, 98, 110
St-Malo, 26
St-Marcellin, 157, 164, 372, 373, 375, 379, 443–4, 461
  Affiné au Vin Blanc, 379, 461
  Lait Cru, 461
  Lait de Mélange, 461
  le Crémeux, 461
  Poivre, 461
  Pur Chèvre, 461
  Sec-en-Feuille, 461
  Surfin, 379
St-Martial-de-Valette, 116, 125
St-Martin, 10, 25, 26
St-Martin-de-Bienfaite, 26
St-Martin-de-Londres, 168
St-Martin-Vésubie, 487, 519
St-Maurice near Gaillefontaine, 40
St-Maximin-la-Ste-Baume, 519
St-Michel, 26, 130, 131, 138, 462
St-Michel-de-Livet, 7, 8
St-Michel-sur-Savasse, 462
St-Moret, 116, 125

St-Morgon, 26
St-Nazaire, 55
St-Nectaire, 161, 205, 210, 211–19, 220, 249, 496, 501
  Fermier, 230, 250
  Laitier, 250
  Petit, 213, 250
St-Palais, 133, 138
St-Paulin, 26, 41, 43, 48, 51, 55, 122, 125, 215, 220, 274, 338, 355
St-Pé, 148
St-Pé-de-Bigorre, 145, 150, 153
St-Philippe, 26
St-Pierre-sur-Dives, 7, 8, 26
St-Pol, 10, 25, 26
St-Pourcain-sur-Sioule, 251
St-Rambert-en-Bugey, Fromage Fort de, 391
St-Raphael, 519
St-Remi, 338
St Remois, Le, 496, 519
St-Rémy, Le, 44, 259, 274, 295, 338, 409, 496, 499, 500
St-Rémy-de-Provence, 492, 495, 519
St-Rieu, 251
St-Saulge, 368
St-Sauveur-sur-Tinée, 487, 519
St-Saviol, 110
St-Sernin, 462
St-Sernin-sur-Rance, 177, 197
St-Simeon, 316, 338
St-Thibaut, 145, 274
St-Tropez, 519
St-Valentin, 379
St-Varent, 110
St-Verand, Fromage de, 462
St-Vincent-sur-Jabron, 519
St-Winocq, 274
Ste-Anne-d'Auray, 44, 51, 55
Ste-Croix, 448, 461
Ste-Foy-de-Montgommery, 26
Ste-Foy-Tarentaise, 436
Ste-Marguerite-de-Viette, 8, 26
Ste-Marie, 352, 368
Ste-Marie-Sicche, 478
Ste-Maure, 58, 66, 70, 72, 82, 87, 98, 108, 110
Ste-Maure-Amy-Bique, 88
Ste-Maure-de-Touraine, 68–71, 87, 88
Ste-Maure Géant, Le, 80
Ste-Maxime, 519
Ste-Mère-Église, 26
Ste-Odile, 294
Saintes, 99, 110
Saintonge, 99–100
Salakis, 198
Salers, 198, 205–7, 251
Saliens, 163
Saligny, 345, 368
Salihès, 252
Salins les Bains, 409
Salon de Provence, 495, 519

Sambuc, Le, 520
Samortein, 161, 163
Sancerre, 65, 66, 88
Sancerrois, 64–6, 88
Santa-Maria-Siche, 478
Sante-Alvère, 125
Santranges, 65, 88
Saône-et-Loire, 343–69, 383
Saou, 462
Sarasson, 252
Sarassou, 252
Sarassoun, 252
Sari d'Orcino, 478
Sarlat, 125
Sarrazins, 391
Sarrebourg, 295
Sartenais, 478
Sartène, 478
Sarteno, 478
Sarthe, 41–9
Sassenage, 442–3, 446, 462
  Bleu de, 462
Saulieu, 368
Saulieu-Brillat-Savarin, 368
Saulx, 409
Saulzet-le-Froid, 216, 252
Saumur, 89
Sauvain, 222, 224, 252
Sauzé-Vaussais, 110
Savaron, 219–20, 252
Savigny, 379
Savigny le Temple, 338
Savoie, 261, 280, 309, 413–38, 436, 485
Savoie Grosse, 438
Schigre, 288, 295
Sechons, 252
Seine-Maritime, 28–40
Seissan, 153
Seix, 157, 158, 163
Select sur Feuille, Le, 89
Selles-sur-Cher, 58, 60, 62, 63, 64, 70, 82, 89, 345
Semur-en-Auxois, 346, 347, 368
Semussac, 110
Sénéchal, Le, 117, 124
  Pur Brebis, 125
Septmoncel, 409
Sérac, 157, 424, 436
  d'Ustou, 163
Seranon, 488, 520
Serans, 26
Sermoyer, 383, 391
Serraval, 417, 418, 437
Sézanne, 315, 338
Sisteron, 489, 520
Sixt, 437
Sixtois, 520
Solignac-sur-Loire, 252
Solitaire de Chartreuse, 462
Sollies-Toucas, 520
Sologne, 64, 89
Sorbais, 259, 262, 264, 274
Sospel, 406, 520
Sost, 151, 153
Souillac, 125
Soule Mauléon-Licharre, La, 137
Soumaintrain, 344, 368

de l'Yonne, 345, 368
Factory, 345–6
Farmhouse, 346–7
Fermier Artisanal, 368
Sourdeval, 26
Sourire, 209, 252
Spécialité du Champsaur, 450, 452
Spécialité Fromagère, 295
Steenvorde, 274
Stoffet, 274
Strasbourg, 295
Su, 26
Sully-sur-Loire, 90
Super Rond, Le, 86
Suppositoire du Diable, Le, 274
Suprême, 26, 40
  des Ducs, 364, 368

Tachoires, 153
Tamié, 420, 437
Tante Mignonne, 111
Tara Crème, 379
  Frais, 379
Tarare, 379
Tarbes, 150, 153
Tardets, 131, 132, 138, 140
Tarentais, Le, 437
Tarn, 33, 164, 166–8, 181
Tartare, 125
Tarte aux Vignes, La, 198
Tartes Bressanes, 391
Taupinière, 93, 100, 111
  Charentaise, 111
Tavaillon, Le, 418–19, 437
Teigny, 368
Tende, 486, 520
Termignon, Bleu de, 437
Terroir, 252
Thenay, 90
Thiérache, 144, 222, 258, 263
Thiers, 220, 252
Thiézac, 210, 252
Thillot, Le, 281, 295
Thimerais, 59, 60, 90
Thionville, Le, 278, 295
Thiviers, 125
Thoiry, 437
Thoissey, 391
Tholy, Le, 295
Thônes, 416, 437
Thonon les Bains, 438
Thorigny, 338
Thymadeuc, 51, 55
Tignard, 438
Timadeuc, 51, 55
Tinée, La, 487, 520
Tome, 72, 119, 253, 285, 295, 391, 462, 517, 520
  à L'Huile de Tournesol, 461
  Blanche, 90, 253
    Père Ségador, 517
  de Chèvre, 121, 457
    Fermière, 503
  de Romans, 460
  de Roure, 518
  de Vache, 72, 515
    de Séranon, 510

des Alpes, 48
du Mazet Bleu, 245
Fraîche, 506
Tomme, 55, 125, 168, 198, 253, 388, 391, 419–20, 462, 520
  Arlésienne, 503
  au Cumin, 454
  au Fenouil, 454
  au Marc de Raisin, 433
  au Raisin, 438
  aux Deux Traites, 450
  Blanche, 55, 120, 125
    du Velay, 222
  Corse, 476
  d'Aligot la Fermière, 204, 227
  d'Alpages, 438
  d'Anceval, 209, 228
  d'Annot, 487, 503
  d'Arles, 493, 503
  de Bairols, 505
  de Belleville, 429
  de Belley, 387
  de Bessans, 430
  de Boudane/Boudanne, 430
  de Brach, 114, 119
  de Brebis, 195, 198
  de Bugey, 388
  de Camargue, 503
  de Capra, 452
  de Champsaur, 446, 450
  de Chèvre, 90, 167, 427, 431, 438, 518
    Fermière, 455
  de Combovin, 453
  de Corps, 446, 453
  de Courchevel, 431
  de Crest, 453
  de Devoluy, 454
  de Fenouil, 438
  de Ferme, 253
    de Castellane, 489, 510
  de la Drôme, 454
  de la Turbie, 520
  de Laye, 456
  de Livron, 456
  de Lize, 54
  de l'Ubaye, 521
  de Lomagne, 152
  de Maurienne, 438
  de Mélange du Champsaur, 450, 452
  de Mont Ventoux, 515
  de Montagne, 162, 163, 166, 242, 253, 434, 438, 457
  de Montagne d'Aubrac, 191
  de Montagne la Genette, 253
  de Montségur, 162
  de Nyons, 457
  de Pralognan, 431
  de Praslin/Pralin, 431
  de Quercy, 118, 125
  de Queyras, 445, 459
  de Rouergue, 197
  de Savoie, 118, 419, 425–6, 427, 436, 437, 438, 486, 487

# INDEX

de Sérac, 427
de Sixt, 438
de Sospel, 520
de Tende, 520
de Thônes, 438
de Vache, 125, 391, 520
de Valberg, 521
de Valdeblore, 521
de Vendée, 111
de Vivarais, 253
des Allues, 421, 427
des Alpages, 427
des Alpes, 461
des Bauges, 428
des Bergers, 429
des Deux Traites du Champsaur, 452
des Neiges, 222
des Préalpes, 459
du Beaufortin, 429
du Champsaur, 452
du Chasseur, 452
du Forez, 240
du Mont Cenis, 434
du Pelvoux, 457
du Quercy, 124
du Revard, 435
du Velay, 253
du Vercors, 463
Fraîche de Laguiole, 204
Fraîche la Fermière, 227
Grise, 27, 55
    de Chèvre, 111
    des Monts, 379
Lait-de-Mélange, 253
Mi-Chèvre, 518
Noire le Roy, 125
Persillée de Coucouron, 238
Persillée du Velay, 253
Tommette, 438
    au Cerron (Ciron), 438
    aux Artisans, 438
    de la Dent du Chat, 432
    de Savoie (affinage Moyen), 438
Torte, 295
Tortora, 520
Toucy de l'Yonne, Le, 344, 369
Toulaux, 462
Toulon, 520
Toulouse, 154, 157
Toummo, 253
Toupin, 438
Tour Eiffel, La, 79, 90
Touraine, 61, 68, 69, 70, 90, 98, 110
Tourette du Père Joseph, 379
Tourgeville, Le, 23, 27
Tournan-en-Brie, 317, 338
Tournesol, 462
Tournon, Le, 90, 225, 253
Tournon-St-Martin, Le, 90
Tournon-St-Pierre, Le, 90
Tournus, 359, 369
Tourol, 165
Tourolades, 165
Tourouillettes, 165
Tourrée de l'Aubier, 462

Tours, 90
Tourton, Le, 125
Trabèche, 111
Traboulin, Le, 379
Tracle, 391
Trang'nat/Trang'natt, 295
Transhumance, 463
Trappe, La, 116, 121, 125
Trappe de Bailleul, 265
Trappe de Ste-Marie du Mont, 265
Trappiste, 27, 55, 296
Trappiste de Bricquebec, 12
Trappiste d'Igny, 318
Trappiste de Melleray, 52
Trappiste d'Oelenberg, 285
Trappistine de Belval, 265
Traque, 409
Trébèche, 100, 109, 111
Tri-Cornes, 100, 109
Tricastin, 448, 481–522
Trident, Le, 493, 502, 504, 520
Trièves, Le, 452, 463
Trinquelin, Le, 353, 361, 369
Triple Bonde, 40
Triple Cœur, 40
Triple-Crème, 353–4
Triple-Crème Duquesne, 332, 339
    aux Raisins de Corinthe, 332, 339
Trizac, 210, 211, 253
Trois Amis, 49
Trois Cornes, 111
Trois-Quarts Livarot, Le, 20
Trôo, 58, 62, 90
    Petit, 91
Trou de Cru, 369
Trou de Murol, 219, 243, 253
Trou du Curé, 219, 239, 243, 253
Trou Tante Mignonne, 111
Troubadour de l'Ermitage, 296
Trouville, Le, 27
Trouville-sur-Mer, 27
Troyen, 319, 329
Troyen, Le, 339
Troyes, 319, 339
Trute, 27
Tumo, La, 253
Tumo de Corse, 478
Turbie, Tomme de la, 486, 520
Tyrou, 27

U Macchione, 472, 476
l'Ubaye, Tomme de, 521
Ugine, 438
Urfé, 253
Urt, 138
Ustou, 157, 163
Ustou, Val de, 157, 163
Uzemain, 296
Uzès, 521

Vachard, 219–20, 253
Vachard-Mélange, 253
Vache, 198, 508
Vachelin, 285, 296, 420

Vachères-en-Quint, 448, 463
Vacherin, 44, 214, 394, 399, 407, 409, 420, 438
    d'Abondance, 414, 427
    des Aillons, 427
    des Bauges, 428
    des Dranses, 427
    du Haut-Doubs, 399–400, 409
    du Mont d'Or, 399–404
Vaison-la-Romaine, 521
Val de Ustou, 163
Valberg, 487, 521
Valbonne, 521
Valchourin au Poivre, 463
Valdeblore, 487, 521
Valembert, 49
Valençay, 58, 61, 64, 67–8, 70, 82, 91, 98
    Cendré, 82
    de l'Indre, 90
Valence, 225, 254, 463
Vallée de Bethmale, 161
Vallée de L'Aspe, 146
Vallée des Merveilles, 486, 514
Vallée de Mixte, 146
Vallée d'Ossau, 148
Vallières, 383, 391
Vallon des Cabrières (Genre Tomme), Le, 498, 499, 512
Valmeuse, 296
Valognes, 27
Valréas, 447, 448, 463, 491, 492, 521
Valromey, 381–91
Vanves, 339
Vanves à la Crème, 339
Var, 487, 488–9, 521
Varacieux, 463
Varella, 170
'Varinière, La', 22
Varzy, 369
Vatan, 67, 91
Vatel, 354, 369
Vaucluse, 447, 490, 492, 521
Vaulx-en-Velin, 378, 379
Velaux, 521
Velay, 201, 209, 221, 222, 225, 254
Venaçais, 478
Venaco, 478
Vence, 521
Vendée, 99, 111
Vendéen, 51, 52, 111, 116
Vendôme, 62, 63, 91, 93
    Bleu, 91
    Cendré, 91
    Fermier, 92
    Petit, 92, 94
Vendôme-Villiers, Le, 63, 94
Vendômois, Le, 58, 59, 61, 62–3, 92, 93
Vendômois Farms, 92
Veneur, 49
Vente de Brebis, 135
Ventoux, 463, 517, 521
    Frais, 517
    Poivre, 517
Vercel, 410

## 562  INDEX

Vercorin, Le, 463
Vercors, 442–3, 444, 445, 463
   Tomme du, 463
Verdun, 280, 339
Véritable Cendré, 329
Véritable Fromage de Gillotons, 355
Véritable Fromage de Langres, 335
Véritable Fromage des Vignerons, 339
Véritable Trappe, 44–5
Vermenton, 344, 345, 353, 369
Vernelle, La, 93
Verneuil, 93
Vernoux, 254
Verruyes, 111
Vers-en-Montagne, 410
Versailles, 339
Vertus, 316, 339
Vesc, 463
Vésubie, 487, 522
Veuve, La, 339
Vexin, 319
Veynes, 446, 463
Vézelay, 345, 369
Vial d'Or, 379
Vialas, 254
Vic-en-Bigorre, 150, 153
Vic-sur-Céré, 209, 254
Vicomte de la Soule, 128–38
Vicomte de Labourd, 128–38
Vidauban, 522
Vieille Mimolette, 272
Vienne, 374, 463
Vierzon, 93

Vieux Bressan, 383, 390, 391
Vieux Cassant, 273
Vieux Gras, 273
Vieux Gris, Le, 262, 273
Vieux Hollande, 270, 272
Vieux Lille, 262, 272, 273, 274
Vieux Pané, Le, 23, 42–3, 49
Vieux Pont, 7, 10
   Affiné au Calvados, Le, 27
   au Calvados, 9–10
Vieux Puant, Le, 262, 273
Vigan, Le, 522
Vignelait, Le, 339
Vigneron, Le, 463
Vignerons, 339
Vignes, 198
Vigneulles-les-Hattonchatel, 280, 296
Vignolas, 379
Vignotte, 339
Villard-de-Lans, 463
Villars-les-Dombes, 391
Ville St-Jacques, 311, 325, 339
Villebarou, 62, 63, 93
Villedieu, 27, 40
Villedieu-les-Poeles, 27, 40
Villefranche-de-Panat, 198
Villefranche-de-Rouergue, 198
Villefranche-en-Beaujolais, 379
Villefranche-le-Château, 409, 463
Villeneuve sur Lot, 125
Villentrois, Le, 339

Villeperdrix, 446, 464
Villiers-sur-Loire, 58, 62, 63, 94
Villiers-sur-Trie, 331, 339
Vimoutiers, 3, 5, 7, 27
Vire, 10, 27
Virieu-sur-Bourbe, 464
Viry-Chatillon, 339
Vitalys, 162, 163
Vitry-le-François, 340
Vivarais, 209, 221, 222, 224, 225–6, 254
Void, 296, 340
Voiron, 443, 464
Vonnas, 391
Vosges, 277–96, 393–410
Vosges-Crème, 296
Vougeot, Le, 369
Vougy, 373, 379
Voulte-sur-Rhône, La, 225, 254
Voves, 61, 94, 340
   au Foin, 94
   Cendré, 61

Walnut, 125
Winzenheim, 296
Wittenheim, 296

Xaintray, 111

Yolo Tomme de Brebis, 138
Yonne, 343–69
Yssingeaux, 254
Yssingelais, 254
Yvetot, 40